EASIER ENGLISH INTERMEDIATE DICTIONARY

second edition

Also published by Bloomsbury Reference:

Easier English™ titles:

Easier English Basic Dictionary	0 7475 6644 5
Easier English Basic Synonyms	0 7475 6979 7
Easier English Dictionary: Handy Pocket Edition	0 7475 6625 9
Easier English Student Dictionary	0 7475 6624 0
English Thesaurus for Students	1 9016 5931 3

Check Your English Vocabulary workbooks:

Business	0 7475 6626 7
Computing	1 9016 5928 3
Academic English	0 7475 6691 7
PET	0 7475 6627 5
IELTS	0 7475 6982 7
FCE +	0 7475 6981 9
TOEFL®	0 7475 6984 3

***Specialist dictionaries*:**

Dictionary of Accounting	0 7475 6991 6
Dictionary of Banking and Finance	0 7475 6685 2
Dictionary of Business	0 7475 6980 0
Dictionary of Computing	0 7475 6622 4
Dictionary of Economics	0 7475 6632 1
Dictionary of Environment and Ecology	0 7475 7201 1
Dictionary of Hotels, Tourism and Catering Management	1 9016 5999 2
Dictionary of Human Resources and Personnel Management	0 7475 6623 2
Dictionary of ICT	0 7475 6990 8
Dictionary of Law	0 7475 6636 4
Dictionary of Marketing	0 7475 6621 6
Dictionary of Medical Terms	0 7475 6987 8
Dictionary of Military Terms	0 7475 7477 4
Dictionary of Nursing	0 7475 6634 8
Dictionary of Politics and Government	0 7475 7220 8
Dictionary of Science and Technology	0 7475 6620 8

EASIER ENGLISH INTERMEDIATE DICTIONARY

second edition

BLOOMSBURY

A BLOOMSBURY REFERENCE BOOK

www.bloomsbury.com/reference

Originally published by Peter Collin Publishing
as *English Study Dictionary*

First published 2000, 2001
Second edition published 2004

Bloomsbury Publishing Plc
38 Soho Square, London W1D 3HB

British Library Cataloguing-in-Publication Data
A catalogue record for this book is available from the British Library

ISBN 0 7475 6989 4

All papers used by Bloomsbury Publishing are natural, recyclable products made from wood grown in well-managed forests. The manufacturing processes conform to the environmental regulations of the country of origin.

Text processed and computer typeset by Bloomsbury
Printed and bound in Great Britain by Clays Ltd, St Ives plc

General Editor
P.H. Collin

Editorial Contributors
Sandra Anderson, Lesley Brown, Stephen Curtis,
Alice Grandison, Isabel Griffiths, Penelope Hands, Imogen Kerr,
Heloise McGuinness, Howard Sargeant

Text Production and Proofreading
Katy McAdam, Heather Bateman,
Emma Harris, Ruth Hillmore

Preface

This dictionary contains the essential words and phrases needed for everyday communication by learners of English and information on how these words and phrases are commonly used. It builds on the *Easier English™ Basic Dictionary* and is especially useful for intermediate learners of all ages who are expanding their vocabulary and knowledge of English.

Each main word, including compound words and phrasal verbs, has its own easy-to-find entry in bold type and a pronunciation in the International Phonetic Alphabet. The relative frequency of the most commonly used words is indicated. Common phrases, verb patterns and idioms associated with the main term are shown in bold type and separately defined within the entry.

The meanings of the main common senses of each word are given clearly and simply, using a limited and easily understood vocabulary. Meanings are grouped together by their part of speech. Examples are given for words that are likely to be used in practice, to provide patterns for the user's own production of English sentences. The prepositions that are regularly used with a word are also shown for common words, in square brackets. Some less frequently encountered words, which may only need to be recognised and understood, are given definitions only. Noted at the end of some entries are words with a different part of speech whose meanings can be easily understood from the rest of the entry.

Extra help is offered in Notes at the end of some entries. These include warnings about words which can be confused with each other and unusual inflected forms. The major differences between US and British spelling are noted.

Parts of Speech

abbr (abbreviation)
adj (adjective)
adv (adverb)
article
conj (conjunction)
interj (interjection)
modal verb
n (noun)
plural noun (always takes a plural verb)
prefix
prep (preposition)
pron (pronoun)
v (verb)

Symbols

① ② ③	indicates words which are commonly used, from ① the most basic and essential, ② frequent and useful to know, to ③ starting to develop a wider vocabulary.
■	before a new part of speech
○	before examples
□	before a phrase or idiom
◇	before an idiom
⇨	an explanation of the word will be found at the place indicated
➧	extra information will be found at the place indicated

Pronunciation

The following symbols have been used to show the pronunciation of the main words in the dictionary.

Stress is indicated by a main stress mark (ˈ) and a secondary stress mark (ˌ). Note that these are only guides, as the stress of the word changes according to its position in the sentence.

Vowels		*Consonants*	
æ	back	b	buck
ɑː	harm	d	dead
ɒ	stop	ð	other
aɪ	type	dʒ	jump
aʊ	how	f	fare
aɪə	hire	g	gold
aʊə	hour	h	head
ɔː	course	j	yellow
ɔɪ	annoy	k	cab
e	head	l	leave
eə	fair	m	mix
eɪ	make	n	nil
əʊ	go	ŋ	sing
ɜː	word	p	print
iː	keep	r	rest
i	happy	s	save
ə	about	ʃ	shop
ɪ	fit	t	take
ɪə	near	tʃ	change
u	annual	θ	theft
uː	pool	v	value
ʊ	book	w	work
ʊə	tour	x	loch
ʌ	shut	ʒ	measure
		z	zone

a[1] /eɪ/, **A** *noun* the first letter of the alphabet, followed by B ○ *Do you mean 'dependant' spelt with an 'a' or 'dependent' with an 'e'?* ◇ **from A to Z** completely, all the way through

a[2] /ə, eɪ/, **an** /ən, æn/ *article* **1.** one ○ *an enormous hole* ○ *a useful guidebook* ○ *She's bought a new car.* ○ *I want a cup of tea.* ○ *We had to wait an hour for the bus.* (NOTE: **an** is used before words beginning with **a, e, i, o, u** and with **h** if the **h** is not pronounced: *an apple* or *an hour.* **a** is used before words beginning with all other letters and also before **u** where **u** is pronounced /juː/ : *a useful guidebook*) **2.** for each or to each ○ *Apples cost £1.50 a kilo.* ○ *The car was travelling at 50 kilometres an hour.* ○ *He earns £100 a day.*

A&E /ˌeɪ ənd ˈiː/ *abbr* accident and emergency

aback /əˈbæk/ *adv* □ **taken aback** surprised and shocked by something unpleasant ○ *She was somewhat taken aback when he told her there was no train that evening*

abacus /ˈæbəkəs/ *noun* an object used for counting consisting of a frame with balls which can be moved on bars

③ **abandon** /əˈbændən/ (**abandons, abandoning, abandoned**) *verb* **1.** to leave someone or something in an unkind way ○ *The dog had been abandoned by its owner.* **2.** to leave somewhere for ever ○ *The village had been abandoned when the dam was built.* **3.** to give up or stop doing something ○ *The company has decided to abandon the project.* ○ *We abandoned the idea of setting up a London office.*

abandoned /əˈbændənd/ *adj* no longer used or lived in

abandonment /əˈbændənmənt/ *noun* the act or process of leaving someone or something without help

abashed /əˈbæʃt/ *adj* ashamed or embarrassed

abate /əˈbeɪt/ (**abates, abating, abated**) *verb* to become less strong or forceful (*formal*)

abattoir /ˈæbətwɑː/ *noun* a place where animals are killed for meat

abbey /ˈæbi/ *noun* **1.** a place where a community of Christian monks or nuns live **2.** a large church ○ *Westminster Abbey*

abbreviated /əˈbriːvieɪtɪd/ *adj* shortened by having something left out

abbreviation /əˌbriːviˈeɪʃ(ə)n/ *noun* a short form of a word. Compare **acronym**

abdicate /ˈæbdɪkeɪt/ (**abdicates, abdicating, abdicated**) *verb* **1.** to give up the position as king or queen of a country **2.** to fail to carry out a duty or responsibility (*formal*) (NOTE: + **abdication** *n*)

abdomen /ˈæbdəmən/ *noun* the space in the front part of your body, containing the stomach and other organs

abdominal /æbˈdɒmɪn(ə)l/ *adj* referring to the abdomen

abduct /æbˈdʌkt/ (**abducts, abducting, abducted**) *verb* to take someone away, usually by force (NOTE: + **abduction** *n*)

aberration /ˌæbəˈreɪʃ(ə)n/ *noun* an action or thing which is not usual or expected (*formal*)

abhorrent /əbˈhɒrənt/ *adj* horrible or disgusting (*formal*)

abide /əˈbaɪd/ (**abides, abiding, abode** or **abided**) *verb* **1.** □ **to abide by** to keep to rules, agreements or customs ○ *You must abide by the rules of the game.* ○ *We have to abide by the decision of the referee.* **2.** □ **can't abide something** to dislike something or someone ○ *I can't abide the smell of cigars.* ○ *If you can't abide him, why do you accept his invitation?*

abiding /əˈbaɪdɪŋ/ *adj* lasting a long time (*formal*)

① **ability** /əˈbɪlɪti/ (*plural* **abilities**) *noun* **1.** a natural tendency to do something well [~in] ○ *I admire his ability to stay calm under pressure.* ○ *We can develop their natural abilities in music further.* □ **I'll do it to the best of my ability** I'll do it as well as I can **2.** the fact of being clever ○ *suitable for different levels of ability* (NOTE: no plural in this sense)

abject /ˈæbdʒekt/ *adj (formal)* **1.** very bad ○ *abject poverty* **2.** making you feel ashamed ○ *an abject apology* ○ *abject terror*

ablaze /əˈbleɪz/ *adv* **1.** on fire ○ *Thirty hectares of trees were ablaze.* **2.** shining brightly ○ *At midnight the house was still ablaze with lights.*

① **able** /ˈeɪb(ə)l/ *adj* **1.** □ **to be able to do something** to be capable of something or have the chance to do something ○ *They weren't able to find the house.* ○ *Will you be able to come to the meeting?* **2.** good at doing something, or good at doing many things ○ *She's a very able manager.* ○ *There are special activities for able children.*

able-bodied /ˌeɪb(ə)l ˈbɒdid/ *adj* fit and healthy

ably /ˈeɪbli/ *adv* in a very competent or efficient way

abnormal /æbˈnɔːm(ə)l/ *adj* not normal

abnormality /ˌæbnɔːˈmælɪti/ (*plural* **abnormalities**) *noun* **1.** the state of being abnormal **2.** something which is abnormal

aboard /əˈbɔːd/ *adv, prep* on a ship or vehicle ○ *The passengers went aboard the 'Queen Elizabeth' at 10 p.m.* ○ *When the ship docked, customs officers came aboard to inspect the cargo.*

abode /əˈbəʊd/ *noun* the place where someone lives (*literary*) □ **of no fixed abode** with no permanent address (*formal*)

abolish /əˈbɒlɪʃ/ (**abolishes, abolishing, abolished**) *verb* to get rid of something such as a law or right

abolition /ˌæbəˈlɪʃ(ə)n/ *noun* the act of abolishing something such as a law or right

abominable /əˈbɒmɪnəb(ə)l/ *adj* very bad (*formal*)

Aboriginal /ˌæbəˈrɪdʒɪn(ə)l/ *adj* referring to Aborigines ■ *noun* same as **Aborigine**

Aborigine /æbəˈrɪdʒɪni/ *noun* an Australian who is a member of the peoples who lived in Australia before Europeans arrived

abort /əˈbɔːt/ (**aborts, aborting, aborted**) *verb* **1.** to stop something taking place **2.** to perform an abortion on a foetus

abortion /əˈbɔːʃ(ə)n/ *noun* the ending of a woman's pregnancy before a live infant can be born

abortive /əˈbɔːtɪv/ *adj* attempted without success

① **about** /əˈbaʊt/ *prep* **1.** referring to something ○ *He told me all about his operation.* ○ *What do you want to speak to the doctor about?* **2.** □ **to be about to do something** to be going to do something very soon ○ *We were about to go home when you arrived.* **3.** not exactly ○ *I've been waiting for about four hours.* ○ *She's only about fifteen years old.* □ **while you're about it** at the same time as the thing you are doing ○ *While you're about it, can you post this letter?* ◇ **how about? 1.** what do you think about? ○ *We can't find a new chairperson for the club – What about Sarah?* **2.** would you like a cup of tea? ◇ **while you're about it** at the same time as the thing you are doing ○ *While you're about it, can you post this letter?*

about-turn /əbaʊtˈtɜːn/, **about-face** *noun* **1.** an order to soldiers to turn to face in the opposite direction **2.** an act of changing your plans or policy to the opposite of what you did before

① **above** /əˈbʌv/ *prep* **1.** higher than ○ *The plane was flying above the clouds.* ○ *The temperature in the street was above 30 degrees.* ○ *At prices above £20, nobody will buy it.* **2.** older than ○ *If you are above 18, you have to pay the full fare.* **3.** louder than ○ *I couldn't hear the telephone above the noise of the drills.*

above board /əˌbʌv ˈbɔːd/ *adj* openly honest and legal

abrasive /əˈbreɪsɪv/ *adj* rude and impatient in dealing with people ■ *noun* a substance which rubs away a surface ○ *Avoid using abrasives to clean this surface.*

abreast /əˈbrest/ *adv* side by side

abridged /əˈbrɪdʒd/ *adj* shortened by removing parts of a text

② **abroad** /əˈbrɔːd/ *adv* in or to another country ○ *I lived abroad for three years.*

abrupt /əˈbrʌpt/ *adj* **1.** sudden **2.** using few words and not being very polite

abruptly /əˈbrʌptli/ *adv* briefly and impolitely

abruptness /əˈbrʌptnəs/ *noun* the fact of using few words and not being very polite

abscess /ˈæbses/ *noun* a collection of pus in the body

abscond /əbˈskɒnd/ (**absconds, absconding, absconded**) *verb (formal)* **1.** to leave somewhere suddenly and secretly [~with] ○ *The sports club's treasurer absconded with their funds.* **2.** to escape from prison

abseil /ˈæbseɪl/ (**abseils, abseiling, abseiled**) *verb* to come down a cliff or wall using a fixed rope wound around your body

② **absence** /'æbsəns/ *noun* the fact of being away from a place [~from] ○ *She did not explain her absence from the meeting.* □ **in the absence of, in someone's absence** because someone or something is not there ○ *In the absence of the chairman* or *In the chairman's absence, his deputy took over.* ○ *In the absence of any official support, we had to raise our own funds.*

③ **absent** /'æbsənt/ *adj* not there ○ *Ten of the staff are absent with flu.*

absentee /ˌæbsən'tiː/ *noun* a person who is not there

absenteeism /ˌæbs(ə)n'tiːɪz(ə)m/ *noun* the act or fact of deliberately staying away from work

absent-minded /ˌæbs(ə)nt 'maɪndɪd/ *adj* often forgetting things

② **absolute** /'æbsəluːt/ *adj* complete or total

① **absolutely** *adv* **1.** /'æbsəluːtli/ completely ○ *I am absolutely sure I left the keys in my coat pocket.* **2.** /ˌæbsə'luːtli/ yes, of course ○ *Did you build it yourself? – Absolutely!*

absolve /əb'zɒlv/ (**absolves, absolving, absolved**) *verb* to remove blame for a sin from someone

③ **absorb** /əb'zɔːb/ (**absorbs, absorbing, absorbed**) *verb* **1.** to take in something such as a liquid ○ *The water should be absorbed by the paper.* ○ *Salt absorbs moisture from the air.* **2.** to reduce a shock ○ *The car's springs are supposed to absorb any shock from the road surface.*

absorbent /əb'zɔːbənt/ *adj* which can absorb something such as a liquid

absorbing /əb'zɔːbɪŋ/ *adj* very interesting

absorption /əb'zɔːpʃən/ *noun* **1.** the act of absorbing something or of being absorbed **2.** the fact of being very interested in something

abstain /əb'steɪn/ (**abstains, abstaining, abstained**) *verb* **1.** deliberately not to do something [~from] ○ *His doctor recommended he should abstain from drinking coffee for six months.* **2.** not to vote on a matter

abstention /əb'stenʃən/ *noun* the act or fact of deliberately not voting on a matter

abstinence /'æbstɪnəns/ *noun* the act or fact of deliberately not doing something, especially not drinking alcohol

abstract /'æbstrækt/ *adj* **1.** which exists only in the mind rather than in the physical world **2.** (*of art*) which does not copy things exactly as they appear

abstract noun /ˌæbstrækt 'naʊn/ *noun* a noun that refers to an idea or quality, e.g. 'truth'

absurd /əb'sɜːd/ *adj* completely unreasonable or impossible to believe ○ *It's absurd to expect you will win the lottery if you only buy one ticket.*

abundance /ə'bʌndəns/ *noun* a large quantity

abundant /ə'bʌndənt/ *adj* existing in large quantities

abundantly /ə'bʌndənt(ə)li/ *adv* in large or more than large enough quantities

② **abuse**[1] /ə'bjuːs/ *noun* **1.** very bad treatment ○ *the sexual abuse of children* ○ *She suffered physical abuse in prison.* (NOTE: no plural in this sense) **2.** a bad use of something ○ *The government's action is an abuse of power.* **3.** rude words ○ *The people being arrested shouted abuse at the police.* (NOTE: no plural in this sense)

abuse[2] /ə'bjuːz/ (**abuses, abusing, abused**) *verb* **1.** to treat someone very badly, usually physically or sexually ○ *She had been abused as a child.* **2.** to make the wrong use of something ○ *He abused his position as finance director.* **3.** to say rude things about someone ○ *The crowd noisily abused the group of politicians as they entered the building.*

abusive /ə'bjuːsɪv/ *adj* **1.** rude and insulting ○ *an abusive letter* ○ *He had too much to drink and became abusive.* **2.** treating someone in a violent or cruel way, or referring to a violent and cruel situation ○ *an abusive father* ○ *an abusive relationship*

abysmal /ə'bɪzm(ə)l/ *adj* extremely bad

abyss /ə'bɪs/ *noun* **1.** a deep hole **2.** a horrible or frightening situation

② **academic** /ˌækə'demɪk/ *adj* **1.** relating to study at a university ○ *Members of the academic staff received a letter from the principal.* **2.** only in theory, not in practice ○ *It is only of academic interest.* ■ *noun* a university teacher ○ *All her friends are academics.*

academy /ə'kædəmi/ *noun* **1.** a college where specialised subjects are taught **2.** a private society for the study of art or science

accelerate /ək'seləreɪt/ (**accelerates, accelerating, accelerated**) *verb* to go faster ○ *Don't accelerate when you get to traffic lights.*

③ **accelerator** /ək'seləreɪtə/ *noun* a pedal which makes a car go faster

accent /'æksənt/ *noun* **1.** a particular way of pronouncing something ○ *He speaks with an American accent.* **2.** the stronger or louder part of a word or sentence ○ *In the word 'letter' the accent is on the first syllable.* **3.** a mark over a letter showing a particular way of pronouncing it ○ *Café has an accent on the 'e'.* **4.** emphasis ○ *The accent is on youth unemployment.*

accentuate /æk'sentʃueɪt/ (**accentuates, accentuating, accentuated**) *verb* to put emphasis on something

① **accept** /ək'sept/ (**accepts, accepting, accepted**) *verb* **1.** to take and keep a present ○ *We hope you will accept this little gift.* **2.** to say 'yes' or to agree to something ○ *She accepted the offer of a job in Australia.* ○ *I invited her to come with us and she accepted.* (NOTE: Do not confuse with **except**.)

③ **acceptable** /ək'septəb(ə)l/ *adj* good enough to be accepted, although not particularly good ○ *Fighting in the street is not acceptable behaviour.* ○ *Smoking is becoming less socially acceptable.* ○ *A small gift of flowers would be very acceptable.* ○ *The offer is not acceptable to the vendor.*

③ **acceptance** /ək'septəns/ *noun* **1.** the act of taking something which is offered **2.** the act or fact of agreeing to do something

③ **accepted** /ək'septɪd/ *adj* which is taken as correct by most people

① **access** /'ækses/ *noun* a way of reaching a place ○ *The concert hall has access for wheelchairs.* ○ *At present there is no access to the site.* □ **to have access to something** to be able to reach a place, meet a person, or obtain something ○ *I'll have access to the studio day and night.* ○ *The company has access to substantial funds.* ■ *verb* (**accesses, accessing, accessed**) to get information from a computer ○ *She tried to access the address list.*

access course /'ækses kɔːs/ *noun* a course of study designed to qualify someone for higher education

accessible /ək'sesɪb(ə)l/ *adj* **1.** easily reached ○ *They live on a farm which is not accessible by car.* **2.** easy to read or understand ○ *Her style of writing is quite accessible.* **3.** suitable for disabled people ○ *accessible toilets* ○ *accessible holidays*

③ **accessory** /ək'sesəri/ (*plural* **accessories**) *noun* **1.** a useful piece of equipment, added to others **2.** a small item of clothing **3.** a person who helps someone commit a crime [~to] ○ *an accessory to the crime*

① **accident** /'æksɪd(ə)nt/ *noun* **1.** an unpleasant thing which happens and causes damage or injury ○ *He lost his leg in an accident at work.* ○ *She was involved in a car accident and had to go to hospital.* **2.** something that happens unexpectedly ○ *Their third baby was an accident.* ◇ **by accident** without being planned or expected ○ *He found the missing papers by accident.*

accidental /ˌæksɪ'dent(ə)l/ *adj* happening without being planned or expected ○ *an accidental meeting* ○ *accidental damage* ○ *His death was not accidental.*

accidentally /ˌæksɪ'dent(ə)li/ *adv* without being planned or expected

acclaim /ə'kleɪm/ *noun* great praise

acclaimed /ə'kleɪmd/ *adj* much praised, especially publicly

accolade /'ækəleɪd/ *noun* a thing given to someone as a sign of praise

③ **accommodate** /ə'kɒmədeɪt/ (**accommodates, accommodating, accommodated**) *verb* to provide someone with a place to live

accommodating /ə'kɒmədeɪtɪŋ/ *adj* taking trouble to help people

② **accommodation** /əˌkɒmə'deɪʃ(ə)n/ *noun* a place to live or somewhere to stay for a short time ○ *Are you still looking for accommodation?* ○ *Visitors have difficulty in finding hotel accommodation during the summer.* (NOTE: In British English, **accommodation** has no plural.)

accompaniment /ə'kʌmp(ə)nimənt/ *noun* **1.** music played to accompany someone singing or playing an instrument ○ *a piece for violin with piano accompaniment* **2.** a thing which accompanies something ○ *They served cranberry sauce as an accompaniment to the turkey.*

② **accompany** /ə'kʌmp(ə)ni/ (**accompanies, accompanying, accompanied**) *verb* **1.** to go with someone or something ○ *She accompanied me to the door.* **2.** to play a musical instrument while someone else plays another instrument or sings ○ *She sang and was accompanied on the piano by her father.* (NOTE: accompanied **by** someone *or* something)

accomplice /ə'kʌmplɪs/ *noun* a person who helps another person to commit a crime

accomplish /ə'kʌmplɪʃ/ (**accomplishes, accomplishing, accomplished**) *verb* to do something successfully ○ *You won't accomplish anything by arguing.*

accomplished /ə'kʌmplɪʃt/ *adj* talented or skilled

accomplishment /ə'kʌmplɪʃmənt/ *noun* the successful finishing of something after a lot of work

accord /ə'kɔːd/ *noun* **1.** an agreement **2.** [~between] ▫ **of your own accord** without being ordered or forced by anyone ○ *Of his own accord he decided to sell the business and retire to a Greek island.* ■ *verb* (**accords, according, accorded**) to give something to someone as an honour

accordingly /ə'kɔːdɪŋli/ *adv* as a result of something just mentioned

① **according to** /ə'kɔːdɪŋ tuː/ *prep* **1.** as someone says or writes ○ *The washing machine was installed according to the manufacturer's instructions.* ○ *According to the police, the car was going too fast.* **2.** in agreement with rules or a system ○ *Everything went according to plan* or *schedule.* **3.** in relation to ○ *The teachers have separated the children into classes according to their ages.*

accost /ə'kɒst/ (**accosts, accosting, accosted**) *verb* to approach or stop someone in an aggressive or suggestive way

① **account** /ə'kaʊnt/ *noun* **1.** same as **bank account 2.** (*in a shop*) an arrangement which a customer makes with a shop to buy goods and pay for them later ○ *Put it on my account* or *Charge it to my account.* ■ *verb* (**accounts, accounting, accounted**) ▫ **to account for** to explain something that has happened (*formal*) ○ *He was asked to account for all his expenditure.* ◇ **by all accounts** as everyone says ○ *By all accounts, she is a very attractive woman.* ◇ **on account of** because of, due to ○ *The trains are late on account of the fog.* ○ *We don't use the car much on account of the price of petrol.* ◇ **on no account** not at all ◇ **on someone's account** for or because of someone ○ *I was worried on her account by the news the letter.* ◇ **take something into account** or **take account of something** to consider something ○ *We have to take the weather into account.*

accountable /ə'kaʊntəb(ə)l/ *adj* having to explain what you have done, especially how you have spent or received money

accountancy /ə'kaʊntənsi/ *noun* the study or the work of being an accountant

③ **accountant** /ə'kaʊntənt/ *noun* a person who deals with financial accounts

accounting /ə'kaʊntɪŋ/ *noun* the work of recording money paid, received, borrowed or owed

accredited /ə'kredɪtɪd/ *adj* given official approval

③ **accumulate** /ə'kjuːmjʊleɪt/ (**accumulates, accumulating, accumulated**) *verb* to increase gradually, or collect something over a period of time ○ *Fat had accumulated in the arteries.* ○ *We've accumulated so many books and papers since we moved into this office.*

accumulation /əˌkjuːmjʊ'leɪʃ(ə)n/ *noun* **1.** the action of accumulating something **2.** an amount of something built up over time

accuracy /'ækjʊrəsi/ *noun* the fact of being correct in every detail

② **accurate** /'ækjʊrət/ *adj* correct in every detail ○ *Are the figures accurate?* ○ *We asked them to make an accurate copy of the plan.*

accurately /'ækjʊrətli/ *adv* correctly ○ *The weather forecast accurately predicted the storm.*

accusation /ˌækjuː'zeɪʃ(ə)n/ *noun* a statement that someone has done something wrong

accusative /ə'kjuːzətɪv/ *adj* in the accusative

③ **accuse** /ə'kjuːz/ (**accuses, accusing, accused**) *verb* to say that someone has done something wrong ○ *The shopkeeper accused her of theft.* ○ *She was accused of stealing the money.* (NOTE: You accuse someone **of** a crime or **of** doing something.)

accusing /ə'kjuːzɪŋ/ *adj* as if you are accusing someone of something ○ *'You forgot to meet me,' she said in an accusing voice.*

accustom /ə'kʌstəm/ (**accustoms, accustoming, accustomed**) *verb* ▫ **to accustom yourself to something** to gradually accept that something is normal or usual ○ *accustomed to doing something* ○ *They had to accustom themselves to working in Swedish.* ○ *It took him some time to become accustomed to driving on the right-hand side of the road.*

accustomed /ə'kʌstəmd/ *adj* **1.** normal or usual **2.** used to [~to] ○ *He is accustomed to assistants and plenty of people to help* ○ *She was accustomed to walking her dog in the park every morning.*

ace /eɪs/ *noun* **1.** a playing card with one spot **2.** someone who is excellent at doing something **3.** a service in tennis which the opponent cannot return

③ **ache** /eɪk/ *noun* a pain that lasts for a while. ◊ **toothache**, **headache** ■ *verb* (**aches, aching, ached**) **1.** to hurt or feel pain that lasts for a while (*formal*) **2.** to feel a painful desire

① **achieve** /ə'tʃiːv/ (**achieves, achieving, achieved**) *verb* to succeed in doing something after trying very hard ○ *Have you achieved all your aims?* ○ *The company has achieved great success in the USA.*

② **achievement** /ə'tʃiːvmənt/ *noun* something which has been done successfully ○ *She is very modest about her achievements.* ○ *Coming sixth was a great achievement, since he had never entered the competition before.*

② **acid** /'æsɪd/ *noun* a chemical substance that is able to dissolve metals

acidic /ə'sɪdɪk/ *adj* having a sour taste

acidity /ə'sɪdɪti/ *noun* **1.** the percentage of acid in something **2.** bitter taste

acid rain /ˌæsɪd 'reɪn/ *noun* polluted rain which kills trees

acid test /ˌæsɪd 'test/ *noun* a test which will show the true value of something

③ **acknowledge** /ək'nɒlɪdʒ/ (**acknowledges, acknowledging, acknowledged**) *verb* **1.** to say that something has been received ○ *She didn't acknowledge receiving my letter.* **2.** to accept that something is true [~that] ○ *She acknowledged that she had seen me there.*

acknowledgement /ək'nɒlɪdʒmənt/ *noun* a letter or note sent to say that something has been received

acne /'ækni/ *noun* spots on the skin, usually on the face, neck and shoulders

acolyte /'ækəlaɪt/ *noun* a person who supports someone else, often without criticising their behaviour or opinions

acorn /'eɪkɔːn/ *noun* the fruit of an oak tree

acoustic /ə'kuːstɪk/ *adj* referring to sound

acoustics /ə'kuːstɪks/ *plural noun* the ability to carry sound without changing its quality ○ *The acoustics in the concert hall are good.*

acquaint /ə'kweɪnt/ (**acquaints, acquainting, acquainted**) *verb* **1.** □ **to be acquainted with someone *or* something** to have some knowledge of someone or something (*formal*) ○ *Is he acquainted with the details of the case?* ○ *She is acquainted with my father.* **2.** to inform someone

acquaintance /ə'kweɪntəns/ *noun* a person you know slightly ○ *She has many acquaintances in the travel industry but no real friends.*

② **acquire** /ə'kwaɪə/ (**acquires, acquiring, acquired**) *verb* to become the owner of something ○ *She has acquired a large collection of old books.*

③ **acquisition** /ˌækwɪ'zɪʃ(ə)n/ *noun* **1.** the act of acquiring something ○ *His acquisition of half the shares in the company surprised the staff.* **2.** a thing which has been acquired

acquisitive /ə'kwɪzɪtɪv/ *adj* always wanting to acquire new things

acquit /ə'kwɪt/ (**acquits, acquitting, acquitted**) *verb* to state formally that someone is not guilty

acquittal /ə'kwɪt(ə)l/ *noun* a decision by a court that someone is not guilty

acre /'eɪkə/ *noun* a measure of land, 4840 square yards or 0.4047 hectares (NOTE: The plural is used with figures, except before a noun: *a farm of 250 acres* or *a 250-acre farm.*)

acrid /'ækrɪd/ *adj* with a bitter smell

acrimonious /ˌækrɪ'məʊniəs/ *adj* angry and bitter

acrobat /'ækrəbæt/ *noun* a person who performs difficult and exciting physical movements for the public

acrobatic /ˌækrə'bætɪk/ *adj* lively and energetic

acrobatics /ˌækrə'bætɪks/ *plural noun* **1.** acrobatic movements **2.** skills used in doing something difficult ○ *We enjoyed the verbal acrobatics as they tried to explain their actions.*

acronym /'ækrənɪm/ *noun* a word made from the first letters of the name of something ○ *NATO and AIDS are both acronyms.* Compare **abbreviation**

① **across** /ə'krɒs/ *prep* **1.** from one side to the other ○ *Don't run across the road without looking to see if there is any traffic coming.* **2.** on the other side of ○ *He saw her across the street.* ■ *adv* from one side to the other ○ *The river is only twenty feet across.* ○ *The stream is very narrow – you can easily jump across.*

across-the-board /əˌkrɒs ðə 'bɔːd/ *adj, adv* having the same effect on everyone or everything

acrylic /ə'krɪlɪk/ *noun* a synthetic substance used to make many products, including fibres ■ *adj* made from acrylic

① **act** /ækt/ *noun* **1.** something which is done ○ *He thanked her for the many acts of friendship she had shown him over the years.* **2.** a part of a play or show ○ *Act 2 of the play takes place in the garden.* **3.** a short performance ○ *The show includes acts by several young singers.* **4.** a law passed by Parliament ○ *an act to ban the sale of weapons* ■ *verb* (**acts, acting, acted**) **1.** to take part in a performance such as a film or play ○ *She's acted on TV many times.* ○ *He acted the part of Hamlet in the film.* **2.** to do something ○ *You will have to act quickly if you want to stop the fire.* □ **to act as someone** or **something** to do the work of someone or something ○ *The thick curtain acts as a screen to cut out noise from the street.* **3.** to behave in a particular way ○ *She's been acting very strangely.* ○ *She acted in a very responsible way.* **4.** to take effect ○ *How long will the drug take to act?* ◇ **to get your act together** to organise yourself properly ○ *If they don't get their act together, they'll miss their train.*

acting /ˈæktɪŋ/ *noun* the profession of an actor

① **action** /ˈækʃən/ *noun* **1.** the fact of doing something ○ *We recommend swift action to prevent the problem spreading.* ○ *What action are you going to take to prevent accidents?* **2.** something that is done ○ *They've shown their commitment by their actions.* **3.** a movement ○ *Avoid sudden actions that could alarm the animals.* **4.** the things that happen in a performance such as a play or film ○ *The action of the play takes place in a flat in London.* **5.** a case in a law court where someone tries to get money from someone else ○ *an action for libel* or *a libel action* ○ *to bring an action for damages against someone* ◇ **out of action** not working ○ *The car has been out of action for a week.*

action-packed /ˈækʃən pækt/ *adj* with a large number of exciting events

action replay /ˌækʃən ˈriːpleɪ/ *noun* a section of a sporting event which is shown again on TV at a slower speed, so that the action can be examined carefully

③ **activate** /ˈæktɪveɪt/ (**activates, activating, activated**) *verb* to make something start to work

② **active** /ˈæktɪv/ *adj* **1.** involved in an activity or activities, especially in an energetic way ○ *He didn't play an active part in the attack on the police station.* ○ *My grandmother is still very active at the age of 88.* **2.** (*of a volcano*) exploding or likely to explode ○ *Scientists think the volcano is no longer active.* ■ *noun* the form of a verb which shows that the subject is doing something (NOTE: If you say 'the car hit him' the verb is active, but in 'he was hit by the car' it is passive.)

activist /ˈæktɪvɪst/ *noun* a person who vigorously supports an organisation that works for social or political change

① **activity** /ækˈtɪvɪti/ (*plural* **activities**) *noun* **1.** the act or fact of being active ○ *There is a possibility of volcanic activity.* **2.** something that someone does to pass time pleasantly ○ *Children are offered various holiday activities – sailing, windsurfing and water-skiing.*

actor /ˈæktə/ *noun* a person who acts in the theatre, in films or on TV

actress /ˈæktrəs/ *noun* a woman who acts in the theatre, in films or on TV (NOTE: Many women prefer to call themselves actors rather than actresses.)

① **actual** /ˈæktʃuəl/ *adj* real ○ *It looks quite small but the actual height is 5 metres.* ○ *Her actual words were much stronger.*

① **actually** /ˈæktʃuəli/ *adv* really ○ *It looks quite small, but actually it is over 5 metres high.* ○ *He said he was ill, but actually he wanted to go to the football match.*

acupuncture /ˈækjʊpʌŋktʃə/ *noun* a treatment in which needles are stuck through the skin in order to reduce pain or other aspects of an illness

acute /əˈkjuːt/ *adj* **1.** (*of serious illness or pain*) which starts suddenly and lasts for a short time ○ *a child with acute bronchitis* ○ *The pain was very acute.* Compare **chronic** **2.** able to notice something easily ○ *Dogs have an acute sense of smell.*

acute accent /əˌkjuːt ˈæksənt/ *noun* a mark sloping forwards over a vowel, indicating a change of sound

③ **ad** /æd/ *noun* an advertisement (*informal*) ○ *If you want to sell your car quickly, put an ad in the paper.*

AD /ˌeɪ ˈdiː/ used before or after a date to show that it is after the birth of Jesus Christ ○ *Claudius invaded Britain in 43 AD.* Full form **Anno Domini**. Compare **BC** (NOTE: Latin for 'in the year of our Lord'. Sometimes PE (Present Era) or CE (Common Era) is used to avoid referring to Jesus Christ.)

adage /ˈædɪdʒ/ *noun* a traditional statement about an aspect of everyday life ○ *According to the old adage, 'time is a great healer'.*

Adam's apple /ˌædəmz ˈæp(ə)l/ *noun* a piece of cartilage that makes a lump in the front of the throat, which can sometimes be seen in men

③ **adapt** /ə'dæpt/ (**adapts, adapting, adapted**) *verb* **1.** to change something to be suitable for a new situation [~for] ○ *She adapted the story for TV.* ○ *The car has been adapted for disabled drivers.* **2.** to change your behaviour to fit into a new situation [~to] ○ *We'll all have to learn to adapt to the new system.*

adaptable /ə'dæptəb(ə)l/ *adj* able to change or be changed easily to deal with new situations or uses

③ **adaptation** /ˌædæp'teɪʃ(ə)n/, **adaption** *noun* **1.** a change which fits new situations or uses **2.** something such as a film or play which has been developed from another

① **add** /æd/ (**adds, adding, added**) *verb* **1.** to make a total of numbers ○ *If you add all these numbers together it should make fifty.* (NOTE: **Adding** is usually shown by the sign + : **10 + 4 = 14**.) **2.** to join one thing to another [~to] ○ *Interest is added to the account monthly.* ○ *Put a teabag into the pot and add boiling water.* ○ *By building the annexe, they have added thirty rooms to the hotel.* **3.** to say or to write something more ○ *I have nothing to add to what I put in my letter.* ○ *She added that we still owed her some money for work she did last month.*

add up *phrasal verb* to make a total □ **the figures do not add up** the total is not correct ◇ **not add up** (*of information*) to be confusing or difficult to accept as true ○ *The story she told the police simply did not add up.*

add up to *phrasal verb* to make a total of something

added /'ædɪd/ *adj* included as well as what there is already

addict /'ædɪkt/ *noun* a person who cannot stop doing something

addicted /ə'dɪktɪd/ *adj* unable to stop doing something

addiction /ə'dɪkʃ(ə)n/ *noun* the fact or state of being unable to stop doing something

addictive /ə'dɪktɪv/ *adj* which people can become addicted to

① **addition** /ə'dɪʃ(ə)n/ *noun* **1.** someone or something added to something else [~to] ○ *the latest addition to the family* ○ *He showed us the recent additions to his collection of paintings.* **2.** the act of adding figures to make a total ○ *You don't need a calculator to do a simple addition.* ◇ **in addition** as well ◇ **in addition to** as well as ○ *There are twelve registered letters to be sent in addition to this parcel.*

② **additional** /ə'dɪʃ(ə)nəl/ *adj* included as well as what there is already

additive /'ædɪtɪv/ *noun* a substance which is added to something, especially to food to preserve it or to alter the taste or colour

① **address** /ə'dres/ *noun* **1.** a set of details of the number of a house, the name of a street and the town where someone lives or works ○ *What is the doctor's address?* ○ *Our address is: 1 Cambridge Road, Teddington, Middlesex.* **2.** the set of letters, symbols and numbers that identify someone's email account ■ *verb* (**addresses, addressing, addressed**) **1.** to write details such as someone's name, street and town on a letter or parcel ○ *That letter is addressed to me – don't open it!* **2.** to speak or write to someone ○ *Please address your questions to the information office.* ○ *Teachers are not normally addressed as 'Sir' here.* **3.** to make a formal speech to a group ○ *The chairman addressed the meeting.*

address book /ə'dres bʊk/ *noun* a notebook or computer file in which you can record people's names, home addresses, telephone numbers and email addresses

③ **adequate** /'ædɪkwət/ *adj* **1.** enough for a purpose ○ *We don't have adequate supplies for the whole journey.* ○ *His salary alone is barely adequate to support his family.* **2.** only just satisfactory

adhere /əd'hɪə/ (**adheres, adhering, adhered**) *verb* to attach physically to something (*formal*)

adhere to *verb* to keep to a rule, agreement or promise

adhesive /əd'hiːsɪv/ *adj* able to stick to things ■ *noun* a substance which sticks things together

ad hoc /ˌæd 'hɒk/ *adj* arranged for a specific case ○ *an ad hoc decision* ○ *We order the books on an ad hoc basis.* ■ *adv* as necessary, without planning in advance ○ *I did it ad hoc.*

adj, adj. *abbr* adjective

adjacent /ə'dʒeɪs(ə)nt/ *adj* very close to or almost touching something [~to] ○ *My office is in an adjacent building.* ○ *Our house is adjacent to the park.*

adjectival /ˌædʒɪk'taɪv(ə)l/ *adj* used like an adjective

① **adjective** /'ædʒɪktɪv/ *noun* a word which describes a noun ○ *In the phrase 'a big black cloud', 'big' and 'black' are both adjectives.*

adjoin /ə'dʒɔɪn/ (**adjoins, adjoining, adjoined**) *verb* to be close to or touching something

adjourn /ə'dʒɜːn/ (**adjourns, adjourning, adjourned**) *verb* to stop something such as a meeting or court proceedings in order to continue at a later time or date (NOTE: + **adjournment** *n*)

adjudicate /ə'dʒuːdɪkeɪt/ (**adjudicates, adjudicating, adjudicated**) *verb* **1.** to give an official decision in a legal matter or a disagreement **2.** to act as a judge in a competition (NOTE: + **adjudicator** *n*)

③ **adjust** /ə'dʒʌst/ (**adjusts, adjusting, adjusted**) *verb* to make a slight change to something ○ *I need to adjust this belt a bit.* □ **to adjust to something** to become used to something ○ *How are you adjusting to being a parent?*

adjustable /ə'dʒʌstəb(ə)l/ *adj* which can be adjusted

③ **adjustment** /ə'dʒʌstmənt/ *noun* a slight change to make something work well

ad-lib /ˌæd 'lɪb/ (**ad-libs, ad-libbing, ad-libbed**) *verb* to speak without a prepared set of words

admin /'ædmɪn/ *noun* **1.** the work of administration **2.** staff dealing with administration (NOTE: singular or plural verb)

administer /əd'mɪnɪstə/ (**administers, administering, administered**) *verb* **1.** to manage or organise something **2.** to give someone a drug or medical treatment (*formal*)

② **administration** /ədˌmɪnɪ'streɪʃ(ə)n/ *noun* **1.** the act of organising something such as a company or office ○ *Hospital administration must be improved.* ○ *Who's in charge of administration here?* **2.** a particular government ○ *the Bush Administration*

③ **administrative** /əd'mɪnɪstrətɪv/ *adj* referring to administration

③ **administrator** /əd'mɪnɪstreɪtə/ *noun* a person who runs an organisation

admirable /'ædm(ə)rəb(ə)l/ *adj* which must be approved of and praised

admiral /'ædm(ə)rəl/ *noun* a high-ranking officer in a country's navy

admiration /ˌædmə'reɪʃ(ə)n/ *noun* respect for someone or something

③ **admire** /əd'maɪə/ (**admires, admiring, admired**) *verb* to consider someone or something with approval ○ *He was admired for his skill as a violinist.* ○ *We admired the view from the balcony.*

admirer /əd'maɪərə/ *noun* a person who loves someone or is attracted by someone

admiring /əd'maɪərɪŋ/ *adj* showing that you admire someone or something

③ **admission** /əd'mɪʃ(ə)n/ *noun* **1.** the act or fact of being allowed to go into a place ○ *Admission to the exhibition is free on Sundays.* ○ *My friend was refused admission to the restaurant because he was not wearing a tie.* **2.** a statement saying that something bad is true ○ *Her admission that she had taken the money led to her arrest.* ◇ **no admission** no one can enter

admission fee /əd'mɪʃ(ə)n fiː/ *noun* an amount of money paid to go into a place such as a museum

① **admit** /əd'mɪt/ (**admits, admitting, admitted**) *verb* to allow someone to go into a place ○ *Children are admitted free, but adults have to pay.* ○ *This ticket admits three people.* □ **to admit (to) doing something** to say that you have done something wrong ○ *They admitted stealing the car.*

admittance /əd'mɪt(ə)ns/ *noun* permission for someone to go into a place (*formal*)

admittedly /əd'mɪtɪdli/ *adv* admitting that something is true

adolescence /ˌædə'les(ə)ns/ *noun* a period between childhood and adulthood, between the ages of 12 and 18

adolescent /ˌædə'les(ə)nt/ *noun* a young person between the ages of 12 and 18

② **adopt** /ə'dɒpt/ (**adopts, adopting, adopted**) *verb* **1.** to take someone legally as a son or daughter ○ *They have adopted a little boy.* **2.** to decide to start using something ○ *We need to adopt a more flexible approach.*

adopted /ə'dɒptɪd/ *adj* taken legally as someone's son or daughter

③ **adoption** /ə'dɒpʃən/ *noun* **1.** the legal taking of someone as a son or daughter **2.** the process of starting to do or have something [~of] ○ *the adoption of a new company name and logo*

adoptive /ə'dɒptɪv/ *adj* having adopted a child as a son or daughter ○ *my adoptive parents*

adorable /ə'dɔːrəb(ə)l/ *adj* attractive and appealing

adoration /ˌædə'reɪʃ(ə)n/ *noun* admiration or love

adore /ə'dɔː/ (**adores, adoring, adored**) *verb* to like someone or something very much

adoring /ə'dɔːrɪŋ/ *adj* who or which adores

adorn /ə'dɔːn/ (**adorns, adorning, adorned**) *verb* to decorate something with ornaments (*formal*)

adrenalin /ə'drenəlɪn/ *noun* a hormone that speeds up the heartbeat and raises the blood pressure when a person or animal is experiencing surprise, shock, fear or excitement

adrift /ə'drɪft/ *adv* floating on the water but not being guided by anyone

ADSL /ˌeɪ diː es 'el/ *abbr* asymmetrical digital subscriber line

adulation /ˌædjʊ'leɪʃ(ə)n/ *noun* excessive praise

② **adult** /'ædʌlt/ *noun* a fully-grown person ■ *adj* **1.** fully grown ○ *an adult tiger* **2.** relating to a mature person or people ○ *adult fiction*

adultery /ə'dʌlt(ə)ri/ *noun* sexual intercourse with someone who is not your husband or wife

adulthood /'ædʌlthʊd/ *noun* the period when someone is an adult

adv, adv. *abbr* **1.** adverb **2.** adverbial

② **advance** /əd'vɑːns/ *verb* (**advances, advancing, advanced**) to move forward ○ *The police slowly advanced across the square.* ■ *noun* **1.** a movement forwards ○ *The police have made some advances in their fight against crime.* ○ *The team made an advance into their opponents' half.* **2.** money paid as a loan or as a part of a payment to be made later ■ *adj* done before something happens ○ *She made an advance payment of £3000.* ◇ **in advance** earlier than the time something happens ○ *You must phone in advance to make an appointment.* ○ *They asked us to pay £200 in advance.*

③ **advanced** /əd'vɑːnst/ *adj* studied at a higher level ○ *He's studying advanced mathematics.* ○ *She's studying for an advanced degree.*

advances /əd'vɑːnsɪz/ *plural noun* attempts to be friendly with someone

① **advantage** /əd'vɑːntɪdʒ/ *noun* something which will help you to be successful ○ *Being able to drive a car is an advantage.* ○ *Knowledge of two foreign languages is an advantage in this job.* ○ *She has several advantages over the other job candidates.* ◇ **to take advantage of something** to profit from something ○ *They took advantage of the cheap fares on offer.* ◇ **to take advantage of someone** to get something unfairly from someone ◇ **to (good *or* best) advantage** in a way that helps someone or something appear especially good ○ *She used her knowledge of Italian to good advantage.*

advantageous /ˌædvən'teɪdʒəs/ *adj* likely to help or make something successful

advent /'ædvent/ *noun* the introduction or appearance of something new

adventure /əd'ventʃə/ *noun* a new, exciting and dangerous experience ○ *I must tell you about our adventures in the desert.*

adventurous /əd'ventʃ(ə)rəs/ *adj* **1.** happy to do something risky **2.** exciting and full of adventure

② **adverb** /'ædvɜːb/ *noun* a word which applies to a verb, an adjective, another adverb or a whole sentence ○ *In the sentence 'He walked slowly, because the snow was very thick.' both 'slowly' and 'very' are adverbs.*

adverbial /æd'vɜːbiəl/ *adj* used like an adverb

adversary /'ædvəs(ə)ri/ (*plural* **adversaries**) *noun* the person you are fighting or opposed to

adverse /'ædvɜːs/ *adj* (*of conditions*) unpleasant and unwanted ○ *an adverse reaction* ○ *adverse effects*

adversity /əd'vɜːsɪti/ *noun* difficult times, when you have to face all sorts of problems

③ **advert** /'ædvɜːt/ *noun* same as **advertisement**

advertise /'ædvətaɪz/ (**advertises, advertising, advertised**) *verb* to make sure that people know that something is for sale, or that something is going to happen [~for] ○ *Did you see that the restaurant is advertising cheap meals on Sundays?* ○ *The company is advertising for secretaries.* ○ *I saw this watch advertised in the paper.*

③ **advertisement** /əd'vɜːtɪsmənt/ *noun* an announcement which tries to make sure that people know that something is for sale, or that something is going to happen

① **advertising** /'ædvətaɪzɪŋ/ *noun* the act of making sure that people know that something is for sale, or that something is going to happen ○ *The company has increased the amount of money it spends on advertising.* ○ *They spent millions on the advertising campaign.*

① **advice** /əd'vaɪs/ *noun* an opinion that someone gives you about what you should do ○ *He went to the bank manager for advice on how to pay his debts.* ○ *They would not listen to the doctor's advice.* ○ *My* *grandfather gave me a very useful piece of advice.* ○ *His mother's advice was to stay in bed.* (NOTE: no plural: use *some advice* or, for one item, *a piece of advice*)

advisable /əd'vaɪzəb(ə)l/ *adj* which is recommended

① **advise** /əd'vaɪz/ (**advises, advising, advised**) *verb* **1.** to suggest to someone what they should do ○ *He advised her to save some of the money.* **2.** to suggest that something should not be done [~against] ○ *He advised against buying the house.* **3.** to tell someone officially that something has happened [~that] (*formal*) ○ *They advised us that the sale of the house had been completed.*

③ **adviser** /əd'vaɪzə/, **advisor** *noun* someone who helps people to make decisions about what to do

advisory /əd'vaɪz(ə)ri/ *adj* giving advice

advocacy /'ædvəkəsi/ *noun* strong support for a cause or policy

advocate[1] /'ædvəkət/ *noun* **1.** a person who strongly supports someone or something **2.** a lawyer in a Scottish court

advocate[2] /'ædvəkeɪt/ (**advocates, advocating, advocated**) *verb* to say that something is a good thing

aerial /'eəriəl/ *noun* a piece of equipment for receiving radio or TV signals

aerobic /eə'rəʊbɪk/ *adj* using or needing oxygen

aerobics /eə'rəʊbɪks/ *noun* active exercises which aim to increase the amount of oxygen taken into the body (NOTE: takes a singular verb)

aerodynamic /ˌeərəʊdaɪ'næmɪk/ *adj* referring to the movement of objects through the air

aerodynamics /ˌeərəʊdaɪ'næmɪks/ *noun* the science of the movement of objects through the air (NOTE: takes a singular verb)

aeronautical /ˌeərə'nɔːtɪk(ə)l/ *adj* referring to the flying of aircraft

③ **aeroplane** /'eərəpleɪn/ *noun* a vehicle which flies in the air, carrying passengers or goods

aerosol /'eərəsɒl/ *noun* tiny particles of a chemical in the air

aerospace /'eərəʊspeɪs/ *noun* earth's atmosphere and space beyond it

aesthetic /iːs'θetɪk/ *adj* pleasant, from an artistic point of view (NOTE: The usual US spelling is **esthetic**.)

aesthetics /iːs'θetɪks/ *noun* the science of and study of beauty, especially in art (NOTE: takes a singular verb. The usual US spelling is **esthetics**.)

affable /'æfəb(ə)l/ *adj* pleasant and easy to talk to

① **affair** /ə'feə/ *noun* **1.** something which is relevant to one person or group of people only ○ *That's his affair – it's nothing to do with me.* ○ *It's an affair for the police.* ○ *His business affairs were very complicated.* **2.** a sexual relationship with someone who is not your husband or wife ○ *He's having an affair with his boss's wife.* **3.** an event ○ *The party is just a family affair.* **4.** an event or situation that shocks people ○ *The whole sorry affair was on the front page of the newspapers for days.* ■ *plural noun* **affairs** situations or activities relating to public or private life □ **the state of affairs** the general situation

① **affect** /ə'fekt/ (**affects, affecting, affected**) *verb* to have an influence on someone or something ○ *The new regulations have affected our business.* ○ *Train services have been seriously affected by the strike.*

affectation /ˌæfek'teɪʃ(ə)n/ *noun* something which someone says or does in a way that does not seem natural or sincere

affected /ə'fektɪd/ *adj* not natural or sincere

affection /ə'fekʃ(ə)n/ *noun* a feeling of liking someone, especially a friend [~for] ○ ' ○ *They had no affection for their former home.* ○ *She always spoke of him with great affection.*

affectionate /ə'fekʃənət/ *adj* showing love

affidavit /ˌæfɪ'deɪvɪt/ *noun* a written statement which is signed and sworn before a solicitor

affiliate /ə'fɪlieɪt/ (**affiliates, affiliating, affiliated**) *verb* to connect something or someone to a larger group

affiliated /ə'fɪlieɪtɪd/ *adj* connected to or with another as an affiliate

affiliation /əˌfɪli'eɪʃ(ə)n/ *noun* the act or fact of being affiliated

affinity /ə'fɪnɪti/ *noun* the fact of being similar in character

affirm /ə'fɜːm/ (**affirms, affirming, affirmed**) *verb* to state publicly that something is true

affirmation /ˌæfə'meɪʃ(ə)n/ *noun* a statement that something is true

affirmative /ə'fɜːmətɪv/ *noun* a word or statement meaning 'yes'

affix /'æfɪks/ *noun* a group of letters added to the beginning or end of a word to make a new word

afflict /ə'flɪkt/ (**afflicts, afflicting, afflicted**) *verb* to make someone suffer (*formal; of a serious problem or illness*)

affliction /ə'flɪkʃ(ə)n/ *noun* (*formal*) **1.** an illness affecting someone physically or mentally **2.** something that causes distress

affluence /'æfluəns/ *noun* wealth

affluent /'æfluənt/ *adj* very rich

① **afford** /ə'fɔːd/ (**affords, affording, afforded**) *verb* **1.** to have enough money to pay for something [to do something] ○ *How will you afford such an expensive holiday?* □ **be unable to afford, can't afford** to be unable to accept something because it might cause you a problem ○ *I can't afford a delay of more than three weeks.* **2.** to have enough time or resources to do something without it causing a problem ○ *We can afford to wait three weeks but no longer.* ○ *They couldn't afford to lose any more public support.* (NOTE: always with **can** or **could**)

affordable /ə'fɔːdəb(ə)l/ *adj* which can be afforded

affront /ə'frʌnt/ *noun* an action which insults someone

afloat /ə'fləʊt/ *adv* **1.** floating, not sinking ○ *She kept afloat by holding on to a piece of wood.* ○ *Our boat was driven onto the beach by the storm, but we managed to get it afloat again.* **2.** (*of a company*) not in financial difficulties ○ *I wonder how they manage to stay afloat when the market is so difficult.*

① **afraid** /ə'freɪd/ *adj* frightened of something or someone ○ *I am afraid of snakes.* ○ *He is too afraid to climb the ladder.* ◇ **to be afraid (that)** to be sorry to say ○ *I'm afraid that all the cakes have been sold.* ○ *You can't see the boss – I'm afraid he's ill.* ○ *Have you got a pocket calculator? – No, I'm afraid not.*

① **African** /'æfrɪkən/ *adj* referring to Africa ■ *noun* a person from Africa

African American /ˌæfrɪkən ə'merɪkən/, **Afro-American** *noun* an American whose ancestors came from Africa

African Caribbean /ˌæfrɪkən kærɪ'biːən/ *noun* someone from the Caribbean whose ancestors came from Africa

Afro- /æfrəʊ/ *prefix* African, or between Africa and another country

Afro-Caribbean /ˌæfrəʊ kærɪ'biːən/ *noun* same as **African Caribbean**

① **after** /'ɑːftə/ *prep* **1.** following or next in order to ○ *If today is Tuesday, the day after tomorrow is Thursday.* ○ *They spoke one after the other.* ○ *What's the letter after Q in the alphabet?* **2.** later than ○ *We arrived after six o'clock.* ○ *We don't let the children go out alone after dark.* ■ *conj* later than a time ○ *After the snow fell, the motorways were blocked.* ○ *Phone me after you get home.* (NOTE: **after** is used with many phrasal verbs: **to look after**, **to take after**, etc.) ◇ **after all 1.** in spite of everything ○ *Everything was all right after all.* **2.** the fact is ○ *He should be OK; after all, he is eighteen now.* ◇ **after you** you go first

after-effects /ˌɑːftə ɪ'fekt/ *plural noun* effects which follow after something ○ *The after-effects of the bomb lasted for years.* ○ *The operation can have some unpleasant after-effects.*

afterlife /'ɑːftəlaɪf/ *noun* **1.** life believed to go on after death **2.** a stage of life that follows a period or event

aftermath /'ɑːftəmɑːθ/ *noun* the period immediately after a bad event when its effects are seen

① **afternoon** /ˌɑːftə'nuːn/ *noun* the time between midday and the evening ○ *He always has a little sleep in the afternoon.* ○ *There is an afternoon flight to Paris.* ○ *Can we meet tomorrow afternoon?*

afters /'ɑːftəz/ *noun* a sweet course of a meal (*informal*)

aftershave /'ɑːftəʃeɪv/, **aftershave lotion** *noun* a lotion for soothing skin after shaving

aftershock /'ɑːftəʃɒk/ *noun* a light earth tremor felt after a major earthquake

aftertaste /'ɑːftəteɪst/ *noun* **1.** a taste that continues after something has been eaten or drunk **2.** an unpleasant feeling after something has happened

afterthought /'ɑːftəθɔːt/ *noun* something which you only think of or do later

① **afterwards** /'ɑːftəwədz/ *adv* later ○ *We'll have lunch first and go shopping afterwards.*

① **again** /ə'gen/ *adv* **1.** another time ○ *He had to take his driving test again.* □ **again and again** several times, usually in a firm or determined way ○ *The police officer asked the same question again and again.* **2.** back as you were before ○ *Although I like going on holiday, I'm always glad to be home again.*

① **against** /ə'genst/ *prep* **1.** so as to touch ○ *He was leaning against the wall.* ○ *She hit her head against the low doorway.* **2.** in opposition to ○ *England is playing against South Africa tomorrow.* ○ *It's hard cycling uphill against the wind.* ○ *They went against his advice.*

① **age** /eɪdʒ/ *noun* the number of years which you have lived ○ *She is thirty years of age.* ○ *He looks younger than his age.* ■ *plural noun* **ages** a very long time (*informal*) ○ *I've been waiting here for ages.* ○ *It took us ages to get served.* ◇ **under age** younger than the legal age to do something ○ *under-age drinkers*

② **aged¹** /eɪdʒd/ *adj* with the age of ○ *a girl aged nine* ○ *She died last year, aged 83.*

aged² /'eɪdʒɪd/ *adj* very old ○ *an aged man*

age group /'eɪdʒ gruːp/ *noun* all the people of a particular age

ageing /'eɪdʒɪŋ/ *adj* which is becoming older (NOTE: The US spelling is **aging**.)

age limit /'eɪdʒ ˌlɪmɪt/ *noun* the youngest or oldest age at which you are allowed to do something

① **agency** /'eɪdʒənsi/ (*plural* **agencies**) *noun* an office which represents another firm ○ *an advertising agency*

③ **agenda** /ə'dʒendə/ *noun* **1.** a list of points for discussion □ **what's on the agenda?** what are we going to discuss? **2.** a set of things that someone plans to do □ **top of your agenda** what someone wants most ○ *A holiday is top of my agenda at present.*

③ **agent** /'eɪdʒənt/ *noun* **1.** a person who works for or represents someone else ○ *Our head office is in London but we have an agent in Paris.* **2.** a person or thing that causes something ○ *an agent of change*

age of consent /ˌeɪdʒ əv kən'sent/ *noun* the age at which someone can legally agree to have sex

age-old /'eɪdʒ əʊld/ *adj, adv* which has existed for a long time

aggravate /'ægrəveɪt/ (**aggravates, aggravating, aggravated**) *verb* **1.** to make something worse **2.** to annoy someone

aggravating /'ægrəveɪtɪŋ/ *adj* who or which annoys someone (*informal*)

③ **aggression** /ə'greʃ(ə)n/ *noun* a feeling of anger against someone that is expressed, especially in physical force □ **an act of aggression** an attack on someone

③ **aggressive** /ə'gresɪv/ *adj* ready to attack someone

aggressively /ə'gresɪvli/ *adv* as if wanting to attack someone

aggressor /ə'gresə/ *noun* a person or country that attacks another

aggrieved /ə'griːvd/ *adj* annoyed because you have been badly treated

aggro /'ægrəʊ/ *noun* violent quarrelling or disagreement

aghast /ə'gɑːst/ *adj* filled with horror and amazement

agile /'ædʒaɪl/ *adj* that can move easily

agitate /'ædʒɪteɪt/ (**agitates, agitating, agitated**) *verb* to stir up public opinion for or against something (NOTE: + **agitator** *n*)

agitated /'ædʒɪteɪtɪd/ *adj* very nervous, worried or upset and often not able to keep still

AGM /ˌeɪ dʒiː 'em/ *abbr* annual general meeting

agnostic /æg'nɒstɪk/ *noun* a person who believes that no one can know if God exists. Compare **atheist**

① **ago** /ə'gəʊ/ *adv* in the past ○ *He phoned a few minutes ago.* ○ *This all happened a long time ago.* (NOTE: **ago** always follows a word referring to time)

agonise /'ægənaɪz/ (**agonises, agonising, agonised**), **agonize** *verb* to spend a lot of time worrying about something

agonising /'ægənaɪzɪŋ/, **agonizing** *adj* **1.** (*of pain*) very strong and painful **2.** very unhappy and difficult

③ **agony** /'ægəni/ *noun* extreme pain

agony aunt /'ægəni ɑːnt/ *noun* a person who writes an agony column

agony column /'ægəni ˌkɒləm/ *noun* a newspaper column giving advice on personal problems

① **agree** /ə'griː/ (**agrees, agreeing, agreed**) *verb* **1.** to say yes or give permission ○ *After some discussion he agreed to our plan.* (NOTE: You agree **to** *or* **on** a plan.) **2.** to say or show that you have the same opinion as someone else ○ *Most of the group agreed with her suggestion.*

agreeable /ə'griːəb(ə)l/ *adj* pleasant

agreed /ə'griːd/ *adj* which has been accepted

① **agreement** /ə'griːmənt/ *noun* **1.** the act or fact of thinking the same ○ *to reach an agreement* or *to come to an agreement on salaries* ○ *Agreement between the two sides is still a long way off.* □ **they are in agreement with our plan** they agree with our plan ○ *We discussed the plan with them and they are in agreement.* **2.** a contract ○ *to draw up* or *to draft an agreement* ○ *We signed an agreement with an Italian company.*

② **agriculture** /ˈægrɪkʌltʃə/ *noun* the practice of growing crops or raising animals on farms

③ **ah** /ɑː/, **aah** *interj* showing surprise ■ *noun* an act of saying 'ah!' ○ *The audience let out 'oohs' and 'ahs' as they watched the lion tamers.*

aha /ɑːˈhɑː/ *interj* showing that something has been discovered, especially expressing satisfaction or excitement

① **ahead** /əˈhed/ *adv* **1.** in front ○ *Our team was losing, but now we are ahead again.* ○ *Run on ahead and find some seats for us.* ○ *You need to go straight ahead, and then turn left.* **2.** in future ○ *My diary is filled with appointments for six weeks ahead.* **3.** before ○ *We try to fill the vacancies at least three weeks ahead.* ◇ **ahead of** /əˈhed ˈɒv/ **1.** in front of ○ *Ahead of us was a steep hill.* ○ *They ran on ahead of the others.* **2.** in a future time ○ *You have a mass of work ahead of you.* **3.** before (*informal*) ○ *They drafted in extra police ahead of the international match.*

② **aid** /eɪd/ *noun* **1.** help, especially money, food or other gifts given to people living in difficult conditions ○ *aid to the earthquake zone* ○ *an aid worker* (NOTE: This meaning of **aid** has no plural.) **2.** something which helps you to do something ○ *kitchen aids* ■ *verb* (**aids, aiding, aided**) **1.** to help something to happen **2.** to help someone ◇ **in aid of** in order to help ○ *We give money in aid of the Red Cross.* ○ *They are collecting money in aid of refugees.*

aide /eɪd/ *noun* a person employed to assist someone important [~to] ○ *The politician came to the meeting with two of his aides.a former aide to the president*

AIDS /eɪdz/ *noun* a viral infection which breaks down the body's immune system ○ *a clinic for people with AIDS* Full form **acquired immunodeficiency syndrome**

ailing /ˈeɪlɪŋ/ *adj* **1.** sick **2.** in financial difficulties

ailment /ˈeɪlmənt/ *noun* an illness, though not generally a very serious one

② **aim** /eɪm/ *noun* what you are trying to do ○ *His aim is to do well at school and then go to university.* ○ *One of our aims is to increase the speed of service.* ■ *verb* (**aims, aiming, aimed**) **1.** to plan to do something ○ *We aim to go on holiday in June.* **2.** to point a gun at someone or something ○ *He was aiming* or *aiming a gun at the policeman.* ○ *He was not aiming at the target.*

aimless /ˈeɪmləs/ *adj* without any particular plan (NOTE: + **aimlessly** *adv*)

ain't /eɪnt/ *short for* is not, has not, have not (*informal*) ○ *It ain't fair.* ○ *He ain't finished yet.*

① **air** /eə/ *noun* **1.** a mixture of gases which cannot be seen, but which is all around us and which every animal breathes ○ *His breath was like steam in the cold air.* **2. the air** the space around things and above the ground ○ *He threw the ball up into the air.* (NOTE: These meanings of **air** have no plural.) **3.** an appearance or feeling ○ *There was an air of gloom over the meeting.* ■ *adj* referring to a method of travelling or sending goods using aircraft ○ *new air routes* ■ *verb* (**airs, airing, aired**) to make a room or clothes fresh by giving them more air ○ *Let's open the windows to air the room.* ◇ **by air** in an aircraft ○ *I don't enjoy travelling by air.* ○ *It's quicker to send the letter by air.*

air bag /ˈeə bæg/ *noun* a bag in a car which inflates if there is an accident and protects the driver or passenger

airborne /ˈeəbɔːn/ *adj* **1.** carried in the air **2.** carried by an aircraft

air-conditioned /ˈeə kənˌdɪʃ(ə)nd/ *adj* having the temperature controlled by an air-conditioner

air-conditioner /ˈeə kənˌdɪʃ(ə)nə/ *noun* a device which filters and cools the air in a room

air-conditioning /ˈeə kənˌdɪʃ(ə)nɪŋ/ *noun* a system of controlling the temperature in a place such as a room or office or a train

② **aircraft** /ˈeəkrɑːft/ (*plural same*) *noun* a vehicle which flies in the air ○ *The passengers got into* or *boarded the aircraft.* ○ *The airline has a fleet of ten aircraft.*

aircraft carrier /ˈeəkrɑːft ˌkæriə/ *noun* a large ship in a navy, which has a large flat deck where aircraft can land and take off

airfare /ˈeəfeə/ *noun* the amount of money a passenger has to pay to travel on an aircraft

airfield /ˈeəfiːld/ *noun* a small, usually military, airport

air force /ˈeə ˌfɔːs/ *noun* a country's military air organisation

air hostess /ˈeə ˌhəʊstəs/ *noun* a woman flight attendant (*dated*)

airing cupboard /ˈeərɪŋ ˌkʌbəd/ *noun* a warm cupboard where clothes can be aired

airless /ˈeələs/ *adj* without any air

airlift /ˈeəlɪft/ *noun* an emergency transporting of something by air (NOTE: + **airlift** *v*)

② **airline** /ˈeəlaɪn/ *noun* a company which takes people or goods to places in aircraft ○ *The airline has been voted the most popular with business travellers.* ○ *He's an airline pilot.*

airliner /ˈeəlaɪnə/ *noun* a large aircraft that carries passengers

③ **airmail** /ˈeəmeɪl/ *noun* a way of sending letters or parcels by air ■ *verb* (**airmails, airmailing, airmailed**) to send letters or parcels by air ○ *We airmailed the documents to New York.*

airplane /ˈeəpleɪn/ *noun US* an aircraft

② **airport** /ˈeəpɔːt/ *noun* a place where aircraft land and take off ○ *You can take the underground to the airport.* ○ *We are due to arrive at Heathrow Airport at midday.*

airspace /ˈeəspeɪs/ *noun* the air above a country

airtight /ˈeətaɪt/ *adj* which does not allow air to get in or out

air time /ˈeə taɪm/ *noun* the amount of time that is given to a programme or subject in radio or TV broadcasting

air traffic controller /ˌeə ˌtræfɪk kənˈtrəʊlə/ *noun* a person on land who gives instructions for the movements of aircraft as they land or take off

airwaves /ˈeəweɪvz/ *plural noun* the way in which radio signals move through the air

airy /ˈeəri/ *adj* full of fresh air

airy-fairy /ˌeəri ˈfeəri/ *adj* not possible to put into practice (*informal*)

aisle /aɪl/ *noun* a space for walking in between seats in something such as a plane, theatre or church, or between shelf units in a shop

ajar /əˈdʒɑː/ *adj* slightly open

aka /ˌeɪ keɪ ˈeɪ/ *abbr* also known as

à la carte /ˌæ læ ˈkɑːt/ *adv, adj* made of several dishes ordered separately from a menu

② **alarm** /əˈlɑːm/ *noun* **1.** a loud warning sound ○ *An alarm will sound if someone touches the wire.* □ **to raise the alarm** to warn everyone of danger **2.** same as **alarm clock** ■ *verb* (**alarms, alarming, alarmed**) to frighten someone ○ *I don't want to alarm you, but there's a police car parked outside your house.*

③ **alarm clock** /əˈlɑːm klɒk/ *noun* a clock which rings a bell to wake you up

alarmed /əˈlɑːmd/ *adj* worried and frightened

alarming /əˈlɑːmɪŋ/ *adj* frightening

alarmist /əˈlɑːmɪst/ *adj* which makes people feel frightened or worried when they do not need to ○ *an alarmist report*

alas /əˈlæs/ *interj* showing sadness ○ *He died in the war, alas.* ○ *Alas, there is no time left to continue the discussion.*

③ **albeit** /ɔːlˈbiːɪt/ *conj* although

③ **album** /ˈælbəm/ *noun* **1.** a large book **2.** a collection of songs on a CD, cassette or record

③ **alcohol** /ˈælkəhɒl/ *noun* a substance in drinks such as beer or wine that can make people drunk ○ *They will not serve alcohol to anyone under the age of 18.*

alcoholic /ˌælkəˈhɒlɪk/ *adj* relating to alcohol

alcoholism /ˈælkəhɒlɪz(ə)m/ *noun* the condition of depending on drinking alcohol regularly

alcove /ˈælkəʊv/ *noun* a part of the wall of a room which is set back

③ **ale** /eɪl/ *noun* a type of British beer, especially bitter beer, but not lager

alert /əˈlɜːt/ *adj* watching or listening carefully, ready to notice something

② **A Level** /ˈeɪ lev(ə)l/ *noun* an examination taken by pupils aged 17 or 18 ○ *If you pass your A Levels, you can go on to higher education.* Full form **advanced level**

algae /ˈældʒiː/ *plural noun* very small organisms living in water or in wet conditions which have no stems or roots or leaves

algebra /ˈældʒɪbrə/ *noun* a type of mathematics where letters are used to represent quantities

alias /ˈeɪliəs/ *noun* a different name that is not the person's own

alibi /ˈælɪbaɪ/ (*plural* **alibis**) *noun* a claim that a person charged with a crime was somewhere else when the crime was committed

alien /ˈeɪliən/ *noun* a person who is from a foreign country

alienate /ˈeɪliəneɪt/ (**alienates, alienating, alienated**) *verb* **1.** to make someone feel unfriendly **2.** to make someone not want to support you

alienated /ˈeɪliəneɪtɪd/ *adj* not feeling included or welcome, especially in society at large

alight /əˈlaɪt/ (**alights, alighting, alighted**) *verb* to get off a vehicle (*formal*)

align /əˈlaɪn/ (**aligns, aligning, aligned**) *verb* to arrange in line with

alike /ə'laɪk/ *adj* very similar ■ *adv* in a similar way ○ *My sister and I just don't think alike.* ○ *The change will affect rich and poor alike.*

② **alive** /ə'laɪv/ *adj* **1.** living ○ *He was still alive when he was rescued from the burning building.* ○ *When my grandfather was alive, there were no supermarkets.* (NOTE: not used in front of a noun: *the fish is alive* but *a live fish*.) **2.** lively ○ *The holiday village really comes alive at night.* ◇ **to come alive** to become busy and active

alkali /'ælkəlaɪ/ *noun* a substance that can make an acid into a salt

alkaline /'ælkəlaɪn/ *adj* containing more alkali than acid

① **all** /ɔːl/ *adj, pron* everything or everyone ○ *They all* or *All of them like coffee.* ○ *All trains stop at Clapham Junction.* ○ *Did you pick all (of) the tomatoes?* ○ *Where are all the children?* ■ *adv* completely ○ *The ground was all white after the snow had fallen.* ○ *I forgot all about her birthday.* ◇ **all along** right from the beginning ◇ **all at once** /'ɔːl ət 'wɒns/ suddenly ◇ **all in 1.** tired out **2.** including everything ◇ **all of a sudden** /'ɔːl ɒv ə 'sʌd(ə)n/ suddenly ◇ **all over 1.** everywhere over something **2.** finished ◇ **all right** /ɔːl 'raɪt/ well ○ *She was ill yesterday but she's all right now.* ◇ **all the same** in spite of this ○ *I'm not really keen on horror films, but I'll go with you all the same.* ◇ **all by yourself** all alone ○ *You can't do it all by yourself.* ○ *I'm all by myself this evening – my girlfriend's gone out.*

Allah /'ælə/ *noun* the Muslim name for God

allay /ə'leɪ/ (**allays, allaying, allayed**) *verb* to calm something

allegation /ˌælə'geɪʃ(ə)n/ *noun* the suggestion that someone may have done something wrong

allege /ə'ledʒ/ (**alleges, alleging, alleged**) *verb* to suggest that someone may have done something wrong

alleged /ə'ledʒd/ *adj* suggested as a fact but not proved

allegiance /ə'liːdʒ(ə)ns/ *noun* the fact of being loyal

allegory /'æləg(ə)ri/ *noun* a painting or story where the characters represent ideas or are symbols of something else

allergen /'ælədʒən/ *noun* a substance which produces an allergic reaction

allergic /ə'lɜːdʒɪk/ *adj* suffering from or referring to an allergy □ **to be allergic to something** to react badly to a substance ○ *Many people are allergic to grass pollen.* ○ *She is allergic to cats.* □ **to be allergic to someone or something** to dislike something or someone very much (*informal*) ○ *He is allergic to jazz.* ○ *She is allergic to men with beards.*

allergy /'ælədʒi/ (*plural* **allergies**) *noun* a bad reaction to a substance which makes you sneeze, or makes your skin itch, e.g. ○ *She has an allergy to household dust.* ○ *The baby has a wheat allergy.*

alleviate /ə'liːvieɪt/ (**alleviates, alleviating, alleviated**) *verb* to make something less painful

③ **alley** /'æli/ *noun* a narrow little street

③ **alliance** /ə'laɪəns/ *noun* a formal agreement between two or more groups or countries

① **allied** /'ælaɪd/ *adj* joined in an alliance

alligator /'ælɪgeɪtə/ *noun* a large reptile like a crocodile, found in the southern parts of the United States

all-important /ɔːl ɪm'pɔːtənt/ *adj* very important or necessary

all-inclusive /ɔːl ɪn'kluːsɪv/ *adj* that includes everything

all-in rate /ˌɔːl ɪn 'reɪt/, **all-in price** /ˌɔːl ɪn 'praɪs/ *noun* a price which covers everything

all-night /'ɔːl naɪt/ *adj* lasting, open or available throughout the night, or throughout a specific night

② **allocate** /'æləkeɪt/ (**allocates, allocating, allocated**) *verb* to give something out to various people

allot /ə'lɒt/ (**allots, allotting, allotted**) *verb* to give something to someone as a share of something

allotment /ə'lɒtmənt/ *noun* **1.** the process of giving out money or other items to different people, groups or activities **2.** a piece of land which belongs to a local council and which can be rented for growing vegetables

all-out /ˌɔːl 'aʊt/ *adj* total, involving a lot of work

① **allow** /ə'laʊ/ (**allows, allowing, allowed**) *verb* to let someone do something ○ *She allowed me to borrow her book.* ○ *Smoking is not allowed in the restaurant.* ○ *You are allowed to take two pieces of hand luggage onto the plane.*

allowance /ə'laʊəns/ *noun* **1.** an amount of money paid to someone regularly ○ *a weekly allowance* **2.** an amount of money which you are allowed to earn without paying tax on it ◇ **to make allowances for** to take something into account ○ *You must make allowances for his age.*

alloy /'ælɔɪ/ *noun* a mixture of metals

all-purpose /ɔːl 'pɜːpəs/ *adj* which can be used in many different situations

all-round /'ɔːl raʊnd/ *adj* able to do many things well, or useful in a number of different ways, not specialised ■ *adv* **1.** considering everything **2.** for, from or involving everyone

all-rounder /ɔːl 'raʊndə/ *noun* a person who is good at anything

all-time /'ɔːltaɪm/ *adj* biggest, best, worst, etc., ever (*informal*)

allude /ə'luːd/ (**alludes, alluding, alluded**) *verb* to refer to something in an indirect way [~to] ○ *He alluded to the issue in his speech, without giving any details.*

allure /ə'lʊə, ə'ljʊə/ *noun* a mysteriously attractive quality

alluring /ə'lʊərɪŋ, ə'ljʊərɪŋ/ *adj* very attractive

allusion /ə'luːʒ(ə)n/ *noun* an indirect reference to something

③ **ally**[1] /'ælaɪ/ (*plural* **allies**) *noun* a country which works together with another, especially in a war

ally[2] /ə'laɪ/ (**allies, allying, allied**) *verb* □ **to ally yourself with** *or* **to someone** to join forces with someone ○ *The unions have allied themselves with the opposition.*

almighty /ɔːl'maɪti/ *adj* very powerful, very loud

almond /'ɑːmənd/ *noun* a type of nut

① **almost** /'ɔːlməʊst/ *adv* nearly ○ *London is almost as far from here as Paris.* ○ *She's almost as tall as I am.* ○ *She'll eat almost anything.* ○ *Hurry up, it's almost time for the train to leave.*

① **alone** /ə'ləʊn/ *adj* **1.** with no one else ○ *She lives alone with her cats.* ○ *He was all alone in the shop.* **2.** only ○ *She alone knew the importance of the message.* ■ *adv* without other people ○ *We don't let the children go out alone after dark.* ○ *I don't like travelling alone.* ◇ **leave alone 1.** not to disturb someone ○ *Leave your sister alone, she's trying to read.* **2.** to stop touching or playing with something ○ *Leave the cat alone, it doesn't like being stroked.* ○ *Leave those keys alone, the noise is annoying me.* ◇ **to go it alone** to do something, especially a business activity, without help from anyone

① **along** /ə'lɒŋ/ *prep* **1.** by the side of ○ *He has planted fruit trees along both sides of the garden path.* ○ *The river runs along one side of the castle.* **2.** in a straight forward direction ○ *She ran along the pavement.* ○ *Walk along the street until you come to the post office.* ○ *I was just driving along when I caught sight of my brother.* **3.** to a place ○ *John came along after about five minutes.* ○ *Is it OK if I bring a friend along?*

③ **alongside** /ə'lɒŋsaɪd/ *prep* at the side of ○ *The ship was tied up alongside the quay.* ■ *adv* so as to be beside or level with something ○ *We had stopped at a red light when a police car pulled up alongside.*

aloof /ə'luːf/ *adj* quiet, private and unfriendly to other people

aloud /ə'laʊd/ *adv* in a voice which can be easily heard

alpha /'ælfə/ *noun* the first letter of the Greek alphabet, or a mark showing the best results. Symbol **α**

alphabet /'ælfəbet/ *noun* a series of letters in a specific order, e.g. A, B, C, etc. ○ *G comes before H in the alphabet.* ○ *If you're going to Greece on holiday, you ought to learn the Greek alphabet.*

alphabetical /ˌælfə'betɪk(ə)l/ *adj* relating to the alphabet □ **in alphabetical order** in order of the first letter of each word ○ *The words in the dictionary are in alphabetical order.* ○ *Sort out the address cards into alphabetical order of the people's names.*

alphabetise /'ælfəbetaɪz/ (**alphabetises, alphabetising, alphabetised**), **alphabetize** *verb* to put words into alphabetical order, especially automatically

① **already** /ɔːl'redi/ *adv* before now or before the time mentioned ○ *I've already done my shopping.* ○ *It was already past ten o'clock when he arrived.*

alright /'ɔːl'raɪt/ *adj, adv* another spelling of **all right**

Alsatian /æl'seɪʃ(ə)n/ *noun* a type of large dog, often used as a guard dog

① **also** /'ɔːlsəʊ/ *adv* in addition to something or someone else that has been mentioned ○ *He's a keen cyclist and his sister also likes to cycle when she can.* ○ *She sings well and can also play the violin.* (NOTE: **also** is usually placed before the main verb or after a modal or auxiliary verb.)

altar /'ɔːltə/ *noun* a table for important objects in religious ceremonies, especially in a church

③ **alter** /'ɔːltə/ (**alters, altering, altered**) *verb* to become different, or make something different, especially in small ways or in parts only ○ *They wanted to alter the* *terms of the contract after they had signed it.* ○ *The shape of his face had altered slightly.* (NOTE: Do not confuse with **altar**.)

③ **alteration** /ˌɔːltəˈreɪʃ(ə)n/ *noun* **1.** the act of becoming different or of making something different **2.** something that has been, or needs, changing ○ *She made some alterations in the design.*

alternate[1] /ɔːlˈtɜːnət/ *adj* every other one ○ *We see each other on alternate Sundays.*

alternate[2] /ˈɔːltəneɪt/ (**alternates, alternating, alternated**) *verb* to keep changing from one particular position or state to another

② **alternative** /ɔːlˈtɜːnətɪv/ *adj* **1.** in place of something else ○ *Do you have an alternative solution?* ○ *If the plane is full, we will put you on an alternative flight.* **2.** following a different way from usual ■ *noun* something which you do instead of something else ○ *Now that she's ill, do we have any alternative to calling the holiday off?*

alternatively /ɔːlˈtɜːnətɪvli/ *adv* used to offer a different possibility ○ *You could go tonight. Alternatively, we could both go tomorrow.*

alternative medicine /ɔːlˌtɜːnətɪv ˈmed(ə)sɪn/ *noun* the treating of diseases by means such as herbal medicines which are not usually used by doctors

① **although** /ɔːlˈðəʊ/ *conj* in spite of the fact that ○ *Although it was freezing, she didn't put a coat on.* ○ *I've never been into that shop although I've often walked past it.*

③ **altitude** /ˈæltɪtjuːd/ *noun* the height above sea level

① **altogether** /ˌɔːltəˈɡeðə/ *adv* taking everything together ○ *The food was £10 and the drinks £5, so that makes £15 altogether.* ○ *The staff of the three shops come to 200 altogether.*

altruistic /ˌæltruˈɪstɪk/ *adj* not selfish

aluminium /ˌæləˈmɪniəm/ *noun* a silver-coloured metal which is extremely light (NOTE: The US spelling is **aluminum**.)

① **always** /ˈɔːlweɪz/ *adv* **1.** every time ○ *She is always late for work.* ○ *Why does it always rain when we want to go for a walk?* **2.** all the time ○ *It's always hot in tropical countries.* **3.** frequently, especially when someone finds it annoying ○ *She's always asking me to lend her money.*

Alzheimer's disease /ˈæltshaɪməz dɪ ˌziːz/ *noun* a disease of the brain that leads to memory loss that gets worse and worse

① **am** /əm, æm/ 1st person present singular of **be**

① **a.m.** /ˌeɪ ˈem/ *adv* before midday ○ *I have to catch the 7 a.m. train to work every day.* ○ *Telephone calls made before 6 a.m. are charged at the cheap rate.* (NOTE: **a.m.** is usually used to show the exact hour and the word **o'clock** is left out. The US spelling is **A.M.**)

amalgamate /əˈmælɡəmeɪt/ (**amalgamates, amalgamating, amalgamated**) *verb* to combine things together [~with] ○ *Our college amalgamated with King's College a few years ago.* (NOTE: + **amalgamation** *n*)

amass /əˈmæs/ (**amasses, amassing, amassed**) *verb* to collect a lot of money, information or things

amateur /ˈæmətə, ˈæmətʃʊə/ *noun* **1.** a person who is not paid to play his or her sport **2.** a person who does something because he or she likes doing it

amateurish /ˈæmətərɪʃ/ *adj* not done well or in a professional way

amaze /əˈmeɪz/ (**amazes, amazing, amazed**) *verb* to surprise someone very much

amazed /əˈmeɪzd/ *adj* very surprised

amazement /əˈmeɪzmənt/ *noun* great surprise ○ *To his amazement he won first prize.*

② **amazing** /əˈmeɪzɪŋ/ *adj* **1.** very surprising ○ *It was amazing that she never suspected anything.* **2.** extremely interesting and unusual ○ *It was an amazing experience, sailing so far from land at night.*

ambassador /æmˈbæsədə/ *noun* a person who is regarded as a representative or a symbol of something

amber /ˈæmbə/ *noun* a yellow to dark brown substance which can be used for making jewellery

ambidextrous /ˌæmbɪˈdekstrəs/ *adj* able to use either the right or left hand equally well

ambience /ˈæmbiəns/ *noun* the character and general feeling of a place

ambiguity /ˌæmbɪˈɡjuːɪti/ *noun* the fact of having two meanings

ambiguous /æmˈbɪɡjuəs/ *adj* having two meanings and therefore not being clear

ambition /æmˈbɪʃ(ə)n/ *noun* a wish to do something special ○ *His great ambition is to ride on an elephant.*

ambitious /æmˈbɪʃəs/ *adj* with high aims

ambivalent /æm'bɪvələnt/ *adj* not sure or decided

amble /'æmb(ə)l/ (**ambles, ambling, ambled**) *verb* to walk in a relaxed way without hurrying

① **ambulance** /'æmbjʊləns/ *noun* a van which carries sick or injured people to hospital ○ *When she fell down the stairs, her husband called an ambulance.*

ambush /'æmbʊʃ/ (**ambushes, ambushing, ambushed**) *verb* to wait hidden and attack someone by surprise (NOTE: + **ambush** *n*)

amen /ɑː'men, eɪ'men/ *interj* meaning 'let this be so' used at the end of Christian prayers

③ **amend** /ə'mend/ (**amends, amending, amended**) *verb* to change for the better

③ **amendment** /ə'mendmənt/ *noun* a change intended to make something better

amenity /ə'miːnɪti/ (*plural* **amenities**) *noun* a feature that makes a place attractive, enjoyable or comfortable to be in

① **American** /ə'merɪkən/ *adj* relating to America or to the United States

American football /əˌmerɪkən 'fʊtbɔːl/ *noun* a type of football played in the United States

American Indian /əˌmerɪkən 'ɪndiən/ *adj* referring to Native Americans

amethyst /'æməθɪst/ *noun* a purple stone which can be used for making jewellery

amiable /'eɪmiəb(ə)l/ *adj* friendly and pleasant

amicable /'æmɪkəb(ə)l/ *adj* done in a friendly way

amid /ə'mɪd/ *prep* in the middle of

amino acid /əˌmiːnəʊ 'æsɪd/ *noun* one of the chemicals that combine to make protein. Humans are only able to produce some amino acids in their bodies, so others have to be absorbed from food.

ammonia /ə'məʊniə/ *noun* a strong poisonous gas or liquid used in cleaning products

ammunition /ˌæmjʊ'nɪʃ(ə)n/ *noun* objects such as bombs and bullets, which can be fired from weapons

amnesia /æm'niːziə/ *noun* a medical state when you forget everything

amnesty /'æmnəsti/ (*plural* **amnesties**) *noun* a period during which criminals will not be punished

amoeba /ə'miːbə/, **ameba** /ə'miːbə/ *noun* a living thing which consists of a single cell

amoebic /ə'miːbɪk/ *adj* caused by an amoeba

among /ə'mʌŋ/, **amongst** /ə'mʌŋst/ *prep* **1.** surrounded by or in the middle of ○ *He was standing among a crowd of tourists.* **2.** between a number of people in a group ○ *Let's share the cake among us.* **3.** in addition to other people or things ○ *Jack was there, among others.*

amoral /eɪ'mɒrəl/ *adj* not caring about right and wrong

amorous /'æmərəs/ *adj* showing sexual love

amorphous /ə'mɔːfəs/ *adj* with no particular shape

① **amount** /ə'maʊnt/ *noun* a quantity of something ○ *The amount in my bank account has reached £1000.* ○ *We spent a large amount of time just waiting.* □ **a certain amount** some but not a lot ○ *Painting the house will take a certain amount of time.*

amount to *phrasal verb* **1.** to make a total of ○ *My year's savings amount to less than £1000.* **2.** to be similar or equal to something ○ *I think what he said amounts to a refusal to take part.* **3.** □ **to amount to the same thing** to mean the same, to be the same ○ *Whether he took cash or free holidays, it all amounts to the same thing.* ○ *The remaining problems don't amount to much.*

amp /æmp/ *noun* a piece of equipment which can make sounds louder

ampersand /'æmpəsænd/ *noun* a printing sign (&) meaning 'and'

amphetamine /æm'fetəmiːn/ *noun* a drug which is supposed to increase the user's energy levels

amphibian /æm'fɪbiən/ *noun* an animal that lives both in water and on land

amphibious /æm'fɪbiəs/ *adj* living both in water and on land

amphitheatre /'æmfɪθɪətə/ *noun* **1.** a circular or oval building without a roof where theatrical events or sports competitions are held **2.** a lecture hall or upper part of a theatre with seats arranged in a semicircle (NOTE: The US spelling is **amphitheater**.)

ample /'æmpəl/ *adj* large enough

amplifier /'æmplɪfaɪə/ *noun* a piece of equipment which makes sound louder

amplify /'æmplɪfaɪ/ (**amplifies, amplifying, amplified**) *verb* **1.** to make a sound louder **2.** to explain something in more detail (NOTE: + **amplification** *n*)

amputate /ˈæmpjʊteɪt/ (**amputates, amputating, amputated**) *verb* to cut off an arm, leg, finger or toe (NOTE: + **amputation** *n*)

amuse /əˈmjuːz/ (**amuses, amusing, amused**) *verb* **1.** to make someone laugh ○ *This story will amuse you.* □ **to amuse yourself** to play or get pleasure from what you are doing ○ *The children amused themselves quietly while their parents talked.* **2.** to make the time pass pleasantly for someone ○ *How can we amuse the children on the journey?*

amused /əˈmjuːzd/ *adj* thinking that something is funny

amusement /əˈmjuːzmənt/ *noun* a feeling of pleasure caused by something that is funny ◇ **to someone's amusement** making someone feel pleasure in a funny situation ○ *Much to her amusement, the band played 'Happy Birthday to you!'.*

amusement arcade /əˈmjuːzmənt ɑːˌkeɪd/ *noun* a place with machines for playing games

amusement park /əˈmjuːzmənt pɑːk/ *noun* an open-air park with various types of entertainment

amusing /əˈmjuːzɪŋ/ *adj* funny

① **an** /ən, æn/ *article* same as **a² 1**

anachronism /əˈnækrənɪz(ə)m/ *noun* a thing which is out of date and does not belong to the present time

anachronistic /əˌnækrəˈnɪstɪk/ *adj* not fitting the period when a play or film is supposed to take place

anaemia /əˈniːmiə/ *noun* a condition where the level of red blood cells is less than normal (NOTE: The US spelling is **anemia**.)

anaesthetic /ˌænəsˈθetɪk/ *noun* a substance given to a patient to remove feeling, so that he or she can have an operation without feeling pain (NOTE: The US spelling is **anesthetic**.)

anaesthetise /əˈniːsθətaɪz/ (**anaesthetises, anaesthetising, anaesthetised**), **anaesthetize** *verb* to give a patient an anaesthetic (NOTE: The US spelling is **anesthetize**.)

anaesthetist /əˈniːsθətɪst/ *noun* a person whose job is to give patients anaesthetics (NOTE: The US term is **anesthesiologist**.)

anagram /ˈænəgræm/ *noun* a word or phrase containing the letters of another word or phrase in a different order, e.g. 'Cathy' is an anagram of 'yacht'

anal /ˈeɪn(ə)l/ *adj* referring to the anus

analgesic /ˌæn(ə)lˈdʒiːzɪk/ *noun* a pain-killing drug

analogous /əˈnæləgəs/ *adj* similar

③ **analogy** /əˈnælədʒi/ *noun* a similarity between two things

analyse /ˈænəlaɪz/ (*3rd person present plural* **analyses**, *present participle* **analysing**, *past participle* **analysed**), **analyze** *verb* to examine closely and scientifically

① **analysis** /əˈnæləsɪs/ (*plural* **analyses**) *noun* a close examination of the parts or elements of something ○ *job analysis* ○ *to make an analysis of the sales* or *a sales analysis* ○ *to carry out an analysis of the market potential*

analyst /ˈænəlɪst/ *noun* **1.** a person who carries out analyses **2.** a doctor who is trained in psychoanalysis

analytical /ˌænəˈlɪtɪk(ə)l/ *adj* examining something in detail

anarchic /əˈnɑːkɪk/, **anarchical** /əˈnɑːkɪkl/ *adj* without any law or order

anarchist /ˈænəkɪst/ *noun* a person who tries to destroy a government by violent means, without planning to replace it in any way

anarchy /ˈænəki/ *noun* a lack of law and order, because the government has lost control or because there is no government

anathema /əˈnæθəmə/ *noun* something which you dislike very much

anatomy /əˈnætəmi/ *noun* the structure of the body or of part of the body

ancestor /ˈænsestə/ *noun* a member of a family who has been dead for a long time

ancestry /ˈænsestri/ *noun* your family going back over many generations

anchor /ˈæŋkə/ *noun* a large metal hook which holds a ship in place ■ *verb* (**anchors, anchoring, anchored**) **1.** (*of a ship*) to drop an anchor to stay in the same place **2.** to hold something firmly in position

anchorman /ˈæŋkəmæn/ (*plural* **anchormen**) *noun* the main presenter on a TV news show

anchovy /ˈæntʃəvi, ænˈtʃəʊvi/ (*plural* **anchovies** or *same*) *noun* a small, very salty fish

② **ancient** /ˈeɪnʃənt/ *adj* very old, or belonging to a time long ago ○ *He was riding an ancient bicycle.*

① **and** /ən, ənd, ænd/ *conj* used to join two words or phrases ○ *All my uncles and aunts live in the country.* ○ *The children were running about and singing.* ○ *Come and sit down next to me.* (NOTE: **and** is used to say numbers after 100: 'seven hundred and two (702)') ◇ **and so on, and so forth, and so on and so forth** with other similar things ○ *He talked about plants, flowers, vegetables, and so on.*

anecdotal /ˌænɪk'dəʊt(ə)l/ *adj* coming from stories told by individual people

anecdote /'ænɪkdəʊt/ *noun* a usually humorous story based on something which has taken place

anemia, anemic US spelling of **anaemia**

anesthesia, anesthetic, anesthetist, anesthetize US spelling of **anaesthetist**

anesthesiologist *noun US* a person whose job is to give patients anaesthetics (NOTE: The US term is **anesthesiologist**.)

angel /'eɪndʒəl/ *noun* **1.** a heavenly being **2.** a sweet, kind person

③ **anger** /'æŋgə/ *noun* a feeling of being very annoyed ○ *He managed to control his anger.* ○ *She couldn't hide the anger she felt.*

③ **angle** /'æŋgəl/ *noun* a corner where two lines meet ○ *She planted the tree in the angle of the two walls.* ◇ **at an angle** not straight ○ *The shop front is at an angle to the road.*

angle for *phrasal verb* to try to get something

angle bracket /ˌæŋgəl 'brækɪt/ *noun* a printed symbol < or >, used around text, especially in instructions for a computer

Anglican /'æŋglɪkən/ *noun* a member of the Anglican Church

angling /'æŋglɪŋ/ *noun* the sport of catching fish with a rod (NOTE: + **angler** *n*)

Anglo- /æŋgləʊ/ *prefix* English, between England and another country

angora /æŋ'gɔːrə/ *adj* made of wool from an angora

angrily /'æŋgrɪli/ *adv* in an angry way ○ *He shouted angrily when the children climbed over the fence.*

① **angry** /'æŋgri/ (**angrier, angriest**) *adj* upset and annoyed, and sometimes wanting to harm someone ○ *The shopkeeper is angry with the children because they broke his window.* ○ *He gets angry if the post is late.* ○ *I am angry that the government is doing nothing to prevent crime.* ○ *When the cashier still hadn't arrived at midday the boss got angrier.*

angst /æŋst/ *noun* great worry about life

anguish /'æŋgwɪʃ/ *noun* great mental suffering

anguished /'æŋgwɪʃt/ *adj* showing or feeling great suffering

angular /'æŋgjʊlə/ *adj* **1.** with sharp corners **2.** with sharp-looking bones

① **animal** /'ænɪm(ə)l/ *noun* a living thing that moves independently ○ *I love having animals as pets.* (NOTE: **animal** may include humans in scientific contexts.)

animated /'ænɪmeɪtɪd/ *adj* full of life and energy

animation /ˌænɪ'meɪʃ(ə)n/ *noun* **1.** being lively **2.** the process of making animated films

animosity /ˌænɪ'mɒsɪti/ *noun* a strong feeling of dislike towards someone

ankle /'æŋkəl/ *noun* the part of the body where your leg joins your foot

annex /ə'neks/ (**annexes, annexing, annexed**) *verb* to take possession of land which belongs to another state (NOTE: + **annexation** *n*)

annexe /'æneks/ *noun* a less important building attached to another building (NOTE: The US spelling is **annex**.)

annihilate /ə'naɪəleɪt/ (**annihilates, annihilating, annihilated**) *verb* to destroy something completely (NOTE: + **annihilation** *n*)

① **anniversary** /ˌænɪ'vɜːs(ə)ri/ (*plural* **anniversaries**) *noun* the same date as an important event that happened in the past

annotate /'ænəteɪt/ (**annotates, annotating, annotated**) *verb* to add notes to a text

annotation /ˌænə'teɪʃ(ə)n/ *noun* a note added to a text

① **announce** /ə'naʊns/ (**announces, announcing, announced**) *verb* to say something officially or in public [~(that)] ○ *She announced the results of the competition.* ○ *She announced that she would stand for election.*

① **announcement** /ə'naʊnsmənt/ *noun* a statement made in public ○ *The managing director made an announcement to the staff.* ○ *There were several announcements concerning flight changes.*

announcer /ə'naʊnsə/ *noun* a person who reads the news or announces programmes on radio or TV

③ **annoy** /ə'nɔɪ/ (**annoys, annoying, annoyed**) *verb* to make someone feel slightly angry, upset or impatient ○ *Their rude behaviour really annoyed us.*

annoyance /ə'nɔɪəns/ *noun* a feeling of being slightly angry, upset or impatient ○ *There was a tone of annoyance in her voice.* ◇ **to someone's annoyance** so that someone is annoyed ○ *I took both sets of keys home with me, much to his annoyance.*

① **annoyed** /ə'nɔɪd/ *adj* slightly angry, upset or impatient ○ *He was annoyed with his neighbour who had cut down one of his trees.* ○ *I was annoyed to find someone had stolen my mobile phone.*

① **annoying** /ə'nɔɪɪŋ/ *adj* making you angry, upset or impatient [~that] ○ *How annoying! I forgot to buy the milk.* ○ *The baby has an annoying cough which won't go away.* ○ *I find it very annoying that the post doesn't come before 10 o'clock.*

② **annual** /'ænjuəl/ *adj* happening once a year ○ *The village fair is an annual event.* ○ *I get annual interest of 6% on my savings account.* (NOTE: + **annually** *adv*)

annul /ə'nʌl/ (**annuls, annulling, annulled**) *verb* to stop something being legally valid ○ *The marriage was annulled* ○ *They want to annul the contract.*

anomaly /ə'nɒməli/ *noun* an unusual thing

anon /ə'nɒn/ *abbr* anonymous

anonymity /ˌænə'nɪmɪti/ *noun* the hiding of your real name

anonymous /ə'nɒnɪməs/ *adj* without stating a name

anorak /'ænəræk/ *noun* someone who is too interested in a particular subject, especially one that seems unfashionable or dull to other people (*informal*)

anorexia /ˌænə'reksiə/ *noun* a condition caused by an extreme fear of becoming fat and marked by ill health as a result of not eating enough

anorexic /ˌænə'reksɪk/ *adj* referring to or affected by anorexia

① **another** /ə'nʌðə/ *adj, pron* **1.** one more ○ *I'd like another cake, please.* ○ *Would you like another?* **2.** a different one ○ *He's bought another car.* ○ *She tried on one dress after another, but couldn't find anything she liked.* ◊ **each other, one another**

① **answer** /'ɑːnsə/ *noun* **1.** something that you say or write when someone has asked you a question ○ *The answer to your question is yes.* **2.** the act of picking up a telephone that is ringing ○ *I phoned his office but there was no answer.* ■ *verb* (**answers, answering, answered**) **1.** to speak or write words to someone who has spoken to you or asked you a question [~that] ○ *He never answers my letters.* ○ *I answered truthfully that the news had surprised me.* **2.** □ **to answer the phone** to speak and listen to a telephone caller ○ *His mother usually answers the phone.* □ **to answer the door** to open the door to someone who knocks or rings the bell ○ *No-one answered the door though I knocked twice.* ◇ **in answer to** as a reply to ○ *I am writing in answer to your letter of October 6th.*

answer back *phrasal verb* to speak to someone in a rude way

① **answerphone** /'ɑːnsəfəʊn/ *noun* a machine which answers the telephone automatically when someone is not in the office or at home, and allows messages to be recorded

ant /ænt/ *noun* a small insect that lives in large groups

antagonise /æn'tægənaɪz/ (**antagonises, antagonising, antagonised**), **antagonize** *verb* to make someone feel angry or impatient

antagonism /æn'tægənɪz(ə)m/ *noun* a strong feeling of dislike towards someone

antelope /'æntɪləʊp/ *noun* an African deer which can run very fast

antenna /æn'tenə/ (*plural* **antennae** or **antennas**) *noun* a person's ability to know something without being told

anthem /'ænθəm/ *noun* a song for a group of singers

anthology /æn'θɒlədʒi/ (*plural* **anthologies**) *noun* a collection of stories or poems

anthrax /'ænθræks/ *noun* a serious disease of cows and sheep, which can be caught by people

anthropoid /'ænθrəpɔɪd/ *adj* similar to a human

anthropology /ˌænθrə'pɒlədʒi/ *noun* the study of people and culture

anti- /ænti/ *prefix* against

antibiotic /ˌæntibaɪ'ɒtɪk/ *noun* a substance which kills harmful organisms such as bacteria

③ **antibody** /'æntɪbɒdi/ (*plural* **antibodies**) *noun* a natural substance produced by the body to fight disease

③ **anticipate** /æn'tɪsɪpeɪt/ (**anticipates, anticipating, anticipated**) *verb* **1.** to expect something to happen [~(that)] ○ *We are anticipating floods* or *that there will be floods.* **2.** to act because you see something is about to happen ○ *He anticipated trouble at the meeting and left early.*

③ **anticipation** /ænˌtɪsɪ'peɪʃ(ə)n/ *noun* excitement because you expect that something will happen

anticlimax /ˌænti'klaɪmæks/ *noun* a feeling of disappointment when something does not turn out as expected

anticlockwise /ˌænti'klɒkwaɪz/ *adv, adj* in the opposite direction to the hands of a clock ○ *an anticlockwise movement* ○ *He was driving anticlockwise round the ring road when the accident took place.*

antics /'æntɪks/ *plural noun* funny or silly behaviour ○ *the antics of the clowns in the circus* ○ *The students' antics cost them their places at university.*

antidepressant /ˌæntidɪ'pres(ə)nt/ *noun* a drug that is used to treat a person suffering from depression

antidote /'æntɪdəʊt/ *noun* **1.** a substance which balances the effect of a poison **2.** something which balances a bad influence

antifreeze /'æntifriːz/ *noun* a liquid you put in the engine of a car to prevent it from freezing in cold weather

antipathy /æn'tɪpəθi/ *noun* a strong dislike

antiquarian bookseller /ˌæntɪˌkweəriən ˌbʊk'selə/ *noun* a person who sells old books

antiquated /'æntɪkweɪtɪd/ *adj* very old and out of date

antique /æn'tiːk/ *noun* an old and valuable object ○ *He collects antiques.* ■ *adj* old and valuable ○ *an antique Chinese vase*

antiquities /æn'tɪkwɪtiːz/ *plural noun* old objects from ancient times

antiquity /æn'tɪkwɪti/ *noun* ancient times

anti-Semitic /ˌænti sə'mɪtɪk/ *adj* showing hate towards Jewish people

③ **antiseptic** /ˌæntɪ'septɪk/ *noun* a substance which prevents infection ■ *adj* preventing infection ○ *an antiseptic dressing* ○ *an antiseptic mouthwash*

antisocial /ˌænti'səʊʃ(ə)l/ *adj* unfriendly, not wanting to meet other people

antithesis /æn'tɪθəsɪs/ (*plural* **antitheses**) *noun* the exact opposite of something

antlers /'æntləz/ *plural noun* the horns of a deer ○ *Deer grow new antlers each summer and then shed them in the winter.*

antonym /'æntənɪm/ *noun* a word which means the opposite of another word

anus /'eɪnəs/ *noun* the opening at the end of the rectum, through which solid waste matter passes from the body

③ **anxiety** /æŋ'zaɪəti/ (*plural* **anxieties**) *noun* **1.** nervous worry about something [~about/over] ○ *Her anxiety about her job prospects began to affect her health.* **2.** the state of being keen to do something ○ *In his anxiety to get away quickly, he forgot to lock the door.*

③ **anxious** /'æŋkʃəs/ *adj* **1.** nervous and very worried about something ○ *She's anxious about the baby.* **2.** keen to do something ○ *The shopkeeper is always anxious to please his customers.*

① **anxiously** /'æŋkʃəsli/ *adv* in a nervous, worried way ○ *They are waiting anxiously for the results of the exam.*

① **any** /'eni/ *adj, pron* **1.** it doesn't matter which ○ *I'm free any day next week except Tuesday.* **2.** (*usually in questions*) a small quantity ○ *Have you got any money left?* ○ *Is there any food for me?* ○ *Would you like any more to eat?* ○ *Will any of your friends be there?* □ **not…any** not even a little more (*used to emphasise comparatives*) ○ *He can't cycle any faster.* ○ *She's been in hospital for two weeks and isn't any better.* ○ *Can't you sing any louder?* ◇ **not…any** none ○ *I don't like any of the paintings in the exhibition.* ○ *Can you lend me some money? – sorry, I haven't got any.*

① **anybody** /'enibɒdi/ *pron* same as **anyone**

① **anyhow** /'enihaʊ/ *adv* **1.** in a careless way **2.** same as **anyway**

③ **anymore** /ˌeni'mɔː/, **any more** ◇ **not … anymore** no longer ○ *We don't go there anymore.*

anyone /'eniwʌn/ *pron* any person at all ○ *Anyone can learn to ride a bike.* □ **anyone else** any other person ○ *Is there anyone else who can't see the screen?*

③ **anyplace** /'enɪpleɪs/ *adv US* same as **anywhere** (*informal*)

① **anything** /'eniθɪŋ/ *pron* **1.** it doesn't matter what ○ *You can eat anything you want.* ○ *Our dog will bite anything that moves.* **2.** (*in questions or negatives*) something ○ *Did you hear anything make a noise during the night?* ○ *Has anything happened to their plans for a long holiday?* ○ *Do you want anything more to drink?* ○ *We didn't do anything interesting at the weekend.*

① **anyway** /'eniweɪ/ *adv* despite something else ○ *I'm not supposed to drink during the daytime, but I'll have a beer anyway.* ○ *I think it's time to leave – anyway, the last bus is at 11.40.*

① **anywhere** /'eniweə/ *adv* **1.** it does not matter where ○ *Put the chair anywhere.* **2.** (*in questions or negatives*) somewhere ○ *Did you go anywhere at the weekend?* ○ *Is there anywhere where I can sit down?* ○ *I can't see your wallet anywhere.*

① **apart** /ə'pɑːt/ *adv* **1.** separated ○ *The two villages are about six miles apart.* **2.** in separate pieces ○ *He took the watch apart.* ◇ **apart from** except for ○ *Do you have any special interests apart from your work?* ○ *I'm feeling fine, apart from a slight cold.*

apartheid /ə'pɑːtheɪt/ *noun* a policy in the past in South Africa of separating black people from the white population

② **apartment** /ə'pɑːtmənt/ *noun* a separate set of rooms for living in ○ *She shares an apartment with a friend.*

apathetic /ˌæpə'θetɪk/ *adj* not caring about anything, not interested in anything

apathy /'æpəθi/ *noun* not having any interest in anything

ape /eɪp/ *noun* a large monkey

aperture /'æpətʃə/ *noun* a little hole

apex /'eɪpeks/ (*plural* **apexes** or **apices**) *noun* the top or highest part of a pointed shape

aphrodisiac /ˌæfrə'dɪziæk/ *noun* a substance which makes people want to have sex ■ *adj* making people want to have sex

apiece /ə'piːs/ *adv* each

aplomb /ə'plɒm/ *noun* a calm and self-confident attitude

apocalyptic /əˌpɒkə'lɪptɪk/ *adj* warning about the end of the world

apocryphal /ə'pɒkrəf(ə)l/ *adj* famous, but probably not true

apologetic /əˌpɒlə'dʒetɪk/ *adj* showing that you are sorry for something

② **apologise** /ə'pɒlədʒaɪz/ (**apologises, apologising, apologised**), **apologize** *verb* to say you are sorry ○ *He shouted at her and then apologised.* ○ *She apologised for being late.*

② **apology** /ə'pɒlədʒi/ *noun* (*plural* **apologies**) an act of indicating that you are sorry ■ *plural noun* **apologies** a statement indicating that you are sorry, especially if you cannot attend a meeting ○ *My apologies for being so late.* ○ *Please give the chairman my apologies.*

apostrophe /ə'pɒstrəfi/ *noun* a printing sign ('), either showing that a letter has been left out, e.g. weren't, or after a noun to show possession, e.g. Ben's coat or the girls' coats

appal /ə'pɔːl/ (**appals, appalling, appalled**) *verb* to shock or offend someone very much (NOTE: The US spelling is **appall**.)

appalled /ə'pɔːld/ *adj* very shocked

appalling /ə'pɔːlɪŋ/ *adj* horrible, shocking

apparatus /ˌæpə'reɪtəs/ *noun* scientific or medical equipment

② **apparent** /ə'pærənt/ *adj* **1.** easy to see or accept as true ○ *It was apparent to everyone that she was annoyed.* **2.** possibly different from what something seems to be ○ *There is an apparent mistake in the accounts.*

① **apparently** /ə'pærəntli/ *adv* according to what you have seen or heard ○ *Apparently she took the last train home and then disappeared.* ○ *He didn't come to work today – apparently he's got a cold.*

apparition /ˌæpə'rɪʃ(ə)n/ *noun* something which you think you see

① **appeal** /ə'piːl/ *noun* **1.** an act of asking for help ○ *The police have made an appeal for witnesses.* ○ *The hospital is launching an appeal to raise £50,000.* **2.** an attractive quality ○ *the strong appeal of Greece as a holiday destination* ■ *verb* **1.** to ask for something [~for] ○ *They appealed for money to continue their work.* **2.** to attract someone [~to] ○ *These CDs appeal to the teenage market.* ○ *The idea of working in Australia for six months appealed to her.* **3.** to make a legal request for a court to look again at a decision [~against] ○ *He has appealed against the sentence.*

appealing /ə'piːlɪŋ/ *adj* **1.** attractive ○ *The design has proved appealing to our older customers.* **2.** wanting help or support ○ *The child gave her an appealing look as she got up to leave.* (NOTE: only used before a noun)

① **appear** /ə'pɪə/ (**appears, appearing, appeared**) *verb* **1.** to start to be seen ○ *A ship appeared through the fog.* **2.** to seem to be or do something [~(that)] ○ *She appeared rather cross.* ○ *There appears to be a mistake.* ○ *He appears to have forgotten the time.* ○ *It appears that they didn't receive the invitation.* **3.** to play a part in a film or play or take part in a TV programme [~in/~on] ○ *She appears regularly in shows on TV.*

① **appearance** /ə'pɪərəns/ *noun* **1.** the way that someone or something looks ○ *You could tell from his appearance that he had been sleeping rough.* **2.** the fact of being present somewhere, especially unexpectedly ○ *The appearance of a teacher caused them to fall silent.* □ **to put in an appearance** to go somewhere where other people are for a short time **3.** the beginning of something new ○ *the rapid appearance of mobile phone shops all over the country* ○ *They were worried by the sudden appearance of a red rash.* **4.** an occasion when someone is performing in a film or play or on TV ○ *This is her second appearance in a film.* ■ *plural noun* looks □ **to keep up appearances** to try to show that you are still as rich or important as you were before

appease /ə'pi:z/ (**appeases, appeasing, appeased**) *verb* **1.** to give someone something that they want, even if it is unreasonable, to try to avoid worse problems arising (NOTE: + **appeasement** *n*) **2.** to try to avoid or prevent something ○ *He ate an apple to appease his hunger.*

appendicitis /ə,pendɪ'saɪtɪs/ *noun* an illness that affects the appendix

③ **appendix** /ə'pendɪks/ (*plural* **appendices**) *noun* **1.** a small part inside the body which has no real purpose but can become infected, causing appendicitis **2.** a section at the back of a book, containing additional information

appetiser /'æpɪtaɪzə/ *noun* a small amount of food before a main meal

appetising /'æpɪtaɪzɪŋ/, **appetizing** *adj* looking or smelling good and making you want to eat

appetite /'æpɪtaɪt/ *noun* **1.** a need or wish to eat ○ *Going for a long walk has given me an appetite.* ○ *He's not feeling well and has lost his appetite.* **2.** a strong wish to do something ○ *She has an appetite for hard work.*

applaud /ə'plɔ:d/ (**applauds, applauding, applauded**) *verb* to clap to show that you like something

applause /ə'plɔ:z/ *noun* the act of clapping your hands together several times to show that you liked a performance

① **apple** /'æp(ə)l/ *noun* a common fruit that is hard, round and sweet, and grows on a tree ○ *Don't eat apples that are not ripe – they'll make you ill.*

appliance /ə'plaɪəns/ *noun* a machine such as a washing machine or cooker used in the home

applicable /ə'plɪkəb(ə)l/ *adj* able to be applied in particular cases

applicant /'æplɪkənt/ *noun* a person who applies for something ○ *job applicants* ○ *Applicants for licences must fill in this form.*

① **application** /,æplɪ'keɪʃ(ə)n/ *noun* **1.** the process of putting something on something else ○ *Several applications of the cream will be necessary.* **2.** the process or act of applying for something such as a job or place on a course [~for] ○ *We've received dozens of applications for the job.* □ **an application to do something** a formal request to do something ○ *She's put in an application to transfer to another department.*

③ **application form** /,æplɪ'keɪʃ(ə)n ,fɔ:m/ *noun* a form which has to be filled in to apply for something

① **apply** /ə'plaɪ/ (**applies, applying, applied**) *verb* **1.** to ask for something formally [~for] ○ *She applied for a job in the supermarket.* ○ *He's applying for a place at university.* □ **to apply to do something** to ask formally if you can do something ○ *No-one has applied to join the club this year.* **2.** to put something onto something ○ *Wait until the first coat of paint is dry before you apply the second.* **3.** to affect or be relevant to someone or something [~to] ○ *This rule only applies to people coming from outside the EU.*

① **appoint** /ə'pɔɪnt/ (**appoints, appointing, appointed**) *verb* to give someone a job ○ *He was appointed (as) manager* or *to the post of manager.* ○ *We want to appoint someone to manage our sales department.* (NOTE: You appoint a person **to** a job.)

① **appointment** /ə'pɔɪntmənt/ *noun* **1.** an agreed time for a meeting ○ *I want to make an appointment to see the doctor.* ○ *She was late for her appointment.* □ **on her appointment as manager** when she was made a manager **2.** the process of being given a job **3.** a job ○ *We are going to make three new appointments.*

③ **appraisal** /ə'preɪz(ə)l/ *noun* a report on the value of someone or something

appraise /ə'preɪz/ (**appraises, appraising, appraised**) *verb* to judge how well someone or something is working

appreciable /ə'pri:ʃəb(ə)l/ *adj* able to be felt or noticed

① **appreciate** /ə'pri:ʃi,eɪt/ (**appreciates, appreciating, appreciated**) *verb* to recognise the value of something ○ *Shoppers always appreciate a bargain.*

appreciation /ə,pri:ʃi'eɪʃ(ə)n/ *noun* **1.** showing that you recognise the value of something **2.** an increase in value

appreciative /ə'pri:ʃətɪv/ *adj* **1.** being very grateful **2.** showing enjoyment

apprehension /,æprɪ'henʃən/ *noun* a worry about what is going to happen. Compare **misapprehension**

apprehensive /,æprɪ'hensɪv/ *adj* worried about the future

apprentice /ə'prentɪs/ *noun* a young person who works as an assistant to a skilled person in order to learn from them ○ *He's started work as a plumber's apprentice.*

apprenticeship /ə'prentɪsʃɪp/ *noun* the time someone spends as an apprentice

② **approach** /ə'prəʊtʃ/ *noun* **1.** the fact of coming nearer ○ *With the approach of winter we need to get the central heating checked.* **2.** a way which leads to something ○ *The approaches to the city were crowded with coaches.* **3.** a way of dealing with a situation ○ *His approach to the question was different from hers.* ■ *verb* (**approaches, approaching, approached**) to come near ○ *The plane was approaching the airport when the lights went out.*

approachable /ə'prəʊtʃəb(ə)l/ *adj* easy to talk to

approaching /ə'prəʊtʃɪŋ/ *adj* coming nearer

① **appropriate** /ə'prəʊpriət/ *adj* suitable for a particular situation ○ *That skirt is not really appropriate for gardening.* ○ *We leave it to you to take appropriate action.*

② **approval** /ə'pruːv(ə)l/ *noun* the act of agreeing ○ *The committee gave their approval to the scheme.* ○ *Does the choice of colour have your approval* or *meet with your approval?*

② **approve** /ə'pruːv/ (**approves, approving, approved**) *verb* **1.** to agree to something officially ○ *The committee approved the scheme.* **2.** to think something is good [~of] ○ *He doesn't approve of loud music.*

approving /ə'pruːvɪŋ/ *adj* showing agreement

approximate /ə'prɒksɪmət/ *adj* more or less correct

① **approximately** /ə'prɒksɪmətli/ *adv* not exactly ○ *It takes approximately 35 minutes to get to the city centre from here.*

apricot /'eɪprɪkɒt/ *noun* a fruit with yellow flesh and a hard stone

① **April** /'eɪprəl/ *noun* the fourth month of the year, the month after March and before May ○ *Her birthday is in April.* ○ *We went on holiday last April.* (NOTE: **April 5th** *or* **April 5**: say 'the fifth of April' or 'April the fifth' or in US English 'April fifth'.)

apron /'eɪprən/ *noun* **1.** a piece of clothing worn over the front of your usual clothes to protect them when cooking **2.** (*at an airport*) a piece of ground on which planes can be parked

apt /æpt/ *adj* fitting well ◇ **to be apt to do something** to be likely to do something regularly ○ *Our old car was apt to break down on motorways.*

aptitude /'æptɪˌtjuːd/ *noun* a natural ability that can be developed further [~for] ○ *She shows real aptitude for teaching.*

aquarium /ə'kweəriəm/ *noun* a tank for keeping tropical fish in

Aquarius /ə'kweəriəs/ *noun* one of the signs of the Zodiac, shaped like a person carrying water, covering the period 20th January to 18th February

aquatic /ə'kwætɪk/ *adj* **1.** living in water, not on land (NOTE: Animals and plants that live on land are **terrestrial**.) **2.** taking place in water

aqueduct /'ækwɪdʌkt/ *noun* a high bridge carrying water over a valley

Arab /'ærəb/ *noun* a person who speaks Arabic and who comes from one of the countries in the Middle East

Arabic /'ærəbɪk/ *noun* the language spoken by Arabs

Arabic numeral /ˌærəbɪk 'njuːmərəl/ *noun* one of the set of written symbols such as 2, 3 or 6 used to represent numbers. Compare **Roman numeral**

arbiter /'ɑːbɪtə/ *noun* a person who decides what is fashionable

arbitrary /'ɑːbɪtrəri/ *adj* done without any reason

arbitration /ˌɑːbɪ'treɪʃ(ə)n/ *noun* the settling of an argument by an official judge, accepted by both sides (NOTE: + **arbitrate** *v*; + **arbitrator** *n*)

③ **arc** /ɑːk/ *noun* a curve, like part of a circle

③ **arcade** /ɑː'keɪd/ *noun* a covered area for walking around a square or an area of shops

arcane /ɑː'keɪn/ *adj* mysterious and secret

③ **arch** /ɑːtʃ/ *noun* a round structure forming a roof or entrance ■ *verb* (**arches, arching, arched**) to make something round like an arch ○ *The cat arched her back and started spitting.*

③ **archaeologist** /ˌɑːki'ɒlədʒɪst/ *noun* a person who studies or is a specialist in archaeology

③ **archaeology** /ˌɑːki'ɒlədʒi/ *noun* the digging up of buried remains of buildings to study ancient civilisations (NOTE: + **archaeological** *adj*)

archaic /ɑː'keɪɪk/ *adj* **1.** dating from ancient times **2.** old-fashioned

archbishop /ɑːtʃ'bɪʃəp/ *noun* a bishop holding the highest rank

archer /'ɑːtʃə/ *noun* a person who shoots with a bow and arrows

archery /'ɑːtʃəri/ *noun* the sport of shooting arrows at targets

archetypal /ˌɑːkɪˈtaɪp(ə)l/ *adj* very typical

archetype /ˈɑːkɪtaɪp/ *noun* a typical example of something

archipelago /ˌɑːkɪˈpeləgəʊ/ (*plural* **archipelagos** or **archipelagoes**) *noun* a group of islands

③ **architect** /ˈɑːkɪtekt/ *noun* a person who designs buildings

③ **architecture** /ˈɑːkɪtektʃə/ *noun* the design of buildings

archive /ˈɑːkaɪv/ *noun* **1.** an organised collection of documents **2.** a place where archives are kept **3.** a copy of computer files stored on tape or disk

archives /ˈɑːkaɪvz/ *plural noun* a collection of documents

archway /ˈɑːtʃweɪ/ *noun* a passage which goes under an arch

arctic /ˈɑːktɪk/ *adj* **1.** referring to the area round the North Pole **2.** extremely cold ■ *noun* **the Arctic** the area round the North Pole ○ *The Arctic is home to polar bears.*

ardent /ˈɑːd(ə)nt/ *adj* very keen

arduous /ˈɑːdjuəs/ *adj* extremely difficult and needing a lot of effort or work

① **are** /ə, ɑː/ 1st person plural present of **be**. 2nd person singular present of **be**. 2nd person plural present of **be**. 3rd person plural present of **be**

① **area** /ˈeəriə/ *noun* **1.** a space ○ *The whole area round the town hall is going to be rebuilt.* ○ *We always sit in the 'no smoking' area.* **2.** a measurement of the space taken up by something, calculated by multiplying the length by the width ○ *The area of the room is four square metres.* ○ *We are looking for a shop with a sales area of about 100 square metres.* **3.** a part of a town or country ○ *Our house is near the commercial area of the town.* ○ *The factory is in a very good area for getting to the motorways and airports.* □ **the London area** the part of England around London ○ *Houses in the London area are more expensive than elsewhere in the country.*

① **area code** /ˈeəriə kəʊd/ *noun* a special telephone number which is given to a particular area

arena /əˈriːnə/ *noun* **1.** a building with seats for people to sit and watch events like sports or fights **2.** a field of activity where something happens

① **aren't** /ɑːnt/ ♦ **be**

arguable /ˈɑːgjuəb(ə)l/ *adj* possibly not true

arguably /ˈɑːgjuəbli/ *adv* quite possibly true

① **argue** /ˈɑːgjuː/ (**argues, arguing, argued**) *verb* to discuss without agreeing, often in a noisy or angry way ○ *They argued over the prices.* ○ *She argued with the waiter about the bill.* ○ *I could hear them arguing in the next room.* (NOTE: You argue **with** someone **about** *or* **over** something.)

① **argument** /ˈɑːgjʊmənt/ *noun* a situation in which people discuss something without agreeing ○ *Nobody would back her up in her argument with the boss.* □ **to get into an argument with someone** to start to argue with someone ○ *He got into an argument with the taxi driver.*

argumentative /ˌɑːgjʊˈmentətɪv/ *adj* liking to argue

arid /ˈærɪd/ *adj* extremely dry because of a regular lack of rain

Aries /ˈeəriːz/ *noun* one of the signs of the Zodiac, shaped like a ram, covering the period 21st March to 19th April

② **arise** /əˈraɪz/ (**arises, arising, arose, arisen**) *verb* to start to appear ○ *The problem arose in the planning department.*

aristocracy /ˌærɪˈstɒkrəsi/ *noun* the people of the highest class in society, usually with titles such as Lord or Duke

aristocrat /ˈærɪstəkræt/ *noun* a member of the aristocracy

aristocratic /ˌærɪstəˈkrætɪk/ *adj* referring to the aristocracy

③ **arithmetic** /əˈrɪθmətɪk/ *noun* calculations with numbers, especially as a subject studied at school

① **arm** /ɑːm/ *noun* **1.** the part of the body which goes from the shoulder to the hand ○ *He held the parcel under his arm.* ○ *She tripped over the pavement and broke her arm.* **2.** the part of a chair which you can rest your arms on ○ *He put his coffee cup on the arm of his chair.* ■ *verb* (**arms, arming, armed**) to give weapons to ○ *The police were armed with guns.* ◇ **arm in arm** with arms linked together ○ *They walked down the street arm in arm.*

armaments /ˈɑːməmənts/ *plural noun* heavy weapons ○ *an important armaments manufacturer* ○ *Britain has been supplying armaments to the Middle Eastern countries.*

armband /ˈɑːmbænd/ *noun* a band of cloth which goes round your arm

armchair /ˈɑːmtʃeə/ *noun* a chair with arms

② **armed** /ɑːmd/ *adj* **1.** provided with weapons ○ *Most British policemen are not armed.* ○ *Armed guards surrounded the house.* **2.** involving weapons ○ *the armed struggle between the two groups* **3.** ready for use as a weapon ○ *The device is already armed.* ◇ **armed with** provided with ○ *Armed with picnic baskets, towels and cameras, we set off for the beach.*

armed forces /ˌɑːmd ˈfɔːsɪz/, **armed services** /ˌɑːmd ˈsɜːvɪsɪz/ *plural noun* the army, navy and air force of a country

armful /ˈɑːmfʊl/ *noun* an amount of things you can carry in your arms

armistice /ˈɑːmɪstɪs/ *noun* an agreement to stop fighting

armour /ˈɑːmə/ *noun* **1.** metal clothing which soldiers wore in the past, to protect their bodies **2.** sheets of thick metal covering on military ships or vehicles, to protect them against attack (NOTE: [all senses] The US spelling is **armor**.)

armoured /ˈɑːməd/ *adj* protected by armour

armpit /ˈɑːmpɪt/ *noun* the part of your body under each arm where it joins the body

arms race /ˈɑːmz reɪs/ *noun* competition between countries to have the largest number of weapons or the most powerful weapons

① **army** /ˈɑːmi/ (*plural* **armies**) *noun* all the soldiers of a country, trained for fighting on land ○ *He left school at 16 and joined the army.* ○ *An army spokesman held a news conference.*

aroma /əˈrəʊmə/ *noun* a pleasant smell of something you can eat or drink ○ *the aroma of freshly baked bread*

aromatherapy /əˌrəʊməˈθerəpi/ *noun* a treatment with pleasant-smelling oils

aromatic /ˌærəˈmætɪk/ *adj* with a strong pleasant smell

arose /əˈrəʊz/ past tense of **arise**

① **around** /əˈraʊnd/ *prep* **1.** going all round something ○ *She had a gold chain around her neck.* ○ *The flood water was all around the village.* **2.** close to or in a place or area ○ *Is there a bus stop around here?* **3.** in various places ○ *We have lots of computers around the office.* **4.** not exactly ○ *It will cost around £200.* ○ *Around sixty people came to the meeting.* ■ *adv* **1.** in various places ○ *Papers were lying around all over the floor.* ○ *The restaurants were all full, so we walked around for some time.* **2.** in a position that is fairly near ○ *We try not to talk about it when she's around.* ○ *It's the only food shop around.* **3.** in existence ○ *She's one of the best eye surgeons around.* ○ *The new coins have been around for some weeks now.*

arousal /əˈraʊz(ə)l/ *noun* a feeling of sexual excitement

arouse /əˈraʊz/ (**arouses, arousing, aroused**) *verb* **1.** to make someone feel a particular emotion **2.** to make someone feel sexually excited. Compare **rouse**

② **arrange** /əˈreɪndʒ/ (**arranges, arranging, arranged**) *verb* **1.** to put in order ○ *The chairs are arranged in rows.* ○ *She arranged the books in alphabetical order.* ○ *The ground floor is arranged as an open-plan area with a little kitchen at the side.* **2.** to make a plan for something ○ *Let's arrange to meet somewhere before we go to the theatre.* ○ *The tour has been arranged by the travel agent.* ○ *She arranged for a taxi to meet him at the airport.* ○ *I've arranged with my mother that she will feed the cat while we're away.* (NOTE: You arrange **for** someone to do something; you arrange **for** something to be done; or you arrange **to** do something.)

② **arrangement** /əˈreɪndʒmənt/ *noun* **1.** the process of putting things in order **2.** a general agreement ○ *We have an arrangement by which we meet for lunch every Tuesday.* ■ *plural noun* **arrangements** the activities involved in making plans for an event ○ *All the arrangements for the party were left to me.*

③ **array** /əˈreɪ/ *noun* a display

③ **arrest** /əˈrest/ *verb* (**arrests, arresting, arrested**) (of the police) to catch and hold someone who has broken the law ○ *The police arrested two men and took them to the police station.* ○ *He ended up getting arrested as he tried to leave the country.* ○ *She was arrested for stealing, but the judge let her off with a fine.* ■ *noun* the act of holding someone for breaking the law ○ *The police made several arrests at the demonstration.* ◇ **under arrest** held by the police ○ *After the fight, three people were under arrest.*

① **arrival** /əˈraɪv(ə)l/ *noun* **1.** the act of reaching a place ○ *We announce the arrival of flight AB 987 from Tangiers.* ○ *We apologise for the late arrival of the 14.25 express from Edinburgh.* ○ *The time of arrival is 5 p.m.* **2.** a person who has arrived ○ *He's a new arrival on our staff.* ■ *plural noun* **arrivals** the part of an airport that deals with passengers who are arriving. Compare **departure** ◇ **on arrival** when you arrive ○ *On arrival at the hotel, members of the party will be allocated rooms.*

① **arrive** /ə'raɪv/ (**arrives, arriving, arrived**) *verb* to reach a place ○ *They arrived at the hotel tired out.* ○ *The train from Paris arrives in London at 5 p.m.* (NOTE: You arrive **in** a town or **in** a country but **at** a place.)

arrogant /'ærəgənt/ *adj* very proud in an unpleasant way ○ *He's such an arrogant young man.* ○ *What an arrogant way to treat customers!*

arrow /'ærəʊ/ *noun* **1.** a weapon made of a piece of wood with a sharp point **2.** a printed sign &rarrowf; which points to something

arsenal /'ɑːsn(ə)l/ *noun* a store of weapons

arsenic /'ɑːsnɪk/ *noun* a very poisonous substance

arson /'ɑːs(ə)n/ *noun* the crime of setting fire to something such as a building or some property

arson attack /'ɑːs(ə)n əˌtæk/ *noun* an act of setting fire to something such as a house

① **art** /ɑːt/ *noun* **1.** the practice of creating objects, e.g. by painting, drawing or sculpture ○ *She is taking art lessons.* ○ *When you're in Washington, don't miss the Museum of Modern Art.* **2.** the objects that are created in this way **3.** a particular skill or ability ○ *He has mastered the art of not answering reporters' questions.*

artefact /'ɑːtɪfækt/, **artifact** *noun* an object such as a tool or a dish that was made by a person in the past

artery /'ɑːtəri/ (*plural* **arteries**) *noun* a tube carrying blood from the heart around the body. Compare **vein**

arthritis /ɑː'θraɪtɪs/ *noun* a painful medical condition affecting a joint, where two bones meet

artichoke /'ɑːtɪtʃəʊk/ *noun* a tall thistle-like plant of which you boil the head and then eat the base of the leaves

① **article** /'ɑːtɪk(ə)l/ *noun* **1.** a report in a newspaper [~about/on] ○ *Did you read the article on skiing in yesterday's paper?* **2.** an object or thing ○ *Several articles of clothing were found near the road.* **3.** a word used before a noun to show whether you are referring to a particular or general example of something. The definite article is 'the' and the indefinite article is 'a' or 'an'.

articulate[1] /ɑː'tɪkjʊleɪt/ (**articulates, articulating, articulated**) *verb* to speak in a clear and careful way

articulate[2] /ɑː'tɪkjʊlət/ *adj* describes someone who expresses thoughts clearly

articulated lorry /ɑːˌtɪkjʊleɪtɪd 'lɒri/ *noun* a large truck with two or more parts which are connected so that they can move in different directions at the same time, e.g. when going around a corner

artifact /'ɑːtɪfækt/ another spelling of **artefact**

③ **artificial** /ˌɑːtɪ'fɪʃ(ə)l/ *adj* not natural ○ *She was wearing artificial pearls.*

artificial intelligence /ˌɑːtɪfɪʃ(ə)l ɪn'telɪdʒəns/ *noun* the use of computer programs to make machines do things which people can do

artificially /ˌɑːtɪ'fɪʃ(ə)li/ *adv* in a way that is not natural

artillery /ɑː'tɪləri/ *noun* the large guns that an army has

artisan /ˌɑːtɪ'zæn/ *noun* a skilled worker who makes things with his or her hands

② **artist** /'ɑːtɪst/ *noun* a person who is skilled in making works of art such as paintings ○ *She collects paintings by 19th-century artists.*

artiste /ɑː'tiːst/ *noun* a professional performer such as a singer or dancer

artistic /ɑː'tɪstɪk/ *adj* **1.** (*of a person*) showing skill or interest in art **2.** arranged or done in a way that shows skill and looks beautiful (NOTE: + **artistically**)

artistry /'ɑːtɪstri/ *noun* skill in a particular art

③ **arts** /ɑːts/ *plural noun* **1.** all work connected with art **2.** a subject of study which is not a science, e.g. history or literature

artwork /'ɑːtwɜːk/ *noun* things such as pictures or designs which are printed in a book or used in advertising

arty /'ɑːti/, **arty-crafty** /ˌɑːti 'krɑːfti/ *adj* pretending to be artistic; making artistic things

① **as** /əz, æz/ *conj* **1.** because ○ *As you can't drive, you'll have to go by bus.* ○ *As it's cold, you should wear an overcoat.* **2.** at the same time that something else happens ○ *As he was getting into the bath, the telephone rang.* ○ *The little girl ran into the road as the car was turning the corner.* **3.** in the same way ○ *Leave everything as it is.* ■ *prep* **1.** in a particular job ○ *She had a job as a bus driver.* **2.** because of being a particular type of person ○ *As a doctor, he has to know the symptoms of all the common diseases.* **3.** in a particular way ○ *She was dressed as a nurse.* ○ *They treated him as a friend of the family.* □ **as...as** used in comparisons ○ *as far as I can see* ○ *She is nearly as tall as I am.* ○ *I can't run as fast as you.* ◇ **as from** from a particular time ○ *as from next Friday* ◇ **as if, as though** in the same way as ◇ **as...as** used in comparisons ○ *She is nearly as tall as I am.* ○ *I can't run as fast as you.* ◇ **as well** in addition to something or someone else that has been mentioned ○ *She came to have tea and brought her sister as well.* ○ *We visited the castle and swam in the pool as well.* ◇ **as well as** in addition to or together with ○ *He has a cottage in the country as well as a flat in town.* ○ *As well as being a maths teacher, he is a part-time policeman.*

asbestos /æs'bestəs/ *noun* a substance which does not burn, formerly used in buildings to protect against fire

③ **ascend** /ə'send/ (**ascends, ascending, ascended**) *verb* to go up ○ *The balloon rapidly ascended to 3000m.*

ascendancy /ə'sendənsi/ *noun* the influence or power that one person or group has over another

③ **ascent** /ə'sent/ *noun* the action of climbing up (NOTE: Do not confuse with **assent**.)

③ **ascertain** /ˌæsə'teɪn/ (**ascertains, ascertaining, ascertained**) *verb* to check facts to see if they are true (*formal*)

asexual /eɪ'sekʃuəl/ *adj* with no sexual organs or without having sex

ash /æʃ/ *noun* **1.** a grey dust left after something has burnt **2.** a type of tree that grows in the northern part of Europe

③ **ashamed** /ə'ʃeɪmd/ *adj* embarrassed and sorry for something that you have done or not done

ashes /'æʃɪz/ *plural noun* the grey dust that remains when the body of a dead person has been cremated

ashore /ə'ʃɔː/ *adv* to or onto land, e.g. from the sea or from a ship. ◊ **shore**

③ **ashtray** /'æʃtreɪ/ *noun* a little dish for cigarette ash

① **Asian** /'eɪʒ(ə)n/ *adj* relating to Asia ■ *noun* a person coming from one of the countries of Asia, especially the Indian subcontinent ○ *More than half the children in the class are Asians.*

③ **aside** /ə'saɪd/ *adv* to one side ○ *He took me aside and whispered in my ear.* ◇ **aside from** except for ○ *Aside from a minor infection, his health had been remarkably good.* ○ *I've got to read these three articles, and that's aside from all my regular work.*

① **ask** /ɑːsk/ (**asks, asking, asked**) *verb* **1.** to put a question to get information ○ *She asked a policeman the way to the hospital.* ○ *Joe went to the station to ask about cheap tickets.* ○ *Ask the assistant how much the shoes cost.* **2.** to put a question to get someone to do something ○ *Ask your father to teach you how to drive.* ○ *Can I ask you not to make so much noise?* **3.** to invite someone to an event or to do something ○ *We asked them to our party.* ○ *She asked me to go skiing with her.* ◇ **to ask after someone** to ask for news about someone, especially about his or her health ○ *Several of your colleagues were asking after you.*

ask for *phrasal verb* to say that you want something ○ *Someone came into the shop and asked for the manager.* □ **ask for something back** to ask someone to give back something which you had lent to him or her

ask out *phrasal verb* to ask someone to go out with you, e.g. to a restaurant or to the cinema ○ *Bill wants to ask my sister out.*

askew /ə'skjuː/ *adv* not straight ○ *That picture's askew.*

① **asleep** /ə'sliːp/ *adj* sleeping ○ *He was asleep and didn't hear the fire alarm.* ○ *They were lying asleep on the ground.* □ **to fall asleep** to begin to sleep

asparagus /ə'spærəgəs/ (*plural same*) *noun* a green vegetable that has long thin stems and pointed tips and which you cook before eating

① **aspect** /'æspekt/ *noun* **1.** a way of considering something such as a situation or a problem ○ *There are several aspects of the problem to be considered before I can decide.* **2.** the direction in which a building or piece of ground faces ○ *The living room has a southerly aspect.*

asphalt /'æsfælt/ *noun* a mixture of tar, small stones and sand, used for making road surfaces

asphyxiate /æs'fɪksieɪt/ (**asphyxiates, asphyxiating, asphyxiated**) *verb* to stop someone breathing, or to die because of being unable to breathe (NOTE: + **asphyxiation** *n*)

aspirate /'æspɪrət/ *noun* a speech sound made by breathing out, e.g. the 'h' in 'horse'

③ **aspiration** /ˌæspɪ'reɪʃ(ə)n/ *noun* something which you want to achieve or to be successful at

aspirational /ˌæspɪ'reɪʃ(ə)n(ə)l/ *adj* typical of people who want to become more successful and be able to afford a more expensive home and way of life

③ **aspire** /ə'spaɪə/ (**aspires, aspiring, aspired**) *verb* □ **to aspire to something** to want to achieve something ○ *He aspires to great success as an actor.*

① **aspirin** /'æsprɪn/ *noun* **1.** a common drug, used in the treatment of minor illnesses to reduce pain **2.** a pill that contains aspirin

aspiring /ə'spaɪərɪŋ/ *adj* hoping to get something

ass /æs/ *noun US* the part of your body that you sit on (*offensive*)

assailant /ə'seɪlənt/ *noun* a person who attacks someone

assassin /ə'sæsɪn/ *noun* a person who kills someone famous for political reasons

assassinate /ə'sæsɪneɪt/ (**assassinates, assassinating, assassinated**) *verb* to kill a famous person, especially for political reasons ○ *Do you remember the day when the President was assassinated?* (NOTE: + **assassination** *n*)

③ **assault** /ə'sɔːlt/ *noun* an attack [~on] ○ *an assault on a police officer* ■ *verb* (**assaults, assaulting, assaulted**) to attack

assemble /ə'semb(ə)l/ (**assembles, assembling, assembled**) *verb* **1.** (*especially of people*) to come together in a place, or to be brought together by someone especially formally or in an ordered way ○ *We'll assemble outside the hotel by the coach at 9 a.m.* ○ *They assembled a panel of experts to renew the project.* **2.** to collect a set of things together ○ *Assemble all the ingredients you need before you start to cook.* **3.** to make something from separate parts ○ *The cupboard can be assembled at home.*

② **assembly** /ə'sembli/ (*plural* **assemblies**) *noun* **1.** a meeting **2.** the process of putting the pieces of something together to make it complete

assembly line /ə'sembli laɪn/ *noun* a moving line in a factory, where the product moves slowly past workers who add pieces to it as it goes past

assent /ə'sent/ *noun* the approval of or agreement with something such as a suggestion

③ **assert** /ə'sɜːt/ (**asserts, asserting, asserted**) *verb* to state something firmly □ **to assert yourself** to state your opinions strongly

③ **assertion** /ə'sɜːʃ(ə)n/ *noun* a statement of something which you believe to be true but of which you have no proof

assertive /ə'sɜːtɪv/ *adj* confident and stating your opinions in a strong way

② **assess** /ə'ses/ (**assesses, assessing, assessed**) *verb* **1.** to consider something or someone in order to make a judgment or decision about it ○ *It's hard to assess how difficult it will be to make the necessary changes.* **2.** to consider someone's achievement or progress in order to decide if it is satisfactory ○ *Students are regularly assessed by their teachers and feedback.* **3.** to calculate an amount to be paid ○ *The cost of the new building is assessed at £1 million.* (NOTE: + **assessment**)

② **asset** /'æset/ *noun* a valuable quality [~to] ○ *Knowing several languages is an asset to a businessperson.*

assign /ə'saɪn/ (**assigns, assigning, assigned**) *verb* □ **to assign someone to something** or **something to someone** to give someone the job of doing something ○ *They assigned her to the accounts department.* ○ *We assigned the job of cleaning the kitchen to Jack.*

① **assignment** /ə'saɪnmənt/ *noun* **1.** a piece of work that has to be done in a specific time ○ *My literature assignment has to be finished by Wednesday.* ○ *He was given the assignment of reporting on the war.* **2.** the act of giving someone a job to do

assimilate /ə'sɪmɪleɪt/ (**assimilates, assimilating, assimilated**) *verb* **1.** to learn and understand **2.** (*of the body*) to change the food that you have just eaten into substances that can be used

③ **assist** /ə'sɪst/ (**assists, assisting, assisted**) *verb* to help someone [~in/with] ○ *He assists me with my income tax forms.* ○ *I will be assisted in my work by Jackie Smith.* □ **to assist someone to do something or with something** to help someone to do something (*formal*) ○ *The money assists young dancers to train.*

② **assistance** /ə'sɪst(ə)ns/ *noun* help ○ *She will need assistance with her luggage.* ○ *He was trying to change the wheel when a truck driver offered his assistance.* ○ *He asked if he could be of any assistance.*

② **assistant** /ə'sɪst(ə)nt/ *noun* a person who helps someone as part of their job ○ *His assistant makes all his appointments.*

associate[1] /ə'səʊsieɪt/ (**associates, associating, associated**) *verb* **1.** to connect different people or things in your mind ○ *I always associate that book with the wonderful holiday when I first read it.* □ **to be associated with** to be connected with or involved in something ○ *This firm has been associated with the project from the start.* **2.** to have contact with or regularly meet someone [~with] ○ *I don't want you to associate with violent people like that.*

associate² /ə'səʊsiət/ *noun* a person who works in the same business as someone else

① **association** /əˌsəʊsi'eɪʃ(ə)n/ *noun* **1.** an official group of people or a group of companies in the same trade ○ *an association offering support to victims of street violence* ○ *the Association of British Travel Agents* **2.** a connection formed in the mind between things ○ *For some people, a black cat has an association with luck.* ■ *plural noun* **associations** feelings produced by memories of particular people or places ○ *Manchester has strong family associations for him.* ◇ **in association with** together with ○ *The guidebook is published in association with the local tourist board.*

assorted /ə'sɔːtɪd/ *adj* various, mixed

assortment /ə'sɔːtmənt/ *noun* a mixture of a lot of things that have some differences, e.g. in shape or colour

① **assume** /ə'sjuːm/ (**assumes, assuming, assumed**) *verb* **1.** to imagine or believe that something is true [~(that)] ○ *Let's assume that he is innocent.* ○ *I assume you have enough money to pay for the meal?* **2.** to take on something such as a job or responsibility ○ *When she was twenty-one, she assumed complete control of the family business.* ○ *He has assumed responsibility for fire safety.*

assumed name /əˌsjuːmd 'neɪm/ *noun* a false name

③ **assuming** /ə'sjuːmɪŋ/ *conj* believing something to be true

② **assumption** /ə'sʌmpʃən/ *noun* a belief that something is true

assurance /ə'ʃʊərəns/ *noun* **1.** an attitude of confidence in your own abilities ○ *He didn't have the assurance to face a press conference* **2.** the fact of being sure that something will happen **3.** a promise ○ *He gave her an assurance that he would not do it again.*

② **assure** /ə'ʃʊə/ (**assures, assuring, assured**) *verb* **1.** to state something definitely **2.** to make sure that something will happen

assured /ə'ʃʊəd/ *adj* very certain and confident

asterisk /'æstərɪsk/ *noun* a printing sign like a star, used to draw attention to something

asteroid /'æstərɔɪd/ *noun* a mass of rock that travels in a path round the sun

asthma /'æsmə/ *noun* a medical condition in which someone suffers breathing difficulties, often because a particular substance has a bad effect on his or her body

asthmatic /æs'mætɪk/ *noun* a person who has asthma

② **astonish** /ə'stɒnɪʃ/ (**astonishes, astonishing, astonished**) *verb* to surprise someone very much [~that] ○ *His success in maths astonished his teacher – he never came to any of her classes.* ○ *It astonishes me that he can't use a computer.*

astonished /ə'stɒnɪʃt/ *adj* very surprised ○ *We were astonished to learn that the head teacher had left.*

astonishing /ə'stɒnɪʃɪŋ/ *adj* very surprising ○ *They spent an astonishing amount of money buying Christmas presents.*

astonishment /ə'stɒnɪʃmənt/ *noun* great surprise

③ **astound** /ə'staʊnd/ (**astounds, astounding, astounded**) *verb* to surprise someone completely

astounded /ə'staʊndɪd/ *adj* very surprised

astounding /ə'staʊndɪŋ/ *adj* very surprising

astride /ə'straɪd/ *adv, prep* with your legs on each side of something ○ *He was sitting astride his bicycle, with both feet on the ground.* ○ *Sit astride and hold tight.*

astrology /ə'strɒlədʒi/ *noun* the practice of saying what the future will be by looking at the position of the planets and the stars

③ **astronaut** /'æstrənɔːt/ *noun* a person who travels into space

astronomical /ˌæstrə'nɒmɪk(ə)l/ *adj* **1.** referring to astronomy **2.** (*of a price or amount*) very large (*informal*)

③ **astronomy** /ə'strɒnəmi/ *noun* the scientific study of the stars, sun and planets

astute /ə'stjuːt/ *adj* clever at understanding things quickly

③ **asylum** /ə'saɪləm/ *noun* **1.** the right to stay in another country if you have been treated badly in your own country ○ *to seek asylum* ○ *to grant someone asylum* ○ *to ask for political asylum* **2.** a hospital for people who have mental illnesses (*old*)

asylum seeker /ə'saɪləm ˌsiːkə/ *noun* a person who asks for permission to stay in another country because the political situation in his or her own country is not safe for him or her to stay there

asymmetrical /ˌeɪsɪˈmetrɪk(ə)l/ *adj* which does not have the same shape or size on both sides

① **at** /ət, æt/ *prep* **1.** used for showing time ○ *We'll meet at eleven o'clock.* ○ *You must put your lights on when you drive at night.* ○ *At the weekend, we went to see my mother.* ○ *We went to Paris at Easter.* **2.** used for showing place ○ *Meet us at the post office.* ○ *She's got a job at the supermarket.* ○ *He's not at home, he's at work.* **3.** used for showing speed ○ *The train was travelling at 200 kilometres an hour.* **4.** showing direction ○ *She threw her slipper at her brother.* **5.** showing cause ○ *She laughed at my old coat.* (NOTE: **at** is often used after verbs, e.g. **to look at, to point at.**)

① **ate** /et, eɪt/ past tense of **eat**

atheist /ˈeɪθiɪst/ *noun* a person who believes there is no god. Compare **agnostic**

athlete /ˈæθliːt/ *noun* a person who takes part in sports especially those such as running

athletic /æθˈletɪk/ *adj* referring to athletics

athletics /æθˈletɪks/ *noun* organised sports such as running which are competitions between individuals (NOTE: no plural)

atlas /ˈætləs/ *noun* a book of maps

ATM /ˌeɪ tiː ˈem/ *abbr* automated teller machine

② **atmosphere** /ˈætməsfɪə/ *noun* **1.** the air around the Earth ○ *The atmosphere surrounds the Earth to a height of several hundred kilometres.* **2.** the air in a particular place ○ *The room had a hot stuffy atmosphere.* **3.** a general feeling [~of] ○ *a friendly atmosphere* ○ *There was an atmosphere of fear everywhere after the bomb attack.*

atmospheric /ˌætməsˈferɪk/ *adj* **1.** referring to the atmosphere **2.** mysterious, beautiful

② **atom** /ˈætəm/ *noun* the smallest part of a chemical element that can exist independently

atom bomb /ˈætəm bɒm/ *noun* a bomb using nuclear energy

③ **atomic** /əˈtɒmɪk/ *adj* relating to the energy produced if an atom is split apart

atomic bomb /əˌtɒmɪk ˈbɒm/ *noun* same as **atom bomb**

atone /əˈtəʊn/ (**atones, atoning, atoned**) *verb* to do something which shows that you are sorry for doing something wrong (*formal*) (NOTE: + **atonement** *n*)

atrocious /əˈtrəʊʃəs/ *adj* very bad

atrocity /əˈtrɒsɪti/ (*plural* **atrocities**) *noun* an extremely evil act

② **attach** /əˈtætʃ/ (**attaches, attaching, attached**) *verb* to fasten something to something else ○ *The gate is attached to the post.* ○ *I am attaching a copy of my previous letter.*

attached /əˈtætʃt/ *adj* having a strong liking for someone or something ○ *She's very attached to her old dog*

attachment /əˈtætʃmənt/ *noun* **1.** something which can be attached to something else **2.** a strong liking for someone or something [~to] ○ *Everyone had known of his attachment to her.* **3.** a document attached to an email

① **attack** /əˈtæk/ *noun* **1.** the act of trying to hurt someone or something ○ *They made an attack on the town.* **2.** a criticism ○ *He launched an attack on the government.* **3.** a sudden return of a particular illness ○ *She had an attack of malaria.* ■ *verb* (**attacks, attacking, attacked**) to try to hurt someone or to hit someone ○ *Three men attacked her as she walked home.* ○ *The old lady was attacked by muggers.* ◇ **under attack** in the situation of being attacked ○ *The town is under attack from rebel guerrillas.*

③ **attacker** /əˈtækə/ *noun* a person who attacks someone or something ○ *Can you describe your attacker?*

③ **attain** /əˈteɪn/ (**attains, attaining, attained**) *verb* to reach a particular status or rank ○ *He attained the position of manager.* ○ *All six students attained full marks in this part of the exam.*

attainment /əˈteɪnmənt/ *noun* success in achieving something or reaching a particular goal

① **attempt** /əˈtempt/ *noun* an act of trying to do something ○ *She attempted to lift the box onto the table.* □ **an attempt on someone's life** the action of trying to kill someone ■ *verb* (**attempts, attempting, attempted**) to try to do something, especially something difficult ○ *I'll attempt another trip to collect the books when my car has been repaired.* ○ *She attempted to lift the box onto the table.*

② **attend** /əˈtend/ (**attends, attending, attended**) *verb* **1.** to be present at an event ○ *Twenty-five people attended the wedding.* ○ *They organised a meeting, but only one or two people attended.* **2.** to listen carefully ○ *Students should attend carefully to the teacher's instructions.*

attend to *phrasal verb* to give careful thought to something and deal with it

attendance /ə'tendəns/ *noun* **1.** the fact of being present at an event **2.** the number of people present at an event (NOTE: no plural)

attendant /ə'tendənt/ *noun* a person on duty in a public place such as a museum

① **attention** /ə'tenʃən/ *noun* **1.** the act of concentrating on what you are doing ○ *Don't distract the driver's attention.* ○ *Please give the talk on safety procedures your full attention.* □ **to pay attention to** to concentrate on something and think about it carefully ○ *Pay attention to the instructions in the leaflet.* □ **Don't pay any attention to something** you can ignore something ○ *Don't pay any attention to what she says – she's making it up.* **2.** special care, help or extra work ○ *The garden is large and needs a lot of attention.* ○ *The children were quiet and shy but responded well to the special attention they were given.* □ **medical attention** treatment by doctors and nurses ○ *That cut needs urgent medical attention.* **3.** the position of a soldier, standing straight, with heels together and looking straight ahead ○ *The guards stood to attention at the entrance to the palace.* ◇ **for the attention of** words written on a letter to show that it is intended for a particular person to deal with it ◇ **to attract (someone's) attention** to make someone notice someone or something ○ *The new play has attracted a lot of press attention* or *attention in the press.*

attention span /ə'tenʃən spæn/ *noun* the length of time that someone can concentrate effectively on a particular job or activity

attentive /ə'tentɪv/ *adj* listening carefully

attic /'ætɪk/ *noun* a room or space at the top of a house under the roof

① **attitude** /'ætɪtjuːd/ *noun* **1.** a way of thinking ○ *What is the government's attitude to the problem?* **2.** the position of your body, e.g. standing or sitting ○ *His portrait shows him in a thoughtful attitude.*

② **attorney** /ə'tɜːni/ (*plural* **attorneys**) *noun* a lawyer (*especially US*)

② **attract** /ə'trækt/ (**attracts, attracting, attracted**) *verb* to make someone want to come to a place or want to become involved in something such as a business ○ *The shops are lowering their prices to attract more customers.* ○ *The exhibition attracted hundreds of visitors.* ○ *We must see if we can attract more candidates for the job.* □ **to be attracted to someone** to feel a sexual interest in someone

③ **attraction** /ə'trækʃən/ *noun* **1.** a reason for liking someone or something ○ *The flat's main attraction is its closeness to the centre of town.* **2.** something which attracts people ○ *The Tower of London is a great tourist attraction.*

② **attractive** /ə'træktɪv/ *adj* **1.** pleasant to look at ○ *They found the mountain scenery very attractive.* ○ *She's an attractive woman.* **2.** having features which people like ○ *There are some attractive bargains in the sale.* ○ *The rival firm made him a very attractive offer.* (NOTE: + **attractiveness**)

attributable /ə'trɪbjʊtəb(ə)l/ *adj* probably the cause of something

attribute[1] /'ætrɪbjuːt/ *noun* a quality that someone has

attribute[2] /ə'trɪbjuːt/ (**attributes, attributing, attributed**) *verb* ○ *The accident was attributed to faulty brakes.* □ **to attribute something to something or someone** to say that something was caused by something else, or that something was done by someone ○ *The accident was attributed to faulty brakes.* ○ *The remark was attributed to his father.*

attributive /ə'trɪbjʊtɪv/ *adj* (*of an adjective*) which comes before a noun and describes it

atypical /eɪ'tɪpɪk(ə)l/ *adj* not typical

aubergine /'əʊbəʒiːn/ *noun* a dark purple shiny fruit of a small plant, used as a vegetable

auburn /'ɔːbən/ *adj* of a dark reddish-brown colour

auction /'ɔːkʃən/ *noun* a public sale in which an object is sold to the person who offers to pay the highest amount of money for it ■ *verb* (**auctions, auctioning, auctioned**) to sell something at an auction

auctioneer /ˌɔːkʃə'nɪə/ *noun* a person who runs an auction

audacious /ɔː'deɪʃəs/ *adj* very brave or involving great risk

audacity /ɔː'dæsɪti/ *noun* audacious behaviour

audible /'ɔːdɪb(ə)l/ *adj* which can be heard

② **audience** /'ɔːdiəns/ *noun* the people watching a performance, e.g. at a theatre or cinema or on television, or listening to a radio programme ○ *Members of the audience cheered.* (NOTE: takes a singular or plural verb)

audio /ɔːdiəʊ/ *adj* referring to sound

audiovisual /ˌɔːdiəʊ ˈvɪʒuəl/ *adj* referring to sound and pictures that have been recorded together

audit /ˈɔːdɪt/ *noun* **1.** an official check of a company's accounts **2.** a careful examination of an organisation or a set of procedures to see how good they are

③ **audition** /ɔːˈdɪʃ(ə)n/ *noun* a test for performers such as actors, singers or dancers, to see if they will be given a part in a play or film ○ *I'm going for an audition for a part in 'Hamlet'.* ■ *verb* (**auditions, auditioning, auditioned**) **1.** to hold an audition for a performer **2.** to do an audition for a part [~for] ○ *Two hundred children auditioned for the lead role in the film.*

auditor /ˈɔːdɪtə/ *noun* someone whose job is to check a company's accounts officially

auditorium /ˌɔːdɪˈtɔːriəm/ (*plural* **auditoriums** or **auditoria**) *noun* a large hall used for events such as concerts

augment /ɔːgˈment/ (**augments, augmenting, augmented**) *verb* to increase the amount or value of something (*formal*)

augur /ˈɔːgə/ (**augurs, auguring, augured**) *verb* to be a sign for the future

① **August** /ˈɔːgəst/ *noun* the eighth month of the year, the month after July and before September ○ *My birthday is in August.* ○ *I left my job last August.* (NOTE: **August 15th** *or* **August 15**: say 'the fifteenth of August' or 'August the fifteenth' or in US English 'August fifteenth'.)

① **aunt** /ɑːnt/, **Aunt** *noun* the sister of your mother or father, or the wife of an uncle ○ *She lives next door to my aunt.* ○ *Say goodbye to Aunt Anne.*

auntie /ˈɑːnti/, **aunty** *noun* an aunt (*informal*)

au pair /əʊ ˈpeə/ *noun* a person, usually a young woman, who lives with a family in another country to learn the language while looking after children and helping to keep the house clean

aura /ˈɔːrə/ *noun* a general feeling or quality in a particular situation

aural /ˈɔːrəl/ *adj* referring to hearing (NOTE: Do not confuse with **oral**.)

auspicious /ɔːˈspɪʃəs/ *adj* likely to be successful

Aussie /ˈɒzi/ (*informal*) *adj* Australian ■ *noun* an Australian ○ *There was a group of Aussies in the restaurant.*

austere /ɔːˈstɪə/ *adj* **1.** with a plain and simple appearance **2.** with only the basic things you need to live

austerity /ɔːˈsterɪti/ *noun* **1.** the quality of being austere **2.** poor living conditions because people do not have much money

authentic /ɔːˈθentɪk/ *adj* original, not false or artificial

authenticate /ɔːˈθentɪkeɪt/ (**authenticates, authenticating, authenticated**) *verb* to prove that something is authentic

② **author** /ˈɔːθə/ *noun* a writer ○ *She is the author of a popular series of children's books.*

authorise /ˈɔːθəraɪz/ (**authorises, authorising, authorised**), **authorize** *verb* to give permission for something to be done

authoritarian /ɔːˌθɒrɪˈteəriən/ *adj* controlling people strictly

authoritative /ɔːˈθɒrɪtətɪv/ *adj* **1.** in a powerful way, so that people will obey **2.** recognised as expert

authorities /ɔːˈθɒrɪtiz/ *plural noun* the government

① **authority** /ɔːˈθɒrɪti/ (*plural* **authorities**) *noun* **1.** power to control something ○ *He has no authority to act on our behalf.* (NOTE: no plural) **2.** an organisation that has control over something ○ *The education authority pays teachers' salaries.* **3.** an expert ○ *He's an authority on Greek literature.*

autism /ˈɔːtɪz(ə)m/ *noun* a mental condition which makes people who have it unable to react in the usual way to other people

autobiography /ˌɔːtəʊbaɪˈɒgrəfi/ (*plural* **autobiographies**) *noun* a story of the life of a person written by himself or herself (NOTE: +**autobiographical** *adj*)

autocrat /ˈɔːtəkræt/ *noun* a person who governs or manages with total power over the people in a country or organisation (*often as criticism*)

autograph /ˈɔːtəgrɑːf/ *noun* a famous person's name written in their own writing for someone to keep (NOTE: + **autograph** *v*)

automate /ˈɔːtəmeɪt/ (**automates, automating, automated**) *verb* to use machines to do work which previously was done by people

automated teller machine /ˌɔːtəmeɪtɪd ˈtelə məˌʃiːn/ *noun* a machine outside a bank from which money can be obtained when a card is inserted. Abbreviation **ATM** (NOTE: The British term is **cashpoint machine**.)

① **automatic** /ˌɔːtəˈmætɪk/ *adj* **1.** working by itself ○ *There is an automatic device which cuts off the electric current.* **2.** done without thinking about it very much ○ *She gave the receptionist an automatic smile as she passed.* **3.** based on an agreement or existing situation ○ *an automatic fine for parking*

① **automatically** /ˌɔːtəˈmætɪkli/ *adv* **1.** by a machine, without people having to do anything **2.** without thinking about it very much ○ *I signed the bill automatically.* **3.** as a result of an agreement or existing situation ○ *The company automatically retires people at 60.*

automation /ˌɔːtəˈmeɪʃ(ə)n/ *noun* the practice of using machines instead of people to carry out work

automobile /ˈɔːtəməbiːl/ *noun especially US* a car

automotive /ˌɔːtəˈməʊtɪv/ *adj* referring to motor vehicles

autonomous /ɔːˈtɒnəməs/ *adj* self-governing

autonomy /ɔːˈtɒnəmi/ *noun* **1.** self-government **2.** the fact of being able to decide what to do by yourself, without asking anyone else

autopsy /ˈɔːtɒpsi/ (*plural* **autopsies**) *noun* the examination of the body of a dead person to find the cause of death

① **autumn** /ˈɔːtəm/ *noun* the season of the year between summer and winter ○ *In autumn, the leaves turn brown.* ○ *We went on a walking holiday last autumn.* ○ *I'll be starting my new job in the autumn term.*

auxiliary /ɔːgˈzɪliəri/ *noun* a person who helps other workers

auxiliary verb /ɔːgˈzɪliəri vɜːb/ *noun* a verb that is used with another verb to show person, number, mood, tense, or aspect

COMMENT: The auxiliary verbs in English are **be**, **do** and **have**.

① **available** /əˈveɪləb(ə)l/ *adj* able to be obtained ○ *The tablets are available from most chemists.* (NOTE: + **availability** *n*)

avalanche /ˈævəlɑːntʃ/ *noun* a sudden fall of a large amount of snow down the side of a mountain

avant-garde /ˌævɒŋ ˈgɑːd/ *adj* describes things such as forms of art or ways of thinking that are new, original and not traditional

Ave *abbr* avenue

avenge /əˈvendʒ/ (**avenges, avenging, avenged**) *verb* to hurt or punish someone because they have done wrong to you or to someone close to you □ **to avenge yourself on someone** to make someone suffer for something wrong that they have done to you ○ *She wanted to avenge herself on her rival.*

③ **avenue** /ˈævənjuː/ *noun* a wide street in a town, often with trees along the side

① **average** /ˈæv(ə)rɪdʒ/ *noun* **1.** the standard that is usual or typical ○ *The journey time today was much slower than the bus company's average.* **2.** a total calculated by adding several quantities together and dividing by the number of different quantities added [/~for] ○ *the average for the last three months* or *the last three months' average* ○ *The temperature has been above the average for the time of year.* ■ *adj* **1.** ordinary or typical ○ *It was an average working day at the office.* ○ *Their daughter is of above average intelligence.* □ **above** *or* **below average** more or less than is usual or typical **2.** not very good ○ *Their results were only average.* **3.** calculated by dividing the total by the number of quantities ○ *His average speed was 30 miles per hour.* ■ *verb* (**averages, averaging, averaged**) to be as an average ○ *Price increases have averaged 10% per annum.*

avert /əˈvɜːt/ (**averts, averting, averted**) *verb* to prevent something happening

aviation /ˌeɪviˈeɪʃ(ə)n/ *noun* the action of flying aircraft

avid /ˈævɪd/ *adj* extremely keen

avocado /ˌævəˈkɑːdəʊ/ (*plural* **avocados**) *noun* a fruit which has a thick green or black skin and pale green flesh with a large seed inside

① **avoid** /əˈvɔɪd/ (**avoids, avoiding, avoided**) *verb* **1.** to keep away from someone or something ○ *Travel early to avoid the traffic jams.* ○ *Aircraft fly high to avoid storms.* **2.** to try to prevent something from happening ○ *How can we avoid a row?* **3.** □ **to avoid doing something** to try not to do something ○ *He's always trying to avoid taking a decision.* ○ *You must avoid travelling on Friday evenings.*

avoidable /əˈvɔɪdəb(ə)l/ *adj* which can be or could have been avoided

await /əˈweɪt/ (**awaits, awaiting, awaited**) *verb* to wait for something

① **awake** /əˈweɪk/ *adj* not asleep ○ *It's 2 o'clock and I'm still awake.* ■ *verb* (**awakes, awaking, awoke, awoken**) **1.** to wake someone up ○ *He was awoken by the sound of the telephone.* **2.** to wake up ○ *He awoke when he heard them knocking on the door.* ○ *They awoke to find a fox in their tent.*

awaken /ə'weɪkən/ (**awakens, awakening, awakened**) *verb* **1.** to wake up **2.** to wake someone up

awakening /ə'weɪk(ə)nɪŋ/ *noun* a waking up

① **award** /ə'wɔːd/ *noun* something such as a prize or a gift of money that is given to someone [~of/~for] ○ *a design award* ○ *He received an award of £1000.* ○ *The school has been nominated for an award for innovation.* ■ *verb* (**awards, awarding, awarded**) to give someone something such as a prize, a degree or diploma, money or a contract to do work ○ *He was awarded first prize.* ○ *She was awarded damages.*

award-winning /ə'wɔːd ˌwɪnɪŋ/ *adj* having won an award or awards

① **aware** /ə'weə/ *adj* knowing something ○ *I'm not aware of any problem.* ○ *Is he aware that we have to decide quickly?* ◇ **not that I am aware of** not as far as I know ○ *Has there ever been an accident here before? – Not that I am aware of.*

① **away** /ə'weɪ/ *adv* **1.** at a particular distance or time ○ *The nearest shop is three kilometres away.* **2.** not here, somewhere else ○ *The managing director is away on business.* ○ *My assistant is away today.* **3.** (*in sports*) at your opponents' sports ground ○ *Our team is playing away next Saturday.* **4.** (*as emphasis, after verbs*) without stopping ○ *The birds were singing away in the garden.*

③ **awe** /ɔː/ *noun* great fear of or respect for someone □ **to be in awe of someone** to be frightened of someone ○ *She is in awe of her father.*

① **awful** /'ɔːf(ə)l/ *adj* very bad or unpleasant ○ *She felt awful about missing the party.* ○ *He's got an awful cold.* ○ *Turn off the television – that programme's awful!*

① **awfully** /'ɔːf(ə)li/ *adv* very (*informal*) ○ *It's awfully difficult to contact her.*

① **awkward** /'ɔːkwəd/ *adj* **1.** embarrassing or difficult to deal with ○ *awkward questions* **2.** difficult to use or deal with because of shape, size or position ○ *The handle's a very awkward shape.* **3.** not convenient ○ *Next Thursday is awkward for me – what about Friday?* **4.** (*of a person*) not relaxed or confident on social occasions **5.** (*of a person*) clumsy and unattractive in appearance or movement (NOTE: + **awkwardly** *adv*; +**awkardness** *n*)

awning /'ɔːnɪŋ/ *noun* a roof made of strong cloth, used to keep the sun or rain off

awoke /ə'wəʊk/ past tense of **awake**

awoken /ə'wəʊkən/ past participle of **awake**

awry /ə'raɪ/ *adj* **1.** not straight **2.** □ **to go awry** not to happen in the expected way

axe /æks/ *noun* a tool with a heavy sharp metal head, used for cutting through something ■ *verb* (*3rd person present plural* **axes,** *present participle* **axing,** *past participle* **axed**) to get rid of something or someone

axis /'æksɪs/ (*plural* **axes**) *noun* an imaginary line through the centre of a round object such as a ball

axle /'æksəl/ *noun* a straight bar, usually made of metal, which connects the wheels in a vehicle

B

b /biː/, **B** *noun* the second letter of the alphabet, between A and C

baa /bɑː/ (**baas, baaing, baaed**) *verb* to make the sound that a sheep makes with its voice

babble /ˈbæb(ə)l/ *noun* the sound of people talking together ○ *a babble of voices in the next room* ■ *verb* (**babbles, babbling, babbled**) to speak in a confused way ○ *She babbled a few words and collapsed.* ○ *What's he babbling on about?*

babe /beɪb/ *noun* **1.** a baby **2.** an attractive young man or woman ○ *She's a real babe!*

baboon /bəˈbuːn/ *noun* a type of large African monkey

① **baby** /ˈbeɪbi/ (*plural* **babies**) *noun* **1.** a very young child ○ *Most babies start to walk when they are about a year old.* ○ *I've known him since he was a baby.* **2.** a very young animal ○ *a baby rabbit* (NOTE: If you do not know if a baby is a boy or a girl, you can refer to it as **it**: *The baby was sucking its thumb.*)

babyish /ˈbeɪbiɪʃ/ *adj* like a baby

③ **baby-sit** /ˈbeɪbi sɪt/ *verb* to look after a child or children in a house, while their parents are out

bachelor /ˈbætʃələ/ *noun* a man who is not married ○ *He's still a bachelor and I'm beginning to wonder if he'll ever get married.*

bachelor's degree /ˈbætʃələz dɪˌgriː/ *noun* a first degree from a university

① **back** /bæk/ *noun* **1.** the part of the body which is behind you, between the neck and top of the legs ○ *She went to sleep lying on her back.* ○ *He carried his son on his back.* ○ *Don't lift that heavy box, you may hurt your back.* **2.** the opposite part to the front of something ○ *He wrote his address on the back of the envelope.* ○ *She sat at the back of the bus and went to sleep.* ○ *The dining room is at the back of the house.* ■ *adj* **1.** on the opposite side to the front ○ *He knocked at the back door of the house.* ○ *The back tyre of my bicycle is flat.* **2.** (of money) owed from an earlier date ○ *back pay* ■ *adv* **1.** towards the back of something ○ *She looked back and waved at me as she left.* **2.** in the past ○ *back in the 1950s* **3.** in the state that something was previously ○ *Put the telephone back on the table.* ○ *She watched him drive away and then went back into the house.* ○ *She gave me back the money she had borrowed.* ○ *I'll phone you when I am back in the office.* (NOTE: **Back** is often used after verbs: **to give back**, **to go back**, **to pay back**, etc.) ■ *verb* (**backs, backing, backed**) **1.** to go backwards, or make something go backwards ○ *He backed* or *backed his car out of the garage.* **2.** to encourage and support a person, organisation, opinion or activity, sometimes by giving money ○ *Her colleagues were willing to back the proposal.* ◇ **to put someone's back up** to annoy someone

back away *phrasal verb* to go backwards from something frightening ○ *The little girl backed away from the dog.*

back out *phrasal verb* **1.** to make a car go backwards out of a place ○ *He backed (the car) out of the garage into the main road.* **2.** to decide not to support a project ○ *We had to cancel the project when the bank backed out.*

back up③ *phrasal verb* **1.** to help or support someone ○ *Nobody would back her up when she complained about the service.* ○ *Will you back me up in the vote?* **2.** to make a copy of a computer file ○ *Don't forget to back up your work before you go home in the evening.* **3.** to make a car go backwards ○ *Can you back up, please – I want to get out of the parking space.*

backache /ˈbækeɪk/ *noun* a pain in the back

③ **backbone** /ˈbækbəʊn/ *noun* **1.** the series of bones which connect together down the back of a person or an animal ○ *If you're careful, you ought to be able to lift the backbone off the fish before eating it.* **2.** strength of character ○ *It takes someone with backbone to stand up to the government.*

backdate /bæk'deɪt/ (**backdates, backdating, backdated**) *verb* to put an earlier date on something

backer /'bækə/ *noun* a person who supports a project with money ○ *One of the company's backers has withdrawn.*

backfire /ˌbæk'faɪə/ (**backfires, backfiring, backfired**) *verb* **1.** (*of a car*) to make a loud noise in the engine ○ *The motorbike backfired several times when I started it this morning.* **2.** (*of a plan*) to go wrong, to turn out exactly the opposite to what was expected ○ *He was sure that everything would go according to plan and had never even thought it could backfire.* ○ *All their holiday plans backfired when their children got chickenpox.*

backgammon /'bækˌgæmən/ *noun* a board game for two people, in which they move their playing pieces after throwing two dice

② **background** /'bækgraʊnd/ *noun* **1.** the part of a picture or view which is behind all the other things that can be seen ○ *The photograph is of a house with mountains in the background.* ○ *His white shirt stands out against the dark background.* Compare **foreground 2.** the experiences, including education and family life, which someone has had ○ *He comes from a working-class background.* ○ *Her background is in the restaurant business.* **3.** information about a situation [~to] ○ *What is the background to the complaint?* ◇ **in the background** while other more obvious or important things are happening

backhand /'bækhænd/ *noun* a backhand shot

③ **backing** /'bækɪŋ/ *noun* **1.** financial support ○ *He has the backing of a French bank.* **2.** music played for a singer ○ *She sings with an Irish backing group.*

backlash /'bæklæʃ/ *noun* a reaction against something

backlog /'bæklɒg/ *noun* a lot of work which someone has not had time to do yet

③ **backpack** /'bækpæk/ *noun* a bag carried on your back

③ **backpacker** /'bækpækə/ *noun* a person who goes walking for pleasure, carrying a backpack

backpedal /'bækˌped(ə)l/ (**backpedals, backpedalling, backpedalled**) *verb* **1.** to move the pedals of a bike backwards **2.** to change your point of view and do the opposite of what you had promised ○ *The government is starting to backpedal over its pledge to cut taxes.* ○ *The minister had to backpedal rapidly when the papers found out about his speech.*

back seat /ˌbæk 'siːt/ *noun* a seat in the back of a vehicle □ **to take a back seat** to take a less important or active position in an organisation from choice

back seat driver /ˌbæk siːt 'draɪvə/ *noun* a passenger in a car who offers the driver advice

backside /'bæksaɪd/ *noun* the part of the body you sit on (*informal*)

backslash /'bækslæʃ/ *noun* a keyboard character (\) in the form of a line that slopes to the left

backstage /bæk'steɪdʒ/ *adv* off the stage in a theatre ○ *The actors gathered backstage to wait for the audience to settle down.*

back-to-back /ˌbæk tə 'bæk/ *adj, adv* **1.** with the back of one person or thing against the back of another ○ *Stand back to-back to see who is the tallest.* ○ *They put the chairs back-to-back.* **2.** happening one after the other ○ *back-to-back meetings*

backtrack /'bæktræk/ (**backtracks, backtracking, backtracked**) *verb* **1.** to go back **2.** to say that you no longer agree with something that you did or said previously

backup /'bækʌp/ *noun* helper, support

backward /'bækwəd/ *adv US* same as **backwards**

① **backwards** /'bækwədz/ *adv* from the front towards the back ○ *Don't step backwards.* ○ *'Tab' is 'bat' spelt backwards.* ◇ **backwards and forwards** in one direction, then in the opposite direction ○ *The policeman was walking backwards and forwards in front of the bank.*

backwater /'bækwɔːtə/ *noun* a quiet country place, away from the capital city

backyard /bæk'jɑːd/ *noun* **1.** an enclosed area behind a house, with a hard surface ○ *We keep our bikes in the backyard.* **2.** the area in which you live ○ *They have no idea of what's going on in their own backyard.* **3.** *US* a piece of land behind a house

③ **bacon** /'beɪkən/ *noun* meat from a pig which has been treated with salt or smoke, usually cut into thin pieces

bacteria /bæk'tɪəriə/ *plural noun* very small living things, some of which can cause disease

bacterial /bæk'tɪəriəl/, **bacteriological** /bæktɪəriə'lɒdʒɪk(ə)l/ *adj* caused by bacteria ○ *a bacterial infection*

① **bad** /bæd/ (**worse, worst**) *adj* **1.** causing problems, or likely to cause problems ○ *Eating too much fat is bad for your health.* ○ *We were shocked at their bad behaviour.* **2.** of poor quality or skill ○ *He's a bad driver.* ○ *She's good at singing but bad at playing the piano.* **3.** unpleasant ○ *He's got a bad cold.* ○ *She's in a bad temper.* ○ *I've got some bad news for you.* ○ *The weather was bad when we were on holiday in August.* **4.** serious ○ *He had a bad accident on the motorway.*

bad debt /ˌbæd 'det/ *noun* an amount of money owed to a person or to a company, which will never be paid

badge /bædʒ/ *noun* a small sign attached to someone's clothes to show something such as who someone is or what company they belong to

badger /'bædʒə/ *noun* a wild animal, with short legs and a black and white mark on the front of its head, which lives in holes in the ground ○ *Farmers say that cows can catch TB from badgers.*

bad language /bæd 'læŋgwɪdʒ/ *noun* swearing and rude words

① **badly** /'bædli/ (**worse, worst**) *adv* **1.** not well or successfully ○ *She did badly in her driving test.* **2.** seriously ○ *He was badly injured in the motorway accident.* **3.** very much ○ *His hair badly needs cutting.*

badly off /ˌbædli 'ɒf/ *adj* not having very much money ○ *When her husband died she was left quite badly off.*

badminton /'bædmɪntən/ *noun* a game for two or four people, similar to tennis, in which the players use rackets to hit a shuttlecock over a net

badmouth /'bædmaʊθ/ (**badmouths, badmouthing, badmouthed**) *verb* to criticise someone in a rude or unpleasant way (*informal*)

bad-tempered /ˌbæd 'tempəd/ *adj* feeling angry

baffle /'bæf(ə)l/ (**baffles, baffling, baffled**) *verb* to be unable to understand something ○ *I'm baffled as to why the car won't start.* ○ *The cause of the common cold has baffled scientists for years.*

① **bag** /bæg/ *noun* **1.** a soft container made of plastic, cloth or paper and used for carrying things ○ *a bag of sweets* ○ *He put the apples in a paper bag.* **2.** same as **handbag** ○ *My keys are in my bag.* **3.** a suitcase or other container used for clothes and other possessions when travelling ○ *Have you packed your bags yet?*

bagel /'beɪg(ə)l/ *noun* a small hard bread roll, shaped like a ring

baggage /'bægɪdʒ/ *noun* cases and bags which you take with you when travelling

baggy /'bægi/ (**baggier, baggiest**) *adj* (*of clothes*) appearing too big for the person who is wearing them

bagpipes /'bægpaɪps/ *plural noun* a musical instrument used especially in Scotland, Ireland and Brittany, which is played by blowing air into a bag and then pumping it through pipes

baguette /bæ'get/ *noun* a stick-shaped loaf of bread

bail /beɪl/ *noun* money which an arrested person, or someone else, pays to a court as a promise that the person will return to court for their trial. If they do not return the court keeps the money. ○ *She was released on bail of £5000.*

bail out *phrasal verb* **1.** to help someone in difficulty ○ *When he couldn't pay his rent, he asked his father to bail him out.* **2.** to pay money to a court to have a prisoner set free ○ *He phoned his lawyer to see if someone could bail him out.* **3.** to remove water from a boat ○ *I'll try to plug the hole, if you start to bail out.*

bailiff /'beɪlɪf/ *noun* a court official who is responsible for making sure that court orders are obeyed ○ *The court ordered the bailiff to seize his property because he had not paid his debt.* ○ *We were having breakfast when the bailiffs arrived and seized our car.*

bait /beɪt/ (**baits, baiting, baited**) *verb* to attach bait to a hook ○ *He baited his line with a worm.*

③ **bake** /beɪk/ (**bakes, baking, baked**) *verb* to cook food such as bread or cakes in an oven ○ *Mum's baking a cake for my birthday.* ○ *Bake the pizza for 35 minutes.*

③ **baked beans** /ˌbeɪkt 'biːnz/ *plural noun* dried white beans cooked in tomato sauce ○ *We had baked beans on toast for supper.* ○ *Can you go to the grocer's and get me a tin of baked beans?*

baked potato /ˌbeɪkt pə'teɪtəʊ/ *noun* a potato which you bake in the oven, often cut open when it is cooked and filled with another food such as cheese or beans

③ **baker** /'beɪkə/ *noun* a person whose job is to make bread and cakes □ **the baker's** a shop that sells bread and cakes ○ *Can you go to the baker's and get a loaf of brown bread?*

bakery /ˈbeɪkəri/ *noun* a place where bread and cakes are made for selling to the public

② **balance** /ˈbæləns/ *noun* **1.** the quality of staying steady ○ *The cat needs a good sense of balance to walk along the top of a fence.* □ **to keep your balance** not to fall over □ **to lose your balance** to fall down ○ *As he was crossing the river on the tightrope he lost his balance and fell.* **2.** an amount of money remaining in an account ○ *I have a balance of £25 in my bank account.* **3.** an amount of money still to be paid from a larger sum owed ○ *You can pay £100 now and the balance in three instalments.* ○ *The balance outstanding is now £5000.* ■ *verb* (**balances, balancing, balanced**) **1.** to stay or stand in position without falling ○ *The cat balanced on the top of the fence.* **2.** to make something stay in position without falling ○ *The waiter balanced a pile of dirty plates on his arm.*

balanced /ˈbælənst/ *adj* **1.** not extreme, having equal quantities ○ *a balanced diet* **2.** sensible ○ *to express a balanced opinion*

balance sheet /ˈbæləns ʃiːt/ *noun* a statement of a company's financial position at the end of a period of time

balancing act /ˈbælənsɪŋ ækt/ *noun* a skilful attempt to deal with opposing groups or opinions, or with a large variety of jobs

balcony /ˈbælkəni/ *noun* **1.** a small flat area that sticks out from an upper level of a building protected by a low wall or by posts ○ *The flat has a balcony overlooking the harbour.* ○ *Breakfast is served on the balcony.* **2.** the upper rows of seats in a theatre or cinema ○ *We booked seats at the front of the balcony.*

bald /bɔːld/ *adj* having no hair where there used to be hair, especially on the head ○ *His grandfather is quite bald.* ○ *He is beginning to go bald.*

balding /ˈbɔːldɪŋ/ *adj* going bald

baldly /ˈbɔːldli/ *adv* done or said in a plain and simple way

bale /beɪl/ *noun* a large block of a substance such as wool, paper or cotton ○ *a bale of cotton* ○ *They used bales of straw to make walls alongside the racetrack.*

balk /bɔːk/ *verb* another spelling of **baulk**

① **ball** /bɔːl/ *noun* **1.** a round object used in playing games, for throwing, kicking or hitting ○ *They played in the garden with an old tennis ball.* ○ *He kicked the ball into the goal.* **2.** any round object ○ *a ball of wool* ○ *He crumpled the paper up into a ball.* **3.** a formal dance ◇ **to have a ball** to enjoy yourself a lot ○ *You can see from the photos we were having a ball.* ◇ **to play ball** to work well with someone to achieve something ○ *I asked them for a little more time but they won't play ball.* ◇ **to start the ball rolling** to start something happening ○ *I'll start the ball rolling by introducing the visitors, then you can introduce yourselves.* ◇ **to be on the ball** to have a lot of skill or knowledge of something ○ *I'll ask Mary to do it – she's been here a long time and is really on the ball.* ◇ **someone won't play ball** someone won't cooperate

ballad /ˈbæləd/ *noun* a simple romantic song

ball boy /ˈbɔːl bɔɪ/ *noun* a boy who picks up the balls during tennis games

ballerina /ˌbæləˈriːnə/ *noun* a woman ballet dancer

ballet /ˈbæleɪ/ *noun* **1.** a type of dance, given as a public entertainment, where dancers perform a story to music **2.** a performance of this type of dance ○ *We went to the ballet last night.*

ball game /ˈbɔːl geɪm/ *noun* **1.** a game played with a ball ○ *football, tennis and other ball games* **2.** *US* a game of baseball

ball girl /ˈbɔːl gɜːl/ *noun* a girl who picks up the balls during tennis games

③ **balloon** /bəˈluːn/ *noun* **1.** a large ball which is blown up with air or gas **2.** a very large balloon which rises as the air inside it is heated, sometimes with a container attached for people to travel in ○ *We went for a ride in a hot-air balloon.* ■ *verb* (**balloons, ballooning, ballooned**) to increase quickly in size or amount

ballot /ˈbælət/ *noun* a way of voting in which voters mark papers with a cross ■ *verb* (**ballots, balloting, balloted**) **1.** to get people to vote on something ○ *The union is balloting its members on the strike.* **2.** to vote by marking papers with a cross ○ *They balloted for the place on the committee.*

ballot box /ˈbælət bɒks/ *noun* a box for putting voting papers into

ballpoint /ˈbɔːlpɔɪnt/, **ballpoint pen** /ˌbɔːlpɔɪnt ˈpen/ *noun* a pen which has a small ball at the tip over which ink flows as you write ○ *Don't write in ballpoint, use a pencil.*

ballroom /ˈbɔːlruːm/ *noun* a large room for formal dances

ballroom dancing /ˈbɔːlruːm ˌdɑːnsɪŋ/ *noun* formal dancing

balm /bɑːm/ *noun* a soothing ointment

balmy /ˈbɑːmi/ *adj* pleasantly mild

Baltic /ˈbɔːltɪk/ *noun* the sea south of Sweden and Finland, and north of Poland ○ *We spent the summer cruising along the Baltic coast.*

bamboo /bæmˈbuː/ *noun* a tall tropical plant whose stems are used as supports or in making furniture

③ **ban** /bæn/ *noun* an official statement which says that people must not do something [~on] ○ *There is a ban on smoking in many public places.* ■ *verb* (**banning, banned, banned**) to say officially that people must not do something [~from] ○ *She was banned from driving for three years.*

banal /bəˈnɑːl/ *adj* quite ordinary and uninteresting

banana /bəˈnɑːnə/ *noun* a long yellow, slightly curved fruit which grows in hot countries

② **band** /bænd/ *noun* **1.** a group of people who play music together ○ *The soldiers marched down the street, following the band.* ○ *My brother's in a rock band.* **2.** a group of people who do something together ○ *Bands of drunken football fans were wandering around the streets.* **3.** a narrow piece of something ○ *Her hair was tied back with a red band.* **4.** a long thin mark of a particular colour ○ *a black tee-shirt with a broad band of yellow across the front* **5.** a range of things taken together ○ *He's in the top salary band.* ○ *We're looking for something in the £10 – £15 price band.*

③ **bandage** /ˈbændɪdʒ/ *noun* a cloth for putting around an injured part of the body ○ *The nurse put a bandage round his knee.* ○ *His head was covered in bandages.*

③ **BandAid** /ˈbændeɪd/ *trademark US* a small strip of cloth with gauze in the middle, which can be stuck to the skin to cover a wound ○ *Let me put a BandAid on your finger.*

B & B *abbr* bed and breakfast

bandit /ˈbændɪt/ *noun* a robber

bandwagon /ˈbændwægən/ *noun* □ **to jump on the bandwagon** to do what everyone else is doing ○ *Once the prince had praised the ecological movement, everyone wanted to jump on the bandwagon.*

bandwidth /ˈbændwɪdθ/ *noun* **1.** a range of radio wavelengths **2.** the amount of electronic data that can be sent through an Internet connection or other communication channel

bandy about *phrasal verb* to speak or write certain words

③ **bang** /bæŋ/ *noun* a sudden noise like that made by a gun ○ *The car started with a series of loud bangs.* ○ *There was a bang and the tyre went flat.* ■ *verb* (**bangs, banging, banged**) to hit something hard, so as to make a loud noise ○ *He banged (on) the table with his hand.* ○ *Can't you stop the door banging?*

banger /ˈbæŋə/ *noun* an old car ○ *I'm surprised his old banger is still on the road.*

bangle /ˈbæŋgəl/ *noun* a metal bracelet worn round the wrist or ankle

③ **banish** /ˈbænɪʃ/ (**banishes, banishing, banished**) *verb* **1.** to send someone to live a long distance away, usually out of the country, or in a distant part of the country, as a punishment [~to] ○ *He was banished to a small island.* **2.** to send someone away from a particular place [~from/~to] ○ *She was banished from the front desk to a little office on the fifth floor.* **3.** to get rid of something bad or unpleasant ○ *The aim is to banish poverty by the year 2010.*

banjo /ˈbændʒəʊ/ (*plural* **banjos** or **banjoes**) *noun* a stringed instrument with a round body and a long neck

① **bank** /bæŋk/ *noun* **1.** a business which holds money for people, and lends them money ○ *I must go to the bank to get some money.* ○ *She took all her money out of the bank to buy a car.* ○ *How much money do you have in the bank?* **2.** land along the side of a river ○ *He sat on the river bank all day, trying to catch fish.* ○ *There is a path along the bank of the canal.* **3.** a long pile of earth, sand, snow or other substance ○ *The road was blocked by banks of snow blown by the wind.* ■ *verb* (**banks, banking, banked**) to store money in a bank ○ *I banked the cheque as soon as it arrived.* ○ *Have you banked the money yet?*

bank on *phrasal verb* to be sure that something will happen

② **bank account** /ˈbæŋk əˌkaʊnt/ *noun* an arrangement which you make with a bank to keep your money safely until you want it □ **to open a bank account** to start keeping money in a bank ○ *He opened a bank account when he started his first job.*

bank balance /ˈbæŋk ˌbæləns/ *noun* the amount of money someone has in a bank account

bank card /ˈbæŋk kɑːd/ *noun* a plastic card you use with a cheque to make a payment

banker /ˈbæŋkə/ *noun* a person who has a senior post in a bank

① **bank holiday** /ˌbæŋk ˈhɒlɪdeɪ/ *noun* a public holiday when most people do not go to work and the banks are closed

③ **banking** /ˈbæŋkɪŋ/ *noun* the work that banks do ○ *Some supermarkets now offer banking services.*

banknote /ˈbæŋknəʊt/ *noun* a piece of paper money

③ **bankrupt** /ˈbæŋkrʌpt/ *noun* a person who cannot pay his or her debts ○ *A bankrupt cannot be a member of parliament.*

bankruptcy /ˈbæŋkrʌptsi/ *noun* being bankrupt

bank statement /ˈbæŋk ˌsteɪtmənt/ *noun* a written document from a bank showing the balance of an account

banquet /ˈbæŋkwɪt/ *noun* a formal dinner for important guests

banter /ˈbæntə/ *noun* talk with joking comments

bap /bæp/ *noun* a soft flat white bread roll

baptise /bæpˈtaɪz/ (**baptises, baptising, baptised**), **baptize** *verb* **1.** to receive someone into the Christian religion in a ceremony involving sprinkling or covering with water **2.** to give a baby a name when it is baptised

baptism /ˈbæptɪz(ə)m/ *noun* a religious ceremony where someone, usually a baby, is welcomed into the Christian church and given a Christian name after being sprinkled with holy water ○ *All the family came together for the baptism.*

① **bar** /bɑː/ *noun* **1.** a long piece of something hard ○ *The yard was full of planks and metal bars.* □ **a bar of soap, a bar of chocolate** a thick piece of soap or chocolate **2.** a solid piece of a substance such as chocolate or soap **3.** a place where you can buy and drink alcohol ○ *Let's meet in the bar before dinner.* ■ *prep* except ○ *All of the suppliers replied bar one.* ○ *All bar two of the players in the team are British.* ■ *verb* (**bars, barring, barred**) **1.** to block something [~to] ○ *The road was barred by the police.* ○ *The path is barred to cyclists.* **2.** □ **to bar someone from doing something** to prevent someone officially from doing something ○ *He was barred from playing football for three months.*

barbarian /bɑːˈbeəriən/ *noun* a wild and uncivilised person

barbaric /bɑːˈbærɪk/ *adj* cruel and uncivilised

barbarous /ˈbɑːbərəs/ *adj* very cruel (*formal*)

③ **barbecue** /ˈbɑːbɪkjuː/ *noun* **1.** a metal grill for cooking food on out of doors ○ *Light the barbecue at least half an hour before you start cooking.* **2.** food cooked on a barbecue ○ *Here is a recipe for chicken barbecue.* **3.** a meal or party where food is cooked out of doors ○ *We had a barbecue for twenty guests.* ○ *They were invited to a barbecue.* ■ *verb* (**barbecues, barbecuing, barbecued**) to cook something on a barbecue ○ *Barbecued spare ribs are on the menu.* ○ *She was barbecuing sausages for lunch when it started to rain.*

barbed /bɑːbd/ *adj* (*of a remark*) sharply critical ○ *He made some barbed comments about her singing.*

③ **barbed wire** /ˌbɑːbd ˈwaɪə/ *noun* a type of wire with sharp spikes, used to make fences

barbell /ˈbɑːbel/ *noun* a long metal bar with a weight at each end which is used in weightlifting

barber /ˈbɑːbə/ *noun* a person who cuts men's hair

barbiturate /bɑːˈbɪtʃʊrət/ *noun* a drug which sends you to sleep

bar chart /ˈbɑː tʃɑːt/ *noun* a diagram where quantities are shown as thick columns of different heights

bar code /ˈbɑː kəʊd/ *noun* printed vertical lines containing information which can be read by a computer

③ **bare** /beə/ (**barer, barest**) *adj* **1.** not covered by clothes or shoes ○ *He walked on the beach in his bare feet.* ○ *I can't sit in the sun with my arms bare.* **2.** without any kind of cover ○ *They slept on the bare floorboards.* ○ *They saw the bare bones of dead animals in the desert.* **3.** without leaves ○ *bare branches* **4.** with just what is really needed and nothing extra ○ *We only took the bare essentials when we went travelling.* ○ *She thought £100 was the bare minimum she would accept.* (NOTE: Do not confuse with **bear**.)

barefoot /ˈbeəfʊt/ *adj, adv* without shoes ○ *She walked barefoot in the grass.* ○ *The children were barefoot.*

③ **barely** /ˈbeəli/ *adv* almost not ○ *She barely had enough money to pay for her ticket.* ○ *He barely had time to get dressed before the police arrived.* ○ *The noise is barely tolerable.*

③ **bargain** /ˈbɑːɡɪn/ *noun* **1.** something bought more cheaply than usual ○ *The car was a real bargain at £500.* **2.** an agreement between two people or groups of people ■ *verb* (**bargains, bargaining, bar-**

gained) to discuss the terms of an agreement or sale ◇ **more than** *or* **not what you bargained for** different, usually worse, than you had expected ◇ **into the bargain** as well as other things ○ *The plane was late and they lost my suitcase into the bargain.*

bargain on *phrasal verb* to expect something ○ *I hadn't bargained on it being so wet.* ○ *She's bargaining on someone dropping out so that she can take their place.*

barge /bɑːdʒ/ (**barging, barged**) *verb*

barge in *phrasal verb* to arrive or intervene in an unwelcome way

bar graph /'bɑː grɑːf/ *noun* same as **bar chart**

baritone /'bærɪtəʊn/ *noun* a singer with a voice which is higher than a bass and lower than a tenor ○ *The baritone sang a duet with the soprano.*

bark /bɑːk/ *noun* **1.** the hard outer layer of a tree **2.** the loud sound a dog makes ○ *The dog gave a bark as we came into the house.* ■ *verb* (**barks, barking, barked**) to be mistaken ○ *They don't know what the real problem is – they're barking up the wrong tree.* ◇ **his bark is worse than his bite** he is not as frightening as he seems ○ *Don't be afraid of Aunt Bessie – her bark is much worse than her bite.*

barley /'bɑːli/ *noun* a common cereal crop grown in temperate areas

barmaid /'bɑːmeɪd/ *noun* a woman who serves drinks in a bar (*dated*)

barman /'bɑːmən/ (*plural* **barmen**) *noun* a man who serves drinks in a bar

bar mitzvah /bɑː 'mɪtsvə/ *noun* a ceremony where a Jewish boy is made a full member of his community at the age of 13

barmy /'bɑːmi/ (**barmier, barmiest**) *adj* not sensible (*informal*)

barn /bɑːn/ *noun* a large farm building for storing produce or for keeping animals or machinery

barometer /bə'rɒmɪtə/ *noun* an instrument which measures changes in atmospheric pressure and can be used to forecast the weather

baron /'bærən/ *noun* **1.** a nobleman of a low rank in the UK **2.** the title given to a life peer in the UK **3.** a powerful person (NOTE: Do not confuse with **barren**.)

barracks /'bærəks/ *noun* a building where soldiers are housed ○ *The soldiers marched into their barracks.*

barrage /'bærɑːʒ/ *noun* **1.** a large amount of questions or complaints [~of] ○ *He faced a barrage of questions from reporters when he arrived at the airport.* **2.** heavy gunfire, or a mass of things thrown ○ *The enemy started an artillery barrage.* ○ *The police were met by a barrage of stones and bottles.* **3.** a dam made of a wall of soil or stones which blocks a river ○ *They built a barrage to help control the water level in the river.*

③ **barrel** /'bærəl/ *noun* **1.** a container with curved sides for storing liquid ○ *a barrel of beer* ○ *a wine barrel* **2.** the tube of a gun out of which a bullet is fired

barren /'bærən/ *adj* (*of living things*) not able to produce young, or not fertile ○ *a barren cow* (NOTE: Do not confuse with **baron**.)

barricade /ˌbærɪ'keɪd/ *noun* a pile of something such as stones or burnt cars, which is used to block a street or entrance ○ *Protesters built barricades across several of the main streets.* ■ *verb* (**barricades, barricading, barricaded**) to build a barricade across somewhere ○ *Protesters barricaded the streets.* ○ *They barricaded the doors and windows.* □ **to barricade yourself in** or **inside** to block a door or window with furniture and other things so that no one else can get inside ○ *He barricaded himself inside the flat.*

③ **barrier** /'bæriə/ *noun* **1.** a bar or fence which blocks a passage ○ *He lifted the barrier and we drove across the border.* **2.** an action or problem that makes it difficult for something to happen [~to] ○ *Lack of qualifications can be a barrier to employment.*

barring /'bɑːrɪŋ/ *prep* unless something is the case

barrister /'bærɪstə/ *noun* a lawyer who can present cases in court. ◊ **bar**

bartender /'bɑːtendə/ *noun* a person who serves behind a bar

barter /'bɑːtə/ (**barters, bartering, bartered**) *verb* to discuss the price for something and try to have it reduced ○ *They had to barter for the things they bought in the market.*

① **base** /beɪs/ *noun* **1.** the bottom part of something ○ *The table lamp has a flat base.* **2.** a place where you work from [~for] ○ *He lives in London but uses Paris as a base for business visits in France.* **3.** something from which something else develops or is produced [~for] ○ *The report will provide a good base for making some changes.* ■ *verb* (**bases, basing, based**) **1.** to use something or somewhere as a base [~on] ○ *The theory is based on research done in*

Russia. **2.** to have a particular place as your main home or place of work [~at/in] ○ *She's based at head office* or *in Edinburgh.* **3.** to use something as a model for something else [~on] ○ *The book is based on her mother's life.* ○ *His theory was based on years of observations.*

② **baseball** /ˈbeɪsbɔːl/ *noun* **1.** an American game for two teams of nine players, in which a player hits a ball with a long, narrow bat and players from the other team try to catch it **2.** the hard ball used in playing baseball

baseball cap /ˈbeɪsbɔːl kæp/ *noun* a soft cotton cap with a large peak

-based /beɪst/ *suffix* **1.** produced or developed from ○ *a milk-based dessert* **2.** living or working at a particular place ○ *a London-based company*

baseline /ˈbeɪslaɪn/ *noun* the line at the back of a tennis court, etc.

basement /ˈbeɪsmənt/ *noun* a floor in a building below ground level

bash /bæʃ/ *noun* **1.** a knock ○ *I see your car has had a bash.* **2.** a party ○ *Are you going to Jane's bash tomorrow?* ■ *verb* (**bashes, bashing, bashed**) to hit hard ○ *When she fell down she bashed her head on the chair.* ○ *He was bashing stakes into the ground with a mallet.*

bashful /ˈbæʃf(ə)l/ *adj* shy and embarrassed

① **basic** /ˈbeɪsɪk/ *adj* very simple, or at the first level ○ *Being able to swim is a basic requirement if you are going canoeing.* ○ *Knowledge of basic Spanish will be enough for the job.*

① **basically** /ˈbeɪsɪkli/ *adv* considering only the most important information and not the details ○ *Basically, he's fed up with his job.*

basil /ˈbæz(ə)l/ *noun* a herb with strongly scented leaves which is used especially in Italian cooking

basilica /bəˈzɪlɪkə/ *noun* an important Catholic church ○ *St Peter's Basilica is the most important church in Rome.*

basin /ˈbeɪs(ə)n/ *noun* **1.** same as **washbasin** **2.** a large or small bowl, especially one for holding or mixing food items

① **basis** /ˈbeɪsɪs/ (*plural* **bases**) *noun* **1.** the general facts on which something is based [~for] ○ *What is the basis for these proposals?* □ **on the basis of** based on ○ *The calculations are done on the basis of an exchange rate of 1.6 dollars to the pound.* **2.** the general terms of an agreement ○ *She is working for us on a temporary basis.* ○ *Many of the helpers at the hospice work on a voluntary basis.*

bask /bɑːsk/ (**basks, basking, basked**) *verb* to lie happily in warm sunshine or in a pleasant atmosphere

② **basket** /ˈbɑːskɪt/ *noun* a container made of thin pieces of wood, wire or fibre woven together

② **basketball** /ˈbɑːskɪtbɔːl/ *noun* a game played by two teams of five players who try to throw the ball through an open net hung high up at each end of the playing area

bass[1] /beɪs/ *noun* **1.** a male singer with a low-pitched voice **2.** a guitar with a low-pitched sound ■ *adj* relating to a low-pitched voice or music ○ *He has a pleasant bass voice.* Compare **tenor**

bass[2] /beɪs/ *noun* a type of edible freshwater fish

bassoon /bəˈsuːn/ *noun* a long wooden wind instrument, with a low tone

③ **bastard** /ˈbɑːstəd/ *noun* **1.** a person whose parents are not married ○ *Technically speaking, many children are born bastards nowadays.* **2.** a nasty person or nasty thing (*generally offensive*) ○ *The bastard walked out of the restaurant without paying.* ○ *The written driving test is a real bastard.*

bastion /ˈbæstiən/ *noun* a place which protects a particular way of living or set of opinions

③ **bat** /bæt/ *noun* **1.** a piece of wood used for hitting a ball ○ *a baseball bat* ○ *a cricket bat* **2.** a small animal with skin flaps like wings that flies at night and hangs upside down when resting

batch /bætʃ/ *noun* a number of things made at one time

② **bath** /bɑːθ/ *noun* (*plural* **baths**) **1.** a large container in which you can sit and wash your whole body ○ *There's a washbasin and a bath in the bathroom.* **2.** the process of washing your whole body □ **to have a bath** to wash your whole body in a bath ■ *verb* (**baths, bathing, bathed**) to wash yourself or someone else in a bath ○ *She's bathing the baby.* ○ *Do you prefer to bath or shower?* (NOTE: Do not confuse with **bathe**.)

bathe /beɪð/ (**bathes, bathing, bathed**) *verb* **1.** to go into water to swim or wash ○ *Thousands of people come to bathe in the Ganges.* **2.** to wash a cut or damaged part of the body carefully ○ *A nurse bathed the wound on his arm.* **3.** *US* to have a bath ○ *I just have enough time to bathe before my* *dinner guests arrive.* (NOTE: Do not confuse with **bath**.)

bathrobe /'bɑːθrəʊb/ *noun* a loose coat of towelling, worn when you get out of a bath ○ *She came out of the bathroom dressed in a pink bathrobe.*

② **bathroom** /'bɑːθruːm/ *noun* **1.** a room in a house with a bath, a washbasin and usually a toilet ○ *The house has two bathrooms.* **2.** *US* a room containing a toilet ○ *Where's the bathroom?* ○ *Can I use your bathroom, please?*

bathtub /'bɑːθtʌb/ *noun US* the container in which you sit and wash your body

baton /'bætɒn/ *noun* **1.** a large stick used to hit with ○ *The crowd was stopped by a row of policemen carrying batons.* **2.** a thin white stick used to conduct an orchestra **3.** a stick which is passed from runner to runner in a relay race

batsman /'bætsmən/ (*plural* **batsmen**) *noun* the player who is batting in a cricket match

battalion /bə'tæljən/ *noun* a section of the army, usually commanded by a lieutenant-colonel

batter /'bætə/ *noun* **1.** a liquid mixture of flour, milk and usually eggs ○ *fish coated in batter and fried* **2.** (*in baseball*) the player who has the bat and hits the ball ■ *verb* (**batters, battering, battered**) to hit often ○ *He was accused of battering the baby to death.*

battered /'bætəd/ *adj* old and in a bad condition ○ *a battered old car*

② **battery** /'bæt(ə)ri/ (*plural* **batteries**) *noun* an object that fits into a piece of electrical equipment to provide it with electric energy ○ *My calculator needs a new battery.* ○ *The battery has given out so I can't use my radio.* ○ *My mobile phone has a rechargeable battery.*

② **battle** /'bæt(ə)l/ *noun* **1.** an occasion when large groups of soldiers fight each other using powerful weapons [~for/~of] ○ *Many soldiers died in the first battle for the bridge.* ○ *Wellington won the Battle of Waterloo.* **2.** an attempt to prevent something unpleasant and difficult to deal with [~against/~for] ○ *a constant battle for better living standards* ○ *He lost his battle against cancer.* ■ *verb* (**battles, battling, battled**) to try to prevent something unpleasant and difficult to deal with [~against/~with/~for]

battlefield /'bæt(ə)lfiːld/, **battleground** /'bæt(ə)lgraʊnd/ *noun* a site of a battle

battlements /'bæt(ə)lmənts/ *plural noun* the top part of a castle wall, with places where soldiers could shoot at attackers ○ *Soldiers were firing from the battlements.*

battleship /'bæt(ə)lʃɪp/ *noun* the largest type of warship, with big guns

baulk /bɔːk/ (**baulks, baulking, baulked**) *verb* to refuse to do something which is dangerous or unpleasant (NOTE: also spelled **balk**)

bawl /bɔːl/ (**bawls, bawling, bawled**) *verb* to shout loudly

③ **bay** /beɪ/ *noun* **1.** an area along a coast where the land curves inwards ○ *a sheltered bay* **2.** a marked or enclosed area used for a particular purpose ○ *a bay marked 'Reserved Parking'*

bay leaf /'beɪ liːf/ *noun* an aromatic leaf of a bay tree which is used in cooking

bayonet /'beɪənɪt/ *noun* a sharp blade fitted at the end of a rifle ○ *The soldiers were ordered to fix bayonets.*

bay window /beɪ 'wɪndəʊ/ *noun* a window which sticks out from a flat wall

bazaar /bə'zɑː/ *noun* a market in South Asia, the Middle East or North Africa ○ *We visited the busy bazaar to try to buy spices.*

BBC *noun* the British national radio and TV company ○ *We were listening to the BBC news* or *to the news on the BBC.* ○ *The BBC broadcasts to many countries in the world.* ○ *A BBC reporter wanted to interview her.* Full form **British Broadcasting Corporation**

BBQ *abbr* barbecue

BC used after a date to show that it is after the birth of Jesus Christ. Full form **before Christ**. Compare **AD** (NOTE: Sometimes BCE (before the Common Era) is used to avoid referring to Jesus Christ.)

① **be** /bɪ, biː/ (*1st person present singular* **am,** *2nd person present singular* **are,** *3rd person present singular* **is,** *1st person present plural* **are,** *2nd person present plural* **are,** *3rd person present plural* **are,** *present subjunctive* **be,** *1st person singular past indicative* **was,** *2nd person singular past indicative* **were,** *3rd person singular past indicative* **was,** *1st person plural past indicative* **were,** *2nd person plural past indicative* **were,** *3rd person plural past indicative* **were,** *past subjunctive* **were,** *past participle* **been**) *verb* **1.** used for describing a person or thing ○ *Our house is older than yours.* ○ *She is bigger than her brother.* ○ *Lemons are yellow.* ○ *The soup is hot.* ○ *Put on your coat – it is cold outside.* ○ *I'm cold after standing waiting for the bus.* ○ *Are* *you tired after your long walk?* **2.** used for showing age or time ○ *He's twenty years old.* ○ *She will be two next month.* ○ *It is nearly ten o'clock.* ○ *It is time to get up.* ○ *September is the beginning of autumn.* **3.** used for showing price ○ *Onions are 80p a kilo.* ○ *The cakes are 50p each.* ○ *My car was worth £10,000 when it was new.* **4.** used for showing someone's job ○ *His father is a bus driver.* ○ *She wants to be a teacher.* **5.** used for showing things such as size, weight, height, etc. ○ *He's 1.70m tall.* ○ *The room is three metres square.* ○ *Our house is ten miles from the nearest station.* **6.** to add up to ○ *Two and two are four.* **7.** used for showing that someone or something exists or is in a particular place ○ *There was a crowd of people waiting for the shop to open.* ○ *There were only two people left on the bus.* ○ *Where are we?* ○ *There's your hat!*

② **beach** /biːtʃ/ *noun* an area of sand or small stones by the edge of the sea

beacon /ˈbiːkən/ *noun* a light which warns about something or shows ships or aircraft the way to go

bead /biːd/ *noun* **1.** a little piece of wood, plastic or glass, with a hole in it, which is used to make a necklace or other decoration ○ *She was wearing a string of red beads.* ○ *Beads are back in fashion again.* **2.** a small drop of liquid ○ *Beads of sweat formed on his brow.*

beagle /ˈbiːg(ə)l/ *noun* a breed of dog used for hunting

③ **beak** /biːk/ *noun* the hard part of a bird's mouth

beaker /ˈbiːkə/ *noun* **1.** a drinking cup with or without a handle, sometimes with a lid and spout if intended for very small children ○ *We'll use these glasses and the children can have the plastic beakers.* ○ *She's just started to drink from a beaker.* **2.** a glass jar used in chemical experiments ○ *You need a beaker and a Bunsen burner for this experiment.*

beam /biːm/ *noun* **1.** a long block of wood or metal which supports a structure, especially a roof ○ *You can see the old beams in the ceiling.* **2.** a ray of light ○ *The beam from the car's headlights shone into the barn.* ○ *Beams of sunlight came through the coloured glass.* ■ *verb* (**beams, beaming, beamed**) to give a big happy smile [~at] ○ *The little girl beamed at him.*

③ **bean** /biːn/ *noun* a seed or the long thin pod of various different plants, that is cooked and eaten

① **bear** /beə/ *noun* a large wild animal covered with fur ■ *verb* (**bears, bearing, bore, borne**) **1.** to carry or support something ○ *The letter bore a London postmark.* ○ *Will this branch bear my weight?* **2.** to accept something bad or unpleasant in a calm way ○ *She bore the bad news bravely.* □ **be unable to bear someone *or* something** to strongly dislike someone or something ○ *I can't bear the smell of cooking fish.* ◇ **to bear something in mind** to remember something that might change a decision ○ *Bear in mind that it takes 2 hours to get there.* ○ *Bear me in mind when you're looking for help.*

bear out *phrasal verb* to confirm something

bear up *phrasal verb* to survive cheerfully

bear with *phrasal verb* to wait patiently for someone to do something

bearable /ˈbeərəb(ə)l/ *adj* which you can accept even though it is unpleasant

③ **beard** /bɪəd/ *noun* the hair growing on a man's chin and cheeks ○ *a long white beard*

bearer /ˈbeərə/ *noun* **1.** a person who carries or brings something [~of] ○ *Flag bearers walked in front of the groups of soldiers.* ○ *He said he was the bearer of bad news.* **2.** a person who owns a legal document such as a cheque ○ *This card entitles the bearer to a discount.*

③ **bearing** /ˈbeərɪŋ/ *noun* **1.** one of a set of little balls inside which an axle turns ○ *The bearings in the bicycle wheel had to be replaced.* **2.** a calculation to show where you are ○ *You need a compass to take a bearing.* □ **to find *or* get your bearings** to find out where you are ○ *Give me a few moments to get my bearings.* **3.** the way a person carries his or her body ◇ **to have a** or **some** or **no bearing on something** a or some or no connection to or effect on something ○ *The letter had no bearing on the result of the trial.* ◇ **to lose your bearings** to get lost ○ *I'm sorry I'm late, but I didn't have a map and lost my bearings.*

bear market /ˈbeə ˌmɑːkɪt/ *noun* a period when prices on the stock market fall as shareholders sell shares, because they think share prices will fall further. Compare **bull market**

③ **beast** /biːst/ *noun* **1.** a wild animal **2.** a nasty person ○ *The beast! He left nothing for anyone else.*

② **beat** /biːt/ *noun* a regular pattern of sound ○ *They danced to the beat of the* *drums.* ◊ **heartbeat** ■ *verb* (**beats, beating, beat, beaten**) **1.** to make a regular sound ○ *His heart was still beating when the ambulance arrived.* ○ *Her heart beat faster as she went into the interview.* **2.** to hit something or someone hard ○ *He was beaten by a gang of youths.* **3.** to win a game against another player or team [~at] ○ *We beat the Australians at cricket last year.* ○ *Their football team beat us by 10 goals to 2.*

beat down *phrasal verb* **1.** to make someone reduce a price ○ *I beat down his price* or *I beat him down.* **2.** to fall hard on ○ *The sun was beating down so we looked for some shade.* ○ *The rain beat down on the marchers.*

beat up② *phrasal verb* **1.** to whip cream, eggs or another food ○ *Beat up the mixture in a big bowl.* **2.** to attack someone ○ *Three muggers beat him up and stole his wallet.*

③ **beating** /ˈbiːtɪŋ/ *noun* the act of hitting or defeating

beautician /bjuːˈtɪʃ(ə)n/ *noun* a person who makes people beautiful by applying makeup

① **beautiful** /ˈbjuːtɪf(ə)l/ *adj* **1.** physically very attractive ○ *We have three beautiful daughters.* **2.** pleasant to look at ○ *a beautiful house* ○ *the beautiful colours of the autumn leaves* **3.** pleasant or enjoyable ○ *What beautiful weather for a walk.*

beautifully /ˈbjuːtɪf(ə)li/ *adv* in a very pleasing way

beautify /ˈbjuːtɪfaɪ/ (**beautifies, beautifying, beautified**) *verb* to make someone or something beautiful

② **beauty** /ˈbjuːti/ (*plural* **beauties**) *noun* **1.** the quality of being beautiful ○ *an object of great beauty* ○ *the beauty of the tall trees against the background of the blue lake* **2.** a beautiful woman or a beautiful thing ○ *At 18 she was a real beauty.* ○ *Look at these apples, they're real beauties.*

beauty spot /ˈbjuːti spɒt/ *noun* a famous beautiful place

beaver /ˈbiːvə/ *noun* an American animal with soft brown fur, sharp teeth and a broad flat tail, which lives in water ○ *Beavers cut down young trees to build their homes.*

became /bɪˈkeɪm/ past tense of **become**

① **because** /bɪˈkɒz/ *conj* for the reason that follows ○ *I was late because I missed the train.* ○ *The dog's wet because he's been in the river.* ◊ **because of** as a result of ○ *The plane was delayed because of bad weather.*

beckon /ˈbekən/ (**beckons, beckoning, beckoned**) *verb* to make a sign with your hand telling someone to come to you [~to] ○ *The nurse beckoned to her to come into the room.*

① **become** /bɪˈkʌm/ (**becomes, becoming, became, become**) *verb* **1.** to change to something different ○ *The sky became dark and the wind became stronger.* ○ *They became good friends.* ○ *As she got older she became rather deaf.* ○ *It soon became obvious that he didn't understand a word of what I was saying.* **2**. to start to work as ○ *He wants to become a doctor.*

① **bed** /bed/ *noun* **1.** a piece of furniture for sleeping on ○ *Lie down on my bed if you're tired.* □ **to go to bed** to get into your bed for the night ○ *She always goes to bed at 9 o'clock.* □ **to make a bed** to make a bed tidy or change the bedclothes after someone has slept in it ○ *You can't go into your hotel room because the beds haven't been made.* ○ *Have you made your bed?* **2.** a piece of ground for particular plants to grow in ○ *a strawberry bed* ○ *a rose bed* **3.** the ground at the bottom of water ○ *the sandy bed of a river* ○ *a river bed*

bedclothes /ˈbedkləʊðz/ *plural noun* sheets and blankets which cover a bed ○ *She woke up when all her bedclothes fell off.*

bedding /ˈbedɪŋ/ *noun* **1.** sheets, blankets and other items for a bed; bedclothes ○ *When you rent a cottage the bedding is usually provided.* **2.** a soft material such as hay for an animal to sleep on

bedraggled /bɪˈdræg(ə)ld/ *adj* dirty, untidy and wet

bedrock /ˈbedrɒk/ *noun* **1.** the bottom layer of rock under the earth **2.** basic principles ○ *Socialism is the bedrock of the party's manifesto.*

① **bedroom** /ˈbedruːm/ *noun* a room where you sleep ○ *My bedroom is on the first floor.* ○ *The hotel has twenty-five bedrooms.* ○ *Shut your bedroom door if you want to be quiet.*

bedside /ˈbedsaɪd/ *noun* the side of a bed

bedspread /ˈbedspred/ *noun* a decorated cloth put over a bed

③ **bedtime** /ˈbedtaɪm/ *noun* the time when you go to bed

bee /biː/ *noun* an insect which makes honey, and can sting you

beech /biːtʃ/ *noun* same as **beech tree**

beech tree /ˈbiːtʃ triː/ *noun* a common hardwood tree ○ *Beech trees are common on the chalk hills in the south of England.*

beef /biːf/ *noun* meat from a cow ○ *roast beef* ○ *beef stew*

beefburger /ˈbiːfbɜːɡə/ *noun* a cake of grilled minced beef, usually served in a roll

beefy /ˈbiːfi/ *adj* big and muscular ○ *a strong, beefy looking man*

beehive /ˈbiːhaɪv/ *noun* a box for bees to make a nest in

① **been** /biːn/ past participle of **be**

beep /biːp/ *noun* an audible warning sound ○ *The printer will make a beep when it runs out of paper.* ■ *verb* (**beeps, beeping, beeped**) to make a beep ○ *The computer beeped when I hit the wrong key.* ◊ **bleep**

② **beer** /bɪə/ *noun* **1.** an alcoholic drink made from grain and water ○ *Can I have a glass of beer?* (NOTE: no plural) **2.** a glass or bottle of beer ○ *Three beers, please.*

beet /biːt/ *noun US* beetroot ○ *Boil young fresh beets, and serve them with butter.*

beetle /ˈbiːt(ə)l/ *noun* an insect with hard covers that protects its folded wings

beetroot /ˈbiːtruːt/ *noun* a vegetable with a dark red root, eaten cooked, usually in a salad

befall /bɪˈfɔːl/ (**befalls, befalling, befell, befallen**) *verb* to happen to (*archaic or literary*)

befit /bɪˈfɪt/ (**befits, befitting, befitted**) *verb* to suit

① **before** /bɪˈfɔː/ *prep* earlier than ○ *They should have arrived before now.* ○ *You must be home before 9 o'clock.* ○ *G comes before H in the alphabet.* ■ *conj* earlier than ○ *The police got there before I did.* ○ *Think carefully before you start to answer the exam questions.* ○ *Wash your hands before you have your dinner.* ○ *Before you sit down, can you switch on the light?* ■ *adv* earlier ○ *I didn't see him last week, but I had met him before.* ○ *Why didn't you tell me before?*

③ **beforehand** /bɪˈfɔːhænd/ *adv* in advance

befriend /bɪˈfrend/ (**befriends, befriending, befriended**) *verb* to become friendly with someone and help them

beg /beɡ/ (**begs, begging, begged**) *verb* **1.** to ask for things like money or food ○ *She sat begging on the steps of the station.* ○ *Children were begging for food.* **2.** to ask someone in an emotional way to do something or give something ○ *His mother begged him not to go.*

① **began** /bɪˈɡæn/ past tense of **begin**

beggar /ˈbeɡə/ *noun* a person who lives by asking for money ○ *There are lots of beggars outside the railway stations.*

① **begin** /bɪˈɡɪn/ (**begins, beginning, began, begun**) *verb* **1.** to start, or start something ○ *The meeting will begin at ten o'clock.* ○ *We began the session with introductions and getting to know each other.* ○ *His surname begins with an S.* □ **to begin again** to start a second time ○ *She played a wrong note and had to begin again.* **2.** to start doing something ○ *The weather is beginning to warm up.* ○ *The children began chasing each other.* ◊ **to begin with** at first ○ *To begin with, I travelled by train but now I cycle every day.*

③ **beginner** /bɪˈɡɪnə/ *noun* a person who is starting to learn something or do something ○ *The course is for absolute beginners.* ○ *I can't paint very well – I'm just a beginner.*

① **beginning** /bɪˈɡɪnɪŋ/ *noun* the first part ○ *The beginning of the film is rather boring.*

begrudge /bɪˈɡrʌdʒ/ (**begrudges, begrudging, begrudged**) *verb* to feel resentment because of something someone has or does

① **begun** /bɪˈɡʌn/ past participle of **begin**

behalf /bɪˈhɑːf/ *noun* □ **on behalf of someone, on someone's behalf** acting for someone ○ *She is speaking on behalf of the trade association.* ○ *He was chosen to speak on the workers' behalf.*

③ **behave** /bɪˈheɪv/ (**behaves, behaving, behaved**) *verb* to act in a particular way [~towards] ○ *He behaved very pleasantly towards his staff.* ○ *She was behaving in a funny way.* □ **to behave (yourself)** to be polite and good ○ *If you don't behave, children, we won't go to see the film.*

① **behaviour** /bɪˈheɪvjə/ *noun* a way of doing things [~towards] ○ *Local people complained about the behaviour of the football fans.* ○ *His behaviour towards her was quite natural.*

behead /bɪˈhed/ (**beheads, beheading, beheaded**) *verb* to cut off someone's head

① **behind** /bɪˈhaɪnd/ *prep* **1.** at the back of ○ *They hid behind the door.* ○ *I dropped my pen behind the sofa.* ○ *He was second, only three metres behind the winner.* **2.** responsible for ○ *The police believe they know who is behind the bombing campaign.* **3.** supporting ○ *All his colleagues were behind his decision.* ○ *We're behind* *you!* ■ *adv* **1.** at the back ○ *He was first, and the rest of the runners were a long way behind.* **2.** later than you should be ○ *I am behind with my correspondence.* ○ *The company has fallen behind schedule with its deliveries.*

beige /beɪʒ/ *adj, noun* very pale brown ○ *He was wearing a beige pullover.*

① **being** /ˈbiːɪŋ/ *noun* **1.** a person **2.** a living thing, especially one that is not easily recognised **3.** a spiritual or magical force ○ *He dreamt he was being supported by supernatural beings.* **4.** a state of existing ◇ **to come into being** to start to exist ○ *The association came into being in 1946.*

belated /bɪˈleɪtɪd/ *adj* coming or happening later than it should

belch /beltʃ/ *noun* the action of allowing air in the stomach to come up through the mouth ○ *He finished his meal and let out a loud belch.* ■ *verb* (**belches, belching, belched**) **1.** to make air in the stomach come up through the mouth ○ *He wiped his mouth and belched.* **2.** *also* **belch out** to produce large amounts of smoke, fumes or flames ○ *Dark smoke belched from the power station.*

beleaguered /bɪˈliːɡəd/ *adj* surrounded by difficulties or by enemies

belie /bɪˈlaɪ/ (**belies, belying, belied**) *verb* **1.** to hide ○ *His brusque manner belies his gentle nature.* **2.** to show that something is false ○ *His exam results belied his teachers' reports.*

② **belief** /bɪˈliːf/ *noun* a strong feeling that something is true [~in] ○ *his firm belief in the power of law* ○ *her strong belief in God* ◇ **beyond belief** incredible ○ *That she did not know that there were drugs in the parcel is quite beyond belief.*

believable /bɪˈliːvəb(ə)l/ *adj* which can be believed

① **believe** /bɪˈliːv/ (**believes, believing, believed**) *verb* **1.** to be sure that something is true, although you can't prove it [~(that)] ○ *I don't believe his story.* ○ *People used to believe that the earth was flat.* **2.** used when you are not absolutely sure of something [~(that)] ○ *I don't believe we've met.*

believer /bɪˈliːvə/ *noun* a person who believes in a particular religion or idea

belittle /bɪˈlɪt(ə)l/ (**belittles, belittling, belittled**) *verb* to make something seem unimportant

② **bell** /bel/ *noun* **1.** a metal object shaped like a cup which makes a ringing noise when hit by a piece of metal inside it ○ *They rang the church bells at the wedding.* **2.** any object designed to make a ringing noise, especially one that uses electricity ○ *The alarm bell rings if you touch the door.* ○ *The postman rang the door bell.* ○ *You ought to have a bell on your bicycle.* ◇ **to ring a bell** *or* **any bells** to sound familiar or remind you of something ○ *Does the name Forsyth ring a bell?*

belligerent /bəˈlɪdʒərənt/ *adj* **1.** wanting to go to war, or being at war ○ *The country has turned increasingly belligerent towards its neighbours.* **2.** aggressive, wanting to argue with other people ○ *Ask the manager about it tomorrow, he's in a belligerent mood at the moment.*

bellow /ˈbeləʊ/ (**bellows, bellowing, bellowed**) *verb* **1.** to make a loud cry ○ *He bellowed with pain.* ○ *The bull was bellowing in the farmyard.* **2.** to shout ○ *He bellowed to the swimmers to come back to the beach.*

③ **belly** /ˈbeli/ (*plural* **bellies**) *noun* the stomach and intestines (*informal*)

belly button /ˈbeli ˌbʌt(ə)n/ *noun* same as **navel** (*informal*)

① **belong** /bɪˈlɒŋ/ (**belongs, belonging, belonged**) *verb* **1.** to be kept in the usual or expected place ○ *That book belongs on the top shelf.* **2.** to be happy to be somewhere or with a group of people ○ *Within a week in my new job I felt I belonged.* **3.** □ **to belong to an organisation** to be a member of an organisation ○ *They still belong to the tennis club.* □ **to belong to someone** to be the property of someone ○ *Does the car really belong to you?* □ **to belong to something** to be part of or connected to something ○ *French belongs to the family of languages that developed from Latin.* **4.** □ **to belong with** to be a part of or connected to something else ○ *These knives belong with the set in the kitchen.*

belongings /bɪˈlɒŋɪŋz/ *plural noun* personal property ○ *Her belongings were scattered all over the room.* ○ *Please be sure to take all your personal belongings with you when you leave the aircraft.*

① **below** /bɪˈləʊ/ *adv* lower down ○ *Standing on the bridge we looked at the river below.* ○ *These toys are for children of two years and below.* ■ *prep* lower down than ○ *The temperature was below freezing.* ○ *In Singapore, the temperature never goes below 25°C.* ○ *Do not write anything below this line.* ○ *These tablets should not be given to children below the age of twelve.* ○ *Can you see below the surface of the water?*

② **belt** /belt/ *noun* a strap which goes round your waist to hold up a skirt or trousers ○ *She wore a skirt with a bright red belt.*

belt up *phrasal verb* (*informal*) **1.** to stop talking **2.** to attach your seat belt ○ *Make sure everyone in the car belts up.*

bemused /bɪ'mjuːzd/ *adj* puzzled and confused

② **bench** /bentʃ/ *noun* a long seat for several people ○ *We sat down on one of the park benches.*

benchmark /'bentʃmɑːk/ *noun* a standard for testing against

② **bend** /bend/ *noun* a curve in something such as a road or a pipe [~in] ○ *Don't drive too fast, there's a sudden bend in the road.* ○ *The pipe under the sink has an awkward bend in it.* ■ *verb* (**bends, bending, bent**) **1.** to move your shoulders and head into a lower position ○ *He bent to pick up the little girl.* ○ *You can reach it if you bend to the left.* **2.** to make something curve ○ *You will have to bend the pipe to fit round the corner.* **3.** to move a jointed part of your body ○ *Bend your knees slightly.* **4.** to have the shape of a curve ○ *The road bends suddenly after the bridge.*

bend down *phrasal verb* to move to a lower position, so that your head is lower than your waist ○ *He bent down to pick up the little girl.*

bend over *phrasal verb* to move to a different or a lower position ○ *You can read it if you bend over to the left.* ○ *Bend over till you can touch your toes.* ◇ **to bend over backwards for someone** *or* **to do something** to do everything you can to help someone ○ *Their friends bent over backwards for* or *to support the family after the accident.*

bendy /'bendi/ *adj* **1.** easily bent ○ *a bendy toy* **2.** having many bends ○ *a bendy road*

② **beneath** /bɪ'niːθ/ *prep* under ○ *There are dangerous rocks beneath the surface of the lake.* ○ *The river flows very fast beneath the bridge.* ■ *adv* underneath (*formal*) ○ *They stood on the bridge and watched the river flowing beneath.*

beneficial /ˌbenɪ'fɪʃ(ə)l/ *adj* having a helpful effect

③ **beneficiary** /ˌbenɪ'fɪʃəri/ (*plural* **beneficiaries**) *noun* **1.** a person who inherits something in a will ○ *The main beneficiaries were his three children.* **2.** someone, or a group, that is helped by something ○ *Who will be the main beneficiaries of this new law?*

① **benefit** /'benɪfɪt/ *noun* **1.** an advantage ○ *What benefit would I get from joining the club?* □ **for someone's benefit** specially for someone ○ *You are not doing it just for my benefit, are you?* **2.** a payment from the government to someone who needs financial help ○ *unemployment benefit* ○ *maternity benefit* ■ *verb* (**benefits, benefiting, benefited**) **1.** to be useful to someone ○ *The book will benefit anyone who is planning to do some house repairs.* **2.** to get an advantage from something

Benelux /'benɪlʌks/ *noun* the countries of Belgium, the Netherlands and Luxembourg as a group

benevolent /bə'nev(ə)lənt/ *adj* good and kind

benign /bə'naɪn/ *adj* kind and pleasant

② **bent**[1] /bent/ *adj* curved or twisted ○ *These nails are so bent we can't use them.*

bent[2] /bent/ ♦ **bend**

bequest /bɪ'kwest/ *noun* the giving of property or money to someone in a will

bereaved /bɪ'riːvd/ *adj* who has a close relative or friend who has died ○ *We sent our condolences to the bereaved families.*

bereavement /bɪ'riːvmənt/ *noun* the loss of a friend or relative through death

beret /'bereɪ/ *noun* a round cap without a peak, worn by men or women

berry /'beri/ (*plural* **berries**) *noun* a small round fruit with several small seeds inside (NOTE: Do not confuse with **bury**.)

berth /bɜːθ/ *noun* **1.** a place where a ship stays in a harbour ○ *There are no berths free – the ferry will have to wait at anchor outside the harbour for a while.* **2.** a bunk bed on a ship or train ○ *Do you want the upper or lower berth?*

② **beside** /bɪ'saɪd/ *prep* at the side of someone or something ○ *Come and sit down beside me.* ○ *The office is just beside the railway station.* ◇ **it's beside the point** it's got nothing to do with the main subject ○ *Whether or not the coat matches your hat is beside the point – it's simply too big for you.*

② **besides** /bɪ'saɪdz/ *prep* as well as ○ *They have two other cars besides the big Ford.* ○ *Besides managing the shop, he also teaches in the evening.* □ **besides being** *or* **doing something** in addition to being or doing something ■ *adv* used for adding another stronger reason for something ○ *I don't want to go for a picnic – besides, it's starting to rain.*

besiege /bɪˈsiːdʒ/ (**besieges, besieging, besieged**) *verb* to surround a building, or a town or city

① **best** /best/ *adj* better than anything else ○ *She's my best friend.* ○ *He put on his best suit to go to the interview.* ○ *What is the best way of getting to London from here?* □ **best regards**, **best wishes** a greeting sent to someone ○ *Give my best wishes to your father.* ■ *noun* the thing which is better than anything else ○ *The picture shows her at her best.* ■ *adv* in the most effective or successful way ○ *The engine works best when it's warm.* ○ *Oranges grow best in hot countries.* ○ *Which of you knows London best?* ◇ **all the best** best wishes for the future ◇ **as best you can** in the best way you can, even though this may not be perfect ◇ **to do your best** to do as well as you can ◇ **to make the best of something** to take any advantage you can from something ◇ **to make the best of a bad job** to accept a bad situation cheerfully ◇ **to the best of someone's ability** as well as possible ○ *I'll help you to the best of my ability.* ◇ **to the best of my knowledge** as far as I know ◇ **best regards, best wishes** a greeting sent to someone ○ *Give my best wishes to your father.* ◇ **as best you can** in the best way you can, even though this may not be perfect ○ *He repaired the dent in the car door as best he could.*

best man /best ˈmæn/ *noun* the man who helps the bridegroom at a wedding

bestow /bɪˈstəʊ/ (**bestows, bestowing, bestowed**) *verb* to give something (*formal*)

bestseller /bestˈselə/ *noun* an item, especially a book, which sells very well

① **bet** /bet/ *noun* a sum of money which is risked by trying to say which horse will come first in a race or which side will win a competition [~on] ○ *I've got a bet on Brazil to win the next World Cup.* ■ *verb* (**bets, betting, bet** or **betted**) to risk money by saying which horse you think will come first in a race or which team will win a competition [~on] ○ *She bet £30 on the horses.* ◇ **I bet (you) (that)** *or* **I'll bet (you) (that)** I'm sure that ○ *I bet you she's going to be late*

betray /bɪˈtreɪ/ (**betrays, betraying, betrayed**) *verb* **1.** to harm someone by telling their secrets ○ *He was betrayed by his best friend.* ○ *The scientist was accused of betraying secrets to the enemy.* **2.** to show a feeling which you want to keep hidden ○ *The tears in her eyes betrayed her emotion.*

betrayal /bɪˈtreɪəl/ *noun* the act of giving someone's secrets to an enemy, or of not doing what you had promised to do

① **better** /ˈbetə/ *adj* **1.** good when compared to something else ○ *The weather is better today than it was yesterday.* ○ *His latest book is better than the first one he wrote.* ○ *She's better at maths than English.* ○ *Brown bread is better for you than white.* ○ *We will shop around to see if we can get a better price.* **2.** healthy again ○ *I had a cold last week but I'm better now.* ○ *I hope your sister will be better soon.* ■ *adv* more successfully than something else ○ *She sings better than her sister.* ○ *My old knife cuts better than the new one.* □ **to think better of something** to decide that something is not a good idea ○ *He was going to drive to London, but thought better of it when he heard the traffic report on the news.* ◇ **for the better** in a way which makes a situation less unpleasant or difficult ○ *Her attitude has changed for the better since we reviewed her responsibilities.* ◇ **had better** *or* **would be better** it would be sensible to ○ *She'd better go to bed if she's got flu.* ○ *It would be better if you phoned your father now.*

better off /ˌbetər ˈɒf/ *adj* in a better position

③ **betting** /ˈbetɪŋ/ *noun* the placing of bets

① **between** /bɪˈtwiːn/ *prep* **1.** with people or things on both sides ○ *There's only a thin wall between his office and mine, so I hear everything he says.* ○ *Don't sit between him and his girlfriend.* **2.** connecting two places ○ *The bus goes between Oxford and London.* **3.** in the period after one time and before another ○ *I'm in a meeting between 10 o'clock and 12.* ○ *Can you come to see me between now and next Monday?* **4.** within a range between two amounts or numbers ○ *The parcel weighs between four and five kilos.* ○ *Cherries cost between £2 and £3 per kilo.* **5.** used for comparing two or more things ○ *Sometimes it's not easy to see a difference between blue and green.* ○ *She could choose between courses in German, Chinese or Russian.* **6.** among ◇ **between you and me** speaking privately ◇ **in between** with things on both sides ○ *There's only a thin wall between his bedroom and mine, so I hear everything he says on the phone.* ◇ **in between** in the middle, with something on both sides

beverage /ˈbev(ə)rɪdʒ/ *noun* a drink (*formal*)

beware /bɪ'weə/ *verb* to be careful about something that might be dangerous or cause a problem ○ *Beware of cheap imitations.* ○ *You need to beware of being persuaded to spend more than you can afford.*

bewilder /bɪ'wɪldə/ (**bewilders, bewildering, bewildered**) *verb* to puzzle someone

bewildered /bɪ'wɪldəd/ *adj* confused or puzzled

bewildering /bɪ'wɪld(ə)rɪŋ/ *adj* confusing or puzzling

bewilderment /bɪ'wɪldəmənt/ *noun* a state of confusion or of being puzzled

bewitch /bɪ'wɪtʃ/ (**bewitches, bewitching, bewitched**) *verb* to cast a spell on someone

① **beyond** /bɪ'jɒnd/ *prep* **1.** further away than ○ *The post office is beyond the bank.* **2.** outside the usual range of something ○ *The delivery date is beyond our control.* ○ *I can't accept new orders beyond the end of next year.* **3.** later than ○ *The party went on beyond midnight.*

bhangra /'bʌŋgrə/ *noun* a style of dance music which mixes Punjabi folk music with Western pop music

biannual /baɪ'ænjuəl/ *adj* happening twice a year (NOTE: Do not confuse with **biennial**.)

bias /'baɪəs/ *noun* a fixed opinion in one direction only

biased /'baɪəst/ *adj* prejudiced

bib /bɪb/ *noun* a little piece of cloth which is tied round a baby's neck, under its chin ○ *Don't forget to put his bib on when he's eating spinach.*

③ **Bible** /'baɪb(ə)l/ *noun* **1.** the holy book of the Christian religion **2. bible** an important and useful reference book ○ *She keeps an old French recipe book in the kitchen – it's her bible.*

bibliography /ˌbɪbli'ɒgrəfi/ *noun* a list of publications about a special subject

biceps /'baɪseps/ *noun* a muscle formed of two parts, especially the muscle in the front of the upper arm

bicker /'bɪkə/ (**bickers, bickering, bickered**) *verb* to quarrel about something

③ **bicycle** /'baɪsɪk(ə)l/ *noun* a vehicle with two wheels which you ride by pushing on the pedals ○ *He goes to school by bicycle every day.* ○ *She's going to do the shopping on her bicycle.* ○ *He's learning to ride a bicycle.*

③ **bid** /bɪd/ *noun* **1.** an offer to buy something at a particular price [~for] ○ *His bid for the painting was too low.* **2.** an attempt to do something [~for] □ **she made a bid for power** she tried to seize power ■ *verb* (**bids, bidding, bade** or **bid, bidden** or **bid**) to make an offer to buy something at an auction [~for] ○ *He bid £500 for the car.*

bidding /'bɪdɪŋ/ *noun* **1.** a command **2.** offers made at an auction ○ *The bidding started at £200 and rose quickly.*

bidet /'biːdeɪ/ *noun* a small low bath for washing your bottom

biennial /baɪ'eniəl/ *adj* (*of an event*) which happens every two years ○ *The athletics competition is a biennial event.* (NOTE: Do not confuse with **biannual**.)

① **big** /bɪg/ (**bigger, biggest**) *adj* of a large size ○ *I don't want a small car – I want a big one.* ○ *His father has the biggest restaurant in town.* ○ *I'm not afraid of him – I'm bigger than he is.* ○ *We had a big order from Germany.*

bigamy /'bɪgəmi/ *noun* the crime of someone going through a ceremony of marriage to someone when they are already married to someone else (NOTE: + **bigamist** *n*)

Big Brother /ˌbɪg 'brʌðə/ *noun* an authority which controls and watches other people

big business /ˌbɪg 'bɪznɪs/ *noun* very large commercial companies, seen as a group

big cheese /ˌbɪg 'tʃiːz/ *noun* an important person (*informal*) (NOTE: no plural)

big money /ˌbɪg 'mʌni/ *noun* a lot of money (*informal*)

big name /ˌbɪg 'neɪm/ *noun* an important person (*informal*)

bigot /'bɪgət/ *noun* a person with a narrow-minded attitude to religion or politics

bigotry /'bɪgətri/ *noun* an attitude where you dislike something strongly for no particular reason

big shot /'bɪg ʃɒt/ *noun* an important person (*informal*)

bigwig /'bɪgwɪg/ *noun* an important person (*informal*)

② **bike** /baɪk/ *noun* a bicycle (*informal*) ○ *She was knocked off her bike by a car.* ○ *He goes to school by bike.* ○ *If the weather's good, we could go for a bike ride.*

biker /'baɪkə/ *noun* a person who rides a motorcycle

bikini /bɪ'kiːni/ *noun* a woman's small two-piece swimsuit

bilateral /baɪ'læt(ə)rəl/ *adj* involving two groups of people

bile /baɪl/ *noun* **1.** a thick bitter brownish-yellow fluid produced by the liver, which helps to digest fatty substances **2.** angry or bitter feelings (*literary*)

bilingual /baɪ'lɪŋgwəl/ *adj* using two languages

① **bill** /bɪl/ *noun* **1.** a piece of paper showing the amount of money you have to pay for something [~for] ○ *a bill for more than £200* ○ *Ask the waiter for the bill.* ○ *Don't forget to pay your gas bill.* **2.** same as **beak 3.** a proposal which, if passed by parliament, becomes law ○ *Parliament will consider the education bill this week.* ○ *He has drafted a bill to ban the sale of guns.* **4.** *US* a piece of paper money ○ *a 10-dollar bill*

billboard /'bɪlbɔːd/ *noun especially US* a large outdoor panel for posters (NOTE: The British term is **hoarding**.)

billiards /'bɪliədz/ *noun* a game played on a table, where two players with long cues hit their own white ball against a red ball or the opponent's ball, scoring points. Compare **snooker** (NOTE: **billiards** loses the 's' when it is used before another noun: *a billiard table*.)

billing /'bɪlɪŋ/ *noun* **1.** the position a performer has on an entertainment programme or advertisement **2.** the preparing and sending out of bills to customers

billion /'bɪljən/ *noun* **1.** one thousand million ○ *The government raises billions in taxes each year.* **2.** one million million (*dated*) **3.** a great many [~of] ○ *Billions of Christmas cards are sent every year.* (NOTE: In US English billion has always meant one thousand million, but in British English it formerly meant one million million, and it is still sometimes used with this meaning. With figures it is usually written **bn**: *$5bn* say 'five billion dollars'.)

billow /'bɪləʊ/ (**billows, billowing, billowed**) *verb* **1.** to become full of air ○ *The sails of the yachts billowed in the breeze.* **2.** to move in large waves ○ *Smoke billowed out of the building.*

bimbo /'bɪmbəʊ/ *noun* an attractive but rather stupid girl (*informal offensive*)

② **bin** /bɪn/ *noun* **1.** a container for putting rubbish in ○ *Don't throw your litter on the floor – pick it up and put it in the bin.* **2.** a container for keeping things in ○ *a bread bin* ■ *verb* (**bins, binning, binned**) to throw something away into a rubbish bin ○ *He just binned the demand for payment.*

② **bind** /baɪnd/ (**binds, binding, bound, bound**) *verb* **1.** to tie someone's hands or feet so they cannot move ○ *They bound her arms with a rope.* **2.** to tie something or someone to something else ○ *Bind the sticks together with strings.* ○ *They bound him to the chair with strips of plastic.* **3.** to force someone to do something ○ *The contract binds him to make regular payments.* **4.** to put a cover on a book ○ *The book is bound in blue leather.*

binder /'baɪndə/ *noun* a stiff cover for papers ○ *Write to the publisher to get a free binder for your magazines.*

binding /'baɪndɪŋ/ *noun* the cover of a book ○ *The book has a leather binding.*

binge /bɪndʒ/ *noun* a time when someone drinks too much alcohol, eats too much or does something else too much ○ *After last night's binge he had to stay in bed.* ○ *She went on a chocolate binge which lasted the whole summer.* ○ *Shopping binges are not uncommon during sales time.* (NOTE: + **binge** *v*)

bingo /'bɪŋgəʊ/ *noun* a game of chance, where each player has a card with numbers on it. Numbers are called out, and when you have marked off a whole row of numbers, you win. ○ *She goes to play bingo every Friday night.* ○ *He won quite a lot at bingo.*

③ **binoculars** /bɪ'nɒkjʊləz/ *plural noun* powerful glasses for looking at things which are too far away to see clearly (NOTE: **binoculars** has no singular. If you want to indicate one item, say 'a pair of binoculars'.)

biochemistry /ˌbaɪəʊ'kemɪstri/ *noun* the science and study of the chemistry of living things (NOTE: + **biochemist** *n*)

biodegradable /ˌbaɪəʊdɪ'greɪdəb(ə)l/ *adj* which can easily be broken down by bacteria, the sun or sea water

biodiversity /ˌbaɪəʊdaɪ'vɜːsɪti/ *noun* the number of species in a certain area

biographer /baɪ'ɒgrəfə/ *noun* a person who writes the story of someone's life

biography /baɪ'ɒgrəfi/ (*plural* **biographies**) *noun* the story of someone's life

biological /ˌbaɪə'lɒdʒɪk(ə)l/ *adj* **1.** referring to living things ○ *the biological balance in the North Sea* **2.** using harmful microorganisms ○ *biological warfare* (NOTE: + **biologically** *adv*)

biologist /baɪ'ɒlədʒɪst/ *noun* a scientist who does research in biology

③ **biology** /baɪ'ɒlədʒi/ *noun* the study of living things

biopsy /'baɪɒpsi/ (*plural* **biopsies**) *noun* an operation to remove a small piece from someone's body for examination

biotechnology /ˌbaɪəʊtekˈnɒlədʒi/ *noun* technology which uses different living materials such as cells for science or industry

birch /bɜːtʃ/ *noun* a northern tree with small leaves and a white outer layer which comes off in strips ○ *the birch forests of Russia*

② **bird** /bɜːd/ *noun* **1.** an animal which has wings and feathers and is usually able to fly **2.** a young woman (*informal; usually used by men and sometimes regarded as offensive by women*)

bird's-eye view /ˌbɜːdz aɪ ˈvjuː/ *noun* a view from high up looking down

Biro /ˈbaɪrəʊ/ *trademark* a type of **ballpoint**

② **birth** /bɜːθ/ *noun* the occasion of being born ○ *He was a big baby at birth.* □ **to give birth to a baby** to have a baby ○ *She gave birth to a boy last week.* ◇ **by birth** according to the country someone's parents come from ○ *He is French by birth.*

birth certificate /ˈbɜːθ səˌtɪfɪkət/ *noun* an official paper showing the date on which someone was born, together with details of the parents

birth control /ˈbɜːθ kənˌtrəʊl/ *noun* the practice of trying to avoid becoming pregnant

② **birthday** /ˈbɜːθdeɪ/ *noun* the date on which someone was born ○ *April 23rd is Shakespeare's birthday.* ○ *My birthday is on 25th June.* ○ *What do you want for your birthday?*

birthmark /ˈbɜːθmɑːk/ *noun* a mark on the skin which a baby has from birth, and which usually cannot be removed

birthplace /ˈbɜːθpleɪs/ *noun* **1.** the place where someone was born ○ *They visited Shakespeare's birthplace in Stratford.* **2.** the place where something was invented ○ *China was the birthplace of gunpowder.*

birth rate /ˈbɜːθ reɪt/ *noun* the number of children born per thousand of the population

③ **biscuit** /ˈbɪskɪt/ *noun* a small flat, usually sweet, hard cake

bisexual /baɪˈsekʃuəl/ *adj* sexually attracted to both men and women. Compare **heterosexual, homosexual**

③ **bishop** /ˈbɪʃəp/ *noun* **1.** a Christian church leader ○ *the Bishop of London* **2.** in chess, a piece which moves diagonally ○ *She took both his bishops in three moves.*

bison /ˈbaɪs(ə)n/ *noun* a large wild animal with long hair, which used to be common in Europe and North America

bistro /ˈbiːstrəʊ/ (*plural* **bistros**) *noun* a small restaurant

① **bit** /bɪt/ *noun* **1.** a little piece ○ *He tied the bundle of sticks together with a bit of string.* ○ *Would you like another bit of cake?* **2.** the smallest unit of information that a computer system can handle ■ *verb* past participle of **bite** ◇ **to bits 1.** into little pieces **2.** very much ○ *thrilled to bits* ◇ **to come** *or* **fall to bits** to fall apart ○ *The chair has come to bits.* ◇ **to take something to bits** to take something apart in order to repair it ○ *He's taking my old clock to bits.* ◇ **a bit** a little ○ *The painting is a bit too dark.* ○ *She always plays that tune a bit too fast.* ○ *Let him sleep a little bit longer.* ○ *Can you wait a bit? I'm not ready yet.* ○ *Have you got a piece of wood a bit bigger than this one?* ◇ **for a bit** for a short period of time ○ *Can you stop for a bit? I'm getting tired.* ◇ **bit by bit** not all at the same time, little by little ○ *He paid back the money he owed, bit by bit.* ○ *He inched forward, bit by bit, towards the edge of the cliff.*

bitch /bɪtʃ/ *noun* **1.** a female animal, especially a female dog ○ *They have two dogs – a male and a bitch.* ○ *The bitch has given birth to five puppies.* **2.** an unpleasant woman (*offensive slang*) ○ *That bitch is going round spreading rumours about me.* ■ *verb* (**bitches, bitching, bitched**) to complain (*slang*)

bitchy /ˈbɪtʃi/ *adj* making unpleasant remarks about someone (*slang*)

① **bite** /baɪt/ *verb* (**bites, biting, bit, bitten**) **1.** to cut someone or something with your teeth [~into] ○ *The dog tried to bite the cat.* ○ *She bit into the pie.* **2.** (*of an insect*) to make a small hole in your skin which turns red and itchy ○ *She's been bitten by a mosquito.* ■ *noun* **1.** a small amount of food that you cut with your teeth in order to eat it ○ *She took a big bite out of the sandwich.* **2. a bite, a bite to eat** a small meal **3.** a place on someone's body where it has been bitten (NOTE: Do not confuse with **byte**.)

bite-sized /ˈbaɪt saɪzd/ *adj* small enough to put in your mouth

biting /ˈbaɪtɪŋ/ *adj* **1.** very cold ○ *A biting wind blew across the valley.* **2.** (*of a criticism*) very unkind ○ *He ended his review with some biting remarks about the costumes.*

① **bitten** /ˈbɪt(ə)n/ past participle of **bite**

③ **bitter** /ˈbɪtə/ *adj* **1.** not sweet ○ *This black coffee is too bitter.* **2.** angry because something is not fair ○ *She was very bitter about the way the company treated her.* **3.** causing great disappointment or unhappiness ○ *Losing her job was a bitter blow.* **4.** cold and unpleasant ○ *a bitter wind*

bitterly /ˈbɪtəli/ *adv* strongly ○ *He bitterly regrets what he said.*

bitterness /ˈbɪtənəs/ *noun* **1.** a bitter taste **2.** angry feelings ○ *His bitterness at being left out of the England team was very obvious.*

bitter-sweet /ˈbɪtə swiːt/ *adj* **1.** smelling or tasting both bitter and sweet **2.** causing feelings of both happiness and sadness

bitty /ˈbɪti/ *adj* made up of unconnected parts

bivouac /ˈbɪvuæk/ *noun* a simple shelter made from branches and leaves

bizarre /bɪˈzɑː/ *adj* very strange

blab /blæb/ (**blabs, blabbing, blabbed**) *verb* to tell someone a secret (*informal*)

① **black** /blæk/ *adj* **1.** having a very dark colour, the opposite to white ○ *a black and white photograph* ○ *He was wearing a black suit.* ○ *She has black hair.* **2.** belonging to a race of people with dark skin, whose families are African in origin ■ *noun* the darkest colour ○ *This picture had a border of black and gold.*

black out *phrasal verb* **1.** to become unconscious ○ *I suddenly blacked out and I can't remember anything more.* **2.** to make all the lights switch off over a large area ○ *The storm blacked out half the town.*

black-and-white /ˌblæk ən ˈwaɪt/ *adj* **1.** (*of an image*) not in colour **2.** clear-cut and simple

black belt /ˈblæk belt/ *noun* a person who has achieved the highest level of skill in an activity such as judo, or the belt which represents this achievement

③ **blackberry** /ˈblækb(ə)ri/ (*plural* **blackberries**) *noun* **1.** a small black fruit that grows on a bush ○ *For dessert we're having blackberry and apple pie.* **2.** the bush this fruit grows on ○ *We had to struggle through blackberry bushes which had grown over the path.* (NOTE: A wild blackberry is also called a **bramble**.)

③ **blackbird** /ˈblækbɜːd/ *noun* a common garden bird with black feathers and a yellow beak

③ **blackboard** /ˈblækbɔːd/ *noun* a dark board which you can write on with chalk, especially on the wall of a classroom (NOTE: now often called a 'chalkboard')

black box /blæk ˈbɒks/ *noun* a piece of equipment carried in an aircraft which records what happens during a flight, including conversations between pilots and the control tower

③ **blackcurrant** /blækˈkʌrənt/ *noun* a small black fruit which is usually eaten cooked ○ *a jar of blackcurrant jam* ○ *The blackcurrants need more sugar – they're very sour.*

blacken /ˈblækən/ (**blackens, blackening, blackened**) *verb* to make black

black eye /ˌblæk ˈaɪ/ *noun* bruising and swelling around an eye, caused by a blow

blackhead /ˈblækhed/ *noun* a blocked area which shows up as a very small black dot on the skin

black hole /blæk ˈhəʊl/ *noun* an area in space which pulls light into it

black ice /blæk ˈaɪs/ *noun* a dangerous layer of thin ice on a road

blacklist /ˈblæklɪst/ *noun* a list of things or people that are not approved of ○ *His name is on the blacklist.* ■ *verb* (**blacklists, blacklisting, blacklisted**) to put someone or something on a blacklist ○ *The company has been blacklisted by the government.*

black magic /blæk ˈmædʒɪk/ *noun* magic used for evil purposes

blackmail /ˈblækmeɪl/ *verb* (**blackmails, blackmailing, blackmailed**) to threaten to do something harmful to someone unless they do what you want ○ *They tried to blackmail the government into releasing prisoners of war.* ■ *noun* the act of blackmailing ○ *The government will not give in to terrorist blackmail.* (NOTE: + **blackmail** *v*)

black mark /blæk ˈmɑːk/ *noun* a bad report

black market /ˌblæk ˈmɑːkɪt/ *noun* buying and selling goods in a way which is not allowed by law

blackout /ˈblækaʊt/ *noun* **1.** an occasion on which you become unconscious ○ *He must have had a blackout while driving.* **2.** a period when there is no electricity, or when there are no lights ○ *The snowstorm caused a blackout.*

black pepper /blæk ˈpepə/ *noun* pepper from whole dried pepper seeds

blacksmith /ˈblæksmɪθ/ *noun* **1.** a person who works with red-hot iron, making it into different shapes with a hammer ○ *She asked the blacksmith to make her a new* *garden gate* **2.** a person who repairs and fits horseshoes ○ *The blacksmith was shoeing a horse.*

black spot /ˈblæk spɒt/ *noun* a place on a road where accidents often happen

black tie /blæk ˈtaɪ/ *noun* a formal style of dress for men that includes a smart black jacket and a black bow tie

bladder /ˈblædə/ *noun* the bag-shaped organ inside the body where urine collects before being passed out of the body ○ *She is taking antibiotics for a bladder infection.*

③ **blade** /bleɪd/ *noun* **1.** a sharp cutting part ○ *the blades of a pair of scissors* ○ *Be careful – that knife has a very sharp blade.* **2.** a thin leaf of grass **3.** one of the long flat parts that spin round on some aircraft engines or that keep a helicopter in the air ○ *a propeller blade*

blah /blɑː/ *noun* boring talk or writing (*informal*)

② **blame** /bleɪm/ *noun* criticism for having done something wrong [~for] ○ *I'm not going to take the blame for something I didn't do.* □ **to get the blame for something** to be accused of something ○ *Who got the blame for breaking the window? Me, of course!* □ **to take the blame for something** to accept that you were responsible for something bad ■ *verb* to say that someone is responsible for something [~for/~on] ○ *Blame my sister for the awful food, not me.* ○ *He blamed the accident on the bad weather.* □ **to be to blame for** to be responsible for something ○ *The manager is to blame for the bad service.* ◇ **I don't blame you** I think you're right to do that ○ *I don't blame you for being annoyed, when everyone else got a present and you didn't.* ◇ **you have only yourself to blame** no one else is responsible for what happened ○ *You have only yourself to blame if you missed the chance of a free ticket.*

blameless /ˈbleɪmləs/ *adj* not guilty

bland /blænd/ *adj* **1.** dull and boring, and often not giving any information ○ *He gave a bland reply.* **2.** without much flavour ○ *Some people don't like avocados because they find them too bland.* ○ *The sauce needs more herbs – it's far too bland.*

③ **blank** /blæŋk/ *adj* (*of paper*) not containing any information, sound or writing, e.g. ○ *She took a blank piece of paper and drew a map.* ○ *Have we got any blank tapes left?* ■ *noun* an empty space, especially on a printed form, for something to be written in ◇ **to go blank** to be unable to remember something ○ *I went blank when they asked what I was doing last Tuesday.* ○ *When he asked for my work phone number, my mind just went blank.*

blank out *phrasal verb* **1.** to cross out or cover a piece of writing ○ *The surname had been blanked out.* **2.** to try to forget something deliberately ○ *She blanked out the days* or *the memory of the days immediately after the car crash.*

blank cheque /ˌblæŋk ˈtʃek/ *noun* **1.** a cheque which has been signed, but without any details ○ *Her father gave her a blank cheque for her birthday and told her to fill in any amount she liked.* **2.** total freedom to do anything ○ *The planners have been given a blank cheque to do what they like with the town centre.*

③ **blanket** /ˈblæŋkɪt/ *noun* **1.** a thick cover which you put over you to keep warm ○ *He woke up when the blankets fell off the bed.* ○ *She wrapped the children up in blankets to keep them warm.* **2.** a thick layer ○ *a blanket of leaves* ○ *A blanket of snow covered the fields.* ○ *The motorway was covered in a blanket of fog.* **3.** a barrier to protect something [~of] ○ *a blanket of secrecy* ■ *adj* affecting everything or everyone ○ *a blanket ban on smoking*

blankly /ˈblæŋkli/ *adv* not showing any reaction or emotion ○ *When the teacher asked him about his homework he just stared at her blankly.*

blank verse /blæŋk ˈvɜːs/ *noun* poetry which does not rhyme

blare /bleə/ (**blares, blaring, blared**) *verb* to make a loud unpleasant noise ○ *The night club has music blaring away in the middle of the night.* ○ *He drives around with his radio blaring.* (NOTE: + **blare** *n*)

blasphemy /ˈblæsfəmi/ *noun* being rude about God, religion or established principles

blast /blɑːst/ *noun* **1.** an explosion ○ *Several windows were shattered by the blast.* **2.** a strong current of wind ○ *an icy blast from the north* **3.** a sharp loud sound from a signal or whistle ○ *Three blasts of the alarm means that passengers should go on deck.* ■ *verb* (**blasts, blasting, blasted**) to damage or remove something with a bomb or explosives ○ *The burglars blasted their way into the safe.* ○ *The road builders blasted through the hill.*

blast off *phrasal verb* (*of a spacecraft*) to leave the ground ○ *The rocket blasted off from Cape Canaveral yesterday morning.*

blast-off /'blɑːst ɒf/ *noun* the time when a spacecraft takes off

blatant /'bleɪt(ə)nt/ *adj* obviously bad

blaze /bleɪz/ *verb* (**blazes, blazing, blazed**) to burn or shine strongly ○ *The fire was blazing.* ○ *The sun blazed through the clouds.* ■ *noun* a large bright fire ○ *The house was burned down in the blaze.* □ **a blaze of colour** a mass of very bright colours ○ *The garden is a blaze of colour.*

blazer /'bleɪzə/ *noun* a jacket, often with a badge to show that the person wearing it belongs to a particular school or club

blazing /'bleɪzɪŋ/ *adj* burning strongly ○ *They sat around the blazing bonfire.*

bleach /bliːtʃ/ *noun* a chemical substance which cleans things and kills harmful bacteria ○ *She poured bleach into the toilet.* ○ *Even a small drop of bleach will remove colour.* ○ *Do not use bleach on this material.* ■ *verb* (**bleaches, bleaching, bleached**) to remove colour from something ○ *He's bleached his hair.* ○ *Her hair was bleached by the sun.*

bleak /bliːk/ *adj* **1.** cold and unpleasant ○ *The path led across bleak mountains.* **2.** showing no sign of hope ○ *She gave him a bleak stare.* ○ *With no qualifications, his job prospects are bleak.*

bleat /bliːt/ (**bleats, bleating, bleated**) *verb* **1.** to make the sound that sheep and goats make ○ *The lambs were bleating in the snow.* **2.** to complain in an annoying voice ○ *What's he bleating on about?*

bleed /bliːd/ (**bleeds, bleeding, bled**) *verb* to lose blood ○ *His chin bled after he cut himself shaving.* ○ *He was bleeding heavily from his wound.*

bleep /bliːp/ *noun* a short high electronic sound made by a computer, radio, etc. ○ *The computer made a bleep and the screen went blank.* ○ *The printer will make a bleep when it runs out of paper.* (NOTE: + **bleep** *v*)

blemish /'blemɪʃ/ *noun* **1.** a mark or small amount of damage that spoils the appearance of something **2.** something that harms someone or something's good reputation

blend /blend/ *noun* something, especially a substance, made by mixing different things together ○ *different blends of coffee* ■ *verb* (**blends, blending, blended**) **1.** to mix things together ○ *Blend the eggs, milk and flour together.* **2.** (*of colours*) to go well together ○ *The grey curtains blend with the pale wallpaper.*

blender /'blendə/ *noun* a piece of kitchen equipment for mixing different foods together thoroughly

③ **bless** /bles/ (**blesses, blessing, blessed** or **blest**) *verb* to make something holy by prayers ○ *The church was blessed by the bishop.* ◇ **to be blessed with** to experience happiness or good things ○ *They were blessed with two healthy children.* ◇ **bless you** said when someone sneezes

blessed /'blesɪd/ *adj* protected by God

③ **blessing** /'blesɪŋ/ *noun* **1.** a prayer which blesses people or things ○ *The priest gave his blessing to the congregation.* **2.** support or official permission for something □ **to give your blessing to something** to approve something officially ○ *The chairman gave his blessing to the new design.* **3.** something which brings happiness ○ *She enjoyed the blessings of good health and a happy family.* ◇ **a mixed blessing** something with advantages and disadvantages ○ *Automation can be a mixed blessing – machines usually tend to be out of order when you need them most.* ◇ **a blessing in disguise** a good thing, even if at first it seemed bad ○ *Breaking his leg was a blessing in disguise – it meant he could spend more time studying.*

② **blew** /bluː/ past tense of **blow**

blight /blaɪt/ *noun* something which causes damage or spoils something [~on] ○ *The news of the car accident was a blight on the family's celebrations.* ■ *verb* (**blights, blighting, blighted**) to spoil something ○ *Knowing that she would have to go into hospital when she got back blighted her holiday.*

② **blind** /blaɪnd/ *adj* not able to see ○ *He went blind in his early forties.* (NOTE: Some people avoid this word as it can cause offence, and prefer terms such as **visually impaired** or **partially sighted**.) ■ *verb* (**blinds, blinding, blinded**) to make someone unable to see, especially for a short time ○ *She was blinded by the bright lights of the oncoming cars.*

blind date /blaɪnd 'deɪt/ *noun* a social meeting arranged with someone you do not know

blindfold /'blaɪndfəʊld/ *noun* a cloth put over someone's eyes to prevent them from seeing ○ *Her kidnappers did not let her take off the blindfold.* ■ *verb* (**blindfolds, blindfolding, blindfolded**) to put a blindfold over someone's eyes to prevent them from seeing ○ *He was blindfolded and bundled into the back of a car.*

blinding /ˈblaɪndɪŋ/ *adj* so bright or strong as to stop you seeing properly

blindly /ˈblaɪndli/ *adv* without being able to see

blindness /ˈblaɪndnəs/ *noun* the state of not being able to see ○ *The disease can cause blindness.* (NOTE: Some people avoid this term as it can cause offence, and prefer **visual impairment**.)

blind spot /ˈblaɪndspɒt/ *noun* an area at the side of a vehicle which the driver cannot see in the mirrors

③ **blink** /blɪŋk/ *noun* to close your eyes and open them again very quickly ○ *The sudden flash of light made him blink.* ■ *verb* (**blinks, blinking, blinked**) (*of lights*) to go on and off ○ *The alarm light is blinking.*

blinkered /ˈblɪŋkəd/ *adj* not interested in unusual things or ideas

blip /blɪp/ *noun* **1.** a small flashing dot on a computer screen ○ *A blip appeared on the radar screen.* **2.** a temporary bad result ○ *We hope that this month's bad export figures are only a blip.*

bliss /blɪs/ *noun* great happiness

blissful /ˈblɪsf(ə)l/ *adj* very pleasant or happy

blister /ˈblɪstə/ *noun* a swelling on the skin containing liquid, caused by rubbing or burning, or by a disease such as chickenpox ○ *I can't run – I've got a blister on my heel.* ■ *verb* (**blisters, blistering, blistered**) to make a swelling on a surface ○ *The heat had blistered the paint.* ○ *His hands were blistered in the fire.*

blistering /ˈblɪst(ə)rɪŋ/ *adj* **1.** very hot ○ *Walking in the blistering desert is impossible.* **2.** very fast (*informal*) ○ *The defence could not keep up with blistering pace of the winger.* **3.** (*of criticism*) very strong ○ *His blistering attack on his host bewildered everyone present.*

blithely /ˈblaɪðli/ *adv* without worrying about anything

blitz /blɪts/ *noun* **1.** □ **to have a blitz on something** to make a sudden effort to do something (*informal*) ○ *We'll have to have a blitz on this pile of orders.* **2.** an act of bombing by planes

blizzard /ˈblɪzəd/ *noun* a snowstorm with strong wind

bloated /ˈbləʊtɪd/ *adj* **1.** fatter or fuller than usual ○ *After the Indian meal she felt bloated.* **2.** swollen with air ○ *Bloated corpses lay in the streets.*

blob /blɒb/ *noun* a small spot of sticky stuff or thick liquid

bloc /blɒk/ *noun* a political group of states

② **block** /blɒk/ *noun* **1.** a large building ○ *They live in a block of flats.* **2.** a large piece ○ *Blocks of ice were floating in the river.* **3.** something that prevents something happening [~on] ○ *a block on making payments* □ **to put a block on something** to stop something happening **4.** same as **blockage 1 5.** *US* a section of buildings surrounded by streets ○ *He lives two blocks away.* ■ *verb* (**blocks, blocking, blocked**) to prevent something from passing along something ○ *The pipe is blocked with dead leaves.* ○ *The crash blocked the road for hours.*

block up *phrasal verb* to close a hole with something

blockade /blɒˈkeɪd/ *noun* preventing supplies arriving ○ *The fishermen decided that a blockade of their harbour would help them in their fight with the EU.* (NOTE: + **blockade** *v*)

blockage /ˈblɒkɪdʒ/ *noun* **1.** something which prevents movement ○ *There's a blockage further down the drain.* **2.** the state of being blocked

blockbuster /ˈblɒkbʌstə/ *noun* a very successful big book or film

③ **bloke** /bləʊk/ *noun* a man (*informal*)

③ **blonde** /blɒnd/ *noun* a woman with fair hair ○ *He came to the party with a gorgeous blonde.*

① **blood** /blʌd/ *noun* the red liquid that flows around the body

blood bank /ˈblʌd bæŋk/ *noun* a place where blood is stored until it is needed by hospitals

bloodbath /ˈblʌdbɑːθ/ *noun* an attack that leads to a lot of deaths and injuries

bloodcurdling /ˈblʌdkɜːdlɪŋ/ *adj* very frightening

blood donor /ˈblʌd ˌdəʊnə/ *noun* a person who gives his or her blood so that it can be used in medical operations

blood group /ˈblʌd gruːp/ *noun* one of the categories into which human blood can be divided

bloodhound /ˈblʌdhaʊnd/ *noun* a large dog which can follow a trail by its sense of smell

bloodless /ˈblʌdləs/ *adj* without violence

② **blood pressure** /ˈblʌd ˌpreʃə/ *noun* the pressure at which someone's heart pumps blood

bloodshed /ˈblʌdʃed/ *noun* a situation which involves killing people

bloodshot /ˈblʌdʃɒt/ *adj* (*of the eyes*) red

bloodsports /ˈblʌdspɔːts/ *plural noun* sports which involve killing animals

bloodstained /ˈblʌdsteɪnd/ *adj* covered with bloodstains

bloodstream /ˈblʌdstriːm/ *noun* the flow of blood round the body

bloodthirsty /ˈblʌdθɜːsti/ *adj* **1.** cruel **2.** full of details about people killing or injuring each other

blood transfusion /ˈblʌd træns ˌfjuːʒ(ə)n/ *noun* an act of putting blood which has been given by another person into a patient's body

blood vessel /ˈblʌd ˌves(ə)l/ *noun* any tube, artery or vein, which carries blood round the body ○ *The wound is bleeding profusely because a blood vessel has been cut.* ◇ **to burst a blood vessel** to get violently angry ○ *The boss will burst a blood vessel when he hears the news.*

③ **bloody** /ˈblʌdi/ *adj* with much blood ○ *a bloody battle* ■ *adj, adv* used as a mild swear word to express anger and annoyance (*informal*) ○ *Stop that bloody noise!*

bloody-minded /ˌblʌdi ˈmaɪndɪd/ *adj* deliberately unhelpful (*informal*)

bloom /bluːm/ *noun* a flower □ **in (full) bloom** covered in flowers ○ *The apple trees are in full bloom.* ■ *verb* (**blooms, blooming, bloomed**) to produce flowers

blossom /ˈblɒs(ə)m/ *noun* **1.** the mass of flowers that appears on trees in the spring ○ *The hedges are covered with hawthorn blossom.* ○ *The trees are in full blossom.* **2.** a single flower ■ *verb* (**blossoms, blossoming, blossomed**) **1.** to produces flowers ○ *The roses were blossoming round the cottage door.* **2.** to improve or become more successful [~into] ○ *The friendship blossomed into romance.*

blot out *phrasal verb* to hide something completely

blotch /blɒtʃ/ *noun* a large area of colour

blotchy /ˈblɒtʃi/ *adj* (*of the face*) covered with red marks

③ **blouse** /blaʊz/ *noun* a woman's shirt

① **blow** /bləʊ/ *verb* (**blows, blowing, blew, blown**) **1.** (*of air or wind*) to move ○ *The wind had been blowing hard all day.* **2.** to push air out from your mouth ○ *Blow on your soup if it's too hot.* □ **to blow your nose** to blow air through your nose into a handkerchief, especially if you have a cold ○ *She has a cold and keeps having to blow her nose.* ■ *noun* **1.** a knock or hit with the hand ○ *He received a blow to the head in the fight.* **2.** a shock, which comes from bad news ○ *The election result was a blow to the government.*

blow away *phrasal verb* **1.** to go away by blowing ○ *His hat blew away.* **2.** to make something go away by blowing ○ *The wind will blow the fog away.*

blow down *phrasal verb* **1.** to make something fall down by blowing ○ *Six trees were blown down in the storm.* **2.** to fall down by being blown ○ *The school fence has blown down.*

blow off *phrasal verb* to make something go away by blowing ○ *The wind blew his hat off.*

blow out① *phrasal verb* to make something go out by blowing ○ *She blew out the candles on her birthday cake.*

blow over *phrasal verb* **1.** (*of a storm or a difficult situation*) to end ○ *We hope the argument will soon blow over.* **2.** to knock something down by blowing ○ *The strong winds blew over several trees.*

blow up *phrasal verb* **1.** to make something get bigger by blowing into it ○ *He blew up balloons for the party.* ○ *Your front tyre needs blowing up.* **2.** to destroy something by making it explode ○ *The soldiers blew up the railway bridge.* **3.** to make a photograph bigger ○ *The article was illustrated with a blown-up picture of the little girl and her stepfather.* **4.** to make something seem more important than it really is ○ *The story has been blown up by the papers.*

blow-by-blow /ˌbləʊ baɪ ˈbləʊ/ *adj* describing an event in great detail

blow-dry /ˌbləʊ ˈdraɪ/ *verb* to dry someone's hair with a hair drier

blown /bləʊn/ past tense and past participle of **blow**

blowout /ˈbləʊaʊt/ *noun* **1.** a very large meal (*informal*) **2.** the bursting of a tyre

blubber /ˈblʌbə/ *noun* the fat of a whale or seal ○ *Whales were killed and their blubber melted down.* ■ *verb* (**blubbers, blubbering, blubbered**) to cry noisily ○ *Stop blubbering, it's only a little scratch.*

bludgeon /ˈblʌdʒən/ (**bludgeons, bludgeoning, bludgeoned**) *verb* to beat with a heavy stick ○ *The young student was bludgeoned and left for dead.* ○ *The rioters bludgeoned him to the ground.*

① **blue** /bluː/ *adj* (**bluer, bluest**) of the colour of the sky ○ *He wore a pale blue* *shirt.* ○ *They live in the house with the dark blue door.* ■ *noun* the colour of the sky ○ *Is there a darker blue than this available?* ◇ **out of the blue** suddenly ○ *Out of the blue came an offer of a job in Australia.*

bluebell /'bluːbel/ *noun* a wild plant with blue flowers like a series of little bells

blueberry /'bluːb(ə)ri/ (*plural* **blueberries**) *noun* a wild fruit, which is dark blue when ripe, eaten raw with sugar and cream, or cooked in pies and jams

blue-blooded /ˌbluː 'blʌdɪd/ *adj* from a royal or upper-class family

blue cheese /bluː 'tʃiːz/ *noun* a cheese with blue mould in it

blueprint /'bluɪprɪnt/ *noun* **1.** a photographic print of a plan which consists of blue lines on a white background or white lines on a blue background ○ *Here's the blueprint of the new engine.* **2.** a plan for doing something [~for] ○ *The deal will act as a blueprint for future cooperation.*

③ **blues** /bluːz/ *plural noun* sad songs from the southern US ○ *Bessie Smith, the great blues singer.*

bluff /blʌf/ *noun* **1.** a threat to do something which you know you will not carry out ○ *Don't believe what he says, it's all just bluff.* **2.** a steep hill made of rock ○ *The soldiers climbed the bluff and found the enemy waiting for them on top.* ■ *verb* (**bluffs, bluffing, bluffed**) to do something by tricking someone ○ *He said he was a naval officer, but he was just bluffing.*

bluish /'bluːɪʃ/ *adj* of a colour that is close to blue

blunder /'blʌndə/ *noun* a big mistake, often one that causes a lot of embarrassment ○ *A dreadful blunder by the goalkeeper allowed their opponents to score.*

blunt /blʌnt/ *adj* **1.** not sharp ○ *He tried to cut the meat with a blunt knife.* **2.** almost rude ○ *His blunt manner often upset people.*

bluntly /'blʌntli/ *adv* in a direct way that may upset people

blur /blɜː/ *noun* an unclear image ○ *He was hit on the head, and everything became a blur.* ○ *You must have moved – the photograph is just a blur.* ■ *verb* (**blurs, blurring, blurred**) to become unclear, to make unclear ○ *His vision became blurred.*

blurb /blɜːb/ *noun* a short piece of text on something which is for sale, encouraging you to buy it (*slang*)

blurred /blɜːd/ *adj* not clearly seen ○ *The paper printed a blurred photograph of the suspect.*

blurt *verb*

blurt out *phrasal verb* to give away a secret suddenly, without intending to

blush /blʌʃ/ (**blushes, blushing, blushed**) *verb* to go red in the face because you are ashamed or embarrassed ○ *She blushed when he spoke to her.*

blusher /'blʌʃə/ *noun* pink or red colouring applied to the cheeks

bluster /'blʌstə/ (**blusters, blustering, blustered**) *verb* **1.** to speak loudly and angrily ○ *He went blustering on about taking us to court.* **2.** (*of wind*) to blow hard (NOTE: + **bluster** *n*)

blustery /'blʌst(ə)ri/ *adj* (*of wind*) blowing strongly

BO *abbr* body odour

boa constrictor /'bəʊə kənˌstrɪktə/ *noun* a large snake found in South America, which kills animals by wrapping itself around them and squeezing them

boar /bɔː/ *noun* a male pig ○ *We have a boar and two sows.* (NOTE: Do not confuse with **bore**.)

① **board** /bɔːd/ *noun* **1.** a long flat piece of something such as wood ○ *The floor of the bedroom was just bare boards.* **2.** a blackboard or chalkboard ○ *The teacher wrote on the board.*

board up *phrasal verb* to cover things such as windows and doors with boards

boarder /'bɔːdə/ *noun* a pupil who lives at his or her school (NOTE: Do not confuse with **border**.)

board game /'bɔːd geɪm/ *noun* any game in which players move pieces on a board

boarding card /'bɔːdɪŋ kɑːd/ *noun* a card which allows you to go on board a plane

boarding house /'bɔːdɪŋ haʊs/ *noun* a house where you pay to live

boarding pass /'bɔːdɪŋ pɑːs/, **boarding card** *noun* same as **boarding card**

boarding school /'bɔːdɪŋ skuːl/ *noun* a school where the children live during term time

boardroom /'bɔːdruːm/ *noun* a room where directors meet

boast /bəʊst/ *verb* (**boasts, boasting, boasted**) **1.** to have something good ○ *The house boasts a large garden and pond.* ○ *The town boasts an 18-hole golf course.* **2.** to say how good or successful you are ■ *noun* the act of talking about things that you are proud of ○ *Their proudest boast is that they never surrendered.*

boastful /ˈbəʊstf(ə)l/ *adj* saying how good or successful you are

① **boat** /bəʊt/ *noun* a small vehicle that people use for moving on water ○ *They sailed their boat across the lake.* ○ *They went to Spain by boat.* ○ *When is the next boat to Calais?* ◇ **in the same boat** in the same difficult situation ○ *Don't expect special treatment – we're all in the same boat.*

boating /ˈbəʊtɪŋ/ *noun* the activity of going in small boats for pleasure

bob /bɒb/ *noun* a woman's or girl's hairstyle, where the hair is cut fairly short so that it is the same length all round ○ *She had her hair in a bob.* ■ *verb* (**bobs, bobbing, bobbed**) to move up and down ○ *Pieces of wood were bobbing about on the water.*

bode /bəʊd/ (**bodes, boding, boded**) *verb* □ **to bode ill** *or* **well** to be a bad or good sign (*formal*) ○ *It bodes ill for their project if the local council has refused them a grant.*

bodily /ˈbɒdɪli/ *adj* referring to the body ○ *The main bodily functions are those of important organs such as the heart, the lungs, etc.*

① **body** /ˈbɒdi/ (*plural* **bodies**) *noun* **1.** the whole of a person or of an animal ○ *He had pains all over his body.* **2.** the main part of an animal or person, but not the head and arms and legs ○ *She had scars on the arms and upper part of her body.* **3.** the body of a dead person or animal ○ *The dead man's body was found in the river.* ○ *Bodies of infected cows were burnt in the fields.* **4.** the main structure of a vehicle ○ *The car has an all-aluminium body.* **5.** the main part of something ○ *You'll find the details in the body of the report.* **6.** the thickness of hair ○ *The shampoo will give your hair body.* (NOTE: no plural)

body blow /ˈbɒdi bləʊ/ *noun* a serious disappointment

body building /ˈbɒdi ˌbɪldɪŋ/ *noun* the practice of developing the muscles of the body through lifting heavy weights and eating particular foods

③ **bodyguard** /ˈbɒdigɑːd/ *noun* **1.** a person who guards someone ○ *The man was stopped by the president's bodyguards.* **2.** a group of people who guard someone ○ *He has a bodyguard of six people* or *a six-man bodyguard.*

body language /ˈbɒdi ˌlæŋgwɪdʒ/ *noun* movements of the body which show what someone is thinking

bodywork /ˈbɒdiwɜːk/ *noun* the metal outer covering of a car

bog /bɒg/ *noun* a marshland

bog standard /bɒg ˈstændəd/ *adj* ordinary, or lacking special features

bogus /ˈbəʊgəs/ *adj* pretending to be real

bohemian /bəʊˈhiːmiən/ *adj* referring to a relaxed way of life, often thought typical of artists ○ *He led a very bohemian existence in Paris as a young man.* ○ *She brought along some of her bohemian friends.*

③ **boil** /bɔɪl/ *verb* (**boils, boiling, boiled**) **1.** (*of water or other liquid*) to form bubbles and change into steam or gas because of being heated ○ *Put the egg in when you see that the water's boiling.* ○ *Don't let the milk boil.* **2.** to heat a liquid until it changes into steam ○ *Can you boil some water so we can make tea?* **3.** to cook food such as vegetables or eggs in boiling water ○ *Boil the potatoes in a large pan.* ■ *noun* an infected swelling ○ *He has a boil on the back of his neck.*

boil down *phrasal verb* **1.** to be reduced through boiling ○ *Let the sauce boil down until it is quite thick.* **2.** to be reduced to ○ *It all boils down to whether he will accept the deal now or not.*

boil over *phrasal verb* (*of liquid*) to rise up when boiling and run over the side of the pan

③ **boiling** /ˈbɔɪlɪŋ/ *adj* **1.** which has started to boil, i.e. for water, at 100°C ○ *Put the potatoes in a pan of boiling water.* **2.** *also* **boiling hot** very hot ○ *It is boiling in this room.*

boiling point /ˈbɔɪlɪŋ pɔɪnt/ *noun* **1.** the temperature at which a liquid boils, i.e. when it turns into steam or gas ○ *100°C is the boiling point of water.* **2.** a point at which a situation becomes very serious ○ *The UN must do something quickly because the situation has reached boiling point.*

boisterous /ˈbɔɪst(ə)rəs/ *adj* energetic and noisy

bold /bəʊld/ *noun* a printing type with thick black letters ○ *The main words in this dictionary are set in bold.*

bollard /ˈbɒlɑːd/ *noun* **1.** a low post for a ship's rope to be tied to **2.** a low post in the road showing where traffic should go ○ *The police have put bollards across the road.*

bolster /ˈbəʊlstə/ (**bolsters, bolstering, bolstered**) *verb* to make something better or stronger ○ *The money from the village fete has bolstered the church funds.* ○

Learning that he will be out of hospital next week has bolstered his spirits.

bolt /bəʊlt/, **boult** *noun* **1.** a long piece of metal with a screw, fastened with a round piece of metal called a nut ○ *The legs of the table are secured to the top with bolts.* **2.** a long piece of metal which you slide into a hole to lock a door ○ *She pulled back the bolts.* **3.** □ **to make a bolt for it** to run away ○ *When the guards weren't looking two prisoners tried to make a bolt for it.* ■ *verb* (**bolts, bolting, bolted**) **1.** to run fast suddenly ○ *The horse bolted.* **2.** to run away from someone or something ○ *When the boys saw him coming, they bolted.* **3.** to fasten something with a bolt ○ *He bolted the door when he went to bed.* ○ *The tables are bolted to the floor.* ◇ **to make a bolt for something** to rush towards something ○ *At the end of the show everyone made a bolt for the door.* ◇ **to make a bolt for it** to run away from someone or something ○ *When the guards weren't looking two prisoners tried to make a bolt for it.*

② **bomb** /bɒm/ *noun* a weapon which explodes, and can be dropped from an aircraft or placed somewhere by hand ○ *The bomb was left in a suitcase in the middle of the station.* ○ *They phoned to say that a bomb had been planted in the main street.* ○ *Enemy aircraft dropped bombs on the army base.* ■ *verb* (**bombs, bombing, bombed**) to drop bombs on something ○ *Enemy aircraft bombed the power station.*

bombard /bɒm'bɑːd/ (**bombards, bombarding, bombarded**) *verb* **1.** to attack again and again with heavy guns or bombs ○ *The town was bombarded for ten days before surrendering.* **2.** to send someone more communications or questions than they can deal with ○ *He was bombarded with offers of jobs.* ○ *She was bombarded with advice from her relatives.* (NOTE: + **bombardment** *n*)

bomber /'bɒmə/ *noun* **1.** a person who puts bombs in places in order to blow them up ○ *The bombers managed to escape after planting the bomb.* **2.** an aircraft for dropping bombs ○ *The bombers were out during the night, attacking enemy targets.*

bombing /'bɒmɪŋ/ *noun* an occasion when someone attacks a place with a bomb or bombs ○ *bombings in the centres of major cities* ○ *a bombing raid by enemy aircraft*

bombshell /'bɒmʃel/ *noun* a very unpleasant surprise (*informal*)

bona fide /ˌbəʊnə 'faɪdi/ *adj* real or true; not deceiving

bonanza /bə'nænzə/ *noun* a situation where you can make a lot of money [~for] ○ *He won £10,000 on the lottery – a real bonanza for the family.*

③ **bond** /bɒnd/ (**bonds, bonding, bonded**) *verb* **1.** (*of two people*) to make a psychological link [~with] ○ *Some mothers find it difficult to bond with their babies.* **2.** to stick together tightly [~with] ○ *Cover the two surfaces with glue and hold them tightly until they bond.*

bondage /'bɒndɪdʒ/ *noun* the state of being a slave

② **bone** /bəʊn/ *noun* one of the solid pieces in the body, which make up the skeleton ○ *He fell over and broke a bone in his leg.* ○ *Be careful when you're eating fish – they have lots of little bones.*

bone marrow /'bəʊn ˌmærəʊ/ *noun* the soft substance inside a bone

bonfire /'bɒnfaɪə/ *noun* a fire made outdoors

③ **bonnet** /'bɒnɪt/ *noun* **1.** the metal cover over the front part of a car, covering the engine ○ *He lifted up the bonnet and looked at the steam pouring out of the engine.* **2.** a hat with strings that tie under the chin

bonsai /'bɒnsaɪ/ *noun* a tree grown in this way ○ *We have a little bonsai oak that is forty years old.*

② **bonus** /'bəʊnəs/ *noun* **1.** extra money ○ *Sales staff earn a bonus if they sell more than their target.* **2.** an advantage ○ *It was a bonus that the plane arrived early, as we were able to catch an earlier bus home.* □ **added bonus** an additional advantage ○ *I prefer this job and it's an added bonus that I can walk to work.*

bony /'bəʊni/ (**bonier, boniest**) *adj* **1.** thin, so that the bones can be seen easily ○ *She was riding a bony horse.* ○ *He grabbed her arm with his bony hand.* **2.** (*of fish*) with many bones ○ *I don't like kippers, they're usually too bony.*

boo /buː/ *interj* showing that you do not like someone such as an actor, singer or politician ○ *Everyone shouted 'boo' when he announced that taxes would have to go up.* ■ *noun* an instance of making the sound 'boo' ○ *The wicked pirate's appearance was greeted with boos and hisses.* ■ *verb* (**boos, booing, booed**) to make a 'boo' sound to show that you do not like someone such as an actor, singer or politician ○ *The crowd booed the referee.*

booby prize /'buːbi praɪz/ *noun* a silly prize given to the last person in a competition

boobytrap /'buːbitræp/ *noun* a hidden bomb

boogie /'buːgi/ (**boogies, boogieing, boogied**) *verb* to dance to disco music

① **book** /bʊk/ *noun* **1.** sheets of printed paper attached together, usually with a stiff cover [~about/on] ○ *I'm reading a book on the history of London.* ○ *He wrote a book about butterflies.* **2.** sheets of paper to write or draw on, attached together in a cover. ◊ **exercise book**, **notebook**, **sketchbook** ■ *verb* (**books, booking, booked**) to reserve a place, a seat, a table in a restaurant or a room in a hotel ○ *We have booked a table for tomorrow evening.* □ **to book someone on** *or* **onto a flight** to order a plane ticket for someone else ○ *I've booked you on the 10 o'clock flight to New York.*

book into *phrasal verb* to reserve a room in a hotel □ **to book someone into a hotel** to reserve a hotel room for someone else

③ **bookcase** /'bʊkkeɪs/ *noun* a cupboard with shelves for keeping books in

book club /'bʊk klʌb/ *noun* **1.** a company which sells books by post, often at reduced prices **2.** a group of people who meet to discuss books and related subjects

bookie /'bʊki/ *noun* same as **bookmaker** (*informal*)

② **booking** /'bʊkɪŋ/ *noun* an arrangement to have something such as a seat, hotel room or a table in a restaurant kept for you □ **to make a booking** to reserve something such as a seat, hotel room or table ○ *We tried to make a booking for the week beginning May 1st, but the hotel was full.*

bookkeeping /'bʊkkiːpɪŋ/ *noun* the activity or job of keeping a company's accounts (NOTE: + **bookkeeper** *n*)

② **booklet** /'bʊklət/ *noun* a book of information with only a few pages

bookmaker /'bʊkmeɪkə/ *noun* a person who takes money from people who want to bet on the result of races (NOTE: The official term is **turf accountant**.)

bookmark /'bʊkmɑːk/ *noun* **1.** something that you put in a book to show the place where you stopped reading **2.** the address of a website or web page, stored for easy access

③ **bookshelf** /'bʊkʃelf/ (*plural* **bookshelves**) *noun* a shelf for keeping books

② **bookshop** /'bʊkʃɒp/ *noun* a shop where you can buy books

book token /'bʊk ˌtəʊkən/ *noun* a card with an amount of money written on it, which can only be used to buy books of that value

bookworm /'bʊkwɜːm/ *noun* someone who enjoys reading books, and reads a lot

③ **boom** /buːm/ *noun* **1.** a sudden increase in a business or activity [~in] ○ *a boom in short holidays* **2.** a loud deep noise, like the sound of an explosion ○ *There was such a loud boom that everyone jumped.* ■ *verb* (**booms, booming, boomed**) **1.** to increase ○ *The economy is booming.* **2.** to make a loud deep noise ○ *His voice boomed across the square.*

boomerang /'buːməræŋ/ *noun* a curved piece of wood, invented in Australia, which twists as it flies and returns to you when you throw it in a special way

boon /buːn/ *noun* a very useful thing [~for/to] ○ *The car has been a real boon to her since the bus company stopped the service to their village.*

boost /buːst/ *noun* help or increase [~for/~in/~to] ○ *It gave a boost to our sales.* ■ *verb* (**boosts, boosting, boosted**) to help to increase something or make something better ○ *The TV commercial should boost our sales.*

booster /'buːstə/ *noun* **1.** a thing which gives extra help or support ○ *Winning the competition was a much needed morale booster for her.* **2.** same as **booster injection**

booster injection /'buːstər ɪn ˌdʒekʃ(ə)n/ *noun* an extra injection of vaccine given some time after the first one so as to make sure it is still effective

booster shot /'buːstə ʃɒt/ *noun* same as **booster injection**

② **boot** /buːt/ *noun* a strong shoe which covers your foot and your ankle or the lower part of your leg ○ *walking boots* ○ *ankle boots* ○ *long black riding boots*

boot up *phrasal verb* to make a computer start, or to be started and ready for use

③ **booth** /buːð/ *noun* **1.** a small room or enclosed space for one person to stand or sit in **2.** *US* a section of a business fair where a company shows its products or services ○ *The American publisher wants us to meet him at his booth.* **3.** *US* an enclosed area in a restaurant with a table in it ○ *We sat in a booth by the bar and listened to the jazz.*

bootleg /'buːtleg/ *adj* sold illegally

boot out *phrasal verb* to make someone leave somewhere (*informal*) ○ *He was booted out of the police force for taking bribes.*

booty /ˈbuːti/ *noun* treasure taken by soldiers, sailors, etc. during fighting (NOTE: no plural)

booze /buːz/ (*informal*) *noun* an alcoholic drink ○ *He's too fond of (the) booze to work well.* ■ *verb* (**boozes, boozing, boozed**) to drink alcohol ○ *He was out all night boozing with his friends.*

② **border** /ˈbɔːdə/ *noun* **1.** an imaginary line between countries or regions [~between/~with] ○ *They crossed the border between Germany and Switzerland.* ○ *The town is near the border with Luxembourg.* ○ *He was questioned by the border guards.* **2.** a pattern around the edge of something ○ *I don't like the pink border on the scarf.* **3.** a patch of soil at the side of a path or an area of grass where flowers or bushes are planted ■ *verb* (**borders, bordering, bordered**) to be along the edge of something ○ *The path is bordered with rose bushes.* ○ *The new houses border the west side of the park.*

border on *phrasal verb* **1.** same as **border** *verb* **2.** to be very similar to or almost the same as something ○ *His excuse was silly, bordering on the ridiculous.*

borderline /ˈbɔːdəlaɪn/ *noun* a line between two things

bore /bɔː/ *noun* a dull person who is not very interesting ○ *I don't want to sit next to him, he's such a bore.* ■ *verb* (**bores, boring, bored**) to make a hole in something

② **bored** /bɔːd/ *adj* not interested in what is happening ○ *You get very bored having to do the same work every day.* ○ *I'm bored – let's go out to the club.*

③ **boredom** /ˈbɔːdəm/ *noun* the state of being bored

② **boring** /ˈbɔːrɪŋ/ *adj* not interesting ○ *I don't want to watch that TV programme – it's boring.*

① **born** /bɔːn/ *verb* to come out of your mother's body and begin to live ○ *He was born in Scotland.* ○ *She was born in 1989.* ○ *The baby was born last week.*

born-again Christian /ˌbɔːn əˌgen ˈkrɪstʃən/ *noun* a person who has been converted to Christianity, after not having been very religious before

③ **borne** /bɔːn/ past participle of **bear**

② **borough** /ˈbʌrə/ *noun* a large town or district that is run by an elected council

② **borrow** /ˈbɒrəʊ/ (**borrows, borrowing, borrowed**) *verb* **1.** to take something for a short time, usually with the permission of the owner ○ *She borrowed three books from the school library.* ○ *He wants to borrow one of my CDs.* **2.** to take money for a time, usually from a bank ○ *Companies borrow from banks to finance their business.* ○ *She borrowed £100,000 from the bank to buy a flat.* Compare **lend**

borrower /ˈbɒrəʊə/ *noun* a person who borrows something, especially money

borrowings /ˈbɒrəʊɪŋz/ *plural noun* money which is borrowed ○ *The company has borrowings of over £200,000.*

bosom /ˈbʊz(ə)m/ *noun* a woman's breasts

② **boss** /bɒs/ *noun* the person in charge, especially the owner of a business ○ *If you want a day off, ask the boss.* ○ *I left because I didn't get on with my boss.*

bossy /ˈbɒsi/ (**bossier, bossiest**) *adj* always telling people what to do

botanist /ˈbɒt(ə)nɪst/ *noun* a scientist who studies plants

botany /ˈbɒt(ə)ni/ *noun* the science and study of plants

botch /bɒtʃ/ (**botches, botching, botched**) *verb* to do or make something badly (*informal*)

① **both** /bəʊθ/ *adj, pron* two people or things together ○ *Hold onto the handle with both hands.* ○ *Both my shoes have holes in them.* ○ *Both her brothers are very tall.* ○ *She has two brothers, both of them in Canada.* ○ *She and her brother both go to the same school.* ○ *I'm talking to both of you.*

① **bother** /ˈbɒðə/ *noun* trouble or worry ○ *We found the shop without any bother.* ○ *It was such a bother getting packed that we nearly didn't go on holiday.* ■ *verb* (**bothers, bothering, bothered**) **1.** to make someone feel slightly angry, especially by disturbing them [~that] ○ *Stop bothering me – I'm trying to read.* ○ *It bothers me that everyone is so lazy.* **2.** to feel worried, or make someone feel worried [~about/~that] ○ *I was bothered about not hearing from her for two weeks.* ○ *It bothers me that it takes so long to get a reply.* **3.** □ **to bother to do something** to take the time or trouble to do something ○ *Don't bother to come with me to the station – I can find my way easily.* ◇ **can't** or **couldn't be bothered to** don't want to ○ *He couldn't be bothered to answer my letters.*

① **bottle** /ˈbɒt(ə)l/ *noun* **1.** a tall plastic or glass container for liquids, usually with a narrow part at the top ○ *He opened two bot-*

tles of red wine. ○ *She drank the water straight out of the bottle.* ○ *He bought his wife a bottle of perfume on the plane.* **2.** confidence (*informal*) ○ *He hasn't got the bottle to do it.* ■ *verb* (**bottles, bottling, bottled**) to put in bottles ○ *The wine is bottled in Germany.* ○ *Only bottled water is safe to drink.*

③ **bottle bank** /'bɒt(ə)l bæŋk/ *noun* a place where you can throw away empty bottles for recycling

bottled /'bɒt(ə)ld/ *adj* sold in bottles

bottleneck /'bɒt(ə)lˌnek/ *noun* **1.** a narrow part of a road where traffic often gets stuck ○ *The roadworks have created a bottleneck and caused jams all through the town.* **2.** a place where things such as production or supplies are held up ○ *There's a bottleneck in the invoicing department and this holds up our deliveries.*

① **bottom** /'bɒtəm/ *noun* **1.** the lowest point ○ *The ship sank to the bottom of the sea.* ○ *Turn left at the bottom of the hill.* ○ *Is there any honey left in the bottom of the jar?* **2.** the far end ○ *Go down to the bottom of the street and you will see the station on your left.* ○ *The shed is at the bottom of the garden.* **3.** the part of the body on which you sit ○ *Does my bottom look big in these trousers?* ■ *plural noun* **bottoms** the lower part of a set of clothes ○ *He was wearing just his track suit bottoms.* ○ *I can't find my bikini bottoms.* ■ *adj* lowest ○ *The jam is on the bottom shelf.* ○ *He was standing on the bottom rung of the ladder.* ◇ **to get to the bottom of a problem** to find the real cause of a problem

bottomless /'bɒtəmləs/ *adj* without any limit

bough /baʊ/ *noun* a branch of a tree (NOTE: Do not confuse with **bow**.)

① **bought** /bɔːt/ past tense and past participle of **buy**

boulder /'bəʊldə/ *noun* a large rock

boulevard /'buːləvɑːd/, **Boulevard** *noun* a wide road in a town, usually with trees along it

③ **bounce** /baʊns/ *noun* **1.** a movement of something such as a ball when it hits a surface and moves away again ○ *He hit the ball on the second bounce.* **2.** energy ○ *She's always full of bounce.* ■ *verb* (**bounces, bouncing, bounced**) to spring up and down or off a surface ○ *The ball bounced down the stairs.* ○ *He kicked the ball but it bounced off the post.* ○ *In this game you bounce the ball against the wall.*

bouncer /'baʊnsə/ *noun* a person whose job is to stop unwanted people getting into a public place, or to make them leave ○ *The bouncers wouldn't let her in because she'd caused trouble before.*

bouncy /'baʊnsi/ *adj* **1.** which bounces ○ *a big bouncy red ball* **2.** full of energy ○ *It's quite tiring working with her because she's so bouncy.*

② **bound** /baʊnd/ *noun* a big jump ■ *adj* **1.** very likely [~to] ○ *They are bound to be late.* **2.** obliged [~to/~by] ○ *He felt bound to help her.* ○ *He is bound by the contract he signed last year.* **3.** tied up ○ *a bundle of old letters bound with pink ribbon* ○ *The boy was left bound to a tree.* ○ *The burglars left him bound hand and foot.* ■ *verb* (**bounds, bounding, bounded**) to make a big jump, or move fast suddenly ○ *She bounded into the room.* ○ *He bounded out of his chair.* ○ *The dog bounded into the bushes.* ◇ **bound for** on the way to ○ *a ship bound for the Gulf*

② **boundary** /'baʊnd(ə)ri/ (*plural* **boundaries**) *noun* an imaginary line or physical barrier separating two things [~between/~with] ○ *The white fence marks the boundary with my neighbour's garden.* ○ *Their behaviour crossed the boundary between unkindness and cruelty.*

boundless /'baʊndləs/ *adj* which seems to have no limit

bounty /'baʊnti/ *noun* money given as a reward

bouquet /buː'keɪ/ *noun* **1.** a beautifully arranged bunch of flowers ○ *He bought a bouquet of white roses.* ○ *A little girl presented the princess with a bouquet.* **2.** the particular smell of a wine ○ *a wine with a delicate bouquet*

bourbon /'bɜːbən/ *noun US* a type of American whisky, or a glass of this drink

bourgeois /'bʊəʒwɑː/ *adj* referring to middle-class people and their views in a disapproving way ○ *They want to go on living their bourgeois existence.* ○ *He accuses his parents of being terribly bourgeois and swears he won't be like them.*

bout /baʊt/ *noun* **1.** a sporting fight or contest ○ *Lewis won that bout.* **2.** an attack of illness ○ *She had a bout of flu.*

boutique /buː'tiːk/ *noun* a small shop, especially for up-to-date fashionable clothes ○ *a jeans boutique* ○ *a ski boutique*

bovine /'bəʊvaɪn/ *adj* **1.** referring to cows **2.** slow and stupid

bow[1] /baʊ/ *noun* **1.** the act of bending your body forwards as a greeting or sign of respect ○ *He made a deep bow to the audience.* □ **to take a bow** to stand on a stage and bend forwards to thank the audience ○ *The actors took their bows one after the other.* **2.** the front part of a ship ■ *verb* (**bows, bowing, bowed**) **1.** to bend your body forward as a greeting or sign of respect [~to] ○ *He bowed to the queen.* **2.** to bend your head forwards ○ *She bowed her head over her books.*

③ **bow²** /bəʊ/ *noun* **1.** a weapon used for shooting arrows ○ *The archers drew their bows and shot arrows into the air.* **2.** a long piece of wood used for playing a stringed instrument ○ *He slowly drew the bow across the strings of his violin.* **3.** a ribbon knotted in a shape like a butterfly ○ *The parcel was tied up with red bows.*

② **bowl** /bəʊl/ *noun* **1.** a wide, round container for something such as food or water ○ *Put the egg whites in a bowl and whisk them.* **2.** the food or liquid contained in a bowl ○ *He was eating a bowl of rice.* ○ *A bowl of hot thick soup is just what you need in this cold weather.* **3.** a large heavy ball used for rolling along the ground in certain games ○ *She picked up the bowl and stepped up to take her turn.* ■ *verb* (**bowls, bowling, bowled**) **1.** (*especially in cricket*) to throw a ball to a batsman **2.** *also* **bowl out** (*especially in cricket*) to throw the ball to a batsman and hit the wicket so that the person cannot continue playing **3.** (*in a game of bowls*) to roll a bowl along the ground to try to get close to the target

bowl over *phrasal verb* **1.** to knock someone down **2.** to surprise someone ○ *He was completely bowled over by the news.*

bow-legged /ˌbəʊ ˈlegɪd/ *adj* with legs which bend out at the knee

bowler /ˈbəʊlə/ *noun* **1.** (*especially in cricket*) a person who throws the ball to a batsman ○ *a fast bowler* **2.** a person who plays bowls **3.** same as **bowler hat**

bowler hat /ˌbəʊlə ˈhæt/, **bowler** *noun* a hat with a rounded top

bowling /ˈbəʊlɪŋ/ *noun* the game of bowls, or the indoor game of knocking down skittles with a large ball. ◊ **ten-pin bowling**

bowls /bəʊlz/ *noun* a game where teams of players roll large balls towards a small ball (a **jack**), trying to get as close to it as possible

bow tie /bəʊ ˈtaɪ/ *noun* a tie which is tied in the shape of a butterfly

① **box** /bɒks/ *noun* **1.** a container made of wood, plastic, cardboard or metal, with a lid ○ *The cakes came in a cardboard box.* **2.** a container and its contents ○ *He took a box of matches from his pocket.* ○ *He gave her a box of chocolates for her birthday.* ■ *verb* (**boxes, boxing, boxed**) to fight by punching, especially when wearing special thick gloves ○ *He learnt to box at a gym in the East End.*

boxer /ˈbɒksə/ *noun* **1.** a person who fights with his fists ○ *The two boxers came together in the ring.* **2.** a type of large dog with short hair

boxing /ˈbɒksɪŋ/ *noun* a sport in which two opponents fight each other in a square area wearing special thick gloves

② **Boxing Day** /ˈbɒksɪŋ deɪ/ *noun* 26th December, the day after Christmas Day

box office /ˈbɒks ˌɒfɪs/ *noun* an office where you buy tickets in a theatre

① **boy** /bɔɪ/ *noun* **1.** a male child ○ *A boy from our school won the tennis match.* ○ *I knew him when he was a boy.* **2.** a son ○ *Her three boys are all at university.* **3.** □ **the boys** men who are friends, or who play sport together (*informal*)

boy band /ˈbɔɪ bænd/ *noun* an all-male pop group aimed at a teenage audience

boycott /ˈbɔɪkɒt/ (**boycotts, boycotting, boycotted**) *verb* to refuse to deal with someone ○ *We are boycotting all food imports from that country.* (NOTE: + **boycott** *n*)

② **boyfriend** /ˈbɔɪfrend/ *noun* a young or older man that someone is having a romantic relationship with ○ *She's got a new boyfriend.* ○ *She brought her boyfriend to the party.*

boyhood /ˈbɔɪhʊd/ *noun* the time of life when someone is, or was, a boy

boyish /ˈbɔɪɪʃ/ *adj* looking or acting like a boy

Boy Scout /bɔɪ ˈskaʊt/ *noun* **1.** in the US, a member of the Boy Scouts of America, an organisation aiming to develop good character and physical fitness, often through community and outdoor activities **2.** a man who is considered to be naive **3.** ♦ **scout**

bra /brɑː/ *noun* a piece of women's underwear worn to support the breasts

brace /breɪs/ *noun* **1.** a support which helps your teeth to grow straight ○ *She wears a brace on her teeth.* **2.** a support for part of the body which has been injured ○ *a knee brace* ■ *verb* [~for] □ **to brace yourself** to prepare yourself for something unpleasant ○ *When the phone rang, she braced herself for the shock of hearing his* *voice again.* ○ *The pilot told us to brace ourselves for a crash landing.*

bracelet /ˈbreɪslət/ *noun* a piece of jewellery worn around your wrist or arm

braces /ˈbreɪsɪz/ *plural noun* a brace for the teeth

bracing /ˈbreɪsɪŋ/ *adj* cool and making you feel healthy

③ **bracket** /ˈbrækɪt/ *noun* **1.** a piece of metal or wood which is attached to a wall to support a shelf ○ *The shelf is held up by two solid brackets.* **2.** a printing sign usually used in pairs, [ ], ( ), < > or { }, used to show that a piece of text is separated from the rest ○ *The words in brackets can be deleted.* ○ *The four words underlined should be put in brackets.* **3.** a group of things or people considered together for administrative purposes

brag /bræg/ (**brags, bragging, bragged**) *verb* to boast about something

braid /breɪd/ *noun* **1.** a decoration made of twisted fibres ○ *Admirals have gold braid on their caps.* **2.** plaited hair ○ *This is a picture of her when she was ten and still had her hair in braids.* ■ *verb* (**braids, braiding, braided**) to plait, e.g. hair or ribbon ○ *She braided her hair before going swimming.*

Braille /breɪl/ *noun* a system of writing using raised dots on paper to represent letters, which allows a blind person to read by passing his or her fingers over the page

② **brain** /breɪn/ *noun* **1.** the nerve centre in the head, which controls all the body ○ *The brain is the most important part of the body.* **2.** intelligence □ **to use your brain** to think sensibly □ **she's got brains, she's got a good brain** she's intelligent

brainchild /ˈbreɪntʃaɪld/ *noun* an original plan that someone has thought of (*informal*)

brainless /ˈbreɪnləs/ *adj* completely stupid (*disapproving*)

brainstorming /ˈbreɪnˌstɔːmɪŋ/ *noun* an intensive group discussion, with no time allowed for thinking, in order to produce ideas or help solve problems

brainwash /ˈbreɪnwɒʃ/ (**brainwashes, brainwashing, brainwashed**) *verb* to make someone believe something is true by repeating it and forcing them to believe it (NOTE: + **brainwashing** *n*)

brainwave /ˈbreɪnweɪv/ *noun* a sudden very good idea

brainy /ˈbreɪni/ (**brainier, brainiest**) *adj* very intelligent (*informal*)

③ **brake** /breɪk/ *noun* a part of a vehicle used for stopping or making it go more slowly ○ *Put the brake on when you go down a hill.* ○ *The brakes aren't working!* ■ *verb* (**brakes, braking, braked**) to slow down by pressing a vehicle's brakes ○ *The driver of the little white van braked, but too late to avoid the dog.*

bran /bræn/ *noun* the outside part of wheat seeds

① **branch** /brɑːntʃ/ *noun* **1.** a thick part of a tree, growing out of the main part ○ *He hit his head against a low branch.* **2.** a local office of an organisation ○ *He's the manager of our local branch of Lloyds Bank.* ○ *The store has branches in most towns in the south of the country.* **3.** one part of something larger ○ *Genetics is a branch of biology.* ○ *I'm not in contact with the Irish branch of my family.* **4.** a section of a road, railway line or river that leads to or from the main part ○ *The town is built on a branch of the Nile.* ■ *verb* (**branches, branching, branched**) to divide into two or more parts

branch out *phrasal verb* to start to do something different, as well as what you normally do

brand /brænd/ *noun* a product with a name, made by a particular company ○ *a well-known brand of soap* ■ *verb* (**brands, branding, branded**) to describe someone or something publicly as something bad [~(as)] ○ *He was branded as a thief.* ○ *The minister was publicly branded a liar in the newspaper.*

brandish /ˈbrændɪʃ/ (**brandishes, brandishing, brandished**) *verb* to wave something about

③ **brand name** /ˈbrænd neɪm/ *noun* the official name of a product

③ **brand-new** /ˌbrænd ˈnjuː/ *adj* completely new

③ **brandy** /ˈbrændi/ *noun* **1.** an alcoholic drink made from wine ○ *I was given a bottle of excellent brandy.* **2.** a glass of this drink ○ *He ordered three brandies.*

brash /bræʃ/ *adj* confident and loud (*technical*)

brass /brɑːs/ *noun* **1.** a shiny yellow metal used for making things such as some musical instruments and door handles ○ *The doctor has a brass nameplate on his door.* **2.** musical instruments made of brass, such as trumpets or trombones ○ *the brass section of the orchestra* ○ *He has composed several pieces of music for brass.*

brass band /brɑːs 'bænd/ *noun* a band of people playing brass instruments

brat /bræt/ *noun* a badly behaved child

bravado /brə'vɑːdəʊ/ *noun* confident actions to show how brave you are

② **brave** /breɪv/ *adj* (**braver, bravest**) not afraid of doing unpleasant or dangerous things ○ *It was very brave of him to dive into the river to rescue the little girl.* ■ *verb* (**braves, braving, braved**) to accept unpleasant or dangerous conditions in order to achieve something ○ *We braved the Saturday crowds in the supermarket because we needed bread and milk.*

bravely /'breɪvli/ *adv* in a brave way

bravery /'breɪvəri/ *noun* the ability to do dangerous or unpleasant things without being afraid ○ *We admired her bravery in coping with the illness.* ○ *He won an award for bravery.*

bravo /brɑː'vəʊ/ *interj* showing approval

brawl /brɔːl/ *noun* a wild fight ○ *Coming out of the pub, he got into a brawl with some soldiers.* (NOTE: + **brawl** *v*)

bray /breɪ/ (**brays, braying, brayed**) *verb* to make a loud noise like a donkey

brazen /'breɪz(ə)n/ *adj* with no shame ○ *What you say is a brazen lie.*

③ **breach** /briːtʃ/ *noun* the act of breaking the law or a promise [~of] ○ *This is a breach of the undertaking they made last year.* ■ *verb* (**breaches, breaching, breached**) to go against rules ○ *The pay settlement has breached the government's guidelines.* ◇ **in breach of** going against an agreement ○ *In breach of their agreement, they started negotiating with our rivals behind our backs.*

① **bread** /bred/ *noun* food made from flour and water baked in an oven ○ *Can you get a loaf of bread from the baker's?* ○ *She cut thin slices of bread for sandwiches.*

bread bin /'bred bɪn/ *noun* a metal box for keeping bread in

breadcrumbs /'bredkrʌmz/ *plural noun* little pieces of dried bread ○ *The fish is covered in breadcrumbs and then fried.*

breadline /'bredlaɪn/ *noun* a very low standard of living

breadth /bredθ/ *noun* **1.** a measurement of how wide something is ○ *The breadth of the piece of land is over 300 m.* **2.** the fact of being full or complete ○ *His answers show the breadth of his knowledge of the subject.* ◇ **the length and breadth of something** everywhere in a place ○ *We walked the length and breadth of the field but found no mushrooms.*

breadwinner /'bredwɪnə/ *noun* a person who earns money to feed the family

① **break** /breɪk/ *verb* (**breaks, breaking, broken**) **1.** to make something divide into pieces accidentally or deliberately ○ *He dropped the plate on the floor and broke it.* ○ *Break the chocolate into four pieces.* **2.** to divide into pieces accidentally ○ *The clock fell on the floor and broke.* **3.** to fail to obey a rule or law **4.** to fail to carry out the terms of a contract or a rule ○ *The company has broken its agreement.* □ **to break a promise** not to do what you had promised to do ○ *He broke his promise and wrote to her again.* **5.** □ **to break it** *or* **to break the news to someone** to tell someone bad news ○ *We will have to break it to her as gently as possible.* (NOTE: Do not confuse with **brake**.) ■ *noun* **1.** a short pause or rest ○ *There will be a 15-minute break in the middle of the meeting.* □ **they worked for three hours without a break** without stopping ○ *They worked without a break.* □ **to take a break** to have a short rest ○ *We'll take a break now, and start again in fifteen minutes.* **2.** a short holiday ○ *a winter break* ◇ **to break your journey** to stop travelling for a while before going on ○ *We'll break our journey in Edinburgh.*

break down *phrasal verb* **1.** (*of a machine*) to stop working ○ *The lift has broken down again.* ○ *The car broke down and we had to push it.* **2.** to show all the items that are included in a total separately ○ *Can you break down this invoice into travel costs and extras?* **3.** to become upset and start crying ○ *When she got her results she just broke down.* **4.** to separate a substance into small parts, or to become separated ○ *Enzymes break down the food.* **5.** to fail ○ *Their relationship quickly broke down when he lost his job.* ○ *The discussions seem likely to break down over the amount of money being offered.*

break in *phrasal verb* **1.** □ **to break in, to break into a building** to use force to get into a building ○ *Burglars broke into the office during the night.* **2.** to interrupt something that is happening ○ *I'm sorry to break in, but I need to speak to Mr McGregor urgently.*

break into *phrasal verb* to start doing something ○ *When they saw the photos, they broke into laughter.*

break off *phrasal verb* **1.** to make something come off by breaking ○ *He broke a piece off his pie and gave it to the dog.* **2.**

to come off by breaking ○ *The handle broke off the cup in the dishwasher.* ○ *Several branches broke off in the wind.* **3.** to stop something suddenly ○ *He broke off in the middle of his story.* ○ *They broke off the discussions.* □ **to break it off** to end a relationship ○ *They were going to get married, but she broke it off.*

break out *phrasal verb* **1.** to start ○ *War broke out between the countries in the area.* **2.** to escape ○ *Three prisoners broke out of jail.*

break up *phrasal verb* **1.** to divide into pieces ○ *The oil tanker was breaking up on the rocks.* **2.** to end ○ *The meeting broke up at 3 p.m.*

breakable /ˈbreɪkəb(ə)l/ *adj* that can break easily

breakaway /ˈbreɪkəweɪ/ *adj* which has become separated from a larger group

③ **breakdown** /ˈbreɪkdaʊn/ *noun* **1.** a situation in which a machine or vehicle stops working ○ *We had a breakdown on the motorway.* ○ *A breakdown truck came to tow us to the garage.* **2.** a failure of a system to work properly ○ *There has been a breakdown in communications between them.* **3.** a situation in which someone cannot continue to live normally any more because they are mentally ill or very tired **4.** a list showing details item by item ○ *Give me a breakdown of the travel costs.*

② **breakfast** /ˈbrekfəst/ *noun* the first meal of the day ○ *I had a boiled egg for breakfast.* ○ *She didn't have any breakfast because she was in a hurry.* ○ *The hotel serves breakfast from 7.30 to 9.30 every day.*

break-in /ˈbreɪk ɪn/ *noun* a burglary

breaking point /ˈbreɪkɪŋ pɔɪnt/ *noun* the point at which a situation reaches a crisis

breakout /ˈbreɪkaʊt/ *noun* an escape from a prison

breakthrough /ˈbreɪkθruː/ *noun* a sudden success

breakup /ˈbreɪkʌp/ *noun* the process of coming to pieces or separating

③ **breast** /brest/ *noun* **1.** one of two parts on a woman's chest which produce milk **2.** meat from the chest part of a bird ○ *Do you want a wing or a slice of breast?* ○ *We bought some chicken breasts to make a stir-fry.*

breastfeed /ˈbrestfiːd/ (**breastfeeds, breastfeeding, breastfed**) *verb* to give a baby milk from the breast

② **breath** /breθ/ *noun* air which goes into and out of the body through the nose or mouth ○ *We could see our breath in the cold air.* □ **to hold your breath** to keep air in your lungs, e.g. in order to go under water ○ *She held her breath under water for a minute.* □ **to take a deep breath** to breathe in as much air as you can ○ *Take a deep breath for the doctor.* ◇ **to take someone's breath away** to surprise someone very much ◇ **under your breath** quietly ○ *He cursed under his breath.* ◇ **don't hold your breath** don't expect it to happen ○ *He said he'll pay us next month, but don't hold your breath!* ◇ **out of breath, gasping for breath** having difficulty in breathing

② **breathe** /briːð/ (**breathes, breathing, breathed**) *verb* to take air into the lungs or let it out ○ *Relax and breathe in and then out slowly.* □ **to breathe deeply** to take a lot of air into the lungs □ **he's breathing down my neck all the time** always watching and judging what someone is doing

breather /ˈbriːðə/ *noun* a time when you can rest (*informal*)

③ **breathing** /ˈbriːðɪŋ/ *noun* the process of taking air in and out of the lungs

breathing apparatus /ˈbriːðɪŋ æpəˌreɪtəs/ *noun* equipment such as a mask and oxygen cylinder which can help a person to breathe

breathing space /ˈbriːðɪŋ speɪs/ *noun* a period when you can rest between activities

breathless /ˈbreθləs/ *adj* finding it difficult to breathe

breathtaking /ˈbreθteɪkɪŋ/ *adj* very impressive

breath test /ˈbreθ test/ *noun* a test for a driver to see if he has been drinking alcohol

③ **breed** /briːd/ *noun* a group of animals or plants specially developed with features that make it different from others of the same type ○ *Alsatians and other large breeds of dog* ■ *verb* (**breeds, breeding, bred**) **1.** to produce young animals ○ *Rabbits breed very rapidly.* **2.** to keep animals which produce young ones ○ *They breed sheep for the meat and the wool.*

breeder /ˈbriːdə/ *noun* a person who breeds animals or plants

③ **breeding** /ˈbriːdɪŋ/ *noun* **1.** the practice of raising animals or plants ○ *Because of the smell, pig breeding is strictly controlled.* ○ *You can't shoot pheasants during the breeding season.* **2.** good education, background and behaviour ○ *It was obvi-*

ous that his secretary was a girl of good breeding.

breeze /briːz/ *noun* a slight wind ○ *A cool breeze is welcome on a hot day like this.* ■ *verb* (**breezes, breezing, breezed**) to walk around looking very pleased with yourself ○ *He breezed into the meeting carrying a cup of coffee.*

breeze through *phrasal verb* to do something without any difficulty ○ *She breezed through the tests in an hour.*

breezy /ˈbriːzi/ *adj* **1.** windy ○ *It is very hot, but slightly breezy which makes it more comfortable.* ○ *It's a little breezy in here, let's shut the French windows.* **2.** happy-go-lucky ○ *A breezy youth looking as if he didn't have a care in the world.*

brevity /ˈbrevɪti/ *noun* (*of time*) the quality of being very short

brewer /ˈbruːə/ *noun* a person or company that makes beer

brewery /ˈbruːəri/ (*plural* **breweries**) *noun* a factory where beer is made

bribe /braɪb/ *noun* an illegal payment to someone to get something done ○ *He offered the witness a bribe to say nothing.* ■ *verb* (**bribes, bribing, bribed**) to give an illegal payment to someone ○ *She planned to customs officials to get the plans approved.*

③ **bribery** /ˈbraɪb(ə)ri/ *noun* the act of bribing

bric-a-brac /ˈbrɪk ə bræk/ *noun* attractive little objects which are not very valuable

② **brick** /brɪk/ *noun* a hard block of baked clay used for building ○ *You'll need more than eighty bricks to build a wall.*

brick up *phrasal verb* to fill a hole with bricks

bricklayer /ˈbrɪkleɪə/ *noun* a person who builds walls with bricks

bridal /ˈbraɪd(ə)l/ *adj* referring to a wedding (NOTE: Do not confuse with **bridle**.)

bride /braɪd/ *noun* a woman who is getting married or has just married

bridegroom /ˈbraɪdgruːm/ *noun* a man who is getting married or has just got married (NOTE: often just called the **groom**)

bridesmaid /ˈbraɪdzmeɪd/ *noun* a girl who is one of the bride's attendants at a wedding

② **bridge** /brɪdʒ/ *noun* **1.** a road or path built over a road or river so that you can walk or drive from one side to the other ○ *There are two bridges across the river near here.* **2.** a connection or helpful link between two things [~between] ○ *A shared interest can be a bridge between old and young.*

bridle /ˈbraɪd(ə)l/ *noun* straps put round a horse's head ○ *She had some difficulty in putting the bridle on the horse.*

② **brief** /briːf/ *adj* short ○ *He wrote a brief note of thanks.* ○ *The meeting was very brief.* ◇ **in brief** in a few words, or without giving details ○ *We have food for only a few days; in brief, the situation is very serious.*

briefcase /ˈbriːfkeɪs/ *noun* a case for carrying papers or documents

briefing /ˈbriːfɪŋ/ *noun* a meeting where information is given

② **briefly** /ˈbriːfli/ *adv* **1.** for a short time **2.** in a few words, or without giving details

briefs /briːfs/ *plural noun* short underwear for men or women ○ *Before the medical, the doctor asked him to strip down to his briefs.*

③ **brigade** /brɪˈgeɪd/ *noun* a section of an army ○ *The general sent an infantry brigade to the region.*

brigadier /ˌbrɪgəˈdɪə/ *noun* an army officer in charge of a brigade

② **bright** /braɪt/ *adj* **1.** full of light or sunlight ○ *a bright day* ○ *a bright room* □ **bright sunshine** *or* **sunlight** strong clear light from the sun **2.** very strong ○ *They have painted their front door bright orange.* **3.** a young person who is bright is intelligent ○ *Both children are very bright.* ○ *She's the brightest student we've had for many years.* **4.** clear and sunny ○ *There will be bright periods during the afternoon.* **5.** happy and pleasant ○ *She gave me a bright smile.*

brighten /ˈbraɪt(ə)n/ (**brightens, brightening, brightened**) *verb* to make something bright, or to become bright

brighten up *phrasal verb* **1.** (*of a person*) to become more cheerful ○ *She brightened up when she saw him.* **2.** (*of weather*) to become sunnier ○ *The weather is brightening up.*

brightly /ˈbraɪtli/ *adv* **1.** in a strong clear light or colour ○ *A children's book with brightly painted pictures.* ○ *The streets were brightly lit for Christmas.* **2.** cheerfully ○ *She smiled brightly as she went into the hospital.*

brightness /ˈbraɪtnəs/ *noun* **1.** strong clear light **2.** strong colour

brilliance /ˈbrɪljəns/ *noun* the fact of being very clever

③ **brilliant** /ˈbrɪljənt/ *adj* **1.** extremely clever ○ *He's the most brilliant student of* *his year.* ○ *She had a brilliant idea.* **2.** strong and clear ○ *She stepped out into the brilliant sunshine.* **3.** very good (*informal*) ○ *The way the information is displayed on this website is brilliant.*

brim /brɪm/ *noun* **1.** the edge ○ *The glass was filled to the brim.* **2.** the flat part around a hat ○ *A hat with a wide brim.*

brim over *phrasal verb* to overflow

① **bring** /brɪŋ/ (**brings, bringing, brought**) *verb* to come with someone or something to this place ○ *She brought the books to school with her.* ○ *He brought his girlfriend home for tea.* ○ *Are you bringing any friends to the party?*

bring about *phrasal verb* to make something happen

bring along *phrasal verb* to bring someone or something with you

bring back *phrasal verb* to carry something back

bring down *phrasal verb* **1.** to carry something down to here ○ *Can you bring down the television from the bedroom?* **2.** to make something less ○ *We've brought down all our prices.*

bring forward *phrasal verb* to arrange something to be done at an earlier date than had been planned

bring off *phrasal verb* to succeed in doing something

bring on *phrasal verb* to produce something ◇ **to have brought it on yourself** you have yourself to blame for what happened to you

bring out *phrasal verb* to make something come out

bring up *phrasal verb* **1.** to look after and educate a child ○ *He was born in the USA but brought up in England.* ○ *He was brought up by his uncle in Scotland.* **2.** to mention a problem ○ *He brought up the question of the noise.* **3.** to vomit something ○ *She's got a stomach upset and brought up all her breakfast.*

brink /brɪŋk/ *noun* the time when something is about to happen ◇ **on the brink of** about to achieve something ○ *The company is on the brink of collapse.* ○ *She was on the brink of a nervous breakdown.*

brisk /brɪsk/ *adj* fairly fast

bristle /ˈbrɪs(ə)l/ *noun* **1.** one of the short stiff hairs on plants, or some animals such as pigs ○ *You could see the bristles on the back of the sow's neck.* **2.** one of the short stiff parts of a brush ○ *The bristles of my toothbrush are coming off – I must get a new one.* ■ *verb* (**bristles, bristling, bristled**) to take offence at something ○ *She bristled at the suggestion that a mistake had been made.*

Brit /brɪt/ *noun* a person from the United Kingdom (*informal*)

① **British** /ˈbrɪtɪʃ/ *adj* relating to the United Kingdom ○ *a British citizen* ○ *the British army* ○ *The British press reported a plane crash in Africa.* ○ *The ship was flying a British flag.*

Briton /ˈbrɪt(ə)n/ *noun* a person from the United Kingdom

brittle /ˈbrɪt(ə)l/ *adj* hard and breaking easily into pieces

broach /brəʊtʃ/ (**broaches, broaching, broached**) *verb* to start talking about a problem

② **broad** /brɔːd/ *adj* very wide ○ *a broad river* ◊ **breadth**

broadband /ˈbrɔːdbænd/ *adj* able to manage large amounts of data quickly ○ *a broadband connection*

③ **broadcast** /ˈbrɔːdkɑːst/ *noun* a radio or TV programme ○ *The broadcast came live from outside Buckingham Palace.*

broadcaster /ˈbrɔːdkɑːstə/ *noun* a person who works on radio or TV but is not an actor

③ **broaden** /ˈbrɔːd(ə)n/ (**broadens, broadening, broadened**) *verb* to make something wider, or to become wider ○ *Part of their plan is to broaden the road.* ○ *The river broadens to form a small lake.*

broadly /ˈbrɔːdli/ *adv* widely

broad-minded /ˌbrɔːd ˈmaɪndɪd/ *adj* not shocked by other people's behaviour or words

broadsheet /ˈbrɔːdʃiːt/ *noun* a newspaper with large pages (NOTE: Small format newspapers are called **tabloids**.)

broadside /ˈbrɔːdsaɪd/ *noun* a strong spoken or written attack

Broadway /ˈbrɔːdweɪ/ *noun* a street in New York, where the major theatres are located ○ *The play was a big hit on Broadway but flopped in London.*

brocade /brəˈkeɪd/ *noun* a thick cloth with a raised pattern

broccoli /ˈbrɒkəli/ *noun* a vegetable of which the green, purple or white flower buds are eaten

brochure /ˈbrəʊʃə/ *noun* a small thin book

broil /brɔɪl/ (**broils, broiling, broiled**) *verb* to grill food

broiler /ˈbrɔɪlə/ *noun* a chicken sold for roasting

② **broke** /brəʊk/ *adj* with no money (*informal*) ■ past tense of **break**

① **broken** /ˈbrəʊkən/ *adj* **1.** in pieces ○ *She tried to mend the broken vase.* **2.** not working ○ *We can't use the lift because it's broken.* ■ past participle of **break**

broken-down /ˌbrəʊkən ˈdaʊn/ *adj* not working

broken-hearted /ˌbrəʊkənˈhɑːtɪd/ *adj* very sad

broker /ˈbrəʊkə/ *noun* a dealer in shares or insurance

brolly /ˈbrɒli/ (*plural* **brollies**) *noun* an umbrella (*informal*)

bronchitis /brɒŋˈkaɪtɪs/ *noun* an illness caused by infection in the bronchial tubes

bronzed /brɒnzd/ *adj* tanned from being in the sun

bronze medal /brɒnz ˈmed(ə)l/ *noun* a medal given to someone who finishes third in a race or competition

brooch /brəʊtʃ/ *noun* a piece of jewellery fixed onto clothes with a pin

brood /bruːd/ *noun* a family of young birds or small children ○ *Some birds raise only one brood of chicks a year.* ○ *Simon and his brood came for lunch yesterday.* ■ *verb* (**broods, brooding, brooded**) to think anxiously about something a lot [~about/over/on] ○ *She's brooding over the possibility that she might lose her job.*

③ **broom** /bruːm/ *noun* **1.** a brush with a long handle, used to clean floors ○ *She swept the kitchen with a broom.* **2.** a bush with yellow flowers, found in sandy places and grown in gardens ○ *Broom flowers early in the summer.*

broth /brɒθ/ *noun* a light meat soup

brothel /ˈbrɒθ(ə)l/ *noun* a house where prostitutes work

① **brother** /ˈbrʌðə/ *noun* a boy or man who has the same mother and father as someone else ○ *My brother John is three years older than me.* ○ *She came with her three brothers.*

brotherhood /ˈbrʌðəhʊd/ *noun* links between people

brother-in-law /ˈbrʌðər ɪn lɔː/ (*plural* **brothers-in-law**) *noun* a brother of your husband or wife; a husband of your sister; or a husband of a husband's or wife's sister

brotherly /ˈbrʌðəli/ *adj* kind or protective like a brother ○ *She was expecting some brotherly advice, instead of which her brother told her she was a fool.*

① **brought** /brɔːt/ past tense and past participle of **bring**

brow /braʊ/ *noun* **1.** the forehead ○ *She wrinkled or knit her brow as she tried to understand the guidebook.* **2.** an eyebrow, the line of hair above the eye ○ *He's instantly recognisable with those dark bushy brows.* **3.** the top of a hill ○ *Having reached the brow of the hill they stopped to look at the view.*

① **brown** /braʊn/ *adj* **1.** with a colour like earth or wood ○ *She has brown hair and blue eyes.* ○ *It's autumn and the leaves are turning brown.* **2.** with skin made dark by the sun ○ *He's very brown – he must have been sitting in the sun.* ■ *noun* a colour like earth or wood ○ *I'd prefer shoes of a lighter brown.*

brownfield /ˈbraʊnfiːld/ *adj* referring to land that previously had industrial building on it but is now available for housing

brownie /ˈbraʊni/ *noun* a small chocolate cake usually with nuts

③ **browse** /braʊz/ (**browses, browsing, browsed**) *verb* **1.** to look through a book, newspaper or magazine, without reading it properly ○ *I browsed through several magazines at the doctor's surgery.* **2.** to wander around a shop looking at things for sale ○ *Do you need any help? – No, I'm just browsing.* **3.** to go to various websites on the Internet without looking for anything in particular

browser /ˈbraʊzə/ *noun* computer software which allows you to browse on the Internet

bruise /bruːz/ *noun* a dark painful area on the skin, where you have been hit ○ *She had bruises all over her arms.* ■ *verb* (**bruises, bruising, bruised**) to make a bruise on the skin by being hit or by knocking yourself on something ○ *She bruised her knee on the corner of the table.*

brunch /brʌntʃ/ *noun* a meal taken from about 10 a.m., a combination of breakfast and lunch

brunette /bruːˈnet/ *noun* a person, usually a woman, with dark brown hair

② **brush** /brʌʃ/ *noun* **1.** a tool made of a handle and hairs or wire, used for doing things such as cleaning or painting ○ *You need a stiff brush to get the mud off your shoes.* ○ *She used a very fine brush to paint the details.* ○ *He was painting the front of the house with a large brush.* **2.** the act of cleaning with a brush ○ *She gave the coat a good brush.* **3.** a short argument or fight with someone ○ *He's had several brushes with the police recently.* ■ *verb* (**brushes, brushing, brushed**) **1.** to clean with a brush ○ *He brushed his shoes before going to the office.* ○ *Always remember to brush your teeth before you go to bed.* **2.** to go past something touching it gently ○ *She brushed against me as she came into the café.*

brush off *phrasal verb* **1.** to clean something off with a brush ○ *He brushed the mud off his boots.* **2.** to ignore something because it is not very important ○ *So far he has managed to brush off all the complaints about his work.*

brush up *phrasal verb* to learn more about something ○ *You'll need to brush up your English if you want to get a job as a guide.*

brusque /brʊsk/ *adj* using very few words and not being very polite

Brussels sprout /ˌbrʌs(ə)lz 'spraʊt/ *noun* a green vegetable like a very small cabbage

brutal /'bruːt(ə)l/ *adj* cruel and violent

brute /bruːt/ *noun* **1.** a violent person ○ *Her husband's such a brute, sometimes I fear for her safety.* **2.** a large animal ○ *Three bears came near our camp and one big brute tried to get into my tent.*

BTW *abbr* by the way

③ **bubble** /'bʌb(ə)l/ *noun* a ball of air or gas contained in a liquid or other substance ○ *Bubbles of gas rose to the surface of the lake.* ○ *He blew bubbles in his drink.* ■ *verb* (**bubbles, bubbling, bubbled**) to make bubbles, or have bubbles inside ○ *The porridge was bubbling in the pan.*

bubble up *phrasal verb* to come to the surface as bubbles

bubble gum /'bʌb(ə)l gʌm/ *noun* **1.** a type of chewing gum that can be blown from the mouth into large bubbles **2.** pop music aimed at the younger teenage market and usually considered to be lacking in originality

bubbly /'bʌbli/ *adj* (**bubblier, bubbliest**) with bubbles ○ *For a really bubbly bath, pour the soap in under running hot water.* ■ *noun* champagne (*informal*) ○ *Come and have a glass of bubbly to celebrate the birth of our son.* (NOTE: no plural)

③ **buck** /bʌk/ *noun* **1.** a male of certain animals such as the hare, rabbit, deer or goat (NOTE: The female is called a **doe**.) **2.** *US* a dollar ○ *It'll cost you ten bucks.* ○ *You couldn't lend me 100 bucks, could you?* ◇ **to pass the buck** to pass responsibility to someone else (*informal*) ○ *The manager is a very weak character, he's always passing the buck.* ◇ **the buck stops here** I am the person who is responsible

② **bucket** /'bʌkɪt/ *noun* **1.** an open container with a handle, used mainly for carrying liquids ○ *He filled a bucket from the tap.* **2.** the contents of a bucket ○ *He brought a bucket of water from the river.* ○ *They threw buckets of water on the fire.* ■ *verb* (**buckets, bucketing, bucketed**) to pour with rain (*informal*) ○ *It's bucketing down outside.*

buckle /'bʌk(ə)l/ (**buckles, buckling, buckled**) *verb* **1.** to bend and collapse ○ *The whole bridge buckled under the weight of the traffic.* **2.** to become bent ○ *The front wheel of my bicycle has buckled.*

buckle down *phrasal verb* to start to work hard (*informal*)

bud /bʌd/ *noun* a place where a new shoot or flower will grow from on a plant ○ *It was spring and the buds on the trees were beginning to open.*

Buddhism /'bʊdɪz(ə)m/ *noun* a religion based on the teaching of the Indian philosopher known as Buddha (NOTE: + **Buddhist** *n*)

budding /'bʌdɪŋ/ *adj* studying to be, hoping to be

buddy /'bʌdi/ (*plural* **buddies**) *noun mainly US* a friend (*informal*)

budge /bʌdʒ/ (**budges, budging, budged**) *verb* to move

budgerigar /'bʌdʒərigɑː/ *noun* a small colourful tropical bird often kept as a pet

② **budget** /'bʌdʒɪt/ *noun* an amount of money that can be spent on something ○ *There isn't enough money in the household budget to pay for a new carpet.* ■ *verb* (**budgets, budgeting, budgeted**) to plan how you will spend money in the future [~for] ○ *They are having to budget carefully before going on holiday.* ○ *We're budgeting for a 5% increase in electricity prices.*

budgie /'bʌdʒi/ *noun* same as **budgerigar** (*informal*)

buff /bʌf/ *noun* **1.** a pale brown colour ○ *This type of envelope comes in blue, green and buff only.* **2.** an enthusiast ○ *This is the best dictionary for crossword buffs.*

buffalo /'bʌfələʊ/ (*plural* **buffaloes** or **buffalos** or *same*) *noun* a large wild animal with long hair, like a large bull, which used to be common in North America but is reduced in numbers (NOTE: For a group, you say **a herd of buffalo**.)

③ **buffer** /'bʌfə/ *noun* **1.** a shock-absorbing pad ○ *The cushion acts as a buffer between the two pieces of machinery.* ○ *The* *train failed to stop and crashed into the buffers.* **2.** something placed between two powerful forces, which prevents problems occurring between them ○ *The UN tried to establish a buffer zone between the two factions.*

buffet /ˈbʊfeɪ/ *noun* a meal where the food is in dishes on a table, and each person helps himself ○ *The hotel serves a buffet breakfast.*

③ **bug** /bʌɡ/ (**bugs, bugging, bugged**) *verb* to make someone feel slightly angry, especially for a long time (*informal*) ○ *I can't remember his name, and it's really bugging me!*

bugging device /ˈbʌɡɪŋ dɪˌvaɪs/ *noun* a hidden microphone

buggy /ˈbʌɡi/ (*plural* **buggies**) *noun* **1.** a little electric car for one or two people ○ *Beach buggies have very large tyres so that they can drive on sand.* ○ *Some people hire buggies when they play golf.* **2.** a light folding chair with wheels for pushing a baby in ○ *She pushed the buggy across the busy road.*

bugle /ˈbjuːɡ(ə)l/ *noun* a brass musical instrument similar to a trumpet, mainly used in the army

① **build** /bɪld/ *verb* (**builds, building, built**) **1.** to make something by putting its parts together ○ *The house was only built last year.* ○ *They are planning to build a motorway across the field.* ○ *The children built sand castles on the beach.* **2.** to develop something ○ *We need to build a good team relationship.* ○ *These games are good for building your vocabulary.* ■ *noun* the particular shape of someone's body ○ *She's a girl of slender build.* ○ *He has the same build as his father.*

build up *phrasal verb* to increase ○ *The pressure is building up on him to resign.* ○ *Gas built up rapidly in the boiler until it exploded.*

③ **builder** /ˈbɪldə/ *noun* a person who builds buildings

① **building** /ˈbɪldɪŋ/ *noun* **1.** something such as a house, railway station or factory which has been built ○ *The flood washed away several buildings.* ○ *His office is on the top floor of the building.* **2.** the action of constructing something ○ *The building of the tunnel has taken many years.*

③ **building society** /ˈbɪldɪŋ səˌsaɪəti/ *noun* an organisation which pays interest on people's savings and lends money to people buying houses or flats

build-up /ˈbɪld ʌp/ *noun* **1.** the preparations for something **2.** a gradual increase in something ○ *a build-up of traffic* **3.** a flattering description of someone or something ○ *We'd expected someone funnier after all the build-up.*

built /bɪlt/ past tense and past participle of **build**

-built /bɪlt/ *suffix* made or constructed

built-in /ˌbɪlt ˈɪn/ *adj* made as part of a room or machine

③ **bulb** /bʌlb/ *noun* **1.** a round part of some plants, which stays under the ground, and from which leaves and flowers grow ○ *She planted spring bulbs all round the house.* **2.** a glass ball which gives electric light ○ *I need to change the bulb in the table lamp.*

bulbous /ˈbʌlbəs/ *adj* fat and round

bulge /bʌldʒ/ *noun* a swelling ○ *There's a little bulge in the carpet – I guess we'll find the missing toy underneath.* ■ *verb* (**bulges, bulging, bulged**) **1.** to be big at one place **2.** to be full of something [~with] ○ *Her pockets were bulging with bundles of notes.* ○ *Father's briefcase bulged not with important papers but with toys for his children.*

bulging /ˈbʌldʒɪŋ/ *adj* sticking out

bulimia /buˈlɪmiə/ *noun* a psychological condition in which the patient eats too much and is incapable of controlling their eating

bulk /bʌlk/ *noun* a large amount ◊ **in bulk** in large quantities ○ *It is cheaper to buy stationery for the school in bulk.* ◇ **the bulk of** most of ○ *The bulk of our sales are in Europe.* ○ *She finished the bulk of the work before lunch.*

bulky /ˈbʌlki/ (**bulkier, bulkiest**) *adj* awkwardly large

bull /bʊl/ *noun* a male animal of the cow family ○ *Be careful when you cross the field – there's a bull in it.* ◇ **to take the bull by the horns** to try to deal with a difficult problem (*informal*) ○ *He decided to take the bull by the horns and tell his father that he was leaving the family firm.*

bulldog /ˈbʊldɒɡ/ *noun* a short strong dog with a flat face

bulldoze /ˈbʊldəʊz/ (**bulldozes, bulldozing, bulldozed**) *verb* **1.** to knock down or to clear using a bulldozer ○ *They bulldozed the old farm buildings.* **2.** to force something to happen □ **he bulldozed his proposal through the committee** he forced the committee to agree to his proposal

bulldozer /ˈbʊldəʊzə/ *noun* a large powerful tractor with a curved plate in front for pushing or moving earth

bullet /ˈbʊlɪt/ *noun* a piece of metal that you shoot from a gun ○ *He loaded his gun with bullets.* ○ *Two bullets had been fired.*

bulletin /ˈbʊlɪtɪn/ *noun* information on a situation

bulletin board /ˈbʊlɪtɪn bɔːd/ *noun* **1.** *US* a board on which notices can be placed **2.** (*on the Internet*) a system of sending messages or advertising events ○ *She advertised the concert on the bulletin board.*

bullet point /ˈbʊlɪt pɔɪnt/ *noun* a printed symbol like a circle before an item in a list

bullet-proof /ˈbʊlɪtpruːf/ *adj* made so that bullets cannot go through

bullfight /ˈbʊlfaɪt/ *noun* entertainment in Spain, where a man fights a bull

bullion /ˈbʊliən/ *noun* gold or silver bars

bull market /ˈbʊl ˌmɑːkɪt/ *noun* a period when prices on the stock market rise as people buy shares because they think share prices will rise still further

bull's eye /ˈbʊlz aɪ/ *noun* the centre of the target which you try to hit in sports such as archery, darts or rifle shooting ○ *This target is not easy, the bull's eye is very small.*

bully /ˈbʊli/ *noun* (*plural* **bullies**) a person who often hurts or is unkind to other people ○ *He's a bully, he's always trying to frighten smaller children.* ■ *verb* (**bullies, bullying, bullied**) to be unkind to someone often ○ *She was bullied by the other children in school.*

bum /bʌm/ *noun* (*informal*) **1.** a person's bottom ○ *He just sits on his bum all day, doing nothing.* **2.** *US* a person who sits around doing nothing ○ *Can't you bums find something to do?* **3.** a person who is very keen on something ○ *a ski bum*

bum bag /ˈbʌ́m bæg/ *noun* a small bag attached to a belt for keeping valuables in

bumblebee /ˈbʌmb(ə)lbiː/ *noun* a large brown furry bee

bumbling /ˈbʌmblɪŋ/ *adj* confused and inefficient (*informal*)

③ **bump** /bʌmp/ *noun* **1.** a slight knock ○ *The boat hit the landing stage with a bump.* **2.** a raised area ○ *Drive slowly, the road is full of bumps.* **3.** a raised area on your body, where something has hit it ○ *He has a bump on the back of his head.* ■ *verb* (**bumps, bumping, bumped**) to hit something or a part of the body ○ *He's crying because he bumped his head on the door.*

bump into *phrasal verb* to hit slightly ○ *Be careful not to bump into the wall when you're reversing.* ◇ **to bump into someone** to meet someone by chance ○ *I bumped into him at the station.*

bump off *phrasal verb* to murder someone (*slang*)

bumper /ˈbʌmpə/ *adj* very large ○ *a bumper crop of corn* ○ *We're publishing a bumper edition of children's stories.* ○ *Last year was a bumper year for sales of mobile phones.* ■ *noun* a protective bar on the front and back of a car ○ *He backed into a lamp-post and dented the rear bumper.* ○ *There was a mile-long traffic jam with cars standing bumper-to-bumper.*

bumpy /ˈbʌmpi/ (**bumpier, bumpiest**) *adj* not smooth

③ **bun** /bʌn/ *noun* **1.** a small round piece of bread or a cake ○ *The burgers are served in a bun.* ○ *These buns are too sweet and sticky.* **2.** hair tied up at the back of the head in a knot ○ *She wears her hair in a bun.*

② **bunch** /bʌntʃ/ *noun* **1.** a group of things taken together ○ *He carries a bunch of keys attached to his belt.* ○ *He brought her a bunch of flowers.* **2.** a group of people ○ *I work with a nice bunch of people* ○ *My friends are a mixed bunch.* **3.** several fruits attached to the same stem ○ *a bunch of grapes* ○ *a bunch of bananas* ■ *verb* (**bunches, bunching, bunched**) to form a group

bundle /ˈbʌnd(ə)l/ *noun* **1.** a parcel of things wrapped up or tied up together ○ *A bundle of clothes was all she owned.* ○ *He produced a bundle of papers tied up with green string.* ○ *She left her clothes in a bundle on the floor.* **2.** a set of things sold or presented together ○ *a bundle of software* ■ *verb* (**bundles, bundling, bundled**) **1.** to put things somewhere quickly without being careful ○ *He bundled the papers into a drawer.* ○ *She bundled the children off to school.* ○ *The police bundled him into the back of their van.* **2.** to sell a software programme at the same time as you sell hardware, both sold together at a special price [~with] ○ *The word-processing package is bundled with the computer.*

bung /bʌŋ/ (**bungs, bunging, bunged**) *verb* to throw (*informal*) ○ *Don't keep that paper – just bung it in the wastepaper basket.*

② **bungalow** /ˈbʌŋgələʊ/ *noun* a house with only a ground floor

bungee-jumping /ˈbʌndʒiː ˌdʒʌmpɪŋ/ *noun* a sport which consists of jumping from a high point such as a bridge when attached by your ankles to a long elastic cable, so that instead of hitting the ground, you bounce up into the air

bungle /ˈbʌŋg(ə)l/ (**bungles, bungling, bungled**) *verb* to do something badly (*informal*)

bunk beds /ˈbʌŋk bedz/ *plural noun* two beds one on top of the other, with a ladder to climb to the top one ○ *We put the children in bunk beds because they take up less space.*

bunker /ˈbʌŋkə/ *noun* **1.** a room with especially strong walls, often underground ○ *The soldiers defended the bunker for several days.* ○ *As the enemy approached, the ministers hid in a bunker under the presidential palace.* **2.** an open pit filled with sand placed on a golf course to trap balls and make difficulties for the players

③ **bunny** /ˈbʌni/ (*plural* **bunnies**) *noun* a child's name for a rabbit (*informal*)

buoyant /ˈbɔɪənt/ *adj* **1.** which can float easily, which helps something float easily ○ *The raft became waterlogged and was no longer buoyant.* ○ *Salt water is more buoyant than fresh water.* **2.** full of confidence ○ *She left the meeting in a very buoyant mood.*

③ **burden** /ˈbɜːd(ə)n/ *noun* **1.** a heavy load ○ *He relieved her of her burden.* **2.** something that is hard to deal with [/~on/to] ○ *I think he finds running the family shop quite a burden on him.*

bureau /ˈbjʊərəʊ/ (*plural* **bureaus** or **bureaux**) *noun* **1.** an office ○ *He filed the report from the New York bureau.* **2.** an antique desk **3.** *US* a chest of drawers ○ *My socks are in the bureau in the bedroom.* **4.** *US* a section of a government department

bureaucracy /bjʊəˈrɒkrəsi/ *noun* **1.** a group of officials working for central or local government, or for an international body ○ *The investigation of complaints is in the hands of the local bureaucracy.* **2.** a complicated official system ○ *Red tape and bureaucracy slow down charitable work.* ○ *I'm fed up with all this bureaucracy, just to get an export licence.*

bureaucrat /ˈbjʊərəkræt/ *noun* a person who runs an office or government department

③ **burger** /ˈbɜːgə/ *noun* same as **hamburger**

③ **burglar** /ˈbɜːglə/ *noun* a person who tries to get into a building to steal things

burglar alarm /ˈbɜːglər əˌlɑːm/ *noun* a piece of equipment which makes a loud noise if someone enters a building illegally

burglary /ˈbɜːgləri/ (*plural* **burglaries**) *noun* a robbery by a burglar

burgle /ˈbɜːg(ə)l/ (**burgles, burgling, burgled**) *verb* to enter a building and steal things from it

burgundy /ˈbɜːgəndɪ/ *adj* dark red

③ **burial** /ˈberiəl/ *noun* a ceremony of burying a dead person

burly /ˈbɜːli/ (**burlier, burliest**) *adj* (*of a person*) with a large strong body

① **burn** /bɜːn/ *noun* a burnt area of the skin or a surface ○ *She had burns on her face and hands.* ○ *There's a burn on the edge of the table where he left his cigarette.* ■ *verb* (**burns, burning, burnt** or **burned**) **1.** to destroy or damage something by fire ○ *She burnt her finger on the hot frying pan.* ○ *The hotel was burnt to the ground last year.* ○ *I've burnt the toast again.* **2.** to feel painful, or to make something feel painful ○ *The sun and wind burnt his face.* **3.** to damage part of the body by heat ○ *She burnt her finger on the hot frying pan.* **4.** to be on fire ○ *The firemen were called to the burning school.*

burn down *phrasal verb* **1.** to destroy something completely by fire ○ *They were playing with matches and burnt the house down.* **2.** to be destroyed completely by fire ○ *The building had burnt down before the firemen arrived.*

burn out *phrasal verb* to destroy the inside completely by fire ○ *The restaurant was completely burnt out.*

burning /ˈbɜːnɪŋ/ *adj* **1.** very hot ○ *The baby must have a temperature – his face is burning.* ○ *Careful, the pan is burning hot.* **2.** painful, as though being touched by something hot ○ *She had a burning pain in her left eye.* **3.** very keen ○ *He had a burning desire to go to Egypt.*

③ **burnt** /bɜːnt/ *adj* destroyed or damaged by fire or heat

burnt-out /ˌbɜːnt ˈaʊt/ *adj* completely tired physically or emotionally through too much hard work, stress, or fast living

burp /bɜːp/ *noun* the noise made when bringing up air from the stomach ○ *When the baby stops drinking, pat him gently on the back until he makes a burp.* ■ *verb* (**burps, burping, burped**) to make a burp ○ *There is nothing like a fizzy drink to make you burp.*

burrow /ˈbʌrəʊ/ *noun* a rabbit hole ○ *The rabbits all popped down into their burrow* *when we came near.* ■ *verb* (**burrows, burrowing, burrowed**) to dig underground ○ *Moles have burrowed under the lawn.*

bursar /'bɜːsə/ *noun* a person in charge of the finances of a school or college

bursary /'bɜːs(ə)ri/ *noun* money given to some students to help them pay for their studies

① **burst** /bɜːst/ *verb* (**bursts, bursting, burst**) to break open or explode suddenly, or cause something to break open or explode suddenly ○ *When she picked up the balloon it burst.* ■ *noun* **1.** a sudden loud sound ○ *There was a burst of gunfire and then silence.* ○ *Bursts of laughter came from the office.* **2.** a sudden effort or activity ○ *She put on a burst of speed.* ○ *In a burst of energy he cleaned the whole house.*

burst into *phrasal verb* **1.** to enter unexpectedly, in a rush ○ *She burst into the meeting waving a bundle of papers.* **2.** to start to do something suddenly ○ *She opened the letter and burst into tears.* ○ *The building burst into flames.*

burst out *phrasal verb* **1.** to suddenly start ○ *She burst out laughing.* **2.** to say something loudly ○ *He burst out into a string of insults.* **3.** to leave quickly ○ *She burst out of the shop, and started running down the street.*

bursting /'bɜːstɪŋ/ *abbr* very full of people ○ *The bar was bursting last night.* ■ *adj* **1.** eager to say something [~to] ○ *He was bursting to tell everyone the news.* **2.** feeling an emotion strongly [~with] ○ *bursting with pride*

bury /'beri/ (**buries, burying, buried**) *verb* to put someone or something into the ground ○ *He was buried in the local cemetery.* ○ *Squirrels often bury nuts in the autumn.*

① **bus** /bʌs/ (*plural* **buses** or **busses**) *noun* a large motor vehicle which carries passengers ○ *He goes to work by bus.* ○ *She takes the 8 o'clock bus to school every morning.* ○ *We missed the last bus and had to walk home.* ○ *The number 6 bus goes to Oxford Street.*

② **bush** /bʊʃ/ *noun* a small tree ○ *a holly bush with red berries* ○ *An animal was moving in the bushes.*

bushel /'bʊʃ(ə)l/ *noun* a measure of dry goods, such as grain (equal to 56 pounds)

bushy /'bʊʃi/ (**bushier, bushiest**) *adj* (*of hair*) growing thickly

① **business** /'bɪznɪs/ *noun* **1.** the work of buying and selling things ○ *They do a lot of business with France.* ○ *She works in the electricity business.* □ **on business** working ○ *The sales director is in Holland on business.* **2.** a company ○ *She runs a photography business.* ○ *He runs a secondhand car business.* **3.** something that affects a particular person □ **it's none of your business** it's nothing to do with you

business class /'bɪznɪs klɑːs/ *noun* travel which is less expensive than first class

businesslike /'bɪznɪslaɪk/ *adj* practical and efficient

businessman /'bɪznɪsmæn/ (*plural* **businessmen**) *noun* a man who works in business, or who runs a business

businessperson /'bɪznɪsˌpɜːs(ə)n/ (*plural* **businesspeople** or **businesspersons**) *noun* a person who works in business, or who runs a business

business plan /'bɪznɪs plæn/ *noun* a plan of the future development of a business

businesswoman /'bɪznɪs ˌwʊmən/ (*plural* **businesswomen**) *noun* a woman who works in business, or who runs a business

busk /bʌsk/ (**busks, busking, busked**) *verb* to entertain people in the street

bus shelter /'bʌs ˌʃeltə/ *noun* a construction with a roof where you can wait for a bus

bust /bʌst/ *noun* **1.** a sculpture of the head and shoulders ○ *Have you seen the bust of the Prime Minister?* **2.** a woman's breasts ■ *verb* (**busts, busting, busted** or **bust**) to break (*informal*) ○ *She's bust my precious vase!* ○ *He hit the ball hard and it bust a window.*

bustle /'bʌs(ə)l/ *noun* a situation where people are hurrying around ○ *It's nice to sit quietly at home after the bustle of the office.* ■ *verb* (**bustles, bustling, bustled**) to hurry around doing things ○ *She bustled around the kitchen getting dinner ready.*

bustling /'bʌs(ə)lɪŋ/ *adj* with a lot of people and activity

bust-up /'bʌst ʌp/ *noun* **1.** the breaking up of something such as a relationship or an organisation **2.** a fight or bad argument

① **busy** /'bɪzi/ (**busier, busiest**) *adj* **1.** working on or doing something ○ *He was busy mending the dishwasher.* ○ *I was too busy to phone my aunt.* **2.** full of people ○ *The shops are busiest during the week before Christmas.* **3.** (*of a phone line*) being used by someone else, so you cannot get an answer when you call ○ *His phone's been busy all day.* (NOTE: + **busily** *adv*)

busybody /ˈbɪzibɒdi/ (*plural* **busybodies**) *noun* a person who is too interested in what other people do (*informal*)

① **but** /bət, bʌt/ *conj* used for showing a difference ○ *He is very tall, but his wife is quite short.* ○ *We would like to come to your party, but we're doing something else that evening.* ■ *prep* except ○ *Everyone but me is allowed to go to the cinema.* ○ *They had eaten nothing but apples.*

③ **butcher** /ˈbʊtʃə/ *noun* a person who prepares and sells meat

butler /ˈbʌtlə/ *noun* the most important male servant in a house, who serves at table, especially dealing with wine

butt /bʌt/ *noun* **1.** a large container for water or wine ○ *It has rained a lot lately and the rainwater butt is overflowing.* **2.** the end of a cigarette which has been smoked ○ *He picked up old butts from the pavement.* **3.** the end of the handle of a gun which presses against the shoulder of the person firing it ○ *The prisoners were beaten with rifle butts.* **4.** a person whom other people laugh at ○ *He will always be the butt of their criticism if he doesn't dress any better.* **5.** a push with the head ○ *The goat came up behind him and gave him a butt with its head.* **6.** *US* buttocks ○ *to give someone a kick in the butt* ■ *verb* (**butts, butting, butted**) to push with the head ○ *The goat lowered its head and butted him.*

butt in *phrasal verb* to interrupt

① **butter** /ˈbʌtə/ *noun* a yellow fat made from the cream of milk, used on bread or for cooking ○ *Could you pass the butter, please?* ○ *Don't spread the butter so thick.* ○ *Fry the mushrooms in butter.* (NOTE: no plural: *some butter, a knob of butter*) ■ *verb* (**butters, buttering, buttered**) to spread butter on something ○ *She was busy buttering slices of bread for the sandwiches.*

buttercup /ˈbʌtəkʌp/ *noun* a common yellow flower found in fields

③ **butterfly** /ˈbʌtəflaɪ/ *noun* an insect with large brightly coloured wings, which flies during the day

buttocks /ˈbʌtəks/ *plural noun* the part of the body on which you sit

① **button** /ˈbʌt(ə)n/ *noun* **1.** a small, usually round piece of plastic, metal or wood, that you push through a hole in clothes to fasten them ○ *The wind is cold – do up the buttons on your coat.* ○ *A button's come off my shirt.* **2.** a small round object which you push to operate something such as a bell ○ *Press this button to call the lift.* ○ *Push the red button to set off the alarm.* ■ *verb* (**buttons, buttoning, buttoned**) to fasten something with buttons ○ *He buttoned (up) his coat because it was cold.*

buttonhole /ˈbʌt(ə)nhəʊl/ *noun* a hole which a button goes through when it is fastened ○ *You've put the button in the wrong buttonhole.*

① **buy** /baɪ/ (**buys, buying, bought**) *verb* to get something by paying money for it ○ *I bought a newspaper on my way to the station.* ○ *She's buying a flat.* ○ *She bought herself a pair of ski boots.* ○ *What did you buy your mother for her birthday?*

buy up *phrasal verb* to buy a large quantity of something

③ **buyer** /ˈbaɪə/ *noun* a person who buys things

buyout /ˈbaɪaʊt/ *noun* same as **takeover**

buzz /bʌz/ *noun* a noise like the sound made by a bee ○ *the buzz of an electric saw in the garden next door* ■ *verb* (**buzzes, buzzing, buzzed**) to make a noise like a bee ○ *Wasps were buzzing round the jam.*

buzz off *phrasal verb* to go away (*informal*)

buzzer /ˈbʌzə/ *noun* a piece of equipment which buzzes as a signal of something

buzzword /ˈbʌzwɜːd/ *noun* a word which is frequently used (*informal*)

① **by** /baɪ/ *prep* **1.** near ○ *The house is just by the bus stop.* ○ *Sit down here by me.* **2.** not later than ○ *They should have arrived by now.* ○ *You must be home by eleven o'clock.* ○ *It must be finished by Friday.* **3.** used for showing the means of doing something ○ *Send the parcel by airmail.* ○ *Get in touch with the office by phone.* ○ *They came by car.* ○ *She caught a cold by standing in the rain.* ○ *You make the drink by adding champagne to orange juice.* ○ *She paid by cheque, not by credit card.* **4.** used for showing the person or thing that did something ○ *a painting by Van Gogh* ○ *a CD recorded by our local group* ○ *'Hamlet' is a play by Shakespeare.* ○ *The postman was bitten by the dog.* ○ *She was knocked down by a car.* **5.** used for showing amounts ○ *We sell tomatoes by the kilo.* ○ *Eggs are sold by the dozen.* ○ *Prices have been increased by 5%.* ○ *They won by 4 goals to 2.* ■ *adv* past ○ *She drove by without seeing us.*

① **bye** /baɪ/, **bye-bye** /ˌbaɪ ˈbaɪ/ *interj* goodbye (*informal*)

by-election /ˈbaɪ ɪˌlekʃən/, **bye-election** *noun* an election for Parliament when an MP has died or retired

bygone /ˈbaɪɡɒn/ *adj* belonging to the past ○ *A painting of a bygone age.*

bypass /ˈbaɪpɑːs/ *noun* a road round a town ○ *Take the bypass if you want to avoid congestion in the town centre.* ■ *verb* (**bypasses, bypassing, bypassed**) to go round a town, avoiding the centre ○ *It would be better if you could bypass the town centre on market day.* ○ *The main road bypasses the town centre.*

by-product /ˈbaɪ ˌprɒdʌkt/ *noun* a product made as a result of manufacturing a main product

bystander /ˈbaɪstændə/ *noun* a person near where something is happening

byte /baɪt/ *noun* a group of eight bits which a computer operates on as a single unit (NOTE: usually used in compounds: **kilobyte**, **megabyte**, etc. Do not confuse with **bite**.)

byway /ˈbaɪweɪ/ *noun* an unimportant road

byword /ˈbaɪwɜːd/ *noun* **1.** somebody or something well known for representing a particular quality **2.** a word or phrase which is in common use

C

c /siː/, **C** *noun* the third letter of the alphabet, between B and D

cab /kæb/ *noun* **1.** a taxi ○ *He took a cab to the airport.* ○ *Can you phone for a cab, please?* ○ *Cab fares are very high in New York.* **2.** a separate part of a large vehicle for a driver ○ *The truck driver climbed into his cab and started the engine.*

cabaret /ˈkæbəreɪ/ *noun* entertainment given in a restaurant or club, with dancing and singing

cabbage /ˈkæbɪdʒ/ *noun* a vegetable with large pale green or red leaves folded into a tight ball

cabin /ˈkæbɪn/ *noun* **1.** a small room on a ship ○ *We booked a first-class cabin on the cruise.* ○ *She felt sick and went to lie down in her cabin.* **2.** the inside of an aircraft ○ *The aircraft is divided into three separate cabins.* ○ *The first-class cabin is in the front of the plane.* **3.** a small hut ○ *He has a cabin by a lake where he goes fishing.*

② **cabinet** /ˈkæbɪnət/ *noun* **1.** a piece of furniture with shelves ○ *a china cabinet* **2.** a committee formed from the most important members of a government ○ *The cabinet met at 10 o'clock this morning.* ○ *There's a cabinet meeting every Tuesday morning.*

③ **cable** /ˈkeɪb(ə)l/ *noun* **1.** a wire for carrying electricity or electronic signals ○ *They've been digging up the pavements to lay cables.* ○ *He ran a cable out into the garden so that he could use the lawnmower.* **2.** a thick rope or wire ○ *The ship was attached to the quay by cables.* **3.** same as **cable television**

cable television /ˌkeɪb(ə)l ˌtelɪ ˈvɪʒ(ə)n/, **cable TV** /ˌkeɪb(ə)l ˌtiːˈviː/ *noun* a television system where the signals are sent along underground cables

cache /kæʃ/ *noun* a hidden store ○ *The police found a cache of explosives in the shed.*

cackle /ˈkæk(ə)l/ (**cackles, cackling, cackled**) *verb* to make a little high-pitched laugh

cacophony /kəˈkɒfəni/ *noun* an unpleasant mixture of loud sounds

cactus /ˈkæktəs/ (*plural* **cacti**) *noun* a plant with thorns which grows in the desert

CAD /kæd/ *abbr* computer aided design

caddie /ˈkædi/ (*plural* **caddies**) *noun* a person who carries the clubs for a golfer ○ *Some of the best golf professionals started as caddies.*

caddy /ˈkædi/ *noun* **1.** a little box for keeping loose tea in **2.** same as **caddie**

cadet /kəˈdet/ *noun* a young person training for the armed services or the police force

caesarean /sɪˈzeəriən/, **caesarean section** /sɪˈzeəriən ˌsekʃən/ *noun* an operation to deliver a baby by cutting through the abdominal wall into the uterus

café /ˈkæfeɪ/ *noun* a small restaurant selling drinks or light meals ○ *We had a snack in the station café.*

cafeteria /ˌkæfəˈtɪəriə/ *noun* a self-service restaurant

cafetiere /ˌkæfəˈtjeə/ *noun* a coffee pot where you push down a filter to make the coffee

caffeine /ˈkæfiːn/ *noun* a chemical found in coffee, chocolate and tea which acts as a stimulant

③ **cage** /keɪdʒ/ *noun* a box made of wire or with metal bars for keeping birds or animals in ○ *The rabbit got out of its cage.*

cagey /ˈkeɪdʒi/ (**cagier, cagiest**) *adj* not wanting to share information (*informal*) ○ *They're being very cagey about their relationship.*

② **cake** /keɪk/ *noun* food made by mixing flour, eggs and sugar, and baking it ○ *a piece of cherry cake* ○ *She had six candles on her birthday cake.* ○ *Have another slice of Christmas cake.* ○ *Would you like some chocolate cake?*

caked /keɪkt/ *adj* covered with something that has become dry and hard

calamity /kəˈlæmɪti/ (*plural* **calamities**) *noun* a disaster

calcium /ˈkælsiəm/ *noun* a chemical element which is found in different forms, e.g. in chalk rocks, shells, bones and teeth, water, milk and some plants, and is an important part of a balanced diet ○ *Their diet has a calcium deficiency* or *is deficient in calcium.*

② **calculate** /ˈkælkjʊˌleɪt/ (**calculates, calculating, calculated**) *verb* to find the answer to a problem using numbers [~(that)/~how/what/when etc] ○ *The bank clerk calculated the rate of exchange for the dollar.* ○ *He calculated that it would take us six hours to finish the job.* ○ *Have you calculated when we'll need to finish?*

calculated /ˈkælkjʊleɪtɪd/ *adj* deliberate

calculating /ˈkælkjʊleɪtɪŋ/ *adj* who makes clever plans in a careful way and thinks about all the possible results

② **calculation** /ˌkælkjʊˈleɪʃ(ə)n/ *noun* **1.** a series of numbers that you obtain when you are calculating something ○ *According to my calculations, we have enough fuel left to do only twenty kilometres.* **2.** the act of calculating

③ **calculator** /ˈkælkjʊleɪtə/ *noun* a small electronic machine for doing calculations

calculus /ˈkælkjʊləs/ *noun* a part of mathematics which is the way of calculating varying rates ○ *Calculus is now taught in sixth forms.*

calendar /ˈkælɪndə/ *noun* a set of pages showing the days and months of the year

③ **calf** /kɑːf/ (*plural* **calves**) *noun* **1.** a young cow or bull ○ *The cow stood in a corner of the field with her two calves.* **2.** the back part of someone's leg between the ankle and the knee

calibrate /ˈkælɪbreɪt/ (**calibrates, calibrating, calibrated**) *verb* to mark the degrees or measurements on a scale

calibre /ˈkælɪbə/ *noun* **1.** the measurement across the inside of a gun barrel ○ *The two bullets come from same calibre guns.* **2.** a quality or ability which something or someone has, particularly when it is of a high standard ○ *It's work which he thinks is beneath a person of his calibre.* (NOTE: [all senses] The US spelling is **caliber**.)

① **call** /kɔːl/ *verb* (**calls, calling, called**) **1.** to say something loudly to someone who is some distance away ○ *Call the children when it's time for tea.* **2.** to telephone someone ○ *If he comes back, tell him I'll call him when I'm in the office.* ○ *Mr Smith is out – shall I ask him to call you back?* ○ *Call the police – the shop has been burgled!* ○ *Can you call me a cab, please?* **3.** to wake someone ○ *Call me at 7 o'clock.* **4.** to give someone or something a name ○ *They're going to call the baby Sam.* ○ *His name is John but everyone calls him Jack.* ○ *What do you call this computer programme?* **5. to be called** to have as a name ○ *Our cat's called Felix.* **6.** to visit someone or somewhere ○ *The doctor called at the house, but there was no one there.* ■ *noun* **1.** a telephone conversation, or an attempt to get in touch with someone by telephone [~for] ○ *Were there any calls for me while I was out?* □ **to make a call** to make contact with and speak to someone on the telephone ○ *She wants to make a (phone) call to Australia.* □ **to take a call** to answer the telephone **2.** a telephone call or short conversation to wake someone ○ *He asked for an early morning call.* □ **I want a call at 7 o'clock** I want someone to wake me at 7 o'clock **3.** a visit to someone's home or place of work [~on] ○ *The doctor made three calls on patients this morning.* □ **to make a call** to visit someone or somewhere, especially on business ◇ **on call** available for duty

call for *phrasal verb* to need a particular skill or ability ○ *Rescuing people with a helicopter calls for particular flying skills.*

call in *phrasal verb* **1.** to ask someone to come and give advice or help **2.** to telephone a place of work in order to collect or leave a message **3.** to ask for a sum of money to be paid back **4.** to arrange for or request that something be returned, e.g. goods that are not suitable for sale **5.** to make a short visit to someone, especially without making an arrangement first

call off *phrasal verb* to decide not to do something which had been planned

call on *phrasal verb* **1.** to visit someone ○ *She called on her mother to see how she was.* **2.** to ask someone to do something ○ *The police have called on everyone to watch out for the escaped prisoner.*

call out *phrasal verb* **1.** to ask a person or an organisation to give help **2.** to tell workers to stop work to show they have an official disagreement with the management of the business **3.** to challenge somebody to a duel or fight **4.** to ask somebody, e.g. a doctor or someone whose job is to repair things, to come to your house and deal with an emergency

call round *phrasal verb* same as **call** *verb* **6** ○ *The whole family called round to see* *if she was better.*

call up *phrasal verb* to tell someone to join the army, navy or air force ○ *Thousands of men were called up at the beginning of the war.*

③ **callbox** /'kɔːlbɒks/ *noun* a public telephone box ○ *I'm phoning from the callbox outside the station.*

call centre /'kɔːl ˌsentə/ *noun* a business that deals with all the telephone calls that people make to a large organisation, e.g. a bank

caller /'kɔːlə/ *noun* **1.** a person who comes to visit ○ *She can't see any callers today.* **2.** a person who telephones ○ *I picked up the phone and the caller asked for my father.*

calligraphy /kə'lɪgrəfi/ *noun* the art of beautiful handwriting, using a special pen

calling /'kɔːlɪŋ/ *noun* a job which someone does because they have a strong feeling that they should do it, especially because it will help other people

callous /'kæləs/ *adj* hard, unfeeling

call-up /'kɔːl ˌʌp/ *noun* an order to join the army

call waiting /ˌkɔːl 'weɪtɪŋ/ *noun* a service offered by a telephone company that allows somebody to answer an additional call from someone without losing their connection to the current call

② **calm** /kɑːm/ *adj* **1.** not anxious or excited ○ *The sea was perfectly calm and no one was seasick.* ○ *Keep calm, everything will be all right.* **2.** not violent or rough ○ *The sea was perfectly calm and no one was seasick.* ■ *noun* a period of quiet ○ *The calm of the Sunday afternoon was broken by the sound of jazz from the house next door.* ■ *verb* (**calms, calming, calmed**) *also* **calm down** to make someone or a situation more peaceful, or to become more peaceful ○ *She stroked his hand to try to calm him (down).* ○ *After shouting for some minutes he finally calmed down.*

calm down *phrasal verb* **1.** to become quieter and less annoyed ○ *After shouting for some minutes he finally calmed down.* **2.** to make someone quieter ○ *She stroked his hand to try to calm him down.*

calmly /'kɑːmli/ *adv* in a way that is not anxious or excited

calorie /'kæləri/ *noun* a unit of measurement of energy in food ○ *She's counting calories to try to lose weight.* ○ *There are 250 calories in a pint of beer.*

calorific /ˌkælə'rɪfɪk/ *adj* containing many calories, and so likely to make you fat

camcorder /'kæmkɔːdə/ *noun* a small portable camera for taking video pictures with sound

① **came** /keɪm/ past tense of **come**

camel /'kæm(ə)l/ *noun* a desert animal with long legs and one or two large round raised parts on its back

cameo /'kæmiəʊ/ *noun* **1.** a small stone with a design of a head which stands out against a darker background ○ *For her birthday, she was given a pair of cameo earrings and a matching brooch.* **2.** a small but important part in a play or film ○ *The film is worth seeing if only for the cameo role played by Gielgud.*

② **camera** /'kæm(ə)rə/ *noun* a piece of equipment for taking photographs ○ *He took a picture of the garden with his new camera.* ○ *They went on holiday and forgot to take their camera.* ○ *Did you remember to put a film in your camera?*

cameraman /'kæm(ə)rəmæn/ (*plural* **cameramen**) *noun* the main film camera operator who is in charge of the lighting and filming of a shot

camouflage /'kæməflɑːʒ/ *noun* a method of using coloured shapes or things such as branches or grass to hide something ○ *We used camouflage to hide the guns.*

② **camp** /kæmp/ *noun* a place where people live in tents or small buildings in the open air ○ *We set up camp halfway up the mountain.* ■ *verb* (**camps, camping, camped**) **1.** to spend a period of time in a tent ○ *They had camped by the side of the lake.* **2. to go camping** to spend a holiday in a tent ○ *We go camping in Sweden every summer.*

① **campaign** /kæm'peɪn/ *noun* **1.** an organised attempt to achieve something [~for/against] ○ *a publicity campaign* ○ *an advertising campaign* ○ *a campaign against the new motorway* **2.** an organised military attack [~against] ○ *Napoleon's campaign against the Russians* ■ *verb* (**campaigns, campaigning, campaigned**) to work in an organised way to achieve something [~for/against] ○ *The group has been campaigning for a ban on land mines.* ○ *They campaign against nuclear reactors.*

camper /'kæmpə/ *noun* a person who goes camping

③ **camping** /'kæmpɪŋ/ *noun* the activity of going on holiday with a tent or caravan

campsite /ˈkæmpsaɪt/ *noun* an area for camping, often including buildings with toilets and showers

campus /ˈkæmpəs/ *noun* land on which a university or college is built, and the buildings on it

① **can** /kæn/ *modal verb* **1.** to be able to do something ○ *He can swim well but he can't ride a bike.* ○ *She can't run as fast as I can.* ○ *Can you remember what the doctor told us to do?* ○ *I can't bear to watch any longer.* **2.** to be allowed to do something ○ *Children under 18 can't drive cars.* ○ *He says we can go in.* ○ *The policeman says we can't park here.* **3.** to ask politely ○ *Can we come in, please?* ○ *Can you shut the door, please?* (NOTE: The negative is **cannot** or, especially in speaking, **can't**. The past tense is **could**. **Can** and **could** are usually used with other verbs, and are not followed by **to**.) ■ *noun* a metal container for food or drink ○ *She opened a can of beans.* ■ *verb* (**cans, canning, canned**) to put food in cans

canal /kəˈnæl/ *noun* an artificial river made between rivers or lakes or from the sea, originally for moving cargo ○ *You can take a boat trip round the canals of Amsterdam.*

canary /kəˈneəri/ (*plural* **canaries**) *noun* a small yellow singing bird

② **cancel** /ˈkænsəl/ (**cancels, cancelling, cancelled**) *verb* to stop something which has been planned ○ *The singer was ill, so the show had to be cancelled.* ○ *There is no refund if you cancel less than three weeks before the date of departure.*

cancellation /ˌkænsəˈleɪʃ(ə)n/ *noun* **1.** the act of cancelling something ○ *The event is subject to cancellation if the weather is bad.* **2.** a seat, ticket or appointment which is available again because the person who bought it cannot use it ○ *If we have a cancellation for next week I'll call and let you know.*

② **cancer** /ˈkænsə/ *noun* a serious disease affecting different parts of the body in which cells grow in a way which is not usual

Cancer /ˈkænsə/ *noun* one of the signs of the Zodiac, shaped like a crab, covering the period 22nd June to 22nd July

candid /ˈkændɪd/ *adj* (*of a person*) direct or open, saying exactly what you think or feel

candidacy /ˈkændɪdəsi/ *noun* the state of being a candidate

② **candidate** /ˈkændɪdeɪt/ *noun* **1.** a person who applies for a job [~for] ○ *We interviewed six candidates for the post of assistant manager.* **2.** a person who has entered for an examination ○ *Candidates are given three hours to complete the exam.* **3.** a person who is taking part in an election or competing for a prize ○ *She accompanied the candidate round the constituency.* **4.** someone or something that is likely to be chosen for or be something [~for] ○ *a city that is a candidate for the next Olympics*

candidature /ˈkændɪdətʃə/ *noun* the act of standing as a candidate

③ **candle** /ˈkænd(ə)l/ *noun* a stick of wax with a string in the centre, which you burn to give light

candlelight /ˈkænd(ə)lˌlaɪt/ *noun* the light given by candles

candlestick /ˈkænd(ə)lˌstɪk/ *noun* a holder for a candle

can-do /ˈkæn duː/ *adj* keen to take on a job or challenge and confident of success

candour /ˈkændə/ *noun* the personal quality of being open and honest in your behaviour towards other people (NOTE: The US spelling is **candor**.)

③ **candy** /ˈkændi/ (*plural* **candies**) *noun* **1.** *US* a sweet food made with sugar ○ *Eating candy is bad for your teeth.* (NOTE: no plural in this sense) **2.** one piece of this food ○ *She bought a box of candies.*

candyfloss /ˈkændiflɒs/ *noun* thin pieces of cooked sugar which are spun in a drum and sold as a mass attached to a stick

cane /keɪn/ *noun* **1.** a strong stem of a plant, especially of tall thin plants like bamboo ○ *a field of sugar cane* **2.** a walking stick cut from the stem of some types of plant ○ *She was leaning heavily on a cane as she walked up the path.*

canine /ˈkeɪnaɪn/ *adj* referring to dogs ○ *Dogs should be vaccinated against various canine illnesses.*

canister /ˈkænɪstə/ *noun* a round metal container for gas, etc.

cannabis /ˈkænəbɪs/ *noun* a drug that is usually smoked for pleasure ○ *In some countries, the sale of cannabis has been legalised.*

canned /kænd/ *adj* preserved in a tin or can

cannibal /ˈkænɪb(ə)l/ *noun* a person who eats people

cannon /ˈkænən/ *noun* a large gun ○ *The sailors hauled a huge cannon across the ship's deck.*

① **cannot** /ˈkænɒt/ *verb* the negative of **can**

③ **canoe** /kəˈnuː/ *noun* a boat with two pointed ends, which is moved forwards by one or more people using long pieces of wood ○ *She paddled her canoe across the lake.* ■ *verb* (**canoes, canoeing, canoed**) to travel in a canoe ○ *They canoed down the river.*

③ **can opener** /ˈkæn ˌəʊp(ə)nə/ *noun* a tool for opening cans

canopy /ˈkænəpi/ *noun* **1.** a cloth cover or light roof over a small area such as a door, window or bed ○ *The porch is covered with a glass canopy.* ○ *The Queen's bedroom is furnished with a 17th-century canopy bed.* **2.** the top parts of a group of trees when considered as a single mass ○ *The trees join to form a canopy over the terrace of the restaurant.*

① **can't** /kɑːnt/ *contr* cannot

cantaloupe /ˈkæntəluːp/, **cantaloup** *noun* a type of melon with pink flesh

③ **canteen** /kænˈtiːn/ *noun* a self-service restaurant for the people who work in a building such as an office block or factory ○ *The food in the office canteen is awful, I prefer to bring my own sandwiches.*

canter /ˈkæntə/ *noun* the movement of a horse when it runs fairly fast ○ *The horses were going through the park at a canter.* ■ *verb* (**canters, cantering, cantered**) to move at a canter ○ *My horse doesn't like cantering, it prefers to gallop.*

canvas /ˈkænvəs/ *noun* a thick cloth for making things such as tents, sails or shoes ○ *He was wearing a pair of old canvas shoes.*

canvass /ˈkænvəs/ (**canvasses, canvassing, canvassed**) *verb* to visit people to ask them to buy goods or to vote or to say what they think (NOTE: Do not confuse with **canvas**.)

canyon /ˈkænjən/, **cañon** *noun* a deep valley with steep sides usually in North America

② **cap** /kæp/ *noun* **1.** a flat hat with a flat hard piece in front ○ *a baseball cap* ○ *an officer's cap with a gold badge* **2.** a lid which covers something ○ *a red pen with a black cap* ○ *Screw the cap back on the medicine bottle.*

③ **capability** /ˌkeɪpəˈbɪlɪti/ (*plural* **capabilities**) *noun* the practical ability to do something ○ *We have the capability to produce a better machine than this.*

② **capable** /ˈkeɪpəb(ə)l/ *adj* able to work well and to deal with problems ○ *She's an extremely capable secretary.* □ **capable of (doing) something** able to do something ○ *He isn't capable of running the conference without help.*

② **capacity** /kəˈpæsɪti/ *noun* **1.** an amount which something can hold ○ *This barrel has a larger capacity than that one.* ○ *The cinema was filled to capacity.* **2.** the amount of something that a machine or person can produce □ **to work at full capacity** to do as much work as possible **3.** the mental or physical ability to do something easily [~for] ○ *a capacity for hard work* **4.** the situation that someone is in or the job they have [~as] □ **acting in his capacity as manager** acting as a manager □ **speaking in an official capacity** speaking officially

cape /keɪp/ *noun* **1.** a long loose piece of clothing like a coat but without sleeves ○ *She wrapped her cape more tightly around her.* **2.** a piece of high land which sticks out into the sea ○ *We rounded the cape on June 21st at 8 a.m.*

capillary /kəˈpɪləri/ (*plural* **capillaries**) *noun* one of the very small tubes in the body which carry blood and other substances around the body

① **capital** /ˈkæpɪt(ə)l/ *noun* **1.** the main city of a country, usually where the government is ○ *The capital is in the eastern part of the country.* ○ *Madrid is the capital of Spain.* **2.** money which is invested ○ *a company with £10,000 capital* or *with a capital of £10,000.* **3.** *also* **capital letter** a letter written as A, B, C, D, etc., rather than a, b, c, d, etc.

capitalise /ˈkæpɪt(ə)laɪz/ (**capitalises, capitalising, capitalised**), **capitalize** (**capitalizes, capitalizing, capitalized**) *verb*

capitalism /ˈkæpɪt(ə)lɪz(ə)m/ *noun* an economic system in which industries and businesses are owned by people or companies and not by the state

capitalist /ˈkæpɪt(ə)lɪst/ *noun* **1.** a person who supports the theory of capitalism ○ *Capitalists are in favour of free enterprise.* **2.** a businessman who invests money in a business ○ *He's a young capitalist who is only twenty-one, but on the way to becoming a millionaire.*

capitalise on *phrasal verb* to take advantage of something

capital punishment /ˌkæpɪt(ə)l ˈpʌnɪʃmənt/ *noun* the act of killing someone as a punishment for a crime

Capitol Hill /ˌkæpɪt(ə)l 'hɪl/ *noun* the hill on which the Capitol stands, used to mean the US Legislature (*informal*)

capitulate /kə'pɪtjʊleɪt/ (**capitulates, capitulating, capitulated**) *verb* to say that you have lost in a situation such as a competition or a war (NOTE: + **capitulation** *n*)

cappuccino /ˌkæpʊ'tʃiːnəʊ/ *noun* an Italian coffee, with hot whipped milk and chocolate on top

capricious /kə'prɪʃəs/ *adj* not fixed or certain, likely to change

Capricorn /'kæprɪkɔːn/ *noun* one of the signs of the Zodiac, shaped like a goat, covering the period 22nd December to 19th January

capsize /kæp'saɪz/ (**capsizes, capsizing, capsized**) *verb* (*of boats*) to overturn

③ **captain** /'kæptɪn/ *noun* **1.** a person in charge of a team ○ *the England captain* ○ *The two captains shook hands at the beginning of the match.* **2.** a person in charge of a ship or aircraft ○ *The captain greeted us as we came on board.* ○ *Captain Smith is flying the plane.* **3.** a rank in the army above a lieutenant and below a major ○ *A lieutenant has to report to his captain.* (NOTE: When used as a title before a surname, it is spelt with a capital letter and is often written as **Capt.**) ■ *verb* (**captains, captaining, captained**) to be the captain of a team ○ *He has captained England three times.*

captaincy /'kæptɪnsi/ *noun* **1.** the position of being captain of a sports team ○ *Because of the scandal, I don't think he will get the England captaincy.* **2.** the rank of captain in the army or navy ○ *Although he had twenty years of service, he never got his captaincy.*

caption /'kæpʃən/ *noun* a phrase printed under a picture

captivate /'kæptɪveɪt/ (**captivates, captivating, captivated**) *verb* to attract someone's interest and attention

captivating /'kæptɪveɪtɪŋ/ *adj* attracting and holding somebody's attention

captive /'kæptɪv/ *noun* a prisoner ○ *The two captives were kept in total darkness for hours.*

captive audience /ˌkæptɪv 'ɔːdiəns/ *noun* a group of people who have to listen to what someone is saying because they cannot leave

captivity /kæp'tɪvɪti/ *noun* the situation of being kept in a place and not allowed to leave

captor /'kæptə/ *noun* a person who captures someone

③ **capture** /'kæptʃə/ (**captures, capturing, captured**) *verb* **1.** to take someone as a prisoner ○ *Four soldiers were captured in the attack.* **2.** to take something by force, especially in war ○ *They captured the enemy capital very quickly.*

① **car** /kɑː/ *noun* **1.** a small private motor vehicle for carrying people ○ *She's bought a new car.* ○ *He drove his car into the garage.* ○ *He goes to his office every morning by car.* **2.** *US* a carriage of a railway train ○ *Is there a restaurant car on the train?*

carafe /kə'ræf/ *noun* a glass container for serving wine or water

caramel /'kærəməl/ *noun* **1.** a sweet made with sugar and butter ○ *I'm a dentist, and I don't like seeing children eating caramel.* **2.** burnt sugar ○ *You can make caramel by heating sugar until it melts and burns.*

carat /'kærət/ *noun* **1.** a measure of the quality of gold. Pure gold is 24 carats. ○ *a 22-carat gold ring* **2.** a measure of the weight of precious stones ○ *a 5-carat diamond*

caravan /'kærəvæn/ *noun* a vehicle which you can live in, especially on holiday, and which, if small enough, can be attached to a car and pulled along ○ *We got stuck behind a caravan on a narrow mountain road.* ○ *We rent a caravan in a caravan park.*

③ **carbohydrate** /ˌkɑːbəʊ'haɪdreɪt/ *noun* a chemical substance containing carbon, hydrogen and oxygen, found in particular in sugar, potatoes and bread; it provides the body with energy

carbon /'kɑːbən/ *noun* a substance found in charcoal, soot or diamonds

carbonated /'kɑːbəneɪtɪd/ *adv* (*of a drink*) containing small bubbles of air

carbon copy /ˌkɑːbən 'kɒpi/ *noun* someone or something that is very similar to another person or thing

car boot sale /kɑː 'buːt seɪl/ *noun* an event organised in a large car park or sports field, where people bring things to sell in their cars

carburettor /kɑːbə'retə/ *noun* a part in a car engine which mixes fuel with air before it is put into the engine (NOTE: The US spelling is **carburetor**.)

carcass /'kɑːkəs/, **carcase** *noun* the body of a dead animal, especially one ready for the butcher

carcinogen /kɑː'sɪnədʒən/ *noun* a substance which produces cancer

carcinogenic /ˌkɑːsɪnə'dʒenɪk/ *adj* which produces cancer

① **card** /kɑːd/ *noun* **1.** a flat piece of stiff paper with a picture on one side, which you can send with a message ○ *They sent us a card from Italy.* ○ *How much does it cost to send a card to Australia?* ◊ **postcard 2.** a piece of stiff paper, folded so that a message can be written inside ○ *She sent me a lovely card on my birthday.* **3.** a piece of stiff paper with a picture or pattern on it, used to play games **4.** a piece of stiff paper with your name and address printed on it ○ *He gave me his business card.* ○ *I've lost my membership card.* **5.** a piece of stiff plastic used for payment ○ *Do you want to pay cash or with a card?* ■ *plural noun* **cards** the entertainment of playing games with a special set of cards with numbers or patterns on them □ **a game of cards** a period of playing with a special set of cards ◇ **on the cards** fairly likely to happen

cardboard /'kɑːdbɔːd/ *noun* thick card, often used for making boxes (NOTE: no plural: *some cardboard*; *a piece of cardboard*)

cardiac /'kɑːdiæk/ *adj* referring to the heart

cardiac arrest /ˌkɑːdiæk ə'rest/ *noun* a serious medical condition in which the heart muscle stops working

cardigan /'kɑːdɪgən/ *noun* a woollen jacket which buttons at the front

cardinal /'kɑːdɪn(ə)l/ *noun* **1.** one of the most important priests in the Catholic Church, after the Pope ○ *The cardinals meet in Rome to elect the Pope.* ○ *Cardinal Lamont has written an article in today's paper.* (NOTE: also used as a title before a surname: *Cardinal Wolsey*) **2.** a bright red bird, which comes from the southern United States

① **care** /keə/ *noun* **1.** serious and careful attention ○ *He handled the glass with great care.* □ **to take care** to be very careful ○ *Take care when you cross the road.* ○ *He took great care with the box of glasses.* ○ *Take care not to be late.* **2.** looking after someone ○ *the care of the elderly* □ **to take care of someone** to look after someone ○ *Will you take care of the children for the weekend for me?* ■ *verb* (**cares, caring, cared**) to be interested in something you think is important [~about/~what/why etc] ○ *She cares a lot about environmental issues.* ○ *I don't care if my car gets dirty.* ◇ **he couldn't care less** used to show that someone does not worry at all about something ○ *Paul couldn't care less about what we think – he's got his own plans.*

care for① *phrasal verb* **1.** to like someone or something ○ *I don't care for this music very much.* ○ *I met her once, but I didn't much care for her.* ○ *Would you care for another cup of coffee?* **2.** to look after people ○ *Nurses cared for the injured people after the accident.* ○ *People who have to care for their elderly relatives need extra help.*

② **career** /kə'rɪə/ *noun* the work someone does throughout their life [~as/~in] ○ *She is starting her career as a librarian.* ○ *He gave up a career in medicine and bought a farm.*

carefree /'keəfriː/ *adj* without any worries

① **careful** /'keəf(ə)l/ *adj* **1.** showing attention to details ○ *We are always very careful to include the most recent information.* ○ *The project needs very careful planning.* **2.** taking care not to make mistakes or cause harm ○ *Be careful not to make any noise – the baby is asleep.* ○ *She is very careful about what she eats.*

① **carefully** /'keəf(ə)li/ *adv* with great care or thought ○ *The holiday had been carefully planned* or *planned carefully.*

② **careless** /'keələs/ *adj* without any care or thought ○ *He is careless about his work.* ○ *He made several careless mistakes when he took his driving test.*

carelessly /'keələsli/ *adv* without taking care or thinking carefully

carelessness /'keələsnəs/ *noun* the fact of being careless or not thinking carefully

carer /'keərə/ *noun* someone who looks after an old or sick person, or children

caress /kə'res/ (**caresses, caressing, caressed**) *verb* to touch gently ○ *She gently caressed the baby's head.* (NOTE: + **caress** *n*)

caretaker /'keəteɪkə/ *noun* a person who looks after a building

cargo /'kɑːgəʊ/ *noun* goods carried on a ship or a plane

caricature /'kærɪkətjʊə/ *noun* a funny drawing or description which exaggerates a person's appearance ○ *He drew a caricature of the Prime Minister.* ○ *Her description of the office is nothing less than a caricature of the system.* (NOTE: + **caricature** *v*)

③ **caring** /'keərɪŋ/ *adj* kind and helpful ○ *a very caring person*

carjacking /ˈkɑːdʒækɪŋ/ *noun* the crime of attacking the driver of a car and stealing the car

carnage /ˈkɑːnɪdʒ/ *noun* a situation in which many people are killed

carnal /ˈkɑːn(ə)l/ *adj* referring to the body (*formal*)

carnation /kɑːˈneɪʃ(ə)n/ *noun* a red, pink or white flower with a strong pleasant smell

carnival /ˈkɑːnɪv(ə)l/ *noun* a festival, often with music, dancing and eating in the open air

carnivore /ˈkɑːnɪvɔː/ *noun* an animal which eats meat

carnivorous /kɑːˈnɪv(ə)rəs/ *adj* meat-eating

carol /ˈkærəl/ *noun* a traditional song, especially one sung at Christmas

carousel /ˌkærəˈsel/ *noun* **1.** a circular machine from which passengers collect their bags at an airport ○ *Baggage from flight AC1 is on carousel number three.* **2.** *US* a roundabout (NOTE: The British term is **merry-go-round**.)

① **car park** /ˈkɑː pɑːk/ *noun* a public place where you can leave a car when you are not using it

carpentry /ˈkɑːpɪntri/ *noun* the art of working with wood

③ **carpet** /ˈkɑːpɪt/ *noun* thick material for covering floors ○ *He spilt his coffee on our new white dining-room carpet.*

carpet-bomb /ˈkɑːpɪt bɒm/ (**carpet-bombs, carpet-bombing, carpet-bombed**) *verb* to destroy an area by dropping very many bombs on it

③ **carriage** /ˈkærɪdʒ/ *noun* **1.** one of the vehicles that are joined together to make a train ○ *Where's the first-class carriage on this train?* **2.** a vehicle, especially an old-fashioned one, that is pulled by a horse **3.** the cost of carrying goods, or the action of carrying goods ○ *Carriage is 15% of the total cost.* ○ *How much do they charge for carriage?*

carriageway /ˈkærɪdʒweɪ/ *noun* the surface of the road on which traffic moves

carried /ˈkærɪd/ past tense and past participle of **carry**

carrier /ˈkæriə/ *noun* **1.** a vehicle that takes people or things from one place to another, or a company with such vehicles **2.** a person who carries the germ of a disease without showing any signs of it, and who can infect others with it ○ *a hepatitis carrier* ○ *Hepatitis A is transmitted by a carrier through food or drink.*

carrier bag /ˈkæriə bæg/ *noun* a large paper or plastic bag with handles, for carrying shopping, often given by a shop, with the shop's name on it

carries /ˈkæriz/ 3rd person singular present of **carry**

carrot /ˈkærət/ *noun* **1.** a vegetable with a long orange root **2.** something good that persuades you to do something (*informal*) ○ *He was offered the carrot of a big pay rise to take on the new project.*

① **carry** /ˈkæri/ (**carries, carrying, carried**) *verb* **1.** to take something and move it to another place ○ *There was no lift, so they had to carry the beds up the stairs.* ○ *The plane was carrying 120 passengers.* ○ *That suitcase is too heavy for me to carry.* **2.** (*of sound*) to be heard at a distance ○ *The sound of the bells carries for miles.* ◇ **to get carried away** to become emotional or excited

carry forward *phrasal verb* (*in bookkeeping*) to take an amount or total on to the next page or column

carry on *phrasal verb* **1.** to continue doing something ○ *When the teacher came in, the students all carried on talking.* ○ *They carried on with their work right through the lunch hour.* **2.** to be very angry ○ *He carried on like anything when he saw his car had been towed away.*

carry out *phrasal verb* to do something, especially something that has been planned ○ *Doctors carried out tests on the patients.* ○ *The police are carrying out a search for the missing man.*

carte blanche /ˌkɑːt ˈblɑːntʃ/ *noun* permission given to someone to do whatever he or she wants ○ *We gave the architect carte blanche to design the bridge.* ○ *He has carte blanche to act on behalf of the government.*

cartel /kɑːˈtel/ *noun* a group of companies which try to fix the price of something

cartilage /ˈkɑːtɪlɪdʒ/ *noun* the thick substance which lines the joints in your body or which forms part of the structure of an organ

carton /ˈkɑːt(ə)n/ *noun* a container made of cardboard

③ **cartoon** /kɑːˈtuːn/ *noun* **1.** a film made of moving drawings ○ *I like watching Tom and Jerry cartoons.* **2.** a funny, often political, drawing in a newspaper ○ *He draws a cartoon for the 'Evening Standard'.*

cartridge /ˈkɑːtrɪdʒ/ *noun* a container for something that fits into a piece of equipment to be used ○ *an ink cartridge* ○ *an explosive cartridge*

carve /kɑːv/ (**carves, carving, carved**) *verb* **1.** to cut up a large piece of meat at a meal ○ *Who's going to carve?* ○ *Father sat at the end of the table, carving a chicken.* **2.** to make a shape by cutting stone or wood ○ *He carved a bird out of wood.* ○ *Chips of stone flew all over the studio as he was carving the statue.*

carving /ˈkɑːvɪŋ/ *noun* **1.** the act of cutting up cooked meat **2.** the art of cutting stone or wood into shapes ○ *Stone carving is an option at art school.* **3.** an object which has been made by carving ○ *He gave me a wood carving for my birthday.* ○ *The stone carvings in the old church date from the 15th century.*

car wash /ˈkɑː wɒʃ/ *noun* a place where cars are washed automatically

cascade /kæˈskeɪd/ (**cascades, cascading, cascaded**) *verb* to fall in large quantities ○ *pale pink roses cascading down the brick wall* (NOTE: + **cascade** *n*)

① **case** /keɪs/ *noun* **1.** a box with a handle, for carrying things such as your clothes when travelling ○ *She was still packing her case when the taxi came.* ○ *The customs made him open his case.* **2.** a special box for an object ○ *Put the gun back in its case.* ○ *I've lost my red spectacle case.* **3.** a large box for a set of goods to be sold ○ *He bought a case of wine.* **4.** a situation, or a way in which something happens ○ *It was a case of having made a poor choice.* ○ *In many cases, we cannot find the owner of the goods.* **5.** same as **court case** ◇ **in case** because something might happen ○ *It's still sunny, but I'll take my umbrella just in case.* ◇ **in any case 1.** whatever may happen ○ *We could move the cabinet upstairs or into the dining room, but in any case we'll need some help.* **2.** used to add something to a statement ◇ **in that case** if that happens or if that is the situation ○ *There is a strike on the underground – In that case, you'll have to take a bus.*

case study /ˈkeɪs ˌstʌdi/ *noun* the study of a certain group or institution or person over a long period of time

① **cash** /kæʃ/ *noun* money in coins and notes, not in cheques ○ *We don't keep much cash in the house.* ○ *I'd prefer to use up my spare cash, rather than pay with a credit card.*

cash in *phrasal verb* to make money from something ○ *The company cashed in on the huge interest in computer games.*

cashback /ˈkæʃbæk/ *noun* money from your bank account which you can get from a shop when you use your bank card to pay for goods

cash card /ˈkæʃ kɑːd/ *noun* a plastic card used to obtain money from a cash dispenser

③ **cash desk** /ˈkæʃ desk/ *noun* a place in a store where you pay for the goods you are buying

cash dispenser /ˈkæʃ dɪˌspensə/ *noun* a machine which gives out money when a special card is put in and instructions given

cashew /ˈkæʃuː/ *noun* a type of nut which you can eat

③ **cash flow** /ˈkæʃ fləʊ/ *noun* the rate at which money comes into and is paid out of a business

cashier /kæˈʃɪə/ *noun* a person who deals with money, e.g. in a bank or supermarket ○ *Ask the cashier if she can give you change.* ○ *Please pay the cashier.*

cash machine /ˈkæʃ məˌʃiːn/ *noun* same as **cash dispenser**

cashmere /ˈkæʃmɪə/ *noun* a soft wool that comes from goats ○ *Cashmere is soft, light and very warm.*

cashpoint /ˈkæʃˌpɔɪnt/ *noun* a place where there are cash dispensers (NOTE: The US term is **automated teller machine** or **ATM**.)

cash register /ˈkæʃ ˌredʒɪstə/ *noun* a machine which shows and adds the prices of things bought in a shop, with a drawer for keeping the money received

casing /ˈkeɪsɪŋ/ *noun* a hard covering which protects something

casino /kəˈsiːnəʊ/ (*plural* **casinos**) *noun* a building where you can gamble

casket /ˈkɑːskɪt/ *noun* **1.** a box for keeping jewels in ○ *The thief stole a casket from beside her bed.* **2.** *mainly US* a long wooden box in which a dead person is buried or cremated

casserole /ˈkæsərəʊl/ *noun* **1.** a covered dish used for cooking food in the oven **2.** food cooked in a covered dish in the oven ○ *chicken casserole* ○ *casserole of lamb*

cassette /kəˈset/ *noun* a plastic case containing magnetic tape which can be used for listening to words or music, or recording sounds ○ *Do you want it on cassette or CD?* ○ *He bought a cassette of folk songs.* ○ *We recorded the poems onto a cassette.*

cassette player /kə'set ˌpleɪə/ *noun* a machine which plays cassettes

③ **cast** /kɑːst/ *noun* all the actors in a play or film ○ *The film has an all-star cast.* ○ *After the first night the cast went out to celebrate in a restaurant.* ■ *verb* (**casts, casting, cast**) to choose actors for a play or film [~as] ○ *In his first film, he was cast as a soldier.*

cast off *phrasal verb* **1.** to untie the ropes holding a boat ○ *The boat is ready to cast off.* **2.** (*in knitting*) to remove the stitches from the needles so that your work is finished ○ *The scarf is long enough, all you have to do is to cast off.*

castaway /'kɑːstəweɪ/ *noun* a person who has been shipwrecked

caste /kɑːst/ *noun* (*in Hindu society*) a group of people who are born with the same social status

castigate /'kæstɪgeɪt/ (**castigates, castigating, castigated**) *verb* to punish, to criticise someone strongly (*formal*)

casting vote /ˌkɑːstɪŋ 'vəʊt/ *noun* a vote used by the person in charge of a meeting in a case where the numbers of votes for and against a proposal are equal

cast iron /ˌkɑːst 'aɪən/ *noun* iron which is shaped in a mould, not bent, and so breaks easily ○ *The pipes are made from cast iron, and are very solid.* ○ *Don't let the cast-iron pan soak in water as it will rust.* Compare **wrought iron**

③ **castle** /'kɑːs(ə)l/ *noun* a large building with strong walls built in the past for protection in war ○ *The Queen is spending the week at Windsor Castle.* ○ *The soldiers shut the castle gate.*

castrate /kæ'streɪt/ (**castrates, castrating, castrated**) *verb* to remove the testicles from a male animal (NOTE: + **castration** *n*)

casual /'kæʒuəl/ *adj* not formal

casually /'kæʒjʊəli/ *adv* in an informal way ○ *He casually mentioned that he had got married last Saturday.*

casualty /'kæʒuəlti/ (*plural* **casualties**) *noun* **1.** a person injured or killed in a battle or in an accident ○ *Casualties were taken to hospital by ambulance and helicopter.* ○ *The radio reported that there had been heavy casualties.* **2.** the Accident and Emergency department in a hospital ○ *The accident victim was rushed into casualty.*

① **cat** /kæt/ *noun* an animal with soft fur and a long tail, kept as a pet ○ *She asked her neighbours to feed her cat when she went on holiday.* ○ *Don't forget to get some tins of cat food.* ◇ **to let the cat out of the bag** to tell a secret (*informal*)

cataclysm /'kætəklɪz(ə)m/ *noun* a sudden event which causes a lot of damage or violence

③ **catalogue** /'kæt(ə)lɒg/ *noun* a list of things for sale or in a library or museum ○ *an office equipment catalogue* ○ *Look up the title in the library catalogue.* ■ *verb* to make a list of things that exist somewhere ○ *She spent months cataloguing the novelist's correspondence.*

catalyst /'kætəlɪst/ *noun* **1.** a substance which produces or helps a chemical process without itself changing ○ *an enzyme that acts as a catalyst in the digestive process* **2.** anything which helps something to take place [~for] ○ *The publication of the report acted as a catalyst for change.*

catapult /'kætəpʌlt/ *noun* a weapon consisting of a piece of strong material which can stretch, attached to a stick shaped like the letter 'Y', used for sending stones through the air ○ *He tried to kill birds with his catapult.*

cataract /'kætərækt/ *noun* **1.** a waterfall on a river ○ *the cataracts on the Nile* **2.** a medical condition in which the lens of the eye gradually becomes covered with a white layer and you lose the ability to see ○ *He has developed a cataract in his right eye.* ○ *The operation to remove the cataract went smoothly.*

③ **catastrophe** /kə'tæstrəfi/ *noun* a sudden violent or harmful event

① **catch** /kætʃ/ *verb* (**catches, catching, caught**) **1.** to take hold of something moving in the air ○ *Can you catch a ball with your left hand?* ○ *He managed to catch the glass before it hit the floor.* **2.** to take hold of something ○ *She caught him by the sleeve as he turned away.* ○ *As he slipped, he caught the rail to stop himself falling.* **3.** to get hold of an animal, especially in order to kill and eat it ○ *He sat by the river all day but didn't catch anything.* ○ *Our cat is no good at catching mice – she's too lazy.* **4.** to get on a vehicle such as a bus, plane or train before it leaves ○ *You will have to run if you want to catch the last bus.* ○ *He caught the 10 o'clock train to Paris.* **5.** to get an illness ○ *He caught a cold from his colleague.* **6.** to find someone doing something wrong ○ *She caught the boys stealing in her shop.* ○ *The police caught the burglar as he was climbing out of the window.* **7.** to hear something ○ *I didn't quite catch what you said.* ■ *noun* **1.** the action of taking and holding a ball as it moves through the air ○ *He made a marvellous catch.* ○ *I dropped an easy catch.* **2.** a hidden disadvantage ○ *It seems such a good deal, but there must be a catch in it somewhere.*

catch on *phrasal verb* **1.** to understand ○ *She caught on very quickly.* **2.** to become fashionable ○ *I don't see silver hair catching on here.*

catch up *phrasal verb* to move to the same level as someone who is in front of you

catch 22 /ˌkætʃ ˌtwenti ˈtuː/ *noun* a circle of events which you cannot escape from

catch-all /ˈkætʃ ɔːl/ *noun* something that covers a wide range of possibilities, meanings, ideas or situations

catching /ˈkætʃɪŋ/ *adj* (*of an illness*) likely to spread from one person to another

catchment area /ˈkætʃmənt ˌeəriə/ *noun* **1.** land from which a river gets its water **2.** an area round a school from which all students must come ○ *We are moving to be in the catchment area of a good school.*

catch phrase /ˈkætʃ freɪz/ *noun* a popular phrase, usually connected with an entertainer or advertisement

categorically /ˌkætəˈɡɒrɪkli/ *adv* definitely

categorise /ˈkætɪɡəraɪz/ (**categorises, categorising, categorised**), **categorize** *verb* to put into classes or categories

② **category** /ˈkætɪɡ(ə)ri/ (*plural* **categories**) *noun* one of the groups that people, animals or things are divided into in a formal system ○ *We grouped the books into categories according to subject.*

③ **catering** /ˈkeɪtərɪŋ/ *noun* the act or practice of supplying food and drink

③ **caterpillar** /ˈkætəpɪlə/ *noun* a small long insect with many legs, which develops into a butterfly ○ *Caterpillars have eaten most of the leaves on our trees.*

catfish /ˈkætfɪʃ/ *noun* a fish with long hairs around its mouth

catharsis /kəˈθɑːsɪs/ *noun* a situation or occasion in which you get rid of strong emotional feelings, e.g. through a particular experience

③ **cathedral** /kəˈθiːdrəl/ *noun* the largest and the most important church in an area

③ **catholic** /ˈkæθ(ə)lɪk/ *adj* having an interest in or liking for many different things ○ *His interests have always been quite catholic.*

Catholic /ˈkæθ(ə)lɪk/ *noun* a member of the Roman Catholic Church

cattle /ˈkæt(ə)l/ *plural noun* animals such as cows and bulls which farmers keep for milk or meat

catty /ˈkæti/ *adj* making unpleasant remarks about someone

catwalk /ˈkætwɔːk/ *noun* **1.** a long raised area down which models walk to show off clothes ○ *The model on the catwalk gave a twirl of her skirt.* ○ *Fashion editors stared at the models on the catwalk.* **2.** an open metal structure for people to walk on, built along the outside of a ship or tall building ○ *He stepped confidently onto the catwalk.*

Caucasian /kɔːˈkeɪziən/ *noun* somebody who has white skin or who is of European origin

① **caught** /kɔːt/ past tense and past participle of **catch**

cauldron /ˈkɔːldrən/ *noun* a large deep pan for cooking (NOTE: The US spelling is **caldron**.)

cauliflower /ˈkɒliflaʊə/ *noun* a vegetable with hard white flowers, which are eaten cooked

① **cause** /kɔːz/ *noun* **1.** something which makes something else happen ○ *What is the main cause of traffic accidents?* ○ *The police tried to find the cause of the fire.* **2.** an aim, organisation or idea which people support ○ *She is fighting for the cause of working mothers.* ■ *verb* (**causes, causing, caused**) to make something happen ○ *The accident caused a traffic jam on the motorway.* ○ *The sudden noise caused her to drop the cup she was carrying.*

causeway /ˈkɔːzweɪ/ *noun* a road or path built up on a bank above wet ground or water

caution /ˈkɔːʃ(ə)n/ *noun* **1.** care ○ *The steps are very slippery – please proceed with great caution.* **2.** a warning not to do something again ○ *The magistrate let him off with a caution.* ■ *verb* (**cautions, cautioning, cautioned**) to warn [~that/~against] ○ *He cautioned them that the strategy had several risks.* ○ *The doctor cautioned him against working too hard.*

cautious /ˈkɔːʃəs/ *adj* not willing to take risks ○ *She's a very cautious driver.*

cavalry /ˈkæv(ə)lri/ *noun* soldiers riding on horses

cave /keɪv/ *noun* a large underground hole in rock or earth ○ *When the tide went out we could explore the cave.*

caveat /ˈkæviæt/ *noun* a warning, especially against doing something

caveman /ˈkeɪvmæn/ (*plural* **cavemen**) *noun* one of the people who lived thousands of years ago in caves

cavern /ˈkævən/ *noun* a very large cave

cavernous /ˈkævənəs/ *adj* with a very large inside space, like a cavern

cavity /ˈkævɪti/ (*plural* **cavities**) *noun* a hole or space ○ *The jewellery was discovered hidden in a cavity in the wall.*

CCTV /ˌsiː siː tiː ˈviː/ *abbr* closed-circuit television

CD a hard, round piece of plastic which can hold a large amount of music or computer information ○ *I don't like his new CD – do you?* ○ *You can get it on CD or cassette.*

CD burner /ˌsiː ˈdiː ˌbɜːnə/ *noun* alternative for CD writer

CD player /ˌsiː ˈdiː ˌpleɪə/ *noun* a machine which plays CDs

② **CD-ROM** /ˌsiː diː ˈrɒm/ *noun* a small plastic disc used as a high capacity ROM storage device which can store 650Mb of data. Full form **compact disc read only memory**

CD-RW /ˌsiː diː ɑː ˈdʌb(ə)ljuː/ *abbr* compact disc rewritable

CD writer /ˌsiː ˈdiː ˌraɪtə/ *noun* a piece of equipment used to record data permanently onto a compact disc

③ **cease** /siːs/ (**ceases, ceasing, ceased**) *verb* to stop, or to stop doing something (*formal*) □ **to cease to exist** to stop being in existence ○ *The pub on the corner ceased to exist some time ago.*

ceasefire /ˈsiːsfaɪə/ *noun* an agreement to stop shooting in a war

ceaseless /ˈsiːsləs/ *adj* without stopping

cedar /ˈsiːdə/ *noun* **1.** a large tree whose leaves do not fall off in winter ○ *There is a large cedar in front of the house.* **2.** the wood from this tree ○ *a cedar chest* ○ *Cedar wood has a pleasant smell.*

cede /siːd/ (**cedes, ceding, ceded**) *verb* to give up something, especially power or land, to someone else (*formal*)

③ **ceiling** /ˈsiːlɪŋ/ *noun* the solid part of a room that is above you ○ *He's so tall, he can easily touch the ceiling.* ○ *Flies can walk on the ceiling.* ○ *He painted the kitchen ceiling.* ○ *Watch out when you go into the bedroom – it has a very low ceiling.*

celeb /səˈleb/ *noun* a celebrity (*informal*)

③ **celebrate** /ˈselɪbreɪt/ (**celebrates, celebrating, celebrated**) *verb* to have a party, or do special things because something good has happened, or because of something that happened at a particular time in the past ○ *Our team won, so we're all going out to celebrate.* ○ *They celebrated their wedding anniversary quietly at home with their children.*

celebrated /ˈselɪbreɪtɪd/ *adj* very famous

③ **celebration** /ˌselɪˈbreɪʃ(ə)n/ *noun* **1.** a party or festival ○ *We had my birthday celebration in the local pub.* ○ *After our team won, the celebrations went on late into the night.* **2.** the activity of celebrating something ○ *a time of celebration* □ **in celebration of something** as an act of celebrating something ○ *an exhibition in celebration of the opening of the new gallery*

③ **celebrity** /sɪˈlebrəti/ (*plural* **celebrities**) *noun* a famous person ○ *The theatre was packed with celebrities from the acting world.* ○ *We hope the new supermarket is going to be opened by a TV celebrity.*

celery /ˈseləri/ *noun* a plant with a white or green stem, eaten as a vegetable or raw in a salad

celestial body /səˌlestiəl ˈbɒdi/ *noun* a star, planet, moon or other natural body in the sky

celibate /ˈselɪbət/ *adj* not having sex, e.g. for religious reasons

① **cell** /sel/ *noun* **1.** a small room in a building such as a prison or monastery ○ *He was arrested in the centre of town and spent the night in the police cells.* **2.** the basic unit of a living thing ○ *You can see the cancer cells under a microscope.* (NOTE: Do not confuse with **sell**.)

③ **cellar** /ˈselə/ *noun* an underground room, or rooms under a house (NOTE: Do not confuse with **seller**.)

cello /ˈtʃeləʊ/ (*plural* **cellos**) *noun* a large stringed musical instrument smaller than a double bass (NOTE: + **cellist** *n*)

cellular /ˈseljʊlə/ *adj* **1.** relating to the cells of an organism **2.** relating to mobile phones

cellular phone /ˌseljʊlə ˈfəʊn/ *noun* a mobile phone that works from a series of radio stations all over the country

cellulite /ˈseljʊlaɪt/ *noun* deposits of fat under the skin, especially in the thighs and buttocks

celluloid /ˈseljʊlɔɪd/ *noun* the thin plastic film which was used in the past for making films

③ **Celsius** /ˈselsiəs/ *noun* a scale of temperature where the freezing point of water is 0° and the boiling point is 100° ○ *The temperature outside is only 6°C (say 'six* *degrees Celsius'). ○ What is 75° Fahrenheit in Celsius?* (NOTE: used in many countries, but not in the USA, where the Fahrenheit system is still preferred. It is usually written as a **C** after the degree sign: *32°C* (say: 'thirty-two degrees Celsius'). It was formerly called **centigrade**.)

Celt /kelt/ *noun* one of an ancient people who lived in parts of Western Europe, e.g. in Scotland, Ireland, Wales and Brittany

Celtic /ˈkeltɪk/ *adj* referring to ancient or modern Celts

cement /sɪˈment/ *noun* grey powder used in building, which is mixed with water and dries hard ○ *He was mixing cement to make a path round the house.*

③ **cemetery** /ˈsemət(ə)ri/ (*plural* **cemeteries**) *noun* an area of ground where the bodies of dead people are buried

censor /ˈsensə/ (**censors, censoring, censored**) *verb* to read books or plays, to watch films, videos or TV programmes to see if they are fit to be published or shown, or to change them, or to say that they cannot be shown or published ○ *The film was censored before being shown on TV.* ○ *He was accused of censoring the article.* (NOTE: + **censor** *n*)

censorship /ˈsensəʃɪp/ *noun* the action to prevent books or newspapers from being published or remove parts of them

censure /ˈsenʃə/ (**censures, censuring, censured**) *verb* to criticise severely (*formal*) ○ *The Opposition put forward a motion to censure the Government.* ○ *The borough architect was censured for failing to consult the engineers.* (NOTE: + **censure** *n*)

census /ˈsensəs/ (*plural* **censuses**) *noun* an official count of a country's population

① **cent** /sent/ *noun US* a small coin of which there are 100 in a dollar ○ *The stores are only a 25-cent bus ride away.* ○ *They sell oranges at 99 cents each.* (NOTE: Do not confuse with **sent, scent**. **Cent** is usually written **c** in prices: **25c**, but not when a dollar price is mentioned: **$1.25**.)

centenary /senˈtiːnəri/ *noun* a hundredth anniversary

centennial /senˈteniəl/ *adj* referring to a centenary ○ *Our college is getting ready for the centennial celebrations next month.*

center /ˈsentə/ *noun, verb* US spelling of **centre**

centilitre /ˈsentɪliːtə/ *noun* a unit of volume equal to one hundredth of a litre (NOTE: The US spelling is **centiliter**.)

③ **centimetre** /ˈsentɪmiːtə/ *noun* a measure of length equal to one hundredth of a metre (NOTE: The US spelling is **centimeter**.)

centipede /ˈsentɪpiːd/ *noun* an insect with a large number of legs

① **central** /ˈsentrəl/ *adj* **1.** in the middle of something ○ *The hall has one central pillar.* **2.** conveniently placed for shops and other facilities ○ *His offices are very central.*

central government /ˌsentrəl ˈɡʌv(ə)nmənt/ *noun* the main government of a country, as opposed to local government

central heating /ˌsentrəl ˈhiːtɪŋ/ *noun* a system of providing heating for a whole house from one main heater and radiators in the various rooms

centralise /ˈsentrəlaɪz/ (**centralises, centralising, centralised**), **centralize** *verb* to organise from a central point

central nervous system /ˌsentrəl ˈnɜːvəs ˌsɪstəm/ *noun* the brain and the spinal cord which link together all the nerves

① **centre** /ˈsentə/ *noun* **1.** the middle of something ○ *chocolates with coffee cream centres* ○ *They planted a rose bush in the centre of the lawn.* ○ *The town centre is very old.* **2.** a large building containing several different sections ○ *an army training centre* **3.** an important place for something [~for] ○ *the regional centre for management training* ■ *verb* (**centres, centring, centred**) to put something in the middle ○ *Make sure you centre the title on the page.* (NOTE: The US spelling is **center**.)

centre around, centre round, centre on, centre upon *verb* to concentrate on something or someone ○ *Our report centres on some aspects of the sales team.*

centrepiece /ˈsentəˌpiːs/ *noun* **1.** the main part of a decoration on a table ○ *A bowl of fruit will be fine as a centrepiece on the dining table.* **2.** the main part of a policy ○ *The project is the centrepiece of the government's policy on pensions.* (NOTE: [all senses] The US spelling is **centerpiece**.)

① **century** /ˈsentʃəri/ (*plural* **centuries**) *noun* one hundred years (NOTE: The number of a century is always one more than the date number, so the period from 1900 to 1999 is the 20th century, and the period starting in the year 2000 is the 21st century.)

CEO *abbr* chief executive officer

ceramic /sə'ræmɪk/ *adj* made from clay which has been baked at a high temperature

ceramics /sə'ræmɪks/ *noun* the art of making objects such as cups or plates from clay ○ *She is taking a course in ceramics at the local art college.*

③ **cereal** /'sɪəriəl/ *noun* **1.** a food made from wheat or similar plants and eaten for breakfast ○ *How much milk do you want on your cereal?* (NOTE: Do not confuse with **serial**.) **2.** a grain crop such as wheat or corn

cerebral palsy /ˌserəbrəl 'pɔːlzi/ *noun* a medical condition of the brain that makes it difficult to control speech and movements of the body

ceremonial /ˌserɪ'məʊniəl/ *adj* referring to a ceremony ○ *A guard of naval officers carrying their ceremonial swords.* ○ *The ceremonial coach is used in the Lord Mayor's Parade.* ■ *noun* a way of performing a ceremony ○ *The ceremonial for the burial of the dead is laid out in the prayer book.*

ceremony /'serɪməni/ *noun* an important official occasion when something special is done in public ○ *They held a ceremony to remember the victims of the train crash.* ◇ **to stand on ceremony** to be formal and not relaxed ○ *Don't stand on ceremony.* ◇ **without ceremony** in an informal and often impolite way

① **certain** /'sɜːt(ə)n/ *adj* **1.** sure about something ○ *Are you certain that you locked the door?* ○ *I'm not certain where she lives.* **2.** definitely going to happen ○ *Our team is certain to win the prize.* **3.** some ○ *There are certain things I feel I need to say to you.* ○ *Certain plants can make you ill if you eat them.* ◇ **to make certain that** to do something in order that something else will definitely happen ○ *He put the money in his safe to make certain that no one could steal it.*

① **certainly** /'sɜːt(ə)nli/ *adv* **1.** (*after a question or order*) of course ○ *Can you give me a lift to the station? – Certainly.* ○ *Tell him to write to me immediately. – Certainly, sir.* ○ *Give me a kiss. – Certainly not!* **2.** definitely ○ *She certainly impressed the judges.* ○ *He certainly knows how to score goals.*

③ **certainty** /'sɜːt(ə)nti/ (*plural* **certainties**) *noun* **1.** being certain ○ *I can't tell who won with any certainty – it was a photo-finish.* ○ *There is no certainty that the weather will stay fine for the whole of next week.* **2.** a sure or certain thing ○ *Fine weather in November is not an absolute certainty.*

③ **certificate** /sə'tɪfɪkət/ *noun* an official document which proves or shows something ○ *She has been awarded a certificate for swimming.* ○ *He has a certificate of aptitude in English.*

certify /'sɜːtɪfaɪ/ (**certifies, certifying, certified**) *verb* **1.** to make an official statement in writing ○ *The document is certified as a true copy.* ○ *He was certified dead on arrival at hospital.* **2.** to send a patient to a mental hospital (*old*) ○ *His parents had him certified.*

cervical /'sɜːvɪk(ə)l/ *adj* **1.** referring to the neck ○ *The bones in the neck are the seven cervical vertebrae.* **2.** referring to the cervix of the womb ○ *What can be done to prevent cervical cancer?* ○ *In your case, you should have a cervical smear test every year.*

cervix /'sɜːvɪks/ (*plural* **cervixes** or **cervices**) *noun* the neck of the womb, the narrow lower part of the uterus leading into the vagina ○ *Cancer of the cervix may not show any symptoms for a very long time.*

cessation /se'seɪʃ(ə)n/ *noun* the process of stopping

CFC *abbr* chlorofluorocarbon, a compound of fluorine and chlorine ○ *CFCs contribute to the destruction of the ozone layer.* ○ *When CFCs are released into the atmosphere, they rise slowly taking about seven years to reach the stratosphere.*

chafe /tʃeɪf/ (**chafes, chafing, chafed**) *verb* to rub something and make it sore

② **chain** /tʃeɪn/ *noun* **1.** a series of metal rings joined together ○ *She wore a gold chain round her neck.* ○ *He stopped when the chain came off his bike.* **2.** a series of businesses such as shops, restaurants or hotels which belong to the same company ○ *a chain of shoe shops* ○ *a chain of hotels* or *a hotel chain* ■ *verb* (**chains, chaining, chained**) to attach with a chain ○ *I chained my bike to the lamppost.*

chain reaction /ˌtʃeɪn ri'ækʃən/ *noun* a series of reactions which follow on from an event

chain store /'tʃeɪn stɔː/ *noun* one of a series of shops owned by the same company

① **chair** /tʃeə/ *noun* **1.** a piece of furniture with a back, which you can sit on **2.** the person who is in charge of a meeting ○ *Please address all your comments to the chair.* □ **in the chair** the position of controlling what happens at a meeting ○ *Mrs*

Smith was in the chair for our first meeting. □ **to take the chair** to be the person controlling a meeting ○ *Mr Jones usually takes the chair at the monthly finance meeting.* ■ *verb* (**chairs, chairing, chaired**) to be the person controlling what happens at a meeting ○ *The meeting was chaired by Mrs Smith.*

① **chairman** /ˈtʃeəmən/ (*plural* **chairmen**) *noun* the person who controls what happens at a meeting ○ *Mrs Jones was the chairman at the meeting.* (NOTE: Many people prefer to say **chair** or **chairperson** because **chairman** suggests that the person is a man.)

chairmanship /ˈtʃeəmənʃɪp/ *noun* the position of being a chairman

chairperson /ˈtʃeəpɜːs(ə)n/ (*plural* **chairpersons**) *noun* the person who controls what happens at a meeting

chairwoman /ˈtʃeəwʊmən/ (*plural* **chairwomen**) *noun* a woman who controls what happens at a meeting

chalet /ˈʃæleɪ/ *noun* a small house, usually made of wood, often one where people stay for a holiday

chalk /tʃɔːk/ *noun* **1.** a type of soft white rock **2.** a stick of a hard white or coloured substance used for writing on a board, e.g. in a classroom ○ *He wrote the dates on the board in coloured chalk.*

chalk up *phrasal verb* to achieve a score or a victory

chalkboard /ˈtʃɔːkbɔːd/ *noun* a dark board which you can write on with chalk, especially on the wall of a classroom

chalky /ˈtʃɔːki/ *adj* like chalk in colour or feel, or containing chalk

② **challenge** /ˈtʃælɪndʒ/ *noun* **1.** a difficult test of someone's skill or strength [~for/~to] ○ *It's a difficult job, but I enjoy the challenge.* ○ *The race will be quite a challenge for me.* ○ *The strike is another challenge to the authority of the government.* □ **to pose** or **present a challenge to someone** to be extremely difficult to do ○ *Getting the piano up the stairs will pose a challenge to the helpers.* **2.** an attempt to win a fight or competition ○ *a challenge for the world title* **3.** an action that shows there are doubts about the truth, accuracy or legality of something [~to/over] ○ *a challenge over her claim on the property* ■ *verb* (**challenges, challenging, challenged**) **1.** to issue an invitation to a contest **2.** to ask someone to prove that they are right ○ *When challenged, he admitted that he had seen her get into a car.* ○ *The committee's conclusions have been challenged by other experts.* ◇ **to take up the challenge 1.** to accept an invitation to take part in a contest ○ *Our team took up the challenge to play another game.* **2.** to decide to prove that you are right about something or able to do something difficult ○ *She decided to take up the challenge of being the first woman to complete the course.*

challenged /ˈtʃælɪndʒd/ *adj* **1.** unable to do a particular activity easily, especially because of physical or mental disadvantages **2.** not having a particular quality (*humorous*) ○ *a scientifically challenged (=not accurate according to science) account of the new cancer treatment*

challenging /ˈtʃælɪndʒɪŋ/ *adj* **1.** difficult to do or achieve but giving a feeling of satisfaction ○ *a challenging job* **2.** refusing to accept someone's authority or the usual way of doing something ○ *challenging behaviour*

③ **chamber** /ˈtʃeɪmbə/ *noun* **1.** an official room **2.** an empty space inside the heart ○ *Blood collects inside the chambers of the heart and is then pumped out.* **3.** a space in a part of a machine, especially one of the spaces for bullets in a gun

chambermaid /ˈtʃeɪmbəmeɪd/ *noun* a woman who cleans bedrooms in a hotel

chamber music /ˈtʃeɪmbə ˌmjuːzɪk/ *noun* music for a few instruments which can be played in a small room

champ /tʃæmp/ *noun* the winner of a competition, especially in sport (*informal*) ○ *He's the champ!*

champagne /ʃæmˈpeɪn/ *noun* a sparkling white wine from the northeast of France

② **champion** /ˈtʃæmpiən/ *noun* **1.** the best one in a particular competition [~in] ○ *a champion swimmer* ○ *He's the world champion in the 100 metres.* **2.** a person who strongly supports something or someone ○ *a champion of free city centre transport* ■ *verb* (**champions, championing, championed**) to support something or someone strongly ○ *They have been championing or championing the cause of children's rights for many years.*

② **championship** /ˈtʃæmpiənʃɪp/ *noun* a contest to find who is the champion ○ *The tennis championship was won by a boy from Leeds.*

① **chance** /tʃɑːns/ *noun* **1.** a possibility [~(that)] ○ *There is little chance of rain in August.* ○ *Is there a chance that we'll get home before 10 p.m.?* □ **a chance of doing**

something a possibility of doing something ○ *Has our team any chance of winning? – Yes, I think they have a good chance.* **2.** an opportunity [~for] ○ *Will there be a chance for a serious talk with her this week?* □ **a *or* the chance to do something** an opportunity to do something ○ *I wish I'd had the chance to visit South Africa.* **3.** luck or accident [~(that)] ○ *The satisfactory outcome owed more to chance than to good planning.* ○ *It was pure chance that we met at the station.* ◇ **by chance** in a way that was not planned or expected ○ *It was quite by chance that we were travelling on the same bus.* ◇ **by any chance** perhaps ○ *Have you by any chance seen my glasses?*

③ **chancellor** /ˈtʃɑːns(ə)lə/ *noun* **1.** an important official ○ *He became chancellor of the university last year.* **2.** (*in Germany or Austria*) the head of the government, equivalent to Prime Minister

③ **Chancellor of the Exchequer** /ˌtʃɑːnsələr əv ðiː ɪksˈtʃekə/, **Chancellor** *noun* the chief finance minister in the British government (NOTE: In most countries, this is called the **Minister of Finance**; the American equivalent is the **Secretary of the Treasury**.)

chandelier /ˌʃændəˈlɪə/ *noun* a light fitting which hangs from the ceiling, with several branches for holding electric bulbs

① **change** /tʃeɪndʒ/ *verb* (**changes, changing, changed**) **1.** to become different, or make something different [~into] ○ *She's changed so much since I last saw her that I hardly recognised her.* ○ *He's changed into a successful executive since I last saw him.* ○ *Living in the country has changed their attitude towards towns.* □ **to change your mind** to have a different opinion about something ○ *I've changed my mind about taking the job.* ○ *You'll change your mind about the charity when you read this article.* **2.** to put on different clothes [~into/out of] ○ *I'm just going upstairs to change* or *to get changed.* ○ *We all changed into our sports gear.* **3.** to use or have something in place of something else [~for] ○ *She's recently changed her job* or *changed jobs.* ○ *Can we change our room for one with a view of the sea?* **4.** to give one country's money for another [~into/out of] ○ *We want to change some traveller's cheques.* ○ *I had to change £1,000 into dollars.* ■ *noun* **1.** an occasion on which something is changed ○ *There was a sudden change of plan.* ○ *We've seen a lot of changes over the years.* **2.** something different ○ *A glass of water is a nice change after all that coffee.We usually go on holiday in summer, but this year we're taking a winter holiday for a change.* ○ *A change of scenery will do you good.* **3.** money in coins ○ *I need some change for the parking meter.* ○ *Have you got change for a £5 note?* **4.** money which you get back when you have given more than the correct price ○ *It cost £3.50, so that's £1.50 change from £5.* ○ *The shopkeeper gave me the wrong change.* ◇ **a change for the better** an improvement ◇ **a change of clothes** a set of clean clothes

change down *phrasal verb* to move to a lower gear when driving a car

change over *phrasal verb* **1.** to exchange places, positions, or roles **2.** (*in sports such as football*) to move to opposite ends of a playing field, usually halfway through a match

change up *phrasal verb* to move to a higher gear when driving a car

changeover /ˈtʃeɪndʒˌəʊvə/ *noun* **1.** a change from one thing to another [~from/~to] ○ *The changeover from the old system to the new one takes place at midnight.* **2.** (*in sports such as football*) the movement of teams to opposite ends of a playing field **3.** the passing of a baton in a relay race

changing room /ˈtʃeɪndʒɪŋ ruːm/ *noun* a room in a public place where you can change into or out of clothes

② **channel** /ˈtʃæn(ə)l/ *noun* **1.** a frequency band for radio or TV or a station using this band ○ *Shall we watch the new show on the other channel?* ○ *We're watching Channel 4.* **2.** a way in which information or goods are passed from one place to another ○ *The request will have to be processed through the normal channels.* **3.** a narrow passage along which water can flow **4.** a piece of water connecting two seas ○ *the English Channel* ■ *verb* (**channels, channelling, channelled**) to send something in a particular direction [~into] ○ *They are channelling their funds into research.*

chant /tʃɑːnt/ (**chants, chanting, chanted**) *verb* to sing or shout to a regular beat ○ *The crowds chanted anti-government slogans.* (NOTE: + **chant** *n*)

chaos /ˈkeɪɒs/ *noun* a state of confusion ○ *There was total chaos when the electricity failed.*

chaotic /keɪˈɒtɪk/ *adj* confused, without order

③ **chap** /tʃæp/ *noun* a man (*informal*) ○ *He's a really nice chap.* ○ *I bought it from a chap at work.*

chapel /ˈtʃæp(ə)l/ *noun* **1.** a room used as a church, e.g. in a hospital or airport **2.** a part of a large church

chaplain /ˈtʃæplɪn/ *noun* a priest attached to a private individual, to a prison or to one of the armed services

① **chapter** /ˈtʃæptə/ *noun* a division of a book ○ *The first chapter is rather slow, but after that the story gets exciting.* ○ *Don't tell me how it finishes – I'm only up to chapter three.*

① **character** /ˈkærɪktə/ *noun* **1.** the part of a person which makes them behave differently from all others ○ *He has a strong, determined character.* □ **a strong character** a person with special qualities such as determination or the ability to influence others **2.** a person in a play or novel ○ *The main character in the film is a woman with a fascinating history.* **3.** a set of features that make something different from other similar things **4.** an attractive quality ○ *The old house was full of character.* **5.** a letter or symbol used in writing or printing ○ *The book is printed in Chinese characters.* **6.** a person with particular qualities ○ *He's an interesting character.* □ **quite a character** or **a real character** an interesting and unusual person ○ *My first head teacher was quite a character.*

characterisation /ˌkærɪktəraɪˈzeɪʃ(ə)n/, **characterization** *noun* an indication of character

③ **characterise** /ˈkærɪktəraɪz/ (**characterises, characterising, characterised**), **characterize** *verb* **1.** to be a typical feature of something ○ *The northern coast is characterised by tall cliffs and tiny beaches.* **2.** to describe someone or something as a particular type of person or thing ○ *He didn't like to be characterised as weak and inefficient.*

② **characteristic** /ˌkærɪktəˈrɪstɪk/ *adj* typical ○ *You can recognise her by her characteristic way of walking.* ○ *The shape is characteristic of this type of flower.* (NOTE: something is characteristic **of** something) ■ *noun* a typical feature ○ *The two cars have very similar characteristics.*

charade /ʃəˈrɑːd/ *noun* a situation which has no meaning or which is simply a pretence ○ *Can you make any sense of this charade?* ○ *Why bother with this charade of consultation when we know that a decision has already been taken?*

charcoal /ˈtʃɑːkəʊl/ *noun* a black fuel formed from wood which has been burnt slowly, used for barbecues and grills ○ *We need a bag of charcoal for the barbecue.*

① **charge** /tʃɑːdʒ/ *noun* **1.** money which you have to pay for something [~for] ○ *There is no charge for delivery.* ○ *We make a small charge for rental.* **2.** a statement that someone has done something bad or wrong [~that] ○ *I completely reject the charge that I had these facts before I made the decision.* **3.** a claim by the police that someone has done something wrong ○ *He was in prison on a charge of trying to shoot a neighbour.* **4.** a sudden rush towards someone or something, especially as part of an attack ○ *The police stood firm against the charge of the crowd.* **5.** an electric current ○ *He was killed by an electric charge from the wires.* ■ *verb* (**charges, charging, charged**) **1.** to ask someone to pay [~for] ○ *The restaurant charged me £10 for two cups of coffee.* ○ *How much did the garage charge for mending the car?* **2.** (*of the police*) to say that someone has done something wrong [~with] ○ *She was charged with stealing the jewels.* **3.** to attack someone while running ○ *The police charged the rioters.* **4.** to run quickly and without care [~into/around etc] ○ *The children charged into the kitchen.* **5.** to give someone responsibility [~with] ○ *She was charged with the organisation of the society's conference.* **6.** to put electricity into a battery ○ *You can charge your phone battery overnight.* ◇ **in charge of something** in control of something ○ *Who's in charge here?* ○ *He is in charge of the sales department.* ◇ **to take charge of something** to start to be responsible for something ○ *She took charge of the class while the teacher was out of the room.*

charge card /ˈtʃɑːdʒ kɑːd/ *noun* a plastic card which you can use to buy things from a particular shop, and pay for them at a later date

charisma /kəˈrɪzmə/ *noun* personal appeal

charitable /ˈtʃærɪtəb(ə)l/ *adj* **1.** referring to a charity ○ *She was famous for her charitable work.* **2.** understanding, or less critical ○ *Commuters ought to be more charitable towards railway staff – they're only doing their best.*

② **charity** /ˈtʃærɪti/ *noun* an organisation which collects money to help the poor or to support some cause ○ *a medical charity*

charity shop /'tʃærɪti ʃɒp/ *noun* a shop run by a charity where you can take things such as old clothes and ornaments, which are then sold and the money given to the charity

charm /tʃɑːm/ *noun* **1.** attractiveness ○ *the charm of the Devon countryside* ○ *She has great personal charm.* **2.** an object which is supposed to have magical powers ○ *She wears a lucky charm round her neck.* ■ *verb* (**charms, charming, charmed**) **1.** to attract someone, or to make someone pleased ○ *He always manages to charm someone into helping him.* ○ *I was charmed by the village and surrounding area.* **2.** to use magic on someone or something ○ *The fairy charmed the trees to grow golden fruit.*

③ **charming** /'tʃɑːmɪŋ/ *adj* attractive

③ **chart** /tʃɑːt/ *noun* **1.** a map of the sea, a river or a lake ○ *You will need an accurate chart of the entrance to the river.* **2.** a diagram showing statistics ○ *A chart showing the increase in cases of lung cancer.* ■ *verb* (**charts, charting, charted**) **1.** to make a map of the sea, a river or lake ○ *He charted the coast of southern Australia in the 18th century.* **2.** to describe or make a diagram of something to show information ○ *The book charts the rise of the new political party.*

③ **charter** /'tʃɑːtə/ *noun* a legal document giving rights or privileges to a public organisation, a group of people, or a town ○ *the United Nations charter* ○ *a shoppers' charter* ○ *The university received its charter in 1846.* ■ *verb* (**charters, chartering, chartered**) to hire an aircraft, bus or boat for a particular trip ○ *We chartered a boat for a day trip to the island.*

chartered accountant /ˌtʃɑːtəd ə 'kaʊntənt/ *noun* a qualified accountant

charter flight /'tʃɑːtə flaɪt/ *noun* a flight in an aircraft which has been hired by the airline for a special occasion

③ **chase** /tʃeɪs/ *verb* (**chases, chasing, chased**) **1.** to go after someone in order to try to catch him or her ○ *The postman was chased by a dog.* ○ *They chased the burglars down the street.* **2.** to find out how work is progressing in order to try to speed it up ○ *We are trying to chase the accounts department for your cheque.* ■ *noun* an occasion on which you run after someone to try to catch them ○ *He was caught after a three-hour chase along the motorway.* □ **to give chase** to run after someone in order to try to catch him or her ○ *The robbers escaped and the police gave chase.*

chase up *phrasal verb* to find out how work is progressing in order to try to speed it up ○ *I'll chase it up for you on Monday.*

chasm /'kæz(ə)m/ *noun* **1.** a very big difference of opinion [~between] ○ *How can we bridge the chasm between the two sides in the dispute?* **2.** a very big crack in the ground ○ *The mountaineers were forced to turn back when they reached a chasm in the glacier.*

chassis /'ʃæsi/ *noun* the metal framework of a vehicle, usually including the wheels and engine ○ *The car's chassis was damaged in the accident.*

② **chat** /tʃæt/ *noun* an informal, friendly talk [~with/~about] ○ *I'd like to have a chat with you about your work.*

chat room /'tʃæt ruːm/ *noun* a facility exchanging messages by computer in real time

② **chat show** /'tʃæt ʃəʊ/ *noun* a TV show where famous people talk to the host

chatter /'tʃætə/ (**chatters, chattering, chattered**) *verb* **1.** *also* **chatter away** *or* **chatter on** to talk quickly and not seriously [~about] ○ *She was chattering about her holiday on the phone, not realising that the boss was standing behind her.* **2.** (*of top and bottom teeth*) to knock together quickly and noisily, because of cold or fear (NOTE: + **chatter** *n*)

chatty /'tʃæti/ *adj* **1.** liking to talk and share information in a friendly way ○ *She's a very chatty person, always stopping to gossip with anyone she meets.* **2.** informal ○ *He has a pleasant chatty style, which goes down well with readers of Saturday papers.*

chauffeur /'ʃəʊfə/ *noun* a person who is paid to drive a car for someone else ○ *The chauffeur brought the Rolls round to the door.*

chauvinist /'ʃəʊvɪnɪst/ *noun* a person who has a strong feeling of pride in his or her native country ○ *Chauvinists insist that British cooking is better than French.*

① **cheap** /tʃiːp/ *adj* not costing a lot of money ○ *If you want a cheap radio you ought to shop around.* ○ *Why do you go by bus? – Because it's cheaper than the train.* ○ *Buses are by far the cheapest way to travel.* ■ *adv* at a low price ○ *I bought them cheap in the local market.*

② **cheaply** /'tʃiːpli/ *adv* **1.** without spending much money ○ *cheaply made fur-*

niture ○ *You can live quite cheaply if you don't go out to eat in restaurants.* **2.** at a low price ○ *They were selling the last few bottles cheaply.*

③ **cheat** /tʃiːt/ *verb* (**cheats, cheating, cheated**) to act unfairly in order to be successful ○ *They are sure he cheated in his exam, but can't find out how he did it.* ■ *noun* a person who acts unfairly in order to win ○ *I won't play cards with him again, he's a cheat.*

① **check** /tʃek/ *noun* **1.** an examination or test [~for/~on] ○ *a routine check of the fire equipment* ○ *The police are carrying out checks for hidden passengers on all lorries arriving at the port.* **2.** US (*in a restaurant*) a bill ○ *I'll ask for the check.* ■ *verb* (**checks, checking, checked**) **1.** to make sure [~that/~if/whether/~with] ○ *Will you go and check that* or *if I locked the door, please.* ○ *I'd better check with the office before I make a firm decision.* **2.** to examine something to see if it is satisfactory [~through/~for/~if/whether/~that] ○ *You must have your car checked regularly.* ○ *Would you just check quickly through this report for any obvious mistakes.* ○ *I The children were very quiet so I went to check that nothing* or *if anything was wrong.* ◇ **in check** under control ○ *We must keep our spending in check.*

check in, check into *phrasal verb* **1.** (*at a hotel*) to arrive at a hotel and sign for a room ○ *He checked in at 12.15.* ○ *We checked into our hotel and then went on a tour of the town.* **2.** (*at an airport*) to give in your ticket to show you are ready to take the flight ○ *Please check in two hours before your departure time.*

check out *phrasal verb* **1.** (*at a hotel*) to leave and pay for a room ○ *We'd better check out before breakfast.* **2.** to take luggage out of safe keeping ○ *The ticket shows that he checked out his bag at 9.15.* **3.** to see if something is all right ○ *I thought I heard a noise in the kitchen – I'll just go and check it out.*

check up on *phrasal verb* to make sure that something has been done correctly

checked /tʃekt/ *adj* with a pattern of small squares

checkers /ˈtʃekəz/ *noun* US a game for two people played on a board with black and white squares and round pieces (NOTE: The British term is **draughts**.)

② **check-in** /ˈtʃek ɪn/ *noun* **1.** *also* **check-in desk** a place where passengers give in their tickets and bags for a flight ○ *Where's the check-in?* **2.** the procedure of dealing with passengers before a flight ○ *Check-in starts at 4.30pm.*

checklist /ˈtʃeklɪst/ *noun* a list of things which have to be done or dealt with before something can be done

② **checkout** /ˈtʃekaʊt/ *noun* (*in a supermarket*) a cash desk in a supermarket where you pay for the goods you have bought ○ *There were huge queues at the checkouts.*

checkpoint /ˈtʃekpɔɪnt/ *noun* a place on a road where the police or army check cars and people passing

② **checkup** /ˈtʃek ʌp/ *noun* **1.** a test to see if someone is fit ○ *He had a heart checkup last week.* **2.** a general examination of a machine ○ *I'm taking the car to the garage for its six-monthly checkup.*

Cheddar /ˈtʃedə/ *noun* a smooth hard light yellow cheese, originally from a village of this name in the west of England

② **cheek** /tʃiːk/ *noun* **1.** the part of the face on each side of the nose and below the eye ○ *a baby with red cheeks* **2.** rudeness ○ *He had the cheek to ask for more money.* ○ *I didn't like his cheek.* (NOTE: no plural in this sense)

cheekbone /ˈtʃiːkbəʊn/ *noun* a bone just below the eye which forms the prominent part of the cheek

cheekily /ˈtʃiːkɪli/ *adv* in a rude way

cheeky /ˈtʃiːki/ (**cheekier, cheekiest**) *adj* rude

③ **cheer** /tʃɪə/ *noun* a shout of praise or encouragement ○ *When he scored the goal a great cheer went up.*

cheer up③ *phrasal verb* to become happier, or make someone happier ○ *I'm sure I'll cheer up once the treatment is over.* ○ *She made him a meal to try to cheer him up.* ◇ **cheer up!** stop being unhappy ○ *Cheer up! It'll all be over tomorrow.*

② **cheerful** /ˈtʃɪəf(ə)l/ *adj* **1.** happy **2.** pleasant ○ *a cheerful smile* ○ *a bright cheerful room*

cheerleader /ˈtʃɪəliːdə/ *noun* a person who directs the cheering of a crowd

cheers /ˈtʃɪəz/ *interj* (*when drinking*) **1.** thank you! **2.** good health! ○ *They all lifted their glasses and said 'cheers!'.*

② **cheese** /tʃiːz/ *noun* a solid food made from milk ○ *She ordered a cheese omelette and chips.* ○ *At the end of the meal we'll have cheese and biscuits.* ◇ **'say cheese!'** used when asking people to smile when their photo is being taken (*informal*) ○ *The* *photographer got us all in a line and then told us to 'say cheese!'.*

cheeseburger /'tʃiːzbɜːɡə/ *noun* a hamburger with melted cheese on top

cheesecake /'tʃiːzkeɪk/ *noun* a tart with a sweet pastry base and cooked cream cheese on top, often covered with fruit

cheesy /'tʃiːzi/ *adj* cheap and without style

cheetah /'tʃiːtə/ *noun* an animal like a small leopard, with black spots on pale fur, which can run faster than any other animal

③ **chef** /ʃef/ *noun* a cook in a restaurant

③ **chemical** /'kemɪk(ə)l/ *noun* a substance which is formed by reactions between chemicals ○ *rows of glass bottles containing chemicals* ○ *Chemicals are widely used in agriculture.* ■ *adj* relating to chemistry ○ *If you add acid it, sets off a chemical reaction.*

③ **chemist** /'kemɪst/ *noun* **1.** a person who prepares and sells medicines ○ *Ask the chemist to give you something for indigestion.* **2.** a scientist who studies chemical substances ○ *She works as a chemist in a nuclear laboratory.*

③ **chemistry** /'kemɪstri/ *noun* the science of chemical substances and their reactions ○ *She's studying chemistry at university.* ○ *He passed his chemistry exam.*

chemotherapy /ˌkiːməʊ'θerəpi/, **chemo** *noun* the process of using chemical drugs to fight a disease, especially using toxic chemicals to destroy rapidly developing cancer cells

① **cheque** /tʃek/ *noun* a form asking a bank to pay money from one account to another [~for] ○ *I paid for the jacket by cheque.* ○ *He made out a cheque for £100 to Mr Smith.*

② **chequebook** /'tʃekbʊk/ *noun* a set of blank cheques attached together in a cover (NOTE: The US spelling is **checkbook**.)

cheque card /'tʃek kɑːd/, **cheque guarantee card** *noun* a plastic bank card that guarantees that a cheque will be paid by the bank

chequered /'tʃekəd/ *adj* **1.** laid out in a pattern of squares **2.** varied, with good and bad parts ○ *She had a chequered career in the police force.*

cherish /'tʃerɪʃ/ (**cherishes, cherishing, cherished**) *verb* **1.** to love ○ *The two people he cherished most died during the year.* ○ *She cherished the old ring given to her by her grandmother.* **2.** to cling onto a hope ○ *She still cherishes the hope of living in a warmer country.*

③ **cherry** /'tʃeri/ (*plural* **cherries**) *noun* a small sweet red or black fruit with a single hard seed in the middle, which grows on a tree

cherub /'tʃerəb/ *noun* a child who looks like an angel

③ **chess** /tʃes/ *noun* a game for two people played on a board with sixteen different-shaped pieces on each side (NOTE: no plural)

chessman /'tʃesmæn/ (*plural* **chessmen**), **chesspiece** *noun* a piece used in the game of chess

② **chest** /tʃest/ *noun* **1.** the top front part of the body, where the heart and lungs are ○ *If you have pains in your chest* or *if you have chest pains, you ought to see a doctor.* ○ *The doctor listened to the patient's chest.* ○ *She was rushed to hospital with chest wounds.* **2.** a measurement around the top part of the body just under the arms ○ *What's his chest size* or *measurement?* ○ *He has a 48-inch chest.* **3.** a piece of furniture, like a large box ○ *He keeps his old clothes in a chest under the bed.* ◇ **to get something off your chest** to speak honestly about a problem

chestnut /'tʃesnʌt/ *noun* **1.** ♦ **horse chestnut**, **sweet chestnut** (*trees*) **2.** the wood from a chestnut tree ○ *a chestnut table* **3.** a red-brown colour ○ *She has beautiful long chestnut hair.* **4.** an old joke ○ *His speech was just a series of not very amusing old chestnuts.*

chew /tʃuː/ (**chews, chewing, chewed**) *verb* to use your teeth to make something soft, usually so that you can swallow it [~on] ○ *You must chew your meat well, or you will get pains in your stomach.* ○ *The dog was lying in front of the fire chewing on a bone.*

chew up *phrasal verb* to ruin something by chewing it a lot

② **chewing gum** /'tʃuːɪŋ ɡʌm/ *noun* a sweet substance which you chew but do not swallow

chewy /'tʃuːi/ *adj* which must be chewed for a long time before being swallowed

chic /ʃiːk/ *adj* elegant and fashionable ○ *It's very chic these days to have an all white sports car.* ○ *We took our visitors to a very chic restaurant in Mayfair.*

chick /tʃɪk/ *noun* a baby bird, especially a baby hen

② **chicken** /'tʃɪkɪn/ *noun* **1.** a bird kept for its eggs and meat ○ *Chickens were running everywhere in the farmyard.* **2.** meat from a chicken ○ *We're having roast chick-*

en for lunch. ○ *Would you like another slice of chicken?* ○ *We bought some chicken sandwiches for lunch.* (NOTE: no plural: *some chicken*; *a piece of chicken*; *a slice of chicken*)

chicken out *phrasal verb* to decide not to do something because you are scared (*slang*)

chickpea /'tʃɪkpiː/ *noun* a round, pale yellow seed that can be cooked and eaten

② **chief** /tʃiːf/ *adj* most important ○ *He's the chief planner in the local authority.* ○ *What is the chief cause of air accidents?* ■ *noun* **1.** the person in control of a group of people or a business ○ *He's been made the new chief of our department.* ○ *The fire chief warned that the building was dangerous.* **2.** the leader of a specific group of people who share a culture and social system ○ *All the chiefs came together at a meeting.*

Chief Executive /ˌtʃiːf ɪg'zekjʊtɪv/ *noun* the main director who runs a company

chiefly /'tʃiːfli/ *adv* mainly ○ *The town is famous chiefly for its cathedral.*

chieftain /'tʃiːftən/ *noun* the leader of a tribe

chiffon /'ʃɪfɒn/ *noun* a type of very thin light silk material

① **child** /tʃaɪld/ (*plural* **children**) *noun* **1.** a young boy or girl ○ *There was no TV when my mother was a child.* ○ *A group of children were playing on the beach.* **2.** a son or daughter ○ *Whose child is that?* ○ *They have six children – two boys and four girls.* ○ *We have two adult children.*

child abuse /'tʃaɪld əˌbjuːs/ *noun* bad treatment of a child by an adult

childbirth /'tʃaɪldbɜːθ/ *noun* the act of giving birth to a child

childcare /'tʃaɪldkeə/ *noun* the care of young children

③ **childhood** /'tʃaɪldhʊd/ *noun* the time when someone is a child

childish /'tʃaɪldɪʃ/ *adj* **1.** silly or foolish **2.** like a child

childlike /'tʃaɪldlaɪk/ *adj* innocent like a child

childminder /'tʃaɪldmaɪndə/ *noun* a person who looks after children in their own home while the parents are working

childproof /'tʃaɪldpruːf/ *adj* difficult for a child to open or operate

children /'tʃɪldrən/ plural of **child**

child support /'tʃaɪld səˌpɔːt/ *noun* a sum of money paid by a divorced person to maintain the normal standard of living of his or her children

③ **chill** /tʃɪl/ *noun* **1.** a short illness causing a feeling of being cold and shivering ○ *You'll catch a chill if you don't wear a coat.* **2.** coldness ○ *The sun came up and soon cleared away the morning chill.* **3.** an atmosphere of gloom ○ *The death of the bride's father cast a chill over the wedding.* ■ *verb* (**chills, chilling, chilled**) **1.** to cool **2.** also **chill out** to relax and be calm (*informal*)

chill out *phrasal verb* to relax

chilli /'tʃɪli/ *noun* a dried seed pod of a type of pepper plant, used to make hot sauces (NOTE: The US spelling is **chili**.)

chilling /'tʃɪlɪŋ/ *adj* frightening

chilly /'tʃɪli/ (**chillier, chilliest**) *adj* quite cold

chime /tʃaɪm/ *noun* the ringing of bells ○ *The chimes of Big Ben start the BBC News.* ■ *verb* (**chimes, chiming, chimed**) (*of bells, doorbells or clocks*) to ring ○ *The church clock has just chimed four.*

chimney /'tʃɪmni/ *noun* a tall brick tube for taking smoke away from a fire

chimpanzee /tʃɪmpæn'ziː/, **chimp** *noun* a type of African ape

② **chin** /tʃɪn/ *noun* the front part of the bottom jaw ○ *She suddenly stood up and hit him on the chin.*

china /'tʃaɪnə/ *noun* things such as cups and plates made of decorated fine white clay (NOTE: no plural)

chink /tʃɪŋk/ *noun* **1.** a very small hole or crack ○ *Even a tiny chink in the curtains will let light into the darkroom.* **2.** a little noise of pieces of something hard hitting each other ○ *the chink of glasses on the waiter's tray*

chinos /'tʃiːnəʊz/ *plural noun* smart but casual thick cotton trousers

② **chip** /tʃɪp/ *noun* **1.** a long thin piece of potato fried in oil ○ *He ordered chicken and chips.* □ **fish and chips** a traditional British food, obtained from special shops, where portions of fish fried in batter are sold with chips ○ *We're having fish and chips for dinner.* **2.** *US* a thin slice of potato or other food, fried till crisp and eaten cold as a snack ○ *a packet of potato* or *corn chips* **3.** a small piece of something hard, such as wood or stone ○ *Chips of wood flew all over the studio as he was carving the statue.* **4.** a small piece of silicon able to store data, used in a computer. Same as **silicon chip** ■ *verb* (**chips, chipping, chipped**) to break a small piece off something hard ○ *He banged the cup down on the plate and chipped it.* ◇ **to have a chip on your shoulder** to feel constantly annoyed because you feel you have lost an advantage ○ *He's got a chip on his shoulder because his brother has a better job than he has.*

chip in *phrasal verb* **1.** to contribute ○ *We all chipped in for the present.* **2.** to interrupt ○ *My assistant suddenly chipped in with a comment.*

chipmunk /ˈtʃɪpmʌŋk/ *noun* a small North American animal, like a little striped squirrel

chiropodist /kɪˈrɒpədɪst/ *noun* a person who specialises in looking after feet

chirp /tʃɜːp/ (**chirps, chirping, chirped**) *verb* (*of birds or grasshoppers*) to call ○ *The little chicks were chirping in their box.* (NOTE: + **chirp** *n*)

chirpy /ˈtʃɜːpi/ *adj* bright and cheerful (*informal*)

chitchat /ˈtʃɪttʃæt/ *noun* conversations about things which are not important (*informal*)

chivalry /ˈʃɪvəlri/ *noun* politeness or courtesy

chives /tʃaɪvz/ *plural noun* a herb of which the leaves are used to decorate dishes or in soups or salads (NOTE: **chives** has no singular.)

chlorinated /ˈklɔːrɪneɪtɪd/ *adj* added to or treated with chlorine

chlorine /ˈklɔːriːn/ *noun* a powerful greenish gas, used to sterilise water and to bleach things

② **chocolate** /ˈtʃɒklət/ *noun* **1.** a sweet brown food made from the crushed seeds of a tropical tree ○ *a bar of chocolate* ○ *Her mother made a chocolate cake.* **2.** a single sweet made from chocolate ○ *There are only three chocolates left in the box.* ○ *Who's eaten the last chocolate?* **3.** a drink made from chocolate powder and milk ○ *I always have a cup of hot chocolate before I go to bed.*

① **choice** /tʃɔɪs/ *noun* **1.** something which is chosen [~for] ○ *Paris was our first choice for our holiday.* **2.** the act of choosing something ○ *We give students plenty of advice on their choice of course.* **3.** a range of things to choose from [~between] ○ *The store has a huge choice of furniture.* ○ *He gave me a choice between full-time or part-time work.* □ **I hadn't any choice, I had no choice** there was nothing else I could do ■ *adj* (**choicer, choicest**) (*of food*) specially selected ○ *choice meat* ○ *choice peaches*

choir /kwaɪə/ *noun* a group of people who sing together ○ *He sings in the church choir.*

choke /tʃəʊk/ (**chokes, choking, choked**) *verb* **1.** to stop breathing properly because something such as a piece of food is blocking the throat [~on] ○ *Don't talk with your mouth full or you'll choke.* ○ *He choked on a piece of bread* or *a piece of bread made him choke.* **2.** to block something such as a pipe [~with] ○ *The canal was choked with weeds.* **3.** to squeeze someone's neck so that they cannot breathe ○ *He felt the tight collar was choking him.* □ **to choke someone to death** to squeeze someone's throat until they die **4.** to find it hard to speak because of emotion [~with] ○ *Her voice was choked with anger.*

choked /tʃəʊkt/ *adj* overcome by emotion such as sadness or anger

cholera /ˈkɒlərə/ *noun* a serious bacterial disease spread through infected food or water

③ **cholesterol** /kəˈlestərɒl/ *noun* a fatty substance found in fats and oils, also produced by the liver and forming an essential part of all cells. Excess amounts can cause blocked arteries.

① **choose** /tʃuːz/ (**chooses, choosing, chose, chosen**) *verb* **1.** to decide which of several things you want to have [~between/~from/~out of/~which/where/whether etc/~as] ○ *I chose a book about sailing.* ○ *I can't choose between the white one or the yellow one.* ○ *There were several good candidates to choose from.* ○ *The girl was chosen out of the thousands of children who applied.* ○ *Have you chosen what you want to eat?* ○ *They chose him as team leader.* ○ *You must give customers plenty of time to choose.* **2.** to decide to do one thing when there are several things you could do ○ *In the end, they chose to go to the cinema.* ◊ **choice**

choosy /ˈtʃuːzi/ *adj* difficult to please (*informal*)

① **chop** /tʃɒp/ *noun* a piece of meat with a bone attached ○ *We had lamb chops for dinner.* ■ *verb* (**chops, chopping, chopped**) to cut something roughly into small pieces with a knife or other sharp tool ○ *He spent the afternoon chopping wood for the fire.* ◇ to do one thing, then another ○ *He keeps chopping and changing and can't make his mind up.*

chop down① *phrasal verb* to cut down a

tree with an axe

chop off① *phrasal verb* to cut something off, e.g. with an axe or knife

chop up① *phrasal verb* to cut something into pieces

chopper /ˈtʃɒpə/ *noun* **1.** an axe, especially one for cutting meat ○ *A butcher armed with a chopper was cutting up carcasses.* **2.** a helicopter (*informal*) ○ *A chopper landed in the middle of the motorway to pick up the accident victims.*

choppy /ˈtʃɒpi/ *adj* (*of water*) quite rough

chopsticks /ˈtʃɒpstɪks/ *noun* a pair of small sticks used in China, Japan, etc., to eat food or to stir food when cooking

choral /ˈkɔːrəl/ *adj* referring to a choir

③ **chord** /kɔːd/ *noun* **1.** several notes played together in harmony ○ *He sat down at the piano and played a few chords.* **2.** a line which joins two points on a curve ○ *Draw a chord across this circle.* (NOTE: Do not confuse with **cord**.)

chore /tʃɔː/ *noun* a piece of routine work, e.g. cleaning in a house, that you have to do ○ *household chores*

choreography /ˌkɒriˈɒɡrəfi/ *noun* the art of arranging the steps for a dance (NOTE: + **choreographer** *n*)

③ **chorus** /ˈkɔːrəs/ *noun* **1.** a part of a song which is repeated later in the song ○ *I'll sing the verses and everyone can join in the chorus.* **2.** a group of people who sing together ○ *All the members of the chorus were on the stage.*

chose /tʃəʊz/ past tense of **choose**

chosen /ˈtʃəʊz(ə)n/ past participle of **choose**

③ **Christ** /kraɪst/ *noun* Jesus Christ, the person on whose life and teachings the Christian religion is based ■ *interj* used for showing you are annoyed (*taboo*) ○ *Christ! It's eight o'clock already and I haven't started cooking dinner.*

christen /ˈkrɪs(ə)n/ (**christens, christening, christened**) *verb* **1.** to give a name to something ○ *She was christened the 'Iron Lady' by the press.* **2.** to use something for the first time ○ *Come and help us christen our new set of champagne glasses.*

christening /ˈkrɪs(ə)nɪŋ/ *noun* a ceremony in church where a baby is given a name

③ **Christian** /ˈkrɪstʃən/ *adj* relating to the religion based on the teachings of Jesus Christ ○ *There are several Christian churches in the town.* ○ *She practises all the Christian virtues.* ■ *noun* a person who believes in the teachings of Jesus Christ and in Christianity

Christianity /ˌkrɪstiˈænɪti/ *noun* a religion based on the doctrine preached by Jesus Christ and followed by Christians ever since

③ **Christian name** /ˈkrɪstʃən neɪm/ *noun* the special name given to someone as a child after birth or at their christening

① **Christmas** /ˈkrɪsməs/, **Christmas Day** *noun* a Christian festival on December 25th, celebrated as the birthday of Jesus Christ, when presents are given ○ *Have you opened your Christmas presents yet?*

Christmas card /ˈkrɪsməs kɑːd/ *noun* a card which is sent to someone at Christmas

Christmas carol /ˌkrɪsməs ˈkærəl/ *noun* a special song sung at Christmas

Christmas Day /ˌkrɪsməs ˈdeɪ/ *noun* December 25th, the day on which Christmas is celebrated

③ **Christmas Eve** /ˌkrɪsməs ˈiːv/ *noun* the evening of December 24th ○ *a Christmas Eve party*

Christmas tree /ˈkrɪsməs triː/ *noun* a fir tree which is brought into the house at Christmas and decorated with coloured lights and ornaments

chrome /krəʊm/ *noun* an alloy of chromium and other metals, used to give a shiny silver surface ○ *a 1960s chair with chrome legs and a plastic seat*

chromosome /ˈkrəʊməsəʊm/ *noun* a rod-shaped structure in the nucleus of a cell, formed of DNA, which carries the genes

chronic /ˈkrɒnɪk/ *adj* **1.** (*of illness or pain*) serious and continuing for a long time ○ *She has chronic bronchitis.* ○ *Chronic asthma sufferers need to use special drugs.* Compare **acute 2.** referring to someone who does a particular activity, especially a harmful one, often ○ *a chronic smoker* **3.** very bad (*informal*) ○ *We have a chronic shortage of skilled staff.*

chronicle /ˈkrɒnɪk(ə)l/ *noun* a record of things which take place ○ *He wrote a chronicle of the war.* (NOTE: + **chronicle** *v*)

chrysanthemum /krɪˈsænθɪməm/ *noun* a type of autumn flower with many small petals

chubby /ˈtʃʌbi/ (**chubbier, chubbiest**) *adj* pleasantly fat

② **chuck** /tʃʌk/ (**chucks, chucking, chucked**) *verb* to throw (*informal*) ○ *Chuck* *me that newspaper, can you?* ○ *She chucked the book out of the window.*

chuckle /ˈtʃʌk(ə)l/ *noun* a quiet laugh ○ *We all had a good chuckle over the chairman's speech.* ■ *verb* (**chuckles, chuckling, chuckled**) to give a quiet laugh ○ *He chuckled when she said she wanted a good steady job.*

chuffed /tʃʌft/ *adj* pleased or proud

chug /tʃʌg/ (**chugs, chugging, chugged**) *verb* to make a regular noise like an engine [~along/up/down etc] (*informal*)

chunk /tʃʌŋk/ *noun* a large thick piece of something

chunky /ˈtʃʌŋki/ (**chunkier, chunkiest**) *adj* made of large or thick pieces

① **church** /tʃɜːtʃ/ *noun* a building where Christians go to pray ○ *We usually go to church on Sunday mornings.* ○ *The oldest building in the village is St Mary's Church.* ○ *The times of the church services are given on the board outside.*

churchgoer /ˈtʃɜːtʃgəʊə/ *noun* a person who goes to church regularly

churchyard /ˈtʃɜːtʃjɑːd/ *noun* a cemetery next to a church

churn /tʃɜːn/ *noun* a large metal container for milk ○ *Churns of fresh milk were lined up at the farm entrance waiting to be picked up.* ■ *verb* (**churns, churning, churned**) **1.** to turn cream to make butter ○ *Do you know of any farm where butter is still churned by hand?* **2.** to buy and sell shares on someone's behalf, in order to earn commission for yourself ○ *Few small investors realise how much money they lose through churning.*

churn out *phrasal verb* to produce something in a series

chute /ʃuːt/ *noun* **1.** a slide into water in a swimming pool ○ *The kids screamed as they slid down the chute into the pool.* **2.** a slide for sending things down to a lower level ○ *The parcels are wrapped and labelled and then sent down a chute to where the delivery vans are waiting.*

chutney /ˈtʃʌtni/ *noun* a highly flavoured sauce usually made with tomatoes, onions, vinegar and spices

cider /ˈsaɪdə/ *noun* an alcoholic drink made from fermented apple juice

cigar /sɪˈgɑː/ *noun* a tight roll of dried tobacco leaves which you can light and smoke

② **cigarette** /ˌsɪgəˈret/ *noun* a roll of very thin paper containing tobacco, which you can light and smoke ○ *a packet* or *pack of cigarettes* ○ *The room was full of cigarette smoke.*

③ **cinema** /ˈsɪnɪmə/ *noun* a building where you go to watch films ○ *We went to the cinema on Friday night.*

cinematic /ˌsɪnɪˈmætɪk/ *adj* referring to films and the cinema

cinnamon /ˈsɪnəmən/ *noun* a spice made from the inner bark of a tropical tree

circa /ˈsɜːkə/ *prep* about (*formal; used of dates*)

② **circle** /ˈsɜːk(ə)l/ *noun* **1.** a line forming a round shape ○ *He drew a circle on the blackboard.* **2.** anything forming a round shape ○ *The children sat in a circle round the teacher.* ○ *The soldiers formed a circle round the prisoner.* **3.** a group of people or a society ○ *She went to live abroad and lost contact with her old circle of friends.* ○ *He moves in the highest government circles.* **4.** a row of seats above the stalls in a theatre ○ *We got tickets for the upper circle.* ■ *verb* (**circles, circling, circled**) to make circular movements [~around/above/over etc] ○ *Large birds were circling above the dead animals.*

③ **circuit** /ˈsɜːkɪt/ *noun* **1.** a fixed or regular way of travelling from one place to another for a particular activity ○ *a familiar speaker on the lecture circuit* **2.** a path on which competitions take place ○ *a race circuit* **3.** a trip around something ○ *His first circuit of the track was very slow.* **4.** the path that electricity flows around ○ *He's designed a circuit for a burglar alarm.*

circuit board /ˈsɜːkɪt bɔːd/ *noun* a board composed of a printed circuit

circuit breaker /ˈsɜːkɪt ˌbreɪkə/ *noun* a safety device in an electrical circuit

② **circular** /ˈsɜːkjʊlə/ *adj* **1.** round in shape ○ *a circular table* **2.** sent to a number of people ○ *The company sent a circular letter to all employees.* (NOTE: only used before a noun) ■ *noun* a document with one or just a few pages sent to a number of people to inform them about something

③ **circulate** /ˈsɜːkjʊleɪt/ (**circulates, circulating, circulated**) *verb* **1.** to send something round to various people ○ *They circulated a new list of prices to all their customers.* **2.** to move round ○ *Blood circulates round the body.* ○ *Waiters circulated round the room carrying trays of drinks.* **3.** to talk to different people at a party ○ *Let's talk later – I've got to circulate.*

③ **circulation** /ˌsɜːkjʊˈleɪʃ(ə)n/ *noun* **1.** the act of circulating ○ *The circulation of* *the new price list to all departments will take several days.* **2.** the movement of blood around the body ○ *Rub your hands together to get the circulation going.* ○ *He has poor circulation.*

circumcise /'sɜːkəmsaɪz/ (**circumcises, circumcising, circumcised**) *verb* to remove the foreskin from a boy's or man's penis (NOTE: + **circumcision** *n*)

circumference /sə'kʌmf(ə)rəns/ *noun* the distance round the outside edge of a circle, an object or an area ○ *We walked the dog around the circumference of the field.*

circumflex /'sɜːkəmfleks/, **circumflex accent** *noun* an accent like an upside down 'v' placed over certain vowels

circumstance /'sɜːkəmstəns/ *noun* the set of conditions that affect a situation ○ *The circumstances surrounding the crash led us to believe it was not an accident.* (NOTE: usually plural) ◇ **in** ***or*** **under the circumstances** if a particular set of conditions exist ○ *It's hard to do a good job under these circumstances.* ○ *In different circumstances, I'd have been willing to stay longer.* ◇ **due to circumstances beyond someone's control** because of something which someone has no power to change ○ *The show had to be cancelled due to circumstances beyond our control.*

circumstantial /ˌsɜːkəm'stænʃ(ə)l/ *adj* giving details of particular circumstances

circumvent /ˌsɜːkəm'vent/ (**circumvents, circumventing, circumvented**) *verb* to avoid something

circus /'sɜːkəs/ *noun* **1.** a travelling show, often given under a large tent, with animals, clowns and other performers ○ *We went to the circus last night.* ○ *The circus is coming to town for the bank holiday weekend.* **2.** a busy road junction in the centre of a large town ○ *Oxford Circus is where Oxford Street crosses Regent Street.*

cistern /'sɪstən/ *noun* a large tank for water

cite /saɪt/ (**cites, citing, cited**) *verb* **1.** to quote a reference or a person as proof ○ *She cited several passages from his latest book.* **2.** to call someone to appear in court ○ *He was cited to appear before the magistrates.* (NOTE: Do not confuse with **sight, site**.)

② **citizen** /'sɪtɪz(ə)n/ *noun* a person who comes from a particular country or has the same right to live there as someone who was born there ○ *All Australian citizens have a duty to vote.* ○ *He was born in Germany, but is now a British citizen.*

③ **citizenship** /'sɪtɪz(ə)nʃɪp/ *noun* the state of being a citizen

citrus fruit /'sɪtrəs fruːt/ *noun* an edible fruit such as an orange, lemon, grapefruit or lime

① **city** /'sɪti/ (*plural* **cities**) *noun* a large town ○ *busy city streets* ○ *Traffic is a problem in big cities.*

city centre /ˌsɪti 'sentə/ *noun* the central part of a town

civic /'sɪvɪk/ *adj* referring to a city

② **civil** /'sɪv(ə)l/ *adj* **1.** relating to general public life rather than to the armed forces ○ *He left the air force and became a civil airline pilot.* **2.** polite ○ *She wasn't very civil to the policeman.* **3.** in court, relating to cases brought by one person against another, as opposed to being brought by the police because it is criminal

civil action /ˌsɪv(ə)l 'ækʃən/ *noun* a court action brought by one citizen against another, as opposed to a criminal action

civil engineering /ˌsɪv(ə)l endʒɪ'nɪərɪŋ/ *noun* the science of building, especially of roads, bridges and railways

civilian /sə'vɪliən/ *noun* an ordinary citizen who is not in the armed forces ○ *It is certain that ordinary civilians will be affected by the war.* ○ *Many civilians were killed in the air raids.*

② **civilisation** /ˌsɪvɪlaɪ'zeɪʃ(ə)n/, **civilization** *noun* a civilised society or civilised way of organising society

civilise /'sɪvɪlaɪz/ (**civilises, civilising, civilised**), **civilize** *verb* to educate people to a higher level of society ○ *Missionaries went out with the idea that they would civilise local tribes.*

civilised /'sɪvɪlaɪzd/, **civilized** *adj* **1.** organised to a high level of social behaviour ○ *How can a civilised nation carry out such barbarous punishments.* **2.** pleasant and polite ○ *We had a very civilised evening, chatting over a good meal.* ○ *Try to greet my parents in a civilised manner if you can.* ○ *It's so good to be in civilised company again.*

civil law /ˌsɪv(ə)l 'lɔː/ *noun* laws relating to people's rights

civil liberties /ˌsɪv(ə)l 'lɪbətiz/ *plural noun* the rights of ordinary people to act freely within the law ○ *a campaign to extend civil liberties* ○ *Security cameras on buildings can be seen as an infringement of civil liberties.* (NOTE: Liberty of the press and liberty of the individual are examples of civil liberties.)

civil rights /ˌsɪv(ə)l 'raɪts/ *plural noun* rights of an ordinary citizen ○ *She campaigned for civil rights in the 1980s.*

③ **civil servant** /ˌsɪv(ə)l 'sɜːvənt/ *noun* a person who works in a government department

③ **civil war** /ˌsɪv(ə)l 'wɔː/ *noun* a war between citizens inside a country

clad /klæd/ *adj* **1.** dressed in a particular way ○ *a group of leather-clad dancers* ○ *The soldiers were clad in winter greatcoats.* **2.** covered ○ *the snow-clad fields* ○ *a white stucco-clad house*

① **claim** /kleɪm/ *noun* **1.** an occasion on which someone asks for money [~for] ○ *His claim for a pay increase was turned down.* **2.** a statement of something which you believe to be true but have no proof [~that] ○ *His claim that the car belonged to him was correct.* **3.** a demand for money against an insurance policy ○ *After the floods, insurance companies received hundreds of claims.* □ **to put in *or* submit a claim** to ask an insurance company officially to pay money for something that has been damaged ○ *I put in a claim for repairs to the car.* ○ *She submitted a claim for £250,000 damages against the driver of the other car.* **4.** a right to something [~on] ○ *He has a legal claim on the property.* ○ *Preparing for my exam was a big claim on my leisure time last year.* ■ *verb* (**claims, claiming, claimed**) **1.** to state something, but without any proof [~(that)] ○ *He claims he never received the letter.* ○ *She claims that the car belongs to her.* **2.** to ask for something that you have a right to receive ○ *If they charged you too much you must claim a refund.* **3.** to say you own something which has been left behind or lost ○ *No one has claimed the umbrella found in my office, so I am going to keep it.*

③ **claimant** /'kleɪmənt/ *noun* **1.** a person who claims something ○ *Benefit claimants will be paid late because of the bank holiday.* **2.** a person who starts a legal action against someone in the civil courts ○ *She's the claimant in a libel action.* ○ *The court decided in favour of the claimant.* (NOTE: The former term was **plaintiff**. The other party in an action is the **defendant**.)

clairvoyant /kleə'vɔɪənt/ *noun* a person who says he or she can see in his or her mind things which are happening elsewhere, or can foretell the future

clam /klæm/ *noun* a large shellfish found in sand, which is dug out with a spade

clam up *phrasal verb* to refuse to talk (*informal*)

clamber /'klæmbə/ (**clambers, clambering, clambered**) *verb* to climb with difficulty

clammy /'klæmi/ (**clammier, clammiest**) *adj* damp and cold

clamour /'klæmə/ *noun* **1.** noise such as shouting ○ *The clamour of the crowd at the rugby ground could be heard for miles around.* **2.** a loud demand [~for] ○ *a clamour for democratic elections* ■ *verb* to demand something or to do something loudly or publicly [~for] ○ *People are clamouring for tickets.* (NOTE: [all senses] The US spelling is **clamor**.)

clamp /klæmp/ *noun* a device that holds something tightly and prevents it from moving ■ *verb* (**clamps, clamping, clamped**) **1.** to hold something in a fixed position [~to/~on/onto] **2.** to prevent an illegally parked car from moving by attaching a clamp to one wheel ○ *I parked on a double yellow line and was clamped.* **3.** to hold something tight with a clamp

clamp down /'klæmp 'daʊn ɒn/ *verb* to try to stop something happening [~on] ○ *Railway staff are clamping down on people travelling without tickets.*

clampdown /'klæmpdaʊn/ *noun* an action by someone in authority to stop something from happening [~on] ○ *a clampdown on smoking in public places*

clan /klæn/ *noun* a family tribe, especially in Scotland

clandestine /klæn'destɪn/ *adj* secret, undercover

clang /klæŋ/ (**clangs, clanging, clanged**) *verb* to make a loud ringing noise ○ *We were woken up by the bells clanging in the churches round us.* (NOTE: + **clang** *n*)

clank /klæŋk/ (**clanks, clanking, clanked**) *verb* to make a noise of metal hitting other metal (NOTE: + **clank** *n*)

clap /klæp/ (**claps, clapping, clapped**) *verb* to beat your hands together to show you are pleased ○ *At the end of her speech the audience stood up and clapped.* ○ *He clapped his hands together in delight.*

clarification /ˌklærɪfɪ'keɪʃ(ə)n/ *noun* the act of making something clear

③ **clarify** /'klærɪfaɪ/ (**clarifies, clarifying, clarified**) *verb* to explain something more clearly [~what/whether/how etc] ○ *We will have to clarify the situation before taking any further decisions.* ○ *Can you clarify what the work will involve?*

clarinet /ˌklærɪ'net/ *noun* a wind instrument in the woodwind group

③ **clarity** /ˈklærɪti/ *noun* clearness

clash /klæʃ/ *noun* **1.** a fight, especially between people who are not soldiers [~between/~with] ○ *There were clashes between supporters of rival football teams.* **2.** an argument or disagreement [~over] ○ *a clash over whose responsibility it was* **3.** a game or competition between two teams or two players **4.** an occasion when two things you want to do are happening at the same time **5.** the shock of two colours seen close together ○ *If you wear red tights with an orange dress there will be a colour clash.* **6.** a loud noise of metal things hitting each other ■ *verb* (**clashes, clashing, clashed**) **1.** to argue violently [~with/~over] ○ *She clashed with her mother over wearing a ring in her nose.* ○ *The opposition deputies clashed with the government during the debate.* **2.** to fight [~with] ○ *Rioting fans clashed with the police.* **3.** to happen at the same time as something else [~with] ○ *The party clashes with a meeting I have to go to.* ○ *Unfortunately, the two meetings clash, so I'll have to miss one.* **4.** (*of colours*) to shock when put side by side [~with] ○ *That bright pink tie clashes with your green shirt.* **5.** to bang things together making a loud noise

③ **clasp** /klɑːsp/ *noun* **1.** a device for holding something shut ○ *My handbag won't close properly – the clasp is broken.* **2.** the act of holding something in your hand ○ *I could feel the firm clasp of his hand on my shoulder.* ■ *verb* (**clasps, clasping, clasped**) to hold something tight ○ *The child clasped his hand anxiously.*

① **class** /klɑːs/ *noun* **1.** a group of children or adults who go to school or college together ○ *There are 30 children in my son's class.* **2.** a lesson ○ *What did you learn in your history class today?* **3.** people of a particular group in society ○ *The college encourages applications from different social classes.* **4.** a group of things, animals or people that share some features ○ *Different standards apply to the five different classes of service you can pay for.* **5.** a particular level of quality ○ *Always buy the best class of product.* ○ *These peaches are Class 1.*

class act /ˌklɑːs ˈækt/ *noun* a person or thing considered to be an example of excellence

Class A drug /ˌklɑːs eɪ ˈdrʌg/ *noun* an illegal drug such as heroin, which is considered to be one of the strongest and most dangerous drugs

③ **classic** /ˈklæsɪk/ *noun* a great book, play or piece of music ○ *'The Maltese Falcon' is a Hollywood classic.* ○ *We have to study several classics of English literature for our course.* ■ *adj* **1.** (*of a style*) elegant and traditional ○ *The classic little black dress is always in fashion.* ○ *The style of the new hotel building is classic, simple and elegant.* **2.** based on Ancient Greek or Roman architecture **3.** typical ○ *It was a classic example of his inability to take decisions.*

③ **classical** /ˈklæsɪk(ə)l/ *adj* **1.** elegant and based on the Ancient Greek or Roman style ○ *a classical eighteenth-century villa* **2.** referring to Ancient Greece and Rome ○ *classical Greek literature* **3.** referring to traditional serious music ○ *a concert of classical music*

classical music /ˌklæsɪk(ə)l ˈmjuːzɪk/ *noun* European music such as that written by Mozart or Bach, based on specific structures

Classics /ˈklæsɪks/ *plural noun* the study of the languages, literature and philosophy of Ancient Greece and Rome ○ *She studied Classics at Oxford.* ○ *He has a Classics degree from Edinburgh.*

classification /ˌklæsɪfɪˈkeɪʃ(ə)n/ *noun* a way of arranging things into categories

classified /ˈklæsɪfaɪd/ *adj* **1.** which has been put into a category **2.** secret

③ **classify** /ˈklæsɪfaɪ/ (**classifies, classifying, classified**) *verb* to arrange things into categories ○ *The hotels are classified according to a system of stars.*

classless /ˈklɑːsləs/ *adj* with no division into social classes

classmate /ˈklɑːsmeɪt/ *noun* a person who is or was in the same class as you at school or college

③ **classroom** /ˈklɑːsruːm/ *noun* a room in a school where children are taught ○ *When the teacher came into the classroom all the children were shouting.*

classy /ˈklɑːsi/ (**classier, classiest**) *adj* stylish and expensive-looking (*informal*)

clatter /ˈklætə/ (**clatters, clattering, clattered**) *verb* to make a loud harsh noise ○ *The wooden cart clattered across the square.* (NOTE: + **clatter** *n*)

② **clause** /klɔːz/ *noun* a paragraph in a legal document ○ *According to clause six, payments will not be due until next year.*

claustrophobia /ˌklɔːstrəˈfəʊbiə/ *noun* a fear of being shut inside a closed place

claustrophobic /ˌklɔːstrəˈfəʊbɪk/ *adj* feeling or causing claustrophobia

claw /klɔː/ *noun* a nail on the foot of an animal or bird ○ *The dog dug a hole with its claws.*

③ **clay** /kleɪ/ *noun* thick heavy soil ○ *The soil in our garden has a lot of clay in it.*

① **clean** /kliːn/ *adj* **1.** not dirty ○ *Wipe your glasses with a clean handkerchief.* ○ *The bedrooms must be spotlessly clean.* ○ *Tell the waitress these cups aren't clean.* **2.** not used ○ *The maid forgot to put clean towels in the bathroom.* ■ *verb* (**cleans, cleaning, cleaned**) to take away the dirt from something ○ *Remember to clean your teeth every morning.* ○ *She was cleaning the car when she saw the damage.* ◇ **to come clean** to confess to, e.g. a crime (*informal*) ○ *He came clean and owned up to stealing the watch.*

clean out *phrasal verb* to make something empty and clean (*informal*)

clean up *phrasal verb* **1.** to make everything clean and tidy, e.g. after a party ○ *It took us three hours to clean up after her birthday party.* **2.** to remove corruption from a place ○ *The police are going to have a hard job cleaning up this town.* **3.** to make a lot of money ○ *He cleaned up at the races.* ○ *In no time he'd cleaned up £50,000.*

clean-cut /ˌkliːn ˈkʌt/ *adj* neat and tidy ○ *a man in a clean-cut suit*

③ **cleaner** /ˈkliːnə/ *noun* **1.** a machine which removes dirt ○ *a carpet cleaner* **2.** a person who cleans a building such as a house or an office ○ *The cleaners didn't empty my wastepaper basket.*

③ **cleaning** /ˈkliːnɪŋ/ *noun* **1.** the action of making something clean ○ *Cleaning the house after the party took hours.* **2.** clothes which are going to be sent for dry-cleaning or which have been returned after dry-cleaning ○ *Could you collect my cleaning for me after work tonight?*

cleanse /klenz/ (**cleanses, cleansing, cleansed**) *verb* to make something very clean

cleanser /ˈklenzə/ *noun* a substance which removes dirt, especially from the face

clean-shaven /ˌkliːn ˈʃeɪv(ə)n/ *adj* with no beard or moustache

clean-up /ˈkliːn ʌp/ *noun* the act of making something clean

① **clear** /klɪə/ *adj* **1.** with nothing in the way ○ *You can cross the road – it's clear now.* ○ *From the window, she had a clear view of the street.* **2.** easily understood ○ *She made it clear that she wanted us to go.* ○ *The instructions on the computer screen are not very clear.* ○ *Will you give me a clear answer – yes or no?*

clear away *phrasal verb* to take something away completely

clear off *phrasal verb* to go away (*informal*)

clear out *phrasal verb* **1.** to empty something completely ○ *Can you clear out your bedroom cupboard?* **2.** to leave somewhere quickly (*informal*) ○ *It's time for me to clear out of here completely.*

clear up *phrasal verb* **1.** to tidy and clean a place completely ○ *The cleaners refused to clear up the mess after the office party.* **2.** to solve a problem ○ *In the end, we cleared up the mystery of the missing computer disk.* **3.** (*of weather*) to improve ○ *I hope the weather clears up because we're going on holiday tomorrow.* **4.** (*of an illness*) to get better ○ *He has been resting, but his cold still hasn't cleared up.*

clearance /ˈklɪərəns/ *noun* **1.** the act of removing obstacles such as trees or old buildings from land ○ *The clearance of the slums from the town centre will make land available for building.* ○ *The government has introduced a programme of slum clearance.* **2.** a space for something to pass through ○ *The lorry can get through the entrance with clearance of about 20 cm on either side.* **3.** permission to do something ○ *The control tower gave the plane clearance to land.*

clear-cut /ˌklɪə ˈkʌt/ *adj* definite or distinct

clearing /ˈklɪərɪŋ/ *noun* **1.** the act of removing obstacles ○ *We don't want the public to interfere with the clearing of the wreckage from the railway track.* **2.** an area in a wood where the trees have been cut down ○ *They set up camp in a clearing in the middle of the forest.*

① **clearly** /ˈklɪəli/ *adv* **1.** in a way which is easily understood or heard ○ *He didn't speak clearly, and I couldn't catch the address he gave.* **2.** obviously ○ *He clearly* or *Clearly he didn't like being told he was too fat.*

cleavage /ˈkliːvɪdʒ/ *noun* the space between the breasts, especially if it can be seen with a low-cut dress ○ *All the ladies were dressed in black and there was not a cleavage in sight.*

clef /klef/ *noun* a sign at the beginning of a written piece of music which shows how high the range of notes is

clemency /'klemənsi/ *noun* forgiveness shown to someone who has done something wrong

clench /klentʃ/ (**clenches, clenching, clenched**) *verb* to close tightly

③ **clergy** /'klɜːdʒi/ *plural noun* priests

cleric /'klerɪk/ *noun* a priest or other clergyman

clerical /'klerɪk(ə)l/ *adj* **1.** referring to office work ○ *A clerical error made the invoice £300.00 when it should have been £3000.00.* ○ *He's looking for part-time clerical work.* **2.** referring to clergy ○ *The newspaper story has been talked about in clerical circles.*

clerk /klɑːk/ *noun* a person who works in an office

② **clever** /'klevə/ *adj* able to think and learn quickly ○ *Clever children can usually do this by the time they are eight years old.*

cleverly /'klevəli/ *adv* in a clever way

cliché /'kliːʃeɪ/ *noun* a saying or phrase which is too frequently used

③ **click** /klɪk/ *noun* **1.** a short sharp sound ○ *She heard a click and saw the door handle turn.* **2.** the act of pressing a key on a computer keyboard or a mouse button ■ *verb* (**clicks, clicking, clicked**) **1.** to make a short sharp sound ○ *The cameras clicked as the film star came out onto the steps.* ○ *He clicked his fingers to attract the waiter's attention.* **2.** to quickly press the button on a mouse to start a computer function ○ *Click twice to start the program.* **3.** to become clear and easily understood ○ *Suddenly something clicked and I realised what his note meant.* **4.** to realise very quickly that you enjoy being with another person and work well together

① **client** /'klaɪənt/ *noun* a person who pays for a service

clientele /kliːɒn'tel/ *noun* all the customers of a shop or business

cliff /klɪf/ *noun* a high steep area of rock usually by the sea

cliffhanger /'klɪfhæŋə/ *noun* **1.** an ending to a part of a story which makes you want to know what happens next **2.** a situation in which people are tense because they do not know what will happen next

climactic /klaɪ'mæktɪk/ *adj* referring to a climax

③ **climate** /'klaɪmət/ *noun* **1.** the general weather conditions in a particular place ○ *The climate in the south of the country is milder than in the north.* **2.** a situation with particular features ○ *The current economic climate makes an interest rate rise very likely.* ○ *The explosions created a climate of fear.*

climatic /klaɪ'mætɪk/ *adj* referring to climate

climax /'klaɪmæks/ *noun* the most important and exciting point

② **climb** /klaɪm/ (**climbs, climbing, climbed**) *verb* **1.** to go up, over or down something using arms and legs [~up/down/over/through etc] ○ *The cat climbed up the apple tree.* ○ *The boys climbed over the wall.* ○ *He escaped by climbing out of the window.* **2.** to go higher [~to] ○ *The road climbs to 500m above sea level.* ○ *House prices have started to climb again.* **3.** to go up mountains as a sport ○ *When you have climbed Everest, there is no higher mountain left to climb.* ○ *He goes climbing every weekend.*

climb down *phrasal verb* **1.** to come down, e.g. a mountain or a ladder ○ *He climbed down from the roof.* ○ *The firemen helped the hotel guests climb down the ladder.* **2.** not to do what you had previously insisted on doing ○ *In the end, the government had to climb down and admit that a mistake had been made.*

climber /'klaɪmə/ *noun* **1.** a person who climbs mountains ○ *The climbers roped themselves together and set off up the slope.* **2.** a plant which climbs ○ *We need a colourful climber to cover that wall.*

climbing /'klaɪmɪŋ/ *noun* the sport of climbing mountains ○ *Climbing is not a sport for young children.* ○ *We had a climbing holiday last Easter.* ○ *She brought her climbing equipment with her.*

climbing frame /'klaɪmɪŋ freɪm/ *noun* a framework of wooden bars and platforms for children to climb on

③ **clinch** /klɪntʃ/ (**clinches, clinching, clinched**) *verb* **1.** (*in boxing*) to hold each other tightly ○ *The referee tried to stop the two boxers clinching.* **2.** to complete a deal ○ *He offered an extra 5% to clinch the deal.*

cling /klɪŋ/ (**clings, clinging, clung**) *verb* to hold tight to something ○ *She survived by clinging on a rope.* ○ *He clung tightly to his mother's arm.* ○ *The girls clung together with cold.*

clingfilm /'klɪŋfɪlm/ *noun* a thin transparent plastic sheet for covering food

clingy /'klɪŋi/ *adj* emotionally dependent on someone

③ **clinic** /ˈklɪnɪk/ *noun* **1.** a medical centre for particular treatment or advice ○ *an eye clinic* **2.** a private hospital

③ **clinical** /ˈklɪnɪk(ə)l/ *adj* medical

clink /klɪŋk/ (**clinks, clinking, clinked**) *verb* to make a little noise, like pieces of metal hitting each other (NOTE: + **clink** *n*)

clip /klɪp/ *noun* a small object that holds things together ○ *a paper clip* ■ *verb* (**clips, clipping, clipped**) **1.** to attach things with a clip [~to/onto/~together] ○ *She clipped the invoice and the cheque together and put them in an envelope.* **2.** to cut something with scissors ○ *He carefully clipped the article out of the newspaper.*

clipboard /ˈklɪpbɔːd/ *noun* a stiff board with a clip at the top so that a piece of paper can be attached to it to allow you to write on it easily

clipping /ˈklɪpɪŋ/ *noun* **1.** a reference to someone or something in a newspaper or magazine which is cut out ○ *Can you file away all these newspaper clippings, please?* **2.** a small piece cut off, e.g. a hedge ○ *Trim the hedge and put the clippings in a black bag.* ○ *Grass clippings can be piled on top of the compost heap.*

clique /kliːk/ *noun* a small select group of people

clitoris /ˈklɪtərɪs/ *noun* the female sex organ at the top of the vulva

cloak /kləʊk/ *noun* a type of long coat which hangs from the shoulders and has no sleeves ○ *She wore a long cloak of black velvet.*

cloakroom /ˈkləʊkruːm/ *noun* **1.** a place where you leave your coat in a public place ○ *I left my coat and briefcase in the cloakroom.* **2.** a room inside a public building with lavatories and washbasins ○ *The ladies' cloakroom is on the first floor.*

clobber /ˈklɒbə/ (**clobbers, clobbering, clobbered**) *verb* to affect badly, especially financially (*informal*) ○ *The new tax will clobber the middle classes.*

clock /klɒk/① *noun* an object which shows the time ○ *Your clock is 5 minutes slow.* ○ *The office clock is fast.* ○ *The clock has stopped.*

clockwise /ˈklɒkwaɪz/ *adj, adv* moving in a circle from left to right, in the same direction as the hands of a clock ○ *Turn the lid clockwise to tighten it.* ○ *He was driving clockwise round the ring road when the accident took place.*

clockwork /ˈklɒkwɜːk/ *noun* a mechanism in a toy, machine, clock, etc which works using a spring which is wound up with a key ◇ **like clockwork** smoothly, with no problems ○ *The whole evening went off like clockwork.*

clog /klɒg/ (**clogs, clogging, clogged**) *verb* to block ○ *Trafalgar Square was clogged with traffic as the protest march arrived.* ○ *Dead leaves are clogging the drains.*

③ **clone** /kləʊn/ *noun* an exact genetic copy of an individual animal or plant ○ *A cutting produces a clone of a plant.* ○ *This sheep was the first mammal to survive as a clone.* ■ *verb* (**clones, cloning, cloned**) to make an exact genetic copy of an individual animal or plant ○ *Biologists have successfully cloned a sheep.*

① **close**[1] /kləʊs/ *adj* (**closer, closest**) **1.** very near, or just next to something [~to] ○ *Our office is close to the station.* ○ *This is the closest I've ever been to a film star!* **2.** near in time ○ *My birthday is close to Christmas.* ■ *adv* (**closer, closest**) **1.** very near ○ *Keep close by me if you don't want to get lost.* ○ *Go further away – you're getting too close.* ○ *They stood so close* or *so close together that she felt his breath on her cheek.* ○ *The sound came closer and closer.* **2.** very near in time ○ *The conference is getting very close.* ■ *noun* a short road, especially of houses ○ *They live in Briar Close.*

close[2] /kləʊz/ *verb* **1.** to shut [~for/~on] ○ *Would you mind closing the window?* ○ *He closed his book and turned on the TV.* **2.** to come to an end, or make something come to an end [~with] ○ *The meeting closed with a vote of thanks.* ■ *noun* an end, the final part ○ *The century was drawing to a close.*

close down *phrasal verb* **1.** to shut a business permanently **2.** (*of a business*) to shut permanently

① **closed** /kləʊzd/ *adj* **1.** changed from being open by being covered or blocked ○ *Make sure all the windows and doors are tightly closed.* ○ *She sat quietly with closed eyes.* ○ *The object was in a closed box.* **2.** not doing business ○ *The shop is closed on Sundays.* ○ *The office will be closed for the Christmas holidays.* ○ *There was a 'closed' sign hanging in the window.*

close-knit /ˌkləʊs ˈnɪt/ *adv* consisting of people who know and rely on each other

① **closely** /ˈkləʊsli/ *adv* with a lot of attention ○ *She studied the timetable very closely.* ○ *The prisoners were closely guarded by armed soldiers.*

closeness /ˈkləʊsnəs/ *noun* the fact of being close to something

closet /ˈklɒzɪt/ *noun US* a cupboard ○ *Will you get my coat from the closet, honey?* ◇ **to come out of the closet** to say publicly that you are homosexual (*informal*)

③ **close-up** /ˈkləʊs ʌp/ *noun* a photograph taken very close to the subject □ **in close-up** taken very close to the subject ○ *a photo of the leaf in close-up*

closing /ˈkləʊzɪŋ/ *adj* final, at the end ○ *the closing days of the election campaign* ■ *noun* the time when something such as a pub or shop closes

closing date /ˈkləʊzɪŋ deɪt/ *noun* the last date by which something can be done [~for] ○ *The closing date for applications is May 1st.*

③ **closure** /ˈkləʊʒə/ *noun* the shutting of something, or the fact of being shut

clot /klɒt/ *noun* a soft mass of thickened blood in a vein or an artery ○ *The doctor diagnosed a blood clot in the brain.* ■ *verb* (**clots, clotting, clotted**) (*of blood*) to thicken, changing from semi-liquid to semi-solid ○ *In people with haemophilia, blood clots very slowly.*

① **cloth** /klɒθ/ *noun* **1.** soft material made from woven fibres ○ *Her dress is made of cheap blue cloth.* ○ *This cloth is of a very high quality.* **2.** a piece of material used for cleaning ○ *He wiped up the milk with a damp cloth.* **3.** a piece of material which you put on a table to cover it ○ *The waiter spread a white cloth over the table.*

clothe /kləʊð/ (**clothes, clothing, clothed** or **clad**) *verb* to dress someone

clothed /kləʊðd/ *adj* dressed or covered in something

② **clothes** /kləʊðz/ *plural noun* things which you wear to cover your body and keep you warm, e.g. trousers, socks, shirts and dresses ○ *The doctor asked him to take his clothes off.* ○ *The children haven't had any new clothes for years.* □ **with no clothes on** naked

clothing /ˈkləʊðɪŋ/ *noun* clothes ○ *a major clothing manufacturer* ○ *Take plenty of warm clothing on your trip to Iceland.* (NOTE: no plural: *some clothing*; *a piece of clothing*)

① **cloud** /klaʊd/ *noun* **1.** a white or grey mass of drops of water floating in the air ○ *Look at those grey clouds – it's going to rain.* ○ *The plane was flying above the clouds.* **2.** a large amount of gas, smoke or dust floating in the air [~of] ○ *Clouds of smoke poured out of the burning shop.* **3.** something that has an unpleasant effect on a situation □ **under a cloud** suspected of having done something wrong ○ *He was under a cloud for some time after the thefts were discovered.*

cloud over *phrasal verb* to become covered with clouds

② **cloudy** /ˈklaʊdi/ (**cloudier, cloudiest**) *adj* **1.** with clouds ○ *The weather was cloudy in the morning, but cleared up in the afternoon.* **2.** not clear ○ *The liquid turned cloudy when I added the flour.*

clout /klaʊt/ *noun* **1.** a blow with the fist ○ *He received a clout on the head.* **2.** power or influence ○ *Because she owns so many shares, she wields a great deal of clout in company meetings.* ○ *Newspaper editors have a lot of political clout.*

clove /kləʊv/ *noun* **1.** a dried flower bud of a tree, used for flavouring ○ *A few cloves stuck into an onion can be used to flavour a stew.* **2.** one of the parts that make up a bulb of garlic ○ *Rub round the salad bowl with a cut clove of garlic.*

clover /ˈkləʊvə/ *noun* a common weed, used as food for cattle ○ *With so much clover in the fields, the bees produce excellent honey.*

① **club** /klʌb/ *noun* **1.** a group of people who have the same interest or who form a team ○ *a youth club* ○ *I'm joining a tennis club.* ○ *Our town has one of the top football clubs in the country.* **2.** a stick for playing golf (NOTE: A **golf club** can either mean the place where you play golf, or the stick used to hit the ball.) **3.** a large heavy stick ■ *verb* (**clubs, clubbing, clubbed**) **1.** to hit with a club ○ *She was clubbed to the ground.* **2.** □ **to club together** (*of several people*) to contribute money jointly ○ *They clubbed together and bought a yacht.*

clubbing /ˈklʌbɪŋ/ *noun* the activity of going out to discos and nightclubs

clubhouse /ˈklʌbhaʊs/ *noun* the house where members of a club meet

cluck /klʌk/ (**clucks, clucking, clucked**) *verb* (*of hens*) to make a low noise in the throat

② **clue** /kluː/ *noun* information which helps you solve a mystery or puzzle [~about/as to/to] ○ *We have no clues about where she has gone.* ○ *The letter gave some vital clues to her state of mind at the time.* ◇ **to not have a clue** to not know something ○ *I don't have a clue how to get there.*

clued up /ˌkluːd ˈʌp/ *adj* well informed about something

clueless /ˈkluːləs/ *adj* stupid (*informal*)

clump /klʌmp/ *noun* a group of trees or bushes ○ *We'll walk as far as that clump of trees and come back.*

clumsy /ˈklʌmzi/ (**clumsier, clumsiest**) *adj* **1.** tending to break things or knock things over **2.** not expressed or done in a good way ○ *a clumsy apology* ○ *a clumsy attempt to hide the situation* (NOTE: + **clumsily** *adv*, **clumsiness** *n*)

③ **clung** /klʌŋ/ past tense and past participle of **cling**

cluster /ˈklʌstə/ *noun* a group of objects or people that are close together ○ *a brooch with a cluster of pearls* ○ *He photographed a cluster of stars.*

clutch /klʌtʃ/ *verb* (**clutches, clutching, clutched**) to grip something tightly ○ *She clutched my arm as we stood on the edge of the cliff.* ■ *noun* a tight grip ○ *She felt the clutch of his fingers on her sleeve.* ■ *plural noun* **clutches** the power that a person or group has over someone else ○ *You can't escape the clutches of your family so easily.* ◇ **in the clutches of, in someone's clutches** under the control of ○ *We want to avoid spending too much and falling into the clutches of the bank* or *the bank's clutches.*

clutter /ˈklʌtə/ *noun* a mass of things left lying about ○ *All this clutter will be cleared away by the weekend.* ■ *verb* (**clutters, cluttering, cluttered**) to fill a room, etc., with a mass of things ○ *Her desk is cluttered with papers and invoices.* ○ *Don't clutter your mind with useless information.*

③ **cm** *abbr* centimetre

③ **Co.** /kəʊ, ˈkʌmp(ə)ni/ *abbr* company ○ *J. Smith & Co.*

co- /kəʊ/ *prefix* together

③ **c/o** *abbr* care of (*used in addresses*) ○ *Jane Smith, c/o Mr & Mrs Jonas, 4 Willowbank Road.*

② **coach** /kəʊtʃ/ *noun* **1.** a large bus for travelling long distances ○ *They went on a tour of southern Spain by coach.* ○ *There's a coach service to Oxford every hour.* **2.** one of the vehicles for passengers that is part of a train ○ *The first four coaches are for London.* **3.** a person who trains sports players ○ *The coach told them that they needed to spend more time practising.* ○ *He's a professional football coach.* ■ *verb* (**coaches, coaching, coached**) **1.** to train sports people ○ *She was coached by a former Olympic gold medallist.* **2.** to give private lessons to someone in a particular sport, subject or activity ○ *He coaches young footballers.*

coagulate /kəʊˈægjʊleɪt/ (**coagulates, coagulating, coagulated**) *verb* to change and thicken from semi-liquid to semi-solid

③ **coal** /kəʊl/ *noun* a hard black substance which produces heat when burnt

③ **coalition** /ˌkəʊəˈlɪʃ(ə)n/ *noun* a combination of several political parties forming a government

coalmine /ˈkəʊlmaɪn/ *noun* a mine where coal is dug

coarse /kɔːs/ *adj* **1.** consisting of large pieces ○ *coarse grains of sand* **2.** rough and hard ○ *coarse cloth* **3.** (*of words or gestures*) rude ○ *He made a coarse gesture and walked out.* ○ *Don't make any coarse remarks in front of my mother.* (NOTE: **coarsely** *adv*; **coarseness** *n*)

② **coast** /kəʊst/ *noun* parts of a country that are by the sea ○ *After ten weeks at sea, Columbus saw the coast of America.* ○ *The south coast is the warmest part of the country.*

coaster /ˈkəʊstə/ *noun* a flat dish or small mat for standing a bottle or glass on ○ *He bought a set of 6 coasters in the museum.*

coastguard /ˈkəʊstgɑːd/ *noun* a person who guards a piece of coast, watching out for wrecks, smugglers, etc.

coastline /ˈkəʊstlaɪn/ *noun* an edge of land along a coast

② **coat** /kəʊt/ *noun* **1.** a piece of clothing which you wear on top of other clothes when you go outside ○ *a winter coat* **2.** a layer of something ○ *a coat of paint* ○ *a thick coat of dust* **3.** the fur of an animal ○ *These dogs have thick shiny coats.*

coat-hanger /ˈkəʊthæŋə/ *noun* a piece of wood, wire or plastic on which you hang a piece of clothing

coating /ˈkəʊtɪŋ/ *noun* a covering of paint, etc.

coax /kəʊks/ (**coaxes, coaxing, coaxed**) *verb* □ **to coax someone into doing something** to persuade someone to do something ○ *He was finally coaxed into paying for two tickets.*

cobalt /ˈkəʊbɔːlt/ *noun* a metallic element used to make alloys ○ *Cobalt 60 is used in radiotherapy.*

cobbler /ˈkɒblə/ *noun* a person who mends shoes ○ *Ask the cobbler how much it will cost to put new heels on these shoes.*

cobra /ˈkəʊbrə/ *noun* a large tropical snake with a poisonous bite

cobweb /ˈkɒbweb/ *noun* a net of fine thread made by a spider to catch flies

③ **cocaine** /kəʊ'keɪn/ *noun* a painkilling drug, which is addictive
cock /kɒk/ *noun* a male bird, especially a male domestic chicken ○ *We were woken by the cocks crowing.*
cockerel /'kɒk(ə)rəl/ *noun* a young cock
cockney /'kɒkni/ (*plural* **cockneys**) *noun* **1.** a person from the East End of London ○ *He was born and brought up as a Cockney.* **2.** a form of English spoken in the East End of London ○ *She spoke in broad cockney.* ○ *'Let's have a butcher's' is cockney for 'let's have a look'.*
cockpit /'kɒkpɪt/ *noun* the place where the pilot sits in an aircraft, racing car or boat
cockroach /'kɒkrəʊtʃ/ *noun* a black or brown beetle, a common household pest
cocktail /'kɒkteɪl/ *noun* **1.** a mixed alcoholic drink ○ *A Bloody Mary is a cocktail of vodka and tomato juice.* **2.** a mixture of various things ○ *She died after taking a cocktail of drugs.*
cocktail party /'kɒkteɪl ˌpɑːti/ *noun* a party where drinks and snacks are served, but not a full meal
cock-up /'kɒk ʌp/ *noun* work which is badly carried out (*informal offensive*)
cocky /'kɒki/ *adj* unpleasantly confident and conceited (*informal*)
③ **cocoa** /'kəʊkəʊ/ *noun* **1.** a brown chocolate powder ground from the seeds of a tree, used for making a drink ○ *a tin of cocoa* ○ *cocoa powder* **2.** a drink made with cocoa and hot water or milk (NOTE: no plural)
coconut /'kəʊkənʌt/ *noun* **1.** a large nut from a type of palm tree ○ *I won a coconut at the fair.* **2.** the white flesh from a coconut ○ *a coconut cake* ○ *I don't like biscuits with coconut in them.*
cocoon /kə'kuːn/ *noun* a case of thread made by a larva before it turns into a moth or butterfly ○ *Silk is taken off the cocoons made by silk worms.* ■ *verb* (**cocoons, cocooning, cocooned**) to wrap something up for protection ○ *The baby was cocooned in blankets.*
cod /kɒd/ (*plural same*) *noun* a large white sea fish
② **code** /kəʊd/ *noun* **1.** secret words or a system agreed as a way of sending messages ○ *We're trying to break the enemy's code.* ○ *He sent the message in code.* **2.** a system of numbers or letters which mean something ○ *The code for Heathrow Airport is LHR.* ○ *What is the code for phoning Edinburgh?* **3.** a set of laws or rules of behaviour ○ *The hotel has a strict dress code, and people wearing jeans are not allowed in.*
code name /'kəʊd neɪm/ *noun* a special name or number used instead of a person's or thing's real name, in order to keep this secret
coerce /kəʊ'ɜːs/ (**coerces, coercing, coerced**) *verb* □ **to coerce someone into doing something** to force someone to do something ○ *They coerced her into signing the contract.*
coercion /kəʊ'ɜːʃ(ə)n/ *noun* the act or practice of forcing someone to do something such as commit a crime
coexist /ˌkəʊɪg'zɪst/ (**coexists, coexisting, coexisted**) *verb* to exist or to live together (*formal*) (NOTE: + **coexistence** *n*)
① **coffee** /'kɒfi/ *noun* **1.** a hot drink made from the seeds of a tropical plant ○ *Would you like a cup of coffee?* ○ *I always take sugar in coffee.* **2.** a cup of coffee ○ *I'd like a white coffee, please.* ○ *Three coffees and two teas, please.*
coffee machine /'kɒfi məˌʃiːn/ *noun* an automatic machine which gives a cup of coffee or other drink when you put in a coin and press a button
③ **coffee shop** /'kɒfi ʃɒp/ *noun* a small restaurant serving drinks and light meals
coffee table /'kɒfi ˌteɪb(ə)l/ *noun* a low table in a sitting room, for putting things such as cups, glasses and newspapers on
coffer /'kɒfə/ *noun* a chest for holding money (*dated*)
③ **coffin** /'kɒfɪn/ *noun* a long box in which a dead person is placed before being buried
cog /kɒg/ *noun* one of a series of little teeth sticking out from a wheel, which connect with teeth on another wheel to make it turn
cognac /'kɒnjæk/ *noun* a brandy made in western France
cognitive /'kɒgnɪtɪv/ *adj* referring to the process of understanding
cohabit /kəʊ'hæbɪt/ (**cohabits, cohabiting, cohabited**) *verb* to live together as man and wife, especially when not married (NOTE: + **cohabitation** *n*)
coherent /kəʊ'hɪərənt/ *adj* (*of a statement*) clear and logical
cohesion /kəʊ'hiːʒ(ə)n/ *noun* the fact or quality of sticking together
coil /kɔɪl/ *noun* a roll of rope, or one loop in something twisted round and round ○ *The sailors stacked the rope in coils on the*

deck. ■ *verb* (**coils, coiling, coiled**) to twist around something or into a coil ○ *The snake had coiled itself up in the basket.* ○ *The sailor coiled the ropes neatly.*

① **coin** /kɔɪn/ *noun* a piece of metal money ○ *This machine only takes 20p coins.*

coincide /ˌkəʊɪn'saɪd/ (**coincides, coinciding, coincided**) *verb* to happen by chance at the same time as something else [~ with] ○ *The conference doesn't coincide with my birthday this year.* ○ *Do our visits to London coincide? – We could meet for lunch.*

③ **coincidence** /kəʊ'ɪnsɪd(ə)ns/ *noun* two things happening at the same time by chance

coincidental /kəʊˌɪnsɪ'dent(ə)l/ *adj* not planned

coke /kəʊk/ *noun* same as **cocaine** (*informal*)

Coke /kəʊk/ *trademark* a type of fizzy soft drink

Col. *abbr* colonel

cola /'kəʊlə/, **kola** *noun* a fizzy sweet drink

colander /'kɒləndə/ *noun* a bowl with holes in it for draining water from vegetables

① **cold** /kəʊld/ *adj* **1.** with a low temperature ○ *It's too cold to go for a walk.* ○ *He had a plate of cold beef and salad.* **2.** not friendly ○ *He got a very cold reception from the rest of the staff.* ○ *She gave him a cold nod.* ■ *noun* **1.** an illness which makes you blow your nose ○ *He caught a cold from his colleague.* ○ *My sister's in bed with a cold.* ○ *Don't come near me – I've got a cold.* **2.** a cold outdoor temperature ○ *He had been waiting in the cold for a bus.* ○ *These plants can't stand the cold.* ◇ **to be left out in the cold** not to be part of a group any more

cold-blooded /ˌkəʊld 'blʌdɪd/ *adj* with no pity ○ *She's a cold-blooded murderess.*

cold-hearted /ˌkəʊld 'hɑːtɪd/ *adj* lacking kindness

coldly /'kəʊldli/ *adv* in an unfriendly way

cold-shoulder /ˌkəʊld 'ʃəʊldə/ *verb* not to give someone a friendly welcome

coleslaw /'kəʊlslɔː/ *noun* a cabbage salad, made with sliced white cabbage and mayonnaise

colic /'kɒlɪk/ *noun* a severe pain in the intestines

③ **collaborate** /kə'læbəreɪt/ (**collaborates, collaborating, collaborated**) *verb* **1.** to work together with someone else [~with/~in/on] ○ *He's collaborating with her on a new book.* **2.** to help rather than resist an enemy

③ **collaboration** /kəˌlæbə'reɪʃ(ə)n/ *noun* the action of working together on something

collaborative /kə'læb(ə)rətɪv/ *adj* involving people working together

collage /'kɒlɑːʒ/ *noun* a picture made from small pieces of paper or other materials, stuck onto a backing

③ **collapse** /kə'læps/ *verb* (**collapses, collapsing, collapsed**) **1.** to fall down suddenly ○ *The roof collapsed under the weight of the snow.* **2.** to fail suddenly ○ *The company collapsed with £25,000 in debts.* **3.** to fall down unconscious ○ *The man in front of me in the queue suddenly collapsed.* ■ *noun* **1.** a sudden fall ○ *The collapse of the old wall buried two workmen.* **2.** a sudden fall in price ○ *the collapse of the dollar on the foreign exchange markets* **3.** the sudden failure of a company ○ *They lost thousands of pounds in the collapse of the bank.*

collapsible /kə'læpsəb(ə)l/ *adj* which can be folded up

② **collar** /'kɒlə/ *noun* **1.** the part of a piece of clothing which goes round your neck ○ *I can't wear this shirt – the collar's too tight.* ○ *She turned up her coat collar because the wind was cold.* ○ *He has a winter coat with a fur collar.* **2.** a leather ring round the neck of a dog or cat ○ *The cat has a collar with her name and address on it.*

collarbone /'kɒləbəʊn/ *noun* a clavicle, one of two long thin bones joining the shoulders to the breastbone

collateral /kə'læt(ə)rəl/ *noun* a security used to provide a guarantee for a loan ○ *He offered his house as collateral.*

② **colleague** /'kɒliːg/ *noun* a person who works with you, especially in the same company or office [~at/in/from] ○ *His colleagues at the college gave him a present when he got married.*

① **collect** /kə'lekt/ (**collects, collecting, collected**) *verb* **1.** to bring things or people together, or to come together ○ *We collected information from all the people who offered to help.* ○ *A crowd collected at the scene of the accident.* **2.** to get things and keep them together ○ *The mail is collected from the postbox twice a day.* ○ *I must collect the children from school at 4 p.m.* ○ *Your coat is ready for you to collect from the cleaner's.* **3.** to buy things or bring things together as a hobby ○ *He collects* *stamps and old coins.* **4.** to gather money to give to an organisation that helps people ○ *They're collecting for Oxfam.*

collected /kə'lektɪd/ *adj* calm

① **collection** /kə'lekʃən/ *noun* **1.** a group of things that have been brought together ○ *He showed me his stamp collection.* ○ *The museum has a large collection of Italian paintings.* **2.** money which has been gathered [~for] ○ *We're making a collection for a shelter for homeless people.*

③ **collective** /kə'lektɪv/ *noun* a business run by a group of workers ○ *The owner of the garage sold out and the staff took it over as a workers' collective*

③ **collector** /kə'lektə/ *noun* **1.** a person who collects things as a hobby ○ *It's an important sale for collectors of 18th-century porcelain.* **2.** a person who collects things as a job

① **college** /'kɒlɪdʒ/ *noun* a teaching institution for adults and young people ○ *She's going on holiday with some friends from college.* ○ *He's studying art at the local college.* ○ *The college library has over 20,000 volumes.*

college of further education /ˌkɒlɪdʒ əv ˌfɜːðə ˌedjʊ'keɪʃ(ə)n/ *noun* a teaching establishment for students after secondary school

collide /kə'laɪd/ (**collides, colliding, collided**) *verb* to bump into something [~with] ○ *The car collided with a bus.*

colliery /'kɒljəri/ (*plural* **collieries**) *noun* a coalmine

collision /kə'lɪʒ(ə)n/ *noun* **1.** an occasion when someone or something hits against something accidentally [~between/~with] ○ *Two people were injured in the collision between a lorry and the bus.* **2.** a disagreement or difference ○ *a collision of ideas* ◇ **in collision with** involved in hitting into ○ *She was in collision with a bike.*

colloquial /kə'ləʊkwiəl/ *adj* used in common speech

colloquialism /kə'ləʊkwiəlɪz(ə)m/ *noun* an expression used in common speech

collusion /kə'luːʒ(ə)n/ *noun* an illegal cooperation or agreement to cheat someone

cologne /kə'ləʊn/ *noun* a type of light perfume. ◊ **eau de cologne**

③ **colon** /'kəʊlɒn/ *noun* **1.** the main part of the part inside your body that removes waste ○ *The intestines are divided into two parts: the small intestine and the large intestine or colon.* **2.** a printing sign (:)

colonel /'kɜːn(ə)l/, **Colonel** *noun* the officer in charge of a regiment, an army rank above lieutenant-colonel (NOTE: also used as a title before a surname: *Colonel Davis*; often shortened to **Col.**: *Col. Davis*. Do not confuse with **kernel**.)

colonial /kə'ləʊniəl/ *adj* referring to a colony

colonialism /kə'ləʊniəlɪz(ə)m/ *noun* the practice of establishing colonies in other lands

colonise /'kɒlənaɪz/ (**colonises, colonising, colonised**), **colonize** *verb* to take possession of an area or country and rule it as a colony

colonist /'kɒlənɪst/ *noun* a person who goes to settle in a new colony

colony /'kɒləni/ (*plural* **colonies**) *noun* **1.** a territory ruled by another country ○ *the former French colonies in Africa* ○ *Roman colonies were established in North Africa and along the shores of the Black Sea.* **2.** a group of animals or humans living together ○ *a colony of ants* ○ *an artists' colony*

color /'kʌlə/ *noun, verb* US spelling of **colour**

colossal /kə'lɒs(ə)l/ *adj* very large, huge

① **colour** /'kʌlə/ *noun* **1.** the appearance which an object has in light, e.g. red, blue or yellow ○ *What colour is your bathroom?* ○ *I don't like the colour of the carpet.* ○ *His socks are the same colour as his shirt.* **2.** not black or white ○ *The book has pages of colour pictures.* ■ *verb* to add colour to something ○ *The children were given crayons and told to colour the trees green and the earth brown.*

colour-blind /'kʌlə blaɪnd/ *adj* not able to tell the difference between certain colours, such as red and green

① **coloured** /'kʌləd/ *adj* in colour ○ *a coloured postcard* ○ *a book with coloured illustrations*

-coloured /kʌləd/ *suffix* with a particular colour ○ *She was wearing a cream-coloured shirt.*

② **colourful** /'kʌləf(ə)l/ *adj* **1.** with bright colours ○ *She tied a colourful silk scarf round her hair.* **2.** full of excitement and adventure ○ *a colourful account of life in Vienna before the First World War*

colouring /'kʌlərɪŋ/ *noun* **1.** the way in which something or a plant or animal is coloured ○ *the bright colouring of parrots* ○ *the brilliant colouring of woods in autumn* **2.** complexion, the colour of your skin and hair ○ *Choose a lipstick that goes with your dress and suits your colouring.* (NOTE: [all senses] The US spelling is **coloring**.)

colt /kəʊlt/ *noun* a young male horse ○ *The Irish colt won the race by two lengths.* (NOTE: A young female horse is a **filly**.)

② **column** /'kɒləm/ *noun* **1.** a tall post, especially one made of stone **2.** a narrow block of printing on a page such as in a newspaper ○ *'Continued on page 7, column 4.'* **3.** a regular article in a newspaper ○ *She writes a gardening column for the local newspaper.* **4.** a series of numbers, one written or printed under the other ○ *to add up a column of figures* ○ *Put the total at the bottom of the column.*

columnist /'kɒləmnɪst/ *noun* a journalist who writes regularly for a paper

com /kɒm/ *noun* a commercial organisation

coma /'kəʊmə/ *noun* a state of unconsciousness from which a person cannot be awakened

comb /kəʊm/ *noun* an object with long pointed pieces that you pull through your hair to make it tidy ○ *Her hair is in such a mess that you can't get a comb through it.* ■ *verb* (**combs, combing, combed**) to smooth your hair with a comb ○ *She was combing her hair in front of the mirror.*

combat /'kɒmbæt/ *noun* fighting ○ *These young soldiers have no experience of combat in the field.*

combatant /'kɒmbətənt/ *noun* a person who is fighting

combative /'kɒmbətɪv/ *adj* who likes to get into quarrels or arguments

② **combination** /ˌkɒmbɪ'neɪʃ(ə)n/ *noun* several things joined or considered together ○ *A combination of bad weather and illness made our holiday a disaster.*

combine /kəm'baɪn/ (**combines, combining, combined**) *verb* to join together, or consider things together [~with] ○ *Let's combine our ideas and then try to work out a plan.* ○ *The cold weather will be combined with high winds next week and the temperature will drop rapidly.*

combined /kəm'baɪnd/ *adj* taken together

combustible /kəm'bʌstɪb(ə)l/ *adj* which can easily catch fire ○ *The warehouse was full of paint and other combustible substances.*

combustion /kəm'bʌstʃən/ *noun* the process of burning

① **come** /kʌm/ (**comes, coming, came, come**) *verb* **1.** to move to or towards a place [~to/into/through etc] ○ *Some of the children come to school on foot.* ○ *Come into my room and we'll talk about the problem.* ○ *She's just coming through the gate now.* □ **to come and do something** to come in order to do something ○ *Come and see us when you're in London.* □ **to come to do something** to come in order to do something ○ *He came to talk to us about the new system.* **2.** to happen [~to/~about] ○ *It came about like this…* ○ *How did the door come to be open?* **3.** to occur in a particular position [~before/after/~first/second etc] ○ *What comes after R in the alphabet?* ○ *P comes before Q.* ○ *She came second in the test.* ◇ **how come?** why?, how? ○ *How come the front door was unlocked?*

come across③ *phrasal verb* to find something by chance ○ *I came across this old photo when I was clearing out a drawer.*

come along③ *phrasal verb* **1.** to go with someone ○ *If you walk, the children can come along with us in the car.* **2.** to hurry ○ *Come along, or you'll miss the bus.*

come apart③ *phrasal verb* to break into pieces

come back③ *phrasal verb* to return ○ *They left the house in a hurry, and then had to come back to get their passports.* ○ *They started to walk away, but the policeman shouted at them to come back.*

come down *phrasal verb* **1.** to get lower ○ *The price of oranges has come down.* **2.** to come downstairs ○ *She was in bed but had to come down to answer the phone.* **3.** to get a disease ○ *The children have come down with measles.*

come in③ *phrasal verb* to enter a place

come in for *phrasal verb* to get or receive something unpleasant

come into *phrasal verb* to enter ○ *Three people came into the restaurant.*

come of *phrasal verb* to happen as a result of

come off③ *phrasal verb* **1.** to stop being attached ○ *The button has come off my coat.* ○ *I can't use the kettle, the handle has come off.* **2.** to be removed ○ *The paint won't come off my coat.* **3.** to do well or badly ○ *Our team came off badly in the competition.* ○ *She came off well in the exam.*

come on③ *phrasal verb* **1.** to hurry ○ *Come on, or we'll miss the start of the film.* **2.** to arrive ○ *A storm came on as we* *were fishing in the bay.* ○ *Night is coming on.* ○ *She thinks she has a cold coming on.*

come out *phrasal verb* **1.** to move outside ○ *Come out into the garden, it's beautifully hot.* **2.** (*of pictures and photographs*) to appear ○ *The church didn't come out very well on the photo.* ○ *Something must be wrong with the camera – half my holiday pictures didn't come out.* **3.** to be removed ○ *The ink marks won't come out of my white shirt.* ○ *Red wine stains don't come out easily.* **4.** to appear for sale ○ *The magazine comes out on Saturdays.* **5.** to state publicly that you are homosexual ○ *He decided to come out before the newspapers started to print stories about him.*

come through *phrasal verb* **1.** to move through something to get to a place ○ *Come through the kitchen into the dining room.* **2.** (*of information*) to arrive by phone, fax, etc. ○ *The message came through this morning.* **3.** to recover from an illness ○ *Do you think she's going to come through?*

come to③ *phrasal verb* **1.** to add up to a particular amount ○ *The bill comes to £10.* **2.** to become conscious again ○ *When he came to, he was in hospital.*

come up *phrasal verb* to come close to someone ○ *The policeman came up to him and asked to see his passport.*

comeback /ˈkʌmbæk/ *noun* **1.** a reaction ○ *Despite the mistakes in the book there has been no comeback yet from the readers.* **2.** a return of someone such as a singer or sportsman after retirement ○ *She is trying to make a comeback.*

comedian /kəˈmiːdiən/ *noun* a person who tells jokes to make people laugh

comedown /ˈkʌmdaʊn/ *noun* a situation making you feel unimportant (*informal*)

comedy /ˈkɒmədi/ (*plural* **comedies**) *noun* **1.** entertainment which makes you laugh **2.** a play or film which makes you laugh

comet /ˈkɒmɪt/ *noun* an object which moves in space, and which you can see at night because of its bright tail

③ **comfort** /ˈkʌmfət/ *noun* **1.** the state of being comfortable ○ *They live in great comfort.* ○ *You expect a certain amount of comfort on a luxury liner.* ○ *She complained about the lack of comfort in the second-class coaches.* **2.** something which helps to make you feel happier [~to] ○ *It was a comfort to me to know that the children were safe.* **3.** a feeling of being less worried or unhappy than you were before ○ *The long-awaited letter gave me some comfort.* ■ *verb* (**comforts, comforting, comforted**) to make someone feel happier ○ *She was comforting the people who had been in the accident.*

① **comfortable** /ˈkʌmf(ə)təb(ə)l/ *adj* **1.** soft and relaxing ○ *These shoes aren't very comfortable.* ○ *There are more comfortable chairs in the lounge.* **2.** □ **to make yourself comfortable** to relax ○ *She made herself comfortable in the chair by the fire.*

comfortably /ˈkʌmf(ə)təbli/ *adv* in a soft, relaxed or relaxing way ○ *If you're sitting comfortably, I'll explain to you what we have to do.* ○ *Make sure you're comfortably dressed because it is rather cold outside.*

comfy /ˈkʌmfi/ (**comfier, comfiest**) *adj* comfortable (*informal*)

comic /ˈkɒmɪk/ *noun* **1.** a children's magazine with pictures and stories **2.** a person who tells jokes to make people laugh ○ *a well-known TV comic* ■ *adj* intended to make people laugh, especially as a performance ○ *a comic poem*

comical /ˈkɒmɪk(ə)l/ *adj* strange or silly in a way that makes people laugh ○ *He looked rather comical wearing his dad's jacket.*

comic strip /ˈkɒmɪk strɪp/ *noun* a series of small pictures telling a story or joke, usually printed in a magazine or newspaper

③ **coming** /ˈkʌmɪŋ/ *adj* which is about to happen ○ *The newspaper tells you what will happen in the coming week in parliament.*

comma /ˈkɒmə/ *noun* a punctuation mark (,) showing a break in a sentence

② **command** /kəˈmɑːnd/ *noun* an order ○ *Don't start until I give the command.* ○ *The general gave the command to attack.* □ **in command of** in control of ○ *They are not fully in command of the situation.* ■ *verb* (**commands, commanding, commanded**) **1.** to order someone to do something ○ *He commanded the troops to open fire on the rebels.* **2.** to be in charge of a group of people, especially in the armed forces ○ *He commands a group of volunteer soldiers.*

commandant /ˈkɒməndænt/ *noun* the officer in charge of something such as a military base

commandeer /ˌkɒmənˈdɪə/ (**commandeers, commandeering, commandeered**) *verb* to take over property to be used by the armed forces

commander /kə'mɑːndə/ *noun* the officer in charge of a group of soldiers or a ship ○ *The commander must make sure that all his soldiers know exactly what they must do.*

commandment /kə'mɑːndmənt/ *noun* a rule

commando /kə'mɑːndəʊ/ (*plural* **commandos** or **commandoes**) *noun* **1.** a group of soldiers who are specially trained to attack under difficult circumstances ○ *They planned a commando attack on the harbour.* **2.** a member of such a group of soldiers ○ *Masked commandos burst in through the door.*

③ **commemorate** /kə'meməreɪt/ (**commemorates, commemorating, commemorated**) *verb* to celebrate the memory of someone, a special occasion, etc.

commemorative /kə'mem(ə)rətɪv/ *adj* which commemorates

③ **commence** /kə'mens/ (**commences, commencing, commenced**) *verb* to begin

commencement /kə'mensmənt/ *noun* the beginning ○ *At the commencement of the service, the priest asked everyone to stand.*

Commencement /kə'mensmənt/ *noun* *US* a day when degrees are awarded at a university or college (NOTE: The British term is **degree day** or **degree ceremony**.)

commend /kə'mend/ (**commends, commending, commended**) *verb* to praise

commendable /kə'mendəb(ə)l/ *adj* which should be praised

① **comment** /'kɒment/ *noun* **1.** words showing what you think about something [~about/on] ○ *His comments were widely reported in the newspapers.* ○ *The man made a rude comment about the food.* **2.** discussion about a particular issue [~about/on] ○ *The scandal aroused considerable comment in the press.* (NOTE: no plural in this meaning) ■ *verb* (**comments, commenting, commented**) to say what you think about something [~on/~that] ○ *The film star refused to comment.* ○ *He commented on the lack of towels in the bathroom.* ○ *The judges commented that the standard had been very high.* ◇ **'no comment'** I refuse to discuss it in public

commentary /'kɒmənt(ə)ri/ (*plural* **commentaries**) *noun* **1.** a spoken report on a football match, horse race, etc. ○ *The match is being shown on Channel 4 with live commentary also on the radio.* **2.** remarks about a book, a problem, etc. ○ *For intelligent commentary on current events you should read the 'Spectator'.*

commentator /'kɒmənteɪtə/ *noun* a person who reports events as they happen, on the radio or TV

commerce /'kɒmɜːs/ *noun* the buying and selling of goods and services

② **commercial** /kə'mɜːʃ(ə)l/ *adj* **1.** relating to business ○ *He is a specialist in commercial law.* **2.** used for business purposes and not private or military purposes ○ *The company makes commercial vehicles such as taxis and buses.* (NOTE: [all adj senses] only used before nouns) ■ *noun* an advertisement on television ○ *Our TV commercial attracted a lot of interest.*

commercialism /kə'mɜːʃ(ə)lɪz(ə)m/ *noun* **1.** the principles and methods of buying and selling goods and services **2.** emphasis on making a profit rather than on quality

commiserate /kə'mɪzəreɪt/ (**commiserates, commiserating, commiserated**) *verb* to sympathise with someone [~with/~about/over] ○ *She was commiserating with me about our theft.*

① **commission** /kə'mɪʃ(ə)n/ *noun* **1.** a group of people which investigates problems of national importance ○ *The government has appointed a commission to look into the problem of drugs in schools.* **2.** an order for something to be made or to be used ○ *He received a commission to paint the portrait of the Prime Minister.* **3.** the percentage of sales value given to the sales representative ○ *She gets 15% commission on everything she sells.* ○ *He charges 10% commission.* **4.** an order making someone an officer ○ *He has a commission in the Royal Marines.* ■ *verb* (**commissions, commissioning, commissioned**) **1.** to authorise someone such as an artist or architect to do a piece of work; to authorise a piece of work to be done ○ *The magazine commissioned him to write a series of articles on Germany.* ○ *The statue was commissioned by the veterans' association.* **2.** to make someone an officer ○ *He was commissioned into the guards.*

commissioner /kə'mɪʃ(ə)nə/ *noun* a representative of authority

② **commit** /kə'mɪt/ (**commits, committing, committed**) *verb* **1.** to carry out a crime ○ *The gang committed six robberies before they were caught.* ○ *He said he was on holiday in Spain when the murder was committed.* **2.** to promise, or make someone promise, something or to do something [~to] ○ *They didn't want to commit £5000 all at once.* ○ *Under my contract I committed to the project three days a week.* ○ *The agreement commits us to check the machine twice a month.*

② **commitment** /kə'mɪtmənt/ *noun* **1.** a responsibility ○ *He has difficulty in meeting his financial commitments.* ○ *She has no family commitments.* **2.** an agreement to do something [~to] ○ *She made a firm commitment to be more punctual in future.* ○ *We have the photocopier on one week's trial, with no commitment to buy.* **3.** determination and enthusiasm ○ *He thanked the staff for their commitment during a difficult period.*

committed /kə'mɪtɪd/ *adj* firmly believing in

① **committee** /kə'mɪti/ *noun* an official group of people who organise or discuss things for a larger group ○ *The company has set up a committee to look into sports facilities.* ○ *Committee members will be asked to vote on the proposal.*

commodity /kə'mɒdɪti/ (*plural* **commodities**) *noun* a product sold in very large quantities, especially raw materials such as silver and tin and food such as corn or coffee

① **common** /'kɒmən/ *adj* happening often, or found everywhere and so not unusual ○ *It's very common for people to get colds in winter.* ○ *The plane tree is a very common tree in towns.*

common ground /ˌkɒmən 'graʊnd/ *noun* the things that two or more people or groups agree upon

common knowledge /ˌkɒmən 'nɒlɪdʒ/ *noun* something that is generally known

common law /ˌkɒmən 'lɔː/ *noun* a law as laid down in decisions of courts, rather than by statute

③ **commonly** /'kɒmənli/ *adv* often

commonplace /'kɒmənpleɪs/ *adj* ordinary, or happening frequently

common room /'kɒmən ruːm/ *noun* a room in which a particular group of people, e.g. senior students, can relax

common sense /ˌkɒmən 'sens/ *noun* the ability to make sensible decisions and do the best thing

commotion /kə'məʊʃ(ə)n/ *noun* noise and confusion

communal /'kɒmjʊn(ə)l, kə'mjuːn(ə)l/ *adj* belonging to, or able to be used by, several people

commune /'kɒmjuːn/ *noun* a group of people who live together sharing everything ○ *What is it like to live in a commune?*

③ **communicate** /kə'mjuːnɪkeɪt/ (**communicates, communicating, communicated**) *verb* **1.** to send or give information to someone [~with] ○ *Communicating with our office in London has been transformed by email.* ○ *Although she is unable to speak, she can still communicate by using her hands.* **2.** to be good at sharing your thoughts or feelings with other people [~with] ○ *He finds it difficult to communicate with his children.*

① **communication** /kəˌmjuːnɪ'keɪʃ(ə)n/ *noun* the act of passing information on to other people [~with/~between] ○ *Email is the most convenient means of communication with our friends abroad.* ○ *There is a lack of communication between the head teacher and the other members of staff.* ■ *plural noun* **communications 1.** a system of sending information between people or places ○ *an improved communications network* ○ *Telephone communications have been restored.* **2.** the ways people use to give information or express their thoughts and feelings to each other [~with/~between] ○ *There's been a breakdown in communications between the agencies dealing with the case.*

communicative /kə'mjuːnɪkətɪv/ *adj* friendly and keen to communicate

③ **communion** /kə'mjuːniən/ *noun* fellowship with someone

communiqué /kə'mjuːnɪkeɪ/ *noun* an official announcement

communism /'kɒmjʊnɪz(ə)m/, **Communism** *noun* a social system in which all property is owned and shared by the society as a whole and not by individual people

communist /'kɒmjʊnɪst/, **Communist** *adj* referring to communism ○ *The Communist Party is holding its annual meeting this weekend.* ■ *noun* a person who believes in communism, especially a member of the Communist Party ○ *He was a Communist all his life.* ○ *The Communists have three seats on the city council.*

① **community** /kə'mjuːnɪti/ (*plural* **communities**) *noun* a group of people living in one area ○ *The local community is worried about the level of violence in the streets.*

community service /kəˌmjuːnɪti 'sɜːvɪs/ *noun* unpaid work for the benefit of the local community, usually done as a sentence for some minor crime

③ **commute** /kə'mjuːt/ (**commutes, commuting, commuted**) *verb* **1.** to travel to work from home each day ○ *He commutes from Oxford to his office in the centre of London.* **2.** to reduce a legal penalty ○ *The prison sentence was commuted to a fine.* ○ *His death sentence was commuted to life imprisonment.* **3.** to exchange one type of payment for another ○ *His pension has been commuted to a lump sum payment.*

③ **commuter** /kə'mjuːtə/ *noun* a person who travels to work in town every day

compact[1] /kəm'pækt/ *adj* small, especially because parts are arranged close together ○ *a compact storage system*

compact[2] /'kɒmpækt/ *noun* **1.** an agreement ○ *The two companies signed a compact to share their research findings.* **2.** a small family car

compact disc /ˌkɒmpækt 'dɪsk/ *noun* same as **CD**

③ **companion** /kəm'pænjən/ *noun* a person who is with someone ○ *She turned to her companion and said a few words.*

companionship /kəm'pænjənʃɪp/ *noun* friendship

① **company** /'kʌmp(ə)ni/ (*plural* **companies**) *noun* **1.** an organisation that offers a service or that buys and sells goods ○ *She runs an electrical company.* ○ *He set up a computer company.* ○ *It is company policy not to allow smoking anywhere in the offices.* (NOTE: usually written **Co.** in names: *Smith & Co.*) **2.** the fact of being together with other people ○ *I enjoy the company of young people.* **3.** a group of people who work together ○ *a theatre company* ◇ **in company with, in the company of** with ○ *She went to Paris in company with* or *in the company of three other girls from college.* ◇ **to be good company** to be a very entertaining person to be with ◇ **to keep someone company** to be with someone so that they are not alone ○ *Would you like to come with me to keep me company?*

comparable /'kɒmp(ə)rəb(ə)l/ *adj* which are similar or which can be compared

comparative /kəm'pærətɪv/ *adj* to a certain extent, when considered next to something else ○ *Judged by last year's performance it is a comparative improvement.* ■ *noun* the form of an adjective or adverb showing an increase in level or strength ○ *'Happier', 'better' and 'more often' are the comparatives of 'happy', 'good' and 'often'.*

③ **comparatively** /kəm'pærətɪvli/ *adv* to a certain extent, more than something else

① **compare** /kəm'peə/ (**compares, comparing, compared**) *verb* **1.** to look at two things side by side to see how they are different ○ *Compare the front with the back.* ○ *The colour of the paint was compared to the sample.* **2.** □ **to compare something to something else** to say how something is like something else ○ *He compared his mother's homemade bread to a lump of wood.*

① **comparison** /kəm'pærɪs(ə)n/ *noun* the act of comparing two or more things [/~with/~between] ○ *He made a comparison of the different methods available.* □ **in comparison with** when one thing is compared with another ○ *This year, July was cold in comparison with last year.* □ **there is no comparison between them** one thing is much better than another

③ **compartment** /kəm'pɑːtmənt/ *noun* **1.** a division inside something ○ *the freezing compartment of a fridge* ○ *The box is divided into several compartments.* **2.** a separate section in a railway carriage, or in a ship ○ *There are no compartments in these trains.* ○ *The hold is divided into watertight compartments.*

③ **compass** /'kʌmpəs/ *noun* an object with a needle that points to the north ○ *They were lost in the mountains without a compass.*

compassion /kəm'pæʃ(ə)n/ *noun* a feeling of sympathy for someone unfortunate

compassionate /kəm'pæʃ(ə)nət/ *adj* showing sympathy with someone who is ill, etc.

compatible /kəm'pætɪb(ə)l/ *adj* **1.** □ **compatible with something** able to fit or work with something ○ *Make sure the two computer systems are compatible.* **2.** □ **compatible with someone** able to live or work happily with someone ○ *How their marriage has lasted so long no one knows – they're not at all compatible.*

compatriot /kəm'pætriət/ *noun* a person from the same country

③ **compel** /kəm'pel/ (**compels, compelling, compelled**) *verb* to force

compelling /kəm'pelɪŋ/ *adj* **1.** which forces you to do something ○ *He used a very compelling argument against capital punishment.* **2.** very exciting or interesting

compensate /'kɒmpənseɪt/ (**compensates, compensating, compensated**) *verb* **1.** to make a bad thing seem less serious or unpleasant [~for] ○ *The high salary compensates for the long hours worked.* **2.** to pay someone for damage or a loss [~for] ○ *The airline refused to compensate him for his cancelled flight.*

③ **compensation** /ˌkɒmpən'seɪʃ(ə)n/ *noun* **1.** something that makes something bad seem less serious or unpleasant [~for] ○ *Working in the centre of London has its compensations.* ○ *Four weeks' holiday is no compensation for a year's work in that office.* **2.** payment for damage or loss [~for] ○ *The airline refused to pay any compensation for his lost luggage.*

③ **compete** /kəm'piːt/ (**competes, competing, competed**) *verb* **1.** to try to win a race or a game [~for/~for/~in/~against] ○ *Teams come from around the world to compete for the cup.* ○ *He is competing in both the 100– and 200-metre races.* ○ *She's competing against some of the best players in the world.* **2.** to try to be more successful than someone or something in an activity, especially in business [~with] ○ *We have to compete with a range of cheap imports.*

③ **competence** /'kɒmpɪt(ə)ns/ *noun* **1.** the quality of being able to do a job or task well enough ○ *Does she have the necessary competence in foreign languages?* ○ *His professional competence was well above the standard required for the job.* **2.** the quality of being legally suitable or qualified to do something ○ *The case falls within the competence of the tribunal.* ○ *This is outside the competence of this court.*

competent /'kɒmpɪt(ə)nt/ *adj* **1.** efficient ○ *She is a very competent manager.* **2.** legally or officially able to do something ○ *The organisation is not competent to deal with this case.*

competing /kəm'piːtɪŋ/ *adj* who or which are in competition

① **competition** /ˌkɒmpə'tɪʃ(ə)n/ *noun* **1.** an event in which several teams or people compete with each other ○ *France were the winners of the competition.* ○ *He won first prize in the piano competition.* **2.** a situation in business in which one person or company is trying to do better than another [~from/~between/among/~for] ○ *We have to keep our prices low because of competition from cheap imports.* ○ *There's strong competition between suppliers for the contract.* (NOTE: no plural in this meaning) **3.** people or companies who are trying to do better than you ○ *We have lowered our prices to try to beat the competition.* ○ *The competition is or are planning to reduce their prices.* (NOTE: singular in this meaning, but can take a plural verb)

② **competitive** /kəm'petɪtɪv/ *adj* **1.** liking to win competitions ○ *He's very competitive.* **2.** having a business advantage, especially by being cheaper ○ *competitive prices* ○ *We must reduce costs to remain competitive.*

competitor /kəm'petɪtə/ *noun* **1.** a person who enters a competition ○ *All the competitors lined up for the start of the race.* **2.** a company which competes with another in the same business ○ *Two German firms are our main competitors.*

compilation /ˌkɒmpɪ'leɪʃ(ə)n/ *noun* **1.** the process of putting things together in a list or book ○ *The compilation of a dictionary is a never-ending task.* **2.** a work which has been compiled ○ *His compilation of jokes from 19th-century magazines has just been published.*

③ **compile** /kəm'paɪl/ (**compiles, compiling, compiled**) *verb* to draw up a list ○ *She compiled a list of all her friends whose names started with the letter 'R'.* ○ *They have compiled a mass of data on space flights.*

complacent /kəm'pleɪs(ə)nt/ *adj* satisfied with yourself

② **complain** /kəm'pleɪn/ (**complains, complaining, complained**) *verb* to say that something is not good or does not work properly [~to/~about/~(that)] ○ *The shop is so cold the staff have started complaining.* ○ *She complained to me about the mistake on her bill.* ○ *They are complaining that our prices are too high.*

② **complaint** /kəm'pleɪnt/ *noun* **1.** an occasion when someone says that something is not good enough or does not work properly [~about/] ○ *She sent her letter of complaint about the standard of service to the directors.* **2.** an illness ○ *She was admitted to hospital with a kidney complaint.*

complement[1] /'kɒmplɪmənt/ *noun* **1.** a thing which adds to or fits in with something else [~to] ○ *Mint sauce is the perfect complement to roast lamb.* **2.** a noun or adjective which follows the verbs 'be' or 'become' ○ *In the sentence 'he's a big boy' the words 'a big boy' are the complement of the verb 'is'.*

complement[2] /'kɒmplɪment/ (**complements, complementing, complemented**) *verb* to fit in with something ○ *The two col-*

ours complement each other perfectly. ○ *Her jewellery complemented the colour of her hair.* (NOTE: Do not confuse with **compliment**.)

complementary /ˌkɒmplɪˈment(ə)ri/ *adj* which fits in with something by offering things which the other thing does not have (NOTE: Do not confuse with **complimentary**.)

① **complete** /kəmˈpliːt/ *adj* **1.** with all its parts ○ *He has a complete set of the new stamps.* **2.** finished ○ *The building is nearly complete.* (NOTE: used after a verb) **3.** used for emphasis ○ *The trip was a complete waste of money.* ■ *verb* (**completes, completing, completed**) **1.** to finish something ○ *The builders completed the whole job in two days.* **2.** to fill in a form ○ *When you have completed the application form, send it to us in the envelope provided.*

① **completely** /kəmˈpliːtli/ *adv* totally ○ *The town was completely destroyed in the earthquake.* ○ *I completely forgot about my dentist's appointment.*

completion /kəmˈpliːʃ(ə)n/ *noun* the act of finishing ○ *With the completion of the Channel Tunnel, travel to France became much easier.* ○ *The bridge is nearing completion.*

② **complex** /ˈkɒmpleks/ *adj* complicated ○ *This really is a complex problem.* ○ *The specifications for the machine are very complex.* ■ *noun* **1.** a group of buildings ○ *The council has built a new sports complex.* **2.** a worry or an unreasonable fear ○ *He has a complex about going bald.*

complexion /kəmˈplekʃən/ *noun* the colour of the skin on your face

③ **complexity** /kəmˈpleksɪti/ *noun* the fact of being complex ○ *The report was delayed because of the complexity of the problems.*

③ **compliance** /kəmˈplaɪəns/ *noun* agreement to do what is ordered

compliant /kəmˈplaɪənt/ *adj* agreeing to do something or to obey the rules

③ **complicate** /ˈkɒmplɪkeɪt/ (**complicates, complicating, complicated**) *verb* to make things complicated

① **complicated** /ˈkɒmplɪkeɪtɪd/ *adj* difficult to understand, with many small details ○ *It is a complicated subject.* ○ *It's all getting too complicated – let's try and keep it simple.* ○ *Chess has quite complicated rules.* ○ *The route to get to our house is rather complicated, so I'll draw you a map.*

complication /ˌkɒmplɪˈkeɪʃ(ə)n/ *noun* **1.** something that causes difficulties **2.** an illness occurring because of or during another illness ○ *She appeared to be getting better, but complications set in.* (NOTE: usually plural)

complicity /kəmˈplɪsɪti/ *noun* the fact of being involved in a crime as an accomplice

compliment[1] /ˈkɒmplɪmənt/ *noun* a nice thing that you say to someone about their appearance or about something good they have done ○ *I've had so many compliments about my new hairstyle today!*

compliment[2] /ˈkɒmplɪment/ (**compliments, complimenting, complimented**) *verb* to praise someone or tell them how nice they look [~on] ○ *She complimented me on my work.* (NOTE: Do not confuse with **complement**.)

② **complimentary** /ˌkɒmplɪˈment(ə)ri/ *adj* full of praise ○ *He was very complimentary about her dress.* ○ *The reviews of his book are very complimentary.*

② **component** /kəmˈpəʊnənt/ *noun* a small part of something larger, especially a small piece of a machine ○ *a manufacturer of computer components* ○ *Each section of the plan is broken down into separate components.* ■ *adj* forming part of something larger

compose /kəmˈpəʊz/ (**composes, composing, composed**) *verb* to write something, thinking carefully about it ○ *He sat down to compose a letter to his family.* ○ *It took Mozart only three days to compose his fifth piano concerto.*

composed /kəmˈpəʊzd/ *adj* not flustered ○ *The accused man sat in the dock looking very calm and composed.*

composer /kəmˈpəʊzə/ *noun* a person who writes music

composite /ˈkɒmpəzɪt/ *adj* made of several different parts

③ **composition** /ˌkɒmpəˈzɪʃ(ə)n/ *noun* **1.** something which has been composed, e.g. a poem or piece of music ○ *We will now play a well-known composition by Dowland.* **2.** an essay or piece of writing on a special subject ○ *We had three hours to write a composition on 'pollution'.*

compost /ˈkɒmpɒst/ *noun* rotted leaves, etc., used as a fertiliser

composure /kəmˈpəʊʒə/ *noun* calmness

compound /ˈkɒmpaʊnd/ *adj* made up of several parts ○ *The word 'address book' is a compound noun.* ■ *noun* **1.** a chemical made up of two or more elements ○ *Water is a compound of two gases, oxygen and hydrogen.* **2.** buildings and land enclosed by a fence ○ *Soldiers were guarding the prison compound.* ○ *Guard dogs patrol the compound at night.*

comprehend /ˌkɒmprɪˈhend/ (**comprehends, comprehending, comprehended**) *verb* to understand (*formal*)

comprehensible /ˌkɒmprɪˈhensəb(ə)l/ *adj* which can be understood

③ **comprehension** /ˌkɒmprɪˈhenʃən/ *noun* understanding ◇ **beyond someone's comprehension** quite impossible for someone to understand ○ *His actions are beyond my comprehension.*

③ **comprehensive** /ˌkɒmprɪˈhensɪv/ *noun* same as **comprehensive school**

comprehensive school /ˌkɒmprɪˈhensɪv skuːl/ *noun* a state school for children of all abilities

compress /kəmˈpres/ (**compresses, compressing, compressed**) *verb* to squeeze into a small space ○ *The garden centre sells peat compressed into large bags.* ○ *I tried to compress the data onto one page, but couldn't do it.*

③ **comprise** /kəmˈpraɪz/ (**comprises, comprising, comprised**) *verb* to be made up of

compromise /ˈkɒmprəmaɪz/ *noun* an agreement between two opposing sides, where each side gives way a little [~on/~with] ○ *They reached a compromise on the price after some discussion.* ○ *There is no question of a compromise with the terrorists.* ■ *verb* (**compromises, compromising, compromised**) **1.** to come to an agreement by giving way a little [~on/~with] ○ *He asked £15 for it, I offered £7 and we compromised on £10.* ○ *The government has refused to compromise with the terrorists.* **2.** to put someone in a difficult position [~over] ○ *Now that he has been compromised over the issue of trust, he has had to withdraw as a candidate.* **3.** to do something which reveals a secret ○ *The security code has been compromised.*

compromising /ˈkɒmprəmaɪzɪŋ/ *adj* embarrassing

compulsion /kəmˈpʌlʃən/ *noun* a force or urge

compulsive /kəmˈpʌlsɪv/ *adj* not able to stop yourself doing something

compulsory /kəmˈpʌlsəri/ *adj* essential, or required by a rule or law ○ *a compulsory charge for admission* ○ *It is compulsory to complete all pages of the form.*

① **computer** /kəmˈpjuːtə/ *noun* an electronic machine which processes and keeps information automatically, and which can be used for connecting to the Internet and sending emails ◇ **on computer** kept in a computer ○ *All our company records are on computer.*

computer-aided design /kəm ˌpjuːtər ˌeɪdɪd dɪˈzaɪn/ *noun* the use of computer software in designing things

computer-literate /kəmˌpjuːtə ˈlɪt(ə)rət/ *adj* able to use a computer

computing /kəmˈpjuːtɪŋ/ *noun* the use of computers

comrade /ˈkɒmreɪd/ *noun* **1.** a friend or companion, especially a soldier ○ *We remember old comrades buried in foreign cemeteries.* **2.** a fellow member of a socialist or communist party ○ *All comrades must attend the party meeting.*

③ **con** /kɒn/ *noun* a trick done to try to get money from someone ○ *Trying to get us to pay him for ten hours' work was just a con.* ◊ **conman** ■ *verb* (**cons, conning, conned**) to trick someone to try to get money ○ *They conned the bank into lending them £25,000.* ○ *He conned the old lady out of all her savings.*

concave /ˈkɒnkeɪv/ *adj* (*of a surface*) rounded inwards like the inside of a spoon

conceal /kənˈsiːl/ (**conceals, concealing, concealed**) *verb* **1.** to hide something or put it where it cannot be seen ○ *He tried to conceal the camera by putting it under his coat.* **2.** to prevent someone from discovering some information ○ *He concealed the fact that he had a brother in prison.*

② **concede** /kənˈsiːd/ (**concedes, conceding, conceded**) *verb* **1.** to admit that you are wrong [~that] ○ *She conceded that this time she had been mistaken.* **2.** □ **to concede defeat** to admit that you have lost ○ *With half the votes counted, the presidential candidate conceded defeat.*

conceit /kənˈsiːt/ *noun* a high opinion of yourself

conceited /kənˈsiːtɪd/ *adj* thinking that you are better, more intelligent, or more talented than other people ○ *He's the most conceited and selfish person I've ever known.*

conceivable /kənˈsiːvəb(ə)l/ *adj* which can be imagined

② **conceive** /kənˈsiːv/ (**conceives, conceiving, conceived**) *verb* **1.** to become pregnant ○ *After two years of marriage she was beginning to think she would never conceive.* **2.** □ **to be conceived** (*of a child*) to start existence in the mother's body ○ *Our little girl was conceived during a power cut in New York.* **3.** to think of a plan ○

They conceived the idea for a big celebration in several countries at the same time. **4.** to imagine something, or imagine doing something [~of/~how/what etc] ○ *I can't conceive of any occasion where I would wear a dress like that.* ○ *It is difficult to conceive how people can be so cruel.*

② **concentrate** /ˈkɒnsəntreɪt/ *verb* (**concentrates, concentrating, concentrated**) **1.** to give your careful attention to something [~on] ○ *The exam candidates were all concentrating on their questions when the electricity went off.* **2.** to put everything together in one place ○ *The enemy guns are concentrated on top of that hill.* ■ *noun* a substance which has been concentrated by extracting some of the water in it ○ *lemon concentrate*

② **concentrated** /ˈkɒnsəntreɪtɪd/ *adj* **1.** from which water has been extracted, so giving a very strong taste ○ *a bottle of concentrated orange juice* **2.** very determined to do something ○ *With a little concentrated effort we should be able to do it.*

② **concentration** /ˌkɒnsənˈtreɪʃ(ə)n/ *noun* **1.** the act of thinking carefully about something ○ *A loud conversation in the next room disturbed my concentration.* ○ *His concentration slipped and he lost the next two games.* **2.** a lot of things together in one area ○ *the concentration of computer companies in the south of Scotland* ○ *The concentration of wild animals round the water hole makes it easy for lions to catch their prey.*

concentration camp /ˌkɒnsən ˈtreɪʃ(ə)n kæmp/ *noun* a harsh camp, often for political prisoners

concentric /kɒnˈsentrɪk/ *adj* used for describing circles and spheres of different sizes with the same centre

② **concept** /ˈkɒnsept/ *noun* an idea about something or about how something works ○ *I'll quickly explain the basic concepts of safe working in this environment.*

③ **conception** /kənˈsepʃən/ *noun* **1.** the fact of becoming pregnant ○ *Birth takes place about nine months after conception.* **2.** an understanding of what something is like ○ *She has no conception of how long it can take to prepare a good lesson.*

① **concern** /kənˈsɜːn/ *verb* (**concerns, concerning, concerned**) **1.** to have a particular thing as a subject ○ *The film concerns* or *is concerned with children growing up in the 1950s.* □ **the letter concerns you** the letter is about you □ **that does not concern him** it has nothing to do with him □ **as far as something is concerned** used for introducing the subject of a comment ○ *The end of June is too soon, as far as delivery is concerned.* □ **to concern yourself with something** to deal with something ○ *You needn't concern yourself with cleaning the shop.* **2.** to make someone worry [~that] ○ *I am concerned that he is always late for work.* ■ *noun* **1.** worry [~about/over/at/~to] ○ *We have a major concern about the late delivery.* ○ *Her health has been a great concern to her family.* **2.** interest [~for] ○ *My main concern is to ensure that we all enjoy ourselves.* ○ *The adults in the group seemed to show no concern at all for the children's safety.* □ **it is not someone's concern** it's nothing to do with someone ○ *I don't care what they do with the money – it's not my concern.* **3.** a company or business ○ *a big German chemical concern*

① **concerned** /kənˈsɜːnd/ *adj* **1.** worried ○ *She looked concerned.* ○ *I could tell something was wrong by the concerned look on her face.* ○ *We are concerned about her behaviour – do you think she is having problems at school?* **2.** involved in or affected by something ○ *I'll speak to the parents concerned.* **3.** showing interest in something ○ *I'm concerned to know what people thought after the information session.*

① **concerning** /kənˈsɜːnɪŋ/ *prep* about; on the subject of (*formal*) ○ *He filled in a questionnaire concerning holidays.* ○ *I'd like to speak to Mr Robinson concerning his application for insurance.* ○ *Anyone with information concerning this person should get in touch with the police.*

② **concert** /ˈkɒnsət/ *noun* an occasion on which music is played in public ○ *I couldn't go to the concert, so I gave my ticket to a friend.*

concerto /kənˈtʃeətəʊ/ (*plural* **concertos** or **concerti**) *noun* a piece of music for a single instrument and orchestra, or for a small group of instruments

concession /kənˈseʃ(ə)n/ *noun* **1.** the act of allowing someone do something you do not really want them to do [~on/~to] ○ *As a concession, we let the children stay out until 11 on Saturdays.* ○ *We have already made concessions on pay and conditions.* ○ *They avoided the subject for a while, as a concession to her feelings of disappointment.* **2.** □ **to make concessions to someone** to change your plans so as to please someone ○ *The Prime Minister has said that no concessions will be made to the ter-*

rorists. **3.** a licence to do something [~to] ○ *a concession to extract oil* or *an oil concession*

concessionary /kən'seʃ(ə)nəri/ *adj* given as a concession ○ *Concessionary rates are offered to OAPs and students.*

conciliation /kən,sɪli'eɪʃ(ə)n/ *noun* the bringing together of the parties in a disagreement with a third party, so that the disagreement can be settled through a series of talks

conciliatory /kən'sɪliət(ə)ri/ *adj* which aims to make people agree to settle a disagreement

concise /kən'saɪs/ *adj* short, using only a few words

② **conclude** /kən'klu:d/ (**concludes, concluding, concluded**) *verb* **1.** to end, or come to an end [~with] ○ *The concert concluded with a piece by Mozart.* ○ *He concluded by thanking all those who had helped arrange the exhibition.* **2.** to come to an opinion from the information available [~(that)] ○ *The police concluded that the thief had got into the building through the broken kitchen window.* **3.** □ **to conclude an agreement with someone** to arrange an agreement with someone

concluding /kən'klu:dɪŋ/ *adj* last

② **conclusion** /kən'klu:ʒ(ə)n/ *noun* **1.** the end of something ○ *At the conclusion of the trial all the accused were found guilty.* **2.** an opinion which you reach after thinking carefully [~that] ○ *She came to* or *reached the conclusion that he had found another girlfriend.* ○ *What conclusions can you draw from the evidence?*

conclusive /kən'klu:sɪv/ *adj* which offers firm proof

concoct /kən'kɒkt/ (**concocts, concocting, concocted**) *verb* **1.** to make up or invent a story ○ *However unbelievable the story is, it is not something which he has concocted.* **2.** to make a dish of food ○ *I'm always a bit dubious about the dishes she concocts for us when she invites us to dinner.* (NOTE: + **concoction** *n*)

concourse /'kɒŋkɔ:s/ *noun* a large entrance area in a railway station or airport

③ **concrete** /'kɒŋkri:t/ *noun* a mixture of a grey powder called cement, and sand, used in building ○ *Concrete was invented by the Romans.* ○ *The pavement is made of slabs of concrete.* ■ *adj* **1.** made of concrete ○ *a concrete path* **2.** firm or definite, rather than vague ○ *The police are sure he is guilty, but they have no concrete evidence against him.* ○ *I need to see some concrete proposals very soon.* **3.** referring to something with a physical structure ○ *A stone is a concrete object.*

concrete noun /,kɒŋkri:t 'naʊn/ *noun* a word which gives the name of a physical thing, e.g. 'clock' or 'elephant'

concur /kən'kɜ:/ (**concurs, concurring, concurred**) *verb* to agree (*formal*) ○ *I concur with your point of view.*

concussion /kən'kʌʃ(ə)n/ *noun* a shock to the brain caused by being hit on the head

condemn /kən'dem/ (**condemns, condemning, condemned**) *verb* **1.** to say strongly that you do not approve of something ○ *She condemned the police for their treatment of the prisoners.* **2.** to sentence a criminal ○ *She was condemned to death.*

condemnation /,kɒndem'neɪʃ(ə)n/ *noun* saying that you do not approve of something

condensation /,kɒnden'seɪʃ(ə)n/ *noun* steam which becomes a film of water on a cold surface

condense /kən'dens/ (**condenses, condensing, condensed**) *verb* **1.** to reduce the size of something ○ *The article was sent back to the author with a note asking her to condense it.* **2.** to make a liquid become thicker ○ *He opened a tin of condensed soup.* **3.** (*of steam*) to form drops of water ○ *Vapour will condense when it is cooled.*

condescending /,kɒndɪ'sendɪŋ/ *adj* behaving in a way which shows you think you are a better person than someone else

① **condition** /kən'dɪʃ(ə)n/ *noun* **1.** a state that something or someone is in ○ *The car is in very good condition.* ○ *He was taken to hospital when his condition got worse.* **2.** something which has to be agreed before something else is done ○ *They didn't agree with some of the conditions of the contract.* ○ *One of conditions of the deal is that the company pays all travel costs.* ◇ **on condition that** only if ○ *I will come on condition that you pay my fare.*

conditional /kən'dɪʃ(ə)n(ə)l/ *adj* **1.** provided that certain things take place **2.** □ **conditional on** subject to certain conditions ○ *The offer is conditional on the board's acceptance.* ■ *noun* a part of a verb which shows that something might happen ○ *'I would come' is a conditional form of 'to come.'*

conditioner /kən'dɪʃ(ə)nə/ *noun* a liquid which you use on hair or clothes after washing them to make them feel smooth and soft ○ *The hairdresser asked me if I* *wanted some conditioner after the shampoo.* ○ *I always use a combined shampoo and conditioner.*

condolences /kən'dəʊlənsɪz/ *plural noun* expressions of feeling sad, especially at the death of someone ○ *He expressed his condolences to the company on the death of their founder.* ○ *We sent our condolences to his wife, whom we know very well.*

condom /'kɒndɒm/ *noun* a rubber covering put over the penis before sex as a protection against infection and also to prevent the woman from becoming pregnant

condominium /ˌkɒndə'mɪniəm/ *noun US* **1.** a building where each apartment is owned by the person who lives in it ○ *They're building a condominium on the site of the old hospital.* **2.** an apartment in a condominium ○ *His cousin has just bought an expensive condominium in Malibu.* (NOTE: often shortened to **condo**)

condone /kən'dəʊn/ (**condones, condoning, condoned**) *verb* to excuse or forgive something such as a fault or crime

conduct[1] /'kɒndʌkt/ *noun* a way of behaving ○ *His conduct in class is becoming worse.* ○ *Her conduct during the trial was remarkably calm.*

conduct[2] /kən'dʌkt/ (**conducts, conducting, conducted**) *verb* **1.** to do something in an organised or particular way (*formal*) ○ *I don't like the way they conduct their affairs.* ○ *They are conducting an experiment into the effect of TV advertising.* □ **to conduct yourself** to behave in a particular way ○ *I was impressed by the calm way in which she conducted herself.* ○ *The children conducted themselves well during the long speeches.* **2.** to direct or take someone to a place ○ *The were conducted to their seats.* **3.** to direct the way in which a musician or singer performs ○ *The orchestra was conducted by a Russian conductor.* **4.** to allow electricity or heat to pass through ○ *Copper conducts electricity very well.*

③ **conductor** /kən'dʌktə/ *noun* **1.** the person who sells tickets on a bus **2.** the person who directs the way an orchestra plays **3.** a metal or other substance through which electricity or heat can pass ○ *Copper is a good conductor but plastic is not.*

③ **cone** /kəʊn/ *noun* a shape which is round at the base, rising to a point above ○ *He rolled the newspaper to form a cone.*

cone off *phrasal verb* to cut off part of a road with cones

confectionery /kən'fekʃən(ə)ri/ *noun* sweets and cakes

confederation /kənˌfedə'reɪʃ(ə)n/ *noun* a group of states or organisations

③ **confer** /kən'fɜː/ (**confers, conferring, conferred**) *verb* **1.** to discuss [~with] ○ *The leader of the Council conferred with the Town Clerk.* **2.** to give something such as a responsibility, legal right or honour to someone [~on] (*formal*) ○ *the powers conferred on the council by law*

① **conference** /'kɒnf(ə)rəns/ *noun* **1.** a large meeting where people who are interested in the same thing come together [~on] ○ *an international conference on the environment* □ **to be in conference** to be in a meeting **2.** a meeting of a group or society [~on] ○ *the annual conference of the Green party* **3.** a meeting to discuss something [~on] ○ *The managers had a quick conference on what action to take.*

conference call /'kɒnf(ə)rəns kɔːl/ *noun* a telephone conversation involving three or more people using special equipment so that they can all talk to each other

confess /kən'fes/ (**confesses, confessing, confessed**) *verb* to admit that you have committed a crime or done something wrong [~to/~(that)] ○ *He confessed to six burglaries.* ○ *She confessed that she had forgotten to lock the door.*

confession /kən'feʃ(ə)n/ *noun* a statement in which someone admits they have committed a crime or done something wrong ○ *The prisoner said his confession had been forced from him by the police.* ○ *I was surprised by her confession of ignorance about the correct procedures to follow.* ○ *I have a confession to make – I forgot to send the cheque.*

confetti /kən'feti/ *noun* small pieces of coloured paper thrown over the bride and bridegroom after a wedding

confidant /'kɒnfɪdænt/ *noun* a person to whom someone tells secrets

confidante /'kɒnfɪdænt/ *noun* a woman to whom someone tells secrets

③ **confide** /kən'faɪd/ (**confides, confiding, confided**) *verb* to tell someone a secret ○ *He has always confided in his mother.*

② **confidence** /'kɒnfɪd(ə)ns/ *noun* **1.** a feeling of being sure about your own or someone else's abilities [~in/~(that)] ○ *He hasn't got much confidence in himself.* ○ *I have confidence that he'll succeed in persuading them to do it.* **2.** the fact of being secret ◇ **in confidence** as a secret ○ *He showed me the report in confidence.*

② **confident** /'kɒnfɪd(ə)nt/ *adj* sure that you or something will be successful ○ *I am confident (that) the show will go off well.* ○ *She's confident of doing well in the exam.*

③ **confidential** /ˌkɒnfɪ'denʃəl/ *adj* secret or private ○ *This information is strictly confidential.*

confidently /'kɒnfɪdəntli/ *adv* in a way which shows that you are confident ○ *She walked confidently into the interview room.*

③ **configuration** /kənˌfɪgjə'reɪʃ(ə)n/ *noun* **1.** the shape or design of something ○ *Just looking at the configuration of the wires on a telephone exchange makes the mind boggle.* **2.** the way in which the hardware and software of a computer system are planned ○ *The machine uses RAM to store system configuration information.*

③ **confine** /kən'faɪn/ (**confines, confining, confined**) *verb* **1.** to keep in one small place ○ *The tigers were confined in a small cage with no room to move around.* **2.** to limit ○ *Make sure you confine your answer to the subject in the question.*

confinement /kən'faɪnmənt/ *noun* the fact of being in prison ○ *He was kept in solitary confinement for seven weeks.*

confines /'kɒnfaɪnz/ *plural noun* **1.** the borders or edges of a place **2.** the limits of something such as an activity or topic of study

② **confirm** /kən'fɜːm/ (**confirms, confirming, confirmed**) *verb* to say that something is certain [~(that)] ○ *The dates of the concerts have been confirmed by the pop group's manager.* ○ *The photograph confirmed that the result of the race was a dead heat.* ○ *We have been told that she left the country last month – can you confirm that?*

confirmed /kən'fɜːmd/ *adj* permanently in a certain state, and not wanting to change

confiscate /'kɒnfɪskeɪt/ (**confiscates, confiscating, confiscated**) *verb* to take away someone's possessions as a punishment (NOTE: + **confiscation** *n*)

conflict[1] /'kɒnflɪkt/ *noun* **1.** a strong disagreement or argument [~over] ○ *conflict over whose responsibility it was to notify the change* **2.** fighting [~with] ○ *The government is engaged in armed conflict with rebel forces.* □ **to come into conflict with someone** to start to disagree strongly with someone ○ *They soon came into conflict over who should be in charge.*

conflict[2] /kən'flɪkt/ (**conflicts, conflicting, conflicted**) *verb* **1.** to disagree with someone or something [~with] ○ *His version of events conflicts with that of his partner.* **2.** □ **they gave conflicting advice** different people gave pieces of advice which were the opposite of each other

③ **conform** /kən'fɔːm/ (**conforms, conforming, conformed**) *verb* to act in the same way as other people

conformist /kən'fɔːmɪst/ *noun* a person who acts in the same way as other people

confound /kən'faʊnd/ (**confounds, confounding, confounded**) *verb* to make someone feel surprised or confused

confront /kən'frʌnt/ (**confronts, confronting, confronted**) *verb* **1.** to threaten someone by approaching them ○ *Don't confront a burglar on your own – he may be armed.* **2.** to be willing to deal with a difficult situation ○ *We need to confront these issues before they get out of control.*

confrontation /ˌkɒnfrʌn'teɪʃ(ə)n/ *noun* an angry meeting between opposing sides [~with] ○ *To avoid confrontation with the fans of the opposing team, the supporters will be kept as far apart as possible.*

confrontational /ˌkɒnfrʌn'teɪʃ(ə)n(ə)l/ *adj* always arguing and causing difficulties

confuse /kən'fjuːz/ (**confuses, confusing, confused**) *verb* **1.** to make someone feel that they cannot understand something ○ *She was confused by all the journalists' questions.* **2.** to mix things or people up ○ *The twins are so alike I am always confusing them.* ○ *I always confuse him with his brother – they are very alike.*

③ **confused** /kən'fjuːzd/ *adj* unable to understand or to think clearly ○ *I'm a bit confused – did we say 8 p.m. or 8.30?* ○ *Grandmother used to get rather confused in her old age.*

③ **confusing** /kən'fjuːzɪŋ/ *adj* difficult to understand ○ *They found the instructions on the computer very confusing.*

③ **confusion** /kən'fjuːʒ(ə)n/ *noun* **1.** a state of not knowing what to do or how to decide something [~about/over/as to] ○ *Her reply just created more confusion over who was responsible.* **2.** a state in which things are not organised in the correct way or are not clear ○ *There were scenes of confusion at the airport when the snow stopped all flights.* ◇ **in confusion** not able to decide what is happening or what to do ○ *He was looking at the letter in great confusion.*

congeal /kən'dʒiːl/ (**congeals, congealing, congealed**) *verb* (*of liquid*) to become solid (NOTE: When referring to blood, the usual word to use is **clot**.)

congenial /kən'dʒiːniəl/ *adj* pleasant or friendly

congenital /kən'dʒenɪt(ə)l/ *adj* (*of an illness or other medical problem*) which exists at or before birth

congested /kən'dʒestɪd/ *adj* blocked or crowded ○ *Following the accident, all the roads round the station soon became congested.* ○ *Something has to be done about London's congested road system.*

congestion /kən'dʒestʃən/ *noun* **1.** a situation where a place is filled with people or traffic **2.** a condition in which a part of your body such as your nose is blocked with mucus ○ *This spray should clear bronchial and nasal congestion.*

conglomerate /kən'glɒmərət/ *noun* a group of companies, each making very different types of products

conglomeration /kənˌglɒmə'reɪʃ(ə)n/ *noun* a mass of things collected together

congratulate /kən'grætʃʊleɪt/ (**congratulates, congratulating, congratulated**) *verb* **1.** to tell someone that you are very pleased that they have been successful [~on] ○ *I want to congratulate you on your promotion.* **2.** to give someone your best wishes on a special occasion [~on] ○ *He congratulated them on their silver wedding anniversary.*

③ **congratulation** /kənˌgrætʃʊ'leɪʃ(ə)n/ *noun* praise for someone who has done well [~on] ○ *His grandparents sent him a letter of congratulation on passing his degree.* ■ *plural noun* **congratulations** an expression of good wishes to someone who has done well or who is celebrating a special occasion ○ *a congratulations card* ○ *Congratulations – you're our millionth customer!* ○ *Congratulations on passing your exam!* ○ *The office sent him their congratulations on his wedding.*

congregate /'kɒŋgrɪgeɪt/ (**congregates, congregating, congregated**) *verb* to gather together

③ **congregation** /ˌkɒŋgrɪ'geɪʃ(ə)n/ *noun* the people who meet together in a church

congress /'kɒŋgres/ *noun* a meeting of a group

③ **Congress** /'kɒŋgres/ *noun* the legislative body of the USA, formed of the House of Representatives and the Senate

conical /'kɒnɪk(ə)l/ *adj* shaped like a cone

conifer /'kɒnɪfə/ *noun* a tree with long thin leaves called needles which stay green all year, and which produces fruit in the form of cones

conjecture /kən'dʒektʃə/ *noun* the process of guessing something when you do not have all the information you need ○ *It was pure conjecture on my part.*

conjugal /'kɒndʒʊg(ə)l/ *adj* referring to marriage

conjugate /'kɒndʒʊgeɪt/ (**conjugates, conjugating, conjugated**) *verb* **1.** to state the forms of a verb **2.** (*of verbs*) to have different grammatical forms

conjunction /kən'dʒʌŋkʃən/ *noun* a word which connects different sections of a sentence. 'and' and 'but' are conjunctions. ◇ **in conjunction with someone *or* something** together with someone or something ○ *The icy road in conjunction with fog made driving very difficult.*

conjure /'kʌndʒə/ (**conjures, conjuring, conjured**) *verb* **1.** to do magic tricks with objects such as cards ○ *Here is a picture of a magician conjuring a rabbit out of a hat.* **2.** to produce something as if by magic **3.** *also* **conjure up** to bring an idea or image into someone's mind ○ *His writing about the south of France conjures up scents of lavender and olive oil.*

conjurer /'kʌndʒərə/, **conjuror** *noun* a person who does magic tricks with objects such as cards

conman /'kɒnmæn/ (*plural* **conmen**) *noun* a person who tricks people in order to get money, by making them believe something (*informal*)

② **connect** /kə'nekt/ (**connects, connecting, connected**) *verb* **1.** to join one thing to another [~to] ○ *The computer should have been connected to the printer.* ○ *Connect the two red wires together.* **2.** to link one person or thing with another [~with] ○ *They found nothing to connect him with the family apart from the fact they had been on holiday in the same hotel.* **3.** to make it possible for a telephone or a computer to be used for communicating with others ○ *Has the telephone been connected yet?* **4.** to arrive before another train, plane, bus or boat leaves, so that you can continue your journey easily ○ *The plane from New York connects with the plane to Athens.*

② **connection** /kə'nekʃən/ *noun* **1.** a relationship between things [~between/~with] ○ *There is a definite connection between smoking and lung cancer.* **2.** a bus, train or plane which you catch after getting off another means of transport [~to] ○ *My train was late and I missed my connection to Birmingham.* **3.** a particular way of communicating remotely ○ *an Internet connection* **4.** a point at which two different pieces of equipment join ○ *There is a loose connection somewhere.* ■ *plural noun* **connections** people you know ○ *He has business connections in Argentina.* ◇ **in connection with** relating to ○ *I'm writing in connection with your visit.*

connector /kə'nektə/, **connecter** *noun* something which connects things, especially two pieces of equipment, or parts of a single object or structure

connoisseur /ˌkɒnə'sɜː/ *noun* an expert, a person who knows a lot about something

connotation /ˌkɒnə'teɪʃ(ə)n/ *noun* an additional meaning

conquer /'kɒŋkə/ (**conquers, conquering, conquered**) *verb* **1.** to defeat people by force ○ *The army had conquered most of the country.* **2.** to change a negative emotion or type of behaviour successfully ○ *I eventually conquered my fear of flying.*

conqueror /'kɒŋkərə/ *noun* a person who takes control of a country by force

③ **conquest** /'kɒŋkwest/ *noun* **1.** the act of taking control of a country or people by force ○ *the Norman Conquest in 1066* **2.** a country or person that has been conquered

③ **conscience** /'kɒnʃəns/ *noun* a feeling that you have done right or wrong

conscientious /ˌkɒnʃi'enʃəs/ *adj* working carefully and well ○ *She's a very conscientious worker.*

② **conscious** /'kɒnʃəs/ *adj* awake and able to know what is happening around you ○ *She was conscious during the minor operation on her toe.* □ **a conscious decision** a decision which you have thought carefully about ○ *Refusing the offer was a conscious decision on his part.* ○ *He made a conscious decision to try to avoid her in future.*

consciously /'kɒnʃəsli/ *adv* in a deliberate or active way ○ *I wasn't consciously ignoring her – I just didn't notice her.* ○ *He doesn't consciously remember locking the door.*

③ **consciousness** /'kɒnʃəsnəs/ *noun* the fact of being conscious □ **to lose consciousness** to become unconscious

conscript[1] /'kɒnskrɪpt/ *noun* a person who is made to join the armed services ○ *The conscripts had hardly any time to train before being sent to the front.*

conscript[2] /kən'skrɪpt/ (**conscripts, conscripting, conscripted**) *verb* to order someone to join the armed services ○ *All men under 35 were conscripted into the armed forces.*

consecrate /'kɒnsɪkreɪt/ (**consecrates, consecrating, consecrated**) *verb* to perform a religious ceremony to make something such as a building or someone such as a king or priest holy ○ *The bishop was consecrated in the cathedral.*

consecutive /kən'sekjʊtɪv/ *adj* following one after the other

③ **consensus** /kən'sensəs/ *noun* an opinion which most people agree on

③ **consent** /kən'sent/ *noun* agreement [~to] ○ *Doctors must obtain a patient's consent to any operation.*

② **consequence** /'kɒnsɪkwəns/ *noun* **1.** something which happens because of something else [/~for] ○ *If we lose this order, the consequences for the firm will be disastrous.* ○ *Smoking has serious health consequences.* **2.** importance (*formal*) ◇ **as a consequence** as a result ○ *We queued for two hours in the rain, and as a consequence all of us got colds.* ◇ **of no consequence** not important ○ *What he thinks about the situation is of no consequence.*

consequent /'kɒnsɪkwənt/ *adj* which follows as a result of something

③ **consequently** /'kɒnsɪkwəntli/ *adv* because of this ○ *We walked all day in the rain and consequently all caught colds.*

③ **conservation** /ˌkɒnsə'veɪʃ(ə)n/ *noun* the careful use of things such as energy or natural resources ○ *The company is spending more money on energy conservation.*

③ **conservationist** /ˌkɒnsə'veɪʃ(ə)nɪst/ *noun* a person who encourages the preservation of the countryside and the careful management of natural resources

conservatism /kən'sɜːvətɪz(ə)m/ *noun* **1.** the fact that someone is conservative ○ *the basic conservatism of British farmers* **2.** the ideas and beliefs of the Conservative political party ○ *Conservatism had a great effect on British society during the 1980s.*

③ **conservative** /kən'sɜːvətɪv/ *adj* not wanting to change ○ *He has very conservative views.*

Conservative /kən'sɜːvətɪv/ *noun* a member of the Conservative Party

conservatoire /kən'sɜːvətwɑː/ *noun* a school or college where music is the only subject of study

conservatory /kən'sɜːvət(ə)ri/ (*plural* **conservatories**) *noun* **1.** a room with large windows, where you keep tropical flowers and plants ○ *With its glass roof and windows, our conservatory becomes very hot in the summer.* **2.** *US* same as **conservatoire**

conserve[1] /kən'sɜːv/ (**conserves, conserving, conserved**) *verb* **1.** to keep, not to waste ○ *a government programme to conserve energy* **2.** to look after and keep in the same state ○ *Our committee aims to conserve the wildlife in our area.*

conserve[2] /'kɒnsɜːv/ *noun* pieces of fruit in a thick sweet liquid ○ *peach conserve*

① **consider** /kən'sɪdə/ (**considers, considering, considered**) *verb* **1.** to think carefully about something [~that/~what/whether etc] ○ *Please consider seriously the offer that we are making.* ○ *We need to consider whether we really need it.* □ **to consider doing something** to think about taking a particular course of action ○ *I considered training as a teacher.* **2.** to regard someone or something in a particular way ○ *Do you consider him the right man for the job?* ○ *She is considered (to be) one of the best lawyers in town.* ◇ **all things considered** used for saying that you have thought about all aspects of a situation, including the bad ones ○ *All things considered, the party went off quite well.*

① **considerable** /kən'sɪd(ə)rəb(ə)l/ *adj* fairly large ○ *He lost a considerable amount of money at the horse race.*

① **considerably** /kən'sɪd(ə)rəbli/ *adv* to a fairly large extent

considerate /kən'sɪd(ə)rət/ *adj* full of feeling or understanding towards someone

① **consideration** /kənˌsɪdə'reɪʃ(ə)n/ *noun* **1.** careful thought ○ *We are giving serious consideration to the possibility of moving the head office to Scotland.* □ **to take something into consideration** to think about something when making a decision ○ *The age of the children has to be taken into consideration.* **2.** something which has an effect on a decision ○ *The safety of the children is more important than all other considerations.* ◇ **under consideration** being thought about ○ *The matter is under consideration.*

① **considering** /kən'sɪd(ə)rɪŋ/ *conj, prep* used to say that one thing affects another ○ *He plays the violin extremely well, considering he's only five.* ○ *He ought to be more grateful, considering the amount of help you have given him.*

consign /kən'saɪn/ (**consigns, consigning, consigned**) *verb* to hand something over to someone

consignment /kən'saɪnmənt/ *noun* **1.** the sending of goods to someone who will sell them for you ○ *The consignment of books to our French distributor was easily organised.* **2.** a quantity of goods sent for sale ○ *A consignment of goods has arrived.* ○ *We are expecting a consignment of cars from Japan.*

③ **consist** /kən'sɪst/ (**consists, consisting, consisted**) *verb* **1.** to be made up of various parts [~of] ○ *The package consists of air travel, six nights in a luxury hotel, and all meals.* ○ *My day consisted of clearing out bedroom and getting ready to paint it.* **2.** to have as the most important element [~in] (*formal*) ○ *Her success consists in her willingness to be flexible.*

③ **consistency** /kən'sɪstənsi/, **consistence** *noun* **1.** the fact of being the same throughout [~in] ○ *I wish there was more consistency in his reports.* **2.** the degree to which a substance is, e.g., thick or smooth ○ *The consistency of the sauce should be that of thick syrup.* ○ *In order to obtain the desired consistency, it may be necessary to add a little water.*

③ **consistent** /kən'sɪstənt/ *adj* always at the same level ○ *Some of his work is very good, but he's not consistent.*

consolation /ˌkɒnsə'leɪʃ(ə)n/ *noun* something which makes you feel less sad or annoyed, e.g. after a loss or a failure

console[1] /'kɒnsəʊl/ *noun* **1.** a unit consisting of a keyboard, screen and usually a printer which allows someone to communicate with a computer system ○ *We have a console which contains both the TV and video.* **2.** a surface containing the controls that operate something ○ *The sound engineer at the console controls the sound coming from the stage.*

console[2] /kən'səʊl/ (**consoles, consoling, consoled**) *verb* to help someone to feel less sad or annoyed ○ *The priest wanted to console her for the loss of her father.* ○ *I tried to console her but she cried herself to sleep.* □ **to console yourself** to do something to make yourself feel less sad or annoyed ○ *After hearing he had failed some of his exams, he consoled himself with the* *thought that his brother had done even worse than he had.*

consolidate /kən'sɒlɪdeɪt/ (**consolidates, consolidating, consolidated**) *verb* **1.** to make firm or sure ○ *Having entered the market, the company spent a year consolidating its position.* ○ *The team consolidated their lead with a second goal.* **2.** to join together to make one single unit ○ *The two businesses consolidated to form one group.* (NOTE: + **consolidation** *n*)

consonant /'kɒnsənənt/ *noun* a letter representing a sound which is produced by partly stopping the air going out of the mouth

consortium /kən'sɔːtiəm/ (*plural* **consortia**) *noun* a group of companies which work together

conspicuous /kən'spɪkjuəs/ *adj* very obvious □ **they were conspicuous by their absence** it was very obvious that they were not there

③ **conspiracy** /kən'spɪrəsi/ (*plural* **conspiracies**) *noun* a secret plan, especially to do something illegal or bad [~to/~against] ○ *a conspiracy to murder the leader* ○ *He's sure there's a conspiracy against him in the office.*

conspirator /kən'spɪrətə/ *noun* a person who is part of a conspiracy

conspiratorial /kən,spɪrə'tɔːriəl/ *adj* like someone who has a secret plan

conspire /kən'spaɪə/ (**conspires, conspiring, conspired**) *verb* to make secret plans or to take part in a conspiracy

constable /'kʌnstəb(ə)l/ *noun* a police officer of the lowest rank

constabulary /kən'stæbjʊləri/ *noun* the police force of a district

② **constant** /'kɒnstənt/ *adj* not changing or stopping ○ *The constant noise of music from the bar next door drives me mad.* ■ *noun* a number or thing which does not change ○ *Death and taxes are the only constants in life.* ○ *The speed of light is a scientific constant.*

② **constantly** /'kɒnstəntli/ *adv* all the time

constellation /ˌkɒnstə'leɪʃ(ə)n/ *noun* a group of stars in the sky, often forming a pattern

consternation /ˌkɒnstə'neɪʃ(ə)n/ *noun* a shock or surprise

constipated /'kɒnstɪpeɪtɪd/ *adj* unable to pass solid waste out of your body easily

constipation /ˌkɒnstɪ'peɪʃ(ə)n/ *noun* the condition of being constipated

③ **constituency** /kən'stɪtjʊənsi/ (*plural* **constituencies**) *noun* an area of the country which elects a Member of Parliament

constituent /kən'stɪtjʊənt/ *noun* **1.** a part which goes to make up a whole ○ *Before starting the experiment, make sure that all the chemical constituents are ready.* **2.** a person who may vote in a constituency ○ *A good MP tries to represent the views of his constituents.* ○ *She has had a mass of letters from her constituents about airport noise.*

③ **constitute** /'kɒnstɪtjuːt/ (**constitutes, constituting, constituted**) *verb* to be or form a particular thing ○ *Selling the photographs to a newspaper constitutes a serious breach of security.* ○ *Women now constitute the majority of the committee.*

② **constitution** /ˌkɒnstɪ'tjuːʃ(ə)n/ *noun* **1.** the ability of a person to stay healthy ○ *She has a very strong constitution.* **2.** the laws and principles under which a country is ruled, which give the people rights and duties, and which give the government powers and duties ○ *Unlike most states, Britain does not have a written constitution.* ○ *Freedom of speech is guaranteed by the American Constitution.* **3.** the written rules of something such as a society or club ○ *Under the society's constitution, the chairman is elected for two years.*

③ **constitutional** /ˌkɒnstɪ'tjuːʃ(ə)n(ə)l/ *adj* according to a country's constitution ○ *Unilateral action by the Minister of Defence is not constitutional.*

③ **constrain** /kən'streɪn/ (**constrains, constraining, constrained**) *verb* to stop someone doing something which they want to do ○ *His movements were constrained by his tight suit.* ○ *Entrepreneurs feel constrained by the mass of bureaucracy and red tape.*

③ **constraint** /kən'streɪnt/ *noun* something which limits your ability to act [~on] ○ *the serious financial constraints on the business*

constrict /kən'strɪkt/ (**constricts, constricting, constricted**) *verb* to make something tighter or smaller (NOTE: + **constriction** *n*)

③ **construct** /kən'strʌkt/ (**constructs, constructing, constructed**) *verb* to build or make something ○ *The airport was constructed in 1995.* ○ *The wings are constructed of aluminium.*

② **construction** /kən'strʌkʃən/ *noun* **1.** the act of building ○ *The construction of* *the new stadium took three years.* **2.** something which has been built ◇ **under construction** being built ○ *The new airport is still under construction.*

constructive /kən'strʌktɪv/ *adj* which aims to help or improve

construe /kən'struː/ (**construes, construing, construed**) *verb* to understand the meaning of words or of a document in a particular way

consul /'kɒnsəl/ *noun* a person who represents a country in a foreign city, and helps his country's citizens and business interests there

consulate /'kɒnsjʊlət/ *noun* the house or office of a consul

③ **consult** /kən'sʌlt/ (**consults, consulting, consulted**) *verb* **1.** to ask someone for advice ○ *He consulted his bank about transferring his account.* **2.** to look at something to get information ○ *After consulting the map they decided to go north.*

consultancy /kən'sʌltənsi/ (*plural* **consultancies**) *noun* the act of giving advice on a subject that you have a lot of knowledge about ○ *He offers a consultancy service.* ○ *She runs a consultancy firm, offering advice on planning.* ○ *Since he's been made redundant, he's been doing consultancy work.*

③ **consultant** /kən'sʌltənt/ *noun* **1.** an expert who gives advice ○ *His tax consultant advised him to sell the shares.* **2.** a senior hospital doctor who is an expert in a particular medical condition or illness ○ *We'll make an appointment for you to see a consultant.*

③ **consultation** /ˌkɒnsəl'teɪʃ(ə)n/ *noun* **1.** the act of consulting someone [~with] ○ *a brief consultation with my lawyer* ○ *After consultations with the police, the government has decided to ban the protest march.* **2.** an act of visiting a doctor for advice [~with] ○ *another consultation with a different eye surgeon*

consume /kən'sjuːm/ (**consumes, consuming, consumed**) *verb* **1.** to eat or drink something ○ *The guests consumed over a hundred hamburgers.* **2.** to use something up ○ *The world's natural resources are being consumed at an alarming rate.* ○ *The new model of car consumes about half the amount of petrol of the previous model.*

② **consumer** /kən'sjuːmə/ *noun* a person or company that buys goods or services ○ *Consumers are buying more from supermarkets and less from small shops.* ○ *Gas consumers are protesting at the increase in prices.*

consuming /kən'sjuːmɪŋ/ *adj* which takes up all your time and energy

③ **consumption** /kən'sʌmpʃən/ *noun* **1.** the act of eating or drinking something ○ *The meat was condemned as unfit for human consumption.* ○ *The consumption of alcohol on the premises is not allowed.* **2.** the quantity of something that someone eats or drinks ○ *Unless you reduce your consumption of fatty foods, you risk having a heart attack.*

② **contact** /'kɒntækt/ *noun* **1.** an act of touching [~between/~with] ○ *Avoid any contact between the acid and the skin.* ○ *Anyone who has been in physical contact with the patient must consult their doctor immediately.* **2.** the act of communicating with someone [~between/~with] ○ *We don't have much contact with our old friends in Australia.* □ **to get in contact with someone** to write to someone or talk to them on the telephone **3.** a person whom you know ○ *He has a lot of contacts in the newspaper world.* ○ *Who is your contact in the ministry?* ■ *verb* (**contacts, contacting, contacted**) to write to someone or talk to them on the telephone ○ *He tried to contact his office by phone.* ○ *Can you contact the ticket office immediately?*

contact lens /'kɒntækt lenz/ *noun* a small piece of glass or plastic which you wear in the eye to help you see more clearly

contagious /kən'teɪdʒəs/ *adj* which can be passed on to someone else ○ *He's a great music teacher and his enthusiasm for music is very contagious.*

① **contain** /kən'teɪn/ (**contains, containing, contained**) *verb* **1.** to hold an amount, or to have an amount inside ○ *The bottle contains acid.* ○ *The envelope contained a cheque for £1,000.* ○ *A barrel contains 250 litres.* ○ *I have lost a briefcase containing important documents.* **2.** to limit or prevent something harmful or unpleasant ○ *The army tried to contain the advance of the enemy forces.* ○ *The party is attempting to contain the revolt among its members.*

③ **container** /kən'teɪnə/ *noun* an object such as a box or bottle which holds something else ○ *We need a container for all this rubbish.* ○ *The gas is shipped in strong metal containers.*

containment /kən'teɪnmənt/ *noun* the process or act of keeping something under control

contaminate /kən'tæmɪneɪt/ (**contaminates, contaminating, contaminated**) *verb* to make something dirty by touching it or by adding something to it (NOTE: + **contamination** *n*)

③ **contemplate** /'kɒntəmpleɪt/ (**contemplates, contemplating, contemplated**) *verb* **1.** to look at something ○ *He stood for several minutes contemplating the painting.* **2.** □ **to contemplate doing something** to plan to do something ○ *He's contemplating retiring from his job and buying a shop.*

② **contemporary** /kən'temp(ə)rəri/ *adj* **1.** of the present time ○ *contemporary art* **2.** existing at the same time as someone or something [~with] ○ *Most of the people I was contemporary with at college have already got jobs.* ■ *noun* (*plural* **contemporaries**) a person who lives at the same time as someone ○ *Shakespeare and his contemporaries* ○ *He is one of my contemporaries from school.*

contempt /kən'tempt/ *noun* the feeling of not respecting someone [~for] ○ *The reviewer had nothing but contempt for the author of the novel.*

contemptuous /kən'temptjuəs/ *adj* showing that you do not respect someone or that you do not believe they are important

③ **contend** /kən'tend/ (**contends, contending, contended**) *verb* **1.** to state that something is true **2.** to be forced to deal with something unpleasant [~with] ○ *We had to contend with rainstorms, floods, and mosquitoes, so the holiday was not a great success.* ○ *Drugs are yet another problem that schools have to contend with.*

contender /kən'tendə/ *noun* a person who takes part in a competition, especially someone who is likely to win [~for] ○ *He's a definite contender for the world title.*

content¹ /'kɒntent/ *noun* the amount of something which is contained in a substance ○ *Dried fruit has a higher sugar content than fresh fruit.* ■ *plural noun* **contents 1.** things which are inside something ○ *The contents of the bottle spilled onto the carpet.* **2.** the list of chapters in a book, usually printed at the beginning

② **content²** /kən'tent/ *adj* **1.** happy with what is happening in your life **2.** satisfied with something [~with] ○ *If you are not content with the way the car runs, bring it back and we will look at it again.* □ **content to do something** happy to do something ○ *She was content to sit in the sun and wait.* ■ *noun* a feeling of satisfaction □ **to your heart's content** as much as you want ○ *You can play the piano to your heart's content.* ○ *Living by the sea, they can go sailing to their heart's content.*

contented /kən'tentɪd/ *adj* satisfied and happy

③ **contention** /kən'tenʃən/ *noun* **1.** an argument **2.** a statement of what you believe ○ *It is his contention that they are trying to ruin our business.*

contentious /kən'tenʃəs/ *adj* which is the cause of a disagreement

contentment /kən'tentmənt/ *noun* a feeling of being satisfied or happy

contest¹ /'kɒntest/ *noun* any event or situation in which people compete with each other ○ *an international sports contest* ○ *Only two people entered the leadership contest.*

contest² /kən'test/ (**contests, contesting, contested**) *verb* **1.** to compete with other people to achieve a position ○ *There are four candidates contesting the championship.* **2.** to say that you disagree with what is written in a legal document

contestant /kən'testənt/ *noun* a person who takes part in a competition ○ *The two contestants shook hands before the match.*

① **context** /'kɒntekst/ *noun* the other words which surround a particular word in a piece of writing and which help to show its meaning ○ *Even if you don't know what a word means, you can sometimes guess its meaning from the context.* □ **taken out of context** showing only part of what someone said or wrote, so that the meaning is changed ○ *My words have been taken out of context – I said the book was 'one of the best' not 'the best' I'd read.*

continent /'kɒntɪnənt/ *noun* one of the seven large land areas in the world, e.g. Africa or Europe

Continent /'kɒntɪnənt/ *noun* the mainland area of Europe, as compared with the islands of the United Kingdom ○ *They go to the Continent on holiday each year, sometimes to France, sometimes to Switzerland.* □ **on the Continent** in the main part of Europe

continental /ˌkɒntɪ'nent(ə)l/ *adj* **1.** referring to a continent **2.** referring to or typical of Europe excluding the United Kingdom

contingency /kən'tɪndʒənsi/ *noun* a possible state of emergency when decisions will have to be taken quickly

contingent /kən'tɪndʒənt/ *noun* a group of people such as soldiers ○ *The army was formed of contingents of freedom fighters from various countries.* ○ *A large contingent of farmers marched to the Parliament building.*

② **continual** /kən'tɪnjuəl/ *adj* **1.** happening many times in a period of time ○ *We have experienced a period of continual change.* **2.** happening frequently in a way that is annoying ○ *The computer has given us continual problems ever since we bought it.*

③ **continuation** /kənˌtɪnju'eɪʃ(ə)n/ *noun* **1.** the process of going on without stopping ○ *How can we ensure the continuation of the peace talks?* **2.** something which has been continued ○ *Broad Street is in fact a continuation of the High Street.*

① **continue** /kən'tɪnjuː/ (**continues, continuing, continued**) *verb* to go on doing something or happening [~with] ○ *The meeting started at 10 a.m. and continued all afternoon.* ○ *The show continued with some children's dances.* ○ *He continued working, even though everyone else had gone home.* ○ *The engine continued to send out clouds of black smoke.*

continuing education /kənˌtɪnjuɪŋ edjʊ'keɪʃ(ə)n/ *noun* education of adults after further or higher education

③ **continuity** /ˌkɒntɪ'njuːɪti/ *noun* the way in which the scenes in a film or television programme continue without a break

② **continuous** /kən'tɪnjʊəs/ *adj* without stopping or without a break ○ *She has been in continuous pain for three days.* ○ *A continuous white line on the road means that you are not allowed to overtake.*

continuously /kən'tɪnjʊəsli/ *adv* without a break

contort /kən'tɔːt/ (**contorts, contorting, contorted**) *verb* to twist something into a position that is not natural [~with] ○ >*His face was contorted with pain.*

contraception /ˌkɒntrə'sepʃən/ *noun* a way of preventing a woman from becoming pregnant by using a device such as a condom or a particular type of drug

contraceptive /ˌkɒntrə'septɪv/ *noun* a drug or condom which prevents pregnancy ○ *an oral contraceptive such as the pill* ○ *The chemist sells various types of contraceptives.*

① **contract**[1] /'kɒntrækt/ *noun* a legal agreement [~with] ○ *I've signed a contract with a new company.*

contract[2] /kən'trækt/ (**contracts, contracting, contracted**) *verb* **1.** to become smaller ○ *Metal contracts when it gets cold, and expands when it is hot.* **2.** to make an official agreement to do some work [~for] ○ *to contract for the supply of spare parts* ○ *to contract to supply spare parts*

③ **contraction** /kən'trækʃən/ *noun* **1.** an act of becoming shorter or smaller ○ *Light will provoke the contraction of the pupil of the eye.* ○ *Cold will cause the contraction of metal rails.* **2.** the movement of the muscles of the womb when a baby is being born ○ *The first strong contractions will come about every twenty minutes.* ○ *She had two contractions in the car on the way to the maternity hospital.*

contractor /kən'træktə/ *noun* a person who does work according to a signed agreement

contradict /ˌkɒntrə'dɪkt/ (**contradicts, contradicting, contradicted**) *verb* **1.** to say that what someone else says is not true ○ *They didn't dare contradict their mother.* **2.** to be different from what has been said before ○ *What you have just said contradicts what you said yesterday.*

③ **contradiction** /ˌkɒntrə'dɪkʃən/ *noun* stating or being the opposite [~between] ○ *There is a basic contradiction between the government's policies and what it actually does.* ◇ **a contradiction in terms** a phrase which is formed of two parts which contradict each other, and so have no meaning ○ *A truthful politician is a contradiction in terms.*

contradictory /ˌkɒntrə'dɪkt(ə)ri/ *adj* which states or is the opposite

contraption /kən'træpʃən/ *noun* an unusual machine or device (*informal*)

contrary /'kɒntrəri/ *adj* opposite ○ *Most people agreed with the speaker, but one or two expressed contrary views.* ◇ **contrary to** in opposition to ○ *Contrary to what you would expect, the desert gets quite cold at night.*

② **contrast**[1] /'kɒntrɑːst/ *noun* a difference between two things [~between] ○ *a big contrast in weather between the north and the south of the country* ○ *The two cities are in sharp contrast.* ◇ **in contrast to** as opposed to ○ *He is quite short, in contrast to his sister who is very tall.* ○ *The north of the country is green and wooded* *in contrast to the south which is dry and sandy.*

② **contrast**[2] /kən'trɑːst/ (**contrasts, contrasting, contrasted**) *verb* to be obviously different from [~with] ○ *His formal letter contrasted with his friendly conversation on the telephone.*

contrasting /kən'trɑːstɪŋ/ *adj* which are very different

contravene /ˌkɒntrə'viːn/ (**contravenes, contravening, contravened**) *verb* to fail to obey a rule or law (NOTE: + **contravention** *n*)

② **contribute** /kən'trɪbjuːt/ (**contributes, contributing, contributed**) *verb* **1.** to help something to happen [~to] ○ *The government's policies have contributed to a feeling of anxiety among teachers.* **2.** to give money to help to pay for something, especially when other people are also giving [~to] ○ *We were asked to contribute to a charity.* ○ *Everyone was asked to contribute to the receptionist's leaving present.*

② **contribution** /ˌkɒntrɪ'bjuːʃ(ə)n/ *noun* **1.** something that someone does to help something to happen [~to] ○ *I want to thank you for your enormous contribution to the success of the project.* **2.** something, usually money, given to help to pay for something [~to] ○ *She makes monthly contributions to the Red Cross.*

contributor /kən'trɪbjʊtə/ *noun* a person or organisation that contributes to something

contrive /kən'traɪv/ (**contrives, contriving, contrived**) *verb* to manage to do something

contrived /kən'traɪvd/ *adj* not natural or reasonable

① **control** /kən'trəʊl/ *noun* **1.** the fact of keeping someone or something in order or being able to direct them ○ *He lost control of his business and resigned.* ○ *The club is under the control of three people.* **2.** the ability to get people to do what you want [~over] ○ *The teacher has no control over the class.* ■ *verb* (**controls, controlling, controlled**) **1.** to keep something in order, to direct or limit something ○ *The police couldn't control the crowds.* ○ *There was nobody there to control the traffic.* ○ *We must try to control the sales of foreign cars.* ○ *The government controls the price of meat.* **2.** □ **to control a business** to have the power to direct the way a business is run ○ *The business is controlled by a company based in Luxembourg.*

control freak /kən'trəʊl friːk/ *noun* a person who wants to be always in control of the situation (*slang*)

controlled /kən'trəʊld/ *adj* kept under control

controller /kən'trəʊlə/ *noun* a person who controls something

control tower /kən'trəʊl ˌtaʊə/ *noun* a high building at an airport with the radio station which directs planes

controversial /ˌkɒntrə'vɜːʃ(ə)l/ *adj* causing strong disagreements ○ *He made a highly controversial speech.* ○ *Legalisation of drugs is a very controversial issue.* ○ *She has controversial views on abortion.*

controversy /'kɒntrəvɜːsi, kən'trɒvəsi/ (*plural* **controversies**) *noun* a sharp discussion ○ *There is a lot of controversy about the funding of political parties.*

conurbation /ˌkɒnɜː'beɪʃ(ə)n/ *noun* a very large built-up area

convalesce /ˌkɒnvə'les/ (**convalesces, convalescing, convalesced**) *verb* to get back to good health after an illness or an operation

convene /kən'viːn/ (**convenes, convening, convened**) *verb* to call a meeting

convenience /kən'viːniəns/ *noun* the fact of being convenient ○ *I like the convenience of working from home.* ○ *We bought the house because of the convenience of the area for shopping.*

convenience food /kən'viːniəns fuːd/ *noun* food which is prepared by the shop before it is sold, so that it needs only heating to be made ready to eat

③ **convenient** /kən'viːniənt/ *adj* not causing any practical problems ○ *Six o'clock in the morning is not a very convenient time for a meeting.* ○ *A bank draft is a convenient way of sending money abroad.*

conveniently /kən'viːniəntli/ *adv* in a convenient way

convent /'kɒnvənt/ *noun* a religious establishment where nuns live; the buildings of such a place (NOTE: The equivalent establishment for men is a **monastery**.)

② **convention** /kən'venʃən/ *noun* **1.** the usual way of doing things ○ *It is a convention that the bride wears white to her wedding.* **2.** a contract or agreement ○ *an international convention on human rights* **3.** a general meeting of a group such as a political party ○ *They are holding their annual convention in Chicago.*

③ **conventional** /kən'venʃ(ə)n(ə)l/ *adj* ordinary or usual ○ *For your interview it's best to wear a conventional suit.*

conventional weapon /kən ˌvenʃ(ə)n(ə)l 'wepən/ *noun* an ordinary weapon such as a gun, not a nuclear weapon

converge /kən'vɜːdʒ/ (**converges, converging, converged**) *verb* to come together at a certain place or point

① **conversation** /ˌkɒnvə'seɪʃ(ə)n/ *noun* an occasion on which two or more people talk to each other about something [~about/~with/~between] ○ *We had a long conversation about loans with the bank manager.* ○ *He heard an interesting conversation between two bus passengers.* □ **to carry on a conversation with someone** to talk to someone ○ *She tried to carry on a conversation with him while he was working.* ○ *It's difficult to carry on a conversation with Uncle Harry because he's deaf.* □ **to make conversation** to talk to someone to be polite rather than because you want to

converse /kən'vɜːs/ (**converses, conversing, conversed**) *verb* to talk ○ *They were conversing seriously in French.*

conversely /'kɒnvɜːsli/ *adv* in the opposite way

conversion /kən'vɜːʃ(ə)n/ *noun* **1.** the act or process of changing one thing into another **2.** the turning of a person to another set of ideas or religion [~to] **3.** the act of converting a try in the game of rugby

convert[1] /'kɒnvɜːt/ *noun* a person who has changed his ideas or religion

convert[2] /kən'vɜːt/ (**converts, converting, converted**) *verb* **1.** to change something into something else [~to/~into] ○ *We are converting the shed into a studio.* ○ *These panels convert the heat of the sun to electricity.* **2.** to turn or to make someone turn from one set of ideas or religion to another [~to/~into] ○ *When she got married she converted to Islam.* ○ *She tried to convert her husband into a vegetarian.* **3.** to change money of one country for money of another [~to/into] ○ *We converted our pounds into Swiss francs.*

convertible /kən'vɜːtəb(ə)l/ *noun* a car with a roof which folds back or can be removed ○ *You can hire a small convertible for $100 a day.*

convex /'kɒnveks/ *adj* which has a shape that curves outwards like the back of a spoon

③ **convey** /kən'veɪ/ (**conveys, conveying, conveyed**) *verb* **1.** to transport, to carry ○ *The supplies were being conveyed in lorries.* **2.** to give a message or to express something ○ *Please convey my congratulations to the team.*

conveyor belt /kən'veɪə belt/, **conveyor** *noun* a moving surface in a factory, which takes something from one part of the factory to another

convict[1] /'kɒnvɪkt/ *noun* a criminal who has been sent to prison ○ *The police are searching for two escaped convicts.*

convict[2] /kən'vɪkt/ (**convicts, convicting, convicted**) *verb* to prove in court that someone is guilty ○ *She was convicted of theft.*

③ **conviction** /kən'vɪkʃən/ *noun* **1.** the fact of being found guilty ○ *His lawyers are appealing against his conviction.* **2.** the fact of being certain that something is true ○ *It was a common conviction in the Middle Ages that the earth was flat.* ○ *Her religious convictions do not allow her to eat shellfish.* **3.** the fact of being likely or being convincing ○ *She gave a string of excuses which completely lacked conviction.*

③ **convince** /kən'vɪns/ (**convinces, convincing, convinced**) *verb* to persuade someone that something is true ○ *The lawyer has to convince the jury of his client's innocence.* ○ *At an interview, you have to convince the employer that you are the right person for the job.*

③ **convinced** /kən'vɪnst/ *adj* very certain ○ *She's convinced that she's right.*

convincing /kən'vɪnsɪŋ/ *adj* easy to accept or believe to be true

convoy /'kɒnvɔɪ/ *noun* a group of vehicles or ships travelling together in a line with armed protection

① **cook** /kʊk/ *noun* a person who gets food ready ○ *He worked as a cook in a pub during the summer.* ■ *verb* (**cooks, cooking, cooked**) to get food ready for eating, especially by heating it ○ *It's my turn to cook the dinner tonight.* ○ *How do you cook cabbage?*

cookbook /'kʊkbʊk/ *noun* a book of recipes

③ **cooker** /'kʊkə/ *noun* a large piece of kitchen equipment, used for cooking food

③ **cookery** /'kʊk(ə)ri/ *noun* the art of cooking

cookery book /'kʊk(ə)ri bʊk/, **cookbook** *noun* a book of recipes

③ **cookie** /'kʊki/ *noun* **1.** *usually US* a small, flat hard sweet cake ○ *She bought a packet of cookies.* (NOTE: The British English term is **biscuit**.) **2.** a computer file sent to your computer by a website when you visit it. It stores information about you which can be used when you next visit the website.

③ **cooking** /'kʊkɪŋ/ *noun* **1.** the action of getting food ready to eat, especially by heating it ○ *He does the cooking, while his wife serves in the restaurant.* **2.** a particular style of preparing food ○ *The restaurant specialises in French provincial cooking.*

① **cool** /kuːl/ *adj* **1.** cold in a pleasant way, or colder than you would like or than you expect ○ *It was hot on deck but cool down below.* ○ *Wines should be stored in a cool cellar.* ○ *It gets cool in the evenings in September.* **2.** not friendly or not enthusiastic [~to/towards] ○ *I got a cool reception when I arrived half an hour late.* ○ *Their proposal got a cool response.* ○ *She was rather cool to me last time we met.* ○ *My colleagues were cool towards the plan unfortunately.* **3.** calm ○ *The nurses remained cool and professional.* **4.** fashionable (*informal*) ○ *They thought it was cool to wear white trainers.* **5.** good (*informal*) ○ *a cool party* ○ *a really cool idea* (NOTE: + **coolly** *adv*; **coolness** *n*) ■ *verb* (**cools, cooling, cooled**) to make something cool; to become cool ○ *She boiled the jam for several hours and then put it aside to cool.* ■ *noun* **1.** a colder area which is pleasant ○ *After the heat of the town centre, it is nice to sit in the cool of the garden.* **2.** the state of being calm ○ *As soon as the reporters started to ask her questions she lost her cool.* ◇ **to be cool with something** to be satisfied with something (*informal*) ○ *We can go tomorrow – I'm cool with that.*

cool down *phrasal verb* **1.** to make something cool or to become cool ○ *Although it is very hot in the desert during the daytime, it always cools down in the evening.* ○ *This coffee is too hot – I'm waiting for it to cool down a bit.* **2.** to calm someone, or to become calmer ○ *He was furious with his secretary, but after a while he cooled down.* ○ *We tried to cool him down but it just made him more angry.*

coolbox /'kuːlbɒks/ *noun* a container which you can carry and which is used for keeping food and drinks cool

cooperate /kəʊ'ɒpəreɪt/ (**cooperates, cooperating, cooperated**) *verb* to work with someone [~with/~in] ○ *Several organisations are cooperating with the government in the fight against international drug smuggling.*

② **cooperation** /kəʊˌɒpə'reɪʃ(ə)n/ *noun* the action of working together with someone else [~with] ○ *Cooperation between team members led to their success.*

③ **cooperative** /kəʊ'ɒp(ə)rətɪv/ *noun* a business which works on a profit-sharing basis ○ *a workers' cooperative*

coordinate[1] /kəʊ'ɔːdɪnət/ *noun* a set of numbers which fix a point on a map or graph ○ *What are the coordinates for that hill? I don't think it is marked on the map.* ○ *Draw the X-Y coordinates.*

coordinate[2] /kəʊ'ɔːdɪneɪt/ (**coordinates, coordinating, coordinated**) *verb* to make people or things work together or fit in with each other ○ *His job is to coordinate the work of the various relief agencies.* ○ *The election campaign was coordinated by the party headquarters.*

coordinates /kəʊ'ɔːdɪnəts/ *plural noun* matching pieces of women's clothing

coordination /kəʊˌɔːdɪ'neɪʃ(ə)n/ *noun* **1.** the action of coordinating ○ *Better coordination between departments would have allowed everyone to know what was happening.* **2.** the ability to move parts of your body properly ○ *She has excellent coordination for a little girl of 18 months.*

coordinator /kəʊ'ɔːdɪneɪtə/ *noun* a person who coordinates

③ **cop** /kɒp/ *noun* a policeman (*informal*)

cop out *phrasal verb* to stop doing an activity, e.g. because of feeling afraid or not wanting to do it

② **cope** /kəʊp/ (**copes, coping, coped**) *verb* to manage to deal with something ○ *She can cope perfectly well on her own.* ○ *We are trying to cope with the backlog of orders.*

copilot /'kəʊpaɪlət/ *noun* a pilot who helps the main pilot to fly an aircraft

copious /'kəʊpiəs/ *adj* in large amounts, in good supply

cop-out /'kɒp aʊt/ *noun* a poor excuse or explanation for refusing to face up to something

copper /'kɒpə/ *noun* a reddish metal which turns green when exposed to air ○ *Copper is a good conductor of electricity.* ○ *The end of the copper wire should be attached to the terminal.*

copulate /'kɒpjʊleɪt/ (**copulates, copulating, copulated**) *verb* to have sex (NOTE: + **copulation** *n*)

① **copy** /'kɒpi/ *noun* (*plural* **copies**) **1.** something made to look the same as something else ○ *This is an exact copy of the* *painting by Picasso.* **2.** a particular book or newspaper ○ *Where's my copy of today's 'Times'?* ○ *I lent my old copy of the play to my brother and he never gave it back.* ■ *verb* (**copies, copying, copied**) **1.** to make something which looks like something else ○ *He stole a credit card and copied the signature.* **2.** to do what someone else does

copycat /'kɒpikæt/ (*informal*) *noun* a person who copies what someone else does ■ *adj* which copies something else ○ *a copycat murder*

copyright /'kɒpiraɪt/ *noun* an author's legal right to do something such as publish a book or put on a play and not to have it copied without permission ○ *Who holds the copyright for the play?* ○ *She is being sued for breach of copyright.*

coral /'kɒrəl/ *noun* a rock-like substance formed of the bones of small animals in the sea

cord /kɔːd/ *noun* a strong thin rope ○ *Pull the cord to open the parachute.* ○ *In an emergency, pull the cord to stop the train.*

cordial /'kɔːdiəl/ *adj* friendly ○ *His greeting was not very cordial.* ■ *noun* to do what someone else does ○ *Fruit cordials such as lemon, orange or lime are popular summer drinks.*

cordless /'kɔːdləs/ *adj* not needing to be connected to an electricity supply

cordon /'kɔːd(ə)n/ *noun* a barrier such as a rope or a line of police or soldiers surrounding an area to prevent people entering or leaving ○ *Police formed a cordon round the referee to protect him from the fans.* ○ *There was a police cordon round the courthouse.*

corduroy /'kɔːdərɔɪ/ *noun* a cloth with raised lines on the surface ○ *He was wearing a corduroy jacket.*

③ **core** /kɔː/ *noun* **1.** the central part of an object □ **the core of an apple, an apple core** the hard part in the middle of an apple, containing the seeds **2.** the most basic or essential part of something ○ *Lack of resources is the core of the problem.* ■ *adj* most important ○ *These are the core points of the report.* □ **core values** the things that a group of people think are most important ○ *Honesty and reliability are among our core values.*

coriander /ˌkɒri'ændə/ *noun* a small herb, whose seeds and leaves are used for flavouring

cork /kɔːk/ *noun* **1.** a small solid tube, used for closing wine bottles **2.** the very light bark of a type of tree, used for making corks and other things ○ *She placed little cork mats on the table to stop the wine glasses marking it.* ■ *verb* (**corks, corking, corked**) to put a cork into a bottle

corkscrew /'kɔːkskruː/ *noun* a special tool for taking corks out of bottles

③ **corn** /kɔːn/ *noun* **1.** cereal plants such as wheat or barley ○ *a field of corn* **2.** maize, a cereal crop which is grown in many parts of the world □ **corn on the cob** the part of maize that has the seeds, boiled and served hot, with butter and salt

① **corner** /'kɔːnə/ *noun* a place where two walls, streets or sides meet ○ *The bank is on the corner of London Road and New Street.* ○ *Put the plant in the corner of the room nearest the window.* ○ *The number is in the top right-hand corner of the page.* ○ *The motorbike went round the corner at top speed.* ◇ **to turn the corner 1.** to go from one street into another by turning left or right ○ *She turned the corner into the main street.* **2.** to get better after being ill or in a difficult situation ○ *Our business affairs seem to have turned the corner.*

corner shop /'kɔːnə ʃɒp/ *noun* a small general store in a town, sometimes on a street corner

cornflakes /'kɔːnfleɪks/ *plural noun* a breakfast food made of small dried pieces of maize ○ *I'll just have a bowl of cornflakes and a cup of coffee for breakfast.*

cornflour /'kɔːnflaʊə/ *noun* a very smooth type of flour made from maize, used in cooking to make sauces thicker

coronary /'kɒrən(ə)ri/ (*plural* **coronaries**) *noun* a coronary thrombosis (*informal*) ○ *He had a coronary and was rushed to hospital.*

coronation /ˌkɒrə'neɪʃ(ə)n/ *noun* the official ceremony at which a king, queen or emperor is crowned

③ **coroner** /'kɒrənə/ *noun* a public official, either a doctor or a lawyer, who tries to find out the reason for a sudden or violent death

corporal /'kɔːp(ə)rəl/ *noun* a rank in the army below sergeant ○ *The major ordered the corporal to take down the flag.*

corporal punishment /ˌkɔːp(ə)rəl 'pʌnɪʃmənt/ *noun* an act of punishment by hitting someone

② **corporate** /'kɔːp(ə)rət/ *adj* relating to a company ○ *Corporate responsibility rests with the whole management.* ○ *Corporate profits are down this year.*

② **corporation** /ˌkɔːpəˈreɪʃ(ə)n/ *noun* a large company ○ *Working for a big corporation can be rather impersonal.*

③ **corps** /kɔː/ (*plural same*) *noun* a military group or organised group

corpse /kɔːps/ *noun* a dead body

corpus /ˈkɔːpəs/ (*plural* **corpora**) *noun* **1.** all the works written by an author or about an author ○ *The library has a huge Dickens corpus which is available to students.* ○ *She is studying references to food in the Shakespeare corpus.* **2.** the mass of text and words stored in a computer ○ *None of the dictionaries in the list state where their corpus comes from.*

① **correct** /kəˈrekt/ *adj* **1.** without any mistakes ○ *You have to give correct answers to all the questions if you want to win first prize.* ○ *If the information you gave us is correct, we can finish the work by Thursday.* **2.** right according to rules or standards ■ *verb* (**corrects, correcting, corrected**) to take away mistakes in something ○ *You must try to correct your driving mistakes, or you will never pass the test.* ○ *The computer keeps switching itself off – can you correct this fault?*

correction /kəˈrekʃən/ *noun* **1.** an action that makes something correct [~to] ○ *He made a few small corrections to the letter.* **2.** the process of correcting something ○ *We drew up a timetable for the correction of minor faults.*

② **correctly** /kəˈrektli/ *adv* without making any mistakes

③ **correlate** /ˈkɒrəleɪt/ (**correlates, correlating, correlated**) *verb* to match or be the same as something else [~with] ○ *The figures in your report do not correlate with those I got from the warehouse.*

③ **correlation** /ˌkɒrəˈleɪʃ(ə)n/ *noun* a connection between things

correspond /ˌkɒrɪˈspɒnd/ *verb* **1.** to fit with [~to] ○ *The findings correspond to my own research.* **2.** to write letters to someone [~with] ○ *She corresponded for years with this man living in New York whom she had never met.*

correspondence /kɒrɪˈspɒndəns/ *noun* **1.** letters ○ *The sisters had been carrying on a correspondence for years.* **2.** the fact that one thing matches or is similar to another [~between] ○ *There isn't much correspondence between theory and practice.*

correspondence course /ˌkɒrɪˈspɒndəns kɔːs/ *noun* lessons given by post

correspondent /ˌkɒrɪˈspɒndənt/ *noun* **1.** a journalist who writes articles for newspapers or reports for television or radio on a particular subject ○ *a report from our football correspondent* ○ *He is the Paris correspondent of the 'Telegraph'.* **2.** a person who writes letters ○ *A correspondent in Australia sent us an email.*

corresponding /ˌkɒrɪˈspɒndɪŋ/ *adj* which relates to something

② **corridor** /ˈkɒrɪdɔː/ *noun* a long narrow passage ○ *The ladies' toilet is straight ahead at the end of the corridor.*

corroborate /kəˈrɒbəreɪt/ (**corroborates, corroborating, corroborated**) *verb* to support a statement, especially a statement made in court, by giving information that shows it is true

corrode /kəˈrəʊd/ (**corrodes, corroding, corroded**) *verb* to damage or change a substance, e.g. by the effects of water, air or chemicals

corrosion /kəˈrəʊʒ(ə)n/ *noun* the damage caused to metals, e.g. by the effects of water, air or chemicals

corrosive /kəˈrəʊsɪv/ *adj, noun* which eats away metal, or a substance which does this

corrugated /ˈkɒrəgeɪtɪd/ *adj* bent into folds like waves

corrupt /kəˈrʌpt/ (**corrupts, corrupting, corrupted**) *verb* **1.** to make someone dishonest or lacking in morals ○ *'Power corrupts, absolute power corrupts absolutely.'* ○ *He was accused of corrupting young people.* ○ *He was corrupted by his rich friends from college.* **2.** to cause mistakes in computer data ○ *The data on this disk has been corrupted.*

corruption /kəˈrʌpʃən/ *noun* **1.** the practice of paying money to someone, usually an official, so that he does what you want ○ *Bribery and corruption are difficult to control.* ○ *Corruption in the civil service will be rooted out.* **2.** the process of damaging data ○ *You have to watch out for corruption of data.*

cortisone /ˈkɔːtɪzəʊn/ *noun* an artificial hormone used against arthritis and skin problems such as allergies

cos /kəz/ *short for also* **'cos** because (*informal*) ○ *You've got to do what I say 'cos I'm bigger than you!*

cosmetic /kɒzˈmetɪk/ *adj* which improves someone's or something's appearance

cosmetics /kɒzˈmetɪks/ *plural noun* substances which improve someone's appearance ○ *My wife keeps all her cosmetics in a little bag.*

cosmetic surgery /kɒzˌmetɪk ˈsɜːdʒəri/ *noun* surgery to improve someone's appearance

cosmic /ˈkɒzmɪk/ *adj* **1.** referring to the universe ○ *Cosmic rays are radiation entering the Earth's atmosphere from outer space.* **2.** very large, affecting the whole world ○ *A war which might reach cosmic proportions.*

cosmopolitan /ˌkɒzməˈpɒlɪt(ə)n/ *adj* **1.** made up of people from different parts of the world ○ *Berlin is a very cosmopolitan city.* **2.** comfortable and confident in different cities or with people of different nationalities ○ *Her cosmopolitan upbringing has made her a very interesting person.* ○ *Born in Canada, brought up in Hong Kong and in England, by the age of ten he was more cosmopolitan than other children.*

① **cost** /kɒst/ *noun* a price which you have to pay for something ○ *What is the cost of a return ticket to London?* ○ *Computer costs are falling each year.* ■ *verb* (**costs, costing, cost**) to have as a price ○ *Potatoes cost 20p a kilo.* ○ *Petrol seems to cost more all the time.* ◇ **at all costs** no matter what happens ○ *At all costs, we have to be in Trafalgar Square by 12 o'clock.* ◇ **to cost an arm and a leg** to be very expensive ○ *The repairs to his car cost him an arm and a leg.*

co-star /ˈkəʊ stɑː/ *noun* the other leading actor or actress in a film or play ○ *His co-star in the film was an Italian actress.* (NOTE: + **co-star** *v*)

cost-cutting /ˈkɒst ˌkʌtɪŋ/ *noun* the process of reducing costs, especially in a business, or the actions taken

cost-effective /ˌkɒstɪ ˈfektɪv/ *adj* which gives value when compared with its cost

costing /ˈkɒstɪŋ/ *noun* a calculation of a selling price, based on the costs of making a product

costly /ˈkɒstlɪ/ *adj* very expensive

costume /ˈkɒstjuːm/ *noun* a set of clothes worn by an actor or actress ○ *The costumes for the film are magnificent.*

costume drama /ˈkɒstjuːm ˌdrɑːmə/ *noun* a play set in a previous historical period

costume jewellery /ˈkɒstjuːm ˌdʒuːəlri/ *noun* jewellery that does not contain precious stones or metals

cosy /ˈkəʊzi/ (**cosier, cosiest**) *adj* comfortable and warm ○ *An open log fire always makes a room feel cosy.* ○ *She wrapped herself up in a blanket and made herself cosy on the sofa.*

cot /kɒt/ *noun US* a folding bed for camping

cot death /ˈkɒt deθ/ *noun* an unexplained death of a sleeping baby (NOTE: The US term is **crib death**.)

cottage /ˈkɒtɪdʒ/ *noun* a little house in the country ○ *We have a weekend cottage in the mountains.* ○ *My mother lives in the little cottage next to the post office.*

cottage cheese /ˌkɒtɪdʒ ˈtʃiːz/ *noun* a very soft lumpy white cheese

cottage industry /ˌkɒtɪdʒ ˈɪndəstri/ *noun* the practice of making products in the workers' homes

cotton /ˈkɒtən/ *noun* **1.** fibres made into thread from the soft seed heads of a tropical plant **2.** cloth made of cotton ○ *I bought some blue cotton to make a skirt.* ○ *He was wearing a pair of cotton trousers.*

cotton on *phrasal verb* to understand [~to] (*informal*) ○ *It was some time before he cottoned on to what I meant.*

③ **cotton wool** /ˌkɒtən ˈwʊl/ *noun* cotton fibres used to clean the skin or wounds or to apply lotion or disinfectant

couch /kaʊtʃ/ *noun* a low bed ○ *She lay down on a couch in the lounge.* ■ *verb* (**couches, couching, couched**) to put something in words ○ *His letter was couched in very formal language.*

couch potato /ˈkaʊtʃ pəˌteɪtəʊ/ *noun* a person who sits watching TV or videos all day (*slang disapproving*)

③ **cough** /kɒf/ *noun* the act of making a noise by sending the air out of your lungs suddenly, e.g. when you are ill ○ *Take some medicine if your cough is bad.* ○ *He gave a little cough to attract the waitress's attention.* ■ *verb* (**coughs, coughing, coughed**) to make a noise by sending air out of your lungs suddenly, e.g. because you are ill ○ *The smoke from the fire made everyone cough.* ○ *People with colds usually cough and sneeze.*

cough up *phrasal verb* **1.** to bring up matter from your throat when coughing ○ *She became worried when the little girl coughed up blood.* **2.** to pay (*informal*) ○ *When he was late with the rent, we sent some people round to get him to cough up.*

① **could** /kəd, kʊd/ *modal verb* **1.** was or would be able to ○ *The old lady fell down* *and couldn't get up.* ○ *You could still catch the train if you ran.* **2.** was allowed to ○ *The policeman said he could go into the house.* **3.** used in asking someone to do something ○ *Could you pass me the salt, please?* ○ *Could you shut the window?* **4.** might ○ *The new shopping centre could be finished by Christmas.* **5.** used in making a suggestion ○ *You could always try borrowing money from the bank.* (NOTE: The negative is **could not** or, especially in speaking, **couldn't**. **Could** is usually used with other verbs and is not followed by **to**. Note also that **could** is used as the past tense of **can**.)

couldn't /ˈkʊd(ə)nt/ *contr* could not

① **council** /ˈkaʊnsəl/ *noun* **1.** an elected committee **2.** an official group chosen to work on or advise about a specific subject ○ *a council set up to promote the arts in the eastern region*

council estate /ˈkaʊnsəl ɪˌsteɪt/ *noun* an area where houses and flats have been built by the local council and are available at low rents

③ **councillor** /ˈkaʊnsələ/ *noun* an elected member of a town council (NOTE: Do not confuse with **counsellor**.)

council tax /ˈkaʊnsəl tæks/ *noun* the tax charged by a local council to help pay for its services

counsel /ˈkaʊnsəl/ *noun* **1.** advice ○ *I should have listened to his wise counsels.* **2.** a lawyer ○ *counsel for the defence* or *defence counsel* ○ *counsel for the prosecution* or *prosecution counsel* ■ *verb* (**counsels, counselling, counselled**) to advise ○ *She counselled us against buying the house.*

counselling /ˈkaʊnsəlɪŋ/ *noun* the practice of giving advice about problems (NOTE: The US spelling is **counseling**.)

counsellor /ˈkaʊnsələ/ *noun* an adviser (NOTE: The US spelling is **counselor**.)

① **count** /kaʊnt/ *verb* (**counts, counting, counted**) **1.** to say numbers in order, e.g. 1, 2, 3, 4 [~(up) to] ○ *She's only two and she can count up to ten.* ○ *Count to five and then start running.* **2.** to find out a total ○ *Did you count how many books there are in the library?* **3.** to include when finding out a total [~as/~towards] ○ *There were sixty people on the boat if you count the children.* ○ *Did you my trip to New York count as holiday?* ○ *Will this training count towards my degree?* □ **not counting** not including ○ *There are three of us, not counting the baby.* ○ *We have three computers, not counting the old ones that don't work any more.* **4.** to be important ○ *Every small improvement we can achieve counts.* □ **to count for a lot** to be very important ○ *Your appearance counts for a lot in an interview.* □ **to count for nothing** not to be important ■ *noun* **1.** the action of counting or of adding **2.** an amount of something, calculated scientifically ○ *Today there is a high pollen count.* ◇ **to lose count** to no longer have any idea of a particular number ○ *I tried to add up all the sales figures but lost count and had to start again.* ○ *I've lost count of the number of times he's left his umbrella on the train.*

count down *phrasal verb* to count backwards, e.g. 9, 8, 7, 6 ○ *He counted down the seconds to the launch.*

count on *phrasal verb* to be sure that someone will do something

countable /ˈkaʊntəb(ə)l/ *adj* **1.** which is able to be counted **2.** describing a noun that is able to form a plural

countdown /ˈkaʊntdaʊn/ *noun* the action of counting time backwards, especially before something takes place

③ **counter** /ˈkaʊntə/ *noun* **1.** a long flat surface in a shop for showing goods for sale, or in a bank for passing over money ○ *She put her bag down on the counter and took out her cheque book.* ○ *The cheese counter is over there.* **2.** a small round disc used in games ○ *You've thrown a six – you can move your counter six places.* ○ *She placed a pile of counters on the board.* ■ *verb* (**counters, countering, countered**) **1.** to act or reply in an opposing way ○ *The adverts are designed to counter familiar opinions about home and family.* **2.** to reply in a way that opposes what has been said ○ *He accused her of laziness and she countered with a list of complaints about his own behaviour.*

counter- /kaʊntə/ *prefix* against, in response

counteract /ˌkaʊntərˈækt/ (**counteracts, counteracting, counteracted**) *verb* to stop the effects of something

counter-attack /ˌkaʊntərəˌtæk/ *noun* an attack against someone who has just attacked you ○ *24 hours after the enemy attack we launched a counter-attack.* ■ *verb* to attack in return ○ *the enemy counter-attacked fiercely*

counterclockwise /ˌkaʊntə ˈklɒkwaɪz/ *adv US* in the opposite direction to the hands of a clock

counterfeit /ˈkaʊntəfɪt/ *adj* (*of money, art or documents*) false, not real ○ *The police have warned shopkeepers that coun-*

terfeit £20 notes are in circulation. ○ *You can see stands in Oxford Street selling counterfeit jewellery.* ■ *verb* (**counterfeits, counterfeiting, counterfeited**) to make imitation money ○ *Are the new £10 notes more difficult to counterfeit than the old ones?* ○ *Only very sophisticated printing machines can be used to counterfeit banknotes.* ■ *noun* a thing which has been forged ○ *There is something wrong with this passport – in fact it may be a counterfeit.*

counterfoil /ˈkaʊntəfɔɪl/ *noun* a slip of paper which you keep after giving someone a cheque

counterpart /ˈkaʊntəpɑːt/ *noun* a person who has a similar job or who is in a similar situation

counter-productive /ˌkaʊntə prəˈdʌktɪv/ *adj* which has the opposite effect to what you want

countess /ˈkaʊntɪs/ *noun* **1.** (*in European aristocracy*) the wife of a count **2.** (*in the British aristocracy*) the wife of an earl

countless /ˈkaʊntləs/ *adj* very many

count noun /ˈkaʊnt naʊn/ *noun* a noun that can be used with 'a' or 'an' and has a plural form

① **country** /ˈkʌntri/ (*plural* **countries**) *noun* **1.** an area of land which is has borders and governs itself ○ *the countries of the EU* ○ *Some African countries voted against the plan.* **2.** land which is not in a town ○ *He lives in the country.* ○ *We went walking in the country.* ○ *Road travel is difficult in country areas.* (NOTE: no plural in this sense)

country club /ˌkʌntri ˈklʌb/ *noun* a club in the country, usually offering special sports facilities such as golf or horse riding

country house /ˌkʌntri ˈhaʊs/ *noun* a large house in the country, with gardens and a park, and sometimes a farm

countryman /ˈkʌntrimən/ (*plural* **countrymen**) *noun* **1.** a person who lives in the country, not in the town ○ *Countrymen are protesting about the new tax.* **2.** a person who comes from the same country as you ○ *He felt ashamed of his countrymen when he saw them fighting at the football stadium.*

country music /ˌkʌntri ˈmjuːzɪk/, **country and western** /ˌkʌntri ən ˈwestən/ *noun* a style of music popular in the southeastern United States, especially Tennessee

② **countryside** /ˈkʌntrisaɪd/ *noun* land which is not in a town ○ *the beautiful English countryside in spring* ○ *The countryside is in danger of being covered in new houses.* (NOTE: no plural)

① **county** /ˈkaʊnti/ (*plural* **counties**) *noun* a district that has some powers of government over local matters

coup /kuː/, **cowp** *noun* **1.** the act of taking over a government by force [~against] ○ *a failed coup against the military regime* Full form **coup d'état 2.** a great success, a successful move [~for] ○ *Getting the Minister of Education to open the school exhibition was a coup for the organisers.*

① **couple** /ˈkʌp(ə)l/ *noun* **1.** two things together **2.** two people together ○ *They are a charming couple.* ○ *Several couples strolled past hand in hand.* ■ *verb* (**couples, coupling, coupled**) **1.** to connect two different things ○ *High tides coupled with strong winds caused flooding along the coast.* **2.** to join two machines together ○ *Couple the trailer to the back of the truck.* ◇ **a couple of 1.** two ○ *They've got a couple of children.* **2.** a few ○ *The film lasted a couple of hours.*

coupon /ˈkuːpɒn/ *noun* a piece of paper which is used in place of money or in place of a ticket

courage /ˈkʌrɪdʒ/ *noun* the ability to deal with a dangerous or unpleasant situation ○ *She showed great courage in attacking the burglar.* ○ *I didn't have the courage to disagree with him.* (NOTE: no plural)

courageous /kəˈreɪdʒəs/ *adj* brave

courgette /kɔːˈʒet/ *noun* the young fruit of the marrow

courier /ˈkʊriə/ *noun* **1.** a person who carries messages ○ *a motorcycle courier* **2.** a guide for tourists on a package tour ○ *We were met at the airport by a courier.* ○ *The courier tried hard to deal with all our complaints about the hotel.*

① **course** /kɔːs/ *noun* **1.** a series of lessons [~in] ○ *I'm taking a maths course.* ○ *The hotel offers weekend courses in a variety of arts and crafts.* **2.** a series of medical treatments ○ *He's taking a course of antibiotics.* **3.** a separate part of a meal ○ *a five-course meal* ○ *The first course is soup, and then you can have either fish or roast lamb.* **4.** the direction in which someone or something, especially a vehicle, is moving in, or will move in ◇ **in due course** after a certain amount of time ○ *If you study for several years at college, in due course you will get a degree.* ○ *Put a coin in the slot and in due course the machine will produce a ticket.* ◇ **in the course of** during a period of time ○ *He's got much richer in the course of the last few years.*

coursebook /ˈkɔːsbʊk/ *noun* a book used by students taking a certain course

coursework /ˈkɔːswɜːk/ *noun* work which students must complete during an academic course

① **court** /kɔːt/ *noun* **1.** a room with a judge who tries criminals, sometimes with a jury ○ *The court was packed for the opening of the murder trial.* ○ *Please tell the court what you saw when you opened the door.* ○ *The defendant was in court for three hours.* □ **to take someone to court** to arrange for someone to come to a court to end an argument **2.** an area where sports such as tennis or basketball are played ○ *The tennis courts are behind the hotel.* □ **to be on court** to be playing tennis **3.** a group of people living round a king or queen

court case /ˈkɔːt keɪs/ *noun* a legal action or trial

courteous /ˈkɜːtiəs/ *adj* polite

courtesy /ˈkɜːtəsi/ *noun* politeness ○ *The hotel staff showed us every courtesy.* ○ *She might have had the courtesy to apologise.* ○ *Children should show some courtesy towards their grandparents.* ◇ **(by) courtesy of** as a gift from, or with the kind permission of ○ *a box of chocolates by courtesy of the management* ○ *He arrived home two hours late, courtesy of the train service.*

court-martial /ˌkɔːt ˈmɑːʃ(ə)l/ (*plural* **courts-martial** or **court-martials**) *noun* **1.** a court which tries someone serving in the armed forces for offences against military discipline ○ *He was found guilty by court-martial and sentenced to imprisonment.* **2.** the trial of someone serving in the armed forces by the armed forces authorities ○ *The court-martial was held in the army headquarters.* (NOTE: + **court-martial** *v*)

court order /ˈkɔːt ˌɔːdə/ *noun* an order issued by a judge

courtroom /ˈkɔːtruːm/ *noun* a room where a judge holds a trial

courtship /ˈkɔːtʃɪp/ *noun* **1.** a period when a man and a woman form a romantic relationship before getting married **2.** a special display put on by animals to attract the opposite sex

courtyard /ˈkɔːtjɑːd/ *noun* a small square area surrounded by buildings

couscous /ˈkuːskuːs/ *noun* **1.** a food made of small grains of wheat **2.** a dish of meat and couscous

③ **cousin** /ˈkʌz(ə)n/ *noun* the son or daughter of your uncle or aunt

cove /kəʊv/ *noun* a small bay ○ *Do you remember the small cove where we loved to go swimming?*

covenant /ˈkʌvənənt/ *noun* a legal contract

① **cover** /ˈkʌvə/ *noun* **1.** something that you put over something else to protect it or keep it clean **2.** the front and back of a book or magazine ○ *She read the book from cover to cover.* **3.** a place where you can hide or shelter ○ *They ran for cover when it started to rain.* □ **to take cover** to find a place to shelter from something such as rain ○ *It started to rain and they took cover under a tree.* ○ *When the robbers started shooting, the policeman took cover behind a wall.* ■ *verb* (**covers, covering, covered**) **1.** to put something over something else to keep it clean ○ *You should cover the furniture with sheets before you start painting the ceiling.* **2.** to hide something [~with] ○ *He covered the hole in the ground with branches.* ○ *She covered her face with her hands.* **3.** to travel a certain distance ○ *They made good progress, covering twenty miles a day.* ◇ **under cover** under a roof, not in the open air ○ *If it rains the meal will be served under cover.*

cover up *phrasal verb* **1.** to cover something completely ○ *He covered up the mark on the wall with white paint.* **2.** to try to hide something that someone has done wrong [~for] ○ *The staff tried to cover up for their boss's absence.*

cover girl /ˈkʌvə ɡɜːl/ *noun* a female model whose picture appears on the front cover of a magazine

covering /ˈkʌv(ə)rɪŋ/ *noun* a thing which covers

covering letter /ˌkʌvərɪŋ ˈletə/ *noun* a letter explaining what is enclosed with it

covert /ˈkəʊvət, ˈkʌvət/ *adj* hidden or secret

cover-up /ˈkʌvər ʌp/ *noun* the hiding of a scandal

cover version /ˈkʌvə ˌvɜːʃ(ə)n/ *noun* a new version of a song, recorded by someone other than the original singer

covet /ˈkʌvət/ (**covets, coveting, coveted**) *verb* to want something which belongs to someone else

coveted /ˈkʌvətɪd/ *adj* which everyone wants

② **cow** /kaʊ/ *noun* a large female farm animal, kept to give milk ○ *a field of cows* ○ *The farmer was milking a cow.*

coward /ˈkaʊəd/ *noun* a person who is not brave

cowardice /ˈkaʊədɪs/ *noun* the state of not being brave

cowardly /ˈkaʊədli/ *adj* not brave

cowboy hat /ˈkaʊbɔɪ hæt/ *noun* a large wide-brimmed hat worn by cowboys

cower /ˈkaʊə/ (**cowers, cowering, cowered**) *verb* to crouch down because you are afraid

co-worker /ˈkəʊ ˌwɜːkə/ *noun* someone who shares their work with one or more people

coy /kɔɪ/ *adj* timid or shy

coyote /kɔɪˈəʊti/ *noun* an American wild animal, like a small wolf

crabby /ˈkræbi/ *adj* bad-tempered

③ **crack** /kræk/ *noun* **1.** a sharp sound ○ *the crack of a whip* ○ *The crack of a twig behind her made her turn round.* **2.** a long thin break in a surface ○ *A crack appeared in the ceiling.* ○ *Her ring fell down a crack in the floorboards.* ○ *The field is so dry it is full of cracks.* ■ *verb* (**cracks, cracking, cracked**) **1.** to make a sharp sound ○ *A twig cracked as he stepped on it.* **2.** to make a long thin break in something ○ *The stone cracked the glass.*

crackdown /ˈkrækdaʊn/ *noun* a campaign against something (*informal*)

cracker /ˈkrækə/ *noun* **1.** a little firework which makes a series of bangs ○ *Crackers were going off all round the procession to the temple.* **2.** a colourful paper tube which makes a little bang when it is pulled, given at Christmas parties

crackle /ˈkræk(ə)l/ (**crackles, crackling, crackled**) *verb* to make little dry sounds, like something burning ○ *The bonfire crackled away in a corner of the garden.*

crackling /ˈkræklɪŋ/ *noun* hard baked pork skin

cradle /ˈkreɪd(ə)l/ *noun* **1.** a baby's bed which can be rocked ○ *She rocked the baby to sleep in its cradle.* **2.** a support for a piece of machinery **3.** a place where something started ○ *Greece is the cradle of Western civilisation.* ■ *verb* (**cradles, cradling, cradled**) to hold something gently in your arms or hands ○ *The little girl was cradling her doll.*

craft /krɑːft/ *noun* **1.** the skill of making something by hand ○ *traditional rural crafts such as thatching* ○ *He learnt the craft of furniture-making as a boy.* **2.** a ship ○ *The sleek craft slipped out of harbour.* ○ *All sizes of craft took part in the rescue.*

craftsman /ˈkrɑːftsmən/ (*plural* **craftsmen**) *noun* an artist who is expert at making things by hand

craftsmanship /ˈkrɑːftsmənʃɪp/ *noun* the skill of a craftsman

craftswoman /ˈkrɑːftswʊmən/ (*plural* **craftswomen**) *noun* a woman who is expert at making things by hand

③ **crafty** /ˈkrɑːfti/ (**craftier, craftiest**) *adj* good at getting the things you want, often in a way that is not completely honest (NOTE: + **craftily** *adv*)

crag /kræg/ *noun* a steep cliff

③ **cram** /kræm/ (**crams, cramming, crammed**) *verb* **1.** to squeeze something into a small space ○ *She crammed all her clothes into a little suitcase.* ○ *Don't try to cram so many interviews into one day.* **2.** to learn facts hurriedly before an examination ○ *Everybody's at home cramming for their finals.*

cramp /kræmp/ *noun* a pain in a tight muscle which will not relax ○ *He went swimming and got cramp in the cold water.* ○ *She woke up with cramp in her right leg.*

cramped /kræmpt/ *adj* too small or too close together ○ *On some planes, the seats are very cramped.*

cranberry /ˈkrænb(ə)ri/ (*plural* **cranberries**) *noun* a bitter wild red berry, used to make a sharp sweet sauce or drink

crane /kreɪn/ *noun* a tall metal piece of equipment for lifting heavy things ○ *The container slipped as the crane was lifting it onto the ship.*

cranium /ˈkreɪniəm/ *noun* the bones covering the top part of the head

crank /kræŋk/ *noun* **1.** a metal arm with a right angle, often mounted on a shaft ○ *You'll need a crank to start the engine.* **2.** a very strange person ○ *She's a bit of a crank when it comes to food, because there are so many things she won't eat.*

crank out *phrasal verb* to produce a series of things as if by a machine (*informal*)

③ **crash** /kræʃ/ *noun* **1.** an accident where vehicles are damaged ○ *He was killed in a train crash.* ○ *None of the passengers was hurt in the coach crash.* ○ *His car was badly damaged in the crash.* **2.** a loud noise when something falls over ○ *The ladder fell down with a crash.* ○ *There was a loud crash in the kitchen.* **3.** the collapse of a company ○ *He lost all his savings in the bank crash.* **4.** the complete breakdown of a computer ■ *verb* (**crashes, crashing, crashed**) **1.** (*of vehicles*) to hit something and be damaged [~against/into/through etc] ○ *The bus crashed into a wall.* **2.** to fall, making a loud noise [~against/into/through etc] ○ *The wall came crashing down.* ○ *The ladder crashed onto the floor.* **3.** (*of a company*) to collapse ○ *He lost all his savings when the bank crashed.* **4.** (*of a computer*) to stop working ○ *The hard disk has crashed but we think the data can be retrieved.*

crash barrier /ˈkræʃ ˌbæriə/ *noun* a strong fence to prevent cars from running off the road

crash course /ˈkræʃ kɔːs/ *noun* a course of fast hard study

crash helmet /ˈkræʃ ˌhelmɪt/ *noun* a hard hat worn by motorcyclists

crash-landing /kræʃ ˈlændɪŋ/ *noun* the act of landing a plane heavily, without using the wheels

crass /kræs/ *adj* rude, stupid or coarse, not caring about what people think

crate /kreɪt/ *noun* **1.** a large wooden box ○ *The dinner set arrived safely, carefully packed in a wooden crate.* **2.** a container for bottles ○ *a beer crate* ○ *The office orders a crate of milk every day.*

crater /ˈkreɪtə/ *noun* **1.** a hole made by a bomb ○ *Over the winter, the bomb craters filled up with rainwater.* **2.** a round hole at the top of a volcano ○ *A group of scientists flew over the crater to monitor the activity of the volcano.* **3.** a round hole on the Moon or a planet, where a meteorite has hit it ○ *A map of the craters of the Moon.*

crave /kreɪv/ (**craves, craving, craved**) *verb* to want something very much

craving /ˈkreɪvɪŋ/ *noun* a strong desire

crawl /krɔːl/ *verb* (**crawls, crawling, crawled**) **1.** to move around on your hands and knees ○ *The baby has just started to crawl.* **2.** to travel along slowly ○ *The traffic was crawling along.* ■ *noun* **1.** a very slow speed ○ *The traffic on the motorway was reduced to a crawl.* **2.** a swimming style where each arm goes over your head in turn ○ *He won the 100m crawl.* (NOTE: no plural)

crayon /ˈkreɪɒn/ *noun* a coloured wax stick, used especially by children for drawing

craze /kreɪz/ *noun* a new fashion [~for] ○ *the current craze for purple shoes*

crazed /kreɪzd/ *adj* behaving wildly

③ **crazy** /ˈkreɪzi/ *adj* **1.** not sensible ○ *It was a crazy idea to go mountain-climbing in sandals.* **2.** very enthusiastic about something or someone [~ about] ○ *He's crazy about her.* ○ *She's crazy about ballroom dancing.* ◇ **to drive someone crazy** to have an effect on someone so that they become very annoyed ○ *The noise is driving me crazy.* ○ *All this work is driving her crazy.*

creak /kriːk/ *verb* (**creaks, creaking, creaked**) to make a squeaky noise ■ *noun* a noise like that of wood moving ○ *She heard a creak on the stairs and sat up in bed.* (NOTE: Do not confuse with **creek**.)

② **cream** /kriːm/ *noun* **1.** the thick yellow part of milk, full of fat ○ *I like strawberries and cream.* **2.** any soft smooth substance used, e.g. for cleaning or for protecting the skin ○ *face cream* ○ *shaving cream* ○ *shoe cream* **3.** the colour of cream ■ *adj* of a yellow-white colour ○ *He was wearing a cream shirt.* ○ *Do you like our new cream carpet?*

cream cheese /kriːm ˈtʃiːz/ *noun* a soft white cheese

crease /kriːs/ *noun* **1.** a mark made in cloth by ironing ○ *Trousers should have a crease in front.* **2.** a mark made by folding accidentally ○ *She ironed his shirts to remove the creases.* ■ *verb* (**creases, creasing, creased**) to make folds accidentally in something ○ *After two hours in the car, my skirt was badly creased and had to be pressed.*

creased /kriːst/ *adj* showing creases from having been crushed or folded ○ *Hang up your clothes as soon as you arrive otherwise everything will stay creased.*

① **create** /kriˈeɪt/ (**creates, creating, created**) *verb* to make or invent something ○ *a government scheme which aims at creating new jobs for young people*

① **creation** /kriˈeɪʃ(ə)n/ *noun* **1.** the act of making or inventing something ○ *Our aim is the creation of new jobs for young unemployed people.* **2.** something which has been made, especially something artistic or unusual

③ **creative** /kriˈeɪtɪv/ *adj* full of ideas, always making something ○ *He's a very creative child.*

creative writing /kriˌeɪtɪv ˈraɪtɪŋ/ *noun* the writing of stories, poems and other works of the imagination

③ **creativity** /ˌkriːeɪˈtɪvɪti/ *noun* being full of ideas, always creating things

creator /kriˈeɪtə/ *noun* a person who makes or invents something

③ **creature** /ˈkriːtʃə/ *noun* **1.** an animal, especially one that you don't know a name for ○ *Lift any stone and you'll find all sorts of little creatures underneath.* ○ *We try not *to harm any living creature.* ○ *Some sea creatures live in holes in the sand.* **2.** an imaginary animal or living being

crèche /kreʃ/ *noun* a special room or building where babies and small children can be looked after, often on a company's premises

credence /ˈkriːd(ə)ns/ *noun* a belief that something is correct or true

credentials /krɪˈdenʃəlz/ *plural noun* letters or documents which describe a person's qualities and skills ○ *The new production manager has very impressive credentials.*

③ **credibility** /ˌkredɪˈbɪlɪti/ *noun* the quality of being able to be believed

credible /ˈkredɪb(ə)l/ *adj* which can be believed

② **credit** /ˈkredɪt/ *noun* **1.** praise for something which is well deserved [~for] ○ *The professor took all the credit for the invention.* **2.** the length of time given to pay for something ○ *We give purchasers six months' credit.* **3.** the side of an account showing money that you have got or which is owed to you ○ *We paid in £100 to the credit of Mr Smith.* ■ *plural noun* **credits** the list of people who helped to make a film or TV programme ○ *Her name appears in the credits.* ■ *verb* (**credits, crediting, credited**) to pay money into an account ○ *to credit an account with £100* or *to credit £100 to an account* ◇ **on credit** without paying immediately ○ *We bought the dining room furniture on credit.*

creditable /ˈkredɪtəb(ə)l/ *adj* which does you credit, which should be praised

credit card /ˈkredɪt kɑːd/ *noun* a plastic card which allows you to borrow money and to buy goods without paying for them immediately

credit limit /ˈkredɪt ˌlɪmɪt/ *noun* the maximum amount of money that a customer is allowed to spend on credit or charge to their credit card

② **creditor** /ˈkredɪtə/ *noun* a person who is owed money

creed /kriːd/ *noun* a statement of what you believe ○ *Retraining for the unemployed is one of the government's creeds.*

creek /kriːk/ *noun US* a small river ◇ **up the creek** in a difficult situation (*informal*) ○ *If we don't get any money by tomorrow evening we'll all be up the creek.*

creep /kriːp/ (**creeps, creeping, crept** or **creeped**) *verb* **1.** to move around quietly ○ *They crept softly down the stairs.* □ **to creep up on someone** to come up close behind someone without that person realising it **2.** to move slowly ○ *The traffic was creeping along the motorway because of the fog.* ◇ **to give someone the creeps** to make someone feel nervous and uncomfortable ○ *I don't like that teacher – he gives me the creeps.*

creepy /ˈkriːpi/ (**creepier, creepiest**) *adj* which makes you feel strangely uncomfortable (*informal*)

cremate /krɪˈmeɪt/ (**cremates, cremating, cremated**) *verb* to burn a dead body (NOTE: + **cremation** *n*)

crematorium /kreməˈtɔːriəm/ *noun* a place where the bodies of dead people are burnt (NOTE: The US term is **crematory**.)

crepe paper /kreɪp ˈpeɪpə/, **crêpe paper** *noun* slightly crinkly coloured paper

crept /krept/ past tense and past participle of **creep**

crescendo /krɪˈʃendəʊ/ *noun* **1.** an increase in sound, especially in music □ **to rise to** *or* **reach a crescendo** to become much louder ○ *The music suddenly rose to a crescendo.* **2.** a rising to reach a high point ○ *A crescendo of complaints came into the office.* ○ *Protests from the public reached a crescendo with a march on Downing Street.*

crescent /ˈkrez(ə)nt/ *noun* **1.** a curved shape, like a new moon ○ *The new moon hung like a silver crescent over the lake.* **2.** a street which forms a semicircle ○ *the beautiful 18th-century houses in Bath's famous crescents*

crest /krest/ *noun* **1.** the highest point along the length of a mountain or a wave ○ *Follow the path along the crest of the hill – the view is splendid.* ○ *The crests of some of the waves reached 30 feet.* **2.** the highest point of something ○ *When the president was elected he was at the crest of his popularity.* **3.** the feathers on the head of a bird ○ *a striking black cockerel with a red crest* ○ *A peacock has a tall coloured crest.* **4.** a coat of arms ○ *His family crest is a red lion.* ○ *His college crest is still hanging on his bedroom wall.*

crevasse /krəˈvæs/ *noun* a deep crack in hard ground

crevice /ˈkrevɪs/ *noun* a small crack in a rock or wall

② **crew** /kruː/ *noun* the people who work on a vehicle such as boat or aircraft ○ *The lifeboat rescued the crew of the sinking ship.* ○ *The plane was carrying 125 passengers and a crew of six.*

crewman /ˈkruːmən/ *noun* a man who is a member of a ship's crew

crew neck /ˈkruː nek/ *noun* a sweater with a tight round neck

crib /krɪb/ *noun* **1.** *US* a baby's bed **2.** a model of the scene of the first Christmas displayed in a church at Christmas **3.** a word-for-word translation or list of answers to help a student with homework

crick /krɪk/ *noun* a pain in the neck or back

③ **cricket** /ˈkrɪkɪt/ *noun* a game played between two teams of eleven players using bats and a hard ball ○ *We haven't played much cricket this year – the weather has been too bad.* ○ *We are going to a cricket match this afternoon.*

cricketer /ˈkrɪkɪtə/ *noun* a person who plays cricket

cried /kraɪd/ past tense and past participle of **cry**

cries /kraɪz/ 3rd person singular present of **cry**

② **crime** /kraɪm/ *noun* **1.** illegal behaviour ○ *We must try to reduce the levels of crime in the inner cities.* ○ *The government is trying to deal with the problem of crime on the streets* or *with the street crime problem.* **2.** a specific illegal act ○ *More crimes are committed at night than during the daytime.*

crime wave /ˈkraɪm weɪv/ *noun* an increase in the number of crimes

② **criminal** /ˈkrɪmɪn(ə)l/ *adj* referring to illegal acts ○ *the criminal justice system* ○ *Stealing is a criminal offence.* ■ *noun* a person who commits a crime

criminalise /ˈkrɪmɪnəlaɪz/ (**criminalises, criminalising, criminalised**), **criminalize** *verb* to make something illegal

criminal law /ˌkrɪmɪn(ə)l ˈlɔː/ *noun* laws which deal with crimes against the law of the land, which are punished by the state. Compare **civil law**

criminal record /ˌkrɪmɪn(ə)l ˈrekɔːd/ *noun* a police record that lists any crimes that a person has been arrested for

crimson /ˈkrɪmzən/ *adj* deep bright red

cringe /krɪndʒ/ (**cringes, cringing, cringed**) *verb* **1.** to bend to avoid a blow ○ *The little boy cringed when he heard his father shouting.* **2.** to be embarrassed ○ *Seeing the boss trying to make jokes just makes me cringe.* ○ *She cringed when her son started to play the violin.*

crinkle /ˈkrɪŋk(ə)l/ (**crinkles, crinkling, crinkled**) *verb* to fold or crush something, making many small creases

cripple /ˈkrɪp(ə)l/ *noun* a person who is disabled or has difficulty in walking (*offensive*) ○ *Cripples sat outside the hotel, begging for money from tourists.* ■ *verb* (**cripples, crippling, crippled**) **1.** to disable someone ○ *He was crippled in a mining accident.* **2.** to prevent something from working ○ *The explosion crippled the supertanker and she drifted towards the rocks.* ○ *The bus and rail strike has crippled the capital's transport system.*

② **crisis** /ˈkraɪsɪs/ (*plural* **crises**) *noun* a serious situation where decisions have to be taken very quickly [~in] ○ *an international crisis* ○ *a crisis in education*

crisp /krɪsp/ *adj* **1.** (*of food*) hard, able to be broken into pieces and making a noise when you bite it ○ *These biscuits are not crisp any more, they have gone soft.* ○ *Pick an apple off the tree, they're really very crisp.* **2.** cold and sunny ○ *It was a beautiful crisp morning, with frost glinting on the grass.* ○ *She could see her breath in the crisp mountain air.*

criss-cross /ˈkrɪs krɒs/ *verb* to go backwards and forwards in different directions ○ *We dodged through the cars, bicycles, carts and pedestrians criss-crossing the street.*

② **criterion** /kraɪˈtɪəriən/ (*plural* **criteria**) *noun* the standard by which things are judged ○ *Does the candidate satisfy all our criteria?*

③ **critic** /ˈkrɪtɪk/ *noun* **1.** a person who examines something and comments on it, especially a person who writes comments on new plays and films for a newspaper ○ *She's the TV critic of the 'Times'.* ○ *The film was praised by all the critics.* **2.** a person who says that something is bad or wrong ○ *The chairman tried to answer his critics at the meeting.*

② **critical** /ˈkrɪtɪk(ə)l/ *adj* **1.** dangerous and difficult ○ *With the enemy attacking on all sides, our position was becoming critical.* **2.** extremely important ○ *He made a critical decision to break off the negotiations.* **3.** very serious ○ *The pilot of the plane was in a critical condition last night.* ○ *The hospital said that her condition was critical.* **4.** criticising someone or something ○ *The report was highly critical of the minister.*

critical mass /ˌkrɪtɪk(ə)l ˈmæs/ *noun* the minimum size that something must reach before it can operate successfully, e.g. the number of customers needed before a business can begin to make money

③ **criticise** /ˈkrɪtɪsaɪz/ (**criticises, criticising, criticised**), **criticize** *verb* to say that something or someone is bad or wrong ○ *She criticised their lack of interest and enthusiasm.* ○ *The design of the new car has been criticised.*

② **criticism** /ˈkrɪtɪsɪz(ə)m/ *noun* an unfavourable comment or comments ○ *There was a lot of criticism of the government's plan.*

③ **critique** /krɪˈtiːk/ *noun* a piece of careful literary criticism

croak /krəʊk/ (**croaks, croaking, croaked**) *verb* to make a deep sound ○ *The frogs started croaking in the pond.* (NOTE: + **croak** *n*)

crochet /ˈkrəʊʃeɪ/ (**crochets, crocheting, crocheted**) *verb* to make something out of wool, using a hooked needle ○ *Who crocheted the beautiful jumper you are wearing?*

crockery /ˈkrɒkəri/ *noun* cups, saucers and plates made from pottery

crocodile /ˈkrɒkədaɪl/ *noun* a large reptile which lives in or near rivers and lakes and eats other animals ○ *Crocodiles lay on the banks of the river waiting for the animals to come to drink.*

crocus /ˈkrəʊkəs/ (*plural* **crocuses** or **croci**) *noun* a little spring flower, in various colours, especially yellow and purple

croissant /ˈkwæsɒŋ/ *noun* a rolled pastry, made in a curved shape

crony /ˈkrəʊni/ (*plural* **cronies**) *noun* an old friend (*disapproving*)

cronyism /ˈkrəʊniɪz(ə)m/ *noun* giving jobs to your old friends (*disapproving*)

crook /krʊk/ *noun* **1.** a dishonest dealer ○ *I don't trust the government – they're a bunch of crooks.* ○ *That secondhand car dealer is a bit of a crook.* **2.** a bend ○ *She held the baby in the crook of her arm.*

crooked /ˈkrʊkɪd/ *adj* bent, not straight ○ *That picture is crooked.*

croon /kruːn/ (**croons, crooning, crooned**) *verb* to sing in a soft voice

③ **crop** /krɒp/ *noun* plants such as vegetables or cereals grown for food ○ *The bad weather has set the crops back by three weeks.* ○ *We had a wonderful crop of potatoes* or *a wonderful potato crop this year.*

crop up *phrasal verb* to happen suddenly (*informal*)

croquet /ˈkrəʊki/ *noun* a game played on grass

② **cross** /krɒs/ *verb* (**crosses, crossing, crossed**) **1.** to go across something to the other side ○ *She just crossed the road without looking to see if there was any traffic coming.* **2.** to put one thing across another ○ *He crossed his arms and looked annoyed.* ○ *She sat down and crossed her legs.* ○ *The road crosses the railway line about 10km from here.* ■ *noun* a shape made where one line has another going across it [~between/] ○ *Write your name where I have put a cross.* ■ *adj* angry ○ *The teacher will be cross with you for missing school.* ○ *Don't be cross – the children were only trying to help.*

cross off, cross out③ *phrasal verb* to draw a line through something which has been written to show that it should not be there

crossbar /ˈkrɒsbɑː/ *noun* **1.** a bar which goes across a space, especially a bar which goes between the posts forming a goal ○ *He kicked the ball over the crossbar and converted the try.* ○ *He almost scored, but the ball hit the crossbar.* **2.** a bar which crosses the frame of a man's bicycle, from the seat to the steering column ○ *She sat on his crossbar.* ○ *Girls' bicycles normally don't have crossbars.*

crossbow /ˈkrɒsbəʊ/ *noun* a weapon which fires bolts

crossed cheque /ˌkrɒst ˈtʃek/ *noun* a cheque which has two lines drawn across it and can only be paid into a bank

cross-examination /ˌkrɒs ɪgzæmɪˈneɪʃ(ə)n/ *noun* the questioning of witnesses called by the other side in a case (NOTE: + **cross-examine** *v*)

cross-eyed /ˌkrɒs ˈaɪd/ *adj* with eyes that do not face forwards, but look inwards towards the nose (*offensive*)

crossfire /ˈkrɒsfaɪə/ *noun* gunfire from two directions, so that the fire crosses

③ **crossing** /ˈkrɒsɪŋ/ *noun* **1.** an occasion of going across to the other side of an area of water ○ *How long is the crossing from England to Germany?* **2.** a place where you go across safely ○ *Cars have to take care at the railway crossing.*

cross-legged /krɒs ˈlegd/ *adj, adv* with one ankle over the other ○ *He was sitting cross-legged on the floor.*

crossover /ˈkrɒsəʊvə/ *noun* the situation where one style mixes with another or becomes popular with a different kind of audience ○ *He made the crossover from pianist to conductor without any difficulty.*

cross-reference /ˌkrɒs ˈref(ə)rəns/ *noun* a note in a reference book telling the reader to look in another part of the book for further information ○ *Please, check all cross-references for accuracy.* ○ *Cross-references are not only useful to readers but also save time.* ■ *verb* to refer to something in another part of a text

crossroads /ˈkrɒsrəʊdz/ *noun* a place where one road crosses another

cross-section /ˈkrɒs ˌsekʃən/ *noun* **1.** a diagram made to show the inside of something, as if it had been cut through ○ *The picture shows a cross-section of the Channel Tunnel.* ○ *Diagram 4 is a cross-section of a diesel engine.* **2.** a typical group of people ○ *The team consulted a cross-section of the public in the shopping centre.*

cross-trainer /krɒs ˈtreɪnə/ *noun* **1.** a shoe designed for more than one sporting activity **2.** an exercise machine intended to develop many different groups of muscles

cross-training /krɒs ˈtreɪnɪŋ/ *noun* training in different sports such as running and weightlifting, usually in order to improve performance in one of the sports

crosswalk /ˈkrɒswɔːk/ *noun US* a place where you can walk safely across a street

crossword /ˈkrɒswɜːd/, **crossword puzzle** *noun* a puzzle where small squares have to be filled with letters to spell words

crotch /krɒtʃ/ *noun* a place between the tops of your legs

crotchety /ˈkrɒtʃiti/ *adj* irritable

③ **crouch** /kraʊtʃ/ (**crouches, crouching, crouched**) *verb* to bend down low ○ *He crouched in the bottom of the boat.* ○ *She crouched down to talk to the child.*

crouton /ˈkruːtɒn/ *noun* a crunchy cube of fried bread used as a garnish

crow /krəʊ/ *noun* a large black bird ○ *The crows make such a noise in the trees that it wakes us up.* ■ *verb* (**crows, crowing, crowed** or **crew, crowed**) **1.** (*of a cock*) to make a loud call ○ *The sound of the cock crowing woke them all up.* **2.** to boast about something [~about] ◇ **as the crow flies** in a straight line ○ *It's only a couple of miles as the crow flies, but since there's no bridge over the river, it takes over half an hour to drive there.*

crowbar /ˈkrəʊbɑː/ *noun* a heavy metal bar for opening boxes and lifting things

② **crowd** /kraʊd/ *noun* a very large number of people together ○ *A crowd of schoolchildren went past.* ○ *Someone in the crowd outside the cinema shouted a warning.* ○ *Let's get an early train home to avoid the crowds after work.* ■ *verb* (**crowds, crowding, crowded**) to group together [~round/around/~into] ○ *The children were crowding round their teacher.* ○ *All the rugby fans crowded into the pub.*

② **crowded** /ˈkraʊdɪd/ *adj* full of a large number of people ○ *The town gets very crowded during the holiday season.* ○ *The stands were crowded before the game started.*

③ **crown** /kraʊn/ *noun* a round metal decoration that a king or queen wears on his or her head ■ *verb* (**crowns, crowning, crowned**) **1.** to make someone king or queen by placing a crown on his or her head ○ *The Queen was crowned in Westminster Abbey.* **2.** to be a very good end to a set of things that happen ○ *He crowned his career by winning a gold medal.* ◇ **to crown it all** used to refer to the last of several bad things to happen ○ *To crown it all, he lost his car keys.*

crowning /ˈkraʊnɪŋ/ *adj* representing outstanding achievement

② **crucial** /ˈkruːʃ(ə)l/ *adj* extremely important ○ *It is crucial that the story be kept out of the papers.*

crucifix /ˈkruːsɪfɪks/ *noun* a cross with a figure of Jesus Christ on it

crucifixion /ˌkruːsɪˈfɪkʃən/ *noun* the act of killing a person by nailing him to a cross

crucify /ˈkruːsɪfaɪ/ (**crucifies, crucifying, crucified**) *verb* **1.** to nail someone to a cross as a punishment ○ *Christ was crucified between two thieves.* **2.** to criticise someone sharply ○ *My brother would crucify me if he knew I had used his car without asking him.* ○ *I can't call her now, she'd crucify me if I woke her up.*

① **cruel** /ˈkruːəl/ (**crueller, cruellest**) *adj* making a person or animal suffer [~to] ○ *You mustn't be cruel to your new puppy.*

② **cruelty** /ˈkruːəlti/ *noun* the act of being cruel [~to] ○ *The zoo keeper was accused of cruelty to animals.*

cruise /kruːz/ *noun* a holiday consisting of a long journey in a ship, stopping at different places ○ *When he retired they went on a cruise round the Mediterranean.* ■ *verb* (**cruises, cruising, cruised**) to go in a boat from place to place ○ *They spent May cruising in the Mediterranean.* ○ *The ship cruised from island to island.*

cruise missile /ˌkruːz ˈmɪsaɪl/ *noun* a long-range guided missile

cruiser /ˈkruːzə/ *noun* a large warship, smaller than a battleship ○ *How many cruisers can the Navy send to the war zone?*

crumb /krʌm/ *noun* a small piece that has broken off some dry food such as bread, cake or biscuits

crumble /ˈkrʌmbəl/ (**crumbles, crumbling, crumbled**) *verb* **1.** to break up into small pieces, or to break something up into small pieces ○ *If you make it too dry it will just crumble when you eat it.* ○ *He picked up a lump of dry earth and crumbled it between his fingers.* **2.** to collapse ○ *As the witness said what he had seen, the defendant's case crumbled.* ○ *All her confidence began to crumble.*

crumple /ˈkrʌmpəl/ (**crumples, crumpling, crumpled**) *verb* **1.** to crush or to screw something up into a ball ○ *I heard him crumple up the paper and throw it into the wastepaper basket.* **2.** to become full of lines or folds ○ *Her shirt was crumpled because she had been lying on the grass.* ○ *The box was full of crumpled bits of paper.*

crunch /krʌntʃ/ *verb* (**crunches, crunching, crunched**) **1.** to bite something hard, making a loud noise ○ *She was crunching an apple when the phone rang.* **2.** to crush something hard or dry ○ *The gravel crunched under his boots.* ■ *noun* **1.** the sound of something hard or dry being crushed **2.** a situation when something must happen or be decided (*informal*) ○ *The crunch will come when the firm has no cash to pay the wages.* ◇ **if** or **when it comes to the crunch** if or when a point of decision is reached ○ *When it came to the crunch, the other side backed down.*

crunchy /ˈkrʌntʃi/ *adj* which makes a noise when you are eating

crusade /kruːˈseɪd/ *noun* a strong action to stop or change something [~against] ○ *The government has launched a crusade against drugs.*

crush /krʌʃ/ *noun* **1.** a mass of people ○ *She was hurt in the crush of people trying to get to the exit.* ○ *He lost his briefcase in the crush on the train.* **2.** □ **to have a crush on someone** to have a feeling of love for someone you do not know very well (*informal*) ○ *She had a crush on her tennis coach.*

crushing /ˈkrʌʃɪŋ/ *adj* which takes away all hope

crust /krʌst/ *noun* **1.** a hard outer layer that covers something softer **2.** the hard outside layer of bread ○ *You can cut the crusts off the sandwiches.* **3.** the layer of pastry on top of a pie **4.** the outer layer of the Earth

crusty /ˈkrʌsti/ (**crustier, crustiest**) *adj* **1.** with a hard outside layer ○ *We had an excellent salad with a glass of wine and a piece of fresh crusty bread.* **2.** getting angry easily ○ *The club is full of crusty old men nodding in leather armchairs.*

crutch /krʌtʃ/ *noun* a strong support for a patient with an injured leg, formed of a stick with a holding bar or a T-bar which fits under the shoulder

crux /krʌks/ *noun* the central point of a problem

① **cry** /kraɪ/ *verb* (**cries, crying, cried**) **1.** to have tears coming out of your eyes ○ *The baby cried when her mother took away her toys.* ○ *Cutting up onions makes me cry.* ○ *Many people were crying when they left the cinema.* **2.** to call out ○ *'Hello there,' she cried.* ■ *noun* (*plural* **cries**) **1.** a loud shout [~of/~for] ○ *a cry of pain* ○ *No one heard her cries for help.* **2.** a sound made by a bird or other animal

crypt /krɪpt/ *noun* a cellar under a church

cryptic /ˈkrɪptɪk/ *adj* secret and mysterious

crystal /ˈkrɪstəl/ *noun* a solid chemical substance with a regular shape ○ *The salt formed crystals at the bottom of the jar.*

crystal ball /ˌkrɪstəl ˈbɔːl/ *noun* a fortune teller's glass ball, regarded as a means of predicting what will happen in the future

crystal clear /ˌkrɪstəl ˈklɪə/ *adj* very clear, simple to understand

crystallise /ˈkrɪstəlaɪz/ (**crystallises, crystallising, crystallised**), **crystallize** *verb* **1.** to form crystals ○ *Water crystallises to form snow.* **2.** to take shape ○ *Following the meeting, our ideas began to crystallise.*

cube /kjuːb/ *noun* **1.** a shape like a box, where all six sides are squares of the same size ○ *The design for the library consists of a series of cubes.* **2.** something shaped like a cube ○ *He put two cubes of sugar in his tea.* ○ *The ice cubes chinked in the glasses.* **3.** (*in mathematics*) the result when a number is multiplied by itself twice ○ *27 is the cube of 3.*

③ **cubic** /ˈkjuːbɪk/ *adj* measured in volume by multiplying length, depth and width (NOTE: Cubic is written in figures as ^{3}: **6m^3** = six cubic metres; **10ft^3** = ten cubic feet.)

cuckoo /ˈkʊkuː/ (*plural* **cuckoos**) *noun* a bird which has a cry that sounds like its name and which lays its eggs in other birds' nests ○ *When you hear the first cuckoo you know that winter is over.* ○ *The cuckoo lays its eggs in the nests of other birds.*

cucumber /'kjuːkʌmbə/ *noun* a long dark green vegetable used mainly in salads

cuddle /'kʌd(ə)l/ *verb* (**cuddles, cuddling, cuddled**) to put your arms round someone and hold them close to you ■ *noun* an act of putting your arms round someone and holding them close to you ○ *She picked up her daughter and gave her a cuddle.*

cuddle up *verb* to stand, sit or lie close to someone [~to] ○ *The children cuddled up to their mother.*

cuddly /'kʌd(ə)li/ *adj* soft and pleasant to hold or hug

cue /kjuː/ *noun* **1.** something that happens or is said which makes something starts happening [~for] ○ *Her announcement was the cue for a general celebration.* **2.** (*in a play*) words after which you have to speak or do something ○ *The gunshot is your cue to rush onto the stage screaming.* **3.** a long stick for playing billiards or snooker

cuff /kʌf/ *noun* **1.** the end of the sleeve round the wrist ○ *The collar and cuffs of his shirt were dirty and frayed.* **2.** *US* a folded part at the bottom of each leg of a pair of trousers ○ *This year, slacks with cuffs are back in fashion.* (NOTE: The British term is **turnup**.) **3.** a hit with an open hand ○ *She gave him a cuff on the back of the head to shut him up.* ■ *verb* (**cuffs, cuffing, cuffed**) to hit someone ○ *The parents said he had cuffed the child on the head.*

cuisine /kwɪ'ziːn/ *noun* a style of cooking ○ *Chinese cuisine is very different from European.* ○ *French cuisine is more and more popular in England.* (NOTE: From the French word for 'kitchen'.)

cul-de-sac /'kʌl də ˌsæk/ (*plural* **culs-de-sac** or **cul-de-sacs**) *noun* a small street which is only open at one end

culinary /'kʌlɪn(ə)ri/ *adj* referring to cooking

cull /kʌl/ *noun* the practice of killing a certain number of animals in order to keep the population under control ○ *The deer cull takes place in early October.* ■ *verb* (**culls, culling, culled**) to kill a certain number of animals in order to keep the population under control ○ *About 10% of the deer population is culled each autumn.*

culminate /'kʌlmɪneɪt/ (**culminates, culminating, culminated**) *verb* to reach a particular result or conclusion [~in] ○ *The race culminated in a win for the Canadian driver.*

culmination /ˌkʌlmɪ'neɪʃ(ə)n/ *noun* a final point, grand ending

culpable /'kʌlpəb(ə)l/ *adj* likely to attract blame

culprit /'kʌlprɪt/ *noun* a person or thing that is responsible for a crime, or for something which has gone wrong

cult /kʌlt/ *noun* a small religious group

cultivate /'kʌltɪveɪt/ (**cultivates, cultivating, cultivated**) *verb* **1.** to dig and water the land to grow plants ○ *Fields are cultivated in early spring, ready for sowing corn.* **2.** to grow plants ○ *This field is used to cultivate new strains of wheat.* **3.** to do everything to get someone's friendship ○ *We are cultivating the new director to try to make sure we get the contract.* (NOTE: + **cultivation** *n*)

cultivated /'kʌltɪveɪtɪd/ *adj* **1.** who has been well educated in subjects such as music, art and literature ○ *A really cultivated person wouldn't be seen dead in a karaoke bar.* **2.** (*of plant*) which is specially grown and is not wild ○ *Wild strawberries have a more intense flavour than cultivated ones.* **3.** (*of land*) prepared for growing crops ○ *From the air, the cultivated fields were like a brown and green quilt.*

② **cultural** /'kʌltʃər(ə)l/ *adj* relating to culture ○ *His cultural interests are very wide-ranging – from Mexican art to 12th-century Greek paintings.* ○ *There will be cultural activities available such as a visit to the museum.*

① **culture** /'kʌltʃə/ *noun* **1.** activities involving things such as music, art and literature ○ *He is taking a course in Russian culture.* **2.** a country's way of thinking or behaving ○ *Is a TV in every home really what we want from Western culture?*

cultured /'kʌltʃəd/ *adj* **1.** civilised, well educated ○ *Our guide was a very cultured lady from Vienna.* ○ *Such behaviour is not acceptable in cultured society.* **2.** which has been grown artificially ○ *Only an expert can tell the difference between a cultured pearl and a real one.*

cumbersome /'kʌmbəs(ə)m/ *adj* large and heavy

cumulative /'kjuːmjʊlətɪv/ *adj* **1.** which is added gradually, especially each year ○ *The interest on this account is cumulative.* ○ *The cumulative effect of a series of late nights finally caught up with him and he fell asleep during the dinner.* **2.** which grows by the addition of new parts ○ *A cu-*

mulative index is made up of several different indexes put together.

cunning /ˈkʌnɪŋ/ *adj* clever at achieving something, especially by tricking people ○ *a cunning plan* ○ *It was cunning of her to ask him to help, as it flattered him.* ■ *noun* cleverness in acting to achieve something ○ *He showed cunning in his attempts to hide his mistake.*

① **cup** /kʌp/ *noun* **1.** a small bowl with a handle, used for drinking from **2.** the liquid in a cup ○ *He drank two cups of coffee.* ○ *Can I have a cup of tea?* **3.** a large silver or gold container given as a prize for winning a competition

① **cupboard** /ˈkʌbəd/ *noun* a piece of furniture with shelves and doors ○ *Put the jam in the kitchen cupboard.* ○ *She painted the cupboard doors white.*

cupful /ˈkʌpfʊl/ *noun* the quantity which a cup can hold

curable /ˈkjʊərəb(ə)l/ *adj* (*of disease*) which can be cured

curate /ˈkjʊərət/ *noun* a priest who helps a parish priest

curator /kjʊˈreɪtə/ *noun* a person in charge of a museum

curb /kɜːb/ *noun* **1.** something which holds something back [~on] ○ *The company needs to put a curb on its spending.* **2.** US the stone edge to a pavement ○ *He sat on the curb and watched the cars go past.* ○ *Try not to hit the curb when you park.* ■ *verb* (**curbs, curbing, curbed**) to hold something back ○ *She needs to curb her enthusiasm to spend money.*

curd /kɜːd/ *noun* a solid food made from sour milk

curdle /ˈkɜːd(ə)l/ (**curdles, curdling, curdled**) *verb* to become or make something become solid and sour ○ *If you add lemon juice to milk it will curdle it.* ○ *Milk will curdle in hot weather.*

③ **cure** /kjʊə/ *noun* something which makes a disease better [~for] ○ *Doctors are still trying to find a cure for colds.* ■ *verb* (**cures, curing, cured**) to make a patient or a disease better ○ *I don't know what's in the medicine, but it cured my cough very fast.*

curfew /ˈkɜːfjuː/ *noun* a period when no one is allowed out into the street

curiosity /ˌkjʊəriˈɒsɪti/ (*plural* **curiosities**) *noun* **1.** a feeling of wanting to know about something **2.** a strange object

③ **curious** /ˈkjʊəriəs/ *adj* **1.** wanting to know things ○ *I'm curious to know what happened at the meeting.* **2.** unusual or strange ○ *We found a curious object that turned out to be an old kitchen tool.* ○ *It's curious that no one knew where he lived.*

③ **curl** /kɜːl/ *verb* (**curls, curling, curled**) to twist, or make something twist ○ *My hair curls naturally.* ○ *Some plants have stems that curl round other plants.* ■ *noun* **1.** a piece of hair which grows in a twist **2.** a curved shape of a particular substance [~of] ○ *a curl of smoke*

curl up *phrasal verb* to bend your body into a round shape ○ *She curled up in the chair and went to sleep.*

curler /ˈkɜːlə/ *noun* a roller for curling hair

③ **curly** /ˈkɜːli/ *adj* with natural curves or twists ○ *curly hair*

currant /ˈkʌrənt/ *noun* **1.** a small round fruit ○ *I have planted some currant bushes.* ◊ **blackcurrant**, **redcurrant** **2.** a small dried black grape ○ *a currant bun* ○ *fruit cake with currants, sultanas and raisins in it* (NOTE: Do not confuse with **current**.)

② **currency** /ˈkʌrənsi/ (*plural* **currencies**) *noun* the money used in a specific country ○ *I want to change my pounds into French currency.*

① **current** /ˈkʌrənt/ *adj* **1.** relating to the present time ○ *What is the current state of the report – will it be finished on time?* ○ *Who is the current prime minister of Japan?* ○ *Do you have a current timetable? – Mine is out of date.* **2.** widely accepted at the present time or at a particular time ○ *current ideas about how to treat children* ○ *The idea that the world was flat was current in the Middle Ages.* ■ *noun* **1.** a flow of water or air ○ *Don't go swimming in the river – the current is very strong.* ○ *A warm westerly current of air is flowing across the country.* ○ *Vultures circle in rising currents of warm air.* **2.** a flow of electricity ○ *Switch the current off at the mains.* (NOTE: Do not confuse with **currant**.)

③ **current account** /ˈkʌrənt əˌkaʊnt/ *noun* a bank account from which you can take money at any time

current affairs /ˌkʌrənt əˈfeəz/ *plural noun* the political situation as it is now ○ *We are studying current affairs as part of our politics course.*

③ **currently** /ˈkʌrəntli/ *adv* at the present time ○ *He is currently the manager of our Paris office.* ○ *We are currently in the process of buying a house.*

② **curriculum** /kəˈrɪkjʊləm/ (*plural* **curricula** or **curriculums**) *noun* **1.** the set of subjects studied in school ○ *I am very glad that music and drama have been added to* *the curriculum.* **2.** the parts of a particular subject that are studied

curriculum vitae /kəˌrɪkjʊləm ˈviːtaɪ/ (*plural* **curricula vitae**) *noun* full form of **CV**

③ **curry** /ˈkʌri/ (*plural* **curries**) *noun* an Indian food prepared with spices ○ *I would like a mild curry, please.* ○ *We ordered chicken curry and rice.*

③ **curse** /kɜːs/ *noun* **1.** a swear word ○ *He threw the letter down with a curse.* **2.** a magic word to make something unpleasant happen to someone ○ *The witch put a curse on the whole family.* **3.** something which causes you problems ○ *Being on call 24 hours a day is the curse of being a doctor.* ○ *Pollution is the curse of industrialised societies.* ■ *verb* (**curses, cursing, cursed**) **1.** to swear ○ *He cursed under his breath and marched out of the room.* **2.** to wish that something bad should happen to someone

cursor /ˈkɜːsə/ *noun* a small flashing line on a computer screen which shows where the next character will appear

cursory /ˈkɜːsəri/ *adj* quick and not very careful

curt /kɜːt/ *adj* abrupt in speaking

curtail /kɜːˈteɪl/ (**curtails, curtailing, curtailed**) *verb* to shorten something; to reduce something

② **curtain** /ˈkɜːt(ə)n/ *noun* **1.** a long piece of cloth hanging in front of a window ○ *Can you close* or *draw the curtains, please?* **2.** a long piece of cloth hanging in front of the stage at a theatre

curtsy /ˈkɜːtsi/ (*plural* **curtsies**), **curtsey** *noun* a respectful movement made by women or girls, by bending the knees and putting one foot forward ○ *She made a curtsy to the queen.* ◊ **bow**[1] (NOTE: + **curtsy** *v*)

③ **curve** /kɜːv/ *noun* a line that is bent like part of a circle ○ *the curve of the coast line* ○ *The road makes a sharp curve to the left.* ■ *verb* (**curves, curving, curved**) to be in the shape of a curve ○ *The road curves round the side of the mountain.*

curved /kɜːvd/ *adj* with a rounded shape

② **cushion** /ˈkʊʃ(ə)n/ *noun* a bag filled with something soft, e.g. feathers, for sitting or leaning on ○ *Put a cushion behind your back if you find your chair is too hard.* ■ *verb* (**cushions, cushioning, cushioned**) to make soft something which could be hard or painful ○ *The bushes cushioned his fall.* □ **to cushion somebody** *or* **something from something** to protect someone or something from the bad effects of something □ **to cushion the blow** or **the shock** to reduce the bad effect of something that happens ○ *She made no attempt to cushion the blow, but just told them straight out that they had all lost their jobs.*

custard /ˈkʌstəd/ *noun* (*in the UK*) a sweet yellow sauce made with milk and a powder containing cornflour ○ *stewed rhubarb and custard* ○ *Would you like some custard with your crumble?*

custodial sentence /kʌˌstəʊdiəl ˈsentəns/ *noun* the fact of being legally sentenced to prison

custodian /kʌˈstəʊdiən/ *noun* a person who is responsible for the care and protection of something or someone

custody /ˈkʌstədi/ *noun* **1.** keeping ○ *The jewels were in the custody of the manager, and he had placed them in the hotel safe.* □ **to take someone into custody** to arrest someone ○ *The three fans were taken into police custody.* **2.** the right of keeping and looking after a child ○ *When they were divorced, she was granted custody of the children.* (NOTE: no plural)

③ **custom** /ˈkʌstəm/ *noun* **1.** something that people usually do, or have done for a long time ○ *the local custom of decorating the wells in spring* ○ *It's their custom to invite all their neighbours to a party at New Year.* **2.** the use of a shop or restaurant ○ *If the assistants are rude to me again I will take my custom elsewhere.* □ **to lose someone's custom** to experience a situation in which a regular customer goes to another place of business, e.g. a restaurant or shop ○ *The little shops will lose a lot of custom when the new supermarket opens.*

customary /ˈkʌstəməri/ *adj* usual (*formal*) ○ *He handled the situation with his customary efficiency.* ○ *It's customary to give taxi drivers a tip.*

custom-built /ˈkʌstəm bɪlt/, **custom-made** /ˌkʌstəm ˈmeɪd/ *adj* made to order for a customer

① **customer** /ˈkʌstəmə/ *noun* **1.** a person who buys something in a shop or restaurant, or from another business ○ *The shops are lowering their prices to attract more customers.* ○ *Customers can order by post on or the Internet.* ○ *His bar is always full of customers.* **2.** a person who uses a service such as a train ○ *We apologise to customers waiting on Platform 5 for the late arrival of their train.*

customise /ˈkʌstəmaɪz/ (**customises, customising, customised**), **customize**

verb to have something changed to fit your special needs

custom-made /ˌkʌstəm 'meɪd/ *adj* alternative for custom-built

② **customs** /'kʌstəmz/ *noun* **1.** □ **H.M. Customs and Excise** the British government department which organises the collection of taxes on goods coming into the country and also collects VAT ○ *He was stopped by customs.* ○ *Her car was searched by customs.* ○ *The customs officer asked her to open her bag.* **2.** an office of this department at a port or airport

① **cut** /kʌt/ *verb* (**cuts, cutting, cut**) **1.** to divide, reduce or remove something using a sharp tool, e.g. a knife or scissors [~into] ○ *The meat is very tough – I can't cut it with my knife.* ○ *She cut the cake into six pieces.* **2.** to damage the skin with something sharp [~on] ○ *She cut her finger on the broken glass.* **3.** to reduce the size of something ○ *We are trying to cut the number of staff.* ○ *Accidents have been cut by 10%.* ○ *The article is too long, so I asked the author to cut 500 words.* ■ *noun* **1.** a place which bleeds when your skin has been broken [~on] ○ *She had a bad cut on her leg.* **2.** a mark made in a surface by something sharp **3.** the sudden lowering of the amount of something [~in] ○ *price cuts* ○ *large cuts in spending* ○ *a cut in working hours* □ **he took a cut in salary** *or* **a salary cut** he accepted a lower salary **4.** a share of something such as profits ○ *Each salesperson gets a cut of what is sold for cash.*

cut across, cut through *phrasal verb* to take a short cut to get somewhere

cut back③ *phrasal verb* to reduce spending ○ *We are having to cut back on staff costs.*

cut down③ *phrasal verb* **1.** to make a tree fall down with a tool such as a saw ○ *He cut the tree down* or *cut down the tree.* **2.** *also* **cut down on** to reduce something ○ *He needs to cut down the number of cigarettes he smokes.* ○ *I'm trying to cut down on chocolate.*

cut in *phrasal verb* **1.** to interrupt someone or something ○ *He would keep on cutting in while I was telling the story.* **2.** to drive suddenly in front of another car ○ *Did you see how the little white car cut in in front of the black one?*

cut off③ *phrasal verb* **1.** to take away a small part of something using a sharp tool such as a knife ○ *She cut off a little piece of string.* ○ *He cut off two slices of ham.* **2.** to stop someone from being with someone else, or from or reaching a place ○ *She was cut off from her friends by a crowd of policemen.* ○ *The village was cut off by the snow.* **3.** to stop a phone call before it is finished ○ *We were cut off in the middle of our conversation.* **4.** to stop electricity or water from reaching someone ○ *He didn't pay the bill, so the company cut off his electricity.* ○ *The lightning hit the generator and caused the power to be cut off.*

cut out③ *phrasal verb* **1.** to remove something from something larger ○ *She cut an advertisement out of the newspaper.* **2.** to remove a part of something larger ○ *We had to cut out all the extras from our order because they cost too much.* **3.** to stop doing or eating something ○ *She's decided to cut out sweet things so as to lose weight.* ◇ **to be cut out for something** to be ideally suited for something ○ *I don't think he's cut out for an office job.* ◇ **cut it out!** stop doing that! (*informal*)

cut up③ *phrasal verb* **1.** to make something into small pieces by cutting it ○ *She cut the old towel up into little pieces.* ○ *Can you cut up the meat for the children?* **2.** to drive suddenly in front of another car ○ *Did you see how the little white car cut up the black one?*

cutback /'kʌtbæk/ *noun* a reduction in spending

③ **cute** /kjuːt/ *adj* nice

cutlery /'kʌtləri/ *noun* knives, forks and spoons (NOTE: no plural)

cutlet /'kʌtlət/ *noun* **1.** a slice of meat, usually with a bone attached ○ *We were served veal cutlets with mushroom sauce.* **2.** a fried dish made with minced meat, fish or vegetables formed into the shape of a piece of meat ○ *She makes delicious fish cutlets.*

cutoff /'kʌtɒf/ *noun* something which marks the end of something ○ *The cutoff point for students going to the next level is 80% marks in the exam.* ○ *What is the cutoff date for applications?*

cut-price /ˌkʌt 'praɪs/ *adj* very cheap

cutter /'kʌtə/ *noun* a tool used for cutting

cut-throat /'kʌt θrəʊt/ *adj* vicious or intense

cutting /'kʌtɪŋ/ *noun* **1.** a small piece of paper cut out of a newspaper **2.** a little piece of a plant which will take root if stuck in the ground ○ *The cuttings I took from your lavender plant are all growing well.*

cutting edge /ˈkʌtɪŋ ˌedʒ/ *noun* the sharp edge of a knife ○ *The cutting edge is blunt and needs sharpening.*

CV /ˌsiː ˈviː/ *noun* a summary of someone's qualifications and experience. Full form **curriculum vitae**

cyanide /ˈsaɪənaɪd/ *noun* a strong poison

cybercafé /ˈsaɪbəˌkæfeɪ/ *noun* a café where you can pay to use the Internet

cyberspace /ˈsaɪbəspeɪs/ *noun* an imaginary place which electronic information such as emails passes through

③ **cycle** /ˈsaɪk(ə)l/ *noun* **1.** a period during which something works or develops and then returns to its starting point ○ *The washing machine broke down in the middle of its cycle.* ○ *Global warming is starting to affect the natural cycle of the seasons.* □ **a business *or* economic *or* trade cycle** a period during which trade expands, then slows down, then expands again **2.** a bicycle ■ *verb* (**cycles, cycling, cycled**) to travel on a bicycle ○ *It's hard to cycle into the wind.*

③ **cyclist** /ˈsaɪklɪst/ *noun* a person who rides a bicycle

cyclone /ˈsaɪkləʊn/ *noun* a tropical storm in the Indian and Pacific Oceans, where the air moves very fast in a circle round a central area ○ *According to the shipping forecasts, a cyclone is approaching Sri Lanka.* (NOTE: In the Far East this is called a **typhoon**; in the Caribbean a **hurricane**.)

cygnet /ˈsɪgnət/ *noun* a baby swan

cylinder /ˈsɪlɪndə/ *noun* an object shaped like a tube closed at both ends

cylindrical /sɪˈlɪndrɪk(ə)l/ *adj* shaped like a cylinder

cymbals /ˈsɪmbəlz/ *plural noun* a pair of round metal plates which are banged together to make a loud noise

cynic /ˈsɪnɪk/ *noun* a person who doubts that anyone has any good points

cynical /ˈsɪnɪk(ə)l/ *adj* believing that people only act for their own benefit

cynicism /ˈsɪnɪsɪz(ə)m/ *noun* the fact of being cynical

cyst /sɪst/ *noun* an unusual growth in the body containing liquid

czar /zɑː/ *noun* **1.** the title of the former emperor of Russia ○ *a photograph of the Czar and his family* **2.** the person in overall charge of some official organisation ○ *He's the new drugs czar, with complete responsibility for fighting drug traffickers and dealing with drug problems.*

D

d /diː/, **D** *noun* the fourth letter of the alphabet, between C and E

③ **DA** *abbr* district attorney

dab /dæb/ *verb* (**dabs, dabbing, dabbed**) to give something a light tap ○ *She dabbed her eyes with her handkerchief.* ○ *She dabbed the cut with cotton wool soaked in antiseptic.* ■ *noun* a small quantity ○ *She put a dab of glue on each corner of the poster.*

dabble /ˈdæb(ə)l/ (**dabbles, dabbling, dabbled**) *verb* to be slightly involved in something [~in] ○ *As a young man he dabbled in politics.*

dachshund /ˈdæksənd/ *noun* a breed of small long low dog, originally from Germany

dad /dæd/ *noun* a father

daffodil /ˈdæfədɪl/ *noun* a bright yellow spring flower

daft /dɑːft/ *adj* silly (*informal*)

dagger /ˈdæɡə/ *noun* a short knife

② **daily** /ˈdeɪli/ *adj* happening every day ○ *daily newspapers such as the Times and the Daily Mail* ○ *The cooker has been in daily use for ten years.* ○ *There's a daily flight to Washington.* ■ *adv* every day ○ *We can deliver milk daily.* □ **twice daily** on two occasions every day ■ *noun* (*plural* **dailies**) a newspaper published every weekday

dainty /ˈdeɪnti/ (**daintier, daintiest**) *adj* delicate and small

dairy /ˈdeəri/ *adj* referring to or involved in producing milk and things made from it such as cream or butter ○ *dairy products* ○ *dairy cattle*

daisy /ˈdeɪzi/ (*plural* **daisies**) *noun* a small white flower with a yellow centre

dam /dæm/ *noun* a wall which blocks a river to make a lake ○ *After the heavy rain people were afraid the dam would burst.* ■ *verb* (**dams, damming, dammed**) to block a river with a wall ○ *When they built the power station, the river had to be dammed.*

② **damage** /ˈdæmɪdʒ/ *noun* **1.** the breaking or physical spoiling of something [~to] ○ *The storm did a lot of damage.* ○ *It will take us months to repair the damage to the restaurant.* **2.** emotional harm done to a person [~to] ○ *I hope the experience of the crash won't cause the children lasting damage.* ○ *There has been serious damage to public confidence as a result of the attack.* ■ *verb* (**damages, damaging, damaged**) **1.** to break or partially destroy something ○ *A large number of shops were damaged in the fire.* ○ *These glasses are easily damaged.* **2.** to affect someone or something in a negative way

damaged /ˈdæmɪdʒd/ *adj* broken or spoiled in some way ○ *a damaged book*

damaging /ˈdæmɪdʒɪŋ/ *adj* causing harm to someone or something

damn /dæm/ *verb* (**damns, damning, damned**) **1.** used to show annoyance ○ *Damn it, we're going to be late!* ○ *Damn him, he's left the front door open!* **2.** to severely criticise someone or something ○ *The new film was damned by the Sunday papers.* **3.** to condemn someone or something in a religious situation ○ *Galileo was damned by the Church for saying that the Earth turned round the Sun.* ■ *interj* used as a mild swear word to show annoyance ○ *Damn! I've left my umbrella on the train.*

damning /ˈdæmɪŋ/ *adj* which clearly proves that someone has done something wrong

③ **damp** /dæmp/ *adj* slightly wet ○ *She'd just had a shower and her hair was still damp.* ○ *The cellar has cold damp walls.* ■ *verb* (**damps, damping, damped**) to wet something slightly

dampen /ˈdæmpən/ (**dampens, dampening, dampened**) *verb* **1.** to make something slightly wet ○ *Dampen the cloth before you wipe the floor.* ○ *She dampened the shirts before ironing them.* **2.** □ **to dampen someone's enthusiasm** to do something to make someone less enthusiastic ○ *The bad weather dampened his enthusiasm for sailing.*

damper /ˈdæmpə/ *noun* something which discourages you ○ *Having just been sacked put a damper on his birthday party.*

② **dance** /dɑːns/ *noun* **1.** a way of moving in time to music ○ *She teaches dance* or *is a dance teacher.* ○ *We learnt a new dance today.* ○ *Scottish dances are very lively.* **2.** an entertainment where people can dance ○ *The club is holding a New Year's dance* ■ *verb* (**dances, dancing, danced**) **1.** to move in time to music [~with/~to] ○ *There he is – he's dancing with that tall girl.* ○ *I like dancing to this music.* **2.** to move or jump around happily [~in/into/around etc] ○ *She danced into the room and announced she'd got the job.* ○ *The football fans were dancing in the streets.*

③ **dancer** /ˈdɑːnsə/ *noun* a person who dances

dandelion /ˈdændɪlaɪən/ *noun* a wild plant with yellow flowers which have a mass of little narrow petals

dandruff /ˈdændrʌf/ *noun* small pieces of dry skin which come off your head

② **danger** /ˈdeɪndʒə/ *noun* the possibility of something bad happening, e.g. damage, failure or getting hurt [~to/~from/~of/~(that)] ○ *danger to health from pollution* ○ *When it rains, there's a danger of flooding.* ○ *There's no danger he'll find out.* ◇ **in danger** /ˈɪn ˈdeɪndʒə/ likely to be harmed or damaged ○ *Get an ambulance – her life is in danger.* ○ *I don't think the children are in any danger.* ○ *The whole building was in danger of catching fire.* ◇ **out of danger** not likely to die ○ *She was very ill, but she's off the danger list now.*

② **dangerous** /ˈdeɪndʒərəs/ *adj* likely to cause injury or damage ○ *Be careful – that old staircase is dangerous!* ○ *Police warned the public not to approach the man as he was dangerous.* ○ *Children are warned that it is dangerous to go out alone at night.*

dangerously /ˈdeɪndʒərəsli/ *adv* in a dangerous way

dangle /ˈdæŋgəl/ (**dangles, dangling, dangled**) *verb* **1.** to hang freely ○ *The fish dangled at the end of his line.* ○ *Dirty sheets were dangling over the balcony.* **2.** to make something hang freely ○ *She dangled the puppet in front of the baby.*

dank /dæŋk/ *adj* cold and damp

dappled /ˈdæp(ə)ld/ *adj* covered with patches of light and dark colour

② **dare** /deə/ *verb* (**dares** or **dare, daring, dared**) **1.** to be brave enough to do something ○ *I wouldn't dare say no – I might lose my job.* □ **to dare not do something** to not be brave enough to do something ○ *I daren't go any faster.* **2.** to try to make someone do something dangerous or unusual in order to see how brave they are ○ *I dare you to jump across that stream.* **3.** used for telling someone how angry you are ○ *Don't you dare do that again!* ○ *How dare you look in my desk drawers!* ■ *noun* an attempt to persuade someone to do something difficult or dangerous ○ *He only climbed on the roof for a dare.* ◇ **I dare say** very probably ○ *I dare say you're right.*

daredevil /ˈdeədev(ə)l/ *noun* a brave person who does not worry about danger ○ *He's a daredevil – he flew his plane under Tower Bridge.*

daring /ˈdeərɪŋ/ *noun* bravery ○ *The helicopter pilot showed great daring in trying to rescue the boy from the cliff.*

① **dark** /dɑːk/ *adj* **1.** with little or no light ○ *The sky turned dark and it started to rain.* ○ *Can you switch the light on? It's getting too dark to see.* ○ *In Scotland in the summer it gets dark very late.* **2.** not a light colour ○ *Her eyes are dark.* ○ *She was wearing a dark blue coat.*

darken /ˈdɑːkən/ (**darkens, darkening, darkened**) *verb* to become dark

dark horse /ˌdɑːk ˈhɔːs/ *noun* a person you know nothing about and who may win something such as an election or a race

darkly /ˈdɑːkli/ *adv* in a threatening or frightening way

③ **darkness** /ˈdɑːknəs/ *noun* the fact of not having any light □ **the building was in complete** ***or*** **total darkness** there were no electric lights on in the building

darling /ˈdɑːlɪŋ/ *noun* **1.** a name used to talk to someone you love ○ *Darling! I'm back from the shops.* **2.** a lovable person ○ *Be a darling and fetch me the newspaper.* **3.** someone who is liked by a particular group ○ *the darling of the art world*

darn /dɑːn/ (**darns, darning, darned**) *verb* to mend holes in clothes ○ *She hates darning socks.*

dart /dɑːt/ *noun* **1.** a small heavy arrow with plastic feathers, used for playing the game of darts ○ *Each player takes a turn to throw his or her three darts.* **2. darts** a game in which players throw small arrows at a round board on a wall, each trying to make their arrow stick closest to the middle ■ *verb* (**darts, darting, darted**) to move quickly ○ *The little boy darted across the street.*

Darwinism /ˈdɑːwɪnɪz(ə)m/ *noun* a theory of evolution developed by the scientist Charles Darwin

dash /dæʃ/ *noun* **1.** a small line in writing or printing, showing a space, or separating items ○ *The reference number is one four six dash seven (146–7).* **2.** a sudden movement towards a place ○ *There was a mad dash to buy tickets.* ○ *While the policeman wasn't looking she made a dash for the door.* ■ *verb* (**dashes, dashing, dashed**) to hurry somewhere ○ *I can't stop now – I must dash to catch the last post.* ○ *I dashed home to watch the football on television.* ○ *She dashed into a shop so that he wouldn't see her.*

dashboard /ˈdæʃbɔːd/ *noun* the instrument panel in a car

① **data** /ˈdeɪtə/ *noun* information involving figures or results of studies ○ *The data is stored in our main computer.* ○ *We spent months gathering data on hospital waiting times.* ○ *The data shows that, on average, flowering takes place after two weeks.* (NOTE: **Data** is often used with a singular verb, except in scientific contexts: *The data is easily available.*)

② **database** /ˈdeɪtəbeɪs/ *noun* a large amount of information stored in a computer in a way that allows particular pieces of information to be found easily

③ **data processing** /ˌdeɪtə ˈprəʊsesɪŋ/ *noun* the selecting and examining of data in a computer to produce information in a special form

① **date** /deɪt/ *noun* **1.** the number of a day in a month or year, or a day when something will happen or has happened ○ *Put today's date on the document.* ○ *What's the date next Wednesday?* ○ *The dates of the exhibition have been changed.* ○ *The date of the next meeting has been fixed for Wednesday, June 10th.* ○ *Do you remember the date of your girlfriend's birthday?* **2.** a small sweet brown fruit ■ *verb* (**dates, dating, dated**) to write the date on something ○ *The letter was dated 15 June.* ○ *You forgot to date the cheque.* ◇ **to date from** *or* **back to** to exist since ○ *This house dates from* or *dates back to the 17th century.*

dated /ˈdeɪtɪd/ *adj* **1.** with a date written on it ○ *Thank you for your letter dated June 15th.* **2.** old-fashioned ○ *That advertisement looks a bit dated now.*

date rape /ˈdeɪt reɪp/ *noun* the act of raping someone you know, especially on a date

daub /dɔːb/ (**daubs, daubing, daubed**) *verb* to put a substance such as paint on a surface in a careless way

① **daughter** /ˈdɔːtə/ *noun* a female child of a parent ○ *They have two sons and one daughter.* ○ *My daughter Mary goes to the local school.*

daughter-in-law /ˈdɔːtər ɪn lɔː/ (*plural* **daughters-in-law**) *noun* the wife of a son

daunting /ˈdɔːntɪŋ/ *adj* which seems very difficult

dawdle /ˈdɔːd(ə)l/ (**dawdles, dawdling, dawdled**) *verb* to do something slowly

dawn /dɔːn/ *noun* the beginning of a day, when the sun rises ○ *We must set off for the Pyramids at dawn, so you'll have to get up very early.* ■ *verb* (**dawns, dawning, dawned**) (*of day*) to begin

dawn on *verb* to begin to realise ○ *The seriousness of the situation finally dawned on him.* □ **it dawned on him that** he began to realise that ○ *It gradually dawned on him that someone else was opening his letters.*

① **day** /deɪ/ *noun* **1.** a period of time lasting 24 hours ○ *There are 365 days in a year and 366 in a leap year.* ○ *New Year's Day is on January 1st.* ○ *They went on a ten-day tour of southern Spain.* ○ *I spoke to him on the phone the day before yesterday.* ○ *We are planning to meet the day after tomorrow.* **2.** the period from morning until night, when it is light ○ *She works all day in the office, and then looks after the children in the evening.* ○ *It took the workmen four days to build the wall.*

daybreak /ˈdeɪbreɪk/ *noun* a time in the very early morning, when the sun is about to rise

day care /ˈdeɪ keə/ *noun* the practice of looking after people, e.g. small children or old people during the daytime in a special centre

daydream /ˈdeɪdriːm/ (**daydreams, daydreaming, daydreamt** or **daydreamed**) *verb* to think about other things; not to concentrate ○ *He was sitting at his desk daydreaming about holidays in Greece.* (NOTE: + **daydream** *n*)

daylight /ˈdeɪlaɪt/ *noun* light that you see during the daytime ◇ **in broad daylight** openly, in the middle of the day ○ *Three men robbed the bank in broad daylight.*

daylight robbery /ˌdeɪlaɪt ˈrɒbəri/ *noun* the practice of charging very high prices (*informal*)

③ **daytime** /ˈdeɪtaɪm/ *noun* the period of light between morning and night ○ *I* *watched a lot of daytime television when I lost my job.*

day-to-day /ˌdeɪ tə ˈdeɪ/ *adj* taking place as part of normal life; which goes on all the time

day trip /ˈdeɪ trɪp/ *noun* a journey lasting one day

dazed /deɪzd/ *adj* confused in the mind

dazzle /ˈdæz(ə)l/ (**dazzles, dazzling, dazzled**) *verb* to shine a strong light in someone's eyes so that they cannot see for a moment ○ *She was dazzled by the lights of the cars coming towards her.*

dazzling /ˈdæzlɪŋ/ *adj* (*of a light*) very bright

deactivate /diːˈæktɪveɪt/ (**deactivates, deactivating, deactivated**) *verb* to make something such as a bomb not active any more

① **dead** /ded/ *adj* **1.** not alive any more ○ *His parents are both dead.* ○ *Dead fish were floating in the water.* **2.** complete ○ *There was dead silence in the exam room.* ○ *The train came to a dead stop.* **3.** not working ○ *We tried to start the car but the battery was dead.* **4.** not lively, not exciting ○ *Seaside towns can be quite dead in winter.* ■ *adv* **1.** completely ○ *He was dead tired after his long walk.* **2.** exactly ○ *You're dead right.* ○ *The train arrived dead on time.* ◇ **wouldn't be seen dead in** would not ever want to be seen in (*informal*) ○ *I wouldn't be seen dead in a hat like that.* ○ *A really cultivated person wouldn't be seen dead in a karaoke bar.*

deaden /ˈded(ə)n/ (**deadens, deadening, deadened**) *verb* to make something less intense, e.g. to make a sound quieter or a pain less painful

dead end /ˌded ˈend/ *noun* **1.** a street or way which leads nowhere ○ *We drove into a little street and found it was a dead end.* **2.** a point at which you can go no further ○ *All their research has come to a dead end.*

dead-end job /ˌded end ˈdʒɒb/ *noun* a job where there is no hope of promotion

dead heat /ded ˈhiːt/ *noun* a race where two people arrive first together

deadline /ˈdedlaɪn/ *noun* a date by which something has to be done [~for] ○ *The deadline for payment of the bill is the end of July.* □ **to meet a deadline** to finish something in time ○ *I don't think we can meet the deadline.* □ **to miss a deadline** not to finish something in time ○ *They worked as fast as they could but missed the deadline by two days.*

deadlock /ˈdedlɒk/ *noun* a point at which two sides in a dispute cannot agree ○ *The negotiations have reached a deadlock.* □ **to break a deadlock** to find a way to start discussions again after being at a point at which no agreement was possible

③ **deadly** /ˈdedli/ *adj* likely to cause people to die ○ *The terrorists turned the car into a deadly weapon.*

deadpan /ˈdedpæn/ *adj* not showing your feelings in your face

dead wood /ˌded ˈwʊd/ *noun* people or things that are considered to be of no worth

② **deaf** /def/ *adj* not able to hear, or having difficulty in hearing ○ *My grandma is going deaf.* ○ *He's deafer than he used to be.* (NOTE: Some people avoid this term as it can cause offence and prefer **hearing-impaired**.)

deafen /ˈdef(ə)n/ (**deafens, deafening, deafened**) *verb* to make someone deaf for a time

deafening /ˈdef(ə)nɪŋ/ *adj* so loud as to make you unable to hear

deafness /ˈdefnəs/ *noun* the state of being deaf (NOTE: no plural)

① **deal** /diːl/ *noun* a business agreement or contract [~with/~to] ○ *We've signed a deal with a German firm.* ○ *They did a deal to supply envelopes.* □ **a bad *or* rough *or* raw deal** bad treatment ○ *She got a rough deal from the firm.* ■ *verb* (**deals, dealing, dealt**) to give out playing cards to players ○ *It's my turn to deal.* ○ *He dealt me two aces.* ◇ **a good *or* great deal** much ○ *He's feeling a good deal better after two days off work.* ○ *She didn't say a great deal.* ◇ **a good *or* great deal of** a lot of ○ *He made a good deal of money from his business.* ○ *There's a great deal of work still to be done.*

deal in *verb* to buy and sell something ○ *She deals in carpets and rugs imported from India.*

deal with③ *phrasal verb* **1.** to do what is necessary to complete a job or solve a problem ○ *The job involves dealing with the public.* ○ *Leave it to the filing clerk – he'll deal with it.* ○ *We will deal with your order as soon as we can.* ○ *The government has to deal with the problem of teenage crime.* **2.** to be about a subject ○ *The report deals with travel insurance.*

③ **dealer** /ˈdiːlə/ *noun* a person who buys and sells things [~in] ○ *She's a dealer in antiques.*

dealing /ˈdiːlɪŋ/ *noun* the practice of buying and selling things

dealt /delt/ past tense and past participle of **deal**

dean /diːn/ *noun* **1.** a person in charge of priests in a cathedral ○ *He was appointed Dean of St Paul's.* **2.** a person in charge of teachers at a university ○ *the Dean of the Arts Faculty*

① **dear** /dɪə/ *adj* **1.** well liked or loved ○ *She's a very dear friend of mine.* **2.** costing a lot of money ○ *Fresh fruit is always dearer in the winter.* ○ *That restaurant is too dear for me.* ■ *interj* used when something has gone slightly wrong ○ *Oh dear! It's started to rain.* ○ *Dear me! Is that how late it is!* ■ *noun* a way of referring to someone you like ○ *Did you have a good day, dear?* ◇ **Dear Sir *or* Madam** used at the beginning of a letter to a man or woman whom you do not know

dearest /ˈdɪərəst/ *adj* most loved (*dated*)

dearly /ˈdɪəli/ *adv* **1.** very much ○ *I'd dearly like to go to Cuba on holiday.* ○ *She loved her old cat dearly, and was very sad when he died.* **2.** at a high cost, especially in terms of pain or suffering ○ *She became a highly paid executive, but paid dearly for the privilege.*

dearth /dɜːθ/ *noun* a shortage of something (*formal*)

① **death** /deθ/ *noun* the act of dying or the state of being dead ○ *She never got over her mother's death.* ○ *Road accidents caused over 1,000 deaths last year.* ◇ **to death** completely (*informal*) ○ *He was bored to death sitting watching football on television.* ○ *I am sick to death of always having to do the housework.* ◇ **to put someone to death** to execute someone

deathbed /ˈdeθbed/ *noun* a bed on which someone is dying

death certificate /ˈdeθ səˌtɪfɪkət/ *noun* a paper signed by a doctor which shows that someone has died and what was the cause of death

death rate /ˈdeθ reɪt/ *noun* the percentage of deaths per thousand of population

death sentence /ˈdeθ ˌsentəns/ *noun* a punishment of a court by which a person is sentenced to be executed

death squad /ˈdeθ skwɒd/ *noun* a group of soldiers or other armed people, who are sent to kill enemies of the people in power

death toll /ˈdeθ təʊl/ *noun* the number of people who have been killed, e.g. in an accident or an earthquake

deathtrap /ˈdeθtræp/ *noun* a dangerous place (*informal*)

death wish /ˈdeθ wɪʃ/ *noun* □ **to have a death wish** to want to die

débâcle /deɪˈbɑːk(ə)l/ *noun* a sudden defeat or collapse

debar /dɪˈbɑː/ (**debars, debarring, debarred**) *verb* to prevent someone from doing something

debase /dɪˈbeɪs/ (**debases, debasing, debased**) *verb* to reduce the worth or the quality of something

debatable /dɪˈbeɪtəb(ə)l/ *adj* not absolutely certain

① **debate** /dɪˈbeɪt/ *noun* **1.** a discussion [~with/~about/on/over] ○ *After his talk the professor had a lively debate with the students about climate change.* **2.** a formal discussion ending with a vote [~on] ○ *a debate on increasing student fees* ■ *verb* (**debates, debating, debated**) **1.** to consider or discuss a subject ○ *We sat in the rain and debated what to do next.* **2.** to discuss something formally before coming to a decision [~what/~whether]

debauchery /dɪˈbɔːtʃəri/ *noun* the fact of living a wild life

debilitating /dɪˈbɪlɪteɪtɪŋ/ *adj* making you weak

debit /ˈdebɪt/ *noun* **1.** money which is paid out or taken out of an account ○ *Your bank statement gives a list of credits and debits at the end of each month.* **2.** money which is owed ○ *a debit balance*

debit card /ˈdebɪt kɑːd/ *noun* a plastic card, similar to a credit card, but which automatically debits your account when you buy something

debrief /diːˈbriːf/ (**debriefs, debriefing, debriefed**) *verb* to ask someone for information about an important job which he or she has just done

debriefing /diːˈbriːfɪŋ/ *noun* a meeting at which someone gives information about an important job which he or she has just done

debris /ˈdebriː/ (*plural same*) *noun* pieces of something, e.g. a demolished building or crashed aircraft

② **debt** /det/ *noun* money owed to someone ○ *After her great success, she was able to repay all her debts.* □ **to be in debt** to owe money ○ *He is in debt to the tune of £2,500.* □ **to get into debt** to start to owe money

③ **debtor** /ˈdetə/ *noun* a person who owes money

debt relief /ˈdet rɪˌliːf/ *noun* the practice of a rich country allowing a poor country not to pay back its debt

debug /diːˈbʌg/ (**debugs, debugging, debugged**) *verb* **1.** to remove hidden microphones from a place **2.** to remove errors from a computer program

debunk /diːˈbʌŋk/ (**debunks, debunking, debunked**) *verb* to show that something is not true

debut /ˈdeɪbjuː/ *noun* the first public appearance of someone such as an actor

② **decade** /ˈdekeɪd/ *noun* a period of ten years ○ *during the last decade of the 20th century*

decadent /ˈdekəd(ə)nt/ *adj* which is declining in moral values

decaf /ˈdiːkæf/, **decaff** *adj* which has had the caffeine removed

decaffeinated /diːˈkæfɪneɪtɪd/ *adj* with all caffeine removed

decapitate /dɪˈkæpɪteɪt/ (**decapitates, decapitating, decapitated**) *verb* to cut off someone's head

decathlon /dɪˈkæθlɒn/ *noun* an athletic contest for men, covering ten events, held over two days

decay /dɪˈkeɪ/ *noun* the natural process of going bad or of becoming damaged, e.g. when things are not looked after properly ○ *The government has plans to deal with inner city decay.* ○ *Tooth decay is especially bad in children who eat sweets.* ○ *You must treat the wood to prevent decay.* (NOTE: no plural) ■ *verb* (**decays, decaying, decayed**) to go bad or to become damaged in this way ○ *Sugar makes your teeth decay.* ○ *The jungle path was blocked by decaying branches.*

deceased /dɪˈsiːst/ *noun* a person who has died (*formal*) ○ *The deceased's will was read out by the solicitor.*

deceit /dɪˈsiːt/ *noun* the practice of trying to trick someone into paying money or trying to make someone believe something which is not true

deceitful /dɪˈsiːtf(ə)l/ *adj* often tricking people

deceive /dɪˈsiːv/ (**deceives, deceiving, deceived**) *verb* to make someone believe something which is not true ○ *They had tried to deceive me, but I realised just in time.*

① **December** /dɪˈsembə/ *noun* the twelfth and last month of the year, after November and before January ○ *She was born last December.* ○ *His birthday is on December 25 – Christmas Day!* ○ *They always go on a skiing holiday in December.* ○ *Today is December 6th.* ○ *The cheque was dated December 6.* (NOTE: **December 6th** *or* **December 6**: say 'the sixth of December' or 'December the sixth' or in US English 'December sixth'.)

decency /ˈdiːs(ə)nsi/ *noun* honour; good morals

② **decent** /ˈdiːs(ə)nt/ *adj* **1.** honest ○ *The boss is a hard-working decent man.* **2.** quite good ○ *She earns a decent salary.* **3.** properly dressed, wearing clothes ○ *You can't come in yet – I'm not decent.*

decentralise /diːˈsentrəlaɪz/ (**decentralises, decentralising, decentralised**), **decentralize** (**decentralizes, decentralizing, decentralized**) *verb* to move power, authority or action from a central point to local areas

③ **deception** /dɪˈsepʃən/ *noun* the practice of telling a lie in order to trick someone, especially into giving you money

deceptive /dɪˈseptɪv/ *adj* not as it seems

decibel /ˈdesɪbel/ *noun* a unit for measuring the loudness of a sound

① **decide** /dɪˈsaɪd/ (**decides, deciding, decided**) *verb* to make a decision about something [~between/~what/whether/how/when etc/~(that)] ○ *I can't decide between the blue one or the green one.* ○ *Have you decided where to go on holiday?* ○ *They decided to stay at home and watch TV.* ○ *He decided the test was too difficult.*

decide against① *phrasal verb* to make up your mind not to do something ○ *She decided against spending her money on a new car.*

decided /dɪˈsaɪdɪd/ *adj* certain or obvious ○ *There's a decided difference between French and Spanish wines.*

deciduous /dɪˈsɪdjuəs/ *adj* (*of a tree*) losing its leaves in the winter. Compare **evergreen**

decimal /ˈdesɪm(ə)l/ *noun* a number in a system based on ten ○ *Three-quarters expressed as a decimal is 0.75.*

decimal point /ˌdesɪm(ə)l ˈpɔɪnt/ *noun* a dot used to show the division between whole numbers and parts of numbers in decimals, such as 2.05

decimal system /ˈdesɪm(ə)l ˌsɪstəm/ *noun* a system of counting based on the number 10

decimate /ˈdesɪmeɪt/ (**decimates, decimating, decimated**) *verb* **1.** to kill people in large numbers **2.** to reduce something by a large amount ○ *German forests have been* *decimated by acid rain.* ○ *Our sales have been decimated by the rise in the value of the pound.*

decipher /dɪ'saɪfə/ (**deciphers, deciphering, deciphered**) *verb* to read or make out something which has been badly written or written in code

① **decision** /dɪ'sɪʒ(ə)n/ *noun* an occasion of thinking carefully what to do [~about/on] ○ *a decision to train as a teacher* ○ *I need to make a decision soon about changing my job.* □ **to come to** *or* **reach** *or* **take a decision** to decide to do something ○ *They talked for hours but didn't come to any decision.* ○ *He thought about the job offer, but, in the end, took the decision to stay where he was.*

③ **decisive** /dɪ'saɪsɪv/ *adj* **1.** firm and confident ○ *He was nervous but tried to sound decisive.* **2.** which brings about a result ○ *The second and decisive round of voting takes place next Sunday.* ○ *Her action was decisive in obtaining the release of the hostages.*

deck /dek/ *noun* a floor of a ship or bus ○ *I'll stay on deck because I'm feeling seasick.* ○ *Let's go up to the top deck – you can see the sights better from there.*

decking /'dekɪŋ/ *noun* pieces of wood used to make a platform outside a house

③ **declaration** /ˌdeklə'reɪʃ(ə)n/ *noun* an official statement

② **declare** /dɪ'kleə/ (**declares, declaring, declared**) *verb* to state something officially [~that] ○ *The Senator declared his intention to run for President.* ○ *She was declared dead on arrival at hospital.* ○ *It was declared that Mrs Broom would be the new chairperson.*

declassified /diː'klæsɪfaɪd/ *adj* (*of information*) which has been officially declared to be no longer secret

② **decline** /dɪ'klaɪn/ *noun* the fact of going downwards [~in] ○ *a welcome decline in the number of cases of pollution* ○ *Sales figures have gone into a sharp* or *steep decline.* ■ *verb* (**declines, declining, declined**) **1.** to refuse or to turn down an invitation or offer to do something ○ *She declined their request.* ○ *He declined to come to lunch.* **2.** to become weaker ○ *He declined rapidly after he went into hospital.* **3.** to become less in numbers or amount ○ *Our sales declined over the last year.* ○ *The fish population has declined sharply.*

decode /diː'kəʊd/ (**decodes, decoding, decoded**) *verb* to translate a coded message into normal writing

decommission /ˌdiːkə'mɪʃ(ə)n/ (**decommissions, decommissioning, decommissioned**) *verb* to stop using something such as a weapon

decompose /ˌdiːkəm'pəʊz/ (**decomposes, decomposing, decomposed**) *verb* (*of organic material*) to rot

decompress /ˌdiːkəm'pres/ (**decompresses, decompressing, decompressed**) *verb* **1.** to reduce the pressure in something **2.** to expand a computer file that has been stored in a smaller space to its full size

③ **decorate** /'dekəreɪt/ (**decorates, decorating, decorated**) *verb* **1.** to put paint or new paper on the walls in a room ○ *She can't come to the phone – she's decorating the kitchen.* **2.** to cover something with pretty or colourful things to make it look attractive or to celebrate an occasion ○ *The streets were decorated with flags.*

③ **decoration** /ˌdekə'reɪʃ(ə)n/ *noun* the act of decorating a place ○ *She is in charge of the decoration of the church for the wedding.*

decorative /'dek(ə)rətɪv/ *adj* pleasant to look at; serving as a decoration

decorator /'dekəreɪtə/ *noun* a person who paints the inside and outside of buildings

decorum /dɪ'kɔːrəm/ *noun* the practice of being well behaved

decoy[1] /'diːkɔɪ/ *noun* an object or a person that is placed to attract and trap something ○ *When they go duck shooting, they use wooden duck decoys which they float on the water.* ○ *They used a woman police officer to act as a decoy to try to trap the mugger.*

decoy[2] /dɪ'kɔɪ/ (**decoys, decoying, decoyed**) *verb* to attract and trap something or someone

decrease[1] /'diːkriːs/ *noun* the fact of becoming less [~of/~in] ○ *a decrease of 20% in applications to join the club* ○ *Sales show a 10% decrease on last year.* □ **to be on the decrease** to be becoming less ○ *Road accidents are on the decrease.*

decrease[2] /dɪ'kriːs/ (**decreases, decreasing, decreased**) *verb* to become less ○ *The number of road accidents is decreasing.* ○ *Applications to join have decreased by 20%.*

decree /dɪ'kriː/ *noun* a legal order which has not been voted by a parliament ○ *The President has issued a decree banning short dresses.*

decrepit /dɪˈkrepɪt/ *adj* old and falling to pieces

dedicate /ˈdedɪkeɪt/ (**dedicates, dedicating, dedicated**) *verb* **1.** to say that something you have produced or done represents a mark of respect or affection for someone ○ *He dedicated his collection of poems to his wife.* **2.** to spend all your life doing something ○ *She dedicated herself or her life to looking after abandoned children.*

dedicated /ˈdedɪkeɪtɪd/ *adj* **1.** giving a lot of time and effort to achieve something ○ *Her life was saved by the dedicated surgical team at the hospital.* **2.** reserved for a particular task ○ *There's one dedicated graphics workstation in the network.*

③ **dedication** /ˌdedɪˈkeɪʃ(ə)n/ *noun* **1.** spending your life doing something ○ *Her dedication and hard work are admirable.* **2.** a note printed at the beginning of a book or play, where the author offers his or her work to someone as a mark of respect or affection

deduce /dɪˈdjuːs/ (**deduces, deducing, deduced**) *verb* to conclude something from examining the evidence (*formal*)

deduct /dɪˈdʌkt/ (**deducts, deducting, deducted**) *verb* to remove an amount from a sum of money

deduction /dɪˈdʌkʃən/ *noun* **1.** a conclusion reached ○ *Their deduction was correct.* □ **by a process of deduction** by looking at the evidence and reaching a conclusion **2.** a sum of money which is taken away ○ *There is an automatic deduction for insurance.* ○ *Net wages are wages after deduction of tax and social security payments.*

③ **deed** /diːd/ *noun* an act, especially a brave one ○ *stories of great deeds performed during the war*

③ **deem** /diːm/ (**deems, deeming, deemed**) *verb* to consider something or someone to be something (*formal*)

① **deep** /diːp/ *adj* (**deeper, deepest**) **1.** going a long way down ○ *The water is very deep in the middle of the river.* ○ *This is the deepest lake in North America.* ○ *In the shallow end of the pool, the water is deep enough to cover your feet.* ◊ **depth 2.** going a long way under the ground ○ *a deep mine* **3.** (*of a voice*) low, not high ○ *Who's been sitting on my chair? said Father Bear in his deep voice.* ■ *adv* a long way down ○ *The mine goes deep under the sea.*

deepen /ˈdiːpən/ (**deepens, deepening, deepened**) *verb* **1.** to become deeper ○ *The water deepened as he walked out into the lake.* **2.** to make something become deeper ○ *They're going to deepen the channel so that bigger boats can use the harbour.* **3.** to become more difficult to understand ○ *The mystery deepened.*

deep-fried /ˌdiːp ˈfraɪd/ *adj* which has been cooked in a deep pan of boiling oil or fat

③ **deeply** /ˈdiːpli/ *adv* **1.** very much ○ *We deeply regret having to make so many people redundant.* **2.** □ **to sleep deeply** to sleep without waking ○ *After taking the drug she slept deeply for ten hours.*

deep-rooted /ˌdiːp ˈruːtɪd/ *adj* which you have had for a long time and which you feel strongly

deep-seated /ˌdiːp ˈsiːtɪd/ *adj* that has lasted a long time and will be difficult to change

deep-set /ˌdiːp ˈset/ *adj* (*of eyes*) which have deep sockets

deer /dɪə/ (*plural same*) *noun* a wild animal, the male of which has long horns called antlers (NOTE: Do not confuse with **dear**. The female is a **doe**, the male is a **stag**, the young are **fawns**. Note also that the meat from a deer is called **venison**.)

deface /dɪˈfeɪs/ (**defaces, defacing, defaced**) *verb* to damage the surface of something by writing on or scratching it

default /dɪˈfɔːlt/ *noun* the situation existing if no change is made ○ *The default for the number of copies is 10.* ◇ **by default 1.** happening because someone else fails to do something ○ *As they didn't reply by the 15th, the agreement ended by default.* **2.** to win a game or competition because another person does not play or cannot finish playing ○ *His opponent withdrew and he won by default.*

default setting /dɪˈfɔːlt ˌsetɪŋ/ *noun* the way in which something is organised to happen unless a change is made ○ *The default setting for the heating is on at 8 a.m. and off at 6 p.m.*

③ **defeat** /dɪˈfiːt/ *noun* the loss of a fight, game or vote ○ *The Government suffered a defeat in Parliament last night.* ○ *It was the team's first defeat for two years.* ■ *verb* (**defeats, defeating, defeated**) to succeed against someone in a fight, game or vote ○ *The ruling party was heavily defeated in the presidential election.* ○ *Our team has not been defeated so far this season.* ○ *The proposal was defeated by 10 votes to 3.*

defect[1] /ˈdiːfekt/ *noun* a fault ○ *There must be a defect in the computer program.*

defect² /dɪ'fekt/ (**defects, defecting, defected**) *verb* to leave your country and join the enemy

defective /dɪ'fektɪv/ *adj* faulty

① **defence** /dɪ'fens/ *noun* **1.** protection against something such as attack or infection ○ *Several people ran to her defence when she was attacked.* ○ *These tablets offer some defence against the disease.* **2.** protection provided by the armed forces ○ *Some countries spend more on defence than on education.* **3.** (*in games*) a part of a team whose job is to protect the goal ○ *The England defence came under attack from the other team's forwards.* **4.** (*in a law court*) the lawyers acting on behalf of an accused person

defenceless /dɪ'fensləs/ *adj* not able to protect yourself

① **defend** /dɪ'fend/ (**defends, defending, defended**) *verb* to protect a person or place that is being attacked ○ *They brought in extra troops to defend the city against attack.*

② **defendant** /dɪ'fendənt/ *noun* (*in a law court*) a person who is accused of doing something illegal or a person who is sued in a civil case

③ **defender** /dɪ'fendə/ *noun* **1.** a person who defends a place such as a castle or town ○ *The defenders surrendered after 90 days, when they ran out of food.* **2.** in team sports, a player who defends the goal ○ *The defenders were continually passing the ball back to the goalkeeper.* **3.** someone who supports something strongly and actively [~of]

defense /dɪ'fens/ *noun* US spelling of **defence**

defensive /dɪ'fensɪv/ *noun* □ **to be on the defensive about something** to feel you need to give reasons for having done something ○ *She's always on the defensive about her decision to resign.*

defer /dɪ'fɜː/ (**defers, deferring, deferred**) *verb* to put something back to a later date, to postpone something ○ *to defer payment* ○ *The decision has been deferred until the next meeting.*

deference /'def(ə)rəns/ *noun* respect

defiance /dɪ'faɪəns/ *noun* a very proud action against an opponent

defiant /dɪ'faɪənt/ *adj* very bold in refusing to obey someone or something

deficiency /dɪ'fɪʃ(ə)nsi/ (*plural* **deficiencies**) *noun* not enough of something needed to make someone or something healthy or complete ○ *Their diet has a deficiency of iron* or *has an iron deficiency.*

deficient /dɪ'fɪʃ(ə)nt/ *adj* lacking something [~in] ○ *The soil is deficient in nutrients.* ○ *Their diet is deficient in calcium.*

deficit /'defɪsɪt/ *noun* an amount by which something is less than it should be ○ *The company announced a deficit of £2 million* or *a £2 million deficit in its accounts.*

② **define** /dɪ'faɪn/ (**defines, defining, defined**) *verb* **1.** to explain something clearly or to give the meaning of something ○ *How would you define the word 'environmental'?* **2.** to indicate the limits of something ○ *The police operate within limits that have been clearly defined.* ○ *The memo tried to define the way in which the two departments should work together.*

③ **definite** /'def(ə)nət/ *adj* very sure ○ *I need a definite answer.* ○ *He was quite definite that he had seen the girl at the bus stop.*

definite article /ˌdef(ə)nət 'ɑːtɪk(ə)l/ *noun* the word 'the' in English, or a word with a similar use in another language

① **definitely** /'def(ə)nətli/ *adv* certainly ○ *I'll definitely be there by 7 o'clock.* ○ *Are you coming? – Definitely not!*

② **definition** /ˌdefɪ'nɪʃ(ə)n/ *noun* an explanation of the meaning of a word ○ *A bilingual dictionary doesn't give definitions, only translations.* ○ *Look up the definition of 'democracy' in the dictionary.*

definitive /dɪ'fɪnɪtɪv/ *adj* final, which cannot be improved on

deflate /diː'fleɪt/ (**deflates, deflating, deflated**) *verb* to let the air out of something, e.g. of a tyre or balloon ○ *Their hot air balloon began to deflate.*

deflated /diː'fleɪtɪd/ *adj* feeling unhappy and lacking confidence in yourself

deflect /dɪ'flekt/ (**deflects, deflecting, deflected**) *verb* to turn aside something, e.g. an arrow or a bullet, so that it goes in another direction

deforestation /diːˌfɒrɪ'steɪʃ(ə)n/ *noun* the act of cutting down trees from an area of land

deformed /dɪ'fɔːmd/ *adj* having a twisted or unattractive shape

deformity /dɪ'fɔːmɪti/ (*plural* **deformities**) *noun* the fact of being deformed

defragment /ˌdiːfræg'ment/ (**defragments, defragmenting, defragmented**) *verb* to arrange the storage space in a computer

defraud /dɪ'frɔːd/ (**defrauds, defrauding, defrauded**) *verb* to cheat someone to get their money ○ *He defrauded the old lady of £10,000.*

defrost /diː'frɒst/ (**defrosts, defrosting, defrosted**) *verb* **1.** to remove ice which has formed in a refrigerator or freezer ○ *I must defrost the freezer.* **2.** (*of frozen food*) to thaw out ○ *A large turkey will take 24 hours to defrost.*

deft /deft/ *adj* very agile or clever with your hands

defunct /dɪ'fʌŋkt/ *adj* no longer functioning

defuse /diː'fjuːz/ (**defuses, defusing, defused**) *verb* **1.** to take the fuse out of a bomb so that it cannot explode ○ *An army unit was brought in to defuse the bomb.* **2.** to make a situation less tense ○ *The chairman made some jokes to try to defuse the situation.* ○ *The UN Secretary General has moved to try to defuse the crisis.*

defy /dɪ'faɪ/ (**defies, defying, defied**) *verb* **1.** to refuse to obey the law ○ *He should never have tried to defy the university authorities.* **2.** □ **to defy description, belief etc** to be almost impossible to describe, believe, etc ○ *His latest film defies description.*

degenerate[1] /dɪ'dʒen(ə)rət/ *adj* which has become morally weak or bad ○ *He was shocked by the student art exhibition which he termed 'degenerate scribbling'.*

degenerate[2] /dɪ'dʒenəreɪt/ (**degenerates, degenerating, degenerated**) *verb* to get worse ○ *Her condition degenerated quickly once she went into hospital.* ○ *The celebrations rapidly degenerated into rioting.*

degrade /dɪ'greɪd/ (**degrades, degrading, degraded**) *verb* **1.** to make someone do something that is humiliating ○ *She had no money but refused to degrade herself by making false social security claims.* **2.** to change a chemical compound into a simpler form, to decompose ○ *Some plastics will degrade if left in the sun.*

degrading /dɪ'greɪdɪŋ/ *adj* which makes a person like an animal

① **degree** /dɪ'griː/ *noun* **1.** a unit for measuring temperature or angles, shown by the symbol (°) ○ *an angle of eighty degrees* ○ *The temperature of the water is above 20°.* (NOTE: With figures, **degree** is usually written as the symbol °: *25° Celsius.*) **2.** a qualification from a university [~in] ○ *a degree in mathematics* **3.** a small amount of something such as a quality or an emotion [~of] ○ *I approached the animal with some degree of fear.* ○ *The degree of public interest in the announcement surprised them.* □ **to some** or **a certain degree** partly ○ *It's his own fault to a certain degree.*

dehydrate /ˌdiːhaɪ'dreɪt/ (**dehydrates, dehydrating, dehydrated**) *verb* **1.** to remove water from something **2.** to lose water from the body

dehydrated /ˌdiːhaɪ'dreɪtɪd/ *adj* (*of food*) having lost water

deity /'deɪɪti/ (*plural* **deities**) *noun* a god

déjà vu /ˌdeɪʒɑː 'vuː/ *noun* a feeling that you have already seen something before ○ *When he came into the room, he immediately had a feeling of déjà vu.*

dejected /dɪ'dʒektɪd/ *adj* very unhappy or discouraged

② **delay** /dɪ'leɪ/ *noun* the length of time by which something is late [~of/~in] ○ *a delay of ten minutes* ○ *We are sorry for the delay in replying to your letter.* ■ *verb* (**delays, delaying, delayed**) **1.** to make someone or something late ○ *The train has been delayed by fog.* ○ *He was delayed because his taxi had an accident.* **2.** to put something off until later ○ *We will delay making a decision until we see the result of the election.* ○ *The company has delayed payment of all invoices.*

delegate[1] /'delɪgət/ *noun* a person who represents others at a meeting ○ *The minister met delegates from the union.*

delegate[2] /'deləˌgeɪt/ (**delegates, delegating, delegated**) *verb* to pass authority or responsibility on to someone else ○ *She finds it difficult to delegate.* ○ *He delegated the job of locking up the shop to the junior manager.*

delegation /delɪ'geɪʃ(ə)n/ *noun* **1.** a group of representatives ○ *The minister met a union delegation.* **2.** the act of passing on authority or responsibility to someone else ○ *The secret of good management is delegation.*

③ **delete** /dɪ'liːt/ (**deletes, deleting, deleted**) *verb* to cut out part of something, e.g. a document or a computer file

deletion /dɪ'liːʃ(ə)n/ *noun* **1.** the action of deleting something ○ *The court asked for the deletion of several sentences from the magazine article.* ○ *She made several deletions to the original text.* **2.** a word or phrase which has been deleted ○ *In spite of all the deletions, the article is still too long.*

deli /'deli/ *noun* same as **delicatessen** (*informal*)

deliberate[1] /dɪ'lɪb(ə)rət/ *adj* **1.** done on purpose ○ *It was a deliberate attempt to spoil her birthday party.* **2.** slow and thoughtful in speaking or doing something ○ *She has a very deliberate way of signing her name.*

deliberate[2] /dɪ'lɪbəreɪt/ (**deliberates, deliberating, deliberated**) *verb* to discuss or think carefully about something ○ *The council were deliberating all morning.* ○ *I'll need some time to deliberate on the possible ways of solving the problem.*

③ **deliberately** /dɪ'lɪb(ə)rətli/ *adv* on purpose ○ *It was an accident – I didn't hit her deliberately.* ○ *He deliberately left the cage door open.*

deliberation /dɪˌlɪbə'reɪʃ(ə)n/ *noun* **1.** great care ○ *He moved his king with great deliberation and leant back with a smile.* **2.** a discussion ○ *After lengthy deliberations the meeting voted on the proposal.* ○ *Did their deliberations produce any result?*

delicacy /'delɪkəsi/ (*plural* **delicacies**) *noun* **1.** sensitivity ○ *It is a question which has to be handled with great delicacy.* **2.** the state of being delicate ○ *The delicacy of the glasses means that they have to be handled very carefully.* **3.** an unusual and tasty thing to eat ○ *They bought all sorts of delicacies for the Christmas party.*

delicate /'delɪkət/ *adj* **1.** made from materials that are thin and light and easily damaged ○ *a delicate china vase* **2.** likely to get ill ○ *Little babies are very delicate.* ○ *She was a delicate child.*

delicatessen /ˌdelɪkə'tes(ə)n/ *noun* a shop selling cold meats and imported food products

delicious /dɪ'lɪʃəs/ *adj* tasting very good ○ *Can I have another piece of that delicious cake?* (NOTE: + **deliciously** *adv*)

delight /dɪ'laɪt/ *noun* **1.** pleasure ○ *The news was greeted with delight by the waiting crowd.* □ **to take (great) delight in something** to enjoy something **2.** something which gives someone pleasure ■ *verb* (**delights, delighting, delighted**) **1.** to give great pleasure to someone ○ *His speech delighted the audience.* **2.** to enjoy something [~in] ○ *She delights in teasing her little brother.*

② **delighted** /dɪ'laɪtɪd/ *adj* very pleased

② **delightful** /dɪ'laɪtf(ə)l/ *adj* very pleasant ○ *What a delightful show of flowers!*

delirious /dɪ'lɪriəs/ *adj* **1.** suffering from delirium ○ *She collapsed and became delirious.* **2.** very excited and happy ○ *They were delirious when they won the lottery.*

delirium /dɪ'lɪriəm/ *noun* a mental state in which a person is confused, restless and very excited and has hallucinations

② **deliver** /dɪ'lɪvə/ (**delivers, delivering, delivered**) *verb* **1.** to bring something to someone [~to] ○ *Has today's newspaper been delivered yet?* ○ *He delivered the letter to her himself so as to be sure she got it.* **2.** □ **to deliver a baby** to help a mother when a baby is being born ○ *The twins were delivered by the midwife.* **3.** □ **to deliver a speech** to make a speech ○ *This is the full text of the speech the President delivered at the meeting.* ◇ **to deliver the goods** to do what you promised to do ○ *You can always rely on him to deliver the goods.*

② **delivery** /dɪ'lɪv(ə)ri/ (*plural* **deliveries**) *noun* the act of bringing something to someone ○ *There is no charge for delivery within the London area.* ○ *Use the back entrance for deliveries.* ○ *The next delivery will be on Thursday.*

delta /'deltə/ *noun* **1.** a triangular piece of land at the mouth of a large river, formed of silt carried by the river ○ *the Mississippi Delta* **2.** the fourth letter of the Greek alphabet. Symbol **δ**

delude /dɪ'luːd/ (**deludes, deluding, deluded**) *verb* to make someone believe something which is wrong

deluge /'deljuːdʒ/ *noun* **1.** a flood of something, e.g. questions or orders ○ *We had a deluge of phone calls after our TV commercial.* **2.** a heavy rainfall ○ *It had been dry for weeks and then last Saturday we had a deluge.* ■ *verb* (**deluges, deluging, deluged**) **1.** to flood a place **2.** to overwhelm someone with a flood of something ○ *We were deluged with phone calls.*

delusion /dɪ'luːʒ(ə)n/ *noun* a false belief which a person holds, which cannot be changed by reason

de luxe /dɪ 'lʌks/ *adj* very expensive or of very high quality

delve /delv/ (**delves, delving, delved**) *verb* **1.** to investigate something [~into] ○ *I remember the case but I might have to delve deeply to get the details.* ○ *He has been delving into the past history of the family.* **2.** to look somewhere for something ○ *She delved in the drawer and produced a small booklet.*

① **demand** /dɪ'mɑːnd/ *noun* **1.** the act of asking for something [~for] ○ *a demand for payment* **2.** the need for particular goods or services [~for] ○ *We cannot keep up with the demand for our new machine.* □ **to meet** *or* **fill a demand** to supply what is needed ○

The factory had to increase production to meet the extra demand. □ **there is not much demand for this item** not many people want to buy this item □ **this item is in great demand** many people want to buy this item ■ *verb* (**demands, demanding, demanded**) to ask firmly for something [~(that)/~to] ○ *I demand an explanation for your behaviour.* ○ *They demanded that more information be made available.* ○ *We demanded to know how long it would be before we received a reply.*

③ **demanding** /dɪ'mɑːndɪŋ/ *adj* which takes up much time and energy

demeaning /dɪ'miːnɪŋ/ *adj* which makes you appear undignified

demeanour /dɪ'miːnə/ *noun* a person's behaviour or manner (NOTE: The US spelling is **demeanor**.)

dementia /dɪ'menʃə/ *noun* a loss of mental ability and memory, causing confusion and changes to the personality, due to a disease of the brain

demise /dɪ'maɪz/ *noun* a death (*formal*)

demo /'deməʊ/ *noun* same as **demonstration**

② **democracy** /dɪ'mɒkrəsi/ *noun* **1.** a country governed by politicians who have been elected by the people **2.** a system of government in which politicians are elected by the people ○ *The people want democracy, not a dictatorship.*

③ **democrat** /'deməkræt/ *noun* a person who believes in democracy ○ *All true democrats will unite against the dictator.*

② **democratic** /ˌdemə'krætɪk/ *adj* relating to democracy ○ *They promised to restore democratic government.*

③ **demolish** /dɪ'mɒlɪʃ/ (**demolishes, demolishing, demolished**) *verb* **1.** to knock something down ○ *We demolished the old church and built a new one.* **2.** to eat something completely ○ *He demolished the whole chocolate cake.* **3.** to show that something is completely wrong ○ *He wrote an article demolishing the professor's theories.*

demolition /ˌdemə'lɪʃ(ə)n/ *noun* the action of knocking down something such as a building

demon /'diːmən/ *noun* a devil ○ *The picture shows red demons throwing people into a fire.*

demonstrable /dɪ'mɒnstrəb(ə)l/ *adj* which can be proved or demonstrated

② **demonstrate** /'demənstreɪt/ (**demonstrates, demonstrating, demonstrated**) *verb* **1.** to show something [~(that)/~what/where/how etc] ○ *This incident demonstrates that nothing has changed.* ○ *He demonstrated how the machine worked.* **2.** to protest against something in public [~against] ○ *A group were demonstrating against the new motorway.*

③ **demonstration** /ˌdemən'streɪʃ(ə)n/ *noun* **1.** the act of showing how something works ○ *Can you give me a demonstration of the new machine?* **2.** a crowd of people who are protesting against something [~against] ○ *a demonstration against the policy on student funding*

demonstrative /dɪ'mɒnstrətɪv/ *adj* (*of a person*) who openly shows his or her feelings ○ *She's not very demonstrative, but I think she appreciated her gift all the same.*

③ **demonstrator** /'demənstreɪtə/ *noun* a person who marches or who forms part of a crowd protesting against something ○ *A crowd of demonstrators blocked the road.* ○ *The police used water cannon to clear demonstrators from in front of the Parliament building.*

demoralised /dɪ'mɒrəlaɪzd/, **demoralized** *adj* unhappy and discouraged

demoralising /dɪ'mɒrəlaɪzɪŋ/, **demoralizing** *adj* which demoralises you or lowers your confidence

demote /dɪ'məʊt/ (**demotes, demoting, demoted**) *verb* to give someone a less important job or reduce an employee to a lower rank or grade (NOTE: + **demotion** *n*)

demure /dɪ'mjʊə/ *adj* quiet and serious

den /den/ *noun* **1.** a place where an animal hides away ○ *a lion's den* **2.** a small room where you can hide away to work ○ *Dad's in his den, so don't disturb him.*

denial /dɪ'naɪəl/ *noun* a statement that something is not true

denigrate /'denɪgreɪt/ (**denigrates, denigrating, denigrated**) *verb* to say that someone or something is not very good

denim /'denɪm/ *noun* a thick cotton cloth, usually blue

denomination /dɪˌnɒmɪ'neɪʃ(ə)n/ *noun* **1.** a unit of money written on a coin, banknote or stamp ○ *Coins of all denominations are put in the church collection box.* ○ *The bank has run out of small denomination notes.* **2.** a religious grouping ○ *The Protestant Church is divided into several denominations.* ○ *What denomination does he belong to?*

③ **denounce** /dɪ'naʊns/ (**denounces, denouncing, denounced**) *verb* **1.** to blame or to accuse someone or something openly ○ *Someone denounced him to the police.* ○

He was denounced as a racist by a fellow professor. **2.** to say you disapprove of someone or something publicly ○ *She denounced the council's policy as short-sighted.*

dense /dens/ *adj* **1.** very thick ○ *Dense fog closed the airport.* **2.** with a lot of trees or plants ○ *They tried to find their way through dense forest.* **3.** containing a lot of information ○ *I find it difficult to read through 100 pages of dense text.*

③ **density** /ˈdensɪti/ *noun* **1.** (*in physics*) the amount of mass per unit of volume ○ *heavy density oils* **2.** the number of things in a certain area ○ *the high traffic density in the centre of Rome* ○ *London suffers from high population density.*

dent /dent/ *noun* a mark that curves inwards, especially in metal, made by hitting something ○ *Someone has made a dent in my car door.* ■ *verb* (**dents, denting, dented**) to make a mark like this in something ○ *He backed into a tree and dented the car.*

dental /ˈdent(ə)l/ *adj* referring to teeth

dental floss /ˈdent(ə)l flɒs/ *noun* a thin waxed thread for pulling between your teeth to remove pieces of food

② **dentist** /ˈdentɪst/ *noun* a person whose job is to look after and provide treatment for your teeth

dentistry /ˈdentɪstri/ *noun* **1.** the profession of a dentist **2.** the branch of medicine dealing with teeth and gums

dentures /ˈdentʃəz/ *plural noun* artificial teeth which fit inside the mouth and are used in place of teeth which have been taken out

denunciation /dɪˌnʌnsiˈeɪʃ(ə)n/ *noun* a public accusation or blame

② **deny** /dɪˈnaɪ/ (**denies, denying, denied**) *verb* to state that something is not true [~(that)] ○ *He flatly denied stealing the car.* ○ *She denied that she had ever seen him.*

deodorant /diˈəʊd(ə)rənt/ *noun* a substance which hides and prevents unpleasant body smells

③ **depart** /dɪˈpɑːt/ (**departs, departing, departed**) *verb* to go away from a place [~for/~from] ○ *The coach departs for Edinburgh from London at 09.00.*

① **department** /dɪˈpɑːtmənt/ *noun* **1.** a section of a large company ○ *He is in charge of the marketing department.* ○ *Write to the complaints department about the service.* **2.** one of the sections of the government ○ *the Department for Education and Skills* ○ *the Department of Transport* **3.** a part of a large shop ○ *If you want cheese you'll need to go to the food department.* ○ *You will find beds in the furniture department.*

③ **department store** /dɪˈpɑːtmənt stɔː/ *noun* a large shop with several different sections

③ **departure** /dɪˈpɑːtʃə/ *noun* the act of leaving a place ○ *The plane's departure was delayed by two hours.* ○ *The departure time is 3 o'clock.* ■ *plural noun* **departures** the part of an airport terminal which deals with passengers who are leaving. Compare **arrival**

① **depend** /dɪˈpend/ (**depends, depending, depended**) *verb* □ **it depends** it is linked to something else ○ *'Are there any seats available for the show?' 'It depends how many people you need tickets for.'* □ **to depend on something** to happen only because of something else happening first ○ *The success of the book will depend on the publicity campaign.* ○ *I'd like to come but it depends what time we can leave work.* □ **to depend on someone *or* something** to be sure that someone will do what they say they will do, or that something will happen as expected ○ *You can't depend on Jack – he's always too busy to help.* ○ *You can depend on her to do her best.* ○ *The company depends on government grants.* ◇ **it (all) depends** it is not certain (*informal*) ○ *We may go to France on holiday, or Spain, it all depends.*

dependable /dɪˈpendəb(ə)l/ *adj* that can be relied on

dependant /dɪˈpendənt/ *noun* a member of the family who is financially supported by another (NOTE: Do not confuse with **dependent**.)

③ **dependence** /dɪˈpendəns/ *noun* the fact of being dependent on someone or something

③ **dependent** /dɪˈpendənt/ *adj* **1.** needing money from someone else in order to live ○ *She has five dependent relatives.* **2.** needing someone else's help in order to live or succeed ○ *The patients become very dependent on the hospital staff.* **3.** caused or affected by something ○ *The success of the project is dependent on getting a government grant.* (NOTE: [all adj senses] Do not confuse with **dependant**.) ■ *noun* US spelling of **dependant**

③ **depict** /dɪˈpɪkt/ (**depicts, depicting, depicted**) *verb* to show or describe something [~as] ○ *Newspapers like to depict him as a lovable crook.*

deplete /dɪ'pliːt/ (**depletes, depleting, depleted**) *verb* to reduce available stocks or stores

depleted /dɪ'pliːtɪd/ *adj* containing less of something than before

deplorable /dɪ'plɔːrəb(ə)l/ *adj* very bad

deplore /dɪ'plɔː/ (**deplores, deploring, deplored**) *verb* to say you strongly dislike an action or an attitude (*formal*) ○ *We deplore the violence that is taking place.*

③ **deploy** /dɪ'plɔɪ/ (**deploys, deploying, deployed**) *verb* to spread out soldiers, etc. ready for action

deport /dɪ'pɔːt/ (**deports, deporting, deported**) *verb* to expel someone from a country (NOTE: + **deportation** *n*)

depose /dɪ'pəʊz/ (**deposes, deposing, deposed**) *verb* to remove a king from the throne or a ruler from office

③ **deposit** /dɪ'pɒzɪt/ *noun* **1.** money kept in a bank ○ *Her deposits in the bank had grown over the years.* **2.** a particular amount of money that you give someone as a first payment for something expensive ○ *She had to pay a deposit on the watch.* ○ *Can you leave £50 as deposit?* ○ *I paid a 30% deposit and don't have to pay anything more for six months.* ■ *verb* (**deposits, depositing, deposited**) to put money into a bank account ○ *She deposited £100 in her current account.* ○ *The cheque arrived at long last, and I deposited it immediately.*

deposit account /dɪ'pɒzɪt əˌkaʊnt/ *noun* an account which pays interest but on which notice usually has to be given to withdraw money

③ **depot** /'depəʊ/ *noun* **1.** a central warehouse for goods ○ *a freight depot* ○ *a goods depot* ○ *an oil storage depot* **2.** a centre for transport ○ *a bus depot* ○ *a tram depot*

depraved /dɪ'preɪvd/ *adj* wicked or immoral

depreciate /dɪ'priːʃiˌeɪt/ (**depreciates, depreciating, depreciated**) *verb* to lose value ○ *The pound has depreciated by 5% against the dollar.*

③ **depress** /dɪ'pres/ (**depresses, depressing, depressed**) *verb* **1.** to make someone sad or miserable ○ *Listening to that particular piece of music always depresses me.* **2.** to push down a button ○ *To activate the alarm, depress both buttons simultaneously.*

③ **depressed** /dɪ'prest/ *adj* so unhappy that you are not able to enjoy life, especially over a long period of time ○ *She's been feeling depressed since the accident.*

③ **depressing** /dɪ'presɪŋ/ *adj* making you feel sad or unhappy

③ **depression** /dɪ'preʃ(ə)n/ *noun* **1.** a mental state where you feel miserable and hopeless ○ *He was in a state of depression after the exams.* ○ *She is subject to fits of depression.* **2.** a low pressure area bringing bad weather ○ *The depression coming from the Atlantic will bring rain to most parts of the country.* ○ *Winds move anticlockwise round a depression.* **3.** an economic crisis ○ *Have many companies here been affected by the current world depression?* **4.** a place which is lower than the area round it ○ *A pool of water had formed in a depression in the rocks.*

deprivation /ˌdeprɪ'veɪʃ(ə)n/ *noun* **1.** a state of being deprived of something **2.** a state of not having enough of the things necessary for a normal life, such as food and housing ○ *They suffered dreadful deprivation(s) during the war.*

deprive /dɪ'praɪv/ (**deprives, depriving, deprived**) *verb* to take something away from someone, or not to let someone have something ○ *We've been deprived of sunshine all month.* ○ *Poverty deprived her of all the usual comforts of life.*

deprived /dɪ'praɪvd/ *adj* not enjoying many of society's benefits

① **depth** /depθ/ *noun* a measurement of how deep something is ○ *The depth of the lake is 20m.* ○ *The submarine dived to a depth of 200m.*

② **deputy** /'depjʊti/ (*plural* **deputies**) *noun* **1.** a person who makes decisions when the manager or boss is away ○ *She's acting as deputy while the managing director is in hospital.* **2.** a person who helps someone in their job ○ *He appointed her as his deputy.*

derail /diː'reɪl/ (**derails, derailing, derailed**) *verb* to make a train leave the rails

derby /'dɑːbi/ (*plural* **derbies**) *noun* **1.** a bowler hat **2.** a sporting contest between local teams ○ *There are always crowds at the local derby.*

deregulation /diːˌregjʊ'leɪʃ(ə)n/ *noun* reducing government control over an industry

derelict /'derɪlɪkt/ *adj* ruined and abandoned ○ *They plan to build the housing development on derelict land near the city centre.* ○ *They bought a derelict cottage to do it up.*

deride /dɪ'raɪd/ (**derides, deriding, derided**) *verb* to laugh at someone or something

derision /dɪ'rɪʒ(ə)n/ *noun* the act of laughing at someone or something because you think they are stupid

derisive /dɪ'raɪsɪv/ *adj* laughing at someone because you think they are stupid

derisory /dɪ'raɪsəri/ *adj* ridiculously small

derivation /ˌderɪ'veɪʃ(ə)n/ *noun* the origin of a word

derive /dɪ'raɪv/ (**derives, deriving, derived**) *verb* to get something from something

dermatologist /ˌdɜːmə'tɒlədʒɪst/ *noun* a doctor who specialises in the study and treatment of diseases of the skin

derogatory /dɪ'rɒgət(ə)ri/ *adj* showing dislike for someone or something

descend /dɪ'send/ (**descends, descending, descended**) *verb* **1.** to go down something such as a ladder ○ *The president seemed to stumble as he descended the steps from the plane.* **2.** □ **to be descended from someone** to have someone as an ancestor ○ *On his mother's side, he is descended from one of William the Conqueror's knights.*

③ **descendant** /dɪ'sendənt/ *noun* a member of a family with a particular ancestor

③ **descent** /dɪ'sent/ *noun* **1.** the process of going down [~into/to] ○ *The descent into the mine takes just under three minutes.* **2.** family ancestry ○ *He can trace his descent back to* or *from William I.* □ **she is of Irish descent** her family is from Ireland **3.** a downhill slope ○ *She successfully completed a tricky descent.* (NOTE: Do not confuse with **dissent**.)

① **describe** /dɪ'skraɪb/ (**describes, describing, described**) *verb* to say or write what someone or something is like [~how/what/who etc/~as] ○ *Can you describe the car which hit the old lady?* ○ *She described how the bus suddenly left the road.* ○ *He described the man as tall with a black beard.*

① **description** /dɪ'skrɪpʃən/ *noun* the act of saying or writing what something or someone is like

descriptive /dɪ'skrɪptɪv/ *adj* which says what something is like

desecrate /'desɪkreɪt/ (**desecrates, desecrating, desecrated**) *verb* to treat a place such as a church or a grave in a disrespectful way (NOTE: + **desecration** *n*)

desegregation /ˌdiːsegrɪ'geɪʃ(ə)n/ *noun* the act of ending the segregation of a group of people or an institution (NOTE: + **desegregate** *v*)

desert[1] /'dezət/ *noun* a very dry area of the world, usually covered with rocks or sand (NOTE: Do not confuse with **dessert**.)

desert[2] /dɪ'zɜːt/ (**deserts, deserting, deserted**) *verb* **1.** to leave the armed forces without permission **2.** to leave someone in a difficult situation

deserted /dɪ'zɜːtɪd/ *adj* with no people ○ *We walked around the deserted town.*

deserter /dɪ'zɜːtə/ *noun* a person who leaves the armed forces without permission

desert island /ˌdezət 'aɪlənd/ *noun* a tropical island with no inhabitants

② **deserve** /dɪ'zɜːv/ (**deserves, deserving, deserved**) *verb* to earn something because of what you have done ○ *He didn't deserve to win because he cheated.* ○ *I've been on my feet all day – I think I deserve a sit-down.* ○ *He deserves a holiday.*

deserving /dɪ'zɜːvɪŋ/ *adj* which should be supported or helped

① **design** /dɪ'zaɪn/ *noun* a plan or drawing of something, before it is made or built [~for] ○ *the designs for the new opera house* ■ *verb* (**designs, designing, designed**) to draw plans for the shape or appearance of something before it is made or built ○ *He designed the new university library.* ○ *She designs garden furniture.*

designate[1] /'dezɪgneɪt/ (**designates, designating, designated**) *verb* to appoint someone to a post ○ *He has been designated as our representative at the meeting.*

designate[2] /'dezɪgnət/ *adj* appointed to a particular job but not doing it yet ○ *the chief executive designate* (NOTE: always after a noun)

③ **designer** /dɪ'zaɪnə/ *noun* an artist who plans the shape or appearance of things such as goods, clothes or rooms

desirable /dɪ'zaɪərəb(ə)l/ *adj* which a lot of people want

② **desire** /dɪ'zaɪə/ *noun* something that you want very much [~for] ○ *It's difficult to satisfy the public's desire for information.* ○ *She had a sudden desire to lie down and go to sleep.* ■ *verb* (**desires, desiring, desired**) to want something (*formal*) ○ *Most of us desire a large comfortable home.* ◇ **to leave a lot to be desired** not to be of the right standard, not to be acceptable ○ *The bathrooms in the hotel leave a lot to be desired.*

desired /dɪ'zaɪəd/ *adj* wanted or required

② **desk** /desk/ *noun* **1.** a table, often with drawers, used for writing ○ *He put the papers away in his desk drawer.* ○ *She was sitting at her desk when the telephone rang.* **2.** a government department ○ *She works on the Central Europe desk in the Foreign Office.*

desk tidy /ˈdesk ˌtaɪdi/ *noun* a small container kept on a desk to keep things such as pens and paper clips tidy

desktop /ˈdesktɒp/ *noun* **1.** the top surface of a desk **2.** a display on a computer screen that shows images representing available programs and files

desktop publishing /ˌdesktɒp ˈpʌblɪʃɪŋ/ *noun* the production of publications using a personal computer

desolate /ˈdesələt/ *adj* bleak and deserted ○ *a desolate mountainside*

despair /dɪˈspeə/ *noun* a feeling that a situation is so bad that there is nothing you can do to make it better ○ *When he lost his job and his girlfriend left him, he was filled with despair.* ■ *verb* (**despairs, despairing, despaired**) to give up all hope of achieving something ◇ **the depths of despair** a situation where there is complete lack of hope

③ **desperate** /ˈdesp(ə)rət/ *adj* **1.** having a strong need for something that you are not able to get, and feeling very worried because you do not know how to solve the problem [~for] ○ *Food ran out and the people were becoming desperate.* ○ *They were desperate for news of their son.* **2.** urgent ○ *There is a desperate need for medical supplies.*

despicable /dɪˈspɪkəb(ə)l/ *adj* unpleasant, which you despise

despise /dɪˈspaɪz/ (**despises, despising, despised**) *verb* to look down on someone, to think someone is not worth much

① **despite** /dɪˈspaɪt/ *prep* although something happened or was done ○ *Despite the wet weather we still enjoyed our holiday.*

despondent /dɪˈspɒndənt/ *adj* discouraged and unhappy

dessert /dɪˈzɜːt/ *noun* a sweet dish at the end of a meal ○ *The meal will end with a dessert of strawberries and cream.* ○ *What's for dessert?* (NOTE: Do not confuse with **desert**. The word **dessert** is mainly used in restaurants. At home, this part of the meal is usually called **the sweet** *or* **afters** *or* **pudding**.)

destabilise /diːˈsteɪbɪlaɪz/ (**destabilises, destabilising, destabilised**), **destabilize** *verb* to make a country or government less stable

destination /ˌdestɪˈneɪʃ(ə)n/ *noun* the place to which a person or vehicle is going ○ *We reached our destination at eight o'clock.* ○ *The destination is shown on the front of the bus.*

destined /ˈdestɪnd/ *adj* **1.** going or being sent to a particular place [~for] ○ *All mail destined for Canada is delayed because of the postal workers' strike.* **2.** certain to have, do or experience something [~for/~to] ○ *She's destined for a great career on TV.* ○ *They were destined to fail in their search for gold.*

destiny /ˈdestɪni/ *noun* **1.** what will happen to you in the future ○ *The war affected the destinies of many people.* **2.** a power that controls what happens to you in the future ○ *You never know what destiny has in store for you.*

destitute /ˈdestɪtjuːt/ *adj* with very little money and very few belongings

② **destroy** /dɪˈstrɔɪ/ (**destroys, destroying, destroyed**) *verb* to damage something so badly that it no longer exists ○ *The bomb destroyed several buildings.* ○ *A lot of private property was destroyed in the war.*

destroyer /dɪˈstrɔɪə/ *noun* a medium-sized naval ship

② **destruction** /dɪˈstrʌkʃən/ *noun* the action of destroying something ○ *the destruction of the village by enemy bombs* ○ *The volcano caused enormous destruction.* ○ *After the bomb attack there was a scene of total destruction.* (NOTE: no plural)

destructive /dɪˈstrʌktɪv/ *adj* which destroys

③ **detach** /dɪˈtætʃ/ (**detaches, detaching, detached**) *verb* to separate something from something or someone

detachable /dɪˈtætʃəb(ə)l/ *adj* which you can detach

detached /dɪˈtætʃt/ *adj* □ **detached house** a house which stands alone, not attached to another

detachment /dɪˈtætʃmənt/ *noun* **1.** indifference, lack of particular interest ○ *He glanced at the advancing policemen with an air of detachment.* **2.** a small group of soldiers ○ *Detachments of marines have been sent to the island.*

① **detail** /ˈdiːteɪl/ *noun* a small piece of information ○ *Send in your CV including full details of your past experience.* ○ *Can you give me further details of when the accident took place?* ○ *I can't make out the details in the photo because the light is* bad. ○ *The policeman noted down the details of the incident.* ■ *verb* (**details, detailing, detailed**) to list all the facts or items ○ *He detailed the work which had to be done.* ◇ **in detail** with as much information as possible ○ *The catalogue lists all the furniture in detail.* ○ *Please describe the circumstances of the accident in as much detail as possible.*

② **detailed** /ˈdiːteɪld/ *adj* giving a lot of details ○ *We need a detailed list of the items which have been stolen.* ○ *The police issued detailed descriptions of the two men.*

detain /dɪˈteɪn/ (**detains, detaining, detained**) *verb* **1.** to keep someone in a police station or prison ○ *The police have detained a man for questioning.* **2.** to stop someone from leaving ○ *I'm sorry I'm late – I was detained by a phone call.*

③ **detect** /dɪˈtekt/ (**detects, detecting, detected**) *verb* **1.** to discover something scientifically ○ *If breast cancer is detected early enough, it can be cured.* **2.** to notice ○ *I detected some unwillingness to agree to the change.*

③ **detective** /dɪˈtektɪv/ *noun* a police officer whose job is to try to find out who committed crimes ○ *Detectives have interviewed four suspects.*

③ **detector** /dɪˈtektə/ *noun* an instrument which checks whether something is present

③ **detention** /dɪˈtenʃ(ə)n/ *noun* **1.** imprisonment ○ *After he was released from detention he committed the same offence again.* ○ *The internees were kept in detention camps.* **2.** keeping children at school as a punishment ○ *The children were kept in detention after school.*

deter /dɪˈtɜː/ (**deters, deterring, deterred**) *verb* □ **to deter someone from doing something** to discourage someone from doing something ○ *The heavy rain didn't deter us from visiting the town.* ○ *We have installed cameras to deter shoplifters.*

detergent /dɪˈtɜːdʒənt/ *noun* a cleaning substance which removes grease and bacteria from things such as clothes or dishes

deteriorate /dɪˈtɪəriəreɪt/ (**deteriorates, deteriorating, deteriorated**) *verb* to go bad; to get worse (NOTE: + **deterioration** *n*)

② **determination** /dɪˌtɜːmɪˈneɪʃ(ə)n/ *noun* a strong wish to do something, and not to let anyone stop you doing it [~in] ○ *The government needs to show more determination in its fight against street crime.* ○ *They admired his determination to win the prize.*

③ **determine** /dɪˈtɜːmɪn/ (**determines, determining, determined**) *verb* **1.** to fix something such as a date ○ *The meeting will be at a date still to be determined.* **2.** □ **to determine to do something** to make a decision to do something (*formal*) ○ *I determined not to make the same mistake again.* **3.** to find out the details of something [~what/whether/why/who etc] ○ *The police have to determine what really happened.* **4.** to affect something in a particular way ○ *His exam results will determine his future.*

③ **determined** /dɪˈtɜːmɪnd/ *adj* having a strong wish to do something, and not letting anyone prevent you from doing it ○ *She's a very determined young woman, and will go far.* ○ *He had a very determined expression on his face.* ○ *She is determined to win the prize.*

determiner /dɪˈtɜːmɪnə/ *noun* a pronoun or article which comes before an adjective or noun, and shows what is being referred to, such as 'this' in 'this old car' (*grammar*)

deterrent /dɪˈterənt/ *noun* something which stops people from wanting to do something ○ *Cameras by the side of the road act as a deterrent to people who drive too fast.*

detest /dɪˈtest/ (**detests, detesting, detested**) *verb* to dislike someone or something intensely

detonate /ˈdetəneɪt/ (**detonates, detonating, detonated**) *verb* **1.** to set off an explosive ○ *The police detonated the package found under the car.* **2.** to explode ○ *A shell landed in their garden but failed to detonate.* (NOTE: + **detonation** *n*)

detonator /ˈdetəneɪtə/ *noun* a small explosive charge which will set off a large explosion

detox /ˈdiːtɒks/ *noun* **1.** medical treatment which helps people to stop taking drugs or drinking too much alcohol **2.** the process of stopping taking drugs or drinking alcohol ■ *verb* (**detoxes, detoxing, detoxed**) to stop taking harmful substances in order to improve your health ○ *No thanks, I'm detoxing after last week's excesses.*

detract /dɪˈtrækt/ (**detracts, detracting, detracted**) *verb* to make something less useful, attractive or interesting [~from] ○ *Her rudeness to the judges detracted from the prize-giving ceremony.*

detriment /ˈdetrɪmənt/ *noun* damage

detrimental /ˌdetrɪˈment(ə)l/ *adj* which can harm

devalue /diːˈvæljuː/ (**devalues, devaluing, devalued**) *verb* to reduce the value of a currency in relation to that of other countries (NOTE: + **devaluation** *n*)

③ **devastate** /ˈdevəsteɪt/ (**devastates, devastating, devastated**) *verb* to wreck something completely

devastated /ˈdevəsteɪtɪd/ *adj* **1.** badly damaged ○ *Relief agencies are trying to help the devastated region.* **2.** upset by something such as bad news ○ *She was devastated when she was made redundant.* ○ *When he read the report in the paper he was completely devastated.*

devastating /ˈdevəsteɪtɪŋ/ *adj* **1.** causing a lot of damage ○ *The country has still not recovered from the devastating effects of the storm.* **2.** shocking, upsetting ○ *The news from Paris was devastating.*

① **develop** /dɪˈveləp/ (**develops, developing, developed**) *verb* **1.** to grow and change [~from/~into] ○ *Eventually, a caterpillar will develop into a butterfly.* ○ *A flower develops from a bud.* **2.** to make something larger ○ *He exercises in order to develop his muscles.* **3.** to get an illness ○ *She developed a cold at the weekend.* **4.** to plan and produce something [~into/~from] ○ *It was eventually developed into a popular game from an idea he'd had as a student.* **5.** to plan and build something [~as/into] ○ *The company is developing a chain of restaurants.* ○ *They are planning to develop the site as* or *into an industrial estate.* **6.** to produce a photograph from film ○ *We can develop your film in an hour.*

developer /dɪˈveləpə/ *noun* a person or company that plans and builds roads, airports, houses, factories or office buildings ○ *The land has been acquired by developers for a housing estate.*

① **development** /dɪˈveləpmənt/ *noun* **1.** growth ○ *The development of the embryo takes place rapidly.* **2.** the planning and production of a new product **3.** the act of planning and building on an area of land **4.** a group of buildings that have been built together at the same time

deviant /ˈdiːviənt/ *adj* different from normal

deviate /ˈdiːvieɪt/ (**deviates, deviating, deviated**) *verb* to be different from what is normal or usual [~from] ○ *The celebrations deviated from their normal pattern by being held on a Sunday.* ○ *He did not deviate from the written version of his speech.*

deviation /ˌdiːviˈeɪʃ(ə)n/ *noun* changing from what is usual

② **device** /dɪˈvaɪs/ *noun* a small tool or piece of equipment that is useful for a particular purpose [~for] ○ *He invented a device for fixing tops on bottles.* ◇ **to be left to your own devices** to be allowed to do whatever you want

devil /ˈdev(ə)l/ *noun* **1.** an evil spirit ○ *He believes in ghosts and devils and all that sort of thing.* **2.** a person ○ *He's won the lottery, lucky devil!* ○ *Poor devil! I must go and see him in hospital.*

devil's advocate /ˌdev(ə)lz ˈædvəkət/ *noun* a person who argues the opposite point of view, in order to stimulate discussion about a widely held opinion

devious /ˈdiːviəs/ *adj* **1.** not honest or straightforward ○ *It's just a very devious plan to avoid paying the staff more money.* **2.** not going straight ○ *The taxi took us on a very devious route to Piccadilly Circus.*

devise /dɪˈvaɪz/ (**devises, devising, devised**) *verb* to think up or invent something ○ *We've devised a new timetable for the summer term.* ○ *He devised a plan for making more money out of the farm.*

devoid /dɪˈvɔɪd/ *adj* without something [~of] ○ *The book is devoid of literary merit.*

devolution /ˌdiːvəˈluːʃ(ə)n/ *noun* the passing of power from a central government to a local or regional authority

devote /dɪˈvəʊt/ (**devotes, devoting, devoted**) *verb* □ **to devote time to something** to spend time on something ○ *Don't you think you've devoted enough time to your model planes?* □ **to devote yourself to something** to spend all your time on something ○ *She devoted herself to looking after refugee children.*

devoted /dɪˈvəʊtɪd/ *adj* **1.** loving [~to] ○ *a devoted father* **2.** showing affection to someone [~to] ○ *He is devoted to his children.* **3.** spending all your time on something [~to] ○ *She's devoted to her flower garden.*

devotion /dɪˈvəʊʃ(ə)n/ *noun* **1.** love **2.** constant work on behalf of someone or something

devour /dɪˈvaʊə/ (**devours, devouring, devoured**) *verb* to eat something greedily

devout /dɪˈvaʊt/ *adj* deeply religious

dew /djuː/ *noun* water which forms at night on objects in the open air (NOTE: Do not confuse with **due**.)

dexterity /dekˈsterɪti/ *noun* skill in using your hands or mind

diabetes /ˌdaɪəˈbiːtiːz/ *noun* a condition in which the body cannot control sugar absorption because the pancreas does not produce enough insulin

diabetic /ˌdaɪəˈbetɪk/ *noun* a person with diabetes ○ *She is a diabetic and has to have regular injections of insulin.*

diabolical /ˌdaɪəˈbɒlɪk(ə)l/ *adj* **1.** evil and wicked ○ *They devised a diabolical plot to assassinate the Prime Minister.* **2.** very bad ○ *The food in the staff canteen is diabolical.*

diagnose /ˈdaɪəgnəʊz/ (**diagnoses, diagnosing, diagnosed**) *verb* to identify a patient's illness by examining him or her and noting symptoms

diagnosis /ˌdaɪəgˈnəʊsɪs/ (*plural* **diagnoses**) *noun* the identification of an illness

diagonal /daɪˈægən(ə)l/ *adj* going straight from one corner to another ○ *He drew a diagonal line on the floor.* ○ *Areas of the map shaded with diagonal lines indicate cultivated land.* ■ *noun* a diagonal line

① **diagram** /ˈdaɪəgræm/ *noun* a plan or accurate drawing ○ *She drew a diagram to show how to get to her house.*

③ **dial** /ˈdaɪəl/ *noun* a round face of a measuring instrument or an old type of telephone ○ *The pilot sits in front of a display of dials.* ■ *verb* (**dials, dialling, dialled**) to call a telephone number using the buttons on a telephone ○ *To call the police you must dial 999.* ○ *Dial 9 to get an outside line.*

③ **dialect** /ˈdaɪəlekt/ *noun* a variety of a language spoken in a particular area ○ *They were speaking in a local dialect.*

dialling code /ˈdaɪəlɪŋ kəʊd/ *noun* a special phone number for a town or country

dialling tone /ˈdaɪəlɪŋ təʊn/ *noun* the noise made by a telephone to show that it is ready for you to dial a number

dialog box /ˈdaɪəlɒg bɒks/ *noun* a small area on a computer screen that presents the user with a choice

② **dialogue** /ˈdaɪəlɒg/ *noun* **1.** a conversation between two people [~between] ○ *The next exercise on the tape is a dialogue between a shopkeeper and a customer.* **2.** the spoken words in a film or TV drama **3.** political talks or negotiations [~between/~with] ○ *They are encouraging more dialogue with consumer groups.* (NOTE: [all senses] The US spelling is **dialog**.)

dial-up /ˈdaɪəl ʌp/ *adj* of a connection between computers that is made by means of a modem and a telephone line

diameter /daɪˈæmɪtə/ *noun* the distance across the centre of a circle

③ **diamond** /ˈdaɪəmənd/ *noun* **1.** a very hard, clear, precious stone ○ *He gave her a diamond ring.* ○ *Diamonds sparkled on her crown.* **2.** one of the red sets in a pack of cards, shaped like a square leaning to one side ○ *He held the ten of diamonds.* (NOTE: The other red suit is **hearts**; **clubs** and **spades** are the black suits.)

③ **diaper** /ˈdaɪəpə/ *noun US* a cloth or thick pad which is wrapped around a baby's bottom

diaphragm /ˈdaɪəfræm/ *noun* **1.** a thin sheet which vibrates with noise ○ *the diaphragm in a hearing aid* **2.** a thin layer of tissue which separates the chest from the abdomen, and pulls air into the lungs when you breathe ○ *The stomach lies in the left upper part of the abdomen, just under the diaphragm.* **3.** a contraceptive device for women

diarrhoea /ˌdaɪəˈriːə/ *noun* a condition in which a patient frequently passes liquid faeces (NOTE: The US spelling is **diarrhea**.)

③ **diary** /ˈdaɪəri/ (*plural* **diaries**) *noun* **1.** a description of what has happened in your life day by day ○ *He kept a diary for years.* ○ *She kept a diary of the places she visited on holiday.* **2.** a small book in which you write notes or make appointments for each day of the week ○ *I've noted the appointment in my desk diary.* ○ *I can't fix the date immediately because I haven't got my diary with me.*

dice /daɪs/ (*plural same*) *noun* a small block with a different number of spots on each side, used for playing games ○ *Shake the dice in the cup and then throw them onto the board.*

dicey /ˈdaɪsi/ *adj* dangerous (*informal*)

dichotomy /daɪˈkɒtəmi/ *noun* a difference between contradictory things

③ **dictate** /dɪkˈteɪt/ (**dictates, dictating, dictated**) *verb* **1.** to say something to someone who writes down your words [~to] ○ *She dictated a letter to her assistant.* **2.** to tell someone what to do [~what/how etc] ○ *She's always trying to dictate how we should run the business.* **3.** to influence what should happen [~that] ○ *His illness dictated that she had to lead a less active life.*

③ **dictation** /dɪkˈteɪʃ(ə)n/ *noun* the act of dictating something to be written down

dictator /dɪkˈteɪtə/ *noun* a person who rules a country alone

dictatorship /dɪk'teɪtəʃɪp/ *noun* the rule of a country by one person

diction /'dɪkʃən/ *noun* a clear and understandable way of speaking

dictionary /'dɪkʃən(ə)ri/ (*plural* **dictionaries**) *noun* a book which lists words in alphabetical order, giving their meanings or translations into other languages

did /dɪd/ past tense of **do**

didn't /'dɪd(ə)nt/ *contr* did not

① **die** /daɪ/ (**dies, dying, died**) *verb* to stop living. ◊ **death** ◇ **dying for something** *or* **to do something** wanting something very much ○ *We're dying for a cold drink.* ○ *I'm dying to read his book.*

die away *phrasal verb* to become less noisy ○ *The sound of police sirens gradually died away.*

die down *phrasal verb* **1.** to get less strong ○ *The wind began to die down.* ○ *The government is waiting for the street protests to die down.* **2.** (*of plants*) to die and lose their stems and leaves ○ *Chrysanthemums will die down during the winter.*

die out③ *phrasal verb* to disappear gradually ○ *If people carry on hunting this animal it will eventually die out.*

diehard /'daɪhɑːd/ *noun* a person who resists change or persists in a particular belief or opinion

③ **diesel** /'diːz(ə)l/ *noun* **1.** □ **diesel (oil)** engine fuel which is thicker than petrol ○ *My new car runs on diesel.* ○ *London taxis have diesel engines.* **2.** a car with a diesel engine ○ *His latest car is a diesel.*

② **diet** /'daɪət/ *noun* **1.** the kind of food you eat ○ *He lives on a simple diet of bread and fruit.* **2.** the practice of eating only certain types of food, either in order to become thinner or to cure an illness ○ *The doctor told her to follow a salt-free diet.* □ **to be on a diet** to eat less food or only some types of food ○ *He's been on a diet for some weeks, but still hasn't lost enough weight.* □ **to go on a diet** to start to eat less food or only some types of food ○ *She went on a diet before going on holiday.* ■ *verb* (**diets, dieting, dieted**) to eat less food or only some types of food ○ *He dieted for two weeks before going on holiday.*

dietary /'daɪət(ə)ri/ *adj* referring to the food people eat in terms of how it affects their health

③ **differ** /'dɪfə/ (**differs, differing, differed**) *verb* **1.** not to be the same as something else [~from] ○ *The weather conditions in the two areas differ considerably.* ○ *This camera differs from the earlier model.* **2.** to have a different opinion about something from someone else ○ *Our views on education differ.* ○ *They differ in several ways in their accounts of what happened.* ◇ **I beg to differ** I do not agree

① **difference** /'dɪf(ə)rəns/ *noun* a way in which two things are not the same [~in/~between] ○ *What is the difference in price between these two cars?* □ **to tell the difference** to see what is different between things or people that are similar ○ *Can you tell the difference between the original picture and the copy?* ◇ **it doesn't make any difference** or **it makes no difference** *or* **little difference** it's not important ○ *You can use any colour you like – it doesn't make any difference.*

① **different** /'dɪf(ə)rənt/ *adj* not the same ○ *Living in London is very different from living in the country.* ○ *I went to three different clothes shops but I couldn't find anything in my size.* ○ *He looks different now that he has a beard.*

differential /ˌdɪfə'renʃəl/ *noun* (*in a motor*) the gears between two drive shafts that allow one shaft to turn at a different speed from the other, while still transmitting power

③ **differentiate** /ˌdɪfə'renʃieɪt/ (**differentiates, differentiating, differentiated**) *verb* **1.** to recognise the difference between two things [~between] ○ *I find it hard to differentiate between the two brands of butter.* ○ *They couldn't differentiate between cheap champagne and really top-quality stuff.* **2.** to treat two things differently [~between] ○ *In this school, we don't differentiate between boys and girls.*

① **difficult** /'dɪfɪk(ə)lt/ *adj* not easy to do or achieve ○ *Finding a parking space is difficult on Saturdays.* ○ *I find it difficult to work when I'm tired.* ◇ **to make things** *or* **life difficult for someone** to create problems for someone ○ *His main aim at the office seems to be to make life as difficult as possible for the secretaries.*

① **difficulty** /'dɪfɪk(ə)lti/ (*plural* **difficulties**) *noun* **1.** a problem [~with] ○ *The difficulty is that nobody in the group can drive.* ○ *He has financial difficulties.* ○ *There is a difficulty with the flight reservation.* □ **to create** *or* **make difficulties for someone** to create problems for someone ○ *She doesn't realise that going on holiday now is going to make difficulties for everyone.* **2.** the amount of effort or skill needed to do something □ **to have difficulty with** *or* **in**

doing something to find something hard, or find it hard to do something ○ *We had difficulty with the directions.* ○ *She has difficulty in paying the rent.* □ **with difficulty** not easily ○ *She walks with difficulty.*

diffident /ˈdɪfɪdənt/ *adj* shy; lacking confidence

diffuse[1] /dɪˈfjuːs/ *adj* vague or unclear ○ *His writing tends to be very diffuse.*

diffuse[2] /dɪˈfjuːz/ (**diffuses, diffusing, diffused**) *verb* to spread something out or to send something out

② **dig** /dɪg/ *verb* (**digs, digging, dug**) to make a hole in the ground with a spade ■ *plural noun* **digs** a furnished room or rooms let to people such as students (*dated informal*)

dig out *phrasal verb* **1.** to take someone or something out by digging ○ *He was dug out of the snow after the avalanche.* **2.** to find something after a lot of searching ○ *They dug out some old photographs of the village.*

dig up *phrasal verb* **1.** to find something by digging ○ *We dug up a Roman coin in the garden.* **2.** to break a solid surface by digging ○ *The workmen had to dig the road up to mend the water main.* **3.** to find information with difficulty ○ *He managed to dig up some old government statistics.*

digest /daɪˈdʒest/ (**digests, digesting, digested**) *verb* **1.** to break down food in the stomach ○ *I find this meat difficult to digest.* **2.** to think about something and understand it fully ○ *Give me time to digest this news.*

digestion /daɪˈdʒestʃən/ *noun* the process by which food is broken down in the stomach

digestive /daɪˈdʒestɪv/ *adj* relating to the digestion of food

digit /ˈdɪdʒɪt/ *noun* **1.** a single number ○ *a seven-digit phone number* **2.** a finger or toe

digital /ˈdɪdʒɪt(ə)l/ *adj* **1.** storing information in an electronic form ○ *a digital radio* **2.** showing the time as a set of numbers

digital camera /ˌdɪdʒɪt(ə)l ˈkæm(ə)rə/ *noun* a camera that stores photographs in digital form so that they can be processed by a computer

digital TV /ˌdɪdʒɪt(ə)l tiːˈviː/ *noun* a TV where the picture has been changed into a form which a computer can process

dignified /ˈdɪgnɪfaɪd/ *adj* solemn and important-looking

dignitary /ˈdɪgnɪt(ə)ri/ (*plural* **dignitaries**) *noun* an important person

③ **dignity** /ˈdɪgnɪti/ *noun* a solemn or serious way of behaving

digress /daɪˈgres/ (**digresses, digressing, digressed**) *verb* to start to talk or write about something else (NOTE: + **digression** *n*)

dilapidated /dɪˈlæpɪdeɪtɪd/ *adj* falling into ruin

dilate /daɪˈleɪt/ (**dilates, dilating, dilated**) *verb* to swell, to become larger

dilemma /dɪˈlemə/ *noun* a difficult choice which has to be made

diligent /ˈdɪlɪdʒənt/ *adj* hard-working

dilute /daɪˈluːt/ (**dilutes, diluting, diluted**) *verb* **1.** to add a liquid, usually water, to another liquid to make it weaker ○ *Dilute the disinfectant with water.* **2.** to make something weaker and less effective ○ *The proposals were thought too radical and were diluted before being announced to the press.*

dim /dɪm/ *adj* (**dimmer, dimmest**) (*of light*) weak ○ *The lights grew dimmer.* ■ *verb* (**dims, dimming, dimmed**) to make a light less bright ○ *They dimmed the cabin lights before takeoff.*

dime /daɪm/ *noun US* a coin that is worth ten cents

③ **dimension** /daɪˈmenʃən/ *noun* the extent of a problem ○ *the international dimension of the refugee problem* ○ *The task is taking on huge dimensions.*

diminish /dɪˈmɪnɪʃ/ (**diminishes, diminishing, diminished**) *verb* **1.** to make something smaller or weaker ○ *Nothing diminishes his enthusiasm for flying.* **2.** to become smaller or weaker ○ *My income has diminished over the last few years.*

diminutive /dɪˈmɪnjʊtɪv/ *adj* very small

dimple /ˈdɪmpəl/ *noun* a small hollow in a part of the body such as the chin or cheeks

din /dɪn/ *noun* a loud noise ○ *The children are making such a din I didn't hear the phone ring.* ○ *What a din! Can't you be a bit quieter, please?* ○ *I couldn't make out what the guide was saying above the din of the machines.*

dine /daɪn/ (**dines, dining, dined**) *verb* to have dinner (*formal*)

dine out *phrasal verb* to have dinner away from home (*formal*)

diner /ˈdaɪnə/ *noun* **1.** a person who is eating an evening meal ○ *When the restaurant caught fire, the diners ran into the street.* **2.** the dining car on a train **3.** *US* a small restaurant selling simple hot food

dinghy /ˈdɪŋi/ (*plural* **dinghies**) *noun* a small boat, either with oars or sails

dingy /ˈdɪndʒi/ *adj* **1.** gloomy and lacking light **2.** dirty or old-looking

③ **dining room** /ˈdaɪnɪŋ ruːm/ *noun* a room in a house or hotel where you usually eat. ◊ **bathroom, bedroom, living room**

① **dinner** /ˈdɪnə/ *noun* **1.** the main meal of the day, usually eaten in the evening ○ *We were having dinner when the telephone rang.* ○ *Would you like to come to dinner on Saturday?* ○ *What are we having for dinner?* or *What's for dinner?* **2.** a formal evening meal ○ *The club is organising a dinner and dance on Saturday.*

dinner jacket /ˈdɪnə ˌdʒækɪt/ *noun* a man's formal jacket

dinosaur /ˈdaɪnəsɔː/ *noun* a large creature that existed on the Earth millions of years ago ○ *At the time when dinosaurs roamed the land, England was covered with tropical forests.*

diocese /ˈdaɪəsɪs/ *noun* an area under the charge of a bishop

③ **dip** /dɪp/ *noun* **1.** a sudden drop in an area of land **2.** a cold sauce into which you can dip biscuits or raw vegetables ■ *verb* (**dips, dipping, dipped**) □ **to dip something into something** to put something quickly into a liquid ○ *She dipped the biscuit into her coffee.* ○ *She dipped her hand into the stream.*

diphtheria /dɪfˈθɪəriə/ *noun* a serious infectious disease of children

diploma /dɪˈpləʊmə/ *noun* a document which shows that a person has reached a certain level of skill in a subject

diplomacy /dɪˈpləʊməsi/ *noun* the art of negotiating, especially between different countries

diplomat /ˈdɪpləmæt/ *noun* a person such as an ambassador who represents his country abroad

diplomatic /ˌdɪpləˈmætɪk/ *adj* **1.** referring to diplomats or diplomacy ○ *We are looking for a diplomatic solution to the crisis, rather than sending in troops.* **2.** careful not to give offence ○ *It wouldn't be very diplomatic to arrive late for the wedding.*

dire /ˈdaɪə/ *adj* very serious

① **direct** /daɪˈrekt/ *adj* straight, without any changes of direction or stops ○ *What's the most direct way of getting to London?* □ **direct line** a telephone line which takes you straight to the person you wish to contact ○ *This phone number will give you a direct line to the minister.* ■ *verb* (**directs, directing, directed**) **1.** to aim something towards a point [~at/to/towards] ○ *I hope you're not directing that gun at me!* **2.** to say something to a particular person [~at/to/towards] ○ *He directed his remarks to the person next to him.* ○ *I hope you're not directing that criticism at me!* **3.** to tell someone how to get to a place [~to] ○ *Can you direct me to the nearest post office?* **4.** to manage or organise something ○ *He directs our London operations.* **5.** to tell someone to do something ○ *The insecticide has to be used as directed on the bottle.* ○ *He did as he had been directed, and took the plane to Birmingham.* ■ *adv* **1.** straight, without stopping ○ *The plane flies direct to Anchorage.* **2.** without passing through an operator ○ *You can telephone New York direct from here.*

direct debit /daɪˌrekt ˈdebɪt/ *noun* a system where a customer allows a company to charge costs to his bank account automatically and where the amount charged can be increased or decreased with the agreement of the customer

① **direction** /daɪˈrekʃən/ *noun* the point towards which you are going ○ *You are going in the wrong direction if you want to get to the station.* ○ *The post office is in the opposite direction.* ■ *plural noun* **directions** instructions on how to do something ◇ **in all directions** everywhere ○ *The wind was blowing bits of old newspapers in all directions.*

③ **directive** /daɪˈrektɪv/ *noun* an official instruction

② **directly** /daɪˈrektli/ *adv* **1.** straight, without anything or anyone between ○ *This door opens directly into the kitchen.* ○ *She reports directly to the managing director himself.* **2.** soon ○ *I'll be with you directly.* ■ *conj* as soon as ○ *I will write the letter directly I get home.*

direct object /ˌdaɪrekt ˈɒbdʒekt/ *noun* a noun or pronoun in a sentence representing the person or thing affected directly by the action of the verb

① **director** /daɪˈrektə/ *noun* **1.** a person who is in charge of all of, or part of, a company ○ *The sales director gave a report on sales to date.* ○ *There are four directors on the board of the company.* **2.** a person who organises the making of a film or play, e.g. giving instructions to the actors, or dealing with the lighting or sound ○ *Who was the first female director to win an Oscar?* Compare **producer**

③ **directory** /daɪˈrekt(ə)ri/ (*plural* **directories**) *noun* a book giving lists of professional people, organisations or businesses with their addresses and telephone numbers

direct tax /daɪˌrekt 'tæks/ *noun* a tax based on income

③ **dirt** /dɜːt/ *noun* **1.** anything that makes something dirty ○ *a washing powder that removes even the worst kinds of dirt* **2.** mud; earth ○ *Children were playing in the dirt.* ○ *His clothes were covered with dirt from handling potatoes.*

dirt cheap /ˌdɜːt 'tʃiːp/ *adv* very cheap

① **dirty** /'dɜːti/ *adj* (**dirtier, dirtiest**) **1.** not clean ○ *Playing rugby gets your clothes dirty.* ○ *Someone has to wash all the dirty plates.* **2.** not honest, or not done according to the rules ■ *verb* (**dirties, dirtying, dirtied**) to make something dirty

disability /ˌdɪsə'bɪlɪti/ (*plural* **disabilities**) *noun* a condition in which a person is unable to use a part of their body because of some permanent injury or illness

③ **disabled** /dɪs'eɪb(ə)ld/ *adj* not able to use part of your body, e.g. because of long-term illness ○ *an association for disabled riders* ○ *The car crash left him permanently disabled.*

disadvantage /ˌdɪsəd'vɑːntɪdʒ/ *noun* something which makes someone or something less likely to succeed ○ *Her main disadvantage is her lack of experience.* ○ *It was a disadvantage not to be able to get to the airport quickly.* ○ *There are certain disadvantages to leaving at 5.30 in the morning.* ◇ **at a disadvantage** less able to do or benefit from something than someone else ○ *We are at a disadvantage compared with our competitors because we have no sales force.*

disadvantaged /ˌdɪsəd'vɑːntɪdʒd/ *adj* **1.** suffering a disadvantage ○ *She was disadvantaged by her lack of experience.* **2.** living in a poor environment, without any facilities ○ *state help for schools in disadvantaged areas*

disaffected /ˌdɪsə'fektɪd/ *adj* discontented or rebellious

② **disagree** /ˌdɪsə'griː/ (**disagrees, disagreeing, disagreed**) *verb* to say that you do not have the same opinion as someone else [~with/~about/on/over] ○ *We all disagreed with the chairperson.* ○ *They disagreed about what to do next.*

② **disagreement** /ˌdɪsə'griːmənt/ *noun* an argument [~over/about/~between/among/~with] ○ *They had a disagreement about who should sit in the front row.* ○ *Nothing could be decided because of the disagreement between the chair and the treasurer.* ○ *She was upset about the disagreement with her sister.*

disallow /ˌdɪsə'laʊ/ (**disallows, disallowing, disallowed**) *verb* to reject something, not to accept something

② **disappear** /ˌdɪsə'pɪə/ (**disappears, disappearing, disappeared**) *verb* **1.** to leave a place, often suddenly and without people noticing or knowing where someone or something has gone [~from] ○ *Half the guests have disappeared already.* ○ *A carton of juice has disappeared from the fridge.* ○ *The figures suddenly disappeared from the screen.* ○ *The two boys disappeared on their way home from school.* **2.** to stop existing ○ *The stain on the carpet soon disappeared.*

③ **disappoint** /ˌdɪsə'pɔɪnt/ (**disappoints, disappointing, disappointed**) *verb* to make someone sad, because things did not turn out as expected

③ **disappointed** /ˌdɪsə'pɔɪntɪd/ *adj* sad, because things have not happened as you hoped ○ *She is disappointed with her exam results.* ○ *He was disappointed because his ticket didn't win a prize.* ○ *You should have seen the disappointed expression on his face.*

③ **disappointing** /ˌdɪsə'pɔɪntɪŋ/ *adj* making you sad because things have not happened as you hoped

③ **disappointment** /ˌdɪsə'pɔɪntmənt/ *noun* **1.** a feeling of sadness that you get when things have not happened as you hoped [~with/~at] ○ *She tried hard not to show her disappointment with the result.* ○ *To his great disappointment, he didn't win anything on the lottery.* (NOTE: no plural in this sense) **2.** something that disappoints someone [~to] ○ *It was a disappointment to his parents when he failed his exam.*

disapproval /ˌdɪsə'pruːv(ə)l/ *noun* the act of disapproving

disapprove /ˌdɪsə'pruːv/ (**disapproves, disapproving, disapproved**) *verb* to show that you do not think something is good ○ *The head teacher disapproves of members of staff wearing jeans to school.*

disarm /dɪs'ɑːm/ (**disarms, disarming, disarmed**) *verb* to remove weapons from someone

disarmament /dɪs'ɑːməmənt/ *noun* reducing the number of arms held by a country

disarming /dɪs'ɑːmɪŋ/ *adj* charming, in such a way that you cannot be annoyed

disarray /ˌdɪsə'reɪ/ *noun* a lack of order

② **disaster** /dɪ'zɑːstə/ *noun* a very bad accident ○ *The disaster was caused by fog or was due to fog.* ○ *Ten people died in the air disaster.* ○ *We're insured against natural disasters such as hurricanes and earthquakes.*

disaster area /dɪ'zɑːstər ˌeəriə/ *noun* **1.** a place that has recently undergone a natural disaster **2.** a very untidy or disorganised place, person or situation

disastrous /dɪ'zɑːstrəs/ *adj* extremely bad

disband /dɪs'bænd/ (**disbands, disbanding, disbanded**) *verb* **1.** to split up an organised group and end their activities ○ *After the successful coup, the former army was disbanded.* ○ *We are disbanding our door-to-door sales team and relying on mail order selling in future.* **2.** to stop working together ○ *The group disbanded and its members started to go solo.*

disbelief /ˌdɪsbɪ'liːf/ *noun* extreme surprise, not being able to believe something

disbelieve /ˌdɪsbɪ'liːv/ (**disbelieves, disbelieving, disbelieved**) *verb* **1.** to not believe someone or something **2.** to have no religious belief

② **disc** /dɪsk/ *noun* a round flat object ○ *The setting sun was a huge orange disc on the horizon.* ◊ **disk**

discard /dɪs'kɑːd/ (**discards, discarding, discarded**) *verb* **1.** to put something or someone on one side because they are no longer useful **2.** to throw something away

discern /dɪ'sɜːn/ (**discerns, discerning, discerned**) *verb* **1.** to see something, to make something out with difficulty ○ *In the fog, we could barely discern the traffic coming in the opposite direction.* ○ *Can you discern any improvement in her pulse rate?* **2.** to understand something, to find out about something ○ *It's hard to discern what her motives might be.*

discerning /dɪ'sɜːnɪŋ/ *adj* with good judgment

discharge[1] /'dɪstʃɑːdʒ/ *noun* **1.** a liquid which comes out of something such as a pipe **2.** pus which comes out of a wound **3.** payment of a debt **4.** the release of a prisoner

discharge[2] /dɪs'tʃɑːdʒ/ (**discharges, discharging, discharged**) *verb* **1.** to get rid of waste ○ *The factory is discharging waste water into the river.* **2.** to send someone away ○ *The judge discharged the jury.* **3.** to let a prisoner go free ○ *The prisoners were discharged by the judge.* ○ *He was discharged after having served eleven months in jail.* **4.** to dismiss somebody, to sack somebody ○ *He was discharged for being late.*

disciple /dɪ'saɪp(ə)l/ *noun* a follower, especially of a religious leader

disciplinarian /ˌdɪsɪplɪ'neəriən/ *noun* a person who believes in strict discipline

disciplinary /ˌdɪsɪ'plɪnəri/ *adj* which keeps someone under control or which punishes someone

② **discipline** /'dɪsɪplɪn/ *noun* **1.** the practice of keeping people under control ○ *The tour leaders are trying to keep discipline among the teenagers.* ○ *We need to enforce stricter discipline in the school.* (NOTE: no plural in this sense) **2.** a subject that people study ○ *biology and other related disciplines* ■ *verb* (**disciplines, disciplining, disciplined**) to punish someone ○ *As a result of the investigation, one employee was dismissed and three were disciplined.* ○ *She was disciplined for swearing at her supervisor.*

disciplined /'dɪsɪplɪnd/ *adj* trained and well controlled

disc jockey /'dɪsk ˌdʒɒki/ *noun* a person who plays music at a disco or on radio. Abbreviation **DJ**

disclaimer /dɪs'kleɪmə/ *noun* **1.** a denial of responsibility **2.** a statement in which a legal right is renounced

③ **disclose** /dɪs'kləʊz/ (**discloses, disclosing, disclosed**) *verb* to reveal a secret [~that] ○ *The bank has no right to disclose details of my account to the tax office.* ○ *She disclosed that she had been offered money for her story.*

disclosure /dɪs'kləʊʒə/ *noun* **1.** a piece of information that had been kept secret before **2.** the action of revealing a secret

disco /'dɪskəʊ/ (*plural* **discos**) *noun* a place or party where people dance to pop music

discomfort /dɪs'kʌmfət/ *noun* a lack of comfort

disconcerted /ˌdɪskən'sɜːtɪd/ *adj* uneasy, or confused

disconcerting /ˌdɪskən'sɜːtɪŋ/ *adj* worrying or surprising

disconnect /ˌdɪskə'nekt/ (**disconnects, disconnecting, disconnected**) *verb* to remove the connection to a mechanical or electrical device

discontent /ˌdɪskən'tent/ *noun* a state of not being satisfied

discontinue /ˌdɪskən'tɪnjuː/ (**discontinues, discontinuing, discontinued**) *verb* to stop stocking, selling or making a product

discord /ˈdɪskɔːd/ *noun* a lack of agreement

③ **discount**[1] /ˈdɪskaʊnt/ *noun* an amount by which a full price is reduced [~on/~for] ○ *The store gives a discount on bulk purchases.* ○ *We give a discount on summer holidays booked before Christmas.* □ **to sell goods at a discount** *or* **discount price** to sell goods below the usual price

discount[2] /dɪsˈkaʊnt/ (**discounts, discounting, discounted**) *verb* **1.** to reduce the price of goods ○ *We are discounting many items in our January sales.* **2.** not to pay any attention to something ○ *Don't discount all his advice – he is very experienced.*

discourage /dɪsˈkʌrɪdʒ/ (**discourages, discouraging, discouraged**) *verb* **1.** not to encourage ○ *We try to discourage people from coming in without tickets.* **2.** to take away all hope ○ *They were completely discouraged by their results.* ○ *Don't be discouraged by the small number of people in the audience.* (NOTE: + **discouragement** *n*)

discouraged /dɪsˈkʌrɪdʒd/ *adj* feeling less confident or optimistic

discouraging /dɪsˈkʌrɪdʒɪŋ/ *adj* not encouraging

discourse /ˈdɪskɔːs/ *noun* a talk, a speech

discourteous /dɪsˈkɜːtiəs/ *adj* rude

① **discover** /dɪˈskʌvə/ (**discovers, discovering, discovered**) *verb* to find something new or to learn something for the first time [~(that)] ○ *New stars are still being discovered.* ○ *The firm discovered some errors in the accounts.* ○ *We discovered that the estate agent had sold the house twice.*

③ **discovery** /dɪˈskʌv(ə)ri/ (*plural* **discoveries**) *noun* **1.** the act of finding something new or learning something for the first time [/~that] ○ *her discovery that someone had been in her house while she was away* ○ *They congratulated him on his discovery of a new planet.* **2.** a new thing which has been found ○ *Look at his latest discovery – an antique oak table which he found in a barn.*

discredit /dɪsˈkredɪt/ (**discredits, discrediting, discredited**) *verb* to make people doubt or lose respect for someone or something ○ *When stories about his private life appeared in the press he was totally discredited as a minister.* ○ *They set out to discredit his research.* (NOTE: + **discredit** *n*)

discreet /dɪˈskriːt/ *adj* **1.** not giving away or trying to find out private information about other people ○ *She never gossips – she is very discreet.* **2.** not intending to attract attention ○ *I had a discreet word with the vicar before the service.*

discrepancy /dɪˈskrepənsi/ (*plural* **discrepancies**) *noun* a lack of agreement between figures or stories

discretion /dɪˈskreʃ(ə)n/ *noun* **1.** the power to decide or choose what to do ○ *at your discretion* **2.** wisdom, tact or good sense ○ *He showed great discretion in his handling of the family crisis.* **3.** the ability to keep a secret, not to give information about someone ○ *You can rely on her – she's known for her discretion.* (NOTE: no plural)

discretionary /dɪˈskreʃ(ə)n(ə)ri/ *adj* which can be done if someone wants it

③ **discriminate** /dɪˈskrɪmɪneɪt/ (**discriminates, discriminating, discriminated**) *verb* **1.** to be biased against someone or something [~against] ○ *She accused the management of discriminating against her because of her age.* **2.** to be able to see that two things are different

discriminating /dɪˈskrɪmɪneɪtɪŋ/ *adj* able to tell the difference between two things, able to tell the value of something

discrimination /dɪˌskrɪmɪˈneɪʃ(ə)n/ *noun* **1.** treating people in different ways because of class, religion, race, language, colour or sex [~against] ○ *We try to avoid discrimination against older applicants.* **2.** good taste ○ *The shop sells gifts which appeal to people with discrimination.* (NOTE: [all senses] no plural)

discriminatory /dɪˈskrɪmɪnət(ə)ri/ *adj* which shows unfair discrimination

① **discuss** /dɪˈskʌs/ (**discusses, discussing, discussed**) *verb* to talk about a serious matter or problem [~how/why/whether etc] ○ *The point of the meeting is to discuss how to save money.*

① **discussion** /dɪˈskʌʃ(ə)n/ *noun* an occasion on which people talk about a serious matter or problem [~about/on/~with] ○ *The next programme will feature a discussion on climate change.* ○ *She had a heated discussion with the bus driver.* ○ *Most problems can be solved by discussion.* □ **the question under discussion** the subject we are talking about

disdain /dɪsˈdeɪn/ *noun* a feeling that someone or something is inferior ○ *She* *showed her disdain by refusing to shake his hand.*

① **disease** /dɪ'ziːz/ *noun* a serious illness ○ *Hundreds of people caught the disease.* ○ *It is a disease that can be treated with antibiotics.*

disembark /ˌdɪsɪm'bɑːk/ (**disembarks, disembarking, disembarked**) *verb* to get off a ship or a plane

disembodied /ˌdɪsɪm'bɒdid/ *adj* without physical presence

disenchanted /ˌdɪsɪn'tʃɑːntɪd/ *adj* not to be as pleased as you used to be with something [~with] ○ *She's very disenchanted with her new job and is thinking of quitting.*

disentangle /ˌdɪsɪn'tæŋgəl/ (**disentangles, disentangling, disentangled**) *verb* **1.** to straighten out things that are tied or knotted together **2.** to clarify something **3.** to free someone from a complicated situation

disfigure /dɪs'fɪgə/ (**disfigures, disfiguring, disfigured**) *verb* to change someone's appearance so as to make it less pleasant

③ **disgrace** /dɪs'greɪs/ *noun* **1.** the loss of someone's respect because of errors, scandal or corruption ○ *The minister's disgrace followed the discovery of the papers in his office.* **2.** a thing which brings shame ○ *He's a disgrace to the teaching profession.* ○ *It was a disgrace to see her lying on the pavement like that.* (NOTE: no plural) ■ *verb* (**disgraces, disgracing, disgraced**) to bring shame on someone ○ *He disgraced all his family by arriving drunk at the tea party.* □ **to disgrace yourself** to do something which brings shame on you ○ *He disgraced himself by throwing sandwiches at the speakers.*

disgraceful /dɪs'greɪsf(ə)l/ *adj* which people should be ashamed of

disgruntled /dɪs'grʌnt(ə)ld/ *adj* annoyed or discontented

disguise /dɪs'gaɪz/ *noun* a set of clothes or something such as false hair or glasses that a persons wears to make them look like someone else ○ *I didn't recognise him as he was wearing a disguise.* ■ *verb* (**disguises, disguising, disguised**) **1.** to dress someone or yourself so as to look like someone else ○ *He entered the country disguised as a fisherman.* ○ *She wore a wig to disguise her hair.* **2.** to make something look or sound different ◇ **in disguise** dressed to look like someone else ○ *The tramp turned out to be a policeman in disguise.*

disgust /dɪs'gʌst/ *noun* **1.** a feeling of dislike that is so strong that you feel angry or slightly ill ○ *Seeing the dead animals filled her with disgust.* **2.** a strong feeling of annoyance ○ *To my disgust, the examiner passed my friend and failed me.* ■ *verb* (**disgusts, disgusting, disgusted**) to give someone a strong feeling of dislike or disapproval ○ *The smell of cooking disgusted her.* ○ *The greediness of these people disgusts me.* ◇ **in disgust** showing that you are upset and annoyed ○ *She walked out of the interview in disgust.*

disgusted /dɪs'gʌstɪd/ *adj* feeling shocked

② **disgusting** /dɪs'gʌstɪŋ/ *adj* that fills you with disgust

② **dish** /dɪʃ/ *noun* **1.** a large plate for serving food ○ *She carefully arranged the slices of meat on a dish.* **2.** food prepared in a particular way ○ *We are trying a new Mexican dish.* **3.** a round aerial, shaped like a plate, used to get signals from satellites

dish out *phrasal verb* to give something out, especially in large quantities (*informal*) ○ *He dished out a piece of bread and a bowl of soup to anyone who asked for it.*

disheartened /dɪs'hɑːt(ə)nd/ *adj* feeling discouraged

disheartening /dɪs'hɑːt(ə)nɪŋ/ *adj* making somebody lose hope or enthusiasm

dishevelled /dɪ'ʃev(ə)ld/ *adj* (*of hair or clothes*) not arranged neatly (NOTE: The US spelling is **disheveled**.)

dishonest /dɪs'ɒnɪst/ *adj* not honest

dishonestly /dɪs'ɒnɪstli/ *adv* not honestly ○ *They were accused of dishonestly obtaining bank loans.*

dishonesty /dɪs'ɒnɪsti/ *noun* a lack of honesty

③ **dishwasher** /'dɪʃwɒʃə/ *noun* a machine for washing dishes

disillusion /ˌdɪsɪ'luːʒ(ə)n/ (**disillusions, disillusioning, disillusioned**) *verb* to make someone feel let down, or sad that something has not turned out as expected (NOTE: + **disillusionment** *n*)

disillusioned /ˌdɪsɪ'luːʒ(ə)nd/ *adj* feeling that something has not turned out as expected

disinfect /ˌdɪsɪn'fekt/ (**disinfects, disinfecting, disinfected**) *verb* to remove germs or bacteria from something

disinfectant /ˌdɪsɪnˈfektənt/ *noun* a substance used to kill germs or bacteria

disintegrate /dɪsˈɪntɪɡreɪt/ (**disintegrates, disintegrating, disintegrated**) *verb* to fall to pieces

disinterested /dɪsˈɪntrəstɪd/ *adj* **1.** quite impartial, not in favour of one side or the other ○ *a totally disinterested observer* **2.** not interested ○ *She seemed quite disinterested in what was going on.* (NOTE: This use is common, but regarded as wrong. The correct word to use in this sense is **uninterested**.)

disjointed /dɪsˈdʒɔɪntɪd/ *adj* with parts that are not linked together

② **disk** /dɪsk/ *noun* a round flat piece of metal in a plastic case, used in computers to record information ○ *How much data do these disks hold?* ◊ **disc**

disk drive /ˈdɪsk draɪv/ *noun* a device which holds a disk in a computer and controls the access of information

③ **dislike** /dɪsˈlaɪk/ *noun* **1.** a feeling of not liking something or someone ○ *She had a great dislike of noisy parties.* **2.** something which you do not like ○ *We try to take account of the likes and dislikes of individual customers.* ■ *verb* (**dislikes, disliking, disliked**) not to like something or someone ○ *He particularly disliked the way they spoke to her.* ○ *I dislike it when the people behind me at the cinema start whispering.* ○ *My father dislikes having to get up early on Monday mornings.*

dislocate /ˈdɪsləkeɪt/ (**dislocates, dislocating, dislocated**) *verb* **1.** to displace a bone from its normal position at a joint, or be displaced ○ *He fell and dislocated his elbow.* ○ *The shoulder joint dislocates easily.* **2.** to disrupt something ○ *Train services have been dislocated by the strike.* (NOTE: + **dislocation** *n*)

dislodge /dɪsˈlɒdʒ/ (**dislodges, dislodging, dislodged**) *verb* to move something which is stuck

disloyal /dɪsˈlɔɪəl/ *adj* not loyal

dismal /ˈdɪzm(ə)l/ *adj* bad in a way that make you feel unhappy

dismantle /dɪsˈmænt(ə)l/ (**dismantles, dismantling, dismantled**) *verb* to take something to pieces

dismay /dɪsˈmeɪ/ *noun* great disappointment ○ *To the dismay of the supporters, the team played extremely badly.* ■ *verb* (**dismays, dismaying, dismayed**) to make someone very upset or shocked ○ *His reaction to her letter dismayed her.* ○ *She was dismayed to find that her passport had been stolen.*

dismember /dɪsˈmembə/ (**dismembers, dismembering, dismembered**) *verb* to cut something up into pieces

③ **dismiss** /dɪsˈmɪs/ (**dismisses, dismissing, dismissed**) *verb* **1.** to tell someone that they can leave ○ *At the end of the interview he dismissed her with a brief 'good afternoon'.* **2.** to refuse to consider an idea ○ *Her plan was dismissed as being quite impractical.* ○ *All his suggestions were dismissed by the MD.* **3.** □ **to dismiss an employee** to remove an employee from a job ○ *He was dismissed for being late.* ○ *When they found him taking money from the petty cash he was dismissed instantly.*

dismissal /dɪsˈmɪs(ə)l/ *noun* removal from a job

dismissive /dɪsˈmɪsɪv/ *adj* showing that you do not consider something or someone important

dismount /dɪsˈmaʊnt/ (**dismounts, dismounting, dismounted**) *verb* to get off something such as a horse or bicycle

disobedience /ˌdɪsəˈbiːdiəns/ *noun* an act of refusing to obey someone

disobedient /ˌdɪsəˈbiːdiənt/ *adj* not obeying

disobey /ˌdɪsəˈbeɪ/ (**disobeys, disobeying, disobeyed**) *verb* not to obey someone or something ○ *She would never disobey her parents.*

③ **disorder** /dɪsˈɔːdə/ *noun* **1.** a lack of order ○ *The whole office is in a state of disorder.* **2.** a disturbance in the streets ○ *Violent public disorders broke out in the streets.* **3.** an illness ○ *a doctor who specialises in disorders of the kidneys* or *in kidney disorders* ○ *She suffers from a stomach disorder.*

disordered /dɪsˈɔːdəd/ *adj* **1.** untidy or confused **2.** not working normally

disorderly /dɪsˈɔːdəli/ *adj* wild and out of order

disorganised /dɪsˈɔːɡənaɪzd/, **disorganized** *adj* not well organised

disorientate /dɪsˈɔːriənteɪt/ (**disorientates, disorientating, disorientated**) *verb* to make someone feel confused, especially so that they do not know where they are (NOTE: The US term is **disorient**.)

disown /dɪsˈəʊn/ (**disowns, disowning, disowned**) *verb* to refuse to accept that something is yours

disparaging /dɪˈspærɪdʒɪŋ/ *adj* saying that something is not very good

disparate /'dɪsp(ə)rət/ *adj* various or different

disparity /dɪ'spærɪti/ *noun* difference (*formal*)

dispatch /dɪ'spætʃ/, **despatch** *noun* **1.** sending ○ *Dispatch of the goods will be delayed until Monday.* **2.** a message sent ○ *The reporters send regular dispatches from the war zone.* ○ *We received a dispatch from our Calcutta office.* ■ *verb* (**dispatches, dispatching, dispatched**) **1.** to send something ○ *They dispatched the message to all commanding officers.* ○ *The goods were dispatched to you first thing this morning.* **2.** to finish doing something quickly ○ *She set to work on the files and dispatched most of them by lunchtime.*

dispel /dɪ'spel/ (**dispels, dispelling, dispelled**) *verb* to clear something away

dispensary /dɪ'spensəri/ *noun* a place where a chemist prepares medicines according to a doctor's prescription

dispensation /ˌdɪspen'seɪʃ(ə)n/ *noun* permission not to follow something such as a rule

dispense /dɪ'spens/ (**dispenses, dispensing, dispensed**) *verb* to provide something (*formal*) ○ *Local magistrates dispense justice in the villages.*

dispenser /dɪ'spensə/ *noun* a machine which automatically provides something when money is put in or a button is pushed

dispense with *phrasal verb* not to use something any more ○ *We've dispensed with the services of an accountant.*

dispersal /dɪ'spɜːs(ə)l/ *noun* the way in which people or things are spread over an area

disperse /dɪ'spɜːs/ (**disperses, dispersing, dispersed**) *verb* **1.** to clear something away ○ *The sun will soon disperse the mist.* ○ *The police were called in to disperse the crowds of angry fans.* **2.** to move quickly in different directions ○ *The crowd dispersed rapidly once the parade was over.*

dispirited /dɪ'spɪrɪtɪd/ *adj* sad or unhappy; feeling disappointed

displace /dɪs'pleɪs/ (**displaces, displacing, displaced**) *verb* to move something from its usual place (NOTE: + **displacement** *n*)

② **display** /dɪ'spleɪ/ *noun* a show, an exhibition ○ *a display of local crafts* ○ *They have a fine display of Chinese porcelain.* ■ *verb* (**displays, displaying, displayed**) to put something in a display ○ *She is displaying her collection of Persian carpets at the antiques fair.*

displeased /dɪs'pliːzd/ *adj* annoyed or dissatisfied

displeasure /dɪs'pleʒə/ *noun* a feeling of being annoyed

disposable /dɪ'spəʊzəb(ə)l/ *adj* which can be used and then thrown away ○ *disposable cups*

disposable income /dɪˌspəʊzəb(ə)l 'ɪnkʌm/ *noun* an amount of income left after the tax has been taken away

disposal /dɪ'spəʊz(ə)l/ *noun* the act of getting rid of something ○ *The disposal of refuse is a problem for large cities.* ◇ **at someone's disposal** available for someone to make use of if they want to ○ *My car is at your disposal all week.* ○ *I am at your disposal – what would you like me to do?*

dispose /dɪ'spəʊz/ (**disposing, disposed**) *verb* □ **to dispose of something** to get rid of something ○ *How are we going to dispose of all this waste paper?* ○ *His objections are easily disposed of.*

disposition /ˌdɪspə'zɪʃ(ə)n/ *noun* **1.** someone's character ○ *He has a pleasant easy-going disposition.* **2.** a tendency ○ *She has a disposition to argue with her husband.*

disproportionate /ˌdɪsprə'pɔːʃ(ə)nət/ *adj* not of a suitable size or amount for a particular purpose

disprove /dɪs'pruːv/ (**disproves, disproving, disproved**) *verb* to prove something is wrong

② **dispute** /dɪ'spjuːt, 'dɪspjuːt/ *noun* an argument [~about/over//~between] ○ *He tried to mediate in the dispute between the two families.* ○ *There was some dispute over who would pay the bill.* ■ *verb* (**disputes, disputing, disputed**) to say that you strongly believe that something is not true or correct ○ *I dispute her version of what happened.* ○ *There is no disputing the fact that Sarah is the best player.*

disqualification /dɪsˌkwɒlɪfɪ'keɪʃ(ə)n/ *noun* an action by which someone is disqualified

disqualify /dɪs'kwɒlɪfaɪ/ (**disqualifies, disqualifying, disqualified**) *verb* to make someone not able to do something

disquiet /dɪs'kwaɪət/ *noun* worry

disregard /ˌdɪsrɪ'gɑːd/ *noun* not feeling that something is important [~for] ○ *He showed a complete disregard for public safety.* ■ *verb* (**disregards, disregarding, disregarded**) to take no notice of ○ *He disregarded the warning signs and went on along the road.*

disreputable /dɪsˈrepjʊtəb(ə)l/ *adj* with a bad reputation, especially for criminal activity

disrepute /ˌdɪsrɪˈpjuːt/ *noun* a bad reputation ▫ **to bring something or someone into disrepute** to give something or someone a bad reputation ○ *He was accused of bringing the club into disrepute by his extraordinary behaviour.*

disrespect /ˌdɪsrɪˈspekt/ *noun* a lack of respect towards someone

disrupt /dɪsˈrʌpt/ (**disrupts, disrupting, disrupted**) *verb* **1.** to stop a service running normally ○ *The snowstorm has disrupted bus services throughout the country.* **2.** to break up or to interrupt a meeting ○ *We are not used to having our meetings disrupted by protesters.* (NOTE: + **disruption** *n*)

disruptive /dɪsˈrʌptɪv/ *adj* which disrupts

dissatisfaction /dɪsˌsætɪsˈfækʃən/ *noun* a lack of satisfaction

dissatisfied /dɪsˈsætɪsfaɪd/ *adj* not satisfied ○ *We were dissatisfied with the service we got from our bank.*

dissect /daɪˈsekt/ (**dissects, dissecting, dissected**) *verb* to cut up a body to examine it (NOTE: + **dissection** *n*)

disseminate /dɪˈsemɪneɪt/ (**disseminates, disseminating, disseminated**) *verb* to spread something around (NOTE: + **dissemination** *n*)

dissent /dɪˈsent/ *noun* lack of agreement ○ *The chairman wished to avoid dissent.* ○ *They received many letters of dissent.* (NOTE: Do not confuse with **descent**.)

dissenting /dɪˈsentɪŋ/ *adj* disagreeing with the beliefs or opinions of a majority

dissertation /ˌdɪsəˈteɪʃ(ə)n/ *noun* a long essay written as part of a university course

disservice /dɪsˈsɜːvɪs/ *noun* an action which damages or harms

dissident /ˈdɪsɪdənt/ *noun* a person who is not in agreement with the state ○ *Several dissidents tried to set up an underground newspaper.* ○ *It was a time when dissidents were being arrested and thrown in jail.*

dissimilar /dɪˈsɪmɪlə/ *adj* not the same

dissipate /ˈdɪsɪpeɪt/ (**dissipates, dissipating, dissipated**) *verb* **1.** to clear something away ○ *The hot sun soon dissipated the morning mist.* ○ *His statement did a lot to dissipate the feeling of annoyance among the members.* **2.** to waste something such as money, time or skill ○ *After winning the lottery he dissipated the lot on drink and expensive cars.*

dissociate /dɪˈsəʊsieɪt/ (**dissociates, dissociating, dissociated**) *verb* **to dissociate yourself from** to say that you want nothing to do with ○ *I wish to dissociate myself from the opinions expressed by my colleague.*

dissolution /ˌdɪsəˈluːʃ(ə)n/ *noun* the ending of a formal relationship, such as a marriage

dissolve /dɪˈzɒlv/ (**dissolves, dissolving, dissolved**) *verb* to make a solid substance become part of a liquid

dissuade /dɪˈsweɪd/ (**dissuades, dissuading, dissuaded**) *verb* ▫ **to dissuade someone from something** to persuade someone not to do something ○ *We tried to dissuade her from entering the beauty competition.*

② **distance** /ˈdɪstəns/ *noun* **1.** the space from one point to another [~from/~to] ○ *a distance of 800 km* ○ *What is the distance from London to Geneva?* ○ *The hotel is only a short distance away.* ▫ **within walking distance** near enough to walk to ○ *The hotel is within walking distance of the town centre.* **2.** ▫ **from a distance** seen from some way away ○ *From a distance, the mountain looks like a sleeping animal.* ▫ **in the distance** a long way away ○ *I caught sight of the mountain in the distance.* ○ *We could hear guns firing in the distance.* ■ *verb* (**distances, distancing, distanced**) ▫ **to distance yourself from someone or something** to show that you do not agree with someone or something

distance learning /ˈdɪstəns ˌlɜːnɪŋ/ *noun* studying in your own time away from the place where the course is organised, using radio or TV

③ **distant** /ˈdɪstənt/ *adj* **1.** far away ○ *We could hear the sound of distant gunfire.* **2.** not close in family relationship ○ *a distant relative/cousin* **3.** not very friendly ○ *The manager was quite helpful but distant.*

distaste /dɪsˈteɪst/ *noun* dislike

distasteful /dɪsˈteɪstf(ə)l/ *adj* unpleasant

distil /dɪˈstɪl/ (**distils, distilling, distilled**) *verb* to make pure water or alcohol by heating it, and collecting the steam (NOTE: The US spelling is **distill**.)

distillery /dɪˈstɪləri/ (*plural* **distilleries**) *noun* a factory for distilling alcohol

③ **distinct** /dɪˈstɪŋkt/ *adj* **1.** separate ○ *There are two distinct varieties of this plant.* ○ *They keep their printing works* *quite distinct from their publishing company.* **2.** that you can clearly see, hear or feel ○ *I got the distinct impression that he was carrying a gun.* ○ *Did you notice the distinct tone of anger in his voice?*

② **distinction** /dɪ'stɪŋkʃən/ *noun* **1.** a difference [~between] ○ *There is a distinction between being interested in politics and joining a political party.* **2.** the highest mark available in an examination ○ *She got a distinction in her exam.* **3.** special excellence ○ *He served in the war with distinction.* ○ *She had the distinction of being the first woman pilot.*

③ **distinctive** /dɪ'stɪŋktɪv/ *adj* very noticeable, which makes one thing different from others

③ **distinctly** /dɪ'stɪŋktli/ *adv* clearly

③ **distinguish** /dɪ'stɪŋgwɪʃ/ (**distinguishes, distinguishing, distinguished**) *verb* **1.** to see or hear clearly, or to see details ○ *We could easily distinguish houses on the other side of the lake.* ○ *I could distinguish at least two birds calling to each other.* **2.** □ **to distinguish between two things** to recognise the difference between two things ○ *Children must be taught to distinguish between right and wrong.* ○ *It's difficult to distinguish by sight between salt and caster sugar.* □ **to distinguish one thing from another** to notice that two things are not the same ○ *I find it difficult to distinguish the blue from the green in the design.* **3.** □ **to distinguish yourself** to do something which makes people notice you ○ *He distinguished himself on the football field.* ○ *She distinguished herself by falling into the river.*

distinguishable /dɪ'stɪŋgwɪʃəb(ə)l/ *adj* which can be distinguished

③ **distinguished** /dɪ'stɪŋgwɪʃt/ *adj* important and well known

distort /dɪ'stɔːt/ (**distorts, distorting, distorted**) *verb* **1.** to twist something ○ *His face was distorted with pain.* **2.** to give a false impression of something ○ *He distorted the meaning of my speech.*

distract /dɪ'strækt/ (**distracts, distracting, distracted**) *verb* to worry or disturb someone when they should be doing something else [~from] ○ *The noise of the planes is bound to distract the students from their work.* ○ *He had been distracted by his mother's illness, and had forgotten the meeting.* □ **to distract someone's attention** to make someone look at or consider something different ○ *The news of her accident distracted their attention from their holiday preparations.*

distracted /dɪ'stræktɪd/ *adj* feeling extremely worried and unable to think clearly

③ **distraction** /dɪ'strækʃən/ *noun* **1.** an entertainment ○ *We went to London to look for some distraction.* **2.** a thing which stops you from concentrating ○ *How can I do my work properly with all the distractions of the family?*

distraught /dɪ'strɔːt/ *adj* feeling extremely worried and unable to think clearly

distress /dɪ'stres/ *noun* a sad or painful feeling which is very strong ○ *I don't want to cause the family any distress.* ○ *The whole family was in distress at grandmother's death.* ■ *verb* (**distresses, distressing, distressed**) to make someone very sad and worried ○ *The news of her grandmother's death distressed her very much.*

distressing /dɪ'stresɪŋ/ *adj* very sad and worrying

③ **distribute** /dɪ'strɪbjuːt/ (**distributes, distributing, distributed**) *verb* to share something between people ○ *She distributed part of her money to the poor.* ○ *The flight attendants came round, distributing immigration forms to non-EU passengers.* ○ *I'll distribute the list to all the committee members.*

② **distribution** /ˌdɪstrɪ'bjuːʃ(ə)n/ *noun* **1.** giving to several people ○ *The staff will organise the distribution of the timetable to the students.* **2.** the act or process of sending out goods from a warehouse to shops

② **distributor** /dɪ'strɪbjʊtə/, **distributer** *noun* a company which sells goods for another company which makes them ○ *Who is the local distributor for this make of lawn mower?*

② **district** /'dɪstrɪkt/ *noun* an area or region ○ *It's a district of the town well known for its Italian restaurants.*

district attorney /ˌdɪstrɪkt ə'tɜːni/ *noun US* a lawyer representing the government in a certain area. Abbreviation **DA**

district council /ˌdɪstrɪkt 'kaʊnsəl/ *noun* a local council

distrust /dɪs'trʌst/ *noun* a lack of trust (NOTE: + **distrust** *v*)

disturb /dɪ'stɜːb/ (**disturbs, disturbing, disturbed**) *verb* **1.** to interrupt what someone is doing ○ *Sorry to disturb you but there's a phone call.* ○ *Don't disturb your mother – she's resting.* **2.** to make someone feel worried ○ *It disturbed me to see that the wheel was wobbling.* **3.** to change the order or arrangement of something ○ *The* *police told us that nothing must be disturbed in the bedroom.* ◇ **'do not disturb'** a notice placed on a hotel room door, to ask the hotel staff not to come into the room

③ **disturbance** /dɪ'stɜːbəns/ *noun* an occasion on which someone is disturbed ○ *I need to work somewhere where there won't be any disturbance.*

disturbed /dɪ'stɜːbd/ *adj* **1.** worried ○ *We are disturbed to hear that the company may be forced to close.* **2.** mentally ill ○ *In her disturbed state of mind, she may do anything.* ○ *Some of the patients are mentally disturbed.* ○ *Highly disturbed children are taught in this special school.*

③ **disturbing** /dɪ'stɜːbɪŋ/ *adj* worrying

disused /dɪs'juːzd/ *adj* not used

ditch /dɪtʃ/ *noun* a long narrow hole cut into the ground for taking away water ○ *After the storm, the ditches were full of rainwater.* ○ *He fell into the ditch beside the road.*

dither /'dɪðə/ (**dithers, dithering, dithered**) *verb* not to be able to make up your mind ○ *Stop dithering and tell me what you want to do.*

diva /'diːvə/ *noun* **1.** an extremely famous woman opera star **2.** a famous woman singer who is thought to behave badly and demand too much attention (*disapproving*)

divan /dɪ'væn/ *noun* a low long chair or a bed with a solid base and no back

dive /daɪv/ (**dives, diving, dived**) *verb* to jump into water head first [~into/in] ○ *He dived in the pool and swam across under water.*

③ **diver** /'daɪvə/ *noun* **1.** a person who dives ○ *the Australian Olympic diver* **2.** a person who swims under water, especially as a job ○ *Police divers searched the canal.*

diverge /daɪ'vɜːdʒ/ (**diverges, diverging, diverged**) *verb* **1.** to go in different directions ○ *The road and the river diverge at the end of the valley.* ○ *They had shared a flat for some time, then their careers diverged and they saw much less of each other.* **2.** to be different from [~ from] ○ *This diverges from the plan I was given originally.*

divergence /daɪ'vɜːdʒəns/ *noun* difference

diverse /daɪ'vɜːs/ *adj* including many different types or things

diversify /daɪ'vɜːsɪfaɪ/ (**diversifies, diversifying, diversified**) *verb* to do other types of work; to add new types of business to your existing one (NOTE: + **diversification** *n*)

diversion /daɪ'vɜːʃ(ə)n/ *noun* **1.** a temporary road system that sends traffic another way ○ *All traffic has to take a diversion and rejoin the motorway 10 km further on.* **2.** an entertainment or an activity that people do for enjoyment ○ *Fishing is one of the most popular diversions for people at weekends.* ○ *It's a quiet country town with very few diversions for teenagers.*

diversity /daɪ'vɜːsɪti/ *noun* great variety

③ **divert** /daɪ'vɜːt/ (**diverts, diverting, diverted**) *verb* **1.** to send something to another place or in another direction ○ *Because of fog in London, flights have been diverted to Manchester.* ○ *Traffic has been diverted to avoid the town centre.* **2.** to entertain someone ○ *A game of snakes and ladders diverted the children for a little while.* **3.** □ **to divert someone's attention** to make someone look away or consider something else ○ *His wife's illness diverted his attention from his business plans for a while.*

① **divide** /dɪ'vaɪd/ (**divides, dividing, divided**) *verb* **1.** to cut something into parts [~between/among/~into/in] ○ *The cake was divided among the children.* ○ *The two companies agreed to divide the market between them.* ○ *Can you divide the cake into seven pieces?* **2.** to calculate how many times one number fits in another [~by] ○ *Ten divided by two gives five.* (NOTE: **Dividing** is usually shown by the sign ÷ : **10 ÷ 2 = 5**: say 'ten divided by two equals five'.)

③ **dividend** /'dɪvɪdend/ *noun* a part of a company's profits shared out among people who own shares in it

dividing line /dɪ'vaɪdɪŋ laɪn/ *noun* something acting as a boundary

divine /dɪ'vaɪn/ *adj* referring to God ○ *He prayed for divine help.*

diving /'daɪvɪŋ/ *noun* **1.** the sport of jumping into water head first from a diving board, with points from 0 – 10 being awarded by a panel of judges ○ *He won a gold medal for diving.* **2.** swimming underwater with special equipment ○ *We went diving in the Red Sea.*

① **division** /dɪ'vɪʒ(ə)n/ *noun* **1.** an important part of a large organisation ○ *The sales division employs twenty people.* ○ *She is the head of the production division.* **2.** a calculation, where one figure is divided by another ○ *My little sister is just learning how to do division.*

divisive /dɪ'vaɪsɪv/ *adj* which produces disagreements

divorce /dɪˈvɔːs/ *noun* a legal separation of a husband and wife where each is free to marry again ○ *Her parents are getting a divorce.* ○ *Since their divorce, they have both married again.* ■ *verb* (**divorces, divorcing, divorced**) **1.** to break off a marriage legally ○ *They divorced last year.* **2.** to separate from your husband or wife ○ *She divorced her husband and married the man next door.*

③ **divorced** /dɪˈvɔːst/ *adj* no longer married ○ *They're both divorced, with children from their previous marriages.*

divorcee /dɪvɔːˈsiː/ *noun* a divorced person, especially a woman who is divorced

divulge /daɪˈvʌldʒ/ (**divulges, divulging, divulged**) *verb* to give away a secret

③ **DIY** *abbr* do it yourself

③ **dizzy** /ˈdɪzi/ *adj* having a feeling that you might fall down, and that everything seems to turn round ○ *Can we stop the car, please, I feel dizzy.* ○ *After standing in the sun, he became dizzy and had to lie down.* ○ *She has started having dizzy spells.*

DJ *abbr* **1.** dinner jacket **2.** disc jockey

DNA /ˌdiː en ˈeɪ/ *noun* the basic genetic material in a cell. Full form **deoxyribonucleic acid**

① **do** /duː/ (**does, doing, did, done**) *verb* **1.** used with other verbs to make questions ○ *Does this train go to London?* ○ *Did the doctor give you any medicine for your cough?* ○ *Where do they live?* ○ *What did you find there?* **2.** used with other verbs and 'not' to make the negative ○ *They didn't laugh at the film.* ○ *It doesn't matter any more.* ○ *His parents don't live in London.* **3.** used to make a verb stronger ○ *Can I sit down? – Please do!* ○ *Why don't you work harder? – I do work hard!* ○ *Why didn't you tell me? – I did tell you!* **4.** used in place of another verb in short answers to questions using the word 'do' ○ *Do you live in London? – Yes I do.* ○ *But your parents don't live there, do they? – No they don't.* ○ *Does the green colour show? – Yes it does.* ○ *Did you go to the concert after all? – Yes I did.* **5.** used in place of another verb at the end of a question or statement ○ *The Russians live here, don't they?* ○ *It looks very nice, doesn't it?* ○ *It doesn't rain a lot in Spain, does it?* ○ *Can you run as fast as he does?* ○ *He speaks German better than I do.* ○ *She asked me to close the door but I'd already done so.* ○ *They got to the pub before we did.* **6.** telling someone not to do something ○ *Don't throw away that letter!* ○ *Don't put your coffee cups on the computer!* **7.** with nouns ending in -ing ○ *She's doing the shopping.* ○ *He always does the washing-up.* ○ *She was doing the ironing.* **8.** to work at something, to arrange something or to clean something ○ *She's doing her hair.* ○ *Have you done the dishes yet?* ○ *I can't do today's crossword.* ○ *What have you been doing all day?* ○ *They're a difficult company to do business with.* **9.** to succeed, to continue ○ *She's doing very well in her new job.* ○ *He did badly in the interview.* ○ *How's your business doing?* **10.** to finish cooking something ○ *The carrots aren't done yet.* **11.** to be satisfactory ○ *Will this size do?* **12.** used when greeting someone ○ *How do you do?* ◇ **that will do** that's enough ◇ **to make do with** to accept something which is not as good as you wanted ○ *The ordinary plates are all dirty, so we will have to make do with paper ones.*

do away with③ *phrasal verb* to get rid of something

do in *phrasal verb* **1.** to kill someone ○ *What happened to the gang boss? – He was done in and dumped in the river.* **2.** to hurt something (*informal*) ○ *I did my back in by digging the garden.*

do up① *phrasal verb* **1.** to attach something ○ *He's still a baby and he can't do his buttons up properly.* ○ *Can you do up the zip at the back of my dress?* **2.** to repair something and make it like new ○ *They bought an old cottage and did it up.* ○ *He's looking for an old sports car to do up.*

do with *phrasal verb* **1.** to be related or connected to ○ *It has nothing to do with us.* ○ *It is something to do with my new book.* **2.** to put something somewhere ○ *What have you done with the newspaper?* **3.** to need something ○ *After that long walk I could do with a cup of tea.* ○ *The car could do with a wash.*

do without① *phrasal verb* not to have something, to manage without something

doc *abbr* document

docile /ˈdəʊsaɪl/ *adj* quiet and well behaved

dock /dɒk/ *noun* **1.** □ **the docks** a harbour where ships are loaded and unloaded ○ *Cars should arrive at the docks 45 minutes before sailing time.* ○ *We used to go down to the docks to watch the ships come in.* **2.** a place in a law court where the prisoner sits ○ *She was in the dock, facing charges of theft.* ■ *verb* (**docks, docking, docked**) (*of a ship*) to arrive in a port ○ *The ship* *docked at 17.00.* ○ *The cruise liner will dock in Bermuda.*

docker /ˈdɒkə/ *noun* a man who works in a port, loading and unloading ships

docking station /ˈdɒkɪŋ ˌsteɪʃ(ə)n/ *noun* a piece of hardware for recharging a portable computer

dockyard /ˈdɒkjɑːd/ *noun* a place where ships are built or repaired

① **doctor** /ˈdɒktə/ *noun* a person whose job is to look after people who are ill ○ *I have a ten o'clock appointment to see the doctor.* ○ *If you have pains in your chest, you ought to see a doctor.* ○ *He went to the doctor's last Friday.*

doctorate /ˈdɒkt(ə)rət/ *noun* the highest degree from a university

③ **doctrine** /ˈdɒktrɪn/ *noun* a statement of what a group of people believe

document[1] /ˈdɒkjʊmənt/ *noun* **1.** a piece of paper with something official or important printed on it ○ *File all the documents away carefully as we may need them again.* ○ *Please read this document carefully and sign at the bottom of page two.* **2.** a separate file in a computer ○ *The letter was saved as a Word document.*

document[2] /ˈdɒkjʊˌment/ (**documents, documenting, documented**) *verb* to note something in official writing ○ *Cases of this disease are well documented in Africa.*

documentary /ˌdɒkjʊˈment(ə)ri/ *noun* (*plural* **documentaries**) a film which shows facts about a real subject [~about/on] ○ *Did you see the documentary about hippos last night?* ■ *adj* referring to documents

③ **documentation** /ˌdɒkjʊmen ˈteɪʃ(ə)n/ *noun* all the papers referring to something

doddle /ˈdɒd(ə)l/ *noun* something that is easy to do (*informal*)

dodge /dɒdʒ/ *noun* a clever trick ○ *He told me a dodge to avoid paying on the Underground.* ■ *verb* (**dodges, dodging, dodged**) **1.** to avoid something, to get out of the way ○ *He ran across the street, dodging the traffic.* ○ *She dodged behind a parked car hoping he wouldn't see her.* **2.** to avoid doing something you should do, in a dishonest way ○ *to dodge payment of your TV licence fee*

dodgy /ˈdɒdʒi/ *adj* **1.** not safe, involving risk ○ *The back wheel on your bike looks a bit dodgy to me.* ○ *I wouldn't go hitch-hiking in Russia – it sounds very dodgy.* **2.** probably dishonest, or dishonestly obtained ○ *He's a bit of a dodgy customer.* ○ *She paid with a dodgy ten-pound note.*

doe /dəʊ/ *noun* a female animal, such as deer or rabbit (NOTE: Do not confuse with **dough**. Male rabbits are called **bucks**, male deer are **stags**.)

does /dʌz/ 3rd person singular present of **do**

doesn't /ˈdʌz(ə)nt/ ♦ **do**

① **dog** /dɒg/ *noun* an animal kept as a pet, or used for hunting ○ *Can you take the dog out for a walk?* ○ *Police with dogs were hunting the gang of escaped prisoners.*

dog-eared /ˈdɒg ɪəd/ *adj* (*of a page or book*) well used or torn

dogged /ˈdɒgɪd/ *adj* not giving in easily, continuing to do something, even though people want you to stop

dogma /ˈdɒgmə/ *noun* an official belief

dogmatic /dɒgˈmætɪk/ *adj* stating firmly that what you say is right

do-gooder /duː ˈgʊdə/ *noun* a person who tries to do good and help others, but in a way that sometimes annoys people (*informal*)

dogsbody /ˈdɒgzbɒdi/ *noun* someone who is employed by other people to do boring and unpleasant jobs for them

doing /ˈduːɪŋ/ present participle of **do**

③ **doll** /dɒl/ *noun* a child's toy which looks like a baby

① **dollar** /ˈdɒlə/ *noun* **1.** the money system used in the United States ○ *a 5-dollar bill* ○ *The country spends millions of dollars on defence.* ○ *There are two dollars to the pound.* **2.** a similar money system used in many other countries ○ *What is the price in Australian dollars?* (NOTE: usually written **$** before figures: *$250*. The currencies used in different countries can be shown by the initial letter of the country: *Can$* (Canadian dollar), *Aus$* (Australian dollar).)

dollop /ˈdɒləp/ *noun* a large lump of something soft (*informal*)

dolphin /ˈdɒlfɪn/ *noun* a large animal with a long nose, that lives in the sea (NOTE: A group of them is a **school of dolphins**.)

③ **domain** /dəʊˈmeɪn/ *noun* **1.** an area of responsibility ○ *I don't do the cooking – that's my husband's domain.* **2.** an area, a group of nodes in a network

domain name /dəʊˈmeɪn neɪm/ *noun* the name of a service provider on the Internet

dome /dəʊm/ *noun* a round roof shaped like half of a ball

② **domestic** /də'mestɪk/ *adj* **1.** relating to the home ○ *She hated having to do all the domestic work.* **2.** inside a country ○ *Sales in the domestic market have risen.* ■ *noun* a servant in a house (*old*) ○ *When the fire broke out all the domestics ran into the house to rescue the furniture.*

domesticated /də'mestɪkeɪtɪd/ *adj* **1.** (*of animals*) kept or used for human requirements **2.** (*of a person*) skilled in doing the work needed to keep a home clean

domesticity /ˌdəʊme'stɪsɪti/ *noun* life at home

③ **dominance** /'dɒmɪnəns/ *noun* being dominant

③ **dominant** /'dɒmɪnənt/ *adj* **1.** most important ○ *The dominant colour in the room is dark red.* ○ *Safety will be the dominant theme of the discussion.* **2.** very powerful [~in] ○ *a dominant personality* ○ *the dominant force in the country's government*

③ **dominate** /'dɒmɪneɪt/ (**dominates, dominating, dominated**) *verb* **1.** to rule somebody or something ○ *He is dominated by his wife.* ○ *The Union party dominates the country's political system.* **2.** to be very important ○ *The conversation was dominated by the subject of the president's wife.* **3.** to be very clearly seen ○ *The volcano dominates the town.*

domination /ˌdɒmɪ'neɪʃ(ə)n/ *noun* control, power, or authority over others or another

domineering /ˌdɒmɪ'nɪərɪŋ/ *adj* forcing your ideas on someone

dominion /də'mɪnjən/ *noun* the power of control ○ *to exercise dominion over a country*

domino /'dɒmɪnəʊ/ (*plural* **dominoes**) *noun* one of a set of small flat blocks used to play a game, each block being divided into two sections, with up to six dots in each section

don /dɒn/ *noun* a university teacher, especially at Oxford or Cambridge ○ *His father was an Oxford don.* ■ *verb* (**dons, donning, donned**) to put on a piece of clothing ○ *Instructions for donning the life jacket are in the pocket in front of your seat.* ○ *Visitors to the factory have to don protective clothing.*

donate /dəʊ'neɪt/ (**donates, donating, donated**) *verb* to give something, especially money, to a charity or similar organisation ○ *He donated a lot of money to a charity for the homeless.*

donation /dəʊ'neɪʃ(ə)n/ *noun* a present, especially of money

① **done** /dʌn/ past participle of **do**

③ **donkey** /'dɒŋki/ *noun* a farm animal with long ears, used for riding or pulling carts

donor /'dəʊnə/ *noun* a person who gives something

① **don't** /dəʊnt/ ♦ **do**

doodle /'duːd(ə)l/ (**doodles, doodling, doodled**) *verb* to draw shapes on paper, usually because you are bored or thinking of something else ○ *She sat at the back of the meeting, doodling on the agenda.* (NOTE: + **doodle** *n*)

doom /duːm/ *noun* an unhappy fate that cannot be avoided

doomed /duːmd/ *adj* condemned to end in ruin

① **door** /dɔː/ *noun* **1.** a solid piece of wood, plastic or metal which closes an entrance ○ *He went into his office and locked the door behind him.* ○ *She opened the car door and hit a passing cyclist.* **2.** used to show where a building is in a street ○ *They live a few doors away from us.*

doorbell /'dɔːbel/ *noun* a bell by a door which you ring to get someone inside to open the door

doorknob /'dɔːnɒb/ *noun* a round handle for opening and shutting a door

doorman /'dɔːmən/ (*plural* **doormen**) *noun* a man who stands at the door of a building such as a restaurant or hotel

doormat /'dɔːmæt/ *noun* a small rough carpet placed in front of or behind a door, on which you wipe your shoes if they are dirty or wet

doorstep /'dɔːstep/ *noun* a block of a hard substance such as stone or wood at the bottom of a door on the outside of a house

door-to-door /ˌdɔː tə 'dɔː/ *adj* going from one house to the next, asking people to buy something, to vote for someone, or asking them questions

doorway /'dɔːweɪ/ *noun* a space where there is a door

dope /dəʊp/ *noun* **1.** illegal drugs **2.** a stupid fool (*informal*) ○ *He's a dope, he should have asked for twice as much!*

dork /dɔːk/ *noun* someone who other people think is not intelligent or does not dress in fashionable clothes (*informal*)

dormant /'dɔːmənt/ *adj* not active ○ *The volcano has been dormant for many years, but has suddenly started to send out clouds of smoke.*

dormitory /ˈdɔːmɪtri/ (*plural* **dormitories**) *noun* a long room full of beds

dosage /ˈdəʊsɪdʒ/ *noun* the amount of a drug calculated by a doctor to be necessary for a patient

dose /dəʊs/ *noun* **1.** a quantity of medicine ○ *Normal daily dose: three tablets.* ○ *Do not exceed the prescribed dose.* **2.** an attack of a disease [~of] ○ *I've had a dose of bronchitis.*

dosh /dɒʃ/ *noun* money (*informal*)

doss /dɒs/ (**dosses, dossing, dossed**), **doss down** *verb* to sleep on something such as a chair or on the floor, because there is no bed available

doss down *phrasal verb* to sleep somewhere where there is no bed available, e.g. on the floor

dossier /ˈdɒsieɪ/ *noun* a file of documents

② **dot** /dɒt/ *noun* **1.** a small round spot ○ *A blue tie with white dots.* **2.** a printing sign (.) used in email addresses ○ *My email address is jane@supertek.com (say 'Jane at Supertek dot com').* ■ *verb* (**dots, dotting, dotted**) **1.** to mark with a spot **2.** to be or be put in many different parts ○ *Vases of flowers dotted the room.* ○ *The wall was dotted with notices.*

dot.com /ˌdɒtˈkɒm/ *noun* a company that does business on the Internet or that provides Internet services

doting /ˈdəʊtɪŋ/ *adj* very fond of someone

dotted line /ˌdɒtɪd ˈlaɪn/ *noun* a line made of a series of dots

dotty /ˈdɒti/ (**dottier, dottiest**) *adj* slightly crazy (*informal*)

① **double** /ˈdʌb(ə)l/ *adj* **1.** containing two of something ○ *The word 'immeasurable' is spelt with a double 'm'.* ○ *The invoice number is six double five double one.* **2.** with two parts, for two people ○ *double doors* ○ *a double bed* **3.** twice the size of that which is considered normal ○ *She asked for a double portion of ice cream.* ■ *plural noun* **doubles** a tennis game for two people on either side ■ *verb* (**doubles, doubling, doubled**) to multiply something by two ○ *Think of a number and then double it.*

double up *phrasal verb* **1.** to bend because of pain ○ *She doubled up in pain when he hit her in the stomach.* **2.** to perform two jobs ○ *The waiter is doubling up as chef because the chef is on holiday.*

double-barrelled /ˌdʌb(ə)l ˈbærəld/ *adj* **1.** used to describe a gun which has two barrels **2.** formed from two names, usually with a hyphen between them

doublebass /ˌdʌb(ə)lˈbeɪs/ *noun* a musical instrument like a very large violin

double bed /ˌdʌb(ə)l ˈbed/ *noun* a bed for two people

double-breasted /ˌdʌb(ə)l ˈbrestɪd/ *adj* describes a coat or jacket which has two rows of buttons down the front

double-check /ˌdʌb(ə)l ˈtʃek/ *verb* to check something carefully, twice

double-click /ˌdʌb(ə)l ˈklɪk/ *verb* to press a mouse button twice quickly, e.g. to give an instruction to a computer

double-cross /ˌdʌb(ə)l ˈkrɒs/ *verb* to trick someone so that they think you are working with them when in fact you are working against them

double-decker /ˌdʌb(ə)l ˈdekə/ *noun* a bus with two levels of seats ○ *Double-decker buses are common in London.*

double figures /ˌdʌb(ə)l ˈfɪgəz/ *plural noun* the numbers with two figures, from 10 to 99

double-glazing /ˌdʌb(ə)l ˈgleɪzɪŋ/ *noun* windows made of two pieces of glass, used to keep out noise or to keep heat inside

double life /ˌdʌb(ə)l ˈlaɪf/ *noun* a situation in which someone has a separate way of life for some of the time, which they keep secret from other people

double-sided /ˌdʌb(ə)l ˈsaɪdɪd/ *adj* having two sides, both of which can be used

double take /ˌdʌb(ə)l ˈteɪk/ *noun* a reaction of surprise, after a slight pause

doubly /ˈdʌbli/ *adv* twice

① **doubt** /daʊt/ *noun* **1.** not being sure ○ *Everyone sometimes has doubts about what they really want to do.* □ **to have doubts about something** to say that you are doubtful about something ○ *I have my doubts about the accuracy of the figures.* □ **to cast doubt on something** to make people feel less sure about something ○ *He cast doubt on the whole proposal.* □ **to give someone the benefit of the doubt** to allow someone to continue doing something, because you are not sure that accusations made against him are correct ○ *The referee gave him the benefit of the doubt.* **2.** □ **there's no doubt about** it is a certain fact ○ *There's no doubt about her commitment to the project.* ○ *There's no doubt that he is guilty.* ■ *verb* (**doubts, doubting, doubted**) not to be sure of something [~(that)/~whether/if] ○ *Did you ever doubt* *that we would win?* ○ *I doubt whether he will want to go to the funeral.* ◇ **no doubt** certainly ○ *No doubt they will be asking for more money soon.* ◇ **in doubt** not yet known or definite, or not yet sure ○ *The result of the game was in doubt until the last minute.* ○ *I'm in doubt about whether I should take the job or not.*

② **doubtful** /ˈdaʊtf(ə)l/ *adj* not sure that something is right or good, or not likely ○ *I am doubtful about whether we should go.* ○ *It is doubtful whether the race will take place because of the snow.*

doubtless /ˈdaʊtləs/ *adv* certainly

dough /dəʊ/ *noun* **1.** a mixture of water and flour for making a food such as bread, before it is cooked ○ *The chef was kneading the dough for the pizza.* **2.** money (*informal*) ○ *Hurry up, give me the dough!* (NOTE: Do not confuse with **doe**.)

doughnut /ˈdəʊnʌt/ *noun* a small round or ring-shaped cake cooked by frying in oil

dour /dʊə/ *adj* not attractive or welcoming in appearance or behaviour

douse /daʊs/ (**douses, dousing, doused**) *verb* to throw water on something

dove[1] /dʌv/ *noun* **1.** a white domesticated pigeon ○ *To celebrate the peace treaty they released hundreds of doves.* **2.** a person who prefers diplomacy and tries to achieve peace ○ *Curiously, it's the military commanders who are the doves while the president and his advisers are the hawks.*

dove[2] /dəʊv/ *US* past tense of **dive**

dowdy /ˈdaʊdi/ (**dowdier, dowdiest**) *adj* old-fashioned and badly dressed

① **down** /daʊn/ *prep* **1.** towards the bottom of ○ *He fell down the stairs and broke his leg.* ○ *The ball ran down the hill.* **2.** away from where the person speaking is standing ○ *He went down the road to the shop.* ○ *The police station is just down the street.* ■ *adv* **1.** towards the bottom, towards a lower position ○ *Put the box down in the corner.* ○ *I looked in the cellar, but there's no one down there.* **2.** in writing ○ *Did you note down the number of the car?* ○ *The policeman took down her address.* **3.** used for showing criticism ○ *Down with the government!* ○ *Down with exams!* (NOTE: **down** is often used with verbs, e.g. **to go down, to fall down, to sit down, to lie down**.)

down-and-out /ˌdaʊn ən ˈaʊt/ *noun* a person with no money who lives on the streets (*informal*)

downcast /ˈdaʊnkɑːst/ *adj* gloomy, depressed

downer /ˈdaʊnə/ *noun* **1.** someone or something that makes you feel depressed **2.** a drug which makes you feel calm

downfall /ˈdaʊnfɔːl/ *noun* a situation in which someone or something fails or is destroyed

downgrade /ˈdaʊngreɪd/ (**downgrades, downgrading, downgraded**) *verb* to reduce the importance of a person or of a job

downhearted /ˌdaʊnˈhɑːtɪd/ *adj* feeling unhappy

downhill /daʊnˈhɪl/ *adv* towards the bottom of a hill ○ *The road goes downhill for a while and then crosses the river.*

Downing Street /ˈdaʊnɪŋ striːt/ *noun* **1.** a street in London with the houses of the British Prime Minister (No. 10) and the Chancellor of the Exchequer (No. 11) ○ *They took the petition to Downing Street.* **2.** the office of the Prime Minister ○ *Downing Street denied the report.*

download /daʊnˈləʊd/ *verb* (**downloads, downloading, downloaded**) to load data or a program into a computer ■ *noun* a computer file that can be downloaded

down-market /ˈdaʊn ˌmɑːkɪt/ *adj* cheaper, appealing to a less wealthy section of the population

down payment /ˌdaʊn ˈpeɪmənt/ *noun* a part of a total payment made in advance

downplay /ˌdaʊnˈpleɪ/ (**downplays, downplaying, downplayed**) *verb* to make something seem less important (NOTE: can also be **to play down**)

downpour /ˈdaʊnpɔː/ *noun* a heavy fall of rain

downright /ˈdaʊnraɪt/ *adj* complete or clear ○ *That's a downright lie.* ○ *The newspaper story was a downright fabrication.* ■ *adv* completely or extremely ○ *The waitress wasn't just unpleasant, she was downright rude.*

downside /ˈdaʊnsaɪd/ *noun* the disadvantages of a situation

downsize /ˈdaʊnsaɪz/ (**downsizes, downsizing, downsized**) *verb* to make a business smaller by cutting the number of jobs

Down's syndrome /ˈdaʊnz ˌsɪndrəʊm/ *noun* a condition caused by the existence of an extra chromosome that affects a person's physical and mental development

② **downstairs** /daʊnˈsteəz/ *adv* on or to the lower part of a building ○ *He heard a noise in the kitchen and went downstairs to see what it was.* ○ *I left my cup of coffee* *downstairs.* ■ *adj* on the ground floor of a building ○ *The house has a downstairs bedroom.* ○ *You can use the downstairs loo.* ■ *noun* the ground floor of a building ○ *The downstairs has three rooms.* ○ *The downstairs of the house is larger than the upstairs.* Compare **upstairs**

downstream[1] /ˈdaʊnstriːm/ *adj* towards the mouth of a river ○ *Downstream communities have not yet been affected.*

downstream[2] /ˌdaʊnˈstriːm/ *adv* towards the mouth of a river ○ *The silt is carried downstream and deposited in the delta.*

down-to-earth /ˌdaʊn tʊ ˈɜːθ/ *adj* sensible or matter-of-fact

② **downtown** /ˈdaʊntaʊn/ *noun* the central district of a town ○ *Downtown will be very crowded at this time of day.*

downtrodden /ˈdaʊntrɒd(ə)n/ *adj* oppressed, badly treated

downturn /ˈdaʊntɜːn/ *noun* a movement towards lower prices, sales or profits

③ **downward** /ˈdaʊnwəd/ *adj* towards the bottom ○ *a downward trend in the unemployment figures* ■ *adv US* same as **downwards**

③ **downwards** /ˈdaʊnwədz/ *adv* towards the bottom

downwind /ˌdaʊnˈwɪnd/ *adv, adj* in the direction in which the wind is blowing

downy /ˈdaʊni/ *adj* **1.** soft and fluffy **2.** covered with soft hairs

dowry /ˈdaʊri/ *noun* money or goods which a bride brings to her husband

doze /dəʊz/ *verb* (**dozes, dozing, dozed**) to sleep a little (*slang*) ○ *She dozed for a while after lunch.* ■ *noun* a short sleep

② **dozen** /ˈdʌz(ə)n/ (*plural same*) *noun* **1.** twelve ○ *I need a dozen eggs for this recipe.* ○ *We ordered two dozen (= 24) chairs.* **2.** □ **dozens of** a lot of ○ *Dozens of people visited the exhibition.* ○ *I've been to New York dozens of times.* ◇ **half a dozen** six ○ *half a dozen apples*

① **Dr** *abbr* doctor

drab /dræb/ (**drabber, drabbest**) *adj* lacking bright colours; brown, grey

② **draft** /drɑːft/ *noun* a rough plan of a document ○ *He quickly wrote out a draft of the agreement.* ○ *It's not the final version, it's just a draft.* ■ *verb* (**drafts, drafting, drafted**) to draw up a rough plan of something

draft in *phrasal verb* to ask someone to do something ○ *The Boy Scouts were drafted in to dig the garden.*

③ **drag** /dræg/ *verb* (**drags, dragging, dragged**) to pull something heavy along the ground [~along/across/out etc] ○ *She dragged her suitcase across the floor.* ○ *The police dragged the men away from the gate.* ■ *noun* something boring, which stops you doing things you really want to do ○ *It's a drag, having to write all the Christmas cards.*

drag on *phrasal verb* to seem to pass slowly ○ *The dinner party seemed to drag on for hours.*

dragon /ˈdrægən/ *noun* an unfriendly woman who seems frightening

dragonfly /ˈdrægənflaɪ/ (*plural* **dragonflies**) *noun* a long insect with bright transparent wings which often flies near water

drain /dreɪn/ *noun* a pipe for carrying waste water away ○ *In the autumn the drains get blocked by leaves.* ○ *We had to phone the council to come and clear the blocked drain.* ■ *verb* (**drains, draining, drained**) to remove a liquid from something

drainage /ˈdreɪnɪdʒ/ *noun* the process of removing water by means of drains

draining board /ˈdreɪnɪŋ bɔːd/ *noun* a slightly sloping surface next to a sink on which dishes can be placed to dry

drainpipe /ˈdreɪnpaɪp/ *noun* a pipe on the outside of a house which takes water down to the drains

③ **drama** /ˈdrɑːmə/ *noun* **1.** a serious performance in a theatre ○ *a new TV drama series about life in Glasgow* ○ *The 'Globe' has put on an unknown Elizabethan drama.* ○ *I'm reading a book on 19th-century French drama.* ○ *She's a drama student* or *She's studying drama.* **2.** a series of serious and exciting events ○ *a day of high drama in the court* ○ *the drama of the rescue by helicopter* ○ *He always makes a drama out of everything.*

③ **dramatic** /drəˈmætɪk/ *adj* sudden, unexpected and very noticeable ○ *the dramatic moment in the film, when the dinosaurs start to attack them* ○ *The door was thrown open and she made a dramatic entrance.* ○ *The TV news showed dramatic pictures of the disaster.*

dramatics /drəˈmætɪks/ *noun* the practice of performing plays, usually by people who are not paid to act

dramatise /ˈdræmətaɪz/ (**dramatises, dramatising, dramatised**), **dramatize** *verb* **1.** to adapt a novel for TV or the theatre ○ *The novel was dramatised by J. Smith.* **2.** to make something seem much more dramatic than it really is ○ *There's no need to dramatise the situation, it's bad enough as it is.*

③ **drank** /dræŋk/ past tense of **drink**

drape /dreɪp/ (**drapes, draping, draped**) *verb* **1.** to hang cloth around something ○ *The statue was draped in a white cloth ready to be unveiled.* ○ *He wore a long scarf draped over his shoulders* **2.** to hang something long over something ○ *He draped his legs over the back of the seat.*

drapes /dreɪps/ *plural noun US* curtains ○ *Open the drapes – it's light outside.*

drastic /ˈdræstɪk/ *adj* severe, which has a sharp effect

③ **draught** /drɑːft/ *noun* a flow of cool air into a room ○ *Don't sit in a draught.*

draughts /drɑːfts/ *noun* a board game played with black and white round pieces ○ *Would you like a game of draughts* or *to play draughts?* ○ *Draughts is a much simpler game than chess.* (NOTE: not plural, and takes a singular verb. The US term is **checkers**.)

draughtsman /ˈdrɑːftsmən/ (*plural* **draughtsmen**) *noun* a person who draws plans for machines or buildings

③ **draughty** /ˈdrɑːfti/ (**draughtier, draughtiest**) *adj* with cool air flowing into it (NOTE: The US spelling is **drafty**.)

① **draw** /drɔː/ *noun* **1.** a game or competition which ends with both teams having the same number of points ○ *The match was a draw: 2–2.* **2.** a competition in which the winner is chosen by a person who takes a ticket out of a container with a name on it ○ *The draw is held on Saturdays.* ○ *We are holding a draw to raise money for the local hospital.* ■ *verb* (**draws, drawing, drew, drawn**) **1.** to make a picture with a pen or pencil ○ *He drew a picture of the house.* ○ *She's drawing a pot of flowers.* **2.** not to have a winner in a game ○ *The teams drew 2 – 2.* □ **the match was drawn** neither side won **3.** to pull curtains open or closed ○ *She drew the curtains and let in the sun.* ○ *Can you draw the curtains – I don't want anyone to see us in here.*

draw up③ *phrasal verb* **1.** to come close and stop ○ *As I was standing at the bus stop, a car drew up and the driver asked if I wanted a lift.* **2.** to write down something, e.g. a plan ○ *They have drawn up a plan to save money.* ○ *Have you drawn up a list of people you want to invite to the party?* **3.** to move something closer ○ *Draw your chairs up to the table.*

drawback /ˈdrɔːbæk/ *noun* a thing which is not convenient or which causes a problem

③ **drawer** /ˈdrɔːə/ *noun* a part of a desk or cupboard like an open box which slides in and out when you pull its handle ○ *I keep my cheque book in the top drawer of my desk.*

② **drawing** /ˈdrɔːɪŋ/ *noun* **1.** a picture that has been drawn ○ *I've bought an old drawing of the church.* **2.** the activity or skill of making pictures with a pencil or pen ○ *He studied drawing in Rome.*

drawing board /ˈdrɔːɪŋ bɔːd/ *noun* a large board used by designers to work on □ **it's back to the drawing board** we'll have to start planning all over again

drawing pin /ˈdrɔːɪŋ pɪn/ *noun* a pin with a large flat head, used for fixing papers to a surface such as a wall

drawing room /ˈdrɔːɪŋ ruːm/ *noun* a sitting room, a room for sitting and talking in, but not eating

drawl /drɔːl/ *noun* a slow way of speaking ○ *He spoke with a southern drawl.* (NOTE: + **drawl** *v*)

③ **drawn** /drɔːn/ *adj* tired and ill ○ *She looked drawn after spending all night with her sick baby.* ■ past participle of **draw**

dread /dred/ *noun* great fear ○ *The sound of her voice filled him with dread.* ○ *She has a dread of meeting him in the street.* □ **in dread of** being very afraid of ○ *They lived in constant dread of being arrested.* ■ *verb* (**dreads, dreading, dreaded**) to fear something very much ○ *I'm dreading taking my driving test.* ○ *She dreads her weekly visit to the doctor.*

dreaded /ˈdredɪd/ *adj* awful, frightening (*humorous*)

② **dreadful** /ˈdredf(ə)l/ *adj* very bad or unpleasant ○ *What a dreadful film!*

② **dreadfully** /ˈdredf(ə)li/ *adv* extremely, in a way that is not good or pleasant

dreadlocks /ˈdredlɒks/ *plural noun* a hairstyle where your hair is plaited into thick strands ○ *He had his hair in dreadlocks.*

② **dream** /driːm/ *noun* **1.** a story or series of events that you think about while you are sleeping [~about] ○ *She had a dream about big pink elephants.* **2.** something which you imagine and hope will happen in the future ○ *All his dreams of wealth collapsed when he lost his job.* ○ *His dream is to appear on Broadway.* ■ *verb* (**dreams, dreaming, dreamt** or **dreamed**) to experience a story or series of events while you are sleeping [~of/about/~(that)] ○ *He was dreaming of white sand and a blue tropical sea.* ○ *I dreamt about you last night.* ○ *Last night I dreamt I was drowning.* ■ *adj* referring to something that is the best you could have ○ *They found their dream house in a small town by the sea.* ○ *Select your dream team for the World Cup.*

dreamer /ˈdriːmə/ *noun* a person who is out of touch with practical things

dreamt /dremt/ past tense and past participle of **dream**

dreamy /ˈdriːmi/ (**dreamier, dreamiest**) *adj* as if you are dreaming

dreary /ˈdrɪəri/ (**drearier, dreariest**) *adj* sad or gloomy; not interesting

dredge /dredʒ/ (**dredges, dredging, dredged**) *verb* **1.** to remove dirt or sand from the bottom of a river or lake ○ *They had to spend weeks dredging the channel so that boats could still get to the harbour.* **2.** to cover something with a substance such as sugar or flour ○ *When the pie is cooked, dredge it with icing sugar.*

dregs /dregz/ *plural noun* the parts of a drink which are left in a cup or glass when you have finished drinking ○ *He poured the dregs down the sink.*

drench /drentʃ/ (**drenches, drenching, drenched**) *verb* to soak something

② **dress** /dres/ *noun* a piece of clothing usually worn by women or girls, covering the body and part or all of the legs ○ *She was wearing a blue dress.* ■ *verb* (**dresses, dressing, dressed**) **1.** to put clothes on someone [~in/~as] ○ *She dressed her little girl in a blue dress.* ○ *He was dressed as a prince.* **2. to get dressed** to put clothes on yourself ○ *He got up, dressed and had breakfast.* **3.** to clean an injury and cover it with a bandage

dress up *phrasal verb* **1.** to put on costumes ○ *The children love dressing up as doctors and nurses.* **2.** to wear your best elegant clothes ○ *Don't dress up – come just as you are.*

③ **dressed** /drest/ *adj* **1.** wearing clothes ○ *I can't come down to see the visitors – I'm not dressed yet.* □ **to get dressed** to dress yourself ○ *Get dressed and come downstairs.* ○ *He got up, got dressed and then had breakfast.* **2. dressed in** wearing a particular colour or type of clothing ○ *She was dressed all in black.* ○ *He was dressed in a teeshirt and shorts.*

dresser /ˈdresə/ *noun* **1.** a piece of kitchen furniture with open shelves above and cupboards below ○ *Put the plates back in the kitchen dresser.* **2.** a person who dresses in a certain way ○ *He's a very smart dresser.*

dressing /ˈdresɪŋ/ *noun* **1.** a sauce for salad **2.** a cover for an injury ○ *The dressings need to be changed every hour.*

dressing gown /ˈdresɪŋ gaʊn/ *noun* a long robe worn over pyjamas or a nightdress

dressing room /ˈdresɪŋ ruːm/ *noun* a room in which you change your clothes, especially a room in a theatre where actors or actresses get dressed in costume, or a room in a sports club where people change into their sports clothes

dressing table /ˈdresɪŋ ˌteɪb(ə)l/ *noun* a piece of bedroom furniture with a mirror or mirrors

dress rehearsal /ˌdres rɪˈhɜːs(ə)l/ *noun* the final practice for an activity such as a play or public event ○ *The attack on the police station was only a dress rehearsal for the coup d'état which took place the following week.*

dressy /ˈdresi/ *adj* (*of person*) wearing formal and fashionable clothes

drew /druː/ past tense of **draw**

dribble /ˈdrɪb(ə)l/ (**dribbles, dribbling, dribbled**) *verb* **1.** to let liquid flow slowly out of an opening, especially out of your mouth ○ *The baby dribbled its food over her dress* **2.** (*of a liquid*) to flow slowly out of an opening [~out/through etc] ○ *Ketchup dribbled onto the tablecloth.* **3.** to kick a football along as you are running, or to move a ball along with one hand as you are running

drier /ˈdraɪə/ *noun* a machine which dries

drift /drɪft/ *noun* **1.** a general meaning ○ *Did you follow the drift of the conversation?* ○ *My Italian isn't very good, but I got the drift of what they were saying.* ○ *I think she got the general drift of my argument.* **2.** a pile of snow blown by the wind ○ *Snow lay in drifts around the farmhouse.* ■ *verb* (**drifts, drifting, drifted**) **1.** to move with the flow of water, without steering ○ *The boat drifted down the river for two miles.* **2.** to move aimlessly ○ *After the match, the spectators drifted towards the exits.* **3.** (*of snow*) to pile up ○ *The snow began to drift in the high wind.* **4.** to behave aimlessly, to avoid taking any decisions ○ *The government lost its sense of purpose and started to drift.* **5.** to move slowly in a certain direction ○ *Prices drifted downwards.*

③ **drill** /drɪl/ *noun* **1.** a tool for making holes in a hard substance such as wood or metal ○ *He used an electric drill to make the holes in the wall.* **2.** the action of practising marching, especially in the armed forces ○ *New recruits spend hours practising their drill.* ■ *verb* (**drills, drilling, drilled**) **1.** to use a drill to make a hole in something [~in/into/~through] ○ *Check how solid the wall is before you drill a hole in it.* ○ *He drilled two holes for the screws.* **2.** to do military practice ○ *The soldiers were drilling on the parade ground.* **3.** to teach someone something by making them do or say it many times [~in/~into] ○ *They were drilled in how to help customers leave the building in an emergency.* ○ *The rule of not speaking to strangers was drilled into the children from an early age.*

① **drink** /drɪŋk/ *noun* **1.** an amount of liquid such as water, juice, tea or coffee which you swallow ○ *If you're thirsty, have a drink of water.* ○ *She always has a hot drink before she goes to bed.* **2.** an alcoholic drink ○ *Would you like a drink?* ○ *Come and have a drink.* ○ *I'll order some drinks from the bar.* ■ *verb* (**drinks, drinking, drank, drunk**) to swallow liquid ○ *He drank water out of a bottle.* ○ *What would you like to drink?*

drink up *phrasal verb* to drink all of a liquid ○ *The baby drank all her milk up.* ○ *Come on, drink up – we're leaving now.*

drink-driving /ˌdrɪŋk ˈdraɪvɪŋ/ *noun* driving a car when drunk

drinker /ˈdrɪŋkə/ *noun* a person who usually drinks a particular quantity or type of alcohol, or a person who drinks too much alcohol regularly ○ *She's only a light drinker.* ○ *They're all beer drinkers.* ○ *Her father was a drinker.*

drinking /ˈdrɪŋkɪŋ/ *noun* the act or process of drinking a lot of alcohol, especially frequently and over a period of time

drinking water /ˈdrɪŋkɪŋ ˌwɔːtə/ *noun* water which is safe to drink

drip /drɪp/ *noun* a small drop of water ○ *There's a hole in the tent – a drip just fell on my nose.* ■ *verb* (**drips, dripping, dripped**) **1.** to fall in small drops ○ *Water was slowly dripping from the ceiling.* **2.** (*of e.g. a tap*) to produce small drops ○ *I must fix that tap – it's dripping.*

① **drive** /draɪv/ *noun* **1.** a journey, especially in a car □ **to go for a drive** to make a short journey in a car for pleasure **2.** a part of a computer which makes a disk work ○ *The disk is stuck in the drive.* **3.** an energetic way of working ○ *We need someone with plenty of drive to run the sales department.* **4.** a little road leading to a house ○ *Visitors can park in the drive.* ■ *verb* (**drives, driving, drove, driven**) to make a motor vehicle travel in a particular direction [~along/down/through etc] ○ *I never learnt to drive.* ○ *He was driving a lorry when the accident happened.* □ **I'll drive your aunt to the airport** I'll take her to the airport in my car ◇ **to drive someone crazy** *or* **mad** to have an effect on someone so that they become very annoyed (*informal*) ○ *The noise is driving me mad.* ○ *All this work is driving her crazy.*

drive away③ *phrasal verb* **1.** to ride away in a motor vehicle ○ *The bank robbers leapt into a car and drove away at top speed.* **2.** to take someone away in a motor vehicle ○ *The children were driven away in a police car.* **3.** to force something or someone to go away ○ *His teaching methods were driving students away.*

drive back③ *phrasal verb* **1.** to go back or to come back in a motor vehicle ○ *We were driving back to London after a day out.* **2.** to force someone or something back ○ *The police drove the demonstrators back from the square.*

drive off③ *phrasal verb* same as **drive away 1, 3**

drive-by /ˈdraɪv baɪ/ *noun* the firing of a gun at somebody from a moving vehicle

drive-in /ˈdraɪv ɪn/ *adj, noun* bank, cinema, restaurant, where cars drive up for service ○ *We went to see the movie at the local drive-in.* ○ *We got a Chinese takeaway at a drive-in restaurant.*

drivel /ˈdrɪv(ə)l/ *noun* rubbish

③ **driven** /ˈdrɪv(ə)n/ past participle of **drive**

① **driver** /ˈdraɪvə/ *noun* a person who drives a vehicle such as a car or train ○ *He's got a job as a bus driver.* ○ *The drivers of both cars were injured in the accident.*

drive-through /ˈdraɪv θruː/, **drive-up** *noun* a business that serves people who wait by a special window in their cars

driveway /ˈdraɪvweɪ/ *noun* a short private road leading to a house

③ **driving** /ˈdraɪvɪŋ/ *adj* (*of rain or snow*) blown horizontally by the wind ○ *They were forced to turn back because of the driving rain.* ■ *noun* the action of driving a motor vehicle ○ *Driving in the centre of London can be very frustrating.* ○ *She's taking driving lessons.*

② **driving licence** /ˈdraɪvɪŋ ˌlaɪs(ə)ns/ *noun* a permit which allows someone to drive a vehicle on public roads

drizzle /ˈdrɪz(ə)l/ *noun* light rain ○ *A thin drizzle was falling so we took our umbrellas.* ■ *verb* (**drizzles, drizzling, drizzled**) to rain a little ○ *It's drizzling outside, so you need a raincoat.*

drone /drəʊn/ *noun* **1.** a male bee ○ *The workers are busy getting pollen, while the drones do nothing.* (NOTE: In a bee colony, the females are **workers**.) **2.** a buzz of an insect, of an engine ○ *I could hear the drone of a small aircraft in the distance.* **3.** a monotonous sound ○ *The drone of the bagpipes sounded across the lake.* ■ *verb* (**drones, droning, droned**) **1.** to buzz ○ *We could hear a small aircraft droning overhead.* **2.** to talk slowly and in a monotonous voice ○ *The lecturer droned on and on about population statistics.*

drool /druːl/ (**drools, drooling, drooled**) *verb* **1.** to slobber ○ *a baby drooling in his high chair* **2.** to show excessive pleasure about something ○ *I absolutely drooled over the painting.*

droop /druːp/ (**droops, drooping, drooped**) *verb* to hang down

① **drop** /drɒp/ *noun* a small amount of liquid which falls ■ *verb* (**drops, dropping, dropped**) **1.** to fall or let something fall [~from/to/into/down/on etc] ○ *He dropped the glass and it broke.* ○ *The plate dropped onto the floor.* **2.** to decrease ○ *Prices are dropping.* ○ *At night the temperature can drop below zero.* **3.** to let someone get off a bus or car at a place [~at/~in] ○ *I'll drop you at your house.* ○ *The bus dropped her in the centre of town.*

drop in *phrasal verb* to call on someone, to visit someone

drop off *phrasal verb* **1.** to fall asleep ○ *She dropped off in front of the TV.* ○ *It took me ages to drop off.* **2.** to let someone who is a passenger in a car get out somewhere ○ *We can drop you off at the station.*

drop out *phrasal verb* **1.** to stop competing or being involved in something ○ *He got as far as the semi-finals but dropped out because of a shoulder injury.* **2.** to decide to give up your ordinary job or studies, usually because you want to live a more simple life ○ *He dropped out and went to live on a beach in India.*

drop-down menu /ˌdrɒp daʊn ˈmenjuː/ *noun* a list of choices which appears on a computer screen, and stays there until you click on one of them

drop-in centre /ˈdrɒp ɪn ˌsentə/ *noun* a place which people can visit without arranging a time, to get advice or information, or to meet other people

droplet /ˈdrɒplət/ *noun* a very small drop of liquid

droppings /ˈdrɒpɪŋz/ *plural noun* solid waste matter from animals ○ *The grass was covered with rabbit and sheep droppings.*

③ **drought** /draʊt/ *noun* a long period when there is no rain and when the land is dry

① **drove** /drəʊv/ past tense of **drive**

③ **drown** /draʊn/ (**drowns, drowning, drowned**) *verb* to die by being unable to breathe in water ○ *He drowned in a shallow pool.*

drowsy /ˈdraʊzi/ (**drowsier, drowsiest**) *adj* sleepy (NOTE: + **drowsily** *adv*, **drowsiness** *n*)

drudgery /ˈdrʌdʒəri/ *noun* hard boring work ○ *Most of the work in the office is sheer drudgery.*

① **drug** /drʌg/ *noun* **1.** a medicine ○ *They have found a new drug for people with arthritis.* **2.** an illegal substance which affects people physically or mentally when they take it ○ *The customs are looking for such things as drugs or alcohol.* ■ *verb* (**drugs, drugging, drugged**) to give a person or animal a drug, or put a drug in their food or drink, to make them unconscious ○ *They drugged him and took him away in a car.* ○ *The dog's food had been drugged with something to make him sleep.*

③ **drugstore** /ˈdrʌgstɔː/ *noun US* a shop where medicines can be bought, as well as many other goods such as shampoo, writing paper, etc.

drum /drʌm/ *noun* **1.** a large round musical instrument which you hit with a stick ○ *He plays the drums in the band.* **2.** a large barrel or container shaped like a cylinder ○ *oil drums* ■ *verb* (**drums, drumming, drummed**) **1.** to play on a drum **2.** to hit something frequently ○ *He drummed his fingers on the table.*

drum into *phrasal verb* □ **to drum something into someone** to make someone learn something ○ *My grandfather drummed it into me that I had to be polite to customers.*

drummer /ˈdrʌmə/ *noun* a person who plays the drums

① **drunk** /drʌŋk/ *adj* excited or ill from drinking too much alcohol ■ *noun* a person who is drunk ■ past participle of **drink**

drunkard /ˈdrʌŋkəd/ *noun* a person who has a habit of drinking too much alcohol

drunken /ˈdrʌŋkən/ *adj* who has drunk too much alcohol. ◊ **driving**

① **dry** /draɪ/ *adj* (**drier** or **dryer, driest** or **dryest**) **1.** not wet ○ *Don't touch the door – the paint isn't dry yet.* ○ *The soil is dry because it hasn't rained for weeks.* **2.** (*of wine*) not sweet ○ *A dry white wine is served with fish.* ■ *verb* (**dries, drying, dried**) **1.** to become dry ○ *The clothes are drying in the sun.* ○ *Leave the dishes on the draining board to dry.* **2.** to wipe something until it is dry ○ *He dried himself with a towel.*

dry out *phrasal verb* **1.** to become completely dry ○ *Hang up your coat to dry out in front of the fire.* **2.** to try to stop drinking alcohol ○ *He went to a clinic in London to dry out.*

dry up *phrasal verb* **1.** to stop flowing ○ *The heatwave has made the rivers dry up.* ○ *The government grants have dried up and it looks as though the theatre will have to close.* **2.** to stop talking, because you can't remember what you were going to say ○ *He dried up in the middle of his speech, and sat down hurriedly.* ○ *As soon as she got on the stage she dried up.*

dry-clean /ˌdraɪ ˈkliːn/ *verb* to clean clothes or other fabric items with chemicals

dry-cleaner's /draɪ ˈkliːnəz/ *noun* a shop where clothes are dry-cleaned

dryer /ˈdraɪə/ *noun* another spelling of **drier**

dry land /draɪ ˈlænd/ *noun* **1.** the land, not the sea **2.** areas of land prone to severe drought, e.g. deserts and savannas

dual /ˈdjuːəl/ *adj* existing as a pair

dual carriageway /ˌdjuːəl ˈkærɪdʒweɪ/ *noun* a road with two lanes in each direction, with a barrier between the two sides (NOTE: The US term is **two-lane highway**.)

③ **dub** /dʌb/ (**dubs, dubbing, dubbed**) *verb* **1.** to give someone a nickname ○ *At college he was dubbed Tom 'Pigpen' Smith because his room was so dirty.* **2.** to add dialogue to a film in a different language from the original ○ *The film has been dubbed into Swedish.*

dubious /ˈdjuːbiəs/ *adj* thinking that something might not be true or good ○ *Everyone else seems to believe her story, but personally I'm dubious about it.* ○ *I'm dubious about getting involved.*

duchess /ˈdʌtʃɪs/ *noun* the wife of a duke

③ **duck** /dʌk/ *noun* **1.** a common water bird (NOTE: The male is a **drake**, the female a **duck** and the young are **ducklings**.) **2.** the meat of this bird ○ *We're having roast duck for dinner.* ■ *verb* (**ducks, ducking, ducked**) to lower your head quickly to avoid hitting something ○ *She didn't duck in time and the ball hit her on the head.* ○ *He ducked as he went through the low doorway.*

duckling /ˈdʌklɪŋ/ *noun* a young duck ○ *a duck with six little ducklings* ○ *roast duckling and orange sauce*

duct /dʌkt/ *noun* **1.** a tube which carries liquids in the body **2.** a tube which carries air or wires in a building ○ *The central heating ducts caught fire.*

dud /dʌd/ *adj* (**dudder, duddest**) false (*informal*) ○ *He paid me with a dud £10 note.* ■ *noun* something which does not work properly ○ *Most of the fireworks in the box were duds.*

dude /djuːd/ *noun US* **1.** a man who is very interested in clothes ○ *that dude, with his stiff collar and wide pink tie* **2.** a visitor from a city on the East coast to a ranch in the Midwest

① **due** /djuː/ *adj* **1.** expected or likely to happen [~for] ○ *The plan is due at 10.30.* ○ *We're due for a thunderstorm after all this hot weather.* □ **due to do something** expected to do something in future ○ *We are due to leave London Airport at 5 o'clock.* ○ *The children are due to arrive this afternoon.* **2.** owed ○ *This payment is due now.* ■ *adv* straight ○ *The plane flew due west.* ■ *noun* what is deserved ○ *The right to answer her critics publicly is her due.* ◇ **due to** because of ○ *The problems are due to lack of training.* ○ *These worries about health are usually due to not being given enough information.* ◇ **in due course** later ◇ **to give someone their due** to be fair to someone ○ *To give him his due, he works very hard.*

duel /ˈdjuːəl/ *noun* a fight between two people with weapons such as swords or guns ○ *They fought a duel over a girl.* ○ *He challenged the doctor to a duel.* (NOTE: Do not confuse with **dual**.)

dues /djuːz/ *plural noun* money owed as a fee or regular payment

duet /djuːˈet/ *noun* a piece of music played or sung by two people

③ **due to** /ˈdjuː tuː/ *prep* because of ○ *The trains are late due to fog.*

duff /dʌf/ *verb*

duff up *phrasal verb* to beat somebody up

(*slang*)

③ **dug** /dʌg/ past tense and past participle of **dig**

dugout /ˈdʌgaʊt/ *noun* **1.** a hole in the ground which is a shelter for soldiers ○ *They sat in a dugout for hours, waiting for the order to advance.* **2.** a bench by the side of a football pitch where the managers and extra team members sit ○ *The manager was yelling instructions from the dugout.*

duke /djuːk/ *noun* a nobleman of the highest rank. ◊ **duchess**

③ **dull** /dʌl/ *adj* **1.** not exciting or interesting ○ *The story is rather dull.* ○ *What's so interesting about old churches? – I find them dull.* **2.** (*of weather*) grey and cloudy ○ *a dull cloudy day* **3.** (*of colours*) not bright ○ *They painted the sitting room a dull green.*

③ **dumb** /dʌm/ *adj* unable to speak (NOTE: Some people avoid this term because it causes offence and prefer to say **speech-impaired.**)

dumbfounded /dʌmˈfaʊndɪd/ *adj* greatly surprised

dummy /ˈdʌmi/ (*plural* **dummies**) *noun* a plastic object, given to a baby to suck in order to stop it from crying ○ *The baby sat sucking a dummy.*

③ **dump** /dʌmp/ *noun* a large area where rubbish is taken ○ *Take your rubbish to the municipal dump.* ■ *verb* (**dumps, dumping, dumped**) **1.** to put something heavy on the ground, especially in a careless way ○ *She just dumped her suitcases in the hall.* **2.** to throw something away, to get rid of something ○ *Someone has dumped an old pram in the car park.*

dumpling /ˈdʌmplɪŋ/ *noun* a small ball of dough served with hot meat

dune /djuːn/ *noun* a hill of sand

dung /dʌŋ/ *noun* solid waste from animals, especially cattle, often used as fertiliser

dungarees /ˌdʌŋgəˈriːz/ *plural noun* working clothes, formed of a pair of trousers and a bib covering the chest, usually of thick blue cloth, and worn over ordinary clothes ○ *The workmen came into the café in their dungarees.*

dungeon /ˈdʌndʒən/ *noun* a dark and unpleasant underground prison

dunk /dʌŋk/ (**dunks, dunking, dunked**) *verb* to dip a biscuit or other food into a liquid

dunno /dəˈnəʊ/ *contr* don't know (*informal*) ○ *Whose car is that? – I dunno.*

duo /ˈdjuːəʊ/ *noun* **1.** two people, usually two performers ○ *a TV comedy duo* **2.** same as **duet**

dupe /djuːp/ *noun* a person who has been tricked ○ *He was the dupe of a Russian businessman.* ■ *verb* (**dupes, duping, duped**) □ **to dupe someone into doing something** to trick someone into doing something ○ *They duped him into giving them all the cash he had in his wallet.*

duplicate[1] /ˈdjuːplɪkət/ *adj* made as a copy of something ○ *Put the duplicate invoices in the file.* ■ *noun* a copy ○ *She sent the invoice and filed the duplicate.*

duplicate[2] /ˈdjuːplɪkeɪt/ (**duplicates, duplicating, duplicated**) *verb* **1.** to make a copy of a document such as a letter ○ *She duplicated the letter and put the copy into a file.* **2.** to do again something which has already been done ○ *Keep a note of where you got to – I don't want to duplicate your work.*

duplication /ˌdjuːplɪˈkeɪʃ(ə)n/ *noun* **1.** the act of copying or repeating something exactly **2.** an exact copy or repeat

durable /ˈdjʊərəb(ə)l/ *adj* staying strong even when used for a long time ○ *You need a really durable floor covering in a kitchen.*

③ **duration** /djʊˈreɪʃ(ə)n/ *noun* the period of time for which something lasts

duress /djʊˈres/ *noun* force or illegal threats of force used to make someone do something

① **during** /ˈdjʊərɪŋ/ *prep* while something is going on ○ *Conditions were bad during the war.*

dusk /dʌsk/ *noun* the period in the evening just before it gets dark

③ **dust** /dʌst/ *noun* a thin layer of dry dirt ○ *The room had never been cleaned – there was dust everywhere.* ○ *A tiny speck of dust got in my eye.* (NOTE: no plural) ■ *verb* (**dusts, dusting, dusted**) to remove dust from something ○ *Don't forget to dust the Chinese bowls carefully.*

③ **dustbin** /ˈdʌstbɪn/ *noun* a large container for rubbish, kept outside a house

duster /ˈdʌstə/ *noun* a cloth for removing dust

dust jacket /ˈdʌst ˌdʒækɪt/ *noun* a paper cover round a book

③ **dustman** /ˈdʌstmən/ (*plural* **dustmen**) *noun* a person employed by a town to collect rubbish

dustpan /ˈdʌstpæn/ *noun* a small flat container for brushing dirt into

dusty /ˈdʌsti/ (**dustier, dustiest**) *adj* covered with dust

dutiful /ˈdjuːtɪf(ə)l/ *adj* who does what should be done

① **duty** /ˈdjuːti/ *noun* (*plural* **duties**) **1.** something which you are legally or morally expected to do ○ *We have a duty to inform the authorities about what we saw.* **2.** a tax which has to be paid [~on] ○ *duty on perfume* ■ *plural noun* **duties** different jobs that have to be done as part of your official work ○ *One of his duties is to see that the main doors are locked at night.* ◇ **on duty** doing official work which you have to do in a job ○ *He's on duty from 9.00 to 6.00.* ○ *She's been on duty all day.*

duty-free /ˌdjuːti ˈfriː/ *adj, adv* sold with no tax to be paid ○ *He bought a duty-free watch at the airport* or *He bought the watch duty-free.*

duvet /ˈduːveɪ/ *noun* a bag full of feathers, used as a covering for a bed

DVD /ˌdiː viː ˈdiː/ *noun* an optical disc that can hold images and sound. Full form **digital video disc**

dwarf /dwɔːf/ *noun* a person of smaller than normal height (NOTE: Some people avoid this term as it can cause offence and prefer **person of short stature** or **person of restricted growth**.) ■ *verb* (**dwarfs, dwarfing, dwarfed**) to make something look very small ○ *His house is dwarfed by the office block next door.*

dwell /dwel/ (**dwells, dwelling, dwelt** or **dwelled**) *verb* **1.** □ **to dwell on something** to keep thinking or talking about a problem ○ *It's best not to dwell too much on your financial situation.* **2.** to live somewhere (*literary*)

dweller /ˈdwelə/ *noun, suffix* a person who lives in a place ○ *Many city-dwellers have cottages in the country where they go for weekends.* ○ *Prehistoric man was a cave-dweller.*

② **dwelling** /ˈdwelɪŋ/ *noun* a place to live (*formal*)

dwindle /ˈdwɪnd(ə)l/ (**dwindles, dwindling, dwindled**) *verb* to get less gradually

dye /daɪ/ *noun* a substance used to colour cloth ○ *synthetic dyes* ○ *vegetable dyes* ■ *verb* (**dyes, dyeing, dyed**) to stain with a colour ○ *She dyed her hair green.* (NOTE: Do not confuse with **die**.)

③ **dying** /ˈdaɪɪŋ/ present participle of **die**

dyke /daɪk/, **dike** *noun* **1.** a long wall of earth to keep water from flooding land ○ *They built dykes along the river.* ○ *With this storm blowing from the east, do you think the dykes will hold?* **2.** a long ditch for rainwater ○ *It rained all month, and the dykes were full.* **3.** a lesbian (*offensive*)

dynamic /daɪˈnæmɪk/ *adj* very energetic and with a strong personality

dynamite /ˈdaɪnəmaɪt/ *noun* **1.** a powerful explosive ○ *They used dynamite to blow up the old building.* **2.** something or someone that has a very powerful effect ○ *This news is dynamite!*

dynamo /ˈdaɪnəməʊ/ *noun* **1.** a small piece of equipment for making electricity ○ *The electric light works by a dynamo attached to the back wheel.* **2.** a very energetic person

dynasty /ˈdɪnəsti/ (*plural* **dynasties**) *noun* **1.** a family of rulers, following one after the other ○ *The Ming dynasty ruled China from 1368 to 1644.* ○ *Henry VII founded the Tudor dynasty in 1487.* **2.** a period of rule by members of the same family ○ *The Great Wall of China was built during the Tsin dynasty.*

dysentery /ˈdɪs(ə)ntri/ *noun* an infection of the intestines, causing bleeding and diarrhoea

dysfunctional /dɪsˈfʌŋkʃən(ə)l/ *adj* **1.** unable to relate to other people emotionally and socially **2.** failing to work properly

dyslexia /dɪsˈleksiə/ *noun* a medical condition in which a person is not able to read and spell correctly

E

e /iː/, **E** *noun* the fifth letter of the alphabet, between D and F

E *abbr* **1.** east **2.** eastern

① **each** /iːtʃ/ *adj* every ○ *Each five pound note has a number.* ○ *He was holding a towel in each hand.* ○ *Each one of us has a separate office.* ■ *pron* **1.** every person ○ *They have two houses each* or *Each of them has two houses.* ○ *She gave them each five pounds* or *She gave them five pounds each* or *She gave each of them five pounds.* **2.** every thing ○ *Each of the books has three hundred pages* or *The books have three hundred pages each.*

① **each other** /ˌiːtʃ ˈʌðə/ *pron* the other one of two people or of two things ○ *They were shouting at each other.* ○ *We always send each other presents on our birthdays.* ○ *The boxes fit into each other.*

eager /ˈiːgə/ *adj* wanting to do something very much

eagerly /ˈiːgəli/ *adv* in a way that shows that you want something very much

eagle /ˈiːg(ə)l/ *noun* a large bird of prey

eagle-eyed /ˌiːg(ə)l ˈaɪd/ *adj* with very good eyesight

① **ear** /ɪə/ *noun* **1.** one of the parts on either side of your head which you hear with ○ *Rabbits have long ears.* ○ *Have you washed behind your ears?* **2.** an ability to sense sound ○ *He has a good ear for music.* □ **to play an instrument by ear** to play without reading the printed notes of music ○ *She can play the piano by ear.* **3.** the top part of a plant such as wheat or barley with the seeds ◇ **to play it by ear** to do what you think is right at the time (*informal*) ○ *We won't make a plan, we'll just play it by ear and see how it goes.* ◇ **to be up to your ears in** to be very busy with (*informal*) ○ *He's up to his ears in work.* ◇ **to have or keep your ear to the ground** to follow what is happening and know all about something

earache /ˈɪəreɪk/ *noun* a pain in your ear

eardrum /ˈɪədrʌm/ *noun* a part of the ear which vibrates with sound and passes the vibrations to the inner ear

earl /ɜːl/ *noun* a nobleman of middle rank, below a marquess and above a viscount. ◊ **countess**

earlier /ˈɜːliə/ *adj* relating to a time before now or before a time being mentioned ○ *an earlier version of the book* ○ *I'll try to catch an earlier train.* ■ *adv* before now or before a time being mentioned ○ *Can't you come any earlier than Tuesday?* ○ *I tried to phone earlier but you were out.*

earliest /ˈɜːliəst/ *adj* the soonest time that something could happen ○ *The earliest I can deliver it is Tuesday.*

earlobe /ˈɪələʊb/ *noun* the lower part of the outside of the ear

① **early** /ˈɜːlɪ/ *adv* **1.** before the usual time ○ *The plane arrived five minutes early.* ○ *We must get up early tomorrow morning if we want to catch the first boat to France.* **2.** at the beginning of a period of time ○ *We went out early in the evening.* ○ *The snow came early in the year.*

early bird /ˈɜːli bɜːd/ *noun* someone who likes to get up early and work before breakfast, and who does not stay up late at night

earmark /ˈɪəmɑːk/ (**earmarks, earmarking, earmarked**) *verb* to reserve something for a special purpose

② **earn** /ɜːn/ (**earns, earning, earned**) *verb* to be paid money for working ○ *He earns £20,000 a year.* ○ *How much does a bus driver earn?*

earner /ˈɜːnə/ *noun* a thing or person that earns money

earnest /ˈɜːnɪst/ *adj* serious ○ *They were engaged in earnest conversation.* ◇ **in earnest** with serious determination ○ *After a slow start the discussions began in earnest in July.*

earnings /ˈɜːnɪŋz/ *plural noun* a salary, the money which you earn from work ○ *His earnings are not enough to pay the rent.*

earphones /ˈɪəfəʊnz/ *plural noun* a piece of equipment which you put on your ears to listen to sounds from a machine such as a radio or telephone ○ *She took off her earphones when I asked her a question.*

earplug /ˈɪəplʌɡ/ *noun* a piece of plastic, rubber or other material which you put in your ears to stop you hearing loud sounds

earring /ˈɪərɪŋ/ *noun* a piece of jewellery worn attached to part of the ear

earshot /ˈɪəʃɒt/ *noun* □ **within** *or* **in earshot** near enough to hear something ○ *Everyone within earshot heard the details of her divorce.* □ **out of earshot** not near enough to hear something ○ *Now that she's out of earshot, you can tell me what really happened.*

ear-splitting /ˈɪə ˌsplɪtɪŋ/ *adj* extremely loud

① **earth** /ɜːθ/ *noun* **1.** *also* **Earth** the planet on which we live ○ *The Earth goes round the Sun once in twenty-four hours.* ○ *The signals from the spacecraft came back to earth.* **2.** the brown substance in which plants grow ○ *Put some earth in the plant pot and then sow your cucumber seeds.* ■ *verb* (**earths, earthing, earthed**) to connect an electrical appliance to the ground ○ *Household appliances should be properly earthed.* (NOTE: The US term is to **ground**.) ◇ **it costs the earth** it costs a great deal of money (*informal*) ○ *It wouldn't cost the earth to have the house repainted.*

earthenware /ˈɜːθ(ə)nweə/ *noun* objects such as pots and dishes, made of clay

earthquake /ˈɜːθkweɪk/ *noun* an occasion on which the earth shakes, caused by movement of the earth's surface (NOTE: also called simply a **quake**)

earth science /ˌɜːθ ˈsaɪəns/ *noun* a science that studies the Earth, e.g. geology

earthy /ˈɜːθi/ (**earthier, earthiest**) *adj* (*of humour*) coarse or rude

ease /iːz/ *noun* a lack of difficulty ○ *He won the first round with the greatest of ease.* ○ *The bottle has a wide mouth for ease of use.* ■ *verb* (**eases, easing, eased**) to make less painful ○ *A couple of aspirins should ease the pain.*

easel /ˈiːz(ə)l/ *noun* a vertical frame on legs to support a blackboard or painting

easier, easiest /ˈiːziə, ˈiːziəst/ ♦ **easy**

① **easily** /ˈiːzɪli/ *adv* **1.** without any difficulty ○ *I passed my driving test easily.* ○ *I can easily get there by 9 o'clock.* **2.** a lot (*for emphasis before comparatives or superlatives*) ○ *Her work was easily better than yours.* ○ *He is easily the tallest man in the team.* ○ *Our shop is easily the biggest in the High Street.*

① **east** /iːst/ *noun* **1.** the direction in which the sun rises ○ *The sun rises in the east and sets in the west.* ○ *Germany is to the east of France.* ○ *The wind is blowing from the east.* **2. East** the countries in the eastern part of the world, e.g. China ■ *adj* relating to the east ○ *The east coast is the coldest part of the country.* ■ *adv* towards the east ○ *The kitchen windows face east, so we get the morning sun.* ○ *Drive east along the motorway for twenty miles.*

eastbound /ˈiːstbaʊnd/ *adj* travelling towards the east

③ **Easter** /ˈiːstə/ *noun* a Christian festival, in March or April, celebrating the occasion on which Jesus Christ died and then came back to life again

Easter egg /ˈiːstər eɡ/ *noun* a chocolate or sugar egg eaten at Easter

easterly /ˈiːstəli/ *adj* **1.** towards the east **2.** (*of a wind*) blowing from the east

② **eastern** /ˈiːst(ə)n/ *adj* from, of or in the east ○ *The best snow is in the eastern part of the mountains.*

easterner /ˈiːstənə/, **Easterner** *noun* a person who lives in or comes from the east of a country or region

easternmost /ˈiːst(ə)nməʊst/ *adj* furthest to the east

eastward /ˈiːstwəd/ *adj, adv* towards the east

eastwards /ˈiːstwədz/ *adv* towards the east

① **easy** /ˈiːzi/ *adj* not difficult, or not needing a lot of effort ○ *The test was easy, in fact much easier than I expected.* ○ *My boss is very easy to get on with.* ◇ **easier said than done** more difficult than you think it will be ○ *Finding the right house was easier said then done.* ◇ **to take things** or **it easy** to rest and not do any hard work ○ *The doctor told him to take things easy for a time after his operation.*

easy chair /ˈiːzi tʃeə/ *noun* a large comfortable armchair

easy-going /ˌiːzi ˈɡəʊɪŋ/ *adj* friendly and not very critical

easy listening /ˌiːzi ˈlɪs(ə)nɪŋ/ *noun* slow or quiet popular music

① **eat** /iːt/ (**eats, eating, ate, eaten**) *verb* **1.** to put food into your mouth and swallow it ○ *I'm hungry – is there anything to eat?* ○ *We haven't eaten anything since breakfast.* ○ *The children ate all the sandwiches.* ○ *Eat as much as you like for £5.95!* ○

You'll get thin if you don't eat. **2.** to have a meal ○ *He was still eating his breakfast when I arrived.* ○ *We are eating at home tonight.* ○ *Have you eaten yet?*

eat away *phrasal verb* to destroy something by gradually wearing it away

eat out *phrasal verb* to have a meal in a restaurant

eat up *phrasal verb* **1.** to eat everything ○ *She ate it all up in a matter of seconds.* ○ *Come on, eat up – it's time to go.* **2.** to use large amounts of something ○ *Buying a car has eaten up my savings.*

eatable /'iːtəb(ə)l/ *adj* which is good enough to eat

eater /'iːtə/ *noun* a person who eats

eatery /'iːtəri/ (*plural* **eateries**) *noun US* a restaurant, a place where you can eat (*informal*)

eating disorder /'iːtɪŋ dɪsˌɔːdə/ *noun* an emotional disorder manifesting as an obsessive attitude to food

eat into *phrasal verb* to use more of something than expected ○ *The delays have eaten into the time we allowed for visiting London.*

eau de cologne /ˌəʊ də kə'ləʊn/ *noun* a type of light perfume

eaves /iːvz/ *plural noun* the edge of a roof which sticks out over the wall beneath it

eavesdrop /'iːvzdrɒp/ (**eavesdrops, eavesdropping, eavesdropped**) *verb* to listen to a conversation which you are not supposed to hear

ebb /eb/ *noun* the regular process of the level of the sea water at a coast becoming lower ■ *verb* (**ebbs, ebbing, ebbed**) **1.** (*of the sea level at a coast*) to become lower ○ *Boats at anchor swing round to point upstream when the tide starts to ebb.* **2.** *also* **ebb away** to become weaker or less gradually ○ *He couldn't hold on to the rope any longer; his strength was ebbing away.* ◇ **to be at a low ebb** to be in a bad state ○ *After his interview, his morale was at a low ebb.* ○ *The manager asked them to try harder, just when their energy was at its lowest ebb.*

e-business /'iː ˌbɪznəs/ *noun* **1.** business that is conducted on the Internet **2.** a company that uses Internet technology

eccentric /ɪk'sentrɪk/ *adj* unusual in a way that is strange ■ *noun* a person who behaves in an unusual way ○ *In his old age, he became something of an eccentric.*

eccentricity /ˌeksen'trɪsɪti/ *noun* strange behaviour

ecclesiastical /ɪˌkliːzi'æstɪk(ə)l/ *adj* referring to the Christian Church

echelon /'eʃəlɒn/ *noun* a group of people at a particular level in an organisation or community ○ *the upper echelons of management* ○ *the lower echelons of the armed forces*

echo /'ekəʊ/ *noun* (*plural* **echoes**) a sound which is repeated such as when you shout in a place such as a tunnel ○ *We could hear the echo of voices in the tunnel.* ○ *If you go to the Whispering Gallery in the dome of St Paul's Cathedral you can hear the echo very clearly.* ■ *verb* (**echoes, echoing, echoed**) **1.** (*of sound*) to make an echo ○ *Their voices echoed down the tunnel.* **2.** to repeat ○ *The newspaper article echoed the opinions put forward in the minister's speech.*

eclectic /ɪ'klektɪk/ *adj* taking ideas from several different sources

eclipse /ɪ'klɪps/ (**eclipsing, eclipsed**) *verb* **1.** to hide the sun or moon by passing in front of it ○ *The sun is eclipsed by the moon.* **2.** to be more successful than someone else ○ *She was eclipsed by her younger sister.*

eco-friendly /'iːkəʊ ˌfrendli/ *adj* intended to have no harmful effect on the natural environment and its inhabitants

ecological /ˌiːkə'lɒdʒɪk(ə)l/ *adj* referring to ecology or the environment

ecology /ɪ'kɒlədʒi/ *noun* the study of the relationship between plants and animals and their environment (NOTE: + **ecologist** *n*)

e-commerce /'iː ˌkɒmɜːs/ *noun* buying and selling things online, especially over the Internet

① **economic** /ˌiːkə'nɒmɪk/ *adj* **1.** relating to the economy ○ *I don't agree with the government's economic policy.* ○ *The government has introduced controls to solve the current economic crisis.* ○ *The country enjoyed a period of economic growth in the 1980s.* **2.** not costing much money ○ *The flat is let at an economic rent.* **3.** using money well ○ *It is hardly economic for us to run two cars.*

economical /ˌiːkə'nɒmɪk(ə)l/ *adj* which saves money or resources

economic migrant /ˌiːkənɒmɪk 'maɪgrənt/ *noun* a person who moves to live in another country where living conditions are better

③ **economics** /ˌiːkə'nɒmɪks/ *noun* the scientific study of how money functions in trade, society and politics ○ *She is studying for an economics degree.*

economise /ɪ'kɒnəmaɪz/ (**economises, economising, economised**), **economize** *verb* to try not to waste something by using as little as possible [~on] ○ *Our bills are too high so we'll have to economise on electricity this winter.*

economist /ɪ'kɒnəmɪst/ *noun* a person who specialises in the study of money and its uses

① **economy** /ɪ'kɒnəmi/ *noun* **1.** the way in which a country makes and uses money, or the financial state of a country **2.** something you do to avoid wasting money or materials ○ *She tried to make a few economies like buying cheaper brands of washing-up liquid.* ■ *adj* cheap, often because of being sold in large sizes or quantities ○ *an economy size notepad* ○ *If you travel midweek you can usually get an economy fare.*

economy class /ɪ'kɒnəmi klɑːs/ *noun* an air fare which is cheaper than first class or business class

economy drive /ɪ'kɒnəmi draɪv/ *noun* an effort to save money or materials

ecosystem /'iːkəʊsɪstəm/ *noun* a system which includes all the organisms of an area and the environment in which they live

ecotourism /'iːkəʊˌtʊərɪz(ə)m/ *noun* tourism that tries to avoid ecological damage to places visited

ecstasy /'ekstəsi/ *noun* **1.** great happiness ○ *She was in sheer ecstasy over her engagement.* ○ *These chocolates are pure ecstasy.* **2.** a dangerous drug which makes you have hallucinations

ecstatic /ɪk'stætɪk/ *adj* very happy or enthusiastic

eczema /'eksɪmə/ *noun* an uncomfortable skin condition with an itchy rash and blisters, but which is not contagious

eddy /'edi/ (*plural* **eddies**) *noun* a circular movement of water or dust ○ *Dust eddies were being raised by the wind.* ○ *He got into an eddy under the waterfall.*

① **edge** /edʒ/ *noun* **1.** the part around the outside of something ○ *He put his plate down on the edge of the table.* ○ *She lay down on the roof and looked over the edge.* ○ *Can you stand this coin on its edge?* **2.** an imaginary line where an area ends [~of/] ○ *He lived in a house at the edge of the forest.* ○ *The factory is built right on the edge of the town.* **3.** the sharp thin part of a knife or tool for cutting **4.** an advantage □ **to have the edge on a rival company** to have a slightly larger share of the market than another company ■ *verb* (**edges, edging, edged**) to move in a slow, careful way ○ *He started edging towards the door.* ◇ **on edge** nervous or worried ○ *Everyone was on edge, waiting for the telephone call.*

edging /'edʒɪŋ/ *noun* a decoration along the edge of something

edgy /'edʒi/ *adj* **1.** nervous or worried **2.** unusual and interesting

③ **edible** /'edɪb(ə)l/ *adj* good enough or safe to eat

edict /'iːdɪkt/ *noun* a public announcement of a law

edifice /'edɪfɪs/ *noun* a large building (*formal*)

edit /'edɪt/ (**edits, editing, edited**) *verb* **1.** to be in charge of a newspaper or magazine ○ *He edited the 'Sunday Express' for more than twenty years.* **2.** to prepare a book for publishing by doing such things as correcting mistakes ○ *I am editing a volume of 20th-century poetry.* **3.** to prepare something such as a film to make it ready to be shown ○ *Once the film has been edited it will run for about 90 minutes.*

③ **edition** /ɪ'dɪʃ(ə)n/ *noun* a number of copies of a book or newspaper printed at the same time ○ *The book of poems was published in an edition of one thousand copies.*

② **editor** /'edɪtə/ *noun* **1.** a journalist in charge of a newspaper or part of a newspaper ○ *He wrote to the editor of 'The Times' asking for a job.* ○ *She is the sports editor of the local paper.* **2.** a person who edits books

editorial /ˌedɪ'tɔːriəl/ *adj* referring to editors or editing ○ *He has overall editorial control of the series.* ■ *noun* a main article written by the editor of a newspaper ○ *Did you read today's editorial in 'The Times'?*

educate /'edjʊkeɪt/ (**educates, educating, educated**) *verb* to teach someone in a school or college, or give them information that they need ○ *She was educated in Switzerland.* ○ *We need to educate young people about the dangers of alcohol.*

educated /'edjʊkeɪtɪd/ *adj* having been to school and university

① **education** /ˌedjʊ'keɪʃ(ə)n/ *noun* the system of teaching, or of being taught or given information about something

① **educational** /ˌedjʊ'keɪʃ(ə)nəl/ *adj* relating to education, teaching and schools ○ *a campaign to improve educational standards* ○ *This game for 3– to 5-year-olds is very educational.*

educator /ˈedjʊkeɪtə/ *noun* a person who teaches, especially someone who teaches people how to teach

Edwardian /edˈwɔːdiən/ *adj* referring to the time of King Edward VII (1901 – 1910)

eel /iːl/ *noun* a long thin fish which looks like a snake

eerie /ˈɪəri/ (**eerier, eeriest**) *adj* strange and frightening (NOTE: + **eerily** *adv*)

① **effect** /ɪˈfekt/ *noun* a result or influence [~on/upon] ○ *The cuts in spending will have a serious effect on the hospital.* ○ *The cream has had no effect on her rash.* ○ *The effects of the shock took some time to wear off.* ■ *plural noun* **1.** sounds, images or displays that are created for a film or event **2.** the things that you own (*formal*) ■ *verb* (**effects, effecting, effected**) to carry something out (*formal*) ○ *She was able to effect a number of changes during her time in charge.* ◇ **in effect** actually ○ *In effect, he gave up trying.* ◇ **or words to that effect** or something with that meaning ○ *She said she wouldn't pay, or words to that effect.* ◇ **to come into** or**take effect** to start to be official or legal ○ *The order comes into effect on 1 January.* ◇ **with effect from** starting from (*formal*) ○ *Prices will be increased by 10% with effect from January 1st.*

① **effective** /ɪˈfektɪv/ *adj* **1.** producing the result that is wanted ○ *His method of keeping the children quiet is very effective.* ○ *Advertising on TV is a very effective way of selling.* **2.** taking effect ○ *an order which is effective from January 1st* (NOTE: + **effectiveness** *n*)

① **effectively** /ɪˈfektɪvli/ *adv* **1.** really, although the situation might appear different ○ *Although there was another game to play in the series, they had effectively won the gold medal.* **2.** in a way which produces the result that is wanted ○ *The floodlighting worked very effectively.*

effeminate /ɪˈfemɪnət/ *adj* referring to a man who behaves in a feminine way (*disapproving*)

effervescent /ˌefəˈves(ə)nt/ *adj* **1.** which makes bubbles ○ *The water will become effervescent if you put this tablet into the glass.* **2.** lively and excited ○ *Her effervescent good humour made the party go with a swing.*

③ **efficiency** /ɪˈfɪʃ(ə)nsi/ *noun* being able to produce a good result without wasting time, money or effort ○ *How can we improve the efficiency of our working methods?* ○ *She is known for her extreme efficiency.*

② **efficient** /ɪˈfɪʃ(ə)nt/ *adj* able to work well and do what is necessary without wasting time, money or effort ○ *He needs an efficient assistant to look after him.* ○ *The new system of printing invoices is very efficient.* □ **a fuel-efficient car** a car which does not use much petrol

efficiently /ɪˈfɪʃ(ə)ntli/ *adv* in an efficient way

effigy /ˈefɪdʒiː/ (*plural* **effigies**) *noun* a rough model of a person, usually someone unpopular

effluent /ˈefluənt/ *noun* liquid waste, especially from factories or industrial processes

① **effort** /ˈefət/ *noun* the use of the mind or body to do something ○ *Lifting the box took considerable physical effort.* ○ *He's made a big effort to learn Spanish.* □ **an effort to do something** an attempt to achieve something ○ *The changes are part of an effort to improve productivity.* ○ *She's already written to three addresses in an effort to contact the owner.* ■ *plural noun* activities for a particular purpose ○ *Thanks to her efforts, we have collected more than £10,000 for the children's hospital.*

effortless /ˈefətləs/ *adj* without needing to use any energy

effrontery /ɪˈfrʌntəri/ *noun* rudeness

effusive /ɪˈfjuːsɪv/ *adj* showing too much emotion when talking about something

EFL *abbr* English as a Foreign Language ○ *She is an EFL teacher.* ○ *He's taking an EFL course.*

e.g., eg *abbr* e.g.

egalitarian /ɪˌgælɪˈteəriən/ *adj* believing in equality or treating all people equally

① **egg** /eg/ *noun* **1.** a round object with a hard shell, produced by a female bird or, e.g. snake, in which a baby bird develops ○ *The owl laid three eggs in the nest.* ○ *Turtles lay their eggs in the sand.* **2.** a chicken's egg, used as food ○ *You need three eggs to make this cake.* ◇ **don't put all your eggs in one basket** don't risk everything on only one project

egg on③ *phrasal verb* to encourage someone to do something, especially something naughty

eggplant /ˈegplɑːnt/ *noun* a dark purple shiny fruit of a small plant, used as a vegetable (NOTE: used mainly in American English. The more common British term is **aubergine**.)

eggshell /'egʃel/ *noun* the hard outside part of an egg

egg white /'eg waɪt/ *noun* the clear liquid found in an egg, which turns solid and white when cooked

ego /'iːgəʊ/ *noun* your high opinion of yourself

egocentric /ˌiːgəʊ'sentrɪk/ *adj* interested only in yourself, not thinking of anyone else

egoism /'iːgəʊɪz(ə)m/ *noun* thinking only about yourself, and not bothering about anyone else

egotism /'iːgəʊtɪz(ə)m/ *noun* thinking that you are better than anyone else

egotist /'iːgətɪst/ *noun* a person who thinks he or she is better than everyone else

egotistic /ˌegə'tɪstɪk/, **egotistical** /ˌegə'tɪstɪk(ə)l/ *adj* thinking you are better than everyone else

ego trip /'iːgəʊ trɪp/ *noun* an activity designed to improve your good opinion of yourself (*informal*)

③ **eh** /eɪ/ *interj* used when asking questions ○ *What a laugh, eh?* ○ *What about a drink, eh?* ○ *Eh? What did he say?*

① **eight** /eɪt/ *noun* the number 8

① **eighteen** /ˌeɪ'tiːn/ *noun* the number 18

① **eighteenth** /eɪ'tiːnθ/, **18th** *adj* relating to number 18 in a series ■ *noun* number 18 in a series

18-wheeler /ˌeɪtiːn 'wiːlə/ *noun* a large lorry with 18 wheels

eighth /eɪtθ/, **8th** *adj* relating to number 8 in a series ■ *noun* number 8 in a series (NOTE: **eighth** is usually written **8th** in dates: *April 8th, 1999; September 8th, 1866* (American style is **8 September 1866**), say: 'the eighth of September' or 'September the eighth' (American style is 'September eighth'). For names of kings and queens, **eighth** is usually written **VIII**: *King Henry VIII*, say: 'King Henry the Eighth'.)

① **eightieth** /'eɪtiəθ/, **80th** *adj* relating to number 80 in a series ■ *noun* number 80 in a series

① **eighty** /'eɪti/ *noun* the number 80 □ **eighties** the numbers between 80 and 89

① **either** /'aɪðə, 'iːðə/ *adj, pron* **1.** one or the other ○ *You can use either computer – it doesn't matter which.* ○ *I don't like either of them.* **2.** each of two; both ○ *There are trees on either side of the road.* ○ *Some people don't take sugar in their coffee, some don't take milk, and some don't take either.* ■ *adv* used with two negatives to show that two people or things are similar in some way ○ *He isn't Irish and he isn't Scottish either.* ○ *She doesn't want to go, and I don't want to go either.* ○ *The report wasn't on the TV news, and it wasn't on the radio either.*

ejaculate /ɪ'dʒækjʊleɪt/ (**ejaculates, ejaculating, ejaculated**) *verb* **1.** to send out semen from the penis **2.** to exclaim (*literary*) (NOTE: + **ejaculation** *n*)

eject /ɪ'dʒekt/ (**ejects, ejecting, ejected**) *verb* **1.** to throw something out ○ *The chairman called in the police to eject the troublemakers from the meeting.* **2.** to escape from an aircraft using an ejector seat ○ *The pilot ejected safely.* (NOTE: + **ejection** *n*)

eke *verb*

eke out *phrasal verb* to use something a little bit at a time, in order to make it last longer ◇ **to eke out a living** to earn or live on very little money ○ *She ekes out a miserable existence as a cleaner.*

elaborate[1] /ɪ'læb(ə)rət/ *adj* very detailed, very complicated ○ *an elaborate dessert of cream, fruit and cake*

elaborate[2] /ɪ'læbəreɪt/ (**elaborates, elaborating, elaborated**) *verb* to go into details ○ *It's a very complicated plan so I won't elaborate.* ○ *He refused to elaborate any further on her reasons for leaving.*

elapse /ɪ'læps/ (**elapses, elapsing, elapsed**) *verb* (*of time*) to pass

elastic /ɪ'læstɪk/ *noun* a material which stretches ■ *adj* able to stretch and contract ○ *She was wearing tight shorts made of some elastic material.*

elastic band /ɪ'læstɪk bænd/ *noun* a thin circle of rubber for holding things together

Elastoplast /ɪ'læstəplɑːst/ *trademark* a small strip of cloth which can be stuck to the skin to cover a wound

elated /ɪ'leɪtɪd/ *adj* very excited and pleased

elation /ɪ'leɪʃ(ə)n/ *noun* a strong feeling of excitement and pleasure

③ **elbow** /'elbəʊ/ *noun* the joint in the middle of your arm ○ *He sat with his elbows on the table.* ○ *She nudged him with her elbow.*

elbow-room /'elbəʊ ruːm/ *noun* space to move about (*informal*)

elder /'eldə/ *adj* older ○ *I have two elder brothers.* ○ *She brought her elder sister.* (NOTE: **elder** is a comparative adjective, used mainly of brothers or sisters. It is never followed by **than**, when **older** should be used.) ■ *noun* an older person ○ *Mary is the elder of the two.* ○ *Which brother is the elder?* ○ *The village elders met to discuss the plan.* ○ *Children should have respect for their elders and betters.*

② **elderly** /'eldəli/ *adj* a more polite word than 'old' used for describing someone who has had a long life ○ *An elderly man sat down beside her.* ○ *My mother is now rather elderly and doesn't drive any more.*

elder statesman /ˌeldə 'steɪtsmən/ *noun* an older and wiser politician

eldest /'eldəst/ *adj* the oldest of a series of people ○ *This is John, my eldest son.*

② **elect** /ɪ'lekt/ (**elects, electing, elected**) *verb* to choose someone by voting ○ *She was elected MP for the town.* ○ *The president is elected for a term of four years.* ○ *The chairman is elected by the members of the committee.*

-elect /ɪlekt/ *suffix* a person who has been elected but has not yet started the job ○ *She is the president-elect.*

① **election** /ɪ'lekʃən/ *noun* the process of choosing by voting [/~for/~to/~as] ○ *the election of a new treasurer for the club* ○ *election to the general council* ○ *We are holding an election for new representatives.* ○ *After her election as president, the crowds were celebrating.*

electioneering /ɪˌlekʃə'nɪərɪŋ/ *noun* the process of working for an election campaign, making speeches, writing pamphlets and meeting voters

elective /ɪ'lektɪv/ *adj* **1.** requiring to be elected **2.** not obligatory

elector /ɪ'lektə/ *noun* a person who votes or who is able to vote in an election

electoral /ɪ'lekt(ə)rəl/ *adj* referring to an election

electoral college /ɪˌlekt(ə)rəl 'kɒlɪdʒ/ *noun* a group who elect someone such as a president

electoral register /ɪˌlekt(ə)rəl 'redʒɪstə/, **electoral roll** *noun* an official list of names and addresses of people living in a particular area who are eligible to vote in local or national elections

electorate /ɪ'lekt(ə)rət/ *noun* all the people in an area who are able to vote

② **electric** /ɪ'lektrɪk/ *adj* **1.** worked by electricity ○ *Is your cooker electric or gas?* ○ *He plays an electric guitar.* ○ *He cut the wood with an electric saw.* ○ *She gave me an electric toothbrush for Christmas.* **2.** making or carrying electricity ○ *Don't touch those electric wires.* ○ *Electric plugs in the USA are different from those in Britain.* **3.** very exciting ○ *The atmosphere was electric as the votes were being counted.*

③ **electrical** /ɪ'lektrɪk(ə)l/ *adj* relating to electricity ○ *a shop selling electrical appliances* ○ *The college offers courses in electrical engineering.* ○ *They are trying to repair an electrical fault.*

electric chair /ɪˌlektrɪk 'tʃeə/ *noun* a chair attached to a powerful electric current, used in some states of the United States to kill criminals as a punishment

electrician /ɪˌlek'trɪʃ(ə)n/ *noun* a person who works on electrical repairs

② **electricity** /ɪˌlek'trɪsɪti/ *noun* energy used to make light, heat or power ○ *We haven't paid the electricity bill this month.* ○ *The electricity was cut off this morning.* ○ *The heating is run by electricity.* ○ *The cottage is in the mountains and doesn't have any electricity.* (NOTE: no plural)

electrics /ɪ'lektrɪks/ *plural noun* the wires and electrical connections in a building or piece of equipment

electric shock /ɪˌlektrɪk 'ʃɒk/ *noun* a sudden pain when an electric current goes through your body

electrify /ɪ'lektrɪfaɪ/ (**electrifies, electrifying, electrified**) *verb* **1.** to connect to an electric source of power ○ *All the most modern railway lines are electrified.* **2.** to startle and excite someone ○ *She gave an electrifying performance.*

electrocute /ɪ'lektrəkjuːt/ (**electrocutes, electrocuting, electrocuted**) *verb* to hurt or kill someone with an electric shock (NOTE: + **electrocution** *n*)

electrode /ɪ'lektrəʊd/ *noun* one of two points on an electric circuit where the current enters or leaves a battery

electron /ɪ'lektrɒn/ *noun* a basic negative particle in an atom

② **electronic** /ˌelek'trɒnɪk/ *adj* using electricity and very small parts which affect the electric current which passes through them ○ *electronic equipment*

electronics /ˌelek'trɒnɪks/ *noun* the science of the movement of electricity in electronic equipment

electronic tag /ˌelektrɒnɪk 'tæg/ *noun* an electronic device attached to someone such as a convicted criminal, so as to be sure where he or she is

elegant /'elɪgənt/ *adj* very fashionable and stylish

elegy /'elədʒi/ *noun* a sad poem or piece of music about someone who is dead

① **element** /'elɪmənt/ *noun* **1.** a basic chemical substance ○ *Magnesium is a metallic element.* **2.** a basic part of something ○ *I think we have all the elements of a settlement.* **3.** a small amount of something ○ *There was an element of jealousy in her decision.* ■ *plural noun* the weather, usually bad weather ■ *noun* a part which produces heat in a piece of equipment such as an electric heater or cooker ○ *I think the element has burnt out.* ◇ **to be in** or **out of your element** to be happy or unhappy in a particular situation

elemental /ˌelɪ'ment(ə)l/ *adj* wild and uncivilised

elementary /ˌelɪ'ment(ə)ri/ *adj* basic or simple

elementary school /elɪ'mentri skuːl/ *noun US* the first school for children up to around eleven years old (NOTE: The British term is **primary school**.)

elephant /'elɪfənt/ *noun* a very large African or Indian animal, with large ears, a trunk and two long teeth called 'tusks'

elevate /'elɪveɪt/ (**elevates, elevating, elevated**) *verb* to lift something or someone into a higher position (*formal*) (NOTE: + **elevation** *n*)

③ **elevator** /'elɪveɪtə/ *noun US* a machine for moving people up or down from floor to floor inside a building ○ *Take the elevator to the 26th floor.* (NOTE: The British term is **lift**.)

① **eleven** /ɪ'lev(ə)n/ *noun* the number 11

elevenses /ɪ'lev(ə)nzɪz/ *noun* a snack served in the middle of the morning at about 11 o'clock

eleventh, 11th *adj* relating to number 11 in a series □ **at the eleventh hour** at the last minute ○ *The contract was finally signed at the eleventh hour.* ○ *His eleventh-hour decision to stand for election.* ■ *noun* number 11 in a series

elf /elf/ (*plural* **elves**) *noun* a little person in fairy stories

elicit /ɪ'lɪsɪt/ (**elicits, eliciting, elicited**) *verb* to obtain something (NOTE: Do not confuse with **illicit**.)

eligible /'elɪdʒɪb(ə)l/ *adj* **1.** qualifying as suitable for something under certain rules [~for] ○ *The previous president is eligible for re-election.* ○ *She is not eligible for a grant.* **2.** very suitable for getting married to ○ *an eligible bachelor*

eliminate /ɪ'lɪmɪneɪt/ (**eliminates, eliminating, eliminated**) *verb* **1.** to remove something that is not wanted ○ *Using a computer should eliminate all possibility of error.* ○ *Smallpox has been eliminated in most parts of the world.* **2.** to remove someone from a competition [~from] ○ *He came last and so was eliminated from the next round of the contest.*

elimination /ɪˌlɪmɪ'neɪʃ(ə)n/ *noun* the act of eliminating

elision /ɪ'lɪʒ(ə)n/ *noun* the omission of an element of a word or phrase

elite /ɪ'liːt/ *noun* a group of people with more privileges than most others

elitism /ɪ'liːtɪz(ə)m/ *noun* a system of giving more privileges to a small group of people

elitist /ɪ'liːtɪst/ *adj* believing that an elite should have most power in a group or society

Elizabethan /ɪˌlɪzə'biːθ(ə)n/ *adj* referring to the time of Queen Elizabeth I (1558 – 1603)

ellipse /ɪ'lɪps/ *noun* an oval shape

elliptical /ɪ'lɪptɪk(ə)l/ *adj* **1.** oval ○ *The comet follows an elliptical orbit round the sun.* **2.** difficult to understand because of a missing word or phrase

elm /elm/ *noun* a large hardwood tree which grows in temperate areas

elocution /ˌelə'kjuːʃ(ə)n/ *noun* the art of speaking in a clear and elegant way

elongated /'iːlɒŋgeɪtɪd/ *adj* longer than normal

elope /ɪ'ləʊp/ (**elopes, eloping, eloped**) *verb* to run away to get married

eloquent /'eləkwənt/ *adj* convincing and persuasive

① **else** /els/ *adv* other (*used after pronouns*) ○ *What else can I say?* ○ *Everyone else had already left.* ○ *Who else was at the meeting?* ◇ **or else** or if not ○ *We could do it now, or else wait till John comes.* ○ *You must have a ticket, or else you will be thrown off the train by the inspector.*

② **elsewhere** /els'weə/ *adv* somewhere else, in another place ○ *This shop doesn't stock maps, so you'll have to try elsewhere.*

ELT *abbr* English Language Teaching ○ *She's an ELT specialist.*

elucidate /ɪ'luːsɪdeɪt/ (**elucidates, elucidating, elucidated**) *verb* to make something clear or easy to understand

elude /ɪ'luːd/ (**eludes, eluding, eluded**) *verb* **1.** (*of a fact or word*) to be difficult to remember ○ *Her name eludes me.* **2.** to avoid being caught ○ *The protestors managed to elude the security guards.*

elusive /ɪ'luːsɪv/ *adj* difficult to find

'em /əm/ *contr* them (*informal*)

emaciated /ɪ'meɪʃieɪtɪd/ *adj* extremely thin

emaciation /ɪˌmeɪsi'eɪʃ(ə)n/ *noun* being emaciated

email /'iːmeɪl/, **e-mail** *noun* **1.** a system of sending messages from one computer to another, using telephone lines ○ *You can contact me by phone or email if you want.* ○ *I'll give you my email address.* **2.** a message sent by email ○ *I had two emails from him this morning.* ■ *verb* (**emails, emailing, emailed, emailing**; **e-mails, e-mailing, e-mailed, e-mailing**) to send a message to someone using email ○ *I emailed him about the meeting.*

emanate /'emәneɪt/ (**emanating, emanated**) *verb* □ **to emanate from** to come from somewhere (*formal*) ○ *the smell of onions emanating from the kitchen* ○ *Some of these ideas emanate from the government's own think tank.*

emancipation /ɪˌmænsɪ'peɪʃ(ə)n/ *noun* the process of making someone free, or giving someone the right to equal status (NOTE: + **emancipate** *v*)

embalm /ɪm'bɑːm/ (**embalms, embalming, embalmed**) *verb* to treat a dead body with chemicals to preserve it

embankment /ɪm'bæŋkmәnt/ *noun* a wall made along a river bank to prevent the river from overflowing ○ *Entire fields were flooded when the river embankment collapsed.*

embargo /ɪm'bɑːgəʊ/ (*plural* **embargoes**) *noun* an official ban on trade ○ *The oil embargo is still in place.* □ **to lift an embargo** to allow trade to start again ○ *The government has lifted the embargo on the export of weapons.* □ **to be under an embargo** to be forbidden

③ **embark** /ɪm'bɑːk/ (**embarks, embarking, embarked**) *verb* **1.** to go on to a ship or an aircraft ○ *The passengers embarked at Southampton.* **2.** □ **to embark on** *or* **upon something** to start a project ○ *The council has embarked on the redevelopment of the town centre.* ○ *We'd better not embark on something new until we have finished this job.*

③ **embarrass** /ɪm'bærәs/ (**embarrasses, embarrassing, embarrassed**) *verb* to make someone feel uncomfortable in front of other people, e.g. by talking about something that they would prefer other people not to know about

② **embarrassed** /ɪm'bærәst/ *adj* uncomfortable or ashamed, and not knowing what to do ○ *She gave an embarrassed laugh, and said she had forgotten to bring the present.* ○ *He was so embarrassed that he turned bright red.*

② **embarrassing** /ɪm'bærәsɪŋ/ *adj* making a person feel embarrassed ○ *It was very embarrassing when he told everyone about my mistake.*

③ **embarrassment** /ɪm'bærәsmәnt/ *noun* a feeling of being worried and ashamed

embassy /'embәsi/ (*plural* **embassies**) *noun* the home or offices of an ambassador

embattled /ɪm'bæt(ə)ld/ *adj* constantly criticised

embed /ɪm'bed/ (**embeds, embedding, embedded**) *verb* to fix something into a mass such as concrete or flesh

embedded /ɪm'bedɪd/ *adj* fixed in a mass of something

embellish /ɪm'belɪʃ/ (**embellishes, embellishing, embellished**) *verb* **1.** to add details which are not true ○ *He embellished the story of the rescue with details of how he had climbed down the cliff.* **2.** to decorate something or to make something beautiful ○ *The ceiling was embellished with gold leaf.*

embellishment /ɪm'belɪʃmәnt/ *noun* a decoration, an improvement to make something look beautiful ○ *The embellishment of the ceiling with gold leaf.*

embers /'embәz/ *plural noun* red hot pieces of wood or coal ○ *She poured water on the embers of the bonfire.*

embezzle /ɪm'bez(ə)l/ (**embezzles, embezzling, embezzled**) *verb* to use money which is not yours, or which you are looking after for someone (NOTE: + **embezzlement** *n*)

embittered /ɪm'bɪtәd/ *adj* made bitter

emblazoned /ɪm'bleɪz(ə)nd/ *adj* decorated in a very noticeable way

emblem /'emblәm/ *noun* a design which is used as the symbol of a country, team or town

embodiment /ɪm'bɒdɪmәnt/ *noun* a physical expression of an idea

embody /ɪm'bɒdi/ (**embodies, embodying, embodied**) *verb* to show an idea in a physical form ○ *She embodies all the best qualities of a children's doctor.*

embolism /'embəlɪz(ə)m/ *noun* the blocking of a blood vessel by a blood clot or a bubble of air

emboss /ɪm'bɒs/ (**embosses, embossing, embossed**) *verb* to raise a design above a flat surface by pressing

embrace /ɪm'breɪs/ (**embraces, embracing, embraced**) *verb* **1.** to hold and kiss someone to show affection ○ *They embraced for several minutes before he got on the train.* **2.** to become a convert to a belief (*formal*) ○ *He embraced communism when he was at university.* (NOTE: + **embrace** *n*)

embroider /ɪm'brɔɪdə/ (**embroiders, embroidering, embroidered**) *verb* **1.** to make artistic patterns by sewing with coloured threads on cloth ○ *She embroidered a tablecloth for her mother.* **2.** to invent extra details and add them to a story ○ *He embroidered the story of his escape from prison with details of how he overpowered three guards and stole their guns.*

embroidery /ɪm'brɔɪdəri/ *noun* **1.** the art of sewing decorations on cloth ○ *She went to embroidery classes.* **2.** sewn decorations ○ *We admired the delicate embroidery on the tablecloth.* ◊ **needlework**

embroiled /ɪm'brɔɪld/ *adj* involved in an awkward situation

embryo /'embriəʊ/ (*plural* **embryos**) *noun* the first state of a living organism ○ *a human embryo*

embryology /ˌembri'ɒlədʒi/ *noun* the study of the development of embryos

embryonic /ˌembri'ɒnɪk/ *adj* at a very early stage of development

emerald /'em(ə)rəld/ *noun* a green precious stone ○ *Her crown was studded with emeralds.*

② **emerge** /ɪ'mɜːdʒ/ (**emerges, emerging, emerged**) *verb* **1.** to come into existence as something [~as] ○ *It was only after the election that he emerged as party leader.* **2.** to become known [~that] ○ *It soon emerged that the Prime Minister knew nothing about what was happening.*

③ **emergence** /ɪ'mɜːdʒəns/ *noun* the act of emerging

② **emergency** /ɪ'mɜːdʒənsi/ *noun* a dangerous situation such as a fire or an accident, where decisions have to be taken quickly ○ *Phone for an ambulance – this is an emergency!*

emergency exit /ɪˌmɜːdʒənsi 'egzɪt/ *noun* a door used in an emergency

emergency room /ɪ'mɜːdʒənsi ruːm/ *noun US* the department of a hospital which treats emergency cases (NOTE: The British term is A&E.)

emergency services /ɪ'mɜːdʒənsi ˌsɜːvɪsɪz/ *plural noun* the police, fire service and ambulance service

emergent /ɪ'mɜːdʒənt/ *adj* in a very early stage of development

emerging /ɪ'mɜːdʒɪŋ/ *adj* starting to appear, occur or develop

emigrant /'emɪgrənt/ *noun* a person who emigrates. Compare **immigrant**

emigrate /'emɪgreɪt/ (**emigrates, emigrating, emigrated**) *verb* to leave your country to live in another. Compare **immigrate** (NOTE: + **emigration** *n*)

émigré /'emɪgreɪ/ *noun* a person who has emigrated for political reasons

eminent /'emɪnənt/ *adj* important and very highly respected

eminently /'emɪnəntli/ *adv* extremely (*formal*)

emission /ɪ'mɪʃ(ə)n/ *noun* **1.** the process of emitting ○ *They are trying to reduce the emission of carbon monoxide from vehicles.* **2.** a substance which is emitted ○ *Gas emissions can cause acid rain.*

emit /ɪ'mɪt/ (**emits, emitting, emitted**) *verb* to send out something such as a sound, a signal or smoke

emoticon /ɪ'məʊtɪkɒn/ *noun* a symbolic picture representing an emotion, made from computer keyboard characters such as :(

③ **emotion** /ɪ'məʊʃ(ə)n/ *noun* a strong feeling ○ *Hatred and love are two of the most powerful emotions.* ○ *He tried to hide his emotions when he made his speech.*

③ **emotional** /ɪ'məʊʃ(ə)n(ə)l/ *adj* causing you to feel emotion, or showing emotion ○ *Saying goodbye was an emotional time for us all.* ○ *The music made her feel very emotional and she started to cry.*

emotive /ɪ'məʊtɪv/ *adj* likely to cause strong feeling

empathise /'empəθaɪz/ (**empathises, empathising, empathised**), **empathize** (**empathizing, empathized**) *verb* to feel empathy

empathy /'empəθi/ *noun* the ability to share the feelings of another person, by imagining yourself as that person

emperor /'emp(ə)rə/ *noun* the ruler of an empire

② **emphasis** /'emfəsɪs/ *noun* **1.** the act of showing the importance of something, usually in speech [~on] ○ *Don't put too much emphasis on his age.* ○ *She banged* *the table for emphasis as she spoke.* **2.** how loud your voice is when you pronounce a word or phrase ○ *Everyone noticed the emphasis he gave to the word 'peaceful'.*

② **emphasise** /ˈemfəsaɪz/ (**emphasises, emphasising, emphasised**), **emphasize** *verb* to show how important you feel something is, by saying it more loudly or slowly ○ *Please emphasise that the meeting must start on time.* ○ *He emphasised the importance of everyone working together.* ○ *She kept on emphasising the same point over and over again.*

emphatic /ɪmˈfætɪk/ *adj* using emphasis

emphysema /ˌemfɪˈsiːmə/ *noun* a condition where the surface of the lungs is reduced, making it difficult to breathe

③ **empire** /ˈempaɪə/ *noun* a group of separate countries ruled by a central government ○ *We're studying the history of the British Empire.* ○ *The Soviet empire covered a huge area from the Pacific Ocean to the middle of Europe.*

empirical /ɪmˈpɪrɪk(ə)l/ *adj* based on practical experiment and not on theory

② **employ** /ɪmˈplɔɪ/ (**employs, employing, employed**) *verb* **1.** to give someone regular paid work ○ *He is employed as a gardener by the duke.* ○ *She is employed in the textile industry.* **2.** to use something (*formal*) ○ *If we were to employ more up-to-date methods, would we make more money?* ○ *How can we best employ our free time on Sunday?*

employed /ɪmˈplɔɪd/ *adj* in regular paid work ○ *Please state the occupations of the employed members of your household.*

① **employee** /ɪmˈplɔɪiː/ *noun* a person who is employed ○ *The company has decided to take on twenty new employees.*

① **employer** /ɪmˈplɔɪə/ *noun* a person or organisation that gives work to people and pays them ○ *Her employer was a Hong Kong businessman.* ○ *The car factory is the biggest employer in the area.*

① **employment** /ɪmˈplɔɪmənt/ *noun* regular paid work

emporium /ɪmˈpɔːriəm/ *noun* a large shop

empower /ɪmˈpaʊə/ (**empowers, empowering, empowered**) *verb* to give someone the power to do something

empowerment /ɪmˈpaʊəmənt/ *noun* the act of giving power to someone

empress /ˈemprɪs/, **Empress** *noun* **1.** a woman who rules an empire ○ *Queen Victoria was Empress of India.* **2.** the wife or widow of an emperor ○ *When the emperor died, the empress decided to rule the country.*

① **empty** /ˈempti/ *adj* (**emptier, emptiest**) with nothing inside, or with no people present ○ *When we opened it, the box was empty.* ○ *Take an empty pot and fill it with soil.* ○ *The fridge is empty – we'll have to go out to eat.* ○ *The ski resorts are empty because there is no snow.* ■ *verb* (**empties, emptying, emptied**) to make something empty ○ *She emptied the clothes out of the suitcase.* ○ *He emptied the bottle into the sink.* ○ *They emptied the contents of the petty cash box into a bag.*

empty-handed /ˌempti ˈhændɪd/ *adj* having obtained nothing

emu /ˈiːmjuː/ *noun* a large Australian bird which cannot fly

emulate /ˈemjʊleɪt/ (**emulates, emulating, emulated**) *verb* to try to do as well as or better than someone else (*formal*)

emulsify /ɪˈmʌlsɪfaɪ/ (**emulsifies, emulsifying, emulsified**) *verb* to mix two liquids which cannot unite completely, such as oil and water

emulsion /ɪˈmʌlʃən/ *noun* a mixture of two liquids which do not unite completely, such as oil and water

① **enable** /ɪnˈeɪb(ə)l/ (**enables, enabling, enabled**) *verb* to make it possible for someone to do something ○ *The dictionary should enable you to understand English better.*

enact /ɪnˈækt/ (**enacts, enacting, enacted**) *verb* to make a law

enamel /ɪˈnæm(ə)l/ *noun* **1.** a very hard covering of colour ○ *The enamel of the painting had begun to crack.* **2.** the hard coating on the teeth ○ *If the enamel of a tooth gets damaged the tooth will soon start to discolour.*

en bloc /ɒŋ ˈblɒk/ *adv* all together as a group

encampment /ɪnˈkæmpmənt/ *noun* a large camp

encapsulate /ɪnˈkæpsjʊleɪt/ (**encapsulates, encapsulating, encapsulated**) *verb* to summarise something; to put something in a shorter form

encase /ɪnˈkeɪs/ (**encases, encasing, encased**) *verb* to completely surround something with a substance ○ *encased in concrete*

enchant /ɪnˈtʃɑːnt/ (**enchants, enchanting, enchanted**) *verb* to delight and attract someone

enchanted /ɪn'tʃɑːntɪd/ *adj* very pleased

enchanting /ɪn'tʃɑːntɪŋ/ *adj* very beautiful

enchantment /ɪn'tʃɑːntmənt/ *noun* a mysterious and magic feeling

encircle /ɪn'sɜːk(ə)l/ (**encircles, encircling, encircled**) *verb* to surround something completely

enclave /'eŋkleɪv/ *noun* a small group of people or small area completely surrounded by another quite different and larger group or area

③ **enclose** /ɪn'kləʊz/ (**encloses, enclosing, enclosed**) *verb* **1.** to put something inside an envelope with a letter ○ *I am enclosing a copy of our current catalogue.* ○ *Please find our cheque enclosed herewith.* **2.** to put a wall or fence round an area of land ○ *The garden is enclosed by high brick walls.*

enclosed /ɪn'kləʊzd/ *adj* surrounded on all sides ○ *an enclosed space*

enclosure /ɪn'kləʊʒə/ *noun* a document enclosed with a letter ○ *Please find details in the accompanying enclosure.*

③ **encode** /ɪn'kəʊd/ (**encodes, encoding, encoded**) *verb* to write something in a code so that it cannot be read or used by other people

encompass /ɪn'kʌmpəs/ (**encompasses, encompassing, encompassed**) *verb* to include something (*formal*)

encore /'ɒŋkɔː/ *noun* **1.** a call by the audience for a performer to repeat a song or a piece of music ○ *The crowd's cries of 'Encore' were simply deafening.* **2.** a song or a piece of music repeated at the request of the audience ○ *At the end of the concert she played* or *sang two encores.*

③ **encounter** /ɪn'kaʊntə/ (**encounters, encountering, encountered**) *verb* to meet someone or something ○ *On the journey we encountered several amusing people.* ○ *I have never encountered such hospitality anywhere else.*

① **encourage** /ɪn'kʌrɪdʒ/ (**encourages, encouraging, encouraged**) *verb* **1.** to make it easier for something to happen ○ *Leaving your credit cards on your desk encourages people to steal* or *encourages stealing.* **2.** to help someone to do something by giving them confidence ○ *He encouraged me to apply for the job.* ○ *I always felt encouraged by his interest in what I was doing.*

encouragement /ɪn'kʌrɪdʒmənt/ *noun* the act of giving someone the confidence to do something

② **encouraging** /ɪn'kʌrɪdʒɪŋ/ *adj* which encourages

encroach /ɪn'krəʊtʃ/ (**encroaches, encroaching, encroached**) *verb* to take over someone else's space [~on/upon] ○ *Their new wall had encroached on our land.* ○ *She accused the professor of encroaching upon her area of study.*

encrusted /ɪn'krʌstɪd/ *adj* covered with a hard substance

encumbrance /ɪn'kʌmbrəns/ *noun* a thing which prevents you from moving or doing something

encyclopedia /ɪnsaɪklə'piːdiə/, **encyclopaedia** *noun* **1.** a reference book containing articles on many subjects of human knowledge, usually presented in alphabetical order **2.** a reference book containing articles on a single subject, arranged usually in alphabetical order ○ *a gardening encyclopedia* ○ *the encyclopedia of sport*

encyclopedic /ɪnsaɪklə'piːdɪk/, **encyclopaedic** *adj* like an encyclopedia

① **end** /end/ *noun* **1.** the last part of something ○ *She tied the two ends of the ribbon together.* ○ *The telephone rang and I missed the end of the TV programme.* ○ *Go down to the end of the road and then turn right.* □ **to come to an end** to be finished ○ *The work should come to an end next month.* **2.** the final part of a period of time ○ *Can you wait until the end of the week?* ■ *verb* (**ends, ending, ended**) when something ends, it reaches the point when it stops happening ○ *The film ends with a wedding.* ○ *The meeting ended with everyone fighting on the floor.* ○ *The concert should end at about 10 o'clock.* ○ *The game ended in a draw.* ◇ **in the end** finally, at last ○ *In the end the teacher let him go home.* ○ *In the end the shop had to call in the police.* ◇ **to make ends meet** to have just enough money to live on ○ *I'm having trouble making ends meet.* ◇ **no end of** very many (*informal*) ○ *The car's caused us no end of problems.*

end up *phrasal verb* to finish in a particular situation

endanger /ɪn'deɪndʒə/ (**endangers, endangering, endangered**) *verb* to put someone or something in danger

endangered species /ɪnˌdeɪndʒəd 'spiːʃiːz/ *noun* a species of animal or plant at risk of dying completely

endear /ɪn'dɪə/ (**endears, endearing, endeared**) *verb* □ **to endear someone to someone** to make someone loved ○ *The old teacher endeared herself to generations of children.*

endearing /ɪn'dɪərɪŋ/ *adj* liked by other people ○ *an endearing manner*

endearment /ɪn'dɪəmənt/ *noun* something that you say that shows that you like or love someone

endeavour /ɪn'devə/ (**endeavours, endeavouring, endeavoured**) *verb* to try very hard to do something (*formal*) ○ *He endeavoured to contact her by both phone and fax.* (NOTE: The US spelling is **endeavor**.)

endemic /en'demɪk/ *adj* **1.** (*of a pest or disease*) very common in certain places ○ *This disease is endemic to Mediterranean countries.* **2.** (*of a plant or animal*) existing in a certain area

③ **ending** /'endɪŋ/ *noun* the way a story finishes ○ *I like films which have a happy ending.* ○ *He told us so much of the story that we could guess the ending.*

endless /'endləs/ *adj* with no apparent end

endorse /ɪn'dɔːs/ (**endorses, endorsing, endorsed**) *verb* **1.** to officially mark or sign the back of a document (NOTE: + **endorsement** *n*) **2.** to show approval of ○ *I heartily endorse what has just been said.* ○ *They asked us to endorse Mrs Martin as the local candidate.*

endow /ɪn'daʊ/ (**endows, endowing, endowed**) *verb* to give money which will provide a regular income for an organisation such as a school or hospital ○ *In her will, she left money to endow a new ward in the children's hospital.*

end product /ˌend 'prɒdʌkt/ *noun* the result at the end of a process or discussion ○ *He works hard, but the end product isn't always satisfactory.*

end result /end rɪ'zʌlt/ *noun* the result at the end of a process or discussion

endurance /ɪn'djʊərəns/ *noun* the ability to accept and live with something difficult or unpleasant

endure /ɪn'djʊə/ (**endures, enduring, endured**) *verb* **1.** to accept and live with something difficult or unpleasant ○ *The prisoners had to endure great hardship.* ○ *The pain was more than she could endure.* **2.** to last ○ *The memory of that day will endure for ever in my mind.*

enduring /ɪn'djʊərɪŋ/ *adj* which continues for a long time

② **enemy** /'enəmi/ (*plural* **enemies**) *noun* a person or country that is not on friendly terms with another, and may try to harm them ○ *Did your husband have many enemies?*

energetic /ˌenə'dʒetɪk/ *adj* active and lively

energise /'enədʒaɪz/ (**energises, energising, energised**), **energize** *verb* to make someone more energetic

① **energy** /'enədʒi/ *noun* **1.** the force or strength of a person ○ *He used up a lot of energy rushing around doing the Christmas shopping.* ○ *She put all her energies into her art gallery.* **2.** a power which makes something work ○ *the use of atomic energy* or *nuclear energy to make electricity* ○ *We try to save energy by switching off the lights when the rooms are empty.* ○ *Trams are an energy-efficient method of public transport.*

energy-saving /'enədʒi ˌseɪvɪŋ/ *adj* designed to use less energy

enforce /ɪn'fɔːs/ (**enforces, enforcing, enforced**) *verb* to make sure a rule is obeyed (NOTE: + **enforcement** *n*)

enfranchise /ɪn'fræntʃaɪz/ (**enfranchises, enfranchising, enfranchised**) *verb* to give someone the right to vote in elections

③ **engage** /ɪn'geɪdʒ/ (**engages, engaging, engaged**) *verb* **1.** to employ a worker (*formal*) ○ *We have engaged a lawyer to represent us.* ○ *The company has engaged twenty new salesmen.* **2.** to make parts of a machine fit into each other ○ *The gears aren't properly engaged.*

③ **engaged** /ɪn'geɪdʒd/ *adj* **1.** having officially stated your intention to marry ○ *She was engaged to Tom and then broke it off.* ○ *John and Sue are engaged: they got engaged last week.* **2.** busy or occupied ○ *You can't speak to the manager – his line is engaged.*

③ **engagement** /ɪn'geɪdʒmənt/ *noun* **1.** a statement that you intend to get married [~to] ○ *My son has announced his engagement to Pam.* ○ *Their engagement was announced in the local paper.* **2.** an appointment ○ *I have no engagements for the rest of the day.* ○ *She noted the appointment in her engagements diary.* □ **to have a prior engagement** to already have an appointment at the same time as one that is being suggested ○ *I can't meet you tonight – I have a prior engagement.*

engaging /ɪn'geɪdʒɪŋ/ *adj* charming

engender /ɪn'dʒendə/ (**engenders, engendering, engendered**) *verb* to produce something such as a feeling (*formal*)

① **engine** /'endʒɪn/ *noun* **1.** a machine which powers or drives something ○ *The car may need a new engine, I'm afraid.* ○ *Early industrial equipment was powered by steam engines.* **2.** a vehicle which pulls a train

③ **engineer** /ˌendʒɪ'nɪə/ *noun* **1.** a person who looks after and repairs technical equipment ○ *There are not enough telephone engineers in the area.* ○ *The photocopier's broken down again – we'll have to call the engineer.* **2.** a person whose job is to design mechanical, electrical or industrial equipment ■ *verb* (**engineers, engineering, engineered**) to arrange something secretly ○ *She engineered the dismissal of one of her colleagues.*

② **engineering** /ˌendʒɪ'nɪərɪŋ/ *noun* the science or study of the design of technical equipment ○ *The college offers courses in electrical engineering.*

England /'ɪŋlənd/ *noun* a country in the southern part of the island of Great Britain, the largest country in the United Kingdom (NOTE: **England** is often used instead of Great Britain, and this is a mistake, as England is only one part of Great Britain; note also the capital: **London;** people: **the English;** language: **English;** currency: **pound sterling**)

① **English** /'ɪŋglɪʃ/ *adj* relating to England (NOTE: **English** is often used instead of British and this is a mistake as England is only one part of Great Britain. Do not say the **English Prime Minister**, say the **British Prime Minister**.) ■ *noun* the English language as a subject of study in school or university ○ *She's good at maths but not so good at English.* ○ *As well as teaching English, he also teaches drama.* ○ *Mr Smith is our English teacher.* ○ *She gives English lessons at home in the evenings.* ○ *There are twenty students in my English class.*

English breakfast /ˌɪŋglɪʃ 'brekfəst/ *noun* a cooked breakfast with bacon, eggs, sausages, mushrooms and tomatoes

Englishman /'ɪŋglɪʃmən/ (*plural* **Englishmen**) *noun* a man from England

Englishwoman /'ɪŋglɪʃwʊmən/ (*plural* **Englishwomen**) *noun* a woman from England

engrave /ɪn'greɪv/ (**engraves, engraving, engraved**) *verb* to cut a pattern or letters onto a hard surface (NOTE: + **engraver** *n*)

engraving /ɪn'greɪvɪŋ/ *noun* a picture made by printing from a plate that has been engraved

engrossed /ɪn'grəʊst/ *adj* totally interested in something

engrossing /ɪn'grəʊsɪŋ/ *adj* very interesting

engulf /ɪn'gʌlf/ (**engulfs, engulfing, engulfed**) *verb* **1.** to completely cover and kill or destroy someone or something ○ *Two villages were engulfed in mud.* **2.** to overwhelm someone or something ○ *She was engulfed by feelings of remorse.*

③ **enhance** /ɪn'hɑːns/ (**enhances, enhancing, enhanced**) *verb* to increase the value or power of something ○ *Slot in this new memory board to enhance your computer memory.* ○ *He took drugs to enhance his performance as an athlete.*

enhancement /ɪn'hɑːnsmənt/ *noun* an improvement in something such as quality or value

enigma /ɪ'nɪgmə/ *noun* a mystery or puzzle

enigmatic /ˌenɪg'mætɪk/ *adj* mysterious and difficult to understand

① **enjoy** /ɪn'dʒɔɪ/ (**enjoys, enjoying, enjoyed**) *verb* **1.** to get pleasure from something ○ *Have you enjoyed the holiday so far?* ○ *When he asked them if they had enjoyed the film they all answered 'no'.* ○ *She doesn't enjoy sailing because it make her seasick.* □ **to enjoy yourself** to have a good time ○ *We enjoyed ourselves so much that we're going to the same place for our holiday next year.* **2.** to have a good feature or quality (*formal*) ○ *The house enjoys beautiful views of the mountains.*

② **enjoyable** /ɪn'dʒɔɪəb(ə)l/ *adj* giving pleasure

③ **enjoyment** /ɪn'dʒɔɪmənt/ *noun* pleasure

enlarge /ɪn'lɑːdʒ/ (**enlarges, enlarging, enlarged**) *verb* to make something bigger ○ *Could you enlarge this photograph?*

enlargement /ɪn'lɑːdʒmənt/ *noun* a bigger photograph than the original

enlightened /ɪn'laɪt(ə)nd/ *adj* without any prejudice; holding modern ideas

enlightenment /ɪn'laɪt(ə)nmənt/ *noun* knowledge, absence of ignorance ○ *In his search for enlightenment he visited the Buddhist monks of the Himalayas.*

enlist /ɪn'lɪst/ (**enlists, enlisting, enlisted**) *verb* to join up voluntarily as a member of the armed forces ○ *He left school at 18 and enlisted as a soldier for five years.*

enliven /ɪn'laɪv(ə)n/ (**enlivens, enlivening, enlivened**) *verb* to make someone or something more lively

en masse /ɒn 'mæs/ *adv* all together in a crowd

enmity /'enmɪti/ *noun* hatred towards someone (NOTE: You experience enmity **towards** someone.)

enormity /ɪ'nɔːmɪti/ *noun* the large size of something which is bad or wrong

② **enormous** /ɪ'nɔːməs/ *adj* of an extremely large size ○ *The house is absolutely enormous.* ○ *He ate an enormous lunch.* ○ *The present was an enormous surprise.*

③ **enormously** /ɪ'nɔːməsli/ *adv* very much

① **enough** /ɪ'nʌf/ *adj* as much as is needed ○ *Have you got enough money for your fare* or *to pay your fare?* ○ *There isn't enough light to take photographs.* ■ *pron* as much of something as is needed ○ *I had £20 in my purse to pay the taxi, but it wasn't enough.* ○ *Have you all had enough to eat?* ■ *adv* as much as is needed ○ *This box isn't big enough for all these books.* ○ *He doesn't work fast enough.*

③ **enquire** /ɪŋ'kwaɪə/ *verb* another spelling of **inquire**

enquiry /ɪn'kwaɪri/ (*plural* **enquiries**) *noun* another spelling of **inquiry**

enrage /ɪn'reɪdʒ/ (**enrages, enraging, enraged**) *verb* to make someone very angry

enrich /ɪn'rɪtʃ/ (**enriches, enriching, enriched**) *verb* **1.** to make someone or something richer ○ *He has no scruples about enriching himself at other people's expense.* **2.** to make something more fertile ○ *Learning French has enriched his life.* ○ *Some crops, such as beans, enrich the soil.* (NOTE: + **enrichment** *n*) **3.** to benefit someone or something

enrol /ɪn'rəʊl/ (**enrols, enrolling, enrolled**) *verb* to admit or be admitted as a new member or new student (NOTE: The US spelling is **enroll**.)

enrolment /ɪn'rəʊlmənt/ *noun* the action of admitting new members or new students ○ *Enrolment starts next Saturday.* (NOTE: no plural in this meaning. The US spelling is **enrollment**.)

en route /ɒn 'ruːt/ *adv* on the way [~to] ○ *We'll eat en route.* ○ *The tanker sank en route to the Gulf.*

ensemble /ɒn'sɒmbəl/ *noun* **1.** a small group of musicians or singers ○ *a jazz ensemble* ○ *An ensemble played music by Mozart.* **2.** a set of women's clothes which match ○ *She lost the hat that went with her ensemble and couldn't find another one to match.* **3.** a group of things which go together to form a whole ○ *The whole ensemble of church, cottages and pub looks just like a postcard.*

enshrine /ɪn'ʃraɪn/ (**enshrines, enshrining, enshrined**) *verb* to make something a legal right that cannot be taken away

enslave /ɪn'sleɪv/ (**enslaves, enslaving, enslaved**) *verb* **1.** make someone into a slave **2.** to control someone, taking away their freedom

ensue /ɪn'sjuː/ (**ensues, ensuing, ensued**) *verb* to follow, or happen as a result of something

ensuing /ɪn'sjuːɪŋ/ *adj* which follows

en-suite /ˌɒn 'swiːt/ *adj, adv* attached to a bedroom ○ *a bedroom with an en-suite shower room*

② **ensure** /ɪn'ʃʊə/ (**ensures, ensuring, ensured**) *verb* to make sure of something [~(that)] ○ *When taking a shower, please ensure that the shower curtain is inside the bath.* (NOTE: Do not confuse with **insure**. Note also: **ensures – ensuring – ensured**.)

entail /ɪn'teɪl/ (**entails, entailing, entailed**) *verb* to involve having or doing something (*formal*)

entangle /ɪn'tæŋgəl/ (**entangles, entangling, entangled**) *verb* **1.** to catch or tie up something in ○ *Her dress became entangled in the machinery.* ○ *The propeller was entangled in seaweed.* **2.** to put someone in a situation from which it is difficult to escape ○ *He became emotionally entangled with a colleague.* ○ *The country is in danger of getting entangled in the war.*

① **enter** /'entə/ *verb* (**enters, entering, entered**) **1.** to go into or to come into a place ○ *He took off his hat as he entered the church.* ○ *Did they stamp your passport when you entered the country?* **2.** to decide to take part in a race or competition ○ *She has entered the 2,000 metres.* **3.** to write information on a book or a form, or to type information into a computer system ○ *We will just enter your name and address on the computer.* ■ *noun* the key on a keyboard which you press when you have finished keying something, or when you want to start a new line ○ *To log on to the system,* *type your password and press enter.* ◊ **entrance**[1], **entry**

② **enterprise** /'entəpraɪz/ *noun* **1.** a business venture, especially something that involves some risk ○ *Their latest enterprise is importing carpets from Turkey.* **2.** a method of organising business ○ *The state should not interfere with free enterprise.* **3.** a commercial firm, a business organisation ○ *They have merged with another huge industrial enterprise.*

enterprising /'entəpraɪzɪŋ/ *adj* using initiative

entertain /ˌentə'teɪn/ (**entertains, entertaining, entertained**) *verb* **1.** to perform, e.g. by telling stories to people or making them laugh ○ *He entertained us with stories of his life in the army.* ○ *We hired a clown to entertain the children.* ○ *The tourists were entertained by the local dance troupe.* **2.** to have someone as a guest and offer them a meal and drinks, and sometimes a place to sleep ○ *They're entertaining some Swedish friends this evening.*

entertainer /ˌentə'teɪnə/ *noun* a person who entertains people, especially as a job

③ **entertaining** /ˌentə'teɪnɪŋ/ *adj* amusing

③ **entertainment** /ˌentə'teɪnmənt/ *noun* things such as films and shows that people enjoy watching ○ *She sang for their entertainment.* ○ *There's not much entertainment in the village – the nearest cinema is 25km away.*

enthral /ɪn'θrɔːl/ (**enthrals, enthralling, enthralled**) *verb* to keep someone's attention (NOTE: The US spelling is **enthrall**.)

③ **enthusiasm** /ɪn'θjuːziæz(ə)m/ *noun* great interest and liking [~for] ○ *We succeeded, thanks to the enthusiasm and hard work of a small group of members.* ○ *She showed a lot of enthusiasm for our new project.*

enthusiast /ɪn'θjuːziæst/ *noun* a person who shows great interest in something

③ **enthusiastic** /ɪnˌθjuːzi'æstɪk/ *adj* showing great interest and approval ○ *The editor was very enthusiastic about my book.* ○ *There were enthusiastic cheers at the end of the performance.*

entice /ɪn'taɪs/ (**entices, enticing, enticed**) *verb* to attract or to tempt someone to do something

② **entire** /ɪn'taɪə/ *adj* whole ○ *We spent the entire day gardening.* ○ *The entire cast came on the stage and bowed to the audience.*

② **entirely** /ɪn'taɪəli/ *adv* completely ○ *I agree with you entirely.* ○ *This is an entirely separate problem.*

entirety /ɪn'taɪərɪti/ *noun* a full amount □ **in its entirety** completely ○ *He read the book in its entirety.*

② **entitle** /ɪn'taɪt(ə)l/ (**entitles, entitling, entitled**) *verb* **1.** to give someone the right to ○ *I am entitled to five weeks' holiday a year.* **2.** to give a title to something ○ *Tolstoy wrote a book entitled 'War and Peace'.*

entitlement /ɪn'taɪt(ə)lmənt/ *noun* a right to have something

③ **entity** /'entɪti/ (*plural* **entities**) *noun* a thing which exists as a separate unit

entourage /'ɒntʊrɑːʒ/ *noun* a group of people such as secretaries, assistants and advisers surrounding an important person

entrance[1] /'entrəns/ *noun* a door for going in ○ *Let's meet at the side entrance of the museum, near the café.*

entrance[2] /ɪn'trɑːns/ (**entrances, entrancing, entranced**) *verb* to make someone very interested and happy ○ *His singing entranced his audience.*

entranced /ɪn'trɑːnst/ *adj* giving all your attention to something enjoyable

entrant /'entrənt/ *noun* a person who takes part in a race, examination or competition ○ *There are over a thousand entrants for the race.*

entrepreneur /ˌɒntrəprə'nɜː/ *noun* a person who directs a company and takes risks commercially

entrust /ɪn'trʌst/ (**entrusts, entrusting, entrusted**) *verb* □ **to entrust something to someone, to entrust someone with something** to give someone the responsibility for looking after something ○ *She entrusted the care of her children to her brother.* ○ *He was entrusted with the keys to the office safe.* ○ *Why did she entrust him with all her money?*

② **entry** /'entri/ (*plural* **entries**) *noun* **1.** the act of going into a place [~to/into] ○ *Her entry into the hall was greeted with applause.* ○ *The sign on the door said 'No Entry'.* **2.** the door or opening where you go into a place [~to/into] ○ *The entry to the cave was blocked by rocks.* **3.** a piece of information in something such as a dictionary, or in a computer system [~to/into] ○ *She looked up the entry on 'roses' in the gardening encyclopedia.*

entwine /ɪn'twaɪn/ (**entwines, entwining, entwined**) *verb* to twist two things together

envelop /ɪn'veləp/ (**envelops, enveloping, enveloped**) *verb* to cover something; to surround something with a covering

③ **envelope** /'envələʊp/ *noun* a folded paper cover for sending letters in ○ *She wrote the address on the envelope and sealed it.* ○ *She wrote down all the information on the back of an envelope.*

enviable /'enviəb(ə)l/ *adj* causing envy

envious /'enviəs/ *adj* feeling or showing in an unhappy way that you would like to have something that someone else has

① **environment** /ɪn'vaɪrənmənt/ *noun* **1.** the conditions in which we live and work ○ *an urban/rural environment* ○ *The environment in the office is stuffy and hot.* □ **the working environment** the general surroundings in which a person works **2.** the natural features and resources of the earth, including animals and plants ○ *The action plan is designed to prevent future damage to the environment.*

① **environmental** /ɪnˌvaɪrən'ment(ə)l/ *adj* relating to the environment ○ *measures taken to protect against environmental pollution* ○ *She's joined an environmental group.*

environmentalist /ɪnˌvaɪrən 'ment(ə)lɪst/ *noun* a person who is concerned with protecting the environment

environmentally friendly /ɪn ˌvaɪrənment(ə)li 'frendli/ *adj* minimising harm to the natural environment

③ **envisage** /ɪn'vɪzɪdʒ/ (**envisages, envisaging, envisaged**) *verb* to imagine something in your mind which could possibly happen in the future

envision /ɪn'vɪʒ(ə)n/ (**envisions, envisioning, envisioned**) *verb US* same as **envisage**

③ **envoy** /'envɔɪ/ *noun* a person sent officially by one country to another

envy /'envi/ *noun* an unhappy feeling that you would like to have something which someone else has ○ *Her beautiful long dark hair filled us all with envy.* ■ *verb* (**envies, envying, envied**) to have the unhappy feeling that you would like to have something that someone else has ○ *I don't envy him with a job like that!* □ **to envy someone something** to want to have something which someone else has ○ *We all envy Sue her new car.*

③ **enzyme** /'enzaɪm/ *noun* a protein produced by living cells which makes other substances change, as when digestion takes place

ephemeral /ɪ'femərəl/ *adj* not lasting for a long time

epic /'epɪk/ *noun* a long poem or film, especially about war ○ *There's an old Hollywood epic on TV this afternoon.* ○ *The reading was an extract from Homer's epic, the 'Iliad'.*

epidemic /ˌepɪ'demɪk/ *noun* **1.** the spread of an infectious disease quickly through a large number of people **2.** a sudden increase in something [~of] ○ *an epidemic of car thefts* ■ *adj* affecting very many people

epilepsy /'epɪlepsi/ *noun* a disorder of the nervous system in which a person suffers convulsions and loss of consciousness

epileptic /ˌepɪ'leptɪk/ *noun* a person who has epilepsy (NOTE: Many people avoid using this word, as it causes offence, and prefer to say *a person with epilepsy*.)

epilogue /'epɪlɒg/ *noun* a short text at the end of a long book or play. Compare **prologue** (NOTE: The US spelling is **epilog**.)

episode /'epɪsəʊd/ *noun* **1.** a short section of a longer story, especially one part of a TV series ○ *Do you remember the episode where the ghost appears?* ○ *The hero's father returns in the third episode.* **2.** a short period of your life ○ *It's an episode in his marriage which he would rather forget.*

epitaph /'epɪtɑːf/ *noun* words written on a gravestone

epitome /ɪ'pɪtəmi/ *noun* a person or thing that shows a particular quality very strongly [~of] ○ *the epitome of good manners*

epoch /'iːpɒk/ *noun* a long period of time ○ *an important epoch in European history*

① **equal** /'iːkwəl/ *adj* having exactly the same amount as something else [~to/~in] ○ *His share is equal to mine.* ○ *Male and female employees must have equal pay.* ○ *The two sticks are of equal length* or *are equal in length.* ■ *verb* (**equals, equalling, equalled**) **1.** to be exactly the same as something else ○ *His time for the 100 metres equals the existing record.* **2.** to give a particular result ○ *Two plus two equals four.* ○ *Ten take away four equals six.* ■ *noun* a person who is on the same level as someone else ○ *I don't consider him your equal.* ○ *We're all equals here.* ◇ **equal to the task** able to carry out the job required ○ *He was put in charge of the prison, but was quickly found not to be equal to the task.* ◇ **all things being equal** assuming nothing else has changed ○ *All things being equal, I'd prefer to go on holiday in June.*

equalise /ˈiːkwəlaɪz/ (**equalises, equalising, equalised**), **equalize** *verb* **1.** (*in a game*) to make a score equal ○ *They equalised just before half-time.* **2.** to make different things equal ○ *We are trying to equalise the availability of medical supplies throughout the region.*

equality /ɪˈkwɒlɪti/ *noun* a situation where people are equal ○ *Policies to ensure equality in the workplace.*

① **equally** /ˈiːkwəli/ *adv* in exactly the same way ○ *They are all equally guilty.* ○ *Here men and women are paid equally badly.* ○ *They were both equally responsible for the mistake.*

equal opportunity /ˌiːkwəl ɒpəˈtjuːnɪti/ *noun* a situation where everyone, regardless of sex, race, class, etc., has the same opportunity to get a job

equals sign /ˈiːkwəlz saɪn/ *noun* a printed or written sign (=) showing that one thing is the same as another

equate /ɪˈkweɪt/ (**equates, equating, equated**) *verb* to consider one thing to be the same as another thing [~with] ○ *They equate lack of complaints with satisfaction.*

③ **equation** /ɪˈkweɪʒ(ə)n/ *noun* a mathematical or chemical formula showing that two parts are equal ○ *Let me show you how this equation can be solved.* ○ *He formulated the equation for converting mass to energy.*

equator /ɪˈkweɪtə/ *noun* the imaginary line running round the circumference of the earth at an equal distance from the North and South Poles

equestrian /ɪˈkwestriən/ *adj* relating to riding horses ○ *The Olympic equestrian events have been postponed because of an outbreak of flu among the horses.*

③ **equilibrium** /ˌiːkwɪˈlɪbriəm/ *noun* **1.** the state of being perfectly balanced ○ *The electromagnetic forces are in a state of equilibrium.* ○ *We do not want to disturb the present political equilibrium in the region.* **2.** the state of being calm ○ *During the argument, she struggled to retain her equilibrium.*

equip /ɪˈkwɪp/ (**equips, equipping, equipped**) *verb* to provide someone or something with something [~with] ○ *a holiday flat equipped with a washing machine and dishwasher* ○ *The course will equip you with all the skills you need to practise scuba-diving.*

② **equipment** /ɪˈkwɪpmənt/ *noun* all the things such as tools, arms and machines which are needed for something ○ *Do you really need all this equipment for a short climb?* ○ *He brought all his camera equipment with him.* (NOTE: no plural: for one item say *a piece of equipment.*)

equitable /ˈekwɪtəb(ə)l/ *adj* fair or just (*formal*)

equity /ˈekwɪti/ *noun* a fair system of justice ○ *She complained about the lack of equity in the company's pay structure.*

③ **equivalent** /ɪˈkwɪvələnt/ *adj* having the same value or the same strength as something else [~to] ○ *Two pints and a litre are roughly equivalent.* ○ *She handed me the equivalent amount in Swiss francs.* ○ *A litre is roughly equivalent to two pints.* ■ *noun* something which has the same value, strength or importance as something else [~of/~to] ○ *What is the American equivalent of the Chancellor of the Exchequer?* ○ *Her salary is more or less equivalent to mine.* ○ *I gave him $2000 and he paid me the equivalent in euros.*

er /ɜː/ *interj* used for showing that you are hesitating

era /ˈɪərə/ *noun* a long period of time ○ *That was an era when there was little public education.*

eradicate /ɪˈrædɪkeɪt/ (**eradicates, eradicating, eradicated**) *verb* to remove something completely (NOTE: + **eradication** *n*)

③ **erase** /ɪˈreɪz/ (**erases, erasing, erased**) *verb* **1.** to rub out writing **2.** to remove recorded material from a tape, or data from a disk ○ *I've erased your recording of the concert by mistake.*

③ **eraser** /ɪˈreɪzə/ *noun US* a piece of rubber for removing writing in pencil

erect /ɪˈrekt/ *adj* standing vertical or sticking up straight ○ *She held herself erect as she walked to the front of the hall.* ■ *verb* (**erects, erecting, erected**) to put up something vertically, such as a mast or a building ○ *They are planning to erect a monument to the princess.* ○ *The civilians rushed to hide in hastily-erected bomb shelters.*

erection /ɪˈrekʃən/ *noun* **1.** a state where the penis becomes stiff and swollen from sexual excitement **2.** the action of putting up (*formal*) ○ *The erection of the tent took about 5 minutes.*

ergonomics /ˌɜːgəˈnɒmɪks/ *noun* the study of how tools or furniture can be best designed to make them easy and comfortable to use

erode /ɪˈrəʊd/ (**erodes, eroding, eroded**) *verb* to wear away gradually (NOTE: + **erosion** *n*)

erotic /ɪ'rɒtɪk/ *adj* strongly sexual

err /ɜː/ (**errs, erring, erred**) *verb* to make a mistake (*formal*) □ **to err on the side of something** to use more of something or do more than is necessary, as a precaution ○ *We erred on the side of caution and ordered 20 course books.*

errand /'erənd/ *noun* a short trip out to buy something

erratic /ɪ'rætɪk/ *adj* irregular or wild

erroneous /ɪ'rəʊniəs/ *adj* wrong (*formal*)

② **error** /'erə/ *noun* something that is wrong, especially a mistake in writing or speaking [~in] ○ *There isn't a single error in the whole document.* ○ *The waiter made an error in calculating the bill.* ◇ **in error** by mistake ○ *The parcel was sent to our Edinburgh office in error.*

erupt /ɪ'rʌpt/ (**erupts, erupting, erupted**) *verb* (*of a volcano*) to throw out fire and other very hot substances ○ *The volcano last erupted in 1968.*

ESC /ɪ'skeɪp/ *abbr* ESCAPE key

escalate /'eskəleɪt/ (**escalates, escalating, escalated**) *verb* **1.** to get worse or more violent ○ *Our financial problems have escalated.* ○ *The conflict escalated into an all-out war.* **2.** to increase steadily ○ *Prices escalated during the year.* (NOTE: + **escalation** *n*)

escalator /'eskəleɪtə/ *noun* a moving staircase

escapade /'eskəpeɪd/ *noun* an exciting adventure

② **escape** /ɪ'skeɪp/ *verb* (**escapes, escaping, escaped**) **1.** to get away from prison or from a difficult situation [~from] ○ *He escaped from the prison by sawing through the bars.* **2.** to get out of a container [~from] ○ *the sound of air escaping from the tyre* ■ *noun* the act of getting away from prison or from a difficult situation [~from] ○ *There were three escapes from this jail last year.* ○ *A weekend by the sea was a wonderful escape from the office.*

ESCAPE key /ɪ'skeɪp kiː/ *noun* the key which stops what is happening on a computer and returns to the main program. Abbreviation **ESC**

escapism /ɪ'skeɪpɪz(ə)m/ *noun* the activity of thinking about something marvellous or fantastic in order to forget about your ordinary daily existence

escapist /ɪ'skeɪpɪst/ *adj, noun* a person who thinks about something marvellous or fantastic in order to forget about his or her ordinary daily existence

escort[1] /'eskɔːt/ *noun* **1.** a person or group of people accompanying someone ○ *The president had a police escort to the airport.* **2.** a person who accompanies someone else to a social event

escort[2] /ɪ'skɔːt/ (**escorts, escorting, escorted**) *verb* to accompany someone ○ *The police escorted the group into the hotel.* ○ *I was escorted around by our local MP.* ○ *The liner entered harbour escorted by a flotilla of yachts.*

Eskimo /'eskɪməʊ/ (*plural* **Eskimos** or *same*) *noun* one of a native people living in the north of Canada and Greenland ○ *Eskimos hunt seals and polar bears.* (NOTE: They are generally called by the name they use themselves: **the Inuit**.)

ESL *abbr* English as a Second Language

ESOL /'iːsɒl/ *abbr* English for Speakers Of Other Languages

esoteric /ˌesəʊ'terɪk/ *adj* understood by very few people

ESP *abbr* English for Special Purposes

① **especially** /ɪ'speʃ(ə)li/ *adv* **1.** used for showing that something is the case to a great degree ○ *This suitcase is especially heavy.* **2.** used for showing that something is more important or true ○ *She does get tired, especially on school day.*

espionage /'espiənɑːʒ/ *noun* the practice of spying

espouse /ɪ'spaʊz/ (**espouses, espousing, espoused**) *verb* to support a cause (*archaic*)

espresso /e'spresəʊ/ *noun* strong black Italian coffee, served in very small cups

② **essay** /'eseɪ/ *noun* a piece of writing on a specific subject [~on/about] ○ *a collection of the writer's most famous essays* ○ *For our homework, we have to write an essay on pollution.*

essence /'es(ə)ns/ *noun* **1.** a pure extract taken from something ○ *custard flavoured with vanilla essence* **2.** the central part of an argument ○ *The essence of what she had to say was very clear.* ◇ **in essence** basically ○ *His plan is in essence the same as the one which we discussed last year.*

② **essential** /ɪ'senʃəl/ *adj* very important or necessary ○ *You can survive without food for some time, but water is essential.* ○ *It is essential that we get the delivery on time.* ■ *noun* something which is very important or which you cannot do without ○ *Sun cream is an essential in the desert.* ■ *plural noun* **essentials** the things that you must have ○ *We've got all the basic essentials – food, water and fuel.* □ **the bare es-**

sentials the most important basic things that are needed ○ *I just packed the bare essentials for my holiday.*

② **essentially** /ɪ'senʃəli/ *adv* used for saying what is the most true, or the most important fact ○ *My new job is essentially not so very different from my old one.* ○ *Although he's essentially a kind man, he does lose his temper sometimes.*

① **establish** /ɪ'stæblɪʃ/ (**establishes, establishing, established**) *verb* **1.** to start something or make something happen ○ *We need to establish a good working relationship with our colleagues.* **2.** to start a company or business activity ○ *The business was established in Scotland in 1823.* **3.** to discover or prove something [~(that)/~whether/how/who etc] ○ *If only the police could establish where the car was parked that evening.* ○ *It's difficult to establish what her reasons are for resigning.*

③ **established** /ɪ'stæblɪʃt/ *adj* which has been shown to be true

② **establishment** /ɪ'stæblɪʃmənt/ *noun* **1.** the act of creating something ○ *She helped them with the establishment of the local drama society.* (NOTE: no plural in this sense) **2.** a business or organisation ○ *It's an establishment which imports radios from China.* ○ *He runs an important teaching establishment.* **3. the Establishment** the most important people in society, especially those who are in authority ○ *He spent a lot of his life fighting against the Establishment.*

② **estate** /ɪ'steɪt/ *noun* **1.** a large area of land belonging to one owner ○ *He owns a 250-acre estate in Norfolk.* **2.** a group of houses on one piece of land, usually all built at the same time

estate agent /ɪ'steɪt ˌeɪdʒənt/ *noun* a person who sells buildings and land

esteem /ɪ'stiːm/ *noun* respect (*formal*) ○ *The staff seem to have very little esteem for the directors.*

esteemed /ɪ'stiːmd/ *adj* admired and respected

esthetic US spelling of **aesthetic**

② **estimate¹** /'estɪmət/ *noun* a calculation or guess which shows the amount of something you think there is, or its worth or cost ○ *I wasn't in when they came to read the gas meter, so this bill is only an estimate.* ○ *Your estimate of two dozen visitors proved to be correct.* □ **she gave me a rough estimate** she gave me an approximate calculation

① **estimate²** /'estɪmeɪt/ (**estimates, estimating, estimated**) *verb* to calculate or guess how much you think something will cost or is worth ○ *I estimate that it will cost £100,000.* ○ *He estimated costs at £50,000.*

estimation /ˌestɪ'meɪʃ(ə)n/ *noun* an opinion or judgment (*formal*)

estuary /'estʃuəri/ (*plural* **estuaries**) *noun* a part of a river where it meets the sea, composed of fresh and salt water

① **etc.** /et'setərə/, **etcetera** *adv* and so on, and other things like this ○ *Fruit such as peaches, apricots, etc.*

etch /etʃ/ (**etches, etching, etched**) *verb* to engrave on metal with acid

eternal /ɪ'tɜːn(ə)l/ *adj* lasting for ever or for a long time

eternity /ɪ'tɜːnɪti/ *noun* a never-ending period of time

ethic /'eθɪk/ *noun* a principle of good and moral behaviour ○ *the Christian ethic*

ethical /'eθɪk(ə)l/ *adj* morally right

③ **ethnic** /'eθnɪk/ *adj* relating to ethnic group ○ *The census shows the ethnic make-up of the population.*

ethnic cleansing /ˌeθnɪk 'klenzɪŋ/ *noun* killing people, or removing people from an area, because of their race or religion

ethnic group *noun* a group of people with the same background and culture

ethnicity /eθ'nɪsɪti/ (*plural* **ethnicities**) *noun* the fact of belonging to a particular ethnic group

ethnic minority /ˌeθnɪk maɪ'nɒrɪti/ *noun* a small part of a population which is of a different ethnic group to the majority

ethos /'iːθɒs/ *noun* beliefs or characteristics, especially those of a group of people

etiquette /'etɪket/ *noun* a correct way of behaving in society

etymological /ˌetɪmə'lɒdʒɪk(ə)l/ *adj* referring to etymology

etymology /ˌetɪ'mɒlədʒi/ (*plural* **etymologies**) *noun* the study of the ways in which words and their meanings have developed

③ **EU** *abbr* European Union (NOTE: formerly called the **European Community**)

eulogy /'juːlədʒi/ (*plural* **eulogies**) *noun* a speech, especially one given at a funeral praising someone

euphemism /'juːfəmɪz(ə)m/ *noun* a word or phrase used in place of a more offensive or unpleasant word

euphoria /juː'fɔːriə/ *noun* a burst of extreme happiness

① **euro** /ˈjʊərəʊ/ (*plural* **euros** or *same*) *noun* the unit of money used by most countries in the European Union ○ *Many articles are priced in euros.* ○ *What's the exchange rate for the euro?* (NOTE: written Ä before numbers: *Ä250:* say: 'two hundred and fifty euros')

Euro- /jʊərəʊ/ *prefix* referring to Europe or the European Union

① **Europe** /ˈjʊərəp/ *proper noun* **1.** the continent of Europe, the part of the world to the west of Asia, extending from Russia to Ireland ○ *Most of the countries of Western Europe are members of the EU.* **2.** Europe not including the UK ○ *Holidays in Europe are less popular than last year.* **3.** the European Union ○ *Canadian exports to Europe have risen by 25%.* Abbreviation **EU**

① **European** /ˌjʊərəˈpiːən/ *adj* relating to Europe

European Union /ˌjʊərəpiːən ˈjuːnjən/ *noun* an organisation which links 25 European countries together based on the four freedoms of movement: movement of goods, of capital, of people and of services. Abbreviation **EU** (NOTE: was formerly called the **European Community** *or* **EC**)

Eurozone /ˈjʊərəʊzəʊn/ *noun* the countries in Europe which use the euro as currency

euthanasia /ˌjuːθəˈneɪziə/ *noun* mercy killing, the killing of a sick person in order to put an end to his or her suffering

③ **evacuate** /ɪˈvækjuˌeɪt/ (**evacuates, evacuating, evacuated**) *verb* to make people leave a dangerous place

evacuee /ɪˌvækjuˈiː/ *noun* a person who has been evacuated

evade /ɪˈveɪd/ (**evades, evading, evaded**) *verb* to avoid or escape something

③ **evaluate** /ɪˈvæljueɪt/ (**evaluates, evaluating, evaluated**) *verb* to make a judgement about something after thinking carefully about it ○ *The students were asked to evaluate the usefulness of the lessons.*

③ **evaluation** /ɪˌvæljuˈeɪʃ(ə)n/ *noun* the act of evaluating something, or the judgement made in this way (NOTE: no plural)

evangelical /ˌiːvænˈdʒelɪk(ə)l/ *adj* referring to certain Protestant churches and their teaching of the Bible

evangelism /ɪˈvændʒəlɪz(ə)m/ *noun* **1.** the act of spreading the teachings of Christ **2.** the enthusiastic promotion of something

evangelist /ɪˈvændʒəlɪst/ *noun* **1.** one of the four men who wrote the Christian Gospels; Matthew, Mark, Luke or John **2.** someone who tries to persuade people to become Christians ○ *The American evangelist is coming to England as part of his world tour.*

evaporate /ɪˈvæpəreɪt/ (**evaporates, evaporating, evaporated**) *verb* (*of liquid*) to turn into steam by being heated ○ *Water gradually evaporates from the soil.*

evasion /ɪˈveɪʒ(ə)n/ *noun* the act of avoiding something

evasive /ɪˈveɪsɪv/ *adj* trying to avoid something

eve /iːv/ *noun* □ **on the eve of** on the day or night before an event, or a short time before ○ *On the eve of the election, the result already seemed clear.* ○ *The flights were cancelled on the eve of our departure.*

① **even** /ˈiːv(ə)n/ *adj* **1.** flat, level ○ *The road has a smooth, even surface.* **2.** not changing ○ *They kept up an even pace for miles.* ○ *The temperature is an even 28° all through the day.* **3.** equal in a competition ○ *At the end of the competition three teams were even with 96 points.* ■ *adv* used for showing surprise or making an expression stronger ○ *He doesn't even like strawberries.* ○ *Even the cleverest businessperson can make mistakes.* ○ *She's tall, but her sister is even taller.* □ **even now** in spite of the passing of time ○ *Even now, he won't admit he was wrong.* □ **even then** in spite of what has happened □ **even worse** worse than before ○ *That film was bad, but this one is even worse.* ◇ **to get even with someone** to try to have your revenge on someone ◇ **even if** it doesn't matter if ○ *We'll try and drive there, even if it's snowing.* ◇ **even so** in spite of something ○ *It was pouring with rain, but even so they decided to go ahead with the village fête.* ◇ **even though** in spite of the fact that ○ *He didn't take an umbrella, even though it was raining quite hard.*

even out *phrasal verb* to make something even or regular with fewer differences ○ *He tried to even out the payments over a period of twelve months.*

even up *phrasal verb* to make something fairer or more balanced ○ *This group needs two more members to even it up.*

① **evening** /ˈiːvnɪŋ/ *noun* the late part of the day, when it starts to get dark ○ *I saw her yesterday evening.* ○ *The accident took place at 8.30 in the evening.* ○ *We arrived in London at breakfast time, having left*

New York the previous evening. ○ *We always go to a restaurant on Sunday evenings.* ○ *They took an evening flight to Madrid.* ○ *The evening meal is served from 7.30 to 10.30.* □ **this evening** today in the evening ○ *We'll all meet this evening after work.*

evening class /ˈiːvnɪŋ klɑːs/ *noun* one of a series of lessons held in the evening, mainly for adults

evening dress /ˈiːvnɪŋ dres/ *noun* clothes worn on special occasions in the evening, consisting of a long dress for women, and a black suit with a black or white bow tie for men

evenly /ˈiːv(ə)nli/ *adv* in an equal way

① **event** /ɪˈvent/ *noun* **1.** something important which happens ○ *the events leading up to the war* ○ *A baby's first birthday is always a very happy event.* □ **in the normal course of events** as things usually happen ○ *In the normal course of events, the winner should get a silver cup.* **2.** a party, meeting or other organised occasion ○ *They're planning a dance event in October.* **3.** a sporting competition, or a part of a sporting competition ○ *It's the biggest golf event of the year.* ○ *The last event was the 100 metres hurdles.* ◇ **in the event** as it happened ○ *In the event, the party went off very well.* ◇ **in the event of** if something should happen ○ *In the event of his refusing the job then we will advertise it again.* ◇ **in the event, at all events** whatever may happen or may have happened ○ *I don't know exactly what happened – in any event, it doesn't matter.*

eventful /ɪˈventf(ə)l/ *adj* with a lot of events taking place

eventual /ɪˈventʃuəl/ *adj* in the end

① **eventually** /ɪˈventʃuəli/ *adv* after a long time ○ *After weeks of hesitation he eventually decided to sell the cottage.*

① **ever** /ˈevə/ *adv* at any time (*used with negatives, in questions and in conditional sentences*) ○ *Nothing ever happens here.* ○ *Did you ever meet my brother?* ○ *If you ever want to borrow my car again, just phone me.* □ **than ever** used for emphasis after comparatives ○ *She is singing better than ever.* ○ *He went on playing the trumpet louder than ever.* ◇ **ever since (then)** from that time on ○ *She was in a road accident and has been afraid to drive ever since.* ◇ **ever so, ever such (a)** extremely (*informal*) ○ *She's been ever so ill.* ○ *I'm ever so grateful.* ○ *He's ever such a kind man.* ◇ **for ever** always ◇ **hardly ever** almost never ○ *I hardly ever go to the theatre.*

evergreen /ˈevəgriːn/ *noun* a tree which keeps its leaves all winter ○ *Holly and other evergreens can be used as decorations in winter.* ■ *adj* (*of a tree or bush*) keeping its leaves all winter ○ *We need an evergreen climber to cover that wall.* Compare **deciduous**

everlasting /ˌevəˈlɑːstɪŋ/ *adj* going on for ever

① **every** /ˈevri/ *adj* **1.** each ○ *It rained every day during the holidays.* ○ *We have a party every New Year's Day.* ○ *Every Wednesday, he goes for a swim in the local pool.* ○ *Every house in the street has a garden.* **2.** with a particular amount of time or distance in between ○ *The medicine is to be taken every four hours.* ○ *Have your car checked every 10,000 kilometres.* ◇ **every other** each alternate one

everybody /ˈevribɒdi/ *pron* same as **everyone**

everyday /ˈevrideɪ/ *adj* ordinary or very common

① **everyone** /ˈevriwʌn/ *pron* all the people involved in a particular situation ○ *Everyone has to die some day.* ○ *If everybody is here, we can start.* ○ *Everyone must show their passport.* (NOTE: **everyone** and **everybody** are followed by **they, their, themselves,** etc., but the verb stays singular: *Is everyone enjoying themselves? Not everybody likes pop music, do they?*) □ **everyone else** all the other people ○ *Only Maggie could come – everyone else was too busy.*

① **everything** /ˈevriθɪŋ/ *pron* **1.** all things ○ *Did you bring everything you need?* ○ *The burglars stole everything of value.* ○ *Everything he says annoys me.* **2.** things in general ○ *Everything was dark in the street.* ○ *Everything is under control.*

① **everywhere** /ˈevriweə/ *adv* in all places ○ *There were papers lying about everywhere.* ○ *We've looked everywhere for the key and can't find it.*

evict /ɪˈvɪkt/ (**evicts, evicting, evicted**) *verb* to force someone, especially a tenant, to leave a property (NOTE: + **eviction** *n*)

① **evidence** /ˈevɪd(ə)ns/ *noun* a fact which proves that something really exists or has happened [~of/~for/~that] ○ *Scientists are still looking for evidence of life on Mars.* ○ *There's no evidence for the existence of dragons.Have you any evidence that he was ever planning to come.*

evident /ˈevɪd(ə)nt/ *adj* obvious

③ **evil** /ˈiːv(ə)l/ *adj* morally very bad ○ *She's considered to be an evil woman.* ○ *His evil intentions were evident as soon as he locked the door.*

evocative /ɪˈvɒkətɪv/ *adj* producing a memory or feeling

evoke /ɪˈvəʊk/ (**evokes, evoking, evoked**) *verb* to produce something in your memory (*formal*)

③ **evolution** /ˌiːvəˈluːʃ(ə)n/ *noun* a gradual development

evolve /ɪˈvɒlv/ (**evolves, evolving, evolved**) *verb* **1.** to work out gradually a scientific theory or a way of working ○ *The research team has evolved its own methods of testing.* **2.** to develop gradually ○ *Modern dance evolved from classical ballet.* ○ *Birds originally evolved from reptiles.*

ewe /juː/ *noun* a female sheep (NOTE: Do not confuse with **yew, you**. The male sheep is a **ram**.)

ex /eks/ *noun* a former boyfriend or girlfriend, or husband or wife (*informal*) ○ *She won't talk to her ex about money.* ○ *How do you get on with your ex?*

ex- /eks/ *prefix* used for showing that a person used to have a particular job or relationship ○ *an ex-soldier* ○ *Tom's my ex-boyfriend.*

exacerbate /ɪgˈzæsəbeɪt/ (**exacerbates, exacerbating, exacerbated**) *verb* to make something worse or more painful

① **exact** /ɪgˈzækt/ *adj* as specified and not different in any way ○ *What is the exact time of arrival?* ○ *The sales assistant asked me if I had the exact sum, since she had no change.*

exacting /ɪgˈzæktɪŋ/ *adj* demanding a lot of effort

① **exactly** /ɪgˈzæktli/ *adv* not more, not less ○ *That comes to exactly ten dollars and fifty cents.* ○ *The time is exactly 16.24.*

exaggerate /ɪgˈzædʒəreɪt/ (**exaggerates, exaggerating, exaggerated**) *verb* to make things seem worse, better, bigger etc than they really are ○ *The wide black belt exaggerates her small waist.* ○ *She exaggerated the importance of my contribution.*

exaggerated /ɪgˈzædʒəreɪtɪd/ *adj* bigger or more important than usual

exaggeration /ɪgˌzædʒəˈreɪʃ(ə)n/ *noun* a statement making things seem worse, better, bigger etc. than they really are □ **without exaggeration** quite truthfully ○ *It was, without any exaggeration, the most perfect summer's day.*

exalted /ɪgˈzɔːltɪd/ *adj* in a high position in authority ○ *In his exalted position he should be able to afford a larger car.*

① **exam** /ɪgˈzæm/ *noun* same as **examination 1** ○ *The exam was very difficult – half the students failed.* ○ *She passed all her exams.*

① **examination** /ɪgˌzæmɪˈneɪʃ(ə)n/ *noun* **1.** a written or spoken test ○ *The examination was very difficult – half the students failed.* ○ *He did badly in his English examination.* ○ *She came first in the final examination for the course.* (NOTE: often shortened to **exam** in this sense) **2.** an occasion on which someone looks at something to see if it works properly, or to see if something is wrong ○ *He had to have an X-ray examination.* ○ *The examination of the car showed that its brakes were faulty.* □ **on examination** when something is examined ○ *On further examination, the newspaper report was shown to be quite untrue.*

① **examine** /ɪgˈzæmɪn/ (**examines, examining, examined**) *verb* **1.** to look carefully at something to see what is in it, or what it is like ○ *The doctor examined her throat.* ○ *We will have to examine the shop's scales to see if they show the correct weight.* ○ *The customs officials wanted to examine the inside of the car.* ○ *The water samples were examined in the laboratory.* **2.** to test a student ○ *They examined everyone in mathematics and computer skills.*

examiner /ɪgˈzæmɪnə/ *noun* a person who conducts an exam

① **example** /ɪgˈzɑːmpəl/ *noun* something chosen to show something ○ *This is a good example of French architecture of the eleventh century.* □ **to set an example** to do things well or properly yourself, so that other people can copy you ○ *He sets everyone a good example by getting into the office before 8.00 every morning.* □ **to make an example of someone** to punish someone so that others will learn not to do what that person did ○ *Her teacher made an example of her by making her miss the class trip.* ◇ **for example** as a typical case ○ *She is keen on getting her weight down – for example, she's stopped eating bread.* ○ *Why don't we sell anything to Eastern Europe – to Poland, for example?*

exasperated /ɪgˈzɑːspəreɪtɪd/ *adj* extremely annoyed with someone or at something [~at/with] ○ *They were exasperated with the waiter who kept bringing them the wrong dishes.* ○ *He was exasperated at getting the engaged tone all the time.*

exasperating /ɪɡ'zɑːspəreɪtɪŋ/ *adj* very annoying

exasperation /ɪɡˌzɑːspə'reɪʃ(ə)n/ *noun* annoyance and frustration

excavate /'ekskəveɪt/ (**excavates, excavating, excavated**) *verb* **1.** to dig a hole in the ground ○ *In order to reinforce the foundations they had to excavate to a depth of 10m.* **2.** to carry out an archaeological investigation of a place ○ *Howard Carter excavated the tomb of Tutankhamen.* (NOTE: + **excavation** *n*)

③ **exceed** /ɪk'siːd/ (**exceeds, exceeding, exceeded**) *verb* to go beyond something ○ *The car was exceeding the speed limit.* ○ *Our expenses have exceeded our income for the first time.* ○ *Did the UN troops exceed their mandate?*

exceedingly /ɪk'siːdɪŋli/ *adv* very (*formal*)

excel /ɪk'sel/ (**excels, excelling, excelled**) *verb* to be very good at something [~at/~in] ○ *At school, she excelled in mathematics.*

③ **excellence** /'eksələns/ *noun* very good quality

① **excellent** /'eksələnt/ *adj* very good ○ *We had an excellent meal in a Chinese restaurant.* ○ *Her handwriting is excellent – it is much clearer than mine.*

① **except** /ɪk'sept/ *prep* not including ○ *She's allowed to eat anything except milk products.* ○ *Everyone was sick on the boat, except (for) me.* ○ *VAT is levied on all goods except books, newspapers, food and children's clothes.* ■ *conj* other than; apart from ○ *He doesn't do anything except sit and watch football on the TV.* ○ *Everything went well, except that James was sick.* ○ *Everyone enjoyed the birthday party, except (that) there wasn't enough to eat.* (NOTE: [all senses] Do not confuse with **accept.**)

② **exception** /ɪk'sepʃən/ *noun* something that is not included [/~to] ○ *All the students failed, with one exception.* ○ *All the books are here, with the exception of the English dictionary.* ○ *Are there any exceptions to this spelling rule?*

exceptional /ɪk'sepʃən(ə)l/ *adj* **1.** extremely good ○ *She's an exceptional athlete.* ○ *His debating skills are really exceptional.* **2.** being an exception ○ *In exceptional cases, the fee may be waived.*

exceptionally /ɪk'sepʃən(ə)li/ *adv* to a very great degree, often so great as to be surprising

excerpt /'eksɜːpt/ *noun* a small part of a larger piece of music or writing

excess *noun* too much of something ○ *He had an excess of alcohol in his bloodstream.* ■ *plural noun* **excesses** bad behaviour such as eating or drinking too much ○ *On Monday mornings he always feels guilty about the weekend's excesses.* ■ *adj* more than necessary ○ *The factory has excess capacity and may sell off some of its machines.* ◇ **in excess of** more than ○ *quantities in excess of 25 kilos* ◇ **to excess** too much ○ *She diets to excess.*

excessive /ɪk'sesɪv/ *adj* more than is usual

① **exchange** /ɪks'tʃeɪndʒ/ *verb* (**exchanges, exchanging, exchanged**) **1.** to give one thing and to get another thing back ○ *The footballers from the two teams exchanged shirts at the end of the match.* **2.** □ **to exchange something for something else** to give one thing and get something else in return ○ *Goods can be exchanged only on production of the sales slip.* ○ *If the trousers are too small you can take them back and exchange them for a larger pair.* ■ *noun* the act of giving one thing for another ○ *the exchange of rings during the wedding ceremony*

③ **exchange rate** /ɪks'tʃeɪndʒ reɪt/ *noun* the rate at which the money of one country can be changed for another

excise /ɪk'saɪz/ (**excises, excising, excised**) *verb* to cut something out ○ *The surgeon decided to excise the growth.*

excitable /ɪk'saɪtəb(ə)l/ *adj* easily excited

excite /ɪk'saɪt/ (**excites, exciting, excited**) *verb* **1.** to make someone lively and happy ○ *His speech excited the crowd.* **2.** to cause a particular feeling ○ *The thought of going to work in Kuala Lumpur excited his imagination.* ○ *The case has excited a lot of interest in the press.*

② **excited** /ɪk'saɪtɪd/ *adj* lively and happy because you think something good is going to happen ○ *She's excited at* or *by the thought of going on holiday.* ○ *The children are excited because it's the Christmas holidays.* ○ *What's everyone so excited about?* ○ *It was lovely to see the children's happy and excited faces.*

② **excitement** /ɪk'saɪtmənt/ *noun* the feeling of being excited ○ *What's all the excitement about?* ○ *The children are always in a state of excitement before the holidays.*

② **exciting** /ɪk'saɪtɪŋ/ *adj* **1.** making you feel excited ○ *The news about the house is really exciting.* **2.** full of activity, sometimes making you a little scared because you do not know what is going to happen ○ *I couldn't sleep after watching an exciting film on TV.*

③ **exclaim** /ɪk'skleɪm/ (**exclaims, exclaiming, exclaimed**) *verb* to say something loudly and suddenly

exclamation /ˌekskləˈmeɪʃ(ə)n/ *noun* the action of shouting out

exclamation mark /ˌekskləˈmeɪʃ(ə)n mɑːk/ *noun* a written or printed sign (!) which shows surprise (NOTE: The usual US term is **exclamation point**.)

② **exclude** /ɪk'skluːd/ (**excludes, excluding, excluded**) *verb* **1.** not to include someone or something ○ *Damage by fire is excluded from the insurance policy.* ○ *Don't exclude his name from your list.* **2.** to stop a child going to school because of bad behaviour ○ *Ten children had to be excluded last term.*

③ **excluding** /ɪk'skluːdɪŋ/ *prep* not including

③ **exclusion** /ɪk'skluːʒ(ə)n/ *noun* **1.** the act of shutting someone or something out [~from] ○ *She was hurt at her exclusion from the guest list.* **2.** the act of being stopped from going to school because of bad behaviour ○ *The school only considers exclusion as a last resort.* ◊ **exclude**

exclusive /ɪk'skluːsɪv/ *adj* not available to everyone ○ *an exclusive Caribbean holiday resort* ○ *The new health club is very exclusive.*

excrement /'ekskrɪmənt/ *noun* solid waste matter produced by the body (*technical*)

excrete /ɪk'skriːt/ (**excretes, excreting, excreted**) *verb* to produce waste matter (*formal*)

excruciating /ɪk'skruːʃieɪtɪŋ/ *adj* extremely painful

excursion /ɪk'skɜːʃ(ə)n/ *noun* a short pleasure trip

② **excuse[1]** /ɪk'skjuːs/ *noun* a reason given for doing something wrong, or for not doing what was expected ○ *His excuse for not coming was that he forgot the date.*

② **excuse[2]** /ɪk'skjuːz/ (**excuses, excusing, excused**) *verb* to forgive someone for making a small mistake ○ *Please excuse my arriving late like this.* ◇ **excuse me** used for attracting someone's attention ○ *Excuse me, is this the right bus for Oxford Circus?* ◇ **excuse me** used meaning 'please forgive me' ○ *Excuse me for arriving so late.* ○ *Excuse me for interrupting, but could you repeat what you have just said?*

execute /'eksɪkjuːt/ (**executes, executing, executed**) *verb* **1.** to kill someone as a punishment ○ *The government's political enemies were executed.* **2.** to do something that has been planned or agreed (*formal*) ○ *As part of the test, drivers are asked to execute an emergency stop.* **3.** in computing, to carry out instructions ○ *Press ENTER to execute the program.*

③ **execution** /ˌeksɪ'kjuːʃ(ə)n/ *noun* **1.** the legal killing of person sentenced to death ○ *In the 19th century there were still public executions.* **2.** the act of carrying something out ○ *The execution of the manoeuvre was more complicated than we imagined.* □ **to put a plan into execution** to carry out a plan ○ *The new government wants its financial strategy to be put into execution as soon as possible.*

executioner /ˌeksɪ'kjuːʃ(ə)nə/ *noun* a public official who executes people

② **executive** /ɪg'zekjʊtɪv/ *noun* a businessperson who makes decisions ○ *You can't leave a decision like that to the junior executives.* ○ *Top executives usually earn very high salaries.*

exemplary /ɪg'zempləri/ *adj* excellent (*formal*)

exemplify /ɪg'zemplɪfaɪ/ (**exemplifies, exemplifying, exemplified**) *verb* to show something as an example, or be an example of something

exempt /ɪg'zempt/ *adj* not forced to obey certain laws or rules ■ *verb* (**exempts, exempting, exempted**) to allow someone not to do something that other people have to do [~from] ○ *Children are exempted from entry charges.* □ **to exempt someone from doing something** to allow someone not to do something that other people have to do ○ *Children and retired people are exempted from paying these charges.*

exemption /ɪg'zempʃ(ə)n/ *noun* the act of exempting someone from something

① **exercise** /'eksəsaɪz/ *noun* practice in using physical or mental powers ○ *She does her piano exercises every morning.* □ **to take exercise** to do physical movements, like walking or running, in order to keep fit ○ *You should take some exercise every day if you want to lose weight.*

exercise bike /'eksəsaɪz baɪk/, **exercise bicycle** *noun* a machine like a bicycle, but which does not move, which you can pedal on as exercise

exercise book /ˈeksəsaɪz bʊk/ *noun* a notebook with lines on each page for writing school work in

③ **exert** /ɪgˈzɜːt/ (**exerts, exerting, exerted**) *verb* to use force or pressure

exertion /ɪgˈzɜːʃ(ə)n/ *noun* an effort

exhale /eksˈheɪl/ (**exhales, exhaling, exhaled**) *verb* to breathe out

exhaust /ɪgˈzɔːst/ *verb* (**exhausts, exhausting, exhausted**) **1.** to wear someone out ○ *The uphill climb had exhausted him.* **2.** to finish a supply of something ○ *We've exhausted our supplies of food.* ■ *noun* **1.** same as **exhaust pipe 2.** gas which is produced by a car engine and is released into the air through the exhaust pipe ○ *We live in the city centre and the children are breathing car exhaust all day.*

exhausted /ɪgˈzɔːstɪd/ *adj* very tired ○ *I'm exhausted after running three miles.* ○ *They staggered back home very late, with three exhausted children.*

exhausting /ɪgˈzɔːstɪŋ/ *adj* extremely tiring

exhaustion /ɪgˈzɔːstʃən/ *noun* the state of being very tired

exhaustive /ɪgˈzɔːstɪv/ *adj* very thorough

exhaust pipe /ɪgˈzɔːst paɪp/ *noun* the tube at the back of a motor vehicle from which gases produced by the engine are sent out into the air (NOTE: The US term is **tailpipe**.)

exhibit /ɪgˈzɪbɪt/ *noun* an object displayed in court or at an exhibition ○ *Exhibit A is the murder weapon.* ○ *The museum has loaned several exhibits to foreign galleries.* ○ *The buyers admired the exhibits on our stand.* ■ *verb* (**exhibits, exhibiting, exhibited**) to display something ○ *They are exhibiting at the Motor Show.* ○ *They have rows of vases exhibited on the shelves of the shop.* ○ *She is exhibiting three paintings in the local art show.*

② **exhibition** /ˌeksɪˈbɪʃ(ə)n/ *noun* a public show of things such as paintings or flowers ○ *The exhibition is open from 10 a.m. to 5 p.m.* ○ *We stood in line for half an hour waiting to get into the Picasso exhibition.*

exhibitor /ɪgˈzɪbɪtə/, **exhibiter** *noun* a person or company that displays something at an exhibition

exhilarated /ɪgˈzɪləreɪtɪd/ *adj* extremely excited and happy

exhilarating /ɪgˈzɪləreɪtɪŋ/ *adj* which makes you full of energy

exile /ˈeksaɪl/ *noun* **1.** the state of being sent away from your home country ○ *The ex-president went into exile in Switzerland.* **2.** a person who is sent away from his or her own country ○ *The former king is now an exile in New York.* ○ *The coup was mounted by exiles living across the border.* ■ *verb* (**exiles, exiling, exiled**) to send someone away from his or her home country as a punishment ○ *The new government exiled the former dictator to Europe.*

① **exist** /ɪgˈzɪst/ (**exists, existing, existed**) *verb* **1.** to be real or present ○ *When I was a child, colour TV didn't exist.* ○ *I don't believe the document exists any more – I think it has been burnt.* **2.** to live in a difficult situation [~for/~on] ○ *They managed to exist for several weeks on berries and roots.*

① **existence** /ɪgˈzɪstəns/ *noun* **1.** the state of existing ○ *Is there anything which proves the existence of life on Mars?* □ **in existence** still existing ○ *The original painting is no longer in existence.* ○ *Only one version of this car is still in existence in a museum in Geneva.* **2.** a way of living ○ *They lived a miserable existence for a few days without heat or light.*

① **existing** /ɪgˈzɪstɪŋ/ *adj* available at this time ○ *Can we modify the existing structure in some way?* ○ *Existing regulations do not allow the sale of food in the street.*

① **exit** /ˈegzɪt/ *noun* **1.** a way out of a building or area ○ *The customers all rushed towards the exits when the fire alarm rang.* ○ *A car bumped into ours at the exit to the car park.* **2.** a road that leads off a motorway, big main road or roundabout ○ *Take the third exit and continue for two miles.* ■ *verb* (**exits, exiting, exited**) **1.** to leave a computer system ○ *Press ESC to exit the system.* **2.** to leave a place (*formal*) ◇ **No Exit!** a sign showing that you must not go out this way

exodus /ˈeksədəs/ *noun* the departure of a crowd of people

exonerate /ɪgˈzɒnəreɪt/ (**exonerates, exonerating, exonerated**) *verb* to state that someone who was previously blamed for something was not responsible for it

exorbitant /ɪgˈzɔːbɪtənt/ *adj* (*of prices*) very high

exorcise /ˈeksɔːsaɪz/ (**exorcises, exorcising, exorcised**), **exorcize** *verb* to say prayers to force evil spirits to leave someone's body, or ghosts to leave a haunted house

exotic /ɪɡ'zɒtɪk/ *adj* **1.** unusual **2.** referring to a strange or foreign place

② **expand** /ɪk'spænd/ (**expands, expanding, expanded**) *verb* to increase the size or extent of something ○ *We have plans to expand our business.*

expanse /ɪk'spæns/ *noun* a large surface covered by something

② **expansion** /ɪk'spænʃən/ *noun* an increase in size

expansive /ɪk'spænsɪv/ *adj* **1.** (*of a person*) who wants to talk freely about things ○ *She was in a very expansive mood when she met the TV reporters.* ○ *You would expect someone who works in public relations to be a bit more expansive than she is.* **2.** covering a wide area ○ *He waved his arms in an expansive gesture of greeting.*

expatriate /eks'pætriət/ *noun* a person who is not living in his or her home country (NOTE: often shortened to **expat**; *expats living in the Far East*)

① **expect** /ɪk'spekt/ (**expects, expecting, expected**) *verb* **1.** to think or guess that something is the case [~(that)] ○ *I expect you are tired after your long train journey.* **2.** to think that it is right that someone should do something ○ *He expects me to do all the housework.* **3.** to be waiting for someone ○ *I can't talk for long – we're expecting visitors.* **4. be expecting** to be pregnant ○ *My sister's expecting twins.*

expectant /ɪk'spektənt/ *adj* expecting; hopeful

② **expectation** /ˌekspek'teɪʃ(ə)n/ *noun* a feeling that something will happen ○ *The performance lived up to our expectations.* ○ *We thought our team would do well, but in the end they exceeded all our expectations.*

② **expected** /ɪk'spektɪd/ *adj* **1.** which you think or hope will happen **2.** due to arrive ○ *Our guests are expected at 10 o'clock.*

expedient /ɪk'spiːdiənt/ *noun* a convenient way of doing something ○ *Registering as a student was a simple expedient to avoid military service.* ■ *adj* convenient ○ *Colleges find it expedient to have students from other countries because they pay higher fees than local students.*

expedition /ˌekspɪ'dɪʃ(ə)n/ *noun* a journey to explore a place ○ *He set off on an expedition to the South Pole.*

expel /ɪk'spel/ (**expels, expelling, expelled**) *verb* **1.** to make someone leave an organisation, school or country ○ *As soon as the generals came to power they expelled all their former allies.* **2.** to send a child away from school ○ *He was expelled for taking drugs.* ◊ **expulsion**

expend /ɪk'spend/ (**expends, expending, expended**) *verb* to spend time or energy doing something (*formal*)

expendable /ɪk'spendəb(ə)l/ *adj* which is not worth keeping; which can be thrown away

② **expenditure** /ɪk'spendɪtʃə/ *noun* an amount of money spent

② **expense** /ɪk'spens/ *noun* an amount of money that you have to pay ○ *I can't afford the expense of a holiday just now.* ○ *The expense of running a household seems to increase every week.* □ **at great expense** having spent a lot of money ○ *The house has been redecorated at great expense.* ■ *plural noun* money spent to do something □ **all expenses paid** with all costs paid by someone else ◇ **at someone's expense** paid for by someone else ◇ **at the expense of something** in a way which has a bad effect on something else ○ *She brought up her three children at the expense of her career.*

① **expensive** /ɪk'spensɪv/ *adj* costing a lot of money ○ *Fresh vegetables are more expensive in winter.* ○ *Send your furniture to Australia by sea – it would be much too expensive by air.*

① **experience** /ɪk'spɪəriəns/ *noun* **1.** knowledge obtained by working or living in various situations [~of/with] ○ *You must write down the full details of your past experience in your CV.* ○ *I have no experience with children.* ○ *Some experience of selling is required for this job.* (NOTE: no plural in this sense) **2.** something that happens to you ○ *Going to the top of the Eiffel Tower was a wonderful experience.* ○ *He wrote a book about his experiences in the desert.* ■ *verb* (**experiences, experiencing, experienced**) to live through something ○ *I'm surprised she's so cheerful after all she experienced in hospital.* ○ *I have experienced a great deal of pleasure and frustration in my career.* ○ *He is experiencing sharp pains in his tooth.*

① **experienced** /ɪk'spɪəriənst/ *adj* good at something because you have learnt a lot from particular experiences you have had ○ *She's a very experienced doctor.* ○ *He's the most experienced member of our staff.* ○ *The police are experienced in crowd control.*

experiment[1] /ɪk'sperɪmənt/ *noun* **1.** a scientific test ○ *to carry out scientific experiments* **2.** a way of finding out about something ○ *We're offering our customers free samples as an experiment.*

experiment[2] /ɪk'sperɪment/ (**experiments, experimenting, experimented**) *verb* **1.** to try something new [~with] ○ *We've been experimenting with a new look for our shop window.* **2.** to carry out a scientific test [~with/~on] ○ *They are experimenting with a new treatment for asthma.* ○ *The laboratory does not experiment on live animals.*

③ **experimental** /ɪkˌsperɪ'ment(ə)l/ *adj* **1.** different from what has been done before **2.** relating to scientific experiments and testing

experimentation /ɪkˌsperɪmen'teɪʃ(ə)n/ *noun* the process of carrying out experiments

② **expert** /'ekspɜːt/ *noun* **1.** a person who knows a great deal about a subject [~in/on] ○ *a leading expert in* or *on tropical diseases* ○ *A rose expert was the judge at the flower show.* **2.** a person who is very good at doing something [~at] ○ *He's an expert at getting the children to go to bed.* ■ *adj* **1.** knowing a lot about a subject ○ *They can give you expert advice on DIY.* **2.** very good at doing something [~at] ○ *I'm not very expert at making pastry.*

③ **expertise** /ekspə'tiːz/ *noun* special knowledge

expire /ɪk'spaɪə/ (**expires, expiring, expired**) *verb* **1.** to come to an end ○ *The lease expires next year.* □ **my passport *or* visa has expired** I need a new passport *or* visa **2.** to die (*formal*)

expiry /ɪk'spaɪəri/ *noun* the fact of coming to an end

expiry date /ɪk'spaɪəri deɪt/ *noun* the last date on which something can be used

① **explain** /ɪk'spleɪn/ (**explains, explaining, explained**) *verb* **1.** to give reasons for something [~(that)/~how/when/what etc] ○ *Can you explain why the weather is cold in winter and warm in summer?* **2.** to make something clear [~to] ○ *He tried to explain the new pension scheme to the staff.*

explain away *phrasal verb* to give excuses for something

② **explanation** /ˌeksplə'neɪʃ(ə)n/ *noun* **1.** a reason for something [~of/~for] ○ *The police officer asked him for an explanation of why the stolen car was in his garage.* ○ *The company has given no explanation for the change of plan.* **2.** information about something [~of/about] ○ *The leaflet gives an explanation of how to apply for a place on the course.*

explanatory /ɪk'splænət(ə)ri/ *adj* explaining something. ◊ **self-explanatory**

expletive /ɪk'spliːtɪv/ *noun* a swear word

explicit /ɪk'splɪsɪt/ *adj* **1.** straightforward and clear ○ *Could you please be more explicit?* ○ *Their intention to sell the shop was not explicit in the letter.* **2.** showing sex or violence very clearly ○ *The film contains explicit sex scenes.*

explode /ɪk'spləʊd/ (**explodes, exploding, exploded**) *verb* **1.** (*of bombs, etc.*) to blow up ○ *A bomb exploded in a crowded train.* **2.** to make a bomb go off ○ *The army cleared the area and then exploded the bomb.* **3.** to increase rapidly

exploit[1] /'eksplɔɪt/ *noun* a great or daring achievement ○ *He told us of his exploits during the war.*

exploit[2] /ɪk'splɔɪt/ (**exploits, exploiting, exploited**) *verb* **1.** to take commercial advantage of something ○ *We are hoping to exploit the mineral resources of the North Sea.* **2.** to make unfair use of someone, usually by paying them very low wages ○ *The company was accused of exploiting children by employing them in its shoe factories.*

③ **exploration** /ˌeksplə'reɪʃ(ə)n/ *noun* **1.** the act of travelling and discovering unknown parts of the world ○ *the exploration of the Antarctic in the early 20th century* ○ *He is famous for his exploration of the Himalayas.* **2.** a careful investigation ○ *We recommend further exploration of possible alternative solutions to the problem.*

exploratory /ɪk'splɒrət(ə)ri/ *adj* forming part of an exploration of something

② **explore** /ɪk'splɔː/ (**explores, exploring, explored**) *verb* **1.** to travel and discover place and things that you have not seen before ○ *It is a part of the jungle which has never been explored before.* ○ *We spent our holidays exploring Holland by canal.* **2.** to investigate something carefully [~how/what/why etc] ○ *We are exploring the possibility of moving the office to London.* ○ *We want to explore how we can improve our service.*

explorer /ɪk'splɔːrə/ *noun* a person who explores unknown parts of the world

③ **explosion** /ɪk'spləʊʒ(ə)n/ *noun* an occasion on which something such as a bomb explodes ○ *Several explosions were* *heard during the night as the army occupied the city.*

explosive /ɪk'spləʊsɪv/ *adj* **1.** likely to blow up ○ *The containers held an explosive mixture.* ○ *The police found an explosive device in the car.* **2.** likely to cause difficulties ○ *The situation in the office was explosive, with the clerical staff demanding to see the manager.* ○ *The paper is running an explosive story about the minister.* ■ *noun* a substance used for destroying things by making them explode ○ *Tests revealed traces of explosive on his hands.* ○ *The box contained explosives.* ○ *Police explosives experts defused the bomb.*

exponent /ɪk'spəʊnənt/ *noun* a person who practises a certain belief or a certain art

② **export**[1] /'ekspɔːt/ *noun* **1.** the business of selling products in other countries ○ *They make cars for export.* ○ *There is a big export trade in wine.* **2.** a product sent to a foreign country to be sold ○ *The country's major export is tea.* ○ *Exports to Africa have increased by 25%.*

③ **export**[2] /ɪk'spɔːt/ (**exports, exporting, exported**) *verb* to send goods to a foreign country for sale ○ *The company exports half of what it produces.*

exporter /ɪk'spɔːtə/ *noun* a person or company that sells goods to foreign countries

③ **expose** /ɪk'spəʊz/ (**exposes, exposing, exposed**) *verb* **1.** to show something which was hidden ○ *He pulled off his shirt, exposing a huge scar across his chest.* ○ *The plastic coating had rubbed off to expose the metal beneath.* **2.** to let light go onto a photographic film ○ *You didn't expose the film for long enough.* **3.** to reveal a shocking fact ○ *He was exposed as the person who wrote the letters.* ○ *The newspaper has exposed several government scandals.*

exposé /ɪk'spəʊzeɪ/ (*plural* **exposés**) *noun* a report which exposes something wrong

③ **exposed** /ɪk'spəʊzd/ *adj* open and not protected

③ **exposure** /ɪk'spəʊʒə/ *noun* **1.** the act of putting someone under the influence of something [~of/~to] ○ *the exposure of young children to violence on television* ○ *the exposure of some workers to radiation* **2.** the state of not being protected, e.g. from cold ○ *The survivors of the crash were all suffering from exposure after spending a night in the snow.* **3.** the time and amount of light needed for a picture to be taken on film ○ *You need a short exposure to photograph a racing car.* **4.** the act of revealing something, e.g. corruption ○ *the newspaper's exposure of the actor's involvement in the scandal* ○ *The council was embarrassed by a string of exposures of irregular financial transactions.*

expound /ɪk'spaʊnd/ (**expounds, expounding, expounded**) *verb* to explain something in detail

① **express** /ɪk'spres/ *verb* (**expresses, expressing, expressed**) to show thoughts or feelings in words, pictures or actions [~in/] ○ *His paintings express his inner thoughts.* ○ *His grief was expressed in fierce anger and constant activity.* ○ *He expressed his gratitude in a short speech.* □ **to express yourself** to make your thoughts or feelings known to other people □ **to express itself** to be shown ○ *His grief expressed itself in fierce anger and constant activity.* ■ *noun* a fast train

① **expression** /ɪk'spreʃ(ə)n/ *noun* **1.** a word, or group of words ○ *'Until the cows come home' is an expression which means 'for a very long time'.* **2.** a look on a person's face which shows a feeling [~of/~on] ○ *His expression showed how miserable he was.* ○ *Everyone noticed the expression of surprise on her face.* **3.** the act of expressing thoughts and feelings

expressionless /ɪk'spreʃ(ə)n(ə)ləs/ *adj* showing no feeling

expressive /ɪk'spresɪv/ *adj* showing feeling

expressly /ɪk'spresli/ *adv* clearly and definitely

expresso /ek'spresəʊ/ *noun* another spelling of **espresso**

expressway /ɪk'spresweɪ/ *noun US* a fast road with few exits

expulsion /ɪk'spʌlʃən/ *noun* the act of making someone leave or sending someone away from an organisation, school or country. ◊ **expel**

exquisite /ɪk'skwɪzɪt/ *adj* very finely made and beautiful

② **extend** /ɪk'stend/ (**extends, extending, extended**) *verb* **1.** to stretch something out ○ *She extended both arms in welcome.* **2.** to cover a particular are area of land [/~over] ○ *The grounds of the house extend over two hectares.* **3.** to make something longer or bigger ○ *We are planning to extend our garden.* ○ *The company has extended my contract for another two years.*

extended family /ɪkˌstendɪd 'fæm(ə)li/ *noun* a family which includes relatives such as aunts and uncles outside the central family group. Compare **nuclear family**

② **extension** /ɪk'stenʃən/ *noun* **1.** the act of extending something [~of/] ○ *I have applied for a short extension to my visa.* **2.** something that makes something bigger or longer ○ *We're building an extension onto our house.* **3.** a telephone in an office which is connected to the company's main line ○ *Can you get me extension 21?* ○ *The manager is on extension 23.*

③ **extensive** /ɪk'stensɪv/ *adj* covering a large area or amount ○ *The grounds of the house are very extensive.* ○ *The church roof needs extensive repair work.*

① **extent** /ɪk'stent/ *noun* the degree, size or area of something ○ *The extent of the earthquake damage was only revealed later.* ○ *He opened up the map to its full extent.* □ **to some extent, to a certain extent** partly; in some way ○ *To some extent, the weather was the cause of the failure of the village fair.*

③ **exterior** /ɪk'stɪəriə/ *noun* the outside parts ○ *The exterior of the house is painted pink.*

exterminate /ɪk'stɜːmɪneɪt/ (**exterminates, exterminating, exterminated**) *verb* **1.** to kill all the living things in a place **2.** to kill a person or a group of people (NOTE: + **extermination** *n*)

② **external** /ɪk'stɜːn(ə)l/ *adj* on the outside ○ *The external walls of the house are quite solid.* ○ *Her injuries were all external.*

extinct /ɪk'stɪŋkt/ *adj* **1.** (*of a type of animal or plant*) no longer in existence, because all of the same kind have died ○ *These birds are in danger of becoming extinct.* **2.** ((*of a volcano*)) no longer active ○ *The mountain is an extinct volcano.* Compare **dormant**

③ **extinction** /ɪk'stɪŋkʃən/ *noun* **1.** (*of a species*) the process of dying out ○ *The last remaining pairs of birds were taken to a zoo for breeding purposes, so as to save the species from extinction.* □ **to face extinction, to be threatened with extinction** to be likely to die out ○ *The tiger is facing extinction unless measures are taken to protect it.* **2.** the act of putting out a fire ○ *The firefighters will stand by until the complete extinction of the blaze.* (NOTE: no plural)

extinguish /ɪk'stɪŋgwɪʃ/ (**extinguishes, extinguishing, extinguished**) *verb* to put out a fire

extinguisher /ɪk'stɪŋgwɪʃə/ *noun* same as **fire extinguisher**

extol /ɪk'stəʊl/ (**extols, extolling, extolled**) *verb* to praise someone or something very highly (*literary*) (NOTE: The US spelling is **extoll**.)

extort /ɪk'stɔːt/ (**extorts, extorting, extorted**) *verb* □ **to extort something from someone** to get money or promises from someone by threats ○ *The secret police extorted very valuable information from him.* ○ *The gang extorted money from small shopkeepers by threatening to burn down their shops.*

extortion /ɪk'stɔːʃ(ə)n/ *noun* the practice of getting money from someone by threats

extortionate /ɪk'stɔːʃ(ə)nət/ *adj* (*of a price*) very high or excessive

① **extra** /'ekstrə/ *adj* more than usual; additional ○ *We need an extra four teachers* or *four extra teachers for this course.* ○ *The charge for delivery is extra.* ○ *Staff get extra pay for working on Sundays.*

extract[1] /'ekstrækt/ *noun* **1.** a thing reduced from something larger ○ *He will be reading extracts from his latest novel.* **2.** something which is reduced to a concentrated form ○ *soup made from meat extract* ○ *Add a drop of vanilla extract to the custard.*

extract[2] /ɪk'strækt/ (**extracts, extracting, extracted**) *verb* **1.** to pull something out ○ *The dentist extracted two teeth.* ○ *We managed to extract £10 from him.* ○ *The police extracted a confession from the accused.* **2.** to produce something from something else ○ *It is no longer viable to extract tin from Cornish mines.* ○ *The oil is extracted from lavender flowers.*

extraction /ɪk'strækʃən/ *noun* **1.** the act of pulling out a tooth ○ *An extraction will cost you £40.* **2.** the production of something from something else ○ *The extraction of iron ore from this mine is becoming too costly.* ◇ **of German** *or* **Japanese** *or* **etc extraction** belonging to a family originally from Germany *or* Japan *or* etc

extracurricular /ˌekstrəkə'rɪkjʊlə/ *adj* outside the normal course of study

extradite /'ekstrədaɪt/ (**extradites, extraditing, extradited**) *verb* to bring an arrested person back from another country to stand trial for a crime committed in his or her home country (NOTE: + **extradition** *n*)

extraordinarily /ɪk'strɔːd(ə)nərəli/ *adv* extremely ○ *Her action was extraordinarily brave.*

① **extraordinary** /ɪk'strɔːd(ə)n(ə)ri/ *adj* **1.** wonderful ○ *Seeing her again gave him an extraordinary thrill.* ○ *A peacock's feathers are quite extraordinary.* **2.** very unusual ○ *It's extraordinary weather for June.*

extrapolate /ɪk'stræpəleɪt/ (**extrapolates, extrapolating, extrapolated**) *verb* to calculate something unknown on the basis of available information (NOTE: + **extrapolation** *n*)

extraterrestrial /ˌekstrətə'restriəl/ *adj* from a planet other than Earth

extravagance /ɪk'strævəgəns/ *noun* unnecessary expense

extravagant /ɪk'strævəgənt/ *adj* **1.** spending a lot of money ○ *They are extravagant when it comes to buying presents for their children.* **2.** expensive and not necessary ○ *an extravagant purchase* **3.** unusual and unreasonable ○ *The company has made some extravagant claims for its new soap powder.*

extravaganza /ɪkˌstrævə'gænzə/ *noun* an expensive and luxurious party, show, film or event

② **extreme** /ɪk'striːm/ *adj* **1.** very great ○ *The device is made to withstand extreme cold.* ○ *He showed extreme reluctance to get involved.* □ **at the extreme end** right at the end **2.** very unusual or serious ○ *an extreme case* **3.** considered unreasonable by some people ○ *He holds extreme views.* ■ *noun* something very unusual or very great ○ *You get extremes of temperature here – very hot summers and very cold winters.* □ **to go from one extreme to the other** to change to something completely different ○ *She can go from one extreme to the other – from being happy and excited one minute to being gloomy and depressed the next.* ◇ **to go to extremes** to do everything in an excessive way

① **extremely** /ɪk'striːmli/ *adv* to a very great degree ○ *It was extremely hot in August.* ○ *The film is extremely long, and some people left before the end.* ○ *It is extremely difficult to spend less than $50.00 a day on meals in New York.*

extreme sport /ɪkˌstriːm 'spɔːt/ *noun* a sport which is very dangerous and exciting, e.g. snowboarding

extremist /ɪk'striːmɪst/ *noun* a person who has very strong opinions, usually about politics, that many other people regard as unreasonable ○ *left-wing extremists* (NOTE: + **extremism** *n*) ■ *adj* having strong, unusual opinions ○ *Members of an extremist group have taken over the post office.*

extremity /ɪk'stremɪti/ *noun* an end point ○ *the northern extremity of the island* ■ *plural noun* **extremities** the fingers, toes, nose and ears ○ *Her extremities became numb in the cold.* (NOTE: plural is **extremities**)

extricate /'ekstrɪkeɪt/ (**extricates, extricating, extricated**) *verb* **1.** to get someone out of a difficult situation ○ *She asked her father to help extricate her from the awkward situation she found herself in.* **2.** to remove something with difficulty ○ *The surgeons extricated the bullet which had lodged itself behind her eye.*

extrovert /'ekstrəvɜːt/, **extravert** *noun* a person who is very friendly and likes to be with other people

exuberant /ɪg'zjuːbərənt/ *adj* lively and energetic

exude /ɪg'zjuːd/ (**exudes, exuding, exuded**) *verb* to send out or to give off a strong smell or a strong feeling

① **eye** /aɪ/ *noun* **1.** the organ in the head which you see with ○ *He has brown eyes.* ○ *Close your eyes and count to ten while we all hide.* ○ *I've got a bit of dust in my eye.* □ **as far as the eye can see** for a very long distance ○ *Grasslands stretch as far as the eye can see.* □ **to keep your eyes open for something** to watch out for something ○ *Keep your eyes open for burglars!* **2.** a small hole in the end of a needle, through which the thread goes ■ *verb* (**eyes, eyeing** or **eying, eyed**) to look at something carefully ○ *She sat in a corner, eyeing the arrivals indicator.* ◇ **to catch someone's eye** to look at someone who is looking at you ○ *She caught his eye and nodded towards the door.* ◇ **to keep an eye on someone** *or* **something** to watch someone or something carefully to see that it is safe ○ *Can you keep an eye on the house while we are away?* ◇ **to keep an eye out for someone** *or* **something** to watch to see if someone or something is available or nearby ○ *I must keep an eye out for Seville oranges to make some marmalade.* ○ *Can you keep an eye out for the traffic warden while I go into the bank?* ◇ **to turn a blind eye to something** not to pay any attention to something bad, even if you know it exists ◇ **not to see eye to eye** not to agree with someone ○ *He doesn't see eye to eye with the boss.* ◇ **to have your eye on someone** to think someone is very good, very attractive or not to be trusted ○ *She's* *got her eye on her best friend's brother.* ○ *The police have had their eye on him for ages.*

eye up *verb* to look at someone showing that you think them attractive (*informal*) ○ *He was eyeing up one of the girls on the other side of the room.*

eyeball /ˈaɪbɔːl/ *noun* a part of the eye, the round ball of tissue through which light passes and which is controlled by various muscles ○ *The retina is a light-sensitive membrane at the back of the eyeball.* ■ *verb* (**eyeballs, eyeballing, eyeballed**) to stare at someone closely (*informal*) ◇ **eyeball to eyeball** facing each other closely ○ *He had an eyeball-to-eyeball confrontation with the referee.*

③ **eyebrow** /ˈaɪbraʊ/ *noun* the line of hair above each of your eyes ◇ **to raise your eyebrows** to look surprised

eye-catching /ˈaɪ ˌkætʃɪŋ/ *adj* very noticeable and attracting attention

eye contact /ˈaɪ ˌkɒntækt/ *noun* the act of looking at someone who is looking at you

③ **eyelash** /ˈaɪlæʃ/ *noun* one of the hairs growing round the edges of your eyes

③ **eyelid** /ˈaɪlɪd/ *noun* a piece of skin which covers the eye

eyeliner /ˈaɪlaɪnə/ *noun* a substance used for drawing a coloured line round your eye

eye-opener /ˈaɪəʊp(ə)nə/ *noun* something which surprises you (*informal*)

eyeshadow /ˈaɪʃædəʊ/ *noun* make-up for colouring the skin round your eye

③ **eyesight** /ˈaɪsaɪt/ *noun* the ability to see

eyesore /ˈaɪsɔː/ *noun* an unpleasant sight

eyewitness /ˈaɪwɪtnəs/ *noun* a person who has seen something happen

e-zine /ˈiː ziːn/ *noun* a magazine which appears in a website on the Internet

F

f /ef/, **F** *noun* the sixth letter of the alphabet, between E and G

fable /ˈfeɪb(ə)l/ *noun* a moral story, usually about animals, making them seem like human beings

fabled /ˈfeɪb(ə)ld/ *adj* well-known in stories

③ **fabric** /ˈfæbrɪk/ *noun* **1.** cloth used for making things such as clothes and curtains ○ *The curtains are made of an expensive fabric.* ○ *We need a fireproof fabric for the chairs.* **2.** the basic structure of society or of an organisation [~of] ○ *During the revolution, the whole fabric of society collapsed.*

fabricate /ˈfæbrɪkeɪt/ (**fabricates, fabricating, fabricated**) *verb* to invent an untrue story

fabrication /ˌfæbrɪˈkeɪʃ(ə)n/ *noun* an invented story that is not true ○ *The newspaper story was a complete fabrication from start to finish.*

fabulous /ˈfæbjʊləs/ *adj* **1.** imaginary, as in fairy stories ○ *unicorns and other fabulous animals* **2.** marvellous or wonderful ○ *It was a fabulous party.*

① **face** /feɪs/ *noun* **1.** the front part of your head ○ *Don't forget to wash your face before you go to the party.* **2.** the front part of something ○ *a clock face* ○ *She put the photograph face down on the desk.* ■ *verb* (**faces, facing, faced**) to have the face or front towards ○ *Can everyone please face the camera?* ○ *The house faces north.* ◇ **to show your face** to come to or be in a place where there are other people ○ *After what he said about my mother he doesn't dare show his face here.* ◇ **to lose face** to be embarrassed by being shown to be wrong or weak ○ *She can't bear being told off in front of the class – it makes her lose face.* ◇ **to make a face** to make a strange expression ○ *He made funny faces and all the children laughed.* ◇ **to try to keep a straight face** to try not to laugh

face up to③ *phrasal verb* to accept an unpleasant situation and try to deal with it

faceless /ˈfeɪsləs/ *adj* anonymous and threatening

facelift /ˈfeɪslɪft/ *noun* **1.** an operation to make your face look younger **2.** the fact of working to make something appear newer ○ *Our website needs a facelift.*

face-saving /ˈfeɪs ˌseɪvɪŋ/ *adj* which avoids causing someone to feel embarrassed and ashamed

facet /ˈfæsɪt/ *noun* one of many aspects of something, e.g. a problem ○ *The problem presents many different facets.* ○ *The film explores several fascinating facets of his life in Africa.*

facetious /fəˈsiːʃəs/ *adj* funny or joking in a way that other people think unsuitable

face to face /ˌfeɪs tə ˈfeɪs/ *adv* looking at each other ○ *He turned a corner and came face to face with a police officer.* ○ *I don't like doing business on the phone – I prefer to make deals face to face.*

face value /ˌfeɪs ˈvæljuː/ ◇ **to take something at (its) face value** to believe that what something appears to mean is true ○ *When we booked our holiday we took what the tour company said about the hotel at face value – but it turned out not to be true.*

facial /ˈfeɪʃ(ə)l/ *noun* a beauty treatment in which your face is cleaned and massaged ○ *She's having a facial.*

facile /ˈfæsaɪl/ *adj* too simple and not carefully considered

③ **facilitate** /fəˈsɪlɪteɪt/ (**facilitates, facilitating, facilitated**) *verb* to make something easy

① **facility** /fəˈsɪlɪti/ (*plural* **facilities**) *noun* **1.** an ability to do something easily ○ *She has a facility for languages.* (NOTE: no plural) **2.** a means of doing something ○ *We offer facilities for payment.* **3.** a large building that enables people to do or have something ○ *We have opened our new warehouse facility.*

facsimile /fækˈsɪmɪli/ *noun* **1.** a perfect copy ○ *This is not the real Magna Carta – it is a facsimile.* ○ *They have published a* *facsimile edition of one of the earliest printed books.* **2.** a fax; a copy of a document or picture sent by telephone ○ *Can you confirm the booking by facsimile?*

① **fact** /fækt/ *noun* something such as a piece of information that is true ○ *He faced up to the fact that he wasn't fit enough for the race.* ○ *Did you check all the facts before you wrote the article?* ◇ **in fact, in actual fact** really; the truth is that ○ *He told the police he had seen a man steal a car but in fact he made the whole story up.* ○ *It rained a lot last month – in fact it rained all month.* ◇ **as a matter of fact** actually; used for saying what is really true, especially when it is surprising ○ *Have you seen John recently? – as a matter of fact I met him yesterday.*

faction /ˈfækʃən/ *noun* a group of people linked together in opposition to a leader or to a government

① **factor** /ˈfæktə/ *noun* **1.** a thing which has influence or importance [~in/~for] ○ *The key factor in our decision is the price.* ○ *The crucial factor for the success of the village fair is the weather.* **2.** one of the numbers which produce a certain other number when multiplied ○ *Four and two are factors of eight.*

① **factory** /ˈfækt(ə)ri/ (*plural* **factories**) *noun* a building where things are made in large quantities using machines ○ *She works in a shoe factory.* ○ *He owns a furniture factory.* ○ *The factory makes computer terminals.*

factory farm /ˈfækt(ə)ri fɑːm/ *noun* a farm where large numbers of animals are kept in small spaces, using modern methods to produce food quickly

factual /ˈfæktʃuəl/ *adj* referring to facts

faculty /ˈfæk(ə)lti/ (*plural* **faculties**) *noun* **1.** a natural ability **2.** a main division of a university ○ *the Faculty of Arts* or *the Arts Faculty* **3.** *US* the teaching staff of a school, university or college ○ *There is a meeting of the faculty tomorrow.*

fad /fæd/ *noun* a strange temporary craze for something

fade /feɪd/ (**fades, fading, faded**) *verb* **1.** to lose colour ○ *The more you wash your jeans, the more they'll fade.* ○ *This teeshirt has faded.* **2.** to become less bright or light ○ *As the light faded, bats came out in the garden.* ○ *The light from the torch began to fade as the batteries ran out.* ○ *The islands faded away into the distance.* **3.** to become less noisy ○ *The sound of the music faded away.*

faeces /ˈfiːsiːz/ *plural noun* solid waste matter passed from the body ○ *The patient's faeces are not solid.* (NOTE: The US spelling is **feces**.)

fag /fæg/ *noun* a cigarette ○ *He cadged a fag off me.* ○ *I bought a packet of fags at the kiosk.*

Fahrenheit /ˈfærənhaɪt/ *noun* a scale of temperatures where the freezing and boiling points of water are 32° and 212°. Abbreviation **F**. Compare **Celsius** (NOTE: used in the USA, but less common in the UK and not usually used in other countries. It is usually written as **F** after the degree sign: *32°F*: say: 'thirty-two degrees Fahrenheit'.)

① **fail** /feɪl/ (**fails, failing, failed**) *verb* **1.** not to succeed [~on] ○ *The examination was very difficult – half the students failed.* ○ *He passed his maths exam but failed English.* ○ *She failed in her attempt to become a contestant in the TV game show.* **2.** □ **to fail to do something** not to do something that should be done ○ *The car failed to stop at the red light.* **3.** not to work properly ○ *The brakes failed and he couldn't stop the car.* ◇ **if all else fails** if you can't do anything else ○ *If all else fails you can always borrow my car.*

failing[1] /ˈfeɪlɪŋ/ *noun* a weakness or bad point of something or someone ○ *She has only one failing – she goes to sleep in front of the TV every night.* ○ *In spite of his failings, we still think he is a wonderful father.*

failing[2] □ **failing that** if that does not work ○ *Try some tape to seal the joint or, failing that, call a plumber.*

② **failure** /ˈfeɪljə/ *noun* **1.** a situation in which something stops working ○ *The accident was caused by brake failure.* ○ *The failure of the plane's engine caused the crash.* **2.** an occasion on a person or event is not successful ○ *His attempts to balance on one leg were a complete failure.* **3.** a person who does not succeed at things ○ *I'm no good at anything – I'm a failure.*

faint /feɪnt/ *adj* difficult to see or hear ○ *They could hear a faint tapping under the wreckage.* ○ *We could just see the faint outline of a man in the fog.* (NOTE: + **faintly** *adv*) ■ *verb* (**faints, fainting, fainted**) to become unconscious for a short time ○ *She fainted when she saw the blood.*

① **fair** /feə/ *adj* **1.** (*of hair or skin*) light-coloured ○ *Her hair is quite fair.* ○ *People with fair skin should use a stronger sun cream.* **2.** not very good ○ *Her work is only fair.* **3.** right, giving someone what they deserve ○ *That's not fair – you must let other children* *play with the ball too.* ○ *It isn't fair if you go on holiday when we have so much work to do.* **4.** (*of weather*) bright and warm ○ *According to the TV the weather will be fair tomorrow.* ■ *noun* **1.** a group of machines for riding on and stalls where you can win things, set up in one place for a short time ○ *The fair is coming to the village for the Easter Bank Holiday.* ○ *He went to the fair and won a prize for shooting.* **2.** an exhibition for selling and advertising goods ○ *We are going to the car fair tomorrow.* (NOTE: Do not confuse with **fare**.)

fair game /feə 'geɪm/ *noun* a person or thing which it is fair to criticise

fairground /'feəgraʊnd/ *noun* a place in the open air where a fair is held

① **fairly** /'feəli/ *adv* **1.** in a way that is right; giving people what they deserve ○ *She complained that she had not been treated fairly in the interview.* **2.** to some degree ○ *I'm fairly certain I have seen this film before.* ○ *She had been working there a fairly short time.* ○ *The hotel is fairly close to the centre of town.* (NOTE: The order of words for **fairly** and **quite** is different: *He's a fairly good worker* but *He's quite a good worker.*)

fairness /'feənəs/ *noun* a tendency or ability to do things in a fair way ○ *Everyone acknowledged her fairness in dealing with staff complaints.*

fairway /'feəweɪ/ *noun* a part of a golf course where the grass is cut, though it is not very short

fairy /'feəri/ (*plural* **fairies**) *noun* a small imaginary creature who can perform magic

fairytale /'feəriteɪl/ *noun* a children's story about fairies, princes, princesses and giants

② **faith** /feɪθ/ *noun* **1.** confidence or trust [~in] ○ *I don't have much faith in these new teaching methods.* **2.** a religious belief ○ *We must respect people of other faiths.* ◇ **in good faith** honestly, even though perhaps wrongly ○ *I sold him the car in good faith – I didn't know it would break down the next day.*

faithful /'feɪθf(ə)l/ *adj* (*of a person or an animal*) trusting or loyal ○ *his faithful old dog* ○ *We must be faithful to father's last wishes.*

fake /feɪk/ *noun* something which is made or designed to look like something else that is, e.g. more valuable ○ *That picture isn't by Picasso, it's a fake.* ■ *adj* not real ○ *She was wearing a fake fur coat.*

falcon /'fɔːlkən/ *noun* a small bird of prey, sometimes trained to catch other birds as a sport

① **fall** /fɔːl/ *verb* (**falls, falling, fell, fallen**) **1.** to drop to a lower level [~down/off/through/into/out of etc] ○ *Snow fell all night* ○ *She fell down the stairs.* ○ *He fell off the ladder.* ○ *Did he fall into the river or did someone push him?* **2.** [~by/~into/onto/~of/~off/through/out of etc/~on/~to/~with] □ **to fall asleep** to go to sleep ○ *We all fell asleep after dinner.* ■ *noun* **1.** an amount of something which has come down ○ *There was a heavy fall of snow during the night.* **2.** the process of going to a lower level [~in] ○ *a welcome fall in the price of oil* ○ *the fall in the exchange rate* **3.** the act of losing your balance [~of] ○ *He had a fall and hurt his back.* ○ *She had a bad fall while skiing.*

fall apart *phrasal verb* **1.** to come to pieces ○ *My shoes are falling apart.* ○ *The porcelain dish just fell apart in my hands.* **2.** to come to an end (in its present form) ○ *When they showed him the letters, his life simply fell apart.* ○ *When our German partners withdrew, the deal fell apart.*

fall away *phrasal verb* to become less

fall back on *phrasal verb* to do or use something only after all other things have failed

fall behind *phrasal verb* to be late in doing something

fall down *phrasal verb* **1.** to drop to the ground ○ *She fell down and hurt her knee.* **2.** to become broken down through age ○ *The place has been deserted for so long it's falling down.*

fall for *phrasal verb* **1.** to fall in love with someone ○ *She always falls for intelligent men.* **2.** to be tricked by something ○ *Don't fall for his sales talk.*

fall off *phrasal verb* to become fewer ○ *The number of customers starts to fall off after 4 o'clock.*

fall out *phrasal verb* **1.** to drop to the ground after having been in something ○ *We put cushions on the floor next to the bed in case she fell out.* **2.** to have an argument ○ *They fell out over the bill for drinks.*

fall over *phrasal verb* to fall down after having been upright

fall through *phrasal verb* not to take place as planned

fallacy /'fæləsi/ (*plural* **fallacies**) *noun* a false argument

fallible /ˈfælɪb(ə)l/ *adj* capable of being wrong

falling-out /ˌfɔːlɪŋ ˈaʊt/ (*plural* **fallings-out**) *noun* the act of having an argument with someone

fallout /ˈfɔːlaʊt/ *noun* an unfortunate result ○ *the fallout from the arrest of the party treasurer*

② **false** /fɔːls/ *adj* not real; designed to look like something real ○ *a set of false nails*

false alarm /fɔːls əˈlɑːm/ *noun* a signal for an emergency when there isn't one

falsehood /ˈfɔːlshʊd/ *noun* a lie (*literary*) ○ *It appears that he had told several falsehoods under oath.*

false start /ˌfɔːls ˈstɑːt/ *noun* a start of a race which is not allowed by the judge

falsify /ˈfɔːlsɪfaɪ/ (**falsifies, falsifying, falsified**) *verb* to change something to make it wrong or not real

falter /ˈfɔːltə/ (**falters, faltering, faltered**) *verb* **1.** to stop happening or working effectively ○ *The engine faltered and then stopped.* ○ *Progress in the talks faltered.* **2.** to speak nervously with pauses ○ *As she ended the speech her voice faltered for a moment.*

fame /feɪm/ *noun* the fact of being famous or well-known

famed /feɪmd/ *adj* well-known

② **familiar** /fəˈmɪliə/ *adj* heard or seen before; that you know ○ *The dog wagged its tail as it heard its master's familiar voice at the door.* ○ *He looked round the room, and saw a couple of familiar faces.*

familiarity /fəˌmɪliˈærɪti/ *noun* **1.** a good knowledge of someone *or* something [~with] ○ *His familiarity with London makes him an excellent guide.* **2.** a very informal way of speaking to someone ○ *The manager told him off for familiarity with the customers.*

① **family** /ˈfæm(ə)li/ (*plural* **families**) *noun* **1.** a group of people who are related to each other, especially mother, father and children ○ *He grew up in a big family of five brothers and sisters.* **2.** a group of animals or plants which are closely related ○ *Lions and tigers are members of the cat family.*

family name /ˈfæm(ə)li neɪm/ *noun* the name of someone's family, shared by all people in the family

family planning /ˌfæm(ə)li ˈplænɪŋ/ *noun* the practice of controlling the number of children in a family by preventing unwanted pregnancies

family tree /ˌfæm(ə)li ˈtriː/ *noun* a table showing a family going back over many generations

famine /ˈfæmɪn/ *noun* a very serious lack of food

famished /ˈfæmɪʃt/ *adj* very hungry

① **famous** /ˈfeɪməs/ *adj* known to many people, especially most people in a place or country ○ *a famous department store* ○ *He's a famous footballer.* ○ *This tea shop is famous for its cakes.*

② **fan** /fæn/ *noun* **1.** a piece of equipment for moving air to make people or things cooler ○ *We put electric fans in the office to try to keep cool.* **2.** an enthusiastic supporter of something or someone, e.g. a team or a pop group ○ *There was a crowd of fans waiting for him outside the theatre.*

fanatic /fəˈnætɪk/ *noun* a person who is extremely enthusiastic about something

fanciful /ˈfænsɪf(ə)l/ *adj* imaginative or unlikely

fan club /ˈfæn klʌb/ *noun* an organised group of supporters of someone, e.g. a pop star or an actor

③ **fancy** /ˈfænsi/ *verb* (**fancies, fancying, fancied**) **1.** to want to have something (*informal*) ○ *I fancy an ice cream – anyone else want one?* ○ *Do you fancy sharing a taxi to the airport?* **2.** to like someone in a sexual way ○ *I'm sure that guy fancies you.* ■ *adj* (**fancier, fanciest**) attractive or decorated ○ *He wore a fancy tie to the party.*

fancy dress /ˌfænsi ˈdres/ *noun* an unusual costume worn to a party

fanfare /ˈfænfeə/ *noun* a short piece of music, played especially on trumpets, when an important person arrives or a show starts

fang /fæŋ/ *noun* an animal's long tooth

fantasise /ˈfæntəsaɪz/ (**fantasises, fantasising, fantasised**), **fantasize** *verb* to imagine

③ **fantastic** /fænˈtæstɪk/ *adj* **1.** wonderful ○ *We had a fantastic time on holiday.* **2.** strange; like a dream ○ *His stories are full of fantastic creatures.*

fantasy /ˈfæntəsi/ (*plural* **fantasies**) *noun* an invented story ○ *Her story of meeting a rich man in Paris was pure fantasy.*

FAQ /fæk, ˌef eɪ ˈkjuː/ *abbr* frequently asked questions

① **far** /fɑː/ *adv* **1.** a certain distance away ○ *The railway station is not far from here.* ○ *How far away is Paris from London?* ○

The road was blocked by cars as far as we could see. **2.** used with comparatives to mean 'much' ○ *It is far cheaper to go by bus than by train.* ○ *Restaurant food is far nicer than the food at college.* ■ *adj* (**farther** or **further, farthest** or **furthest**) a long way away; distant ○ *The shop is at the far end of the High Street.* ◇ **as far as I know** *or* **can tell** I think, but I am not completely sure ○ *As far as I know, the train is on time.* ○ *As far as I can tell, the engine is working normally.*

faraway /ˌfɑːrəˈweɪ/ *adj* which is a long way away

farce /fɑːs/ *noun* **1.** a funny play based on silly situations ○ *We went to see a 19th-century French farce.* **2.** a silly situation ○ *The meeting rapidly became a farce.*

farcical /ˈfɑːsɪk(ə)l/ *adj* silly

③ **fare** /feə/ *noun* a price which you have to pay for a journey ○ *Rail fares have been increased by 10%.* ○ *The tourist-class fare is much less than the first class one.* ○ *If you walk to work, you will save £5 a week on bus fares.* (NOTE: Do not confuse with **fair**.)

fare dodger /ˈfeə ˌdɒdʒə/ *noun* a person who travels on public transport without a ticket

farewell /feəˈwel/ *interj, noun* goodbye ○ *It's time to say farewell.* ■ *adj* at which you say goodbye ○ *We gave a farewell party for our neighbours who were going to live in Canada.*

far-fetched /ˌfɑː ˈfetʃt/ *adj* difficult to believe

far from /ˈfɑː frɒm/ *adv* not at all ○ *The food here is far from cheap.*

② **farm** /fɑːm/ *noun* an area of land used for growing crops and raising animals ○ *He runs a pig farm.* ○ *We're going to work on a farm during the holidays.* ○ *You can buy eggs and vegetables at the farm shop.* ■ *verb* (**farms, farming, farmed**) to grow crops or raise animals on a farm ○ *He farms dairy cattle in Devon.*

farm out③ *phrasal verb* **1.** to hand over work to another person to do **2.** to hand over a child for someone else to look after ○ *The children were farmed out to their grandparents for a week.*

② **farmer** /ˈfɑːmə/ *noun* a person who manages or owns a farm

farmhouse /ˈfɑːmhaʊs/ *noun* the house where a farmer and his or her family live

farming /ˈfɑːmɪŋ/ *noun* the work of managing a farm, e.g. growing crops or keeping animals for sale

farmland /ˈfɑːmlænd/ *noun* land which is used for growing crops or raising animals for food

farmyard /ˈfɑːmjɑːd/ *noun* an area around farm buildings, where tractors are sometimes kept

③ **far off** /ˌfɑːr ˈɒf/ *adv* a long way away ○ *We could see the house far off beside the lake.*

far-off /ˈfɑːr ɒf/ *adj* which is a long way away

far-reaching /ˌfɑː ˈriːtʃɪŋ/ *adj* which has wide effects or results

far-sighted /ˌfɑː ˈsaɪtɪd/ *adj* **1.** having the ability to make wise plans for the future ○ *They were far-sighted enough to save money for their children's tuition fees.* **2.** *US* unable to see clearly things that are a short distance away

fart /fɑːt/ (**farts, farting, farted**) *verb* to pass wind from the intestines through the anus (*vulgar*)

farther /ˈfɑːðə/ *adv* at or to a longer way away

③ **fascinate** /ˈfæsɪneɪt/ (**fascinates, fascinating, fascinated**) *verb* to make someone very interested

fascinated /ˈfæsɪneɪtɪd/ *adj* very interested

③ **fascinating** /ˈfæsɪneɪtɪŋ/ *adj* very interesting ○ *A microscope gives you a fascinating glimpse of life in a drop of water.* ○ *The book gives a fascinating description of London in the 1930s.* ○ *It was fascinating to hear her talk about her travels in India.*

fascination /ˌfæsɪˈneɪʃ(ə)n/ *noun* great interest or attraction

fascism /ˈfæʃɪz(ə)m/ *noun* an extreme right-wing political movement

fascist /ˈfæʃɪst/ *noun* a person who supports fascism ○ *when the fascists came to power*

② **fashion** /ˈfæʃ(ə)n/ *noun* the most popular style at a particular time [~for] ○ *the fashion for short skirts worn worn boots* □ **in fashion** popular; following the current style ○ *High heels are in fashion this year.* □ **out of fashion** unpopular; not the current style ○ *Red cars are out of fashion at the moment.*

fashionable /ˈfæʃ(ə)nəb(ə)l/ *adj* **1.** of a style which is popular at a particular time ○ *These loose trousers are really fashionable at the moment.* **2.** popular with rich or glamorous people ○ *She lives in the fashionable West End of London.* ○ *It's a fash-*

ionable restaurant for film stars and journalists.

② **fast** /fɑːst/ *adj* **1.** quick ○ *I just love driving fast cars.* **2.** not stopping anywhere ○ *This is the fast train to London.* **3.** (*of a clock*) to show a time which is later than the correct time ■ *adv* **1.** quickly ○ *Walk faster if you want to catch up with the children in front.* ○ *Don't go so fast – you almost hit that man on the zebra crossing.* **2.** tightly fixed in a particular position ○ *The window was stuck fast and I couldn't open it.* ■ *verb* (**fasts, fasting, fasted**) to eat nothing for religious or health reasons ○ *Many people fast during Lent.* ○ *He fasted for a week.*

fasten /ˈfɑːs(ə)n/ (**fastens, fastening, fastened**) *verb* to close or attach something tightly ○ *Please fasten your seatbelts.* ○ *These shoes fasten with a buckle.*

fastener /ˈfɑːs(ə)nə/, **fastening** *noun* an object which fastens something such as a piece of clothing

fastening /ˈfɑːs(ə)nɪŋ/ *noun* a device which fastens something

③ **fast food** /fɑːst ˈfʊd/ *noun* food which is prepared and served quickly

fast-forward /fɑːst ˈfɔːwəd/ (**fast-forwards, fast-forwarding, fast-forwarded**) *verb* to make something such as a DVD or a videotape move forward quickly

fastidious /fæˈstɪdiəs/ *adj* hard to please, careful about tidiness and cleanliness

fast-track /ˌfɑːst ˈtræk/ *adj* (*of a process*) which is faster than normal ○ *They have started a fast-track application scheme.*

① **fat** /fæt/ *adj* (**fatter, fattest**) having too much flesh or weighing too much ○ *Two fat men got out of the little white car.* ○ *You'll have to eat less – you're getting too fat.* ○ *He's fatter than me.* ■ *noun* a part of meat which is yellowish-white ○ *If you don't like the fat, cut it off.*

fatal /ˈfeɪt(ə)l/ *adj* causing people to die ○ *There were three fatal accidents on this road last year.*

fatalism /ˈfeɪt(ə)lɪz(ə)m/ *noun* the belief that fate decides what happens to you and that you cannot change this

fatality /fəˈtælɪti/ (*plural* **fatalities**) *noun* a death in an accident

fat cat /fæt ˈkæt/ *noun* a rich person (*informal*)

fate /feɪt/ *noun* **1.** destiny; what is certain to happen to you ○ *They met by chance in a bar in New Zealand, and got married – it must have been fate!* **2.** what happens to someone, especially in the end ○ *The people of the country have the right to decide their own fate.* (NOTE: Do not confuse with **fete**.) ◇ **to tempt fate** to do something which could have bad results ○ *It's tempting fate to ask him to look after your girlfriend while you are away.*

fateful /ˈfeɪtf(ə)l/ *adj* important because of its serious results for the future

① **father** /ˈfɑːðə/ *noun* a man who has a son or daughter ○ *Ask your father if he will lend you his car.* ○ *She is coming to tea with her mother and father.*

③ **Father Christmas** /ˌfɑːðə ˈkrɪsməs/ *noun* a man in a long red coat, with a big white beard, who is supposed to bring presents to children on Christmas Day

father figure /ˈfɑːðə ˌfɪɡə/ *noun* a man who helps and advises a younger person who is not his child

fatherhood /ˈfɑːðəhʊd/ *noun* the fact of being a father

father-in-law /ˈfɑːðər ɪn lɔː/ (*plural* **fathers-in-law**) *noun* the father of your wife or husband

fatherly /ˈfɑːðəli/ *adj* like a father

fathom /ˈfæðəm/ (**fathoms, fathoming, fathomed**) *verb also* **fathom out** to understand something *or* someone

fatigue /fəˈtiːɡ/ *noun* the fact of being tired (*formal*) ○ *After a long day walking in the mountains, the group were showing signs of fatigue.*

fatten /ˈfæt(ə)n/; /ˌfæt(ə)n ˈʌp/ (**fattens, fattening, fattened**) *verb* to give animals more food to make them fat for slaughter

fatten up *phrasal verb* to give animals more food to make them fat for slaughter

fattening /ˈfæt(ə)nɪŋ/ *adj* which makes you fat

fatty /ˈfæti/ (**fattier, fattiest**) *adj* (*of food or tissue*) which has a lot of fat in it ○ *I don't like fatty bacon.*

fatuous /ˈfætjuəs/ *adj* silly and thoughtless

③ **faucet** /ˈfɔːsɪt/ *noun US* an object which, when you twist it, lets liquid or gas come out

② **fault** /fɔːlt/ *noun* **1.** the fact of making a mistake or of being to blame for something going wrong ○ *It isn't my fault if there's nothing in the fridge.* ○ *It's all your fault – if you hadn't stayed in bed all morning we would be at the seaside by now.* **2.** an instance of something not working properly [~in] ○ *The invoice was wrong because of a fault in the computer system.* ○

The engineers are trying to mend an electrical fault. **3.** a mistake in serving in tennis ○ *He served two double faults.* ◇ **at fault** having made a mistake ○ *The shop is at fault if they sent you the wrong table.*

faultless /ˈfɔːltləs/ *adj* perfect

③ **faulty** /ˈfɔːlti/ *adj* **1.** not working correctly or not made correctly ○ *The lights are flickering – there must be a faulty connection somewhere.* **2.** with mistakes in planning or judgment ○ *a faulty argument*

fauna /ˈfɔːnə/ (*plural* **faunas** or **faunae**) *noun* wild animals, or all the wild animals of a specific area. Compare **flora**

faux pas /ˌfəʊ ˈpɑː/ *noun* an embarrassing mistake, especially in something you do (*literary*)

favor /ˈfeɪvə/ *noun, verb* US spelling of **favour**

favorable /ˈfeɪv(ə)rəb(ə)l/ *adj* US spelling of **favourable**

favorite /ˈfeɪv(ə)rət/ *noun, verb* US spelling of **favourite**

① **favour** /ˈfeɪvə/ *noun* **1.** a friendly act done to help someone ○ *Can I ask a favour – will you look after my bike while I'm in the post office?* □ **to do someone a favour** to do something to help someone ○ *He won't charge for it – he did it as a favour.* ○ *Will you do me a favour and look after my cat when I'm away?* **2.** approval or popularity ○ *She tried to win the favour of the committee.* □ **in favour** liked or approved of □ **out of favour** disliked ■ *verb* (**favours, favouring, favoured**) **1.** to like or prefer something ○ *The managers favour moving to a bigger office.* **2.** to make things easier for someone ○ *The conditions favour Australian bowlers.* ◇ **in favour of something** preferring something ○ *We were all in in favour of a change of venue.*

favourable /ˈfeɪv(ə)rəb(ə)l/ *adj* good

③ **favourite** /ˈfeɪv(ə)rət/ *adj* which you like best ○ *Which is your favourite TV programme?* (NOTE: The US spelling is **favorite**.) ■ *noun* **1.** something or someone you like best ○ *Which ice cream is your favourite?* ○ *This game is a favourite with the children.* ○ *The singer was a favourite in the fifties.* (NOTE: The US spelling is **favorite**.) **2.** someone who is treated better than other people by a particular person ○ *She was always her father's favourite.*

favouritism /ˈfeɪv(ə)rətɪz(ə)m/ *noun* the practice of showing support for one group or one person at the expense of others (NOTE: The US spelling is **favoritism**.)

fawn /fɔːn/ *noun* a young deer ○ *a female deer with two little fawns* ■ *adj* of a brownish-cream colour

③ **fax** /fæks/ *noun* a copy of a document or picture sent to someone using telephone lines ○ *Post it to me, or send a fax.* ○ *Can you confirm the booking by fax?* ■ *verb* (**faxes, faxing, faxed**) to send a document or picture by telephone ○ *I will fax the design to you* or *I will fax you the design as soon as it is ready.*

faze /feɪz/ (**fazes, fazing, fazed**) *verb* to surprise or shock someone

① **fear** /fɪə/ *noun* the feeling of being afraid [~of/~that] ○ *Fear of the dark is common in small children.* ○ *She had a real fear that she would not recover fully from the illness.* ■ *verb* (**fears, fearing, feared**) **1.** to be afraid of something (*formal*) ○ *What do you fear most?* **2.** to worry that something bad might happen [~(that)/~for] ○ *The family feared homelessness and hunger.* ○ *Climate experts fear that the ice will melt making the sea level rise.* □ **to fear for someone or something** to worry about someone or something ○ *Most parents fear for their child's safety.*

fearful /ˈfɪəf(ə)l/ *adj* terrible

fearless /ˈfɪələs/ *adj* with no feeling of fear

fearsome /ˈfɪəs(ə)m/ *adj* frightening (*literary*)

feasible /ˈfiːzɪb(ə)l/ *adj* which can be done

feast /fiːst/ *noun* **1.** a very large meal for a group of people, especially one eaten to celebrate a special occasion **2.** a special religious day ○ *Today is the Feast of St Nicholas.*

feat /fiːt/ *noun* an particularly difficult act

③ **feather** /ˈfeðə/ *noun* one of many light soft parts which cover a bird's body

feathery /ˈfeðəri/ *adj* light and delicate like a feather

① **feature** /ˈfiːtʃə/ *noun* **1.** a part of the face such as the nose or mouth ○ *His unusual features make him easy to recognise.* **2.** an important part or aspect of something ○ *The main feature of the castle is its huge tower.* ○ *Fjords are a feature of the coastline of Norway.* **3.** an important story or article in a TV news programme or in a newspaper ○ *a feature on nuclear power* ■ *verb* (**features, featuring, featured**) **1.** to have someone as the main performer of a film, a TV programme or a play ○ *The film featured Charlie Chaplin as the tramp.* ○ *The circus features Russian clowns.* **2.** to have something as the most important part ○ *The tour features a visit to the Valley of the Kings.* ○ *The next programme will feature a discussion between environmental experts.* **3.** to appear as the main actor in, or as the subject of a film or a TV programme [~in] ○ *She has featured in many TV series.*

feature film /ˈfiːtʃə fɪlm/ *noun* a full length film

① **February** /ˈfebruəri/ *noun* the second month of the year, between January and March ○ *My birthday is in February.* ○ *He died on February 17th.* ○ *We are moving to new offices next February.* (NOTE: **February 17th**: say 'the seventeenth of February' or 'February the seventeenth', or in US English 'February seventeenth'.)

feckless /ˈfekləs/ *adj* having no determination or strength of character

③ **fed** /fed/ past tense and past participle of **feed**

③ **federal** /ˈfed(ə)rəl/ *adj* **1.** relating to the central government of the United States ○ *Most federal offices are in Washington.* ○ *Federal law is more important than state law.* **2.** relating to a system where a group of states exist under a central government ○ *the former Federal Republic of Germany*

federalism /ˈfed(ə)rəlɪz(ə)m/ *noun* a type of government in which the state is a group of provinces or states with a central government

federation /ˌfedəˈreɪʃ(ə)n/ *noun* a group of states or organisations which have joined together

③ **fed up** /ˌfed ˈʌp/ *adj* feeling bored and unhappy [~with] (*informal*) ○ *She went back to school last Tuesday and she's already fed up.* ○ *I'm fed up with watching TV – let's go out.*

② **fee** /fiː/ *noun* money paid to someone such as a doctor or lawyer for work done ○ *Private school fees are very high.* ○ *The lawyer's fee for two days' work was more than I earn in a month!*

feeble /ˈfiːb(ə)l/ (**feebler, feeblest**) *adj* **1.** physically weak, especially because of illness or age ○ *He gave a feeble wave with his hand.* ○ *The voice on the phone sounded feeble.* **2.** not strong or able to be seen or heard well ○ *She replied in a feeble voice.*

① **feed** /fiːd/ *verb* (**feeds, feeding, fed**) **1.** to give food to a person or an animal ○ *I'd better just feed the baby before we go out.* ○ *Could you feed the cat while we're away?* **2.** to take milk from its mother ○ *Please don't disturb the baby while she's feeding.* ■ *noun* food given to animals ○ *a bag of cattle feed*

① **feedback** /ˈfiːdbæk/ *noun* information or comments about something which has been done [~on/~from]

① **feel** /fiːl/ *verb* (**feels, feeling, felt**) **1.** to touch something, usually with your fingers ○ *Feel how soft the bed is.* **2.** to seem soft, cold, etc., when touched ○ *The bed feels hard.* ○ *The stone floor felt cold.* **3.** to experience something with your body or mind [~(that)/~about] ○ *Did you feel the table move?* ○ *I felt the lift go down suddenly.* ○ *Do you feel warmer now that you've had a cup of tea?* ○ *They felt happy when they saw that all was well.* ○ *By twelve o'clock she was feeling hungry.* **4.** to think something [~(that)] ○ *He feels it would be wrong to leave the children alone in the house.* ○ *The police felt that the accident was due to fog.* ■ *noun* how something seems when touched ○ *the rough feel of the wooden floor* ○ *Velvet has a soft feel.*

feel for *phrasal verb* to be sympathetic towards someone

feel up to *phrasal verb* to be strong or well enough to do something

feel-good /ⁿ, ˈfiːl gʊd/ *adj* causing people to feel happy

① **feeling** /ˈfiːlɪŋ/ *noun* an opinion that you have formed about something [/~against/~on/about//~about/~that] ○ *a feeling of security* ○ *a feeling that someone is watching you* ○ *What is your feeling about the idea?* ■ *plural noun* **feelings** someone's emotions □ **to hurt someone's feelings** to upset someone ○ *I didn't want to hurt her feelings.*

③ **feet** /fiːt/ plural of **foot**

feign /feɪn/ (**feigns, feigning, feigned**) *verb* to pretend to feel an emotion

feisty /ˈfaɪsti/ *adj* energetic and brave (*informal*)

feline /ˈfiːlaɪn/ *adj* like a cat

③ **fell** /fel/ (**fells, felling, felled**) past tense of **fall**

③ **fellow** /ˈfeləʊ/ *noun* **1.** a man ○ *A young fellow came up to me and asked me the time.* ○ *Who's that fellow with a beard?* **2.** a person who belongs to the same group ○ *I was OK on the boat, but several of my fellow passengers were sick.*

③ **fellowship** /ˈfeləʊʃɪp/ *noun* **1.** a friendly feeling ○ *He developed a feeling of fellowship with the other hostages.* **2.** a grant to continue studying ○ *She has a fellowship to research into the causes of skin cancer.*

③ **felt** /felt/ *noun* a thick material made of wool fibres pressed together

felt-tip /ˈfelt tɪp/ *noun* a pen which has a tip made from felt

② **female** /ˈfiːmeɪl/ *adj* **1.** relating to women or girls ○ *a female athlete* **2.** relating to the sex of an animal, insect or bird which gives birth to young or produces eggs ○ *a female kitten* **3.** relating to a flower which produces seeds

③ **feminine** /ˈfemɪnɪn/ *adj* like a woman or suitable for a woman ○ *Her long white silk dress was very feminine.*

femininity /ˌfemɪˈnɪnɪti/ *noun* female qualities

feminism /ˈfemɪnɪz(ə)m/ *noun* the fact of being a feminist

③ **fence** /fens/ *noun* a type of wall made of wood or wire, used to keep people or animals in or out of a place ○ *The fence was blown down.* ○ *The boys looked through the hole in the fence.* ○ *The builders put up a fence round the construction site.* ◇ **to sit on the fence** to avoid giving a definite answer to a question or giving support to one particular side ○ *He never takes sides – he just sits on the fence.*

fencing /ˈfensɪŋ/ *noun* **1.** material which makes a fence ○ *The crowd surged forward and flattened the fencing around the football ground.* **2.** the sport of fighting with swords ○ *Fencing is one of the sports in the pentathlon.*

fend /fend/ (**fends, fending, fended**) *verb* □ **to fend for yourself** to look after yourself ○ *We went to Spain and left the children to fend for themselves.*

fend off *phrasal verb* to push someone away ○ *He spent the morning fending off newspaper reporters.*

③ **fender** /ˈfendə/ *noun* **1.** a low guard around a fireplace to stop coal or wood falling out into the room ○ *She sat by the fender, poking the fire.* **2.** *US* a guard over the wheels of a car or bicycle, to prevent mud splashing ○ *She ran into a tree and bent a fender.*

feng shui /ˌfʌŋ ˈʃweɪ/ *noun* a way of arranging buildings and the furniture in them to bring happiness and good luck, according to the principles of a Chinese system based on energy flow

ferment[1] /ˈfɜːment/ *noun* a disturbance or upset ○ *The university was in a ferment.*

ferment[2] /fəˈment/ (**ferments, fermenting, fermented**) *verb* to change into alcohol by the effect of yeast on sugar ○ *Cider has to ferment for at least ten weeks before it is ready to drink.*

fern /fɜːn/ *noun* a green plant with feathery leaves which does not have flowers or seeds

ferocious /fəˈrəʊʃəs/ *adj* wild and angry ○ *a ferocious dog*

ferocity /fəˈrɒsɪti/ *noun* the fact of being fierce

ferret /ˈferɪt/ *noun* a small animal similar to a weasel, which is half-tamed and used to drive rabbits or rats from holes ○ *As boys we used to go rat-catching with ferrets.*

③ **ferry** /ˈferi/ (*plural* **ferries**) *noun* a boat which carries cars and trucks or people across a stretch of water ○ *We are going to take the night ferry to Belgium.* ○ *There's a ferry across the Rhine here.*

fertile /ˈfɜːtaɪl/ *adj* **1.** ((*of land*)) able to produce good crops **2.** (*of a female or an egg*) able to produce young ○ *The zoo hopes the female panda is fertile, so that she can have cubs.* ○ *The eagle laid several eggs but only two were fertile.* **3.** producing many good ideas

fertilise /ˈfɜːtəlaɪz/ (**fertilises, fertilising, fertilised**), **fertilize** *verb* **1.** to spread fertiliser on land ○ *The soil is poor and needs to be heavily fertilised.* **2.** to join male and female cells together, so that a new animal or plant will be made ○ *The sheep was fertilised in the laboratory.*

③ **fertiliser** /ˈfɜːtəlaɪzə/, **fertilizer** *noun* a chemical or organic material spread over the soil to make it richer and more able to produce crops

③ **fertility** /fɜːˈtɪlɪti/ *noun* the fact of being fertile, or of being able to produce crops or young

fervour /ˈfɜːvə/ *noun* a strong enthusiasm (NOTE: The US spelling is **fervor**.)

fester /ˈfestə/ (**festers, festering, festered**) *verb* **1.** (*of a wound*) to become infected ○ *His legs were covered with festering sores.* **2.** to become worse and more bitter ○ *The resentment of the staff continued to fester.*

③ **festival** /ˈfestɪv(ə)l/ *noun* **1.** a religious celebration which is celebrated at the same time each year and is usually a public holiday ○ *The tour will visit Hong Kong for the Lantern Festival.* **2.** an event, often lasting several days, where entertainment is provided ○ *We saw some excellent plays at the Edinburgh Festival this year.*

festive /ˈfestɪv/ *adj* referring to a celebration

festoon /fe'stuːn/ (**festoons, festooning, festooned**) *verb* to hang a place with decorations ○ *The streets were festooned with flags.*

② **fetch** /fetʃ/ (**fetches, fetching, fetched**) *verb* to go to a place and bring someone or something back ○ *It's your turn to fetch the children from school.* ○ *Can you fetch me the atlas?*

fete /feɪt/, **fête** *noun* a small public event, usually in the open air, with stalls, sideshows and competitions ○ *I hope it doesn't rain for the village fête.* (NOTE: Do not confuse with **fate**.)

fetish /'fetɪʃ/ *noun* **1.** a strong sexual interest in a certain object or material ○ *a rubber fetish* **2.** a very strong interest in or liking for something

feud /fjuːd/ *noun* a bitter quarrel ○ *I don't want to get involved in their family feud.* (NOTE: + **feud** *v*)

feudal /'fjuːd(ə)l/ *adj* referring to the feudal system

fever /'fiːvə/ *noun* a state in which the body's temperature is higher than normal ○ *You must stay in bed until the fever goes down.*

feverish /'fiːvərɪʃ/ *adj* **1.** suffering from fever ○ *He felt feverish and took an aspirin.* **2.** nervously quick or excited ○ *In a burst of feverish activity he finally finished writing the book on time.*

① **few** /fjuː/ *adj* (**fewer, fewest**), *noun* not many ○ *She has very few friends at work.* ○ *We go to fewer concerts than last year.* ◇ **few and far between** not very frequent ○ *Trains are few and far between on Sundays.*

fiancé /fɪ'ɒnseɪ/, **fiancée** *noun* a man or woman who is engaged to be married ○ *Her fiancé is a French lawyer.* ○ *He brought his fiancée to the party.*

fiasco /fi'æskəʊ/ (*plural* **fiascos**) *noun* a total failure

fib /fɪb/ *noun* a lie about something unimportant (*informal*) ○ *That was a little fib, wasn't it?*

fibre /'faɪbə/ *noun* **1.** a small thread of material ○ *From the fibres left at the scene of the murder, the police could work out what the murderer had been wearing.* **2.** thin threads in foods such as vegetables and bread, which cannot be digested, but which helps food to pass through your body ○ *You need to eat more fibre.*

fibreglass /'faɪbəglɑːs/ *noun* a material made from glass fibres, used to make boats and car bodies ○ *He's bought a new fibreglass boat.* (NOTE: The US spelling is **fiberglass**.)

fickle /'fɪk(ə)l/ *adj* likely to change often; not steady

fiction /'fɪkʃən/ *noun* novels ○ *fiction writers such as Graham Greene* ○ *To find the latest novels you must look in the fiction section of the library.*

fictional /'fɪkʃən(ə)l/ *adj* **1.** (*of a character*) who exists in fiction ○ *Mr Pickwick, Sam Weller and other fictional characters from Dickens may have been based on real people.* **2.** written as a novel ○ *The book is a fictional account of a real murder.*

fictitious /fɪk'tɪʃəs/ *adj* not true or not real

③ **fiddle** /'fɪd(ɔ)l/ *verb* (**fiddles, fiddling, fiddled**) to keep information about money in a dishonest way ○ *The company caught him fiddling his expense account.* ○ *She tried to fiddle her tax return.* ■ *noun* dishonest or illegal dealings (*informal*) ○ *The whole thing's a fiddle to get money from the EU.* ◇ **on the fiddle** trying to make money illegally

fiddly /'fɪdli/ *adj* small and awkward to use (*informal*)

fidelity /fɪ'delɪti/ *noun* **1.** the fact of being faithful ○ *He was rewarded for his fidelity to the president.* **2.** the quality of the sound produced by an electronic machine such as a CD player ○ *a high fidelity CD player*

fidget /'fɪdʒɪt/ (**fidgets, fidgeting, fidgeted**) *verb* to move all the time ○ *After an hour he started to fidget in his seat.* ○ *Sit still and stop fidgeting!*

① **field** /fiːld/ *noun* **1.** a piece of ground on a farm, used for keeping animals or growing crops ○ *a field of potatoes* ○ *The sheep are in the field.* **2.** a piece of ground for playing a game ○ *a football field* ○ *The two teams ran onto the field.*

field day /'fiːld deɪ/ *noun* a busy and exciting time

fielder /'fiːldə/ *noun* a member of a cricket side which is not batting

field event /'fiːld ɪˌvent/ *noun* a sport involving throwing or jumping, e.g. the high jump or the javelin

field marshal /ˌfiːld 'mɑːʃ(ə)l/ *noun* an officer of the highest rank in the army (NOTE: can be used as a title with a name: *Field Marshal Haig*)

field test /'fiːld test/ *noun* a test of a new piece of equipment in a real environment

field trip /'fiːld trɪp/ *noun* a trip taken in order to study a subject

fieldwork /ˈfiːldwɜːk/ *noun* the practice of doing some work in a real environment as part of a course of study

fiend /fiːnd/ *noun* **1.** an evil person ○ *the fiend who attacked the old lady* **2.** a person who is very enthusiastic about something ○ *He's a car fiend.* ○ *She's a health-food fiend.*

fiendish /ˈfiːndɪʃ/ *adj* **1.** very unpleasant **2.** very difficult ○ *You have to pass a fiendish exam to become an accountant.*

fierce /fɪəs/ *adj* very angry and likely to attack ○ *Watch out – that dog looks fierce.*

fiercely /ˈfɪəsli/ *adv* strongly ○ *She is fiercely independent.*

fiery /ˈfaɪəri/ *adj* **1.** burning ○ *a fiery chariot* **2.** fierce or angry ○ *She has a fiery temper.*

① **fifteen** /fɪfˈtiːn/ *noun* the number 15

① **fifteenth** /fɪfˈtiːnθ/ *adj* relating to number 15 in a series ■ *noun* number 15 in a series

① **fifth** /fɪfθ/ *adj* relating to number 5 in a series ■ *noun* **1.** number 5 in a series **2.** one part of five equal parts

① **fiftieth** /ˈfɪftiəθ/ *adj* relating to number 50 in a series ■ *noun* number 50 in a series

① **fifty** /ˈfɪfti/ *noun* the number 50

fifty-fifty /ˌfɪfti ˈfɪfti/ *adj, adv* divided into two equal amounts

fig /fɪɡ/ *noun* the juicy sweet fruit of the fig tree ○ *We sat under the tree and ate figs and goat's cheese.*

① **fight** /faɪt/ *noun* **1.** an occasion on which people try to hurt each other or knock each other down [~with/~between] ○ *He got into a fight with boys who were bigger than him.* ○ *Fights broke out between the demonstrators and the police.* □ **to pick a fight with someone** to start a fight with someone **2.** a situation in which people do everything they can to stop something from happening [~against/for] ○ *a fight against the new developments* ■ *verb* (**fights, fighting, fought**) **1.** to be involved in a situation in which people try to hurt each other or knock each other down ○ *Rival gangs fought in the street.* **2.** to do everything you can try to stop something from happening ○ *We are committed to fighting crime.* ○ *Doctors are fighting to control the disease.*

fight off *phrasal verb* to get rid of an attacker or an illness

③ **fighter** /ˈfaɪtə/ *noun* **1.** a person who fights ○ *The referee stopped the fight when one of the fighters had a cut eye.* **2.** a person who is strong ○ *She's a real fighter – she'll pull through this illness.* **3.** a fast attacking aircraft ○ *Two fighters went up to attack the enemy bombers.*

figment /ˈfɪɡmənt/ *noun* □ **a figment of someone's imagination** something which a person has imagined but which is not real

figurative /ˈfɪɡərətɪv/ *adj* **1.** (*of art*) which shows something as it really is ○ *He's a well-known figurative artist.* **2.** which is not the literal meaning of a word ○ *Calling him a 'lump of jelly' was a figurative use of the phrase.* ○ *You didn't mean that literally, did you? – No, I was speaking in a figurative sense.*

① **figure** /ˈfɪɡə/ *noun* **1.** a written number, e.g. 35 ○ *I can't read the figure on the order – is it 250?* ○ *He added up the figures on the bill.* ○ *Cheques have to be made out in both words and figures.* ◊ **double**, **single 2.** the shape of a person ○ *the figures at the front of the painting* ○ *We could see some figures through the mist.* ■ *verb* (**figures, figuring, figured**) *especially US* to consider or think something [~(that)/] ○ *We figured that you'd be late because of the show.* ○ *I figure the costs will be high.* □ **to figure on doing something** to plan to do something ○ *Had you figured on being there before two o'clock?* ◊ **that figures** that makes sense (*informal*)

figure out *phrasal verb* to try to think of an answer to a problem ○ *Try to figure out the answer yourself, instead of asking someone else.*

figurehead /ˈfɪɡəhed/ *noun* a person who seems important but who has no real power ○ *The President is just a figurehead; the Minister of the Interior has the real power.*

① **file** /faɪl/ *noun* **1.** a metal tool used for making rough surfaces smooth ○ *Use a file to round off the edges of the metal.* **2.** a set of records or information about something or someone [~on] ○ *The police have a file on him.* **3.** a container similar to an envelope, used for keeping documents in ○ *When you have finished with the papers, put them back in the file.* **4.** a set of information held in a computer ○ *Type the name of the file and then press 'enter'.* **5.** a line of people □ **in single file** one standing behind the other ○ *The children entered the hall in single file.* ■ *verb* (**files, filing, filed**) **1.** to put papers away in a file ○ *File that letter under SALES.* **2.** to walk in a line [~in/out/past/through etc] ○ *They filed past the place where the boy had been shot.* **3.** to make an official request or complaint **4.** to smooth a surface with a file ○ *File down the rough edges.*

file extension /ˈfaɪl ɪkˌstenʃən/ *noun* the second part of a computer file name,e.g. '.doc', which shows what type of file it is.

filing cabinet /ˈfaɪlɪŋ ˌkæbɪnət/ *noun* a piece of office furniture; a tall box with drawers for putting files in

filings /ˈfaɪlɪŋz/ *plural noun* small pieces of metal removed by using a file ○ *You can demonstrate magnetic fields with iron filings and a magnet.*

① **fill** /fɪl/ (**fills, filling, filled**) *verb* to make something full; to become full ○ *He filled the bottle with water.* ○ *She was filling the boxes with presents.* ○ *The bucket filled slowly.*

fill in *phrasal verb* **1.** to fill up a hole ○ *He dug a hole in the garden, put the box inside, and then filled it in.* **2.** to write in the empty spaces on a form ○ *Just fill in your name and address.* ○ *To win the prize you have to fill in the missing words.* **3.** □ **to fill in for someone** to do something which someone else normally does but cannot do ○ *I'm filling in for the manager who is on holiday.* **4.** □ **to fill someone in on something** to tell or to inform someone about something (*informal*) ○ *Just fill me in on what happened at the meeting.*

fill out *phrasal verb* **1.** to write in all the empty spaces on a form ○ *Could you please fill out this form?* **2.** (*of a person*) to become less thin

fill up *phrasal verb* **1.** to make something completely full; to become completely full ○ *He filled the bottle up with fresh water.* **2.** *US* to write in all the empty spaces on a form ○ *Fill up the form and send it back to this address.*

fillet /ˈfɪlɪt/ *noun* **1.** a piece of good-quality meat, with no bones ○ *She bought a fillet of lamb.* **2.** a piece of fish from which the bones have been removed ○ *We ordered fried fillet of sole.* ■ *verb* (**fillets, filleting, filleted**) to remove the bones from a fish ○ *Ask the fishmonger to fillet the fish for you.*

filling /ˈfɪlɪŋ/ *noun* **1.** metal put into a hole in your tooth by a dentist ○ *I had to go to the dentist because one of my fillings came out.* **2.** food used to put into something such as a sandwich or cake ○ *a cake with a jam filling*

① **film** /fɪlm/ *noun* **1.** moving pictures shown at a cinema or on TV ○ *Have you seen this old Laurel and Hardy film?* ○ *We've seen the film already on TV.* **2.** a roll of material which you put into a camera to take photographs or to record moving pictures ○ *I must buy another film before the wedding.* ○ *Do you want a colour film or a black and white one?* **3.** a thin layer of something [~of] ○ *A film of moisture formed on the cold metal surface.* ○ *Everywhere was covered with a film of dust.* ○ *A film of grease had formed on the walls around the oven.* ■ *verb* (**films, filming, filmed**) to take pictures of something or someone with a camera ○ *Security cameras filmed him robbing the bank.* ○ *'Star Wars' was filmed in 1977.*

filming /ˈfɪlmɪŋ/ *noun* the action of making a film

film-maker /ˈfɪlm ˌmeɪkə/ *noun* a person who makes films

③ **film star** /ˈfɪlm stɑː/ *noun* a well-known film actor or actress

filter /ˈfɪltə/ *noun* **1.** a piece of equipment or material through which liquids or air can pass in order to remove any substances which are not wanted ○ *The filters in the swimming pool have to be cleaned regularly.* **2.** a piece of glass on a camera which allows only certain colours or levels of light to pass through ○ *I use an orange filter to give a warm colour to the picture.* **3.** material at the end of a cigarette, used to remove nicotine

filth /fɪlθ/ *noun* **1.** dirt ○ *They were horrified at the filth in the streets.* **2.** offensive words or pictures, especially because they deal with sex in an unpleasant way (*informal*) ○ *I don't want you to read any more of this filth.*

③ **filthy** /ˈfɪlθi/ *adj* very dirty ○ *Your hands are absolutely filthy!*

fin /fɪn/ *noun* a thin part on the body of a fish which sticks out and helps it to swim ○ *From the beach they could see a shark's fin in the sea.*

① **final** /ˈfaɪn(ə)l/ *adj* last; coming at the end ○ *This is your final warning – if your work doesn't improve you will have to go.* ○ *The competition is in its final stages.* ■ *noun* the last competition in a series between several teams or competitors ○ *I thought they would win a couple of rounds, but I never imagined they would get to the final.*

finale /fɪˈnɑːli/ *noun* the last part of a piece of music or of a show

finalise /ˈfaɪnəlaɪz/ (**finalises, finalising, finalised**), **finalize** (**finalizes, finaliz-**

ing, finalized) *verb* to finish making plans for something

finalist /ˈfaɪn(ə)lɪst/ *noun* a person taking part in the final of a competition

① **finally** /ˈfaɪn(ə)li/ *adv* at last; in the end ○ *The police finally cleared up the mystery.* ○ *The little boy finally turned up in Edinburgh.*

② **finance** /ˈfaɪnæns/ *noun* money, especially money which belongs to the public or to a company ○ *How are you going to raise the finance for the project?* ○ *My finances are in a poor state at the moment.* ■ *verb* (**finances, financing, financed**) to provide money for something ○ *How are you going to finance your course at university if you don't have a grant?* ○ *The redevelopment of the city centre is being financed locally.*

① **financial** /faɪˈnænʃəl/ *adj* relating to money ○ *What is our financial position?* ○ *The company has got into financial difficulties.*

financial year /faɪˌnænʃəl ˈjɪə/ *noun* the 12-month period for which accounts are calculated

financier /faɪˈnænsiə/ *noun* a person who deals with money on a large scale

finch /fɪntʃ/ *noun* a small seed-eating bird

① **find** /faɪnd/ (**finds, finding, found**) *verb* **1.** to see where something hidden or lost is after looking for it ○ *I found a £2 coin behind the sofa.* ○ *Did she find the book she was looking for?* **2.** to discover something which was not known before [~(that)] ○ *No one has found a cure for the common cold yet.* ○ *She found that she was allergic to tomatoes.*

find out *phrasal verb* to discover information ○ *I found out something very interesting last night.* ○ *Where can I find out about my family's history?*

② **findings** /ˈfaɪndɪŋz/ *plural noun* **1.** facts discovered ○ *The two companies signed an agreement to share their research findings.* **2.** actions which someone suggests should be done ○ *The findings of the committee of inquiry will be published next week.*

① **fine** /faɪn/ *adj* (**finer, finest**) **1.** (*of the weather*) dry and sunny ○ *We'll go for a walk tomorrow if the weather stays fine.* ○ *Let's hope it's fine for the village fair next week.* **2.** healthy ○ *I was ill in bed yesterday, but today I'm feeling fine.* **3.** with no problems ○ *How are things at home? – Fine!* **4.** acceptable ○ *It's fine to wear casual clothes for this meeting.* **5.** very thin or very small ○ *Use a sharp pencil if you want to draw fine lines.* ○ *I can't read the notice – the print is too fine.* ■ *adv* satisfactorily or well ○ *It's working fine.* ■ *noun* money which you have to pay as a punishment for having done something wrong ○ *I had to pay a £25 fine for parking in a No Parking area.* ○ *He was found guilty of embezzlement and got off with a fine.* ■ *verb* (**fines, fining, fined**) to make someone pay money as a punishment for having done something wrong ○ *He was fined £25 for parking on double yellow lines.*

fine art /ˌfaɪn ˈɑːt/ *noun* art such as painting or sculpture

finely /ˈfaɪn(ə)li/ *adv* **1.** in very small pieces ○ *Cook some finely chopped onions in a little butter.* **2.** in a beautiful and delicate way ○ *She bought some finely carved ivory figures.*

finesse /fɪˈnes/ *noun* skill in dealing with awkward situations

fine-tune /faɪn ˈtjuːn/ (**fine-tunes, fine-tuning, fine-tuned**) *verb* **1.** to make changes to the way an engine works, in order to improve its performance **2.** to get something just right

① **finger** /ˈfɪŋgə/ *noun* **1.** one of the parts at the end of your hand, sometimes not including the thumb ○ *He wears a ring on his little finger.* ○ *He pressed the button with his finger.* **2.** one of the parts of a glove that cover the fingers ○ *I must mend my glove – there's a hole in one of the fingers.* ○ *Gloves without fingers are called 'mittens'.* **3.** a piece of food shaped like a finger ○ *a box of chocolate fingers* ◇ **to keep your fingers crossed** to hope that something will happen as you want it to happen ○ *Have you heard the exam results yet? – No, but I'm keeping my fingers crossed.*

fingernail /ˈfɪŋgəneɪl/ *noun* the hard thin part covering the end of a finger

fingerprint /ˈfɪŋgəprɪnt/ *noun* a mark left by a finger when you touch something

fingertip /ˈfɪŋgətɪp/ *noun* the end of the finger □ **to have information at your fingertips** to know all about something

finicky /ˈfɪnɪki/ *adj* **1.** (*of a person*) too concerned with details **2.** (*of an object*) too detailed

① **finish** /ˈfɪnɪʃ/ (**finishes, finishing, finished**) *verb* **1.** to do something completely ○ *Haven't you finished your homework yet?* ○ *Tell me when you've finished reading the paper.* ○ *You can't go out until you've finished doing the washing up.* **2.** to come to an end ○ *The game will finish at about four o'clock.*

finish off *phrasal verb* to do something completely

finish up *phrasal verb* **1.** to be somewhere in the end ○ *We got lost and finished up miles from our hotel.* **2.** to eat something completely ○ *You must finish up all your vegetables.*

finish with *phrasal verb* to finish using something

finite /ˈfaɪnaɪt/ *adj* with an end; with a limit ○ *The world's coal resources are finite and are forecast to run out soon.*

fir /fɜː/ *noun* □ **fir tree** a tree with needle-shaped leaves ○ *Fir trees are often used as Christmas trees.*

① **fire** /faɪə/ *noun* **1.** something which is burning and gives off heat ○ *They burnt the dead leaves on a fire in the garden.* □ **to catch fire** to start to burn because of something else which is burning ○ *The office block caught fire.* ○ *Take those papers away – they might catch fire.* □ **to set fire to something** to make something start burning ○ *His cigarette set fire to the carpet.* **2.** something which heats ○ *We have an electric fire in the living room.* **3.** an emergency in which something such as a building burns ○ *They lost all their belongings in the fire.* **4.** shooting with guns ○ *The soldiers came under fire.* ■ *verb* (**fires, firing, fired**) **1.** to shoot a gun [~at/on/upon] ○ *The gunmen fired at the police car.* **2.** to tell someone that they must leave their job because of something wrong they have done ○ *She was fired for being late.* ◇ **on fire** burning ○ *Call the fire brigade – the house is on fire!*

fire away *phrasal verb* to ask someone questions (*informal*)

③ **fire alarm** /ˈfaɪər əˌlɑːm/ *noun* a bell or siren which gives a warning that a fire has started

③ **fire brigade** /ˈfaɪə brɪˌgeɪd/ *noun* a public service organisation for preventing or putting out fires

firecracker /ˈfaɪəkrækə/ *noun* a small tube containing chemicals which explode with a loud noise and bright lights when you light it

fire drill /ˈfaɪə drɪl/ *noun* a practice to escape from a burning building

fired-up /ˌfaɪəd ˈʌp/ *adj* feeling very excited or eager to do something

③ **fire engine** /ˈfaɪər ˌendʒɪn/ *noun* the large red truck used by firefighters, together with all the equipment they need

fire escape /ˈfaɪər ɪˌskeɪp/ *noun* stairs or a ladder which can be used by people to get out of burning buildings

fire extinguisher /ˈfaɪər ɪkˌstɪŋgwɪʃə/ *noun* a large metal container, usually painted red, containing chemicals which can be sprayed on to a fire to put it out

firefighter /ˈfaɪəˌfaɪtə/ *noun* someone whose job is to put out fires and save people from dangerous situations (NOTE: + **firefighting** *n*)

firefly /ˈfaɪəflaɪ/ (*plural* **fireflies**) *noun* a type of little insect which glows in the dark

fire hydrant /ˈfaɪə ˌhaɪdrənt/ *noun* a large pipe in a street which provides water for fighting fires

firelight /ˈfaɪəlaɪt/ *noun* the light which a fire makes

fireplace /ˈfaɪəpleɪs/ *noun* a hole in the wall of a room where you can light a fire for heating

fireproof /ˈfaɪəpruːf/ *adj* which will not burn

fire service /ˈfaɪə ˌsɜːvɪs/ *noun* the organisation that deals with fires and other emergency situations

fireside /ˈfaɪəsaɪd/ *noun* the area around a fireplace in a room

③ **fire station** /ˈfaɪə ˌsteɪʃ(ə)n/ *noun* a centre where fire engines are based

firewall /ˈfaɪəwɔːl/ *noun* a piece of software that prevents unauthorised people from getting access to a computer system

firewood /ˈfaɪəwʊd/ *noun* wood for making fires

③ **firework** /ˈfaɪəwɜːk/ *noun* a small tube holding chemicals which will shine brightly or explode when lit

firing squad /ˈfaɪərɪŋ skwɒd/ *noun* a group of soldiers who kill someone by shooting

① **firm** /fɜːm/ *adj* **1.** solid or fixed ○ *Make sure that the ladder is firm before you climb up.* ○ *My back hurts – I think I need a firmer mattress.* **2.** strong and definite ○ *There is no firm evidence that he stole the money.* ○ *She is a firm believer in hard work.* ■ *noun* a business or company ○ *When he retired, the firm presented him with a watch.* ○ *The firm I work for was taken over last year.*

firmly /ˈfɜːmli/ *adv* in a firm way

firmness /ˈfɜːmnəs/ *noun* **1.** the quality of being strong or firm **2.** determination

① **first** /fɜːst/ *noun* number 1 in a series ○ *Our house is the first on the left.* ■ *adj* relating to number 1 in a series ○ *That was the* *first time I ever saw him.* (NOTE: As a number can be written **1st**.) ■ *adv* **1.** at the beginning ○ *She came first in the exam.* **2.** before doing anything else ○ *Wash your hands first, and then you can eat.* ◇ **at first** at the beginning ○ *At first he didn't like the work, but later he got used to it.* ◇ **first come, first served** dealing with things such as requests in the order in which they are received ○ *Applications will be dealt with on a first come, first served basis.*

③ **first aid** /ˌfɜːst ˈeɪd/ *noun* the help given to a person who is hurt before a doctor or the emergency services arrive

first aid kit /ˌfɜːst ˈeɪd ˌkɪt/ *noun* a box with bandages and dressings kept to be used in an emergency

first class *noun* travel in the most expensive seats on a train or plane ○ *First class is always much more comfortable than tourist or business class.*

first-class /ˌfɜːst ˈklɑːs/ *adj* **1.** very good quality ○ *You can get a first-class meal in that hotel.* **2.** using the most expensive seats on a plane or train ○ *Can I have a first-class return to Paris, please?*

first cousin /fɜːst ˈkʌz(ə)n/ *noun* someone who is the child of your uncle or aunt

first-degree burn /ˌfɜːst dɪˌgriː ˈbɜːn/ *adj* the least serious type of burn

first-degree murder /ˌfɜːst dɪˌgriː ˈmɜːdə/ *noun* in the USA, the most serious type of murder

firsthand /ˈfɜːsthænd/ *adj* which comes directly from someone who has experienced something ○ *We have some firsthand reports of the coup from our reporter in the capital.*

first language /fɜːst ˈlæŋgwɪdʒ/ *noun* **1.** the first language that you learn to speak **2.** a country's main language

② **firstly** /ˈfɜːstli/ *adv* to start with

③ **first name** /ˈfɜːst neɪm/ *noun* someone's personal name, as opposed to their surname or family name

first-rate /ˌfɜːst ˈreɪt/ *adj* excellent

fiscal /ˈfɪskəl/ *adj* referring to tax or to government revenues

① **fish** /fɪʃ/ *noun* (*plural same* or **fishes**) an animal which lives in water and swims; it has fins and no legs, ○ *I sat by the river all day and only caught two little fish.* ■ *verb* (**fishes, fishing, fished**) to try to catch a fish ○ *We often go fishing in the lake.* ○ *They fished all day but didn't catch anything.*

③ **fishing** /ˈfɪʃɪŋ/ *noun* the sport or industry of catching fish

fishing rod /ˈfɪʃɪŋ rɒd/ *noun* a long stick with a line attached, used for fishing

fishmonger /ˈfɪʃmʌŋgə/ *noun* a person who sells fish in a shop

fishy /ˈfɪʃi/ *adj* **1.** like a fish ○ *These eggs have a fishy taste.* **2.** strange or unusual ○ *There's something fishy about the whole business.* ○ *What was she doing there at 2 o'clock in the morning? – It's very fishy if you ask me.*

fissure /ˈfɪʃə/ *noun* a crack or split, especially in a rock or in the ground

fist /fɪst/ *noun* a tightly closed hand

① **fit** /fɪt/ *adj* (**fitter, fittest**) **1.** healthy and having a lot of physical energy ○ *He isn't fit enough to go back to work.* ○ *You'll have to get fit if you're going to run in that race.* **2.** suitable for something ○ *These containers aren't fit for the purpose.* □ **fit to do something** in good enough condition to do something ○ *That car isn't fit to be driven – its brakes don't work and the tyres are worn.* ○ *He looks very tired – is he fit to drive?* ■ *noun* a sudden sharp occurrence of illness, of an emotion such as anger, or of activity [~of] ○ *She had a coughing fit* or *a fit of coughing.* ○ *In a fit of anger he threw the plate across the kitchen.* ○ *She's having one of her periodic fits of efficiency.* ■ *verb* (**fits, fitting, fitted**) to be the right size or shape [~into/~with/] ○ *He's grown so tall that his jackets don't fit him any more.* ○ *These shoes don't fit me – they're a size too small.*

fitful /ˈfɪtf(ə)l/ *adj* happening several times, but only for short periods of time

③ **fitness** /ˈfɪtnəs/ *noun* **1.** being physically fit ○ *She does fitness exercises every morning.* ○ *Physical fitness is important in the marines.* **2.** being suitable [~for] ○ *Doubts were expressed about her fitness for the job.*

③ **fitted** /ˈfɪtɪd/ *adj* made to fit into a certain space

fitting /ˈfɪtɪŋ/ *adj* suitable; right ○ *It's fitting that grandmother should sit at the head of the table – it's her birthday party, after all.*

fitting room /ˈfɪtɪŋ ruːm/ *noun* a small room in a shop where you can try on clothes before you buy them

① **five** /faɪv/ *noun* the number 5

fiver /ˈfaɪvə/ *noun* a five pound note (*informal*)

① **fix** /fɪks/ (**fixes, fixing, fixed**) *verb* **1.** to fasten or to attach one thing to another ○

Fix one end of the cord to the tree and the other to the fence. **2.** to organise a time for something such as a meeting ○ *We'll try to fix a time for the meeting.* **3.** to repair something ○ *Someone's coming to fix the telephone this afternoon.* ○ *Can you fix the dishwasher?* ○ *Does anyone know how to fix the photocopier?* **4.** *US* to prepare a drink or some food for someone ○ *Let me fix you something to drink.* ○ *She fixed them some tuna sandwiches.*

fixation /fɪk'seɪʃ(ə)n/ *noun* a state of only thinking about one thing

③ **fixed** /fɪkst/ *adj* attached firmly ○ *The sign is fixed to the post with nails.*

fixture /'fɪkstʃə/ *noun* a sports match ○ *Their next fixture is against Liverpool on Saturday.* ○ *Season ticket holders are sent a list of fixtures at the beginning of the season.*

fizz /fɪz/ *noun* a sound like that made by bubbles ○ *the fizz of the rocket as it went up into the air*

fizzle /'fɪz(ə)l/ (**fizzles, fizzling, fizzled**) *verb* **1.** to make a hissing sound **2.** to gradually become less strong or successful after a good start

fizzle out *phrasal verb* to come to nothing

fizzy /'fɪzi/ *adj* full of small balls of gas (NOTE: Drinks which are not fizzy are **still**. A drink which is no longer fizzy is **flat**.)

fjord /'fiːɔːd/, **fiord** *noun* a long arm of the sea among mountains in Norway

flab /flæb/ *noun* excess flesh on your body (*informal*)

flabbergasted /'flæbəgɑːstɪd/ *adj* extremely surprised (*informal*)

flabby /'flæbi/ (**flabbier, flabbiest**) *adj* soft and fat (*informal*)

flag /flæg/ *noun* a piece of brightly coloured material with the symbol of a country or an organisation on it ○ *The French flag has blue, red and white stripes.* ○ *The ship was flying the British flag.* ○ *The flags were blowing in the wind.*

flagpole /'flægpəʊl/, **flagstaff** *noun* a tall pole on which large flags are flown

flagrant /'fleɪgrənt/ *adj* clear, obvious and shocking

flagship /'flægʃɪp/ *noun* the most important or best thing in a group ○ *the flagship of the range* ○ *the company's flagship store*

flail /fleɪl/ (**flails, flailing, flailed**) *verb* to wave your arms about ○ *He lay on his back flailing with his arms at his opponent.*

flair /fleə/ *noun* a natural ability for doing something, especially in a skilful or interesting way [~for] ○ *She has a distinct flair for dress design.* ○ *He has a flair for languages.* (NOTE: Do not confuse with **flare**.)

flak /flæk/ *noun* strong criticism ○ *The play has taken a lot of flak from the reviewers.* ○ *He came in for a lot of flak for missing the penalty.*

flake /fleɪk/ *noun* **1.** a small, very thin piece of something ○ *The paint came off in little flakes.* **2.** a small piece of snow which falls from the sky ○ *Snow fell in large soft flakes all night.*

flaky /'fleɪki/ *adj* **1.** made up of thin loose pieces **2.** not sensible or reliable

flamboyant /flæm'bɔɪənt/ *adj* very noticeable and unusual in a way that attracts attention

flame /fleɪm/ *noun* a brightly burning part of a fire, or the light that burns on a candle ○ *Flames could be seen coming out of the upstairs windows.*

flamenco /flə'meŋkəʊ/ *noun* a fast Spanish dance, to guitar music

flamingo /flə'mɪŋgəʊ/ (*plural* **flamingos** or **flamingoes** or *same*) *noun* a tropical water bird with long legs and neck, often with pink feathers

flammable /'flæməb(ə)l/ *adj* easily set on fire (NOTE: means the same as **inflammable**)

flan /flæn/ *noun* an open pastry case with a filling of food such as eggs and fruit

flank /flæŋk/ *noun* a side, especially of an animal or of an army ○ *He patted the horse's flank.* ○ *The right flank of the army moved forward.*

flannel /'flæn(ə)l/ *noun* a small square of soft material for washing the face or body ○ *He put his flannel under the hot tap and wiped his face.*

flap /flæp/ *noun* a flat part which is attached to an object and has a special type of fastening allowing it to move up and down ○ *The pilot tested the wing flaps before taking off.* ■ *verb* (**flaps, flapping, flapped**) to move up and down like a bird's wing ○ *Flags were flapping in the breeze.* ○ *The swans stood by the edge of the water, flapping their wings.*

③ **flare** /fleə/ *noun* an object which gives a sudden burst of light, especially as a signal ○ *The lifeboat sent up flares.* ○ *We knew the ship was in distress when we saw the flares.*

flare up *phrasal verb* **1.** to suddenly start burning ○ *The bonfire flared up when he poured petrol on it.* ○ *The flames died down and then flared up again.* **2.** to get angry suddenly ○ *She flared up when he suggested it was her fault.*

flared /fleəd/ *adj* with a shape that becomes wider at one end

flare-up /'fleər ʌp/ *noun* a sudden return, sudden beginning (*informal*)

③ **flash** /flæʃ/ *noun* **1.** a short sudden burst of light ○ *Flashes of lightning lit up the sky.* **2.** a piece of equipment used for making a bright light, allowing you to take photographs in the dark ○ *People sometimes have red eyes in photos taken with a flash.* ■ *verb* (**flashes, flashing, flashed**) **1.** to light up quickly and suddenly [~across/through/into] ○ *Lightning flashed over the hills.* **2.** to move or to pass by quickly [~across/by/on/past] ○ *The champion flashed past to win in record time.*

flashback /'flæʃbæk/ *noun* a scene in a film, showing what happened at an earlier date

flashcard /'flæʃkɑːd/ *noun* a card that has words or numbers printed on it, used to help someone to learn something

flash flood /flæʃ 'flʌd/ *noun* a sudden flood after heavy rain

③ **flashlight** /'flæʃlaɪt/ *noun* a torch; a small electric light that you can carry

flashpoint /'flæʃpɔɪnt/ *noun* the stage in something such as a process or situation at which violence or some other serious problem is likely to develop

flashy /'flæʃi/ (**flashier, flashiest**) *adj* showy and bright but of poor quality

flask /flɑːsk/ *noun* a small glass bottle for liquids

② **flat** /flæt/ *adj* (**flatter, flattest**) **1.** level, not sloping or curved ○ *a house with a flat roof* **2.** (*of a battery*) with no electric power left ○ *The car wouldn't start because the battery was flat.* ■ *noun* a set of rooms on one floor, usually in a building with several similar sets of rooms ○ *They live in the block of flats next to the underground station.* ○ *Their flat is on the ground floor.*

flatly /'flætli/ *adv* in a firm way

flat-mate /'flæt meɪt/ *noun* a person who shares a flat with you

flat-pack /'flæt pæk/ *noun* furniture which is sold as a set of pieces packed flat for the customer to put it together

flatten /'flæt(ə)n/ (**flattens, flattening, flattened**) *verb* to make flat

flatter /'flætə/ (**flatters, flattering, flattered**) *verb* to praise in order to please them ○ *Just flatter the boss a bit, tell him how good his golf is, and he'll give you a rise.*

flattered /'flætəd/ *adj* feeling honoured

flattery /'flætəri/ *noun* praising someone too much

flaunt /flɔːnt/ (**flaunts, flaunting, flaunted**) *verb* to show something in a deliberate way because you want to attract people's attention

flautist /'flɔːtɪst/ *noun* a person who plays the flute

flavor /'fleɪvə/ *noun, verb* US spelling of **flavour**

flavour /'fleɪvə/ *noun* a particular taste ○ *The tomato soup had an unusual flavour.* ○ *What flavour of ice cream do you want?* ■ *verb* (**flavours, flavouring, flavoured**) to add things such as salt or pepper to food, to give it a special taste ○ *soup flavoured with herbs* ○ *Use rosemary to flavour lamb.*

flavoured /'fleɪvəd/ *adj* which tastes of something (NOTE: The US spelling is **flavored**.)

flavouring /'fleɪvərɪŋ/ *noun* a substance added to food to give a particular taste (NOTE: The US spelling is **flavoring**.)

flaw /flɔː/ *noun* **1.** a fault in something which makes it appear less attractive or causes a problem ○ *The expert examined the Chinese vase, looking for flaws.* ○ *There must be a flaw in the computer program.* **2.** a mistake in an argument ○ *There's a flaw in your reasoning.* ○ *There was a fundamental flaw in their calculations.*

flawed /flɔːd/ *adj* with mistakes

flawless /'flɔːləs/ *adj* perfect

flea /fliː/ *noun* a very small insect that jumps and sucks blood (NOTE: Do not confuse with **flee**.)

flea market /'fliː ˌmɑːkɪt/ *noun* an open-air market for objects which have been owned by other people

fleck /flek/ *noun* a small spot ○ *She tried to brush the flecks of powder off her dress.* ○ *He had flecks of plaster in his hair.*

flecked /flekt/ *adj* marked with a pattern of small stripes or spots

fled /fled/ past tense and past participle of **flee**

flee /fliː/ (**flees, fleeing, fled**) *verb* to run away from something ○ *As the fighting spread, the village people fled into the jungle.* ○ *She tried to flee but her foot was caught in the rope.* (NOTE: Do not confuse with **flea**.)

fleece /fliːs/ *noun* a coat of wool covering a sheep ○ *After shearing, the fleeces are taken away to market.*

fleet /fliːt/ *noun* **1.** a group of ships belonging together ○ *When the fleet is in port, the pubs are full of sailors.* **2.** a collection of vehicles ○ *the airline's fleet of Boeing 747s* ○ *The company replaces its car fleet or fleet of cars every two years.*

fleeting /ˈfliːtɪŋ/ *adj* lasting for a very short time only ○ *She only caught a fleeting glimpse of the princess.*

③ **flesh** /fleʃ/ *noun* **1.** a soft part of the body covering the bones **2.** a soft part of a fruit ○ *a melon with pink flesh* (NOTE: no plural) ◇ **in the flesh** not on TV or in photographs, but here and now ○ *It was strange to see the TV newsreader in the flesh.*

fleshy /ˈfleʃi/ *adj* fat or soft and thick

③ **flew** /fluː/ past tense of **fly** (NOTE: Do not confuse with **flu, flue**.)

flex /fleks/ *noun* a plastic covered wire that bends easily, used for carrying electricity ○ *He tripped over a flex.* ○ *We bought a roll of flex to rewire the office.* ■ *verb* (**flexes, flexing, flexed**) to bend something, or be bent

③ **flexibility** /ˌfleksɪˈbɪlɪti/ *noun* the ability to change when your situation changes

flexible /ˈfleksɪb(ə)l/ *adj* **1.** easy to bend ○ *Soft rubber soles are very flexible.* **2.** able to change easily ○ *My timetable is very flexible – we can meet whenever you want.*

flick /flɪk/ *noun* a little sharp blow or movement (*informal*) ○ *He shook off the wasp with a flick of his hand.* ■ *verb* (**flicks, flicking, flicked**) to hit or move something gently, with a short quick movement ○ *The horse flicked its tail to get rid of the flies.*

flick through *phrasal verb* to look quickly at the pages of a newspaper or book

flicker /ˈflɪkə/ *noun* **1.** a movement of something such as a light which seems to shake or to burn for only a short time ○ *They saw the flicker of a light in the forest.* **2.** a small amount ○ *There is still a flicker of hope that someone may still be alive under the ruins.* ■ *verb* (**flickers, flickering, flickered**) to shake; to burn unsteadily ○ *The candles flickered in the draught.* ○ *We could see the flickering lights of the old harbour in the distance.*

flier /ˈflaɪə/, **flyer** *noun* another spelling of **flyer**

③ **flies** /flaɪz/ 3rd person singular present of **fly**

② **flight** /flaɪt/ *noun* a journey in a plane ○ *Go to gate 25 for flight AB198.* ○ *All flights to Paris have been cancelled.* ○ *She sat next to me on a flight to Montreal.*

flight attendant /ˈflaɪt əˌtendənt/ *noun* a person whose job is to look after passengers on a plane

flimsy /ˈflɪmzi/ *adj* likely to break because of being badly made ○ *The shelter was a flimsy construction of branches covered with grass and leaves.*

flinch /flɪntʃ/ (**flinches, flinching, flinched**) *verb* to move back in pain or fear ○ *The reporters flinched at the sight of the corpses.* ◇ **not to flinch from** to do something, even though it is extremely difficult or painful ○ *He didn't flinch from his duty.*

fling /flɪŋ/ (**flings, flinging, flung**) *verb* to throw something carelessly and with a lot of force ○ *He flung the empty bottle into the sea.*

flint /flɪnt/ *noun* a very hard type of rock which was used to make tools in the past ○ *Flints are found in chalky soil.* ○ *Prehistoric people used flints to make knives.*

flip /flɪp/ (**flips, flipping, flipped**) *verb* **1.** to hit something such as a control on a machine without using a lot of force ○ *She flipped a switch and the lights went off.* **2.** to get very angry (*informal*) ○ *He flipped when they told him how much the bill came to.*

flipchart /ˈflɪptʃɑːt/ *noun* a stand with large sheets of paper fixed together at the top, used for showing pictures or writing when speaking to a group of people

flippant /ˈflɪpənt/ *adj* not taking seriously things which should be taken seriously

flipper /ˈflɪpə/ *noun* **1.** a long flat piece of rubber which you can attach to your foot to help you swim faster ○ *You need flippers and a snorkel to go scuba diving.* **2.** the flat arm or leg of a sea animal, used for swimming ○ *The seal walked across the rock on its flippers.*

flip side /ˈflɪp saɪd/ *noun* the side of a record which has the less popular piece of music on it

flirt /flɜːt/ *noun* a man or woman who often behaves in a way that shows sexual interest towards another person ○ *His new secretary is a bit of a flirt.* ■ *verb* (**flirts, flirting, flirted**) to behave in a way that shows sexual interest towards another person ○ *He flirted a lot at the office party.*

flirt with *phrasal verb* **1.** to behave in a way that shows sexual interest towards another person ○ *She flirted with all the boys at the party.* **2.** to consider a course of action in a way that is not serious ○ *We've been flirting with the idea of going to live in the States.* **3.** to be close to something risky ○ *She's flirting with danger in standing so close to the fireworks.*

flirtation /flɜː'teɪʃ(ə)n/ *noun* a love affair which is not serious and lasts for only a short time

flit /flɪt/ (**flits, flitting, flitted**) *verb* to move quickly and quietly ○ *A thought flitted through my mind.* ○ *Bats were flitting around the church tower.*

③ **float** /fləʊt/ (**floats, floating, floated**) *verb* **1.** to lie on the top of a liquid [~on/in] ○ *Dead fish were floating in the river.* **2.** to put something on the top of a liquid [~on] ○ *He floated a paper boat on the lake.* **3.** to stay in the air without any effort [~in] ○ *little white clouds floating in the sky*

flock /flɒk/ *noun* a group of similar animals together ○ *a flock of birds* ○ *A flock of sheep were grazing on the hillside.* (NOTE: **flock** is usually used with sheep, goats, and birds such as hens or geese. For cattle, the word to use is **herd**.) ■ *verb* (**flocks, flocking, flocked**) to move in large numbers ○ *Tourists flocked to see the changing of the guard.* ○ *Holidaymakers have been flocking to the resorts on the south coast.*

flog /flɒg/ (**flogs, flogging, flogged**) *verb* **1.** to sell (*informal*) ○ *I flogged my car to my brother.* ○ *They've been trying to flog the boat for months.* **2.** to beat hard, usually with a whip ○ *When he was a little boy he was often flogged at school.*

flogging /'flɒgɪŋ/ *noun* the act of beating someone as a punishment

③ **flood** /flʌd/ *noun* **1.** a large amount of water over an area of land which is usually dry ○ *The floods were caused by heavy rain.* **2.** a large amount of something, e.g. tears or letters [~of] ○ *The TV station received a flood of complaints after the ad was shown.* ○ *She was in floods of tears when they told her that she had to leave her house.* ■ *verb* (**floods, flooding, flooded**) **1.** to cover something with water ○ *They are going to build a dam and flood the valley.* ○ *Fields were flooded after the river burst its banks.* ○ *He forgot to turn the tap off and flooded the bathroom.* **2.** to become covered with water [~in/out/down etc/~into/out of/across etc/] ○ *She left the tap on and the bathroom flooded.* **3.** to come in large numbers [~with] ○ *The office was flooded with complaints.*

flooding /'flʌdɪŋ/ *noun* a situation in which an area is covered with water

floodlight /'flʌdlaɪt/ *noun* a strong electric light used to light an area in the open air ○ *They switched on the floodlights for the evening match.*

floodlit /'flʌdlɪt/ *adj* lit by floodlights

① **floor** /flɔː/ *noun* **1.** the part of a room on which you walk ○ *He put the books in a pile on the floor.* ○ *If there are no empty chairs left, you'll have to sit on the floor.* **2.** all the rooms on one level in a building ○ *The bathroom is on the ground floor.* ○ *His office is on the fifth floor.* ○ *There is a good view of the town from the top floor.*

floorboard /'flɔːbɔːd/ *noun* a long flat piece of wood used for making wooden floors

flooring /'flɔːrɪŋ/ *noun* material used to make a floor

flop /flɒp/ *noun* something that is not successful ○ *His new play was a complete flop and closed after only ten performances.* ○ *The film was a big hit in New York but it was a flop in London.* ■ *verb* (**flops, flopping, flopped**) **1.** to fall or sit down suddenly, with your body relaxed ○ *She got back from the sales and flopped down on the sofa.* **2.** to be unsuccessful ○ *The play was a big hit on Broadway but it flopped in London.*

floppy /'flɒpi/ (**floppier, floppiest**) *adj* which hangs down loosely ○ *a floppy red hat* ○ *a white rabbit with long floppy ears*

③ **floppy disk** /ˌflɒpi 'dɪsk/ *noun* a small disk which can be put into a computer and removed

flora /'flɔːrə/ (*plural* **floras** or **florae**) *noun* the wild plants that grow in a particular area. Compare **fauna**

floral /'flɔːrəl/ *adj* referring to flowers

florist /'flɒrɪst/ *noun* a person who sells flowers

flotation /fləʊ'teɪʃ(ə)n/ *noun* an act of selling shares in a company on the stock exchange for the first time

③ **flour** /flaʊə/ *noun* wheat grain crushed to powder, used for making food such as bread or cakes

flourish /'flʌrɪʃ/ (**flourishes, flourishing, flourished**) *verb* **1.** to grow well; to be successful ○ *Palms flourish in hot countries.* **2.** to wave something in the air ○ *She came in with a big smile, flourishing a cheque.*

flout /flaʊt/ (**flouts, flouting, flouted**) *verb* to pay no attention to something such as a rule

② **flow** /fləʊ/ *verb* (**flows, flowing, flowed**) to move along smoothly [~into//] ○ *Traffic on the motorway is flowing smooth-*

ly. ○ *The river flows into the sea.* ■ *noun* the movement of things such as liquid or air, or of people [~of] ○ *She tried to stop the flow of blood with a tight bandage.* ○ *There was a steady flow of visitors to the exhibition.* (NOTE: Do not confuse with **floe**.)

flow chart /ˈfləʊ tʃɑːt/, **flow diagram** *noun* a drawing which shows all the different operations in a process

② **flower** /ˈflaʊə/ *noun* the colourful part of a plant, which attracts insects and produces fruit or seeds ○ *a plant with bright yellow flowers* ■ *verb* (**flowers, flowering, flowered**) to produce flowers ○ *a plant which flowers in early summer* ○ *The cherry trees flowered very late this year.* ◇ **in flower** covered with flowers ○ *Go to Japan when the cherry trees are in flower.*

flowerbed /ˈflaʊəbed/ *noun* a piece of ground where flowers grow

flowery /ˈflaʊəri/ *adj* **1.** decorated with a pattern of flowers ○ *a flowery dress* ○ *She chose some very flowery wallpaper.* **2.** using literary or emotional language ○ *He wrote the most flowery thank-you letter.* (NOTE: Do not confuse with **floury**.)

③ **flown** /fləʊn/ past participle of **fly**

③ **flu** /fluː/ *noun* a common illness like a bad cold, often with a high temperature (NOTE: Do not confuse with **flew, flue**. Note also that the full word is **influenza**.)

fluctuate /ˈflʌktʃueɪt/ (**fluctuates, fluctuating, fluctuated**) *verb* to rise and fall (NOTE: + **fluctuation** *n*)

fluent /ˈfluːənt/ *adj* able to speak easily; spoken easily

fluff /flʌf/ *noun* a soft mass of fibres or hair ○ *She pulled the sofa away from the wall and saw all the fluff which had collected under it.* ■ *verb* (**fluffs, fluffing, fluffed**) to do something badly (*informal*) ○ *He fluffed his speech, and everyone laughed.*

fluffy /ˈflʌfi/ *adj* like fluff; covered with fluff

fluid /ˈfluːɪd/ *noun* a liquid ○ *You need to drink plenty of fluids in hot weather.*

fluid ounce /ˌfluːɪd ˈaʊns/ *noun* **1.** a US unit of liquid measurement equal to ⅟₁₆ of a US pint or 29.57 ml **2.** a UK unit of liquid measurement equal to ⅟₂₀ of an imperial pint or 28.41 ml

fluke /fluːk/ *noun* a chance; lucky event ○ *It was a pure fluke that I happened to be there when the phone rang.*

flung /flʌŋ/ past tense and past participle of **fling**

flunk /flʌŋk/ (**flunks, flunking, flunked**) *verb US* to fail an examination or to make someone fail an examination (*informal*)

fluorescent /flʊəˈres(ə)nt/ *adj* **1.** giving off light when electric current is applied ○ *We have fluorescent lighting in the office.* **2.** which seems to glow ○ *She's bought a fluorescent pink tracksuit.*

fluorescent light /flʊəˈres(ə)nt ˌlaɪt/ *noun* a very bright light consisting of a long glass tube containing fluorescent gas

fluoride /ˈflʊəraɪd/ *noun* a chemical substance which is sometimes added to water or to toothpaste because it can protect your teeth

flurry /ˈflʌri/ (*plural* **flurries**) *noun* **1.** hurried excitement ○ *In his flurry to leave he forgot to take his keys.* **2.** a sudden small fall of snow when there is a strong wind blowing ○ *There will be snow flurries during the morning.*

flush /flʌʃ/ *noun* **1.** a red colour on the face ○ *a flush of anger* **2.** a quick flow of water **3.** (*at cards*) a hand in which all the cards are of the same suit ○ *She is holding a flush.* ■ *verb* (**flushes, flushing, flushed**) **1.** to go red in the face ○ *She flushed with pleasure when she heard the results.* **2.** □ **to flush the toilet *or* a lavatory** to wash it out by moving a handle which makes water rush through ○ *She told the children not to forget to flush the toilet.* ■ *adj* level [~with] ○ *The door must be flush with the wall.*

flushed /flʌʃt/ *adj* red in the face

flustered /ˈflʌstəd/ *adj* confused

flute /fluːt/ *noun* a tall narrow wine glass on a stem, used for serving champagne

flutter /ˈflʌtə/ (**flutters, fluttering, fluttered**) *verb* **1.** to move wings quickly but with not a lot of force ○ *The little bird fell out of its nest and fluttered to the ground.* **2.** to move softly and quickly ○ *Dead leaves fluttered from the trees.* ○ *The flags fluttered in the breeze.* (NOTE: + **flutter** *n*)

flux /flʌks/ *noun* a situation which is not settled ○ *The company seems to be in a state of flux.*

① **fly** /flaɪ/ *noun* (*plural* **flies**) a small insect with wings which eats food and spreads diseases ○ *Cover the food to protect it from flies.* ■ *verb* (**flies, flying, flew, flown**) **1.** to move through the air using wings ○ *When the cat came into the garden, the birds flew away.* ○ *Some birds fly to Africa for the winter.* **2.** to travel in a plane ○ *I'm flying to China next week.* ○ *He flies across the Atlantic twice a month.* **3.** to be quick [~around/about/~at/~by/~into/along/through/out/~past/~past/over/up etc//] ○ *I must fly if I want to get home by 6 o'clock.* ◇ **time flies** time passes quickly ○ *His daughter is already two – how time flies!*

flyer /ˈflaɪə/ *noun* **1.** a person who flies an aircraft ○ *He was one of the first flyers to cross the Atlantic.* **2.** a paper advertising something ○ *They sent us a flyer about their home delivery service.*

③ **flying** /ˈflaɪɪŋ/ *adj* flying in the air ○ *flying ants* ■ *noun* the act of travelling in a plane ○ *He has a fear of flying.*

flying saucer /ˌflaɪɪŋ ˈsɔːsə/ *noun* a flying object which people claim to see and which they think comes from another planet

flying start /ˌflaɪɪŋ ˈstɑːt/ *noun* a good beginning to something such as a race, game or piece of work

flying visit /ˌflaɪɪŋ ˈvɪzɪt/ *noun* a very short visit

fly-on-the-wall /ˌflaɪ ɒn ðə ˈwɔːl/ *adj* filmed in a way that shows something as it really is or as it actually happens

flyover /ˈflaɪəʊvə/ *noun* a road which passes over another

foal /fəʊl/ *noun* a young horse ○ *The mare gently nudged her foal.*

foam /fəʊm/ *noun* a mass of small bubbles ○ *This soap makes a large amount of foam.*

fob off *verb* to persuade someone to accept something which they do not really want [~with] ○ *They fobbed her off with an out-of-date model.*

focal point /ˈfəʊk(ə)l pɔɪnt/ *noun* a point which everything is focused on

② **focus** /ˈfəʊkəs/ *noun* (*plural* **focuses** or **foci**) **1.** a point where rays of light from an object meet ○ *The focus of the beam is a point 20 metres from the spotlight.* **2.** (*of a photograph*) a point where the details of the photograph are clear and sharp ○ *Adjust the focus so as to get a clear picture.* □ **in focus** clear □ **out of focus** not clear **3.** the centre of attention ○ *The director brought the star actress to the front of the stage, so that the focus of the audience's attention would be on her.* ■ *verb* (**focuses** or **focusses, focusing** or **focussing, focused** or **focussed**) **1.** to change something so as to be able to see clearly ○ *He focused his telescope on a ship on the horizon.* **2.** to concentrate on something [~on] ○ *The paper is focusing on the problems of the TV star's marriage.* ○ *The editorial focuses on the economic situation.* **3.** to point a camera at something [~on] ○ *There were cameras focussed on all the exits.*

focused /ˈfəʊkəst/ *adj* concentrating on one thing and giving it all your attention

focus group /ˈfəʊkəs gruːp/ *noun* a representative group of people who are questioned about their opinions as part of political or market research

fodder /ˈfɒdə/ *noun* plants such as grass which are grown and given to animals as food

foe /fəʊ/ *noun* an enemy or opponent (*formal*)

foetus /ˈfiːtəs/ *noun* a baby human or animal which has not been born but is developing from an embryo inside the womb (NOTE: The US spelling is **fetus**.)

③ **fog** /fɒg/ *noun* a thick mist made up of many tiny drops of water

foible /ˈfɔɪb(ə)l/ *noun* a particular way of behaving which someone has and which may seem unusual or annoying to other people

foil /fɔɪl/ *noun* **1.** a thin metal sheet **2.** a person who is quite different from another and so makes the other's qualities stand out ○ *Laurel and Hardy were perfect foils for each other.* ■ *verb* (**foils, foiling, foiled**) to stop a plan from being put into effect ○ *The bank robbery was foiled by the police.*

foist /fɔɪst/ (**foists, foisting, foisted**) *verb* □ **to foist something on someone** to force someone to accept something which they do not want

① **fold** /fəʊld/ *noun* a piece of something such as cloth or skin which hangs down loosely ○ *She wanted the surgeon to remove the folds of skin under her chin.* ■ *verb* (**folds, folding, folded**) to bend something such as a piece of paper so that one part is on top of the other ○ *Fold the piece of paper in half.* ○ *He folded the newspaper and put it into his briefcase.*

fold up *phrasal verb* to bend something over to make it take up a smaller area than before

-fold /fəʊld/ *suffix* times ○ *twofold*

folder /ˈfəʊldə/ *noun* an envelope made of thin card or plastic and used for holding papers

foliage /ˈfəʊliɪdʒ/ *noun* leaves on a tree or plant

② **folk** /fəʊk/ *noun* people (NOTE: **Folk** takes a plural verb. The plural form **folks** is also used.)

folklore /ˈfəʊklɔː/ *noun* traditional stories and beliefs

folk music /ˈfəʊk ˌmjuːzɪk/ *noun* the traditional music of a people

① **follow** /ˈfɒləʊ/ (**follows, following, followed**) *verb* **1.** to come after or behind someone or something ○ *What letter follows B in the alphabet?* ○ *The dog followed me all the way home.* **2.** to walk or drive behind someone, e.g. in order to see where they are going [~with/] ○ *I had the impression I was being followed.* **3.** to do what someone tells you to do ○ *She followed the instructions on the tin of paint.* ○ *He made the cake following a recipe in the newspaper.* **4.** to be certain because of something [~(that)] ○ *Just because I lent you money yesterday, it doesn't follow that I will lend you some every time you ask.* ○ *If the owner of the shop is arrested by the police, it follows that his business is likely to close.* **5.** to understand ○ *I don't quite follow you – you want me to drive you all the way to Edinburgh?* **6.** to go along a certain route ○ *Follow the path and turn left at the crossroads.* □ **to follow a career in medicine** to train as a doctor ◇ **as follows ...** as in the information given next ◇ **follow suit** to do what someone else does ○ *She jumped into the pool and everyone else followed suit.*

follow up *phrasal verb* to find out more about something or to research something further ○ *The police followed up their enquiries by interviewing the woman's husband.* ○ *That's an interesting idea – it might be worth following it up.*

follower /ˈfɒləʊə/ *noun* a supporter

① **following** /ˈfɒləʊɪŋ/ *adj* which comes next ○ *They arrived on Friday and the following day she became ill.* ○ *Look at the following picture.* ■ *prep* after ○ *Following his death, his son sold the family house.*

follow-up /ˈfɒləʊ ʌp/ *adj* which follows something sent earlier

folly /ˈfɒli/ (*plural* **follies**) *noun* **1.** silly behaviour ○ *It was utter folly to go out in a small boat in a storm like that.* **2.** a strange building, built to create an effect and with no practical use ○ *He built a gothic folly on the hill overlooking his house.*

③ **fond** /fɒnd/ *adj* liking someone or something ○ *I'm fond of my sister's children.* ○ *Michael's very fond of playing golf.*

fondle /ˈfɒnd(ə)l/ (**fondles, fondling, fondled**) *verb* to stroke someone or something in a loving way

fondly /ˈfɒndli/ *adv* in a way which shows you are fond of someone or something

font /fɒnt/, **fount** *noun* **1.** a bowl holding holy water for the ceremony of baptism in a church ○ *The church has an 11th century font.* **2.** (*in printing*) a set of characters all of the same size and appearance

① **food** /fuːd/ *noun* things which you eat ○ *This hotel is famous for its food.* ○ *Do you like German food?* ◇ **to give someone food for thought** to make someone think carefully

food chain /ˈfuːd tʃeɪn/ *noun* a series of living things which pass energy from one to another as each is eaten by the next. For example, grass is eaten by small animals, which are then eaten by larger animals, and so on.

food poisoning /ˈfuːd ˌpɔɪz(ə)nɪŋ/ *noun* an illness caused by eating food which is contaminated with bacteria

food processor /ˈfuːd ˌprəʊsesə/ *noun* a machine used in preparing food, e.g. for cutting or mixing it

fool /fuːl/ *noun* a stupid person ○ *You fool! Why didn't you put the brakes on?* ○ *I was a fool to think that I could make her change her mind.* ■ *verb* (**fools, fooling, fooled**) to trick someone ○ *They fooled the old lady into letting them into her house.* ○ *You can't fool me – I know you're not really ill.* ◇ **to make a fool of yourself** to behave in a silly way ◇ **you could have fooled me** I find it hard to believe ○ *She says she did her best – well, you could have fooled me!*

fool about, fool around *phrasal verb* to act in a silly way ○ *Stop fooling around with that knife – you're going to have an accident.*

foolhardy /ˈfuːlhɑːdi/ *adj* brave, but taking unnecessary risks

foolish /ˈfuːlɪʃ/ *adj* showing a lack of intelligence or good judgment ○ *That was a rather foolish thing to do.* ○ *I felt rather foolish.*

foolproof /ˈfuːlpruːf/ *adj* extremely simple, so that anyone could use it safely and successfully

① **foot** /fʊt/ (*plural* **feet**) *noun* **1.** the part at the end of your leg on which you stand ○ *She has very small feet.* ○ *Watch out, you trod on my foot!* **2.** the bottom part; the end ○ *There is a door at the foot of the stairs.* ○ *There are traffic lights at the foot of the hill.* ○ *Sign the document at the foot of the page.* **3.** a unit of measurement equal to about 30 centimetres ○ *The table is four foot or four feet long.* ○ *She's almost six foot tall.* ○ *I'm five foot seven (5' 7").* ◊ **inch** (NOTE: As a measurement **foot** often has no plural form: *six foot tall; three foot wide*. With numbers **foot** is also often written with the symbol ' *a 6' ladder; he is 5' 6*: say 'he's five foot six'.) ◇ **on foot** walking ○ *They completed the rest of the journey on foot.* ◇ **to find your feet** to become confident (*informal*) ○ *She's been with us three months now and has really found her feet.* ◇ **to put your foot in it** to say something embarrassing ○ *He really put his foot in it when he said that the mayor's wife was fat.* ◇ **to put your feet up** to rest

footage /'fʊtɪdʒ/ *noun* a piece of film showing an event (NOTE: no plural)

① **football** /'fʊtbɔːl/ *noun* **1.** a game played between two teams of eleven players with a round ball which can be kicked or headed, but not carried ○ *They went to a football match.* ○ *The children were playing football in the street.* ○ *Let's have a game of football.* ○ *He spends all his time watching football on TV.* ○ *He's got a new pair of football boots.* **2.** a ball used for kicking; the ball used in the various games of football ○ *They were kicking a football around in the street.*

footballer /'fʊtbɔːlə/ *noun* a person who plays football

footbridge /'fʊtbrɪdʒ/ *noun* a small bridge for people to walk across, and not for vehicles

foothills /'fʊthɪlz/ *plural noun* the lower slopes of a group of mountains

foothold /'fʊthəʊld/ *noun* **1.** a place where you can put your foot when climbing ○ *He hung in the air at the end of a rope, trying to get a foothold.* **2.** a small position on which you can build ○ *They gained a foothold in the Spanish market.*

footing /'fʊtɪŋ/ *noun* a safe place for your feet ○ *She lost her footing on the cliff path, and fell fifty feet into the sea.* ◇ **to be on an equal footing with someone** to be at the same stage or level as someone ○ *All applicants are on an equal footing.* ◇ **to put things on a firm footing** to make things solid ○ *We want to make sure the business is on a firm footing.*

footlights /'fʊtlaɪts/ *plural noun* a row of lights along the front of the stage in a theatre

footnote /'fʊtnəʊt/ *noun* an explanation at the bottom of a page, referring to something on the page

footpath /'fʊtpɑːθ/ *noun* a path for people to walk on, but not to ride on

footprint /'fʊtprɪnt/ *noun* a mark left by someone's foot on the ground ○ *They followed the footprints in the snow to the cave.*

footstep /'fʊtstep/ *noun* a sound made by a foot touching the ground ○ *We heard soft footsteps along the corridor.*

footstool /'fʊtstuːl/ *noun* a small piece of furniture in the shape of a box on which you can rest your feet

footwear /'fʊtweə/ *noun* articles of clothing worn on your feet, such as boots or shoes

footwork /'fʊtwɜːk/ *noun* a way of using your feet, especially in sports

① **for** /fə, fɔː/ *prep* **1.** showing the purpose or use of something ○ *This plastic bag is for the apples.* ○ *What's that key for?* **2.** showing the occasion on which or the reason why something is given ○ *What did you get for your birthday?* ○ *What did you win for coming first?* **3.** showing the person who receives something ○ *There was no mail for you this morning.* ○ *I'm making a cup of tea for my mother.* **4.** showing how long something takes ○ *He has gone to France for two days.* ○ *We've been waiting here for hours.* **5.** showing distance ○ *You can see for miles from the top of the hill.* ○ *The motorway goes for kilometres without any service stations.* **6.** showing where someone or something is going ○ *Is this the plane for Edinburgh?* ○ *When is the next bus for Oxford Circus?* **7.** in the place of someone ○ *Can you write this letter for me?*

forage /'fɒrɪdʒ/ (**forages, foraging, foraged**) *verb* to search for food or supplies ○ *They spent the day foraging for food in the jungle.*

foray /'fɒreɪ/ *noun* a sudden attack

forbade /fə'bæd/ past tense of **forbid**

forbid /fə'bɪd/ (**forbids, forbidding, forbade, forbidden**) *verb* to tell someone that they are not allowed to do something ○ *The staff are forbidden to use the front entrance.*

forbidden /fə'bɪd(ə)n/ *adj* which is not allowed ○ *Father's new rock garden is forbidden territory to the children.*

forbidding /fə'bɪdɪŋ/ *adj* which looks frightening or dangerous

① **force** /fɔːs/ *noun* **1.** strength or power ○ *The force of the wind blew tiles off the roof.* ○ *The police had to use force to restrain the crowd.* **2.** an organised group of people ○ *He served in the police force for twenty years.* ■ *verb* (**forces, forcing, forced**) to make someone do something ○ *He was* *forced to stop smoking.* ○ *You can't force me to go if I don't want to.*

forced /fɔːst/ *adj* **1.** done because someone made you do it ○ *His lawyer said that his confession was forced.* **2.** artificial; not real ○ *He gave a rather forced laugh.*

forceful /ˈfɔːsf(ə)l/ *adj* strong or powerful

forceps /ˈfɔːseps/ *plural noun* a medical tool consisting of two long flat pieces joined together, used by doctors in medical operations ○ *He needed forceps to deliver the baby.*

forcible /ˈfɔːsɪb(ə)l/ *adj* done by or with force

forearm /ˈfɔːrɑːm/ *noun* the part of the arm between the hand and the elbow ○ *The dog put his paw on her forearm.*

forebears /ˈfɔːbeəz/ *plural noun* all the people in your family who have lived before you (*formal*) ○ *His forebears came from Russia in the 18th century.*

foreboding /fɔːˈbəʊdɪŋ/ *noun* a feeling that something bad will happen

forecast /ˈfɔːkɑːst/ *noun* what you think will happen in the future ○ *His forecast of sales turned out to be completely accurate.* ■ *verb* (**forecasts, forecasting, forecast**) to say what will happen in the future ○ *They are forecasting storms for the south coast.* ○ *They forecast a rise in the number of tourists.*

forecaster /ˈfɔːkɑːstə/ *noun* a person who says what will happen in the future, especially what sort of weather there will be

foreclose /fɔːˈkləʊz/ (**forecloses, foreclosing, foreclosed**) *verb* to take away property because the owner cannot pay back money which he has borrowed to buy it (*formal*)

forecourt /ˈfɔːkɔːt/ *noun* an open area in front of a building

forefinger /ˈfɔːfɪŋgə/ *noun* the index finger; the first finger next to the thumb

forefoot /ˈfɔːfʊt/ *noun* the front foot of an animal

foregone conclusion /ˌfɔːgɒn kən ˈkluːʒ(ə)n/ *noun* something which will definitely happen as a result of something else

foreground /ˈfɔːgraʊnd/ *noun* a part of a picture which seems nearest the front

forehand /ˈfɔːhænd/ *adj* played with the palm of the hand facing forwards, in sports such as tennis

forehead /ˈfɔːhed/ *noun* the part of the front of the head above the eyes and below the line of the hair

① **foreign** /ˈfɒrɪn/ *adj* not from your own country ○ *There are lots of foreign medical students at our college.*

foreign body /ˌfɒrɪn ˈbɒdi/ *noun* something which should not be there, such as a piece of dust in your eye

foreigner /ˈfɒrɪnə/ *noun* a person who does not come from the same country as you

foreign exchange /ˌfɒrən ɪks ˈtʃeɪndʒ/ *noun* the process or practice of changing the money of one country for money of another

Foreign Secretary /ˌfɒrɪn ˈsekrɪt(ə)ri/ *noun* the British government minister in charge of the Foreign Office (NOTE: In other countries this is **the Foreign Minister**, and in the USA **the Secretary of State**.)

foreleg /ˈfɔːleg/ *noun* the front leg of an animal

foreman /ˈfɔːmən/ (*plural* **foremen**) *noun* (*in a factory*) a skilled worker in charge of several other workers ○ *The foreman came to make a complaint to the manager.*

foremost /ˈfɔːməʊst/ *adj, adv* first; most important ◇ **first and foremost** first of all, the most important thing is ○ *First and foremost we need to get the costs under control.*

forensic /fəˈrensɪk/ *adj* referring to the scientific solving of crimes

forensics /fəˈrensɪks/ *noun* scientific methods used for solving crimes

forerunner /ˈfɔːrʌnə/ *noun* a person or thing coming earlier than another more important or advanced one

foresee /fɔːˈsiː/ (**foresees, foreseeing, foresaw, foreseen**) *verb* to have a strong feeling that something will happen in the future although you cannot be sure that it will

foreseeable /fɔːˈsiːəb(ə)l/ *adj* which can be foreseen ◇ **for the foreseeable future** as far in the future as you can imagine ○ *I will certainly stay here for the foreseeable future.*

foreshadow /fɔːˈʃædəʊ/ (**foreshadows, foreshadowing, foreshadowed**) *verb* to be a warning or sign of something that may happen

foresight /ˈfɔːsaɪt/ *noun* the ability to see what will probably happen in the future; the ability to plan for emergencies

foreskin /ˈfɔːskɪn/ *noun* the fold of skin covering the tip of the penis

② **forest** /ˈfɒrɪst/ *noun* a large area covered with trees ○ *The country is covered with thick forests.* ○ *In dry weather there's a danger of forest fires.* ○ *In winter bears come out of the forest to search for food.*

forestall /fɔːˈstɔːl/ (**forestalls, forestalling, forestalled**) *verb* to think about what someone may do and try to stop them

forestry /ˈfɒrɪstri/ *noun* the work of looking after a forest

foretell /fɔːˈtel/ (**foretells, foretelling, foretold**) *verb* to say what will happen in the future (*literary*)

forethought /ˈfɔːθɔːt/ *noun* the practice of planning for the future; thinking ahead

forever /fɔːrˈevə/, **for ever** /fər ˈevə/ *adv* **1.** always in the future ○ *I will love you forever.* **2.** a very long time ○ *It took us forever to get to the hotel.*

forewarn /fɔːˈwɔːn/ (**forewarns, forewarning, forewarned**) *verb* to warn about something that is going to happen

foreword /ˈfɔːwɜːd/ *noun* a short section at the beginning of a book, usually written by a person who is not the author, introducing the book and its author to the reader

forfeit /ˈfɔːfɪt/ *noun* a thing taken away as a punishment ○ *You have to pay a forfeit if you answer wrongly.* ■ *verb* (**forfeits, forfeiting, forfeited**) to lose something, especially as a punishment ○ *She forfeited her deposit.*

③ **forgave** /fəˈgeɪv/ past tense of **forgive**

forge /fɔːdʒ/ (**forges, forging, forged**) *verb* to copy something illegally ○ *He forged the signature on the cheque.* ○ *The new design of the banknotes makes them difficult to forge.*

forge ahead *phrasal verb* to go forward or make progress quickly ○ *The wind blew harder and the yacht forged ahead.* ○ *We are forging ahead with our new project.*

forger /ˈfɔːdʒə/ *noun* a person who copies something illegally

forgery /ˈfɔːdʒəri/ (*plural* **forgeries**) *noun* **1.** the action of making an illegal copy ○ *He was sent to prison for forgery.* **2.** an illegal copy ○ *The signature proved to be a forgery.*

① **forget** /fəˈget/ (**forgets, forgetting, forgot, forgotten**) *verb* **1.** not to remember [/~how/why/where/when etc/~about/~(that)] ○ *He's forgotten the name of the restaurant.* ○ *I've forgotten how to play chess.* ○ *She forgot all about her doctor's appointment.* ○ *Don't forget we're having lunch together tomorrow.* **2.** to leave something behind ○ *When he left the office he forgot his car keys.*

forgetful /fəˈgetf(ə)l/ *adj* often unable to remember

② **forgive** /fəˈgɪv/ (**forgives, forgiving, forgave, forgiven**) *verb* to stop being angry with someone ○ *Don't worry about it – I forgive you!* ○ *Will she ever forgive me for forgetting her birthday?*

forgiveness /fəˈgɪvnəs/ *noun* the act of forgiving

forgiving /fəˈgɪvɪŋ/ *adj* **1.** having a tendency to forgive **2.** allowing for some imperfection

forgo /fɔːˈgəʊ/ (**forgoes, forgoing, forwent, forgone**), **forego** *verb* to do without something

forgot /fəˈgɒt/ past tense of **forget**

forgotten /fəˈgɒt(ə)n/ past participle of **forget**

③ **fork** /fɔːk/ *noun* an object with a handle at one end and several sharp points at the other, used for picking up food and putting it in your mouth ○ *Don't try to eat Chinese food with a knife and fork.* ○ *It's polite to use a fork to eat cake – don't use your fingers.* ■ *verb* (**forks, forking, forked**) to become two parts ○ *The railway line forks at Crewe and one branch goes to the coast.*

forked /fɔːkt/ *adj* divided, particularly into two branches

forlorn /fəˈlɔːn/ *adj* left alone and feeling sad ○ *She stood all forlorn on the platform, watching the train leave.*

① **form** /fɔːm/ *noun* **1.** an official paper with spaces, in which you are asked to write information such as your name and address ○ *Could you please fill in this form with your details?* **2.** a state or condition ○ *Their team wasn't in top form and lost.* □ **in good form** in a good mood; well ○ *She's in good form today.* □ **off form, out of form** not performing very well ○ *He's off form at the moment – he needs more practice.* **3.** a class, usually in a secondary school ○ *She's in the third form.* ■ *verb* (**forms, forming, formed**) **1.** to sit or stand with others so as to make a particular shape ○ *The children formed a circle.* ○ *Form a queue here, please.* **2.** □ **formed of** made of ○ *The team is formed of ex-students.*

② **formal** /ˈfɔːm(ə)l/ *adj* **1.** done according to certain rules ○ *The formal opening ceremony was performed by the mayor.* **2.** serious in style; suitable for special or official occasions ○ *'Good afternoon' is a formal way of saying 'Hello' in the afternoon.*

③ **formality** /fɔː'mælɪti/ (*plural* **formalities**) *noun* a thing which has to be done to obey the law or because it is the custom

formally /'fɔːməli/ *adv* according to rules; done or spoken in a serious way

③ **format** /'fɔːmæt/ *noun* a shape, size or style that something is made in ○ *What format do you want your invitations printed in?* ■ *verb* (**formats, formatting, formatted**) to arrange the way text appears in a computer file ○ *Style sheets are used to format documents.*

② **formation** /fɔː'meɪʃ(ə)n/ *noun* the act of forming something ○ *The formation of ice occurs at temperatures below zero.*

formative /'fɔːmətɪv/ *adj* important for the development of someone or something

① **former** /'fɔːmə/ *adj* referring to a person's or a thing's job or position at an earlier time ○ *a former army officer* ○ *The former champion came last in the race.*

formerly /'fɔːməli/ *adv* at an earlier time ○ *He was formerly head of our department.*

formidable /'fɔːmɪdəb(ə)l/ *adj* causing admiration but also a little fear

③ **formula** /'fɔːmjʊlə/ (*plural* **formulae**) *noun* **1.** a statement of a scientific fact, often shown by means of symbols ○ *The chemical formula of carbon dioxide is CO_2.* ○ *The drug is made to a secret formula.* **2.** a set of plans for achieving something [~for]

formulaic /ˌfɔːmjʊ'leɪɪk/ *adj* **1.** expressed as, or having the nature of, a formula **2.** created according to existing models or ideas, and therefore not very original or exciting

③ **formulate** /'fɔːmjʊleɪt/ (**formulates, formulating, formulated**) *verb* **1.** to express an idea clearly ○ *He had some difficulty in formulating his ideas.* **2.** to develop carefully something such as a plan or way of doing something

forsake /fə'seɪk/ (**forsakes, forsaking, forsook, forsaken**) *verb* to leave someone or something behind. ◊ **god-forsaken**

fort /fɔːt/ *noun* a strong army building which can be defended against enemy attacks ○ *The soldiers rode out of the fort.* ○ *He was posted to a fort in the desert.*

forte /'fɔːteɪ/ *noun* a particular ability, or the subject you are best in ○ *History is not my forte.*

② **forth** /fɔːθ/ *adv* forwards

forthcoming /fɔːθ'kʌmɪŋ/ *adj* **1.** soon to come ○ *His forthcoming novel will be about London.* ○ *No government grant is forthcoming.* **2.** talkative; full of information ○ *She wasn't very forthcoming about her plans.*

forthright /'fɔːθraɪt/ *adj* direct and blunt

forthwith /fɔːθ'wɪθ/ *adv* immediately

fortieth /'fɔːtiəθ/ *adj* relating to the number 40 in a series ■ *noun* number 40 in a series

fortifications /ˌfɔːtɪfɪ'keɪʃ(ə)nz/ *plural noun* walls or towers built to defend a city ○ *Archaeologists have uncovered remains of the Roman fortifications.*

fortify /'fɔːtɪfaɪ/ (**fortifies, fortifying, fortified**) *verb* **1.** to make a place strong, so that it can be defended against attack **2.** □ **to fortify yourself with something** to eat or drink something to make you able to continue

fortitude /'fɔːtɪtjuːd/ *noun* bravery and determination (*formal*)

③ **fortnight** /'fɔːtnaɪt/ *noun* two weeks (NOTE: not used in US English)

fortnightly /'fɔːtnaɪtli/ *adj, adv* once every two weeks ○ *a fortnightly visit to the doctor*

fortress /'fɔːtrəs/ *noun* a strong castle

fortuitous /fɔː'tjuːɪtəs/ *adj* happening by chance and having a good result

③ **fortunate** /'fɔːtʃənət/ *adj* having better things happen to you than happen to other people ○ *You are very fortunate to have such a lovely family.*

② **fortunately** /'fɔːtʃənətli/ *adv* by good luck ○ *Fortunately, he had remembered to take an umbrella.* ○ *He was late getting to the airport, but fortunately the flight had been delayed.*

③ **fortune** /'fɔːtʃən/ *noun* **1.** a large amount of money ○ *He won a fortune on the lottery.* ○ *She made a fortune on the stock market.* ○ *She left her fortune to her three children.* **2.** what will happen in the future ○ *She claims to be able to tell your fortune using cards.* ◇ **to cost a fortune** to cost a lot of money ○ *That shop has shoes that cost a fortune.* ◇ **to tell someone's fortune** to say what will happen to someone in the future ○ *She tells fortunes from cards.*

fortune-teller /'fɔːtʃən ˌtelə/ *noun* a person who says what will happen in the future, e.g. by looking at cards or lines on your hand

① **forty** /'fɔːti/ *noun* the number 40 □ **forties** the numbers between 40 and 49

.45 /ˌfɔːti ˈfaɪv/ *noun* a gun with a .45 calibre.

③ **forum** /ˈfɔːrəm/ *noun* an occasion when matters of general interest can be discussed

① **forward** /ˈfɔːwəd/ *adj* confident ○ *She was always very forward as a child.* ■ *adv* **1.** in the direction that someone or something is facing ○ *She bent forward to hear what he had to say.* ○ *He took two steps forward.* ○ *The policeman made a sign with his hand and the cars began to go forward.* **2.** towards the future ○ *We need to do some forward planning.* ■ *noun* a player in a team whose job is to attack the other side ○ *The England defence came under attack from the other team's forwards.*

forwarding address /ˈfɔːwədɪŋ əˌdres/ *noun* an address to which mail can be sent

forward-looking /ˈfɔːwəd ˌlʊkɪŋ/ *adj* planning for or thinking about the future

forwards /ˈfɔːwədz/ *adv* in the direction that someone or something is facing ○ *She bent forwards to hear what he had to say.* ○ *He took two steps forwards.* ○ *The policeman made a sign with his hand and the cars began to go forwards.*

forward slash /ˈfɔːwəd slæʃ/ *noun* an ordinary slash used in printing or writing text

fossil /ˈfɒs(ə)l/ *noun* the mark of an animal or plant left in a rock, formed over millions of years

fossil fuel /ˈfɒs(ə)l ˌfjuːəl/ *noun* a fuel which has developed from the ancient remains of plants or animals over many centuries

fossilised /ˈfɒsəlaɪzd/, **fossilized** *adj* referring to something which has become a fossil

foster /ˈfɒstə/ (**fosters, fostering, fostered**) *verb* **1.** to bring up a child who is not your own, without adopting it ○ *They have fostered several children.* **2.** to encourage an idea, etc. ○ *Tourism fosters interest in other countries.* ○ *We are trying to foster the children's interest in the history of the village.*

③ **fought** /fɔːt/ past tense and past participle of **fight**

foul /faʊl/ *adj* **1.** smelling or tasting unpleasant ○ *A foul-smelling drain ran down the centre of the street.* **2.** very unpleasant ○ *What foul weather we're having!* ○ *The boss has been in a foul temper all day.* ■ *noun* an action which is against the rules of a game ○ *The referee gave a free kick for a foul on the goalkeeper.* ○ *Look at the action replay to see if it really was a foul.* (NOTE: Do not confuse with **fowl**.) ■ *verb* (**fouls, fouling, fouled**) to do something to another player which is against the rules of a game ○ *He was fouled inside the penalty box so the ref gave a penalty.*

foul play /faʊl ˈpleɪ/ *noun* murder

foul-up /ˈfaʊl ʌp/ *noun* a bad situation which has happened because of a mistake someone has made

① **found** /faʊnd/ *verb* (**founds, founding, founded**) to establish something; to begin something ○ *The business was founded in 1900.* ■ past tense and past participle of **find**

② **foundation** /faʊnˈdeɪʃ(ə)n/ *noun* **1.** the act of establishing something or of setting something up ○ *Ever since its foundation in 1892, the company has been a great success.* **2.** a charitable organisation which provides money for certain projects ○ *a foundation for educational research*

foundation course /faʊnˈdeɪʃ(ə)n kɔːs/ *noun* a basic course at a university, which allows you to go on to a more advanced course

founder /ˈfaʊndə/ *noun* a person who establishes or sets up something ○ *He was one of the founders of the National Trust.*

foundry /ˈfaʊndri/ *noun* a place for melting and moulding metal or glass

fountain /ˈfaʊntɪn/ *noun* an object or a structure with a pump which makes a stream of water come out, usually found in a street or a large garden

fountain pen /ˈfaʊntɪn pen/ *noun* a pen which can be filled with ink

4 /fɔː/ *prep* for (*informal*)

① **four** /fɔː/ *noun* the number 4 ◇ **on all fours** on hands and knees ○ *He was creeping around under the desk on all fours.*

four-by-four /ˌfɔː baɪ ˈfɔː/, **4x4** *noun* a four-wheel-drive vehicle. Abbreviation **4x4**

four-poster /fɔː ˈpəʊstə/, **four-poster bed** *noun* an old-fashioned bed with a post at each corner, that can be used to support a canopy or curtains

foursome /ˈfɔːs(ə)m/ *noun* a group of four people ○ *The foursome stole a car and drove to Las Vegas.*

① **fourteen** /ˌfɔːˈtiːn/ *noun* the number 14

① **fourteenth** /ˌfɔːˈtiːnθ/ *adj, noun* relating to the number 14 in a series ■ *noun* number 14 in a series

① **fourth** /fɔːθ/ *adj* relating to the number 4 in a series ■ *noun* **1.** number 4 in a series **2.** one part of four equal parts

Fourth of July /ˌfɔːθ əv dʒʊ'laɪ/ *noun* the national day in the United States ○ *We're having a Fourth of July party.*

4WD *noun* a vehicle with four-wheel drive

four-wheel drive /ˌfɔː wiːl 'draɪv/ *noun* **1.** a system in which engine power drives all four wheels of a vehicle **2.** a vehicle working by this system. Abbreviation **4WD**

fowl /faʊl/ *noun* a domestic bird which is kept for its eggs or to be killed for food, such as a chicken, duck, turkey or goose

③ **fox** /fɒks/ *noun* a wild animal with reddish fur and a long thick tail. Compare **vixen**

foyer /'fɔɪeɪ/ *noun* a large entrance hall at the front of a hotel, restaurant or theatre

fracas /'frækɑː/ *noun* a noisy disturbance

fraction /'frækʃən/ *noun* **1.** (*in mathematics*) a unit that is less than a whole number ○ *0.25 and 0.5 are ¼ and ½ expressed as fractions.* **2.** a small part or amount ○ *Only a fraction of the stolen money was ever found.* ○ *Sales are up a fraction this month.* ○ *Move the camera a fraction to the right, and you'll all get in the picture.*

fracture /'fræktʃə/ *noun* a break, especially in a bone ○ *The X-ray showed up the fracture clearly.* ■ *verb* (**fractures, fracturing, fractured**) to break a bone ○ *He fractured his leg in the accident.* ○ *They put her fractured leg in plaster.*

fragile /'frædʒaɪl/ *adj* made from materials that are easily broken ○ *Be careful when you're packing these plates – they're very fragile.*

fragment[1] /'frægmənt/ *noun* a small piece ○ *When digging on the site of the house they found fragments of very old glass.*

fragment[2] /fræg'ment/ (**fragments, fragmenting, fragmented**) *verb* to separate into small pieces ○ *As soon as the founder died the whole organisation fragmented.*

fragrance /'freɪgrəns/ *noun* **1.** a pleasant smell **2.** a pleasant-smelling liquid which is put on the skin

fragrant /'freɪgrənt/ *adj* with a sweet smell

frail /freɪl/ *adj* physically weak, especially because of age ○ *His grandmother is now rather frail.*

frailty /'freɪlti/ (*plural* **frailties**) *noun* being weak ○ *the frailty of human existence* ○ *the frailty of my father's health*

② **frame** /freɪm/ *noun* a border around something such as a pair of glasses, a picture, a mirror or a window ○ *He has glasses with gold frames.* ○ *I think the frame is worth more than the painting.* ■ *verb* (**frames, framing, framed**) to put a frame round a picture ○ *The photograph has been framed in red.*

③ **framework** /'freɪmwɜːk/ *noun* **1.** the structure supporting a building, etc. ○ *The framework of the shed is sound – it just needs some paint.* **2.** the basis of a plan ○ *They are working within the framework of the United Nations resolution.* ○ *They are negotiating the framework of the agreement.*

③ **franchise** /'fræntʃaɪz/ *noun* **1.** a right to vote ○ *In some countries women do not have the franchise.* **2.** a permit to sell a company's products in a certain region or to trade using a well-known brand name ○ *He bought a pizza franchise.*

frank /fræŋk/ *adj* saying what you think ○ *To be really frank with you – I think the plan stinks.* ○ *He gave her some frank advice.* (NOTE: Do not confuse with **franc**.) ■ *verb* (**franks, franking, franked**) to stamp a letter with a special machine, instead of using a postage stamp ○ *The letters were all franked before they left the office.*

frankfurter /'fræŋkfɜːtə/, **frankfurt** *noun* a long sausage which is boiled and sometimes eaten inside a roll. ◊ **hot dog**

③ **frankly** /'fræŋkli/ *adv* telling the truth

frantic /'fræntɪk/ *adj* wild, worried and doing things fast

fraternal /frə'tɜːn(ə)l/ *adj* brotherly ○ *He started going out with his brother's girlfriend – there's fraternal feeling for you!*

fraternise /'frætənaɪz/ (**fraternises, fraternising, fraternised**), **fraternize** *verb* to spend time with other people socially, especially people who are considered unsuitable

fraternity /frə'tɜːnɪti/ *noun* **1.** a group of people with similar interests or occupations ○ *Members of the banking fraternity have criticised the Chancellor of the Exchequer.* **2.** a brotherly feeling ○ *The slogan of the French state is 'Liberty, Equality, Fraternity'.*

fraud /frɔːd/ *noun* **1.** obtaining money by making people believe something which is not true ○ *He is facing trial for fraud.* **2.** a person pretending to be something which he or she is not ○ *She's a fraud – she has no legal qualifications.* ○ *He's an old fraud – he didn't build that car himself.*

fraudulent /ˈfrɔːdjʊlənt/ *adj* dishonest

fraught /frɔːt/ *adj* **1.** full of problems or danger ○ *The whole building project has been fraught with problems.* **2.** worried, or causing anxiety

frayed /freɪd/ *adj* having a worn edge, with loose threads

freak /friːk/ *noun* **1.** an unusual type of person, animal or plant ○ *A white whale is a freak of nature.* **2.** a person who is extremely interested in something (*informal*) ○ *My brother's a computer freak.*

freckles /ˈfrek(ə)lz/ *plural noun* small brown marks on the skin, often caused by the sun ○ *You'll recognise her at once, she's tall with fair hair and freckles.* ○ *She was trying to get rid of the freckles on her arms.*

① **free** /friː/ *adj* (**freer, freest**) **1.** not costing any money ○ *Send in four tokens from cereal boxes and you can get a free toy.* ○ *I got a free ticket for the exhibition.* **2.** not busy; available ○ *Will you be free next Tuesday?* ○ *There is a table free in the corner of the restaurant.* ○ *Do you have any free time next week?* **3.** able to do what you want; not forced to do anything ○ *He's free to do what he wants.* **4.** not in prison or a cage ○ *After six years in prison he's a free man again.* □ **to set someone** *or* **something free** to allow someone to leave prison, or to let an animal out of a cage ○ *The young birds were raised in the zoo and then set free in the wild.* ■ *verb* (**frees, freeing, freed**) to release someone who is trapped ○ *It took the fire service some time to free the passengers in the bus.*

free agent /friː ˈeɪdʒənt/ *noun* someone who is able to do what they want

freebie /ˈfriːbi/ *noun* something supplied free of charge, especially as a gift to a customer or journalist (*informal*)

② **freedom** /ˈfriːdəm/ *noun* **1.** the state of being free, rather than being forced to stay somewhere or being in prison ○ *She felt a sense of freedom being in the country after working all week in the city.* ○ *His lawyer pleaded for his client's freedom.* **2.** the state of being allowed to do what you want ○ *They are trying to restrict our freedom of movement.*

freedom fighter /ˈfriːdəm ˌfaɪtə/ *noun* a guerilla fighting against an oppressive government

free enterprise /ˌfriː ˈentəpraɪz/ *noun* a system of business where there is no interference from the government

free-for-all /ˈfriː fər ɔːl/ *noun* a general fight or argument among several people (*informal*)

free kick /friː ˈkɪk/ *noun* a kick which a footballer is allowed to make without anyone opposing him, to punish the other side for something which they have done

freelance /ˈfriːlɑːns/ (**freelances, freelancing, freelanced**) *verb* to work independently ○ *She freelances for several newspapers.*

freelancer /ˈfriːlɑːnsə/ *noun* a freelance worker

freely /ˈfriːli/ *adv* in an open manner, without being forced

free market /ˌfriː ˈmɑːkɪt/ *noun* a situation in which trade takes place without government control

Freemason /ˈfriːmeɪs(ə)n/ *noun* a member of a secret society whose members help each other and protect each other (NOTE: also simply called **Masons**)

free-range /ˌfriː ˈreɪndʒ/ *adj* (*of animals, birds*) kept in the open, not in cages or boxes

free speech /ˌfriː ˈspiːtʃ/ *noun* the ability to say what you think without danger of being prosecuted

③ **free trade** /ˌfriː ˈtreɪd/ *noun* a system where goods can go from one country to another without any restrictions

freeware /ˈfriːweə/ *noun* free computer software

② **freeway** /ˈfriːweɪ/ *noun US* a fast motorway with few junctions

free will /friː ˈwɪl/ *noun* the ability to choose your own actions

③ **freeze** /friːz/ (**freezes, freezing, froze, frozen**) *verb* **1.** to become solid because of the cold ○ *The winter was mild, and for the first time ever the river did not freeze over.* ○ *It's so cold that the lake has frozen solid.* **2.** to make food very cold so that it does not decay ○ *We froze the raspberries we picked this morning.* **3.** to become very cold ○ *The forecast is that it will freeze tonight.* ○ *Put a hat on or you'll freeze!*

③ **freezer** /ˈfriːzə/ *noun* a piece of equipment like a large box, which is very cold inside, used for freezing food and keeping it frozen

③ **freezing** /ˈfriːzɪŋ/ *adj* very cold, or close to the temperature at which water freezes

freezing point /ˈfriːzɪŋ pɔɪnt/ *noun* a very low temperature at which a liquid becomes solid

freight /freɪt/ *noun* **1.** the action of transporting goods by air, sea or land ○ *We sent the order (by) air freight.* **2.** goods transported ○ *The government is encouraging firms to send freight by rail.*

freight car /ˈfreɪt kɑː/ *noun US* a goods wagon on a train

freighter /ˈfreɪtə/ *noun* an aircraft or ship which carries goods

① **French** /frentʃ/ *adj* referring to France ■ *noun* the language spoken in France

French horn /frentʃ ˈhɔːn/ *noun* a brass musical instrument with a tube which is coiled round

frenetic /frəˈnetɪk/ *adj* wildly excited

frenzied /ˈfrenzid/ *adj* wild and uncontrollable

frenzy /ˈfrenzi/ *noun* a wild excitement

③ **frequency** /ˈfriːkwənsi/ *noun* the number of times that something happens over a particular period of time ○ *The government is becoming alarmed at the frequency of accidents in the construction industry.* (NOTE: no plural)

frequent[1] /ˈfriːkwənt/ *adj* happening or appearing often ○ *He was a frequent visitor to the library.* ○ *Skin cancer is becoming more frequent.* ○ *How frequent are the planes to Birmingham?*

frequent[2] /frɪˈkwent/ (**frequents, frequenting, frequented**) *verb* to go somewhere very often ○ *He frequents the bar at the corner of the street.*

② **frequently** /ˈfriːkwəntli/ *adv* often ○ *The ferries don't run as frequently in the winter.* ○ *She could frequently be seen walking her dog in the park.*

fresco /ˈfreskəʊ/ (*plural* **frescoes** or **frescos**) *noun* a painting done on wet plaster on a wall or ceiling

② **fresh** /freʃ/ *adj* **1.** not used or not dirty ○ *I'll get you a fresh towel.* **2.** made recently ○ *a basket of fresh rolls* ○ *Let's ask for a pot of fresh coffee.* **3.** new and different ○ *The police produced some fresh evidence.* **4.** not in a tin or frozen ○ *The fishmonger sells fresh fish.* ○ *Fresh fruit salad is better than tinned.* ○ *Fresh vegetables are difficult to get in winter.*

fresh air /ˌfreʃ ˈeə/ *noun* the open space outside buildings where the air flows freely ○ *After ten hours in the office they were glad to come out into the fresh air.*

freshen /ˈfreʃ(ə)n/ (**freshens, freshening, freshened**) *verb* **1.** to make something fresh ○ *The hot air in the valley was freshened by a mountain breeze.* **2.** to become cooler or fresher ○ *The wind freshened as night came on.*

freshen up *verb* to wash your hands and face, and tidy your hair ○ *I must just go to freshen (myself) up before the guests arrive.*

fresher /ˈfreʃə/ *noun* a new student in his or her first year at college or university (*informal*)

freshman /ˈfreʃmən/ (*plural* **freshmen**) *noun* a new student in his or her first year at college or university. Compare **senior**

freshwater /ˈfreʃwɔːtə/ *adj* referring to river or lake water, not salt water

fret /fret/ (**frets, fretting, fretted**) *verb* to worry or be unhappy ○ *She's fretting about her exams.*

fretful /ˈfretf(ə)l/ *adj* always complaining and unhappy

friar /ˈfraɪə/ *noun* a member of a Christian religious order who went out to collect money or to preach

friction /ˈfrɪkʃən/ *noun* **1.** one thing rubbing against another ○ *You need more oil to reduce friction in the motor.* **2.** a disagreement between two or more people ○ *There has been a good deal of friction between the members of the board.*

① **Friday** /ˈfraɪdeɪ/ *noun* the fifth day of the week, the day between Thursday and Saturday ○ *We all had a meal together last Friday.* ○ *We always go to the cinema on Friday evenings.* ○ *We normally have our meetings on Fridays.* ○ *Friday is a day of rest for Muslims.* ○ *Today is Friday, June 20th.*

② **fridge** /frɪdʒ/ *noun* a kitchen machine for keeping things cold ○ *The fridge is empty – we must buy some more food.* ○ *Shall I put the milk back in the fridge?*

fridge-freezer /frɪdʒ ˈfriːzə/ *noun* a kitchen machine consisting of both a fridge and a freezer in a single unit

③ **fried** /fraɪd/ past tense and past participle of **fry** ■ *adj* cooked in oil or fat

① **friend** /frend/ *noun* a person that you know well and like ○ *She's my best friend.* ○ *We're going on holiday with some friends from work.* □ **to make friends with someone** to get to know and like someone ○ *We made friends with some French people on holiday.*

② **friendly** /ˈfrendli/ (**friendlier, friendliest**) *adj* pleasant and kind, wanting to make friends ○ *Don't be frightened of the dog – he's very friendly.* ○ *We're not on friendly terms with the people who live next door.*

③ **friendship** /ˈfrendʃɪp/ *noun* the state of being friends ○ *He formed several lasting friendships at school.*

fries /fraɪz/ 3rd person singular present of **fry**

frieze /friːz/ *noun* a decorated band around a room just below the ceiling

frigate /ˈfrɪgət/ *noun* a small fast-moving naval ship

fright /fraɪt/ *noun* fear

frighten /ˈfraɪt(ə)n/ (**frightens, frightening, frightened**) *verb* to make someone afraid ○ *Take off that horrible mask – you'll frighten the children.* ○ *The cat has frightened all the birds away.*

② **frightened** /ˈfraɪtn(ə)d/ *adj* afraid [~of] ○ *The frightened children ran out of the building.* ○ *Don't be frightened of the dog – he won't hurt you.*

③ **frightening** /ˈfraɪt(ə)nɪŋ/ *adj* making you feel afraid ○ *a frightening sound of footsteps in the corridor* ○ *He had a frightening thought – what if no one heard his cries for help?*

frightful /ˈfraɪtf(ə)l/ *adj* terrible or awful

frightfully /ˈfraɪtf(ə)li/ *adv* extremely (*dated or humorous*)

frigid /ˈfrɪdʒɪd/ *adj* **1.** unfriendly, not showing any warm feelings ○ *His frigid response did not give us much hope.* **2.** (*of a woman*) not responsive in sexual relations (*insulting*) ○ *After his marriage he discovered that she was frigid.*

frill /frɪl/ *noun* a piece of material gathered together and sewn onto a dress, etc.

fringe /frɪndʒ/ *noun* **1.** the hair lying over the forehead **2.** the edging of something such as a shawl or carpet, consisting of loose threads hanging down ○ *a lampshade with a yellow fringe* **3.** an outer edge of an area ○ *Round the fringe of the crowd people were selling souvenirs.*

fringe benefit /ˈfrɪndʒ ˌbenɪfɪt/ *noun* an additional advantage which someone gets from doing a particular job or activity

frisk /frɪsk/ (**frisks, frisking, frisked**) *verb* **1.** to search someone by running your hands over his or her body ○ *When they frisked him at the airport, they found a knife hidden under his shirt.* **2.** to jump about happily ○ *little lambs frisking in the field*

frisky /ˈfrɪski/ *adj* feeling lively, or behaving in a lively way

fritter *verb*

fritter away *verb* to waste time, money, etc. on unimportant things ○ *He inherited a fortune from his grandfather but had frittered it all away by the time he was thirty.*

frivolity /frɪˈvɒlɪti/ *noun* silliness; lack of seriousness

frivolous /ˈfrɪvələs/ *adj* silly; not serious

frizzy /ˈfrɪzi/ *adj* (*of hair*) in a mass of tight curls

③ **frog** /frɒg/ *noun* a small greenish-brown animal with long legs, which jumps, and lives both on land and in water ○ *He kept some tadpoles in a jar hoping they would turn into frogs.* ○ *Can you hear the frogs croaking round the pond?*

frogman /ˈfrɒgmən/ (*plural* **frogmen**) *noun* a diver working underwater

frolic /ˈfrɒlɪk/ (**frolics, frolicking, frolicked**) *verb* to play happily ○ *The lambs were frolicking in the fields.*

① **from** /frəm, frɒm/ *prep* **1.** away **2.** showing the place where something starts or started ○ *He comes from Germany.* ○ *The bees went from flower to flower.* ○ *We've had a letter from the bank.* ○ *He read the book from beginning to end.* ○ *Take three from four and you get one.* ○ *I took a book from the pile on his desk.* **3.** showing the time when something starts or started ○ *I'll be at home from 8 o'clock onwards.* ○ *The hours of work are 9.30 to 5.30, from Monday to Friday.* ○ *From now on I'm going to get up early.* **4.** showing distance ○ *It is not far from here to the railway station.* **5.** showing difference ○ *Can you tell butter from margarine?* ○ *His job is totally different from mine.* **6.** showing a cause ○ *He died from the injuries he received in the accident.* ○ *She suffers from coughs every winter.*

frond /frɒnd/ *noun* a large leaf divided into many thin sections, as, e.g., on a palm tree

① **front** /frʌnt/ *noun* a part of something which is furthest forward ○ *The front of the house is on London Road.* ○ *She spilt coffee down the front of her dress.* ■ *adj* which is in front ○ *She sat in the front seat, next to the driver.* ◇ **in front** further forwards ○ *Her mother sat in the back seat and she sat in front.* ◇ **in front of someone *or* something** before or further forwards than something ○ *Don't stand in front of the car – it may start suddenly.* ○ *There are six people in front of me in the queue.* ○ *You can park your car in front of the shop.*

frontal /ˈfrʌnt(ə)l/ *adj* of or in the front ○ *a frontal attack on the enemy*

③ **front door** /ˌfrʌnt ˈdɔː/ *noun* the main door to a house or building

frontier /frʌnˈtɪə/ *noun* the boundary line between two countries ○ *The customs men at the frontier didn't even bother to look at our passports.*

front line /ˌfrʌnt ˈlaɪn/ *noun* the line where two armies meet in war

front page /frʌnt ˈpeɪdʒ/ *noun* the first page of a newspaper or magazine

front-runner /frʌnt ˈrʌnə/ *noun* the person who is currently first in a race or contest (*informal*)

frost /frɒst/ *noun* **1.** a white covering on the ground that appears when the temperature is below freezing ○ *The garden was white with frost.* **2.** an occasion on which the temperature outside is below freezing ○ *There was a hard frost last night.* ○ *There's a touch of frost in the air.* ○ *A late frost can damage young plants.*

frostbite /ˈfrɒstbaɪt/ *noun* an injury caused by very severe cold which freezes your flesh

frosted glass /ˌfrɒstɪd ˈɡlɑːs/ *noun* glass with a rough or textured surface which makes it opaque

frosting /ˈfrɒstɪŋ/ *noun* icing on a cake

froth /frɒθ/ *noun* a mass of bubbles on top of a liquid ○ *Wait until the froth has settled before drinking your beer.* ■ *verb* (**froths, frothing, frothed**) to make masses of bubbles ○ *He was lying on the floor, frothing at the mouth.*

frown /fraʊn/ *verb* (**frowns, frowning, frowned**) to make lines in the skin on your forehead because you are concentrating or worried ○ *He frowned as he tried to do the calculation.* ■ *noun* pulling your eyebrows together as a sign that you are angry or worried ○ *Take that frown off your face – everything's going to be all right.*

frown on *phrasal verb* to disapprove of something ○ *The teachers frown on singing in the corridors.* ○ *The company frowns on people who bring food into the office.*

③ **froze** /frəʊz/ past tense of **freeze**

③ **frozen** /ˈfrəʊz(ə)n/ past participle of **freeze** ■ *adj* **1.** very cold ○ *Come inside – you must be frozen out there.* **2.** at a temperature below freezing point ○ *We went skating on the frozen lake.*

frugal /ˈfruːɡ(ə)l/ *adj* **1.** small and plain ○ *He had a frugal meal of bread and cheese.* **2.** careful when you spend money or use resources ○ *He lived a frugal life and died a millionaire.* ○ *The frugal use of the heating system will cut down on your electricity bills.*

② **fruit** /fruːt/ *noun* a food that grows on trees or plants, which is often eaten raw and is usually sweet ○ *You should eat five pieces of fruit every day.* ○ *He has six fruit trees in his garden.*

fruitful /ˈfruːtf(ə)l/ *adj* which produces good results

fruition /fruːˈɪʃ(ə)n/ *noun* □ **to come to fruition** to be finished with good results ○ *After ten years' work, the project finally came to fruition.* □ **to bring something to fruition** to finish something with good results

fruitless /ˈfruːtləs/ *adj* producing no result

fruit salad /ˌfruːt ˈsæləd/ *noun* pieces of different fruit, cut up and mixed together

fruity /ˈfruːti/ *adj* **1.** tasting of fruit ○ *a dark fruity red wine* **2.** (*of a voice or laugh*) deep and attractive

frustrate /frʌˈstreɪt/ (**frustrates, frustrating, frustrated**) *verb* **1.** to make someone annoyed because they cannot do what they want to **2.** to prevent someone or something from being successful

frustrated /frʌˈstreɪtɪd/ *adj* **1.** annoyed because of not being able to do something ○ *She was frustrated in her attempt to get an honest answer.* **2.** having the desire to be something, but not having the talent or the opportunity ○ *a frustrated artist* ○ *When he gets behind the wheel of his car you can see the frustrated Grand Prix driver coming out.*

frustrating /frʌˈstreɪtɪŋ/ *adj* annoying, because someone or something stops you doing what you want to do

③ **frustration** /frʌˈstreɪʃ(ə)n/ *noun* a feeling of anger and impatience when you cannot do what you want to do

③ **fry** /fraɪ/ (**fries, frying, fried**) *verb* to cook something in oil or fat ○ *Fry the onions over a low heat so that they don't burn.* ○ *Fry the eggs in some fat.*

③ **frying pan** /ˈfraɪɪŋ pæn/ *noun* an open pan with low sides, used for frying

③ **ft** /fʊt/ *abbr* foot *or* feet

fuchsia /ˈfjuːʃə/ *noun* a garden plant with colourful bell-shaped hanging flowers

fudge /fʌdʒ/ *noun* **1.** a soft sweet made from butter, sugar and milk **2.** an informal way of avoiding a problem ○ *The report on* *the scandal was a fudge.* ■ *verb* (**fudges, fudging, fudged**) to avoid giving a clear answer or making a definite decision about something ○ *We can't wait for those details to arrive, we'll have to fudge it.* □ **to fudge the issue** to avoid making a clear decision about a difficult situation (*informal*) ○ *For years, they have been fudging the issue of legalising drugs.*

② **fuel** /ˈfjuːəl/ *noun* a substance such coal, gas, oil, petrol or wood which can be burnt to give heat or power ○ *What fuel do you use to heat the house?* ○ *What's the fuel consumption of your car?* ○ *We ran out of fuel on the motorway.* ◇ **to add fuel to the flames** to make matters worse ○ *Just to add fuel to the flames the union leader sent the minister's letter to the newspapers.*

fugitive /ˈfjuːdʒɪtɪv/ *noun* a person who is running away ○ *The two fugitives were captured by the police.*

③ **fulfil** /fʊlˈfɪl/ *verb* to complete something in a satisfactory way ○ *He died before he could fulfil his ambition to fly a plane.* ○ *We are so busy that we cannot fulfil any more orders before Christmas.* (NOTE: The US spelling is **fulfill**.)

fulfilled /fʊlˈfɪld/ *adj* satisfied with what you are doing, or happy because of the things you have achieved

fulfilling /fʊlˈfɪlɪŋ/ *adj* which gives satisfaction

fulfilment /fʊlˈfɪlmənt/ *noun* carrying something out in a satisfactory way (NOTE: The US spelling is **fulfillment**.)

① **full** /fʊl/ *adj* **1.** with as much inside as is possible ○ *Is the box full?* ○ *The bag is full of potatoes.* ○ *We couldn't get on the first bus because it was full.* ○ *All the hotels were full.* **2.** complete ○ *You must give the police full details of the accident.* ○ *Write your full name and address at the top of the paper.* ■ *adv* completely ○ *The story has never been told in full.* ◇ **to be full of yourself** to think a lot of yourself, or to be always talking about how successful you are

full-blown /ˌfʊl ˈbləʊn/ *adj* **1.** (*of a flower*) completely open ○ *a full-blown rose* **2.** fully qualified **3.** (*of a disease*) complete; with all the symptoms ○ *He developed full-blown AIDS.*

full board /ˌfʊl ˈbɔːd/ *noun* a rate for bedroom and all meals in a hotel

full-fledged /ˌfʊl ˈfledʒd/ *adj US* fully-fledged

full-grown /ˌfʊl ˈgrəʊn/ *adj* same as **fully-grown**

full house /ˌfʊl ˈhaʊs/ *noun* an audience for a theatre or cinema performance that fills all the seats

full-length /ˌfʊl ˈleŋθ/ *adj* **1.** covering or showing the whole of someone ○ *a full-length evening gown* ○ *a full-length portrait* **2.** referring to a long film or novel ○ *It was his first full-length film, made when he was 21.*

full moon /ˌfʊl ˈmuːn/ *noun* the time when the moon appears as a complete circle

full-on /ˌfʊl ˈɒn/ *adj* having a particular quality to the highest degree

③ **full-scale** /ˈfʊl skeɪl/ *adj* **1.** the same size as in real life ○ *a full-scale model of a dinosaur* **2.** complete ○ *It started as a dispute over a few islands and soon developed into a full-scale war.*

③ **full stop** /ˌfʊl ˈstɒp/ *noun* a punctuation mark like a small dot, showing the end of a sentence or an abbreviation

③ **full-time** /ˈfʊl taɪm/ *adj, adv* working for all the usual working time, i.e. about seven hours a day, five days a week ○ *She is in full-time work.* or *She works full-time.* ○ *We have eight full-time and two part-time teachers at our school.* Compare **part-time**

② **fully** /ˈfʊli/ *adv* completely ○ *He was fully aware that he had made a mistake.* ○ *She still hasn't fully recovered from her accident.* ○ *The hotel is fully booked for the Christmas week.* ○ *When fully grown, an elephant can weigh several tons.*

fully-fledged /ˌfʊli ˈfledʒd/ *adj* experienced or qualified

fully-grown /ˌfʊli ˈgrəʊn/ *adj* adult-sized

fumble /ˈfʌmbəl/ (**fumbles, fumbling, fumbled**) *verb* to touch or feel clumsily

③ **fume** /fjuːm/ (**fumes, fuming, fumed**) *verb* to be angry ○ *After he had read the report he was absolutely fuming.*

fumes /fjuːmz/ *plural noun* smoke or gas ○ *They must have inhaled the fumes from the gas cooker.*

fumigate /ˈfjuːmɪ geɪt/ (**fumigates, fumigating, fumigated**) *verb* to clean a building or a room by burning chemicals to produce smoke which kills germs and insects

② **fun** /fʌn/ *noun* enjoyment from an activity ○ *Having to stay in bed on my birthday is not much fun.* □ **to have fun** to enjoy yourself ○ *We had a lot of fun on the river.* ◇ **to make fun of someone, to poke fun at someone** to laugh at someone ○ *Don't make fun of her – she's trying her best.* ○ *He poked fun at the Prime Minister.* ◇ **for**

fun as a joke or for enjoyment ○ *She poured water down his neck for fun.* ○ *Just for fun, he drove the car through town dressed as a gorilla.* ○ *Why did you do that? – Just for the fun of it!*

① **function** /ˈfʌŋkʃən/ *noun* **1.** a party, or a gathering of people ○ *We have two wedding functions in the main restaurant this weekend.* ○ *The Prime Minister busy up with official functions all week.* **2.** the work done by someone or something ○ *The function of a goalkeeper is to stop the ball going into the net.* ○ *What's the function of that red switch?* ■ *verb* (**functions, functioning, functioned**) **1.** to work ○ *The computer is still functioning well after years of use.* **2.** to serve as something [~as] ○ *The sofa functions as a bed if we have visitors.*

functional /ˈfʌŋkʃən(ə)l/ *adj* **1.** useful but not decorative ○ *These old saucepans are not works of art but they're functional.* **2.** working properly ○ *The heating system will be functional again in an hour or so.*

function key /ˈfʌŋkʃən kiː/ *noun* one of a row of keys along the top of a computer keyboard which activates a set of instructions

① **fund** /fʌnd/ *noun* an amount of money intended for a particular purpose ○ *She contributes to a pension fund.* ■ *verb* (**funds, funding, funded**) to provide money for a special purpose ○ *We have asked the government to fund the building of the new library.* ○ *The company is funding her manager's course.*

② **fundamental** /ˌfʌndəˈment(ə)l/ *adj* basic; essential ○ *The fundamental difference between us is that I apologise for my mistakes and you don't.* ○ *Good air quality is fundamental for children's health.*

fundamentalism /ˌfʌndəˈment(ə)lɪz(ə)m/ *noun* an approach to religion which involves following religious rules very strictly

fundamentalist /ˌfʌndəˈment(ə)lɪst/ *noun* a person who follows religious rules very strictly

③ **funding** /ˈfʌndɪŋ/ *noun* money for something

fundraiser /ˈfʌndreɪzə/ *noun* **1.** a person who raises money for a charity or voluntary group **2.** a money-raising activity or event for a charity or voluntary group

fund-raising /ˈfʌnd ˌreɪzɪŋ/ *noun* the activity of raising money for a charity or voluntary group

funds /fʌndz/ *noun* money which is available for spending ○ *He started a course at college and then ran out of funds.* ○ *The company has the funds to set up the research programme.* ○ *Funds are available to get the project off the ground.*

③ **funeral** /ˈfjuːn(ə)rəl/ *noun* a ceremony at which a dead person is buried or cremated ○ *The church was packed for her funeral.* ○ *The funeral will take place on Friday morning.*

funeral director /ˈfjuːn(ə)rəl daɪˌrektə/ *noun* a person who arranges funerals in return for payment

funfair /ˈfʌnfeə/ *noun* a group of amusements, sideshows, food stalls, etc., set up in one place for a short time

fungus /ˈfʌŋgəs/ (*plural* **fungi**) *noun* a plant which has no green leaves or flowers and which lives on decaying matter or on other plants

funk /fʌŋk/ *noun* a style of African dance music with a strong rhythm ○ *The crowd of teenagers were dancing to funk music.*

funky /ˈfʌŋki/ (**funkier, funkiest**) *adj* fashionable, modern (*informal*)

funnel /ˈfʌn(ə)l/ *noun* a tube with a wide opening and a narrow tube, used when pouring liquids from one container into another

① **funny** /ˈfʌni/ *adj* **1.** making people laugh ○ *He made funny faces and all the children laughed.* ○ *That joke isn't funny.* **2.** strange ○ *She's been behaving in a funny way recently.* ○ *There's a funny smell in the bathroom.*

fur /fɜː/ *noun* the soft covering of an animal's body ○ *This type of cat has very short fur.* ○ *She was wearing a fur coat.* ○ *Have you got any fur-lined boots?* (NOTE: Do not confuse with **fir**.)

furious /ˈfjʊəriəs/ *adj* very angry

furl /fɜːl/ (**furls, furling, furled**) *verb* to roll up a flag or sail when it is out of use, or to become tightly rolled up

furlong /ˈfɜːlɒŋ/ *noun* a measure of length, equal to 220 yards (NOTE: It is only used when referring to the length of a track for horse-racing.)

furnace /ˈfɜːnɪs/ *noun* **1.** a large brick or metal oven which can be heated to a very high temperature **2.** a heater which warms the water for central heating

furnish /ˈfɜːnɪʃ/ (**furnishes, furnishing, furnished**) *verb* **1.** to put furniture into a house, office, etc. ○ *His house is furnished with antiques.* **2.** to provide with something ○ *He furnished the police with a complete list of addresses.* ○ *The town council furnished details of the improvement plan.*

furnishings /ˈfɜːnɪʃɪŋz/ *plural noun* the furniture, carpets, curtains and fittings in a house ○ *All the furnishings were removed before the house was demolished.*

② **furniture** /ˈfɜːnɪtʃə/ *noun* objects in, e.g. a house or an office such as tables, chairs, beds and cupboards ○ *The burglars stole all our office furniture.* ○ *You should cover up all the furniture before you start painting the ceiling.* (NOTE: no plural: *some furniture*; *a lot of furniture*; *a piece of furniture*)

furore /fjʊˈrɔːri/ *noun* an outburst of anger or excitement (NOTE: The US spelling is **furor**.)

furrow /ˈfʌrəʊ/ *noun* **1.** a long trench cut in the soil by a plough ○ *Seagulls followed the plough, looking for food in the furrows.* **2.** a deep line in the surface of something ○ *As he grew older, the furrows on his face deepened.*

furry /ˈfɜːri/ *adj* covered with fur

① **further** /ˈfɜːðə/ *adv* at or to a greater distance ○ *Can you all move further back – I can't get you in the picture.* ○ *The police station is quite close, but the post office is further away.* ○ *Edinburgh is further from London than Newcastle.* ■ *adj* more ○ *The bank needs further information about your salary.* ○ *Please send me further details of holidays in Greece.*

③ **furthest** /ˈfɜːðəst/ *adv, adj* at or to the greatest distance ○ *Some of the staff live quite close to the office – James lives furthest away.* ○ *The furthest distance I have ever flown is to Hong Kong.*

furtive /ˈfɜːtɪv/ *adj* as if trying not to be noticed

fury /ˈfjʊəri/ *noun* very strong anger ○ *He shouted at us in fury.*

③ **fuse** /fjuːz/ *noun* a small piece of wire in an electrical system which breaks if too much power tries to pass through it, so preventing further damage ○ *The plug has a 13-amp fuse.* ○ *If the lights go out, the first thing to do is to check the fuses.*

fuselage /ˈfjuːzəlɑːʒ/ *noun* the body of an aircraft

③ **fusion** /ˈfjuːʒ(ə)n/ *noun* **1.** the melting together of two pieces of metal **2.** the joining together of two or more groups, such as political parties ○ *The new party has been formed by the fusion of two existing parties.*

③ **fuss** /fʌs/ *noun* unnecessary excitement or complaints [~about/over] ○ *What's all the fuss about?* □ **to make a fuss *or* to kick up a fuss about something** to complain for a long time about something which is not important ○ *Don't make such a fuss – it's only a little scratch.* ■ *verb* (**fusses, fussing, fussed**) to worry about things that are unimportant [~over] ○ *Don't fuss -everything's ready and there are no problems.* ○ *Stop fussing over your hair.* ◇ **to make a fuss of someone** to pay great attention to someone ○ *The children made a fuss of their mother on her birthday.*

fussy /ˈfʌsi/ (**fussier, fussiest**) *adj* **1.** too concerned about details or unimportant things ○ *She's fussy about what she eats* or *She's a fussy eater.* **2.** with too many small decorations ○ *I don't like the fussy pattern on this carpet.*

futile /ˈfjuːtaɪl/ *adj* certain to fail, and therefore not worth doing

futon /ˈfuːtɒn/ *noun* a thick mattress that can be folded, used as a seat or simple bed, on the floor or on a folding wooden frame

① **future** /ˈfjuːtʃə/ *noun* a time which has not yet happened ○ *What are his plans for the future?* ○ *You never know what the future will bring.* ○ *Can you imagine what London will be like in the future?* ■ *adj* which is coming; which has not happened yet ○ *They are spending all their time preparing for their future retirement.* ○ *I try to save something each week for future expenses.*

futuristic /ˌfjuːtʃəˈrɪstɪk/ *adj* very modern, or relating to the future

fuzz /fʌz/ *noun* **1.** a mass of short hair **2. the fuzz** the police (*dated slang offensive*)

fuzzy /ˈfʌzi/ (**fuzzier, fuzziest**) *adj* **1.** fluffy and curly ○ *She's got dark fuzzy hair, which is difficult to comb.* **2.** blurred; not clear ○ *The security camera produced a fuzzy photograph of the bank robbers.*

FYI /ˌef waɪ ˈaɪ/ *abbr* for your information

G

g /dʒiː/, **G** *noun* the seventh letter of the alphabet, between F and H

gabble /ˈgæb(ə)l/ (**gabbles, gabbling, gabbled**) *verb* to speak very quickly ○ *He gabbled a few words in Spanish.*

gable /ˈgeɪb(ə)l/ *noun* the top part of a wall where it forms a triangle with the roof

gadget /ˈgædʒɪt/ *noun* a small useful tool

Gaelic /ˈgeɪlɪk/; *in Scotland* /ˈgælɪk/ *noun* a Celtic language spoken in some parts of Scotland, Ireland and the Isle of Man

gag /gæg/ *noun* **1.** something put into or over a person's mouth to stop him or her speaking ○ *The burglars tied him up and put a gag in his mouth.* **2.** a joke ○ *The audience laughed at most of his gags.* ■ *verb* (**gags, gagging, gagged**) **1.** to put something over a person's mouth to try to stop him or her talking ○ *He was gagged and put into the boot of the car.* **2.** to try to stop someone talking or writing ○ *The government tried to gag the press.* **3.** to choke; to try to vomit but be unable to do so ○ *Every time the doctor tries to examine her throat, she gags.* ○ *He gagged on the hamburger.*

gaggle /ˈgæg(ə)l/ *noun* a flock of geese, or a group of noisy people

② **gain** /geɪn/ *verb* (**gains, gaining, gained**) **1.** to achieve something, or get it with some work or effort ○ *The army gained control of the country.* ○ *She gained some useful experience working for a computer company.* **2.** (*of a clock or watch*) to move ahead of the correct time ○ *My watch gains five minutes a day.* ■ *noun* **1.** an increase in weight, quantity or size [~in] ○ *There was no gain in weight over three weeks* **2.** benefit or profit ○ *He doesn't do the job for financial gain.*

gait /geɪt/ *noun* a way of walking (NOTE: Do not confuse with **gate**.)

gala /ˈgɑːlə/ *noun* a festive public occasion or performance

galaxy /ˈgæləksi/ (*plural* **galaxies**) *noun* an extremely large group of stars ○ *There are vast numbers of galaxies in the universe.*

Galaxy, the /ˈgæləksi/ *noun* the large group of stars and planets that the Earth forms part of

gale /geɪl/ *noun* a very strong wind

gallant /gəˈlænt, ˈgælənt/ *adj* **1.** brave **2.** polite to women ○ *It was very gallant of him to offer to take her home.* (NOTE: **Gallant** is used only of men.)

gall bladder /ˈgɔːl ˌblædə/ *noun* a sac underneath the liver, in which bile produced by the liver is stored

③ **gallery** /ˈgæləri/ (*plural* **galleries**) *noun* **1.** □ **(art) gallery** a place where objects such as pictures and sculptures are shown to the public **2.** the highest rows of seats in a theatre or cinema ○ *We managed to get two seats in the gallery.*

gallon /ˈgælən/ *noun* a measure of quantity of liquid, equal to 4.55 litres ○ *The car was empty and I had to put in seven gallons of petrol.* ○ *An economical car does 40 miles to the gallon.*

③ **gallop** /ˈgæləp/ *verb* (**gallops, galloping, galloped**) to go fast, especially on horseback ■ *noun* the fastest running speed of a horse ○ *The horse went off at a gallop.*

gallows /ˈgæləʊz/ (*plural same*) *noun* a wooden support from which criminals are executed by hanging

galore /gəˈlɔː/ *adj* in large quantities ○ *This autumn we had pears galore.* (NOTE: always follows the noun)

gambit /ˈgæmbɪt/ *noun* something said or done which should give you an advantage in an argument

gamble /ˈgæmbəl/ *noun* a risk ○ *This investment is a bit of a gamble.* ○ *He took a gamble with the weather in planning his picnic for the beginning of March.* ■ *verb* (**gambles, gambling, gambled**) to bet money on cards, horses, etc. ○ *He lost all his money gambling on dog races.* (NOTE: + **gambling** *n*) □ **to gamble on something happening** to do something, hoping that something will happen ○ *We're gambling on fine weather for the village fête.*

① **game** /geɪm/ *noun* **1.** an activity in which people compete with each other using skill, strength or luck ○ *She's not very good at games like chess.* **2.** a single match between two opponents or two opposing teams ○ *Everyone wanted to watch the game of football.* ○ *Do you want a game of snooker?* ○ *Our team have won all their games this year.* **3.** a single session in an activity or sport such as tennis or cards ○ *She's winning by six games to three.* **4.** wild animals and birds such as deer, rabbits and pheasants, which are killed for sport or food ■ *plural noun* **Games** a large organised sports competition ○ *the Olympic Games*

gamekeeper /ˈgeɪmkiːpə/ *noun* a person working on a private estate who protects wild birds and animals so that they can be hunted

game show /ˈgeɪm ʃəʊ/ *noun* a TV show, where teams play games

gammon /ˈgæmən/ *noun* meat from the lower part of a side of bacon

gamut /ˈgæmət/ *noun* the complete range of things of the same type

gander /ˈgændə/ *noun* a male goose (NOTE: The females are **geese** and the young are **goslings**.)

③ **gang** /gæŋ/ *noun* **1.** a group of criminals ○ *a drugs gang* **2.** a group of young people who do things together, especially one that causes trouble ○ *Gangs of football fans wandered the streets after the match.* **3.** a group of workers ○ *Gangs of men worked all night to repair the railway track.*

gangster /ˈgæŋstə/ *noun* a criminal belonging to a violent gang

gangway /ˈgæŋweɪ/ *noun* **1.** (*in a theatre, cinema, etc.*) a passage between rows of seats ○ *Don't block the gangway.* **2.** a little movable bridge for going on board a ship ○ *We went up the gangway carrying our cases.*

gaol /dʒeɪl/, **gaoler** /ˈdʒeɪlə/ another spelling of **jail**, **jailer**

② **gap** /gæp/ *noun* a space between two things or in the middle of something [~between/~in] ○ *There's a gap between the two planks.* ○ *The sheep all rushed through the gap in the hedge.*

gape /geɪp/ (**gapes, gaping, gaped**) *verb* **1.** to open your mouth wide in surprise or shock **2.** to be wide open ○ *The entrance to the cave gaped before us.*

gaping /ˈgeɪpɪŋ/ *adj* wide

② **garage** /ˈgærɪdʒ, ˈgærɑːʒ/ *noun* **1.** a building where you can keep a car ○ *He put the car into the garage overnight.* ○ *She drove the car out of the garage.* ○ *Don't forget to lock the garage door.* ○ *The hotel has garage space for thirty cars.* **2.** a place where petrol is sold and where cars are repaired or sold ○ *Where's the nearest garage? I need some petrol.* ○ *I can't drive you to the station – my car is in the garage for repair.* ○ *You can hire cars from the garage near the post office.*

garb /gɑːb/ *noun* clothes worn by a particular category of person

③ **garbage** /ˈgɑːbɪdʒ/ *noun* **1.** nonsense ○ *I don't believe a word of what he said – it's just garbage.* **2.** (*mainly US*) household waste

garbled /ˈgɑːb(ə)ld/ *adj* confusingly expressed and difficult to understand

① **garden** /ˈgɑːd(ə)n/ *noun* an area of land near a house, used for growing such things as vegetables and flowers ○ *We grow all the vegetables we need in the back garden.* ○ *Your sister's outside, sitting in the garden.*

garden centre /ˈgɑːd(ə)n ˌsentə/ *noun* a place which sells things such as plants, seeds and equipment for gardening

gardener /ˈgɑːd(ə)nə/ *noun* a person who looks after a garden either as a hobby or as a job

gardening /ˈgɑːd(ə)nɪŋ/ *noun* the activity of looking after a garden

garden party /ˈgɑːd(ə)n ˌpɑːti/ *noun* a social occasion held in a garden or in a house's grounds

garden shed /ˌgɑːd(ə)n ˈʃed/ *noun* a small building where tools, equipment, and supplies for gardening are kept

gargle /ˈgɑːg(ə)l/ (**gargles, gargling, gargled**) *verb* to clean your mouth by taking liquid into your mouth and blowing air through it before spitting it out

garish /ˈgeərɪʃ/ *adj* too colourful

garland /ˈgɑːlənd/ *noun* a circle of flowers or paper decorations ○ *She wore a garland of flowers in her hair.* ○ *The room was decorated with paper garlands.*

③ **garlic** /ˈgɑːlɪk/ *noun* a round white vegetable with a strong smell, which can be separated into sections and used to give flavour to food

garment /ˈgɑːmənt/ *noun* a piece of clothing (*formal*)

garnish /ˈgɑːnɪʃ/ *noun* something used to decorate food ○ *ham with a garnish of pickled cucumbers* (NOTE: + **garnish** *v*)

garrison /'gærɪs(ə)n/ *noun* soldiers defending a castle or town ○ *The attackers promised the garrison safe passage if they surrendered.*

① **gas** /gæs/ *noun* **1.** a chemical substance which has no form and which becomes liquid if it is cooled ○ *Air is made up of several gases, mainly nitrogen and oxygen.* ○ *Rubbish gives off a type of gas called methane as it rots.* **2.** a chemical substance which is burnt to make heat, e.g. for cooking

gas chamber /'gæs ˌtʃeɪmbə/ *noun* a room where people are killed using poison gas

gash /gæʃ/ *noun* a deep cut ○ *He received a gash on his forehead.* (NOTE: + **gash** *v*)

gasoline /'gæsəliːn/ *noun US* a liquid, made from petrol, used to drive a car engine (NOTE: usually shortened to **gas**)

gasp /gɑːsp/ *verb* (**gasps, gasping, gasped**) to take a short deep breath ○ *He gasped when he saw the bill.* ■ *noun* a sudden loud breath that you take when you are surprised or in pain ○ *She gave a gasp when she saw the face at the window.*

gas station /'gæs ˌsteɪʃ(ə)n/ *noun US* a place where you can buy gasoline

gastric /'gæstrɪk/ *adj* referring to the stomach

② **gate** /geɪt/ *noun* **1.** a low outside door made of bars of wood or metal ○ *Shut the gate – if you leave it open the sheep will get out of the field.* ○ *There is a white gate leading into the garden.* **2.** a door which leads to an aircraft at an airport ○ *Flight AZ270 is now boarding at Gate 23.*

gâteau /'gætəʊ/ (*plural* **gâteaux**) *noun* a large cake with several layers decorated with cream, chocolate etc.

gatecrash /'geɪtkræʃ/ (**gatecrashes, gatecrashing, gatecrashed**) *verb* to get into a party without being invited ○ *A group of students tried to gatecrash* or *gatecrash her party.*

gateway /'geɪtweɪ/ *noun* **1.** an opening where a gate is fitted **2.** a place which leads to a larger area ○ *Washington, gateway to the south*

② **gather** /'gæðə/ (**gathers, gathering, gathered**) *verb* **1.** to bring things or people together ○ *He gathered his papers together after the lecture.* ○ *She has been gathering information on the history of the local school.* **2.** (especially of people) to come together in one place, or be brought together by someone ○ *Groups of people gathered outside the government building.* ○ *They gathered together a team of experienced people for the new project.* **3.** to understand from what someone has told you ○ *I gather that his father is in hospital.* ○ *We gather he has left the office.* **4.** to pick plants, flowers or fruit ○ *The children were gathering blackberries.* ○ *The grape harvest has been gathered.*

② **gathering** /'gæðərɪŋ/ *noun* a group of people who have come together ○ *A speaker from another association will address the gathering.*

gaudy /'gɔːdi/ (**gaudier, gaudiest**) *adj* very brightly coloured (NOTE: + **gaudily** *adv*)

② **gauge** /geɪdʒ/ *noun* **1.** an instrument to measure depth, pressure, etc. **2.** the distance between the two rails in a railway line

gaunt /gɔːnt/ *adj* very thin

gauntlet /'gɔːntlət/ *noun* a strong glove

gauze /gɔːz/ *noun* a thin material

③ **gave** /geɪv/ past tense of **give**

gawp /gɔːp/ (**gawps, gawping, gawped**) *verb* to gaze stupidly or rudely at something

③ **gay** /geɪ/ *adj* **1.** attracted to people of the same sex, or relating to people like this ○ *It's a club where gay men and women meet.* ○ *They met in a gay bar.* **2.** bright and lively (*dated*) ○ *The houses along the street are all painted in gay colours.* ■ *noun* a person who is attracted to someone of the same sex ○ *a club for gays*

gaze /geɪz/ *verb* (**gazes, gazing, gazed**) to look steadily ○ *She gazed into his eyes.* ○ *He stood on the cliff, gazing out to sea.* ■ *noun* a steady look ○ *She refused to meet his gaze.*

GCSE *noun* a British school exam taken at the age of around 16. Full form **General Certificate of Secondary Education**

③ **gear** /gɪə/ *noun* **1.** equipment for a particular purpose ○ *He took all his climbing gear with him.* ○ *She was carrying her painting gear in a rucksack.* **2.** clothing for a particular purpose ○ *She was putting on her tennis gear.* **3.** a part of an engine that makes it possible to change the amount of work the engine has to do to turn the wheels

gear up *phrasal verb* to get someone or something ready, or get yourself ready

gearbox /'gɪəbɒks/ *noun* a case for gears in a car

geek /giːk/ *noun* a person who is a proud or enthusiastic user of computers or other technology, especially one who is interested in few other things or is socially awkward (*informal*)

③ **geese** /giːs/ plural of **goose**

gel /dʒel/ *noun* a thick substance similar to a jelly ■ *verb* (**gels, gelling, gelled**) to become more certain or more clear ○ *The details of the plan began to gel.*

gelatine /ˈdʒelətiːn/, **gelatin** *noun* a substance made from boiling animal bones, and used to make foods such as jelly

gem /dʒem/ *noun* **1.** a precious stone ○ *She wore a crown set with pearls and gems.* **2.** an amusing or interesting item ○ *Here are some gems from yesterday's paper.* **3.** a person who is very useful and important to you

Gemini /ˈdʒemɪnaɪ/ *noun* one of the signs of the Zodiac, shaped like twins, covering the period 21st May to 21st June

gender /ˈdʒendə/ *noun* **1.** the fact of being male or female ○ *Everyone has the same rights, regardless of race, religion or gender.* **2.** (*in grammar*) a system where nouns and adjectives have different forms to show if they are masculine, feminine or neuter

② **gene** /dʒiːn/ *noun* a set of chemicals in a cell which carries information about features that are passed from parent to child

① **general** /ˈdʒen(ə)rəl/ *adj* not specific; covering a wide range of subjects ○ *He had a good general education, but didn't specialise in any particular field.* ■ *noun* an army officer of high rank ○ *He has only recently been promoted to general.* ◇ **in general** normally ○ *In general, the weather is warmer in the south.*

general anaesthetic /ˌdʒen(ə)rəl ænəsˈθetɪk/ *noun* a substance given to make a patient lose consciousness so that a major surgical operation can be carried out

general election /ˌdʒen(ə)rəl ɪ ˈlekʃən/ *noun* an election where all voters can vote for a new government

generalisation /ˌdʒen(ə)rəlaɪ ˈzeɪʃ(ə)n/, **generalization** *noun* a general statement

generalise /ˈdʒen(ə)rəlaɪz/ (**generalises, generalising, generalised**), **generalize** *verb* to make a general statement about something

① **generally** /ˈdʒen(ə)rəli/ *adv* usually ○ *The office is generally closed between Christmas and the New Year.*

general strike /ˌdʒen(ə)rəl ˈstraɪk/ *noun* a strike of all or many of the workers in a country

② **generate** /ˈdʒenəreɪt/ (**generates, generating, generated**) *verb* to produce something such as power ○ *We use wind to generate electricity.*

② **generation** /ˌdʒenəˈreɪʃ(ə)n/ *noun* **1.** the production of something such as power ○ *the generation of electricity from waves* **2.** all people born at about the same time ○ *The 1960s generation had an easier life than we did.* ○ *Many people of my father's generation cannot understand computer technology.* **3.** members of a family born at about the same time **4.** a series of machines made at about the same time ○ *They are developing a new type of engine for the next generation of aircraft.*

② **generator** /ˈdʒenəreɪtə/ *noun* a machine which makes electricity

generic /dʒəˈnerɪk/ *adj* referring to a range or class of things

generosity /ˌdʒenəˈrɒsɪti/ *noun* willingness to give money or your time to help someone

generous /ˈdʒen(ə)rəs/ *adj* **1.** giving more money or presents than people usually do ○ *Thank you! You're so generous!* **2.** large ○ *a generous helping of pudding*

generously /ˈdʒen(ə)rəsli/ *adv* in a generous way

② **genetic** /dʒəˈnetɪk/ *adj* relating to those things that are controlled by genes

genetic engineering /dʒəˌnetɪk endʒɪˈnɪərɪŋ/ *noun* techniques used to change the genetic composition of a cell so as to change certain characteristics

geneticist /dʒəˈnetɪsɪst/ *noun* a person who specialises in the study of genetics

genetics /dʒəˈnetɪks/ *noun* the science and study of the way genes are involved in passing features from parents to children

genial /ˈdʒiːniəl/ *adj* cheerful and friendly

③ **genius** /ˈdʒiːniəs/ *noun* **1.** a very intelligent person; a person who has great ability ○ *She's a chess genius.* ○ *Napoleon was a military genius.* ○ *She came top of the class – she's a real genius.* **2.** great ability ○ *He has a genius for keeping people amused.*

genocide /ˈdʒenəʊsaɪd/ *noun* the killing of an entire racial group

genome /ˈdʒiːnəʊm/ *noun* **1.** all the genes in an individual **2.** a set of genes which are inherited from one parent

genre /ˈʒɒnrə/ *noun* a type of something artistic such as art, literature or theatre ○

the three main literary genres of prose, poetry and drama

genteel /dʒen'tiːl/ *adj* refined and respectable

③ **gentle** /'dʒent(ə)l/ (**gentler, gentlest**) *adj* **1.** soft and kind ○ *The nurse has gentle hands.* **2.** not very strong ○ *After a little gentle persuasion, she agreed to the plan.* ○ *He gave the door a gentle push.* **3.** not very steep ○ *There is a gentle slope down to the lake.*

② **gentleman** /'dʒent(ə)lmən/ (*plural* **gentlemen**) *noun* a man, especially a well-behaved or upper-class man ○ *He's such a gentleman, he always opens the door for me.*

③ **gently** /'dʒentli/ *adv* **1.** softly and carefully ○ *He gently put the blanket over her.* ○ *She rocked the cradle gently.* **2.** not steeply ○ *The path rises gently to the top of the hill.*

gentrification /ˌdʒentrɪfɪ'keɪʃ(ə)n/ *noun* the action of making a poor part of a town more popular with rich people

③ **genuine** /'dʒenjuɪn/ *adj* real; true ○ *The painting was not a genuine Picasso.* ○ *A genuine leather purse will cost a lot more than that.*

genus /'dʒiːnəs/ (*plural* **genera**) *noun* a group of related species of animals or plants

③ **geography** /dʒi'ɒgrəfi/ *noun* the study of the earth's surface, its climate and the plants and animals that live on it

③ **geology** /dʒi'ɒlədʒi/ *noun* the science and study of the rocks that form the earth's crust

③ **geometry** /dʒi'ɒmətri/ *noun* the mathematical science of lines, surfaces and solids

geranium /dʒə'reɪniəm/ *noun* a brightly coloured summer flower, usually red or pink

geriatric /ˌdʒeri'ætrɪk/ *adj* referring to old people, or old age ○ *geriatric medicine*

geriatrics /ˌdʒeri'ætrɪks/ *noun* the study of old people and their health

③ **germ** /dʒɜːm/ *noun* an organism which causes disease ○ *Wash your hands after emptying the dustbin so you don't spread any germs.*

① **German** /'dʒɜːmən/ *adj* referring to Germany or its inhabitants ■ *noun* **1.** the language spoken in Germany, Austria and parts of Switzerland and Italy **2.** a person from Germany

German measles /ˌdʒɜːmən 'miːz(ə)lz/ *noun* a usually mild disease which gives a red rash but which can affect an unborn child if caught by a pregnant woman

germinate /'dʒɜːmɪneɪt/ (**germinates, germinating, germinated**) *verb* (*of a plant seed*) to start to grow (NOTE: + **germination** *n*)

gerund /'dʒerənd/ *noun* a noun formed from the present participle of a verb (NOTE: In English, gerunds are formed from the '-ing' form of verbs, as in *Cycling is good exercise*; *Choral singing is very popular in Wales*.)

gestation /dʒe'steɪʃ(ə)n/ *noun* **1.** a period when a baby is carried in its mother's womb **2.** a period when something such as a book is being worked on ○ *The gestation period is almost over and the book should be published next month.*

gesticulate /dʒe'stɪkjʊleɪt/ (**gesticulates, gesticulating, gesticulated**) *verb* to make signs with your hands or arms

③ **gesture** /'dʒestʃə/ *noun* a movement of a part of the body such as the hands to show feeling ○ *She made a slight gesture of impatience with her hand.* ■ *verb* (**gestures, gesturing, gestured**) to make a movement with your hands [~at/to/towards] ○ *He gestured to the audience to sit down.*

① **get** /get/ (**gets, getting, got**) *verb* **1.** to receive something ○ *We got a letter from the bank this morning.* ○ *She gets more money than I do.* **2.** [~from/to/~how/what etc/~into/out of/on/off/~off/~on/~on/onto/~to/~without] □ **to get to a place** ***or*** **situation** to arrive at a place or situation ○ *We only got to the hotel at midnight.* ○ *When does your train get to London?* ○ *The plane gets to New York at 4 p.m.* ○ *When you get to my age you'll understand!* **3.** to start to be in a particular state ○ *I'm getting too old for rugby.* ○ *He's got much fatter over the last year or so.* ○ *The sun got hotter and hotter.* ○ *The carpet's getting dirty.* **4.** to have something done ○ *I must get my suit cleaned.* ○ *We got the car mended in time to go on holiday.* **5.** to make someone do something ○ *Can you get the garage to mend the brakes?* ○ *I'll try and get her to bring some CDs.*

get across② *phrasal verb* **1.** to manage to cross something ○ *They got across the river on rafts.* **2.** to make someone understand something ○ *I'm trying to get across to the people in the office that they* *all have to work harder.* ○ *We just can't seem to get our message across.*

get along② *phrasal verb* to manage ○ *She got along quite well when her mother was away on holiday.* ○ *We seem to get along very happily without the telephone.* ○ *How are you getting along?*

get around *phrasal verb* **1.** to move from place to place ○ *Since he had his accident he gets around on two sticks.* **2.** (*of news*) to be heard by a lot of people ○ *The news soon got around that they were married.*

get at③ *phrasal verb* **1.** to reach something ○ *You'll need to stand on a chair to get at the books on the top shelf.* **2.** to criticise someone all the time (*informal*) ○ *She thinks she's being got at.* **3.** to suggest or try to say something ○ *What was he really getting at when he said that some people were not working hard enough?*

get away② *phrasal verb* to escape ○ *The robbers got away in a stolen car.*

get back① *phrasal verb* **1.** to return ○ *They got back home very late.* ○ *When did they get back from the cinema?* **2.** to get something again which you had before ○ *I got my money back after I had complained to the manager.* **3.** to phone back or reply by post ○ *I'll find out what the situation is and get back to you as soon as I can.*

get by③ *phrasal verb* **1.** to manage to do something with difficulty ○ *I can just get by in German.* ○ *How are you going to get by without a car?* **2.** to manage to live ○ *It is difficult for them to get by in New York on only $30 a day.*

get down② *phrasal verb* **1.** to go back down onto the ground ○ *The cat climbed up the tree and couldn't get down.* ○ *He got down off the ladder.* **2.** to bring something down ○ *Can you get my suitcase down for me?* **3.** to make someone sad ○ *Rainy weather always gets me down.*

get going② *phrasal verb* to start doing something, or to leave ○ *Come on, let's get going!*

get in① *phrasal verb* **1.** to go inside a place or a vehicle ○ *Get in! – the train's going to leave.* ○ *The burglars must have got in through the bathroom window.* **2.** to arrive home or at the office ○ *What time did you get in last night?* ○ *Because of the train strike, we didn't get in until eleven o'clock.* **3.** to ask someone to come to do a job ○ *We'll get a builder in to mend the wall.*

get into① *phrasal verb* to go inside a place or a vehicle ○ *They got into the back of the car.* ○ *I was just getting into bed when the phone rang.* ○ *The burglars got into the building through a window on the ground floor.*

get off① *phrasal verb* **1.** to come down from or out of a form of transport such as a car, bus, train or plane ○ *She got off her bicycle at the red light.* ○ *If you want the post office, you should get off at the next stop.* ○ *You have to get off the Underground at South Kensington.* **2.** not to be punished, or only receive a light punishment ○ *She was lucky to get off so lightly.* ○ *He was found guilty of embezzlement and got off with a fine.*

get on① *phrasal verb* **1.** to go onto a form of transport such as a car, bus, train or plane ○ *They got on the bus at the bank.* ○ *The policeman got on his bike and rode away.* **2.** to become old ○ *He's getting on and can't work as hard as he used to.* **3.** to manage ○ *How's your new assistant getting on?* **4.** to be friendly with someone ○ *They don't get on at all well.*

get out① *phrasal verb* **1.** to take something out ○ *I'll get the book out of the library.* ○ *She's getting the car out of the garage.* **2.** to go out of a place or a vehicle ○ *The bus stopped and the driver got out.* ○ *The burglars got out through the front door.*

get over② *phrasal verb* **1.** to climb over something ○ *They got over the wall into the garden.* **2.** to recover from an illness ○ *He's got over his flu.* **3.** to recover from a shock ○ *She never got over the death of her father.*

get round *phrasal verb* to persuade someone to like you or to do what you want ○ *She got round the boss by giving him a bottle of wine.*

get through③ *phrasal verb* **1.** to manage to go through something ○ *The cows got through the hole in the fence.* **2.** to be successful ○ *He got through his exams, so he is now a qualified engineer.*

get to③ *phrasal verb* to arrive at or reach a place

get up① *phrasal verb* **1.** to get out of bed ○ *He went to bed so late that he didn't get up until 11 o'clock.* **2.** to make someone get out of bed ○ *You must get everyone up by 7.30 if we are going to leave on time.* **3.** to stand up ○ *When he had finished his meal, he got up from the table and walked out of the room.*

get up to③ *phrasal verb* to reach something ○ *Stop reading when you get up to page 23.*

getaway /ˈɡetəweɪ/ *noun* an escape

get rid of ♦ **rid**

get-together /ˈɡet təˌɡeðə/ *noun* a meeting of friends (*informal*)

geyser /ˈɡiːzə/ *noun* a natural spring of hot water ○ *There are famous geysers in Yellowstone National Park.*

ghastly /ˈɡɑːstli/ (**ghastlier, ghastliest**) *adj* horrible

ghetto /ˈɡetəʊ/ (*plural* **ghettos** or **ghettoes**) *noun* a poor area in a city in which people of a particular race, religion or nationality live

ghost /ɡəʊst/ *noun* an image of a dead person which some people believe they have seen ○ *They say the house is haunted by the ghost of its former owner.* ○ *Her face is white – she looks as if she has seen a ghost.*

ghostly /ˈɡəʊstli/ *adj* like a ghost

ghost town /ˈɡəʊst taʊn/ *noun* an abandoned town where no one lives

ghoul /ɡuːl/ *noun* **1.** a person who is interested in unpleasant things **2.** an evil and frightening spirit

GI /ˌdʒiː ˈaɪ/ *noun* an American soldier

giant /ˈdʒaɪənt/ *noun* (*in fairy tales and myths*) a very large man ○ *a story about a giant who lived in a castle at the top of a mountain* ■ *adj* very large ○ *He's grown a giant cabbage.* ○ *They are planning to build a giant car factory in South Wales.*

gibberish /ˈdʒɪbərɪʃ/ *noun* nonsense; words that do not seem to mean anything

gibe /dʒaɪb/ *noun* a nasty remark ○ *He went on with his experiments, disregarding the gibes of the press.*

giddy /ˈɡɪdi/ (**giddier, giddiest**) *adj* feeling that everything is turning round, and that you could lose your balance

② **gift** /ɡɪft/ *noun* **1.** something given to someone as a present ○ *The wedding gifts were displayed on a table.* ○ *She was wrapping up gifts to put under the Christmas tree.* **2.** a natural ability for doing something well [~for] ○ *She has a gift for making people feel welcome.* ○ *He has a gift for maths.*

gifted /ˈɡɪftɪd/ *adj* with a special talent ○ *He was a gifted musician.*

gift token /ˈɡɪft ˌtəʊkən/, **gift voucher** /ˈɡɪft ˌvaʊtʃə/ *noun* a card bought in a shop which is given as a present and which must be exchanged in that shop for goods

gift-wrap /ˈɡɪft ræp/ *verb* to wrap something in coloured paper to give as a present

gift-wrapped /ˈɡɪft ræpt/ *adj* (*of a gift*) packaged in attractive paper

③ **gig** /ɡɪɡ/ *noun* a performance of pop music (*informal*)

gigabyte /ˈɡɪɡəbaɪt/ *noun* a unit of computer data equal to 1,024 megabytes

gigantic /dʒaɪˈɡæntɪk/ *adj* extremely large

② **giggle** /ˈɡɪɡ(ə)l/ *noun* a little laugh, often showing you are embarrassed ■ *verb* (**giggles, giggling, giggled**) to laugh in an embarrassed way [~about/at] ○ *The girls were giggling about the letter.*

gild /ɡɪld/ (**gilds, gilding, gilded**) *verb* to cover something with a layer of gold (NOTE: Do not confuse with **guild**.)

gill /dʒɪl/, **ghyll** *noun* a measure of liquids, equal to a quarter of a pint

gilt /ɡɪlt/ *adj* covered with gold ○ *a picture in a gilt frame* (NOTE: Do not confuse with **guilt**.)

gimme /ˈɡɪmi/ *verb* give me (*informal*)

gimmick /ˈɡɪmɪk/ *noun* a thing which is intended to attract attention

gin /dʒɪn/ *noun* a colourless alcoholic drink, flavoured with juniper ○ *a cocktail made with gin*

ginger /ˈdʒɪndʒə/ *noun* a plant whose root has a sharp burning taste and is used in cooking ○ *Fry the meat with spring onions and slices of ginger.* ○ *Add a pinch of powdered ginger to the cake mixture.* ■ *adj* (*of hair*) orange in colour ○ *She has ginger hair and green eyes.* ○ *A ginger cat lay sleeping in the sun.*

gingerly /ˈdʒɪndʒəli/ *adv* carefully, in case you might get hurt

gipsy /ˈdʒɪpsi/ another spelling of **gypsy**

③ **giraffe** /dʒɪˈrɑːf/ *noun* a large African animal with a very long neck

girder /ˈɡɜːdə/ *noun* a strong metal beam to hold up a wall or roof

girdle /ˈɡɜːd(ə)l/ *noun* **1.** a belt round a dress **2.** a tight piece of underwear worn by women in the past to support their bodies

① **girl** /ɡɜːl/ *noun* a female child ○ *a crowd of girls waiting at the bus stop* ○ *They have four children – two boys and two girls.* ○ *My sister goes to the local girls' school.*

③ **girlfriend** /ˈɡɜːlfrend/ *noun* **1.** a girl or woman that someone is having a romantic relationship with ○ *He's broken up with his girlfriend.* **2.** a friend who is a girl ○ *On Saturdays she always has lunch with a group of girlfriends.*

girlish /ˈgɜːlɪʃ/ *adj* like a young girl

girth /gɜːθ/ *noun* a measurement round something, especially round your stomach

git /gɪt/ *noun* an annoying person (*informal insult*)

① **give** /gɪv/ (**giving, gave, given**) *verb* **1.** to pass something to someone [~(to)] ○ *I'll give the letter to her tonight* or *I'll give her the letter tonight.* ○ *Can you give me some information about holidays in Greece?* **2.** to send or pass something to someone as a present [~(to)] ○ *We gave her flowers for her birthday.* ○ *What are you going to give him when he gets married?* ○ *We gave ten pounds to the Red Cross.* **3.** to do something to someone or something [~to] ○ *He gave me a broad smile.* ○ *He gave her a kiss.* ○ *She gave the ball a kick.* **4.** to organise something such as a party ○ *They gave a reception for the visiting Foreign Minister.* ○ *We gave a party to celebrate her twenty-first birthday.*

give away① *phrasal verb* **1.** to give something as a present ○ *We are giving away a pocket calculator with each £10 of purchases.* **2.** to throw things out by giving them to charity **3.** to lead the bride to the bridegroom at a wedding ○ *She was given away by her father.* **4.** to reveal something which you are trying to keep secret ○ *His accent gave him away.* ○ *She gave herself away by saying that she had never been to France.*

give back① *phrasal verb* to hand something back to someone

give in③ *phrasal verb* to agree to do something that you had refused to do earlier

give off *phrasal verb* to produce something such as steam or a smell

give out③ *phrasal verb* **1.** to give something to everyone ○ *She gave out presents to all the children.* **2.** to come to an end ○ *The battery has given out so I can't use my watch.*

give up① *phrasal verb* **1.** to stop doing something ○ *She's trying to give up smoking.* **2.** □ **to give yourself up** to surrender to an enemy, the police, etc. ○ *He gave himself up to the police.* ○ *They shouted to the gang to come out of the store and give themselves up.*

give way③ *phrasal verb* **1.** to let someone go first ○ *Give way to traffic coming from the right.* **2.** to break under a heavy weight ○ *The chair gave way when he sat on it.* **3.** to stop opposing something ○ *In the end, our dad gave way and let us go camping by ourselves.*

giveaway /ˈgɪvəweɪ/ *noun* **1.** a gift which is given to a customer **2.** a thing which reveals something ○ *Her beaming smile was an absolute giveaway that she'd got the job.*

② **given** /ˈgɪv(ə)n/ *adj* (*of a specific time*) already arranged or specified ○ *There is no given time for departure.* □ **at any given time** at any particular time ■ *conj* considering [~that] ○ *He plays the violin very well given his age.* ○ *Given that it's his birthday, it's a shame he couldn't get to the party.*

glacial /ˈgleɪʃ(ə)l/ *adj* **1.** referring to glaciers **2.** very cold **3.** very unfriendly

glacier /ˈglæsiə/ *noun* a mass of ice like a frozen river which moves slowly down a mountain

② **glad** /glæd/ *adj* pleased ○ *Aunt Jane was glad to get your postcard.* ○ *After shopping all day, she was glad to find somewhere to sit down.*

glade /gleɪd/ *noun* an open grassy place in a wood

gladiator /ˈglædieɪtə/ *noun* an ancient Roman fighter

gladly /ˈglædli/ *adv* with great pleasure

glamorise /ˈglæməraɪz/ (**glamorises, glamorising, glamorised**), **glamorize** *verb* to make something seem to be more attractive or glamorous than it really is

glamorous /ˈglæmərəs/ *adj* attractive; enchanting

glamour /ˈglæmə/ *noun* an attractive, dazzling appearance (NOTE: no plural. Another US spelling is **glamor**.)

③ **glance** /glɑːns/ *noun* a quick look ○ *She gave him an admiring glance.* ■ *verb* (**glances, glancing, glanced**) to look quickly ○ *He glanced over his shoulder to see who was following him.* ○ *She glanced suspiciously at the waiter.* ◇ **at a glance** after a quick look at something ○ *At a glance, I'd say these rugs are Chinese.*

gland /glænd/ *noun* an organ in the body which produces a chemical substance

glandular fever /ˌglændjʊlə ˈfiːvə/ *noun* an infectious disease, where the body has an excessive number of white blood cells

glare /gleə/ *noun* **1.** a very bright light ○ *The glare of the sun on the wet road blinded me.* **2.** an angry look ○ *He gave her a glare and walked on.* ■ *verb* (**glares, glaring, glared**) to look angrily ○ *She glared at me and went on reading her book.*

glaring /ˈgleərɪŋ/ *adj* **1.** very bright ○ *the glaring headlights of the cars* **2.** obvious ○ *The book is full of glaring mistakes.*

① **glass** /glɑːs/ *noun* **1.** a hard, smooth material which you can see through, used to make things such as windows, vases and bowls [~of] ○ *a bowl made of glass* or *a glass bowl* ○ *They found some very old pieces of glass in the earth.* (NOTE: no plural) **2.** a container to drink out of, usually made of glass ○ *She put the dirty glasses in the dishwasher.* ○ *We took plastic wine glasses on the picnic.* **3.** the liquid contained in a glass ○ *Would you like a large glass or a small glass?* ○ *He was so thirsty he drank three glasses.* ○ *Add a glass of red wine to the sauce.* ■ *plural noun* **glasses** two plastic or glass lenses in a frame which you wear in front of your eyes to help you see better ○ *She has to wear glasses for reading.* (NOTE: no singular: for one item, say 'a pair of glasses'.)

glass ceiling /glɑːs ˈsiːlɪŋ/ *noun* a system which prevents certain people, especially women, from progressing in their career

glasshouse /ˈglɑːshaʊs/ *noun* a large greenhouse

glassware /ˈglɑːsweə/ *noun* things made of glass

glassy /ˈglɑːsi/ *adj* **1.** resembling glass **2.** (*of eyes*) dull ○ *a glassy stare*

glaze /gleɪz/ *noun* a shiny surface on pottery ○ *The pot has a green-blue glaze.* (NOTE: + **glaze** *v*)

glazed /gleɪzd/ *adj* **1.** with a shiny surface ○ *a floor of glazed tiles* **2.** with glass windows ○ *We have built a glazed porch.*

gleam /gliːm/ *noun* **1.** a small light ○ *He saw the gleam of a flashlight in the distance.* **2.** a slight sign ○ *He saw a gleam of recognition in the boy's eyes.* ○ *There was a wild gleam in her eyes.* ■ *verb* (**gleams, gleaming, gleamed**) to shine as if polished ○ *a line of gleaming black cars*

glean /gliːn/ (**gleans, gleaning, gleaned**) *verb* to collect scraps of information

glee /gliː/ *noun* great happiness

glen /glen/ *noun* (*in Scotland*) a narrow valley

glib /glɪb/ *adj* easily said, but insincere

③ **glide** /glaɪd/ (**glides, gliding, glided**) *verb* to move in a smooth way ○ *Skaters were gliding across the ice.* ○ *A bird went gliding past.*

glider /ˈglaɪdə/ *noun* an aircraft which flies without a motor

gliding /ˈglaɪdɪŋ/ *noun* the sport of flying a glider

glimmer /ˈglɪmə/ *noun* **1.** a small weak light ○ *There was a glimmer of light in one of the upstairs windows.* **2.** a very small amount ○ *The news brought a glimmer of hope to the families of the trapped miners.* ■ *verb* (**glimmers, glimmering, glimmered**) to shine weakly ○ *A light glimmered some distance away in the trees.*

glimpse /glɪmps/ *noun* a quick sight of something ○ *We caught a glimpse of the princess as she drove past.* ○ *There was a brief glimpse of the sun during the afternoon.* ■ *verb* (**glimpses, glimpsing, glimpsed**) to catch sight of someone or something ○ *We only glimpsed the back of her head as she was leaving.*

glint /glɪnt/ (**glints, glinting, glinted**) *verb* to flash ○ *The soldiers' swords glinted in the sunshine.* (NOTE: + **glint** *n*)

glisten /ˈglɪs(ə)n/ (**glistens, glistening, glistened**) *verb* to shine brightly, as if wet

glitch /glɪtʃ/ *noun* a small problem which suddenly arises

glitter /ˈglɪtə/ (**glitters, glittering, glittered**) *verb* to shine brightly with small points of light, as the stars in the sky seem to shine ○ *The jewels in her crown were glittering in the light of the candles.* ○ *Her eyes glittered hopefully as she spoke.*

glittering /ˈglɪtərɪŋ/ *adj* **1.** which shines brightly ○ *a glittering diamond crown* **2.** very brilliant; very successful ○ *They threw a glittering reception at the golf club.* ○ *He had a glittering career in the Foreign Office.*

glitz /glɪts/ *noun* a quality which makes something seem to be very exciting and glamorous

gloat /gləʊt/ (**gloats, gloating, gloated**) *verb* to be happy about something, especially someone else's bad luck

③ **global** /ˈgləʊb(ə)l/ *adj* **1.** relating to the whole world ○ *We offer a global parcel delivery service.* **2.** relating to the whole of something ○ *We are carrying out a global review of salaries.*

globalisation /ˌgləʊbəlaɪˈzeɪʃ(ə)n/, **globalization** *noun* the process by which world economy and culture merge, as a result of telecommunications and multinational companies

③ **global warming** /ˌgləʊb(ə)l ˈwɔːmɪŋ/ *noun* a gradual rise in temperature over the whole of the earth's surface, caused by the greenhouse effect

globe /gləʊb/ *noun* **1.** ◻ **the globe** the world ○ *He is trying to be the first person to fly round the globe in a balloon.* **2.** a map of the world on a ball ○ *He spun the globe round and pointed to Canada.*

globule /ˈglɒbjuːl/ *noun* a small round drop, especially of oil or another thick liquid

gloom /gluːm/ *noun* **1.** darkness ○ *It was difficult to see in the gathering gloom.* **2.** deep despair ○ *A feeling of deep gloom came down on the family.* ○ *When the exam results came out everyone sank into gloom.*

③ **gloomy** /ˈgluːmi/ (**gloomier, gloomiest**) *adj* **1.** unhappy ○ *She was gloomy about her chances of passing the exam.* ○ *He's very gloomy about his job prospects.* **2.** dark ○ *a gloomy Sunday afternoon in November*

glorified /ˈglɔːrɪfaɪd/ *adj* seeming more important or special than it really is

glorify /ˈglɔːrɪfaɪ/ (**glorifies, glorifying, glorified**) *verb* to make something seem more important or special than it really is (NOTE: + **glorification** *n*)

glorious /ˈglɔːriəs/ *adj* splendid

glory /ˈglɔːri/ (*plural* **glories**) *noun* **1.** fame ○ *I did it for the glory of the school, not for myself.* **2.** a wonderful sight ○ *It is one of the glories of ancient Rome.*

gloss /glɒs/ *noun* **1.** a shine on the surface of something ○ *The metal is polished to give a brilliant gloss.* **2.** a note which explains or gives a meaning to a word, phrase or whole text ○ *his glosses on the plays of Shakespeare*

gloss over *phrasal verb* to try to hide a mistake or fault ○ *She tried to gloss over the fact that they had failed.* ○ *The report glosses over the mistakes made by officials.*

glossary /ˈglɒsəri/ (*plural* **glossaries**) *noun* a list of specialist words and their meanings or translations

gloss paint /ˈglɒs peɪnt/ *noun* a paint which is shiny when dry

glossy /ˈglɒsi/ (**glossier, glossiest**) *adj* shiny ○ *the glossy coat of a horse*

glove /glʌv/ *noun* a piece of clothing worn on your hand

glove compartment /ˈglʌv kəmˌpɑːtmənt/ *noun* a little cupboard with a door in front of the passenger's seat in a car

glow /gləʊ/ *verb* (**glows, glowing, glowed**) to shine in a dull way ○ *The logs glowed in the fireplace.* ○ *Her face glowed with pride.* ■ *noun* a soft bright light ○ *the warm glow of the fire*

glower /ˈglaʊə/ (**glowers, glowering, glowered**) *verb* to look angrily

glowing /ˈgləʊɪŋ/ *adj* **1.** bright; shining with fire ○ *the glowing charcoal in the barbecue* **2.** full of praise or enthusiasm ○ *He had a glowing report from his boss.*

glucose /ˈgluːkəʊz/ *noun* a widely occurring simple sugar

③ **glue** /gluː/ *noun* a substance which sticks things together ○ *She spread the glue carefully onto the back of the poster.* ○ *The glue on the envelope doesn't stick very well.* ■ *verb* (**glues, gluing, glued**) to stick things together ○ *He glued the label to the box.*

glum /glʌm/ (**glummer, glummest**) *adj* miserable (NOTE: + **glumly** *adv*)

glut /glʌt/ *noun* too much of something ○ *There's a glut of poultry on the market.*

glutinous /ˈgluːtɪnəs/ *adj* unpleasantly thick and sticky

glutton /ˈglʌt(ə)n/ *noun* a person who eats too much ○ *He's just a glutton – look at him finishing off that trifle!*

gluttony /ˈglʌt(ə)ni/ *noun* eating and drinking too much

GM *abbr* genetically modified

GMO *abbr* genetically modified organism

GMT *abbr* Greenwich Mean Time

gnat /næt/ *noun* a small fly which bites

gnaw /nɔː/ (**gnaws, gnawing, gnawed, gnawed** or **gnawn**) *verb* to bite something again and again

gnawing /ˈnɔːɪŋ/ *adj* (*of worries*) persistent and troubling

gnome /nəʊm/ *noun* a little man with a beard and pointed hat, in children's fairy stories

① **go** /gəʊ/ *verb* (**goes, going, went, gone**) **1.** to move from one place to another [*I/////*] ○ *The plane goes to Frankfurt, then to Rome.* ○ *She is going to London for the weekend.* ○ *It's time the children went to bed.* ○ *He has gone to work in Washington.* ○ *They are going on a tour of southern Spain.* ○ *She was going downstairs when she fell.* **2.** to leave [*I/////*] ○ *Get your coat, it's time to go.* ○ *The last bus goes at half past two.* **3.** to work ○ *Can you phone the garage? – the car won't go.* ○ *He's trying to get his motorbike to go.* **4.** to fit ○ *It's too big to go into the box.* ○ *This case won't go into the back of the car.* **5.** to be placed ○ *The date should go at the top of the letter.* **6.** to become ○ *Her face went red from sit-*

ting in the sun. ○ *He went pale and rushed out of the room.* ○ *You have to shout, my father's going deaf.* ○ *She's going grey, but it suits her.* **7.** to happen in a particular way ○ *The party went very well.* ○ *Things are going badly at work.* **8.** to make a particular sound ○ *The balloon landed on a candle and went 'pop'.* ○ *Do you remember the song that goes: 'There's no place like home'?* ■ *noun* (*plural* **gos**) a try; an attempt ○ *He won the lottery at the first go.* ○ *She had three goes at the test and still didn't pass.* ○ *We'll give it one more go, and if the car doesn't start I'll call the garage.*

go about *phrasal verb* to deal with something

go ahead *phrasal verb* to take place as planned ○ *The project went ahead even though there were not enough staff.*

go along with *phrasal verb* to agree with someone or something

go away *phrasal verb* to leave

go back *phrasal verb* to return

go back on *phrasal verb* not to do what has been promised

go down① *phrasal verb* **1.** to go to a lower level ○ *There are thirty-nine steps which go down to the beach.* ○ *Be careful when going down the hill.* ○ *After having a rest in her bedroom, she went down to the hotel bar.* ○ *Prices have gone down.* **2.** to catch a disease ○ *Half the crew went down with flu.* **3.** to be received in a particular way ○ *The speech went down well today.*

go in *phrasal verb* to enter a place ○ *You don't need to knock – just go in.*

go in for *phrasal verb* **1.** to take an examination ○ *She went in for her proficiency exam.* **2.** to take something up as a career ○ *He's going in for medicine.*

go into① *phrasal verb* **1.** to enter a place ○ *She went into the bedroom.* **2.** (*in maths*) to be able to divide a number to give a figure ○ *Seven into three won't go.* **3.** to examine something; to look at something carefully ○ *The bank wants to go into the details of his account.* **4.** to explain something in detail ○ *She said she had a job offer but wouldn't go into any details.*

go off① *phrasal verb* **1.** to go to another place ○ *He went off to look for a parking space.* ○ *She went off muttering something about buying cheese.* **2.** (*of an alarm*) to start making its noise ○ *The burglar alarm went off in the middle of the night.* **3.** to explode ○ *The bomb went off when there were still lots of people in the building.* ○ *Fireworks were going off everywhere on Bonfire Night.* **4.** to become rotten ○ *Throw that meat away – it's gone off.* ○ *Fish goes off quickly in hot weather.* **5.** not to like something any more ○ *I've gone off modern music.* ○ *She went off her new boyfriend quite quickly.*

go on① *phrasal verb* **1.** to continue ○ *Please go on, I like hearing you sing.* ○ *They went on working in spite of the fire.* ○ *She went on speaking for two hours.* **2.** to happen ○ *What's been going on here?* **3.** to base your opinion and actions on something ○ *The police investigating the murder don't have much to go on.* ○ *We have to go on the assumption that the festival will start on time.* **4.** to talk all the time about something [~about] ○ *She will keep going on about her operation.* **5.** used for showing you do not believe someone ○ *Go on! She's not as old as that!*

go out① *phrasal verb* **1.** to leave a building ○ *I don't go out often at night.* ○ *He forgot to lock the door when he went out.* **2.** to go to parties ○ *We used to go out every Friday and Saturday night.* **3.** not to be burning or lit any more ○ *The fire went out and the room got cold.* ○ *All the lights in the building suddenly went out.* **4.** □ **to go out of business** to stop trading ○ *The firm went out of business last week.*

go over *phrasal verb* **1.** to cross to the other side ○ *Go over the bridge and turn left.* **2.** to examine something carefully ○ *She went over the contract with her solicitor.*

go round① *phrasal verb* **1.** to turn ○ *The merry-go-round went round and round.* **2.** to turn round something ○ *We went round the roundabout and took the third road on the left.* ○ *We didn't go far, we just went round the block.* **3.** to visit a place ○ *You'll need at least two hours to go round the museum.* **4.** to be enough for a particular number of people ○ *There wasn't enough ice cream to go round all twelve of us.* **5.** to go to somewhere near ○ *Let's go round to your sister's.* ○ *We all went round to the pub for a drink.*

go up① *phrasal verb* **1.** to go to a higher place ○ *Take the lift and go up to the fourth floor.* **2.** to increase; to rise to a higher level ○ *The price of bread has gone up.*

go with① *phrasal verb* **1.** to match something ○ *Blue shoes won't go with a green* *dress.* ○ *Red wine goes best with meat.* **2.** to be linked to something ○ *That remote control goes with the TV.* ○ *He has a big house that goes with his job.* **3.** to accompany someone ○ *Who are you going to the party with?*

go without① *phrasal verb* not to have something which you usually have ○ *We often went without lunch.*

goad /gəʊd/ (**goads, goading, goaded**) *verb* to take pleasure in making someone feel upset ○ *She goaded him with taunts of his failure.* □ **to goad someone into doing something** to push someone into doing something by making them upset ○ *Her laughter goaded him into action.*

② **go-ahead** /ˈgəʊ əˌhed/ *noun* □ **to give something the go-ahead** or **get the go-ahead** to give or get permission for something to start (*informal*) ○ *We got the council's go-ahead to build the new supermarket.*

① **goal** /gəʊl/ *noun* **1.** (*in games*) two posts between which you have to send the ball to score a point ○ *He was unlucky to miss the goal with that shot.* **2.** (*in games*) a point scored by sending the ball between the posts ○ *He scored a goal before being sent off.* ○ *Our team scored three goals.* **3.** an aim ○ *Our goal is to open a new pizza restaurant every month.* ○ *He achieved his goal of becoming a millionaire before he was thirty.*

goalie /ˈgəʊli/ *noun* a goalkeeper (*informal*)

goalkeeper /ˈgəʊlkiːpə/ *noun* a player who stands in front of the goal to stop the ball going in

goalpost /ˈgəʊlpəʊst/ *noun* one of the two posts between which you have to send the ball to score a point

goat /gəʊt/ *noun* a small farm animal with horns and a beard, giving milk and wool ○ *a herd of goats*

goatee /gəʊˈtiː/ *noun* a small pointed beard

gobble /ˈgɒb(ə)l/ (**gobbles, gobbling, gobbled**) *verb* **1.** to eat something greedily ○ *He gobbled up his dinner.* **2.** to make a noise like a turkey ○ *We could hear the turkeys gobbling away in the farmyard.*

gobbledegook /ˈgɒb(ə)ldiˌguːk/ *noun* nonsense or technical language that you do not understand

go-between /ˈgəʊ bɪˌtwiːn/ *noun* a person who takes messages between two people

goblet /ˈgɒblət/ *noun* a large wine glass with a long stem, or a similar container made of metal or pottery

goblin /ˈgɒblɪn/ *noun* an ugly little man in fairy stories

god /gɒd/ *noun* a being with special powers that humans do not have, who is believed in and worshipped by some people ○ *Bacchus was the Roman god of wine.*

① **God** /gɒd/ *noun* the spiritual Christians, Jews and Muslims believe in and worship ○ *Do you believe in God?* ○ *We pray to God that the children will be found alive.* ■ *interj* used for showing that you are surprised or annoyed ○ *God, what awful weather!* ○ *My God, have you seen how late it is?*

godchild /ˈgɒdtʃaɪld/ (*plural* **godchildren**) *noun* a child who has a godparent

goddess /ˈgɒdes/ *noun* a female god

godfather /ˈgɒdfɑːðə/ *noun* **1.** a male godparent ○ *He was godfather to four children.* **2.** the head of a mafia gang ○ *The godfather's word is law.*

god-forsaken /ˈgɒd fəˌseɪkən/ *adj* desolate

godmother /ˈgɒdmʌðə/ *noun* a female godparent

godparent /ˈgɒdpeərənt/ *noun* a person who promises to take a special interest in a child at his or her baptism

godsend /ˈgɒdsend/ *noun* a helpful thing which arrives just in time

goes /gəʊz/ 3rd person singular present of **go**

go-getter /gəʊ ˈgetə/ *noun* a person who works hard and is determined to succeed

goggles /ˈgɒg(ə)lz/ *plural noun* close-fitting glasses worn to protect your eyes ○ *You should wear goggles when you use a drill.* ○ *He wore goggles when going scuba diving.*

① **going** /ˈgəʊɪŋ/ present participle of **go**

going concern /ˌgəʊɪŋ kənˈsɜːn/ *noun* a business that is operating successfully and is likely to continue to do so ○ *The business is being sold as a going concern.*

going-over /ˌgəʊɪŋ ˈəʊvə/ (*plural* **goings-over**) *noun* a thorough check

goings-on /ˌgəʊɪŋz ˈɒn/ *plural noun* strange things that happen (*informal*)

going to /ˈgəʊɪŋ tuː/ *phrase* used for showing future ○ *We're going to win.* ○ *I hope it's going to be fine tomorrow.* ○ *When are you going to wash your hair?* ○ *He's going to be a great tennis player when* *he's older.* ○ *Is she going to sing at the concert?*

go-kart /ˈgəʊ kɑːt/ *noun* a little racing car made of a simple metal frame with an engine

② **gold** /gəʊld/ *noun* a very valuable yellow-coloured metal ○ *That ring isn't made of gold.* ○ *Gold is worth more than silver.* ○ *He wears a gold ring on his little finger.* (NOTE: no plural: *some gold, a bar of gold*) ■ *adj* of the colour of gold ○ *a gold carpet*

③ **golden** /ˈgəʊld(ə)n/ *adj* coloured like gold; made from gold ○ *She has beautiful golden hair.*

golden age /ˈgəʊld(ə)n eɪdʒ/ *noun* a period of wealth or success

golden opportunity /ˌgəʊld(ə)n ɒpəˈtjuːnɪti/ *noun* a marvellous chance to do something which may not happen again

golden rule /ˌgəʊld(ə)n ˈruːl/ *noun* an important rule that must be obeyed

golden wedding /ˌgəʊld(ə)n ˈwedɪŋ/ *noun* a day when you have been married for fifty years ○ *It's my parents' golden wedding next Tuesday.*

goldfish /ˈgəʊldfɪʃ/ (*plural same* or **goldfishes**) *noun* a small orange fish, kept as a pet

③ **gold medal** /gəʊld ˈmedl/ *noun* the medal given to someone who finishes first in a race or competition

gold medallist /gəʊld ˈmed(ə)lɪst/ *noun* the person who wins the gold medal in a race or competition

goldmine /ˈgəʊldmaɪn/ *noun* a mine which produces gold

② **golf** /gɒlf/ *noun* a game played on a large open course, by hitting a small ball into 18 separate holes with a variety of clubs, using as few attempts as possible ○ *He plays golf every Saturday.* ○ *Do you want a game of golf?*

golf ball /ˈgɒlf bɔːl/ *noun* a small hard white ball used when playing golf

③ **golf club** /ˈgɒlf klʌb/ *noun* **1.** an organisation for people who play golf together ○ *He's joined his local golf club.* **2.** a place with a golf course and a restaurant and bar, where people go to play golf and meet socially

golf course /ˈgɒlf kɔːs/ *noun* a large area of ground for playing golf

③ **gone** /gɒn/ past participle of **go**

gonna /ˈgɒnə/ *contr* going to (*informal*) ○ *I'm gonna get you before you get me!*

goo /guː/ *noun* sticky stuff (*informal*)

① **good** /gʊd/ *adj* (**better, best**) **1.** sensible, enjoyable or of a high standard ○ *We had a good breakfast and then started work.* ○ *Did you have a good time at the party?* ○ *It would be a good idea to invest in these shares.* ○ *Her Spanish is better than his.* **2.** skilful at doing something [~with/~at] ○ *She's good with young children* ○ *He is good at football.* ○ *He's good at making things out of wood.* **3.** well-behaved ○ *Be a good girl and I'll give you a sweet.* ○ *Have you been good while we've been away?* ■ *noun* advantage or benefit ○ *The medicine didn't do me any good.* ○ *He decided to give up smoking for the good of his health.* ○ *What's the good of having a big garden if you don't like gardening?* ○ *Governments should work for the good of the people.*

① **good afternoon** /ˌgʊd ˌɑːftəˈnuːn/ *interj* used when meeting or leaving someone in the afternoon

① **goodbye** /ˌgʊdˈbaɪ/ *noun, interj* used when leaving someone ○ *Say goodbye to your teacher.* ○ *Goodbye! We'll see you again on Thursday.* (NOTE: often shortened to **bye**)

① **good evening** /ˌgʊd ˈiːvnɪŋ/ *interj* used as a greeting when meeting someone or sometimes when leaving someone in the evening

good-for-nothing /ˈgʊd fə ˌnʌθɪŋ/ *noun* a lazy person

good-humoured /ˌgʊd ˈhjuːməd/ *adj* cheerful and friendly (NOTE: The US spelling is **good-humored.**)

goodies /ˈgʊdiz/ *plural noun* **1.** sweet food ○ *The children looked at all the goodies on the table.* **2.** presents ○ *What goodies did Father Christmas bring you?*

good-looking /ˌgʊd ˈlʊkɪŋ/ *adj* (*of a person*) having an attractive face ○ *His sister is a very good-looking girl.* ○ *He's not especially good-looking.*

good looks /ˌgʊd ˈlʊks/ *plural noun* pleasing and beautiful appearance ○ *His good looks and charm attracted many women.*

① **good morning** /ˌgʊd ˈmɔːnɪŋ/ *interj* used when meeting someone, or sometimes when leaving someone in the morning

good-natured /ˌgʊd ˈneɪtʃəd/ *adj* with a pleasant and cooperative character

goodness /ˈgʊdnəs/ *noun* being good ○ *She did it out of pure goodness of heart.* ■ *interj* used for showing surprise ○ *Goodness! is that the time?* ◇ **thank goodness!**

used for showing relief ○ *Thank goodness the ambulance arrived quickly!* ◇ **for goodness' sake** used for showing you are annoyed, or that something is important ○ *What are you screaming for? – It's only a little mouse, for goodness' sake.* ○ *For goodness' sake try to be quiet, we don't want the guards to hear us!*

① **good night** /ˌɡʊd'naɪt/ *interj* used when leaving someone late in the evening

② **goods** /ɡʊdz/ *plural noun* **1.** things that are produced for sale ○ *The company sells goods from various European countries.* **2.** possessions; things which you own ○ *She carried all her worldly goods in a bag.*

goodwill /ɡʊd'wɪl/ *noun* **1.** a kind feeling ○ *The charity relies on the goodwill of people who give money regularly.* **2.** a value given to things such as the customers of a business, its reputation and its site ○ *He paid £10,000 for the goodwill of the restaurant and £40,000 for the fittings.*

goody /'ɡʊdi/, **Goody** *interj* I'm glad (*dated informal*)

goody-goody /'ɡʊdi ˌɡʊdi/ *adj* a person who is not liked because they are always trying to please people such as their teacher or their boss

gooey /'ɡuːi/ *adj* soft and sticky

goofy /'ɡuːfi/ *adj* stupid (*informal*)

③ **goose** /ɡuːs/ (*plural* **geese**) *noun* a large bird, living near water, which can be eaten (NOTE: The males are **ganders**, the young are **goslings**.)

gooseberry /'ɡʊzb(ə)ri/ *noun* a little green hairy fruit, with a sharp taste

gore /ɡɔː/ *noun* blood ○ *The final scene of the play was very violent, with lots of gore.* ■ *verb* (**gores, goring, gored**) to wound with a horn ○ *He was gored by a bull.*

gorge /ɡɔːdʒ/ *noun* a rocky valley ○ *The walkers climbed down into the gorge.* ■ *verb* (**gorges, gorging, gorged**) to eat too much ○ *Look at her gorging herself on cakes.*

③ **gorgeous** /'ɡɔːdʒəs/ *adj* magnificent

gorilla /ɡə'rɪlə/ *noun* a large black African ape (NOTE: Do not confuse with **guerrilla**.)

gorse /ɡɔːs/ *noun* a wild prickly shrub with bright yellow flowers

gory /'ɡɔːri/ *adj* **1.** covered in blood **2.** terrible; awful (*humorous*) ○ *She told me all the gory details of her interview.*

gosh /ɡɒʃ/ *interj* used for showing surprise (*dated informal*)

gosling /'ɡɒzlɪŋ/ *noun* a baby goose

gospel /'ɡɒspəl/ *noun* the part of the Bible which tells the life of Jesus Christ

② **gossip** /'ɡɒsɪp/ *noun* stories or news about someone, which may or may not be true ○ *Have you heard the latest gossip about Sue?* ■ *verb* (**gossips, gossiping, gossiped**) to talk about people's private lives ○ *They spent hours gossiping about the people working in the office.*

③ **got** /ɡɒt/ past tense and past participle of **get**

gotta /'ɡɒtə/ *contr* got to (*informal*) ○ *I'm sick – I've gotta go to the doctor.*

③ **gotten** /'ɡɒt(ə)n/ *US* past participle of **get**

gouge /ɡaʊdʒ/ (**gouges, gouging, gouged**) *verb* to cut something out ○ *He gouged out a hole in the plank.* ○ *The waves have gouged out a cave in the cliff.* (NOTE: + **gouge** *n*)

gourd /ɡʊəd/ *noun* a round fruit of a climbing plant, dried and used as a bottle or as a decoration

gourmet /'ɡʊəmeɪ/ *noun* **1.** a person who knows about and appreciates good food and drink **2.** referring to good food ○ *We had a gourmet dinner in a three-star restaurant.* ○ *This recipe comes from a gourmet cookbook.*

③ **govern** /'ɡʌv(ə)n/ (**governs, governing, governed**) *verb* to rule a country ○ *The country is governed by three generals.*

governess /'ɡʌvənəs/ *noun* a private female teacher

① **government** /'ɡʌv(ə)nmənt/ *noun* the people or a political party which rules a country ○ *The president asked the leader of the largest party to form a new government.* ○ *The government controls the price of bread.* ○ *He has an important job in the government.*

③ **governor** /'ɡʌv(ə)nə/ *noun* a person who runs a state, a colony or an institution

gown /ɡaʊn/ *noun* **1.** a woman's long formal dress ○ *a ball gown* **2.** a robe worn by someone such as a judge or a person with a degree

③ **GP** /ˌdʒiː 'piː/ *noun* a family doctor who does not specialise in any particular branch of medicine. Full form **general practitioner**

③ **grab** /ɡræb/ (**grabs, grabbing, grabbed**) *verb* **1.** to pick something up suddenly ○ *He grabbed his suitcase and ran to the train.* **2.** to get something quickly (*informal*) ○ *Let's grab some lunch before the meeting starts.*

grace /greɪs/ *noun* **1.** elegance and attractiveness ○ *We admired the grace of the deer as they ran off into the woods.* **2.** a prayer before a meal ○ *Father always says grace before dinner.* **3.** extra time to pay ○ *We gave the creditors two weeks' grace to pay.* ■ *verb* (**graces, gracing, graced**) to honour ○ *She graced the ceremony with her presence.*

graceful /ˈgreɪsf(ə)l/ *adj* moving in a smooth and beautiful way ○ *She crossed the stage with graceful steps.* ○ *We admired the swimmer's graceful strokes across the pool.*

graceless /ˈgreɪsləs/ *adj* **1.** not elegant **2.** not dignified

gracious /ˈgreɪʃəs/ *interj* used for showing surprise ○ *Gracious! Is that the time?*

gradation /grəˈdeɪʃ(ə)n/ *noun* **1.** a series of degrees or stages **2.** one of a series of degrees or stages **3.** the act of arranging things according to size, or quality

③ **grade** /greɪd/ *noun* **1.** a level of quality ○ *I always buy grade 2 eggs.* ○ *What grade of vegetables do you sell most of?* **2.** an examination mark ○ *She got top grades in maths.* **3.** *US* a class in school ○ *students in fifth grade* ○ *She's a fifth-grade student.* ■ *verb* (**grades, grading, graded**) to sort things according to size or quality ○ *a machine for grading fruit* ○ *Hotels are graded with two, three, four or five stars.* ◇ **to make the grade** to succeed; to do well

gradient /ˈgreɪdiənt/ *noun* a slope in a road or railway,

③ **gradual** /ˈgrædʒuəl/ *adj* which changes a little at a time

② **gradually** /ˈgrædʒuəli/ *adv* little by little ○ *His condition improved gradually day by day.* ○ *She gradually learnt how to deal with customers' complaints.*

graduate[1] /ˈgrædʒuət/ *noun* a person with a degree from a university or college ○ *He's a graduate of London University.* ○ *She's a physics graduate.*

graduate[2] /ˈgrædʒuˌeɪt/ (**graduates, graduating, graduated**) *verb* to get a degree ○ *She graduated from Edinburgh University last year.*

graduated /ˈgrædʒueɪtɪd/ *adj* **1.** rising in stages ○ *graduated income tax* **2.** with quantities marked on it ○ *a graduated measuring jar*

graduation /ˌgrædʒuˈeɪʃ(ə)n/ *noun* **1.** the ceremony at which you get a degree from a university or college ○ *Graduation will take place on June 10th.* **2.** *US* leaving high school or college with a diploma **3.** a mark showing quantities

graffiti /grəˈfiːti/ *noun* words which have been written or painted on walls in public places

graft /grɑːft/ *noun* very hard work that needs a lot of physical energy (*informal*) ○ *She has succeeded through sheer hard graft.*

grain /greɪn/ *noun* **1.** a crop such as wheat or corn ○ *a field of grain* ○ *the grain harvest* **2.** a very small piece ○ *a grain of sand*

③ **gram** /græm/, **gramme** *noun* a unit of weight; there are 1000 grams in a kilogram (NOTE: usually written **g** after figures: *50 g.*)

③ **grammar** /ˈgræmə/ *noun* **1.** the rules of a language ○ *I'm finding Russian grammar very difficult.* ○ *He's been learning English for years, and still makes basic grammar mistakes.* **2.** a book of rules of a language ○ *I'll look it up in my new German grammar.*

grammar school /ˈgræmə skuːl/ *noun* a secondary school where students have to pass an exam to enter

grammatical /grəˈmætɪk(ə)l/ *adj* referring to correct grammar

gran /græn/ *noun* a grandmother (*informal*)

granary /ˈgrænəri/ *noun* a place where grain is stored

② **grand** /grænd/ *adj* **1.** big and important ○ *his grand plan for making a lot of money* **2.** impressive ○ *We went to a very grand wedding.*

grandad /ˈgrændæd/ *noun* **1.** a grandfather (*informal*) **2.** a common name used for addressing a grandfather

③ **grandchild** /ˈgræntʃaɪld/ (*plural* **grandchildren**) *noun* a child of a son or daughter

③ **granddaughter** /ˈgrændɔːtə/ *noun* the daughter of a son or daughter

grandeur /ˈgrændʒə/ *noun* splendour

③ **grandfather** /ˈgrænˌfɑːðə/ *noun* the father of your mother or father ○ *Tomorrow is grandfather's hundredth birthday.* ○ *My grandfather always tells us fascinating stories about his childhood.* (NOTE: often called **grandad** or **grandpa** by children)

grandfather clock /ˈgrænfɑːðə klɒk/ *noun* a tall clock which stands on the floor

grandiose /ˈgrændiəʊs/ *adj* impressive, but too big and complicated

grandma /ˈgrænmɑː/ *noun* a grandmother (*informal*)

③ **grandmother** /ˈgrænmʌðə/ *noun* the mother of your mother or father ○ *It will be grandmother's ninetieth birthday next month.* ○ *My grandmother taught me how to make bread.* (NOTE: often called **gran** *or* **granny** *or* **grandma** *or* **nan** by children)

grandpa /ˈgrænpɑː/ *noun* a grandfather (*informal*)

grandparent /ˈgrænpeərənt/ *noun* the mother or father of one of your parents

grand piano /grænd piˈænəʊ/ *noun* a large horizontal piano (NOTE: A smaller piano, with a vertical body, is called an **upright**.)

Grand Prix /grɒn ˈpriː/ *noun* a race for large and powerful racing cars

grand slam /grænd ˈslæm/ *noun* winning a series of competitions, such as all the main tennis competitions held in a year

③ **grandson** /ˈgrænsʌn/ *noun* the son of a son or daughter

grandstand /ˈgrændstænd/ *noun* a stand with seats for spectators at games or races

grand total /ˌgrænd ˈtəʊt(ə)l/ *noun* a final total made by adding several items

granite /ˈgrænɪt/ *noun* a hard grey stone

granny /ˈgræni/ (*plural* **grannies**) *noun* a grandmother (*informal*)

① **grant** /grɑːnt/ *noun* an amount of money given to help someone to pay for something, or to live while they are doing something such as studying ○ *Not many students get a full grant.* ○ *My grant only pays for a few books.* ○ *We have applied for a grant to plant trees by the side of the road.* ■ *verb* (**grants, granting, granted**) to give someone something, especially officially (*formal*) ○ *The council has granted the school permission to build a new hall.* ◇ **to take someone for granted** to accept what someone does for you without showing them that you are grateful ◇ **to take something for granted** to assume that you will get something, or will keep something, and so not to appreciate it ○ *The children seem to take it for granted that I will give them big presents every birthday.*

granule /ˈgrænjuːl/ *noun* a very small particle

grape /greɪp/ *noun* a small green or red fruit which grows on low plants, often used to make wine

③ **grapefruit** /ˈgreɪpfruːt/ (*plural* **grapefruits** or *same*) *noun* a large yellow citrus fruit, like an orange but not as sweet

grapevine /ˈgreɪpvaɪn/ *noun* a plant on which grapes grow □ **I heard it on the grapevine** someone told me about it when gossiping

graph /grɑːf/ *noun* a chart showing how amounts rise and fall in the form of a line

graphic /ˈgræfɪk/ *adj* **1.** drawn in symbols or letters ○ *The results are shown in graphic form.* **2.** vivid ○ *He gave a graphic description of the accident.*

graphic design /ˌgræfɪk dɪˈzaɪn/ *noun* the art or practice of designing things involving images and text

③ **graphics** /ˈgræfɪks/ *plural noun* pictures on a computer screen or designed on a computer ○ *The graphics on this game are brilliant.*

graphite /ˈgræfaɪt/ *noun* natural carbon

grapple /ˈgræp(ə)l/ (**grapples, grappling, grappled**) *verb* **1.** to fight ○ *The two men were grappling on the floor.* **2.** □ **to grapple with something** to struggle to solve something difficult ○ *He's grappling with the company accounts.*

grasp /grɑːsp/ *noun* an understanding ○ *She has a good grasp of physics.* ■ *verb* (**grasps, grasping, grasped**) to understand something ○ *They didn't seem to grasp my meaning.*

② **grass** /grɑːs/ *noun* a low green plant, which is eaten by sheep and cows in fields, or used in gardens to cover the area that you walk or sit on ○ *The grass is getting too long – it needs cutting.*

grasshopper /ˈgrɑːshɒpə/ *noun* a green insect which jumps and makes a rubbing noise

grassland /ˈgrɑːslənd/ *noun* an area of land covered in wild grass

grate /greɪt/ *noun* a metal frame for holding coal in a fireplace ■ *verb* (**grates, grating, grated**) to make something into small pieces by rubbing against a grater ○ *She grated nutmeg over the pudding.* ○ *Sprinkle grated cheese over your pasta.* ○ *We made a salad of grated carrots and spring onions.* (NOTE: Do not confuse with **great**.)

③ **grateful** /ˈgreɪtf(ə)l/ *adj* feeling that you want to thank someone for something that they have done for you ○ *We are most grateful to you for your help.*

grater /ˈgreɪtə/ *noun* a kitchen instrument with a rough surface and little holes for grating

gratify /ˈgrætɪfaɪ/ (**gratifies, gratifying, gratified**) *verb* (*formal*) **1.** to satisfy someone ○ *It gratifies her need for luxury.* **2.** to please someone ○ *We were gratified to see that our work was prominently displayed.*

grating /ˈɡreɪtɪŋ/ *noun* a metal frame which covers a hole ○ *They lifted up the grating to look into the drain.*

gratitude /ˈɡrætɪtjuːd/ *noun* thankfulness

gratuitous /ɡrəˈtjuːɪtəs/ *adj* unnecessary; unjustified

grave /ɡrɑːv/ *noun* a hole in the ground where a dead person is buried ○ *At the funeral, the whole family stood by the grave.* ■ *adj* serious ○ *She looked at him with a grave expression.*

gravel /ˈɡræv(ə)l/ *noun* small stones

gravestone /ˈɡreɪvstəʊn/ *noun* a large stone placed on a grave with the name of the dead person written on it

graveyard /ˈɡreɪvjɑːd/ *noun* a cemetery

gravitate /ˈɡrævɪteɪt/ (**gravitates, gravitating, gravitated**) *verb* to move in a particular direction [~towards] ○ *In the evening the students gravitate towards the bars.*

③ **gravity** /ˈɡrævɪti/ *noun* the force which pulls things towards the ground ○ *Apples fall to the ground because of the earth's gravity.*

gravy /ˈɡreɪvi/ *noun* sauce made from the juices of cooked meat (NOTE: no plural)

gray /ɡreɪ/ *noun, adj* US spelling of **grey**

graze /ɡreɪz/ *noun* a slight skin injury ○ *He had a graze on his knee.* ■ *verb* (**grazes, grazing, grazed**) (*of animals*) to feed on grass ○ *The sheep were grazing on the hillside.*

grease /ɡriːs/ *noun* thick oil ○ *Put some grease on the hinge.* ■ *verb* (**greases, greasing, greased**) to cover with oil ○ *Don't forget to grease the wheels.* ○ *She greased the pan before cooking the eggs.*

greasy /ˈɡriːsi/ (**greasier, greasiest**) *adj* covered with oil or grease ○ *He wiped his greasy hands on a piece of rag.* ○ *I don't like the chips they serve here – they're too greasy.*

① **great** /ɡreɪt/ *adj* **1.** large ○ *She was carrying a great big pile of sandwiches.* ○ *The guide showed us into the Great Hall.* **2.** important or famous ○ *the greatest tennis player of all time* ○ *New York is a great city.* ○ *Picasso was a great artist.* **3.** wonderful; very good ○ *We had a great time at the party.* ○ *What did you think of the film? – It was great!* ○ *It was great of you to help.* ○ *It was great that they could all get to the picnic.*

great-grandchild /ɡreɪt ˈɡræntʃaɪld/ *noun* the son or daughter of a grandchild

③ **greatly** /ˈɡreɪtli/ *adv* very much

greatness /ˈɡreɪtnəs/ *noun* importance or respect

greed /ɡriːd/ *noun* too much love of food, money or power

greedy /ˈɡriːdi/ (**greedier, greediest**) *adj* wanting more food or other things than you need (NOTE: + **greedily** *adv*)

① **green** /ɡriːn/ *adj* **1.** of a colour like the colour of grass ○ *He was wearing a bright green shirt.* **2.** relating to, interested in or concerned about the environment ○ *She's very worried about green issues.* ○ *He's a leading figure in the green movement.* ■ *noun* **1.** a colour like that of grass and leaves ○ *The door was painted a very dark green.* **2.** an area of public land covered with grass in the middle of a village ○ *They were playing cricket on the village green.*

green bean /ɡriːn ˈbiːn/ *noun* a long thin green vegetable

green belt /ˈɡriːn ˈbelt/ *noun* an area of farming land or woods and parks, which surrounds a town, and on which building is restricted or completely banned

green card /ˌɡriːn ˈkɑːd/ *noun* a work permit for someone who is going to live in the USA

greenery /ˈɡriːnəri/ *noun* the leaves of trees and plants

greenfield site /ˈɡriːnfiːld saɪt/ *noun* a site for a factory which is in the country, and not surrounded by other factories

greengrocer /ˈɡriːnɡrəʊsə/ *noun* a person who sells fruit and vegetables

③ **greenhouse** /ˈɡriːnhaʊs/ (*plural* **greenhouses**) *noun* a glass building for growing plants

green light /ɡriːn ˈlaɪt/ *verb* to give approval or permission for something to proceed

② **greet** /ɡriːt/ (**greets, greeting, greeted**) *verb* to meet someone and say hello

greeting /ˈɡriːtɪŋ/ *noun* the words that people say to each other when they meet

gregarious /ɡrɪˈɡeəriəs/ *adj* enjoying the company of other people

grenade /ɡrɪˈneɪd/ *noun* a small bomb, usually thrown by hand

③ **grew** /ɡruː/ past tense of **grow**

② **grey** /ɡreɪ/ *noun* a colour that is a mixture of black and white ○ *He was dressed all in grey.* ■ *adj* of a colour that is a mixture of black and white ○ *Her hair has turned quite grey.* ○ *She was wearing a* *light grey suit.* ○ *Look at the grey clouds – I think it is going to rain.* (NOTE: The US spelling is **gray**.)

grey area /ˈgreɪ ˌeəriə/ *noun* a situation, subject, or category of something that is unclear or hard to define

greyhound /ˈgreɪhaʊnd/ *noun* a racing dog

③ **grid** /grɪd/ *noun* **1.** a set of parallel bars ○ *We have fitted a metal grid over the top of the well.* **2.** the numbered squares on a map ○ *What's the grid reference of the church?*

gridlock /ˈgrɪdlɒk/ *noun* a traffic jam

② **grief** /griːf/ *noun* a feeling of great sadness ◇ **to come to grief** to have an accident; to fail ○ *His horse came to grief at the first fence.* ○ *The project came to grief when the council refused to renew their grant.*

grievance /ˈgriːv(ə)ns/ *noun* a reason for complaint

grieve /griːv/ (**grieves, grieving, grieved**) *verb* **1.** to be sad, especially because someone has died ○ *She is grieving for her fiancé who was killed in the war.* **2.** to make someone sad (*formal*) ○ *It grieves me to say this, but we are going to arrest your daughter.*

grievous /ˈgriːvəs/ *adj* severe; very bad (*formal*)

grievous bodily harm /ˈgriːvəs ˈbɒdɪli hɑːm/ *noun* the crime of causing serious physical injury to someone. Abbreviation **GBH**

③ **grill** /grɪl/ *noun* a part of a cooker where food is cooked under the heat ○ *Cook the chops under the grill.* ■ *verb* (**grills, grilling, grilled**) to cook something in this part of the cooker ○ *We're having grilled sardines for dinner.*

grille /grɪl/ *noun* a structure of metal bars in front of a window or on the front of a car, with the radiator behind

② **grim** /grɪm/ *adj* **1.** serious and not smiling ○ *His expression was grim.* ○ *He gave a grim laugh and went on working.* **2.** grey and unpleasant ○ *The town centre is really grim.*

grimace /ˈgrɪməs/ (**grimaces, grimacing, grimaced**) *verb* to make a twisted expression ○ *She grimaced as the dentist started up his drill.* (NOTE: + **grimace** *n*)

grime /graɪm/ *noun* black dirt

grimy /ˈgraɪmi/ *adj* covered with old dirt that is difficult to remove ○ *The furniture was broken and the windows were grimy.*

② **grin** /grɪn/ *verb* (**grins, grinning, grinned**) to smile widely ○ *He grinned when we asked him if he liked his job.* ■ *noun* a wide smile ○ *She gave me a big grin.*

② **grind** /graɪnd/ (**grinds, grinding, ground**) *verb* **1.** to crush something to powder ○ *to grind coffee* ○ *a cup of ground coffee* **2.** to rub surfaces together

grip /grɪp/ *noun* a firm hold ○ *He has a strong firm grip.* ○ *Radial tyres give a better grip on the road surface.* ■ *verb* (**grips, gripping, gripped**) **1.** to hold something tight ○ *She gripped the rail with both hands.* **2.** to be very interesting to someone ○ *The story gripped me from the first page.*

gripe /graɪp/ *noun* a complaint ○ *his list of gripes about the work* (NOTE: + **gripe** *v*)

gripping /ˈgrɪpɪŋ/ *adj* which holds your interest or attention

grisly /ˈgrɪzli/ (**grislier, grisliest**) *adj* horrible (NOTE: Do not confuse with **grizzly** or **gristly**.)

grit /grɪt/ (**grits, gritting, gritted**) *verb* to put sand on a road that is covered with ice ○ *Lorries have been out all night, gritting the motorway.*

gritty /ˈgrɪti/ *adj* full of strength

grizzled /ˈgrɪz(ə)ld/ *adj* with lots of grey hairs

groan /grəʊn/ (**groans, groaning, groaned**) *verb* to make a long low noise ○ *She groaned when she saw how much work had to be done.*

grocer /ˈgrəʊsə/ *noun* a person who sells goods such as sugar, butter and tins of food

groceries /ˈgrəʊsəriz/ *plural noun* things you buy at a grocer's ○ *a heavy bag of groceries*

groggy /ˈgrɒgi/ *adj* not having a clear head

groin /grɔɪn/ *noun* the place where the legs join the body

groom /gruːm/ (**grooms, grooming, groomed**) *verb* **1.** to make someone or a horse look smart ○ *a well-groomed young man* ○ *She was grooming her horse.* **2.** to train someone for a particular role ○ *He is being groomed to take his father's place in the family business.*

groove /gruːv/ *noun* a wide line cut into a surface

grope /grəʊp/ (**gropes, groping, groped**) *verb* to feel with your hands

③ **gross** /grəʊs/ *adj* total; with nothing taken away ○ *What's your gross salary?* ■

adv with nothing taken away ○ *His salary is paid gross.*

gross domestic product /ɡrəʊs də ˌmestɪk ˈprɒdʌkt/ *noun* the value of goods and services paid for inside a country. Abbreviation **GDP**

gross national product /ɡrəʊs ˌnæʃ(ə)nəl ˈprɒdʌkt/ *noun* the value of goods and services paid for in a country, including income earned in other countries. Abbreviation **GNP**

gross profit /ɡrəʊs ˈprɒfɪt/ *noun* a profit calculated as income from sales less the cost of the goods sold, before paying for any other expenses

grotesque /ɡrəʊˈtesk/ *adj* **1.** strange and ugly ○ *We got a really grotesque present from our Spanish landlady.* **2.** unnatural and unpleasant ○ *It was grotesque to see her at the funeral.* ○ *Grotesque abuses of justice were commonplace during the civil war.*

① **ground** /ɡraʊnd/ *noun* **1.** the surface of the earth ○ *The factory was burnt to the ground.* ○ *There were no seats, so we had to sit on the ground.* ○ *She lay down on the ground and went to sleep.* **2.** soil or earth ○ *You should dig the ground in the autumn.* ○ *The house is built on wet ground.* ○ *It has been so dry that the ground is hard.* **3.** an area of land used for a special purpose ○ *a football ground* ○ *a sports ground* ○ *a cricket ground* ○ *a show ground* ■ *plural noun* **grounds 1.** a large area of land around a big house or institution ○ *The police searched the school grounds for the weapon.* ○ *The village fair is held in the grounds of the hospital.* **2.** reasons ○ *Does he have any grounds for complaint?* ○ *What grounds have you got for saying that?* ○ *Do they have sufficient grounds to sue us?*

groundbreaking /ˈɡraʊndbreɪkɪŋ/ *adj* involving new ideas

③ **ground floor** /ˌɡraʊnd ˈflɔː/ *noun* a floor in a building which is level with the street

grounding /ˈɡraʊndɪŋ/ *noun* basic instruction

groundless /ˈɡraʊndləs/ *adj* without any reason

groundswell /ˈɡraʊndswel/ *noun* a general feeling

groundwork /ˈɡraʊndwɜːk/ *noun* preliminary work

ground zero /ˌɡraʊnd ˈzɪərəʊ/ *noun* **1.** the point just above or below a nuclear explosion **2.** the most basic possible level or starting point **3.** the huge debris field left following the terrorist attacks on the World Trade Center towers in New York City on 11 September 2001

① **group** /ɡruːp/ *noun* **1.** a number of people together ○ *a group of houses in the valley* ○ *Groups of people gathered in the street.* ○ *She is leading a group of businessmen on a tour of Italian factories.* ○ *There are reduced prices for groups of 30 and over.* **2.** a way of classifying things ○ *These drugs belong to the same group.* **3.** people playing music together ○ *He plays in a jazz group.* ○ *She's the lead singer in a pop group.*

groupie /ˈɡruːpi/ *noun* a girl follower of a singer or pop group (*informal*)

grouping /ˈɡruːpɪŋ/ *noun* the process of putting things or people together in a group

grouse /ɡraʊs/ *noun* (*plural* **grouses** or *same*) **1.** a complaint ○ *All we heard at dinner were his grouses about the office.* **2.** a small dark game bird, found in the north of England and Scotland ○ *We had grouse for supper.* ○ *They shot six brace of grouse yesterday.* ○ *Grouse shooting starts on August 12th.* (NOTE: Two of the birds are called **a brace of grouse.**) ■ *verb* (**grouses, grousing, groused**) to complain [~about] (*informal*) ○ *He's always grousing about his salary.*

grove /ɡrəʊv/ *noun* a small group of trees

grovel /ˈɡrɒv(ə)l/ (**grovels, grovelling, grovelled**) *verb* to behave towards someone in a way that shows respect or admiration too obviously

① **grow** /ɡrəʊ/ (**grows, growing, grew, grown**) *verb* **1.** (*of plants*) to live and develop ○ *There was grass growing in the middle of the road.* ○ *Roses grow well in our garden.* **2.** to make plants grow ○ *He grows all his vegetables in his garden.* ○ *We are going to grow some cabbages this year.* **3.** to become taller or bigger ○ *He's grown a lot taller since I last saw him.* ○ *The profit has grown to £1m.* ○ *The town's population is growing very fast.*

grow into *phrasal verb* to become

grow out of *phrasal verb* **1.** to become bigger so that something such as an item of clothing does not fit ○ *He's grown out of his coat.* **2.** to become older, and so stop some bad habit ○ *He plays the drums all day long, but we hope it's something he'll grow out of.*

grow up ③ *phrasal verb* to become an adult

growing /'grəʊɪŋ/ *adj* **1.** becoming bigger in size or amount **2.** becoming stronger or more extreme ○ *growing fear of war*

growl /graʊl/ (**growls, growling, growled**) *verb* to make an angry sound ○ *The dog growled when he tried to take away its bone.* ○ *When we asked the doorman if we could go in, he just growled 'yes'.* (NOTE: + **growl** *n*)

③ **grown** /grəʊn/ *adj* full size ○ *What silly behaviour from a grown man!* (NOTE: Do not confuse with **groan**.)

③ **grown-up** /ˌgrəʊn 'ʌp/ *noun, adj* adult ○ *a grown-up taste in books* ○ *The family consists of three grown-ups and ten children.* ○ *She has a grown-up daughter.* ○ *The grown-ups had wine with their meal.*

② **growth** /grəʊθ/ *noun* an increase in size [~in] ○ *The table showed the rapid growth in population since 1980.* ○ *They measured the tree's growth over the last fifty years.*

growth industry /'grəʊθ ˌɪndəstri/ *noun* an industry that is expanding

grub /grʌb/ *noun* **1.** a little worm which is a young insect ○ *Birds were searching for grubs under the bushes.* **2.** food (*informal*) ○ *The grub in the canteen is so awful that I take sandwiches to work.*

grubby /'grʌbi/ (**grubbier, grubbiest**) *adj* so dirty as to be unpleasant ○ *Grubby children were playing in the street.* ○ *He was wearing a grubby old shirt.*

grudge /grʌdʒ/ *noun* □ **to have *or* bear a grudge against someone** to have bad feelings about someone because of something they did to you in the past ○ *Since her bag was snatched in Rome, she has a grudge against Italians.* ○ *He has been nursing a grudge against his boss for the last six years.* ■ *verb* (**grudges, grudging, grudged**) □ **to grudge someone something** to be unwilling to give someone something or be angry that they have something ○ *I grudge having to pay so much for so-called expert advice.* ○ *No one grudges him his success in the tennis championship.*

grudging /'grʌdʒɪŋ/ *adj* unwilling

gruelling /'gruːəlɪŋ/ *adj* tiring

gruesome /'gruːs(ə)m/ *adj* horrific and shocking in the way violence or death is shown

gruff /grʌf/ *adj* rough and unfriendly

grumble /'grʌmbəl/ (**grumbles, grumbling, grumbled**) *verb* to complain in a bad-tempered way, especially regularly and often about unimportant things ○ *He's always grumbling about the music from the flat above.*

grumpy /'grʌmpi/ (**grumpier, grumpiest**) *adj* bad-tempered (NOTE: + **grumpily** *adv*)

grunt /grʌnt/ (**grunts, grunting, grunted**) *verb* **1.** (*of a pig*) to make a noise ○ *The pigs were grunting and squealing in their pen.* **2.** to make a bad-tempered noise ○ *I asked if we could have a glass of water and the waiter just grunted.* ○ *She grunted something and slammed the door.* (NOTE: + **grunt** *n*)

② **guarantee** /ˌgærən'tiː/ *noun* **1.** a legal document in which someone states that something is going to happen [~(that)//] ○ *The travel agent could not give a guarantee that we would be accommodated in the hotel mentioned in the brochure.* **2.** a promise [///~of] ○ *I can't give you any guarantee of success.* ■ *verb* (**guarantees, guaranteeing, guaranteed**) to give a firm promise that something will work, that something will be done [~(that)] ○ *I can guarantee that the car will give you no trouble.* ○ *We can almost guarantee good weather in the Caribbean at this time of year.*

② **guaranteed** /ˌgærən'tiːd/ *adj* which has been promised legally

② **guard** /gɑːd/ *noun* **1.** [~against/~over] □ **to catch someone off guard** to catch someone by surprise, when they are not expecting it **2.** a person who protects, often a soldier ○ *Security guards patrol the factory at night.* ○ *Our squad is on guard duty tonight.* **3.** the man in charge of a train ○ *The guard helped my put my bike into his van.* ■ *verb* (**guards, guarding, guarded**) to watch someone or somewhere carefully to prevent attacks or escapes ○ *The prison is guarded at all times.* ◇ **to be on your guard** to try to be ready for an unpleasant surprise ○ *You always have to be on your guard against burglars.*

guard against *verb* to try to prepare for something or prevent it happening [~against] ○ *I need to guard against the likelihood that prices will rise.*

guarded /'gɑːdɪd/ *adj* reluctant to share information

② **guardian** /'gɑːdiən/ *noun* a person who protects, especially a person who legally looks after someone else's child

guardian angel /ˌgɑːdiən 'eɪndʒəl/ *noun* a person who looks after and protects someone

guerrilla /gə'rɪlə/, **guerilla** *noun* a soldier who is not part of a regular national army (NOTE: Do not confuse with **gorilla**.)

① **guess** /ges/ *noun* an attempt to give the right answer or amount [~at] ○ *Go on – make a guess at the answer!* ○ *At a guess, I'd say it weighs about 10 kilos.* ■ *verb* (**guesses, guessing, guessed**) **1.** to try to give the right answer or amount [~(that)///~what/how etc] ○ *I would guess that it's about six o'clock.* ○ *Neither of them guessed the right answer.* ○ *He guessed right.* ○ *I've bought you a present – shut your eyes and guess what it is.* **2.** *especially US* to have an opinion about something ○ *I guess the plane's going to be late.*

guessing game /'gesɪŋ geɪm/ *noun* an annoying situation which could end in different ways

guesstimate /'gestɪmət/ *noun* an estimate based on a guess

guesswork /'geswɜːk/ *noun* the process or end result of guessing

② **guest** /gest/ *noun* **1.** a person who is invited to come to your home or to an event ○ *We had a very lively party with dozens of guests.* ○ *None of the guests left the party early.* **2.** a person staying in a hotel ○ *Guests are requested to vacate their rooms before midday.*

guesthouse /'gesthaus/ *noun* a private house which takes several guests, like a small hotel

③ **guidance** /'gaɪd(ə)ns/ *noun* advice

② **guide** /gaɪd/ *noun* **1.** a person who shows you the way ○ *They used local farmers as guides through the forest.* **2.** a person who shows tourists round a place ○ *The guide showed us over the castle* or *showed us round the castle.* ○ *The museum guide spoke so fast that we couldn't understand what she was saying.* **3.** a book which gives information [~to] ○ *a guide to Athens* ○ *a guide to the butterflies of Europe* ■ *verb* (**guides, guiding, guided**) **1.** to show someone the way to somewhere ○ *She guided us up the steps in the dark.* **2.** to show tourists round a place ○ *He guided us round the castle and told us about its history.*

③ **guidebook** /'gaɪdbʊk/ *noun* a book with information about a place

guide dog /'gaɪd dɒg/ *noun* a dog which has been trained to lead a blind person

guidelines /'gaɪdlaɪnz/ *plural noun* general advice on what to do ○ *If you follow the government guidelines, you should not have any trouble.* ○ *The minister has issued a new set of guidelines about city planning.*

guild /gɪld/ *noun* an association of craftsmen (NOTE: Do not confuse with **gild**.)

guile /gaɪl/ *noun* the use of trickery to deceive people

guillotine /'gɪlətiːn/ *noun* **1.** a machine which was used in France for punishing criminals by cutting off their heads **2.** a machine for cutting paper

guilt /gɪlt/ *noun* **1.** the state of having committed a crime ○ *The prisoner admitted his guilt.* **2.** a feeling of being responsible for doing something bad ○ *The whole group bears the guilt for his death.* (NOTE: Do not confuse with **gilt**.)

② **guilty** /'gɪlti/ (**guiltier, guiltiest**) *adj* **1.** who has committed a crime ○ *He was found guilty of murder.* ○ *The jury decided she was not guilty.* **2.** feeling unhappy because you have done something wrong ○ *I feel very guilty about not having written to you.*

guinea pig /'gɪni pɪg/ *noun* **1.** a little furry animal, kept as a pet ○ *She keeps guinea pigs in a hutch in the garden.* **2.** a person used in an experiment ○ *The hospital is advertising for guinea pigs to test the new drug.* ○ *We're using her as a guinea pig to see if the instructions for making the cake work.*

guise /gaɪz/ *noun* an appearance, which is sometimes misleading

③ **guitar** /gɪ'tɑː/ *noun* a musical instrument with six strings, played with the fingers ○ *He plays the guitar in a pop group.*

③ **gulf** /gʌlf/ *noun* an area of sea partly surrounded by land ○ *the Gulf of Mexico*

gull /gʌl/ *noun* a large common white seabird

gullibility /ˌgʌlɪ'bɪlɪti/ *noun* a willingness to believe something or trust someone very easily

gullible /'gʌlɪb(ə)l/ *adj* ready to believe anything

gully /'gʌli/ *noun* a small narrow valley

gulp /gʌlp/ (**gulps, gulping, gulped**) *verb* to swallow fast ○ *She gulped and went onto the stage.* ○ *He gulped down his drink and ran for the bus.* (NOTE: + **gulp** *n*)

③ **gum** /gʌm/ *noun* **1.** glue ○ *She spread gum on the back of the photo and stuck it onto a sheet of paper.* **2.** the flesh around the base of your teeth ○ *Brushing your teeth every day is good for your gums.* ■ *verb* (**gums, gumming, gummed**) to stick something with glue ○ *She gummed the pictures onto a sheet of paper.*

gumption /ˈɡʌmpʃən/ *noun* **1.** good common sense **2.** the courage to take action

② **gun** /ɡʌn/ *noun* **1.** a weapon which shoots bullets ○ *The robber pulled out a gun.* ○ *She grabbed his gun and shot him dead.* **2.** a small piece of equipment which you hold in your hand to spray a substance such as paint or glue ○ *A spray gun gives an even coating of paint.* ◇ **to jump the gun** to start too quickly ○ *The new law comes into effect in a month's time, but some shops have already jumped the gun.*

gunboat /ˈɡʌnbəʊt/ *noun* a small ship with guns on it

gun control /ˈɡʌn kənˌtrəʊl/ *noun* legal measures to control the ownership of guns by members of the public

gunfire /ˈɡʌnfaɪə/ *noun* the shooting of guns

gunge /ɡʌndʒ/ *noun* an unpleasant sticky substance

③ **gunman** /ˈɡʌnmən/ (*plural* **gunmen**) *noun* a man armed with a gun ○ *The gunman pulled out a revolver and started shooting.*

gunpoint /ˈɡʌnpɔɪnt/ *noun* □ **at gunpoint** with a gun being pointed at you ○ *He was held at gunpoint by robbers.*

gunshot /ˈɡʌnʃɒt/ *noun* the firing of a gun

gurgle /ˈɡɜːɡ(ə)l/ (**gurgles, gurgling, gurgled**) *verb* to make a bubbling sound ○ *The water gurgled in the pipes.* ○ *The baby was gurgling in his pram.* (NOTE: + **gurgle** *n*)

guru /ˈɡʊruː/ *noun* **1.** a respected teacher, often a religious or spiritual teacher ○ *He was the great guru of the civil disobedience movement.* **2.** a person who gives advice ○ *She's one of the Prime Minister's media gurus.*

gush /ɡʌʃ/ *noun* **1.** a sudden fast flow of liquid ○ *A sudden gush of water came out of the pipe.* **2.** lots of praise ○ *I can't stand all this gush about babies.* ■ *verb* (**gushes, gushing, gushed**) **1.** to flow out very quickly and suddenly ○ *Oil gushed from the hole in the pipeline.* **2.** to speak in a very enthusiastic way ○ *She tends to gush over babies.*

gushing /ˈɡʌʃɪŋ/ *adj* **1.** flowing fast or in large quantities **2.** speaking or behaving in an extremely enthusiastic or emotional way that embarrasses other people

gust /ɡʌst/ (**gusts, gusting, gusted**) *verb* to blow in gusts ○ *The wind was gusting at up to 70 miles an hour.*

gusto /ˈɡʌstəʊ/ *noun* energy and enthusiasm

③ **gut** /ɡʌt/ *noun* the tube in which food is digested as it passes through the body ○ *He complained of a pain in the gut.*

gut reaction /ɡʌt riˈækʃən/ *noun* an instinctive reaction

guts /ɡʌts/ *plural noun* courage (*informal*) ○ *She had the guts to tell the boss he was wrong.*

gutsy /ˈɡʌtsi/ *adj* brave

gutter /ˈɡʌtə/ *noun* **1.** the side of a road where water can flow ○ *Pieces of paper and leaves were blowing about in the gutter.* **2.** an open pipe under the edge of a roof for catching rain ○ *It rained so hard the gutters overflowed.*

① **guy** /ɡaɪ/ *noun* **1.** a man (*informal*) ○ *She married a guy from Texas.* ○ *The boss is a very friendly guy.* ○ *Hey, you guys, come and look at this!* **2.** a model of a man burnt on Bonfire Night, November 5th ○ *The children are collecting clothes to make a guy.* ○ *Penny for the guy!*

guzzle /ˈɡʌz(ə)l/ (**guzzles, guzzling, guzzled**) *verb* to eat or drink greedily (*informal*)

③ **gym** /dʒɪm/ *noun* **1.** a place with special equipment, or a large hall as in a school, for indoor sports and physical training ○ *I go to the gym twice a week to exercise.* **2.** physical exercises, especially as an activity at school

gymnasium /dʒɪmˈneɪziəm/ *noun* a hall for indoor sports and athletics

gymnast /ˈdʒɪmnæst/ *noun* an athlete who is expert at gymnastics

gymnastics /dʒɪmˈnæstɪks/ *noun* physical exercises, as a competitive sport

gynaecology /ˌɡaɪnɪˈkɒlədʒi/ *noun* the study of female sex organs and the treatment of diseases of women in general (NOTE: The US spelling is **gynecology**.)

gypsy /ˈdʒɪpsi/ *noun* someone who travels a lot

gyrate /dʒaɪˈreɪt/ (**gyrates, gyrating, gyrated**) *verb* to turn round and round fast

h /eɪtʃ/, **H** *noun* the eighth letter of the alphabet, between G and I

③ **ha** /hɑː/ *interj* an expression showing surprise ○ *Ha! There's a mistake on page one of the book!*

③ **habit** /ˈhæbɪt/ *noun* something that someone does regularly ○ *He has the habit of biting his fingernails.* □ **to develop** *or* **get into the habit of doing something** to start to do something regularly ○ *He's getting into the habit of playing football every week.* □ **to break the habit** to stop doing something which you used to do regularly ○ *I haven't had a cigarette for six months – I think I've broken the habit!*

habitable /ˈhæbɪtəb(ə)l/ *adj* fit to live in

habitat /ˈhæbɪtæt/ *noun* a place where an animal or plant lives

habitation /ˌhæbɪˈteɪʃ(ə)n/ *noun* a place where someone lives

habitual /həˈbɪtʃuəl/ *adj* regular, who does something by habit ○ *a habitual liar* ○ *a habitual offender*

hack /hæk/ *noun* a badly paid journalist ○ *A bunch of hacks followed her everywhere.* ■ *verb* (**hacks, hacking, hacked**) **1.** to cut something roughly ○ *He hacked at the tree with an axe.* **2.** to enter a computer system illegally ○ *He hacked into the bank's computer.*

hacker /ˈhækə/ *noun* a person who enters a computer system illegally

hackles /ˈhæk(ə)lz/ ◇ **feel** *or* **make your hackles rise** to begin to feel or to make you feel angry

hackneyed /ˈhæknid/ *adj* used too often

had /əd, həd, hæd/ past tense and past participle of **have**

haddock /ˈhædək/ *noun* a white sea fish

hadn't /ˈhæd(ə)nt/ *abbr for* had not

haemophilia /ˌhiːməˈfɪliə/ *noun* a blood disorder, usually of men, that can lead to death from the smallest cut because the bleeding will not stop quickly enough

haemophiliac /ˌhiːməˈfɪliæk/ *noun* a person who has haemophilia (NOTE: The US spelling is **hemophiliac**.)

haemorrhage /ˈhem(ə)rɪdʒ/ *noun* **1.** bleeding where a large quantity of blood is lost, especially bleeding from a burst blood vessel ○ *She had a haemorrhage and was rushed to hospital.* ○ *He died of a brain haemorrhage.* **2.** loss of money, members or other resources ○ *We are trying to stem the haemorrhage of the company's resources.* (NOTE: [all senses] The US spelling is **hemorrhage**.)

haggard /ˈhægəd/ *adj* thin and tired

haggis /ˈhægɪs/ *noun* a Scottish dish, made of the inner parts of a sheep cooked in a bag made from the sheep's stomach

haggle /ˈhæg(ə)l/ (**haggles, haggling, haggled**) *verb* to argue about prices and terms to try to reduce them (NOTE: You haggle **with** someone **over** something.)

ha ha /hɑː ˈhɑː/ *interj* **1.** showing that you find something funny ○ *Ha ha! What a funny hat!* **2.** showing that you find something surprising ○ *Ha ha! I've caught you stealing from the cash box again!*

hail /heɪl/ *noun* frozen rain ○ *I thought the hail was going to break the windscreen.* ■ *verb* (**hails, hailing, hailed**) to fall as frozen rain ○ *It hailed for ten minutes and then the sun came out.*

① **hair** /heə/ *noun* **1.** a mass of long fibres growing on your head ○ *She has long brown hair* or *her hair is long and brown.* ○ *She always brushes her hair before washing it.* ○ *You must get your hair cut.* ○ *He's had his hair cut short.* ○ *Use some hair spray to keep your hair in place.* **2.** one of the fibres growing on the body of a human or animal ○ *Waiter, there's a hair in my soup!* ○ *The cat has left hairs all over the cushion.* ○ *He's beginning to get some grey hairs.* ◇ **to split hairs** to try to find very small differences between things when arguing ○ *Stop splitting hairs, you know you're in the wrong.*

③ **haircut** /ˈheəkʌt/ *noun* **1.** the cutting of the hair on your head ○ *You need a haircut.* ○ *He went to get a haircut.* **2.** a style of cutting hair ○ *Have you seen his new haircut?*

hairdo /ˈheəduː/ (*plural* **hairdos**) *noun* a hairstyle (*informal*) (NOTE: usually refers to a woman's hair)

③ **hairdresser** /ˈheədresə/ *noun* a person who cuts and washes your hair

hair grip /ˈheə grɪp/ *noun* a small bent metal or plastic pin, used to keep the hair in place

hairline /ˈheəlaɪn/ *noun* **1.** the line where your hair meets your forehead ○ *He's very worried about his receding hairline.* **2.** a very thin line or crack ○ *Hairline cracks appeared in the metal.*

hairpin /ˈheəpɪn/ *noun* a piece of bent wire used to keep your hair in place

hairpin bend /ˌheəpɪn ˈbend/ *noun* a sharp bend on a mountain road

hair-raising /ˈheə ˌreɪzɪŋ/ *adj* frightening

hair's breadth /ˈheəz bredθ/ *noun* a very small distance

hairstyle /ˈheəstaɪl/ *noun* the way in which your hair has been cut or arranged

hairy /ˈheəri/ (**hairier, hairiest**) *adj* **1.** covered with hairs ○ *a hairy dog* ○ *He's got hairy arms.* **2.** frightening and dangerous (*informal*) ○ *Driving across that mountain road in a snowstorm was the hairiest ride I've ever had.*

halal /həˈlɑːl/ *adj* describes meat from animals killed according to Islamic law

① **half** /hɑːf/ (*plural* **halves**) *noun* **1.** one of two parts which are the same in size ○ *She cut the orange in half.* ○ *One half of the apple fell on the carpet.* ○ *Half of six is three.* **2.** (*in sport*) one of two parts of a match ○ *Our team scored a goal in the first half.* ○ *We thought we were going to win, and then they scored in the final minutes of the second half.*

half-baked /hɑːf ˈbeɪkd/ *adj* not properly planned and therefore not practical

half board /hɑːf ˈbɔːd/ *noun* a rate for breakfast and dinner at a hotel, but not lunch

half-brother /ˈhɑːf ˌbrʌðə/ *noun* a brother who has only one parent the same as another brother or sister

half-hearted /ˌhɑːf ˈhɑːtɪd/ *adj* not very enthusiastic

② **half-hour** /ˌhɑːf ˈaʊə/ *noun* a period of thirty minutes

half-hourly /ˌhɑːf ˈaʊəli/ *adj, adv* every thirty minutes ○ *We have a half-hourly bus service to town.*

half measures /hɑːf ˈmeʒəz/ *plural noun* an plan or action which is begun but not completed

② **half past** /ˌhɑːf ˈpɑːst/ *phrase* 30 minutes after an hour

half-sister /ˈhɑːf ˌsɪstə/ *noun* a sister who has only one parent the same as another brother or sister

② **half-term** /ˌhɑːf ˈtɜːm/ *noun* a short holiday in the middle of a school term. Compare **midterm**

half-time /ˌhɑːf ˈtaɪm/ *noun* a rest period in the middle of a game

③ **halfway** /ˌhɑːfˈweɪ/ *adv* in the middle ○ *Come on, we're more than halfway there!* ○ *The post office is about halfway between the station and our house.* ◇ **to meet someone halfway, to go halfway to meet someone** to compromise ○ *I'll meet you halfway: I write the report and you present it at the meeting.*

halibut /ˈhælɪbət/ *noun* a large flat white fish

① **hall** /hɔːl/ *noun* **1.** a room just inside the entrance to a house, where you can leave your coat ○ *Don't wait in the hall, come straight into the dining room.* ○ *She left her umbrella in the hall.* **2.** a large room where large numbers of people can come together ○ *The children have their dinner in the school hall.*

hallmark /ˈhɔːlmɑːk/ *noun* a mark put on gold or silver items to show that the metal is of the correct quality ○ *The hallmark on this old silver spoon has almost been worn away.*

③ **hallo** /həˈləʊ/ another spelling of **hello**

hallucinate /həˈluːsɪneɪt/ (**hallucinates, hallucinating, hallucinated**) *verb* to imagine seeing or hearing someone or something

hallway /ˈhɔːlweɪ/ *noun* a hall; a passage at the entrance to a house or flat

halo /ˈheɪləʊ/ *noun* the ring of light round the head of a holy person in a painting ○ *A painting of an archbishop with two saints, each with a golden halo.*

③ **halt** /hɔːlt/ *noun* (*plural same*) a complete stop □ **to come to a halt** to stop completely ○ *The lorry came to a halt just before the wall.* □ **to call a halt to something** to make something stop ○ *He tried to call a halt to arguments inside the party.* □ **to grind to a halt** to stop working gradually ○ *The whole plan ground to a halt for lack* *of funds.* ■ *verb* (**halts, halting, halted**) to stop something ○ *The cars halted when the traffic lights went red.* ○ *We are trying to halt experiments on live animals.*

halting /ˈhɔːltɪŋ/ *adj* not sure

halve /hɑːv/ (**halves, halving, halved**) *verb* to reduce something by half ○ *Because the town has no cash, its budget has been halved.*

③ **halves** /hɑːvz/ plural of **half**

ham /hæm/ *noun* meat from a pig which has been treated, e.g. with salt ○ *She cut three slices of ham.* ○ *We had a ham and tomato salad.* ○ *She had a ham sandwich for lunch.*

③ **hamburger** /ˈhæmbɜːɡə/ *noun* a piece of minced beef grilled and served in a toasted roll

hamlet /ˈhæmlət/ *noun* a little village

③ **hammer** /ˈhæmə/ *noun* a tool with a heavy head for knocking nails ○ *She hit the nail hard with the hammer.* ■ *verb* (**hammers, hammering, hammered**) **1.** to knock something such as a nail into something such as a piece of wood with a hammer ○ *It took him a few minutes to hammer the tent pegs into the ground.* **2.** to hit something hard, as with a hammer ○ *He hammered the table with his fist.* ○ *She hammered on the door with her stick.*

hammer out *verb* to go through long and difficult discussions in order to reach agreement on something

hammock /ˈhæmək/ *noun* a bed made from a piece of fabric hanging between two hooks

hamper /ˈhæmpə/ *noun* a large basket ○ *We packed the hamper with food for the picnic.* ■ *verb* (**hampers, hampering, hampered**) to prevent something from happening or moving normally ○ *Lack of funds is hampering our development project.* ○ *The heavy bags hampered her progress.*

hamstring /ˈhæmstrɪŋ/ *noun* the group of tendons behind the knee, which connect the thigh muscle to the bones in the lower leg

hamstrung /ˈhæmstrʌŋ/ *adj* not able to do what you want to

① **hand** /hænd/ *noun* **1.** the part of the body at the end of each arm, which you use for holding things ○ *She was carrying a cup of tea in each hand.* ○ *She held out her hand, asking for money.* □ **they walked along hand in hand** they walked holding each other by the hand **2.** one of the two long parts on a clock which move round and show the time. The minute hand is longer than the hour hand. ■ *verb* (**hands, handing, handed**) to pass something to someone ○ *Can you hand me that box?* ○ *She handed me all her money.* ◇ **to give or lend someone a hand with something** to help someone with something ○ *Can you lend a hand with moving the furniture?* ○ *He gave me a hand with the washing up.* ◇ **to shake hands** to hold someone's hand to show you are pleased to meet them or to show that an agreement has been reached ○ *The visitors shook hands and the meeting started.*

hand down *phrasal verb* **1.** to pass something from one generation to a younger one ○ *This is one of those folk tales which have been handed down over the centuries.* ○ *The house has been handed down from father to son since the sixteenth century.* **2.** to announce something publicly ○ *The judge handed down his verdict.*

hand in① *phrasal verb* to give something to someone such as a teacher or a policeman ○ *We handed in the money we had found.*

hand out *phrasal verb* to distribute something ○ *Protesters were handing out leaflets at the station.*

hand over① *phrasal verb* to give something to someone ○ *She handed over all the documents to the lawyers.*

③ **handbag** /ˈhændbæɡ/ *noun* a small bag which a woman carries to hold small things such as money or make-up

hand baggage /ˈhænd ˌbæɡɪdʒ/ *noun* small cases carried by passengers onto a plane

handbook /ˈhændbʊk/ *noun* a book which gives instructions on how to use or repair something

handbrake /ˈhændbreɪk/ *noun* a lever in a vehicle which works the brakes

handcuff /ˈhændkʌf/ (**handcuffs, handcuffing, handcuffed**) *verb* to attach something with handcuffs

handcuffs /ˈhændkʌfs/ *plural noun* two metal rings connected by a chain, which are locked round the wrists of someone who is being arrested ○ *He came out of the court house in handcuffs.*

③ **handful** /ˈhændfʊl/ *noun* **1.** as much as you can hold in your hand ○ *She paid with a handful of loose change.* **2.** a very few ○ *Only a handful of people came to the wedding.* **3.** a difficult child ○ *Their son is a bit of a handful.*

hand grenade /ˈhænd ɡrɪˌneɪd/ *noun* a small bomb usually thrown by hand

handgun /ˈhændɡʌn/ *noun* a small gun which is carried in the hand

hand-held /ˌhænd ˈheld/ *adj* which can be held in the hand

③ **handicap** /ˈhændikæp/ *noun* **1.** a physical or mental condition which makes ordinary activities difficult (*dated*) ◊ **disability 2.** something which puts you at a disadvantage ○ *Not being able to drive is a handicap in this job.* ■ *verb* (**handicaps, handicapping, handicapped**) to cause someone difficulty ○ *She was handicapped on the trip by not being able to speak Russian.*

③ **handicapped** /ˈhændikæpt/ *adj* not able to use part of the body or mind because of a permanent illness or injury ○ *a school for handicapped children* (NOTE: Many people avoid this term as it can cause offence and prefer to say **disabled**.)

handiwork /ˈhændiwɜːk/ *noun* work done or made by yourself

③ **handkerchief** /ˈhæŋkətʃɪf/ (*plural* **handkerchieves**) *noun* a piece of cloth or thin paper for wiping your nose

② **handle** /ˈhænd(ə)l/ *noun* a part of something which you hold in your hand to carry something or to use something ○ *I turned the handle but the door didn't open.* ○ *Be careful, the handle of the frying pan may be hot.* ○ *The handle has come off my suitcase.* ○ *He broke the handle off the cup.* ■ *verb* (**handles, handling, handled**) to move by hand ○ *Be careful when you handle the bottles of acid.*

handlebars /ˈhænd(ə)lbɑːz/ *plural noun* a bar for steering a bicycle or motorcycle ○ *The handlebars are too low, can you alter their height?*

handling /ˈhændlɪŋ/ *noun* **1.** the way in which a person deals with something ○ *a situation that needs careful handling* **2.** the way in which something can be controlled or used **3.** the transport and packaging of goods **4.** the buying or selling of goods known to be stolen ○ *convicted of handling stolen goods*

hand luggage /ˈhænd ˌlʌɡɪdʒ/ *noun* same as **hand baggage**

handmade /ˈhændmeɪd/ *adj* made by hand, without using a machine

handout /ˈhændaʊt/ *noun* **1.** a gift such as clothes or money, given to poor people ○ *The support group exists on handouts from the government.* **2.** a printed information sheet ○ *You will all get handouts after the lecture.*

handover /ˈhændəʊvə/ *noun* the passing of power to someone else

handpicked /ˌhændˈpɪkt/ *adj* carefully chosen

handset /ˈhændset/ *noun* the part of a telephone which you hold in your hand

hands-free /ˌhændz ˈfriː/ *adj* able to be used or operated without the use of the hands

handshake /ˈhændʃeɪk/ *noun* the act of shaking hands when meeting someone

handsome /ˈhæns(ə)m/ *adj* a handsome man or boy has an attractive face ○ *Her boyfriend is very handsome.* (NOTE: usually used of men rather than women)

hands-on /ˌhændz ˈɒn/ *adj* practical and done by yourself

hand-to-mouth /ˌhænd tə ˈmaʊθ/ *adv* with only just enough money or food for what is necessary to live each day

③ **handwriting** /ˈhændraɪtɪŋ/ *noun* writing done by hand

handwritten /ˌhændˈrɪt(ə)n/ *adj* written by hand

③ **handy** /ˈhændi/ *adj* practical and useful ◇ **to come in handy** to be useful ○ *The knife will come in handy when we are camping.*

handyman /ˈhændimæn/ (*plural* **handymen**) *noun* someone who is skilled at doing small jobs such as repairs

① **hang** /hæŋ/ (**hangs, hanging, hung**) *verb* to attach one thing to another so that it does not touch the ground [~from/on/over etc] ○ *Hang your coat on the hook behind the door.* ○ *He hung his umbrella over the back of his chair.* ○ *We hung the painting in the hall.* ○ *The boys were hanging upside down from a tree.*

hang around③ *phrasal verb* to wait in a certain place without doing anything much

hang back③ *phrasal verb* to stay behind when others go on

hang on③ *phrasal verb* **1.** to wait ○ *If you hang on a few minutes you will be able to see her.* **2.** to hold something tight [~to] ○ *Hang on to the ladder and don't look down.* **3.** to keep something [~to] (*informal*) ○ *I've decided to hang on to my shares until the price goes up.*

hang out③ *phrasal verb* **1.** to hang things outside on a string ○ *They hung out flags all around the square.* ○ *Mother's hanging out her washing to dry.* **2.** to wait in a certain place without doing anything much (*informal*) ○ *Teenagers like to hang out round the internet café.*

hang up③ *phrasal verb* **1.** to put something on a hanger or on a hook ○ *Don't leave your jacket on the back of your chair – hang it up!* **2.** to stop a telephone conversation by putting the telephone back on its hook ○ *When I asked him when he was going to pay, he hung up.*

hangar /ˈhæŋə/ *noun* a large shed for keeping aircraft in (NOTE: Do not confuse with **hanger**.)

hanger /ˈhæŋə/ *noun* a device for hanging things on

hang-glider /ˈhæŋ ˌɡlaɪdə/ *noun* **1.** a large cloth wing stretched over a light frame, under which a person hangs, holding onto a bar which is used for steering (NOTE: + **hang-gliding** *n*) **2.** a person who flies a hang-glider

hanging /ˈhæŋɪŋ/ *noun* the act of killing someone by hanging them off the ground ○ *The hangings took place in front of the prison.*

hangover /ˈhæŋəʊvə/ *noun* **1.** an unpleasant feeling after having drunk too much alcohol ○ *Last night's party was good but I've got a dreadful hangover this morning.* **2.** a thing which is left over from the past ○ *This is a hangover from the old days when inns always provided stables for horses.*

hang-up /ˈhæŋ ʌp/ *noun* a worry or anxious feeling (*informal*)

hanker /ˈhæŋkə/ (**hankers, hankering, hankered**) *verb* to want something over a long time

hanky-panky /ˌhæŋki ˈpæŋki/ *noun* **1.** activity which is strange or suspicious **2.** sexual behaviour

Hanukkah /ˈhɑːnəkə/ *noun* a Jewish religious festival in November or December

haphazard /hæpˈhæzəd/ *adj* done without any plan

① **happen** /ˈhæpən/ (**happens, happening, happened**) *verb* **1.** to take place ○ *The accident happened at the traffic lights.* ○ *How did the accident happen?* ○ *Something happened to make all the buses late.* ○ *He's late – something must have happened to him.* **2.** □ **to happen to someone or something** to have an effect on someone or something ○ *What's happened to his brother since he left school?* ◇ **as it happens, as it happened** completely by chance ○ *As it happens I have the car today and can give you a lift.* ○ *It so happened that my wife bumped into her at the supermarket.*

② **happening** /ˈhæp(ə)nɪŋ/ *noun* an event

happily /ˈhæpɪli/ *adv* in a happy way

happiness /ˈhæpinəs/ *noun* a feeling of being happy

① **happy** /ˈhæpi/ *adj* **1.** (*of people*) very pleased ○ *I'm happy to say we're getting married next month.* ○ *I'm so happy to hear that you are better.* ○ *She's very happy in her job.* **2.** (*of events*) pleasant ○ *It was the happiest day of my life.*

happy-go-lucky /ˌhæpi ɡəʊ ˈlʌki/ *adj* without any worries

happy hour /ˈhæpi aʊə/ *noun* a period when drinks are cheaper in a bar

happy medium /ˌhæpi ˈmiːdiəm/ *noun* an agreement that includes something for everyone

harangue /həˈræŋ/ (**harangues, haranguing, harangued**) *verb* to make a loud speech to someone ○ *The president harangued the crowd for three hours.* (NOTE: + **harangue** *n*)

harass /ˈhærəs, həˈræs/ (**harasses, harassing, harassed**) *verb* to bother and worry someone

harassed /ˈhærəst/ *adj* bothered and worried

harassment /ˈhærəsmənt, həˈræsmənt/ *noun* pestering and worrying

harbour /ˈhɑːbə/ *noun* a place where boats can come and tie up ○ *The ship came into harbour last night.*

① **hard** /hɑːd/ *adj* **1.** not soft ○ *If you have back trouble, you ought to get a hard bed.* ○ *The ice cream is rock hard* or *hard as a rock.* ○ *The cake she made is so hard I can't bite into it.* **2.** not easy ○ *Some of the questions were very hard.* ○ *It's hard to stay happy when bad things happen.* ■ *adv* strongly ○ *He hit the nail hard.* ○ *It's snowing very hard.* ◇ **it's hard to say** it's difficult to know ○ *It's hard to say if it's going to rain or not.*

hardback /ˈhɑːdbæk/, **hardcover** *noun* a book bound in stiff card. Compare **paperback**

hardboard /ˈhɑːdbɔːd/ *noun* artificial board, made of little bits of wood mixed with glue and pressed together

hard-boiled /ˌhɑːd ˈbɔɪld/ *adj* **1.** (*of an egg*) which has been boiled until the inside is solid ○ *Do you prefer your egg hard-boiled or soft-boiled?* **2.** tough; not showing any emotion ○ *She's pretty hard-boiled, that sort of thing doesn't bother her.*

hard copy /ˌhɑːd ˈkɒpi/ *noun* computer data which has been printed on paper

hard core /ˈhɑːd kɔː/ *noun* a central group ○ *Most of the guests left before eleven, but the hard core of drinkers stayed till two.*

hard currency /ˌhɑːd ˈkʌrənsi/ *noun* the currency of a country with a strong economy, which can be changed into other currencies easily

hard disk /ˌhɑːd ˈdɪsk/, **hard drive** *noun* a disk which is fixed inside a computer

harden /ˈhɑːd(ə)n/ (**hardens, hardening, hardened**) *verb* **1.** to become hard ○ *Leave the cement for a couple of days to harden.* ○ *Attitudes are hardening as the transport strike continues.* **2.** to make something harder ○ *We use specially hardened steel in the construction.* **3.** to make someone more experienced ○ *a hardened criminal*

hardened /ˈhɑːdənd/ *adj* so experienced that something that most people would find unpleasant or difficult seems ordinary

hard-headed /ˌhɑːd ˈhedɪd/ *adj* practical or sensible

hard-hearted /ˌhɑːd ˈhɑːtɪd/ *adj* cruel

hard-hitting /ˌhɑːd ˈhɪtɪŋ/ *adj* very critical

hardline /ˈhɑːdlaɪn/ *adj* strict over policy

② **hardly** /ˈhɑːdli/ *adv* almost not ○ *Do you know her? – Hardly at all.* ○ *We hardly slept a wink last night.* ○ *She hardly eats anything at all.*

hard-nosed /ˈhɑːd nəʊzd/ *adj* tough; determined

hard-pressed /ˌhɑːd ˈprest/ *adj* acting under a lot of pressure

hard sell /ˌhɑːd ˈsel/ *noun* aggressive selling

hardship /ˈhɑːdʃɪp/ *noun* difficult conditions, suffering

hard shoulder /ˌhɑːd ˈʃəʊldə/ *noun* a hard strip along the edge of a motorway, used for stopping in an emergency

③ **hard up** /ˌhɑːd ˈʌp/ *adj* with very little money (*informal*)

hardware /ˈhɑːdweə/ *noun* tools and pans used in the home ○ *I bought the paint in a hardware shop.*

hard-wired /hɑːd ˈwaɪəd/ *adj* physically connected to a computer system or network

hard-won /ˈhɑːd wʌn/ *adj* achieved after a big effort

hardwood /ˈhɑːdwʊd/ *noun* a slow-growing tree, such as oak or teak, which produces a hard wood

hardworking /ˌhɑːdˈwɜːkɪŋ/ *adj* who works hard

hardy /ˈhɑːdi/ *adj* able to survive in cold weather

hare /heə/ *noun* a wild mammal like a large rabbit ○ *In the spring mountain hares lose their white winter coats.*

harebrained /ˈheəbreɪnd/ *adj* not serious; not concentrating on essential things

harem /ˈhɑːriːm/ *noun* **1.** a group of women who are the wives of the same man in some Muslim societies, especially in the past **2.** the part of a Muslim house where only women live

harlot /ˈhɑːlət/ *noun* a woman who has sex for money (*dated*)

③ **harm** /hɑːm/ *noun* damage done to people or animals ○ *He didn't mean to do any harm* or *He meant no harm.* ○ *There's no harm in having a little drink before you go to bed.* ■ *verb* (**harms, harming, harmed**) to physically affect something or someone in a bad way ○ *Luckily, the little girl was not harmed.* ○ *The bad publicity has harmed our reputation.*

③ **harmful** /ˈhɑːmf(ə)l/ *adj* which causes damage

③ **harmless** /ˈhɑːmləs/ *adj* which does not upset or hurt anyone

harmonica /hɑːˈmɒnɪkə/ *noun* a mouth-organ; a small musical instrument which you play by blowing and sucking, and moving across your mouth to get different notes

harmonious /hɑːˈməʊniəs/ *adj* **1.** sounding or looking good together **2.** friendly and cooperative ○ *a harmonious discussion between the heads of state.*

harmonise /ˈhɑːmənaɪz/ (**harmonises, harmonising, harmonised**), **harmonize** *verb* to go well together ○ *Make sure the colours of the curtains harmonise with the carpet.*

harmony /ˈhɑːməni/ (*plural* **harmonies**) *noun* **1.** agreeable musical sounds ○ *The group sang in harmony.* **2.** agreeable colours, etc. ○ *We are aiming to create a pleasant harmony in the decoration of the room.* **3.** a general peace ○ *They want to live in harmony with their neighbours.*

harness /ˈhɑːnɪs/ *noun* **1.** straps used to hold a horse to a cart **2.** straps used to attach something to a person ○ *a parachute harness* ○ *Make sure that you buy a pushchair with a reliable baby harness.*

harp /hɑːp/ *noun* a musical instrument shaped like a large triangle, played by the fingers plucking the strings ○ *She plays the harp in the local orchestra.*

harpoon /hɑːˈpuːn/ *noun* a long sharp weapon used to kill whales (NOTE: + **harpoon** *v*)

harrowing /ˈhærəʊɪŋ/ *adj* which causes mental pain

harsh /hɑːʃ/ *adj* **1.** severe ○ *The prosecutor asked for a harsh sentence to fit the crime.* **2.** rough ○ *He shouted in a harsh voice.*

harvest /ˈhɑːvɪst/ *noun* picking crops ○ *The corn harvest is in August.* ■ *verb* (**harvests, harvesting, harvested**) to pick crops ○ *The corn will be ready to harvest next week.* ○ *They have started harvesting the grapes in the vineyard.*

has /əz, həz, hæz/ 3rd person singular present of **have**

has-been /ˈhæz biːn/ *noun* a person no longer as well-known or important as before (*informal*)

hash /hæʃ/ *noun* **1.** a dish prepared from chopped meat and vegetables **2.** hashish

hasn't /ˈhæz(ə)nt/ *short for* has not

③ **hassle** /ˈhæs(ə)l/ (*informal*) *noun* irritating trouble ○ *It was quite a hassle getting tickets.* ○ *I got to the station early to avoid all the hassle with the luggage.* ■ *verb* (**hassles, hassling, hassled**) to bother someone ○ *Her boss is always hassling her to work faster.*

haste /heɪst/ *noun* the speed of doing something (*formal*)

hasten /ˈheɪs(ə)n/ (**hastens, hastening, hastened**) *verb* **1.** to go fast ○ *The chief of police hastened into the room.* **2.** to do something fast ○ *The government has hastened to deny the report in the paper.* **3.** to make something go faster ○ *Several weeks' rest after your operation will hasten your recovery.*

hasty /ˈheɪsti/ (**hastier, hastiest**) *adj* carelessly fast (NOTE: + **hastily** *adv*)

② **hat** /hæt/ *noun* a piece of clothing which you wear on your head ○ *Take your hat off when you go into a church.* ○ *He's bought a Russian fur hat for the winter.*

hatch /hætʃ/ *noun* an opening in the deck of a ship, or a cover for this opening ○ *He opened the hatch and went down into the cabin.* ■ *verb* (**hatches, hatching, hatched**) to plan ○ *They hatched a plot to kidnap the Prime Minister's daughter.*

hatchback /ˈhætʃbæk/ *noun* a type of car where the back opens upwards as a door

hatchet /ˈhætʃɪt/ *noun* a small axe

① **hate** /heɪt/ *verb* (**hates, hating, hated**) to dislike someone or something very much ○ *I think she hates me, but I don't know why.* ○ *I hate being late.* ■ *noun* a very strong feeling of not liking someone ○ *Her eyes were full of hate.*

hateful /ˈheɪtf(ə)l/ *adj* which makes people dislike it

hate mail /ˈheɪt meɪl/ *noun* letters showing that the writer hates someone

hatred /ˈheɪtrɪd/ *noun* a very strong feeling of not liking someone or something ○ *a campaign against racial hatred* ○ *She had a hatred of unfair treatment.*

hat trick /ˈhæt trɪk/ *noun* a score of three goals or wins by the same person in a sport

haughty /ˈhɔːti/ (**haughtier, haughtiest**) *adj* extremely proud and unpleasant (NOTE: + **haughtily** *adv*; **haughtiness** *n*)

haul /hɔːl/ (**hauls, hauling, hauled**) *verb* to pull something with effort ○ *They hauled the boat up onto the beach.*

haunt /hɔːnt/ *noun* a place which you visit frequently ○ *I went back to some of my old haunts.* ○ *The pub is a favourite haunt of actors.* ■ *verb* (**haunts, haunting, haunted**) (*of ghosts*) to visit something frequently ○ *The castle is supposed to be haunted by the ghost of a soldier.*

haunted /ˈhɔːntɪd/ *adj* visited by ghosts

haunting /ˈhɔːntɪŋ/ *adj* sad and wonderful

① **have** /həv, əv, hæv/ (**has, having, had**) *verb* **1.** to own something ○ *She has a lot of money.* ○ *They have a new green car.* ○ *She has long dark hair.* ○ *The house has no telephone.* ○ *Do you have a table for three, please?* **2.** to take or eat something ○ *Have you had any tea?* ○ *She has sugar in her coffee.* ○ *They had a meal of bread and cheese.* ○ *She had her breakfast in bed.* ○ *They had a game of tennis.* ○ *I had a long walk.* **3.** to arrange for something to be done for you ○ *I must have my hair cut.* ○ *She's having the house painted.* **4.** used to form the present and past perfect form of verbs ○ *Have they finished their work?* ○ *She has never been to Paris.* ○ *They had finished supper when we arrived.* ○ *I haven't seen him for two days.* ○ *If she had asked me I would have said no.* **5.** used to introduce good wishes to someone ○ *Have a nice day!* ○ *Have a good trip!*

have got *phrasal verb* **1.** to own something ○ *She's got dark hair.* ○ *Have you got a table for three, please?* ○ *They've got a new green car.* ○ *The house hasn't* *got a telephone.* ○ *They haven't got enough to eat.* **2.** used to mean 'must' ○ *Why have you got to go so early?* ○ *She's got to learn to drive.*

have on *phrasal verb* **1.** □ **to have** or **have got something on** to be wearing something ○ *What did she have on at the party?* **2.** □ **to have something on** to have something planned (*informal*) ○ *I haven't anything on tonight so I'll be able to finish painting the bathroom.* **3.** □ **to have someone on** to trick someone (*informal*) ○ *I think he's having you on.*

haven /ˈheɪv(ə)n/ *noun* a safe port or safe place

③ **haven't** /ˈhæv(ə)nt/ *short for* have not

havoc /ˈhævək/ *noun* damage

hawk /hɔːk/ *noun* a person who prefers military action to diplomacy ○ *Curiously, it's the military commanders who are the doves and the president and his advisers are the hawks.*

③ **hay** /heɪ/ *noun* dried grass used to feed animals such as cows

hayfever /ˈheɪfiːvə/ *noun* an inflammation of the nose and eyes caused by an allergy to flowers, pollen, scent or dust

hazard /ˈhæzəd/ *noun* a dangerous situation ○ *Don't leave those cardboard boxes in the passage – they're a fire hazard.* ■ *verb* (**hazards, hazarding, hazarded**) to risk something

hazardous /ˈhæzədəs/ *adj* risky or dangerous

haze /heɪz/ *noun* **1.** mist, smoke or dust suspended in the atmosphere, reducing visibility **2.** not being able to think or remember clearly ○ *He was in a haze when he came round after the operation.*

hazy /ˈheɪzi/ (**hazier, haziest**) *adj* **1.** misty ○ *It was too hazy for us to get a good view from the top of the cliff.* **2.** vague ○ *I have a hazy recollection of the party.* ○ *He reported the accident to the police but was very hazy about some of the details.*

① **he** /hi, hiː/ *pron* referring to a man or boy, and some animals ○ *He's my brother.* ○ *He and I met in Oxford.* ○ *He's eaten all my pudding.* ○ *Don't be frightened of the dog – he won't hurt you.* ◊ **him**, **his** (NOTE: When it is the object, **he** becomes **him**: *He hit the ball or The ball hit him.* When it follows the verb **to be**, **he** usually becomes **him**: *Who's that? – It's him, the man who borrowed my knife.*)

① **head** /hed/ *noun* **1.** the top part of the body, where your eyes, nose, mouth and brain are ○ *He says he can relax by standing on his head.* ○ *She hit her head on the cupboard door.* **2.** your brain; intelligence ○ *She has a good head for figures.* ○ *He tried to do the sum in his head.* ○ *If we all put our heads together we might come up with a solution.* **3.** the first place ○ *An old lady was standing at the head of the queue.* ○ *His name comes at the head of the list.* **4.** the most important person ○ *She's head of the sales department.* ○ *The head waiter showed us to our table.* **5.** one person, or one animal, when counting ○ *She counted heads as the children got onto the coach.* ○ *There are fifty head of sheep in the flock.* ■ *verb* (**heads, heading, headed**) to go towards something ○ *She headed immediately for the manager's office.* ○ *The car headed east along the motorway.* ○ *He's heading towards the Channel ports.* ○ *She's heading for trouble.* ◇ **to shake your head** to move your head from side to side to mean 'no' ○ *She asked him if he wanted any more coffee and he shook his head.*

head off *phrasal verb* **1.** to prevent something from taking place ○ *They offered the staff more pay in order to head off a strike.* **2.** to go away in a certain direction ○ *They headed off into the jungle.*

headache /ˈhedeɪk/ *noun* a pain in your head ○ *I've got a bad headache.*

headcount /ˈhedkaʊnt/ *noun* the process of counting the people in a group one by one

header /ˈhedə/ *noun* **1.** the act of hitting a ball with your head ○ *He scored with a header.* **2.** a dive ○ *He took a header into the waves.* **3.** words or page numbers at the top of a page of a book or document

head-first /ˌhed ˈfɜːst/ *adv* **1.** with your head first ○ *He tripped and fell head-first down the stairs.* **2.** hastily ○ *Don't rush head-first into a deal with someone you hardly know.*

headgear /ˈhedgɪə/ *noun* something which is worn on the head

headhunter /ˈhedhʌntə/ *noun* a person or company that looks for top managers and offers them jobs in other companies

heading /ˈhedɪŋ/ *noun* words at the top of a piece of text. ◊ **subheading**

③ **headline** /ˈhedlaɪn/ *noun* words in large letters on the front page of a newspaper ○ *Did you see the headlines about the accident?*

headlong /ˈhedlɒŋ/ *adj* rushing ○ *the headlong flight of the people of the villages in front of the advancing army* ■ *adv* rushing ○ *The soldiers rushed headlong into the crowd.*

③ **headmaster** /hed'mɑːstə/ *noun* a man who is in charge of a school

headmistress /hed'mɪstrəs/ *noun* a woman who is in charge of a school

head office /ˌhed 'ɒfɪs/ *noun* the main office where the directors work and meet

② **head-on** /hed 'ɒn/ *adj, adv* **1.** with the front first; direct ○ *We had a head-on confrontation with the police.* **2.** directly ○ *He decided to meet the objections head-on.*

headphones /'hedfəʊnz/ *plural noun* equipment which you put on your ears to listen to sounds privately

headquarters /hed'kwɔːtəz/ *noun* the main offices of a large organisation ○ *Several people were arrested and taken to police headquarters.* Abbreviation **HQ**

headrest /'hedrest/ *noun* a cushion on top of a car seat against which you can lean your head

headroom /'hedruːm/ *noun* the amount of space needed to be able to sit or walk upright

headset /'hedset/ *noun* a set of headphones for listening to something such as the telephone, the radio or a CD, which fits over your ears with a band across the top of your head, and sometimes has a microphone attached

headstone /'hedstəʊn/ *noun* a piece of stone standing at the end of a grave with the name of the dead person written on it

headstrong /'hedstrɒŋ/ *adj* determined to do what you want

head teacher /ˌhed 'tiːtʃə/ *noun* a man or woman who is in charge of a school

head-to-head /ˌhed tə 'hed/ *adv, adj* competing directly with someone or something ○ *a head-to-head contest* ○ *The winner of this game will go head-to-head with the reigning champion.*

headwind /'hedwɪnd/ *noun* a wind blowing towards you

heady /'hedi/ (**headier, headiest**) *adj* strong and likely to affect your senses, such as making you drunk or excited

heal /hiːl/ (**heals, healing, healed**) *verb* to make someone or something healthy again, or to become healthy again ○ *She claims to be able to heal people through touch.* ○ *This should help the wound to heal.* (NOTE: Do not confuse with **heel**.)

healing /'hiːlɪŋ/ *noun* the action of making something or someone healthy ○ *The healing of the sick is her vocation.*

① **health** /helθ/ *noun* the fact of being well or being free from any illness ○ *He has enjoyed the best of health for years.* ○ *Smoking is bad for your health.*

health care /'helθkeə/ *noun* the services which take care of people's health, e.g. doctors and dentists

health centre /'helθ ˌsentə/ *noun* a building with various doctors and specialists

health club /'helθ klʌb/ *noun* a club for people who want to improve their health, e.g. by taking exercise and dieting

health insurance /'helθ ɪnˌʃʊərəns/ *noun* insurance which pays the cost of medical treatment if you are ill

health service /'helθ ˌsɜːvɪs/ *noun* an organisation in a district or country which is in charge of providing health care to the public

③ **healthy** /'helθi/ *adj* **1.** not ill ○ *He's healthier than he has ever been.* **2.** making you stay fit and well ○ *the healthiest place in England* ○ *She's keeping to a healthy diet.*

heap /hiːp/ *noun* a pile ○ *a heap of coal* ○ *Step over that heap of rubbish.* ■ *verb* (**heaps, heaping, heaped**) to pile things up ○ *A pile of presents were heaped under the Christmas tree.* ○ *Boxes were heaped up on the station platform.*

① **hear** /hɪə/ (**hears, hearing, heard**) *verb* **1.** to notice sounds with your ears ○ *He heard footsteps behind him.* ○ *You could hear the sound of church bells in the distance.* ○ *I heard her drive up in the car.* ○ *Can you hear him singing in the bath?* **2.** to listen to something ○ *Did you hear the talk on the radio?* ○ *I heard it on the BBC news.* **3.** to get information [~(that)/~about/~from/] ○ *I hear he's got a new job.* ○ *Have you've heard about Joe's promotion?* ○ *We have not heard from them for some time.*

hear of③ *phrasal verb* to know about something ○ *I've heard of a new restaurant in the High Street.* ○ *She's never heard of the Rolling Stones.*

② **hearing** /'hɪərɪŋ/ *noun* the ability to hear ○ *Bats have a very sharp sense of hearing.* ○ *She has hearing difficulties.*

hearing aid /'hɪərɪŋ eɪd/ *noun* an electric device put in your ear to make you hear better

hearing-impaired /ˌhɪərɪŋ ɪm'peəd/ *adj* not able to hear properly

hearsay /'hɪəseɪ/ *noun* what people say, rather than what is true

hearse /hɜːs/ *noun* a vehicle for carrying a coffin

① **heart** /hɑːt/ *noun* **1.** a main organ in the body, which pumps blood around it ○ *She isn't dead – her heart's still beating.* ○ *The doctor listened to his heart.* ○ *He has had heart trouble for years.* **2.** your feelings and emotions ○ *My heart sank when I realised that he hadn't read my letter.* **3.** a centre or middle ○ *The restaurant is in the heart of the old town.* **4.** one of the red sets in a game of cards, with a symbol shaped like a heart ○ *My last card was the ten of hearts.* (NOTE: The other red suit is **diamonds**; **clubs** and **spades** are the black suits.)

heartache /ˈhɑːteɪk/ *noun* great sadness and worry

① **heart attack** /ˈhɑːt əˌtæk/ *noun* a condition where the heart suffers from a reduced blood supply because an artery has become blocked

heartbeat /ˈhɑːtbiːt/ *noun* a regular noise made by the heart as it pumps blood

heartbreak /ˈhɑːtbreɪk/ *noun* great sadness and worry

heartbreaking /ˈhɑːtbreɪkɪŋ/ *adj* very sad and worrying

heartbroken /ˈhɑːtbrəʊkən/ *adj* very sad and upset

heartburn /ˈhɑːtbɜːn/ *noun* indigestion causing a burning feeling in the stomach

③ **heart disease** /ˈhɑːt dɪˌziːz/ *noun* any disease affecting the heart

heartened /ˈhɑːtənd/ *adj* feeling more cheerful or encouraged

heart failure /ˈhɑːt ˌfeɪljə/ *noun* a dangerous condition when the heart has stopped beating

heartfelt /ˈhɑːtfelt/ *adj* sincere

hearth /hɑːθ/ *noun* a hole in the wall of a room where you can light a fire for heating

heartland /ˈhɑːtlænd/ *noun* a region where certain activities are concentrated

heartless /ˈhɑːtləs/ *adj* cruel; not having any pity

heartrending /ˈhɑːtrendɪŋ/ *adj* very sad for someone

heart-stopping /ˈhɑːt ˌstɒpɪŋ/ *adj* very frightening or shocking

heart-to-heart /ˌhɑːt tə ˈhɑːt/ *noun* a serious private talk ○ *I will have a heart-to-heart with him.*

heartwarming /ˈhɑːtwɔːmɪŋ/ *adj* making you feel happy

hearty /ˈhɑːti/ (**heartier, heartiest**) *adj* big (NOTE: + **heartily** *adv*)

② **heat** /hiːt/ *noun* **1.** the state of being hot ○ *The heat of the sun made the ice cream melt.* **2.** one part of a sports competition ○ *There are two heats before the final race.* ■ *verb* (**heats, heating, heated**) to make something hot ○ *Can you heat the soup while I'm getting the table ready?* ○ *The room was heated by a small electric fire.* ○ *Heat the milk to room temperature.*

② **heated** /ˈhiːtɪd/ *adj* **1.** made warm ○ *The car has a heated rear window.* **2.** angry ○ *There was a heated discussion after the meeting.* ○ *The students became very heated during the debate.*

② **heater** /ˈhiːtə/ *noun* a machine for heating a room

heath /hiːθ/ *noun* an area of dry sandy acid soil with low plants such as heather and gorse growing on it

heather /ˈheðə/ *noun* a low plant with mainly purple or pink flowers common in hilly areas

② **heating** /ˈhiːtɪŋ/ *noun* a way of keeping a place such as a house or an office warm

heatwave /ˈhiːtweɪv/ *noun* a period of very hot weather

③ **heave** /hiːv/ *noun* a strong hard pull ○ *One more heave, and we should pull down the tree.* ■ *verb* (**heaves, heaving, heaved**) **1.** to pull something hard ○ *They heaved on the anchor to pull it up.* **2.** to throw something ○ *He heaved a brick through the window.* **3.** to breathe heavily ○ *She heaved a sigh, and picked up the phone.* ○ *We all heaved a collective sigh of relief when he left.*

③ **heaven** /ˈhev(ə)n/ *noun* **1.** a beautiful place believed by some people to be where good people go after death ○ *She believes that when she dies she will go to heaven.* **2.** □ **good heavens** an expression showing you are surprised ○ *Good heavens! It's almost 10 o'clock!* ◇ **for heaven's sake** an expression showing you are annoyed, or that something is important ○ *What are you screaming for? – It's only a little mouse, for heaven's sake.* ○ *For heaven's sake try to be quiet, we don't want the guards to hear us!* ◇ **good heavens** an expression showing you are surprised ○ *Good heavens! It's almost 10 o'clock!*

③ **heavily** /ˈhevɪli/ *adv* **1.** with force ○ *He sat down heavily on the little chair.* **2.** to a great extent; very much ○ *The company was heavily criticised in the press.* ○ *She is heavily in debt.* ○ *It rained heavily during the night.*

① **heavy** /ˈhevi/ *adj* **1.** weighing a lot ○ *This suitcase is so heavy I can hardly lift it.* ○ *She's heavier than I am.* **2.** in large amounts ○ *There has been a heavy demand for the book.* ○ *There was a heavy fall of snow during the night.* ○ *The radio says there is heavy traffic in the centre of town.* □ **to be a heavy smoker** to smoke a lot of cigarettes □ **to be a heavy drinker** to drink a lot of alcohol

heavy-duty /ˌhevi ˈdjuːti/ *adj* made for rough work

heavy-handed /ˌhevi ˈhændɪd/ *adj* not delicate

heavy industry /ˌhevi ˈɪndəstri/ *noun* industry which makes large products such as steel bars, ships or railway lines

heavy metal /ˌhevi ˈmet(ə)l/ *noun* a type of loud music with electric guitars

heavyweight /ˈheviweɪt/ *noun* **1.** the largest and heaviest class of boxer ○ *the heavyweight champion* ○ *a heavyweight title fight* **2.** a person who has a lot of influence ○ *He's the director of the National Theatre – a heavyweight in the theatre world.*

Hebrew /ˈhiːbruː/ *noun* **1.** the official language of Israel **2.** a Jewish person who lived in Israel in ancient times

heckle /ˈhek(ə)l/ (**heckles, heckling, heckled**) *verb* to call out and interrupt a public speaker (NOTE: + **heckler** *n*)

③ **hectare** /ˈhekteə/ *noun* an area of land measuring 100 metres by 100 metres, i.e. 10,000 square metres, or 2.47 acres

hectic /ˈhektɪk/ *adj* very active

he'd /hid, hiːd/ *short form* **1.** he had **2.** he would

hedge /hedʒ/ *noun* a row of bushes planted and kept in an even shape to form a screen round a field or garden ○ *There is a thick hedge round the churchyard.*

hedgehog /ˈhedʒhɒg/ *noun* a small animal with its back covered in spines

hedgerow /ˈhedʒrəʊ/ *noun* a line of bushes forming a hedge round a field or along a country road

hedonist /ˈhiːd(ə)nɪst/ *noun* a person who only lives for pleasure

heed /hiːd/ (**heeds, heeding, heeded**) *verb* to pay attention to something ○ *She didn't heed the doctor's warning.*

heel /hiːl/ *noun* **1.** the back part of the foot ○ *After walking, she got sore heels.* **2.** the back part of a sock or shoe ○ *He's got a hole in the heel of his sock.* ○ *She always wears shoes with high heels* or *high-heeled shoes.*

hefty /ˈhefti/ (**heftier, heftiest**) *adj* **1.** strong ○ *We need a couple of hefty lads to move the table.* **2.** large ○ *He had a hefty pay increase.* ○ *You'll pay a hefty fine if you get caught.*

heifer /ˈhefə/ *noun* a young cow which has not had a calf

② **height** /haɪt/ *noun* **1.** a measurement of how high something is or how tall someone is ○ *The height of the bridge is only three metres.* **2.** the highest point ○ *looking down on the city from the heights around*

heighten /ˈhaɪt(ə)n/ (**heightens, heightening, heightened**) *verb* to increase something

heinous /ˈheɪnəs/ *adj* very bad (*formal*)

heir /eə/ *noun* a man or woman who will inherit something from someone after that person's death ○ *He's the heir to the banking fortune.* ○ *Her heirs divided the estate between them.*

heiress /ˈeəres/ *noun* a woman who will inherit something from someone after that person's death

heirloom /ˈeəluːm/ *noun* a valuable object which has belonged to a family for a long time

③ **held** /held/ past tense and past participle of **hold**

helicopter /ˈhelɪkɒptə/ *noun* an aircraft with a set of large flat blades on top that spin round, making it rise straight up in the air

helium /ˈhiːliəm/ *noun* a light inert gas, often used in balloons

① **hell** /hel/ *noun* **1.** a place where some people believe bad people are sent after they die ○ *Medieval pictures show hell as a burning place.* **2.** a very unpleasant place or experience ○ *It's hell working in the office these days.* **3.** used to emphasise what you are saying (*informal*) ○ *What the hell's been going on here?* ○ *Am I going to lend you £50? Am I hell!* (NOTE: Using expressions that include the word **hell** is offensive to some people.)

he'll /hil, hiːl/ *short form* he will

① **hello** /həˈləʊ/ *interj* used as a greeting ○ *She called hello from the other side of the street.* ○ *Hello Mary! I'm glad to see you.* ○ *When you see her, say hello to her from me.* (NOTE: also spelled **hallo**, **hullo**.)

helm /helm/ *noun* a wheel or bar with which a ship or boat is steered ○ *He put the* *helm hard to starboard as soon as he saw the iceberg.*

helmet /ˈhelmɪt/ *noun* a solid hat used as a protection

① **help** /help/ *noun* **1.** something which makes it easier for you to do something [~with/~in] ○ *Do you need any help with moving the furniture?* ○ *She finds the word-processor a great help in writing her book.* **2.** the act of making it easier for someone to do something ○ *People were calling for help from the ruins of the house.* ○ *The nurses offered help to people injured in the accident.* ■ *verb* (**helps, helping, helped**) to make it easier for someone to do something ○ *The government wants to help small businesses.* ○ *Your father can help you with your homework.* □ **to help somebody (to) do something** to do something with somebody else so that it is easier for them ○ *One of my friends helped me move the piano into the bedroom.*

help out *phrasal verb* to help someone in an emergency

help desk /ˈhelp desk/ *noun* a service which helps people with computer problems

helper /ˈhelpə/ *noun* a person who helps someone do a particular job or task, especially without being paid

② **helpful** /ˈhelpf(ə)l/ *adj* useful or giving help to someone ○ *She made some helpful suggestions.* ○ *They were very helpful when we moved house.*

③ **helping** /ˈhelpɪŋ/ *noun* an amount of food for one person ○ *The helpings in this restaurant are very small.* ○ *Children's helpings are not as large as those for adults.*

② **helpless** /ˈhelpləs/ *adj* not able to do anything to make a bad situation better

helpline /ˈhelplaɪn/ *noun* a special phone number for people to call when they need help

hem /hem/ *noun* the sewn edge of a piece of clothing, e.g. a skirt or dress ○ *She was wearing a long skirt, with the hem touching the floor.* ■ *verb* (**hems, hemming, hemmed**) to make the hem of a piece of clothing, e.g. a skirt or dress ○ *I've almost finished the skirt, it just needs to be hemmed.*

hemisphere /ˈhemɪsfɪə/ *noun* half of a sphere

hemp /hemp/ *noun* a plant used to make ropes and sacks

hen /hen/ *noun* an adult female chicken ○ *The hens were scared by the fox.* ○ *Look, one of the hens has laid an egg!*

② **hence** /hens/ *adv* in the future ○ *Five months hence, the situation should be better.*

henchman /ˈhentʃmən/ (*plural* **henchmen**) *noun* a political assistant or bodyguard; a person who assists or protects an important person

hen night /ˈhen naɪt/, **hen party** *noun* a party for women only (NOTE: A party for men only, is a **stag party** *or* **stag night**.)

hepatitis /ˌhepəˈtaɪtɪs/ *noun* an infectious disease of the liver

① **her** /ə, hə, hɜː/ *object pronoun* referring to a female ○ *There's a parcel for her in reception.* ○ *Did you see her?* ○ *He told her to go away.* ■ *adj* belonging to a female, a ship or a country ○ *Someone has stolen all her luggage.* ○ *Have you seen her father?* ○ *The dog doesn't want to eat her food.* ○ *France is helping her businesses to sell more abroad.*

herald /ˈherəld/ (**heralds, heralding, heralded**) *verb* to be a sign of something coming ○ *dark clouds that herald stormy weather* ○ *The statistics seem to herald an end to the recession.*

herb /hɜːb/ *noun* a plant used to give flavour to food, or as a medicine

herbicide /ˈhɜːbɪsaɪd/ *noun* a chemical which kills plants, especially weeds

herbivore /ˈhɜːbɪvɔː/ *noun* an animal which eats plants

herd /hɜːd/ *noun* a group of animals, especially cows ○ *Herds of cattle were grazing on the hillside.* (NOTE: Do not confuse with **heard**. The word **herd** is usually used with cattle; for sheep, goats, and birds, the word to use is **flock**.)

① **here** /hɪə/ *adv* **1.** in this place ○ *I'll sit here in the shade and wait for you.* ○ *Here are the keys you lost.* ○ *I'll put the book down here next to your computer.* ○ *They have been living here in England for a long time.* **2.** to this place ○ *Come here at once!* ○ *Can you bring the chairs here, please?* ○ *Here comes the bus!* ◇ **here you are** take this ○ *Here you are, today's newspaper!*

hereditary /həˈredɪt(ə)ri/ *adj* **1.** passed from parent to child biologically **2.** passed from parent to child as a legal right ○ *a hereditary title*

heredity /həˈredɪti/ *noun* the occurrence of physical or mental characteristics in children which are inherited from their parents

heresy /'herəsi/ *noun* a wrong opinion or belief, especially wrong religious belief

heretic /'herətɪk/ *noun* a person who holds wrong religious beliefs

heritage /'herɪtɪdʒ/ *noun* the national treasure passed from one generation to the next

hermit /'hɜːmɪt/ *noun* a person who chooses to live alone outside the community

hernia /'hɜːniə/ *noun* a medical condition in which an organ bulges through a hole or weakness in the wall which surrounds it

③ **hero** /'hɪərəʊ/ (*plural* **heroes**) *noun* **1.** a brave man ○ *The hero of the fire was the man who managed to rescue the children from an upstairs room.* **2.** the main male character in something such as a book, play or film ○ *The hero of the story is a little boy.*

heroic /hɪ'rəʊɪk/ *adj* like a hero

heroics /hɪ'rəʊɪks/ *plural noun* very brave actions

heroin /'herəʊɪn/ *noun* a strong addictive illegal drug made from poppies (NOTE: Do not confuse with **heroine**.)

heroine /'herəʊɪn/ *noun* **1.** a brave woman ○ *The heroine of the accident was a passing cyclist who pulled the children out of the burning car.* **2.** the main female character in something such as a book, play or film ○ *The heroine of the film is a school teacher.* (NOTE: Do not confuse with **heroin**.)

heroism /'herəʊɪz(ə)m/ *noun* bravery

heron /'herən/ *noun* a tall, usually grey, water bird with a long neck and long legs

herpes /'hɜːpiːz/ *noun* a disease caused by a virus, which causes small blisters

herring /'herɪŋ/ *noun* a small silver sea fish ○ *She had grilled herrings for dinner.*

① **hers** /hɜːz/ *pron* belonging to her ○ *That watch is hers, not mine.*

① **herself** /ə'self, hə'self/ *pron* used for referring back to a female subject ○ *The manager wrote to me herself.* ○ *Did your sister enjoy herself?* ○ *She's too young to be able to dress herself.*

hertz /hɜːts/ *noun* the standard unit of frequency of radio waves (NOTE: no plural)

③ **he's** /hiz, hiːz/ *short form* **1.** he has **2.** he is

hesitant /'hezɪt(ə)nt/ *adj* slow and cautious

hesitate /'hezɪteɪt/ (**hesitates, hesitating, hesitated**) *verb* to be slow to speak or make a decision ○ *He hesitated for a moment and then said 'no'.* ○ *She's hesitating about whether to accept the job.*

hesitation /ˌhezɪ'teɪʃ(ə)n/ *noun* the act of waiting and not deciding

heterosexual /ˌhetərəʊ'sekʃuəl/ *adj, noun* sexually attracted to people of the opposite sex. Compare **bisexual**, **homosexual**

heterosexuality /ˌhetərəʊsekʃu'ælɪti/ *noun* the fact of being heterosexual

hexagon /'heksəgən/ *noun* (*in geometry*) a shape with six sides

hey! /heɪ/ *interj* showing a greeting or surprise ○ *Hey, you! What are you doing there?* ○ *Hey! That's my chair!*

heyday /'heɪdeɪ/ *noun* a time of greatest success, popularity or power

③ **HGV** *abbr* heavy goods vehicle

hi /haɪ/ *interj* showing a greeting ○ *Hi! I'm your tour leader.* ○ *Hi, Mary! How are you today?* ○ *Say hi to her from me.*

hiatus /haɪ'eɪtəs/ (*plural* **hiatuses** or *same*) *noun* a gap or interruption

hibernate /'haɪbəneɪt/ (**hibernates, hibernating, hibernated**) *verb* (*of an animal*) to sleep during the winter, either completely unconscious or semi conscious (NOTE: + **hibernation** *n*)

hiccup /'hɪkʌp/, **hiccough** *noun* **1.** a sudden high sound that you sometimes make in your throat, e.g. if you have been eating too quickly ○ *She had an attack of hiccups.* ○ *He got the hiccups from laughing too much.* **2.** a small thing which goes wrong ○ *There has been a slight hiccup in the delivery of our supplies.* ■ *verb* (**hiccups, hiccupping, hiccupped**) to make a hiccup ○ *She patted him on the back when he suddenly started to hiccup.* ○ *He hiccupped so loudly that everyone in the restaurant stared at him.*

① **hid** /hɪd/ past tense of **hide**

① **hidden** /'hɪd(ə)n/ *adj* which cannot be seen or found easily ○ *There's a hidden safe in the wall behind his desk.* ○ *They say there's some hidden treasure in the castle.* ◊ **hide**

hidden agenda /ˌhɪd(ə)n ə'dʒendə/ *noun* a secret reason for doing something which will be to your advantage

① **hide** /haɪd/ (**hides, hiding, hid, hidden** or **hid**) *verb* **1.** to put something where no one can see or find it [~behind/under/in etc] ○ *She hid the presents in the kitchen.* ○ *Someone has hidden my car keys.* **2.** to put yourself where no one can see or find you [~behind/under/in etc/~from] ○ *The children hid from us behind the bushes.*

hide away *phrasal verb* to go to a place

where you can be away from other people

hide-and-seek /ˌhaɪd ən 'siːk/ *noun* a children's game, in which one person hides and the others try to find him or her

hideous /'hɪdiəs/ *adj* extremely unpleasant to look at ○ *Where did she get that hideous dress?*

hide-out /'haɪdaʊt/ *noun* a secret place where you cannot be found

② **hiding** /'haɪdɪŋ/ *noun* a situation in which you have put yourself where no one can find you ○ *He stayed in hiding for three days until the soldiers left the village.* ○ *They decided to go into hiding for a time until the police called off their search.*

③ **hierarchy** /'haɪərɑːki/ *noun* **1.** arrangement in ranks ○ *There is a strict hierarchy in the army.* **2.** the people in the upper ranks of an organisation ○ *The party hierarchy met to elect a new leader.* ○ *The church hierarchy has condemned the attack.*

hi-fi /ˌhaɪ'faɪ/ (*plural* **hi-fis**) *noun* **1.** a very accurate reproduction of sound by equipment such as a CD player and amplifier ○ *The company is a leading manufacturer of hi-fi audio equipment.* **2.** a set of equipment for playing CDs or cassettes or for listening to the radio ○ *He played the CD on his hi-fi.*

① **high** /haɪ/ *adj* **1.** far above other things ○ *Everest is the highest mountain in the world.* ○ *The new building is 20 storeys high.* ○ *The kitchen has a high ceiling.* ○ *The door is not high enough for us to get the wardrobe into the bedroom.* ◊ **height** (NOTE: **High** is used with figures: *the mountain is 1,000 metres high.* **High** also refers to things that are a long way above the ground: *a high mountain, high clouds.* For people and narrow things like trees use **tall**: *a tall man.*) **2.** large in quantity ○ *the high level of unemployment in the country* ○ *He earns a high income.* ○ *High prices put customers off.* ○ *The car shakes when going at high speeds.* ○ *The price of petrol is higher every year.* ■ *adv* above; up in the air ○ *The sun rose high in the sky.* ○ *The bird flew higher and higher.*

highbrow /'haɪbraʊ/ *adj* with a high intellectual content

high chair /haɪ 'tʃeə/ *noun* a baby's chair at a level with a table, sometimes with a tray in front of the baby

high-class /ˌhaɪ 'klɑːs/ *adj* of very good quality

Higher /'haɪə/ *noun* (*in Scotland*) an examination in various subjects taken in fifth or sixth year at secondary school

③ **higher education** /ˌhaɪər edjʊ'keɪʃ(ə)n/ *noun* education in universities and colleges

high five /haɪ 'faɪv/ *noun* a greeting in which two people each raise an arm and slap palms

high-flyer /haɪ 'flaɪə/ *noun* a person who has great potential and ambition

high-grade /'haɪ greɪd/ *adj* of a very good quality

high-handed /ˌhaɪ 'hændɪd/ *adj* with no respect for other people or customs

high heels /haɪ 'hiːlz/ *plural noun* very high thin heels, on women's shoes ○ *You are not allowed to walk on the polished floor of the museum in high heels.*

highlands /'haɪləndz/ *plural noun* a mountain region ○ *the Malaysian Highlands* ○ *the Scottish Highlands*

high-level /'haɪ ˌlev(ə)l/ *adj* important; composed of important people

③ **highlight** /'haɪlaɪt/ *noun* the most important or interesting event ○ *The highlight of our tour of Greece was our visit to the Parthenon.* ■ *verb* (**highlights, highlighting, highlighted**) **1.** to draw attention to something ○ *The report highlights various problems.* **2.** to make part of a text stand out from the rest ○ *The headings are highlighted in bold.* ○ *The report highlights various problems.*

③ **highlighter** /'haɪlaɪtə/ *noun* a marker pen; a coloured felt pen used to highlight text

highlights /'haɪlaɪts/ *plural noun* **1.** a selection of the best parts of a sporting event which are repeated on TV ○ *highlights of this afternoon's game* **2.** streaks in your hair which have been dyed a pale colour **3.** characters which stand out from the text on a screen by being brighter than the rest

② **highly** /'haɪli/ *adv* used before some adjectives to mean 'very well' ○ *highly priced meals* ○ *The restaurant has been highly recommended.* ○ *Their employees are not very highly paid.*

high-pitched /ˌhaɪ 'pɪtʃt/ *adj* making a shrill sound

high point /'haɪ pɒɪnt/ *noun* the best moment

high-powered /ˌhaɪ 'paʊəd/ *adj* very powerful

high-profile /ˌhaɪ 'prəʊfaɪl/ *adj* who is often in the news

high-rise /'haɪ raɪz/ *adj* with many storeys

high school /'haɪ skuːl/ *noun* **1.** a secondary school for children aged from 11 to 18 **2.** *US* a secondary school, from grade 9 to grade 12 ○ *He's in grade 10* or *tenth grade at high school.*

high season /ˌhaɪ 'siːz(ə)n/ *noun* a period when there are lots of travellers and when fares are high, usually the period from July to September. Compare **low season**

① **high street** /'haɪ striːt/, **High Street** *noun* the most important street in a village or town, where shops and banks are (NOTE: often written **High St.** The US term is **Main Street**.)

③ **high tech** /ˌhaɪ 'tek/ *adj* referring to high technology

high technology /ˌhaɪ tek'nɒlədʒi/ *noun* advanced technology as used in industry, e.g. the use of electronics and robots

high tide /ˌhaɪ 'taɪd/, **high water** *noun* the points when the level of the sea is at its highest or at its lowest

② **highway** /'haɪweɪ/ *noun* a main public road ○ *A footbridge was built over the highway.*

hijack /'haɪdʒæk/ (**hijacks, hijacking, hijacked**), **highjack** *verb* to take control of a vehicle by force ○ *The men hijacked the lorry and left the driver by the road.* ○ *They hijacked an aircraft and ordered the pilot to fly to Moscow.* (NOTE: + **hijacker** *n*)

hike /haɪk/ *noun* **1.** a vigorous walk ○ *We went for a 10-mile hike in the mountains.* **2.** an increase ○ *a price hike* ■ *verb* (**hikes, hiking, hiked**) **1.** to go for a vigorous walk ○ *They were hiking in the Pyrenees when the accident happened.* **2.** to increase prices ○ *Petrol companies have hiked up their prices.*

hiking /'haɪkɪŋ/ *noun* the practice of going for long walks for pleasure

hilarious /hɪ'leəriəs/ *adj* very funny ○ *I thought the play was hilarious.*

② **hill** /hɪl/ *noun* a piece of high land (*informal*) ○ *The hills are covered with spring flowers.* ○ *If you climb to the top of the hill you will get a good view of the valley.*

hillside /'hɪlsaɪd/ *noun* the sloping side of a hill

hilltop /'hɪltɒp/ *noun* the top of a hill

hilt /hɪlt/ *noun* a sword handle ○ *He stood for the photograph with his hand on the hilt of his sword.*

① **him** /ɪm, hɪm/ *object pronoun* referring to a male ○ *Tell him there's a letter waiting for him.* ○ *Have you spoken to him today?* ○ *That's him! – The man with the beard.*

① **himself** /ɪm'self, hɪm'self/ *pron* used for referring back to a male subject ○ *I was served by the manager himself.* ○ *The doctor has got flu himself.* ○ *Did your brother enjoy himself?*

hinder /'hɪndə/ (**hinders, hindering, hindered**) *verb* to make it difficult for someone to do something ○ *Snow hindered the efforts of the rescuers.* ○ *This hostile situation is hindering plans for peace in the region.*

hindrance /'hɪndrəns/ *noun* something which hinders

hindsight /'haɪndsaɪt/ *noun* the act of realising something too late, after it has happened

Hinduism /'hɪnduːɪz(ə)m/ *noun* the main religion of India, in which people worship several gods

hinge /hɪndʒ/ *noun* a piece of metal used to hold something, e.g. a door, window or lid, so that it can swing open and shut ○ *That hinge squeaks – it needs some oil.* ○ *They lifted the door off its hinges.*

hint /hɪnt/ *noun* **1.** something you say that reveals information in an indirect way ○ *He didn't give a hint as to where he was going on holiday.* □ **to drop a hint** to make a suggestion ○ *She's been dropping hints about what she wants for her birthday.* □ **to take a hint** to accept a suggestion ○ *He took the hint and offered to pay for the lamp he broke.* **2.** a piece of advice or a suggestion ○ *She gave me some useful hints about painting furniture.* ○ *I don't know what to give her for her birthday – have you any hints?* ■ *verb* (**hints, hinting, hinted**) to say something in a way that makes people guess what you mean ○ *She hinted that her sister was pregnant.*

hinterland /'hɪntəlænd/ *noun* an area inland from a sea port or around a large town

hip /hɪp/ *noun* the part of the body where your legs join your waist ○ *The tailor measured him round the hips.* ■ *adj* (**hipper, hippest**) very fashionable (*slang*) ○ *That's a very hip shirt she's wearing.*

hip hop /'hɪp hɒp/ *noun* a kind of popular culture which started among African-Americans and which involves rap and graffiti art

hippo /ˈhɪpəʊ/ (*plural* **hippos**) *noun* same as **hippopotamus**

hippopotamus /hɪpəˈpɒtəməs/ (*plural* **hippopotamuses** or **hippopotami**) *noun* a large heavy African animal which spends most of its time submerged in water, but comes onto dry land to graze

③ **hire** /ˈhaɪə/ *verb* (**hires, hiring, hired**) **1.** (*of a borrower*) to pay money to use something for a time ○ *She hired a car for the weekend.* ○ *He was driving a hired car when the accident happened.* **2.** to employ someone to work for you ○ *We've hired three more sales assistants.* ○ *They hired a small company to paint their offices.* ■ *noun* the act of paying money to rent something such as a car, a boat or a piece of equipment

① **his** /ɪz, hɪz/ *adj* belonging to him ○ *He's lost all his money.* ○ *Have you met his mother?* ○ *Our dog wants his food.* ■ *pron* belonging to him ○ *That watch is his, not mine.*

③ **hiss** /hɪs/ (**hisses, hissing, hissed**) *verb* **1.** to make a hissing sound ○ *The snake hissed as we came nearer.* **2.** to show disapproval of someone or something by making an 's' sound ○ *The audience began to hiss.* ○ *She was hissed off the stage.*

③ **historian** /hɪˈstɔːriən/ *noun* a person who studies or writes history

③ **historic** /hɪˈstɒrɪk/ *adj* important in the life of a person or place and likely to be remembered (NOTE: can be preceded by **an** in formal style: *The opening of the new bridge was an historic event for the town.*)

② **historical** /hɪˈstɒrɪk(ə)l/ *adj* relating to history ○ *He likes books of historical interest.*

① **history** /ˈhɪst(ə)ri/ *noun* **1.** the study of the past ○ *He is studying Greek history.* ○ *She failed her history exam.* ○ *She teaches history at London University.* **2.** a book which tells the story of what happened in the past ○ *He wrote a history of the French Revolution.*

① **hit** /hɪt/ *noun* someone or something that is very popular, e.g. a song, a film or a performer [~with] ○ *The song rapidly became a hit.* ○ *She was a hit with the old people's club.* ■ *verb* (**hits, hitting, hit**) **1.** to knock something or someone [~at/~for/~with] ○ *The car hit the tree.* ○ *She hit him on the head with a bottle.* ○ *She hit the ball so hard that we couldn't find it.* ○ *I hit my head on the cupboard door.* **2.** to cause someone to realise something [~(that)] ○ *It suddenly hit her that now she was divorced she would have to live alone.*

hit back③ *phrasal verb* **1.** to hit someone who has hit you ○ *They hit him so hard that he was unable to hit back.* **2.** to do something as a reaction to something ○ *When the supermarket chain lowered their prices, the other chains hit back by lowering prices too.* ○ *He hit back at the inspectors, saying that their report was biased.*

hit-and-run /ˌhɪt ən ˈrʌn/ *noun* an accident in which a driver knocks someone down and does not stop to give help

hitch /hɪtʃ/ *noun* an unexpected temporary problem ○ *There's a hitch, and the wedding has been postponed.* ■ *verb* (**hitches, hitching, hitched**) to attach one thing to another ○ *The caravan was hitched to the car.*

HIV *noun* the virus which causes AIDS. Full form **human immunodeficiency virus**

hiya /ˈhaɪə/ *interj* showing a greeting

hm, hmm *interj* showing a pause while the speaker thinks about something

hoard /hɔːd/ *noun* a store of something such as food or money, which has been collected ○ *They discovered a hoard of gold coins in the field.* ■ *verb* (**hoards, hoarding, hoarded**) to buy and store supplies of something essential that you think you will need in a crisis ○ *Everyone started hoarding fuel during the strike.* (NOTE: Do not confuse with **horde**.)

hoarding /ˈhɔːdɪŋ/ *noun* **1.** the act of buying stocks of something, e.g. food or money, in case supply may be difficult **2.** a large advertising board in a street

hoarse /hɔːs/ *adj* (*of a voice*) which sounds rough (NOTE: Do not confuse with **horse**.)

hoax /həʊks/ *noun* a trick played on someone as a joke or to annoy him or her ○ *The police and fire brigade arrived but the bomb was just a hoax.* ○ *The ambulance answered a hoax telephone call.*

hob /hɒb/ *noun* a flat top on a cooker ○ *Our new cooker has a ceramic hob.* ○ *Do not use abrasive cleaner on the hob.*

hobble /ˈhɒb(ə)l/ (**hobbles, hobbling, hobbled**) *verb* **1.** to walk with difficulty ○ *He hobbled into the room on crutches.* **2.** to attach a horse's legs together ○ *The horses were hobbled so that they couldn't run away.*

③ **hobby** /ˈhɒbi/ (*plural* **hobbies**) *noun* an enjoyable activity which you do in your spare time

hockey /ˈhɒki/ *noun* a team game played on grass, where you try to hit a small ball into your opponents' goal using a long stick which is curved at the end ○ *He played in the hockey team at school.*

hoe /həʊ/ *noun* a garden tool with a long handle and small sharp blade, used to break up the surface of soil or cut off weeds ○ *Use a sharp hoe to remove the weeds between your peas.* (NOTE: + **hoe** *v*)

hog /hɒg/ *noun* **1.** a castrated male pig **2.** *US* any pig ○ *Hogs are traded on the Chicago exchange.* ■ *verb* (**hogs, hogging, hogged**) to monopolise something; to take more of something than you should (*informal*) ○ *He was hogging the middle of the road.* ○ *Stop hogging the biscuits – we'd like some too!* ○ *She's always hogging the limelight.*

hoist /hɔɪst/ (**hoists, hoisting, hoisted**) *verb* to lift something or someone using special equipment or a lot of force ○ *The box was hoisted up on a rope.* ○ *It's time to hoist the flag.*

① **hold** /həʊld/ *verb* (**holds, holding, held**) **1.** to keep something or someone tight, especially in your hand ○ *She was holding the baby in her arms.* ○ *She held her ticket between her teeth as she was carrying suitcases in both hands.* ○ *Hold tight – the machine is going to start.* ○ *He held the bag close to his chest.* **2.** to be large enough to contain a certain quantity of things or people ○ *The bottle holds two litres.* ○ *The box will hold four pairs of shoes.* ○ *Will the car hold eight people?* ○ *The plane holds 250 passengers.* **3.** to make an event happen ○ *They are holding a party for their wedding anniversary.* ○ *The meeting will be held next Tuesday in the town hall.* ○ *We are holding the village fete next week.* **4.** to own something ○ *She holds a valid driving licence.* ○ *He holds the record for the 2000 metres.* **5.** to keep someone inside ○ *The prisoners were held in police cells overnight.* □ **to hold your breath** to keep air in your lungs, e.g. in order to go under water ○ *She held her breath under water for a minute.* ○ *We're all holding our breath to see if he wins a gold medal.* ■ *noun* **1.** the bottom part of a ship or an aircraft, in which goods or luggage are stored ○ *You can't take all that luggage with you – it has to go in the hold.* **2.** the act of keeping something tightly in your hand ○ *He lost his hold on the ladder.* ○ *Keep tight hold of the bag, we don't want it stolen.* □ **to get hold of someone** to manage to contact someone by telephone ○ *I tried to get hold of the doctor but he was out.* □ **to get hold of something** to find something which you want to use ○ *Do you know where I can get hold of a ladder?* □ **to take hold** to take control ○ *The fire took hold rapidly.* □ **to take hold of something** to grip something ○ *Take hold of my hand.*

hold back③ *phrasal verb* **1.** not to go forwards, or stop someone or something from going forwards ○ *Most of the crowd held back until they saw it was safe.* **2.** not to tell someone something ○ *She held back important information from the police.*

hold down③ *phrasal verb* to keep something at a low level ○ *We are holding our prices down.*

hold on① *phrasal verb* **1.** to hold something tightly ○ *She held on to the rope with both hands.* ○ *Hold on to your purse in the crowd.* ○ *Hold on tight, we're turning!* **2.** to wait ○ *Hold on a moment, I'll get my umbrella.* ○ *Do you want to speak to the manager? Hold on, I'll find him for you.*

hold out③ *phrasal verb* **1.** to move something towards someone ○ *Hold out your plate to be served.* ○ *He held out his hand but she refused to shake it.* **2.** to manage to be strong enough ○ *The castle held out for ten weeks against a huge enemy army.*

hold over *phrasal verb* to postpone something

hold up① *phrasal verb* **1.** to lift someone or something ○ *He held up his hand.* ○ *He held the little boy up so that he could see the procession.* **2.** to support something ○ *The roof is held up by those pillars.* **3.** to make someone or something late ○ *The planes were held up by fog.* ○ *Government ministers are holding up the deal.* **4.** to use a gun to make someone give up all their money ○ *Six gunmen held up the security van.*

holdall /ˈhəʊldɔːl/ *noun* a soft bag for carrying things such as clothes when travelling

② **holder** /ˈhəʊldə/ *noun* **1.** something which holds things ○ *Put the pen back into its holder.* **2.** a person who holds something ○ *She is a British passport holder* or *the holder of a British passport.* ○ *He is the world record holder in the javelin.*

③ **holding** /ˈhəʊldɪŋ/ *noun* an investment owned

holding company /ˈhəʊldɪŋ ˌkʌmp(ə)ni/ *noun* a company which owns shares in other companies

③ **hold-up** /ˈhəʊld ʌp/ *noun* **1.** a delay; an occasion on which something is later than planned ○ *Long hold-ups are expected because of road works on the motorway.* ○ *There's been a hold-up and the goods won't arrive till next week.* **2.** an occasion on which a person with a gun steals money from someone ○ *The gang carried out three hold-ups in the same day.*

① **hole** /həʊl/ *noun* an opening or a space in something [~in] ○ *You've got a hole in your sock.* ○ *We all peeped through the hole in the fence.* ○ *Rabbits live in holes in the ground.*

hole up *phrasal verb* to hide from someone (*slang*)

hole-in-the-wall /ˌhəʊl ɪn ðə ˈwɔːl/ (*plural* **holes-in-the-wall**) *noun* a machine in the outside wall of a bank where customers can get money from their account

① **holiday** /ˈhɒlɪdeɪ/ *noun* **1.** a period when you do not work, and sometimes go and stay in a different place ○ *When are you taking your holiday* or *When are you planning to go on holiday?* ○ *He's going to Spain on holiday.* ○ *We always spend our holidays in the mountains.* ○ *How many days' holiday do you have each year?* **2.** a day on which most people do not work because of laws or religious rules ○ *The office is closed for the Christmas holiday.*

holidaymaker /ˈhɒlɪdeɪmeɪkə/ *noun* a person who is on holiday

holistic /həʊˈlɪstɪk/ *adj* dealing with a medical or social problem as a whole rather than only looking at one aspect of it ○ *The committee has been calling for a more holistic approach to learning.*

hollow /ˈhɒləʊ/ *adj* with a hole inside ○ *a hollow log* ○ *If you tap the box it sounds hollow.*

hollow out *phrasal verb* to remove the inside part of something so as to make it hollow

holly /ˈhɒli/ *noun* a small evergreen tree with shiny dark green prickly leaves and bright red berries

Hollywood /ˈhɒliwʊd/ *noun* a town in California, the centre of the American film industry

holocaust /ˈhɒləkɔːst/ *noun* total destruction, especially by fire or nuclear war ○ *A nuclear holocaust would cause unimaginable suffering.*

Holocaust /ˈhɒləkɔːst/ *noun* the mass killing of the Jews during the Second World War (NOTE: always written with **the**)

hologram /ˈhɒləgræm/ *noun* a three-dimensional picture made using laser beams

holster /ˈhəʊlstə/ *noun* a leather holder for a revolver

③ **holy** /ˈhəʊli/ *adj* relating to religion or the church ○ *They went to ask a holy man his advice.*

homage /ˈhɒmɪdʒ/ *noun* **1.** respect for someone **2.** an action or work of art that is made to show respect to someone ○ *This song is a homage to my parents.*

① **home** /həʊm/ *noun* **1.** the place where you live or where your parents live ○ *Their home is a flat in the centre of London.* ○ *Will you be at home tomorrow evening?* ○ *When do you leave home for work in the morning?* ○ *I like to go home for the holidays.* □ **to make yourself at home** to behave as if you were in your own home ○ *He lay down on my sofa, opened a bottle of beer, and made himself at home.* **2.** a house ○ *They are building fifty new homes on the edge of the village.* **3.** a house where people are looked after ○ *My aunt has moved to an old people's home.* **4.** [~for/~of] □ **at home** (*in sports*) on the local sports ground ○ *Our team is playing at home next Saturday.* ■ *adv* towards the place where you usually live ○ *We've got to go home now.* ○ *He usually gets home by 7 o'clock.* ○ *Don't send it – I'll take it home with me.* ○ *If you don't want to walk, you can always take the bus home.* (NOTE: used without a preposition: *He went home* or *She's coming home.*) ■ *adj* referring to where you live or where you were born ○ *My home town is Birmingham.* ○ *Send the letter to my home address, not to my office.*

homecoming /ˈhəʊmkʌmɪŋ/ *noun* the act of coming home

homegrown /ˈhəʊmgrəʊn/ *adj* grown in your own garden

home improvement /həʊm ɪm ˈpruːvmənt/ *noun* a change which you make to your home to make it better

homeland /ˈhəʊmlænd/ *noun* the home of a people

home language /həʊm ˈlæŋgwɪdʒ/ *noun* the language which you first learn to speak as a child (*US*)

homeless /ˈhəʊmləs/ *adj* with nowhere to live ○ *The council has a duty to house homeless families.*

homely /ˈhəʊmli/ *adj* **1.** simple but pleasant ○ *The accommodation was homely and* *unpretentious.* ○ *The pub serves good homely food.* **2.** US (*of a person*) not attractive ○ *She's a homely girl.*

homemade /ˌhəʊm'meɪd/ *adj* made at home and not bought

③ **home page** /'həʊm peɪdʒ/ *noun* the first page of a website, which gives details of the person or organisation that the website belongs to

home rule /ˌhəʊm 'ruːl/ *noun* a system of government in which a country is ruled by itself rather than by another country

Home Secretary /ˌhəʊm 'sekrət(ə)rɪ/ *noun* the British government minister in charge of the Home Office (NOTE: In other countries, this minister is usually called the **Minister of the Interior**. In the USA, he is the **Secretary of the Interior**.)

homesick /'həʊmsɪk/ *adj* feeling sad because you are away from home

homestead /'həʊmsted/ *noun* a farmhouse and land

home town /həʊm 'taʊn/ *noun* the town where you live or where you were born

home truths /həʊm 'truːðz/ *plural noun* unpleasant facts about someone, which someone else tells him or her ○ *I had to tell her a few home truths.*

② **homework** /'həʊmwɜːk/ *noun* work which you take home from school to do in the evening ○ *Have you finished your maths homework?* ○ *I haven't got any homework today, so I can watch TV.* (NOTE: no plural)

homicidal /ˌhɒmɪ'saɪd(ə)l/ *adj* likely to kill someone

homicide /'hɒmɪsaɪd/ *noun* murder, the killing of someone

homogeneous /ˌhəʊməʊ'dʒiːniəs/ *adj* all of the same type

homonym /'hɒmənɪm/ *noun* a word spelled and pronounced the same as another but which has a different meaning

homophobia /ˌhəʊməʊ'fəʊbiə/ *noun* a fear of and hostility towards homosexuals

homophone /'hɒməfəʊn/ *noun* a word which is pronounced the same as another, but which is spelt differently or has a different meaning

homosexual /ˌhəʊməʊ'sekʃuəl/ *adj* sexually attracted to people of the same sex. Compare **bisexual**, **heterosexual**

hone /həʊn/ (**hones, honing, honed**) *verb* **1.** to improve something over a long period ○ *His technique has been honed through years of practice.* **2.** to sharpen and smooth something

① **honest** /'ɒnɪst/ *adj* **1.** telling the truth ○ *He was honest with the police and told them what he had done.* **2.** tending to tell people the truth; treating people fairly ○ *I wouldn't buy a car from that garage – I'm not sure they're completely honest.*

① **honestly** /'ɒnɪstli/ *adv* **1.** in an open and honest way **2.** used to express a feeling of being annoyed ○ *Honestly, you might have told me sooner!*

honesty /'ɒnɪsti/ *noun* the quality of being honest ○ *I admire him for his honesty in saying the job was too difficult for him.*

③ **honey** /'hʌni/ *noun* a sweet substance produced by bees ○ *I like honey on toast.* ○ *Greek cakes are often made with honey.*

③ **honeymoon** /'hʌnimuːn/ *noun* a holiday taken immediately after a wedding ○ *They went on their honeymoon to Corsica.*

honk /hɒŋk/ (**honks, honking, honked**) *verb* to make a noise like a goose or with a car horn ○ *Geese flew overhead, honking loudly.* ○ *He honked as he drove past.* (NOTE: + **honk** *n*)

honor /'ɒnə/ *noun, verb* US spelling of **honour**

honorary /'ɒnərəri/ *adj* **1.** not paid a salary ○ *She's the honorary secretary of the society.* **2.** a title which shows respect ○ *He's the honorary president of the company.*

③ **honour** /'ɒnə/ *noun* **1.** the practice of acting according to what you think is right ○ *He's a man of honour.* **2.** something that you are proud of ○ *It is an honour for me to be invited here today.* ■ *verb* **1.** to show your respect for someone ○ *to honour the dead* **2.** to give someone an award to show that you respect them ○ *He was honoured by the university.* **3.** to do what you promised ○ *He honoured the agreement and gave the staff a pay rise.*

honourable /'ɒn(ə)rəb(ə)l/ *adj* **1.** who or which can be respected ○ *He lived the rest of his life in honourable retirement.* ○ *He did the honourable thing and resigned.* (NOTE: The US spelling is **honorable**.) **2.** a title used when one MP addresses another in Parliament ○ *The honourable Member for Putney would do well to remember the conditions in his constituency.* (NOTE: usually shortened to **Hon.** in this meaning)

honoured /'ɒnəd/ *adj* pleased and proud (NOTE: The US spelling is **honored**.)

Hons *abbr* honours degree

hood /hʊd/ *noun* **1.** a loose piece of clothing to cover your head ○ *He has a blue coat with a hood.* **2.** a folding roof on something such as a car or pram ○ *Let's put down the hood, it's very hot.* **3.** *US* a metal cover for the front part of a car, covering the engine ○ *He lifted the hood to see what was wrong with the motor.*

hoof /huːf/ (*plural* **hooves**) *noun* the part of the foot of a horse, cow and many other animals

③ **hook** /hʊk/ *noun* **1.** a bent piece of metal for hanging things on ○ *Hang your coat on the hook behind the door.* **2.** a very small piece of thin bent metal, attached to a line for catching fish ○ *The fish ate the worm but didn't swallow the hook.*

hooker /ˈhʊkə/ *noun* **1.** a player in the centre of a rugby scrum, who has to try to kick the ball backwards ○ *The English hooker got the ball and from there they scored a try.* **2.** a prostitute; a woman who receives money for sexual intercourse ○ *hookers standing on street corners* .

hooligan /ˈhuːlɪgən/ *noun* a wild young man (*informal*)

hoop /huːp/ *noun* a ring, often a large one (NOTE: Do not confuse with **whoop**.)

hooray! /hʊˈreɪ/ *interj* showing enthusiasm ○ *Hooray, it's the first day of the holidays!* ○ *Hip, hip, hooray!*

hoot /huːt/ *noun* **1.** a call made by an owl ○ *the ghostly hoot of the owl in the night* **2.** the sound of a car horn ○ *The sudden hoot of a car horn made her jump.* ■ *verb* (**hoots, hooting, hooted**) **1.** (*of an owl*) to make a loud cry ○ *An owl hooted in the distance.* **2.** to sound a car horn ○ *He hooted at the sheep to get them to move.*

Hoover /ˈhuːvə/ *trademark* a type of vacuum cleaner ○ *We need a bigger Hoover – this one isn't powerful enough.*

hooves /huːvz/ plural of **hoof**

③ **hop** /hɒp/ *verb* (**hops, hopping, hopped**) **1.** to jump on one leg ○ *He hurt his toe and had to hop around on one foot.* **2.** (*of a bird or animal*) to jump with both feet together ○ *Magpies were hopping across the grass.* ○ *The frog hopped onto the lily pad.* ■ *noun* **1.** a little jump ○ *Magpies walk in a series of little hops.* **2.** a short flight ○ *It's only a short hop from London to Paris.*

① **hope** /həʊp/ *verb* (**hopes, hoping, hoped**) to want and expect something to happen [~(that)] ○ *We all hope our team wins.* ○ *She's hoping she will soon be able to drive a car.* ○ *I hope it doesn't rain.* □ **to hope for something** to want something to happen ○ *We are hoping for better weather next week.* □ **to hope to do something** to expect to do something ○ *The chairman hopes to be at the meeting tomorrow.* ○ *They said they hoped to be back home by 6 o'clock.* ○ *I had hoped to go to the party but in the end I couldn't.* ■ *noun* the fact of wanting and expecting something to happen [~(that)/] ○ *They have given up all hope of rescuing any more earthquake victims.* ○ *They expressed a hope that past disagreements could be forgotten.* □ **in the hope that something happens** wanting something to happen ○ *I rang in the hope that you might have a table free for tonight.* ◇ **I hope so** I want it to happen ○ *Are you coming to the party? – Yes, I hope so.* ◇ **I hope not** I don't want it to happen ○ *It's going to rain tomorrow, isn't it? – I hope not!*

② **hopeful** /ˈhəʊpf(ə)l/ *adj* confident that something will happen ○ *We are hopeful that the company will accept our offer.*

① **hopefully** /ˈhəʊpf(ə)li/ *adv* **1.** confidently ○ *He looked hopefully at the list of lottery winners.* **2.** let us hope ○ *Hopefully, the rain will stop in time for the picnic.*

② **hopeless** /ˈhəʊpləs/ *adj* **1.** unlikely to get better; impossible to improve ○ *The invoices are in a hopeless mess.* **2.** not at all skilful at something ○ *She's hopeless at tennis.* ○ *He's hopeless when it comes to mending cars.*

hopelessly /ˈhəʊpləsli/ *adv* very much ○ *The company is hopelessly in debt.*

horde /hɔːd/ *noun* a large crowd (NOTE: Do not confuse with **hoard**.)

③ **horizon** /həˈraɪz(ə)n/ *noun* the line in the distance where the earth and the sky meet

horizons /həˈraɪz(ə)nz/ *plural noun* □ **to broaden someone's horizons** to increase someone's range of interests and experiences ○ *Travel broadens your horizons*

③ **horizontal** /ˌhɒrɪˈzɒnt(ə)l/ *adj* flat; level with the ground

hormone /ˈhɔːməʊn/ *noun* a substance produced by glands in the body and carried to other parts of the body by the bloodstream to stimulate certain cells into action

③ **horn** /hɔːn/ *noun* **1.** a sharp pointed bone growing out of an animal's head ○ *That bull's horns look very dangerous.* **2.** a piece of equipment on a car that makes a loud noise to warn people of something **3.** a metal musical instrument which you blow into ○ *a piece of music for horn and orchestra*

horoscope /ˈhɒrəskəʊp/ *noun* a forecast of what will happen, according to the stars

horrendous /hɒ'rendəs/ *adj* horrible and unpleasant

② **horrible** /'hɒrɪb(ə)l/ *adj* extremely unpleasant ○ *The victims of the fire had horrible injuries.* ○ *He's a horrible little boy.* ○ *We had a horrible meal at the restaurant.*

horrid /'hɒrɪd/ *adj* bad and unpleasant

③ **horrific** /hɒ'rɪfɪk/ *adj* which makes you shocked

③ **horrified** /'hɒrɪfaɪd/ *adj* frightened or shocked

horrify /'hɒrɪfaɪ/ (**horrifies, horrifying, horrified**) *verb* to frighten or shock someone

③ **horror** /'hɒrə/ *noun* the fact or feeling of being very frightened ○ *He couldn't hide his horror at hearing the news.* ○ *She has a horror of spiders.* ○ *Everyone watched in horror as the planes collided.*

① **horse** /hɔːs/ *noun* a large animal used for riding or for pulling vehicles ○ *She was riding a black horse.* ○ *The coach was pulled by six white horses.* ○ *He's out on his horse every morning.*

horse around, horse about *phrasal verb* to play roughly

horse chestnut /hɔːs 'tʃesnʌt/ *noun* a tree with large leaves and upright white or pink flowers that produces large shiny brown seeds

horsepower /'hɔːspaʊə/ *noun* a unit for measuring the power of a motor engine

horse-riding /'hɔːsraɪdɪŋ/ *noun* the practice of riding horses for pleasure

horseshoe /'hɔːsʃuː/ *noun* an iron shoe nailed to the hard part of a horse's hoof, also used as a sign of luck

horticulture /'hɔːtɪkʌltʃə/ *noun* the practice of growing fruit, flowers and vegetables for food or decoration

hose /həʊz/ *noun* a long flexible tube, either of rubber or plastic ○ *There is a ban on using garden hoses during the summer.* ○ *The firefighters turned their hoses on the burning building.*

hosiery /'həʊziəri/ *noun* (*in a shop*) stockings, socks and tights

hospice /'hɒspɪs/ *noun* a hospital which cares for terminally ill patients

hospitable /hɒ'spɪtəb(ə)l/ *adj* welcoming and friendly to guests

① **hospital** /'hɒspɪt(ə)l/ *noun* a place where sick or hurt people are looked after ○ *She was taken ill at work and sent to hospital.* ○ *When is she due to go into hospital?* ○ *He was in hospital for several days after the accident.*

hospitalise /'hɒspɪt(ə)laɪz/ (**hospitalises, hospitalising, hospitalised**), **hospitalize** *verb* to put someone in hospital

③ **hospitality** /ˌhɒspɪ'tælɪti/ *noun* a welcome to guests

③ **host** /həʊst/ *noun* **1.** a person who has invited guests ○ *The host asked his guests what they wanted to drink.* **2.** the landlord of a hotel or inn, also sometimes of a restaurant **3.** the person who introduces and talks to the guests on a TV or radio show ○ *He had been a host on a Saturday evening TV show.* **4.** □ **a host of** a large number of ○ *We face a host of problems.* ■ *verb* (**hosts, hosting, hosted**) **1.** to act as host at a party ○ *The company hosted a reception for two hundred guests.* **2.** to be the centre where something takes place ○ *Barcelona hosted the Olympic Games.* **3.** to organise and manage websites for other people

hostage /'hɒstɪdʒ/ *noun* a person who is captured and held by someone or an organisation, which threatens to kill him or her unless their demands are met ○ *Three of the hostages will be released tomorrow.* ◇ to keep someone as a hostage ○ *He was held hostage for more than a year by the rebels.*

hostel /'hɒst(ə)l/ *noun* a cheap place where people can live

hostess /'həʊstɪs/ *noun* a woman who has invited guests

hostile /'hɒstaɪl/ *adj* **1.** referring to an enemy ○ *Hostile forces are moving towards the airport.* **2.** showing a dislike of someone ○ *The crowd seemed hostile, so the President decided not to go on his planned walkabout.*

③ **hostility** /hɒ'stɪlɪti/ (*plural* **hostilities**) *noun* opposition [/~to/towards] ○ *The board's hostility towards the plan.*

① **hot** /hɒt/ *adj* **1.** very warm; with a high temperature ○ *The weather is very hot in June, but August is the hottest month.* ○ *If you're too hot, take your coat off.* ○ *Plates should be kept hot before serving the meal.* ◊ **heat 2.** (*of food*) full of spices, giving you a burning feeling in your mouth ○ *This curry is particularly hot.* ○ *He chose the hottest dish on the menu.*

hot-air balloon /hɒt 'eə bəˌluːn/ *noun* a very large balloon which rises into the air as the air inside it is heated, with people travelling in a basket attached underneath

hotbed /'hɒtbed/ *noun* a place where a lot of some activity takes place ○ *a hotbed of crime*

hot chocolate /hɒt 'tʃɒklət/ *noun* a drink made from chocolate powder and hot milk

③ **hot dog** /'hɒt dɒg/ *noun* a snack consisting of a hot sausage in a long piece of bread

① **hotel** /həʊ'tel/ *noun* a building where travellers can rent a room for the night, eat in a restaurant or drink in a bar ○ *They are staying at the Grand Hotel.* ○ *I'll meet you in the hotel lobby.* ○ *All the hotel rooms in the town are booked.* ○ *It's the only five-star hotel in town.*

hotelier /həʊ'telieɪ/ *noun* a person who owns or manages a hotel

hot key /'hɒt kiː/ *noun* a computer key that you press as a quick way to perform a set of actions

hotline /'hɒtlaɪn/ *noun* a phone line for giving urgent messages or for placing urgent orders ○ *We get thousands of orders on our Christmas hotline.* ○ *Call the ticket hotline for reservations.*

hotly /'hɒtli/ *adv* **1.** angrily ○ *He hotly denied the reports which had been published in the newspapers.* **2.** close behind ○ *The enemy fled, hotly pursued by government troops.*

hotplate /'hɒtpleɪt/ *noun* a flat heated surface on a cooker

hot potato /hɒt pə'teɪtəʊ/ *noun* a subject which is difficult to deal with

hot spot /'hɒt spɒt/ *noun* **1.** a place which is exciting ○ *This café is one of the hottest spots in town.* **2.** a place where fighting is taking place ○ *He was sent to report from one of the hot spots in the Middle East.*

hot-water bottle /hɒt 'wɑːtə ˌbɒt(ə)l/ *noun* a container filled with hot water which is placed in a bed to warm it

hound /haʊnd/ *noun* a dog used for hunting ○ *He has a pack of hounds for hunting.* ■ *verb* (**hounds, hounding, hounded**) to attack or victimise someone ○ *When he came out of prison he was hounded by the press.*

① **hour** /aʊə/ *noun* a period of time which lasts 60 minutes ○ *The train journey takes two hours.* ○ *It's a three-hour flight to Greece.* ○ *The train travels at over 150 miles an hour.*

hourly /'aʊəli/ *adj, adv* happening every hour

house¹ /haʊs/ *noun* **1.** a building in which someone lives ○ *He has bought a house in London.* ○ *He has a small flat in town and a large house in the country.* ○ *All the houses in our street look the same.* **2.** a part of a Parliament ○ *The British Parliament is formed of the House of Commons and the House of Lords.* ○ *The American Congress is formed of the House of Representatives and the Senate.*

house² /haʊz/ (**houses, housing, housed**) *verb* to provide a place for someone or something to stay or be kept ○ *His collection of old cars is housed in a barn.* ○ *We have been asked if we can house three students for the summer term.*

houseboat /'haʊsbəʊt/ *noun* a boat moored on a river, arranged for living in, not for travelling

housebound /'haʊsbaʊnd/ *adj* not able to leave your house

② **household** /'haʊshəʊld/ *noun* the people living together in a house

householder /'haʊshəʊldə/ *noun* a person who owns a private house

house husband /haʊz 'hʌzbənd/ *noun* a man who does not go out to work but stays at home to look after his house and family

housekeeper /'haʊskiːpə/ *noun* **1.** a person who looks after a house ○ *He employs a housekeeper, a chauffeur and two gardeners.* **2.** a person employed to look after the rooms in a hotel, being responsible for the people who do the cleaning, and for providing clean sheets, etc. ○ *The housekeeper is responsible for the cleanliness of the rooms.*

housekeeping /'haʊskiːpɪŋ/ *noun* the work of looking after a house

housemate /'haʊsmeɪt/ *noun* a person who is not a member of your family, but who shares a house with you

houseproud /'haʊspraʊd/ *adj* taking great pride in the appearance of your house, and very concerned with keeping it tidy

house-to-house /ˌhaʊs tə 'haʊs/ *adj* going from one house to the next, in order to ask people to buy something or vote for someone, or to ask them questions ○ *The police carried out house-to-house checks to try to find the gunman.* ○ *He has a job selling cleaning products house-to-house.*

house-trained /haʊz treɪnd/ *adj* (*of animals*) having been taught not to urinate or defecate on the floor in houses

housewarming /'haʊswɔːmɪŋ/, **housewarming party** *noun* a party that people have when they move into a new house

③ **housewife** /'haʊswaɪf/ (*plural* **housewives**) *noun* a woman who looks after the house, and does not go out to work

housework /'haʊswɜːk/ *noun* the work of keeping a house clean (NOTE: no plural)

② **housing** /'haʊzɪŋ/ *noun* houses ○ *Public housing has to meet certain standards.*

housing estate /'haʊzɪŋ ɪˌsteɪt/ *noun* a large group of flats or houses of a similar type built at the same time ○ *She lives on the Bellevue Estate.*

hover /'hɒvə/ (**hovers, hovering, hovered**) *verb* to hang in the air without moving forward ○ *flies hovering over the surface of a pool*

hovercraft /'hɒvəkrɑːft/ *noun* a type of boat which moves over the surface of the water on a cushion of air

① **how** /haʊ/ *adv* **1.** showing or asking the way in which something is done ○ *How do you switch off the cooker?* ○ *Can you tell me how to get to the railway station from here?* ○ *I don't know how he does it.* **2.** showing or asking about things such as the age, size or quantity of something ○ *How big is their house?* ○ *How many people are there in your family?* ○ *She showed us how good she was at skiing.* ○ *How old is your little boy?* ○ *How far is it to the church?* **3.** showing surprise ○ *How cold it is outside!* ○ *How different it is from what I remember!*

① **however** /haʊ'evə/ *adv* but ○ *We never go out on Saturdays – however, this week we're going to a wedding.* ■ *conj* in whatever way ○ *Do it however you like.*

howl /haʊl/ *verb* (**howls, howling, howled**) to make a long loud high sound like a wolf ○ *The wolves howled outside the cabin.* ○ *The wind howled in the chimney.* ■ *noun* a long loud cry ○ *Howls of disappointment came from the fans.*

HQ *abbr* headquarters

hr *abbr* hour

HTML /ˌeɪtʃ tiː em 'el/ *noun* a system of codes used to prepare a document for the World Wide Web

hub /hʌb/ *noun* **1.** the centre of a wheel ○ *The spokes of a wheel meet at the hub.* **2.** the centre of some activity, especially business activity ○ *Frankfurt is hoping to take the place of the City of London as the financial hub of Europe.* **3.** a central airport, where domestic flights connect with international flights ○ *Chicago is the airline's American hub.*

hubbub /'hʌbʌb/ *noun* the confused sound of voices

huddle /'hʌd(ə)l/ (**huddles, huddling, huddled**) *verb* to crowd together, or to be crowded together ○ *The refugees huddled in the shade of some trees.* ○ *The children were huddled together in one room.*

hue /hjuː/ *noun* a colour (*formal*) ○ *The garden is filled with flowers of every hue.* (NOTE: Do not confuse with **hew**.)

hue and cry /ˌhjuː ən 'kraɪ/ *noun* a loud protest

hug /hʌg/ *noun* the act of putting your arms round someone and holding them close to you ○ *She ran to the little girl and gave her a hug.* ■ *verb* (**hugs, hugging, hugged**) to throw your arms around someone ○ *The players hugged each other when the goal was scored.*

② **huge** /hjuːdʒ/ *adj* of a very large size ○ *Huge waves battered the ship.* ○ *The concert was a huge success.* ○ *Failing the test was a huge disappointment for him.*

huh /hʌ, hə/ *interj* **1.** used for showing that you did not hear or understand what someone has just said **2.** used for showing a reaction such as surprise or disgust ○ *Huh, you think you can sneak out without paying, do you?*

hulk /hʌlk/ *noun* **1.** a big and awkward person or thing ○ *Watch where you're treading, you lumbering great hulk!* **2.** a rotten old ship ○ *Rusting hulks blocked the approaches to the harbour.*

hull /hʌl/ *noun* the main body of a ship ○ *The liner is in dry dock for repairs to her hull.*

hum /hʌm/ (**hums, humming, hummed**) *verb* **1.** to make a low sound like a bee ○ *Bees were humming around the hive.* **2.** to sing without words ○ *If you don't know the words of the national anthem, you can always hum the tune.*

① **human** /'hjuːmən/ *adj* relating to people

humane /hjuː'meɪn/ *adj* kind to people or animals

human error /ˌhjuːmən 'erə/ *noun* a mistake made by a person, and not by a machine

human interest /ˌhjuːmən 'ɪntrəst/ *noun* the power to make people interested or sympathetic

humanitarian /hjuːˌmænɪ'teəriən/ *adj* helping other human beings

humanity /hjuː'mænɪti/ *noun* **1.** all people ○ *a crime against humanity* **2.** great kindness ○ *She showed great humanity to the refugees.*

humankind /ˌhjuːmən'kaɪnd/ *noun* all human beings

human nature /ˌhjuːmən 'neɪtʃə/ *noun* natural feelings which are found in all people

human resources /ˌhjuːmən rɪ 'sɔːsɪz/ *plural noun* the employees of a company, seen as a group

① **human rights** /ˌhjuːmən 'raɪts/ *plural noun* rights which each member of society should enjoy, such as freedom of speech and freedom of movement ○ *Demonstrators are protesting against abuses of human rights in various parts of the world.*

humble /'hʌmbəl/ *adj* feeling or acting as if you are not as important as other people ○ *Seeing how much work she does for charity makes me feel very humble.* ◊ **pie**

humdrum /'hʌmdrʌm/ *adj* dull and boring

humid /'hjuːmɪd/ *adj* (*of the air*) warm and damp

③ **humidity** /hjuː'mɪdɪti/ *noun* a measurement of how much water vapour is contained in the air

humiliate /hjuː'mɪlieɪt/ (**humiliates, humiliating, humiliated**) *verb* to make someone feel unimportant or stupid (NOTE: + **humiliation** *n*)

humiliating /hjuː'mɪlieɪtɪŋ/ *adj* which makes you feel embarrassed, unimportant or stupid

humility /hjuː'mɪlɪti/ *noun* the quality of being humble

humor /'hjuːmə/ *noun* US spelling of **humour**

humorous /'hjuːmərəs/ *adj* funny in a quiet way, making people smile rather than laugh ○ *humorous stories* ○ *Some of her comments were rather humorous.*

humorously /'hjuːmərəsli/ *adv* in a humorous

humour /'hjuːmə/ *noun* **1.** the ability to make situations seem funny ○ *He has a good sense of humour.* ○ *She has absolutely no sense of humour.* ○ *Want to meet male, aged 30 – 35, with a good sense of humour (GSOH).* **2.** a general feeling or mood ○ *I am in no humour to talk about holidays just now.* ○ *His good humour lasted until the end of the party.*

humourless /'hjuːmələs/ *adj* lacking an ability to find things funny (NOTE: The US spelling is **humorless**.)

hump /hʌmp/ *noun* **1.** a raised part on the back of a person or animal ○ *One type of camel has only one hump, while another type has two.* **2.** a small raised part in the ground ○ *They have built humps in the road to slow down the traffic.*

hunch /hʌntʃ/ *noun* a feeling that something is going to happen ○ *I've got a hunch that we will win.* ○ *The detective acted purely on a hunch.* ■ *verb* (**hunches, hunching, hunched**) to bend forwards ○ *We hunched down behind the wall to get out of the wind.*

hunchback /'hʌntʃbæk/ *noun* a person with a hunched back (*offensive*)

① **hundred** /'hʌndrəd/ *noun* the number 100 (NOTE: In numbers above one hundred, **hundred** does not become 'hundreds' and is followed by **and** when speaking: **491** = four hundred and ninety-one; **102** = a hundred and two. Note also: **a hundred and one** (101), **three hundred and six** (306) but **the hundred and first** (101st), **the three hundred and sixth** (306th), etc.) □ **in the hundreds** less than 1000 ○ *The visitors were numbered in the hundreds.* ○ *They came in their hundreds to visit the grave.* ◇ **hundreds of** very many ○ *Hundreds of birds were killed by the cold weather.*

hundredth /'hʌndrədθ/ *adj* relating to number 100 in a series ■ *noun* number 100 in a series

hundredweight /'hʌndrədweɪt/ *noun* a weight of dry goods, equal to 112 pounds or approximately 50 kilos

① **hung** /hʌŋ/ past tense and past participle of **hang**

hunger /'hʌŋgə/ *noun* the state of wanting or needing to eat

hunger strike /'hʌŋgə straɪk/ *noun* a continuing refusal to eat, as a form of protest

hungover /hʌŋ'əʊvə/ *adj* feeling ill as a result of having been drunk a few hours earlier

② **hungry** /'hʌŋgri/ *adj* feeling that you need to eat ○ *You must be hungry after that game of football.* ○ *I'm not very hungry – I had a big lunch.* ○ *Hurry up with the food – we're getting hungry.*

hunk /hʌŋk/ *noun* **1.** a rough piece of something ○ *We each had a hunk of bread and a bowl of soup.* **2.** a strong athletic man (*informal*) ○ *Sophie came to the party with that gorgeous hunk of hers.*

hunt /hʌnt/ *verb* (**hunts, hunting, hunted**) **1.** to try to find someone or something [~for] ○ *We're hunting for a cheap flat* ○ *The police are hunting for the driver of the car.* **2.** to chase wild animals for food or sport ○ *Our cat is not very good at hunting mice.* ○

They go to Scotland every year to hunt deer. (NOTE: You hunt animals, but you hunt **for** things.) ■ *noun* a search ○ *The hunt for new offices has just started.*

hunter /ˈhʌntə/ *noun* a person who hunts animals

③ **hunting** /ˈhʌntɪŋ/ *noun* **1.** the sport of chasing wild animals and killing them ○ *Many people are opposed to fox hunting.* **2.** the action of looking for something

hurdle /ˈhɜːd(ə)l/ *noun* **1.** a small fence which you have to jump over in a race ○ *She fell at the first hurdle.* **2.** an obstacle in the way of something ○ *Only one more hurdle to clear and the house will be ours.*

hurl /hɜːl/ (**hurls, hurling, hurled**) *verb* to throw something

hurricane /ˈhʌrɪkən/ *noun* a tropical storm with strong winds and rain (NOTE: In the Far East called a **typhoon**; in the Indian Ocean called a **cyclone**.)

③ **hurried** /ˈhʌrid/ *adj* done in a rush, or too quickly

③ **hurry** /ˈhʌri/ (**hurries, hurrying, hurried**) *verb* to go somewhere or do something fast ○ *She hurried across the room.* ○ *You'll have to hurry if you want to catch the last post.* ○ *There's no need to hurry – we've got plenty of time*

hurry up③ *phrasal verb* to go or do something faster ○ *Hurry up – we'll be late for the film.* ○ *Can't you get the cook to hurry up? I'm getting hungry!*

② **hurt** /hɜːt/ (**hurts, hurting, hurt**) *verb* **1.** to have pain, or to cause someone to feel pain ○ *My tooth hurts.* ○ *No one was badly hurt in the accident.* ○ *Where did you hurt yourself?* **2.** to harm or damage something ○ *The bad publicity did not hurt our sales.* ○ *This news report will surely hurt his reputation.*

hurtful /ˈhɜːtf(ə)l/ *adj* which is upsetting, and which makes someone sad

hurtle /ˈhɜːt(ə)l/ (**hurtles, hurtling, hurtled**) *verb* to go dangerously fast

① **husband** /ˈhʌzbənd/ *noun* a man to whom a woman is married ○ *Her husband is Scottish.* ○ *He's the doctor's husband.*

hush /hʌʃ/ (**hushes, hushing, hushed**) *verb* to make someone quiet ○ *She eventually managed to hush the children to sleep.*

hushed /hʌʃt/ *adj* quiet, so as not to make too much noise

hush-hush /hʌʃ ˈhʌʃ/ *adj* secret (*informal*)

hush up *phrasal verb* to hide something so that no one knows about it ○ *They tried to hush up the scandal.*

husky /ˈhʌski/ (*plural* **huskies**) *noun* a dog used to pull sledges ○ *Each sled was pulled by a team of huskies.*

hustle /ˈhʌs(ə)l/ *noun* a movement of people ○ *the hustle of the commuters trying to get home on the Underground* ■ *verb* (**hustles, hustling, hustled**) to hurry someone along roughly ○ *The police tried to hustle the crowd of protesters away.* ○ *Don't hustle me – I'm going as fast as I can!*

③ **hut** /hʌt/ *noun* a small rough wooden house

hutch /hʌtʃ/ *noun* a box or cage for animals such as rabbits

hyacinth /ˈhaɪəsɪnθ/ *noun* a bulb which produces spikes of bright pink, white or blue scented flowers

hybrid /ˈhaɪbrɪd/ *noun* a cross between two varieties of plant or animal ○ *She is well known for growing hybrid roses.*

hydraulic /haɪˈdrɔːlɪk/ *adj* worked by fluid pressure

hydrofoil /ˈhaɪdrəʊfɔɪl/ *noun* a type of boat which skims fast over the surface of the water

hydrogen /ˈhaɪdrədʒən/ *noun* a common gas which combines with oxygen to form water

③ **hygiene** /ˈhaɪdʒiːn/ *noun* the science of being and keeping things clean

hygienic /haɪˈdʒiːnɪk/ *adj* clean and safe because all germs have been destroyed

hype /haɪp/ *noun* an excessive claim in advertising ○ *No one really believes all the hype surrounding the pop group.* ○ *There was a lot of hype about the festival and in the end it turned out to be very small.* ■ *verb* (**hypes, hyping, hyped**) to make excessive claims in publicity ○ *The show was hyped (up) in all the newspapers.*

hyper- /haɪpə/ *prefix* higher, or to a greater degree

hyperactive /ˌhaɪpərˈæktɪv/ *adj* very active

hyperbole /haɪˈpɜːbəli/ *noun* an exaggerated statement

hyperlink /ˈhaɪpəlɪŋk/ *noun* a link in hypertext

hypermarket /ˈhaɪpəmɑːkɪt/ *noun* a very large supermarket, usually on the outskirts of a large town

hypersensitive /ˌhaɪpəˈsensɪtɪv/ *adj* **1.** very easily upset or insulted **2.** having a strong physical reaction to a drug or other substance

hypertension /ˌhaɪpəˈtenʃən/ *noun* high blood pressure; a condition where the pressure of the blood in the arteries is too high

hypertext /ˈhaɪpətekst/ *noun* a system of storing computer files that gives the user direct access to related electronic information

hyperventilate /ˌhaɪpəˈventɪleɪt/ (**hyperventilates, hyperventilating, hyperventilated**) *verb* to breathe so fast or deeply that you start to feel dizzy

③ **hyphen** /ˈhaɪf(ə)n/ *noun* a printing sign (-) used to show that two words are joined

hyphenated /ˈhaɪfəneɪtɪd/ *adj* (*of a word*) spelled with one or more hyphens

hypnosis /hɪpˈnəʊsɪs/ *noun* a state like sleep, but caused artificially, where the patient can remember forgotten events in the past or will do whatever the hypnotist tells him or her to do

hypnotise /ˈhɪpnətaɪz/ (**hypnotises, hypnotising, hypnotised**), **hypnotize** *verb* to make someone go into a state where he or she appears to be asleep and will do anything the hypnotist suggests

hypnotist /ˈhɪpnətɪst/ *noun* a person who practises hypnosis (NOTE: + **hypnotism** *n*)

hypoallergenic /ˌhaɪpəʊæləˈdʒenɪk/ *adj* unlikely to start off an allergic reaction

hypochondriac /ˌhaɪpəʊˈkɒndriæk/ *noun* a person who is always worried about his or her health

hypocrisy /hɪˈpɒkrɪsi/ *noun* pretending to be what you are not

hypocrite /ˈhɪpəkrɪt/ *noun* a person who says one thing and acts in a different way

hypocritical /ˌhɪpəˈkrɪtɪk(ə)l/ *adj* referring to hypocrisy

hypothermia /ˌhaɪpəʊˈθɜːmiə/ *noun* a state where the temperature of the body is dangerously low

③ **hypothesis** /haɪˈpɒθəsɪs/ (*plural* **hypotheses**) *noun* something which is probably true, though it cannot be proved

hypothetical /ˌhaɪpəˈθetɪk(ə)l/ *adj* suggested as possible, but not an actual happening

hysterectomy /ˌhɪstəˈrektəmi/ *noun* the surgical removal of a woman's womb, either to treat cancer or because of some other problem

hysteria /hɪˈstɪəriə/ *noun* a neurotic state, where the patient is in a fit of panic or excitement

hysterical /hɪˈsterɪk(ə)l/ *adj* **1.** very excited and emotional in an uncontrolled way **2.** very funny

hysterics /hɪˈsterɪks/ *plural noun* laughter which you cannot control ○ *The children were in hysterics as they watched the clown tearing up pieces of paper.*

I

i /aɪ/, **I** *noun* the ninth letter of the alphabet, between H and J

① **I¹** /aɪ/ *pron* used by a speaker when talking about himself or herself ○ *She said, 'I can do it', and she did it.* ○ *He told me I could go home early.* ○ *She and I come from the same town.* ○ *I said I was going to be late.* (NOTE: When it is the object of a verb, **I** becomes **me**: *I gave it to him – he gave it to me*; *I hit him – he hit me.* When it follows the verb **be**, **I** usually becomes **me**: *Who is it? – It's me!*)

① **I²** /aɪ/ *noun* the Roman numeral for one or first ○ *King Charles I*

② **ice** /aɪs/ *noun* water which is frozen and has become solid ○ *When water freezes, it turns into ice.* ○ *Would you like ice in your drink?* (NOTE: no plural: *some ice, a lump of ice*)

ice up③ *phrasal verb* to become covered with ice

iceberg /ˈaɪsbɜːɡ/ *noun* a huge block of ice floating on the sea

icebox /ˈaɪsbɒks/ *noun US* same as **refrigerator** (*dated*)

ice-breaker /ˈaɪs ˌbreɪkə/ *noun* a game at the start of a party or other event with a lot of people, to help everyone to get to know one another

ice cap /aɪs kæp/ *noun* a thick layer of ice and snow that never melts, such as at the North and South Poles or on the top of some high mountains

ice-cold /aɪs kəʊld/ *adj* extremely cold

② **ice cream** /aɪs ˈkriːm/ *noun* a frozen sweet food made from cream and fruit, chocolate, nuts, etc.

ice cube /ˈaɪs kjuːb/ *noun* a little block of ice, used to cool a drink

ice hockey /ˈaɪs ˌhɒki/ *noun* a form of hockey played on ice using a hard rubber disc called a puck (NOTE: The US term is **hockey**.)

ice lolly /ˈaɪs ˌlɒli/ *noun* a mixture of water and flavouring, frozen until solid with a stick in it (NOTE: The US term is **popsicle**.)

ice pack /ˈaɪs pæk/ *noun* a bag of ice placed on your forehead to cure a headache, etc.

ice rink /ˈaɪs rɪŋk/ *noun* a special area for ice skating, or for playing ice hockey, etc.

ice skate /ˈaɪs skeɪt/ *noun* a boot with a steel blade fitted to the sole for skating on ice

icicle /ˈaɪsɪk(ə)l/ *noun* a long piece of ice hanging from a roof, etc., formed by water dripping in freezing weather

③ **icing** /ˈaɪsɪŋ/ *noun* a covering of sugar and flavouring, spread over a cake or biscuits

③ **icon** /ˈaɪkɒn/ *noun* **1.** a little picture used as a symbol on a computer screen ○ *Click twice on the icon of a key to enter the program.* ○ *To print your text, point your cursor at the printer icon and click twice.* **2.** a picture of Christ or a saint in the Eastern Christian Church ○ *There is an exhibition of Russian icons in the British Museum.* ○ *The icon of the Virgin Mary is carried in procession round the church.* **3.** a person who is admired as a good example of a certain type ○ *She has become something of a feminist icon.*

icy /ˈaɪsi/ *adj* covered with ice ○ *Be careful, the pavement is icy.*

ID card /ˈaɪ ˈdiː kɑːd/ *noun* an identity card; a card which shows a photograph of the holder, with their name, date of birth and other details, carried by citizens of a country or members of a group to prove who they are

① **idea** /aɪˈdɪə/ *noun* **1.** a thought or opinion which you have about something [~about/on/~of] ○ *I like his ideas about co-operation and working as a team.* ○ *He has unusual ideas on food and diet.* ○ *The description gave us no idea of what the hotel was really like.* □ **to have an idea** to think of something ○ *She had a good idea for a new specialist course.* ○ *I've had an idea about how to change our presentation.* ○ *I've had an idea – let's all go for a picnic!* □ **to have no idea**, **not to have the faintest**

idea not to know ○ *Where's your brother? – I've no idea* or *I haven't the faintest idea.* ○ *I had no idea it was as late as that.* **2.** a plan which you make in your mind [~for] ○ *Free entry for children – that's a good idea!* ○ *Her ideas for the new hotel were unusual and exciting.* □ **it's a good idea to do something** you should do something (*used to give someone advice*) ○ *It's a good idea to book a ticket in advance at busy times.*

② **ideal** /aɪˈdɪəl/ *adj* extremely suitable ○ *This is the ideal site for a factory.* ○ *The cottage is an ideal place for watching birds.* ■ *noun* the highest point of perfection, which people try to reach ○ *My ideal would be to work for six months of the year and travel for the other six months.*

idealise /aɪˈdɪəlaɪz/ (**idealises, idealising, idealised**), **idealize** *verb* to make someone or something seem perfect

idealism /aɪˈdɪəlɪz(ə)m/ *noun* aiming at achieving an ideal

idealist /aɪˈdɪəlɪst/ *noun* **1.** a person who aims at achieving an ideal ○ *She's an idealist, and is upset when anyone suggests a solution which is less than perfect.* **2.** an impractical person ○ *He's too much of an idealist to be a government minister.*

idealistic /aɪˌdɪəˈlɪstɪk/ *adj* aiming at an ideal; too perfect

③ **ideally** /aɪˈdɪəli/ *adv* **1.** in an ideal way ○ *She is ideally suited to the job of chef.* **2.** if everything were perfect ○ *Ideally, I'd take three weeks' holiday, but there's too much work at the office.*

identical /aɪˈdentɪk(ə)l/ *adj* exactly the same [~to] ○ *The twins wore identical clothes for the party.* ○ *Her political opinions are identical to mine.*

identifiable /aɪˈdentɪfaɪəb(ə)l/ *adj* which can be identified

identification /aɪˌdentɪfɪˈkeɪʃ(ə)n/ *noun* **1.** the act of saying who someone is by giving their name, personal details, etc. ○ *The formal identification of the body was made by the victim's sister.* **2.** a document which shows who someone is ○ *The bank manager asked him for identification.*

① **identify** /aɪˈdentɪfaɪ/ (**identifies, identifying, identified**) *verb* **1.** to recognise a person or thing and to be able to say who or what they are ○ *Can you identify what sort of rock this is?* ○ *She was able to identify her attacker.* **2.** to state that something belongs to you ○ *Each person was asked to identify his or her baggage.*

identify with *phrasal verb* to have the same feelings as someone, or to have a feeling of sympathy for someone or something [~with] ○ *I can identify with the heroine who spends her life trapped in a small rural town.*

② **identity** /aɪˈdentɪti/ *noun* someone's name and personal details ○ *He changed his identity when he went to work for the secret services.*

identity card /aɪˈdentɪti ˌkɑːd/ *noun* a card which shows a photograph of the holder, with the name, date of birth and other details, carried by citizens of a country or members of a group to prove who they are

③ **ideology** /ˌaɪdiˈɒlədʒi/ (*plural* **ideologies**) *noun* a theory of life based not on religious belief, but on political or economic philosophy

idiocy /ˈɪdiəsi/ *noun* total stupidity (*offensive*)

③ **idiom** /ˈɪdiəm/ *noun* **1.** an expression which means something different as a whole from what the individual parts of it usually mean ○ *'It's raining cats and dogs' is an idiom meaning 'it is raining hard'.* **2.** a characteristic way of speaking or of writing ○ *'How now, what news?' was a common greeting in the idiom of Shakespeare's England.*

idiomatic /ˌɪdiəˈmætɪk/ *adj* referring to a natural colloquial way of speaking a language

idiosyncrasy /ˌɪdiəʊˈsɪŋkrəsi/ *noun* a particularly odd way of behaving

idiosyncratic /ˌɪdiəʊsɪŋˈkrætɪk/ *adj* odd or peculiar; particular to one person

③ **idiot** /ˈɪdiət/ *noun* a person who behaves in a stupid way (*insult*)

idiotic /ˌɪdiˈɒtɪk/ *adj* stupid

idle /ˈaɪd(ə)l/ *adj* (**idler, idlest**) **1.** not doing anything ○ *He's the idlest man I know – he never does any work at all.* **2.** not operating ○ *The machines lay idle for days when the factory closed.* (NOTE: Do not confuse with **idol**.) ■ *verb* (**idles, idling, idled**) (*of a machine*) to run at a low speed ○ *He waited for her in the car with the engine idling.*

idol /ˈaɪd(ə)l/ *noun* **1.** someone such as a star performer or sportsperson who is very popular and admired ○ *The England captain is many boys' idol.* **2.** the statue of a god which is worshipped

idolise /ˈaɪdəlaɪz/ (**idolises, idolising, idolised**), **idolize** *verb* to admire someone very much

idyllic /ɪ'dɪlɪk/ *adj* happy and pleasant in a romantic way

① **if** /ɪf/ *conj* **1.** showing what might happen ○ *If it freezes tonight, the paths will be slippery tomorrow.* ○ *If I'm in London, I'll come and see you.* ○ *If he had told me you were ill, I'd have come to see you in hospital.* ○ *If I won the lottery, I would take a long holiday.* **2.** used in asking questions ○ *Do you know if the plane is late?* ○ *I was wondering if you would like to have some tea.*

iffy /'ɪfi/ *adj* doubtful, not at all certain

igloo /'ɪgluː/ *noun* a dome-shaped shelter built out of blocks of snow

ignite /ɪg'naɪt/ (**ignites, igniting, ignited**) *verb* **1.** to catch fire ○ *There was a loud explosion as the gas ignited.* **2.** to set fire to something ○ *The teacher showed us how to ignite the Bunsen burner.*

ignition /ɪg'nɪʃ(ə)n/ *noun* (*in a car*) the process which starts the burning of the compressed air-fuel mixture

ignominious /ˌɪgnə'mɪniəs/ *adj* shameful (*formal*)

ignorance /'ɪgnərəns/ *noun* a state of not knowing

ignorant /'ɪgnərənt/ *adj* not knowing anything

② **ignore** /ɪg'nɔː/ (**ignores, ignoring, ignored**) *verb* not to notice someone or something deliberately ○ *She ignored the red light and just drove straight through.* ○ *When we met he just ignored me.*

iguana /ɪg'wɑːnə/ *noun* a large type of plant-eating lizard

① **ill** /ɪl/ *adj* sick; not well ○ *Stress can make you ill.* ○ *If you're feeling ill you ought to see a doctor.* □ **to fall ill** to become ill ○ *She fell seriously ill and we thought she was going to die.* □ **to be taken ill** to become ill suddenly ○ *He was taken ill while on holiday in Greece.*

③ **I'll** /aɪl/ *short for* I will

ill-advised /ˌɪl əd'vaɪzd/ *adj* not sensible, or not a good idea

ill-conceived /ɪl kən'siːvd/ *adj* foolish or badly planned

illegal /ɪ'liːg(ə)l/ *adj* against the law ○ *It is illegal to serve alcohol to people under 16.*

illegal immigrant /ɪˌliːg(ə)l 'ɪmɪgrənt/ *noun* a person who has entered a country illegally and wants to settle there

illegally /ɪ'liːgəli/ *adv* in an illegal way

illegible /ɪ'ledʒɪb(ə)l/ *adj* (*of writing*) which cannot be read

illegitimate /ˌɪlɪ'dʒɪtɪmət/ *adj* **1.** born to parents who are not married to each other ○ *He failed in his attempt to hide his illegitimate child from the press.* **2.** forbidden by certain rules; against the law ○ *We should all be concerned at the illegitimate use of certain prescription drugs.* ○ *The government is cracking down on the illegitimate ownership of firearms.*

ill-equipped /ɪl ɪ'kwɪpt/ *adj* not having the right equipment or preparation

ill-fated /ˌɪl 'feɪtɪd/ *adj* unlucky and bound to fail

ill-fitting /ɪl 'fɪtɪŋ/ *adj* which fits badly

ill-gotten gains /ˌɪl gɒt(ə)n 'geɪnz/ *plural noun* money made illegally or dishonestly (*humorous*) ○ *Thinking of them sitting there with their ill-gotten gains makes me envious.*

illicit /ɪ'lɪsɪt/ *adj* against the law (NOTE: Do not confuse with **elicit**.)

ill-informed /ɪl ɪn'fɔːmd/ *adj* having a lack of knowledge in a particular area

illiteracy /ɪ'lɪt(ə)rəsi/ (*plural* **illiteracies**) *noun* the state of being unable to read or write

illiterate /ɪ'lɪt(ə)rət/ *adj* not able to read or write ○ *With so few schools or teachers it is hardly surprising so many children are illiterate.*

ill-mannered /ɪl 'mænəd/ *adj* rude

② **illness** /'ɪlnəs/ *noun* a medical condition which makes you unwell ○ *She developed a serious illness.* ○ *A lot of the staff are absent because of illness.*

illogical /ɪ'lɒdʒɪk(ə)l/ *adj* not sensible; not reasonable

ill-treat /ˌɪl 'triːt/ *verb* to treat a person or animal badly

illuminate /ɪ'luːmɪneɪt/ (**illuminates, illuminating, illuminated**) *verb* **1.** to make something bright with lights ○ *The pitch was illuminated by giant floodlights.* ○ *The town looked magical, illuminated with strings of lights along the edge of the sea.* **2.** to explain something to make it clearer ○ *His talk illuminated several points which I hadn't understood before.*

illuminating /ɪ'luːmɪneɪtɪŋ/ *adj* interesting and educational, particularly in the case of something that explains or emphasises facts that were previously difficult to understand

illumination /ɪˌluːmɪ'neɪʃ(ə)n/ *noun* **1.** the state of being brightly lit, or the act of lighting something brightly **2.** the action of giving information about something ○ *I* *turned to the encyclopedia for illumination.* **3.** a coloured illustration in a manuscript ○ *The chapter illuminations are real works of art.*

illusion /ɪ'luːʒ(ə)n/ *noun* an impression which is not true

illusory /ɪ'luːsəri/ *adj* not real; which is an illusion

② **illustrate** /'ɪləstreɪt/ (**illustrates, illustrating, illustrated**) *verb* to put pictures into a book ○ *The book is illustrated with colour photographs of birds.*

③ **illustration** /ˌɪlə'streɪʃ(ə)n/ *noun* a picture in a book ○ *The book has 25 colour illustrations.*

illustrator /'ɪləstreɪtə/ *noun* a person who draws the pictures for a book

illustrious /ɪ'lʌstriəs/ *adj* very famous (*formal*)

ill will /ɪl 'wɪl/ *noun* dislike and unpleasantness towards someone

③ **I'm** /aɪm/ *short for* I am

① **image** /'ɪmɪdʒ/ *noun* **1.** the opinion which other people have of a person or of an organisation ○ *They are spending a lot of money to improve the company's image.* **2.** a picture produced by something such as a computer or television screen ○ *Can this software handle images in that format?* ○ *Can you adjust the projector? The image on the screen is out of focus.* **3.** a picture of someone or something, especially one that you have in your mind ○ *He suddenly had an image of her saying goodbye the last time they had met.*

③ **imagery** /'ɪmɪdʒəri/ *noun* the use of comparisons or symbols in writing as a way of making people imagine things

imaginable /ɪ'mædʒɪnəb(ə)l/ *adj* which you can imagine

imaginary /ɪ'mædʒɪn(ə)ri/ *adj* not real; part of a story

③ **imagination** /ɪˌmædʒɪ'neɪʃ(ə)n/ *noun* the ability to think of things that are not part of your own immediate life ○ *She let her imagination run riot in her stories for children.*

imaginative /ɪ'mædʒɪnətɪv/ *adj* having or showing a lot of imagination

② **imagine** /ɪ'mædʒɪn/ (**imagines, imagining, imagined**) *verb* **1.** to think of something that is not part of your own immediate life [~(that)/~what/why/how etc] ○ *Imagine yourself sitting on a beach in the hot sun.* ○ *He had never imagined that cooking could be so enjoyable.* ○ *I can't imagine why she said that to you.* **2.** to think that something exists when it does not ○ *She thought she had heard footsteps, and then decided she had imagined it.*

imaging /'ɪmɪdʒɪŋ/ *noun* a technique for creating pictures using scanners attached to computers

imbalance /ɪm'bæləns/ *noun* a lack of balance

imbecile /'ɪmbəsiːl/ *noun* a person who behaves in a stupid way (*insult*) ○ *You imbecile, you threw the envelope with the cheque in it into the rubbish!* (NOTE: not used by doctors)

imbue /ɪm'bjuː/ (**imbues, imbuing, imbued**) *verb* to fill someone with a feeling

imitate /'ɪmɪteɪt/ (**imitates, imitating, imitated**) *verb* **1.** to copy something or someone ○ *The company imitates its competitors by making very similar products.* **2.** to behave as someone else does, often to make other people laugh ○ *He made us all laugh by imitating the head teacher's way of walking.*

imitation /ˌɪmɪ'teɪʃ(ə)n/ *noun* **1.** a copy made of something **2.** an act of copying someone's behaviour in order to make other people laugh ○ *She does a very good imitation of the Queen.* ■ *adj* made to appear to be something else more valuable ○ *a necklace of imitation pearls* ○ *The bag is made of imitation leather.*

immaculate /ɪ'mækjʊlət/ *adj* **1.** extremely clean or tidy ○ *The car looked absolutely immaculate – there wasn't a spot of dirt on it.* ○ *The nurses all wore immaculate white uniforms.* ○ *The last house we visited was in immaculate condition, while all the others needed a lot of repairs.* **2.** perfect; with no errors ○ *She did an immaculate driving test.*

immaterial /ˌɪmə'tɪəriəl/ *adj* not relevant

immature /ˌɪmə'tʃʊə/ *adj* **1.** not mature; still developing ○ *Two immature swans followed their parents across the lake.* **2.** not sensible; not adult ○ *I wish she would grow up and stop being so immature!*

immeasurable /ɪ'meʒ(ə)rəb(ə)l/ *adj* too enormous to be measured

② **immediate** /ɪ'miːdiət/ *adj* **1.** very soon ○ *He wrote an immediate letter of complaint.* ○ *You didn't expect an immediate reply, did you?* ○ *Your order will receive immediate attention.* **2.** closest, or right next to you ○ *He had to share his book with his immediate neighbour.*

① **immediately** /ɪ'miːdɪətli/ *adv* very soon, or very soon after an event ○ *He got* *my letter, and wrote back immediately.* ○ *As soon as he heard the news he immediately phoned his wife.*

immense /ɪ'mens/ *adj* very big; enormous

immensely /ɪ'mensli/ *adv* very much

immensity /ɪ'mensɪti/ *noun* a huge size

immerse /ɪ'mɜːs/ (**immerses, immersing, immersed**) *verb* **1.** to plunge something into a liquid ○ *He lowered the box into the water until it was completely immersed.* ○ *To sterilise the bottle, immerse in water and boil for four minutes.* **2.** to be completely involved in something you are doing [~in] ○ *She was immersed in her book and didn't hear me come in.* □ **to immerse yourself in something** to concentrate on, or get fully involved in, something ○ *He immersed himself in the study of Latin literature.*

immigrant /'ɪmɪgrənt/ *noun* a person who comes to a country to live

immigrate /'ɪmɪgreɪt/ (**immigrates, immigrating, immigrated**) *verb* to come to live in a new country

immigration /ˌɪmɪ'greɪʃ(ə)n/ *noun* the process of settling in a new country ○ *The government is encouraging immigration because of the shortage of workers in key industries.*

imminent /'ɪmɪnənt/ *adj* which is about to happen

immobile /ɪ'məʊbaɪl/ *adj* not moving; not able to move

immoral /ɪ'mɒrəl/ *adj* not following the usual principles of good behaviour

immortal /ɪ'mɔːt(ə)l/ *adj* very famous; which will always be remembered ○ *that immortal line from 'Casablanca': 'play it again, Sam'* ○ *And now, another song from the immortal Frank Sinatra.*

immortalise /ɪ'mɔːt(ə)laɪz/ (**immortalises, immortalising, immortalised**), **immortalize** *verb* to make someone or something be remembered for ever

immovable /ɪ'muːvəb(ə)l/ *adj* which cannot be moved

immune /ɪ'mjuːn/ *adj* **1.** protected against infection ○ *I seem to be immune to colds – I just never have any.* ○ *This injection should make you immune to yellow fever.* **2.** legally protected against, or not liable to, something ○ *She believed she would be immune from prosecution.* (NOTE: You are immune **to** a disease, and **from** prosecution.)

immune system /ɪ'mjuːn ˌsɪstəm/ *noun* a complex network of cells which protects the body from disease

immunisation /ˌɪmjʊnaɪ'zeɪʃ(ə)n/, **immunization** *noun* injections, etc., to make a person immune to a disease

immunise /'ɪmjʊnaɪz/ (**immunises, immunising, immunised**), **immunize** *verb* to give someone immunity to a disease (NOTE: You immunise someone **against** a disease.)

③ **immunity** /ɪ'mjuːnɪti/ *noun* **1.** the ability to resist attacks of a disease because of antibodies produced in your body **2.** protection from something such as following a rule or being punished for a crime

imp /ɪmp/ *noun* a small devil ○ *When you go into the cathedral, look out for the little imp carved high up near the choir.*

impact[1] /'ɪmpækt/ *noun* **1.** a strong effect ○ *The TV documentary had an strong impact on the viewers.* **2.** an instance of two things coming together with force ○ *The car was totally crushed by the impact of the collision.* ◇ **on impact** as soon as contact is made ○ *The plane burst into flames on impact with the ground.*

impact[2] /ɪm'pækt/ (**impacts, impacting, impacted**) *verb* to have a strong effect on something [~on] ○ *The fall in the value of the currency will impact strongly on businesses.*

impair /ɪm'peə/ (**impairs, impairing, impaired**) *verb* to damage something so that it does not work properly

impaired /ɪm'peəd/ *adj* damaged or not very good, either temporarily or permanently

impairment /ɪm'peəmənt/ *noun* damage to or poor functioning of something, particularly a physical or mental ability

impale /ɪm'peɪl/ (**impales, impaling, impaled**) *verb* to jab a sharp object through the body

impart /ɪm'pɑːt/ (**imparts, imparting, imparted**) *verb* to pass on information to someone; to communicate something to someone ○ *The news imparted a sense of excitement to the meeting.*

impartial /ɪm'pɑːʃ(ə)l/ *adj* not biased

impassable /ɪm'pɑːsəb(ə)l/ *adj* which you cannot go through or across

impasse /æm'pɑːs/ *noun* a state where two sides cannot agree

impassioned /ɪm'pæʃ(ə)nd/ *adj* showing very deep feelings

impassive /ɪm'pæsɪv/ *adj* showing no expression of feelings

impatience /ɪm'peɪʃ(ə)ns/ *noun* a lack of the ability to wait for things in a calm way

impatient /ɪm'peɪʃ(ə)nt/ *adj* unable to wait for something in a calm way; in a hurry to do something ○ *We were all impatient for the film to start.* ○ *He's very impatient with anyone who works slowly.*

impatiently /ɪm'peɪʃ(ə)ntli/ *adv* in an impatient way

impeccable /ɪm'pekəb(ə)l/ *adj* perfect

impede /ɪm'piːd/ (**impedes, impeding, impeded**) *verb* to make it difficult for someone or something to go forwards or make progress (*formal*)

impediment /ɪm'pedɪmənt/ *noun* an obstacle; a situation which stops something happening ○ *Is there any just impediment why these two people should not be joined together in matrimony?* ○ *He finds that not having a car is no impediment to his job as a salesman.*

impel /ɪm'pel/ (**impels, impelling, impelled**) *verb* to force someone to do something (*formal*)

impending /ɪm'pendɪŋ/ *adj* which will happen soon

impenetrable /ɪm'penɪtrəb(ə)l/ *adj* which you cannot go through or into, or see through

imperative /ɪm'perətɪv/ *noun* **1.** a thing which has to be done ○ *Profitability is an imperative with most companies.* **2.** (*in grammar*) the form of a verb when used as a command ○ *'Come here!' is an example of a verb used in the imperative.*

imperceptible /ˌɪmpə'septɪb(ə)l/ *adj* which you cannot notice

imperfect /ɪm'pɜːfɪkt/ *adj* not perfect, or not complete ○ *It's an imperfect world we live in.* ○ *We only have an imperfect understanding of the origins of the universe.* ■ *noun* (*in grammar*) the form of a verb which shows that something was not finished in the past ○ *'He was cycling' is the imperfect past of 'to cycle'.*

imperialism /ɪm'pɪəriəlɪz(ə)m/ *noun* **1.** (*often as a criticism*) the idea or practice of having an empire formed of colonies **2.** control of other countries as if they were part of an empire ○ *Multinational businesses are accused of economic imperialism.*

imperil /ɪm'perəl/ (**imperils, imperilling, imperilled**) *verb* to put someone or something in danger (*formal*)

impersonal /ɪm'pɜːs(ə)n(ə)l/ *adj* not personal; without any personal character ○ *Just stick to the facts and keep the interview impersonal.* ○ *The waiting-room was cold and impersonal.*

impersonate /ɪm'pɜːsəneɪt/ (**impersonates, impersonating, impersonated**) *verb* to dress like someone, or to pretend to be that person (NOTE: + **impersonation** *n*)

impertinent /ɪm'pɜːtɪnənt/ *adj* rude and lacking respect

impetuous /ɪm'petʃuəs/ *adj* referring to an action done without thinking

impetus /'ɪmpɪtəs/ *noun* energy which encourages rapid progress

implacable /ɪm'plækəb(ə)l/ *adj* strong; which cannot be satisfied or changed

implant[1] /ɪm'plɑːnt/ *noun* a thing which has been fixed inside a person's body ○ *She has had silicone breast implants.*

implant[2] /'ɪmplɑːnt/ (**implants, implanting, implanted**) *verb* **1.** to fix something inside a person's mind very deeply ○ *A love of his native country was implanted in him from a very early age.* **2.** to fix something inside a person's body ○ *Surgeons implanted a pacemaker in his chest.*

implausible /ɪm'plɔːzɪb(ə)l/ *adj* difficult or impossible to believe

implement[1] /'ɪmplɪmənt/ *noun* a tool or instrument ○ *The plumber brought an implement for bending pipes.*

implement[2] /'ɪmplɪˌment/ (**implements, implementing, implemented**) *verb* to put something into effect ○ *The changes must be implemented immediately.*

implicate /'ɪmplɪkeɪt/ (**implicates, implicating, implicated**) *verb* □ **to implicate someone in something** to suggest that someone is connected with a crime or something morally wrong ○ *The documents seemed to implicate his boss in the scandal.*

② **implication** /ˌɪmplɪ'keɪʃ(ə)n/ *noun* **1.** the possible effect of an action [~of/~for] ○ *What will be the implications of the election results for public spending?* **2.** the fact of being involved in a crime or something that is morally wrong [~in] ○ *The newspaper revealed his implication in the affair of the stolen diamonds.* **3.** a suggestion that something such as a criticism is true although it has not been expressed directly [~that] ○ *I resent the implication that I knew anything about the report in advance.*

implicit /ɪm'plɪsɪt/ *adj* **1.** referring to something which is not definitely said, but is suggested ○ *It was implicit in his tone of voice that he wasn't going to agree.* ○ *Implicit in the inspectors' report was the possibility that the restaurant might have to* *close permanently.* **2.** complete and unquestioning ○ *He has implicit faith in his teacher's advice.*

implode /ɪm'pləʊd/ (**implodes, imploding, imploded**) *verb* to burst inwards

implore /ɪm'plɔː/ (**implores, imploring, implored**) *verb* to ask someone in an emotional way to do something (*formal*)

② **imply** /ɪm'plaɪ/ (**implies, implying, implied**) *verb* to suggest something without saying it directly [~(that)] ○ *He implied that he knew where the papers had been hidden.* ○ *The lawyer implied that the witness had not in fact seen the accident take place.*

impolite /ˌɪmpə'laɪt/ *adj* rude; not polite

import¹ /'ɪmpɔːt/ *noun* a product that has come from another country (NOTE: usually plural) ■ *adj* relating to products from another country ○ *import controls*

import² /ɪm'pɔːt/ (**imports, importing, imported**) *verb* to bring goods into a country ○ *The company imports television sets from Japan.* ○ *This car was imported from France.*

① **importance** /ɪm'pɔːtəns/ *noun* the fact of being important [/~for] ○ *He recognized the importance of her contribution to the success of the deal.* ○ *This decision has great importance for everyone here.*

① **important** /ɪm'pɔːtənt/ *adj* **1.** having a great effect; mattering very much ○ *It's important to be in time for the interview.* ○ *I have to go to London for an important meeting.* ○ *He left a file containing important papers in the taxi.* **2.** (*of a person*) in a high position ○ *He has an important job.* ○ *She's an important government official.* ○ *He was promoted to a more important position.*

importantly /ɪm'pɔːtəntli/ *adv* referring to something that is important ○ *He understood the facts, and, more importantly for a teacher, he was able to explain them.*

② **impose** /ɪm'pəʊz/ (**imposes, imposing, imposed**) *verb* **1.** to put something into action officially [~on] ○ *They have tried to impose a ban on smoking.* **2.** to ask someone to pay a tax or because they have done something wrong [~on] ○ *The government imposed a tax increase on electrical items.* ○ *The judge imposed a fine on the shoplifter.* **3.** to cause someone trouble or inconvenience [~on] ○ *I hope it's not imposing on you too much, but I need to have the report today.*

③ **imposing** /ɪm'pəʊzɪŋ/ *adj* grand or solemn

imposition /ˌɪmpə'zɪʃ(ə)n/ *noun* **1.** the action of making people pay a tax or of laying down conditions ○ *the imposition of a tax on tea* **2.** an unfair duty or punishment ○ *She felt it was something of an imposition.*

② **impossible** /ɪm'pɒsɪb(ə)l/ *adj* which cannot be done ○ *It's impossible to do all this work in two hours.* ○ *Getting skilled staff is becoming impossible.*

impossibly /ɪm'pɒsɪbli/ *adv* to such an extent that something is impossible

impotent /'ɪmpət(ə)nt/ *adj* **1.** not able to do anything ○ *We were impotent in the face of the typhoon.* **2.** (*of a man*) physically unable to have sexual intercourse

impound /ɪm'paʊnd/ (**impounds, impounding, impounded**) *verb* to take something away and keep it until the owner claims it

impoverished /ɪm'pɒvərɪʃt/ *adj* made poor

impractical /ɪm'præktɪk(ə)l/ *adj* **1.** which is not easy to put into practice ○ *It is quite impractical to expect three people to move all the furniture in two hours.* **2.** not good at doing things with your hands ○ *He's totally impractical – he can't even change a light bulb.*

imprecise /ˌɪmprɪ'saɪs/ *adj* not precise; not accurate

impregnable /ɪm'pregnəb(ə)l/ *adj* which cannot be captured

impregnate /'ɪmpregneɪt/ (**impregnates, impregnating, impregnated**) *verb* **1.** to soak with something, usually with a liquid ○ *She wiped the floor with a cloth impregnated with insecticide.* **2.** (*of a male animal*) to make a female animal pregnant

③ **impress** /ɪm'pres/ (**impresses, impressing, impressed**) *verb* to make someone feel admiration or respect ○ *Her rapid response to the request impressed her boss.* ○ *She was impressed by his skill with the paintbrush.* ○ *The military government organised the display to impress the neighbouring states.*

② **impression** /ɪm'preʃ(ə)n/ *noun* an effect on someone's mind ○ *Blue walls create an impression of coldness.* ○ *The exhibition made a strong impression on her.*

impressionable /ɪm'preʃ(ə)nəb(ə)l/ *adj* easily influenced by others

impressionistic /ɪmˌpreʃ(ə)'nɪstɪk/ *adj* **1.** giving a general rather than a detailed idea of something **2.** (*of art or music*) in, or having elements of, the Impressionist style

③ **impressive** /ɪm'presɪv/ *adj* impressing people ○ *He had a series of impressive wins in the chess tournament.* ○ *The government staged an impressive display of military hardware.*

imprint[1] /'ɪmprɪnt/ *noun* **1.** a mark made by something pressed down **2.** the name and address of the publisher or printer, which must appear on most printed matter

imprint[2] /ɪm'prɪnt/ (**imprints, imprinting, imprinted**) *verb* to stamp; to mark ○ *The outline of a child's hand was left imprinted on the door.* ○ *The scene of devastation remained indelibly imprinted on her memory.*

imprison /ɪm'prɪz(ə)n/ (**imprisons, imprisoning, imprisoned**) *verb* to put or to keep someone in prison (NOTE: + **imprisonment** *n*)

improbable /ɪm'prɒbəb(ə)l/ *adj* not probable, not likely

impromptu /ɪm'prɒmptjuː/ *adj* done without any rehearsal or practice ○ *He gave an impromptu interview on his doorstep.* ■ *adv* without any rehearsal or practice ○ *They gave her five minutes' notice to speak impromptu in front of six hundred delegates.*

improper /ɪm'prɒpə/ *adj* **1.** not according to the normal rules of society or of an organisation ○ *It was a quite improper use of our company name.* **2.** rude or shocking ○ *The old man made some very improper suggestions to the girl.* **3.** used in a wrong way ○ *The improper use of a drug can cause serious damage to health.*

impropriety /ˌɪmprə'praɪəti/ *noun* the quality of being socially wrong, or an act which is socially wrong

① **improve** /ɪm'pruːv/ (**improves, improving, improved**) *verb* **1.** to make something better ○ *We are trying to improve our image with a series of TV commercials.* **2.** to get better ○ *The general manager has promised that the bus service will improve.* ○ *It poured down all morning, but in the afternoon the weather improved a little.*

improve on *or* **upon** *verb* to try to do better than something ○ *She tried to improve on her previous performance.*

① **improvement** /ɪm'pruːvmənt/ *noun* **1.** a process of becoming better, or of making something better [~in] ○ *There has been no improvement in the train service since we complained.* **2.** a change that you make so that something is better than before [~on/to] ○ *They carried out some improvements to the house.* ○ *We are planning some home improvements such as a new kitchen.* ○ *The new software is a great improvement on the old version.*

improvise /'ɪmprəvaɪz/ (**improvises, improvising, improvised**) *verb* **1.** to do or to make something without any proper planning ○ *Without a tent, we improvised a shelter using leaves and branches.* **2.** to speak without having any text to read from ○ *Having forgotten the notes for her speech she had to improvise as best as she could.*

impudent /'ɪmpjʊd(ə)nt/ *adj* rude and without showing respect

impulse /'ɪmpʌls/ *noun* **1.** a sudden feeling or decision ○ *He had a sudden impulse to take the car and drive to France.* □ **to do something on impulse** to do something because you have just thought of it, not because it was planned **2.** a shock which makes something move or work ○ *Electrodes attached to his head measure brain impulses.* ○ *Neurons are cells in the nervous system which transmit nerve impulses.*

impulsive /ɪm'pʌlsɪv/ *adj* acting because of a sudden decision, without thinking

impure /ɪm'pjʊə/ *adj* which is not pure, having another substance mixed with it

impurity /ɪm'pjʊərɪti/ (*plural* **impurities**) *noun* a substance which is impure

① **in** /ɪn/ *prep, adv* **1.** used for showing place ○ *He lives in the country.* ○ *In Japan it snows a lot during the winter.* ○ *She's in the kitchen.* ○ *He's still in bed.* ○ *Don't stand outside in the pouring rain.* **2.** at home, in an office, at a station ○ *Is the boss in?* ○ *He isn't in yet.* ○ *My husband usually gets in from work about now.* ○ *The train from Birmingham is due in at 6.30.* **3.** used for showing time ○ *In autumn the leaves turn brown.* ○ *On holiday there was nothing to do in the evenings.* ○ *She was born in 1999.* ○ *He ate his meal in five minutes.* ○ *We went for a skiing holiday in January.* **4.** used for showing time in the future ○ *I'll be back home in about two hours.* ○ *She should arrive in twenty minutes' time.* **5.** fashionable ○ *This year, short skirts are in.* **6.** used for showing a state or appearance ○ *He was dressed in black.* ○ *She ran outside in her dressing gown.* ○ *We're in a hurry.* ○ *The words are set out in alphabetical order.*

inability /ˌɪnə'bɪlɪti/ *noun* the state of being unable to do something ○ *His inability to make decisions causes problems.*

inaccessible /ˌɪnək'sesɪb(ə)l/ *adj* **1.** impossible to reach or to get to ○ *They live in a farm which is inaccessible by car.* ○

The explorers were lost in an inaccessible mountain region. ○ *The valley is inaccessible to motorists.* **2.** difficult to read or understand ○ *He writes in a rather inaccessible style.*

inaccuracy /ɪn'ækjʊrəsi/ (*plural* **inaccuracies**) *noun* **1.** the state of not being exact ○ *the inaccuracy of the data* **2.** something that is not correct, but usually only slightly incorrect ○ *I found several inaccuracies in the report.*

inaccurate /ɪn'ækjʊrət/ *adj* not accurate, not exact

inaction /ɪn'ækʃən/ *noun* a lack of activity

inactive /ɪn'æktɪv/ *adj* not active or not doing anything

inadequacy /ɪn'ædɪkwəsi/ (*plural* **inadequacies**) *noun* **1.** a feeling of being inadequate ○ *Being compared with his brother all the time gave him feelings of inadequacy.* (NOTE: no plural in this meaning) **2.** a feature of something which is not good enough or which does not work well enough ○ *The report mentions inadequacies in the system used for counting votes*

inadequate /ɪn'ædɪkwət/ *adj* **1.** not enough ○ *The island has inadequate supplies of water in the summer months.* **2.** not good enough compared with what is expected ○ *Being compared to his brother made him feel quite inadequate.*

inadvisable /ˌɪnəd'vaɪzəb(ə)l/ *adj* (*of a plan or idea*) unwise or foolish

inalienable /ɪn'eɪliənəb(ə)l/ *adj* which cannot be taken away or refused (*formal*)

inane /ɪ'neɪn/ *adj* silly, senseless

inanimate /ɪn'ænɪmət/ *adj* not alive

inappropriate /ˌɪnə'prəʊpriət/ *adj* not suitable, not fitting the circumstances

inarticulate /ˌɪnɑː'tɪkjʊlət/ *adj* not speaking clearly ○ *an inarticulate exam candidate*

inasmuch as /ˌɪnəz'mʌtʃ əz/ *conj* seeing that, owing to the fact that

inaudible /ɪn'ɔːdɪb(ə)l/ *adj* which cannot be heard

inaugural /ɪ'nɔːgjʊrəl/ *adj* **1.** being the first of a series **2.** referring to an official beginning

inaugurate /ɪ'nɔːgjʊreɪt/ (**inaugurates, inaugurating, inaugurated**) *verb* **1.** to open officially a new building or a festival, etc. ○ *The Minister was invited to inaugurate the new computer system.* **2.** □ **to inaugurate someone as something** to swear in someone as the new holder of a particular post ○ *Each new US president is inaugurated on January 20th.*

inborn /ˌɪn'bɔːn/ *adj* which you have since birth

inbox /'ɪnbɒks/ *noun* (*computers*) the folder in an email package into which mail is delivered

③ **Inc** *abbr US* incorporated ○ *We're dealing with a company called John Doe, Inc.*

incandescent /ˌɪnkæn'des(ə)nt/ *adj* **1.** shining brightly **2.** showing extreme emotion, especially anger

incapable /ɪn'keɪpəb(ə)l/ *adj* not able to do something

incapacitate /ˌɪŋkə'pæsɪteɪt/ (**incapacitates, incapacitating, incapacitated**) *verb* to make someone unable to do something

incapacity /ˌɪnkə'pæsɪti/ *noun* **1.** a lack of ability to do something **2.** a physical or mental disability

incarcerate /ɪn'kɑːsəreɪt/ (**incarcerates, incarcerating, incarcerated**) *verb* to put someone in prison (*formal*)

incarnation /ˌɪnkɑː'neɪʃ(ə)n/ *noun* an appearance in human form ○ *To many people, he was the incarnation of evil.*

incendiary /ɪn'sendiəri/ *adj* which causes fire ○ *Terrorists left incendiary devices in the shopping centre.*

incense[1] /'ɪnsens/ *noun* powder which when burnt gives a strong smell ○ *The priests burnt incense round the shrine.*

incense[2] /ɪn'sens/ (**incenses, incensing, incensed**) *verb* to make someone angry ○ *His speech incensed the crowd who went on the rampage in the centre of the town.*

incensed /ɪn'senst/ *adj* very angry

③ **incentive** /ɪn'sentɪv/ *noun* something which encourages someone to do something ○ *The possibility of a bonus is an incentive to the sales force.*

inception /ɪn'sepʃən/ *noun* the start of something (*formal*)

incessant /ɪn'ses(ə)nt/ *adj* continuous, not stopping

incest /'ɪnsest/ *noun* the offence of a person's having sexual intercourse with a close relative such their daughter, son, mother or father

② **inch** /ɪntʃ/ *noun* a measure of length equal to 2.54 centimetres ○ *a three-and-a-half-inch disk* ○ *Snow lay six inches deep on the ground.* ○ *She is five foot six inches tall (5'6").* ◊ **foot** (NOTE: With numbers **inch** is usually written with the symbol ": *a 3½"* *disk; He is 5' 9".*; say: 'a three and a half inch disk', 'He's five foot nine')

② **incident** /'ɪnsɪd(ə)nt/ *noun* **1.** something which happens, especially something unpleasant ○ *Last year six hundred incidents of oil pollution were reported.* **2.** a violent action or disturbance that occurs somewhere ○ *There were several incidents during the demonstration.*

incidental /ˌɪnsɪ'dent(ə)l/ *adj* happening in connection with something else, but not important ○ *Breaking the Olympic record was almost incidental – winning the gold medal was the important thing.*

② **incidentally** /ˌɪnsɪ'dent(ə)li/ *adv* used for mentioning something new in a conversation

incinerate /ɪn'sɪnəreɪt/ (**incinerates, incinerating, incinerated**) *verb* to destroy something by burning

incinerator /ɪn'sɪnəreɪtə/ *noun* a furnace for burning rubbish

incipient /ɪn'sɪpiənt/ *adj* which is beginning or starting

incision /ɪn'sɪʒ(ə)n/ *noun* a cut in a patient's body made by a surgeon

incisive /ɪn'saɪsɪv/ *adj* very perceptive, sharp or cutting

incite /ɪn'saɪt/ (**incites, inciting, incited**) *verb* to encourage something □ **to incite someone to something** to encourage or persuade someone to do something bad ○ *He was accused of inciting racial hatred.*

③ **inclination** /ˌɪŋklɪ'neɪʃ(ə)n/ *noun* **1.** a tendency ○ *After a big lunch he had a strong inclination to go to sleep.* **2.** a slope, or angle of a slope ○ *The hill has an inclination of 1 in 15.* **3.** a slight movement forwards ○ *She acknowledged my presence with a slight inclination of her head.*

incline[1] /'ɪnklaɪn/ *noun* a slope ○ *A steep incline leads to the garage.*

incline[2] /ɪn'klaɪn/ (**inclines, inclining, inclined**) *verb* **1.** to slope ○ *The garden inclines gradually down to the river.* **2.** to encourage someone to do something ○ *The results of the poll inclined newspaper reporters to try to forecast the result of the general election.* **3.** □ **to be inclined to do something** to be likely to do something ○ *She is inclined to try to excuse everything her son does.* ○ *Our washing machine is inclined to overheat.* **4.** to bend or to bow ○ *He inclined his head and murmured a greeting.*

③ **inclined** /ɪn'klaɪnd/ *adj* **1.** sloping ○ *An inclined plane gives easy access to the warehouse.* **2.** likely to do something ○ *She is inclined to get very annoyed when anyone criticises her golf strokes.*

① **include** /ɪn'kluːd/ (**includes, including, included**) *verb* to count someone or something along with others ○ *The waiter did not include service in the bill.* ○ *The total is £140, not including insurance and handling charges.* ○ *There were 120 people at the wedding if you include the children.*

① **including** /ɪn'kluːdɪŋ/ *prep* taking something together with something else ○ *The total comes to £25.00 including VAT.*

③ **inclusion** /ɪn'kluːʒ(ə)n/ *noun* the act of counting someone or something in among others

inclusive /ɪn'kluːsɪv/ *adj* **1.** which counts something in with other things ○ *The bill is not inclusive of VAT.* **2.** (*giving figures or dates*) referring to a period of time or a passage of writing that includes the first and last items mentioned ○ *The conference runs from the 12th to the 16th inclusive.* ○ *For the next lesson, you need to study pages 23 to 31 inclusive.*

incoherent /ˌɪnkəʊ'hɪərənt/ *adj* not able to speak in a way which makes sense

① **income** /'ɪnkʌm/ *noun* an amount of money which you receive, especially as pay for your work ○ *Their weekly income is not really enough to live on.*

③ **income tax** /'ɪnkʌm tæks/ *noun* a tax on money earned as wages or salary

incoming /'ɪnkʌmɪŋ/ *adj* **1.** arriving or coming in **2.** recently elected or appointed ○ *The chairman welcomed the incoming committee.* ○ *The incoming government has the job of trying to deal with the worsening economic situation.*

incomparable /ɪn'kɒmp(ə)rəb(ə)l/ *adj* which cannot be compared to anything else

incompatible /ˌɪnkəm'pætɪb(ə)l/ *adj* not able to live, work or fit together, or with something else [~with] ○ *The two computer systems are incompatible.* ○ *John and Susan are quite incompatible: I don't know how they can stay married.* ○ *His behaviour is quite incompatible with his position as a manager.*

incompetent /ɪn'kɒmpɪt(ə)nt/ *adj* who cannot work well, who is not able to do something ○ *She was dismissed for being incompetent.*

incomplete /ˌɪnkəm'pliːt/ *adj* not complete, not finished

incomprehensible /ɪnˌkɒmprɪ'hensɪb(ə)l/ *adj* which cannot be understood

inconceivable /ˌɪnkən'siːvəb(ə)l/ *adj* very unlikely, which cannot be imagined

inconclusive /ˌɪnkən'kluːsɪv/ *adj* without any definite result

incongruous /ɪn'kɒŋgruəs/ *adj* which does not fit with the rest, which seems out of place

inconsequential /ɪnˌkɒnsɪ'kwenʃəl/ *adj* not important

inconsiderate /ˌɪnkən'sɪdərət/ *adj* not thinking of other people

inconsistent /ˌɪnkən'sɪstənt/ *adj* whose behaviour changes often and is unpredictable ○ *He's inconsistent – sometimes he works hard, sometimes he doesn't.* ○ *The team's form has been inconsistent of late.*

inconspicuous /ˌɪnkən'spɪkjuəs/ *adj* not at all obvious

incontinent /ɪn'kɒntɪnənt/ *adj* unable to control the body's waste products

inconvenience /ˌɪnkən'viːniəns/ *noun* awkwardness ○ *The inconvenience of the date of the business conference, on the day before Christmas Day, meant that few people turned up.* ■ *verb* (**inconveniences, inconveniencing, inconvenienced**) to bother someone ○ *I don't want to inconvenience you.*

inconvenient /ˌɪnkən'viːniənt/ *adj* awkward, causing difficulties

③ **incorporate** /ɪn'kɔːpəreɪt/ (**incorporates, incorporating, incorporated**) *verb* **1.** to bring something into something else to make one main whole ○ *We are trying to incorporate the suggestions from the committees into the main proposal.* **2.** to form an official body or a registered company ○ *The company was incorporated three years ago.*

incorporated /ɪn'kɔːpəreɪtɪd/ *adj US* showing that a company has been officially registered

incorrect /ˌɪnkə'rekt/ *adj* wrong, not correct

incorrigible /ɪn'kɒrɪdʒɪb(ə)l/ *adj* badly behaved and unlikely to improve

increase¹ /ɪn'kriːs/ *noun* an instance of something becoming larger [~in] ○ *an increase in tax* or *a tax increase* ○ *an increase in the cost of living*

increase² /'ɪnkriːs/ (**increasing, increased**) *verb* **1.** to rise or grow [~in] ○ *Oil has increased in price twice in the past year.* **2.** to make a level or amount higher ○ *The boss increased her salary.* ○ *Rail fares have been increased by 10%.*

① **increased** /ɪn'kriːst/ *adj* larger or higher than before ○ *These increased rail fares mean that we cannot afford to travel so much.*

② **increasingly** /ɪn'kriːsɪŋli/ *adv* more and more ○ *He found it increasingly difficult to keep up with the workload at the office.* ○ *His future with the company looks increasingly doubtful.*

incredible /ɪn'kredɪb(ə)l/ *adj* **1.** which you find difficult to believe ○ *It is absolutely incredible that anyone as rich as he is can avoid paying tax.* **2.** of remarkable size, quantity, etc. ○ *Over the years he has amassed an incredible fortune.* ○ *You should go to see 'Jaws' – it's an incredible film.*

③ **incredibly** /ɪn'kredɪbli/ *adv* very, extremely ○ *She's incredibly tall.* ○ *It is incredibly difficult to find a parking space near my office in the middle of the day.*

incredulous /ɪn'kredjʊləs/ *adj* who does not believe what someone says or what is happening

increment /'ɪŋkrɪmənt/ *noun* a regular automatic addition to salary

incremental /ˌɪŋkrɪ'ment(ə)l/ *adj* gradually increasing

incriminate /ɪn'krɪmɪneɪt/ (**incriminates, incriminating, incriminated**) *verb* to show that a person has committed a criminal act □ **to incriminate yourself** to say something which makes you seem to be guilty ○ *He refused to testify in case he incriminated himself.*

incumbent /ɪn'kʌmbənt/ *noun* a person who holds an official post ○ *Mrs Jones is our new librarian – she is taking over from the present incumbent next month.* ○ *There will be no changes in the governor's staff while the present incumbent is still in office.*

③ **incur** /ɪn'kɜː/ (**incurs, incurring, incurred**) *verb* to get into a position where you have to pay money or will be in danger ○ *The company has incurred considerable losses in the USA.* ○ *He incurred many debts during his time at college.*

incurable /ɪn'kjʊərəb(ə)l/ *adj* unable to be cured

incursion /ɪn'kɜːʃ(ə)n/ *noun* an attack on another country's territory

indebted /ɪn'detɪd/ *adj* owing something to someone

indecent /ɪn'diːs(ə)nt/ *adj* **1.** rude, offensive ○ *He was prosecuted for indecent exposure.* **2.** not polite ○ *As soon as the* *speeches ended, there was an indecent rush to find something to eat.*

indecision /ˌɪndɪˈsɪʒ(ə)n/ *noun* hesitation, the inability to decide

indecisive /ˌɪndɪˈsaɪsɪv/ *adj* **1.** without any positive result ○ *The result of the election was indecisive as no party had a majority.* **2.** who cannot decide anything ○ *He was criticised for being indecisive.*

① **indeed** /ɪnˈdiːd/ *adv* (*for emphasis*) really ○ *Thank you very much indeed for inviting me to stay.* ○ *They have been very kind indeed to their daughter.*

indefensible /ˌɪndɪˈfensɪb(ə)l/ *adj* which cannot be defended or excused

indefinable /ˌɪndɪˈfaɪnəb(ə)l/ *adj* which cannot be defined or explained

③ **indefinite** /ɪnˈdef(ə)nət/ *adj* without a definite end ○ *He has been suspended for an indefinite period, pending an inquiry.*

indefinite article /ɪnˌdef(ə)nət ˈɑːtɪk(ə)l/ *noun* the word 'a' or 'an' in English, or a word with a similar use in another language

indelible /ɪnˈdelɪb(ə)l/ *adj* which cannot be removed

indelicate /ɪnˈdelɪkət/ *adj* rude and embarrassing

indemnity /ɪnˈdemnɪti/ (*plural* **indemnities**) *noun* compensation for a loss or a wrong

indent /ɪnˈdent/ (**indents, indenting, indented**) *verb* to start a line several spaces in from the left-hand side of the page

indentation /ˌɪndenˈteɪʃ(ə)n/ *noun* **1.** a hole or space in the surface or edge of something **2.** a space at the beginning of a line of text

② **independence** /ˌɪndɪˈpendəns/ *noun* **1.** a state of not needing help from anyone else [~from] ○ *She's eighteen and is looking forward to a life of independence from her family.* **2.** freedom from rule by another country

② **independent** /ˌɪndɪˈpendənt/ *adj* **1.** free, not ruled by anyone else ○ *Slovenia has been independent since 1991.* **2.** not owned by a group, not controlled by the state ○ *The big chains are forcing the independent shops to close down.* **3.** not needing help from anyone else ○ *She's eighteen and wants to be independent of her family.*

in-depth /ɪn ˈdepθ/ *adj* very serious and thorough

indescribable /ˌɪndɪˈskraɪbəb(ə)l/ *adj* which cannot be described

indestructible /ˌɪndɪˈstrʌktəb(ə)l/ *adj* which cannot be destroyed

indeterminate /ˌɪndɪˈtɜːmɪnət/ *adj* **1.** not exact or clear **2.** not having a predictable result

③ **index** /ˈɪndeks/ *noun* **1.** a list, usually in alphabetical order, showing the pages on which different subjects appear in a book ○ *Look up the references to London in the index.* (NOTE: The plural in this sense is **indexes**) **2.** a regular report which shows rises and falls in things such as prices and unemployment ○ *The economic indices look very promising at the moment.* (NOTE: The plural in this sense is **indices**)

index card /ˈɪndeks kɑːd/ *noun* a card used to make a card index

index finger /ˈɪndeks ˌfɪŋgə/ *noun* the first finger, next to the thumb

① **indicate** /ˈɪndɪkeɪt/ (**indicates, indicating, indicated**) *verb* to show something [~(that)] ○ *He indicated the position of the hotel on this map?* ○ *The latest figures indicate that not as many people are now unemployed.*

③ **indication** /ˌɪndɪˈkeɪʃ(ə)n/ *noun* a sign

indicative /ɪnˈdɪkətɪv/ *adj* that shows or indicates something ○ *Repeated attacks on tourists are indicative of a general breakdown of law and order in the country.*

indicator /ˈɪndɪkeɪtə/ *noun* **1.** something which indicates how good or bad, hot or cold, etc. something is ○ *The inflation rate is a good indicator of the strength of the economy.* **2.** a flashing light on a car which shows which way the driver is going to turn ○ *His left indicator was flashing and then he turned right!*

indict /ɪnˈdaɪt/ (**indicts, indicting, indicted**) *verb* to charge someone with a crime (*formal*)

indictment /ɪnˈdaɪtmənt/ *noun* a written statement of the details of the crime with which someone is charged (*formal*)

indifferent /ɪnˈdɪf(ə)rənt/ *adj* **1.** not caring, not interested ○ *The world cannot remain indifferent to the problems of the starving refugees in central Africa.* **2.** not particularly good, not special ○ *In view of the school's indifferent exam results, the governors have set up a review of teaching practices.* ○ *They served us a bottle of very indifferent champagne.*

indigenous /ɪnˈdɪdʒɪnəs/ *adj* born in or belonging to a place

indigestion /ˌɪndɪˈdʒestʃən/ *noun* a pain caused when your stomach has difficulty in digesting food

indignant /ɪnˈdɪgnənt/ *adj* feeling offended or angry because of an unfair situation ○ *I was really indignant when I found out how much my colleague earned.*

indignation /ˌɪndɪgˈneɪʃ(ə)n/ *noun* a feeling of something not being fair or reasonable ○ *The crowd showed their indignation at the referee's decision by whistling.*

indignity /ɪnˈdɪgnɪti/ *noun* a shameful action which causes embarrassment

indirect /ˌɪndaɪˈrekt/ *adj* not direct ○ *The taxi took us to the airport by a very indirect route.*

indirectly /ˌɪndɪˈrektli/ *adv* not directly

indirect object /ˌɪndɪrekt ˈɒbdʒekt/ *noun* a person or thing to whom or which an action is done

indirect speech /ˌɪndɪrekt ˈspiːtʃ/ *noun* the reporting of what someone has said

indiscreet /ˌɪndɪˈskriːt/ *adj* very obvious, not discreet

indiscretion /ˌɪndɪˈskreʃ(ə)n/ *noun* **1.** carelessness about what you do or say ○ *the minister's indiscretion in talking to the journalist* **2.** a mildly immoral action ○ *We must forget his youthful indiscretions.*

indiscriminate /ˌɪndɪˈskrɪmɪnət/ *adj* widespread; not choosing carefully

indispensable /ˌɪndɪˈspensəb(ə)l/ *adj* which you cannot do without

indisputable /ˌɪndɪˈspjuːtəb(ə)l/ *adj* which cannot be argued about (*formal*)

indistinct /ˌɪndɪˈstɪŋkt/ *adj* vague or unclear

indistinguishable /ˌɪndɪˈstɪŋgwɪʃəb(ə)l/ *adj* not able to be told apart from something [~from] ○ *To some people margarine is indistinguishable from butter.*

① **individual** /ˌɪndɪˈvɪdʒuəl/ *noun* a single person ○ *We welcome private individuals as well as groups.* ■ *adj* single, for a particular person ○ *We treat each individual case on its merits.* ○ *We provide each member of the tour group with an individual itinerary.*

individualism /ˌɪndɪˈvɪdʒuəlɪz(ə)m/ *noun* a liking for doing things in your own way, not as other people do

individuality /ˌɪndɪvɪdʒuˈælɪti/ *noun* the quality which makes each person different from all others

individually /ˌɪndɪˈvɪdʒuəli/ *adv* separately, singly

indoctrinate /ɪnˈdɒktrɪneɪt/ (**indoctrinates, indoctrinating, indoctrinated**) *verb* to teach political or religious ideas and force someone to accept them (NOTE: + **indoctrination** *n*)

indoor /ˈɪndɔː/ *adj* inside a building ○ *an indoor swimming pool*

③ **indoors** /ɪnˈdɔːz/ *adv* inside a building ○ *Let's go indoors.* ○ *Mum was indoors, reading.*

③ **induce** /ɪnˈdjuːs/ (**induces, inducing, induced**) *verb* **1.** to persuade someone to do something ○ *Do you think an extra 10% will induce them to sign the contract?* ○ *They induced him to steal the plans by offering him a large amount of money.* **2.** to make something, such as the birth of a child, happen ○ *The baby was ten days late, so had to be induced.*

inducement /ɪnˈdjuːsmənt/ *noun* something which is used to persuade someone to do something

induction /ɪnˈdʌkʃən/ *noun* the process of starting a new person in a new job ○ *Induction for all trainees will take place over two weeks in May.*

indulge /ɪnˈdʌldʒ/ (**indulges, indulging, indulged**) *verb* **1.** to have or do something you enjoy [~in] ○ *On holiday I indulged my passion for chocolate.* ○ *I like to indulge in a sauna once in a while.* **2.** to give someone little luxuries ○ *She always indulges her little grandson with sweets and presents.* □ **to indulge yourself** to give yourself a little luxury ○ *I love Greek cakes, but I don't often get the chance to indulge myself.*

indulgence /ɪnˈdʌldʒəns/ *noun* a pleasant activity, especially eating or drinking

indulgent /ɪnˈdʌldʒənt/ *adj* kind, too generous towards someone

① **industrial** /ɪnˈdʌstriəl/ *adj* relating to the production of goods ○ *The Midlands is the main industrial region in Britain.*

industrial action /ɪnˌdʌstriəl ˈækʃən/ *noun* a strike or protest by workers

industrial estate /ɪnˈdʌstriəl ɪˌsteɪt/ *noun* an area of land near a town specially for factories and warehouses

industrialisation /ɪnˌdʌstriəlaɪˈzeɪʃ(ə)n/, **industrialization** *noun* another spelling of **industrialisation**

industrialise /ɪnˈdʌstriəˌlaɪz/, **industrialize** *verb* another spelling of **industrialise**

industrialised, **industrialized** *adj* another spelling of **industrialised**

industrialist /ɪn'dʌstriəlɪst/ *noun* an owner or director of a factory

industrial park /ɪn'dʌstriəl pɑːk/ *noun* an area especially for factories and businesses

industrial relations /ɪn,dʌstriəl rɪ'leɪʃ(ə)nz/ *plural noun* the relations between management and workers ○ *He carried out a study of industrial relations over the last 10 years.* ○ *We aim to promote good industrial relations.*

industrial tribunal /ɪn,dʌstriəl traɪ'bjuːn(ə)l/ *noun* a court which decides in disputes between employers and workers

industrious /ɪn'dʌstriəs/ *adj* who works steadily and hard

① **industry** /'ɪndəstri/ *noun* the production of goods and the provision of services, or the companies involved in this activity ○ *Oil is a key industry.* ○ *The car industry has had a good year.* ○ *The government is helping industry to sell more products abroad.* ○ *The tourist industry brings in a lot of foreign currency.*

inebriated /ɪ'niːbrieɪtɪd/ *adj* drunk

inedible /ɪn'edɪb(ə)l/ *adj* which you cannot eat

ineffective /,ɪnɪ'fektɪv/ *adj* which does not have any effect

ineffectual /,ɪnɪ'fektʃuəl/ *adj* **1.** which does not have the right effect ○ *Her ineffectual attempts to open the door.* **2.** weak, unable to show any authority ○ *He's a nice man but quite ineffectual as a salesman.*

inefficient /,ɪnɪ'fɪʃ(ə)nt/ *adj* not efficient

ineligible /ɪn'elɪdʒɪb(ə)l/ *adj* who is not qualified for something or to do something

inept /ɪ'nept/ *adj* not able to do much; lacking any skill

③ **inequality** /,ɪnɪ'kwɒlɪti/ (*plural* **inequalities**) *noun* the state of not being equal

inertia /ɪ'nɜːʃə/ *noun* **1.** a lack of desire to move, a lack of ability to do anything ○ *A feeling of inertia came over the committee as the meeting continued.* **2.** a physical force which makes a stationary body remain still, or a moving body remain moving ○ *An astronaut who pushes himself away from his spaceship will continue to drift away into space under inertia if he is not attached to a safety line.* **3.** a lack of energy, laziness ○ *He became manager of the shop through sheer inertia on the part of everyone else.*

inescapable /,ɪnɪ'skeɪpəb(ə)l/ *adj* which you cannot avoid

③ **inevitable** /ɪn'evɪtəb(ə)l/ *adj* which must happen, which cannot be avoided ○ *It was inevitable that the younger children would want to leave home.*

inexcusable /,ɪnɪk'skjuːzəb(ə)l/ *adj* which cannot be excused or forgiven

inexhaustible /,ɪnɪg'zɔːstɪb(ə)l/ *adj* **1.** impossible to finish or use up **2.** never becoming tired

inexpensive /,ɪnɪk'spensɪv/ *adj* cheap

inexperienced /,ɪnɪk'spɪəriənst/ *adj* who does not have much experience

inexplicable /,ɪnɪk'splɪkəb(ə)l/ *adj* which cannot be explained

infamous /'ɪnfəməs/ *adj* famous for being bad or unpleasant ○ *Tourists were warned not to go near the infamous back street bars.*

infancy /'ɪnfənsi/ *noun* young childhood ○ *Two of her children died in infancy.*

③ **infant** /'ɪnfənt/ *noun* a young baby

infantile /'ɪnfəntaɪl/ *adj* (*(of behaviour)*) very silly and annoying

infantry /'ɪnfəntri/ *noun* soldiers who fight on foot

infatuated /ɪn'fætjueɪtɪd/ *adj* wildly in love

infatuation /ɪn'fætjueɪʃ(ə)n/ *noun* a sudden strong feeling of love for someone, especially someone you do not know very well or someone who does not love you

infect /ɪn'fekt/ (**infects, infecting, infected**) *verb* to pass on a disease or infection to someone ○ *He was infected with the disease when he was abroad on holiday.*

③ **infection** /ɪn'fekʃən/ *noun* a disease which spreads from one person to another ○ *Her throat infection keeps coming back.* ○ *He was sneezing and spreading infection to other people in the office.* ○ *She seems to catch every little infection there is.*

③ **infectious** /ɪn'fekʃəs/ *adj* (*of an illness or an emotion such as fear*) likely to be passed from one person to another ○ *This strain of flu is highly infectious.* ○ *He's a great music teacher and his enthusiasm for jazz is very infectious.* Compare **contagious**

③ **infer** /ɪn'fɜː/ (**infers, inferring, inferred**) *verb* to reach an opinion about something from facts [~from/~(that)] ○ *He inferred from the letter that the accused knew the murder victim.* ○ *Counsel inferred that the witness had not been present at the time of the accident.*

③ **inference** /ˈɪnf(ə)rəns/ *noun* an understanding or conclusion

inferior /ɪnˈfɪəriə/ *noun* a person of a lower rank ○ *He always addressed his inferiors in a very abrupt way.*

inferiority complex /ɪnˌfɪəriˈɒrɪti ˌkɒmpleks/ *noun* a feeling that you are not as good as others

inferno /ɪnˈfɜːnəʊ/ (*plural* **infernos**) *noun* a very great fire ○ *By the time help arrived there was a raging inferno at the plastics factory.*

infertile /ɪnˈfɜːtaɪl/ *adj* (*of living things*) not able to reproduce ○ *Over the last few years there has been an alarming increase in the number of infertile couples.*

infest /ɪnˈfest/ (**infests, infesting, infested**) *verb* (*of parasites*) to be present in large numbers

infidelity /ˌɪnfɪˈdelɪti/ *noun* being unfaithful

infighting /ˈɪnfaɪtɪŋ/ *noun* bitter arguments between members of a group

infiltrate /ˈɪnfɪltreɪt/ (**infiltrates, infiltrating, infiltrated**) *verb* to become, or to make someone become, a member of an organisation secretly, without the officials knowing

infinite /ˈɪnfɪnət/ *adj* with no end

③ **infinitive** /ɪnˈfɪnɪtɪv/ *noun* the basic form of a verb, usually shown with 'to'

infinity /ɪnˈfɪnɪti/ *noun* a space or quantity that never ends

infirmary /ɪnˈfɜːməri/ (*plural* **infirmaries**) *noun* an old word for a hospital, now used in names ○ *the Glasgow Royal Infirmary*

inflame /ɪnˈfleɪm/ (**inflames, inflaming, inflamed**) *verb* **1.** to make more violent ○ *His speech was calculated to inflame public opinion.* **2.** to make part of the body react by becoming red and sore ○ *His eyes had become inflamed from the chlorine in the water.*

inflamed /ɪnˈfleɪmd/ *adj* red and sore

inflammable /ɪnˈflæməb(ə)l/ *adj* which can easily catch fire

inflammation /ˌɪnfləˈmeɪʃ(ə)n/ *noun* the process or state of being sore, red and swollen as a reaction to an infection, an irritation or an injury

inflammatory /ɪnˈflæmət(ə)ri/ *adj* which makes people behave violently ○ *His inflammatory speeches caused riots.*

inflatable /ɪnˈfleɪtəb(ə)l/ *adj* which can be inflated or blown up

inflate /ɪnˈfleɪt/ (**inflates, inflating, inflated**) *verb* to fill with air ○ *He used a small pump to inflate the dinghy.*

② **inflation** /ɪnˈfleɪʃ(ə)n/ *noun* a state of the economy where prices and wages are rising to keep up with each other ○ *The government is trying to keep inflation down below 3%.* ○ *We have 15% inflation or inflation is running at 15%.*

inflationary /ɪnˈfleɪʃ(ə)n(ə)ri/ *adj* which tends to increase inflation

inflection /ɪnˈflekʃən/, **inflexion** *noun* the ending of a word which changes to indicate the plural, the gender, etc.

inflexible /ɪnˈfleksɪb(ə)l/ *adj* **1.** which cannot be bent or changed ○ *The rules on this point are quite inflexible.* ○ *Negotiation is pointless if everyone maintains an inflexible position.* **2.** determined not to change your mind ○ *She had a reputation for being totally inflexible in her talks with her EU counterparts.*

③ **inflict** /ɪnˈflɪkt/ (**inflicts, inflicting, inflicted**) *verb* □ **to inflict pain *or* damage on someone** to cause pain or damage to someone or something ○ *Drugs can inflict serious harm on young people.* ○ *The bombs inflicted heavy damage on the capital.*

① **influence** /ˈɪnfluəns/ *noun* the ability to change someone or something; an effect [~on] ○ *He has had a good influence on the other staff in the department.* ○ *The influence of the moon on the tides.* ○ *He was charged with driving under the influence of alcohol.* ■ *verb* (**influences, influencing, influenced**) to make someone or something change ○ *She was deeply influenced by her old teacher.* ○ *The moon influences the tides.* ○ *The price of oil has influenced the price of industrial goods.*

③ **influential** /ˌɪnfluˈenʃəl/ *adj* **1.** which causes change ○ *Her speech was influential in changing the opinion of the other members of the committee.* **2.** powerful ○ *She has influential friends who got the police to drop the charges.*

influx /ˈɪnflʌks/ *noun* a sudden flow into

info /ˈɪnfəʊ/ *abbr* information

② **inform** /ɪnˈfɔːm/ (**informs, informing, informed**) *verb* to tell someone something officially ○ *Have you informed the police that your watch has been stolen?* ○ *I regret to inform you that your father has died.* ○ *We are pleased to inform you that your offer has been accepted.*

② **informal** /ɪnˈfɔːm(ə)l/ *adj* **1.** relaxed, not formal ○ *Dress casually – the party will* *be informal.* ○ *The guide gave us an informal talk on the history of the castle.* **2.** (*of language*) used when talking to friends and family

informant /ɪn'fɔːmənt/ *noun* a person who informs or who gives information to someone

① **information** /ˌɪnfə'meɪʃ(ə)n/ *noun* a set of facts about something [~about/on/as to/regarding] ○ *She couldn't give the police any information about how the accident happened.* ○ *She gave me a very useful piece* or *bit of information.*

informative /ɪn'fɔːmətɪv/ *adj* which tells you a lot, which provides a lot of information

informed /ɪn'fɔːmd/ *adj* having a lot of information, or having the latest information

informer /ɪn'fɔːmə/ *noun* a person who gives information to the police about a crime or criminals, sometimes someone who is himself a criminal

infraction /ɪn'frækʃən/ *noun* the act of breaking the law

③ **infrastructure** /'ɪnfrəˌstrʌktʃə/ *noun* the basic structure of roads, railways and other connections in a country

infrequent /ɪn'friːkwənt/ *adj* not frequent, not happening very often

infringe /ɪn'frɪndʒ/ (**infringes, infringing, infringed**) *verb* to break a law or a right (NOTE: + **infringement** *n*)

infuriate /ɪn'fjʊərieɪt/ (**infuriates, infuriating, infuriated**) *verb* to make someone very angry ○ *Slow service in restaurants always infuriates him.*

infuriating /ɪn'fjʊərieɪtɪŋ/ *adj* which makes you very annoyed

infusion /ɪn'fjuːʒ(ə)n/ *noun* **1.** an addition of something new which will make an improvement ○ *The football club needs an infusion of capital to buy new players.* **2.** a drink made by pouring boiling water onto a dry substance such as tea or flowers

ingenious /ɪn'dʒiːniəs/ *adj* very clever ○ *It was an ingenious plan.* (NOTE: Do not confuse with **ingenuous**.)

ingenuity /ˌɪndʒɪ'njuːɪti/ *noun* skill in inventing new things

ingest /ɪn'dʒest/ (**ingests, ingesting, ingested**) *verb* to take into the body as if it were food

ingrained /ˌɪn'greɪnd/ *adj* deeply fixed

ingratiate /ɪn'greɪʃieɪt/ (**ingratiates, ingratiating, ingratiated**) *verb* □ **to ingratiate yourself with someone** to make yourself liked by someone

ingratiating /ɪn'greɪʃieɪtɪŋ/ *adj* which will help make someone like you

ingratitude /ɪn'grætɪtjuːd/ *noun* not being grateful

ingredient /ɪn'griːdiənt/ *noun* a material or substance which you use to make something ○ *Make sure you've got all your ingredients together before you start cooking.*

inhabit /ɪn'hæbɪt/ (**inhabits, inhabiting, inhabited**) *verb* to live in a place

inhabitant /ɪn'hæbɪt(ə)nt/ *noun* a person who lives in a particular place

inhabited /ɪn'hæbɪtɪd/ *adj* lived in, especially by humans

inhale /ɪn'heɪl/ (**inhales, inhaling, inhaled**) *verb* to breathe in, to draw something into your lungs when breathing

inherent /ɪn'hɪərənt/ *adj* natural, which belongs to someone or something naturally

inherit /ɪn'herɪt/ (**inherits, inheriting, inherited**) *verb* **1.** to receive money or property from a person who has died ○ *She inherited a small fortune from her father.* ○ *When her grandfather died she inherited the shop.* **2.** to have characteristics passed on from a parent ○ *I think she has inherited her father's grumpy character.* **3.** to take over a client or a problem from someone ○ *When they bought the shop they inherited a lot of ancient equipment.* ○ *The new manager had inherited a lot of financial problems.*

③ **inheritance** /ɪn'herɪt(ə)ns/ *noun* property which is received from a dead person

③ **inhibit** /ɪn'hɪbɪt/ (**inhibits, inhibiting, inhibited**) *verb* to prevent an action happening

inhibited /ɪn'hɪbɪtɪd/ *adj* not being able to express yourself freely or to do what you want to do

③ **inhibition** /ˌɪnhɪ'bɪʃ(ə)n/ *noun* the action of some mental influence which prevents normal reactions

inhospitable /ˌɪnhɒ'spɪtəb(ə)l/ *adj* not welcoming

inhuman /ɪn'hjuːmən/ *adj* cruel, not human

inhumane /ˌɪnhjuː'meɪn/ *adj* not humane; barbarous

inhumanity /ˌɪnhjuː'mænɪti/ *noun* the cruel treatment of people or animals

② **initial** /ɪ'nɪʃ(ə)l/ *adj* first ○ *The initial stage of the project went off smoothly.* ○ *My* *initial reaction was to say 'no'.* ○ *He started the business with an initial sum of £500.* ■ *verb* (**initials, initialling, initialled**) to write the first letters of your name on a document to show you have read and approved it ○ *Can you initial each page of the contract to show that you have approved it?* ○ *Please initial the agreement at the place marked with an X.*

③ **initially** /ɪ'nɪʃ(ə)li/ *adv* at the beginning ○ *Initially we didn't like the new flat, but we have got used to it now.*

initiate /ɪ'nɪʃieɪt/ (**initiates, initiating, initiated**) *verb* **1.** to start something ○ *He initiated the new project last year.* **2.** to introduce someone into something secret ○ *He initiated her into the secrets of digging for gold.* **3.** to show someone the basic information about something

② **initiative** /ɪ'nɪʃətɪv/ *noun* a decision which is intended to solve a problem ○ *The government has proposed various initiatives to get the negotiations moving again.* □ **to take the initiative** to decide to do something which other people are reluctant to do ○ *The manager decided to take the initiative and ask for a meeting with the boss.* ○ *The president took the initiative in asking the rebel leader to come for talks.*

inject /ɪn'dʒekt/ (**injects, injecting, injected**) *verb* **1.** to force a liquid into something under pressure ○ *The nurse injected the drug using a needle and syringe.* ○ *He injected himself with a drug.* **2.** to put something new into something ○ *to inject some cash into a company* ○ *Come on, let's try to inject some life into these rehearsals!*

③ **injection** /ɪn'dʒekʃən/ *noun* the act of putting a liquid into the body using a needle ○ *The doctor gave him a flu injection.*

injunction /ɪn'dʒʌŋkʃ(ə)n/ *noun* **1.** a court order forcing someone to stop doing something or not to do something ○ *He got an injunction preventing his ex-wife from selling his car.* ○ *The company applied for an injunction to stop their rivals marketing a product which was similar to theirs.* **2.** an instruction, order ○ *The children were given strict injunctions not to open the door.* ○ *Most people ignored the government's injunction to spend less and save more.*

injure /'ɪndʒə/ (**injures, injuring, injured**) *verb* to cause pain or damage to a part of the body ○ *He injured his back playing rugby.* ○ *He was badly injured in a car accident.*

③ **injured** /'ɪndʒəd/ *noun* hurt ○ *The injured girl had fallen off her bike.*

② **injury** /'ɪndʒəri/ (*plural* **injuries**) *noun* damage to your body ○ *He never really recovered from his football injury.* ○ *She received severe back injuries in the accident.*

injustice /ɪn'dʒʌstɪs/ *noun* a lack of justice

ink /ɪŋk/ *noun* the liquid in a pen ○ *He has ink marks on his shirt.* ○ *The ink won't come off the tablecloth.* ○ *She wrote comments on his work in red ink.*

ink-jet printer /'ɪnk dʒet ˌprɪntə/ *noun* a computer printer that prints characters by sending out little jets of ink

inkling /'ɪŋklɪŋ/ *noun* a small idea

inland /'ɪnlənd/ *adv* away from the coast of a country ○ *If you go inland from the port, you soon get into the forest.*

in-laws /'ɪn lɔːz/ *plural noun* the parents of your wife or husband ○ *He visited his in-laws while his wife was in hospital.*

inlet /'ɪnlet/ *noun* a small branch of water off a large stretch of water ○ *The smugglers could have used any one of the numerous inlets along this stretch of coastline.*

in-line skating /ˌɪn laɪn 'skeɪtɪŋ/ *noun* same as **rollerblading**

inmate /'ɪnmeɪt/ *noun* a person living in a home or in a prison

inn /ɪn/ *noun* a small hotel

② **inner** /'ɪnə/ *adj* inside ○ *Go through that arch and you will come to the inner courtyard.* ○ *Heat is conducted from the inner to the outer layer of the material.*

inner circle /ˌɪnə 'sɜːk(ə)l/ *noun* a small group of people closely associated with an important person such as a president

③ **inner city** /ˌɪnə 'sɪti/ *noun* the central part of a city

innermost /'ɪnəməʊst/ *adj* **1.** furthest inside ○ *A long dark corridor led to the innermost part of the bank vault.* **2.** deepest, most private ○ *His poems reveal his innermost feelings.*

innings /'ɪnɪŋz/ (*plural same*) *noun* (*in cricket*) the time when a team or a player is batting (NOTE: In US English, in baseball, the singular **inning** is used.)

innocence /'ɪnəs(ə)ns/ *noun* **1.** not being guilty ○ *The lawyers tried to prove his innocence.* **2.** not having any experience or particular knowledge ○ *In my innocence, I believed them when they said they were police officers.*

innocent /'ɪnəs(ə)nt/ *adj* not guilty ○ *He was found to be innocent of the crime.* ○ *In English law, the accused is always pre-*

sumed to be innocent until he is proved to be guilty.

innocuous /ɪ'nɒkjuəs/ *adj* harmless

③ **innovation** /ˌɪnə'veɪʃ(ə)n/ *noun* a new invention, a new way of doing something

innovative /'ɪnəveɪtɪv/ *adj* new in a way that has not been tried before ○ *a very innovative design*

innuendo /ˌɪnju'endəʊ/ (*plural* **innuendoes** or **innuendos**) *noun* a remark that suggests someone has done something wrong, but without giving direct details

innumerable /ɪ'njuːm(ə)rəb(ə)l/ *adj* very many, which cannot be counted

inoffensive /ˌɪnə'fensɪv/ *adj* harmless

③ **input** /'ɪnpʊt/ *noun* **1.** a contribution to a discussion ○ *Thank you very much for your input during the seminar.* **2.** information that is put into a computer [~from/~into/to] ○ *The input from the various branches is fed automatically into the head office computer.*

inquest /'ɪŋkwest/ *noun* a legal inquiry into how someone died

③ **inquire** /ɪn'kwaɪə/ (**inquires** /ɪŋ'kwaɪə/, **inquiring, inquired**), **enquire** *verb* **1.** to ask questions about something ○ *The chef inquired if anything was wrong with the meal.* ○ *She phoned the travel agent to inquire about air fares to Australia.* ○ *She inquired about my mother's health.* **2.** to investigate, to try to find out about something ○ *The police are inquiring into his background.* ○ *The social services are inquiring about the missing girl.*

inquiring /ɪn'kwaɪərɪŋ/ *adj* interested in finding out information

③ **inquiry** /ɪn'kwaɪəri/ *noun* **1.** a formal investigation into a problem ○ *a government inquiry into the police force* ○ *A public inquiry will be held about plans to build another airport.* **2.** a question about something ○ *I refer to your inquiry of May 25th.* ○ *All inquiries should be addressed to this department.* ○ *He made an inquiry about trains to Edinburgh.* (NOTE: also spelt **enquiry**.)

inquisitive /ɪn'kwɪzɪtɪv/ *adj* asking a lot of questions

insane /ɪn'seɪn/ *adj* with a mental disorder

insanity /ɪn'sænɪti/ *noun* a severe mental disorder or illness

insatiable /ɪn'seɪʃəb(ə)l/ *adj* which cannot be satisfied

inscribe /ɪn'skraɪb/ (**inscribes, inscribing, inscribed**) *verb* **1.** to write, especially to write a note inside a book when giving it to someone ○ *The book is inscribed 'with best wishes to John, from the author'.* **2.** to write permanently, as on stone ○ *The names of the dead soldiers are inscribed on the walls of the cemetery.*

inscription /ɪn'skrɪpʃən/ *noun* **1.** words cut on a surface such as stone ○ *The tomb has an inscription in Latin.* **2.** a note written in a book which is given to someone ○ *The inscription in the front of the book is by the author who gave it to his mother.*

insect /'ɪnsekt/ *noun* a small animal with six legs and a body in three parts ○ *A butterfly is a kind of insect.* ○ *Insects have eaten the leaves of the cabbages.* ○ *She was stung by an insect.*

insecticide /ɪn'sektɪsaɪd/ *noun* a liquid or powder which kills insects

insecure /ˌɪnsɪ'kjʊə/ *adj* **1.** not safe ○ *She felt insecure when walking down the High Street alone at night.* **2.** not firmly fixed ○ *Be careful! that scaffolding looks insecure.*

insemination /ɪnˌsemɪ'neɪʃ(ə)n/ *noun* the process of making a woman or female animal pregnant

insensitive /ɪn'sensɪtɪv/ *adj* not worrying how other people feel, not sensitive to other people's feelings

insert[1] /ɪn'sɜːt/ (**inserts, inserting, inserted**) *verb* to put something inside something else ○ *She inserted another sentence into the letter.* ○ *He inserted each leaflet into an envelope.* ○ *Insert a coin into the slot.*

insert[2] /'ɪnsɜːt/ *noun* a paper which is put inside something ○ *The invitation card had an insert with a map showing how to get to the hotel.*

inset /'ɪnset/ *noun* a small piece which is put into something larger, such as a small picture inside a larger one

① **inside** /ɪn'saɪd/ *adv* in a house or other building ○ *Come on inside – it's cold in the street.* ○ *It rained all afternoon, so we just sat inside and watched TV.* ○ *Is there anyone there? – The house seems quite dark inside.* ■ *prep* in ○ *There was nothing inside the bottle.* ○ *She was sitting inside the car, reading a book.* ○ *I've never been inside his office.*

inside leg /'ɪnˌsaɪd leg/ *noun* the measurement of an inside trouser leg seam

inside out /ˌɪnsaɪd 'aʊt/ *adv* **1.** turned with the inner part facing outwards ○ *He* *put his pyjamas on inside out.* **2.** □ **to know something inside out** to know something very well ○ *She knows Central London inside out.*

insider /ɪn'saɪdə/ *noun* a person who works in an organisation and therefore knows secret information

insider dealing /ɪnˌsaɪdə 'diːlɪŋ/ *noun* the illegal buying or selling of shares by people who have inside information about a company

insidious /ɪn'sɪdiəs/ *adj* working secretly to do harm

insight /'ɪnsaɪt/ *noun* clear ideas or knowledge

insignificant /ˌɪnsɪg'nɪfɪkənt/ *adj* very small and unimportant

insincere /ˌɪnsɪn'sɪə/ *adj* not sincere

insinuate /ɪn'sɪnjueɪt/ (**insinuates, insinuating, insinuated**) *verb* **1.** to suggest by hinting at something in an unpleasant way ○ *The finance director seemed to be insinuating that the boss was incompetent.* **2.** □ **to insinuate yourself** to work your way gradually into a favourable position ○ *He managed to insinuate himself into the MD's good books.*

insipid /ɪn'sɪpɪd/ *adj* with no particular taste ○ *They served us some insipid tomato soup.*

② **insist** /ɪn'sɪst/ (**insists, insisting, insisted**) *verb* to state firmly [~(that)] ○ *He insisted that he had never touched the car.* ○ *I insist on an immediate explanation.*

insistence /ɪn'sɪstəns/ *noun* firm demands for something

insistent /ɪn'sɪstənt/ *adj* stating or demanding something firmly

③ **in so far as** /ɪn 'səʊ 'fɑː 'æz/, **insofar as** *conj* to the extent that

insolent /'ɪnsələnt/ *adj* rude and lacking in respect

insoluble /ɪn'sɒljʊb(ə)l/ *adj* **1.** (*of a substance*) which will not dissolve in water **2.** (*of a problem*) which cannot be solved

insolvent /ɪn'sɒlvənt/ *adj* (*especially of a business*) not able to pay debts

insomnia /ɪn'sɒmniə/ *noun* the condition of not being able to sleep

③ **inspect** /ɪn'spekt/ (**inspects, inspecting, inspected**) *verb* to look at something closely ○ *She inspected the room to see if it had been cleaned properly.*

③ **inspection** /ɪn'spekʃ(ə)n/ *noun* the process of examining something closely ○ *They carried out an inspection of the drains.*

③ **inspector** /ɪn'spektə/ *noun* a senior official who examines something closely

inspiration /ˌɪnspɪ'reɪʃ(ə)n/ *noun* **1.** a sudden urge to create something ○ *Her inspiration comes from the countryside of her native Cornwall.* **2.** a sudden good idea ○ *We had run out of sugar and all the shops were closed, but she had an inspiration and tried the railway station snack bar.*

③ **inspire** /ɪn'spaɪə/ (**inspires, inspiring, inspired**) *verb* to make someone feel a wish to do something

inspired /ɪn'spaɪəd/ *adj* filled with a desire to do something

instability /ˌɪnstə'bɪlɪti/ *noun* the condition of not being steady (NOTE: The adjective is **unstable**.)

③ **install** /ɪn'stɔːl/ (**installs, installing, installed**) *verb* to put a piece of equipment into the place where it will operate ○ *It took the plumber a week to install the new central heating system.*

③ **instalment** /ɪn'stɔːlmənt/ *noun* **1.** a payment of part of a total amount of money, which is made regularly ○ *They are paying for the kitchen by monthly instalments.* ○ *You pay £25 down and twelve monthly instalments of £20.* **2.** a part of something which is being broadcast or delivered in parts ○ *The next instalment of the thriller will be shown on Monday evening.* (NOTE: [all senses] The US spelling is **installment**.)

② **instance** /'ɪnstəns/ *noun* an example ○ *There have been several instances of bullying in our local school.* ○ *In this instance, we will pay for the damage.* ◇ **for instance** as an example ○ *Why don't you take up a new sport – golf, for instance?*

② **instant** /'ɪnstənt/ *noun* a moment or second ○ *For an instant, he stood still and watched the policemen.* ■ *adj* immediate ○ *A savings account can give you instant access to your money.*

instantaneous /ˌɪnstən'teɪniəs/ *adj* immediate

instantly /'ɪnstəntli/ *adv* so soon after an event that no time appears to have passed in between

instant messaging /ˌɪnstənt 'mesɪdʒɪŋ/ *noun* a system for communicating directly by electronic means such as e-mail

instead /ɪn'sted/, **instead of** *adv* in place of ○ *We haven't any coffee – would you like some tea instead?* ○ *If you can't go, can I go instead?* ○ *I'm going instead of him, be-*

cause he's ill. ○ *Instead of stopping when the police officer shouted, he ran away.*

instep /'ɪnstep/ *noun* the arched middle part of your foot (NOTE: Do not confuse with **in step**.)

instigate /'ɪnstɪgeɪt/ (**instigating, instigated**) *verb* to make something happen (NOTE: + **instigation** *n*)

instil /ɪn'stɪl/ (**instils, instilling, instilled**) *verb* to put an idea into someone's mind gradually

instinct /'ɪnstɪŋkt/ *noun* something which you have from birth and have not learnt ○ *Many animals have a hunting instinct.*

instinctive /ɪn'stɪŋktɪv/ *adj* (*of a reaction*) natural

② **institute** /'ɪnstɪtjuːt/ *noun* an organisation set up for a special purpose ○ *They are proposing to set up a new institute of education.* ○ *She goes to the research institute's library every week.*

① **institution** /ˌɪnstɪ'tjuːʃ(ə)n/ *noun* **1.** an organisation or society set up for a special purpose ○ *A prison is an institution which houses criminals.* **2.** a permanent custom ○ *British institutions such as cream teas and the royal family* ○ *The lottery has rapidly become a national institution.* **3.** the process of setting something up ○ *the institution of legal action against the president*

③ **instruct** /ɪn'strʌkt/ (**instructs, instructing, instructed**) *verb* to show someone how to do something (*formal*) ○ *We were all instructed in the use of the fire safety equipment.*

instruction /ɪn'strʌkʃən/ *noun* **1.** a statement telling someone what they must do **2.** something which explains how something is to be done or used ○ *She gave us detailed instructions how to get to the church.*

instructive /ɪn'strʌktɪv/ *adj* which gives a lot of information

instructor /ɪn'strʌktə/ *noun* a teacher, especially of a sport

② **instrument** /'ɪnstrʊmənt/ *noun* a piece of equipment or a tool ○ *The technical staff have instruments which measure the flow of electricity.*

instrumental /ˌɪnstrʊ'ment(ə)l/ *adj* **1.** playing an important part in getting something done ○ *The mayor was instrumental in getting our building proposals passed by the planning committee.* **2.** referring to a musical instrument ○ *I prefer instrumental music to choral music.*

insubordinate /ˌɪnsə'bɔːdɪnət/ *adj* not obeying orders

insubstantial /ˌɪnsəb'stænʃəl/ *adj* **1.** not very solid or strong **2.** not seeming real

insufficient /ˌɪnsə'fɪʃ(ə)nt/ *adj* not enough

insular /'ɪnsjʊlə/ *adj* **1.** thinking only of your own local interests ○ *Opponents of the UK joining the euro were accused of being insular.* **2.** referring to an island ○ *The insular flora and fauna of the Galapagos are unique.*

insulate /'ɪnsjʊleɪt/ (**insulates, insulating, insulated**) *verb* to prevent heat or cold or sound escaping or entering

insulation /ˌɪnsjʊ'leɪʃ(ə)n/ *noun* **1.** the process of preventing heat or cold or sound escaping or entering ○ *Good insulation saves energy.* **2.** materials used to insulate something ○ *The previous owners had used straw in the roof for insulation.*

insulin /'ɪnsjʊlɪn/ *noun* a hormone which controls the way in which the body converts sugar into energy and controls the level of sugar in the blood

insult[1] /'ɪnsʌlt/ *noun* a rude word said to or about a person ○ *That is an insult to the government.* ○ *The crowd shouted insults at the police.*

insult[2] /ɪn'sʌlt/ (**insults, insulting, insulted**) *verb* to say rude things about someone ○ *He was accused of insulting the president's wife.*

③ **insulting** /ɪn'sʌltɪŋ/ *adj* rude ○ *I'm used to hearing insulting things about my business.*

② **insurance** /ɪn'ʃʊərəns/ *noun* an agreement with a company by which you are paid money for loss or damage in return for regular payments of money [~for] ○ *Do you have insurance for your travel?*

insure /ɪn'ʃʊə/ (**insures, insuring, insured**) *verb* to agree with a company that if you pay them a regular amount of money, they will pay you for loss or damage to property or persons (NOTE: Do not confuse with **ensure**.)

insurmountable /ˌɪnsə'maʊntəb(ə)l/ *adj* which cannot be solved or dealt with successfully

insurrection /ˌɪnsə'rekʃən/ *noun* a rebellion against a government

intact /ɪn'tækt/ *adj* in one piece, not broken

intake /'ɪnteɪk/ *noun* **1.** a thing or things which are taken in ○ *She is trying to reduce her calorie intake* or *her intake of calories.*

2. a group of new students, soldiers, etc. ○ *We are increasing our intake of mature students again this year.* ○ *This year's intake of recruits has more potential officers than usual.*

intangible /ɪn'tændʒɪb(ə)l/ *adj* which cannot be defined

integral /'ɪntɪgrəl/ *adj* which forms part of something

integrate /'ɪntɪgreɪt/ (**integrates, integrating, integrated**) *verb* to link up to form a whole (NOTE: + **integration** *n*)

integrity /ɪn'tegrɪti/ *noun* honesty, moral principles ○ *His integrity is in doubt since the report on the company loan scandal.*

intellect /'ɪntɪlekt/ *noun* the power of the brain to think or reason ○ *You could see at once that she was a person of superior intellect.*

③ **intellectual** /ˌɪntɪ'lektʃuəl/ *noun* a person who uses his or her brain to make a living ○ *Left-wing intellectuals have criticised the Prime Minister.*

intellectual property /ɪntɪˌlektjuəl 'prɒpəti/ *noun* original creative work or ideas which can be protected by law

③ **intelligence** /ɪn'telɪdʒəns/ *noun* **1.** the ability to think and understand ○ *His intelligence is well above average.* **2.** information provided by the secret services ○ *Intelligence gathered by our network of agents is very useful to us in planning future strategy.*

③ **intelligent** /ɪn'telɪdʒənt/ *adj* able to understand and learn things very well ○ *He's the most intelligent child in his class.*

intelligible /ɪn'telɪdʒɪb(ə)l/ *adj* which can be understood

① **intend** /ɪn'tend/ (**intends, intending, intended**) *verb* [~that] □ **to intend to do something** to plan to do something ○ *We intended to get up early but we all overslept.* ○ *The company intends to sue for damages.*

③ **intense** /ɪn'tens/ *adj* very strong or extreme ○ *There was a period of intense activity to try to finish the work before they went on holiday.* ○ *She had an intense period of study before the exams.*

intensify /ɪn'tensɪfaɪ/ (**intensifies, intensifying, intensified**) *verb* **1.** to become stronger ○ *The rain intensified and continued all night.* **2.** to make something become stronger ○ *He intensified his attacks on the government.* (NOTE: + **intensification** *n*)

intensive /ɪn'tensɪv/ *adj* with a lot of effort ○ *He took a two-week intensive course in German.*

intensive care /ɪnˌtensɪv 'keə/ *noun* the close care and treatment of patients who are very ill or badly injured so that essential action can be taken with a minimum of delay if it is needed

intent /ɪn'tent/ *noun* an aim

② **intention** /ɪn'tenʃən/ *noun* an aim or plan to do something [~of] ○ *I have no intention of going to the party.* ○ *The fans came with the deliberate intention of stirring up trouble.*

intentional /ɪn'tenʃən(ə)l/ *adj* done on purpose

interact /ˌɪntər'ækt/ (**interacts, interacting, interacted**) *verb* □ **to interact with someone** to work in a friendly way with someone ○ *She is interacting well with her teachers.* □ **to interact with something** to have an effect on something

interactive /ˌɪntər'æktɪv/ *adj* each having an effect on the others ○ *We teach drama through interactive groups.*

intercept /ˌɪntə'sept/ (**intercepts, intercepting, intercepted**) *verb* to stop something as it is passing (NOTE: + **interception** *n*)

interchangeable /ˌɪntə'tʃeɪndʒəb(ə)l/ *adj* which can be exchanged for each other

intercom /'ɪntəkɒm/ *noun* a radio for speaking to people over a short distance inside a building

intercontinental /ˌɪntəkɒntɪ'nent(ə)l/ *adj* from one continent to another, between continents

intercourse /'ɪntəkɔːs/ *noun* **1.** same as **sexual intercourse** ○ *They had intercourse on the first night they met.* **2.** communication between people ○ *'How do you do?' is a polite expression used in normal social intercourse.*

interdependent /ˌɪntədɪ'pendənt/ *adj* **1.** needing each other to exist **2.** relying on each other's help or support

① **interest** /'ɪntrəst/ *noun* **1.** special attention to something [~in] ○ *She takes a lot of interest in politics.* ○ *He has no interest in what his sister is doing.* ○ *Why doesn't he take more interest in local affairs?* **2.** a thing that you enjoy doing ○ *Her main interest is canoeing.* ○ *List your special interests on your CV.* **3.** a payment made to someone who lends money [~on] ○ *He was hoping to get 5% interest on his savings.* ○ *How much interest do I have to pay if I borrow £1000?* ■ *verb* (**interests, interesting,**

interested) to attract someone ○ *The book didn't interest me at all.* ○ *He tried to interest several companies in his new invention.*

① **interested** /'ɪntrəstɪd/ *adj* with a personal interest in something ○ *He's interested in old churches.* ○ *She's interested in crime fiction.*

① **interesting** /'ɪntrəstɪŋ/ *adj* attracting your attention; enjoyable ○ *There's an interesting article in the newspaper on European football.* ○ *She didn't find the TV programme very interesting.* ○ *What's so interesting about old cars? – I find them dull.*

interest rate /'ɪntrəst reɪt/ *noun* a percentage charged for borrowing money

interface /'ɪntəfeɪs/ *noun* **1.** a point where two computer systems connect or a program which allows two computer systems to be connected **2.** an area where two different systems meet and interact ○ *Great progress is being made at the interface between medical science and genetic engineering.*

interfere /ˌɪntə'fɪə/ (**interferes, interfering, interfered**) *verb* **1.** to try to become involved in a situation that is not your concern [~in] ○ *His mother was always interfering in his private life.* **2.** to be treat something in such a way that it does not work well [~with] ○ *Stop interfering with the TV controls.*

③ **interference** /ˌɪntə'fɪərəns/ *noun* **1.** an involvement with someone else's life or business [~in] ○ *His parents' interference in his travel plans annoyed him.* **2.** a noise which affects radio or TV programmes

interim /'ɪntərɪm/ *noun* □ **in the interim** meanwhile ○ *We are still redecorating the offices: in the interim you will have to share an office with your boss.*

interior /ɪn'tɪəriə/ *noun* an inner part of a building, car, etc. ○ *She cautiously walked into the interior of the cave.* ○ *The interior of the building is fine, but the exterior needs repainting.*

③ **interior designer** /ɪnˌtɪəriə dɪ'zaɪnə/ *noun* a person who designs the inside of a building, including wall coverings, paint colours, furniture, fabrics, etc.

interject /ˌɪntə'dʒekt/ (**interjects, interjecting, interjected**) *verb* to interrupt with a comment

③ **interjection** /ˌɪntə'dʒekʃən/ *noun* an exclamation, a word used to show an emotion such as surprise

interlude /'ɪntəluːd/ *noun* a short break between two parts of an activity when something different happens ○ *There was a short interlude, then the noise started again.*

intermediary /ˌɪntə'miːdiəri/ (*plural* **intermediaries**) *noun* a person who is the link between parties who do not agree or who are negotiating ○ *He refused to act as an intermediary between the two directors.*

intermediate /ˌɪntə'miːdiət/ *adj* **1.** between two points ○ *We are at an intermediate stage in our research work.* **2.** between beginners and advanced ○ *She has passed her intermediate level English.*

interminable /ɪn'tɜːmɪnəb(ə)l/ *adj* which never ends, which is boring

intermission /ˌɪntə'mɪʃ(ə)n/ *noun especially US* an interval in a performance

intermittent /ˌɪntə'mɪt(ə)nt/ *adj* stopping and starting in an irregular way ○ *Intermittent showers are expected over the weekend.*

intern[1] /'ɪntɜːn/ *noun US* a medical school graduate who is working in a hospital while at the same time finishing his studies ○ *Hospital interns work very long hours.*

intern[2] /ɪn'tɜːn/ (**interns, interning, interned**) *verb* to put someone in a prison or in a camp without trial, usually for political reasons ○ *Many intellectuals and opponents of the military regime have been interned.*

② **internal** /ɪn'tɜːn(ə)l/ *adj* inside

① **international** /ˌɪntə'næʃ(ə)nəl/ *adj* between countries ○ *an international conference on the environment* ○ *an important international company* ■ *noun* a sportsperson who has played for his or her country's team against another country ○ *There are three England internationals in our local team.*

Internet /'ɪntənet/ *noun* an international network allowing people to exchange information on computers using telephone lines ○ *We send messages over the Internet to hundreds of users of our products.* ○ *He searched the Internet for information on cheap plane tickets.* (NOTE: also called simply **the Net**)

interpersonal /ˌɪntə'pɜːs(ə)n(ə)l/ *adj* between people

interplay /'ɪntəpleɪ/ *noun* a reaction between two things

③ **interpret** /ɪn'tɜːprɪt/ (**interprets, interpreting, interpreted**) *verb* to translate what someone is saying into a different language ○ *His brother knows Greek, so he will interpret for us.*

② **interpretation** /ɪnˌtɜːprɪ'teɪʃ(ə)n/ *noun* **1.** a meaning ○ *A poem can have many interpretations.* ○ *The book puts quite a different interpretation on the meaning of the rule.* **2.** the act of translating what someone is saying into a different language ○ *She is taking a course in simultaneous interpretation.* **3.** a way of playing a piece of music ○ *Two of the young musicians were praised for their interpretations of Bach.*

③ **interpreter** /ɪn'tɜːprɪtə/ *noun* a person who translates what someone is saying into a different language

interrelated /ˌɪntərɪ'leɪtɪd/ *adj* in a relationship in which each depends on or is affected by the other or others

interrogate /ɪn'terəgeɪt/ (**interrogates, interrogating, interrogated**) *verb* to ask someone questions to get information, often unpleasantly and for a long period of time (NOTE: + **interrogation** *n*)

interrogative /ˌɪntə'rɒgətɪv/ *adj* which asks a question

interrupt /ˌɪntə'rʌpt/ (**interrupts, interrupting, interrupted**) *verb* to start talking when someone else is talking ○ *Excuse me for interrupting, but have you seen the office keys anywhere?*

③ **interruption** /ˌɪntə'rʌpʃən/ *noun* something that interrupts or stops you from working

intersect /ˌɪntə'sekt/ (**intersects, intersecting, intersected**) *verb* to cut across each other

intersection /'ɪntəˌsekʃən/ *noun* **1.** a place where two or more roads cross ○ *The accident occurred at one of the busiest intersections in the city.* **2.** a place where lines cut across each other ○ *The intersection on the graph shows when the pound became weaker than the dollar.*

intersperse /ˌɪntə'spɜːs/ (**intersperses, interspersing, interspersed**) *verb* **1.** to interrupt one activity with another for short periods of time **2.** to put various things in or among something else

interstate[1] /ɪntə'steɪt/ *adj* **1.** between two countries ○ *Interstate negotiations are continuing to decide on the expansion of the EU.* **2.** *US* between two states ○ *We took the interstate freeway to San Diego.*

interstate[2] /'ɪntəsteɪt/ *noun US* a road between two states ○ *They took Interstate 80 to Nevada.*

③ **interval** /'ɪntəv(ə)l/ *noun* **1.** a period of time between two events or points in time ○ *There will be bright intervals during the morning, but it will rain in the afternoon.* ○ *There will be a short interval during which the table will be cleared.* **2.** a period of time between two acts in a play ○ *Anyone arriving late won't be allowed in until the first interval.*

③ **intervene** /ˌɪntə'viːn/ (**intervenes, intervening, intervened**) *verb* **1.** to be between two things ○ *After they left Singapore, several years intervened before they went to Australia.* **2.** to try to change something that is happening [~in] ○ *Six or seven boys had joined in the fight before the teachers intervened.* ○ *The government refused to intervene in the dispute.*

intervening /ˌɪntə'viːnɪŋ/ *adj* coming between two things ○ *We knew each other at school but haven't met often in the intervening years.*

③ **intervention** /ˌɪntə'venʃən/ *noun* an act of intervening between two things, or an action to make a change in a system

② **interview** /'ɪntəvjuː/ *noun* **1.** a conversation between a famous or interesting person and a journalist, broadcast on radio or TV, or printed in a newspaper ○ *She gave an interview to the Sunday magazine.* **2.** a formal meeting in which one or more people ask you questions to find out if you are suitable for something such as a particular job or a course at university ○ *We asked six candidates for interview.* ○ *He's had eight interviews, but still no job offers.* ○ *When will you attend your first interview?* ■ *verb* (**interviews, interviewing, interviewed**) **1.** to ask a famous or interesting person questions about themselves and their work in order to publish or broadcast what they say ○ *The journalist interviewed the Prime Minister.* **2.** to meet a person who is applying for something such as a job or a place on a university course, to see if he or she is suitable ○ *We interviewed ten candidates, but did not find anyone we liked.*

intimacy /'ɪntɪməsi/ *noun* a sexual relationship with someone

intimate[1] /'ɪntɪmət/ *adj* **1.** very close ○ *She is an intimate friend from my schooldays.* ○ *They had intimate knowledge of the layout of the house.* **2.** sexual ○ *an intimate relationship* **3.** very detailed ○ *They had intimate knowledge of the layout of the house.*

intimate[2] /'ɪntɪmeɪt/ (**intimates, intimating, intimated**) *verb* to announce or to suggest ○ *He intimated that he was going to resign and go to work in Australia.*

intimidate /ɪn'tɪmɪdeɪt/ (**intimidates, intimidating, intimidated**) *verb* to frighten someone by threatening them or appearing to threaten them (NOTE: + **intimidation** *n*)

intimidated /ɪn'tɪmɪdeɪtɪd/ *adj* feeling frightened or feeling that someone is better than you at doing something

intimidating /ɪn'tɪmɪdeɪtɪŋ/ *adj* frightening

① **into** /'ɪntə, 'ɪntʊ, 'ɪntuː/ *prep* **1.** used for showing movement towards the inside ○ *She went into the shop.* ○ *He fell into the lake.* ○ *Put the cards back into their box.* ○ *You can't get ten people into a taxi.* ○ *We all stopped talking when he came into the room.* ○ *The bus is going into the town centre.* **2.** hitting against something ○ *The bus drove into a lamp post.* **3.** used for showing a change ○ *The tadpole changed into a frog.* ○ *Water turns into steam when it is heated.* **4.** used for showing that you are dividing something ○ *Try to cut the cake into ten equal pieces.*

intolerable /ɪn'tɒlərəb(ə)l/ *adj* which you cannot bear

intolerance /ɪn'tɒlərəns/ *noun* a refusal to accept the points of view of other people

intolerant /ɪn'tɒlərənt/ *adj* refusing to accept the points of view of other people

③ **intonation** /ˌɪntə'neɪʃ(ə)n/ *noun* a rise or fall of the voice in speech or singing

intoxicated /ɪn'tɒksɪkeɪtɪd/ *adj* **1.** drunk, under the effects of alcohol ○ *He was charged with driving while intoxicated.* **2.** extremely excited ○ *Intoxicated with their success, they decided to go out to celebrate.*

intractable /ɪn'træktəb(ə)l/ *adj* very difficult to deal with; which is impossible to solve

intranet /'ɪntrənet/ *noun* a computer network within an organisation

intransigent /ɪn'trænsɪdʒənt/ *adj* determined not to change your mind

intransitive /ɪn'trænsɪtɪv/ *adj* describes a verb that does not need a direct object to complete its meaning

intravenous /ˌɪntrə'viːnəs/ *adj* put into a vein

intrepid /ɪn'trepɪd/ *adj* without fear, very brave (*literary or humorous*)

intricacy /'ɪntrɪkəsi/ *noun* the state of being very complicated

intricate /'ɪntrɪkət/ *adj* very complicated, made of many different parts

intrigue /'ɪntriːg/ *noun* a secret plan ○ *The story is one of intrigues at the court of Mary Queen of Scots.* ■ *verb* (**intrigues, intriguing, intrigued**) **1.** to make secret plans, especially to harm someone ○ *She intrigued to get the ambassador assassinated.* **2.** to make someone interested ○ *The girl's story intrigued him.*

intriguing /ɪn'triːgɪŋ/ *adj* which makes you interested

intrinsic /ɪn'trɪnsɪk/ *adj* forming a basic part of something

intro /'ɪntrəʊ/ *noun* an introduction, especially to a piece of music

① **introduce** /ˌɪntrə'djuːs/ (**introduces, introducing, introduced**) *verb* to tell someone another person's name when they meet for the first time ○ *He introduced me to a friend of his called Anne.* ○ *She introduced me to her new teacher.*

① **introduction** /ˌɪntrə'dʌkʃən/ *noun* **1.** a part at the beginning of a book which describes the subject of the book ○ *Read the introduction which gives an explanation of the book's layout.* **2.** a book which gives basic information about a subject ○ *He's the author of an introduction to mathematics.*

introductory /ˌɪntrə'dʌkt(ə)ri/ *adj* introducing something

introspective /ˌɪntrə'spektɪv/ *adj* thinking a lot about yourself

introvert /'ɪntrəvɜːt/ *noun* a person who does not like to be with other people

intrude /ɪn'truːd/ (**intrudes, intruding, intruded**) *verb* to go in or become involved where you are not wanted

③ **intruder** /ɪn'truːdə/ *noun* a person who has got into a place, usually illegally

③ **intrusion** /ɪn'truːʒ(ə)n/ *noun* the act of intruding

intrusive /ɪn'truːsɪv/ *adj* which intrudes and is not wanted

intuition /ˌɪntju'ɪʃ(ə)n/ *noun* thinking of something or knowing something naturally, without it being explained

intuitive /ɪn'tjuːɪtɪv/ *adj* based on intuition

Inuit /'ɪnuɪt/ *noun* a member of a group of people living in the north of Canada and Greenland (NOTE: also called **Eskimo** *or* **Eskimos**, though this may be offensive)

inundate /'ɪnʌndeɪt/ (**inundates, inundating, inundated**) *verb* **1.** to have more things or people than you can deal with ○ *We have been inundated with requests for tickets.* ○ *The relief camps were inundated with refugees.* **2.** to flood a place ○ *Acres of* *farmland were inundated when the banks of the river gave way.*

invade /ɪn'veɪd/ (**invades, invading, invaded**) *verb* **1.** to attack and enter a country with an army ○ *William the Conqueror invaded England in 1066.* **2.** □ **to invade someone's privacy** when people such as journalists try to find out details of someone's private life ○ *She claimed that the photographers had invaded her privacy by climbing over the wall.*

③ **invalid** /'ɪnvəlɪd/ *adj* sick or disabled ○ *Her invalid mother lives in a nursing home.* ■ *noun* a sick or disabled person ○ *She's been an invalid since her operation.*

invaluable /ɪn'væljuəb(ə)l/ *adj* extremely valuable

invariably /ɪn'veəriəbli/ *adv* always

invasion /ɪn'veɪʒ(ə)n/ *noun* entering a country by force with an army ○ *The invasion took place in early June.*

③ **invent** /ɪn'vent/ (**invents, inventing, invented**) *verb* **1.** to create a new process or a new machine ○ *She invented a new type of computer terminal.* ○ *Who invented this communication system?* **2.** to make up an excuse ○ *When she asked him why he was late he invented some story about the train not arriving.*

③ **invention** /ɪn'venʃən/ *noun* **1.** the act of creating a new process or a new machine ○ *The invention of computers was made possible by developments in electronics.* **2.** a machine or process that someone has invented

inventive /ɪn'ventɪv/ *adj* which creates something in a way that shows imagination

③ **inventor** /ɪn'ventə/ *noun* a person who invents new processes or new machines

③ **inventory** /'ɪnvənt(ə)ri/ *noun* **1.** a list of all the things in a place such as a house ○ *The landlord checked the inventory when the tenants left.* **2.** *US* all the goods in a warehouse ○ *Our whole inventory was destroyed by fire.* ○ *We are carrying a high inventory.*

invert /ɪn'vɜːt/ (**inverts, inverting, inverted**) *verb* to turn something upside down or back to front ○ *Invert the mould and ease the jelly onto the dish.*

inverted commas /ɪnˌvɜːtɪd 'kɒməz/ *plural noun* printed or written marks (or) showing that a quotation starts or finishes

③ **invest** /ɪn'vest/ (**invests, investing, invested**) *verb* **1.** to use your money for buying things such as property or shares in a company, so that you will make a profit [~in] ○ *She was advised to invest in government bonds.* ○ *He invested all his money in a restaurant.* **2.** to spend money on something which you believe will be useful [~in] ○ *We have invested in a new fridge.*

② **investigate** /ɪn'vestɪgeɪt/ (**investigates, investigating, investigated**) *verb* to try to find out about something [~what/why/whether etc] ○ *We are investigating the possibility of going to live abroad.* ○ *She asked me to investigate why she had had no response to her complaint.*

② **investigation** /ɪnˌvestɪ'geɪʃ(ə)n/ *noun* a close examination [/~into] ○ *a police investigation into the causes of the crash* □ **on investigation** when it was examined ○ *On further investigation, the newspaper report was shown to be quite untrue.*

investigative /ɪn'vestɪgətɪv/ *adj* who or which investigates

① **investment** /ɪn'vestmənt/ *noun* **1.** money which has been invested in something such as shares or property, and is expected to make a profit [~in] ○ *He has been very successful with his investments in property.* **2.** money spent by a government or a company to improve it or make it more successful [~in] ○ *The economy is suffering from a lack of investment in training.*

invigorate /ɪn'vɪgəreɪt/ (**invigorates, invigorating, invigorated**) *verb* to make someone feel healthy and full of energy

invincible /ɪn'vɪnsɪb(ə)l/ *adj* which cannot be defeated

invisible /ɪn'vɪzɪb(ə)l/ *adj* which cannot be seen ○ *The message was written in invisible ink and hidden inside the pages of a book.*

③ **invitation** /ˌɪnvɪ'teɪʃ(ə)n/ *noun* a letter or card, asking someone to do something or go somewhere [~to] ○ *He received an invitation to his sister's wedding.* ○ *She had an invitation to dinner.* □ **at someone's invitation** invited by someone ○ *She spoke to the meeting at the invitation of the committee.*

② **invite** /ɪn'vaɪt/ (**invites, inviting, invited**) *verb* to ask someone to do something, especially to come to a social event such as a party ○ *We invited two hundred people to the party.* ○ *She invited us to come in.* ○ *She's been invited to talk to the club.*

③ **inviting** /ɪn'vaɪtɪŋ/ *adj* which attracts

② **invoice** /'ɪnvɔɪs/ *noun* a note sent to ask for payment for services or goods ○ *Our invoice dated November 10th has still not been paid.* ○ *They sent in their invoice* *six weeks late.* ○ *Ask the sales assistant to make out an invoice for £250.*

invoke /ɪn'vəʊk/ (**invokes, invoking, invoked**) *verb* to call on someone or something for help or support

involuntary /ɪn'vɒlənt(ə)ri/ *adj* **1.** done suddenly in a way that you cannot control ○ *His leg gave an involuntary jerk when the doctor tapped his knee.* ○ *Her cry was the involuntary reaction of a mother protecting her young.* **2.** not done willingly ○ *Does the travel insurance cover the involuntary cancellation of the holiday?*

① **involve** /ɪn'vɒlv/ (**involves, involving, involved**) *verb* **1.** to include someone or something in an activity or situation ○ *a competition involving teams from ten different countries* ○ *We want to involve the local community in the decision about the bypass.* ○ *Members of the local council are involved in the company which has won the contract for the new road.* **2.** to make an activity necessary ○ *Going to Cambridge from here involves taking a bus and then the train.*

② **involved** /ɪn'vɒlvd/ *adj* complicated

③ **involvement** /ɪn'vɒlvmənt/ *noun* the fact of being connected with someone, or involved in something [~in/with//] ○ *Did she have any involvement with the music festival?* ○ *The police were unable to prove his involvement in the crime.*

inward /'ɪnwəd/ *adj* on the inside

inwardly /'ɪnwədli/ *adv* **1.** to or inside yourself **2.** on or to the inside of something

inwards /'ɪnwədz/ *adv* towards the inside ○ *These doors open inwards.*

in-your-face /ɪn jə/ *adj* direct or obvious in a way that is designed to attract attention

iodine /'aɪədiːn/ *noun* a chemical put on cuts in the skin to prevent infection

IOU /ˌaɪ əʊ 'juː/ *noun* a paper promising that you will pay back money which you have borrowed (NOTE: It spells the words **I owe you**.)

IPA *abbr* International Phonetic Alphabet

③ **IQ** *abbr* intelligence quotient ○ *She has an IQ of 110.*

irate /aɪ'reɪt/ *adj* very angry

Ireland /'aɪələnd/ *noun* a large island forming the western part of the British Isles, containing the Republic of Ireland and Northern Ireland ○ *These birds are found all over Ireland.*

iris /'aɪrɪs/ *noun* **1.** a plant with tall flat leaves and usually yellow or purple flowers ○ *Irises grow well in damp soil.* **2.** a coloured ring in the eye, with the pupil at its centre ○ *The iris has muscles that adjust the size of the pupil.*

① **Irish** /'aɪrɪʃ/ *adj* referring to Ireland ○ *The Irish Sea lies between Ireland and Britain.*

② **iron** /'aɪən/ *noun* **1.** a common grey metal ○ *The old gates are made of iron.* ◊ **cast iron, wrought iron** (NOTE: no plural in this sense: *some iron, lumps of iron, pieces of iron*) **2.** an object with a flat metal bottom, which is heated and used to make clothes smooth after washing ○ *Don't leave the iron there – it will burn the clothes.* ○ *If your iron is not hot enough it won't take the creases out.* ■ *verb* (**irons, ironing, ironed**) to make cloth smooth using an iron ○ *She was ironing shirts when the telephone rang.* ○ *Her skirt doesn't look as if it has been ironed.*

③ **ironing** /'aɪənɪŋ/ *noun* clothes which have been washed and are ready to be ironed

③ **ironing board** /'aɪənɪŋ bɔːd/ *noun* a special narrow table used when ironing clothes

irony /'aɪrəni/ *noun* **1.** a way of referring to something where you say the opposite of what you mean ○ *Do I detect a note of irony in his letter?* **2.** a situation when something happens at the wrong moment, as if deliberately planned ○ *The irony of it was that the rain finally stopped on the last day of our holiday.*

irrational /ɪ'ræʃ(ə)n(ə)l/ *adj* not sensible or reasonable

irreconcilable /ɪˌrekən'saɪləb(ə)l/ *adj* which cannot be made to agree

irregular /ɪ'regjʊlə/ *adj* **1.** not happening in a regular way ○ *An irregular pattern of lines and circles.* ○ *His heart had an irregular beat.* **2.** not level ○ *An irregular stone path leads across the garden.* **3.** not happening always at the same time ○ *His payments are very irregular.* ○ *He makes irregular visits to his mother in hospital.* **4.** not according to rules or a usual way of doing something ○ *This procedure is highly irregular.*

irregularity /ɪˌregjʊ'lærɪti/ (*plural* **irregularities**) *noun* a thing which goes against the rules or the law

irrelevant /ɪ'reləvənt/ *adj* with no connection to the present subject

irreparable /ɪ'rep(ə)rəb(ə)l/ *adj* which cannot be repaired

irreplaceable /ˌɪrɪ'pleɪsəb(ə)l/ *adj* which cannot be replaced

irrepressible /ˌɪrɪˈpresəb(ə)l/ *adj* which cannot be held back

irresistible /ˌɪrɪˈzɪstəb(ə)l/ *adj* which cannot be controlled, which you cannot refuse

irrespective /ˌɪrɪˈspektɪv/ *prep* □ **irrespective of** taking no account of ○ *Anyone parking on a double yellow line will be fined, irrespective of who they are.* ○ *The appointment will be made on merit, irrespective of age or sex.*

irresponsible /ˌɪrɪˈspɒnsɪb(ə)l/ *adj* acting or done in a way that shows a lack of good sense

irreverent /ɪˈrev(ə)rənt/ *adj* not showing respect, often in a humorous way

irreversible /ˌɪrɪˈvɜːsɪb(ə)l/ *adj* which cannot be changed back to how it was before

irrevocable /ɪˈrevəkəb(ə)l/ *adj* which cannot be changed

irrigate /ˈɪrɪgeɪt/ (**irrigates, irrigating, irrigated**) *verb* to supply water to land to allow plants to grow, usually through a system of little channels (NOTE: + **irrigation** *n*)

irritable /ˈɪrɪtəb(ə)l/ *adj* easily annoyed ○ *He was tired and irritable, and snapped at the children.*

irritant /ˈɪrɪt(ə)nt/ *noun* **1.** a thing which annoys ○ *The mosquitoes were a minor irritant, the big problem was the alligators.* **2.** a substance which can irritate ○ *Irritants like chlorine in swimming pool water can make the eyes inflamed.*

irritate /ˈɪrɪteɪt/ (**irritates, irritating, irritated**) *verb* to make someone feel angry or impatient ○ *It irritates me when the trains run late.*

irritated /ˈɪrɪteɪtɪd/ *adj* annoyed

irritating /ˈɪrɪteɪtɪŋ/ *adj* which annoys

③ **irritation** /ˌɪrɪˈteɪʃ(ə)n/ *noun* a feeling of being annoyed and impatient ○ *She watched with irritation as he tried to fix the wheel again.*

③ **is** /ɪz/ 3rd person singular present of **be**

-ish /ɪʃ/ *suffix* **1.** having the quality of, like, tending to **2.** almost, nearly

Islam /ˈɪzlɑːm/ *noun* the religion of the Muslims, founded by the prophet Muhammad

② **island** /ˈaɪlənd/ *noun* a piece of land with water all around it ○ *They live on a little island in the middle of the river.* ○ *The Greek islands are favourite holiday destinations.*

islander /ˈaɪləndə/ *noun* a person who lives on an island

isle /aɪl/ *noun* an island (*literary*)

③ **isn't** /ˈɪz(ə)nt/ *short for* is not

③ **isolate** /ˈaɪsəleɪt/ (**isolates, isolating, isolated**) *verb* **1.** to put something or someone in a place alone ○ *Violent prisoners are usually isolated from the others.* **2.** to separate a chemical substance from a compound, to identify a single microorganism among many ○ *Doctors have isolated a new form of the flu virus.* ○ *Scientists have been able to isolate the substance which causes the disease.*

③ **isolated** /ˈaɪsəleɪtɪd/ *adj* **1.** separated from others ○ *They live in an isolated village in the hills.* **2.** one only

③ **isolation** /ˌaɪsəˈleɪʃ(ə)n/ *noun* the state of being cut off from communication with other people ○ *He lived for six months on the island in complete isolation.*

isolationism /ˌaɪsəˈleɪʃ(ə)nɪz(ə)m/ *noun* a country's policy of deliberately not becoming involved in international relations

ISP /ˌaɪ es ˈpiː/ *abbr* Internet service provider

① **issue** /ˈɪʃuː/ *noun* **1.** a subject or problem that people talk or write about ○ *The main issues will be discussed at the meeting.* **2.** an occasion when something is officially given out ○ *The issue of identity cards has been delayed.* **3.** a newspaper or magazine which is published at a particular time ○ *We bought the January issue of the magazine.* ■ *verb* (**issues, issuing, issued**) **1.** to make something available for use ○ *The new set of stamps will be issued next week.* ○ *Initially the euro was issued alongside the former national currencies.* **2.** to give something out officially ○ *The government issued a report on city centre traffic.* ○ *Each soldier was issued with a gun.* **3.** to come out of somewhere [~from] ○ *Smoke began to issue from the hole in the ground.* ◇ **to make an issue of something** to have a big discussion about something ○ *She's apologised so don't try to make an issue of it.* ◇ **to take issue with someone or something** to disagree with someone or something

① **it** /ɪt/ *pron* **1.** used to refer to something which has just been mentioned ○ *What do you want me to do with the box? – Put it down.* ○ *Where's the box? – It's here.* ○ *She picked up a potato and then dropped it on the ground.* ○ *I put my book down somewhere and now I can't find it.* ○ *Where's the newspaper? – It's on the chair.* **2.** used for talking about the weather, the date or time or another situation ○ *Look! – It's snowing.* ○ *It's miles from here to the railway station.* ○ *Is it the 30th today?* ○ *It's almost impossible to get a ticket at this time of year.* ○ *What time is it? – It's ten o'clock.* ○ *It's dangerous to use an electric saw when it's wet.* (NOTE: **It's = it is** or **it has**. Do not confuse with **its**.)

③ **IT** *abbr* information technology

italic /ɪ'tælɪk/ *noun* a printing type with sloping letters

italics /ɪ'tælɪks/ *plural noun* sloping letters ○ *This example is printed in italics.* Compare **Roman**

itch /ɪtʃ/ *noun* a place on the skin where you want to scratch ○ *I've got an itch in the middle of my back that's driving me mad!* ■ *verb* (**itches, itching, itched**) to make someone want to scratch ○ *The cream made his skin itch more than before.*

itchy /'ɪtʃi/ *adj* which makes a person want to scratch ○ *The main symptom of the disease is an itchy red rash.*

it'd /'ɪtəd/ *short form* **1.** it had **2.** it would

① **item** /'aɪtəm/ *noun* a thing shown in a list ○ *We are discussing item four on the agenda.* ○ *Please find enclosed an order for the following items from your catalogue.* ○ *I couldn't buy several items on the shopping list because the shop had sold out.*

itemise /'aɪtəmaɪz/ (**itemises, itemising, itemised**), **itemize** *verb* to make a detailed list of things

itinerary /aɪ'tɪnərəri/ (*plural* **itineraries**) *noun* a list of places to be visited on one journey

③ **it'll** /ɪt(ə)l/ *contr* it will

① **its** /ɪts/ *adj* belonging to 'it' ○ *I can't use the car – one of its tyres is flat.* ○ *The company pays its staff very badly.* (NOTE: Do not confuse with **it's**.)

① **it's** /ɪts/ *short for* **1.** it is **2.** it has (NOTE: Do not confuse with **it's**.)

① **itself** /ɪt'self/ *pron* **1.** used for referring back to a thing or an animal ○ *The dog seems to have hurt itself.* ○ *The screw had worked itself loose.* **2.** used for emphasis ○ *If the plug is all right there must be something wrong with the computer itself.* ◇ **all by itself** alone, with no one helping ○ *The church stands all by itself in the middle of the street.* ○ *The bus started to move all by itself.*

IV /ˌaɪ 'viː/ *noun* the Roman numeral for four or fourth

③ **I've** /aɪv/ *short form* I have

ivory /'aɪvəri/ *noun* a hard whitish substance from an elephant's tusk ○ *She bought some finely carved ivory chessmen.* ○ *Trade in ivory has been banned.*

ivy /'aɪvi/ (*plural* **ivies** or *same*) *noun* an evergreen plant which climbs up walls and trees

J

j /dʒeɪ/, **J** *noun* the tenth letter of the alphabet, between I and K

jab /dʒæb/ (**jabs, jabbing, jabbed**) *verb* to suddenly push something with a sharp object ○ *He jabbed the piece of meat with his fork.* ○ *She jabbed me in the back with her umbrella.*

jack /dʒæk/ *noun* **1.** a tool for raising something heavy, especially a car ○ *I used the jack to lift the car up and take the wheel off.* **2.** (*in playing cards*) the card with the face of a young man, with a value between the queen and the ten ○ *I won because I had the jack of hearts.*

jack up *phrasal verb* **1.** to lift up something heavy with a jack ○ *They jacked up the car to remove the exhaust pipe.* **2.** to raise profits or prices ○ *The newspaper article alleged that dealers had jacked up prices to make bigger profits.*

jackal /ˈdʒæk(ə)l/ *noun* an African wild animal, similar to a dog, which feeds mainly on dead flesh

② **jacket** /ˈdʒækɪt/ *noun* a short coat ○ *He was wearing a blue jacket and brown trousers.* ○ *Take your jacket off if you are hot.* ○ *This orange jacket shows up in the dark when I ride my bike.*

jacket potato /ˌdʒækɪt pəˈteɪtəʊ/ *noun* a potato cooked in an oven with its skin on

jack-in-the-box /ˈdʒæk ɪn ðə ˌbɒks/ *noun* a toy in which a doll jumps up out of a box when the lid is opened

jackknife /ˈdʒæknaɪf/ (**jackknifes, jackknifing, jackknifed**) *verb* (*of an articulated vehicle*) to go out of control, when the two parts bend in half so that they are pointing in different directions ○ *The section of the motorway is closed where a lorry has jackknifed.*

Jacuzzi /dʒəˈkuːzi/ *trademark* a type of bath which has bubbly water ○ *The health club has two Jacuzzis and a whirlpool.*

jade /dʒeɪd/ *noun* a hard green stone used for making jewellery and other attractive objects

jaded /ˈdʒeɪdɪd/ *adj* worn out, tired

jagged /ˈdʒægɪd/ *adj* with edges which are rough and not even

jaguar /ˈdʒægjuə/ *noun* a large wild cat with marks like spots on its skin, which lives in Central and South America

③ **jail** /dʒeɪl/, **gaol** *noun* a prison ○ *She was sent to jail for three months.* ■ *verb* (**jails, jailing, jailed; gaols**) to put someone in prison ○ *He was jailed for six years.*

jailer /ˈdʒeɪlə/, **jailor, gaoler** *noun* a person who guards prisoners in a jail (*dated*)

Jain /dʒaɪn/, **Jaina** *noun* a member of a Hindu group which believes that people should have deep respect for any living creature (NOTE: + **Jainism** *n*)

③ **jam** /dʒæm/ *noun* **1.** a sweet food made by boiling fruit and sugar together ○ *a pot of apricot jam* ○ *Do you want jam or honey on your bread?* ○ *We made jam with the fruit in the garden.* ○ *Have you any more jam – the jar is empty?* **2.** a situation in which too many things block something ○ *a traffic jam* ○ *There is a paper jam in the printer.* ■ *verb* (**jams, jamming, jammed**) **1.** (*of machines*) to stick and not be able to move ○ *Hold on – the paper has jammed in the printer.* **2.** to force things into a small space ○ *Don't try to jam all those boxes into the car boot.* ○ *The switchboard was jammed with calls.*

jamboree /ˌdʒæmbəˈriː/ *noun* a large gathering of people for a celebration

Jan. *abbr* January

jangle /ˈdʒæŋgəl/ (**jangles, jangling, jangled**) *verb* to make a noise of pieces of metal hitting together ○ *He jangled the keys in his pocket.*

janitor /ˈdʒænɪtə/ *noun especially US* a person who looks after a building, e.g. by making sure it is clean and that the rubbish is cleared away

① **January** /ˈdʒænjuəri/ (*plural* **Januarys**) *noun* the first month of the year, followed by February ○ *He was born on January 26th.* ○ *It's his birthday on January 26.* ○ *We never go on holiday in January because it's too cold.* ○ *We all went skiing* *last January.* (NOTE: **January 26th** *or* **January 26**: say 'the twenty-sixth of January' or 'January the twenty-sixth'; American English: 'January twenty-sixth'.)

③ **jar** /dʒɑː/ *noun* a container for food such as jam, usually made of glass ○ *There was some honey left in the bottom of the jar.* ○ *Use a jam jar for the water you collect.* ■ *verb* (**jars, jarring, jarred**) to produce an unpleasant effect ○ *The drilling sound jarred on my ears.* ○ *Orange curtains will jar with purple cushions.* ○ *He tripped over the step, jarring his knee.*

jargon /ˈdʒɑːɡən/, **jargoon** *noun* a special type of language used by a trade or profession or a particular group of people ○ *People are confused by computers because they don't understand the jargon.*

jaundice /ˈdʒɔːndɪs/ *noun* a condition where there is too much bile in the blood, and the skin and the whites of the eyes become yellow

jaundiced /ˈdʒɔːndɪst/ *adj* negative and tending to criticise things

jaunt /dʒɔːnt/ *noun* a short journey, especially for pleasure

jaunty /ˈdʒɔːnti/ (**jauntier, jauntiest**) *adj* happy and confident

javelin /ˈdʒæv(ə)lɪn/ *noun* a long spear used in battle or in sport

jaw /dʒɔː/ *noun* the bones in the face which hold the teeth and form the mouth

jazz /dʒæz/ *noun* a type of music with a strong rhythm, and in which the players often make the music up as they play; jazz was first played in the southern United States

jazz up *phrasal verb* to make bright and attractive (*informal*)

jealous /ˈdʒeləs/ *adj* feeling annoyed because you want something which belongs to someone else ○ *John was jealous of Mark because all the girls fancied him.* ○ *She was jealous of his new car.* ○ *Her new boyfriend is very handsome – I'm jealous!*

jealousy /ˈdʒeləsi/ *noun* the feeling of being annoyed because someone has something which you want but do not have

② **jeans** /dʒiːnz/ *plural noun* trousers made of a type of strong cotton, often blue ○ *She came into the office in jeans.* ○ *He bought a new pair of jeans.*

jeep /dʒiːp/ *trademark* a strong four-wheel drive vehicle used for travelling over rough ground, especially used by the army ○ *The convoy of jeeps and tanks crossed slowly over the bridge.*

jeer /dʒɪə/ (**jeers, jeering, jeered**) *verb* to laugh in a unpleasant way [~at] ○ *'You'll never win', he jeered.* ○ *The other children often jeered at him because he was fat.*

③ **jelly** /ˈdʒeli/ (*plural* **jellies**) *noun* a type of sweet food made with fruit, which shakes when you touch it or move it ○ *The children had fish fingers and chips followed by jelly and ice-cream.*

jellyfish /ˈdʒelifɪʃ/ (*plural* **jellyfishes** or *same*) *noun* an animal with a body like jelly, which lives in the sea

jeopardise /ˈdʒepədaɪz/ (**jeopardises, jeopardising, jeopardised**), **jeopardize** *verb* to be likely to harm

jeopardy /ˈdʒepədi/ *noun* □ **in jeopardy** in danger ○ *The management's attitude to safety has put us all in jeopardy.* ○ *The sale of the company has put thousands of jobs in jeopardy.*

jerk /dʒɜːk/ *noun* a sudden sharp pull ○ *He felt a jerk on the fishing line.* ■ *verb* (**jerks, jerking, jerked**) to suddenly pull something hard, often causing pain or injury ○ *He jerked the rope.*

jerky /ˈdʒɜːki/ *adj* abrupt, sudden

jersey /ˈdʒɜːzi/ *noun* **1.** a warm piece of clothing which covers the top part of your body and your arms ○ *She was knitting a pink jersey for the new baby.* **2.** a special shirt worn by a member of a sports team ○ *After every game the players swapped jerseys with the other team.*

jet /dʒet/ *noun* **1.** a long narrow stream of liquid or gas ○ *A jet of water put out the flames.* **2.** an aircraft with jet engines ○ *Jets flew low overhead.*

jet black /ˌdʒet ˈblæk/ *adj* very black and shiny

③ **jet engine** /ˈdʒet ˌendʒɪn/ *noun* an engine which gets its power from a stream of gas

jet lag /ˈdʒet læɡ/ *noun* the feeling of being extremely tired after a long journey by plane

Jet Ski /ˈdʒet skiː/ *trademark* a jet-propelled vehicle for one person which travels across water

jettison /ˈdʒetɪs(ə)n/ (**jettisons, jettisoning, jettisoned**) *verb* to throw fuel from a plane, or goods from a ship into the sea to make it lighter

jetty /ˈdʒeti/ (*plural* **jetties**) *noun* a small structure, e.g. at the side of a river, where boats can tie up

Jew /dʒuː/ *noun* a member of the group of people who lived in Israel in ancient times or who believe in Judaism

jewel /ˈdʒuːəl/ *noun* a valuable stone such as a diamond

jeweller /ˈdʒuːələ/ *noun* a person who makes or sells jewellery, and usually watches as well (NOTE: The US spelling is **jeweler**.)

② **jewellery** /ˈdʒuːəlri/ *noun* things that you wear as decoration round your neck, fingers, etc., made from things such as valuable stones, gold and silver ○ *The burglar stole all her jewellery.* (NOTE: no plural)

Jewish /ˈdʒuːɪʃ/ *adj* **1.** of Judaism **2.** of Jews

jibe /dʒaɪb/ *noun* an unpleasant remark

jig /dʒɪg/ *noun* **1.** a type of fast lively dance ○ *When he heard the news he did a little jig around the office.* **2.** music for this dance ○ *The band started to play an Irish jig and everyone got up to dance.*

jiggle /ˈdʒɪg(ə)l/ (**jiggles, jiggling, jiggled**) *verb* **1.** to move quickly or nervously **2.** to move something a little ○ *If you jiggle the top a bit, it should come off fairly easily.*

jigsaw /ˈdʒɪgsɔː/ *noun* □ **jigsaw puzzle** a picture made of shaped pieces of wood or cardboard that you have to try to fit together ○ *As it's raining, let's stay indoors and try to do this huge jigsaw of the Houses of Parliament.*

jingle /ˈdʒɪŋg(ə)l/ (**jingles, jingling, jingled**) *verb* to make a sound like pieces of metal knocking together ○ *The doorbell jingled as he went into the shop.*

jinx /dʒɪŋks/ *noun* something which brings bad luck

jittery /ˈdʒɪtəri/ *adj* nervous and unable to concentrate

① **job** /dʒɒb/ *noun* **1.** regular work which you get paid for [~as] ○ *She's got a job as a shop assistant in the local supermarket.* ○ *When the factory closed, hundreds of people lost their jobs.* **2.** a specific piece of work ○ *Don't sit down, there are a couple of jobs I want you to do.* ○ *He does all sorts of little electrical jobs around the house.* **3.** difficulty (*informal*) ○ *I had a job trying to find your house.* ○ *What a job it was getting a hotel room at the time of the music festival!*

job description /ˈdʒɒb dɪˌskrɪpʃən/ *noun* an official document from a company which says what a job involves

③ **jobless** /ˈdʒɒbləs/ *adj* with no job

job security /ˈdʒɒb sɪˌkjʊərɪti/ *noun* a situation in which an employee is likely to keep his or her job until he retires

job-share /ˈdʒɒb ʃeə/ *verb* to share a single job with another person so that each of you works for part of the day or week

jockey /ˈdʒɒki/ *noun* a person who rides horses in races ○ *He's an experienced jockey and knows how to handle a horse over a muddy racecourse.* ○ *He's the youngest jockey to ride in the Grand National.* ■ *verb* (**jockeys, jockeying, jockeyed**) □ **to jockey for position** to try to improve your position in relation to other people ○ *There's a vacancy for managing director, and the sales director and the production director are jockeying for position.*

jocular /ˈdʒɒkjʊlə/ *adj* in a humorous way, treating things as a joke

③ **jog** /dʒɒg/ (**jogs, jogging, jogged**) *verb* **1.** to run fairly slowly, especially for exercise ○ *He jogged along the river bank for two miles.* ○ *She was listening to her personal stereo as she was jogging.* **2.** to push someone or something slightly ○ *Someone jogged my elbow and I spilt my drink.* ◇ **to jog someone's memory** to make someone remember something ○ *The police are hoping that the film from the security camera will jog people's memories.*

③ **jogging** /ˈdʒɒgɪŋ/ *noun* the practice of running in slow steady way for exercise

① **join** /dʒɔɪn/ (**joins, joining, joined**) *verb* **1.** to come together ○ *Go on for about two hundred metres, until the road joins the motorway.* ○ *The two rivers join about four kilometres beyond the town.* **2.** to become a member of a club or other organisation ○ *After university, he is going to join the police.* ○ *She joined the army because she wanted to travel.* **3.** to do something with someone ○ *We're going to have a cup of coffee – would you like to join us?* ○ *Won't you join us for a game of golf?*

join in③ *phrasal verb* to take part in something done as a group

join up③ *phrasal verb* **1.** to link things together ○ *She's getting better at writing, and can do joined-up letters.* **2.** to join the army, navy or air force ○ *He joined up when he was 18 and soon rose to become an officer.*

joined-up /ˈdʒɔɪnd ʌp/ *adj* **1.** used to describe handwriting in which each letter of a word is joined to the next, especially by children learning to write in this way **2.** well-planned or with all its separate parts working well together, e.g. of government or a policy

joiner /ˈdʒɔɪnə/ *noun* a person who builds things out of wood, especially windows and doors for houses

① **joint** /dʒɔɪnt/ *noun* **1.** a place where bones come together and can move, such as the knee or the elbow ○ *Her elbow joint hurt after her game of tennis.* **2.** a large piece of meat, especially for cooking in an oven ○ *The joint of lamb was very tender.* ○ *We all sat round the table while Father carved the joint.* ■ *adj* combined, with two or more things connected together

② **joke** /dʒəʊk/ *noun* a thing said or done to make people laugh [~about] ○ *She poured water down his neck as a joke.* ○ *They all laughed at his jokes about student life in the 1960s.*

joker /ˈdʒəʊkə/ *noun* an extra card, with the picture of a clown on it, used as a bonus in some card games

③ **jolly** /ˈdʒɒli/ *adj* (**jollier, jolliest**) happy, pleasant, enjoyable ○ *It was marvellous to see all the jolly faces of the children.* ○ *Her birthday party was a very jolly affair.* ■ *adv* very (*used for emphasis*) ○ *It's jolly hard work carrying all those boxes up to the attic.*

jolt /dʒəʊlt/ *noun* a sudden shake or shock, or violent push ○ *The train stopped with a jolt.* ■ *verb* (**jolts, jolting, jolted**) **1.** to move with sudden movements ○ *The train jolted twice before moving off.* **2.** to push or to shake suddenly ○ *The people in the back of the truck were jolted about from side to side as we bumped over the rocky track.* **3.** to give a sudden shock to ○ *The sound of the whistle jolted her into action.*

jostle /ˈdʒɒs(ə)l/ (**jostles, jostling, jostled**) *verb* to push or to knock into people, especially in a crowd □ **to jostle for position** to push others so as to get into a good position ○ *The cars on the starting line were jostling for position.*

jot /dʒɒt/ (**jots, jotting, jotted**) *verb also* **jot down** to make quick notes about something ○ *He jotted her address on an envelope.* ○ *He jotted down her phone number.*

journal /ˈdʒɜːn(ə)l/ *noun* a book where you write details of things that have happened which you want to remember ○ *He kept a journal during his visit to China.* ○ *She wrote a journal of the gradual progress of her illness.*

③ **journalism** /ˈdʒɜːn(ə)lɪz(ə)m/ *noun* the profession of writing for newspapers or magazines, or reporting on events for radio or TV

③ **journalist** /ˈdʒɜːn(ə)lɪst/ *noun* a person who writes for newspapers or magazines, or reports on events for radio or TV ○ *Journalists asked the policeman some very awkward questions.* ○ *Film stars were greeted by journalists from around the world at the première of the new film.*

② **journey** /ˈdʒɜːni/ *noun* an occasion when you travel somewhere, usually a long distance ○ *It's at least two days' journey from here.* ○ *They went on a train journey across China.* ○ *She has a difficult journey to work every day – she has to change buses twice.*

jovial /ˈdʒəʊviəl/ *adj* good-humoured, happy

③ **joy** /dʒɔɪ/ *noun* very great happiness ○ *The birth of our baby son filled us with joy.*

joypad /ˈdʒɔɪpæd/ *noun* a control for a computer game which you hold in your hand

joyriding /ˈdʒɔɪraɪdɪŋ/ *noun* the crime of high-speed driving in a stolen car

joystick /ˈdʒɔɪstɪk/ *noun* **1.** a rod which controls the movements of an aircraft ○ *Pull on the joystick to make the plane rise.* **2.** a device that allows the user to move the cursor round a screen by moving an upright arm

jubilant /ˈdʒuːbɪlənt/ *adj* full of happiness, e.g. because of winning something

jubilee /ˈdʒuːbɪliː/ *noun* a celebration on the date of an important event which happened in the past

Judaism /ˈdʒuːdeɪɪz(ə)m/ *noun* the religion of the Jewish people, which is based on the texts called the Torah and Talmud

② **judge** /dʒʌdʒ/ *noun* **1.** a person whose job is to make legal decisions in a court of law ○ *He was convicted for stealing, but the judge let him off with a small fine.* **2.** a person who decides who should win a competition ○ *The three judges of the beauty contest couldn't agree.* ■ *verb* (**judges, judging, judged**) **1.** to make decisions in situations such as a court of law or a competition ○ *He was judged guilty.* ○ *Her painting was judged the best and she won first prize.* **2.** to make a assessment of a situation [~what/whether/when etc/~(that)] ○ *It's hard to judge whether he likes the job or not.* ○ *The Senator judged it would be impossible for him to win the Presidency so he dropped out of the race.*

judgment /ˈdʒʌdʒmənt/, **judgement** *noun* **1.** a legal decision by a judge or court

○ *The judgment of the tribunal was fair.* ○ *We will appeal against the judgment.* **2.** the ability to make good decisions ○ *He trusted his wife's judgment in everything.*

judgmental /dʒʌdʒ'mənt(ə)l/ *adj* tending to judge or criticise people

judicial /dʒuː'dɪʃ(ə)l/ *adj* referring to a legal process or to a court of law

judicious /dʒuː'dɪʃəs/ *adj* based on good judgment

judo /'dʒuːdəʊ/ *noun* an Olympic sport, derived from the traditional Japanese art of fighting without weapons between two people

③ **jug** /dʒʌg/ *noun* a container with a handle, used for pouring liquids

juggle /'dʒʌg(ə)l/ (**juggles, juggling, juggled**) *verb* **1.** to throw and catch several things such as balls, so that most of them are in the air at the same time ○ *Try and juggle four balls at once.* **2.** to keep changing things or arranging them in a complicated way ○ *I will have to juggle my meetings so that I can fit everyone in.* ○ *She's trying to juggle her investments to get the best interest rate.*

juggler /'dʒʌglə/ *noun* a person who juggles

② **juice** /dʒuːs/ *noun* a liquid from fruit, vegetables or meat ○ *They charged me £1 for two glasses of orange juice.* ○ *She had a glass of grapefruit juice for breakfast.*

juicy /'dʒuːsi/ (**juicier, juiciest**) *adj* full of juice

jukebox /'dʒuːkbɒks/ *noun* a coin-operated machine which plays records or CDs

① **July** /dʒʊ'laɪ/ *noun* the seventh month of the year, between June and August ○ *July 23* ○ *We went to Spain last July.* ○ *July is always one of the busiest months for holidays.* (NOTE: **July 23rd** *or* **July 23**: say 'July the twenty-third' or 'the twenty-third of July'; American English: 'July twenty-third'.)

jumble /'dʒʌmbəl/ *noun* a confused mess ○ *His clothes were lying in a jumble on the floor.* ○ *A jumble of thoughts raced through my mind.* ■ *verb* (**jumbles, jumbling, jumbled**) *also* **jumble up** to mix or confuse things ○ *The books are all jumbled up – can you sort them out?* ○ *His thoughts were all jumbled in his head.*

jumble sale /'dʒʌmbəl seɪl/ *noun* a sale of old clothes and other things which people no longer want, organised by a club or organisation to raise money (NOTE: The US term is **rummage sale**.)

jumbo /'dʒʌmbəʊ/ *adj* very large ○ *He ordered jumbo sausages and chips.* ○ *She bought a jumbo box of fireworks.*

① **jump** /dʒʌmp/ *noun* **1.** a sudden movement up or down into the air ○ *The jump was higher than she thought and she hurt her leg.* **2.** a sudden increase [~in] ■ *verb* (**jumps, jumping, jumped**) **1.** to go suddenly into the air from or towards the ground [//////~down/up/over etc] ○ *She jumped down from the chair.* ○ *The horse jumped over the fence.* **2.** to make a sudden movement because you are frightened ○ *She jumped when I came up behind her quietly and said 'Boo!'.* ○ *When they fired the gun, it made me jump.*

jump at③ *phrasal verb* to accept enthusiastically

③ **jumper** /'dʒʌmpə/ *noun* a warm piece of clothing, usually made of wool, which covers the top part of your body and your arms

jumpy /'dʒʌmpi/ (**jumpier, jumpiest**) *adj* nervous and excited

③ **junction** /'dʒʌŋkʃən/ *noun* a place where railway lines or roads meet ○ *Go as far as the next junction and you will see the library on your right.* ○ *Leave the motorway at Junction 5.*

juncture /'dʒʌŋktʃə/ *noun* a point in time

① **June** /dʒuːn/ *noun* the sixth month of the year, between May and July ○ *June 17* ○ *Last June we had a holiday in Canada.* (NOTE: **June 17th** *or* **June 17**: say 'June the seventeenth' or 'the seventeenth of June' or in US English: 'June seventeenth'.)

jungle /'dʒʌŋgəl/ *noun* an area of thick tropical forest which is difficult to travel through

③ **junior** /'dʒuːniə/ *adj* intended for younger children ○ *She sings in the junior choir.* ○ *He plays for the junior hockey team.*

junior high school /'dʒuːniə haɪ/ *noun* a school in the US for children from 12 to 15 years old

junior school /'dʒuːniə skuːl/ *noun* a school for children from 7 to 11 years old

③ **junk** /dʒʌŋk/ *noun* useless articles, rubbish ○ *Don't keep that – it's junk.* ○ *You should throw away all that junk you keep under your bed.*

junk food /'dʒʌŋk fuːd/ *noun* prepared food which is not healthy, e.g. because it contains a lot of fat or sugar

junkie /'dʒʌŋki/ *noun* (*slang*) **1.** a person who is addicted to an illegal drug ○ *The* *park is full of junkies and dossers at night.* **2.** a person who is very enthusiastic about something and cannot get enough of it ○ *I'm something of a crossword junkie.* ○ *Some Internet junkies spend a fortune on telephone bills.*

junk mail /ˈdʒʌŋk meɪl/ *noun* advertising material sent through the post, often thrown away immediately by the people who receive it because they do not want it

junta /ˈdʒʌntə/ *noun* a ruling group of ministers, a government which has taken power by force (NOTE: used mainly of military governments. The word is correctly pronounced as /ˈhʊntə/ but this pronunciation is not often used in English.)

jurisdiction /ˌdʒʊərɪsˈdɪkʃən/ *noun* legal power over someone or something

juror /ˈdʒʊərə/ *noun* a member of a jury

jury /ˈdʒʊəri/ (*plural* **juries**) *noun* **1.** a group of twelve citizens who are sworn to decide whether someone is guilty or innocent after hearing the evidence given in a court of law ○ *The jury brought in a verdict of not guilty.* **2.** a group of judges in a competition ○ *He's been chosen to serve on the jury for the literary prize.* ◇ **the jury is still out (on this)** no one is sure what the result will be

① **just** /dʒʌst/ *adv* **1.** exactly ○ *Is that too much sugar? – No, it's just right.* ○ *Thank you, that's just what I was looking for.* ○ *Just how many of students have got computers?* ○ *What time is it? – It's just seven o'clock.* ○ *He's just fifteen – his birthday was yesterday.* **2.** showing the very recent past ○ *The train has just arrived from Paris.* ○ *She had just got into her bath when the phone rang.* ○ *Thanks for calling – I was just going to phone you.* **3.** only ○ *We're just good friends, nothing more.* ○ *I've been to Berlin just once.*

② **justice** /ˈdʒʌstɪs/ *noun* fair treatment in law ○ *Justice must always be seen to be done.*

justifiable /ˈdʒʌstɪfaɪəb(ə)l/ *adj* which can be justified

② **justification** /ˌdʒʌstɪfɪˈkeɪʃ(ə)n/ *noun* **1.** a reason which shows that something has been done correctly [~for] ○ *What was his justification for doing that?* ○ *They tried to find some justification for what they had done.* **2.** (*in typing and printing*) arranging the words so that the ends of the lines are straight ○ *An American hyphenation and justification program will not work with British English spellings.*

justified /ˈdʒʌstɪfaɪd/ *adj* shown to be right

② **justify** /ˈdʒʌstɪfaɪ/ (**justifies, justifying, justified**) *verb* to show that something is fair, to prove that something is right ○ *How can you justify spending all that money?* ○ *How can you justify your behaviour?*

jut /dʒʌt/ (**juts, jutting, jutted**) *verb also* **jut out** to stick out, usually horizontally ○ *My hotel room has a balcony jutting out over a busy main road.* ○ *The cliff juts out into the lake.*

③ **juvenile** /ˈdʒuːvənaɪl/ *adj* **1.** referring to young people ○ *Young offenders are tried before a juvenile court.* **2.** silly and annoying ■ *noun* a young person, officially, one under eighteen years of age ○ *The police entered the club and arrested four people, two of them juveniles.*

juvenile delinquent /ˌdʒuːvənaɪl dɪˈlɪŋkwənt/ *noun* a young person who commits minor crimes, especially crimes against property

juxtapose /ˌdʒʌkstəˈpəʊz/ (**juxtaposes, juxtaposing, juxtaposed**) *verb* to place side by side, so as to show a difference (NOTE: + **juxtaposition** *n*)

K

k /keɪ/, **K** *noun* the eleventh letter of the alphabet, between J and L

③ **K** /keɪ/ *abbr* one thousand

kaleidoscope /kə'laɪdəskəʊp/ *noun* **1.** a toy formed of a tube with mirrors which reflect small pieces of coloured material and make patterns when you move it while looking into it **2.** something which has a series of patterns and colours ○ *The kaleidoscope of autumn colours which you only see in parts of North America.*

kangaroo /ˌkæŋgə'ruː/ *noun* a large Australian animal, of which the female carries its young in a pouch

karaoke /ˌkæri'əʊki/ *noun* entertainment, coming originally from Japan, in which people sing to recorded music

karate /kə'rɑːti/ *noun* a Japanese style of fighting, where you hit sharp quick blows with the side of the hand or kicks with the feet

karma /'kɑːmə/ *noun* **1.** the Hindu and Buddhist belief that the quality of people's current and future lives is determined by their behaviour in this and past lives **2.** the atmosphere which some people can feel is present in a place, situation, person, or object **3.** destiny or fate

kayak /'kaɪæk/ *noun* a type of small boat which is pointed at both ends, and almost completely covered, with only a narrow opening for one person to sit in

kebab /kɪ'bæb/ *noun* small pieces of meat or vegetables, cooked on a long metal stick

② **keen** /kiːn/ **(keener, keenest)** *adj* **1.** enthusiastic about doing something or wanting to do something ○ *I wanted to see the film but my friend wasn't keen.* ○ *We're keen to keep the cost as low as possible.* **2.** **keen on something/someone** liking something or someone a lot [~on] ○ *I am not very keen on classical music.* ○ *I don't think she's very keen on her new maths teacher.* ○ *He's keen on keeping fit – he goes running every morning.* **3.** very strong ○ *She has a keen interest in politics.* ○ *Our product has keen competition but it's selling well.* **4.** very sensitive ○ *Bats have a keen sense of hearing.*

① **keep** /kiːp/ **(keeps, keeping, kept)** *verb* **1.** to continue to have something ○ *Can I keep the newspaper I borrowed from you?* ○ *I don't want that book any more, you can keep it.* ○ *The police kept my gun and won't give it back.* **2.** to continue to do something ○ *The clock kept going even after I dropped it on the floor.* ○ *He had to keep smiling so that people would think he was pleased.* ○ *Keep quiet or they'll hear you.* ○ *Luckily the weather kept fine for the fair.* ○ *The food will keep warm in the oven.* **3.** to have or to put something in a particular place ○ *I keep my car keys in my pocket.* ○ *Where do you keep the paper for the laser printer?* **4.** to make someone or something stay in a place or state ○ *It's cruel to keep animals in cages.* ○ *I was kept late at the office.* ○ *They kept us waiting for half an hour.* ○ *We put the plates in the oven to keep them warm.* **5.** to stay ○ *Keep close to me.*

keep back *phrasal verb* **1.** to hold on to something which you should give to someone ○ *They kept back £20 from the deposit to cover damage to the carpet.* **2.** □ **to keep something back from someone** not to tell someone information which you could give to them ○ *I have the feeling that she's keeping something back from us.*

keep down *phrasal verb* **1.** to keep at a low level ○ *Keep your voice down, the police will hear us!* **2.** to bend down in order to hide from someone ○ *Keep down behind the wall so that they won't see us.*

keep off *phrasal verb* **1.** not to walk on something ○ *Keep off the grass!* **2.** not to use ○ *If he can keep off drink, his health will improve.*

keep on① *phrasal verb* to continue doing something ○ *My computer keeps on breaking down.* ○ *The cars kept on moving, though very slowly.* ○ *Keep on trying!*

keep on at③ *phrasal verb* to criticise someone all the time [~about] (*informal*) ○ *She keeps on at me about going to visit her.*

keep out① *phrasal verb* **1.** to stop someone going in ○ *We put up notices telling people to keep their dogs out of the field where the lambs are.* **2.** not to go in ○ *There were 'Keep Out!' notices round the building site.* **3.** not to get involved ○ *He kept out of the quarrel.* ○ *Try to keep out of trouble with the police.*

keep to *phrasal verb* **1.** to follow the same direction when you are going somewhere ○ *Keep to this road until you come to the library, then turn left.* **2.** to make something stay inside a limit ○ *Keep your speed to 30 miles per hour in towns.* **3.** to do what you have agreed to do, or what a rule or law says you must do ○ *Don't worry I'll keep to my promise to pay back the money.* ○ *The company kept to the regulations and had good records.* **4.** not to move away from the main subject being discussed ○ *Let's keep to the subject of widening the motorway.* ○ *Keep to the point.*

keep up① *phrasal verb* **1.** to make something stay at the same high level ○ *He finds it very difficult to keep up his German.* ○ *They won't be able to keep up that speed for very long.* **2.** to prevent someone from going to sleep or to bed ○ *The noise from the street kept us up all night.*

keep up with① *phrasal verb* **1.** to go at the same speed as someone ○ *My foot hurts, that's why I can't keep up with the others.* ○ *His salary hasn't kept up with the cost of living.* **2.** to keep yourself informed about ○ *Have you been keeping up with the news from Russia?*

keeper /'kiːpə/ *noun* **1.** a person in charge of a certain type of animal in a zoo ○ *an elephant keeper* **2.** a person in charge of a section of a museum ○ *The keeper of Roman coins in the British Museum.* **3.** same as **goalkeeper** (*sport*)

keeping /'kiːpɪŋ/ *noun* □ **in** *or* **out of keeping with** in or not in the same style as something else ○ *The dinner plates are antiques, in keeping with the furniture in the dining room.*

keg /keg/ *noun* a small round container for liquid, especially alcohol

kennel /'ken(ə)l/ *noun* a small house for a dog

③ **kept** /kept/ past tense and past participle of **keep**

kerb /kɜːb/ *noun* the stone edge of a path along the side of a road

kernel /'kɜːn(ə)l/ *noun* **1.** the softer inside part of a nut which you can eat ○ *Squirrels bite into nuts to get at the kernel.* **2.** the centre, the essential part ○ *At the heart of every classical myth is a kernel of truth.* (NOTE: Do not confuse with **colonel**.)

kerosene /'kerəsiːn/ *noun especially US* a type of thin oil, e.g. used in lights or heaters

ketchup /'ketʃəp/ *noun* a type of tomato sauce

kettle /'ket(ə)l/ *noun* a container used for boiling water

① **key** /kiː/ *noun* **1.** a shaped piece of metal that you use to open a lock or to start a car ○ *I can't start the car, I've lost the key.* ○ *Where did you put the front door key?* **2.** one of the moving parts which you push down with your fingers on a typewriter, a computer or a musical instrument such as a piano ○ *The 'F' key always sticks.* ○ *There are 64 keys on the keyboard.* **3.** a system of musical tones ○ *This piece of music is written in the key of F major.* ■ *adj* most important ○ *The key person in the team is the goalkeeper.* ○ *The key person in the company is the sales manager.* ○ *Oil is a key industry.*

③ **keyboard** /'kiːbɔːd/ *noun* a set of keys on something such as a computer or piano ○ *She spilled her coffee on the computer keyboard.* ○ *He practises on the keyboard every day.* ■ *verb* (**keyboards, keyboarding, keyboarded**) to put information into a computer using a keyboard ○ *She was keyboarding the figures.*

keyhole /'kiːhəʊl/ *noun* a hole in a lock which you put a key into

keynote /'kiːnəʊt/ *noun* a main subject ○ *The keynote of the meeting was the need for political compromise.*

keypad /'kiːpæd/ *noun* a set of special keys on a computer keyboard, e.g. the number keys

keyword /'kiːwɜːd/ *noun* **1.** a word used as a reference point for further information or as a guide to show you what is contained in a document **2.** a series of letters and numbers, often in the form of a common word, which has a special meaning for a computer database or programming or command language

khaki /'kɑːki/ *adj* of a dull yellow-brown colour, like that sometimes worn by soldiers ○ *I don't like those dull khaki cushions in the living room.*

② **kick** /kɪk/ *noun* **1.** the act of hitting something with your foot ○ *The goalkeeper gave the ball a kick.* **2.** a feeling of excitement ○ *He gets a kick out of watching a football match on TV.* ■ *verb* (**kicks, kicking, kicked**) to hit something with your foot ○ *He kicked the ball into the net.* ○ *She kicked her little brother.*

kick in *phrasal verb* **1.** to make something open by kicking it ○ *The police kicked the door in.* **2.** to start to have an effect ○ *The car really moves when the turbocharger kicks in.*

kick off③ *phrasal verb* **1.** to start a game of football ○ *They kicked off at 3.00 and by half-time there was still no score.* **2.** to start ○ *Let's kick off with a discussion about modern painters.*

kick out③ *phrasal verb* to get rid of someone (*informal*)

kick-off /ˈkɪk ɒf/ *noun* the start of a football game

kick start /ˈkɪk stɑːt/ *verb* to make something start or start again ○ *The government's plans to kick start the economy.*

① **kid** /kɪd/ *noun* **1.** a child (*informal*) ○ *There were a few school kids on their bicycles.* ○ *They're married with two kids.* **2.** a young goat ■ *verb* (**kids, kidding, kidded**) to make someone believe something which is not true ○ *Are you kidding?* ○ *She tried to kid me that she'd had an accident.*

kiddie /ˈkɪdi/ *noun* a small child (*informal*)

③ **kidnap** /ˈkɪdnæp/ (**kidnaps, kidnapping, kidnapped**) *verb* to take someone away illegally and keep them prisoner (NOTE: + **kidnapper** *n*)

③ **kidney** /ˈkɪdni/ *noun* one of a pair of organs in animals that clean the blood and remove waste from it

kidney bean /ˈkɪdni biːn/ *noun* a type of bean with reddish seeds which look a little like kidneys

① **kill** /kɪl/ (**kills, killing, killed**) *verb* to make someone or something die ○ *Sixty people were killed in the plane crash.* ○ *A long period of dry weather could kill all the crops.*

killer /ˈkɪlə/ *noun* **1.** a person who kills ○ *The police are still hunting for the killer.* **2.** which kills ○ *a killer flu virus*

killing /ˈkɪlɪŋ/ *noun* the process of putting a person or animal to death ○ *The police are investigating the killing of the tourists.* ○ *There have been reports of killings in the villages.* ○ *The killing of rhinos has been banned.*

kiln /kɪln/ *noun* an oven for making objects from clay hard enough to last

③ **kilo** /ˈkiːləʊ/ *abbr* kilogram

kilobyte /ˈkɪləʊbaɪt/ *noun* a unit of storage for a computer equal to 1,024 bytes

③ **kilogram** /ˈkɪləgræm/, **kilogramme** *noun* a measure of weight equal to one thousand grams (NOTE: written **kg** after figures: *20kg*)

③ **kilometre** /ˈkɪləˌmiːtə/ *noun* a measure of distance equal to one thousand metres

kilt /kɪlt/ *noun* a skirt, usually of tartan cloth, worn by men in Scotland, and also by women

kin /kɪn/ *noun* □ **next of kin** a person's nearest relative ○ *After the fatal accident, the police informed the next of kin.* ○ *Names of the victims will not be released until their next of kin have been informed.*

① **kind** /kaɪnd/ *adj* friendly and helpful ○ *It's very kind of you to offer to help.* ○ *How kind of you to invite him to your party!* ○ *You should always be kind to little children.* ○ *He's a kind old gentleman.* ■ *noun* a type [~of] ○ *A butterfly is a kind of insect.* ○ *We have several kinds of apples in our garden.* ○ *We discussed all kinds of things.* ◇ **of a kind** similar ○ *The three sisters are three of a kind.* ◇ **it's nothing of the kind** that's not correct at all ◇ **kind of** in a certain way (*informal*) ○ *I was kind of annoyed when she told me that.*

kindergarten /ˈkɪndəgɑːt(ə)n/ *noun* a school for little children

kindle /ˈkɪnd(ə)l/ (**kindles, kindling, kindled**) *verb* **1.** to make something catch fire ○ *A cigarette end must have kindled the dead leaves.* **2.** to make someone start to feel something ○ *The aim of the class is to kindle an interest in art.*

kindling /ˈkɪndlɪŋ/ *noun* material such as small pieces of wood, used for starting a fire

③ **kindness** /ˈkaɪndnəs/ *noun* **1.** the quality of being kind ○ *She was touched by his kindness.* **2.** a kind act

① **king** /kɪŋ/ *noun* **1.** a man who governs a country by right of birth ○ *The king and queen came to visit the town.* (NOTE: **king** is spelt with a capital letter when used with a name or when referring to a particular person: *King Henry VIII.*) **2.** the main piece in chess ○ *She moved her knight to place his king in check.* **3.** (*in cards*) the card with the face of a man, coming before the ace and after the queen in value ○ *He knew he could* *win when he drew the king of spades.* **4.** a person in the top position

③ **kingdom** /ˈkɪŋdəm/ *noun* **1.** the land ruled over by a king or queen ○ *England is part of the United Kingdom.* ○ *He gave her a book of fairy stories about a magic kingdom.* **2.** a part of the world of nature ○ *the animal kingdom*

kingpin /ˈkɪŋpɪn/ *noun* the main person in an organisation (*informal*)

king-size /ˈkɪŋ saɪz/ *adj* bigger than the usual size

kink /kɪŋk/ *noun* **1.** a twist in something that should be straight ○ *Can you straighten the flex, it's got a kink in it.* **2.** a peculiar mental state ○ *He has a kink about women's underwear.*

kinship /ˈkɪnʃɪp/ *noun* the relationship that exists between people in the same family

kiosk /ˈkiːɒsk/ *noun* a small shelter, for selling goods out of doors

kipper /ˈkɪpə/ *noun* a split herring, salted and smoked

③ **kiss** /kɪs/ *noun* the act of touching someone with your lips to show that you are pleased to see them or that you like them [~on] ○ *She gave the baby a kiss on the cheek.* □ **to blow someone a kiss** to touch your lips with your hand and then hold out your hand to a person at a distance ○ *As the train left, she blew him a kiss.* ■ *verb* (**kisses, kissing, kissed**) to touch someone with your lips to show that you are pleased to see them or that you like them [~on] ○ *They kissed each other on both cheeks.*

③ **kit** /kɪt/ *noun* clothes and personal equipment, usually kept in a bag ○ *Did you bring your tennis kit?*

① **kitchen** /ˈkɪtʃɪn/ *noun* a room where you can cook food ○ *She put the meat down on the kitchen table.* ○ *If you're hungry, have a look in the kitchen to see if there's anything to eat.*

③ **kite** /kaɪt/ *noun* a toy made of light wood and paper or cloth which is flown in the wind on the end of a string ○ *He was flying his kite from the top of the hill.*

③ **kitten** /ˈkɪt(ə)n/ *noun* a young cat

kitty /ˈkɪti/ *noun* money which has been collected from each member of a group of people to be used for everyone later ○ *We each put £5 into the kitty for the office party.*

knack /næk/ *noun* an ability or tendency to do something, often something wrong (*informal*) ○ *She has a knack for talking to strangers.* ○ *He has this knack of accidentally offending people.*

knackered /ˈnækəd/ *adj* very tired (*slang*)

knead /niːd/ (**kneads, kneading, kneaded**) *verb* to press and fold dough before it is cooked to make bread

② **knee** /niː/ *noun* **1.** the part on your body where the upper and the lower leg join, where your leg bends ○ *She sat the child on her knee.* ○ *He was on his knees looking under the bed.* **2.** the part of a pair of trousers that covers the knee ○ *My jeans have holes in both knees.*

kneecap /ˈniːkæp/ *noun* the little bone in front of the knee ○ *He hurt his kneecap when he fell.*

knee-jerk /ˈniː dʒɜːk/ *adj* tending to react without thinking, or happening as a result of such a reaction

② **kneel** /niːl/ (**kneels, kneeling, kneeled, knelt**) *verb* to go down on your knees

③ **knew** /njuː/ past tense of **know**

knickers /ˈnɪkəz/ *plural noun* a piece of a woman's or girl's underwear for the lower body ○ *She bought a pair of blue knickers.*

① **knife** /naɪf/ *noun* (*plural* **knives**) an instrument used for cutting, with a sharp metal blade fixed in a handle ○ *Put out a knife, fork and spoon for each person.* ○ *You need a sharp knife to cut meat.* ■ *verb* (**knifes, knifing, knifed**) to injure someone using a knife ○ *He was knifed in the back during the fight.*

knighthood /ˈnaɪthʊd/ *noun* the position of being a knight

③ **knit** /nɪt/ (**knits, knitting, knitted** or **knit**) *verb* to make cloth out of wool by joining threads together using two long needles ○ *My mother is knitting me a pullover.* ○ *She was wearing a blue knitted hat.*

③ **knitting** /ˈnɪtɪŋ/ *noun* **1.** the action of making something out of wool with knitting needles ○ *Her great hobby is knitting.* **2.** a piece of work which is in the process of being made by knitting ○ *She brought her knitting with her to the conference.*

knitwear /ˈnɪtweə/ *noun* knitted clothes such as jumpers and pullovers

knives /naɪvz/ plural of **knife**

knob /nɒb/ *noun* **1.** a rounded handle that you turn, e.g. on a door or drawer ○ *To open the door, just turn the knob.* **2.** a round object which you turn to operate a radio or TV, etc. ○ *Turn the knob to increase the volume.*

① **knock** /nɒk/ *noun* a sound made by hitting something ■ *verb* (**knocks, knocking, knocked**) to hit something ○ *Knock twice before going in.* ○ *You'll need a heavy hammer to knock that nail in.*

knock about③ *phrasal verb* **1.** to wander about doing nothing ○ *He spent several years knocking about the back streets of New Orleans.* **2.** □ **to knock someone about** to beat someone ○ *He was badly knocked about in the fight.* □ **to knock something about** to damage something ○ *The cathedral was badly knocked about in the bombardment.* **3.** to be in a place (*informal*) ○ *Can you see my hammer knocking about anywhere?*

knock back③ *phrasal verb* **1.** to drink a drink quickly ○ *He knocked back his drink and ran outside.* **2.** □ **to knock someone back a sum** to cost someone an amount of money ○ *It will knock me back a few hundred pounds.*

knock down③ *phrasal verb* **1.** to make something fall down ○ *They are going to knock down the old house to build a factory.* **2.** to hit someone or something ○ *She was knocked down by a car.* **3.** to reduce a price ○ *They knocked the price down to £50.* **4.** to sell something to someone at an auction ○ *It was knocked down to a German buyer for £250.*

knock off③ *phrasal verb* **1.** to make something fall off by hitting it ○ *The cat knocked the glass off the shelf.* **2.** to stop work ○ *The workmen all knocked off at 4.30.* **3.** to reduce the price of something by an amount ○ *He knocked £1000 off the price of the car.*

knock out③ *phrasal verb* **1.** to hit someone so hard that they are no longer conscious ○ *She was knocked out by a blow on the head.* ○ *The boxer was knocked out in the third round.* **2.** to make someone go to sleep ○ *The doctor gave her something which knocked her out.*

knock up *phrasal verb* **1.** to wake someone up ○ *Can you knock me up early tomorrow morning?* **2.** to put something together rapidly ○ *She knocked up a dinner for six people at half an hour's notice.* ○ *He knocked up a garden shed out of old pieces of timber.*

knocker /ˈnɒkə/ *noun* **1.** a knob or ring attached to a door which can be hit against it to call attention ○ *The bell on the front door doesn't work, so you have to use the knocker.* **2.** a person who is always criticising something ○ *The letter in the paper should silence the government's knockers.*

knock-on effect /ˈnɒk ɒn ɪˌfekt/ *adj* an effect which follows on from something [~on] ○ *The airport strike had a knock-on effect on the tourist industry.*

knockout /ˈnɒkaʊt/ *noun* (*in boxing*) the action of hitting someone so hard that they lose consciousness ○ *He won by a knockout (KO) in the third round.*

③ **knot** /nɒt/ *noun* **1.** one or more pieces of string, rope, or other fibre, twisted and fastened together ○ *Boy Scouts are supposed to be able to tie knots.* ○ *Is the knot of my tie straight?* **2.** a measure of the speed of a ship, or of the wind ○ *The ship was doing 22 knots when she hit the rocks.* ○ *There's a wind speed of 60 knots.*

① **know** /nəʊ/ (**knows, knowing, knew, known**) *verb* **1.** to have learned something, or have information about something [~(that)/~what/whether/if/ why/ how etc] ○ *Do you know all the words to this song?* ○ *He didn't know that she had died.* ○ *You knew it would be expensive.* ○ *His secretary doesn't know where he is.* ○ *Do you know how to start the computer?* ○ *Do you know the Spanish for 'one – two – three'?* **2.** to have met someone ○ *I know your sister – we were at school together.* ○ *I used to know a man called Peter Jones who worked in your company.* □ **to know someone by sight** to know who someone is, even though you have never spoken to him or her **3.** to have been to a place often ○ *I know Paris very well.* ○ *She doesn't know Germany at all.* □ **to know somewhere like the back of your hand** to be very familiar with a place ◇ **as far as I know** all I know is that ○ *As far as I know, he left by car at 6 p.m.* ○ *Is she in trouble? – Not as far as I know.* ◇ **in the know** knowing something that most people do not know ○ *Those in the know say that's the best restaurant in town.* ○ *Someone in the know gave me the tip.* ◇ **to know better than** to have the experience to avoid making a mistake ○ *You should know better than to wake grandfather up when he's having his afternoon nap.* ◇ **you never know** perhaps ○ *You never know, she may still turn up.*

know-all /ˈnəʊ ɔːl/ *noun* a person who claims he knows everything (*informal*)

know-how /ˈnəʊ haʊ/ *noun* knowledge about how something is made or is done (*informal*)

knowing /ˈnəʊɪŋ/ *adj* showing that you know about something

knowingly /ˈnəʊɪŋli/ *adv* **1.** deliberately, on purpose ○ *He is accused of knowingly handling stolen goods.* **2.** showing that you know about something ○ *He glanced knowingly in her direction.*

① **knowledge** /ˈnɒlɪdʒ/ *noun* the general facts or information that people know ○ *No encyclopedia can contain all human knowledge.*

knowledgeable /ˈnɒlɪdʒəb(ə)l/ *adj* who knows a lot about something

③ **known** /nəʊn/ past participle of **know**

knuckle /ˈnʌk(ə)l/ *noun* a part where two bones join in a finger

knuckle down *phrasal verb* to start working hard (*informal*)

knuckle under *phrasal verb* to give in to someone

koala /kəʊˈɑːlə/, **koala bear** *noun* a small Australian animal which carries its young in a pouch and lives in trees

kosher /ˈkəʊʃə/ *adj* (*of food*) prepared according to Jewish law

Kremlin /ˈkremlɪn/ *noun* the Russian government and its building in Moscow

kudos /ˈkjuːdɒs/ *noun* glory, fame

kung fu /ˌkʌŋ ˈfuː/ *noun* a Chinese style of fighting, where you can kick as well as punch

L

l /el/, **L** *noun* the twelfth letter of the alphabet, between K and M

③ **lab** /læb/ *noun* same as **laboratory** (*informal*)

③ **label** /'leɪb(ə)l/ *noun* a note attached to something to give information about, e.g. its price, its contents or someone's name and address ○ *She stuck a label on the parcel.* ○ *The price on the label is £25.00.* ■ *verb* (**labels, labelling, labelled**) to put a label on something ○ *All the goods are labelled with the correct price.*

labor /'leɪbə/ *noun, verb* US spelling of **labour**

③ **laboratory** /lə'bɒrət(ə)ri/ (*plural* **laboratories**) *noun* a place where scientific experiments, testing and research are carried out ○ *She's a chemist working in the university laboratories.* ○ *All our products are tested in our own laboratories.*

laborious /lə'bɔːriəs/ *adj* difficult, involving a lot of work over a period of time, and often boring ○ *Moving the pile of sand to the back of the house was a laborious task*

③ **labor union** /'leɪbə ˌjuːnjən/ *noun US* a trade union

① **labour** /'leɪbə/ *noun* **1.** work, especially hard work ○ *Does the price include the cost of labour?* **2.** the people who do work ○ *Cheap labour is difficult to find.* **3.** the process of giving birth to a baby ○ *She went into labour at home, and her husband drove her to the hospital.* ○ *She was in labour for 12 hours.* ■ *verb* (**labours, labouring, laboured**) **1.** to work hard ○ *They laboured night and day to finish the project in time.* **2.** to do something with difficulty ○ *She laboured across the room to me.* □ **to labour under an impression** *or* **a delusion** to have a wrong impression, to assume something which is quite wrong ○ *He was labouring under the delusion that air fares were cheaper in Europe than in the USA.* □ **to labour the point** to discuss something for too long ○ *I don't want to labour the point, but may I raise the question for the third time?*

laboured /'leɪbəd/ *adj* showing signs of too much effort (NOTE: The US spelling is **labored**.)

labourer /'leɪbərə/ *noun* a person who does heavy work with his hands

labour force /'leɪbə fɔːs/ *noun* the total number of workers employed in a country, an industry or an organisation

labour-intensive /ˌleɪbər ɪn'tensɪv/ *adj* involving a high number of employees or greater costs for labour than for other areas such as materials, machines or design

labour market /'leɪbə ˌmɑːkɪt/ *noun* a supply of workers ready and available for work

labour movement /'leɪbə ˌmuːvmənt/ *noun* organisations whose aims are to improve conditions for workers and get political power

labyrinth /'læbərɪnθ/ *noun* a system of complicated paths, alleys or corridors which it is difficult to find your way out of

③ **lace** /leɪs/ *noun* **1.** a thin strip of material for tying up a shoe or other piece of clothing ○ *His laces kept coming undone.* ○ *She's too little to be able to do up her laces herself.* **2.** cloth made with open patterns of threads, like a net ○ *a lace tablecloth* ○ *Her wedding dress was trimmed with lace.* (NOTE: no plural in this sense)

laceration /ˌlæsə'reɪʃ(ə)n/ *noun* a place where flesh has been torn

② **lack** /læk/ *noun* the fact that you do not have something ○ *The children are suffering from a lack of food.* ○ *The project was cancelled because of lack of funds.* (NOTE: no plural) ■ *verb* (**lacks, lacking, lacked**) not to have enough of something ○ *The sales staff lack interest in what they are doing.*

③ **lacking** /'lækɪŋ/ *adj* not having any [~in] ○ *Support for people looking after elderly relatives has been sadly lacking.* ○ *She's completely lacking in business sense.*

lacquer /ˈlækə/ *noun* **1.** a type of hard shiny varnish or paint, often used on wood or metal ○ *The coating of lacquer on the chest had begun to crack.* **2.** a spray for keeping hair in place (*old*) ○ *Cover your eyes if you're using hair lacquer anywhere near your face.* (NOTE: + **lacquer** *v*)

lactose /ˈlæktəʊs/ *noun* a sugar contained in milk

③ **lad** /læd/ *noun* a boy or young man

③ **ladder** /ˈlædə/ *noun* an object made of several bars between two posts, used for climbing up to high places ○ *The ladder was leaning against the wall.* ○ *He was climbing up a ladder.* ○ *She got down off the ladder.*

ladle /ˈleɪd(ə)l/ *noun* a large deep spoon for serving liquid foods such as soup ○ *The cook stood by the soup bowl, with her ladle in her hand.* ■ *verb* (**ladles, ladling, ladled**) *also* **ladle out** to serve with a ladle

② **lady** /ˈleɪdi/ (*plural* **ladies**) *noun* a polite way of referring to a woman ○ *There are two ladies waiting to see you.*

ladybird /ˈleɪdibɜːd/ *noun* a type of small beetle, usually red with black spots (NOTE: The US term is **ladybug**.)

lag /læg/ *noun* an interval of time between two linked happenings ○ *There's often a long time lag between setting up in business and seeing any results.* ◊ **jet lag** ■ *verb* (**lags, lagging, lagged**) **1.** to be behind, to fall behind ○ *She was lagging 10m behind the leaders.* **2.** to cover water pipes to prevent them losing heat or freezing ○ *Make sure your pipes are lagged before the winter.*

③ **lager** /ˈlɑːgə/ *noun* a type of light beer ○ *He came to the bar and ordered six pints of lager.*

lagoon /ləˈguːn/ *noun* a shallow part of the sea in the tropics, surrounded by reefs

③ **laid** /leɪd/ past tense and past participle of **lay**

③ **laid-back** /ˌleɪd ˈbæk/ *adj* relaxed, not in a hurry (*informal*)

lain /leɪn/ past participle of **lie** *verb* **2**

lair /leə/ *noun* a place where a wild animal sleeps (*informal*)

② **lake** /leɪk/ *noun* an area of water surrounded by land ○ *Let's take a boat out on the lake.* ○ *We can sail across the lake.* ○ *The hotel stands on the shores of Lake Windermere.*

③ **lamb** /læm/ *noun* **1.** a young sheep ○ *In spring, the fields are full of sheep and their little lambs.* **2.** meat from a lamb or sheep ○ *a leg of lamb* ○ *roast lamb* (NOTE: no plural in this sense)

lambast /læmˈbæst/ *verb* to be very critical of someone or something

lame /leɪm/ *adj* (**lamer, lamest**) **1.** not able to walk properly ○ *He is lame in his left leg.* **2.** weak or unsatisfactory ○ *He produced a very lame excuse for not coming to the meeting.* ■ *verb* (**lames, laming, lamed**) to injure someone so that he or she cannot walk properly

lame duck /ˌleɪm ˈdʌk/ *noun* someone or something that is regarded as weak and unsuccessful

lame-duck /ˈleɪm ˌdʌk/ *adj* regarded as weak and unsuccessful ○ *lame-duck company* ○ *lame-duck president* (NOTE: only used before a noun)

lament /ləˈment/ (**laments, lamenting, lamented**) *verb* to be very sad about ○ *We are still lamenting the closure of our local post office.* (NOTE: + **lament** *n*)

lamentable /ˈlæməntəb(ə)l/ *adj* very bad

laminate[1] /ˈlæmɪnət/ (**laminates, laminating, laminated**) *verb* **1.** to cover something with a thin protective sheet **2.** to bond layers together

laminate[2] /ˈlæmɪneɪt/ *noun* a hard material made up of bonded layers

② **lamp** /læmp/ *noun* an object which produces light ○ *The hall is lit by large electric lamps.*

lampoon /læmˈpuːn/ (**lampoons, lampooning, lampooned**) *verb* to use humour as a way of attacking somebody or something in a piece of writing

lamppost /ˈlæmpˌpəʊst/ *noun* a tall post by the side of a road, holding a lamp

③ **lampshade** /ˈlæmpʃeɪd/ *noun* a cover put over a lamp

LAN /læn/ *abbr* local area network

lance /lɑːns/ *noun* a long pointed stick carried by a knight in armour

① **land** /lænd/ *noun* earth, as opposed to water ○ *They were glad to be back on (dry) land again after two weeks at sea.* (NOTE: no plural) ■ *verb* (**lands, landing, landed**) to arrive on the ground, or on another surface [~at/~on/in/under] ○ *The flight from Amsterdam has landed.* ○ *We will be landing at London Airport in five minutes.* ○ *The ducks tried to land on the ice.*

land up③ *phrasal verb* to end in a place (*informal*) ○ *I got the wrong train and landed up in Scotland.*

landfill /'lændfɪl/ *noun* a way of disposing of rubbish by putting it into holes in the ground and covering it with earth

landing /'lændɪŋ/ *noun* **1.** (*especially of aircraft*) an instance of arriving on the ground or on a surface ○ *The plane made a smooth landing.* ◊ **crash-landing 2.** a flat area at the top of a set of stairs ○ *She was waiting for me on the landing.*

③ **landlady** /'lændleɪdi/ (*plural* **landladies**) *noun* a woman from whom you rent a place to live ○ *You must pay your rent to the landlady every month.*

landline /'læn(d)ˌlaɪn/ *noun* a telephone which sends sound by cable rather than by satellite. Compare **mobile phone**

landlocked /'lændlɒkt/ *adj* more or less surrounded by land

③ **landlord** /'lændlɔːd/ *noun* a man or company from whom you rent property such as a house, room or office ○ *Tell the landlord if your roof leaks.* ○ *The landlord refused to make any repairs to the roof.*

landmark /'lændmɑːk/ *noun* a building or large object on land which you can see easily ○ *The statue is a famous landmark.*

landmass /'lændmæs/ *noun* a large area of land

landmine /'lændmaɪn/ *noun* a small bomb hidden under the surface of the soil, which explodes if disturbed

landowner /'lændəʊnə/ *noun* a person who owns land, and may rent it out

③ **landscape** /'lændskeɪp/ *noun* **1.** the appearance of the countryside ○ *the beautiful landscape of the West Country* **2.** a painting of a country scene ○ *He collects 18th century English landscapes.*

landslide /'lændslaɪd/ *noun* **1.** a sudden fall of large amounts of soil and rocks down the side of a mountain ○ *Landslides have blocked several roads through the mountains.* **2.** an large majority obtained in an election ○ *The Socialists won in a landslide* or *won a landslide victory.*

② **lane** /leɪn/ *noun* **1.** a narrow road, often in the country ○ *a lane with hedges on both sides* **2.** a part of a road for traffic going in a particular direction or at a certain speed ○ *Motorways usually have three lanes on either side.* ○ *One lane of the motorway has been closed for repairs.*

① **language** /'læŋgwɪdʒ/ *noun* a way of speaking or writing used in a country or by a group of people ○ *We go to English language classes twice a week.* ○ *She can speak several European languages.*

language laboratory /'læŋgwɪdʒ ləˌbɒrət(ə)ri/ *noun* a room with tape recorders and monitors where students listen to lessons in foreign languages in order to practise their language skills

languid /'læŋgwɪd/ *adj* moving slowly, without any energy

languish /'læŋgwɪʃ/ (**languishes, languishing, languished**) *verb* to become weaker or more ill, to be in a bad situation

lanky /'læŋki/ (**lankier, lankiest**) *adj* tall, thin and awkward

lantern /'læntən/ *noun* an oil or gas lamp which can be carried in the hand

lap /læp/ *noun* **1.** the part of your body from your waist to your knees when you are sitting ○ *She listened to the story, sitting in her father's lap.* **2.** one turn round a racetrack ○ *He's finished lap 23 – only two laps to go!* ■ *verb* (**laps, lapping, lapped**) **1.** (*of animals*) to drink with the tongue ○ *The dog lapped the water in the pond.* **2.** to go so fast that you are one whole lap ahead of another person in a race ○ *The winner had lapped three other runners.*

lap up *phrasal verb* **1.** (*of animals*) to drink greedily with the tongue ○ *The cat was lapping up the milk.* **2.** to accept something enthusiastically ○ *She told him how good his book was, and he just sat there lapping it up.*

lapel /lə'pel/ *noun* one of the two parts of a coat or jacket which are folded back, just above the top button that fastens it

lapse /læps/ *noun* **1.** an interval of time, especially when something does not take place ○ *There is a lapse of two seconds between touching the switch and the screen lighting up.* ○ *They have started work on the motorway again after a considerable lapse of time.* **2.** a failure of something to work properly ○ *I must have had a lapse of memory.* ■ *verb* (**lapses, lapsing, lapsed**) **1.** to stop ○ *All rubbish collections lapsed during the strike.* **2.** to stop being valid ○ *My parking permit has lapsed, I must get it renewed.*

lapse into *phrasal verb* to fall into a worse state than before ○ *The country lapsed into anarchy when the president was assassinated.* ○ *After the brain operation, she lapsed into a coma from which she never recovered.*

③ **laptop** /'læptɒp/ *noun* a small computer which can be held on your knees

lard /lɑːd/ *noun* pork fat used in cooking

larder /'lɑːdə/ *noun* a cool room or cupboard for storing food

① **large** /lɑːdʒ/ *adj* big ○ *She ordered a large cup of coffee.* ○ *Our house has one large bedroom and two very small ones.* ○ *How large is your garden?* ○ *Why has she got an office which is larger than mine?*

② **largely** /ˈlɑːdʒli/ *adv* mainly, mostly ○ *The price rises are largely due to increased demand.*

③ **large-scale** /ˈlɑːdʒ skeɪl/ *adj* involving large numbers of people or large amounts of money

lark /lɑːk/ *noun* a bird which sings and flies high in the sky ○ *Larks were singing high up above the fields.*

larva /ˈlɑːvə/ (*plural* **larvae**) *noun* the early stage of development of an insect, like a fat worm and different in form from the adult

lasagne /ləˈzænjə/ *noun* a type of flat pasta, served cooked with meat or vegetable sauce

laser /ˈleɪzə/ *noun* an instrument which produces a concentrated beam of light; lasers can be used to cut through hard materials, and to carry out some medical operations

laser printer /ˈleɪzə ˌprɪntə/ *noun* an office printing machine which prints using a laser beam

lash /læʃ/ (**lashes, lashing, lashed**) *verb* **1.** to beat something with a whip ○ *She lashed at the horse to make it go faster.* **2.** to beat against something, as if with a whip ○ *The rain was lashing against the windows.* **3.** to fasten or tie down tightly with rope ○ *Containers carried on the deck of a ship must be securely lashed down.*

lass /læs/ *noun* (*in the North of England & Scotland*) a girl or young woman

① **last** /lɑːst/ *adj* **1.** coming at the end of a list, line or period of time ○ *The post office is the last building on the right.* ○ *The invoice must be paid by the last day of the month.* □ **at last, at long last** in the end, after a long time **2.** most recent ○ *She's been ill for the last ten days.* ○ *The last three books I read were rubbish.* ■ *adv* **1.** at the end ○ *Out of a queue of twenty people, I was served last.* ○ *I'll print the labels last.* **2.** most recently ○ *When did you see her last?* ○ *She was looking ill when I saw her last* or *when I last saw her.* ■ *verb* (**lasts, lasting, lasted**) to continue for some time [~for/until/through etc] ○ *The storm lasted all night.* ○ *The meeting lasted for three hours.* ○ *The fine weather won't last until the weekend.* ◇ **last but one** the one before the last one ○ *My last car but one was a Rolls Royce.*

last-ditch /ˌlɑːst ˈdɪtʃ/ *adj* final, last before something unpleasant happens

lasting /ˈlɑːstɪŋ/ *adj* which lasts for a long time

lastly /ˈlɑːstli/ *adv* at the end

③ **last-minute** /ˌlɑːst ˈmɪnɪt/ *adj* very late

last name /ˈlɑːst neɪm/ *noun* a person's surname

last orders /lɑːst ˈɔːdəz/ *plural noun, interj* the final opportunity to buy drinks before a pub or bar closes

last word /lɑːst ˈwɜːd/ *noun* the very latest fashion

latch /lætʃ/ *noun* the fastening for a door consisting of a small bar which fits into a catch ○ *The burglars pushed on the door and broke the latch.*

① **late** /leɪt/ *adj* **1.** after the usual or expected time ○ *The plane is thirty minutes late.* ○ *It's too late to change your ticket.* ○ *Hurry or you'll be late for the show.* ○ *We apologise for the late arrival of the plane from Amsterdam.* **2.** at the end of a period of time ○ *The traffic was bad in the late afternoon.* ○ *He moved to London in the late 1980s.* **3.** a word used about people instead of 'dead' in order to be polite ○ *His late father was a director of the company.* (NOTE: only used before a noun in this meaning)

latecomer /ˈleɪtkʌmə/ *noun* a person who arrives late

lately /ˈleɪtli/ *adv* during recent days or weeks

late-night /ˈleɪt naɪt/ *adj* happening late at night

latent /ˈleɪt(ə)nt/ *adj* present but not yet developed; hidden

later /ˈleɪtə/ *adv* at a time after the present; at a time after a time which has been mentioned ○ *The family came to live in England and she was born a month later.* ○ *Can we meet later this evening?* ◇ **see you later!** I hope to see you again later today ◇ **later (on)** afterwards, at a later time ○ *I'll do it later on.* ○ *We were only told later that she was very ill.*

lateral /ˈlæt(ə)rəl/ *adj* referring to the side

latest /ˈleɪtɪst/ (*informal*) *adj* the most recent ○ *Have you seen his latest film?* ○ *He always drives the latest model car.* ○ *The latest snow reports are published each day in the papers.* ■ *noun* □ **the latest** the most recent news ○ *Have you heard the latest about Gina?* ◇ **at the latest** no later than the time stated ○ *I'll ring back before 7 o'clock at the latest.*

latex /ˈleɪteks/ *noun* the milky juice from a rubber tree ○ *The raw latex is collected and then heated to make rubber.*

lather /ˈlɑːðə/ *noun* **1.** a mass of soap bubbles ○ *The barber covered my chin with lather.* **2.** (*especially on horses*) a sweat like froth

Latin /ˈlætɪn/ *noun* the language spoken by the ancient Romans ○ *We learnt Latin at school.* ○ *The inscription on the tomb is in Latin.*

latitude /ˈlætɪtjuːd/ *noun* **1.** a position on the earth's surface measured in degrees north or south of the equator ○ *Pine trees grow in temperate latitudes.* ◊ **longitude 2.** freedom to do what you want to do ○ *The management allows the heads of department considerable latitude in selecting staff.*

latte /ˈlæteɪ/ *noun* a coffee made with hot milk

② **latter** /ˈlætə/ *adj* **1.** used for referring to the second of two people or things mentioned **2.** towards the end of the period of time mentioned ○ *I'm busy on Monday and Tuesday, but I'll be free during the latter part of the week.* ■ *noun* □ **the latter** the second person or thing mentioned of two people or things ○ *Which do you prefer, apples or pears? – I prefer the latter.*

② **laugh** /lɑːf/ *noun* a sound you make when you think something is funny ○ *He's got a lovely deep laugh.* ○ *'That's right,' she said with a laugh.* ■ *verb* (**laughs, laughing, laughed**) to make a sound to show you think something is funny [/~at] ○ *Everyone was laughing at his jokes.* ◇ **to do something for a laugh** to do something as a joke or for fun ○ *Don't be angry – they only did it for a laugh.*

laughable /ˈlɑːfəb(ə)l/ *adj* ridiculous or unreasonable

laughing stock /ˈlɑːfɪŋ stɒk/ *noun* a person who is laughed at by everyone

laughter /ˈlɑːftə/ *noun* the sound or act of laughing ○ *As soon as he opened his mouth, the audience burst into laughter.* (NOTE: no plural)

② **launch** /lɔːntʃ/ *noun* **1.** the act of starting off a boat or a spacecraft ○ *The launch of the new car went off successfully.* ○ *The rocket launch has been delayed by two weeks.* **2.** the act of starting off the sale of a new product ○ *The launch of the new car went off successfully.* ■ *verb* (**launches, launching, launched**) **1.** to put a boat into the water, especially for the first time and with a lot of ceremony ○ *The Queen launched the new ship.* **2.** to send a spacecraft into space ○ *The spacecraft was launched from Cape Kennedy.* **3.** to start selling a new product ○ *We're launching the new perfume in the spring.*

launderette /ˌlɔːndəˈret/, **laundrette** *noun* a shop with washing machines which anyone can pay to use (NOTE: The US term is **laundromat**.)

③ **laundry** /ˈlɔːndri/ *noun* **1.** clothes that need to be washed ○ *Please put any laundry into the bag provided.* (NOTE: no plural) **2.** a place where clothes are washed ○ *The hotel's sheets and towels are sent to the laundry every day.*

laurel /ˈlɒrəl/ *noun* a large bush with smooth shiny evergreen leaves

lava /ˈlɑːvə/ *noun* the hot liquid rock flowing from a volcano which becomes solid when it cools

lavatory /ˈlævətri/ (*plural* **lavatories**) *noun* same as **toilet** ○ *The gents' lavatory is to the right.* ○ *The lavatories are situated at the rear of the plane.*

lavender /ˈlævɪndə/ *noun* **1.** a shrub with small lilac-coloured flowers and narrow leaves, grown for perfume ○ *My grandmother puts bags filled with dried lavender flowers in her wardrobe to make her clothes smell nice.* **2.** a bluish-purple colour ■ *adj* bluish purple

lavish /ˈlævɪʃ/ *adj* **1.** very generous ○ *He bought all the children lavish presents.* **2.** larger than necessary ○ *Grandmother always gives us lavish portions.* ■ *verb* (**lavishes, lavishing, lavished**) □ **to lavish something on someone** to give lots of something to someone ○ *He lavished presents on his grandchildren.* ○ *She lavishes a lot of care on her collection of orchids.*

① **law** /lɔː/ *noun* one of the rules governing a country, usually in the form of an act of parliament [~on] ○ *Parliament has passed a new law on environmental protection.* ◇ **to be a law unto yourself** to do exactly what you want

law-abiding /ˈlɔː əˌbaɪdɪŋ/ *adj* who obeys the law

lawcourt /ˈlɔːkɔːt/ *noun* a court where cases are heard by a judge and jury, or by a magistrate

lawful /ˈlɔːf(ə)l/ *adj* allowed by the law (*formal*) ○ *Their behaviour was perfectly lawful.*

lawless /ˈlɔːləs/ *adj* not controlled by the law or by the police

law-making /ˈlɔː ˌmeɪkɪŋ/ *noun* the process of making laws

lawn /lɔːn/ *noun* a part of a garden covered with short grass

lawsuit /ˈlɔːsuːt/ *noun* a case brought to a court □ **to bring a lawsuit against someone** to tell someone to appear in court because you think they have acted wrongly towards you ○ *The parents of the victims brought a lawsuit against the tour company.*

② **lawyer** /ˈlɔːjə/ *noun* a person who has studied law and can advise you on legal matters ○ *If you are arrested you have the right to speak to your lawyer.*

lax /læks/ *adj* not strict

laxative /ˈlæksətɪv/ *noun* medicine which causes a bowel movement ○ *The doctor prescribed a laxative to help his constipation.*

① **lay** /leɪ/ (**lays, laying, laid**) *verb* **1.** to put something down flat [~on/against/over etc] ○ *He laid the papers on the table.* ○ *A new carpet has been laid in the dining room.* **2.** □ **to lay the table** to arrange knives, fork, spoons, plates and glasses on a table for a meal ○ *The table is laid for four people.* **3.** (*of birds, turtles, etc.*) to produce an egg ○ *The hens laid three eggs.*

lay off *phrasal verb* **1.** to dismiss employees for a time, until more work is available ○ *The factory has had to lay off half its workforce because of a temporary lack of orders.* **2.** to stop doing or using something ○ *You should lay off bread and potatoes if you want to reduce weight.*

lay on *phrasal verb* to provide something

lay out *phrasal verb* **1.** to arrange something in an organised way ○ *The plans were laid out on the table.* ○ *They laid out the children's presents under the Christmas tree.* **2.** to design a plan for a garden, a book, etc. ○ *The grounds of the hotel are laid out with trees and flowerbeds.* **3.** to spend ○ *She laid out thousands of pounds on her wedding dress.*

layby /ˈleɪbaɪ/ *noun* a place at the side of a road where vehicles can park

③ **layer** /ˈleɪə/ *noun* an amount of a substance that lies on a flat surface ○ *She put a layer of chocolate on the cake, then one of cream.*

layman /ˈleɪmən/ (*plural* **laymen**) *noun* a person who does not belong to a particular profession, who is not an expert in something

layout /ˈleɪaʊt/ *noun* a design, e.g. of a garden or a book

laze /leɪz/ (**lazes, lazing, lazed**) *verb* to relax, to do nothing or very little

laziness /ˈleɪzinəs/ *noun* the state of being lazy

② **lazy** /ˈleɪzi/ (**lazier, laziest**) *adj* not wanting to do any work ○ *She's just lazy – that's why the work never gets done on time.* ○ *He is so lazy he does not even bother to open his mail.* (NOTE: + **lazily** *adv*)

③ **lb** /paʊndz/ *abbr* pound ○ *take 6lb of sugar* ○ *It weighs 26 lbs.*

① **lead**[1] /led/ *noun* **1.** a very heavy soft metal ○ *Tie a piece of lead to your fishing line to make it sink.* **2.** the black part in the middle of a pencil

lead on③ *phrasal verb* **1.** to go first ○ *Lead on, we will all follow!* **2.** □ **to lead someone on** to mislead someone by promising something ○ *He's just leading you on.* ○ *They promised him a new car, but they were just leading him on.*

lead up to③ *phrasal verb* to happen in a way that makes something else important happen ○ *the events that led up to the First World War*

lead[2] /liːd/ *noun* **1.** an electric wire which joins a machine to the electricity supply ○ *The lead is too short to go across the room.* **2.** first place during a race ○ *He went into the lead* or *he took the lead.* ○ *Who's in the lead at the halfway mark?* ○ *She has a lead of 20m over her nearest rival.* **3.** a long piece of leather or other material used to hold a dog ○ *All dogs must be kept on a lead in the park.* ■ *verb* (**leads, leading, leaded**) **1.** to be in first place during a race or match ○ *Our side was leading at half time.* ○ *They were leading by three metres.* **2.** to go in front to show someone the way ○ *She led us into the hall.* **3.** (*of a path or road*) to go in a particular direction ○ *The road leads you to the top of the hill.* **4.** to be the main person in a group ○ *She is leading a group of businesswomen on a tour of Chinese factories.*

① **leader** /ˈliːdə/ *noun* a person who is in charge of an organisation or group of people ○ *He is the leader of our tour group.*

② **leadership** /ˈliːdəʃɪp/ *noun* **1.** the ability to manage or direct others ○ *We think he has certain leadership qualities.* **2.** the position of a leader ○ *Under his leadership the party went from strength to strength.* **3.** a group of leaders of an organisation ○ *The leadership was weaker after the president's resignation.*

② **leading** /ˈliːdɪŋ/ *adj* most important ○ *He took the leading role in the play.*

leading-edge /ˈliːdɪŋ edʒ/ *noun* the most modern developments in technology, science or some other field

leading question /ˌliːdɪŋ ˈkwestʃən/ *noun* a question which is worded in order to get a particular answer

② **leaf** /liːf/ (*plural* **leaves**) *noun* one of the flat green parts of a plant ○ *The leaves of the trees turn brown or red in autumn.* ○ *Caterpillars have eaten the leaves of the roses.*

② **leaflet** /ˈliːflət/ *noun* a sheet of paper, often folded, giving information

leafy /ˈliːfi/ *adj* **1.** with lots of leaves ○ *These lettuces are really leafy.* **2.** with lots of trees ○ *We strolled along the leafy avenue.*

② **league** /liːg/ *noun* a group of sports clubs which play matches against each other ○ *He plays for one of the clubs in the local football league.*

③ **leak** /liːk/ *noun* **1.** a hole in an object where liquid or gas can escape [~in] ○ *I can smell gas – there must be a gas leak in the kitchen.* **2.** an occasion on which secret information is given to the public ○ *She was embarrassed by the leak of the news.* ○ *The leak of the report led to the minister's resignation.* (NOTE: Do not confuse with **leek**.) ■ *verb* (**leaks, leaking, leaked**) **1.** (*of liquid or gas, etc.*) to flow away, to escape from its container [~from/out of/into/through etc] ○ *Water must have been leaking through the ceiling for days.* **2.** to pass on secret information to the public [~to] ○ *Governments don't like their plans to be leaked to the press.* ○ *We found that the sales director was leaking information to a rival company.*

leakage /ˈliːkɪdʒ/ *noun* an escape of liquid or gas ○ *There's a smell of gas – there must a leakage somewhere.*

leaky /ˈliːki/ *adj* which leaks

② **lean** /liːn/ *adj* **1.** (*of a person*) thin ○ *He's a lean athletic man.* **2.** (*of meat*) with little fat ○ *a slice of lean bacon* ■ *verb* (**leans, leaning, leant** or **leaned**) **1.** to move your body from the waist [~over/forward/on] ○ *He leaned over and picked up the cushion.* ○ *It's dangerous to lean out of car windows.* ○ *She felt dizzy and leant on a chair for support.* **2.** to be in or to put into a sloping position [~against] ○ *The ladder was leaning against the shed.* ○ *She leant her bike against the wall.*

lean on③ *phrasal verb* **1.** to try to force someone to do what you want ○ *They leant on him to get him to agree.* **2.** to depend on someone ○ *If things get difficult she always has her father to lean on.*

leaning /ˈliːnɪŋ/ *noun* a tendency towards ○ *She has socialist leanings.* ○ *He has a leaning towards a career in the church.*

leant /lent/ past tense and past participle of **lean**

leap /liːp/ (**leaps, leaping, leapt** or **leaped**) *verb* to jump ○ *He leapt over the ditch.* ○ *She leapt with joy when she heard the news.* ○ *He leapt into the train as it was leaving.*

leap at③ *phrasal verb* to accept eagerly something which is suggested

leap-frog /ˈliːp frɒg/ *verb* to advance more quickly than someone else

leapt /lept/ past tense and past participle of **leap**

③ **leap year** /ˈliːp jɪə/ *noun* every fourth year, in which February has 29 days

① **learn** /lɜːn/ (**learns, learning, learned** or **learnt**) *verb* **1.** to get knowledge of something, or about how to do something ○ *We learn French and German at school.* □ **to learn to do something** to become able to do something new ○ *He's learnt to speak more slowly and clearly when giving talks.* □ **to learn how to do something** to get the skill of doing something new ○ *Everyone needs to learn how to cook simple things.* □ **to learn something by heart** to learn and remember something ○ *She learnt the poem by heart.* □ **to learn from your mistakes** to make mistakes and because of them learn how something should be done ○ *He doesn't want to ask advice, so I only hope he learns from his mistakes.* **2.** to hear news or find out about something [~about/of/~(that)] ○ *How did you come to learn about the product?* ○ *Her boss learned that she was planning to leave the company.*

learned /ˈlɜːnɪd/ *adj* who has a lot of knowledge ○ *Learned professors have written to the paper contradicting the government's calculations.*

③ **learner** /ˈlɜːnə/ *noun* a person who is learning how to do something ○ *The evening swimming classes are specially for adult learners.* ○ *The new dictionary is good for advanced learners of English.*

② **learning** /ˈlɜːnɪŋ/ *noun* the process of gaining knowledge, especially by formal study ○ *different methods of language learning*

learning curve /ˈlɜːnɪŋ kɜːv/ *noun* a gradual process of learning □ **a steep learning curve** the need to learn new skills fast ○ *Being promoted into a new department involved a steep learning curve.*

learnt past tense and past participle of **learn**

③ **lease** /liːs/ *noun* a written contract, allowing someone to use a building or piece of land for a particular period ○ *We're renting our offices on a twenty-year lease.* ■ *verb* (**leases, leasing, leased**) to give or hold something on a lease ○ *He leases the shop from an Australian company.* ○ *My landlord leases out six other flats.*

leash /liːʃ/ *noun* a strap for holding a dog

① **least** /liːst/ *adj* **1.** used for describing the smallest amount ○ *This car uses by far the least petrol.* **2.** having less of a particular quality than anything else of its type ○ *These people are the least well-off, yet they have to pay the most.* ■ *pron* □ **the least** the smallest or the most unimportant amount ○ *She was the one who spent the least during their trip round Holland.* ■ *adv* less than everyone or everything else ○ *I liked that part of the book least.* ○ *He was the least conceited man she had ever met.* ◇ **at least 1.** mentioning one good thing in a bad situation **2.** to correct a statement **3.** as the smallest thing **4.** not less than ◇ **least of all** absolutely less than everyone or everything else ○ *No one was interested in what I said, least of all my son.* ○ *There's nothing much to do here, least of all in the evenings.* ◇ **not in the least** not at all ○ *It doesn't bother me in the least to work on Sundays.* ◇ **to say the least** which was more than I expected ○ *I thought he was in the office so when I saw him in the supermarket I was surprised to say the least.*

③ **leather** /ˈleðə/ *noun* the skin of certain animals used to make things such as shoes and bags ○ *a leather bag* ○ *My shoes have leather soles.*

① **leave** /liːv/ (**leaves, leaving, left**) *verb* **1.** to go away from a place [~for] ○ *When they couldn't find what they wanted, they left the shop.* ○ *When does the next bus leave for Oxford?* **2.** to forget to take something with you ○ *I left my toothbrush at home.* **3.** to allow something to stay in a particular condition ○ *Did you leave the light on when you locked up?* ○ *Yesterday she left the iron on, and burnt a hole in the ironing board.* ○ *Someone left the door open and the dog got out.* □ **leave me alone** don't disturb me **4.** not to take something ○ *Leave some pizza for your brother.* **5.** to choose to stop being in a relationship with someone ○ *She's left her husband.* **6.** not to do something ○ *She went out leaving all the washing up.* □ **to leave somebody to do something** not to do something, so that someone else has to do it ○ *He left to arrange the holiday.*

leave behind③ *phrasal verb* not to take someone or something with you

leave off *phrasal verb* **1.** to stop doing something **2.** to forget to include ○ *She left the postcode off the address.* ○ *The waitress left the drinks off the bill.*

leave out① *phrasal verb* **1.** to forget something or someone **2.** not to put something in

③ **leaves** /liːvz/ **1.** ♦ **leaf 2.** ♦ **leave**

lecherous /ˈletʃərəs/ *adj* only interested in sexual intercourse

③ **lecture** /ˈlektʃə/ *noun* a talk on a particular subject given to people such as students [~on] ○ *She gave a lecture on Chinese art.* ■ *verb* (**lectures, lecturing, lectured**) **1.** to give a lecture on something [~on] ○ *He will lecture on Roman history next Thursday.* **2.** to teach a subject, by giving lectures [~on] ○ *She lectures on history at Birmingham University.*

lecturer /ˈlektʃərə/ *noun* **1.** a person who gives a talk on a particular subject ○ *This week's lecturer is talking about modern art.* **2.** a teacher in a university or college ○ *He has been a lecturer in biology for five years.*

③ **led** /led/ past tense and past participle of **lead**

ledge /ledʒ/ *noun* a narrow flat part which sticks out from a cliff or a building

ledger /ˈledʒə/ *noun* a large book in which accounts are written

leech /liːtʃ/ *noun* a type of parasitic worm which lives in water and sucks the blood of animals by attaching itself to the skin

leek /liːk/ *noun* a vegetable of the onion family, with a white stem and long green leaves (NOTE: Do not confuse with **leak**.)

leer /lɪə/ (**leers, leering, leered**) *verb* to look with a leer at someone ○ *The men were sitting in the pavement café, leering at girls passing in the street.* (NOTE: + **leer** *n*)

leeway /ˈliːweɪ/ *noun* the time or space available

① **left** /left/ *adj* **1.** relating to the side of the body which has the hand that most people do not use for writing ○ *I can't write with my left hand.* ○ *The post office is on the left side of the street as you go towards the church.* **2.** (*in politics*) relating to people with left-wing opinions ○ *His politics are left of centre.* Compare **right** ■ *noun* the side towards the left ○ *Remember to drive on the left when you are in Britain.* ○ *The school is on the left as you go towards the town centre.* ○ *She was sitting on the chairman's left.* ■ *adv* towards the left ○ *Go straight ahead and turn left at the traffic lights.*

left-click /'left klɪk/ *verb* (*in computing*) to click with the left mouse button

left-hand /ˌleft 'hænd/ *adj* on the left side ○ *The book is in the left-hand drawer of his desk.* ○ *In England cars drive on the left-hand side of the road.*

left-handed /ˌleft 'hændɪd/ *adj* using the left hand more often than the right for doing things ○ *She's left-handed, so we got her a left-handed cup for her birthday.*

left-luggage office /left 'lʌgɪdʒ ˌɒfɪs/ *noun* a place where suitcases can be left and collected later for a fee (NOTE: The US term is **baggage room**.)

leftover /'leftəʊvə/ *adj* which is not used ○ *I've finished painting the kitchen – what shall I do with the leftover paint?*

leftovers /'leftəʊvəz/ *plural noun* food which is left after a meal ○ *The children will eat the leftovers tomorrow morning.*

③ **left-wing** /ˌleft 'wɪŋ/ *adj* in politics, relating to people who believe that money and property should be shared more equally

lefty /'lefti/ *noun* a person with left-wing beliefs

① **leg** /leg/ *noun* **1.** one of the parts of the body with which a person or animal walks ○ *The bird was standing on one leg, asleep.* ○ *Some animals can't stand on their back legs.* ○ *She fell down the steps and broke her leg.* **2.** one of the parts of a chair or table which touch the floor ○ *The table has four legs.* **3.** a leg of an animal used for food ○ *roast leg of lamb* ○ *Would you like a chicken leg?* ◇ **to pull someone's leg** to try to make someone believe something that is not true for a joke ○ *Don't worry, she will get here on time – I was only pulling your leg.*

legacy /'legəsi/ (*plural* **legacies**) *noun* **1.** what is left to a person after someone's death ○ *He received a large legacy from his uncle.* ○ *The legacy can be paid only to the rightful claimant.* **2.** what is left behind by someone ○ *The company's overdraft is a legacy of the previous finance director.*

① **legal** /'liːg(ə)l/ *adj* **1.** allowed by the law ○ *It's legal to drive at 17 years old in the UK* **2.** relating to the law

legal aid /ˌliːg(ə)l 'eɪd/ *noun* free legal work done for people without enough money to pay lawyers' fees

legalisation, legalization *noun* the action of making something legal

legalise (**legalises, legalising, legalised**), **legalize** (**legalizes, legalizing, legalized**) *verb* to make something legal

legality /lɪ'gælɪti/ *noun* being allowed by law

legally /'liːgəli/ *adv* according to the law

legend /'ledʒənd/ *noun* **1.** a story, or group of stories, from the past which may not be based on fact ○ *The legend of Jason and the Golden Fleece.* **2.** a famous person whose name often appears in the news ○ *Marilyn Monroe, the Hollywood legend*

legendary /'ledʒənd(ə)ri/ *adj* **1.** famous, often talked about ○ *His meanness is legendary.* ○ *Her legendary dislike of men with beards.* **2.** referring to legends ○ *A legendary tale of witches and good fairies.*

legible /'ledʒɪb(ə)l/ *adj* able to be read easily

legion /'liːdʒən/ *noun* a group, especially of soldiers

legislate /'ledʒɪsleɪt/ (**legislates, legislating, legislated**) *verb* to make a law or laws

② **legislation** /ˌledʒɪ'sleɪʃ(ə)n/ *noun* laws, written rules which are passed by Parliament and applied in the courts

legislative /'ledʒɪslətɪv/ *adj* referring to laws or to law-making

legislature /'ledʒɪslətʃə/ *noun* a body which makes laws ○ *Members of the legislature voted against the proposal.*

legitimate /lɪ'dʒɪtɪmət/ *adj* fair and reasonable, or allowed by the law ○ *They have legitimate concerns about the project.* ○ *He acted in legitimate defence of his rights.*

leisure centre /'leʒə ˌsentə/ *noun* a building where people can play sports, put on plays, dance, act, etc.

leisurely /'leʒəli/ *adj* without any hurry

lemon /'lemən/ *noun* a pale yellow fruit with a sour taste ○ *Oranges are much sweeter than lemons.*

③ **lemonade** /ˌlemə'neɪd/ *noun* a usually fizzy lemon-flavoured drink

① **lend** /lend/ (**lends, lending, lent**) *verb* to let someone use something for a certain period of time ○ *He asked me if I would lend him £5 till Monday.* ○ *I lent her my dictionary and now she won't give it back.* Compare **borrow**

lender /'lendə/ *noun* a person who lends money

② **length** /leŋθ/ *noun* **1.** a measurement of how long something is from end to end ○ *The table is at least twelve feet in length.* **2.** a long piece of something ○ *She bought a length of curtain material in the sale.* ○ *We need two lengths of piping for the new central heating system.*

lengthen /'leŋθən/ (**lengthens, lengthening, lengthened**) *verb* **1.** to make longer ○ *You can lengthen the skirt by turning down the hem.* **2.** to become longer ○ *The shadows began to lengthen across the lawn as the sun sank slowly down in the west.*

③ **lengthy** /'leŋθi/ (**lengthier, lengthiest**) *adj* very long

lenient /'liːniənt/ *adj* not strict or severe

lens /lenz/ *noun* a curved piece of glass or plastic, used for looking through to make things clearer or bigger ○ *My eyesight is not very good, and I have to have glasses with strong lenses.* ◊ **contact lens**

③ **lent** /lent/ past tense and past participle of **lend**

lentil /'lentɪl/ *noun* a small round dried seed, used especially in soups and stews

Leo /'liːəʊ/ *noun* one of the signs of the Zodiac, shaped like a lion, covering the period 23rd July to 22nd August

leopard /'lepəd/ *noun* a large wild spotted cat, living in Africa

leotard /'liːətɑːd/ *noun* a skin-tight one-piece costume covering the top of the body, worn by ballet dancers

leper /'lepə/ *noun* a person who has leprosy

leprosy /'leprəsi/ (*plural* **leprosies**) *noun* a serious infectious disease which slowly destroys flesh and nerves

lesbian /'lezbiən/ *adj* who is sexually attracted to other women ○ *They went to the Lesbian and Gay Pride march in London.* ■ *noun* a woman who is lesbian

lesion /'liːʒ(ə)n/ *noun* a wound or sore, or other damage to the body

① **less** /les/ *adj, pron* a smaller amount (of) ○ *You will get thinner if you eat less bread.* ○ *The total bill came to less than £10.* ○ *She finished her homework in less than an hour.* ○ *He sold it for less than he had paid for it.* ■ *adv* not as much ○ *I like that one less than this one.* ○ *The second film was less interesting than the first.* ○ *I want a car which is less difficult to drive.* ■ *prep* with a certain amount taken away ○ *We pay £10 an hour, less 50p for insurance.* ◇ **more or less** almost ○ *I've more or less finished painting the kitchen.* ◇ **less and less** diminishing all the time ○ *I enjoy my work less and less.* ○ *He's less and less able to look after his garden.*

lessen /'les(ə)n/ (**lessens, lessening, lessened**) *verb* to become less, or to make something become less ○ *Wearing a seat belt lessens the risk of injury.* (NOTE: Do not confuse with **lesson**.)

lesser /'lesə/ *adj* smaller, not as large or important ◇ **the lesser of two evils** one of two things which is not quite as bad as the other ○ *Faced with the choice of taking a taxi or waiting in the rain for a bus, we chose the lesser of two evils and decided to take the taxi.*

② **lesson** /'les(ə)n/ *noun* **1.** a period of time, especially in school, when you are taught something [~in] ○ *He went to sleep during the French lesson.* ○ *We have six lessons of history a week.* ○ *She's taking* or *having driving lessons.* ○ *He gives Spanish lessons at home in the evenings.* **2.** something which you learn from experience and which makes you wiser □ **to learn a lesson, to learn your lesson** to learn something from experience ◇ **to teach someone a lesson** to punish someone for doing something wrong ○ *I refused to pay her bill this time – that will teach her a lesson.*

① **let** /let/ (**lets, letting, let**) *verb* **1.** to allow someone to do something [~on//] ○ *He let her borrow his car.* ○ *Will you let me see the papers?* **2.** to allow someone to use a house or office in return for payment [~to] ○ *We're letting our cottage to some friends for the weekend.*

let down③ *phrasal verb* **1.** to lower something or someone ○ *They let him down into the mine on a rope.* **2.** to make the air go out of something such as a tyre or balloon ○ *Someone had let down my front tyre.* **3.** not to help when someone expects you to help ○ *I asked three people to speak at the meeting but they all let me down.*

let go③ *phrasal verb* to stop holding on to something

let in③ *phrasal verb* to allow to come in

let off③ *phrasal verb* **1.** to make something such as a gun or bomb fire explode ○ *They let off fireworks in the town centre.* **2.** to not punish someone severely ○

He was charged with stealing, but the judge let him off with a fine. **3.** to agree that someone need not do something ○ *She let the class off their homework.*

let on *phrasal verb* to tell a secret

let out① *phrasal verb* **1.** to allow to go out ○ *The boys let the pigs out of the field.* ○ *We let the dogs out into the garden in the evening.* ○ *She let the air out of my front tyre.* **2.** to make a piece of clothing bigger ○ *Can you let out these trousers, they're getting too tight?* (NOTE: In this meaning the opposite is to **take in**.)

let up *phrasal verb* to do less, to become less ○ *The snow didn't let up all day.* ○ *She's working too hard – she ought to let up a bit.*

letdown /ˈletdaʊn/ *noun* a disappointment

③ **lethal** /ˈliːθ(ə)l/ *adj* dangerous and able to kill ○ *She took a lethal overdose.*

lethargic /lɪˈθɑːdʒɪk/ *adj* showing lethargy

lethargy /ˈleθədʒi/ *noun* a tired feeling, when your movements are extremely slow and you are almost unable to do anything

① **letter** /ˈletə/ *noun* **1.** a piece of writing sent from one person to another to pass on information ○ *There were two letters for you in the post.* ○ *Don't forget to write a letter to your mother to tell her what we are doing.* ○ *We've had a letter from the bank manager.* **2.** one of the signs which make up the alphabet, a sign used in writing which corresponds to a particular sound ○ *Z is the last letter of the alphabet.* ○ *I'm trying to think of a word with ten letters beginning with A and ending with R.* ◇ **to the letter** exactly as shown or stated ○ *They followed his instructions to the letter.*

letterbox /ˈletəbɒks/ *noun* **1.** a box in the road where you post letters ○ *There's a letterbox at the corner of the street.* **2.** a hole in a front door through which letters are delivered ○ *The Sunday paper is too big to go through the letterbox.*

lettuce /ˈletɪs/ *noun* a plant with large green leaves which are used in salads (NOTE: no plural except when referring to several plants: *a row of lettuces*)

leukaemia /luːˈkiːmiə/ *noun* any of several serious illnesses where an unusual number of white blood cells form in the blood (NOTE: The US spelling is **leukemia**.)

① **level** /ˈlev(ə)l/ *noun* **1.** a position relating to height or amount [/~with] ○ *I want to lower the level of our borrowings.* ○ *The water reached a level of 5m above normal during the flood.* ○ *The ground floor is level with the street.* **2.** a floor in a building ○ *Go up to the next level.* ○ *The toilets are at street level.* ■ *adj* **1.** flat and even ○ *Are these shelves level, or do they slope to the left?* **2.** equal, the same ○ *At half-time the scores were level.*

③ **level crossing** /ˌlev(ə)l ˈkrɒsɪŋ/ *noun* a place where a road crosses a railway line without a bridge or tunnel (NOTE: The US term is **grade crossing**.)

level-headed /ˌlev(ə)lˈhedɪd/ *adj* sensible

level playing-field /ˌlev(ə)l ˈpleɪɪŋ/ *noun* a situation in which all the conditions are the same for everyone who is involved, so that nobody has an unfair advantage

③ **lever** /ˈliːvə/ *noun* an object like a bar, which helps you to lift a heavy object, or to move part of a machine ○ *Lift the lever, then push it down again to make the machine work.* ○ *We used a pole as a lever to lift up the block of stone.* ■ *verb* (**levers, levering, levered**) to move with a lever ○ *They levered the door open with an iron bar.*

leverage /ˈliːvərɪdʒ/ *noun* **1.** the power to move something heavy by using a lever ○ *They used a longer bar to get better leverage.* ○ *You'll need a longer pole to increase the leverage.* **2.** an influence which you can use to get what you want ○ *His business contacts were useful leverage in discussing terms for the contract.* ○ *She has a majority of the shares in the company and therefore can exert a lot of leverage over the directors.*

levitate /ˈlevɪteɪt/ (**levitates, levitating, levitated**) *verb* to rise into the air, as if by magic

levy /ˈlevi/ *noun* (*plural* **levies**) an official tax or other payment ○ *I think the import levies on luxury goods are too high.* ○ *We paid the levy on time.* ■ *verb* (**levies, levying, levied**) to order a person to pay a tax or other payment, or to collect it ○ *The customs levied a large fine.*

lewd /luːd/ *adj* rude because of referring to sex in an unpleasant way

② **liability** /ˌlaɪəˈbɪlɪti/ (*plural* **liabilities**) *noun* **1.** a legal responsibility ○ *Make sure you understand your legal liabilities before you sign the contract.* **2.** a tendency to do something ○ *a liability to burst into tears when criticised* **3.** something or someone who causes problems or makes you feel embarrassed [~for/~to]

liable /ˈlaɪəb(ə)l/ *adj* **1.** legally responsible for something [~for] ○ *Parents can be made liable for their children's debts.* ○ *You will be liable for payment of the fine.* **2.** likely to have or do something [~to] ○ *The figures are liable to error.* ○ *The trains are liable to be late at present.*

liaise /liˈeɪz/ (**liaises, liaising, liaised**) *verb* to inform someone of what is being done or planned so that everyone who is involved can work together well [~with] ○ *Can you liaise with each individual manager regarding the move to new offices?*

③ **liaison** /liˈeɪz(ə)n/ *noun* **1.** the process of keeping someone informed of what is happening [~between/~with] ○ *There has been a total lack of liaison between the police and the customs department on this case.* **2.** a sexual relationship [~between/~with] ○ *His liaison with the singer was soon well-known.*

liar /ˈlaɪə/ *noun* a person who tells lies

Lib Dem /ˌlɪb ˈdem/ *abbr* Liberal Democrat ○ *Delegates at the Lib Dem party conference.*

③ **libel** /ˈlaɪb(ə)l/ *noun* a written statement about someone which is not true and may damage their reputation ○ *I will sue you for libel.* ■ *verb* (**libels, libelling, libelled**) to damage someone's reputation in writing ○ *He accused the newspaper of libelling him.* Compare **slander** (NOTE: US spelling is **libeling – libeled**)

② **liberal** /ˈlɪb(ə)rəl/ *adj* not strict, willing to accept other people's views ○ *The liberal view would be to let the teenagers run the club themselves.*

Liberal /ˈlɪb(ə)rəl/ *noun* (*in politics*) referring to or supporting the Liberal Party

liberalise /ˈlɪb(ə)rəlaɪz/ (**liberalises, liberalising, liberalised**), **liberalize** *verb* to make things such as laws more liberal

liberate /ˈlɪbəreɪt/ (**liberates, liberating, liberated**) *verb* to set someone or something free from something (NOTE: + **liberation** *n*)

liberated /ˈlɪbəreɪtɪd/ *adj* **1.** not influenced by a society's traditional ideas about how people should behave e.g. the way women should behave **2.** set free from enemy control

liberating /ˈlɪbəreɪtɪŋ/ *adj* which liberates you

liberty /ˈlɪbəti/ *noun* freedom ○ *When he was in prison he wrote poems about his lost liberty.* ○ *Anti-terrorist legislation can be seen as an infringement of the liberty of the individual.* ◇ **at liberty** free; not in prison ○ *Two of the escaped prisoners are still at liberty.* ◇ **to be at liberty to do something** to be free to do something ○ *You are at liberty to go now.*

libido /lɪˈbiːdəʊ/ *noun* the feeling of wanting to have sex

Libra /ˈliːbrə/ *noun* one of the signs of the zodiac, shaped like a pair of scales, covering the period 22nd September to 23rd October

librarian /laɪˈbreəriən/ *noun* a person who works in a library

① **library** /ˈlaɪbrəri/ *noun* **1.** a place where books are kept, especially ones which you can borrow ○ *He forgot to take his books back to the library.* ○ *You can't keep it, it's a library book.* **2.** a collection of things such as books or records ○ *He has a big record library.*

lice /laɪs/ plural of **louse**

① **licence** /ˈlaɪs(ə)ns/ *noun* a document which gives official permission to own something or to do something ○ *She has applied for an export licence for these paintings.*

① **license** /ˈlaɪs(ə)ns/ (**licenses, licensing, licensed**) *verb* to give someone official permission to do something ○ *The restaurant is licensed to serve beer, wines and spirits.* ○ *She is licensed to run an employment agency.*

licensed /ˈlaɪs(ə)nst/ *adj* given official permission to do something

licensee /ˌlaɪs(ə)nˈsiː/ *noun* a person who has a licence for a particular activity, especially a person who is in charge of a public house

license plate /ˈlaɪs(ə)ns pleɪt/ *noun US* a number plate on a vehicle

lichen /ˈlaɪkən, ˈlɪtʃən/ *noun* a very small plant which grows on the surface of stones or trunks of trees

③ **lick** /lɪk/ (**licks, licking, licked**) *verb* to make a gentle movement with your tongue across the surface of something ○ *You shouldn't lick the plate when you've finished your pudding.*

③ **lid** /lɪd/ *noun* a covering for a container, sometimes with a handle ○ *Where's the lid for the black saucepan?* ○ *He managed to get the lid off the jam jar.*

① **lie** /laɪ/ *verb* (**lies, lying, lied**) **1.** to say something which is not true [~about/~to] ○ *She was lying when she said she had been at home all evening.* ○ *He lied about the accident to the headmaster.* **2.** to be in a flat position ○ *Six soldiers lay dead on the ground.* ○ *The dog spends the evening lying* *in front of the fire.* **3.** to be in a particular place ○ *There were bits of paper and cigarette packets lying all over the pavement.* ○ *The city of Quito lies near the equator.* ■ *noun* something that is not true ○ *That's a lie! – I didn't say that!* □ **to tell lies** to say things that are not true ◇ **to lie in wait for someone** to hide and wait for someone to come so as to attack him

lie down③ *phrasal verb* to put yourself in a flat position, e.g. on a bed

lie in③ *phrasal verb* to stay in bed late in the morning (*informal*) ○ *I think I'll lie in this morning.*

lie detector /ˈlaɪ dɪˌtektə/ *noun* a machine which is used to check if someone is telling the truth, e.g. when the police are questioning them

③ **lie-in** /ˈlaɪɪn/ *noun* □ **to have a lie-in** to stay in bed longer than usual (*informal*) ○ *I can't wait until Saturday comes, then I can have a lie-in*

lieu /ljuː/ *noun* □ **in lieu of** in place (of) ○ *When she was sacked she was given four weeks' pay in lieu of notice.* ○ *He accepted a car in lieu of payment.*

③ **lieutenant** /lefˈtenənt/ *noun* **1.** a rank in the armed forces below a captain ○ *The lieutenant has to report to his captain.* **2.** someone whose job is to help an important person ○ *The mayor came into the room with two of his lieutenants.*

① **life** /laɪf/ (*plural* **lives**) *noun* **1.** the period during which you are alive ○ *He spent his whole life working on the farm.* □ **for life** for as long as someone is alive ○ *They put him behind bars for life.* ○ *His pension gives him a comfortable income for life.* **2.** the fact of being a living person [~of] ○ *Life is a precious thing; don't waste it.* **3.** a particular experience of life ○ *I think I'd enjoy the life of a celebrity.* ○ *She had a hard life as a child.* **4.** living things [~of] ○ *animal and plant life* ○ *Scientists are still looking for life on Mars.* □ **there's no sign of life in the house** it looks as though there is no one in **5.** enthusiasm or energy ○ *The young actors injected some life into the old play.* ○ *The film comes to life when she appears on the screen.* ○ *She's always full of life.* ◇ **to lose your life** to die ○ *Several lives were lost when the ship sank.* ◇ **to take your life** or **your own life** to kill yourself ○ *In a fit of despair she took her life.*

lifebelt /ˈlaɪfbelt/ *noun* a large ring which helps to prevent you from sinking in water

lifeboat /ˈlaɪfbəʊt/ *noun* a special boat used to save people from danger at sea

lifebuoy /ˈlaɪfˌbɔɪ/ *noun* a float used in an emergency to keep somebody's head and shoulders above water until help arrives

life cycle /ˈlaɪf ˌsaɪk(ə)l/ *noun* all the changes which a living creature goes through during its life

life expectancy /ˈlaɪf ɪkˌspektənsi/ *noun* **1.** the number of years that a person or animal is likely to live ○ *Average life expectancy has increased to over 80 for women.* **2.** the length of time that something is expected to continue ○ *The life expectancy of this government is short – it only has a majority of one in Parliament.*

lifeguard /ˈlaɪfɡɑːd/ *noun* a person who is on duty on a beach or at a swimming pool, and who saves people who get into difficulty in the water

life insurance /ˈlaɪf ɪnˌʃʊərəns/ *noun* a type of insurance paying an amount of money to your family if you die

life jacket /ˈlaɪf ˌdʒækɪt/ *noun* something which you wear when you are on a boat and which will prevent you from sinking if you fall into the water

lifeless /ˈlaɪfləs/ *adj* **1.** not alive, or appearing not to be alive ○ *Her lifeless body was lying across the bed.* **2.** not lively or interesting ○ *The dancers' performance was dull and lifeless.*

lifelike /ˈlaɪflaɪk/ *adj* just like a living person

lifeline /ˈlaɪflaɪn/ *noun* **1.** a rope thrown to a person who is sinking in water ○ *They threw him a lifeline from the boat.* **2.** the help given to someone in difficulties ○ *The scholarship offers a lifeline to young writers.* ○ *The government grant is a lifeline which helps them put on exhibitions of young painters' work at their gallery.*

lifelong /ˈlaɪflɒŋ/ *adj* lasting your whole life

life saving /ˈlaɪf ˌseɪvɪŋ/ *adj* able to prevent someone from dying

life sentence /ˌlaɪf ˈsentəns/ *noun* the punishment of being sent to prison for many years for committing murder

life-size /laɪf saɪz/ *adj* the same size as the real thing

③ **life-span** /ˈlaɪf spæn/ *noun* the length of time something exists

life story /laɪf ˈstɔːri/ *noun* a detailed account of all the events of someone's life

③ **lifestyle** /ˈlaɪfstaɪl/ *noun* the way in which someone or a group of people live

life-threatening /ˌlaɪf ˌθret(ə)nɪŋ dɪ ˈziːz/ *adj* which may kill

lifetime /ˈlaɪftaɪm/ *noun* the time when you are alive

② **lift** /lɪft/ *noun* **1.** a machine which takes people up or down from one floor to another in a building ○ *Take the lift to the tenth floor.* ○ *Push the button to call the lift.* ○ *Your room is on the fifteenth floor, so you may wish to use the lift.* **2.** a ride in a car that you give to someone ○ *She gave me a lift to the station.* ■ *verb* (**lifts, lifting, lifted**) to take something, often off the ground, and put it in a higher position ○ *My briefcase is so heavy I can hardly lift it.* ○ *He lifted the little girl up so that she could see the procession.*

lift-off /ˈlɪft ɒf/ *noun* the act of sending a spacecraft up into the air

ligament /ˈlɪɡəmənt/ *noun* a thick band of fibrous tissue which connects the bones at a joint

① **light** /laɪt/ *noun* **1.** brightness, the opposite of darkness ○ *I can't read the map by the light of the moon.* ○ *There's not enough light to take a photo.* **2.** a piece of electrical equipment which gives light ○ *Turn the light on – I can't see to read.* ○ *It's dangerous to ride a bicycle with no lights.* ○ *In the fog, I could just see the red lights of the car in front of me.* ■ *verb* (**lights, lighting, lit** or **lighted**) to start to burn, or make something start to burn ○ *He is trying to get the fire to light.* ○ *Can you light the candles on the birthday cake?* ■ *adj* **1.** not heavy ○ *I can lift this box easily – it's quite light.* ○ *You need light clothing for tropical countries.* ○ *She's just been ill, and can only do light work.* **2.** pale ○ *He was wearing a light green shirt.* ○ *I prefer a light carpet to a dark one.* **3.** having a lot of light so that you can see well ○ *The big windows make the kitchen very light.* ○ *It was six o'clock in the morning and just getting light.* ◇ **to cast *or* throw light on something** to make something easier to understand ○ *The papers throw light on how the minister reached his decision.* ◇ **to come to light** to be discovered ○ *Documents have come to light which could help the police in their investigations.* ◇ **in the light of something** when something is considered ○ *In the light of the reports in the press, can the minister explain his decision?*

light up③ *phrasal verb* **1.** to make something bright ○ *The flames from the burning petrol store lit up the night sky.* ○ *The firework display lit up the gardens and the lake.* **2.** to become bright and happy ○ *Her face lit up when she saw the presents under the Christmas tree.* **3.** to start to smoke ○ *Please do not light up until coffee has been served.*

light aircraft /laɪt ˈeəˌkrɑːft/ *noun* a small plane

③ **light bulb** /ˈlaɪt bʌlb/ *noun* a glass ball which gives electric light

lighten /ˈlaɪt(ə)n/ (**lightens, lightening, lightened**) *verb* **1.** to make or become less dark ○ *You can lighten the room by painting it white.* ○ *The sky lightened as dawn broke.* **2.** to become less heavy, or to make something become less heavy ○ *I'll have to lighten my suitcase – it's much too heavy.*

light entertainment /laɪt ˌentə ˈteɪnmənt/ *noun* entertainment that is not serious, usually involving things such as telling jokes, singing, dancing or popular music

lighter /ˈlaɪtə/ *noun* a small object used for lighting things such as cigarettes ○ *Can I borrow your lighter? – mine has run out of gas.*

light-headed /ˌlaɪt ˈhedɪd/ *adj* with the feeling that you are going to fall down

light-hearted /ˌlaɪt ˈhɑːtɪd/ *adj* happy, not very serious

light industry /ˌlaɪt ˈɪndəstri/ *noun* an industry which makes small products, such as clothes, books or things you use in the home

③ **lighting** /ˈlaɪtɪŋ/ *noun* the light in a place

lightly /ˈlaɪtli/ *adv* **1.** gently, without force ○ *She touched my arm lightly.* ○ *I always sleep lightly and wake up several times each night.* **2.** not severely **3.** without much rich food ○ *She always eats lightly at lunchtime.* **4.** not very much ○ *some lightly cooked vegetables*

② **lightning** /ˈlaɪtnɪŋ/ *noun* a flash of electricity in the sky in a storm ○ *The storm approached with thunder and lightning.*

lightweight /ˈlaɪtweɪt/ *noun* a weight of a boxer between featherweight and welterweight ○ *the lightweight champion* ○ *a lightweight title fight*

③ **light year** /ˈlaɪt jɪə/ *noun* the distance travelled by light during one year,equal to about 9.3 billion kilometres ○ *Stars are light years from earth.*

① **like** /laɪk/ *prep* **1.** similar to, in the same way as ○ *He's like his mother in many ways, but he has his father's nose.* ○ *Like you, I don't get on with the new boss.* ○ *The picture doesn't look like him at all.* ○ *He* *can swim like a fish.* ○ *It tastes like strawberries.* ○ *What's that record? – it sounds like Elgar.* **2.** used for asking someone to describe something ○ *What was the weather like when you were on holiday?* ○ *What's he like, her new boyfriend?* ■ *verb* (**likes, liking, liked**) **1.** to have pleasant feelings about someone or something ○ *Do you like the new manager?* ○ *She doesn't like eating meat.* ○ *How does he like his new job?* ○ *No one likes driving in rush hour traffic.* ○ *In the evening, I like to sit quietly and read the newspaper.* **2.** to want ○ *Take as many apples as you like.* ◇ **would like** used for telling someone what you want in a polite way ○ *I'd like you to meet one of our sales executives.* ○ *I'd like to go to Paris next week.*

likeable /'laɪkəb(ə)l/ *adj* pleasant

likelihood /'laɪklihʊd/ *noun* being likely to happen

① **likely** /'laɪkli/ (**likelier, likeliest**) *adj* probably going to happen ○ *It's likely to snow this weekend.* ○ *He's not likely to come to the party.* ○ *Is that at all likely?*

like-minded /ˌlaɪk 'maɪndɪd/ *adj* who has the same opinions

liken /'laɪkən/ (**likens, likening, likened**) *verb* □ **to liken something or someone to something or someone else** to compare two things, by showing how one is similar to the other ○ *Can I liken her to a ray of sunlight?* ○ *He likened being tackled by the South African forward to being hit by a rhino.*

likeness /'laɪknəs/ *noun* **1.** a picture or other object which looks like someone ○ *The sketch is an astonishing likeness of grandmother.* **2.** the fact of being like someone else ○ *There is a strong family likeness in all the children.*

likewise /'laɪkwaɪz/ *adv* in the same way

③ **liking** /'laɪkɪŋ/ *noun* a feeling of enjoying something [~for] ○ *She has a liking for chocolate.* ◇ **for someone's liking** not being what someone likes in a particular way ○ *This drink is too sweet for my liking.* ◇ **to take a liking to someone or something** to start to like someone or something ○ *The manager has taken a liking to her.* ◇ **to someone's liking** being the kind of thing someone likes ○ *Is this type of music to your liking?*

lilac /'laɪlək/ *noun* **1.** a tree with purple or white flowers ○ *They have a pretty lilac in their front garden.* **2.** a pale purple colour ■ *adj* pale purple

lilt /lɪlt/ *noun* a way of speaking or singing with a light well-marked rhythm

lily /'lɪli/ (*plural* **lilies**) *noun* a type of flower shaped like a trumpet, which grows from a bulb

③ **limb** /lɪm/ *noun* a leg or arm ○ *He was lucky not to break a limb in the accident.*

limbo /'lɪmbəʊ/ (*plural* **limbos**) *noun* the position of being halfway between two stages ○ *After losing his seat in the election he now finds himself in political limbo.*

lime /laɪm/ *noun* **1.** a white substance containing calcium, used in making cement ○ *The builder ordered some bags of lime.* **2.** a small yellowish-green tropical fruit like a lemon or the tree which bears such fruit ○ *You need the juice of two limes to make this recipe.*

limerick /'lɪmərɪk/ *noun* a type of funny poem with five lines

② **limit** /'lɪmɪt/ *noun* the furthest point beyond which you cannot go [~of/~on/~to] ○ *We were never allowed to go beyond the limits of the garden.* ○ *What's the limit on your credit card?* ○ *Is there a limit to how much we can use at one time?* ■ *verb* (**limits, limiting, limited**) not to allow something to go beyond a certain point [~to] ○ *Her parents limited the number of evenings she could go out.* ○ *The amount we can spend on entertainment is limited to £500 each month.*

③ **limitation** /ˌlɪmɪ'teɪʃ(ə)n/ *noun* **1.** the act of limiting someone or something **2.** a thing which stops you going further [~of/~on] ○ *the limitations of a machine*

② **limited** /'lɪmɪtɪd/ *adj* which has a limit

limiting /'lɪmɪtɪŋ/ *adj* which limits

limitless /'lɪmɪtləs/ *adj* without any limit

limousine /lɪmə'ziːn/, **limo** *noun* a large expensive car, especially one that is longer than usual

limp /lɪmp/ *verb* to walk in a way which is affected by having an injured leg or foot ○ *After the accident she limped badly.* ■ *noun* a way that someone walks, when one leg hurts or is shorter than the other ○ *His limp has improved since his operation.* ■ *adj* soft, not strong ○ *All we had as a salad was two limp lettuce leaves.* ○ *He gave me a limp handshake.* ○ *She went limp and we had to give her a glass of water.*

① **line** /laɪn/ *noun* **1.** a long thin mark ○ *She drew a straight line across the sheet of paper.* ○ *The tennis ball went over the line.* **2.** a row of written or printed words ○ *He printed the first two lines and showed them to me.* ○ *Can you read the bottom line on* *the chart?* □ **to drop someone a line** to send someone a short letter (*informal*) ○ *I'll drop you a line when I get to New York.* **3.** a long row of people or things ○ *We had to stand in (a) line for half an hour to get into the exhibition.* ○ *The line of lorries stretched for miles at the frontier.* **4.** a long string or wire with a particular use ○ *a fishing line* **5.** a wire along which telephone messages are sent ○ *Can you speak louder – the line is bad.* □ **to be on the line** to be talking to someone on the telephone ○ *Don't interrupt – I'm on the line to New York.* ○ *Do you want to speak to Charles while he's on the line?* **6.** metal rails on which trains run ○ *A tree had blown onto the line.* **7.** a part of a railway system ○ *the west coast line* **8.** a way of doing things □ **to take a hard line** not to be weak ○ *The headmaster takes a hard line with boys who sell drugs in the playground.* ◇ **in line with** according to ○ *We acted in line with the decision taken at the meeting.* ◇ **to draw the line at** to refuse to do something ○ *I don't mind having a cup of coffee with the boss, but I draw the line at having to invite him for a meal at home.* ◇ **to be on the right lines** to be doing things the right way

line up③ *phrasal verb* to stand in a line ○ *Line up over there if you want to take the next boat.*

linear /'lɪniə/ *adj* **1.** referring to lines ○ *a linear diagram* **2.** referring to length ○ *A metre is a linear measurement.*

line manager /'laɪn ˌmænɪdʒə/ *noun* a manager in a company who is involved in production or the central part of the business and who is in charge of the employees in that part of the company

linen /'lɪnɪn/ *noun* a strong cloth made from natural fibres ○ *a linen tablecloth* ○ *He bought a white linen suit.*

liner /'laɪnə/ *noun* a large passenger ship ○ *They went on a cruise round the Caribbean on an American liner.*

line-up /'laɪn ʌp/ *noun* a group or list of people

③ **linger** /'lɪŋgə/ (**lingers, lingering, lingered**) *verb* to stay longer than necessary or than expected

lingerie /'lænʒəri/ *noun* women's underwear

lingering /'lɪŋgərɪŋ/ *adj* which remains for some time

③ **linguist** /'lɪŋgwɪst/ *noun* **1.** a person who knows foreign languages well ○ *Only the very best linguists can hope to become interpreters for the EU.* **2.** a person who studies linguistics ○ *Linguists have discovered similarities between Sanskrit and ancient Greek.*

③ **linguistic** /lɪŋ'gwɪstɪk/ *adj* referring to language or languages

③ **linguistics** /lɪŋ'gwɪstɪks/ *noun* the science of language

lining /'laɪnɪŋ/ *noun* material sewn onto the inside of something such as a piece of clothing ○ *You'll need a coat with a warm lining if you're going to Canada in winter.* ○ *She has a pair of boots with a fur lining.*

② **link** /lɪŋk/ *noun* **1.** something which connects two things or places [~between/~with] ○ *The Channel Tunnel provides a fast rail link between England and France.* **2.** one of the rings in a chain ○ *a chain with solid gold links* ■ *verb* (**links, linking, linked**) **1.** to join places or things together [~to/with] ○ *Eurostar links London with Paris and Brussels.* **2.** to be related in some way [~to] ○ *His salary is linked to the cost of living.*

link up③ *phrasal verb* to join two or more things together ○ *We have been able to link up all our computers to form a network.*

link-up /'lɪŋk ʌp/ *noun* a connection between two things

linoleum /lɪ'nəʊliəm/ *noun* a hard smooth floor covering, made in large rolls

lion /'laɪən/ *noun* a large wild yellowish-brown animal of the cat family (NOTE: The female is a **lioness** and the young are **cubs**.)

lioness /'laɪənes/ *noun* a female lion

② **lip** /lɪp/ *noun* **1.** one of the two pink or red parts forming the outside of the mouth ○ *Put some cream on your lips to stop them getting chapped.* **2.** the edge of a round deep hole in the ground ○ *They stood on the lip of the crater and looked down into the volcano.*

lip-read /'lɪp riːd/ (**lip-reads, lip-reading, lip-read**) *verb* (*of a deaf person*) to understand what someone says by watching the movements of his or her lips

② **lipstick** /'lɪpstɪk/ *noun* a substance for colouring the lips

liquefy /'lɪkwɪfaɪ/ (**liquefies, liquefying, liquefied**) *verb* to become liquid

liqueur /lɪ'kjʊə, lɪ'kɜː/ *noun* strong sweet alcohol, made from fruit or herbs

liquid /'lɪkwɪd/ *noun* a substance such as water, which flows easily and which is neither a gas nor a solid ○ *You will need to drink more liquids in hot weather.* ■ *adj* in a form which flows easily ○ *a bottle of liquid soap*

liquor /ˈlɪkə/ *noun* an alcoholic drink

liquor store /ˈlɪkə stɔː/ *noun US* a shop which sells alcohol (NOTE: The British term is **off-licence**.)

lisp /lɪsp/ *noun* a speech difficulty in which ‘s’ is pronounced as ‘th’ ○ *She speaks with a lisp.* (NOTE: + **lisp** *v*)

① **list** /lɪst/ *noun* a number of things such as names or addresses, written or said one after another ○ *We've drawn up a list of people to invite to the party.* ○ *He was ill, so we crossed his name off the list.* ○ *The names on the list are in alphabetical order.* ■ *verb* (**lists, listing, listed**) to say or to write a number of things one after the other ○ *The contents are listed on the label.* ○ *She listed the ingredients on the back of an envelope.* ○ *The catalogue lists twenty-three models of washing machine.*

① **listen** /ˈlɪs(ə)n/ (**listens, listening, listened**) *verb* to pay attention to someone who is talking or to something which you can hear [~to/~for] ○ *Don't make a noise – I'm trying to listen to a music programme.* ○ *I was listening for the sound of a car stopping outside.* □ **to listen out for something** to wait to see if you hear something ○ *Can you listen out for the telephone while I'm in the garden?*

listener /ˈlɪs(ə)nə/ *noun* a person who listens

listing /ˈlɪstɪŋ/ *noun* a published list of information

listless /ˈlɪst(ə)ləs/ *adj* with no energy, weak and tired

listserv /ˈlɪstˌsɜːv/ *noun* an Internet service allowing users to have online discussions

③ **lit** /lɪt/ past tense and past participle of **light**

-lit /lɪt/ *suffix* showing where light comes from

lite /laɪt/ *adj* low in calories, sugar, fat, or alcohol

liter /ˈliːtə/ *noun* US spelling of **litre**

literacy /ˈlɪt(ə)rəsi/ *noun* being able to read and write. Compare **illiteracy, numeracy**

③ **literal** /ˈlɪt(ə)rəl/ *adj* keeping to the exact meaning of the original words ○ *A literal translation usually sounds odd.*

② **literary** /ˈlɪt(ə)rəri/ *adj* relating to literature

literate /ˈlɪt(ə)rət/ *adj* able to read and write ○ *Most people in Britain are literate.* ○ *When he left school he was barely literate.* Compare **illiterate, numerate**

② **literature** /ˈlɪt(ə)rətʃə/ *noun* **1.** books or writing, especially when considered to be of high quality ○ *She's studying English and American literature.* **2.** written information about something [~on] ○ *Do you have any literature on holidays in Greece?* (NOTE: no plural)

lithe /laɪð/ *adj* able to bend your body easily

litigation /ˌlɪtɪˈgeɪʃ(ə)n/ *noun* an act of bringing a legal case against someone in order to have a disagreement settled

③ **litre** /ˈliːtə/ *noun* a unit of measurement for liquids, equal to 1000 millilitres (NOTE: usually written **l** or **L** after figures: *25 l*, say ‘twenty-five litres’.)

litter /ˈlɪtə/ *noun* **1.** rubbish on streets or in public places ○ *The council tries to keep the main street clear of litter.* (NOTE: no plural in this sense) **2.** a group of young animals born at one time ○ *She had a litter of eight puppies.*

① **little** /ˈlɪt(ə)l/ *adj* (**less, least**) **1.** small ○ *They have two children – a baby boy and a little girl.* (NOTE: no comparative or superlative forms in this sense) **2.** not much ○ *We drink very little milk.* ○ *A TV uses very little electricity.* ○ *He looked at it for a little while.* ■ *adv* not much, not often ○ *It's little more than two miles from the sea.* ○ *We go to the cinema very little these days.*

little by little /ˌlɪt(ə)l baɪ ˈlɪt(ə)l/ *adv* gradually

little finger /ˌlɪt(ə)l ˈfɪŋgə/ *noun* the smallest of the five fingers

live[1] /laɪv/ *adj* **1.** living, not dead ○ *There are strict rules about transporting live animals.* **2.** carrying electricity ○ *Don't touch the live wires.* **3.** not recorded; being broadcast at the same time as events take place ○ *a live radio show* ■ *adv* at the same time as events take place ○ *The show was broadcast live.*

live down *phrasal verb* to stop being embarrassed by something which has finally been forgotten by everyone □ **he'll never live it down** it will never be forgotten

live in③ *phrasal verb* to live in the building where you work

live off③ *phrasal verb* to earn money from

live on③ *phrasal verb* to use food or money to stay alive ○ *They lived on bread and water for two weeks.*

live through③ *phrasal verb* to experience something dangerous

live together③ *phrasal verb* (*of two people*) to live in the same house and have a sexual relationship

live with③ *phrasal verb* to put up with something ○ *As for aircraft noise – you'll just have to live with it.* ■ *verb* to live in the same house as someone else as if married ○ *He lives with a writer of children's books.*

live[2] /lɪv/ (**lives, living, lived**) *verb* **1.** to have your home in a place ○ *They have gone to live in France.* ○ *Do you prefer living in the country to the town?* ○ *He lives next door to a film star.* ○ *Where does your daughter live?* **2.** to be alive ○ *King Henry VIII lived in the 16th century.* ○ *The doctor doesn't think she will live much longer.*

livelihood /ˈlaɪvlihʊd/ *noun* a way of earning your living

③ **lively** /ˈlaɪvli/ (**livelier, liveliest**) *adj* very active

liver /ˈlɪvə/ *noun* **1.** a large organ in the body which helps you to process food and cleans the blood **2.** animal's liver used as food ○ *I'll start with chicken liver pâté.* ○ *He looked at the menu and ordered liver and bacon.*

③ **lives** /laɪvz/ 3rd person singular present of **life**

livestock /ˈlaɪvstɒk/ *noun* farm animals, which are kept to produce meat, milk or other products

livid /ˈlɪvɪd/ *adj* extremely angry ○ *Her father was livid when he heard she had spent the night with her boyfriend.*

② **living** /ˈlɪvɪŋ/ *adj* having the signs such as breathing or growing of not being dead ○ *Does she have any living relatives?* ■ *noun* money that you need for things such as food and clothes ○ *He earns his living by selling postcards to tourists.*

② **living room** /ˈlɪvɪŋ ruːm/ *noun* (*in a house or flat*) a comfortable room for sitting in

living standards /ˈlɪvɪŋ ˌstændədz/ *plural noun* the quality of personal home life, such as the amount and quality of food or clothes you can buy or the type of car you own ○ *As long as living standards continue to improve, everyone is happy.* (NOTE: also the **standard of living**)

③ **lizard** /ˈlɪzəd/ *noun* a small animal with a long tail and rough skin

② **load** /ləʊd/ *noun* a number of heavy objects which are carried in a vehicle such as truck ○ *The lorry delivered a load of bricks.* ■ *verb* (**loads, loading, loaded**) **1.** to put something, especially something heavy, into or on to a vehicle such as a truck or van [~with] ○ *They loaded the van with furniture and personal belongings.* **2.** to put bullets into a gun, or a film into a camera [~with] ○ *They loaded their guns and hid behind the wall.* **3.** to put a program into a computer ○ *Load the word-processing program before you start keyboarding.*

loaded /ˈləʊdɪd/ *adj* **1.** having a lot of money ○ *Chris is loaded – he won the lottery!* **2.** referring to a gun which contains bullets or a camera which contains a film

loaf /ləʊf/ (*plural* **loaves**) *noun* bread made in a large round shape, which you can cut into slices before eating it ○ *He bought a loaf of bread at the baker's.* ○ *We eat about 10 loaves of bread per week.*

② **loan** /ləʊn/ *noun* **1.** a thing lent, especially an amount of money ○ *He bought the house with a £100,000 loan from the bank.* **2.** the act of lending something to someone ○ *I had the loan of his car for three weeks.* ◇ **on loan** being lent ○ *The picture is on loan to the National Gallery.*

loath /ləʊθ/ *adj* □ **to be loath to do something** to be unwilling to do something ○ *Personally, I'm very loath to get involved.*

loathe /ləʊð/ (**loathes, loathing, loathed**) *verb* to hate very much (NOTE: + **loathing** *n*)

loaves /ləʊvz/ plural of **loaf**

lob /lɒb/ (**lobs, lobbing, lobbed**) *verb* to throw or hit a ball slowly high into the air ○ *He lobbed a ball at his sister.*

lobby /ˈlɒbi/ *noun* **1.** an entrance hall ○ *I'll meet you in the hotel lobby in half an hour.* **2.** a group of people who try to influence important people, especially members of parliament ○ *The MPs met members of the anti-abortion lobby.* ■ *verb* (**lobbies, lobbying, lobbied**) to try to influence someone, especially in order to get a bill through Parliament ○ *She lobbied her MP with a detailed letter and other documents.*

lobbyist /ˈlɒbiɪst/ *noun* a person who is paid to represent a pressure group

lobster /ˈlɒbstə/ *noun* the flesh of this shellfish used as food

① **local** /ˈləʊk(ə)l/ *adj* relating to a place or district near where you are or where you live ○ *She works as a nurse in the local hospital.* ○ *The local paper comes out on Fridays.* ○ *She was formerly the headmistress of the local school.*

local anaesthetic /ˌləʊk(ə)l ænəsˈθetɪk/ *noun* a substance which removes the feeling in a certain part of the body only

local area network /ˌləʊk(ə)l ˌeəriə ˈnetwɜːk/ *noun* a network of personal computers within a small area

local authority /ˌləʊk(ə)l ɔːˈθɒrɪti/ *noun* a section of elected government which runs a town or district

③ **local government** /ˌləʊk(ə)l ˈɡʌv(ə)nmənt/ *noun* organisations dealing with the matters of small areas of the country, such as towns and counties

locality /ləʊˈkælɪti/ *noun* an area of the country or district of a town (*formal*) □ **in the locality** near by ○ *There are two theatres and four cinemas in the locality.*

② **locally** /ˈləʊk(ə)li/ *adv* in the district near where you are

local time /ˈləʊk(ə)l ˌtaɪm/ *noun* the time of day in a particular place

③ **locate** /ləʊˈkeɪt/ (**locates, locating, located**) *verb* to find the position of something ○ *Divers are trying to locate the Spanish galleon.*

② **location** /ləʊˈkeɪʃ(ə)n/ *noun* a place or position ○ *The hotel is in a very central location.*

loch /lɒx/ *noun* (*in Scotland*) an inland lake or arm of the sea

② **lock** /lɒk/ *noun* a part of a door or container such as a box, used for fastening it so that you can only open it with a key ○ *She left the key in the lock, so the burglars got in easily.* ○ *We changed the locks on the doors after a set of keys were stolen.* ■ *verb* (**locks, locking, locked**) **1.** to close a door or a container such as a box, using a key ○ *I forgot to lock the safe.* ○ *We always lock the front door before we go to bed.* **2.** to fix something or to become fixed in a certain position ○ *The wheels suddenly locked as he went round the corner.* ◇ **under lock and key** locked up firmly ○ *We keep our jewels safely under lock and key.*

lock in③ *phrasal verb* to make someone stay inside a place by locking the door

lock out③ *phrasal verb* to make someone stay outside a place by locking the door

lock up③ *phrasal verb* **1.** to close a building by locking the doors ○ *He always locks up before he goes home.* ○ *She was locking up the shop when a man walked in.* **2.** to keep a person or thing inside a place or container by locking the door or lid ○ *Lock up the jewels in the safe* or *lock the jewels up in the safe.* **3.** to put someone in prison ○ *They locked him up for a week.*

③ **locker** /ˈlɒkə/ *noun* a small cupboard for personal things which you can close with a key

locket /ˈlɒkɪt/ *noun* a piece of jewellery which consists of a small case that you can keep a picture in, attached to a chain which is worn round the neck

locomotive /ˌləʊkəˈməʊtɪv/ *noun* the engine of a train

lodge /lɒdʒ/ *noun* a small house at the gates of a large building ○ *If the lodge is as big as that, just imagine the size of the main house!* ■ *verb* (**lodges, lodging, lodged**) **1.** to rent a room in a house ○ *He lodges with Mrs Bishop in London Road.* **2.** to become stuck ○ *A piece of bread was lodged in her windpipe.* ○ *The bullet was lodged in his spine.* **3.** to leave something with someone to look after for you [~with] ○ *They lodged all the documents with the solicitor.* **4.** to make an official complaint about someone or something [~with] ○ *They lodged a complaint with the local electricity company.*

lodger /ˈlɒdʒə/ *noun* a person who pays to stay in a room in a house

lodging /ˈlɒdʒɪŋ/ *noun* a place where someone lodges

③ **loft** /lɒft/ *noun* the top part of a house right under the roof ○ *They converted their loft into a bedroom.*

lofty /ˈlɒfti/ (**loftier, loftiest**) *adj* **1.** very high ○ *From the lofty height of the church tower the boys could see for miles.* ○ *The lofty ceiling and wide windows gave the studio a wonderful feeling of space.* **2.** proud ○ *Her lofty attitude towards her colleagues does not make her many friends.*

③ **log** /lɒɡ/ *noun* a thick piece of a tree ○ *He brought in a load of logs for the fire.*

log in, log on *phrasal verb* (*in computing*) to start to use a computer system, usually by typing a particular word

log off, log out *phrasal verb* to finish using a computer system, usually by typing a particular word

loggerheads /ˈlɒɡəhedz/ *noun* □ **to be at loggerheads with someone** to always arguing with someone ○ *He has been at loggerheads with the town council for some months.*

logic /ˈlɒdʒɪk/ *noun* **1.** formal reasoning ○ *Your logic is flawed – just because she's an MA doesn't mean she's a good teacher.* **2.** sensible thinking, good reason ○ *I don't see the logic of owning two cars and not being able to drive.*

③ **logical** /ˈlɒdʒɪk(ə)l/ *adj* **1.** clearly reasoned ○ *a logical conclusion* **2.** (*of a person*) able to reason clearly ○ *She's a very logical person and thinks everything through carefully.*

login /ˈlɒɡɪn/ *noun* the act of logging in to a computer system

logistics /ləˈdʒɪstɪks/ *noun* the organisation of the movement of large numbers of people and things such as vehicles and supplies

③ **logo** /ˈləʊɡəʊ/ (*plural* **logos**) *noun* a symbol or design used by a company in order for people to recognise its products

loins /lɔɪnz/ *plural noun* the part of the body between the hips

loiter /ˈlɔɪtə/ (**loiters, loitering, loitered**) *verb* to stand or walk slowly about doing nothing

loll /lɒl/ (**lolls, lolling, lolled**) *verb* to sit or lie in a lazy way ○ *They spent the afternoon lolling about in armchairs, watching the cricket.*

lolly /ˈlɒli/ *noun* **1.** a lollipop, a sweet on the end of a stick **2.** money ○ *What happened to the lolly, then?*

lone /ləʊn/ *adj* single, one alone. ◊ **wolf** (NOTE: Do not confuse with **loan**.)

loneliness /ˈləʊnlinəs/ *noun* **1.** a feeling of sadness you can get from being alone ○ *After his wife died it took him a long time to get over his feelings of loneliness.* **2.** the state of being alone ○ *He was attracted by the loneliness of the hotel, all by itself on the top of the cliff.*

③ **lonely** /ˈləʊnli/ (**lonelier, loneliest**) *adj* **1.** feeling sad because of being alone ○ *It's odd how lonely you can be in a big city full of people.* **2.** (*of a place*) with few or no people around ○ *The cliff top is a lonely place at night.* ○ *We spent the weekend in a lonely cottage in the Welsh hills.*

loner /ˈləʊnə/ *noun* a person who prefers to be alone

lonesome /ˈləʊns(ə)m/ *adj especially US* lonely, sad because of being alone

① **long** /lɒŋ/ *adj* **1.** not short in length ○ *a long piece of string* ○ *The Nile is the longest river in the world.* ○ *My hair needs cutting – it's getting too long.* **2.** not short in time ○ *What a long programme – it lasted almost three hours.* ○ *They've been waiting for the bus for a long time.* ○ *We don't approve of long holidays in this job.* **3.** used for asking about an amount of time ○ *How long is it before your holiday starts?* ■ *adv* a long time ○ *Have you been waiting long?* ○ *I didn't want to wait any longer.* ■ *noun* a long time □ **long ago** many years before the present time ○ *Long ago this was a wealthy farming area.* ■ *verb* to want something very much [~for] ○ *I'm longing for a cup of tea.* ○ *Everyone was longing to be back home.* ◇ **as long as, so long as** provided that, on the condition that ○ *I like going on picnics as long as it doesn't rain.* ◇ **no longer** not any more ○ *I no longer have that car.* ◇ **before long** in a short time ○ *She'll be boss of the company before long.* ◇ **for long** for a long time ○ *He wasn't out of a job for long.*

long-awaited /ˌlɒŋ əˈweɪtɪd/ *adj* for which people have been waiting for a long time

long-distance /lɒŋˈdɪstəns/ *adj* **1.** (*of a sports race*) between two places which are far apart ○ *She was over fifty when she took up long-distance running.* ○ *You'll have to get fit if you're going to run a long-distance race.* **2.** made over a long distance ○ *We spent three days walking along one of the long-distance paths in the hills.* ○ *Long-distance telephone calls cost less after 6 p.m.*

long-drawn-out /ˌlɒŋ drɔːn ˈaʊt/ *adj* which continues for a long period of time

long-haul /ˌlɒŋ ˈhɔːl/ *adj* over a large distance, especially between continents

③ **longing** /ˈlɒŋɪŋ/ *noun* a strong wish to have something

longitude /ˈlɒŋɡɪtjuːd/ *noun* a position on the earth's surface measured in degrees east or west of an imaginary line running north-south through Greenwich, a town just to the east of London

③ **long-lasting** /ˌlɒŋ ˈlɑːstɪŋ/ *adj* which lasts a long time

long-life /lɒŋ laɪf/ *adj* (*of food and drink*) treated with a special process so that it will stay fresh for a long time

long-lost /lɒŋ lɒst/ *adj* who or which is not seen for a long time

③ **long-range** /ˌlɒŋ ˈreɪndʒ/ *adj* which covers a long distance or a long time. ◊ **short-range**

long-running /ˌlɒŋ ˈrʌnɪŋ/ *adj* which has been going on for a long time ○ *Our long-running dispute with our neighbours.*

longsighted /ˌlɒŋˈsaɪtɪd/ *adj* able to see things clearly things which are far away but not things which are close. ◊ **short-sighted**

longstanding /ˌlɒŋˈstændɪŋ/ *adj* which has been in existence for a long time

long-suffering /ˌlɒŋ ˈsʌf(ə)rɪŋ/ *adj* patient with problems caused by other people

② **long-term** /ˌlɒŋ ˈtɜːm/ *adj* planned to last for a long time

long-time /ˈlɒŋ taɪm/ *adj* who has existed for a long time

③ **long wave** /ˈlɒŋ weɪv/ *noun* a radio wave with a wavelength longer than 1000 metres. ◊ **medium wave**, **short wave**

long weekend /ˌlɒŋ wiːkˈend/ *noun* a weekend, including Friday night

long-winded /ˌlɒŋ ˈwɪndɪd/ *adj* (*of a person*) talking too much in a boring way

③ **loo** /luː/ (*plural* **loos**) *noun* a toilet or a room in which there is a toilet (*informal*)

① **look** /lʊk/ *verb* (**looks, looking, looked**) **1.** to turn your eyes to see something [~at/~through/under/in/outetc] ○ *I want you to look carefully at this photograph.* ○ *Look in the restaurant and see if there are any tables free.* ○ *If you look out of the office window you can see our house.* ○ *He opened the lid of the box and looked inside.* **2.** to appear to be ○ *Those pies look good.* ○ *He looks much older than forty.* **3.** used as an interjection ○ *Look! if we don't sort this out now, we'll never do it.* ■ *noun* **1.** the way someone or something appears ○ *There is a French look about her clothes.* **2.** the act of seeing something with your eyes ○ *Have a good look at this photograph and tell me if you recognise anyone in it.* ○ *We only had time for a quick look round the town.* **3.** a search for something [~for/~around] ○ *I didn't see him at the concert though I had a good look around.* ○ *We had a look for the ring and couldn't find it anywhere.*

look after① *phrasal verb* to take care of someone or something

look ahead③ *phrasal verb* to make plans for the future

look back③ *phrasal verb* to turn your head to see what is behind you ○ *He looked back and saw a police car was following him.*

look for① *phrasal verb* to search for something, to try to find something

look forward to① *phrasal verb* to think happily about something which is going to happen

look into① *phrasal verb* to try to find out about a matter or problem

look on *phrasal verb* **1.** to watch without doing anything ○ *The police beat up the demonstrators while the tourists just looked on.* **2.** to consider, to think of something as ○ *We look on trade fairs as a bit of relaxation after the office.* ○ *He looks on his secretary as simply someone to make coffee and answer the phone.*

look out① *phrasal verb* to be careful ○ *Look out! – the car is going backwards!*

look out for③ *phrasal verb* **1.** to try to see or find someone or something ○ *We're looking out for new offices because ours are too small.* ○ *I'll look out for his sister at the party.* **2.** to be careful about ○ *Look out for ice on the pavement.*

look over③ *phrasal verb* **1.** to examine quickly ○ *She looked over the figures and said they seemed to be OK.* **2.** to have a view over something ○ *The office looks over a disused warehouse.*

look up① *phrasal verb* **1.** to turn your eyes upwards ○ *She looked up and saw clouds in the sky.* **2.** to try to find some information in a book ○ *I'll look up his address in the telephone book.* ○ *Look up the word in the dictionary if you don't know what it means.* **3.** to get in touch with ○ *Look me up when you're next in London.* **4.** to get better ○ *Things are looking up.*

look up to③ *phrasal verb* to admire or respect someone

lookalike /ˈlʊkəlaɪk/ *noun* a person who look like someone else, especially someone famous (*informal*)

③ **lookout** /ˈlʊkaʊt/ *noun* **1.** a careful watch ○ *Keep a sharp lookout for pickpockets.* ○ *From their lookout post they could see across the square.* **2.** a person who is on watch ○ *The captain posted a lookout in the bows.* ◊ **to be on the lookout for** to watch carefully for ○ *She's always on the lookout for bargains.* ○ *The police are on the lookout for car thieves.*

loom /luːm/ (**looms, looming, loomed**) *verb* to appear in a rather threatening way ○ *A storm loomed on the horizon.* ○ *A bus suddenly loomed out of the fog.*

loony /ˈluːni/, **looney** *noun* a person who is regarded as silly or crazy (*insult*) ○ *Whoever invented bungee-jumping was a bit of a loony.*

loop /luːp/ *noun* a curve formed by a piece of something such as string, which crosses over itself ○ *To tie your laces, start by making a loop.*

loophole /ˈluːphəʊl/ *noun* a means of avoiding a law

③ **loose** /luːs/ (**looser, loosest**) *adj* **1.** (*of a garment*) not tight ○ *Wear loose trousers and a teeshirt for the dance class.* **2.** not attached to anything ○ *The front wheel is loose and needs tightening.* ○ *The boat came loose and started to drift away.* ○

Once he was let loose, the dog ran across the park.

loose cannon /luːs 'kænən/ *noun* someone who is not easily controlled and may do or say things which are not officially approved (*slang*)

loose change /ˌluːs 'tʃeɪndʒ/ *noun* money in coins only

loose end /luːs end/ *noun* one of the details in something such as a problem or situation which has not yet been dealt with

loosely /'luːsli/ *adv* **1.** not tightly ○ *The skirt fits loosely round her waist.* ○ *He tied his horse loosely to the post.* **2.** in a way which is not completely accurate ○ *The word can be loosely translated as 'hanging down'.*

loosen /'luːs(ə)n/ (**loosens, loosening, loosened**) *verb* to make something less tight ○ *He loosened his shoelaces and relaxed.*

loot /luːt/ *noun* **1.** things which have been stolen ○ *The police discovered the rest of the loot under his bed.* **2.** money (*informal*) ○ *He's got plenty of loot.* ■ *verb* (**loots, looting, looted**) to steal, especially from shops and houses, during a riot or other emergency ○ *Some houses were looted during the floods.* (NOTE: + **looter** *n*; **looting** *n*)

lope /ləʊp/ (**lopes, loping, loped**) *verb* to run with long easy steps

lopsided /lɒp'saɪdɪd/ *adj* leaning to one side, with one side lower than the other

② **lord** /lɔːd/ *noun* **1.** a man who has a high social rank ○ *He was born a lord.* ○ *Powerful lords forced King John to sign the Magna Carta.* **2.** an expression of surprise or shock ○ *Good lord! I didn't realise it was so late!*

lore /lɔː/ *noun* traditional beliefs and knowledge. ◊ **folklore** (NOTE: no plural)

③ **lorry** /'lɒri/ *noun* a large motor vehicle for carrying goods

① **lose** /luːz/ (**loses, losing, lost**) *verb* **1.** to put or drop something somewhere and not to know where it is ○ *I can't find my wallet – I think I lost it on the train.* ○ *If you lose your ticket you'll have to buy another one.* **2.** not to have something any longer ○ *We lost money on the lottery.* **3.** not to win ○ *We lost the match 10 – 0.* ○ *Did you win? – No, we lost.* ◇ **to lose your way** to not know where you are or which direction to go in ○ *They lost their way in the fog on the mountain.*

③ **loser** /'luːzə/ *noun* a person who does not win

① **loss** /lɒs/ *noun* **1.** the state of no longer having something ○ *He was very unhappy at the loss of his house.* ○ *The loss of a child is almost unbearable to a parent.* **2.** money which you have spent and have not got back through earnings ○ *Companies often make losses in their first year of operations.* ◇ **to be at a loss (to do something)** not to know what to do ○ *We are at a loss to know how to proceed since our appeal has been rejected.* ○ *I'm at a loss for something to do now that the party has been cancelled.*

② **lost** /lɒst/ past tense and past participle of **lose**

lost cause /lɒst kɔːz/ *noun* something such as a plan or activity which cannot succeed

① **lot** /lɒt/ *noun* □ **a lot of, lots of** a large number or a large quantity ○ *I've been to the cinema quite a lot recently.* ○ *She's feeling a lot better now.* ○ *What a lot of cars there are in the car park!* ○ *Lots of people are looking for jobs.* ○ *There's lots of time before the train leaves.* ◇ **the lot** everything ○ *That's the lot – there's nothing left.* ○ *There were old pots and books and newspapers – we sold the lot for £50.* ○ *We picked a kilo of strawberries and ate the lot for dinner.*

lotion /'ləʊʃ(ə)n/ *noun* a liquid used on the skin to make it smooth or to protect it

③ **lottery** /'lɒtəri/ (*plural* **lotteries**) *noun* a game of chance in which tickets with numbers on are sold with prizes given for certain numbers

② **loud** /laʊd/ *adj* very easy to hear ○ *Can't you stop your watch making such a loud noise?* ○ *Turn down the radio – it's too loud.* ■ *adv* loudly ○ *I can't sing any louder.* ○ *She laughed out loud in church.*

loudly /'laʊdli/ *adv* in a way which is easy to hear

loudness /'laʊdnəs/ *noun* the state of being loud, being noisy

loudspeaker /laʊd'spiːkə/ *noun* the part of an object such as a radio or CD player which allows sound to be heard

lounge /laʊndʒ/ *noun* a comfortable room for sitting in ○ *Let's go and watch TV in the lounge.*

louse /laʊs/ (*plural* **lice**) *noun* a small insect which sucks blood and lives on the skin as a parasite on animals and humans

lousy /'laʊzi/ (**lousier, lousiest**) *adj* extremely bad or unpleasant

lout /laʊt/ *noun* a rude and badly behaved young man (*insult*) ◊ **lager**

lovable /ˈlʌvəb(ə)l/ *adj* pleasant, easy to love

① **love** /lʌv/ *noun* **1.** a strong feeling of liking someone or something very much ○ *his love for his children* ○ *Her great love is opera.* **2.** (*in games such as tennis*) a score of zero points ○ *She lost the first set six – love (6–0).* ■ *verb* (**loves, loving, loved**) **1.** to have strong feelings of affection for someone or something ○ *'I love you!,' he said.* ○ *She loves little children.* ○ *The children love their teacher.* ○ *His wife thinks he loves someone else.* **2.** to like something very much ○ *I love chocolate ice cream.* □ **to love doing something** to enjoy doing something very much ○ *We love going on holiday by the seaside.* □ **to love to do something** to like or want to do something very much ○ *He loved to watch the birds in the garden.* ○ *I'd love to come with you, but I've got too much work to do.* ◇ **to be in love** to love someone or to love each other ○ *I told her I was in love with her.*

love affair /ˈlʌv əˌfeə/ *noun* a sexual relationship between two people who are not married to each other

loved ones /lʌvd wʌns/ *plural noun* your family and friends

love life /ˈlʌv laɪf/ *noun* someone's sexual relationships

② **lovely** /ˈlʌvli/ (**lovelier, loveliest**) *adj* **1.** very pleasant to look at ○ *She looks lovely in that dress.* ○ *There's a lovely garden behind the house.* **2.** pleasant or enjoyable ○ *I had a lovely time on holiday.* ○ *It was lovely to have all those visitors when I was in hospital.*

③ **lover** /ˈlʌvə/ *noun* **1.** a person, especially a man, who is having a sexual relationship with someone ○ *Her lover was arrested when the woman's body was found on the beach.* **2.** a person who loves something ○ *a lover of French food*

loving /ˈlʌvɪŋ/ *adj* affectionate, showing love

① **low** /ləʊ/ *adj* (**lower, lowest**) not high ○ *She hit her head on the low branch.* ○ *The town is surrounded by low hills.* ○ *We shop around to find the lowest prices.* ○ *The engine works best at low speeds.* ○ *The temperature here is too low for oranges to grow.* ○ *Sales were lower in December than in November.* ■ *adv* (**lower, lowest**) towards the bottom; not high up ○ *The plane was flying too low – it hit the trees.*

lowbrow /ˈləʊbraʊ/ *adj* not difficult to understand and of a low quality

low-calorie /ˌləʊ ˈkæləri/ *adj* containing few calories

low-cut /ləʊ ˈkʌt/ *adj* used to describe women's clothing which has a low neckline and shows the top part of the chest

③ **lower** /ˈlaʊə/ *adj* not as high ○ *They booked a cabin on the lower deck.* ■ *verb* (**lowers, lowering, lowered**) to make something go down ○ *They lowered the boat into the water.*

lower case /ˌləʊə ˈkeɪs/ *noun* small letters such as a, b and c as opposed to capitals such as A, B and C

lower class /ˌləʊə ˈklɑːs/ *noun* a group of people in society who are not rich, aristocratic or middle-class (*dated*)

low-fat /ˌləʊ ˈfæt/ *adj* containing very little fat ○ *Do you have any low-fat yoghurt?*

low-key /ˌləʊ ˈkiː/ *adj* quiet, without much excitement

lowlands /ˈləʊləndz/ *plural noun* a low-lying area of the country ○ *the Lowlands of Scotland*

low-level /ˌləʊ ˈlev(ə)l/ *adj* **1.** positioned or done at lower than the usual level **2.** low in status or degree

low-lying /ˌləʊ ˈlaɪɪŋ/ *adj* which is near to sea level, or to the level of a river

low-paid /ˌləʊ ˈpeɪd/ *adj* not being paid much for a job ○ *She has a low-paid job as a cleaner* or *her job as a cleaner is very low-paid.*

low point /ˈləʊ pɔɪnt/ *noun* the least enjoyable or successful period of something

low profile /ˌləʊ ˈprəʊfaɪl/ *noun* behaviour that avoids public attention

low-rise /ˈləʊ raɪz/ *adj* (*of buildings*) consisting of only a few levels

low season /ˌləʊ ˈsiːz(ə)n/ *noun* a time of year, usually during the winter, when few people go on holiday, and when air fares and hotel prices are cheaper

low-tech /ləʊ ˈtek/ *noun* simple and not highly developed technically ○ *a low-tech solution*

low tide /ˌləʊ ˈtaɪd/, **low water** *noun* the lowest level of the sea the land, or the time when the sea is at this level

loyal /ˈlɔɪəl/ *adj* who supports someone or something for along time without changing ○ *Dogs are very loyal to their owners.*

loyalist /ˈlɔɪəlɪst/ *noun* a person who is loyal to someone or something

loyalties /ˈlɔɪəltiz/ *plural noun* the strong feelings of support and friendship which you have for someone or something

loyalty /ˈlɔɪəlti/ *noun* the quality of being loyal

lozenge /ˈlɒzɪndʒ/ *noun* **1.** a diamond shape, especially when used in heraldry ○ *The shield has a pattern of red lozenges.* **2.** a sweet medicine in the form of a pill ○ *She was sucking cough lozenges to get rid of her cough.*

LSD /ˌel es ˈdiː/ *noun* an illegal drug which has a powerful effect, e.g. making people see things which are not real

① **Ltd** *abbr* limited company

lubricate /ˈluːbrɪkeɪt/ (**lubricates, lubricating, lubricated**) *verb* to cover something with a lubricant to make it run smoothly (NOTE: + **lubrication** *n*)

lucid /ˈluːsɪd/ *adj* **1.** clear, easily understood ○ *The old lady gave a clear and lucid account of the incident to the police.* **2.** able to think clearly ○ *For most of the time he was delirious but in his few lucid moments he seemed to recognise me.*

② **luck** /lʌk/ *noun* something, usually good, which happens to you ○ *The bus is empty – that's a bit of luck!* ◇ **to do something for luck** because I hope it will bring me luck ○ *I'll wear this ring for luck.*

③ **luckily** /ˈlʌkɪli/ *adv* used for showing that you think an event was lucky

② **lucky** /ˈlʌki/ (**luckier, luckiest**) *adj* **1.** having good things happening to you, especially if they are unexpected ○ *He's lucky not to have been sent to prison.* ○ *How lucky you are to be going to Spain!* **2.** bringing good luck ○ *Fifteen is my lucky number.*

lucrative /ˈluːkrətɪv/ *adj* bringing in a lot of money or profit

ludicrous /ˈluːdɪkrəs/ *adj* ridiculous, which makes you laugh

lug /lʌg/ (**lugs, lugging, lugged**) *verb* to carry or pull something heavy ○ *I had to lug my cases up two flights of stairs.* ○ *Lugging those boxes up into the attic has worn me out.*

② **luggage** /ˈlʌgɪdʒ/ *noun* suitcases or bags for carrying your clothes and other things when travelling

lukewarm /ˌluːkˈwɔːm/ *adj* **1.** not very hot ○ *The soup was only lukewarm.* ○ *We sent back the coffee because it was lukewarm.* **2.** not enthusiastic ○ *He was only lukewarm about our project.*

lull /lʌl/ *noun* a quiet period ○ *After last week's hectic rushing around this week's lull was welcome.* ■ *verb* (**lulls, lulling, lulled**) to make someone calmer, to soothe someone ○ *She sang a song to lull the baby to sleep.* ○ *The report was not very critical and that lulled them into a false sense of security.*

lumber /ˈlʌmbə/ (**lumbers, lumbering, lumbered**) *verb* **1.** to give someone something he or she doesn't want to do [~with] (*informal*) ○ *You always manage to lumber me with the worst jobs.* ○ *Why do I always get lumbered with doing the shopping?* **2.** to move slowly and heavily ○ *The tractor lumbered across the field pulling a trailer full of hay.* ○ *Watch where you're treading, you lumbering great hulk!* (NOTE: Do not confuse with **lumbar**.)

lumberjack /ˈlʌmbədʒæk/ *noun* a person who cuts down trees

luminous /ˈluːmɪnəs/ *adj* which gives out light in the dark

② **lump** /lʌmp/ *noun* **1.** a piece of something, often with no particular shape ○ *a lump of sugar* **2.** a hard or swollen part on the body [~on] ○ *She went to the doctor because she had found a lump on her neck.*

lump sum /ˌlʌmp ˈsʌm/ *noun* money paid in one payment, not in several small payments

lumpy /ˈlʌmpi/ (**lumpier, lumpiest**) *adj* with solid lumps in it

lunacy /ˈluːnəsi/ *noun* madness, idiotic behaviour

lunar /ˈluːnə/ *adj* referring to the moon

lunatic /ˈluːnətɪk/ *noun* a person who acts in a mad way (*informal insult*) ○ *Don't be such a lunatic – try to talk to her!* ○ *He drove like a lunatic to catch the ferry.*

① **lunch** /lʌntʃ/ *noun* the meal eaten in the middle of the day ○ *Come on – lunch will be ready soon.* ○ *We always have lunch at 12.30.* ○ *We are having fish and chips for lunch.* ○ *I'm not hungry so I don't want a big lunch.* ○ *The restaurant serves 150 lunches a day.*

③ **lunchtime** /ˈlʌntʃtaɪm/ *noun* the time when you usually have lunch

lung /lʌŋ/ *noun* one of two organs in the chest with which you breathe

lunge /lʌndʒ/ (**lunges, lunging, lunged**) *verb* to make a sudden movement forwards ○ *The baby suddenly lunged at the candles on the cake.* (NOTE: + **lunge** *n*)

lupin /ˈluːpɪn/ *noun* a plant with tall flowers in different colours

lurch /lɜːtʃ/ *noun* a sudden unsteady movement ○ *The ship gave a sudden lurch.* ■ *verb* (**lurches, lurching, lurched**) to make a sudden unsteady movement ○ *When the taxi finally lurched to a stop I* *was shaking all over.* ○ *He lurched over to the bar and ordered another drink.*

lure /ljʊə/ *noun* a thing which attracts a person or animal ○ *The white beaches are a lure for tourists.* ■ *verb* (**lures, luring, lured**) to attract someone, especially into something bad ○ *She was lured to the club by reports of high wages for bar staff.*

lurid /ˈljʊərɪd/ *adj* **1.** glowing with brilliant colours ○ *The flames gave a lurid glow to the scene.* ○ *She was wearing a lurid pink tracksuit.* **2.** (*of a book or film*) sensational, meant to shock ○ *There were several lurid descriptions of conditions in the refugee camps.*

lurk /lɜːk/ (**lurks, lurking, lurked**) *verb* to be hidden

luscious /ˈlʌʃəs/ *adj* very sweet and juicy

lush /lʌʃ/ *adj* ((*of plants*)) very green and growing well ○ *The cattle were put to graze on the lush grass by the river.* ○ *Lush tropical vegetation rapidly covered the clearing.*

lust /lʌst/ *noun* **1.** strong sexual desire ○ *He looked at her with eyes full of lust.* **2.** a great desire for something ○ *She is driven by a lust for power.*

luxurious /lʌɡˈzjʊəriəs/ *adj* very comfortable and expensive

luxury /ˈlʌkʃəri/ (*plural* **luxuries**) *noun* **1.** great comfort ○ *He lived a life of great luxury.* ○ *A hot bath is a real luxury after two weeks camping in the mountains.* **2.** a thing which is pleasant to have, but not necessary ○ *She often buys little luxuries for dessert on Friday nights.*

③ **lying** /ˈlaɪɪŋ/ present participle of **lie**

lynch /lɪntʃ/ (**lynches, lynching, lynched**) *verb* (*of a mob*) to catch an accused person and execute him or her, especially by hanging, without a trial

lyrics /ˈlɪrɪks/ *plural noun* the words of a song ○ *He wrote the lyrics for the musical.*

M

m /em/, **M** *noun* the thirteenth letter of the alphabet, between L and N

③ **ma** /mɑː/ *noun* a mother (*informal*)

ma'am *noun* a formal or polite way of referring to a lady

mac /mæk/, **mack** *noun* a coat which keeps off water, which is worn when it is raining (*informal*) (NOTE: short for **mackintosh**)

macabre /məˈkɑːbrə/ *adj* very strange and horrifying, especially referring to dead bodies

macaroni /ˌmækəˈrəʊni/ *noun* an Italian food made of short thick tubes of flour paste

machete /məˈʃeti/ *noun* a large sharp knife

① **machine** /məˈʃiːn/ *noun* a piece of equipment that uses power ○ *We have bought a machine for putting leaflets in envelopes.* ○ *There is a message on my answering machine.* ○ *She made her dress on her sewing machine.* ○ *The washing machine has broken and flooded the kitchen.*

machine gun /məˈʃiːn ɡʌn/ *noun* a gun which automatically fires many bullets rapidly, one after the other

machine-readable /məˈʃiːn ˈriːdəb(ə)l/ *adj* which can be used by a computer

③ **machinery** /məˈʃiːnəri/ *noun* **1.** machines in general ○ *The factory has got rid of a lot of old machinery.* **2.** a way of organising something [~for] ○ *a review of local government machinery* ○ *the machinery for awarding government contracts*

macho /ˈmætʃəʊ/ *adj* behaving in a way that is thought to be typical of a man (*disapproving*)

mackerel /ˈmækrəl/ (*plural* **mackerels** or *same*) *noun* a sea fish with dark flesh, eaten grilled or smoked; also canned and made into pâté

macro /mækrəʊ/ (*plural* **macros**), **macroinstruction** *noun* a block of instructions for a computer identified by one or more keystrokes ○ *I do the page layouts using a macro.*

macro- /mækrəʊ/ *prefix* on a large scale

② **mad** /mæd/ (**madder, maddest**) *adj* **1.** silly or crazy ○ *Everyone thought he was mad to try to cross the Atlantic in a rowing boat.* **2.** very angry (*informal*) ○ *She's mad at* or *with him for borrowing her car.* ○ *He was hopping mad when they told him his car had been stolen.* **3.** having a serious medical condition which affects the brain (*offensive*) (NOTE: + **madly** *adv*) ◇ **mad about someone** ***or*** **something** very keen on someone or something (*informal*) ○ *He's mad about jigsaw puzzles.*

madam /ˈmædəm/ (*plural* **mesdames**) *noun* **1.** a polite way of addressing a woman, often used by people who are providing a service such as waiters or shop assistants ○ *Can I help you, madam?* **2.** used when writing a letter to a woman whom you do not know ○ *Dear Madam*

mad cow disease /mæd ˈkaʊ dɪˌziːz/ *noun* bovine spongiform encephalopathy, a disease affecting the brains of cattle (*informal*)

maddening /ˈmæd(ə)nɪŋ/ *adj* exasperating or annoying

① **made** /meɪd/ past tense and past participle of **make** (NOTE: Do not confuse with **maid**.)

madhouse /ˈmædhaʊs/ *noun* a place where there is a lot of confused activity (*informal*)

③ **madman** /ˈmædmən/ (*plural* **madmen**) *noun* a person who is mentally ill (*offensive*)

③ **madness** /ˈmædnəs/ *noun* stupid behaviour which may be dangerous ○ *It's sheer madness to go out in a little boat in this weather.*

maestro /ˈmaɪstrəʊ/ *noun* a musical genius

mag /mæɡ/ *noun* an illustrated publication which comes out regularly ○ *He found a pile of old car mags in a corner of the shop.*

② **magazine** /ˌmægəˈziːn/ *noun* a large thin book with a paper cover, which is published regularly ○ *The gardening magazine comes out on Fridays.*

maggot /ˈmægət/ *noun* a white caterpillar of a fly, which eats rotting meat

magic /ˈmædʒɪk/ *noun* **1.** a mysterious imaginary power to make things happen **2.** a special enjoyable atmosphere [~of] ○ *the magic of a summer's evening* **3.** tricks such as making things appear and disappear, performed by an entertainer called a 'magician' ■ *adj* with mysterious imaginary qualities ○ *The children found themselves in a magic wood.* ◇ **as if by magic** suddenly, without any possible explanation ○ *He pushed a button and, as if by magic, lights came on all over the garden.*

magical /ˈmædʒɪk(ə)l/ *adj* as if produced by magic

magic bullet /ˌmædʒɪk ˈbʊlɪt/ *noun* **1.** a medicine which can quickly cure a serious illness **2.** a quick solution to a difficult problem

magician /məˈdʒɪʃ(ə)n/ *noun* **1.** a wizard ○ *Merlin was the great magician in medieval legends.* **2.** a conjurer ○ *They hired a magician to entertain the children at the party.*

③ **magistrate** /ˈmædʒɪstreɪt/ *noun* a judge who tries cases in a minor court

magnanimous /mægˈnænɪməs/ *adj* very kind and generous to someone you have defeated or to someone who is weaker than you

magnate /ˈmægneɪt/ *noun* an important and powerful businessman

magnesium /mægˈniːziəm/ *noun* a white metal which is used in making alloys and is also an essential element in biological life

③ **magnet** /ˈmægnɪt/ *noun* **1.** a piece of metal which attracts iron and steel ○ *She has a Mickey Mouse which sticks to the fridge door with a magnet.* **2.** anything which attracts people or things [~for] ○ *The big city is a magnet for teenagers running away from home.*

magnetic /mægˈnetɪk/ *adj* which attracts metal

magnetism /ˈmægnətɪz(ə)m/ *noun* **1.** the quality of being magnetic **2.** being charming and attractive ○ *The princess had enormous personal magnetism.*

magnification /ˌmægnɪfɪˈkeɪʃ(ə)n/ *noun* **1.** the action of making something appear larger ○ *Magnification enables us to see things that are too small to be visible to the naked eye.* **2.** the degree to which things appear larger when magnified ○ *What magnification do you get with these binoculars?*

magnificent /mægˈnɪfɪs(ə)nt/ *adj* very impressive or beautiful

magnify /ˈmægnɪfaɪ/ (**magnifies, magnifying, magnified**) *verb* to make something appear larger

③ **magnitude** /ˈmægnɪtjuːd/ *noun* importance ○ *They did not underestimate the magnitude of the task.* ○ *We will need more staff if we take on a project of this magnitude.*

magnolia /mægˈnəʊliə/ *noun* a large tree with huge white or pink flowers

mag tape /ˈmæg teɪp/ *noun* same as **magnetic tape**

mahogany /məˈhɒgəni/ *noun* a dark red tropical hardwood, now becoming rare

maid /meɪd/ *noun* a female servant ○ *The maid forgot to change the towels.* ○ *The chalet has a daily maid to do the cleaning.*

maiden /ˈmeɪd(ə)n/ *noun* an unmarried girl or woman ○ *The village maidens danced at the wedding.*

maiden name /ˈmeɪd(ə)n neɪm/ *noun* the surname of a woman before she is married

② **mail** /meɪl/ *noun* **1.** letters which are delivered or which are sent ○ *The mail hasn't come yet.* ○ *The receipt was in this morning's mail.* **2.** a service provided by the post office ○ *We sent the parcel by sea mail.* ○ *It's cheaper to send the order by surface mail than by air.*

mailbox /ˈmeɪlbɒks/ *noun US* **1.** one of several boxes where incoming mail is put in a large building ○ *I checked the mailbox to see if I had any letters.* **2.** a box for putting letters and packets in which you want to mail ○ *I posted the letter in the mailbox at the corner of the street.*

③ **mailing list** /ˈmeɪlɪŋ lɪst/ *noun* a list of names and addresses of people to whom information can be sent

maim /meɪm/ (**maims, maiming, maimed**) *verb* to injure someone very badly, sometimes causing permanent damage

① **main** /meɪn/ *adj* most important ○ *The main thing is to get to work on time.* ○ *Their main factory is in Scotland.* ○ *January is the main month for skiing holidays.* ○ *A car will meet you at the main entrance.*

main clause /meɪn ˈklɔːz/ *noun* the main part of a sentence

main course /ˈmeɪn kɔːs/ *noun* the most important part of a meal, usually a dish of meat and vegetables or fish and vegetables

mainframe /ˈmeɪnfreɪm/ *noun* a large computer

main line /meɪn laɪn/ *noun* an important main railway line

② **mainly** /ˈmeɪnli/ *adv* most often ○ *We sell mainly to businesses.* ○ *People mainly go on holiday in the summer.*

main road /meɪn ˈrəʊd/ *noun* the largest and busiest road in a place

mainstay /ˈmeɪnsteɪ/ *noun* a main support that plays the most important part in keeping something going

mainstream /ˈmeɪnstriːm/ *adj* (*of a group*) most important

② **maintain** /meɪnˈteɪn/ (**maintains, maintaining, maintained**) *verb* **1.** to make something stay the same ○ *We like to maintain good relations with our customers.* **2.** to keep something in good working order ○ *The boiler needs to be regularly maintained.* **3.** to continue to state something as a fact [~(that)] ○ *Throughout the trial he maintained that the car was not his.*

② **maintenance** /ˈmeɪntənəns/ *noun* **1.** the act of keeping something in working order ○ *We offer a full maintenance service.* **2.** the act of keeping things going or working ○ *the maintenance of contacts with government officials* **3.** money for upkeep, especially paid by a divorced or separated person to help pay for living expenses for children ○ *to pay maintenance for the children*

maisonette /ˌmeɪzəˈnet/ *noun* a flat on two floors in a larger house

maize /meɪz/ *noun* a widely grown cereal crop, with tall plants bearing large yellow seeds (NOTE: Do not confuse with **maze**. The US term is **corn**.)

majestic /məˈdʒestɪk/ *adj* grand or stately

majesty /ˈmædʒəsti/ *noun* **1.** a beautiful or impressive sight ○ *The majesty of the snow-covered mountains took his breath away.* **2.** used as a title for a king or queen ○ *Her Majesty, Queen Elizabeth II*

② **major** /ˈmeɪdʒə/ *adj* important ○ *Smoking is a major cause of lung cancer.* ○ *Computers are a major influence on modern industrial society.* ○ *Many small roads are blocked by snow, but the major roads are open.* □ **the major part of something** most of something ○ *The major part of the film takes place in Scotland.* ■ *noun* a rank of an officer in the army below colonel ○ *A major came up in a truck with six soldiers.* (NOTE: also used as a title before a surname: *Major Smith*)

② **majority** /məˈdʒɒrɪti/ *noun* **1.** the larger part of a group ○ *The majority of the members of the club don't want to change the rules.* □ **in the majority** being more than half of the members ○ *Women are in a majority on the committee.* **2.** a number of voters which is larger than half ○ *She was elected with a majority of 10,000.* **3.** the age when you become legally adult ○ *He will inherit money from his grandfather when he reaches his majority.*

① **make** /meɪk/ (**makes, making, made**) *verb* **1.** to produce or build something [~with/~of/out of] ○ *These knives are made of steel.* ○ *He made a boat out of old pieces of wood.* ○ *She's making a birthday cake.* **2.** to get something ready [~with] ○ *Do you want me to make some tea?* **3.** to add up to a total ○ *Six and four make ten.* **4.** to give someone a particular feeling ○ *The smell of curry makes me hungry.* ○ *The rough sea made him feel sick.* ○ *Looking at old photographs made her sad.* ○ *He made himself comfortable in the armchair.* **5.** to force someone to do something ○ *His mother made him clean his room.* ○ *The teacher made us all stay in after school.* ○ *I can't make the car go any faster.* ○ *What on earth made you do that?* ◇ **to make do (with something)** to use something because there is nothing else available ◇ **to make sense 1.** to be understood ○ *The message doesn't make sense.* **2.** to be a good idea ○ *It makes sense to put a little money into your savings account every week.*

make for③ *phrasal verb* **1.** to go towards a place ○ *The army was making for the capital.* ○ *As soon as the film started, she made straight for the exit.* **2.** to help something to happen ○ *Non-stick pans make for easier washing up.*

make of③ *phrasal verb* to have an impression or opinion about something

make off with③ *phrasal verb* to steal something

make out① *phrasal verb* **1.** to be able to see clearly ○ *Can you make out the house in the dark?* **2.** to be able to understand ○ *I can't make out why he doesn't want to come.* **3.** to claim something which is probably not true ○ *The English weather isn't really as bad as it is made out to be.* ○ *She tries to make out that she's very poor.* **4.** to write something, such as a name ○ *The cheque is made out to Mr*

Smith. **5.** *US* to be successful ○ *He tried opening a fish restaurant but it didn't make out.* ○ *How is Bobby making out at school?*

make up① *phrasal verb* **1.** to invent a story ○ *He said he had seen a man climbing into the house, but in fact he made the whole story up.* **2.** □ **to make yourself up** to put on makeup, e.g. powder and lip stick **3.** to form something ○ *The staff is made up of secretaries and drivers.* **4.** □ **to make up your mind** to decide on something ○ *They can't make up their minds on where to go for their holiday.* **5.** □ **to make up for lost time** to act quickly because you did not act earlier ○ *It's June already – we'll have to plant our beans now to make up for lost time.* **6.** to become friends again ○ *They quarrelled, and then made it up.* **7.** □ **to make it up to someone** to compensate someone for something, e.g. for something lost or damaged ○ *Don't worry about the paint on your carpet – we'll make it up to you.*

make-believe /ˈmeɪk bɪˌliːv/ *noun* the practice of pretending that something is true when it is not

makeshift /ˈmeɪkʃɪft/ *adj* used temporarily in place of something else

③ **makeup** /ˈmeɪkʌp/ *noun* substances, e.g. face powder and lipstick, which people put on their face to make it more beautiful or change their appearance in some way ○ *She wears no makeup apart from a little eye shadow.* ○ *He spent hours over his makeup for the part of the monster.*

③ **making** /ˈmeɪkɪŋ/ present participle of **make**

malaise /məˈleɪz/ *noun* **1.** a feeling of being slightly ill ○ *She had a feeling of malaise but couldn't say what caused it.* **2.** a feeling of being slightly worried ○ *There is a general malaise among the middle-class which might make them vote against the government.*

malaria /məˈleəriə/ *noun* a tropical disease caused by a parasite which enters the body after a bite from a female mosquito

② **male** /meɪl/ *adj* relating to the sex which does not give birth to young ○ *A male deer is called a stag.* (NOTE: Do not confuse with **mail**.)

malevolent /məˈlevələnt/ *adj* who wants to harm other people

malfunction /mælˈfʌŋkʃən/ *noun* the fact of not working properly ○ *The data was lost due to a software malfunction.* (NOTE: + **malfunction** *v*)

malice /ˈmælɪs/ *noun* an unfriendly or spiteful feeling towards someone

malicious /məˈlɪʃəs/ *adj* done because you want to harm someone ○ *There has been some malicious gossip about her.* ○ *It was a malicious attempt to make her lose her job.*

malignant /məˈlɪgnənt/ *adj* likely to be cause death

mallet /ˈmælɪt/ *noun* a large wooden hammer

malnourished /mælˈnʌrɪʃt/ *adj* suffering from malnutrition

malnutrition /ˌmælnjʊˈtrɪʃ(ə)n/ *noun* the state of not having enough to eat

malpractice /mælˈpræktɪs/ *noun* the practice of acting in an unprofessional or illegal way (*by a doctor, lawyer, accountant, etc.*)

malt /mɔːlt/ *noun* barley grains which have been through the malting process and are used in breweries to make beer and in distilleries to make whisky

maltreat /mælˈtriːt/ (**maltreats, maltreating, maltreated**) *verb* to treat someone badly

mama /məˈmɑː/, **mamma** *noun* a child's name for mother (*informal dated*)

③ **mammal** /ˈmæm(ə)l/ *noun* a type of animal which gives birth to live young and feeds them with milk

mammoth /ˈmæməθ/ *noun* a very large hairy elephant living in prehistoric times ○ *There's a full-size model of a mammoth in the museum.* ○ *The woolly mammoth is thought to have become extinct during the last Ice Age.*

① **man** /mæn/ *noun* (*plural* **men**) a male human being ○ *That tall man is my brother.* ○ *There's a young man at reception asking for Mr Smith.* ■ *verb* (**mans, manning, manned**) to provide staff to work something ○ *The switchboard is manned all day.* ○ *She sometimes mans the front desk when the receptionist is ill.*

① **manage** /ˈmænɪdʒ/ (**manages, managing, managed**) *verb* to be in charge of something ○ *She manages all our offices in Europe.* ○ *We want to appoint someone to manage the new shop.*

manageable /ˈmænɪdʒəb(ə)l/ *adj* which can be dealt with easily

① **management** /ˈmænɪdʒmənt/ *noun* **1.** a group of people who direct workers ○ *The management has decided to move to new offices.* **2.** the practice of directing and controlling work ○ *He's taking a course in* *management.* ○ *If anything goes wrong now it's just a case of bad management.*

① **manager** /'mænɪdʒə/ *noun* **1.** the person in charge of a department in a shop or in a business ○ *The bank manager wants to talk about your account.* ○ *The sales manager organised a publicity campaign.* ○ *She's the manager of the shoe department.* **2.** a person in charge of a sports team ○ *The club have just sacked their manager.*

manageress /ˌmænɪdʒə'res/ *noun* a woman who manages a shop or department (*dated*)

managerial /mænə'dʒɪəriəl/ *adj* referring to managers

③ **managing director** /ˌmænədʒɪŋ daɪ'rektə/ *noun* a director in charge of a company

Mandarin /'mændərɪn/ *noun* the principal spoken form of Chinese, the official language of China

mandate /'mændeɪt/ *noun* the power given to a person to act on behalf of someone else

mandatory /'mændət(ə)ri/ *adj* which has to be done or has to take place because of a rule or law

mane /meɪn/ *noun* the long hair on the neck of a lion or horse (NOTE: Do not confuse with **main**.)

manger /'meɪndʒə/ *noun* a box for food for farm animals, e.g. horses or cows

mangle /'mæŋgəl/ (**mangles, mangling, mangled**) *verb* **1.** to squash something or chop something up ○ *The mangled remains of a dog run over by a lorry.* **2.** to spoil something by doing it badly ○ *He mangled his part so much that the audience laughed.* ○ *The poem was completely mangled in translation.*

mangrove /'mæŋˌgrəʊv/ *noun* a tree which grows beside water in hot countries and which has roots above the ground

manhandle /'mænhænd(ə)l/ (**manhandles, manhandling, manhandled**) *verb* **1.** to move something large and heavy by hand ○ *Ten men were needed to manhandle the statue into place.* **2.** to handle someone roughly ○ *The protesters complained they had been manhandled by the police.*

manhole /'mænhəʊl/ *noun* a hole in the road or pavement through which you go below the ground, e.g. into the sewers

manhood /'mænhʊd/ *noun* the state of being a man (NOTE: no plural)

manhunt /'mænˌhʌnt/ *noun* a search for someone, especially by the police

mania /'meɪniə/ *noun* **1.** a form of mental illness where the patient is very excited and violent **2.** a passion for something ○ *He has a mania for collecting old cars.* ○ *She has a mania for white clothes.*

maniac /'meɪniæk/ *noun* a crazy person ○ *We were nearly killed by some maniac driving a sports car.*

manic /'mænɪk/ *adj* wildly energetic ○ *The scene of manic activity in the office as everyone rushed to finish the work before the deadline.*

manicure /'mænɪkjʊə/ *noun* the act of looking after the hands and nails

manifest /'mænɪfest/ (**manifests, manifesting, manifested**) *verb* to show something ○ *The cat manifested no interest in her food whatsoever.* □ **to manifest itself as something** to show itself as something ○ *The disease first manifests itself as a slight skin rash.*

③ **manifestation** /ˌmænɪfe'steɪʃ(ə)n/ *noun* an appearance

manipulate /mə'nɪpjʊleɪt/ (**manipulates, manipulating, manipulated**) *verb* **1.** to influence people or situations so that you get what you want ○ *By manipulating the media the government made sure its message got across to the people.* **2.** to handle something ○ *She found it difficult to manipulate the instruments when wearing protective clothing.*

manipulative /mə'nɪpjʊlətɪv/ *adj* controlling and using people, so as to get them to do what you want

③ **mankind** /mæn'kaɪnd/ *noun* the human race, all human beings (*dated*)

manly /'mænli/ *adj* looking or behaving as a man should look or behave

man-made /ˌmæn 'meɪd/ *adj* which has been made by human beings

② **manner** /'mænə/ *noun* a way of behaving ○ *The staff don't like the new manager's manner.* ○ *She has a very abrupt manner of speaking to you.* ■ *plural noun* **manners** a way of behaving in public ○ *It's bad manners to speak with your mouth full.* ○ *Those boys need to be taught some manners.*

mannerism /'mænərɪz(ə)m/ *noun* a gesture or way of speaking which is particular to one person

manoeuvre /mə'nuːvə/ *noun* a planned action to avoid something or to deceive someone ○ *The captain had to make a sudden manoeuvre to avoid hitting the smaller ship.* ○ *The company has carried out various manoeuvres to avoid bankruptcy.* ■

verb **1.** to move something heavy or difficult to handle ○ *We manoeuvred the piano into position on the stage.* ○ *A big lorry is difficult to manoeuvre round corners.* **2.** to work to put yourself in a good position ○ *She managed to manoeuvre herself onto the board of the company.* (NOTE: [all senses] The US spelling is **maneuver**.)

③ **manor** /ˈmænə/ *noun* a country house and the land surrounding it (NOTE: Do not confuse with **manner**.)

manpower /ˈmænpaʊə/ *noun* the number of workers in a country or industry or organisation

③ **mansion** /ˈmænʃən/ *noun* a very large private house ○ *He's bought a mansion overlooking the golf course.* ○ *They live in a mansion in Hampstead with its own swimming pool and tennis courts.*

manslaughter /ˈmænslɔːtə/ *noun* the offence of killing someone without having intended to do so or of killing someone intentionally but with mitigating circumstances. Compare **murder**

mantra /ˈmæntrə/ *noun* a phrase which is chanted many times, as in a prayer

manual /ˈmænjuəl/ *noun* a book of instructions ○ *Look in the manual to see if it tells you how to change the toner cartridge.*

manufacture /ˌmænjʊˈfæktʃə/ (**manufactures, manufacturing, manufactured**) *verb* to make products for sale ○ *We no longer manufacture tractors here.*

② **manufacturer** /ˌmænjʊˈfæktʃərə/ *noun* a person or company producing industrial products

③ **manufacturing** /ˌmænjʊˈfæktʃərɪŋ/ *noun* the business of making things in large quantities for sale ○ *Only 25% of the nation's workforce is now engaged in manufacturing.*

manure /məˈnjʊə/ *noun* animal dung used as fertiliser on land ○ *The farmers were out in the field, spreading manure.*

manuscript /ˈmænjʊskrɪpt/ *noun* **1.** a document, letter or poem which has been written by hand ○ *the sale of several manuscript letters by King Charles II* ○ *One of the original manuscripts of the Domesday Book is kept in London.* **2.** a handwritten or typed version of a book which has not been printed or published ○ *He sent his manuscript to several publishers, but no one wanted to publish it.*

① **many** /ˈmeni/ *adj* **1.** a large number of things or people ○ *Many old people live on the south coast.* ○ *So many people wanted rooms that the hotel was booked up.* ○ *She ate twice as many cakes as her sister did.* **2.** asking a question ○ *How many times have you been to France?* ○ *How many passengers were there on the plane?* ■ *pron* a large number of people ○ *Many of the students knew the lecturer when he was a student himself.* ○ *Many would say that smoking should be banned in all public places.*

Maori /ˈmaʊri/ *noun* **1.** a person of the race of the original inhabitants of New Zealand ○ *The Maoris decorated the prows of their war canoes.* **2.** the language spoken by the race of the original inhabitants of New Zealand

② **map** /mæp/ *noun* a drawing which shows a place such as a town, a country or the world as if it is seen from the air ○ *Here's a map of Europe.* ○ *The village where they live is so small I can't find it on the map.* ○ *Show me on the map where the mountains are.* ○ *They lost their way because they'd forgotten to take a map.*

maple /ˈmeɪp(ə)l/ *noun* a northern tree, growing mainly in Canada and the USA, with sweet sap

mar /mɑː/ (**mars, marring, marred**) *verb* to spoil something

marathon /ˈmærəθ(ə)n/ *noun* a race, often run on roads in a city, covering a distance of 42 kilometres ○ *She's training for the New York marathon.*

marauding /məˈrɔːdɪŋ/ *adj* moving from place to place to steal and destroy things

marble /ˈmɑːb(ə)l/ *noun* a very hard type of stone which can be polished so that it shines ○ *The entrance hall has a marble floor.* ○ *The table top is made from a single slab of green marble.*

march /mɑːtʃ/ *noun* the act of walking so that your legs move at exactly the same times as everyone else's, especially by soldiers ○ *The soldiers were tired after their long march through the mountains.* ■ *verb* (**marches, marching, marched**) **1.** to walk in this way ○ *The guards marched after the band.* ○ *We were just in time to see the soldiers march past.* **2.** to walk in a protest march ○ *Thousands of workers marched to the parliament building.* (NOTE: + **marcher** *n*)

① **March** /mɑːtʃ/ *noun* the third month of the year, between February and April (NOTE: **March 6th** *or* **March 6**: say 'March the sixth' or 'the sixth of March' or in US English: 'March sixth'.)

mare /meə/ *noun* a female horse

margarine /ˌmɑːdʒəˈriːn/ *noun* a substance made from animal or vegetable oil which is used instead of butter

③ **margin** /ˈmɑːdʒɪn/ *noun* a white space at the edge of a page of writing ○ *Write your comments in the margin.* ○ *We left a wide margin so that you can write notes in it.*

marginalise /ˈmɑːdʒɪnəlaɪz/ (**marginalises, marginalising, marginalised**), **marginalize** *verb* to make someone or something less important

marijuana /ˌmærɪˈwɑːnə/ *noun* a drug made from hemp

marina /məˈriːnə/ *noun* a special harbour with floating jetties where a large number of yachts and pleasure boats can be tied up

marinade /ˈmærɪneɪd/ *noun* a mixture of wine and herbs, etc., in which meat or fish is soaked before cooking ○ *The marinade gives a delicious flavour to the meat.*

marinate /ˈmærɪneɪt/ (**marinates, marinating, marinated**) *verb* same as **marinade**

marine /məˈriːn/ *adj* referring to the sea ○ *marine plants and animals*

marital /ˈmærɪt(ə)l/ *adj* referring to a marriage

marital status /ˌmærɪt(ə)l ˈsteɪtəs/ *noun* the position of being married, divorced or not married

maritime /ˈmærɪtaɪm/ *adj* referring to the sea or ships

① **mark** /mɑːk/ *noun* **1.** a small spot of a different colour [~on] ○ *The red wine has made a mark on the tablecloth.* ○ *She has a mark on her forehead where she hit her head.* **2.** the points given to a student [~for/in] ○ *What mark did you get for your homework?* ○ *She got good marks in English and history.* ○ *No one got full marks – the top mark was 8 out of 10.* **3.** a particular point or level ○ *His income has reached the £100, 000 mark.* ■ *verb* (**marks, marking, marked**) **1.** to make a mark or write on something ○ *The box was marked 'Fragile'* **2.** to correct and give points to work ○ *The teacher hasn't finished marking our homework.* ○ *Has the English exam been marked yet?* **3.** (*in games*) to follow an opposing player closely, so as to prevent him or her getting the ball

mark down③ *phrasal verb* to reduce the price of something ○ *We have marked all prices down by 30% for the sale.*

mark up③ *phrasal verb* to increase the price of something ○ *These prices have been marked up by 10%.* ○ *If retailers find the discount too low they mark the prices up to make a better margin.*

③ **marked** /mɑːkt/ *adj* very obvious, definite ○ *This month's sales showed a marked improvement.* ○ *His performance was first class – in marked contrast to his game last week.*

③ **marker** /ˈmɑːkə/ *noun* **1.** a thing which marks something ○ *The golfer put down a marker before moving his ball.* **2.** a person who gives a mark to something, e.g. a piece of work, an examination or an entry in a competition ○ *Our teacher is a very hard marker – nobody gets more than seven out of ten.*

① **market** /ˈmɑːkɪt/ *noun* **1.** a place where products such as fruit and vegetables are sold from small tables, often in the open air **2.** a place where a product is required or where a product could be sold [~for/~in] ○ *The potential global market for this product is enormous.* **3.** the activity of trading in goods ○ *the market in luxury imported goods* ■ *verb* (**markets, marketing, marketed**) to sell products using marketing techniques ○ *This product is being marketed in all European countries.*

marketable /ˈmɑːkɪtəb(ə)l/ *adj* which can be sold easily

market economy /ˌmɑːkɪt ɪˈkɒnəmi/ *noun* a system of economy in which prices and earnings are controlled by the people's demands rather than by the government

market forces /ˌmɑːkɪt ˈfɔːsɪz/ *plural noun* commercial influences which have an effect on the success of a product or firm ○ *Market forces decide which firms succeed and which fail.*

market garden /ˌmɑːkɪt ˈɡɑːd(ə)n/ *noun* a small farm which grows vegetables or fruit which are sold in a nearby town

③ **marketing** /ˈmɑːkɪtɪŋ/ *noun* the methods used by a company to encourage people buy a product

③ **marketplace** /ˈmɑːkɪtpleɪs/ *noun* **1.** an open space in the middle of a town where a market is held ○ *The marketplace is usually right in the centre of a town.* **2.** the activity of selling goods or services ○ *Our sales staff find life difficult in the marketplace.* ○ *What is the reaction to the new car in the marketplace?*

market research /ˌmɑːkɪt rɪˈsɜːtʃ/ *noun* the activity of examining the possible sales of a product and the possible customers before it is put on the market

③ **market share** /ˌmɑːkɪt ˈʃeə/ *noun* the percentage of possible sales which a company or product has

③ **marking** /ˈmɑːkɪŋ/ *noun* **1.** the action of making marks **2.** the action of correcting something, e.g. exercises or homework ○ *Marking is not a job I like.*

marksman /ˈmɑːksmən/ (*plural* **marksmen**) *noun* a person who shoots well

mark-up /ˈmɑːk ʌp/ *noun* an amount added to the cost price to give the selling price

③ **marmalade** /ˈmɑːməleɪd/ *noun* a jam made from fruits such as oranges, lemons or grapefruit and eaten at breakfast

maroon /məˈruːn/ *adj* deep purple red ■ *noun* a deep purple-red colour

marquee /mɑːˈkiː/ *noun* a very large tent

marquess /ˈmɑːkwɪs/ *noun* a member of the nobility, the rank below a duke

② **marriage** /ˈmærɪdʒ/ *noun* **1.** the state of being legally joined as husband and wife ○ *A large number of marriages end in divorce.* ○ *She has two sons by her first marriage.* **2.** a wedding, the ceremony of being married ○ *They had a simple marriage, with just ten guests.* ○ *The marriage took place at the registry office.*

② **married** /ˈmærid/ *adj* joined as husband and wife ○ *Are you married or single?* ○ *Married life must suit him – he's put on weight.*

marrow /ˈmærəʊ/ *noun* a large green vegetable of the pumpkin family, similar to a large cucumber ○ *His marrow was the biggest exhibit in the vegetable show.*

① **marry** /ˈmæri/ (**marries, marrying, married**) *verb* **1.** to make two people husband and wife ○ *They were married in church.* **2.** to become the husband or wife of someone ○ *She married the boy next door.* ◇ **to get married to someone** to be joined as husband and wife in a ceremony ○ *They're getting married next Saturday.*

marsh /mɑːʃ/ *noun* an area of wet land

marshal /ˈmɑːʃ(ə)l/ *noun* **1.** a military officer of the highest rank **2.** an organiser of a race or a show ○ *Marshals tried to direct the crowds to the grandstands.* ○ *Some marshals rushed to the scene of the crash and others waved flags to try to stop the race.* **3.** *US* an officer of a court ○ *Federal marshals raided several houses looking for a prisoner who had escaped from jail.* **4.** *US* the chief of police or chief of the fire brigade in an area ■ *verb* (**marshals, marshalling, marshalled**) to organise people or things into order ○ *Extra police were brought in to marshal the crowds of fans.* ○ *He tried to marshal the facts but was too sleepy to think clearly.* (NOTE: The US spelling is **marshaling – marshaled**)

marshmallow /mɑːʃˈmæləʊ/ *noun* a soft white or pink sweet

marsupial /mɑːˈsuːpiəl/ *noun* a type of animal found in Australia, which carries its young in a pouch in the front of its body

martial /ˈmɑːʃ(ə)l/ *adj* referring to war (*formal*)

martial law /ˌmɑːʃ(ə)l ˈlɔː/ *noun* maintenance of law by the army instead of the police

Martian /ˈmɑːʃ(ə)n/ *noun* an imaginary person living on or coming from the planet Mars ○ *A story about Martians who come to invade the Earth.*

martyr /ˈmɑːtə/ *noun* **1.** a person killed or made to suffer because of his or her beliefs ○ *St Stephen, the first Christian martyr* ○ *Christian martyrs were killed by the Romans.* ○ *She was a martyr in the cause of national liberation.* **2.** a person who pretends to suffer in order to get sympathy ○ *She sat at the switchboard all day, looking a real martyr.*

martyrdom /ˈmɑːtədəm/ *noun* the fact of suffering death for your beliefs

marvel /ˈmɑːv(ə)l/ *noun* a thing which you think is wonderful ○ *The building is one of the marvels of the modern age.* ○ *It's a marvel that she managed to remember my birthday.* ■ *verb* (**marvels, marvelling, marvelled**) to show wonder or surprise at someone or something ○ *Everyone marvelled at the sheer size of the statue.* (NOTE: **marvelling – marvelled** but American spelling is **marveling – marveled**)

② **marvellous** /ˈmɑːvələs/ *adj* wonderful (NOTE: The US spelling is **marvelous**.)

Marxism /ˈmɑːksˌɪz(ə)m/ *noun* the political theories of Karl Marx, which led to communism and socialism

marzipan /ˈmɑːzɪpæn/ *noun* a paste made from ground almonds, sugar and egg, used to cover a fruit cake before icing or to make individual little sweets

mascara /mæˈskɑːrə/ *noun* a substance for making eyelashes dark

mascot /ˈmæskɒt/ *noun* an object or animal which you think brings good luck

③ **masculine** /ˈmæskjʊlɪn/ *adj* suitable for or typical of a man ○ *She had a very masculine hair style.*

masculinity /ˌmæskjʊˈlɪnɪti/ *noun* male qualities, what is typical of a male

mash /mæʃ/ (**mashes, mashing, mashed**) *verb* to crush something into a paste ○ *Mash the ingredients together before adding water.* ○ *She mashed the potatoes with butter and milk.*

mask /mɑːsk/ *noun* something which covers or protects your face ○ *The burglars wore black masks.* ○ *He wore a mask to go diving.*

masochism /ˈmæsəkɪz(ə)m/ *noun* **1.** a condition in which a person takes sexual pleasure in being hurt or badly treated **2.** the practice of doing something painful and enjoying it ○ *Taking all those children to France sounds more like masochism than a holiday to me.* (NOTE: + **masochist** *n*)

masonry /ˈmeɪsənri/ *noun* the stones used to make a building

masquerade /ˌmæskəˈreɪd/ (**masquerades, masquerading, masqueraded**) *verb* to pretend to be someone else [~as] ○ *The thief was masquerading as a policeman.*

② **mass** /mæs/ *noun* **1.** a large number or large quantity of things ○ *Masses of people went to the exhibition.* ○ *A mass of leaves blew onto the pavement.* ○ *I have a mass of letters* or *masses of letters to write.* **2.** a Catholic church service ■ *adj* involving a large number of people ○ *They found a mass grave on the hillside.* ○ *The group is organising a mass protest to parliament.* ■ *verb* (**masses, massing, massed**) to gather in large numbers

massacre /ˈmæsəkə/ *noun* the killing of a large number of people or animals ○ *Witnesses to the massacre led reporters to a mass grave in the hillside.* (NOTE: + **massacre** *v*)

massage /ˈmæsɑːʒ/ *noun* a rubbing of the body to relieve pain or to get someone to relax ○ *She gave me a massage.* (NOTE: + **massage** *v*)

② **massive** /ˈmæsɪv/ *adj* very large ○ *He had a massive heart attack.* ○ *The company has massive losses.* ○ *A massive rock came hurtling down the mountainside towards them.*

mass-market /mæs ˈmɑːkɪt/ *adj* made in large quantities for a wide market

mass media /ˌmæs ˈmiːdiə/ *plural noun* the means of passing information to a large number of people, e.g. newspapers, TV and radio

mass-produced /ˌmæs prəˈdjuːst/ *adj* manufactured in large quantities

mast /mɑːst/ *noun* **1.** a tall pole on a ship which carries the sails ○ *The gale was so strong that it snapped the ship's mast.* **2.** a tall metal structure for broadcasting TV, radio or mobile phone signals ○ *They have put up a television mast on top of the hill.*

master /ˈmɑːstə/ (**masters, mastering, mastered**) *verb* to become skilled at something ○ *She has mastered the art of TV newscasting.* ○ *Although he passed his driving test some time ago, he still hasn't mastered the art of motorway driving.*

mastermind /ˈmɑːstəmaɪnd/ *noun* a very clever person ○ *a criminal mastermind* ■ *verb* (**masterminds, masterminding, masterminded**) to be the brains behind a plan ○ *The escape was masterminded by two convicted murderers.*

masterpiece /ˈmɑːstəpiːs/, **masterwork** *noun* a very fine painting, book, piece of music, etc.

master's degree /ˈmɑːstəz dɪˌgriː/ *noun* a degree for further study after a Bachelor of Arts degree

mastery /ˈmɑːst(ə)ri/ *noun* **1.** the complete understanding of a subject or great skill at a game ○ *The French side showed their complete mastery of the game.* ○ *Her mastery of Italian is well-known.* **2.** having control over someone or something

masturbate /ˈmæstəbeɪt/ (**masturbates, masturbating, masturbated**) *verb* to rub your own sex organs to excite them and get pleasure (NOTE: + **masturbation** *n*)

mat /mæt/ *noun* a small piece of something such as carpet, used as a floor covering ○ *Wipe your shoes on the mat before you come in.*

② **match** /mætʃ/ *noun* **1.** a single occasion when two teams or players compete with each other in a sport ○ *We watched the football match on TV.* ○ *He won the last two tennis matches he played.* **2.** a small piece of wood with a one end which catches fire when you rub it against a special surface ○ *He bought a packet of cigarettes and a box of matches.* ○ *She struck a match and lit a candle.* ■ *verb* (**matches, matching, matched**) to fit or to go with something ○ *The yellow wallpaper doesn't match the bright green carpet.*

matchbox /ˈmætʃbɒks/ *noun* a small box with matches inside

③ **matching** /ˈmætʃɪŋ/ *adj* which fits or goes with something

③ **mate** /meɪt/ *noun* **1.** a friend, especially a man's friend ○ *He's gone down to the pub with his mates.* **2.** one of a pair of people or animals, especially where these can produce young together ■ *verb* (**mates, mating, mated**) (*of animals*) to breed ○ *A mule* *is the result of a donkey mating with a horse.*

① **material** /mə'tɪəriəl/ *noun* **1.** something which can be used to make something ○ *You can buy all the materials you need in the DIY shop.* **2.** cloth ○ *I bought three metres of material to make curtains.* ○ *What material is your coat made of?* (NOTE: no plural) **3.** facts or information ○ *She's gathering material for a TV programme on drugs.* (NOTE: no plural)

materialise (**materialises, materialising, materialised**), **materialize** (**materializes, materializing, materialized**) *verb* **1.** to become real ○ *His planned holiday never materialised.* ○ *She promised the staff an extra week's holiday but it never materialised.* **2.** to appear ○ *A man on horseback suddenly materialised out of the mist.* ○ *After a couple of phone calls, the money we were owed duly materialised.*

materialism /mə'tɪəriəlɪz(ə)m/ *noun* an interest only in physical things, especially money and property, not in spiritual ones

maternal /mə'tɜːn(ə)l/ *adj* referring to a mother

mathematician /ˌmæθ(ə)mə'tɪʃ(ə)n/ *noun* an expert at mathematics

① **mathematics** /ˌmæθə'mætɪks/, **maths** /mæθs/ *noun* the science of numbers and measurements

matinée /'mætɪneɪ/, **matinee** *noun* an afternoon performance of a play or film

matriarch /'meɪtriɑːk/ *noun* a respected old woman

matrimony /'mætrɪməni/ *noun* the state of being married

① **matter** /'mætə/ *noun* **1.** a problem or difficulty [~with] ○ *You look worried – what's the matter?* ○ *What's the matter with your leg?* □ **there's something the matter with my phone** my phone is not working properly **2.** a concern or business [~for] ○ *a serious matter affecting every family with young children* ○ *This is a matter for discussion with your financial adviser.* **3.** a particular type of material ○ *We put rotting vegetable matter on the garden as fertiliser.* ○ *Take some reading matter for the journey.* **4.** the substances that everything that exists is made of ■ *verb* (**matters, mattering, mattered**) to be important [~that/~which/whether/how etc] ○ *It doesn't matter if you're late.* ○ *His job matters a lot to him.* ○ *Does it matter if we sit by the window?* ◇ **as a matter of fact** to tell you the truth ○ *I know Paris quite well, as a matter of fact I go there every month on business.* ◇ **as a matter of course** in the usual way ○ *The police checked his driving licence as a matter of course.* ◇ **no matter what** whatever ○ *No matter what time it is, call the doctor immediately the symptoms appear.* ◇ **no matter how** however ○ *No matter how hard he tried he couldn't ride a bike.*

matter-of-fact /ˌmætər əv 'fækt/ *adj* practical, not showing any emotion

matting /'mætɪŋ/ *noun* large mats, or strong material from which mats are made

mattress /'mætrəs/ *noun* a thick pad forming the part of a bed that you lie on

mature /mə'tʃʊə/ (**matures, maturing, matured**) *verb* **1.** to become mature ○ *Whisky is left to mature for years.* ○ *He matured a lot during his year in Germany.* ○ *Girls are supposed to mature faster than boys.* **2.** to become due for payment ○ *The policy will mature in 20 years' time.*

maturity /mə'tʃʊərɪti/ *noun* **1.** the state of being an adult or of doing things like an adult ○ *He's only twelve, yet his painting already shows signs of considerable maturity.* **2.** the time when a bond becomes due to be paid ○ *The bonds have reached maturity.*

maul /mɔːl/ (**mauls, mauling, mauled**) *verb* **1.** to attack or handle someone roughly ○ *He was badly mauled by the tiger.* **2.** to criticise someone severely ○ *The minister was mauled by the tabloid press.* (NOTE: Do not confuse with **mall**.)

mausoleum /ˌmɔːsə'liːəm/ *noun* a special building in which an important person is buried

mauve /məʊv/ *noun* a light pinkish-purple colour ○ *She had the dining room walls painted in mauve.* ■ *adj* light pinkish purple

maverick /'mævərɪk/ *noun* a person who is unusual and does not fit into a normal pattern ○ *She's a political maverick.*

max /mæks/ *abbr* maximum

maxim /'mæksɪm/ *noun* a wise saying

② **maximum** /'mæksɪməm/ *adj* the greatest possible ○ *What is the maximum number of guests the hotel can take?* ■ *noun* the greatest possible number or amount ○ *The maximum we are allowed to charge per person is £10.* ◇ **at the maximum** not more than ○ *We can seat 15 at the maximum.*

① **may** /meɪ/ *modal verb* **1.** it is possible ○ *Take your umbrella, they say it may rain.* ○ *Here we are sitting in the bar, and he may be waiting for us outside.* ○ *If you don't hurry you may not catch the train.* **2.** it is allowed ○ *Guests may park in the hotel car* *park free of charge.* ○ *You may sit down if you wish.* **3.** asking questions politely ○ *May I ask you a question?* ○ *May we have breakfast early tomorrow as we need to leave the hotel before 8 o'clock?* (NOTE: The negative is **may not**. **May** is usually used with other verbs and is followed by **to**.)

① **May** /meɪ/ *noun* the fifth month of the year, after April and before June ○ *Her birthday's in May.* ○ *Today is May 15th.* ○ *She was born on May 15.* ○ *We went on holiday last May.* (NOTE: **May 15th** *or* **May 15**: say 'the fifteenth of May' or 'May the fifteenth' or in US English: 'May fifteenth'.)

① **maybe** /ˈmeɪbi/ *adv* possibly, perhaps ○ *Maybe the next bus will be the one we want.* ○ *Maybe you should ask a policeman.* ○ *Maybe the weather forecast was right after all.* ◇ **maybe not** possibly not ○ *Are you coming? – Maybe not.*

mayhem /ˈmeɪhem/ *noun* wild confusion (*informal*)

mayonnaise /ˌmeɪəˈneɪz/ *noun* a sauce for cold dishes, made of oil, eggs and lemon juice or vinegar

mayor /meə/ *noun* a person who is chosen as the official head of a town, city or local council

maze /meɪz/ *noun* **1.** a network of puzzling paths in which you can get lost ○ *We couldn't find our way out of the Hampton Court maze.* ○ *He led me along a maze of corridors.* **2.** a complicated network of things ○ *We have to try to find our way through the maze of European regulations.* (NOTE: Do not confuse with **maize**.)

MB *abbr* megabyte

③ **MD** /ˌem ˈdiː/ *noun* a director who is in charge of a whole company. Full form **managing director**

① **me** /miː/ *pron* used by the person who is speaking to talk about himself or herself ○ *give me that book* ○ *Could you give me that book, please?* ○ *I'm shouting as loud as I can – can't you hear me?* ○ *She's much taller than me.* ○ *Who is it? – It's me!* ○ *Can you hear me?* ○ *She's taller than me.*

meadow /ˈmedəʊ/ *noun* a large field of grass

meagre /ˈmiːgə/ *adj* small, not enough (NOTE: The US spelling is **meager**.)

② **meal** /miːl/ *noun* an occasion when people eat food, or the food that is eaten ○ *Most people have three meals a day – breakfast, lunch and dinner.* ○ *You sleep better if you only eat a light meal in the evening.* ○ *When they had finished their evening meal they watched TV.* ○ *You can have your meals in your room at a small extra charge.*

mealtime /ˈmiːltaɪm/ *noun* a time when you usually eat

① **mean** /miːn/ *adj* **1.** not liking to spend money or to give people things ○ *Don't be mean – let me borrow your car.* ○ *She's very mean with her money.* **2.** nasty or unpleasant [~to] ○ *The other children were being mean to him.* ○ *That was a mean thing to say.* ○ *He played a mean trick on his mother.* ■ *verb* (**means, meaning, meant**) **1.** used when you have not understood something ○ *Did he mean me when he was talking about fat old men?* ○ *What do you mean when you say she's old-fashioned?* **2.** to show or represent something [~(that)] ○ *'Zimmer' means 'room' in German.* ○ *When a red light comes on it means that you have to stop.* ◊ **meant** □ **to mean a lot** or **nothing to someone** to be very important or not important at all ○ *His family means a lot to him.* **3.** □ **to mean to do something** to plan to do something ○ *I meant to phone you but I forgot.*

meander /miˈændə/ (**meanders, meandering, meandered**) *verb* **1.** to wind about ○ *From the top of the hill you can see how the river meanders around the town.* ○ *The road meanders through several little villages.* **2.** to continue without any aim ○ *The negotiations meandered on without any decision being reached.*

① **meaning** /ˈmiːnɪŋ/ *noun* what something represents ○ *If you want to find the meaning of the word, look it up in a dictionary.* ○ *The meaning of a red light is pretty clear to me.*

meaningful /ˈmiːnɪŋf(ə)l/ *adj* full of meaning, significant

meaningless /ˈmiːnɪŋləs/ *adj* not meaning anything

② **means** /miːnz/ *noun* **1.** a way or method of doing something ○ *We'll have to write – we can't contact her by any other means.* ○ *Do we have any means of copying all these documents quickly?* ○ *The bus is the cheapest means of getting round the town.* **2.** money ○ *They'd like to buy a flat but they don't have the means.* □ **beyond someone's means** too expensive for someone to buy ◇ **by all means** of course ○ *By all means use my phone if you want to.* ◇ **by no means** not at all ○ *She's by no means sure of getting the job.* ◇ **by means of** by using something ○ *He got her money by means of a trick.*

means test /'miːnz test/ *noun* an inquiry to find out how much money someone has, to see whether he or she should qualify for a benefit or grant

③ **meant** /ment/ *verb* ▫ **to be meant to do something** should do something, or ought to do something ○ *We're meant to be at the station at 11 o'clock.* ○ *This medicine is not meant to be used by children.* ○ *Trains are meant to leave every half-hour.* ◊ **mean**

② **meantime** /'miːntaɪm/ ◇ **in the meantime** meanwhile, during this time ○ *We waited for her for hours in the rain, and in the meantime, she was happily sitting at home watching TV.* ○ *The new stadium will be finished by Easter but in the meantime we will still have to use the old one.*

② **meanwhile** /'miːnwaɪl/ *adv* during this time ○ *She hid under the table – meanwhile, the footsteps were coming nearer.*

② **measure** /'meʒə/ *noun* **1.** an action ○ *a safety measure* ○ *What measures are you planning to fight air pollution?* ○ *The government has taken measures to reduce street crime.* **2.** a certain amount or size ○ *We have no accurate measure of the pressure inside the volcano.* ○ *There was a measure of truth in what she said.* ■ *verb* (**measures, measuring, measured**) **1.** to find out the length or quantity of something ○ *She measured the window for curtains.* ○ *He measured the size of the garden.* **2.** to be of a certain size or quantity ○ *a package which measures* or *a package measuring 10cm by 25cm* ○ *How much do you measure round your waist?* ○ *The table measures four foot long by three foot wide.*

measured tread /'meʒəd tred/ ◇ **with measured tread** in a slow and stately way

② **measurement** /'meʒəmənt/ *noun* a quantity or size, found by measuring ○ *He took the measurements of the room.* ○ *The piano won't go through the door – are you sure you took the right measurements?* ○ *The measurements of the box are 25cm x 20cm x 5cm.*

② **meat** /miːt/ *noun* food from an animal or bird ○ *Can I have some more meat, please?* ○ *Would you like meat or fish for your main course?* ○ *I like my meat very well cooked.*

meaty /'miːti/ *adj* with a lot of details or information ○ *a meaty report*

mecca /'mekə/ *noun* a place which attracts a large number of people ○ *It's a mecca for motor-racing enthusiasts.*

mechanic /mɪ'kænɪk/ *noun* a person who works on machines

mechanical /mɪ'kænɪk(ə)l/ *adj* relating to machines ○ *Engineers are trying to fix a mechanical fault.*

mechanism /'mekənɪz(ə)m/ *noun* **1.** the working parts of a machine ○ *If you take the back off the watch you can see the delicate mechanism.* **2.** a way in which something works ○ *The mechanism for awarding government contracts.*

medal /'med(ə)l/ *noun* a round metal object, made to represent an important occasion or battle, and given to people who have performed well

medallion /mə'dæliən/ *noun* a round piece of metal worn round the neck on a chain as an ornament

medallist /'med(ə)lɪst/ *noun* a person who wins a medal in a competition (NOTE: The US spelling is **medalist**.)

meddle /'med(ə)l/ (**meddles, meddling, meddled**) *verb* to interfere in something that is nothing to do with you [~in/with] ○ *Don't meddle in matters that don't concern you.* (NOTE: do not confuse with **medal**)

② **media** /'miːdiə/ *noun* newspapers, TV and radio ○ *The book attracted a lot of interest in the media.* ◊ **mass media** ■ plural of **medium**

mediate /'miːdieɪt/ (**mediates, mediating, mediated**) *verb* to intervene to try to bring agreement between two opponents (NOTE: + **mediator** *n*)

medic /'medɪk/ *noun* a doctor (*informal*)

② **medical** /'medɪk(ə)l/ *adj* relating to medicine ○ *She's a medical student.* ○ *The Red Cross provided medical help.*

medication /ˌmedɪ'keɪʃ(ə)n/ *noun* **1.** drugs taken by a patient ○ *Are you taking any medication?* **2.** treatment by giving drugs ○ *The doctor prescribed a course of medication.*

medicinal /mə'dɪs(ə)n(ə)l/ *adj* referring to medicine ○ *He has a drink of whisky before he goes to bed for medicinal purposes.*

② **medicine** /'med(ə)s(ə)n/ *noun* **1.** a drug taken to treat a disease ○ *If you have a cough you should take some cough medicine.* ○ *The chemist told me to take the medicine four times a day.* ○ *Some cough medicines make you feel sleepy.* **2.** the study of diseases and how to cure or pre[illegible] vent them ○ *He went to university to* [illegible] *medicine.* (NOTE: no plural in this [illegible]

③ **medieval** /ˌmedi'iːv([illegible] to the Middle Ages

mediocre /ˌmiːdi'əʊkə/ *adj* ordinary, not particularly good

meditate /'medɪteɪt/ (**meditates, meditating, meditated**) *verb* **1.** to remain in a calm, silent state, without thought ○ *Don't disturb him – he's meditating.* **2.** to think deeply about something [~on/about] ○ *The accident made them spend some time meditating on how they spent their lives.*

Mediterranean /ˌmedɪtə'reɪniən/ *adj* referring to the Mediterranean Sea, between Europe and Africa, and the countries surrounding it ○ *The Mediterranean climate is good for olives.* ○ *She has bought a villa on one of the Mediterranean islands.*

③ **medium** /'miːdiəm/ *adj* middle, average ○ *He is of medium height.*

medium-sized /'miːdiəm saɪzd/ *adj* which is neither very large nor very small

medium wave /'miːdiəm weɪv/ *noun* a radio frequency range between 200 and 1000 metres

medley /'medli/ *noun* a mixture of different things, such as pieces of music

meek /miːk/ *adj* humble, always willing to do what other people want, feeling you are not important

① **meet** /miːt/ (**meets, meeting, met**) *verb* **1.** to come together with someone [~for] ○ *He met her at the railway station.* ○ *We'll meet for lunch before we go to the cinema.* □ **to meet to do something** to come together with someone to discuss something or make a decision ○ *We met the builder yesterday to discuss the plans for our new house.* **2.** to get to know someone ○ *I've never met your sister. – Come and meet her then!* ○ *Have you met our sales manager? – Yes, we have already met.* **3.** to produce a particular response ○ *The school's proposal met strong opposition from parents.* **4.** to satisfy what is necessary ○ *Does the car now meet the standards set by the motor racing authorities?* ○ *The company will meet your expenses.* **5.** to join at a particular point ○ *Several streets meet at Piccadilly Circus.* ○ *If you draw a diagonal line from each corner of a square to the opposite corner, the two lines will meet in the centre.*

meet up③ *phrasal verb* (*of several people*) to come together

meet with③ *phrasal verb* **1.** to find or to come up against a problem ○ *The advancing soldiers met with stiff resistance.* ○ *She met with an accident on the escalator.* **2.** to have an accident ○ *She met with an accident on the escalator.* **3.** *usually US* to meet someone ○ *He met with the sales people in New York.*

① **meeting** /'miːtɪŋ/ *noun* an occasion on which people come together, especially in order to discuss something [~of/~about/on/~with] ○ *The next meeting of the club will be next month.* ○ *There will be another meeting about safety procedures soon.* ○ *I had a meeting with my boss this morning.*

megabyte /'megəbaɪt/ *noun* a unit of storage for a computer equal to 1,048,576 bytes. Abbreviation **MB**

megahertz /'megəˌhɜːts/ (*plural same*) *noun* a unit equal to one million hertz

megalomaniac /ˌmegələʊ'meɪniæk/ *adj* a person who enjoys having power over other people

megaphone /'megəfəʊn/ *noun* a metal trumpet which makes the voice sound louder

melancholy /'melənk(ə)li/ *noun* great sadness ○ *There was an air of melancholy as the contents of the house were auctioned.*

melanin /'melənɪn/ *noun* a substance that gives colour to skin, hair and eyes

melanoma /ˌmelə'nəʊmə/ *noun* a malignant type of skin tumour

melee /'meleɪ/, **mêlée** *noun* **1.** a noisy confused fight **2.** a confused mixture of people or things

mellow /'meləʊ/ (**mellows, mellowing, mellowed**) *verb* **1.** to become soft or rich ○ *Time has mellowed the brickwork to a soft deep red.* **2.** to become ripe, to mature ○ *You should leave the wine to mellow for some years.*

melodrama /'meləʊdrɑːmə/ *noun* a play or event that is full of excitement and violent emotions

melodramatic /ˌmelədrə'mætɪk/ *adj* full of violent and exaggerated emotions

melody /'melədi/ (*plural* **melodies**) *noun* a tune

③ **melon** /'melən/ *noun* a large round fruit which grows on a plant which grows near the ground

③ **melt** /melt/ (**melts, melting, melted**) *verb* **1.** to change from a solid to a liquid by heating, or to cause a solid to do this ○ *If the sun comes out your snowman will melt.* ○ *The heat of the sun melted the road.* ○ *Glass will melt at very high temperatures.* **2.** to disappear

melt down *phrasal verb* to heat metal and make it into blocks so that it can be used again ○ *They stole the rings and melted them down into gold bars.*

melt away *verb* to go gradually ○ *The rioters melted away when the police appeared.*

meltdown /ˈmeltdaʊn/ *noun* the collapse of a nuclear power station because of overheating (*informal*)

melting pot /ˈmeltɪŋ pɒt/ *noun* a place where people of different origins come to live together

① **member** /ˈmembə/ *noun* **1.** a person who belongs to a group ○ *The two boys went swimming while the other members of the family sat on the beach.* ○ *Three members of staff are away sick.* **2.** an organisation or country which belongs to a group ○ *the members of the United Nations* ○ *the member states of the EU*

③ **Member of Parliament** /ˌmembər əv ˈpɑːləmənt/ *noun* a person elected to represent a constituency in Parliament (NOTE: often abbreviated to **MP**)

② **membership** /ˈmembəʃɪp/ *noun* **1.** the state of belonging to a group ○ *I must remember to renew my membership.* ○ *Membership costs £50 a year.* **2.** the members of a group ○ *The club has a membership of five hundred.*

③ **membrane** /ˈmembreɪn/ *noun* **1.** a thin layer of tissue which lines or covers part of the inside of the body ○ *A membrane connecting the tongue to the bottom of the mouth.* **2.** a thin material ○ *The metal is covered with a waterproof membrane.*

memento /məˈmentəʊ/ (*plural* **mementos** or **mementoes**) *noun* a thing kept to remind you of something

③ **memo** /ˈmeməʊ/ *noun* a note or short message between people working in the same organisation

memoirs /ˈmemwɑːz/ *plural noun* an autobiographical work, written in a less formal way than a full autobiography ○ *The general spent his retirement writing his memoirs.*

memorabilia /ˌmem(ə)rəˈbɪliə/ *noun* things which used to belong to a famous person or organisation and are kept to remind you of them

memorable /ˈmem(ə)rəb(ə)l/ *adj* which you cannot forget easily

memorandum /ˌmeməˈrændəm/ (*plural* **memorandums** or **memoranda**) *noun* a short note (NOTE: often shortened to **memo**)

memorial /mɪˈmɔːriəl/ *noun* a monument to remind you of something or someone ○ *The mayor unveiled the memorial to the dead poet.*

memorise (**memorises, memorising, memorised**), **memorize** *verb* to learn something thoroughly so that you know and can repeat all of it

① **memory** /ˈmem(ə)ri/ (*plural* **memories**) *noun* **1.** (*in people*) the ability to remember [/~for] ○ *I have a clear memory of my first visit to France.* ○ *My memory for faces is poor.* **2.** (*in computers*) the capacity for storing information ○ *This computer has a much larger memory than the old one.*

③ **men** /men/ plural of **man**

menace /ˈmenɪs/ *noun* **1.** someone or something which can harm people ○ *She's an absolute menace on the motorway.* **2.** a tone which threatens ○ *The menace in his voice made her shiver.* ■ *verb* (**menaces, menacing, menaced**) to threaten ○ *The members of the gang were menaced with imprisonment.* ○ *Several regions are menaced by drought.*

③ **mend** /mend/ (**mends, mending, mended**) *verb* to make something work which has a fault ○ *She's trying to mend the washing machine.*

meningitis /ˌmenɪnˈdʒaɪtɪs/ *noun* an inflammation of the membranes which surround the brain and spinal cord, where the patient has violent headaches, fever, and stiff neck muscles, and can become delirious

menopause /ˈmenəpɔːz/ *noun* the time when a woman stops menstruating and can no longer have children

menstrual /ˈmenstruəl/ *adj* referring to menstruation

menstruate /ˈmenstrueɪt/ (**menstruates, menstruating, menstruated**) *verb* to bleed from the uterus during menstruation (NOTE: + **menstruation** *n*)

② **mental** /ˈment(ə)l/ *adj* relating to the mind ○ *I've lost my calculator – how's your mental arithmetic?*

mentality /menˈtælɪti/ *noun* a way of thinking which is typical of someone or of a group

mentally /ˈment(ə)li/ *adv* concerning the ability to think ○ *They were tested mentally and physically.*

① **mention** /ˈmenʃən/ (**mentions, mentioning, mentioned**) *verb* to refer to something [~(that)] ○ *The press has not mentioned the accident.* ○ *Can you mention to everyone that the date of the next meeting has been changed?*

mentor /ˈmentɔː/ *noun* a person who teaches, or helps younger people starting their careers

③ **menu** /ˈmenjuː/ *noun* **1.** a list of food available in a restaurant ○ *The lunch menu changes every week.* ○ *Some dishes are not on the menu, but are written on a blackboard.* **2.** a list of choices available on a computer program

MEP *abbr* Member of the European Parliament

mercenary /ˈmɜːs(ə)n(ə)ri/ (*plural* **mercenaries**) *noun* a soldier who is paid to fight for a foreign country ○ *He was one of a group of mercenaries hired to protect the president.* ○ *The national army was mainly formed of foreign mercenaries.*

③ **merchandise** /ˈmɜːtʃəndaɪz/ *noun* goods for sale

merchandising /ˈmɜːtʃ(ə)nˌdaɪzɪŋ/ *noun* products such as toys and clothes which are related to a popular film, TV programme, sports team, or event

merchant /ˈmɜːtʃənt/ *noun* a businessman who buys and sells a particular product ○ *a tobacco merchant* ○ *a wine merchant*

③ **merchant bank** /ˈmɜːtʃənt bæŋk/ *noun* a bank which lends money to companies, not to people

merchant navy /ˌmɜːtʃənt ˈneɪvi/, **merchant marine** *noun* a country's commercial ships

merciful /ˈmɜːsɪf(ə)l/ *adj* kind and forgiving, showing mercy ○ *They decided to confess their crime and hope the king would be merciful.*

merciless /ˈmɜːsɪləs/ *adj* showing no mercy

mercy /ˈmɜːsi/ *noun* **1.** kindness towards unfortunate people ○ *The parents of the little boy pleaded with the kidnappers for mercy.* **2.** a gift of fate ◇ **at the mercy of** dependent on ○ *Cricket games are always at the mercy of the weather.* ○ *The success of the garden party is very much at the mercy of the weather.*

③ **mere** /mɪə/ *adj* simply, only

② **merely** /ˈmɪəli/ *adv* simply, only ○ *I'm not criticising you – I merely said I would have done it differently.*

merge /mɜːdʒ/ (**merges, merging, merged**) *verb* to join together with something

merger /ˈmɜːdʒə/ *noun* the joining together of two companies

meridian /məˈrɪdiən/ *noun* an imaginary line running from the North Pole to the South Pole at right angles to the equator (*literary*)

meringue /məˈræŋ/ *noun* a sweet baked dessert made of egg whites and sugar

③ **merit** /ˈmerɪt/ *noun* the quality of being good or excellent ○ *There is some merit in what he says, but I can't agree with all of it.* ○ *This picture has no artistic merit whatsoever.* ■ *verb* (**merits, meriting, merited**) to be worthy of or to deserve something ○ *The plan merits further discussion.* ○ *Her essay only merited a 'B+'.*

mermaid /ˈmɜːmeɪd/ *noun* an imaginary creature, half woman and half fish

merry /ˈmeri/ (**merrier, merriest**) *adj* **1.** happy and cheerful ○ *I wish you a Merry Christmas.* **2.** slightly drunk ○ *We all got a bit merry that evening.*

merry-go-round /ˈmeri ɡəʊ ˌraʊnd/ *noun* (*in a fairground*) a large machine, which turns round and plays music, usually with horses to sit on which move up and down

mesh /meʃ/ *noun* an arrangement of threads with spaces in between like a net ○ *We put wire mesh round the chicken pen to keep foxes out.* ■ *verb* (**meshes, meshing, meshed**) (*of gears*) to link together with cogs on another wheel ○ *For some reason the gears on my bike don't mesh together properly.*

③ **mess** /mes/ *noun* dirt or disorder ○ *The milk bottle broke and made a mess on the floor.* ○ *We had to clear up the mess after the party.*

mess about③ *phrasal verb* **1.** to spend your spare time doing something without having planned what to do ○ *He spends his weekends messing about in the garden.* **2.** □ **to mess someone about** to treat someone badly (*informal*) ○ *If you start messing me about, there'll be trouble.* ○ *The garage has messed me about so much I'm going to take my car somewhere else for servicing.*

mess up③ *phrasal verb* **1.** to make dirty ○ *You've messed up your brand new school uniform!* ○ *I hope it doesn't mess up your arrangements.* **2.** to spoil something ○ *I'm sorry we can't come – I hope it doesn't mess up your arrangements.*

① **message** /ˈmesɪdʒ/ *noun* information which is sent to someone ○ *I will leave a message with his secretary.* ○ *Can you give the director a message from his wife?* ○ *We got his message by e-mail.*

messaging /ˈmesɪdʒɪŋ/ *noun* the process of sending a message using an electronic messaging system

③ **messenger** /ˈmesɪndʒə/ *noun* a person who brings a message

messiah /mɪˈsaɪə/ *noun* **1.** a person who has a great impact on something ○ *the messiah of the ecological movement* **2. Messiah** a name Christians use for Jesus Christ ○ *For Christians, Christmas celebrates the birth of the Messiah.* **3.** a person whom the Jews expect will come to free them ○ *The coming of the Messiah is prophesied in the Book of Isaiah.*

③ **messy** /ˈmesi/ (**messier, messiest**) *adj* **1.** dirty ○ *Making pottery is a messy business.* ○ *Little children are always messy eaters.* **2.** unpleasant and disorganised ○ *It was a long messy divorce case.*

③ **met** /met/ past tense and past participle of **meet**

metabolism /məˈtæbəlɪz(ə)m/ *noun* chemical processes which are continually taking place in organisms and which are essential to life

② **metal** /ˈmet(ə)l/ *noun* a material, such as iron, which can carry heat and electricity and is used for making things ○ *a metal frying pan* ○ *These spoons are plastic but the knives are metal.*

metallic /meˈtælɪk/ *adj* like metal, referring to metal ○ *Suddenly we heard a quiet metallic sound, like a chain being moved.*

metamorphosis /ˌmetəˈmɔːfəsɪs/ (*plural* **metamorphoses**) *noun* a change to something quite different, especially an insect's change of form

metaphor /ˈmetəfə/ *noun* a way of describing something by giving it the qualities of something else, as in 'our eagle-eyed readers soon spotted the mistake.' Compare **simile**

mete *verb*

mete out *phrasal verb* to give a punishment

meteor /ˈmiːtiə/ *noun* a solid body which enters the earth's atmosphere from outer space, usually burning up and shining brightly as it does so

meteoric /ˌmiːtiˈɒrɪk/ *adj* sudden, unexpected and very noticeable

meteorite /ˈmiːtiəraɪt/ *noun* a piece of solid rock which falls from outer space onto the earth's surface

meteorology /ˌmiːtiəˈrɒlədʒi/ *noun* the study of climate and weather (NOTE: + **meteorologist** *n*)

③ **meter** /ˈmiːtə/ *noun* **1.** a piece of equipment for counting how much of something such as time, water or gas has been used ○ *He came to read the gas meter.* **2.** US spelling of **metre**

methadone /ˈmeθədəʊn/ *noun* a synthetic painkilling drug, used as a substitute for heroin in the treatment of addiction

① **method** /ˈmeθəd/ *noun* a way of doing something ○ *We use the most up-to-date manufacturing methods.* ○ *What is the best method of payment?*

methodical /mɪˈθɒdɪk(ə)l/ *adj* done carefully, in an orderly way ○ *The police carried out a methodical search of the house room by room.*

methodology /ˌmeθəˈdɒlədʒi/ *noun* methods used in a certain process or study

meticulous /mɪˈtɪkjʊləs/ *adj* being very careful about details □ **to be meticulous in doing something** *or* **about something** to pay great attention to detail when you do something ○ *He is very meticulous in sending off his tax return on time.* ○ *They were not very meticulous about their payments.*

② **metre** /ˈmiːtə/ *noun* a standard measurement of length, equal to 100 centimetres

metric /ˈmetrɪk/ *adj* using the metre as a basic measurement

metro /metrəʊ/, **Metro** *noun* (*in some towns*) an underground railway system

metropolis /mɪˈtrɒpəlɪs/ *noun* a large capital city

metropolitan /ˌmetrəˈpɒlɪt(ə)n/ *adj* referring to a large capital city ○ *She spent her childhood in a little village and found it difficult to get used to the metropolitan bustle of central London.*

Mexican wave /ˌmeksɪkən ˈweɪv/ *noun* an action when people watching an event stand up, raise their arms in turn, and then sit down, giving the impression of a wave running through the crowd

miaow /mjaʊ/ *noun* a call made by a cat ○ *We heard plaintive miaows coming from inside the cupboard.* ■ *verb* (**miaows, miaowing, miaowed**) to make a miaow ○ *The cat was miaowing to be let in.* (NOTE: [all senses] The US spelling is **meow**.)

③ **mice** /maɪs/ plural of **mouse**

microbe /ˈmaɪkrəʊb/ *noun* a very small organism which can only be seen with a microscope

microchip /ˈmaɪkrəʊtʃɪp/ *noun* a very small part, used in computers, with electronic connections on it

microcosm /ˈmaɪkrəʊkɒz(ə)m/ *noun* a miniature version

microorganism /ˌmaɪkrəʊ ˈɔːɡənɪz(ə)m/ *noun* a very small organism which can only be seen with a microscope

③ **microphone** /ˈmaɪkrəfəʊn/ *noun* a piece of electrical equipment used for making someone's voice louder, or for recording sound ○ *He had difficulty in making himself heard without a microphone.*

microprocessor /ˈmaɪkrəʊˌprəʊsesə/ *noun* the central processing unit inside a microcomputer

microscope /ˈmaɪkrəskəʊp/ *noun* a piece of equipment which makes things look much bigger than they really are, allowing you to examine things which are very small

microscopic /ˌmaɪkrəˈskɒpɪk/ *adj* extremely small, or so small that you need to use a microscope to see it

microwave /ˈmaɪkrəweɪv/ *noun* a small oven which cooks very quickly using very short electric waves ○ *Put the dish in the microwave for three minutes.* ■ *verb* (**microwaves, microwaving, microwaved**) to cook something in a microwave ○ *You can microwave those potatoes.*

mid-air /ˌmɪd ˈeə/ *adj, adv* in the air, flying ○ *The two planes collided in mid-air.* ○ *A mid-air collision between the two planes.*

③ **midday** /ˌmɪdˈdeɪ/ *noun* twelve o'clock in the middle of the day

① **middle** /ˈmɪd(ə)l/ *adj* in the centre; halfway between two ends ○ *They live in the middle house, the one with the green door.* ◇ **in the middle 1.** in the centre ○ *She was standing in the middle of the road, trying to cross over.* ○ *Chad is a country in the middle of Africa.* **2.** halfway through a period of time ○ *We were woken in the middle of the night by a dog barking.* ○ *We were just in the middle of eating our supper when they called.* ○ *His telephone rang in the middle of the meeting.* ○ *The house was built in the middle of the eighteenth century.*

③ **middle-aged** /ˌmɪd(ə)l ˈeɪdʒd/ *adj* between approximately 40 and 60 years old

① **middle class** /ˌmɪd(ə)l ˈklɑːs/ *noun* a social or economic group of people who usually have more than enough money to live on, and who often own their own property

Middle England /ˌmɪd(ə)l ˈɪŋɡlənd/ *noun* the section of English society which is regarded as socially traditional

middle ground /ˈmɪd(ə)l ɡraʊnd/ *noun* a position between extremes of opinion

middleman /ˈmɪd(ə)lˌmæn/ (*plural* **middlemen**) *noun* a businessman who buys from the manufacturer and sells to customers

middle management /ˌmɪd(ə)l ˈmænɪdʒmənt/ *noun* departmental managers who are not as important as directors

middle name /ˈmɪd(ə)l neɪm/ *noun* a second given name of someone

middle-of-the-road /ˌmɪd(ə)l əv ðə ˈrəʊd/ *adj* (*in politics*) of the centre, moderate

middle school /ˈmɪd(ə)l skuːl/ *noun* a state school for children in the UK from age 8 to 13

midfield /ˈmɪdfiːld/ *noun* **1.** the central section of a football pitch ○ *The goalkeeper kicked the ball to midfield.* **2.** the players who play in the midfield ○ *The midfield is the most important section of a football team.*

midfielder /ˈmɪdˌfiːldə/ *noun* a member of a football team active in the central area of the playing field, often both in attack and defence

midget /ˈmɪdʒɪt/ *noun* a very short person (*offensive*)

③ **midnight** /ˈmɪdnaɪt/ *noun* twelve o'clock at night ○ *I must go to bed – it's after midnight.* ○ *We only reached the hotel at midnight.*

midriff /ˈmɪdrɪf/ *noun* the front part of your body above the waist and below the chest

③ **midst** /mɪdst/ *noun* middle

midsummer /ˌmɪdˈsʌmə/ *noun* the middle of the summer

midterm /ˌmidˈtɜːm/ *noun* a point halfway through an academic term, or through a term of office ○ *midterm elections* ○ *We have our midterm exam next week.* Compare **half-term**

midway /ˌmɪdˈweɪ/ *adv* half-way ○ *We arranged to meet them midway between London and Oxford.* ○ *The lights went out midway through the performance.*

midweek /ˌmɪdˈwiːk/ *adj, adv* in the middle of the week ○ *If you travel midweek, the fares are higher than if you travel at the weekend.*

midwife /ˈmɪdwaɪf/ (*plural* **midwives**) *noun* a professional nurse who helps a woman give birth, often at home (*formal*)

midwinter /mɪdˈwɪntə/ *noun* the middle of the winter

miffed /mɪfd/ *adj* feeling annoyed or offended

① **might** /maɪt/ *modal verb* **1.** it is possible ○ *Take an umbrella – it might rain.* ○ *If he isn't here, he might be waiting outside.* ○ *I might call in to see you tomorrow if I have time.* ○ *That was a stupid thing to do – you might have been killed!* ○ *They might win, but I wouldn't bet on it.* **2.** should (have done) ○ *You might try and stay awake next time.* □ **he might have done something to help** it would have been better if he had done something to help □ **you might have told me** I wish you had told me ○ *You might have told me you'd invited her as well.* **3.** making a request politely ○ *Might I have another cup of tea?* **4.** used for suggesting something ○ *You might like to read this book.* ○ *We haven't got any bread left, but you might try the shop on the corner.* (NOTE: The negative is **might not** or, especially in speaking, **mightn't**. **might** is usually used with other verbs and is not followed by **to**. Note also that **might** is used as the past tense of **may**: *They said they might cancel the event if the weather was wet.*) ■ *noun* strength ○ *She pulled at it with all her might, and still could not move it.* ○ *All the might of the armed forces is displayed during the National Day parade.* ◇ **might (just) as well** used to refer to a different course of action ○ *They said the photos will be ready in 20 minutes, so we might as well wait.* ○ *The letter was too late for the post, so I might as well have left it until tomorrow.*

mightn't *short for* might not

mighty /'maɪti/ (**mightier, mightiest**) *adj* having a lot of force or strength (*literary*) ○ *With one mighty heave he lifted the sack onto the lorry.* ○ *All she could remember was getting a mighty blow on the head, and then everything went black.*

migraine /'miːgreɪn, 'maɪgreɪn/ *noun* a sharp headache often associated with vomiting and seeing bright lights

migrant /'maɪgrənt/ *noun* a worker who moves from one job to another or from one country to another to look for work ○ *The government is trying to prevent migrants coming into the country.*

migrate /maɪ'greɪt/ (**migrates, migrating, migrated**) *verb* to move from one place to another as the weather becomes warmer or colder (NOTE: + **migration** *n*)

mike /maɪk/ *abbr* microphone (*informal*)

③ **mild** /maɪld/ *adj* **1.** not severe ○ *There was some mild criticism, but generally the plan was welcomed.* ○ *He had a mild heart attack and was soon back to work again.* **2.** not strong-tasting ○ *We'll choose the mildest curry on the menu.*

① **mile** /maɪl/ *noun* a measure of length, equal to 1.61 kilometres ○ *He thinks nothing of cycling ten miles to work every day.* ○ *The car can't go any faster than sixty miles per hour.* ○ *The line of cars stretched for three miles from the road works.*

mileage /'maɪlɪdʒ/ *noun* **1.** the distance travelled in miles **2.** □ **to get a lot of** *or* **more mileage out of something** to take as much advantage as possible of something ○ *Can we get any more mileage out of his appearance on TV?*

mileometer /maɪ'lɒmɪtə/, **milometer** *noun* a device in a vehicle for recording the distance travelled

milestone /'maɪlstəʊn/ *noun* an important point in time ○ *This year marks an important milestone in the firm's history.*

milieu /'miːljɜː/ *noun* a society which surrounds someone

militant /'mɪlɪtənt/ *noun* **1.** a person who is very active in supporting a cause or a political party ○ *The party must keep its militants under control.* **2.** a person who supports a policy of using violence to achieve aims ○ *A few militants in the march started throwing stones at the police.* (NOTE: + **militancy** *n*)

① **military** /'mɪlɪt(ə)ri/ *adj* relating to the armed forces ○ *The two leaders discussed the possibility of military intervention.* ○ *Military spending has fallen over the past three years.*

militia /mɪ'lɪʃə/ *noun* an emergency police force organised like an army

① **milk** /mɪlk/ *noun* a white liquid produced by some female animals to feed their young, especially the liquid produced by cows ○ *Do you want milk with your coffee?* ○ *Can we have two glasses of milk, please?* ○ *Don't forget to buy some milk, there's none in the fridge.*

milkman /'mɪlkmən/ (*plural* **milkmen**) *noun* a man who brings milk to each house in the morning

milk shake /mɪlk 'ʃeɪk/ *noun* a drink made by beating milk with sweet liquid or fruit

③ **mill** /mɪl/ *noun* **1.** a small machine for turning seeds into powder ○ *There is a pepper mill on the table.* **2.** a large factory ○ *a paper mill*

millennium /mɪ'leniəm/ (*plural* **millennia**) *noun* a period of a thousand years

milligram /ˈmɪlɪɡræm/ *noun* one thousandth of a gram

millilitre /ˈmɪlɪˌliːtə/ *noun* a unit of measurement of liquid, equal to one thousandth of a litre (NOTE: usually written **ml** after figures. The US spelling is **millimeter**.)

③ **millimetre** /ˈmɪlɪmiːtə/ *noun* one of a thousand parts of a metre (NOTE: usually written **mm** after figures: *35mm*. The US spelling is **millimeter**.)

① **million** /ˈmɪljən/ *noun* the number 1,000,000

③ **millionaire** /ˌmɪljəˈneə/ *noun* a person who has more than a million pounds or a million dollars (NOTE: To show the currency in which a person is a millionaire, say 'a dollar millionaire', 'a sterling millionaire', etc.)

① **millionth** /ˈmɪljənθ/, **1,000,000th** *adj, noun* relating to 1,000,000 in a series ■ *noun* number 1,000,000 in a series

millisecond /ˈmɪlɪˌsekənd/ *noun* a unit of measurement of time, equal to one thousandth of a second

mime /maɪm/ (**mimes, miming, mimed**) *verb* to tell a story or show emotions through gestures ○ *He mimed getting into a car and driving off.* (NOTE: + **mime** *n*)

mimic /ˈmɪmɪk/ *noun* a person who imitates ○ *A good mimic imitates a person's body language as well as their voice.* ■ *verb* (**mimics, mimicking, mimicked**) to copy the way someone speaks or behaves, especially to amuse other people

min *abbr* **1.** minimum **2.** minute

③ **mince** /mɪns/ ◇ **he didn't mince his words** he said what he had to say in a straightforward way

① **mind** /maɪnd/ *noun* the part of the body which controls memory and reasoning ○ *His mind always seems to be on other things.* ○ *I've forgotten her name – it just slipped my mind.* ○ *I think about her night and day – I just can't get her out of my mind.* ○ *My mind went blank as soon as I saw the exam paper.* □ **to bear in mind** to remember something that might change a decision ○ *Bear in mind that it takes 2 hours to get there.* ○ *Bear me in mind when you're looking for help.* ■ *verb* (**minds, minding, minded**) **1.** to be careful [~(that)] ○ *Mind the plate – it's hot!* ○ *Mind that you don't forget the meeting starts early at 4 o'clock.* **2.** to be annoyed or upset by something [~if/~(that)] ○ *There aren't enough chairs, but I don't mind standing up.* ○ *Nobody will mind if you're late.* ○ *He didn't mind that his daughter had forgotten his birthday.* **3.** to look after someone or something for someone, or while the owner is away ○ *Have you got anyone to mind the children when you start work?* ◇ **never mind** don't worry ○ *Never mind – you'll get another chance to enter the competition next year.* ◇ **would** *or* **do you mind** asking politely ○ *Do you mind if I open the window?* ○ *Would you mind shutting the door?* ◇ **wouldn't mind** would rather like ○ *I wouldn't mind a cup of coffee.* ◇ **mind your own business!** don't interfere with other people's affairs ◇ **to have something in mind** to be planning a decision about something or someone ○ *Let's do something unusual this weekend – what do you have in mind?* ◇ **to have something on your mind** to be worrying about something ○ *She's not her usual cheery self today – I think she's got something on her mind.* ◇ **to take someone's mind off something** to try to stop someone worrying about something ○ *Let's go out to take your mind off your interview.* ◇ **to make up your mind (to do something)** to decide (to do something) ○ *I can't make up my mind whether to take the afternoon off to do some shopping or stay in the office and work.* ○ *She couldn't make up her mind what clothes to wear to the wedding.* ◇ **to change your mind** to decide to do something different ○ *He was going to go by car but then changed his mind and went by bus.* ○ *He has decided to go on holiday next week and nothing will make him change his mind.* ◇ **to be in two minds about something** not to be sure about something, to be undecided ○ *I'm in two minds about his proposal.*

mind-blowing /maɪnd ˈbləʊɪŋ/ *adj* extremely impressive, surprising or shocking

minder /ˈmaɪndə/ *noun* a person who protects someone (*informal*) ◊ **bodyguard 1**

mindful /ˈmaɪndf(ə)l/ *adj* remembering or thinking about something carefully when doing something ○ *He is mindful of his responsibilities as a parent, even though his job often takes him away from home.* ○ *You should be mindful of the risks you are taking in not following the guidelines.*

mindless /ˈmaɪndləs/ *adj* stupid, done without thinking

mindset /ˈmaɪndset/ *noun* a way of thinking, general attitude to things

① **mine** /maɪn/ *pron* belonging to me ○ *That book is mine.* ○ *Can I borrow your bike, mine's been stolen.* ○ *She's a great friend of mine.* ■ *noun* a deep hole in the ground from which substances such as coal are taken ○ *The coal mine has stopped working after fifty years.* ○ *He has shares in an African gold mine.*

minefield /'maɪnfiːld/ *noun* **1.** an area of land or sea where mines have been laid ○ *Minefields lay along both sides of the road.* **2.** a difficult and dangerous situation ○ *Trying to find your way round EU agriculture regulations is an absolute minefield.* ○ *The company got caught up in the minefield of government tax regulations.*

miner /'maɪnə/ *noun* a person who works in a mine (NOTE: Do not confuse with **minor**.)

mineral /'mɪn(ə)rəl/ *noun* a substance, such as rock, which is dug out of the earth, or which is found in food ○ *What is the mineral content of spinach?* ○ *The company hopes to discover valuable minerals in the mountains.*

mineral water /'mɪn(ə)rəl ˌwɔːtə/ *noun* water from a spring

mingle /'mɪŋgəl/ (**mingles, mingling, mingled**) *verb* **1.** to mix together ○ *The flavours of chocolate and lemon mingle deliciously.* **2.** to mix, to join in a party ○ *The host and hostess started to mingle with their guests.*

mini- /mɪni/ *adj, prefix* very small

miniature /'mɪnɪtʃə/ *adj* much smaller than the usual size ○ *He has a miniature camera.*

minibar /'mɪniˌbɑː/ *noun* a refrigerator in a hotel room containing cold drinks

minibus /'mɪnibʌs/ *noun* a small bus holding about twelve passengers

minicab /'mɪniˌkæb/ *noun* a car which a person drives as a taxi

minimal /'mɪnɪm(ə)l/ *adj* very low or small, the smallest possible

minimalism /'mɪnɪm(ə)lˌɪz(ə)m/ *noun* **1.** a movement of abstract artists who produce paintings and sculptures that make use of basic colours and geometric shapes in impersonal arrangements. The movement started in New York in the 1960s. **2.** a simple style in art, design or literature **3.** a style in music with a simplicity of rhythm and tone

minimise /'mɪnɪmaɪz/ (**minimises, minimising, minimised**), **minimize** (**minimizes, minimizing, minimized**) *verb* to reduce to the smallest amount; to make something seem very small

② **minimum** /'mɪnɪməm/ *adj* smallest possible ○ *The minimum amount you can save is £25 per month.* ○ *The minimum age for drivers is 18.* ■ *noun* the smallest possible amount ○ *We try to keep expenditure to a minimum.* ○ *She does the bare minimum of study, just enough to pass her exams.*

minimum wage /ˌmɪnɪməm 'weɪdʒ/ *noun* the lowest hourly wage which a company can legally pay its workers

mining /'maɪnɪŋ/ *noun* **1.** the action of taking coal and other minerals out of the land ○ *We used a Welsh mining village as a base for climbing in the mountains.* ○ *The company is engaged in mining for diamonds* or *in diamond mining.* **2.** the process of placing mines underground or under water ○ *The mining of the harbour was carried out by marines.*

miniskirt /'mɪniˌskɜːt/ *noun* a skirt which is very short

① **minister** /'mɪnɪstə/ *noun* **1.** the member of a government in charge of a department ○ *The inquiry is to be headed by a former government minister.* ○ *He was the Minister of Defence in the previous government.* **2.** a clergyman

ministerial /ˌmɪnɪ'stɪəriəl/ *adj* referring to a government minister

① **ministry** /'mɪnɪstri/ (*plural* **ministries**) *noun* a government department ○ *He works in the Ministry of Defence.* (NOTE: In the UK and the USA, important ministries are also called **departments**: *the Department of Work and Pensions, the Commerce Department.*)

mink /mɪŋk/ *noun* a small animal whose fur is very valuable ○ *Mink are now found in the wild in Britain.*

minnow /'mɪnəʊ/ *noun* a very small freshwater fish

② **minor** /'maɪnə/ *adj* not very serious or important ○ *It was just a minor injury.* ○ *She has a minor role in the film.* ○ *He played a minor part in the revolution.* ■ *noun* a person under the age of 18, who is not considered to be an adult ○ *We are forbidden to serve alcohol to minors.* (NOTE: Do not confuse with **miner**.)

② **minority** /maɪ'nɒrɪti/ *noun* **1.** a number or quantity which is less than half of a total ○ *A large minority of members voted against the proposal.* □ **in the minority** being less than half of the members ○ *The men are in the minority.* **2.** the period when a person is less than 18 years old ○ *During the king's minority the country was ruled by his uncle.*

mint /mɪnt/ (**mints, minting, minted**) *verb* to make coins ○ *British coins are minted by the Royal Mint.*

③ **minus** /ˈmaɪnəs/ *prep* **1.** reduced by ○ *Ten minus eight equals two (10 – 8 = 2).* ○ *Net salary is gross salary minus tax and National Insurance deductions.* **2.** below ○ *It was minus 10 degrees (-10°) outside.*

minuscule /ˈmɪnɪskjuːl/ *adj* very small

minus sign /ˈmaɪnəs saɪn/, **minus** *noun* a symbol, (-), used to show a negative quantity or subtraction

minute[1] /ˈmɪnɪt/ *noun* **1.** one of 60 parts of an hour ○ *There are sixty minutes in an hour, and sixty seconds in a minute.* ○ *The doctor can see you for ten minutes only.* ○ *The house is about ten minutes' walk* or *is a ten-minute walk from the office.* **2.** a very short space of time ○ *I'll be ready in a minute.* ○ *Why don't you wait for a minute and see if the dentist is free?* ◇ **I won't be a minute** I'll be very quick ○ *I'm just going to pop into the bank – I won't be a minute.* ◇ **at any minute, any minute now** very soon ○ *I expect the train to arrive at any minute.*

minute[2] /maɪˈnjuːt/ *adj* extremely small ○ *A minute piece of dust must have got into the watch.*

minutes /ˈmɪnɪts/ *plural noun* notes taken of what has been said at a meeting ○ *Who volunteers to take the minutes of the meeting?* ○ *Copies of the minutes of the last meeting will be sent to all members of the committee.*

miracle /ˈmɪrək(ə)l/ *noun* **1.** a very lucky event ○ *It was a miracle she was not killed in the accident.* **2.** an event which you cannot explain, and which people believe happens by the power of God ○ *She went to the shrine and was cured – it must have been a miracle.*

miraculous /mɪˈrækjʊləs/ *adj* wonderful, which cannot be explained

mirage /ˈmɪrɑːʒ/ *noun* an imaginary sight caused by hot air, such as an oasis seen in a desert

③ **mirror** /ˈmɪrə/ *noun* a piece of glass with a metal backing which reflects an image ○ *They looked at themselves in the mirror.*

mirth /mɜːθ/ *noun* enjoyment, especially shown by laughter

misapprehension /ˌmɪsæprɪˈhenʃ(ə)n/ *noun* an incorrect understanding

misbehave /ˌmɪsbɪˈheɪv/ (**misbehaves, misbehaving, misbehaved**) *verb* to behave badly

misbehaviour /mɪsbɪˈheɪvjə/ *noun* bad behaviour (NOTE: The US spelling is **misbehavior**.)

misc. *abbr* miscellaneous

miscalculate /mɪsˈkælkjʊleɪt/ (**miscalculates, miscalculating, miscalculated**) *verb* to calculate wrongly (NOTE: + **miscalculation** *n*)

miscarriage /ˈmɪskærɪdʒ/ *noun* the loss of a baby during pregnancy ○ *She had two miscarriages before having her first child.*

miscarry /mɪsˈkæri/ (**miscarries, miscarrying, miscarried**) *verb* **1.** (*of a plan*) to go wrong **2.** to produce a baby which is not sufficiently developed to live ○ *She miscarried three months into her pregnancy.*

miscellaneous /mɪsəˈleɪniəs/ *adj* various or mixed, not all of the same sort

mischief /ˈmɪstʃɪf/ *noun* behaviour, especially by children, which causes trouble ◇ **to make mischief** to make trouble for other people ○ *She's always trying to make mischief between me and the boss.*

mischievous /ˈmɪstʃɪvəs/ *adj* enjoying annoying people and causing trouble ○ *He's a very mischievous little boy.* ○ *She had a mischievous look in her eyes.*

misconception /ˌmɪskənˈsepʃən/ *noun* a mistaken idea

misconduct /mɪsˈkɒndʌkt/ *noun* a wrong action by a professional person or worker

misdeed /mɪsˈdiːd/ *noun* a wicked action

misdemeanour /ˌmɪsdɪˈmiːnə/ *noun* a minor crime (NOTE: The US spelling is **misdemeanor**.)

miserable /ˈmɪz(ə)rəb(ə)l/ *adj* **1.** very sad ○ *She's been really miserable since her boyfriend left her.* **2.** (*of weather*) bad or unpleasant ○ *What miserable weather – will it ever stop raining?*

③ **misery** /ˈmɪzəri/ *noun* great unhappiness

misfire /mɪsˈfaɪə/ (**misfires, misfiring, misfired**) *verb* not to fire properly

misfit /ˈmɪsfɪt/ *noun* a person who does not fit in with a group, who does not fit into society

③ **misfortune** /mɪsˈfɔːtʃən/ *noun* **1.** bad luck ○ *It was his misfortune to be born in the year when his father was declared bankrupt.* **2.** a piece of bad luck ○ *Misfortunes never come singly.*

misgiving /mɪsˈɡɪvɪŋ/ *noun* a doubt or fear that something will go wrong

misguided /mɪs'gaɪdɪd/ *adj* based on wrong decisions

mishandle /mɪs'hænd(ə)l/ (**mishandles, mishandling, mishandled**) *verb* **1.** to deal with a situation badly **2.** to treat something roughly

mishap /'mɪshæp/ *noun* a little accident

mishmash /'mɪʃˌmæʃ/ *noun* a confusing mixture

misinform /ˌmɪsɪn'fɔːm/ (**misinforms, misinforming, misinformed**) *verb* to give someone the wrong information

misinterpret /ˌmɪsɪn'tɜːprɪt/ (**misinterprets, misinterpreting, misinterpreted**) *verb* not to understand correctly

misjudge /mɪs'dʒʌdʒ/ (**misjudges, misjudging, misjudged**) *verb* **1.** to judge wrongly ○ *He misjudged the distance he had to jump and fell into the ditch.* **2.** to form a wrong opinion about someone or something ○ *I thought he was lazy, but I obviously misjudged him.*

mislay /mɪs'leɪ/ (**mislays, mislaying, mislaid**) *verb* to put something down and not to remember where it is

mislead /mɪs'liːd/ (**misleads, misleading, misled**) *verb* to give someone wrong information

mismanagement /mɪs'mænɪdʒmənt/ *noun* bad organisation and management (NOTE: + **mismanage** *v*)

mismatch /'mɪsmætʃ/ *noun* a badly matched pair

misnomer /mɪs'nəʊmə/ *noun* a wrong name

misogynist /mɪ'sɒdʒənɪst/ *noun* a man who hates women

misplaced /ˌmɪs'pleɪst/ *adj* directed at the wrong person or thing

misprint /'mɪsprɪnt/ *noun* a mistake in printing

mispronounce /ˌmɪsprə'naʊns/ (**mispronounces, mispronouncing, mispronounced**) *verb* to pronounce a sound or word wrongly

misquote /mɪs'kwəʊt/ (**misquotes, misquoting, misquoted**) *verb* to quote someone or something incorrectly

misread /mɪs'riːd/ (**misreads, misreading, misread**) *verb* **1.** to read something incorrectly **2.** to misinterpret something

misrepresent /ˌmɪsreprɪ'zent/ (**misrepresents, misrepresenting, misrepresented**) *verb* to report what someone thinks wrongly (NOTE: + **misrepresentation** *n*)

① **miss** /mɪs/ *verb* (**misses, missing, missed**) **1.** not to hit something that you are trying to hit ○ *He missed the target.* ○ *She tried to shoot the rabbit but missed.* **2.** not to see, hear or notice someone or something ○ *We missed the road in the dark.* ○ *I missed the article about books in yesterday's evening paper.* ○ *I arrived late, so missed most of the discussion.* **3.** not to catch something that you are trying to catch ○ *He tried to catch the ball but he missed it.* ○ *She missed the last bus and had to walk home.* **4.** to be sad because someone is not there any more ○ *We'll all miss Jack when he retires.* □ **to miss doing something** to be sad because you are not doing something any more ○ *I miss living by the sea.* ■ *noun* an instance of not hitting something that you are trying to hit ○ *He hit the target twice and then had two misses.*

miss out on③ *phrasal verb* not to enjoy something because you are not there

miss out③ *phrasal verb* to leave out, to forget to put in

① **Miss** /mɪs/ *noun* a polite title given to a girl or woman who is not married ○ *Have you met Miss Jones, our new sales manager?* ○ *The letter is addressed to Miss Anne Smith.* (NOTE: used before a surname, or a first name and surname)

missile /'mɪsaɪl/ *noun* a weapon which is sent or thrown ○ *They think the plane was brought down by an enemy missile.* ○ *They threw missiles at the police.*

③ **missing** /'mɪsɪŋ/ *adj* lost, which is not there ○ *I'm looking for my missing car keys.* ○ *They found there was a lot of money missing.* ○ *The police searched everywhere for the missing children.*

③ **mission** /'mɪʃ(ə)n/ *noun* **1.** an aim or purpose for which someone is sent ○ *The students were sent on a mission to find the best place to camp.* **2.** a group of people sent somewhere with a particular aim ○ *a United Nations peace mission* ○ *Several firms took part in a business mission to Japan.* ○ *A rescue mission was sent out into the mountains.*

missionary /'mɪʃ(ə)n(ə)ri/ (*plural* **missionaries**) *noun* a person who tries to convert people to his or her religion ○ *European missionaries tried to convert the inhabitants of the Pacific Islands.*

mission statement /'mɪʃ(ə)n ˌsteɪtmənt/ *noun* a statement which gives the aims of an organisation

misspell /mɪsˈspel/ (**misspells, misspelling, misspelt**) *verb* to spell wrongly

mist /mɪst/ *noun* tiny drops of water that hang in the air ○ *Early morning mist covered the fields.*

② **mistake** /mɪˈsteɪk/ *noun* an act or belief that is wrong ○ *There are lots of mistakes in this essay.* ○ *You've made a mistake – my name is David, not John.* ■ *verb* (**mistakes, mistaking, mistook, mistaken**) to not understand or not realise something ○ *There's no mistaking him, with his red hair and purple anorak.* ◇ **by mistake** as an accident ○ *They sent the wrong items by mistake.* ○ *By mistake she put my letter into an envelope for the chairman.* ○ *We took the wrong bus by mistake.* ○ *He put my coat on by mistake in the cloakroom.*

② **mistaken** /mɪˈsteɪkən/ *adj* wrong

mister /ˈmɪstə/ *noun* a way of addressing a man (= Mr.) ○ *What's the time, mister?*

③ **mistook** /mɪˈstʊk/ past tense of **mistake**

mistreat /mɪsˈtriːt/ (**mistreats, mistreating, mistreated**) *verb* to treat something or someone badly or roughly

mistress /ˈmɪstrəs/ *noun* **1.** a woman who has a sexual relationship with a man without being married to him ○ *She had engaged a detective to follow her husband and photograph him with his mistress.* **2.** a woman teacher ○ *the geography mistress* **3.** a woman in charge of or who owns an animal ○ *The dog chased after a rabbit but came back when his mistress whistled.*

mistrust /mɪsˈtrʌst/ *noun* not having any confidence ○ *The occupying army aroused considerable mistrust in the local population.* (NOTE: + **mistrust** *v*)

misunderstand /ˌmɪsʌndəˈstænd/ (**misunderstands, misunderstanding, misunderstood**) *verb* not to understand correctly

misunderstanding /ˌmɪsʌndəˈstændɪŋ/ *noun* a situation where something has not been understood correctly

misunderstood /ˌmɪsʌndəˈstʊd/ *adj* not appreciated because people do not understand you. ◊ **misunderstand**

misuse¹ /mɪsˈjuːs/ *noun* a wrong use ○ *The directors of the charity were accused of misuse of funds.*

misuse² /mɪsˈjuːz/ (**misuses, misusing, misused**) *verb* to use something in a wrong way ○ *She misused the money which she had been given to look after.* ○ *He felt misused when the company refused to help him.*

mite /maɪt/ *noun* **1.** a tiny animal of the spider family which lives in soil or is a parasite on animals or plants ○ *House mites can cause allergies.* **2.** a very small child ○ *The poor little mite looks half-starved.*

mitigate /ˈmɪtɪgeɪt/ (**mitigates, mitigating, mitigated**) *verb* to make less serious (NOTE: + **mitigation** *n*)

mitt /mɪt/ *noun* a padded glove worn by a baseball player

② **mix** /mɪks/ (**mixes, mixing, mixed**) *verb* to combine things ○ *She made the cake by mixing eggs and flour.*

mix up③ *phrasal verb* to think that a person or thing is someone or something else ○ *I always mix her up with her sister.*

② **mixed** /mɪkst/ *adj* **1.** made up of different things put together ○ *The recipe uses mixed herbs.* **2.** involving different age groups, ethnic groups or sexes ○ *The reaction to the proposal has been rather mixed – some people approve, but others disapprove.* **3.** involving some good things and some bad things ○ *There has been a mixed reaction to our proposal.* ◇ **in mixed company** when both men and women are together ○ *That's not the sort of joke you can tell in mixed company.*

mixed blessing /mɪkst ˈblesɪŋ/ *noun* something which can have advantages and disadvantages as well

mixed salad *noun* a salad that includes lettuce, cucumbers, tomatoes and other vegetables

mixed school /ˈmɪkst skuːl/ *noun* a school for both boys and girls

mixed up /ˌmɪkst ˈʌp/ *adj* confused in your mind ◇ **to be mixed up in** *or* **with** to be part of or involved in something ○ *He was mixed up in the bank scandal.* ○ *How did she get mixed up with those awful people?*

mixer /ˈmɪksə/ *noun* a machine for mixing

③ **mixture** /ˈmɪkstʃə/ *noun* **1.** a number of things mixed together ○ *a mixture of flour, fat and water* **2.** something made up of different types of thing ○ *His latest paintings are a strange mixture of shapes and colours.*

mix-up /ˈmɪks ʌp/ *noun* a confusion

moan /məʊn/ *noun* a low sound made by someone who is in pain or upset ○ *The rescue team could hear moans from under the wreckage.* ○ *When she read the news she gave a loud moan.* ■ *verb* (**moans, moaning, moaned**) to make a low sound as if you are in pain ○ *I could hear someone* *moaning in the bathroom.* ○ *They could hear someone moaning in the cellar.*

moat /məʊt/ *noun* a wide ditch with water in it, made as a protection round a castle or town

mob /mɒb/ *noun* a large number of people behaving in a noisy, angry or uncontrolled way ○ *Mobs of looters ran through the streets.* ○ *An angry mob surged towards the factory gates.*

② **mobile** /ˈməʊbaɪl/ *adj* able to move or be moved ○ *a mobile library* ■ *noun* **1.** a mobile phone ○ *I'll call him on his mobile.* ○ *He gave me the number of his mobile.* **2.** an object made of small pieces of metal, card etc., which when hung up move around with the movements of the air ○ *They bought a mobile of clowns to hang over the baby's cot.*

mobile home /ˌməʊbaɪl ˈhəʊm/ *noun US* a large caravan in which people can live permanently, which is usually based in a special park

② **mobile phone** /ˌməʊbaɪl ˈfəʊn/ *noun* a small telephone which you can carry around. Compare **landline**

mobility /məʊˈbɪlɪti/ *noun* being able to move easily

mobster /ˈmɒbstə/ *noun especially US* a member of a criminal gang (*informal*)

mocha /ˈmɒkə/ *noun* **1.** a type of strong dark coffee **2.** a coffee and chocolate flavouring used in baking

mock /mɒk/ (**mocks, mocking, mocked**) *verb* to laugh at someone or something in an unkind way ○ *Don't mock the singer – he's doing the best he can.*

mockery /ˈmɒkəri/ *noun* **1.** a thing which is only a bad imitation, which is of no use ○ *The trial was a mockery of justice.* **2.** the action of laughing at someone or something in an unkind way ○ *He could see the mockery in her eyes.* ◇ **to make a mockery of something** to make something seem useless ○ *The exam makes a mockery of the government's insistence on educational standards.*

mock-up /ˈmɒk ʌp/ *noun* a scale model of a new product for testing purposes

modal verb /ˈməʊd(ə)l vɜːb/ *noun* a verb such as 'can', which is used with another verb to express an idea such as possibility

③ **mode** /məʊd/ *noun* a way of doing something

① **model** /ˈmɒd(ə)l/ *noun* **1.** a small version of something larger ○ *The exhibition has a model of the new town hall.* ○ *He spends his time making model planes.* **2.** a good example of something [/~for] ○ *The conference was a model of good organisation.* ○ *Their report can be used as a model for all the other departments.* **3.** a person who wears new clothes to show them to customers ○ *He used only top models to show his designs during the London Fashion Week.* **4.** a particular type of product produced at a particular time ○ *This is this year's model.* ○ *He bought a 1979 model Mini.* ■ *verb* (**models, modelling, modelled**) **1.** to wear newly designed clothes to show to customers ○ *She is modelling the autumn collection by Dior.* **2.** to make shapes in clay ○ *He modelled a statue of the little girl.* **3.** to copy something [~on] ○ *The garden is modelled on the famous one at Versailles.*

modelling /ˈmɒd(ə)lɪŋ/ *noun* **1.** the job of being a fashion model ○ *With your looks you could take up modelling as a career.* **2.** the process of making models (NOTE: [all senses] The US spelling is **modeling**.)

② **modem** /ˈməʊdem/ *noun* a device which links a computer to the telephone lines, so as to send data. Full form **modulator-demodulator**

moderate[1] /ˈmɒd(ə)rət/ *adj* not excessive ○ *She had moderate success in her exams.* ○ *The economy has ended a period of steady moderate growth.* ○ *The union's wage demands are really quite moderate.* ■ *noun* a person whose political ideas are not very violent ○ *After years of struggle the moderates have gained control of the party.*

moderate[2] /ˈmɒdəreɪt/ (**moderates, moderating, moderated**) *verb* to make or become less strong ○ *They moderated their demands.* ○ *As the wind moderated, the waves became smaller.*

moderation /ˌmɒdəˈreɪʃ(ə)n/ *noun* the fact of not being excessive

① **modern** /ˈmɒd(ə)n/ *adj* referring to the present time ○ *It is a fairly modern invention – it was patented only in the 1980s.* ○ *You expect really modern offices to have air-conditioning systems.*

modern-day /ˈmɒd(ə)n deɪ/ *adj* **1.** at the present time ○ *Modern-day living is becoming more and more stressful.* **2.** existing now, but very similar to somebody or something that existed in the past ○ *The army needs a modern-day Napoleon to lead it.* ○ *He's a modern-day equivalent of a Victorian factory owner.*

modernity /mɒˈdɜːnəti/ *noun* the quality or idea of being modern or up-to-date

modern languages /ˌmɒd(ə)n ˈlæŋɡwɪdʒɪz/ *plural noun* languages which are spoken today ○ *She's studying German and Italian in the modern languages department.*

modest /ˈmɒdɪst/ *adj* not telling other people about your achievements ○ *He was very modest about his gold medal.*

modesty /ˈmɒdɪsti/ *noun* **1.** the quality of being modest ○ *Modesty forbids me to mention all my other achievements.* **2.** the quality of not being excessive, being quite small ○ *We think he stole some money from the petty cash box, but in view of the modesty of the sum involved, we won't report it to the police.* **3.** a reservation about showing parts of your body

modicum /ˈmɒdɪkəm/ *noun* a fairly small amount

③ **modification** /ˌmɒdɪfɪˈkeɪʃ(ə)n/ *noun* an alteration

modifier /ˈmɒdɪˌfaɪə/ *noun* a word or phrase that affects the meaning of another, usually describing it or restricting its meaning. 'Pink' in the phrase 'the pink ribbon' and 'fire' in the compound 'fire alarm' are modifiers.

modify /ˈmɒdɪfaɪ/ (**modifies, modifying, modified**) *verb* to change something to suit a different situation ○ *The design was modified to make the car faster.*

modular /ˈmɒdjʊlə/ *adj* made of various modules

② **module** /ˈmɒdjuːl/ *noun* a part of something such as a course of study, which is made up of various sections ○ *The science course is made up of a series of modules.*

mogul /ˈməʊɡ(ə)l/ *noun* the boss of a large business organisation, especially a film or a TV company

mohair /ˈməʊheə/ *noun* a very soft wool from a type of goat

③ **moist** /mɔɪst/ *adj* slightly wet, often in a pleasant way ○ *To clean the oven, just wipe it with a moist cloth.* ○ *The cake should be moist, not too dry.*

moisten /ˈmɔɪs(ə)n/ (**moistens, moistening, moistened**) *verb* to make slightly wet

③ **moisture** /ˈmɔɪstʃə/ *noun* small drops of water in the air or on a surface (NOTE: no plural)

moisturise (**moisturises, moisturising, moisturised**), **moisturize** (**moisturizes**) *verb* to rub a cream or liquid onto your skin to prevent it from being dry

molar /ˈməʊlə/ *noun* a large back tooth used for grinding food

molasses /məˈlæsɪz/ *noun* a thick black syrup removed from sugar as it is being refined (NOTE: The usual British term is **black treacle**.)

mold /məʊld, ˈməʊldi/, **moldy** US spelling of **mould, mouldy**

③ **mole** /məʊl/ *noun* **1.** a small animal with soft dark grey fur, which lives under the ground **2.** a small dark spot on the skin ○ *She has a little mole on her cheek.* ○ *The doctor removed a mole from the back of her hand.*

molecule /ˈmɒlɪkjuːl/ *noun* the smallest unit in a substance that can exist by itself

molest /məˈlest/ (**molests, molesting, molested**) *verb* to attack a child or a woman, especially in a sexual way

mollify /ˈmɒlɪfaɪ/ (**mollifies, mollifying, mollified**) *verb* to make someone less annoyed or less upset

mollusc /ˈmɒləsk/ *noun* an animal with no backbone, but usually with a soft body and a shell, such as a snail or an oyster (NOTE: The US spelling is **mollusk**.)

mollycoddle /ˈmɒliˌkɒd(ə)l/ (**mollycoddles, mollycoddling, mollycoddled**) *verb* to treat someone in an overprotective and overindulgent way

molten /ˈməʊltən/ *adj* which has become liquid with heat ○ *molten lava*

① **mom** /mɒm/ *noun US* a child's name for mother (*informal*) ○ *His mom always waits for him outside school.* (NOTE: The British term is **mum** or **mummy**.)

① **moment** /ˈməʊmənt/ *noun* a very short time ○ *Can you please wait a moment – the doctor is on the phone?* ○ *I only saw her for a moment.* ◇ **in a moment** in a short time from now

momentary /ˈməʊmənt(ə)ri/ *adj* which only lasts for a short time

momentous /məʊˈmentəs/ *adj* very important

momentum /məʊˈmentəm/ *noun* a forward movement

Mon. *abbr* Monday

monarch /ˈmɒnək/ *noun* the king or queen

monarchy /ˈmɒnəki/ (*plural* **monarchies**) *noun* **1.** a system of government with a hereditary ruler such as a king or queen ○ *There's a big debate about whether we should get rid of the monarchy and* *become a republic.* **2.** a country ruled by a monarch ○ *All European countries with kings or queens are constitutional monarchies.*

monastery /'mɒnəst(ə)ri/ (*plural* **monasteries**) *noun* a religious establishment where monks live; the buildings of such a place. Compare **convent**

① **Monday** /'mʌndeɪ/ *noun* the first day of the working week, the day between Sunday and Tuesday ○ *Some stores are shut on Mondays.* ○ *She had to go to the doctor last Monday.* ○ *The 15th is a Sunday, so the 16th must be a Monday.*

③ **monetary** /'mʌnɪt(ə)ri/ *adj* referring to money or currency

① **money** /'mʌni/ *noun* **1.** coins or notes which are used for buying things ○ *How much money have you got in the bank?* ○ *He doesn't earn very much money.* ○ *We spent more money last week than in the previous month.* ○ *We ran out of money in Spain and had to come home early.* **2.** the type of coins and notes used in a country ○ *I want to change my British pounds into Mexican money.* **3.** □ **to make money** to make a profit

money market /'mʌni ˌmɑːkɪt/ *noun* a market for buying and selling short-term loans

money order /'mʌni ˌɔːdə/ *noun* a document which can be used for passing money from one person to another through the post

mongrel /'mʌŋgrəl/ *adj, noun* a dog of mixed breed ○ *They've bought a mongrel puppy.*

③ **monitor** /'mɒnɪtə/ *noun* the screen of a computer, or a small television screen used for checking what is happening ○ *My computer has a colour monitor.* ○ *Details of flight arrivals and departures are displayed on monitors around the airport.* ■ *verb* (**monitors, monitoring, monitored**) to check or to watch over the progress of something ○ *Doctors are monitoring her heart condition.* ○ *How do you monitor the performance of the sales staff?*

monk /mʌŋk/ *noun* a man who is a member of a religious group who live together in a monastery, away from other people. Compare **friar** (NOTE: The equivalent women are **nuns**.)

monkey /'mʌŋki/ *noun* a tropical animal which lives in trees and normally has a long tail ○ *Monkeys ran up the trees looking for fruit.*

monkey business /'mʌŋki ˌbɪznəs/ *noun* tricks, cheating

monkey wrench /'mʌŋki rentʃ/ *noun* a large spanner with an adjustable grip

monochrome /'mɒnəkrəʊm/ *adj* appearing only in black, white or grey

monogamous /mə'nɒgəməs/ *adj* where a person has only one husband or wife

monogamy /mə'nɒgəmi/ *noun* the system of marriage to only one person at a time

monogram /'mɒnəgræm/ *noun* the initials of a name linked together artistically

monolingual /ˌmɒnəʊ'lɪŋgwəl/ *adj* **1.** speaking only one language **2.** written or made in only one language

monolith /'mɒnəlɪθ/ *noun* **1.** a tall rock standing by itself **2.** something large, unchangeable and out-of-date, especially a long-established organisation

monolithic /ˌmɒnə'lɪθɪk/ *adj* **1.** built using very large stones or blocks of some other material **2.** large, uniform in character, and slow to change

monologue /'mɒnəlɒg/ *noun* a long speech by one actor or other person alone (NOTE: The US spelling is **monolog**.)

monopolise /mə'nɒpəlaɪz/ (**monopolises, monopolising, monopolised**), **monopolize** *verb* to use something entirely for yourself ○ *Don't monopolise the computer – let some of the others have a go.*

monopoly /mə'nɒpəli/ (*plural* **monopolies**) *noun* a system where one person or company supplies all of a product in one area without any competition

monorail /'mɒnəʊˌreɪl/ *noun* a railway in which trains travel along a single rail

monosyllabic /ˌmɒnəʊsɪ'læbɪk/ *adj* **1.** (*of words*) with only one syllable ○ *monosyllabic words such as 'hat' and 'cat'* **2.** using short simple words and not saying much ○ *In answer to the reporters' questions he gave a series of monosyllabic replies.*

monosyllable /'mɒnəʊˌsɪləb(ə)l/ *noun* a word which only has one syllable

monotone /'mɒnətəʊn/ *noun* **1.** a sound that stays at the same pitch without rising or falling **2.** a lack of variety in colour, or some other quality

monotonous /mə'nɒt(ə)nəs/ *adj* boring and never changing

monotony /mə'nɒt(ə)ni/ *noun* a lack of variety, which leads to boredom

monsoon /mɒn'suːn/ *noun* a season of wind and rain in tropical countries ○ *At last the monsoon brought relief after the hot dry summer.*

monster /'mɒnstə/ *noun* a strange and frightening animal ○ *The Loch Ness Monster is said to be a large dinosaur living in the bottom of Loch Ness in Scotland.* ○ *She drew a picture of a green monster with purple horns and huge teeth.* ■ *adj* very large ○ *Look at the monster cabbage Dad's grown in the garden.* ○ *What a monster sandwich!*

monstrosity /mɒn'strɒsɪti/ *noun* a horrible, large, ugly thing

monstrous /'mɒnstrəs/ *adj* **1.** huge and ugly ○ *a monstrous sea serpent* **2.** very shocking or unfair ○ *That's a monstrous accusation.*

① **month** /mʌnθ/ *noun* one of the twelve parts that a year is divided into ○ *December is the last month of the year.* ○ *What day of the month is it today?* ○ *There was a lot of hot weather last month, in fact it was hot all month long.* ○ *She's taken a month's holiday to visit her parents in Australia.* ○ *We haven't had any homework for months.*

③ **monthly** /'mʌnθli/ *adj, adv* happening every month ○ *He is paying for his car by monthly instalments.* ○ *My monthly salary cheque is late.* ○ *She gets paid monthly.*

monument /'mɒnjʊmənt/ *noun* a stone, building or statue, built in memory of someone who is dead ○ *They put up a monument to the people from the village who died in the war.*

monumental /ˌmɒnjʊ'ment(ə)l/ *adj* **1.** very large and impressive ○ *Brahms' monumental Fourth Symphony* **2.** very serious ○ *He made a monumental error.*

moo /muː/ (**moos, mooing, mooed**) *verb* to make a noise like a cow ○ *The cows were mooing because they wanted to be milked.* (NOTE: + **moo** *n*)

② **mood** /muːd/ *noun* **1.** the way you are feeling at a particular time ○ *Wait until she's in a good mood and then ask her.* ○ *The boss is in a terrible mood this morning.* ○ *Her mood changed as soon as she opened the letter.* ○ *A mood of gloom fell over the office.* **2.** a period of bad temper ○ *Don't talk to the boss – he's in one of his moods.*

moody /'muːdi/ (**moodier, moodiest**) *adj* often in a bad temper; changing quickly from being in a good mood to a bad one (NOTE: + **moodily** *adv*)

② **moon** /muːn/ *noun* an object in the sky like a planet which goes round the Earth and shines at night ○ *The first man walked on the moon in 1969.* ○ *The moon is shining very brightly tonight.* ○ *There's no moon because it's cloudy.* ◇ **once in a blue moon** very rarely (*informal*) ○ *We only go to the theatre once in a blue moon.* ◇ **to be over the moon about something** to be very happy and excited ○ *She's over the moon about her exam results.* ○ *They're absolutely over the moon with their first baby.*

moonbeam /'muːnbiːm/ *noun* a ray of light from the moon

③ **moonlight** /'muːnlaɪt/ *noun* the light from the moon ○ *We could see the path clearly in the moonlight.*

moonlighting /'muːnlaɪtɪŋ/ *noun* the activity of doing a second job, usually in the evening, separate from your regular job (*informal*)

moonlit /'muːnlɪt/ *adj* lit by light from the moon

③ **moor** /mʊə/ *noun* a large area of poor land covered with grass and small bushes ○ *The horsemen galloped across the moor.* ○ *The Lake District is wild country, full of moors and forests.* ■ *verb* (**moors, mooring, moored**) to attach a boat to something ○ *The boat was moored to the river bank.* ○ *He moored his boat with a piece of rope.*

mooring /'mʊərɪŋ/ *noun* **1.** a place where a boat, ship, or aircraft can be held still or tied up **2.** a chain or rope used for holding still or tying up a boat, ship, or aircraft

moose /muːs/ (*plural same*) *noun* a large deer from North America

moot /muːt/ (**moots, mooting, mooted**) *verb* to raise a question ○ *The idea was first mooted in 1967.*

mop /mɒp/ (**mops, mopping, mopped**) *verb* to wash something with a mop ○ *She was mopping the kitchen floor.*

mop up③ *phrasal verb* **1.** to clear up spilt liquid ○ *Use a cloth to mop up the water on the floor.* ○ *We spent days mopping up after the floods.* **2.** to overcome small groups of enemy fighters ○ *It took our soldiers several days to mop up the last pockets of enemy resistance in the mountains.*

mope /məʊp/ (**mopes, moping, moped**) *verb* to sit miserably, thinking about how bad things are

moped /'məʊped/ *noun* a two-wheeled cycle with a low-powered engine (NOTE: Do not confuse with the verb **moped** /'məʊpd/ .)

② **moral** /'mɒrəl/ *adj* **1.** relating to right and wrong behaviour ○ *Judges have a mor-*

al obligation to be impartial. ○ *He refused to join the army on moral grounds.* **2.** relating to good behaviour ○ *She's a very moral person.* ■ *noun* something which you can learn from a story [~of] ○ *There must be a moral in this somewhere.* ○ *The moral of the story is that if you always tell lies, no one will believe you when you tell the truth.*

③ **morale** /məˈrɑːl/ *noun* a confident feeling

moralise /ˈmɒrəlaɪz/ (**moralises, moralising, moralised**), **moralize** *verb* to draw a lesson from a story or event

moralistic /ˌmɒrəˈlɪstɪk/ *adj* attempting or intending to teach people the difference between right and wrong

morality /məˈrælɪti/ *noun* a sense of moral standards

morally /ˈmɒrəli/ *adv* according to the principles of correct human behaviour

moral support /ˌmɒrəl səˈpɔːt/ *noun* encouragement and support intended to give someone more confidence

moratorium /ˌmɒrəˈtɔːriəm/ (*plural* **moratoriums** or **moratoria**) *noun* a temporary stop, such as to repayments of money owed

morbid /ˈmɔːbɪd/ *adj* showing an unhealthy interest in death or unpleasant things ○ *Even as a little boy he showed a morbid curiosity in skeletons.* ○ *All this talk about death and decomposition seems distinctly morbid to me.*

① **more** /mɔː/ *adj* extra, which is added ○ *Do you want any more tea?* ○ *There are many more trains during the week than at the weekend.* ■ *adv* used with adjectives to make the comparative form ○ *The dog was more frightened than I was.* ○ *She is much more intelligent than her sister.* ○ *The dinner was even more unpleasant than I had thought it would be.* ■ *pron* an extra thing or amount ○ *Is there any more of that soup?* ○ *£300 for that suit – that's more than I can afford!* ○ *We've only got nine men, we need two more to make a football team.*

② **moreover** /mɔːrˈəʊvə/ *adv* in addition ○ *Its freezing cold, and moreover you're too young to go out in the dark.*

morgue /mɔːg/ *noun* a building where dead bodies are kept before being buried

① **morning** /ˈmɔːnɪŋ/ *noun* the first part of the day, before 12 o'clock ○ *Every morning he took his briefcase and went to the office.* ○ *Tomorrow morning we will be meeting our Japanese agents.* ○ *Have you read the morning paper?* ○ *If we want to be in Paris for lunch you have to get the early morning train.*

moron /ˈmɔːrɒn/ *noun* a very stupid person (*insult*)

morose /məˈrəʊs/ *adj* miserable and bad-tempered

morphine /ˈmɔːfiːn/ *noun* a drug made from opium, used to relieve pain

morsel /ˈmɔːs(ə)l/ *noun* a small piece, particularly of food

mortal /ˈmɔːt(ə)l/ *adj* **1.** human and therefore bound to die **2.** referring to injury serious enough to cause someone to die ○ *He suffered a mortal blow in the fight.* ■ *noun* an ordinary human being (*informal*)

③ **mortality** /mɔːˈtælɪti/ *noun* the state of being a human, and knowing that all human beings must die ○ *Having a heart attack makes you acutely aware of your own mortality.*

mortally /ˈmɔːt(ə)li/ *adv* ending in death ○ *He was mortally wounded in battle.*

mortar /ˈmɔːtə/ *noun* a bowl for crushing things with a pestle ○ *Crush the seeds with a mortar and pestle.*

③ **mortgage** /ˈmɔːgɪdʒ/ *noun* an agreement by which someone lends money on the security of a property [~on] ○ *He took out a mortgage on the house.* ○ *She bought a house with a £200,000 mortgage.* ■ *verb* (**mortgages, mortgaging, mortgaged**) to give a property as security for a loan ○ *He mortgaged his house to set up his business.* ○ *Because his house was already mortgaged, he had to take out a second mortgage to pay for his car.*

mortified /ˈmɔːtɪfaɪd/ *adj* feeling extreme embarrassment or shame

mortuary /ˈmɔːtjuəri/ (*plural* **mortuaries**) *noun* a place where dead bodies are kept before burial

mosaic /məʊˈzeɪɪk/ *noun* a picture made of tiny pieces of coloured stone, glass, etc., stuck to a wall or floor, etc.

② **mosque** /mɒsk/ *noun* a building where Muslims meet for prayer

③ **mosquito** /mɒˈskiːtəʊ/ *noun* a small flying insect which bites people and animals and sucks their blood

moss /mɒs/ *noun* a small green plant like fur, growing in compact low clumps in damp places on the ground or on stones

① **most** /məʊst/ *adj* the largest number of ○ *Most people go on holiday in the summer.* ○ *He spends most evenings watching TV.* ○ *Most apples are sweet.* ■ *pron* a very large number or amount ○ *Most of the work* *was done by my wife.* ○ *She spent most of the evening on the phone to her sister.* ○ *It rained for most of our holiday.* ○ *Most of the children in the group can ride bikes.* ■ *adv* used with adjectives and 'the' for making the superlative form ○ *She's the most intelligent child in the class.* ○ *The most important thing if you are a sales representative is to be able to drive a car.* ◇ **to make the most of something** to get as much profit or value from something as possible ○ *You should make the most of the warm weather before the snows come.* ◇ **at (the) most** no more than ○ *There were twenty people at the most in the theatre.*

② **mostly** /ˈməʊstli/ *adv* **1.** usually, most often ○ *We sometimes go to France for our holidays, but we mostly stay in Britain.* **2.** almost all ○ *The staff are mostly women of about twenty.*

MOT /ˌem aʊ ˈtiː/ *noun* in the United Kingdom, an annual test to check that a car or other vehicle is safe on the roads

motel /məʊˈtel/ *noun* a hotel for car drivers which is near a main road and where there are plenty of parking spaces

moth /mɒθ/ *noun* a flying insect similar to a butterfly, but which has brown wings and flies mainly at night

① **mother** /ˈmʌðə/ *noun* a woman who has children ○ *He's twenty-two but still lives with his mother.* ○ *Her mother's a dentist.* ○ *Mother! There's someone asking for you on the telephone.*

motherboard /ˈmʌðəbɔːd/ *noun* the main circuit board in a computer

motherhood /ˈmʌðəhʊd/ *noun* the state of being a mother

mother-in-law /ˈmʌðər ɪn lɔː/ (*plural* **mothers-in-law**) *noun* the mother of your wife or husband

motherly /ˈmʌðəli/ *adj* like a mother

mother-of-pearl /ˌmʌðər əv ˈpɜːl/ *noun* a shiny substance found on the inside of oyster shells

Mother's Day /ˈmʌðəz deɪ/ *noun* a day in the spring when mothers get presents or cards or flowers from their children

mother tongue /ˈmʌðə tʌŋ/ *noun* the language which you spoke when you were a little child

③ **motif** /məʊˈtiːf/ *noun* a particular pattern which is repeated in a design or in a piece of music

③ **motion** /ˈməʊʃ(ə)n/ *noun* the act of moving ○ *The motion of the ship made him feel ill.* ◇ **in motion** moving ○ *Do not try to get on or off while the train is in motion.* ◇ **to set something in motion** to make something start to happen ○ *Now that we have planning permission for the new sports hall, we can set things in motion to get the foundations laid.*

motionless /ˈməʊʃ(ə)n(ə)ləs/ *adj* not moving

motion picture /ˌməʊʃ(ə)n ˈpɪktʃə/ *noun US* a cinema film

motivate /ˈməʊtɪveɪt/ (**motivates, motivating, motivated**) *verb* to encourage someone to do something

motivated /ˈməʊtɪˌveɪtɪd/ *adj* having enough interest or determination to do something

motivation /ˌməʊtɪˈveɪʃ(ə)n/ *noun* encouragement or determination to do something

motive /ˈməʊtɪv/ *noun* a reason for doing something ○ *The police are trying to find a motive for the murder.*

motley /ˈmɒtli/ *adj* of varied types or colours

② **motor** /ˈməʊtə/ *noun* the part of a machine which makes it work ○ *The model plane has a tiny electric motor.*

motorbike /ˈməʊtəbaɪk/ *noun* a motorcycle

motorboat /ˈməʊtəbəʊt/ *noun* a boat driven by a motor

motorcade /ˈməʊtəkeɪd/ *noun US* an official procession of cars

motorcycle /ˈməʊtəsaɪk(ə)l/ *noun* a type of large bicycle driven by a motor

motoring /ˈməʊtərɪŋ/ *noun* the driving of a car (*dated*) ○ *The costs of motoring or motoring costs seem to increase year by year.*

motorised /ˈməʊtəraɪzd/, **motorized** *adj* driven by, or working with the help of a motor

② **motorist** /ˈməʊtərɪst/ *noun* a person who drives a car

motor neurone disease /ˌməʊtə ˈnjʊərəʊn dɪˌziːz/ *noun* an illness that affects the motor neurons, gradually affecting all the body's physical functions

motor racing /ˌməʊtə ˈreɪsɪŋ/ *noun* the sport of racing fast cars

motor vehicle /ˌməʊtə ˈviːɪk(ə)l/ *noun* any road vehicle that works by means of an engine

② **motorway** /ˈməʊtəweɪ/ *noun* a road with several lanes, on which traffic can travel at high speeds

mottled /ˈmɒt(ə)ld/ *adj* marked with an uneven pattern of different colours

motto /ˈmɒtəʊ/ *noun* a short phrase which is used to sum up an attitude ○ *'Be Prepared' is the motto of the Scouts.*

③ **mould** /məʊld/, **mold** *noun* **1.** a type of soft earth **2.** a hollow shape into which a liquid is poured, so that when the liquid becomes hard it takes that shape ○ *Gold bars are made by pouring molten gold into moulds.* **3.** a grey fungus which looks like powder ○ *Throw that bread away – it's got mould on it.* (NOTE: [all noun senses] The US spelling is **mold**.) ■ *verb* (**moulds, moulding, moulded**) to shape something ○ *She moulded a little dog out of clay.*

moulding /ˈməʊldɪŋ/ *noun* a thing which has been moulded, especially plaster decorations on the ceiling of a room (NOTE: The US spelling is **molding**.)

mouldy /ˈməʊldi/ *adj* covered with mould (NOTE: The US spelling is **moldy**.)

moult /məʊlt/ (**moults, moulting, moulted**), **molt** *verb* to lose feathers or hair at a certain period of the year (NOTE: The US spelling is **molt**.)

mound /maʊnd/ *noun* **1.** a small hill ○ *They built a mound of stones to mark the farthest point they reached.* ○ *The castle is built on top of a mound.* ○ *Stonehenge is surrounded by burial mounds.* **2.** a heap of things ○ *There's a mound of letters waiting to be signed.*

mount /maʊnt/ (**mounts, mounting, mounted**) *verb* **1.** to climb on to something; to climb up something ○ *They mounted their horses and rode off.* ○ *He mounted the stairs two at a time.* ○ *The car turned, mounted the pavement, and hit a wall.* **2.** to increase ○ *Tension is mounting as the time for the football final approaches.*

② **mountain** /ˈmaʊntɪn/ *noun* a very high piece of land, rising much higher than the land which surrounds it ○ *Every weekend we go climbing in the Scottish mountains.*

mountain bike /ˈmaʊntɪn baɪk/ *noun* a strong bike with thick tyres, used for country cycling

mountaineer /ˌmaʊntɪˈnɪə/ *noun* a person who climbs mountains as a sport

mountaineering /ˌmaʊntɪˈnɪərɪŋ/ *noun* the sport of climbing mountains

mountainous /ˈmaʊntɪnəs/ *adj* with many high mountains ○ *It is a mountainous region, and very difficult for tanks and artillery.* ○ *Parts of Scotland are very mountainous.*

③ **mounting** /ˈmaʊntɪŋ/ *adj* increasing

mourn /mɔːn/ (**mourns, mourning, mourned**) *verb* to feel very sad about someone or something

mourner /ˈmɔːnə/ *noun* a person who mourns someone who has died

mournful /ˈmɔːnf(ə)l/ *adj* very sad

mourning /ˈmɔːnɪŋ/ *noun* **1.** a period of time when you grieve over the death of a person ○ *The official period of mourning for the dead president was one week.* **2.** dark clothes worn as a mark of respect for someone who has died ○ *Only the close family members wore mourning to the funeral.* (NOTE: Do not confuse with **morning**.)

② **mouse** /maʊs/ (*plural* **mice**) *noun* **1.** a small animal with a long tail, often living in holes in the walls of houses ○ *I saw a mouse sitting in the middle of the kitchen floor.* ○ *Our cat is good at catching mice.* **2.** a piece of computer equipment which is held in the hand and moved across a flat surface, used to control activity on the screen ○ *You can cut, paste and copy using the mouse.* ○ *Using the mouse, move the cursor to the start button and click twice.* ○ *Click twice on the mouse to start the program.*

mouse mat /maʊs mæt/, **mouse pad** /maʊs pæd/ *noun* a soft plastic mat on which you move a mouse around

mousse /muːs/ *noun* a light food made of whipped eggs, cream and flavouring

moustache /məˈstɑːʃ/ *noun* the hair grown on the upper lip (NOTE: The US spelling is **mustache**.)

mouth[1] /maʊθ/ *noun* **1.** the opening in your face through which you take in food and drink, and which has your teeth and tongue inside ○ *It's not polite to talk with your mouth full.* ○ *He snored because he slept with his mouth open.* ○ *The cat was carrying a mouse in its mouth.* **2.** a wide or round entrance ○ *The mouth of the cave is hidden by bushes.* ○ *The train came out of the mouth of the tunnel.* ○ *New York is built on the mouth of the Hudson river.*

mouth[2] /maʊð/ (**mouths, mouthing, mouthed**) *verb* to speak without making any sound ○ *She mouthed 'No' across the room.*

mouthful /ˈmaʊθfʊl/ *noun* **1.** an amount which you can hold in your mouth ○ *He took a mouthful of meat and chewed hard.* ○ *The baby took a mouthful and immediately spat it out.* ○ *She dived into the waves and got a mouthful of salt water.* **2.** a complicated word or phrase ○ *I'll spell the* *name of the Welsh village for you – it's a bit of a mouthful.*

mouth-organ /ˈmaʊθ ˌɔːgən/ *noun* a small musical instrument which you play by blowing and moving across your mouth to get different notes

mouthpiece /ˈmaʊθpiːs/ *noun* **1.** a part of a musical instrument which goes into the mouth ○ *There is a reed attached to the mouthpiece of a clarinet.* **2.** the part of a telephone that you speak into ○ *He put his hand over the mouthpiece so she couldn't hear what he was saying.* **3.** a person who speaks on behalf of someone, especially a political party ○ *She acts as the mouthpiece for the party.*

mouthwash /ˈmaʊθwɒʃ/ *noun* an antiseptic solution used to treat infection in the mouth or bad breath

mouth-watering /ˈmaʊθ ˌwɔːtərɪŋ/ *adj* which looks and smells so delicious that it makes your mouth water

① **move** /muːv/ *noun* **1.** a change in position ○ *The police were watching every move he made.* **2.** an action done to achieve something [~towards/~into] ○ *It was a clever move to get here early before the crowds arrive.* ○ *The agreement is a move towards a fairer system.* ○ *The company is planning a move into children's clothes.* □ **what's the next move?** what do we have to do next? □ **who will make the first move?** who will act first? **3.** a change of house or office ■ *verb* (**moves, moving, moved**) **1.** to change the place of something ○ *Move the chairs to the side of the room.* ○ *Who's moved my drink?* ○ *He moved his hand to show he had heard.* **2.** to change your position ○ *Some animal was moving about outside the tent.* ○ *The only thing moving was the tip of the cat's tail.* ◇ **get a move on!** hurry up! ◇ **on the move** being active and moving around ○ *After I've been on the move all day I just want to get home and go to bed.* ◇ **to make a move** to leave somewhere ○ *It's time to make a move.*

move in③ *phrasal verb* **1.** to put your possessions into a new house and start to live there ○ *They only moved in last week.* ○ *They got married and moved in with her parents.* **2.** to come together as a group ○ *The lions moved in for the kill.* ○ *When everything is ready the police will move in on the gang.*

move on③ *phrasal verb* **1.** to go forward ○ *We stopped for a quick visit to the cathedral and then moved on to the next town.* **2.** to make people move ○ *The police moved the crowd on.* **3.** to deal with the next item ○ *We will now move on to item 10 on the agenda.*

① **movement** /ˈmuːvmənt/ *noun* an act of moving, not being still ○ *There was hardly any movement in the trees.* ○ *All you could see was a slight movement of the tiger's tail.*

② **movie** /ˈmuːvi/ *noun especially US* a cinema film ○ *We watch a movie most weekends.*

movie star /ˈmuːvi stɑː/ *noun US* a very successful film actor

movie theater /ˈmuːvi ˌθɪətə/ *noun US* a building where films are shown

② **moving** /ˈmuːvɪŋ/ *adj* making you feel emotion ○ *a moving story* ○ *The funeral was very moving.*

mow /məʊ/ (**mows, mowing, mowed, mown** or **mowed**) *verb* to cut grass, hay, etc.

mow down *phrasal verb* to kill

mower /ˈməʊə/ *noun* a machine which cuts grass

① **MP** *abbr* member of parliament

MP3 /ˌem piː ˈθriː/ *noun* **1.** a computer file standard which you can use to get and play music from the Internet **2.** a file which contains music in MP3 format

mpg /ˈempiːˈdʒiː/ *abbr* miles per gallon

mph *abbr* miles per hour

MPV /ˌem piː ˈviː/ *noun* a car similar to a van, which usually has three rows of seats

① **Mr** /ˈmɪstə/ *noun* the polite title given to a man ○ (at the beginning of a letter) *Dear Mr Smith,* ○ *Mr Jones is our new sales manager.* ○ *Here are Mr and Mrs Smith.* (NOTE: used before a surname, sometimes with both the first name and surname)

MRI *abbr* magnetic resonance imaging

① **Mrs** /ˈmɪsɪz/ *noun* the title given to a married woman ○ (at the beginning of a letter) *Dear Mrs Jones,* ○ *Mrs Jones is our manager.* (NOTE: used before a surname, sometimes with both the first name and surname.)

① **Ms** /məz, mɪz/ *noun* (*at the beginning of a letter*) a way of referring to a woman without saying whether or not she is married (NOTE: **Ms** is used with a surname, sometimes with both the first name and surname.)

① **much** /mʌtʃ/ *adj* a lot of ○ *with much love from Aunt Mary* ○ *How much sugar do you need?* ○ *I never take much money with me when I go on holiday.* ○ *She eats too much meat.* ■ *adv* a lot ○ *He's feeling much* *better today.* ○ *It's much less cold in the south of the country.* ○ *Does it matter very much?* ○ *Much as I like her, I don't want to share an office with her.* ■ *pron* a lot ○ *He didn't write much in his exam.* ○ *Much of the work has already been done.* ◇ **as much as** the same quantity of something as ○ *You haven't eaten as much fruit as she has.*

muck /mʌk/ *noun* farmyard manure

muck in *phrasal verb* to do work together (*informal*)

muck up *phrasal verb* to ruin something (*informal*)

mucky /ˈmʌki/ (**muckier, muckiest**) *adj* very dirty (*informal*)

mucus /ˈmjuːkəs/ *noun* a slippery liquid secreted by mucous membranes inside the body, which protects the membranes (NOTE: Do not confuse with **mucous**.)

③ **mud** /mʌd/ *noun* wet earth

muddle /ˈmʌd(ə)l/ *noun* a confused mess ○ *The papers were lying all over the floor in a muddle.* ○ *She tried to put up the tent on her own but she got into a muddle.* ○ *There was some muddle over the tickets.* ■ *verb* (**muddles, muddling, muddled**) to confuse, to mix up ○ *Don't muddle the papers up – I've just put them in order.* ○ *Granny often muddles up our names.* ○ *I always muddle him with his brother – they are very alike.*

muddle through *phrasal verb* to get through your work, to succeed in a confused way

muddled /ˈmʌd(ə)ld/ *adj* confused, not clear and not well organised

③ **muddy** /ˈmʌdi/ (**muddier, muddiest**) *adj* full of mud; covered with mud

mudflap /ˈmʌdflæp/ *noun* a flap hanging behind the wheel of a car to protect the bodywork from damage by dirt or stones

muesli /ˈmjuːzli/ *noun* a breakfast food of flakes of cereal, dried fruit, etc., eaten with milk

muffin /ˈmʌfɪn/ *noun* a small round cake eaten warm with butter

muffle /ˈmʌf(ə)l/ (**muffles, muffling, muffled**) *verb* **1.** to wrap someone up in cloth for warmth ○ *She muffled herself in a big woollen shawl.* **2.** to make a loud noise quieter ○ *She wrapped a cloth around the hammer to muffle the sound of the blows.*

③ **mug** /mʌg/ *noun* a large cup with a handle ○ *She passed round mugs.* ■ *verb* (**mugs, mugging, mugged**) to attack and steal from someone in the street ○ *She was mugged as she was looking for her car keys.* ○ *She's afraid of going out at night for fear of being mugged.* ○ *The gang specialises in mugging tourists.*

muggy /ˈmʌgi/ *adj* (*of weather*) warm and wet

mug shot /ˈmʌg ʃɒt/ *noun* a photograph of someone's face

mule /mjuːl/ *noun* **1.** a cross between a donkey and a horse ○ *He entered the town riding on a mule.* **2.** a light shoe with no back part at the heel

mull /mʌl/ (**mulls, mulling, mulled**) *verb*

mull over *phrasal verb* to think about or consider something

mullah /ˈmʌlə/ *noun* a title of respect for a learned Muslim man

multicultural /ˌmʌltiˈkʌltʃərəl/ *adj* referring to several cultures together

multigym /ˈmʌltɪˌdʒɪm/ *noun* a piece of exercise equipment with a range of weights

multilateral /ˌmʌltiˈlæt(ə)rəl/ *adj* between several people or groups

multimedia /ˈmʌltiˌmiːdiə/ *noun* a means of communication using several different media, such as sound, moving images, computer screens, etc. ○ *The company gave a multimedia presentation to show off its new product range.* ○ *The pop concert was a spectacular multimedia event.*

multimillionaire /ˌmʌltimɪljəˈneə/ *noun* a person who has several million pounds or dollars

multinational /ˌmʌltiˈnæʃ(ə)nəl/ *noun* a company which operates in several different countries ○ *Our business has been bought by one of the big multinationals.*

③ **multiple** /ˈmʌltɪp(ə)l/ *adj* involving many people or things ○ *She was taken to hospital suffering from multiple injuries.*

multiple-choice /ˈmʌltɪp(ə)l tʃɔɪs/ *adj* (*of an exam question*) in which the task is to choose the correct answer from a list of usually 4 possible answers, marked A, B, C and D

multiplex /ˈmʌltɪpleks/ *noun* **1.** a large cinema building containing several separate projection rooms **2.** the sending of several different signals along one communications line

multiplicity /ˌmʌltɪˈplɪsəti/ *noun* a large variety of things

③ **multiply** /ˈmʌltɪplaɪ/ (**multiplies, multiplying, multiplied**) *verb* to calculate the result when several numbers are added together a certain number of times ○ *Square measurements are calculated by multiply-*

ing length by width. ○ *Ten multiplied by five gives fifty.*

multi-purpose /ˌmʌlti ˈpɜːpəs/ *adj* having several different uses

multiracial /ˌmʌltiˈreɪʃ(ə)l/ *adj* referring to various races

multi-storey /ˌmʌltiˈstɔːri/ *adj* with several storeys (NOTE: The US spelling is **multi-story**.)

multitasking /ˈmʌltiˌtɑːskɪŋ/ *noun* the activity of doing two or more jobs at the same time

multitude /ˈmʌltɪtjuːd/ *noun* **1.** a very large number **2.** a crowd of people ○ *He stood up to address the assembled multitude.*

① **mum** /mʌm/ same as **mummy**

mumble /ˈmʌmbəl/ (**mumbles, mumbling, mumbled**) *verb* to speak in a low voice which is not clear ○ *He mumbled an excuse and left the room.* ○ *She mumbled something about the telephone and went to the back of the shop.*

mumbo-jumbo /ˌmʌmbəʊ ˈdʒʌmbəʊ/ *noun* **1.** complicated and confusing language that is difficult to understand **2.** language or practices that are regarded as unusual or strange

① **mummy** /ˈmʌmi/ (*plural* **mummies**) *noun* **1.** a child's name for mother ○ *Tell your mum I want to see her.* ○ *Hello, John, is your mummy at home?* ○ *Mummy! can I have a biscuit?* **2.** a dead body which has been treated with chemicals to stop it decaying ○ *We went to see the Egyptian mummies in the British Museum.*

munch /mʌntʃ/ (**munches, munching, munched**) *verb* to eat noisily something such as an apple or raw carrot, with a regular movement of your mouth

mundane /mʌnˈdeɪn/ *adj* ordinary, not exciting

② **municipal** /mjuːˈnɪsɪp(ə)l/ *adj* referring to a town which has its own local government

munitions /mjuːˈnɪʃ(ə)nz/ *plural noun* weapons and ammunition ○ *She works in a munitions factory.*

mural /ˈmjʊərəl/ *noun* a painting on a wall ○ *The murals were painted by Giotto in the fourteenth century.* ◊ **fresco**

② **murder** /ˈmɜːdə/ *noun* the act of deliberately killing someone ○ *The murder was committed during the night.* ○ *She was accused of murder.* ○ *They denied the murder charge.* Compare **manslaughter** ■ *verb* (**murders, murdering, murdered**) to kill someone deliberately ○ *He was accused of murdering a policeman.*

② **murderer** /ˈmɜːdərə/ *noun* a person who has committed a murder

murderous /ˈmɜːdərəs/ *adj* likely to kill

murky /ˈmɜːki/ (**murkier, murkiest**) *adj* dark and dirty

murmur /ˈmɜːmə/ *noun* a low sound of people talking ○ *There was a murmur of voices in the hall.* ■ *verb* (**murmurs, murmuring, murmured**) to speak very quietly ○ *She murmured something and closed her eyes.*

② **muscle** /ˈmʌs(ə)l/ *noun* one of the part of the body which makes other parts move ○ *He has very powerful arm muscles.*

muscular /ˈmʌskjʊlə/ *adj* **1.** referring to muscles ○ *She suffered from muscular pain after working in the garden.* **2.** with big muscles ○ *He has very muscular arms.* ○ *A couple of muscular bouncers stood at the door of the club.*

muse /mjuːz/ (**muses, musing, mused**) *verb* to think deeply ○ *She spent hours musing about her youth.* ○ *He was sitting in his garden musing on the beauty of the autumn colours.*

② **museum** /mjuːˈziːəm/ *noun* a building which you can visit to see a collection of valuable or rare objects ○ *The National Museum of Art* ○ *The museum has a rich collection of Italian paintings.*

mush /mʌʃ/ *noun* **1.** a soft, semi-liquid substance **2.** over-emotional or soppy words or ideas

③ **mushroom** /ˈmʌʃruːm/ *noun* a round white or brown fungus which can be eaten ○ *Do you want fried mushrooms with your steak?* ○ *She ordered a mushroom omelette.* (NOTE: Fungi which are poisonous are called **toadstools**.)

① **music** /ˈmjuːzɪk/ *noun* **1.** the sound made when you sing or play an instrument ○ *Do you like Russian music?* ○ *She's taking music lessons.* ○ *Her music teacher says she plays the violin very well.* **2.** written signs which you read to play an instrument ○ *Here's some music, see if you can play it on the piano.* ○ *He can play the piano by ear – he doesn't need any music.*

③ **musical** /ˈmjuːzɪk(ə)l/ *adj* relating to music ○ *Do you play any musical instrument?*

musician /mjʊˈzɪʃ(ə)n/ *noun* a person whose job is to play music ○ *a group of young musicians playing the street* ○ *The actors applauded the group of musicians who had played during 'Twelfth Night'.*

② **Muslim** /ˈmʊzlɪm/ *adj* relating to the religion of the prophet Muhammad ■ *noun* a person who follows the religion of the prophet Muhammad

muslin /ˈmʌzlɪn/ *noun* a very fine thin cotton cloth

mussel /ˈmʌs(ə)l/ *noun* a small shellfish, with a blue black shell (NOTE: Do not confuse with **muscle**.)

① **must** /məst, mʌst/ *modal verb* **1.** it is necessary that ○ *You must go to bed before eleven, or your mother will be angry.* ○ *We mustn't be late or we'll miss the last bus.* ○ *You must hurry up if you want to see the TV programme.* ○ *Must you really go so soon?* (NOTE: The negative is **must not** or, especially in speaking, **mustn't**; **needn't** is also used. Note also the meanings: **mustn't** = not allowed; **needn't** = not necessary: *We mustn't be late; You needn't hurry.*) **2.** used for showing that you think something is very likely ○ *I must have left my briefcase on the train.* ○ *There is someone knocking at the door – it must be the postman.* ○ *You must be wet through after walking in the rain.* (NOTE: The negative is **can't**: *It can't be the doctor.* The past tense is **had to**: *I must go to the dentist; Yesterday I had to go to the dentist.* The negative is **didn't have to**. The perfect tense is **must have**: *I must have left it on the train.* The negative is **can't have**: *I can't have left it on the train.* Note also that **must** is usually used with other verbs and is not followed by **to**.) **3.** used for encouraging someone to do something ○ *You must go and see this film -it's excellent.* ■ *noun* something important ○ *When in Florida, a trip to the Everglades is a must.*

muster /ˈmʌstə/ (**musters, mustering, mustered**) *verb* to gather something, or a number of things or people, together ○ *He tried to muster all his supporters before the vote.* ○ *I find it difficult to muster enough energy to go for a walk after lunch.*

mustn't /ˈmʌs(ə)nt/ *short for* must not

musty /ˈmʌsti/ (**mustier, mustiest**) *adj* smelling damp, rotten or stale; smelling old

mutant /ˈmjuːt(ə)nt/ *noun* an organism carrying a gene in which mutation has occurred ○ *This plant appears to be a mutant.*

mutate /mjuːˈteɪt/ (**mutates, mutating, mutated**) *verb* to undergo a change in structure which changes a gene or chromosome (NOTE: + **mutation** *n*)

mute /mjuːt/ *adj* **1.** not speaking ○ *A look of mute horror crossed her face.* **2.** which is not pronounced ○ *In the word 'crumb' the letter 'b' is mute.*

muted /ˈmjuːtɪd/ *adj* **1.** quiet, not noisy ○ *The press gave the proposal a muted welcome.* ○ *Criticism of the government's proposals has been muted.* **2.** not bright ○ *I prefer muted colours for the sitting room.*

mutilate /ˈmjuːtɪleɪt/ (**mutilates, mutilating, mutilated**) *verb* to damage something by cutting off part of it (NOTE: + **mutilation** *n*)

mutinous /ˈmjuːtɪnəs/ *adj* likely to take part in a mutiny, likely not to obey

mutiny /ˈmjuːtɪni/ *noun* a rebellion against someone in a position of authority such as the officers in the army or navy ○ *The officers kept a lookout for any signs of mutiny among the crew.* (NOTE: + **mutiny** *v*)

mutter /ˈmʌtə/ (**mutters, muttering, muttered**) *verb* to mumble, to speak in a low and indistinct voice ○ *Don't mutter, I can't understand you.* ○ *He muttered something about the telephone and went to the back of the shop.*

mutton /ˈmʌt(ə)n/ *noun* the meat of a sheep (NOTE: not very often used: **lamb** is generally used for all meat from sheep as well as lambs)

mutual /ˈmjuːtʃuəl/ *adj* referring to what is done by two people, countries, companies, etc., to each other □ **by mutual agreement, by mutual consent** with the agreement of both parties ○ *By mutual agreement they have decided to sell the flat and split the money between them.*

mutually /ˈmjuːtʃuəli/ *adv* to two people; by two people

muzzle /ˈmʌz(ə)l/ *noun* **1.** the front part of an animal's head, especially the mouth, jaws and nose ○ *She stroked the horse's long, silky muzzle.* **2.** a system of straps placed round the mouth of a dog to prevent it from biting ○ *Our dog has to wear a muzzle when he's taken for a walk.* **3.** the mouth of a gun ○ *She found herself looking down the muzzle of a gun.* ○ *The army was equipped with muzzle-loading rifles.* ■ *verb* (**muzzles, muzzling, muzzled**) **1.** to stop someone from saying what they want to publicly **2.** to put a muzzle on a dog to prevent it biting ○ *I always muzzle my dog when I walk him through the children's playground.*

① **my** /maɪ/ *adj* belonging to me ○ *Is that my pen you're using?* ○ *Have you seen my glasses anywhere?* ○ *We went skiing and I broke my leg.*

myriad /ˈmɪriəd/ *noun* a very large number ○ *There are myriads of islands in the mouth of the river.* ○ *The sky was bright with a myriad of stars.*

① **myself** /maɪˈself/ *pron* used for referring back to ‘I’ ○ *I hurt myself climbing down the ladder.* ○ *It’s true – I saw it myself.* ○ *I enjoyed myself a lot at the party.* ◇ **all by myself** all alone, with no one else ○ *I built the house all by myself.* ○ *I don’t like being all by myself in the house at night.*

③ **mysterious** /mɪˈstɪəriəs/ *adj* which cannot be explained

③ **mystery** /ˈmɪst(ə)ri/ (*plural* **mysteries**) *noun* something that cannot be explained ○ *The police finally cleared up the mystery of the missing body.* ○ *It’s a mystery how the box came to be hidden under her bed.*

mystic /ˈmɪstɪk/ *noun* a person who attempts to achieve union with God through prayer, meditation, etc.

mystical /ˈmɪstɪk(ə)l/ *adj* in contact with spiritual forces by some process which cannot be understood

mysticism /ˈmɪstɪsɪz(ə)m/ *noun* a religion based on attempts to achieve union with God by prayer and meditation

mystify /ˈmɪstɪfaɪ/ (**mystifies, mystifying, mystified**) *verb* to puzzle someone

mystique /mɪˈstiːk/ *noun* a mysterious atmosphere about a person or thing

myth /mɪθ/ *noun* an ancient story about gods ○ *poems based on the myths of Greece and Rome*

mythical /ˈmɪθɪk(ə)l/ *adj* **1.** referring to ancient tales of gods ○ *The unicorn is a mythical animal.* **2.** untrue, which does not exist ○ *He keeps talking about some mythical order from Japan.*

mythology /mɪˈθɒlədʒi/ *noun* ancient folk stories from a particular source ○ *The floor was covered with mosaics showing scenes from Greek mythology.* ○ *According to ancient Scandinavian mythology, he cut off the head of the dragon.*

N

n /en/, **N** *noun* the fourteenth letter of the alphabet, between M and O

N *abbr* **1.** north **2.** northern

nab /næb/ (**nabs, nabbing, nabbed**) *verb* **1.** to snatch something quickly (*informal*) ○ *When we came down to the pool we found that the others had nabbed all the best seats.* ○ *Pass me that bottle before anyone else nabs it.* **2.** to arrest someone ○ *The police nabbed him as he was coming out of the bank.*

naff /næf/ *adj* attempting to be stylish, but instead appearing boring or silly

nag /næg/ (**nags, nagging, nagged**) *verb* **1.** to ask someone over and over again for something or to do something ○ *They been nagging me about changing the date for weeks.* ○ *She's been nagging me to buy a new car.* **2.** to keep worrying someone [~at] ○ *The feeling that he had met her somewhere before kept nagging at him.*

nagging /ˈnægɪŋ/ *adj* that worries you over a long period of time

③ **nail** /neɪl/ *noun* **1.** a small thin metal object which you use for attaching two pieces of a hard material such as wood ○ *Hit the nail hard with the hammer.* ○ *You need a hammer to knock that nail in.* **2.** the hard part at the end of your fingers and toes ○ *She painted her nails red.* ■ *verb* (**nails, nailing, nailed**) to attach something with nails ○ *He nailed the notice to the door.* ◇ **to hit the nail on the head** to judge something accurately (*informal*)

nail down *phrasal verb* to attach something flat with nails ○ *They nailed down the floorboards* or *they nailed the floorboards down.*

nail file /ˈneɪl faɪl/ *noun* a flat stick covered with sandpaper, used to smooth your fingernails

nail polish /neɪl ˈpɒlɪʃ/ *noun* same as **nail varnish**

nail varnish /ˈneɪl ˌvɑːnɪʃ/ *noun* a liquid which is put on fingernails or toenails, and which dries quickly to form a hard, shiny surface

naive /naɪˈiːv/ *adj* innocent, lacking experience

naked /ˈneɪkɪd/ *adj* not wearing clothes ○ *The little children were playing in the river stark naked.* ○ *A naked man was standing on the balcony.*

① **name** /neɪm/ *noun* a special way of calling someone or something ○ *Hello! My name's James.* ○ *What's the name of the shop next to the post office?* □ **to put your name down for something** to apply for something ○ *She put her name down to join the club.* ■ *verb* (**names, naming, named**) to call someone or something by a name ○ *They named him Nicholas.* ○ *They have a black cat named Jonah.* □ **to name someone after someone** to give someone the same name as someone else ○ *They named their son Peter after his grandfather.*

name-dropping /ˈneɪmˌdrɒpɪŋ/ *noun* the practice of mentioning the names of famous people whom you know, with the intention of impressing those who are listening

nameless /ˈneɪmləs/ *adj* **1.** with no name **2.** not to be mentioned because it is disgusting or frightening

namely /ˈneɪmli/ *adv* that is to say

namesake /ˈneɪmseɪk/ *noun* a person with the same name as another

nan /næn/ *noun* a type of flat bread, often eaten with curry

nap /næp/ *noun* a short sleep ○ *After lunch he always takes a little nap.* (NOTE: + **nap** *v*)

nape /neɪp/ *noun* the back of the neck

napkin /ˈnæpkɪn/ *noun* **1.** a small square of cloth or paper provided for each person at a meal table, and may be used for cleaning fingers or mouth, or to protect clothes **2.** a nappy ○ *The baby must have his napkin changed.*

③ **nappy** /ˈnæpi/ (*plural* **nappies**) *noun* a cloth which is wrapped round a baby's bottom to absorb urine and faeces

narcissism /ˈnɑːsɪsɪz(ə)m/ *noun* a tendency to admire yourself, especially your own appearance

narcotic /nɑːˈkɒtɪk/ *noun* a pain-relieving drug which makes a patient sleep ○ *The doctor put her to sleep with a powerful narcotic.*

narrate /nəˈreɪt/ (**narrates, narrating, narrated**) *verb* to tell a story

narration /nəˈreɪʃ(ə)n/ *noun* speaking or writing about things that have happened

narrative /ˈnærətɪv/ *noun* a written story ○ *He's writing a narrative about their journeys in South America.*

narrator /nəˈreɪtə/ *noun* a person who tells a story

② **narrow** /ˈnærəʊ/ *adj* not wide ○ *Why is your bicycle seat so narrow?* ○ *We went down a narrow passage to the shop.* ■ *verb* (**narrows, narrowing, narrowed**) to become less wide ○ *The road narrows suddenly, and there is hardly enough room for two cars to pass.*

narrowly /ˈnærəʊli/ *adv* only just

narrow-minded /ˌnærəʊ ˈmaɪndɪd/ *adj* not tolerant of others' views, not capable of seeing many points of view

nasal /ˈneɪz(ə)l/ *adj* **1.** referring to the nose ○ *She used nasal drops to try to cure her cold.* **2.** speaking as if through the nose ○ *He speaks with a nasal accent.*

② **nasty** /ˈnɑːsti/ *adj* unpleasant

② **nation** /ˈneɪʃ(ə)n/ *noun* **1.** a country ○ *the member nations of the EU* **2.** the people living in a country ○ *The whole nation was shocked by the terrible events.*

① **national** /ˈnæʃ(ə)nəl/ *adj* belonging to a country ○ *We want to celebrate our national culture.* ○ *The story appeared in the national newspapers.*

national anthem /ˌnæʃ(ə)nəl ˈænθəm/ *noun* a piece of music which is used to represent the nation officially, and is played at official ceremonies

national curriculum /ˌnæʃ(ə)nəl kəˈrɪkjʊləm/ *noun* the subjects studied at school by all children aged between 5 and 16 in England and Wales (NOTE: The National curriculum is made up of three 'core' subjects – English, maths and science; and seven 'foundation' subjects – art, design and technology, geography, history, music, physical education, and a foreign language.)

National Insurance /ˌnæʃ(ə)nəl ɪnˈʃʊərəns/ *noun* a government-run insurance which provides for state medical care, unemployment payments, etc.

nationalise (**nationalises, nationalising, nationalised**), **nationalize** (**nationalizes, nationalizing, nationalized**) *verb* to put a privately-owned industry under state ownership and control

nationalism /ˈnæʃ(ə)nəˌlɪz(ə)m/ *noun* **1.** the political opinion of wanting independence for your country ○ *During the occupation, all feelings of nationalism had to be suppressed.* **2.** a feeling of great pride in your country, or a feeling that your country is better than others ○ *Danish nationalism as shown by their football supporters.*

nationalist /ˈnæʃ(ə)nəlɪst/ *noun* a person who wants his or her country to be independent ○ *a Welsh nationalist* ○ *The nationalists have not been invited to the negotiations.*

nationalistic /ˌnæʃ(ə)nəˈlɪstɪk/ *adj* strongly supporting your own country

nationality /ˌnæʃəˈnælɪti/ (*plural* **nationalities**) *noun* the status of being a citizen of a state ○ *He is of German nationality.*

national park[1] /ˌnæʃ(ə)nəl ˈpɑːk/ *noun* an area of land protected by the government for people to enjoy ○ *The Peak District in Derbyshire is a national park.* ○ *We went camping in the national park.*

③ **national park**[2] /ˌnæʃ(ə)nəl ˈpɑːk/ *noun* an area of land protected by the government for people to enjoy ○ *The Peak District in Derbyshire is a national park.*

national security /ˌnæʃ(ə)nəl sɪˈkjʊərəti/ *noun* the systems that are intended to protect a nation from danger

national service /ˌnæʃ(ə)nəl ˈsɜːvɪs/ *noun* in some countries, a period that citizens must spend working in their national armed forces

nation-state /ˌneɪʃ(ə)n ˈsteɪt/ *noun* a country which is an independent political unit, formed of people with the same nationality and often the same language and traditions

nationwide /ˈneɪʃ(ə)nwaɪd/ *adj* all over the country ○ *The union called for a nationwide strike.* ○ *We offer a nationwide delivery service.*

③ **native** /ˈneɪtɪv/ *noun* **1.** a person born in a particular place ○ *She's a native of Cornwall.* **2.** a flower, bird, etc., which has always been in a place ○ *The robin is a native of the British Isles.* ■ *adj* belonging to a country ○ *The tiger is native to India.*

Native American /ˌneɪtɪv əˈmerɪkən/ *noun* a member of any of the peoples who were living in North, Central, and South America before the arrival of Europeans

③ **native speaker** /ˌneɪtɪv 'spiːkə/ *noun* a person who speaks a language from childhood

natter /'nætə/ *noun* a casual friendly talk (*informal*) ○ *Come round for coffee tomorrow and we can have a natter.* (NOTE: + **natter** *v*)

① **natural** /'nætʃ(ə)rəl/ *adj* **1.** ordinary, not unusual ○ *Her behaviour at the meeting was quite natural.* ○ *It's natural to worry about your first baby.* **2.** coming from nature, and not produced or caused by people ○ *Do you think the colour of her hair is natural? ○ Yes, she's a natural blonde.* ○ *The inquest decided that he died from natural causes.*

natural gas /ˌnætʃ(ə)rəl 'gæs/ *noun* gas which is found in the earth and not made in a gasworks

natural history /ˌnætʃ(ə)rəl 'hɪst(ə)ri/ *noun* the study of plants and animals

naturalist /'nætʃ(ə)rəlɪst/ *noun* a person who is interested in and studies natural history

① **naturally** /'nætʃ(ə)rəli/ *adv* of course ○ *Naturally the top team beat the bottom team.* ○ *Do you want to watch the game? – Naturally!*

natural resources /ˌnætʃ(ə)rəl rɪ 'zɔːsɪz/ *plural noun* minerals, energy sources, etc., which can be used commercially, such as coal or water power ○ *Canada is a country which is very rich in natural resources.*

① **nature** /'neɪtʃⁿə/ *noun* **1.** plants and animals ○ *We must try to protect nature and the environment.* **2.** the character of a person, thing, or animal ○ *By living there, you discover the true nature of the country.* ○ *He has a very aggressive nature.*

nature reserve /'neɪtʃə rɪˌzɜːv/ *noun* an area of land where animals and plants are protected

③ **naughty** /'nɔːti/ (**naughtier, naughtiest**) *adj* (*usually of a child*) causing trouble and not obedient to adults ○ *Children who are naughty should be punished.* ○ *It was very naughty of you to put glue on your daddy's chair.* (NOTE: + **naughtily** *adv*; **naughtiness** *n*)

nausea /'nɔːziə/ *noun* a feeling of sickness, a desire to vomit

nauseating /'nɔːzieɪtɪŋ/ *adj* which makes you sick or disgusted

nauseous /'nɔːziəs/ *adj US* feeling sick, feeling about to vomit

nautical /'nɔːtɪk(ə)l/ *adj* referring to ships and the sea

naval /'neɪv(ə)l/ *adj* referring to the navy

navel /'neɪv(ə)l/ *noun* a depression in the middle of the abdomen, just below the waist, where the umbilical cord was detached after birth (NOTE: In children's language a navel is called a **belly button** or **tummy button**. Do not confuse with **naval**.)

navigate /'nævɪgeɪt/ (**navigates, navigating, navigated**) *verb* **1.** to guide a ship or aircraft ○ *The pilot navigated the boat into the harbour.* **2.** to give directions to the driver of a car ○ *Can you navigate as far as Marble Arch? – I know my way from there.*

③ **navigation** /ˌnævɪ'geɪʃ(ə)n/ *noun* **1.** the job of finding out or deciding how to get to a place, e.g. using a map ○ *In the sixteenth century, navigation was done by the stars.* ○ *Thanks to Jim's bad navigation we lost our way twice.* **2.** the movement of ships or aircraft ○ *The canal is open to navigation again.*

navigator /'nævɪgeɪtə/ *noun* a person who calculates the distances and direction taken by an aircraft or ship ○ *The navigator estimates that we should reach the coast in about ten minutes.*

③ **navy** /'neɪvi/ *noun* (*plural* **navies**) **1.** a military force which fights battles at sea ○ *He left school and joined the navy.* ○ *The navy has many ships.* **2.** *also* **navy blue** a very dark blue colour ■ *adj also* **navy blue** of a very dark blue colour

Nazi /'nɑːtsi/ *noun* a member or supporter of Adolf Hitler's fascist German National Socialist Party

① **near** /nɪə/ *adv, prep, adj* **1.** close to, not far away from ○ *Our house is near the post office.* ○ *Bring your chair nearer to the table.* ○ *He lives quite near* or *quite near here.* ○ *Which is the nearest chemist's?* **2.** soon, not far off in time ○ *Her birthday is on December 21st – it's quite near to Christmas.* ○ *Can you phone again nearer the day and I'll see if I can find a few minutes to see you?* ■ *verb* (**nears, nearing, neared**) to get closer to a place or time ○ *We're nearing the end of the year.*

nearby /nɪə'baɪ/ *adv, adj* not far away ○ *He lives just nearby.* ○ *They met in a nearby restaurant.*

① **nearly** /'nɪəli/ *adv* almost ○ *He's nearly 18 – he'll be going to university next year.* ○ *The film lasted nearly three hours.* ○ *The book isn't nearly as good as the last one I read.* ○ *Hurry up, it's nearly time for breakfast.* ○ *We haven't got nearly enough time to get to London.*

② **neat** /niːt/ *adj* tidy, without any mess ○ *a blouse with a neat lace collar* ○ *Leave your bedroom neat and tidy.* ○ *Her handwriting is very neat.*

① **necessarily** /ˌnesɪˈserɪli/ *adv* which cannot be avoided ○ *Going to Newcastle from here necessarily means changing trains twice.*

① **necessary** /ˈnesɪs(ə)ri/ *adj* which has to be done ○ *Don't phone me in the evening unless it's absolutely necessary.* ○ *Is it necessary to finish the work today?*

necessitate /nɪˈsesɪteɪt/ (**necessitates, necessitating, necessitated**) *verb* to make something necessary

necessity /nəˈsesɪti/ (*plural* **necessities**) *noun* **1.** an essential thing, or thing that is needed ○ *A car is a necessity if you live in the country.* ○ *Can they afford the simple necessities of life?* **2.** the fact that it is necessary to do or have something [~for] ○ *There's no necessity for identification – we know everyone here.*

② **neck** /nek/ *noun* **1.** a part which joins your head to your body ○ *She was sitting in a draught and got a stiff neck.* ○ *The mayor wears a gold chain round his neck.* **2.** the part of a piece of clothing which goes round your neck ○ *I can't wear this shirt – the neck is too tight.*

③ **necklace** /ˈnekləs/ *noun* a piece of jewellery which you wear round your neck ○ *a diamond necklace*

neckline /ˈnekˌlaɪn/ *noun* the line formed by the edge of an item of clothing where it goes around the neck

nectar /ˈnektə/ *noun* a liquid produced by flowers to attract bees ○ *Honey is made from the nectar collected by bees.*

nectarine /ˈnektəriːn/ *noun* a fruit like a peach with a smooth skin

① **need** /niːd/ *verb* (**needs, needing, needed**) **1.** to require something, or have to have something ○ *We shall need some euros for our holiday in Spain.* ○ *Painting needs a lot of skill.* ○ *I need someone to help me with the cooking.* **2.** to want something ○ *Does anyone need any more coffee?* ■ *modal verb* used with other verbs meaning to be necessary ○ *Need you make so much noise in the bath?* ○ *Need you go now?* ○ *The living room needs painting* or *needs to be painted.* ○ *You don't need to come if you have a cold.* ○ *The police need to know who saw the accident.* ○ *You needn't bother waiting for me.* (NOTE: The negative is **need not** or, especially in speaking, **needn't**.) ■ *noun* the fact that something is necessary or wanted [~for] ○ *There's no need for you to wait – I can find my own way.* ◇ **in need** requiring food and help ○ *The Red Cross is bringing supplies to families in need.* ◇ **to be in need of** to want something ○ *They're in urgent need of medical supplies.*

needle /ˈniːd(ə)l/ *noun* **1.** a long thin sharp object with a hole at one end, used for sewing ○ *This needle hasn't got a very sharp point.* ○ *You must try to put the piece of wool through the hole in the needle.* □ **knitting needle** a thin pointed plastic or metal stick used for knitting **2.** a long thin sharp piece of medical equipment, used for putting medicine into your body **3.** a small thin part on a piece of equipment, which points to something such as a number ○ *He looked at the dial and saw the needle was pointing to zero.* **4.** one of the thin leaves of a pine tree ○ *She had lots of pine needles stuck in her hair.*

needless /ˈniːdləs/ *adj* not necessary ◇ **needless to say** as you might expect ○ *Needless to say, they can't pay for it themselves.*

needlework /ˈniːd(ə)lwɜːk/ *noun* decorative sewing

③ **needn't** /ˈniːd(ə)nt/ *modal verb* it is not necessary ○ *She needn't come if she has a cold.* ○ *You needn't have made a cake – I'm not hungry.* ○ *She needn't make such a fuss about a little spider.* (NOTE: **Needn't** is usually used with other verbs and is not followed by **to**. Note also the difference between **needn't** = not necessary and **mustn't** = not allowed: *You needn't hurry; We mustn't be late.*)

negate /nɪˈgeɪt/ (**negates, negating, negated**) *verb* to cancel something out, to remove the effect of something (*formal*) (NOTE: + **negation** *n*)

② **negative** /ˈnegətɪv/ *adj* **1.** meaning 'no' ○ *a negative response* **2.** showing that something is not there ○ *Her blood test was negative.* ■ *noun* **1.** a statement meaning 'no' ○ *The answer was in the negative.* **2.** developed film with an image where the light parts are dark and dark parts light ○ *Don't touch the negatives with your dirty fingers.*

neglect /nɪˈglekt/ (**neglects, neglecting, neglected**) *verb* not to do something ○ *He neglected to tell the police that he had been involved in an accident.*

neglectful /nɪˈglektf(ə)l/ *adj* not doing anything about something that is your responsibility

negligence /ˈneglɪdʒəns/ *noun* a lack of suitable care in carrying out a duty or activity

negligent /ˈneglɪdʒ(ə)nt/ *adj* showing negligence, not taking proper care

negligible /ˈneglɪdʒɪb(ə)l/ *adj* very small, not worth bothering about

negotiable /nɪˈgəʊʃiəb(ə)l/ *adj* **1.** which can be changed or decided by discussions between the people involved ○ *The salary for the job is negotiable.* **2.** which can be exchanged for cash

③ **negotiate** /nɪˈgəʊʃieɪt/ (**negotiates, negotiating, negotiated**) *verb* **1.** to discuss with someone ○ *We are negotiating with the travel agent about a refund.* **2.** to go round something which is in the way ○ *We had to negotiate several boulders in the road.* ○ *The burglars managed to negotiate the alarm system successfully.*

② **negotiation** /nɪˌgəʊʃiˈeɪʃ(ə)n/ *noun* the process of discussing something

neigh /neɪ/ (**neighs, neighing, neighed**) *verb* to make the sound of a horse ○ *We could hear the horses neighing in the stables.* (NOTE: + **neigh** *n*)

neighbor /ˈneɪbə/ *noun* US spelling of **neighbour**

② **neighbour** /ˈneɪbə/ *noun* **1.** a person who lives near you ○ *He doesn't get on with his neighbours.* **2.** a person who is sitting next to you ○ *Help yourself and then pass the plate on to your neighbour.* **3.** another person (*old*) ○ *'Love of your neighbour' is one of the essentials of Christian doctrine.*

neighbourhood /ˈneɪbəhʊd/ *noun* a small area and the people who live in it ○ *This is a quiet neighbourhood – we don't like noisy parties.* ○ *The doctor knows everyone in the neighbourhood.*

neighbouring /ˈneɪbərɪŋ/ *adj* which is close to you (NOTE: The US spelling is **neighboring**.)

neighbourly /ˈneɪbəli/ *adv* friendly to the people near you ○ *It's very neighbourly of you to lend us your lawnmower.* ○ *People in this street aren't very neighbourly.* (NOTE: The US spelling is **neighborly**.)

② **neither** /ˈnaɪðə, ˈniːðə/ *adj, pron* not either of two people or things ○ *Neither car* or *neither of the cars passed the test.* ○ *Neither sister is dark* or *neither of the sisters is dark.* ■ *adv* not either; used for showing that a negative statement applies to two things or people ○ *He doesn't eat meat and neither does his wife.* ○ *She isn't fat but neither is she really very thin.*

neon /ˈniːɒn/ *noun* an inert gas found in very small quantities in the atmosphere and used in illuminated signs

③ **nephew** /ˈnefjuː/ *noun* a son of your sister or brother, or a son of your husband's or wife's brother or sister

nepotism /ˈnepətɪz(ə)m/ *noun* the unfair practice of giving jobs to members of your own family rather than to people who deserve to have them

nerd /nɜːd/ *noun* a person who is very interested in technical things, especially computers, and who other people sometimes think is boring

③ **nerve** /nɜːv/ *noun* **1.** one of the fibres in your body which take messages to and from the brain ○ *Nerves are very delicate and easily damaged.* **2.** over-confidence or rude behaviour ○ *He's got a nerve to ask for a day off, when he was away all last week.* **3.** the ability to keep your fear under control in order to achieve something ○ *It takes a lot of nerve to disagree with your friends.* ○ *He went over to speak to her but at the last minute he lost his nerve.*

nerve-racking /ˈnɜːv rækɪŋ/ *adj* which is extremely frightening or worrying

nerve-wracking /nɜːv ˈrækɪŋ/ *adj* same as **nerve-racking**

③ **nervous** /ˈnɜːvəs/ *adj* **1.** worried and easily frightened ○ *She's always been of a nervous disposition* ○ *She gets nervous if she is alone in the house at night.* ○ *He's nervous about driving in London.* **2.** referring to the nerves ○ *the nervous system*

nervous breakdown /ˌnɜːvəs ˈbreɪkdaʊn/ *noun* a non-medical expression for a condition where a patient becomes so worried or upset that he or she is not able to do anything

nervousness /ˈnɜːvəsnəs/ *noun* a state of worry and tension

nervous system /ˈnɜːvəs ˌsɪstəm/ *noun* the system of nerves in the body

③ **nest** /nest/ *noun* a structure built by birds, and by some animals and insects, to lay their eggs in ○ *an ants' nest* ○ *The birds built their nests among the trees.* ○ *The blackbirds have laid three eggs in their nest.*

nestle /ˈnes(ə)l/ (**nestles, nestling, nestled**) *verb* to be in a safe and sheltered place ○ *Their cottage nestles at the bottom of the valley.* ○ *A church nestling in the hills.*

② **net** /net/, **nett** *noun* **1.** a woven material with large holes ○ *A long skirt made of pink net.* **2.** a piece of this material used for a special purpose ○ *a fishing net* **3.** same as

Internet ■ *adj* after all payments such as tax have been considered ○ *That figure is net, not gross.*

netball /ˈnetbɔːl/ *noun* a team game similar to basketball, played by two teams of seven players, usually women, in which the aim is to score points by throwing the ball through a horizontal ring into a high net

netting /ˈnetɪŋ/ *noun* a loosely woven material

③ **network** /ˈnetwɜːk/ *noun* **1.** a system of things such as roads or railways connecting different places ○ *the British rail network* ○ *a satellite TV network* ○ *There is a network of tunnels under the castle.* **2.** a system of computers which are connected together ○ *How does this network operate?* ○ *You can book at any of our hotels throughout the country using our computer network.* **3.** a group of people connected with each other ○ *his rapidly developing network of contacts in government* ■ *verb* (**networks, networking, networked**) to connect two or more computers in order to allow them to exchange information ○ *Workstations within an office are usually networked and share resources.*

neural /ˈnjʊərəl/ *adj* referring to a nerve or the nervous system

neurology /njʊˈrɒlədʒi/ *noun* the study of nerves and the illnesses which affect them

neurosis /njʊˈrəʊsɪs/ (*plural* **neuroses**) *noun* a mental state in which a patient thinks all the time about something in an excessive way and experiences strong emotions about it, such as fear of empty spaces

neurotic /njʊˈrɒtɪk/ *adj* worried or always thinking about something in an excessive way ○ *She has a neurotic dislike of cats.* ○ *Don't get neurotic about the change in the firm's logo.*

neuter /ˈnjuːtə/ (**neuters, neutering, neutered**) *verb* to remove an animal's sex organs ○ *We took our tomcat to the vet to have him neutered.*

neutral /ˈnjuːtrəl/ *noun* (*of motor vehicles*) not in gear ○ *The car is in neutral.*

neutralise /ˈnjuːtrəlaɪz/ (**neutralises, neutralising, neutralised**), **neutralize** *verb* to work against the effect of something ○ *We acted immediately to neutralise the threat from their navy.*

neutrality /njuːˈtrælɪti/ *noun* the fact of being neutral in a war

neutron /ˈnjuːtrɒn/ *noun* a neutral particle in the nucleus of an atom

① **never** /ˈnevə/ *adv* not at any time; not ever ○ *We'll never forget that restaurant.* ○ *I've never bought anything in that shop although I've often been inside it.* ○ *He never eats meat.*

② **nevertheless** /ˌnevəðəˈles/ *adv* although a particular situation exists ○ *I know it is raining, but nevertheless I'd like to go for a walk along the beach.* ○ *She had a cold, but went to the meeting nevertheless.*

① **new** /njuː/ *adj* **1.** made very recently, or never used before ○ *Put some new paper in the printer.* ○ *The new version of the software is now available.* **2.** which arrived recently ○ *There are two new secretaries in the office.* **3.** completely different from what was before ○ *We need someone with new ideas.* ○ *They put some new wallpaper in the bedroom.*

New Age /njuː eɪdʒ/ *adj* of modern ideas about spiritual and medical matters

newborn /ˈnjuːbɔːn/ *adj* which has been born recently ○ *The mother and her newborn baby survived the crash.*

newcomer /ˈnjuːkʌmə/ *noun* a person who has just come to a place

newfangled /ˌnjuːˈfæŋgəld/ *adj* modern and complicated (*informal*)

new-found /ˈnjuː faʊnd/ *adj* that has been found recently

③ **newly** /ˈnjuːli/ *adv* recently

newly-weds /ˈnjuːli wedz/ *plural noun* two people who have just got married

① **news** /njuːz/ *noun* spoken or written information about what has happened ○ *What's the news of your sister?* ○ *I don't want to hear any bad news.* ○ *He was watching the 10 o'clock news on TV.* ◇ **to break the news to someone** to tell someone the bad news ○ *He broke the news to his daughters.*

newsagent /ˈnjuːzeɪdʒənt/ *noun* a person who sells newspapers (NOTE: **Newsagent** has no connection with **news agency**.)

newsflash /ˈnjuːzflæʃ/ *noun* a short piece of news broadcast at an unexpected time

newsgroup /ˈnjuːzˌgruːp/ *noun* an Internet discussion group

newsletter /ˈnjuːzletə/ *noun* a printed sheet or small newspaper giving news about a company, a club or other organisation

① **newspaper** /ˈnjuːzpeɪpə/ *noun* a set of loose folded sheets of paper, containing news of what has happened, especially in the last 24 hours ○ *He was so absorbed in his newspaper that he didn't notice that the toast had burnt.* ○ *We saw your picture in the local newspaper.* ○ *The newspapers are full of news of the election.*

newsprint /ˈnjuːzprɪnt/ *noun* cheap paper used for newspapers and magazines

③ **newsreader** /ˈnjuːzriːdə/ *noun* a person who reads the news on radio or TV

newsworthy /ˈnjuːzwɜːði/ *adj* interesting enough to be in the newspapers or on radio or TV

new wave /njuː weɪv/ *noun* an original movement in the arts

③ **New Year's Day** /ˌnjuː jɪəz ˈdeɪ/ *noun* 1st January

③ **New Year's Eve** /ˌnjuː jɪəz ˈiːv/ *noun* 31st December

① **next** /nekst/ *adj, adv* **1.** coming after in time ○ *On Wednesday we go to Paris, and the next day we travel to Italy.* ○ *First you put the eggs into a bowl and next you add some sugar.* ○ *Don't forget to give me a call when you're next in town.* ○ *Next week is the start of our holiday.* ○ *The next time you go to the supermarket, can you get some coffee?* **2.** nearest in place ○ *The ball went over the fence into the next garden.* ○ *She took the seat next to mine.* ■ *pron* the thing or person following ○ *After two buses went past full, the next was almost empty.* ○ *I'll be back from holiday the week after next.* ○ (asking the next person in the queue to come) *Next, please!*

③ **next door** /ˌnekst ˈdɔː/ *adj, adv* in the house next to this one ○ *Who lives next door to your mother?* ○ *The shop is next door to a bank.*

nib /nɪb/ *noun* the point of a pen, from which the ink flows

nibble /ˈnɪb(ə)l/ (**nibbles, nibbling, nibbled**) *verb* to eat something by taking small bites ○ *She was nibbling a biscuit.* ○ *The mice have nibbled into the flour sacks.* (NOTE: + **nibble** *n*)

① **nice** /naɪs/ *adj* **1.** pleasant, enjoyable ○ *We had a nice time at the seaside.* ○ *If the weather's nice let's have a picnic.* ○ *The nicest thing about the town is that it is on the sea.* **2.** pleasant, polite ○ *That wasn't a very nice thing to say.* ○ *Try and be nice to your grandfather.*

nice-looking /naɪs ˈlʊkɪŋ/ *adj* attractive or pleasing to look at

nicety /ˈnaɪsəti/ (*plural* **niceties**) *noun* a slight or exact detail

niche /niːʃ/ *noun* a place which curves inwards in a wall ○ *There are statues in niches all round the garden.*

nick /nɪk/ *noun* **1.** a small cut in something ○ *He made a nick in the stick.* **2.** a prison ○ *He's been in the nick for the last year.* ■ *verb* (**nicks, nicking, nicked**) **1.** to make a small cut in something ○ *He nicked his finger with a razor blade.* **2.** to steal something (*informal*) ○ *A group of young lads who went around nicking things from the local shops.* ○ *Who's nicked my umbrella?* ◇ **in the nick of time** just in time (*informal*)

nickel /ˈnɪk(ə)l/ *noun* **1.** a metallic element, used in making special metal alloys ○ *nickel-plated handlebars* ○ *We use an alloy of copper and nickel.* **2.** *US and Canada* a 5-cent coin ○ *Can you lend me a nickel?*

nickname /ˈnɪkneɪm/ *noun* a short or informal name given to someone ○ *Her real name's Henrietta, but everyone calls her by her nickname 'Bobbles'.* ■ *verb* to give a nickname to someone ○ *He was nicknamed 'Camel' because of his big nose.*

nicotine /ˈnɪkətiːn/ *noun* a harmful substance in tobacco, also used for killing insects

③ **niece** /niːs/ *noun* a daughter of a brother or sister, or a daughter of your husband's or wife's brother or sister

nifty /ˈnɪfti/ *adj* very good or effective

niggle /ˈnɪg(ə)l/ (**niggles, niggling, niggled**) *verb* **1.** to criticise someone or something in an annoying way **2.** to be a cause of worry to somebody, especially in a small way over a long period of time

niggling /ˈnɪg(ə)lɪŋ/ *adj* small and not very important

① **night** /naɪt/ *noun* the time when it is dark ○ *It's dangerous to walk alone in the streets at night.* ○ *Burglars got into the office during the night.* ○ *He is on night duty three days a week.* ○ *They're planning to have a night out tomorrow.*

nightclub /ˈnaɪtklʌb/ *noun* a club which is only open at night

nightdress /ˈnaɪtdres/ *noun* a long loose dress which you wear in bed (NOTE: usually called a **nightie**)

nightfall /ˈnaɪtfɔːl/ *noun* the time when night starts

nightgown /ˈnaɪtˌgaʊn/ *noun* a nightdress or nightshirt

nightie /ˈnaɪti/ *noun* a nightdress (*informal*)

nightingale /ˈnaɪtɪŋgeɪl/ *noun* a small singing bird which sings at night

night life /ˈnaɪt laɪf/ *noun* entertainment in a town at night

nightly /ˈnaɪtli/ *adv* every night ○ *Car thefts are a nightly occurrence around here.*

nightmare /ˈnaɪtmeə/ *noun* a very frightening dream

nightshirt /ˈnaɪtˌʃɜːt/ *noun* a piece of clothing like a long loose shirt for wearing in bed

night-time /ˈnaɪt taɪm/ *noun* a period when it is night

③ **nil** /nɪl/ *noun* **1.** the number 0 (*used in giving the result of a game*) ○ *We lost three nil.* **2.** nothing ○ *Our advertising budget has been cut to nil.*

nimble /ˈnɪmbəl/ (**nimbler, nimblest**) *adj* able to move quickly

① **nine** /naɪn/ *noun* the number 9

9/11 /ˌnaɪn ɪˈlev(ə)n/ *noun* the events of 9 September 2001, when terrorists flew aircraft into the two towers of the World Trade Center in New York, destroying them and causing thousands of deaths

999 /ˌnaɪn naɪn ˈnaɪn/ *noun* a telephone number to call the emergency services in Britain ○ *The firemen came quickly when we called 999.* ○ *The ambulance answered the 999 call.*

① **nineteen** /ˌnaɪnˈtiːn/ *noun* the number 19

① **nineteenth** /naɪnˈtiːnθ/, **19th** *adj* relating to number 19 in a series ■ *noun* number 19 in a series

① **ninetieth** /ˈnaɪntiəθ/, **90th** *adj* relating to number 90 in a series ○ *It's his ninetieth birthday tomorrow.* ■ *noun* number 90 in a series

① **ninety** /ˈnaɪnti/ *noun* number 90 □ **nineties** the numbers between 90 and 99

① **ninth** /naɪnθ/ *adj* relating to number 9 in a series ○ *You're the ninth person in the queue.* ■ *noun* number 9 in a series

nip /nɪp/ (**nips, nipping, nipped**) *verb* **1.** to squeeze sharply ○ *We nipped off the end of the stalk to stop the plant growing any taller.* ○ *The crab nipped his thumb as he picked it up.* ◊ **bud 2.** to bite sharply ○ *The dog nipped the postman in the leg.* **3.** to go very quickly ○ *I'll just nip round to the newsagent's and get the evening paper.* ○ *We'll nip down to the pub for a drink.*

③ **nipple** /ˈnɪp(ə)l/ *noun* the darker part in the centre of a woman's breast, through which the milk passes ○ *She held the baby to her nipple.*

nirvana /nɪəˈvɑːnə/ *noun* a state of spiritual enlightenment in religions such as Hinduism, Buddhism and Jainism

nitrate /ˈnaɪtreɪt/ *noun* a chemical compound containing nitrogen and oxygen, existing in all plants

③ **nitrogen** /ˈnaɪtrədʒən/ *noun* an important gas which is essential for life, and which forms most of the atmosphere

nitwit /ˈnɪtwɪt/ *noun* a stupid idiot (*insult*)

① **no** /nəʊ/ *adj, adv* **1.** used for giving a negative answer ○ *I asked my mother if we could borrow her car but she said 'no'.* ○ *Do you want another cup of coffee? – No, thank you.* **2.** not any ○ *There's no milk left in the fridge.* ○ *We live in a little village, and there's no post office for miles around.* ○ *We had no reply to our fax.* ◇ **no entry** you may not go in this way ◇ **no exit** you may not go out this way ◇ **no parking** you may not park ◇ **no smoking** you may not smoke

③ **no.** /ˈnʌmbə/ *abbr* number

nobility /nəʊˈbɪlɪti/ *noun* **1.** all noble families, taken as a group ○ *The king invited members of the nobility to the meeting.* ○ *The nobility fought hard to protect their privileges.* **2.** the quality of being extremely polite, being impressive and brave ○ *The nobility of his actions is not in doubt.*

noble /ˈnəʊb(ə)l/ *noun* a person of high rank ○ *The nobles forced the king to sign the treaty.*

nobleman /ˈnəʊb(ə)lmən/ (*plural* **noblemen**) *noun* a man of high rank

noblewoman /ˈnəʊb(ə)lwʊmən/ (*plural* **noblewomen**) *noun* a woman of high rank

① **nobody** /ˈnəʊbədi/ *pron* same as **no one**

nocturnal /nɒkˈtɜːn(ə)l/ *adj* relating to the night ○ *The nocturnal habits of the badger.*

② **nod** /nɒd/ *verb* (**nods, nodding, nodded**) **1.** to move the head slightly up and down, meaning 'yes' ○ *When he asked her if she understood, she nodded (her head).* ○ *He nodded in agreement.* (NOTE: The opposite is to **shake** your head, meaning 'no'.) **2.** to move the head slightly up and down, to mean 'hello' or 'goodbye' [~at] ○ *She nodded at me as I went past.* ■ *noun* a movement of the head up and down, meaning 'yes' ○ *He gave me a nod as I came in.*

nod off *phrasal verb* to go to sleep ○ *She was nodding off in front of the television.* (NOTE: **nodding – nodded**)

nodule /ˈnɒdjuːl/ *noun* a small lump or swelling

no-go area /ˌnəʊ gəʊ ˈeəriə/ *noun* an area of a town where ordinary people or the police cannot go

② **noise** /nɔɪz/ *noun* **1.** a loud or unpleasant sound ○ *I can't hear you for the noise of the workmen in the street.* ○ *Let's not invite the children – I can't stand noise.* **2.** sound in general ○ *There was a noise of running water in the bathroom.* ○ *The washing machine is making a funny noise.* ○ *He woke up when he heard a noise in the kitchen.*

noise pollution /ˈnɔɪz pəˌluːʃ(ə)n/ *noun* spoiling people's enjoyment of the outdoors by making a lot of noise

noisily /ˈnɔɪzɪli/ *adv* making a lot of noise

③ **noisy** /ˈnɔɪzi/ (**noisier, noisiest**) *adj* who or which makes a lot of noise ○ *a crowd of noisy little boys* ○ *Unfortunately, the hotel overlooks a noisy crossroads.* ○ *This lawn mower is noisier than our old one.*

nomad /ˈnəʊmæd/ *noun* a person who moves from place to place in a large area of land without settling in any one spot

no-man's-land /ˈnəʊ mænz ˌlænd/ *noun* land between two countries or armies, which does not belong to either

nominal /ˈnɒmɪn(ə)l/ *adj* **1.** in name, not in fact ○ *He's the nominal head of the company, but his secretary does all the work.* ○ *His appointment as director is entirely nominal – I will continue to be in charge.* **2.** involving a small amount of money ○ *We pay a nominal fee.* ○ *The subscription is really nominal.* ○ *We make a nominal charge for our services.*

nominate /ˈnɒmɪneɪt/ (**nominates, nominating, nominated**) *verb* to suggest someone for a post (NOTE: + **nomination** *n*)

nominee /ˌnɒmɪˈniː/ *noun* a person who has been suggested for something such as a job

non- /nɒn/ *prefix* not

non-aggression /ˌnɒn əˈgreʃ(ə)n/ *noun* a government's policy of not attacking other countries

nonchalant /ˈnɒnʃ(ə)lənt/ *adj* not showing any excitement or worry about anything

non-combatant /nɒn ˈkɒmbətənt/ *noun* **1.** a person who is not in the armed forces during a war **2.** a chaplain, medical officer, or other member of the armed forces who does not take part in battle

non-committal /ˌnɒn kəˈmɪt(ə)l/ *adj* not deciding on a definite course of action, not agreeing with either side in an argument

nonconformist /ˌnɒnkənˈfɔːmɪst/ *adj, noun* not following the usual social conventions ○ *His nonconformist attitude to staff relations.*

non-count /ˈnɒn kaʊnt/ *adj* same as **uncountable**

nondescript /ˈnɒndɪskrɪpt/ *adj* very ordinary, without any special qualities

① **none** /nʌn/ *pron* **1.** not any ○ *How many dogs have you got? – None.* ○ *Can you buy some milk? We've none left in the fridge?* ○ *A little money is better than none at all.* **2.** not one ○ *None of my friends smokes.* ○ *None of the group can speak Chinese.*

nonentity /nɒˈnentɪti/ *noun* a person who is completely unimportant

nonetheless /ˌnʌnðəˈles/ *adv* although a particular situation exists

non-event /nɒn ɪˈvent/ *noun* an occasion or event which makes you feel disappointed because it is not as good as you expected

nonexistent /ˌnɒnɪgˈzɪstənt/ *adj* which does not exist, which is not real

non-fiction /nɒn ˈfɪkʃən/ *noun* books which are about real things, events or people, and are not stories

non-flammable /nɒn ˈflæməb(ə)l/ *adj* which does not burn easily

non-intervention /ˌnɒn ˌɪntəˈvenʃ(ə)n/ *noun* a decision or policy to avoid becoming involved in disagreements between two other people or countries

non-member /nɒn ˈmembə/ *noun* not a member of a particular organisation

no-no /ˈnəʊ nəʊ/ *noun* a thing which is not allowed (*informal*)

no-nonsense /ˌnəʊ ˈnɒnsəns/ *adj* sensible, serious and honest

non-payment /ˌnɒn ˈpeɪmənt/ *noun* a failure to pay

nonplussed /nɒnˈplʌst/ *adj* confused

non-proliferation /nɒn prəˌlɪfəˈreɪʃ(ə)n/ *noun* the practice of limiting the production or spread of something, especially nuclear weapons or other weapons of mass destruction

non-resident /ˌnɒn ˈrezɪd(ə)nt/ *noun* a person who is not living in a place or not staying there very long

③ **nonsense** /ˈnɒnsəns/ *noun* silly ideas ○ *I'm too fat – nonsense!* ○ *He talked a lot* *of nonsense. ○ It's nonsense to expect people to pay money for that.* (NOTE: no plural)

non sequitur /ˌnɒn ˈsekwɪtə/ *noun* a statement which appears to have no connection to what was said immediately before it

non-smoker /nɒn ˈsməʊkə/ *noun* a person who does not smoke

non-standard /nɒn ˈstændəd/ *adj* not meeting the requirements of an accepted standard

nonstarter /nɒnˈstɑːtə/ *noun* a project or plan which is never going to be accepted

non-stick /ˌnɒn ˈstɪk/ *adj* with a surface which prevents food sticking to it

non-stop /ˌnɒn ˈstɒp/ *adj* which does not stop ○ *a non-stop train to Paris* ○ *They took a non-stop flight to Australia.* ○ *All our flights to Toronto are non-stop.* ■ *adv* without stopping ○ *The planes flies to Hong Kong non-stop.* ○ *They worked non-stop to finish the job on time.*

noodles /ˈnuːd(ə)lz/ *plural noun* long flat pieces of pasta ○ *I ordered spicy meatballs with noodles.* ○ *We started with chicken noodle soup.*

nook /nʊk/ *noun* a small hiding place

noon /nuːn/ *noun* twelve o'clock in the middle of the day

① **no one** /ˈnəʊ wʌn/ *pron* no person ○ *We met no one we knew.* ○ *No one here takes sugar in their tea.* ○ *There was nobody in the café.* ○ *Nobody wants to do her job.* □ **no one else** no other person ○ *No one else's child behaved as badly as ours on the plane!*

noose /nuːs/ *noun* a circle in a piece of rope which becomes tight as you pull on it

nope /nəʊp/ *interj* no ○ *Any luck? – Nope!*

① **nor** /nɔː/ *conj* and not ○ *'I don't want to go' – 'Nor me!'* ○ *I did not meet him that year nor in subsequent years.* ○ *I never went there again, nor did my wife.* ◊ **neither**

③ **norm** /nɔːm/ *noun* the standard

① **normal** /ˈnɔːm(ə)l/ *adj* usual or expected ○ *We hope to restore normal service as soon as possible.* ○ *Look at the rain – it's just a normal British summer.* ○ *What's the size of a normal swimming pool?* ○ *At her age, it's only normal for her to want to go to parties.*

normalise /ˈnɔːməlaɪz/ (**normalises, normalising, normalised**), **normalize** *verb* to make normal again

normality /nɔːˈmælɪti/ *noun* the fact of being normal

① **normally** /ˈnɔːm(ə)li/ *adv* usually ○ *The bus is normally late.* ○ *She doesn't normally drink wine.*

① **north** /nɔːθ/ *noun* the direction to your left when you are facing the direction in which the sun rises ○ *There will be snow in the north of the country.* ○ *It's cold when the wind blows from the north.* ■ *adj* relating to the north ○ *We went on holiday to the north coast of Scotland.* ○ *The north side of our house never gets any sun.* ○ *When the north wind blows, you can expect snow.* ■ *adv* towards the north ○ *They were travelling north at the time.* ○ *Go north for three miles and then you'll see the road to London.* ○ *Our office windows face north.*

northbound /ˈnɔːθbaʊnd/ *adj* travelling towards the north

③ **north-east** /ˌnɔːθ ˈiːst/ *adv* the direction between north and east

north-easterly /nɔːθ ˈiːstəli/ *adj* **1.** towards the north-east **2.** (*of a wind*) blowing from the north-east ■ *noun* a wind from the north-east

north-eastern /ˌnɔːθ ˈiːstən/ *adj* from, of or in the north-east

northerly /ˈnɔːðəli/ *adj* **1.** towards the north **2.** (*of a wind*) blowing from the north

② **northern** /ˈnɔːð(ə)n/ *adj* from, of or in the north ○ *They live in the northern part of the country.*

northerner /ˈnɔːð(ə)nə/, **Northerner** *noun* a person who lives in or comes from the north of a country or region

northern hemisphere /ˌnɔːð(ə)n ˌhemɪˈsfɪə/ *noun* the part of the earth above the equator

northernmost /ˈnɔːð(ə)nməʊst/ *adj* furthest to the north

North Pole /ˈnɔːθ ˈpəʊl/ *noun* the furthest point north on the earth

northward /ˈnɔːθwəd/ *adj* towards the north

northwards /ˈnɔːθwədz/ *adv* towards the north

③ **north-west** /ˌnɔːθ ˈwest/ *adv* the direction between west and north

north-westerly /nɔːθ ˈwestəli/ *adj* **1.** towards the north-west **2.** (*of a wind*) lowing from the north-west

north-western /ˌnɔːθ ˈwestən/ *adj* from, of or in the north-west

① **nose** /nəʊz/ *noun* a part of the body on your face which you breathe through and smell with ○ *He has a cold, and his nose is red.* ○ *Dogs have wet noses.* ○ *She's got flu – her nose is running.* ○ *Don't wipe your* *nose on your sleeve, use a tissue.* ◇ **under his, her, etc. very nose** in front of him, her, etc. ○ *I did it under his very nose and he didn't notice a thing.* ◇ **to blow your nose** to blow air through your nose into a handkerchief to remove liquid from your nose ◇ **to speak through your nose** to talk as if your nose is blocked, so that you say 'b' rather than 'm' and 'd' rather than 'n' ◇ **to look down your nose at something** to look at something as if you don't think it is very good ○ *She's got a degree and looks down her nose at the other secretaries.* ◇ **to turn your nose up at something** to show that you don't feel something is good enough for you ○ *It's a marvellous deal, I don't see why you should turn your nose up at it.*

nosebleed /ˈnəʊzbliːd/ *noun* blood coming from the nose

nosedive /ˈnəʊzdaɪv/ *noun* (*of something flying*) a steep movement downwards (NOTE: + **nosedive** *v*)

nostalgia /nɒˈstældʒə/ *noun* a sad feeling of wanting things to be the same as they were in the past

nostalgic /nɒˈstældʒɪk/ *adj* referring to nostalgia

nostril /ˈnɒstrɪl/ *noun* one of the two holes in your nose, which you breathe through

① **not** /nɒt/ *adv* used with verbs to show the negative ○ *A service charge is not included.* ○ *It isn't there.* ○ *She can't come.* ○ *He didn't want any meat.* ○ *We couldn't go home because of the fog.* ○ *Don't you like coffee?* ◇ **not exactly 1.** not completely ○ *Was it a disaster? – Not exactly a disaster, but it didn't go very well.* ○ *It's not exactly the colour I wanted.* **2.** used for emphasising a negative ○ *He's not exactly pleased at having to pay out so much money.* ◇ **not...either** and not...also ○ *She doesn't eat meat, and she doesn't eat fish either.* ○ *It wasn't hot, but it wasn't very cold either.* ◇ **not only...but also** not just this...but this as well ○ *The film wasn't only very long, but it was also very bad.*

notable /ˈnəʊtəb(ə)l/ *adj* which is worth noticing ○ *It was a notable achievement.* ○ *She was notable by her absence.* ○ *The town is notable for its currant cakes.* ■ *noun* an important person ○ *a meeting of local notables*

③ **notably** /ˈnəʊtəbli/ *adv* **1.** especially ○ *Some Western countries, notably Canada and the United States, have a very high standard of living.* **2.** in a way that is easily noticed ○ *The food was notably better than the last time we ate there.*

notation /nəʊˈteɪʃ(ə)n/ *noun* a system of symbols used to show notes in music, or to show signs used in mathematics

notch /nɒtʃ/ *noun* a small V-shaped cut ○ *He cut two notches in the stick with his penknife.*

① **note** /nəʊt/ *noun* **1.** a few words in writing to remind yourself of something ○ *She made a note of what she needed to buy before she went to the supermarket.* ○ *She made a few notes before she gave her speech.* ○ *He left us a note to say he'd be back later.* **2.** a short message ○ *She left a note for the managing director with his secretary.* ○ *He wrote me a note to say he couldn't come.* **3.** a piece of paper money ○ *I tried to pay with a £10 note.* **4.** a musical sound or a written sign meaning a musical sound ○ *He can't sing high notes.* ■ *verb* (**notes, noting, noted**) **1.** to write down something in a few words ○ *The policeman noted in his notebook all the details of the accident.* **2.** to take notice of something [~(that)] ○ *Please note that our prices were raised on January 1st.* ◇ **to take note of** to pay attention to ○ *We have to take note of public opinion.*

notebook /ˈnəʊtbʊk/ *noun* a small book for making notes ○ *The policeman wrote down the details in his notebook.*

③ **noted** /ˈnəʊtɪd/ *adj* famous

notepad /ˈnəʊtpæd/ *noun* **1.** a block of paper for writing notes ○ *I took a notepad to jot down any interesting points from the lecture.* **2.** (*in computing*) a part of the screen used to store information even if the terminal is switched off ○ *Use the notepad to make changes to your file.*

③ **notepaper** /ˈnəʊtpeɪpə/ *noun* **1.** a paper for writing letters ○ *It must be an official order, it's written on the company's headed notepaper.* ○ *You'll find some notepaper in the hotel bedroom.* **2.** *US* paper for writing rough notes on

noteworthy /ˈnəʊtwɜːði/ *adj* worth noticing because it is interesting or special

① **nothing** /ˈnʌθɪŋ/ *pron* not anything ○ *There's nothing interesting on TV.* ○ *She said nothing about what she had seen.* ○ *There's nothing more we can do.* ◇ **for nothing** free, without having to pay ○ *We're friends of the woman running the show and she got us in for nothing.*

① **notice** /ˈnəʊtɪs/ *noun* **1.** a piece of writing giving information, usually put in a place where everyone can see it ○ *He* *pinned up a notice about the staff tennis match.* **2.** an official warning that something has to be done, that something is going to happen ○ *They gave us five minutes' notice to leave the office.* ○ *If you want to resign, you have to give a month's notice.* ○ *The train times were changed without notice.* ■ *verb* (**notices, noticing, noticed**) to see; to take note of [~(that)/~how/what/who etc] ○ *I didn't notice you had come in.* ○ *Did you notice how tired John was looking?* ○ *I wore one blue and one white sock all day and nobody noticed.* ◇ **at short notice** with very little warning ○ *It had to be done at short notice.* ○ *The bank manager will not see anyone at such short notice.* ◇ **until further notice** until different instructions are given ○ *You must pay £200 on the 30th of each month until further notice.*

③ **noticeable** /ˈnəʊtɪsəb(ə)l/ *adj* which is easily noticed

noticeboard /ˈnəʊtɪsbɔːd/ *noun* a board which is fixed to a wall, on which notices can be attached

notification /ˌnəʊtɪfɪˈkeɪʃ(ə)n/ *noun* the act of informing someone

notify /ˈnəʊtɪfaɪ/ (**notifies, notifying, notified**) *verb* to tell someone about something formally [~of/about] ○ *They were notified of the arrival of the shipment.* ○ *We will notify you of the exact fee at a later date.*

③ **notion** /ˈnəʊʃ(ə)n/ *noun* an idea ○ *She has this strange notion that she ought to be a TV star.*

notoriety /ˌnəʊtəˈraɪəti/ *noun* a bad reputation

notorious /nəʊˈtɔːriəs/ *adj* well known for bad qualities, or for doing bad things

nougat /ˈnuːgɑː/ *noun* a type of white sweet made with nuts, honey and the white parts of eggs

nought /nɔːt/ *noun* **1.** the number 0 ○ *One million can be written as '1m' or as one and six noughts.* (NOTE: **nought** is more common in British English; in US English, **zero** is more usual.) **2.** nothing

③ **noun** /naʊn/ *noun* (*in grammar*) a word which can be the subject or object of a verb and is used to refer to a person, thing or animal ○ *nouns such as 'brick' and 'elephant'* ○ *In 'the cat caught a mouse', 'cat' and 'mouse' are both nouns.*

noun phrase /naʊn freɪz/ *noun* a word or group of which is used in the same way as a noun, e.g. as the subject, object, or topic, in a sentence

nourish /ˈnʌrɪʃ/ (**nourishes, nourishing, nourished**) *verb* **1.** to give food to someone ○ *All the children look very well nourished.* **2.** to keep things such as ideas or hopes alive ○ *The news nourished their hopes that their son might still be alive.*

nourishing /ˈnʌrɪʃɪŋ/ *adj* which provides people, animals, or plants with the substances they need to live, grow and remain fit and healthy

nourishment /ˈnʌrɪʃmənt/ *noun* food in general ○ *She just lies in bed and refuses to take any nourishment.*

③ **novel** /ˈnɒv(ə)l/ *noun* a long story with imaginary characters and events ○ *'Pickwick Papers' was Dickens' first major novel.* ■ *adj* new and unusual ○ *Visiting New York is a novel experience for me.*

novelist /ˈnɒv(ə)lɪst/ *noun* a person who writes novels

③ **novelty** /ˈnɒv(ə)lti/ (*plural* **novelties**) *noun* **1.** a new thing you have not experienced before ○ *Flying in a plane is still a novelty for them.* **2.** the fact of being new ○ *The novelty of the new job soon wore off.* **3.** an unusual little object, usually with no practical use ○ *Small shops selling novelties and souvenirs.*

① **November** /nəʊˈvembə/ *noun* the eleventh month of the year, the month after October and before December ○ *November 5* ○ *Today is November 5th.* ○ *She was born in November.* ○ *We never go on holiday in November.* (NOTE: **November 5th** *or* **November 5**: say 'November the fifth' or 'the fifth of November' or in US English: 'November fifth'.)

novice /ˈnɒvɪs/ *noun* a person who has very little experience or skill, e.g. in a job or sport ○ *He's still a novice at rowing.* ○ *A competition like this is not for novices.*

① **now** /naʊ/ *adv* at or around this point in time ○ *I can hear a train coming now.* ○ *Please can we go home now?* ○ *The flight is only two hours – he ought to be in Berlin by now.* ○ *Now's the best time for going skiing.* ○ *A week from now we'll be sitting on the beach.* ■ *interj* showing a warning ○ *Now then, don't be rude to the teacher!* ○ *Come on now, work hard!* ○ *Now, now! Nobody wants to hear you crying.* ◇ **now and then** from time to time, not continuously ◇ **until now, up to now** until this point in time ○ *Until now, I've never had to see a doctor.*

② **nowadays** /ˈnaʊədeɪz/ *adv* at the present time ○ *Nowadays lots of people go to Spain on holiday.* ○ *The traffic is so bad* *nowadays that it takes us an hour to drive to Piccadilly Circus.*

① **nowhere** /ˈnəʊweə/ *adv* not in or to any place ○ *My wallet was nowhere to be found.* ○ *Where are you going? – Nowhere.* ○ *There is nowhere else for them to live.* ◇ **to get nowhere** not to have any success ○ *I rang six shops to try and find a spare part, but got nowhere.*

no-win situation /nəʊ wɪn/ *noun* a situation in which you are likely to fail or suffer, whatever you do

noxious /ˈnɒkʃəs/ *adj* harmful or poison ous

nozzle /ˈnɒz(ə)l/ *noun* a fitting at the end of a pipe which controls the flow of liquid

nuance /ˈnjuːɒns/ *noun* a slight shade of meaning

③ **nuclear** /ˈnjuːkliə/ *adj* relating to energy made from parts of atoms ○ *a nuclear power station*

nuclear family /ˌnjuːkliə ˈfæm(ə)li/ *noun* a family consisting simply of parents and children. ◊ **extended family**

nuclear reactor /ˌnjuːkliə riˈæktə/ *noun* a machine which creates heat and energy by starting and controlling atomic fission

③ **nucleus** /ˈnjuːkliəs/ (*plural* **nuclei**) *noun* **1.** the central part of an atom, formed of neutrons and protons ○ *Electrons orbit the nucleus of the atom.* **2.** the central body in a cell, containing DNA and RNA, and controlling the way that the cell works ○ *First the nucleus divides, then the whole cell splits in two.* **3.** a centre around which something gathers ○ *The six experienced players form the nucleus of the new team.*

nude /njuːd/ *adj* not wearing clothes, especially in situations where people are expected to wear some clothes ○ *Nude sunbathing is not allowed on this beach.* ○ *She has appeared nude on stage several times.*

nudge /nʌdʒ/ *noun* a little push, usually with the elbow ○ *She gave me a nudge to wake me up.* ■ *verb* (**nudges, nudging, nudged**) to give a little push, usually with the elbow ○ *He nudged me when it was my turn to speak.*

nudism /ˈnjuːdɪz(ə)m/ *noun* a belief in the physical and mental advantages of not wearing any clothes

nudist /ˈnjuːdɪst/ *noun* a person who chooses not wear clothes ■ *adj* relating to nudists

nudity /ˈnjuːdɪti/ *noun* nakedness

nugget /ˈnʌgɪt/ *noun* **1.** a lump of gold in its natural state **2.** a little lump of food fried with others ○ *chicken nuggets*

③ **nuisance** /ˈnjuːs(ə)ns/ *noun* a thing which annoys people

nuke /njuːk/ *verb* (**nukes, nuking, nuked**) to attack with nuclear weapons ■ *noun* a nuclear weapon

nullify /ˈnʌlɪfaɪ/ (**nullifies, nullifying, nullified**) *verb* **1.** to make something no longer legal or official ○ *This new amendment to the contract will nullify the conditions we have just agreed.* ○ *It nullified all our attempts at negotiation.* **2.** to make useless ○ *His speech has nullified all our attempts at negotiation.*

numb /nʌm/ *adj* not able to feel things that you touch ○ *The tips of his fingers went numb.* ○ *His hands were numb with cold.*

① **number** /ˈnʌmbə/ *noun* **1.** a sign that represents an amount ○ *13 is not a lucky number.* ○ *Their house is number 49.* ○ *Can you give me your telephone number?* ○ *A number 6 bus goes to Oxford Street.* ○ *Please quote your account number.* **2.** a quantity of people or things ○ *The number of tickets sold was disappointing.* ○ *A large number of children* or *large numbers of children will be sitting the exam.* ○ *There were only a small number of people at the meeting.* ■ *verb* (**numbers, numbering, numbered**) to give something a number ○ *The raffle tickets are numbered 1 to 1000.* ○ *I refer to our invoices numbered 234 and 235.* ○ *All the seats are clearly numbered.* ◇ **his days are numbered** he hasn't much time left to live

number one /ˌnʌmbə ˈwɒn/ *noun* **1.** yourself, your own interests **2.** the most important thing or person ○ *His latest single is number one in the charts.* ○ *She's number one in the organisation.*

③ **number plate** /ˈnʌmbə pleɪt/ *noun* one of two signs fixed on the front and back of a vehicle which shows the official number of the vehicle (NOTE: The US term is **license plate**.)

numbing /ˈnʌmɪŋ/ *adj* causing a lack of feeling in a part of the body

numbness /ˈnʌmnəs/ *noun* having no feeling

numeracy /ˈnjuːm(ə)rəsi/ *noun* the ability to work with numbers

numeral /ˈnjuːm(ə)rəl/ *noun* a written sign representing a number

numerate /ˈnjuːm(ə)rət/ *adj* able to work with numbers

③ **numerous** /ˈnjuːm(ə)rəs/ *adj* very many ○ *He has been fined for speeding on numerous occasions.*

nun /nʌn/ *noun* a woman member of a religious group who live together (NOTE: Do not confuse with **none**. Note: the equivalent men are **monks**.)

③ **nurse** /nɜːs/ *noun* a person who looks after sick people (*woman or man*) ○ *She has a job as a nurse in the local hospital.* ■ *verb* (**nurses, nursing, nursed**) to look after people who are ill ○ *When she fell ill her daughter nursed her until she was better.*

nursery /ˈnɜːs(ə)ri/ (*plural* **nurseries**) *noun* a school for very young children, or a place where very young children are looked after ○ *My sister went to a nursery every day from the age of 18 months.*

nursery rhyme /ˈnɜːs(ə)ri raɪm/ *noun* a little piece of poetry for children

nursery school /ˈnɜːs(ə)ri skuːl/ *noun* a school for very small children, for children under five years old

nursing /ˈnɜːsɪŋ/ *noun* the profession of being a nurse ○ *She decided to go in for nursing.* ○ *Have you considered nursing as a career?*

③ **nursing home** /ˈnɜːsɪŋ həʊm/ *noun* a small private hospital

nurture /ˈnɜːtʃə/ (**nurtures, nurturing, nurtured**) *verb* to care for children, plants or ideas and encourage them to develop

③ **nut** /nʌt/ *noun* **1.** a dry fruit with a hard shell, that grows on trees **2.** a metal ring which screws on a bolt to hold it tight ○ *Screw the nut on tightly.* ◇ **the nuts and bolts of something** the main details of something (*informal*) ○ *You'll need to master the nuts and bolts of the stock market before going to work in the city.*

nutcracker /ˈnʌtˌkrækə/ *noun* a bird that eats pine nuts

nutrient /ˈnjuːtriənt/ *noun* a substance in food which encourages the growth of living things

nutrition /njuːˈtrɪʃ(ə)ⁿn/ *noun* **1.** the way in which food affects health ○ *A scheme to improve nutrition in the poorer areas.* **2.** the study of food ○ *We are studying nutrition as part of the food science course.*

nutritionist /njuːˈtrɪʃ(ə)nɪst/ *noun* a person who is an expert in the study of nutrition and who advises people about what to eat in order to be healthy

nutritious /njuːˈtrɪʃəs/ *adj* valuable as food

③ **nuts** /nʌts/ *adj* crazy (*informal*) ◇ **nuts about someone *or* something** very keen on someone or something ○ *He's nuts about old cars.* ◇ **to drive someone nuts** to make someone crazy ○ *I wish they'd turn the music down – it's driving me nuts.*

nutshell /ˈnʌtʃel/ *noun* the hard outside part of a nut ◇ **in a nutshell** as concisely as possible ○ *It's a long and complicated story, but, in a nutshell, he left his wife and set fire to the house.*

nutter /ˈnʌtə/ *noun* a person who other people think is extremely strange or crazy (*offensive informal*)

nutty /ˈnʌti/ *adj* **1.** full of nuts ○ *a nutty chocolate bar* **2.** crazy ○ *He's a typical nutty professor.* ○ *I think it's a bit of a nutty idea myself.*

nuzzle /ˈnʌz(ə)l/ (**nuzzles, nuzzling, nuzzled**) *verb* to press your nose up to

③ **nylon** /ˈnaɪlɒn/ *noun* a type of strong artificial material used to make things such as clothing or sheets

nymphomaniac /ˌnɪmfəˈmeɪniæk/ *noun* an offensive word for a woman who is always thinking about sex or wanting to have sex

O

o /əʊ/, **O** *noun* the fifteenth letter of the alphabet, between N and P

③ **oak** /əʊk/ *noun* **1.** a type of large tree which loses its leaves in winter ○ *a forest of oak trees* ○ *Oaks produce thousands of acorns each year.* **2.** wood from this tree ○ *an oak table*

oar /ɔː/ *noun* a long wooden pole with a flat part at the end, used for moving a boat along

oasis /əʊ'eɪsɪs/ (*plural* **oases**) *noun* **1.** a place in the desert where there is water, and where plants grow ○ *After crossing the desert for days they finally arrived at an oasis.* **2.** a quiet pleasant place which is different from everything else around it ○ *Golden Square is an oasis of calm in the middle of London's West End.*

③ **oath** /əʊθ/ *noun* a swear word ○ *As the police grabbed him, he let out a long string of oaths.*

oatmeal /'əʊtmiːl/ *noun* small rough pieces of crushed oats, used especially to make porridge

obedient /ə'biːdiənt/ *adj* doing what you are told to do ○ *Our old dog is very obedient – he always comes when you call him.*

obese /əʊ'biːs/ *adj* someone who is obese is so fat that it is dangerous for their health

obesity /əʊ'biːsɪti/ *noun* the medical condition of being extremely fat

③ **obey** /ə'beɪ/ (**obeys, obeying, obeyed**) *verb* to do what someone tells you to do ○ *If you can't obey orders you shouldn't be a policeman.* ○ *Everyone must obey the law.*

obituary /ə'bɪtʃuəri/ (*plural* **obituaries**) *noun* a written account of someone's life, published after his or her death

object[1] /'ɒbdʒekt/ *noun* **1.** a thing ○ *They thought they saw a strange object in the sky.* **2.** an aim ○ *Their object is to take control of the radio station.* **3.** a noun, pronoun or phrase which follows directly from a verb or preposition ○ *In the phrase 'the cat caught the mouse', the word 'mouse' is the object of the verb 'caught'.*

object[2] /əb'dʒekt/ (**objects, objecting, objected**) *verb* to say that you do not like something or you do not want something to happen ○ *I object to being treated like a child.* ○ *He objected that the pay was too low.*

③ **objection** /əb'dʒekʃən/ *noun* a reason for refusing to agree to [~to] ○ *Do you have any objection to me smoking?* ○ *Any objections to the plan?* □ **to raise an objection to something** to object to something ○ *She raised several objections to the proposal.*

③ **objective** /əb'dʒektɪv/ *adj* considering things from a general point of view and not from your own ○ *You must be objective when planning the future of your business.* ■ *noun* something that you are trying or intending to achieve ○ *Our main objective is to make the club financially sound.* ○ *The company has achieved all its objectives.*

objectivity /ˌɒbdʒek'tɪvɪti/ *noun* the fact of being objective

objector /əb'dʒektə/ *noun* a person who objects

③ **obligation** /ˌɒblɪ'geɪʃ(ə)n/ *noun* **1.** something that you must do, e.g. for legal reasons [~to] ○ *You have an obligation to attend the meeting.* **2.** a feeling of being grateful to someone because they have done something for you [~to/towards] ○ *He felt an obligation towards his older sister for the way she had always supported his plans.*

obligatory /ə'blɪgət(ə)ri/ *adj* which has to be done according to rules or laws

③ **oblige** /ə'blaɪdʒ/ (**obliges, obliging, obliged**) *verb* **1.** to force someone to do something ○ *He was obliged to hand the money back.* □ **to feel obliged to do something** to feel it is your duty to do something ○ *He felt obliged to study medicine at university because his father was a doctor.* **2.** to do something useful or helpful ○ *He wanted to oblige you by weeding your garden for you.* **3.** □ **to be obliged to someone** to be grateful to someone for having done something (*formal*) ○ *Thank you – I'm* *much obliged to you for your help.* ○ *I'd be obliged if you could shut the window.*

obliging /ə'blaɪdʒɪŋ/ *adj* ready to help

obliterate /ə'blɪtəreɪt/ (**obliterates, obliterating, obliterated**) *verb* to destroy completely (NOTE: + **obliteration** *n*)

oblivion /ə'blɪviən/ *noun* **1.** the fact of being completely forgotten ○ *After being famous during the war the town fell into complete oblivion.* **2.** the fact of not noticing what is going on around you ○ *He sat there in a state of complete oblivion.*

oblivious /ə'blɪviəs/ *adj* not noticing

oblong /'ɒblɒŋ/ *noun* a shape with two pairs of equal sides, one pair being longer than the other ○ *The screen is an oblong, approximately 30cm by 40cm.*

obnoxious /əb'nɒkʃəs/ *adj* very unpleasant or very offensive

oboe /'əʊbəʊ/ *noun* a woodwind instrument, with a smaller range than the clarinet

obscene /əb'siːn/ *adj* offensive to moral standards or normal feelings ○ *He earns an obscene amount of money.*

obscenity /əb'senɪti/ (*plural* **obscenities**) *noun* **1.** the fact of being obscene ○ *The artist narrowly escaped being prosecuted for obscenity.* **2.** something which is obscene ○ *She regards the mere existence of nuclear weapons as an obscenity.*

obscure /əb'skjʊə/ (**obscures, obscuring, obscured**) *verb* to hide, especially by covering ○ *During a solar eclipse, the moon obscures the sun.*

obscurity /əb'skjʊərɪti/ *noun* the fact of being obscure, not being well-known

observance /əb'zɜːv(ə)ns/ *noun* the action of obeying a law or rule

observant /əb'zɜːvənt/ *adj* who notices many details

③ **observation** /ˌɒbzə'veɪʃ(ə)n/ *noun* **1.** the action of observing ○ *By careful observation, the police found out where the thieves had hidden the money.* □ **under observation** being carefully watched ○ *The patient will be kept under observation for a few days.* **2.** a remark [~about/on] ○ *He made several observations about the government.*

observatory /əb'zɜːvətri/ *noun* a place from which stars and planets can be watched

② **observe** /əb'zɜːv/ (**observes, observing, observed**) *verb* **1.** to follow or to obey something such as a law, rule or custom ○ *His family observes all the religious festivals strictly.* ○ *The local laws must be observed.* **2.** to watch something with a lot of attention ○ *They observed and recorded all the changes carefully.* **3.** to make a remark [~that] ○ *I merely observed that the bus was late as usual.*

observer /əb'zɜːvə/ *noun* a person who goes to an event and watches but does not take part

obsess /əb'ses/ (**obsesses, obsessing, obsessed**) *verb* to think about someone or something all the time, especially in a way that seems extreme to other people ○ *He is obsessed by money.*

obsessed /əb'sest/ *adj* thinking about someone or something all the time in a way which seems extreme to other people

obsession /əb'seʃ(ə)n/ *noun* **1.** a fixed idea which you think about all the time ○ *Making money is an obsession with him.* **2.** an idea or problem which worries you all the time, often connected with mental illness ○ *She has an obsession with cleanliness.*

obsessive /əb'sesɪv/ *adj* showing an obsession

obsolete /'ɒbsəliːt/ *adj* no longer used

obstacle /'ɒbstək(ə)l/ *noun* something which prevents someone from moving forward or making progress ○ *Outdated computer systems can be an obstacle to success.* ○ *Drivers have to negotiate obstacles in the road.*

obstetrician /ˌɒbstə'trɪʃ(ə)n/ *noun* a doctor who is an expert in obstetrics

obstetrics /əb'stetrɪks/ *noun* a branch of medicine dealing with pregnancy, childbirth and the period immediately after childbirth

obstinate /'ɒbstɪnət/ *adj* **1.** determined not to change your mind or not to change your opinion or course of action, whatever other people say ○ *She's such an obstinate person, that you can never make her change her mind.* ○ *Stop being so obstinate and do what I say!* **2.** difficult to remove ○ *She tried to get rid of the obstinate red wine stain on the tablecloth.*

obstruct /əb'strʌkt/ (**obstructs, obstructing, obstructed**) *verb* to put something in the way, so that nothing can pass through ○ *The artery was obstructed by a blood clot.* ○ *A large black car was obstructing the entrance.*

obstruction /əb'strʌkʃən/ *noun* **1.** the act of obstructing ○ *The fullback was penalised for obstruction.* **2.** a thing which gets in the way ○ *His car broke down and caused an obstruction on the motorway.*

obstructive /əb'strʌktɪv/ *adj* causing difficulties and not cooperating

② **obtain** /əb'teɪn/ (**obtains, obtaining, obtained**) *verb* to manage to get something ○ *She obtained a copy of the will.* ○ *He obtained control of the business.*

obtainable /əb'teɪnəb(ə)l/ *adj* which can be obtained

obtrusive /əb'tru:sɪv/ *adj* which sticks out or which is in the way

② **obvious** /'ɒbviəs/ *adj* clear; easily seen ○ *It's obvious that we will have to pay for the damage.* ○ *It was obvious to everyone that the shop was not making any money.*

① **obviously** /'ɒbviəsli/ *adv* clearly ○ *Obviously we will need to borrow various pieces of equipment.*

① **occasion** /ə'keɪʒ(ə)n/ *noun* **1.** □ **a special occasion** a special event such as a wedding ○ *The baby's first birthday was a special occasion.* ○ *It's an extra-special occasion – she's one hundred years old today!* **2.** a time when something happens ○ *I didn't meet him on that particular occasion.* ◇ **on occasion** from time to time ○ *On occasion, we spend a weekend in the country.*

③ **occasional** /ə'keɪʒ(ə)n(ə)l/ *adj* happening sometimes, but not very often ○ *He was an occasional visitor to my parents' house.* ○ *We make the occasional trip to London.*

② **occasionally** /ə'keɪʒ(ə)nəli/ *adv* sometimes, not very often ○ *Occasionally he has to work late.* ○ *We occasionally go to the cinema.*

occupancy /'ɒkjʊpənsi/ *noun* the act of moving into a property, such as a house, an office or a room in a hotel, either permanently or for a short stay

③ **occupant** /'ɒkjʊpənt/ *noun* the person or company occupying a property

③ **occupation** /ˌɒkjʊ'peɪʃ(ə)n/ *noun* **1.** the act of taking control of a place, or the fact of being in such a situation ○ *the occupation of the country by enemy soldiers* ○ *The city had been under enemy occupation for a week.* **2.** a job, position, employment ○ *What is her occupation?* ○ *His main occupation is running a small engineering works.*

③ **occupational** /ˌɒkjʊ'peɪʃ(ə)nəl/ *adj* referring to a job

③ **occupied** /'ɒkjupaɪd/ *adj* **1.** being used ○ *All the rooms in the hotel are occupied.* ○ *All the toilets are occupied, so you'll have to wait.* **2.** busy with an activity [~with] ○ *The manager is occupied just at the moment.* ○ *Keeping a class of 30 little children occupied is difficult.* ○ *He is occupied with sorting out the mail.*

occupier /'ɒkjʊpaɪə/ *noun* a person who lives in a particular house or flat

② **occupy** /'ɒkjʊpaɪ/ (**occupies, occupying, occupied**) *verb* **1.** to live in or work in ○ *They occupy the flat on the first floor.* ○ *The firm occupies offices in the centre of town.* **2.** (*of time, thoughts or attention*) to use or fill ○ *Dealing with the office occupies most of my time.* **3.** to take control of a place by being inside it ○ *Protesters occupied the TV station.* **4.** to hold a post ○ *Who occupies the post of company secretary.* (NOTE: **occupies – occupying – occupied**)

① **occur** /ə'kɜː/ (**occurs, occurring, occurred**) *verb* **1.** to happen ○ *When did the accident occur?* **2.** to come to your mind [~to] ○ *Did it never occur to you that she was lying?* ○ *It's just occurred to me that I didn't bring the keys.* **3.** to exist ○ *Iron ore occurs in several parts of the country.*

③ **occurrence** /ə'kʌrəns/ *noun* a happening

② **ocean** /'əʊʃ(ə)n/ *noun* a very large area of sea surrounding the large areas of land on the Earth ○ *Ocean currents can be very treacherous.* ○ *Ocean liners used to dock here.*

① **o'clock** /ə'klɒk/ *adv* used with numbers to show the time ○ *Get up – it's 7 o'clock.* ○ *We never open the shop before 10 o'clock.* ○ *By 2 o'clock in the morning everyone was asleep.* (NOTE: **O'clock** is only used for the exact hour, not for times which include minutes. It can also be omitted: *We got home before eight.* or *We got home before eight o'clock.*)

octagon /'ɒktəgən/ *noun* a geometrical figure with eight sides

octave /'ɒktɪv/ *noun* (*in music*) the eight notes between the first and last notes of a scale

① **October** /ɒk'təʊbə/ *noun* the tenth month of the year, between September and November ○ *October 18* ○ *Do you ever go on holiday in October?* ○ *Today is October 18th.* ○ *Last October we moved to London.* (NOTE: **October 18th** *or* **October 18**: say 'October the eighteenth' or 'the eighteenth of October'; in US English: 'October eighteenth'.)

octopus /'ɒktəpəs/ *noun* a sea animal with eight long arms called 'tentacles.' ◊ **squid**

OD /aʊ 'diː/ *noun* a large amount of a drug taken at one time and causing illness or death

① **odd** /ɒd/ *adj* **1.** unusual and not normal ○ *It's odd that she can never remember how to get to their house.* ○ *He doesn't like chocolate – Really, how odd!* **2.** □ **odd numbers** numbers such as 17 or 33 which cannot be divided by two ○ *The buildings with odd numbers are on the opposite side of the street.* **3.** (*of an amount*) almost, not exact or accurate ○ *She had 200 odd records in cardboard boxes* **4.** one forming part of a pair **5.** done only rarely or occasionally ○ *I've only been to the odd concert in the last few years.* ○ *On the odd occasions I've met him, he's seemed very nice.*

oddity /'ɒdɪti/ (*plural* **oddities**) *noun* **1.** the state of being odd ○ *I was struck by the oddity of the situation, sitting at the same table as my two former wives.* **2.** an unusual person or thing ○ *This symphony is a bit of an oddity, it only has two movements.*

odd jobs /ɒd 'dʒɒbz/ *plural noun* small pieces of work, especially repairs, done in the house ○ *He does odd jobs for us around the house.*

① **odds** /ɒdz/ ◇ **to be at odds with someone** to disagree with someone all the time

ode /əʊd/ *noun* a long poem often addressed to a person or thing

odour /'əʊdə/ *noun* a smell, especially an unpleasant smell ○ *the odour of rotten eggs* (NOTE: The US spelling is **odor**.)

odyssey /'ɒdɪsi/ *noun* a long journey with many exciting or unusual events

oestrogen /'iːstrədʒən/ *noun* a hormone produced in the ovaries which controls sexual development and the reproductive system (NOTE: The US spelling is **estrogen**.)

① **of** /əv, ɒv/ *prep* **1.** used for showing a connection ○ *She's the sister of the girl who you met at the party.* ○ *Where's the top of the jam jar?* ○ *What are the names of Henry VIII's wives?* **2.** used for showing a part or a quantity ○ *a litre of orange juice* ○ *How much of the cloth do you need?* ○ *Today is the sixth of March.* ○ *There are four boys and two girls – six of them altogether.* ○ *Half of the staff are on holiday.* **3.** used for giving a specific age, amount, etc ○ *The school takes children of ten and over.* ○ *He earns a salary of over £30,000.* **4.** showing position, material, cause ○ *He lives in the north of the town.* ○ *The jumper is made of cotton.* ○ *She died of cancer.* (NOTE: **Of** is often used after verbs or adjectives: *to think of, to be fond of, to be tired of, to smell of, to be afraid of*, etc.)

① **of course** /əv 'kɔːs/ *adv* **1.** used to say 'yes' or 'no' more strongly ○ *Are you coming with us? – Of course I am!* ○ *Do you want to lose all your money? – Of course not!* **2.** used for stating something that is not surprising ○ *He is rich, so of course he lives in a big house.*

① **off** /ɒf/ *adv, prep* **1.** showing movement or position away from a place ○ *We're off to the shops.* ○ *The office is just off the main road.* ○ *They spent their holiday on an island off the coast of Wales.* ○ *The children got off the bus.* ○ *Take your boots off before you come into the house.* **2.** away from work ○ *She took the week off.* ○ *It's my day off today.* ○ *Half the staff are off with flu.* **3.** not switched on ○ *Switch the light off before you leave the office.* ○ *Is the TV off?*

offal /'ɒf(ə)l/ *noun* organs such as the heart or liver of an animal used as food

off and on /ˌɒf ənd 'ɒn/ *adv* not continuously, with breaks in between

off-balance /ɒf 'bæləns/ *adv* not standing steadily ○ *The sudden movement of the bus threw her off-balance.*

offbeat /ɒf'biːt/ *adj* unusual

off-centre /ɒf 'sentə/ *adj* not at the centre of something (NOTE: The US spelling is **off-center**.)

off-chance /'ɒf tʃɑːns/ *noun* a slight possibility ◇ **on the off-chance** in case something happens

③ **off-colour** /ɒf'kʌlə/ *adj* not well (NOTE: The US spelling is **off-color**.)

off-duty /ˌɒf 'djuːti/ *adj* who is not on duty

③ **offence** /ə'fens/ *noun* **1.** the state of being offended ○ *He took offence when I said he looked bigger than before.* **2.** a crime, an act which is against the law ○ *He was charged with committing an offence.* ○ *Since it was his first offence, he was let off with a fine.* ◇ **to take offence at** to be offended by ○ *He took offence at being called a coward.* ○ *Don't take offence – I didn't really mean it.*

offend /ə'fend/ (**offends, offending, offended**) *verb* **1.** to do or say something that makes someone angry or upset ○ *He offended the whole village by the article he wrote in the paper.* ○ *That wallpaper offends my sense of taste.* **2.** to commit a crime ○ *He was released from prison and immediately offended again.*

offender /ə'fendə/ *noun* a person who commits an offence against the law

offense /ə'fens/ *noun* US spelling of **offence**

offensive /ə'fensɪv/ *adj* **1.** unpleasant ○ *What an offensive smell!* **2.** not polite; rude ○ *The waiter was quite offensive.*

① **offer** /'ɒfə/ *noun* a thing which is suggested ○ *She accepted his offer of a job in Paris.* ○ *He turned down her offer to drive him to the station.* ■ *verb* (**offers, offering, offered**) to suggest doing something for someone or giving someone something ○ *She offered to drive him to the station.* ◇ **on offer** which has been offered ○ *There are several good holiday bargains on offer.*

offering /'ɒf(ə)rɪŋ/ *noun* a thing which is offered; a present

off-guard /ɒf 'gɑːd/ *adj* not prepared and therefore surprised when something such as an attack happens

offhand /ɒf'hænd/ *adv* immediately, without thinking carefully ○ *I can't say offhand whether I'll be able to go.*

① **office** /'ɒfɪs/ *noun* a room or building where you do work such as writing, telephoning and working at a computer ○ *I'll be working late at the office this evening.* ○ *We bought some new office furniture.* ○ *Dad has his office at the top of the house.*

office block /'ɒfɪs blɒk/ *noun* a large building containing many offices

office hours /ˌɒfɪs 'aʊəz/ *plural noun* the time when an office is open ○ *Staff are not allowed to make private calls during office hours.*

① **officer** /'ɒfɪsə/ *noun* a person who holds an official position ○ *The customs officer asked me to open my suitcase.*

② **official** /ə'fɪʃ(ə)l/ *adj* **1.** relating to an organisation, especially one which is part of a government or some other authority ○ *He left official papers in his car.* ○ *We had an official order from the local authority.* ○ *He represents an official body.* **2.** done or approved by someone in authority ○ *She received an official letter of explanation.* ○ *The strike was made official by the union headquarters.* ■ *noun* a person holding a recognised position ○ *They were met by an official from the embassy.* ○ *I'll ask an official of the social services department to help you.*

officially /ə'fɪʃ(ə)li/ *adv* **1.** in an official way ○ *He has been officially named as a member of the British team.* ○ *She has been officially named as our representative at the meeting.* **2.** according to what is said in public ○ *Officially, you are not supposed to go in through this door, but everyone does.* ○ *Officially he knows nothing about the problem, but unofficially he has given us a lot of advice about it.*

officious /ə'fɪʃəs/ *adj* very ready to give advice or tell people what to do, especially when the advice is not wanted

off-licence /'ɒf ˌlaɪs(ə)ns/ *noun* a shop which has a licence to sell alcoholic drinks to be taken away

off-limits /ɒf 'lɪmɪts/ *adj* (*of a place*) where you are not allowed to go

offline /ɒf'laɪn/ *adj* not connected to a computer

off-peak /ˌɒf 'piːk/ *adj* not at the most busy time ○ *Off-peak fares are considerably less expensive.*

off-putting /ˌɒf 'pʊtɪŋ/ *adj* rather unpleasant or annoying

offset /ɒf'set/ (**offsets, offsetting, offset**) *verb* to balance one thing against another ○ *Losses in France more than offset our profits in the domestic market.*

offshoot /'ɒfʃuːt/ *noun* something which branches from something else

offside /ɒf'saɪd/ *adv* (*in football*) between the ball and the opposing team's goal ○ *The goal was disallowed because he was offside.* ■ *adj* referring to the side of a car nearest to the middle of the road ○ *Your offside rear light isn't working.*

③ **offspring** /'ɒfsprɪŋ/ (*plural same*) *noun* **1.** the young of an animal ○ *The mother deer produces her offspring in early spring.* **2.** a child or children ○ *Her offspring are all very musical.*

offstage /ɒf'steɪdʒ/ *adv* outside the area of a stage used for acting

off-the-cuff /ˌɒf ðə 'kʌf/ *adj, adv* made without notes ○ *He was only asked to speak at the last minute, and for an off-the-cuff speech, it was excellent.*

off-the-peg /ˌɒf ðə 'peg/ *adj, adv* (*of clothes*) which are mass-produced, ready to fit any person of a certain size

off-the-record /ɒf ðiː/ *adj* (*of a statement*) said privately and not to be repeated as an official statement or to have the speaker's name published

off-the-wall /ˌɒf ðə 'wɔːl/ *adj* very unusual and strange (*informal*)

off-white /ˌɒf 'waɪt/ *adj* yellowish white

① **often** /'ɒf(ə)n/ *adv* on many occasions ○ *I often have to go to town on business.* ○ *Do you eat beef often?* ○ *How often is there a bus to Richmond?* ◇ **every so often** from time to time ○ *We go to the cinema every so often.*

ogle /ˈəʊg(ə)l/ (**ogles, ogling, ogled**) *verb* to look at someone in a way that shows a sexual interest in them

ogre /ˈəʊgə/ *noun* an imaginary person in children's stories, who is very large and cruel and eats people ○ *Puss in Boots knocked at the door of the ogre's castle.*

① **oh** /əʊ/ *interj* showing surprise, interest or excitement

0800 number /ˌəʊ eɪt ˈhʌndrəd ˌnʌmbə/ *noun* a telephone number that can be rung free of charge

000 *noun* blood clotting which blocks an artery or vein

② **oil** /ɔɪl/ *noun* **1.** a liquid taken from plants and animals, which flows smoothly and is used in cooking ○ *Cook the vegetables in hot oil.* **2.** a thick mineral liquid found mainly underground and used as a fuel or to make something move smoothly ○ *The door squeaks – it needs some oil.* ○ *Some of the beaches are covered with oil.* ○ *The company is drilling for oil in the desert.*

oilfield /ˈɔɪlfiːld/ *noun* an area of rock under which oil lies and which can be drilled to take out oil

oil paint /ˈɔɪl peɪnt/ *noun* paint made with colours and oil

oil painting /ˈɔɪl ˌpeɪntɪŋ/ *noun* a picture painted in oil paints

oil rig /ˈɔɪl rɪg/ *noun* a structure for drilling for oil

oil slick /ˈɔɪl slɪk/ *noun* a layer of oil which has spilled into the sea from a tanker or oil rig and which floats on the water

oil tanker /ˈɔɪl ˌtæŋkə/ *noun* a large ship specially constructed for carrying oil

oil well /ˈɔɪl wel/ *noun* a hole in the ground from which oil is pumped

ointment /ˈɔɪntmənt/ *noun* a smooth healing cream which you spread on the skin

OK /əʊˈkeɪ/, **okay** *interj* **1.** used for answering 'yes' to a question ○ *Would you like a coffee? – OK!* **2.** used for starting to talk about something after a pause ○ *'It's ten o'clock' – 'OK, let's get going'.* ■ *adj* all right ○ *He was off ill yesterday, but he seems to be OK now.* ○ *Is it OK for me to bring the dogs?*

① **old** /əʊld/ *adj* **1.** having had a long life ○ *My uncle is an old man – he's eighty-four.* ○ *She lives in an old people's home.* **2.** having existed for a long time ○ *He collects old cars.* ○ *Play some old music, I don't like this modern stuff.* ○ *She's an old friend of mine.* **3.** relating to something which has been used for a long time ○ *Put on an old shirt if you're going to wash the car.* ○ *He got rid of his old car and bought a new one.* **4.** used with a number to talk about someone's age ○ *He's six years old today.* ○ *How old are you?*

old age /əʊld ˈeɪdʒ/ *noun* a period of your life when you are old

old age pension /ˌəʊld eɪdʒ ˈpenʃən/ *noun* a government pension given to a person who is past retirement age

old age pensioner /ˌəʊld eɪdʒ ˈpenʃ(ə)nə/ *noun* a person who has retired and lives on a pension. Abbreviation **OAP**

old-fashioned /ˌəʊld ˈfæʃ(ə)nd/ *adj* no longer in fashion ○ *She wore old-fashioned clothes.*

old flame /əʊld ˈfleɪm/ *noun* a former boyfriend or girlfriend

old hand /əʊld ˈhænd/ *noun* a person who is very skilled and experienced at doing something

old hat /əʊld ˈhæt/ *adj* old-fashioned or out of date (*informal*)

old-time /ˈəʊld taɪm/ *adj* done in an old-fashioned way

old wives' tale /əʊld ˈwaɪvz teɪl/ *noun* an old, and often silly, idea

old-world /ˈəʊld wɜːld/ *adj* old-fashioned in a way that is liked ○ *This hotel still provides old-world hospitality.*

olive /ˈɒlɪv/ *noun* a small black or green fruit from which oil is made for use in cooking ○ *Olives are grown in Mediterranean countries like Spain, Greece and Italy.* ○ *Which do you prefer – green or black olives?*

olive branch /ˈɒlɪv brɑːntʃ/ *noun* a sign of peace

olive oil /ˌɒlɪv ˈɔɪl/ *noun* an oil made from olives

omelette /ˈɒmlət/ *noun* a dish made of beaten eggs, cooked in a frying pan and folded over before serving, with various fillings inside (NOTE: The US spelling is **omelet**.)

omen /ˈəʊmən/ *noun* a thing that indicates what will happen in the future

ominous /ˈɒmɪnəs/ *adj* threatening bad results

③ **omission** /əʊˈmɪʃ(ə)n/ *noun* **1.** the act of omitting ○ *We were surprised at the omission of his name from the list of candidates.* **2.** a thing which has been omitted ○ *I can think of at least two obvious omis-*

sions from your list of famous playwrights: Shakespeare and Shaw!

omit /əʊ'mɪt/ (**omits, omitting, omitted**) *verb* to leave something out ○ *She omitted the date when she signed the contract.*

omnipotent /ɒm'nɪpət(ə)nt/ *adj* all-powerful

① **on** /ɒn/ *prep* **1.** on the top or surface of something ○ *Put the box down on the floor.* ○ *Flies can walk on the ceiling.* **2.** hanging from ○ *Hang your coat on the hook.* **3.** showing movement or place ○ *A crowd of children got on the train.* ○ *The picture's on page three.* ○ *The post office is on the left-hand side of the street.* **4.** doing something ○ *I have to go to Germany on business.* ○ *We're off on holiday tomorrow.* **5.** referring to a time, date or day ○ *The shop is open on Sundays.* ○ *We went to see my mother on my birthday.* **6.** a means of travel ○ *You can go there on foot – it only takes five minutes.* ○ *She came on her motorbike.* **7.** using an instrument or machine ○ *He played some music on the piano.* ○ *The song is available on CD.* ○ *He was on the telephone for most of the morning.* ○ *The film was on TV last night.* ■ *adv* **1.** being worn ○ *Have you all got your wellingtons on?* ○ *The central heating was off, so he kept his coat on in the house.* **2.** operating ○ *Have you put the kettle on?* ○ *The heating is on.* ○ *She left all the lights on.* ○ *She turned the engine on.* ○ *He switched the TV on.* **3.** being shown or played ○ *What's on at the theatre this week?*

on and off /ˌɒn ənd 'ɒf/ *adv* not continuously but with breaks in between

① **once** /wʌns/ *adv* **1.** one time ○ *Take the tablets once a day.* ○ *The magazine comes out once a month.* ○ *'How many times did you go to the cinema last year?' – 'Only once'.* **2.** at a time in the past ○ *Once, when it was snowing, the car skidded into a ditch.* ○ *He's someone I knew once when I worked in London.* ■ *conj* as soon as ○ *Once he starts talking you can't get him to stop.* ○ *Once we've moved house I'll give you a phone call.* ◇ **once and for all** finally ○ *I'll tell you once and for all 'stop talking!'.* ○ *The government wants to eradicate poverty once and for all.* ◇ **once in a while** from time to time ○ *It's nice to go and have an Indian meal once in a while.*

oncoming /'ɒnkʌmɪŋ/ *adj* coming towards you

① **one** /wʌn/ *noun* **1.** the number 1 **2.** a single item ○ *Have a toffee – oh dear, there's only one left!* ■ *pron* a single thing ○ *Which hat do you like best – the black one or the red one?* ○ *One of the staff will help you carry the box to your car.* ○ *I've lost my map – have you got one?* ○ *Small cars use less petrol than big ones.* ◇ **one or two** a few ○ *One or two people stayed behind to chat.* ◇ **in ones and twos** a few at a time ○ *The guests were arriving in ones and twos.* ◇ **last but one** the one before the last ○ *This is the last weekend but one before Christmas.* ◇ **one by one** one after another ○ *He ate all the chocolates one by one.* ○ *They came in one by one and sat in a row at the back of the hall.*

one another /wʌn ə'nʌðə/ *adj, pron* each other ○ *We write to one another every week.*

1471 /ˌwʌn fɔː sev(ə)n 'wʌn/ *noun* a telephone number that you can use to find out who was the last person to telephone you

one-man /wɒn 'mæn/ *adj* consisting of, designed for, featuring or performed, run or worked by only one person

one-night stand /ˌwʌn naɪt 'stænd/ *noun* **1.** a stop for a single performance of a play or by a pop group, before moving to another theatre the following night **2.** a sexual relationship which lasts for only one night (*informal*)

one-off /wɒn'ɒf/ *adj* which is done, happens or is made only once ○ *It's a one-off bargain.*

one-on-one /wʌn ɒn 'wʌn/ *adj US* same as **one-to-one**

one-person /wʌn 'pɜːs(ə)n/ *adj* consisting of, designed for, featuring or performed, run or worked by only one person

③ **oneself** /wʌn'self/ *pron* referring to the person speaking as an indefinite subject

one-sided /ˌwʌn 'saɪdɪd/ *adj* dealing with or favouring one side only

one-time /'wʌn taɪm/ *adj* former

one-to-one /ˌwʌn tə 'wʌn/ *adj* where one person has to deal with one other person only ○ *The two presidents had a one-to-one conversation.* ○ *She is taking a one-to-one Spanish conversation course.*

one-track mind /ˌwʌn træk 'maɪnd/ *noun* □ **to have (got) a one-track mind** to think too much about one thing, especially sex

one-upmanship /wʌn 'ʌpmənʃɪp/ *noun* the practice of trying to do better than another person so as to appear superior to him or her

③ **one-way** /ˌwʌn 'weɪ/ *adj* going in one direction only

one-woman /wʌn 'wʊmən/ *adj* consisting of, designed for, featuring or performed, run or worked by only one person

ongoing /'ɒngəʊɪŋ/ *adj* which is continuing

③ **onion** /'ʌnjən/ *noun* a round, strong-tasting vegetable which is made up of many layers

online /'ɒnlaɪn/ *adj, adv* directly connected to a computer ○ *You need to know the password to access the data online.*

onlooker /'ɒnlʊkə/ *noun* a person who watches an event

① **only** /'əʊnli/ *adj* without others of the same type ○ *Don't break it – it's the only one I've got.* ■ *adv* **1.** with no one or nothing else ○ *We've only got ten pounds between us.* ○ *Only an accountant can deal with this problem.* ○ *This lift is for staff only.* **2.** as recently as ○ *We saw her only last week.* ○ *Only yesterday the bank phoned for information.* ■ *conj* but, except ○ *I would have arrived on time, only the train was late.* ◇ **only just** almost not ◇ **only too** very much

only child /ˌəʊnli 'tʃaɪld/ *noun* son or daughter who has no other brothers or sisters

on-off /ɒn 'ɒf/ *adj* something which keeps on starting and stopping

on-screen /ˌɒn 'skriːn/ *adj, adv* on a computer screen rather than on paper ○ *Most of our design work is done on-screen.*

③ **onset** /'ɒnset/ *noun* beginning

onslaught /'ɒnslɔːt/ *noun* a sudden severe attack

① **onto** /'ɒntə, 'ɒntʊ, 'ɒntuː/ *prep* on or to something ○ *The speaker went up onto the platform.* ○ *The door opens directly onto the garden.* ○ *Turn the box onto its side.*

onus /'əʊnəs/ *noun* a responsibility for doing something difficult

onward /'ɒnwəd/ *adj* further forward ○ *Nothing can stop the onward march of computer technology.*

onwards /'ɒnwədz/ *adv* further forwards

ooh! /uː/ *interj* showing surprise or shock (*informal*)

oops! /uːps/ *interj* showing surprise or that you are sorry (*informal*)

ooze /uːz/ (**oozes, oozing, oozed**) *verb* (*of liquid*) to flow slowly

opal /'əʊp(ə)l/ *noun* a semi-precious white stone with changing colours

opaque /əʊ'peɪk/ *adj* **1.** which you cannot see through, but which does allow light through ○ *The surface of the glass is treated to make it opaque.* ○ *Opaque black tights are the fashion this winter.* **2.** difficult to understand ○ *The meaning of the document is completely opaque to me.* ○ *Her writings are notorious for being opaque to non-specialists.*

① **open** /'əʊpən/ *adj* **1.** not shut ○ *The safe door is open.* ○ *Leave the window open – it's very hot in here.* **2.** available for use by or the enjoyment of the public ○ *Is the supermarket open on Sundays?* ○ *The show is open from 9 a.m. to 6 p.m.* ○ *The competition is open to anyone over the age of fifteen.* ■ *verb* (**opens, opening, opened**) **1.** to make something open ○ *Can you open the door for me, I'm trying to carry these heavy boxes?* ○ *Don't open the envelope until tomorrow.* **2.** to start doing something, to start a business ○ *A new restaurant is going to open next door to us.* ○ *Most shops open early in the morning.*

open up *phrasal verb* **1.** to start working ○ *A new bookshop has opened up next door.* **2.** to make available for use ○ *We are opening up the park to visitors.*

open air /ˌəʊpən 'eə/ *noun* a place outside which is not covered or hidden ○ *We keep the plants in the greenhouse during the winter, but bring them out into the open air in the summer.*

open-air /'əʊpən eə/ *adj* in the open, not in a building

open day /'əʊpən deɪ/ *noun* a day when a building is open to the public

open-ended /ˌəʊpən 'endɪd/ *adj* with no fixed limit and with some items not specified

③ **opener** /'əʊp(ə)nə/ *noun* a piece of equipment for opening things such as tins or bottles

open house /əʊpən 'haʊs/ *noun* a situation when people are welcome to visit at any time

③ **opening** /'əʊp(ə)nɪŋ/ *noun* **1.** the action of becoming open ○ *The opening of the exhibition has been postponed.* ○ *The office opening times are 9.30 to 5.30.* **2.** a hole or space [~in] ○ *The cows got out through an opening in the wall.*

opening hours /'əʊp(ə)nɪŋ aʊəz/ *plural noun* the times that a business such as a shop or bank is working and open to the public

opening night /ˌəʊp(ə)nɪŋ 'naɪt/ *noun* the first evening performance when a new film or play is shown (NOTE: for a play also **first night**)

open invitation /ˌəʊpən ˌɪnvɪ'teɪʃ(ə)n/ *noun* **1.** an invitation to visit someone or somewhere at any time **2.** something which encourages someone to do something wrong or to commit a crime ○ *Leaving the garage door open was an open invitation to car thieves.*

③ **openly** /'əʊpənli/ *adv* in a frank and open way

open market /ˌəʊpən 'mɑːkɪt/ *noun* a market where anyone can buy or sell

open-minded /ˌəʊpən 'maɪndɪd/ *adj* not having prejudices or fixed opinions and willing to listen to other people's ideas

open-mouthed /ˌəʊpən 'maʊðd/ *adj* with the mouth open in surprise or shock

openness /'əʊpənəs/ *noun* the state of being open

open-plan /ˌəʊpən 'plæn/ *adj* describing a building or an area of a building with no internal walls to divide it up ○ *an open-plan school* ○ *open-plan offices*

opera /'ɒp(ə)rə/ *noun* a performance on a stage with music in which the words are sung and not spoken

opera house /'ɒp(ə)rə haʊs/ *noun* a theatre in which operas are performed

② **operate** /'ɒpəreɪt/ (**operates, operating, operated**) *verb* **1.** to make something work ○ *He knows how to operate the machine.* ○ *She is learning how to operate the new telephone switchboard.* **2.** to treat a patient by cutting open the body [~on] ○ *She was operated on by our top surgeons*

③ **operating system** /'ɒpəreɪtɪŋ ˌsɪstəm/ *noun* basic software that controls the running of the hardware on a computer, and the management of data files, without the user having to operate it

operating theatre /'ɒpəreɪtɪŋ ˌθɪətə/ *noun* a special room in a hospital where surgeons carry out operations

① **operation** /ˌɒpə'reɪʃ(ə)n/ *noun* **1.** an organised action to achieve a specific goal ○ *The rescue operation was successful.* **2.** a treatment when a surgeon cuts open the body [~on] ○ *She's had three operations on her leg.* ○ *The operation lasted almost two hours.* ◇ **to come into operation** to begin to be applied ○ *The new schedules came into operation on June 1st.*

operational /ˌɒpə'reɪʃ(ə)nəl/ *adj* **1.** referring to the working of something ○ *The operational procedure is described in the manual.* **2.** ready for use ○ *The new set-up will be fully operational by next year.*

operative /'ɒp(ə)rətɪv/ *adj* working or in operation ■ *noun* a worker, especially one who operates a machine, etc. ○ *The factory used to employ two hundred operatives.*

③ **operator** /'ɒpəreɪtə/ *noun* **1.** a person who works instruments, etc. ○ *He's a computer operator.* ○ *She's a machine operator.* **2.** a person who works a telephone switchboard ○ *Dial 0 for the operator.* ○ *You can place a call through* or *via the operator.* **3.** a person who organises things

ophthalmologist /ˌɒfθæl'mɒlədʒɪst/ *noun* a doctor who treats diseases of the eye. Compare **optician**, **optometrist**

① **opinion** /ə'pɪnjən/ *noun* what someone thinks about something [~on/~of] ○ *She has an opinion on every subject.* ○ *What's your opinion of their latest album?* ○ *In my opinion, we should wait until the weather gets warmer before we go on holiday.*

opinionated /ə'pɪnjəneɪtɪd/ *adj* with strong fixed opinions

③ **opinion poll** /ə'pɪnjən pəʊl/ *noun* asking a sample group of people questions, so as to get the probable opinion of the whole population

opium /'əʊpiəm/ *noun* a drug made from a type of poppy, used in the preparation of codeine and heroin

③ **opponent** /ə'pəʊnənt/ *noun* **1.** a person or group which is against something [~of] ○ *Opponents of the planned motorway have occupied the site.* **2.** (*in boxing, an election, etc.*) a person who fights someone else ○ *His opponent in the election is a local councillor.* ○ *He knocked out his last three opponents.*

opportune /'ɒpətjuːn/ *adj* happening by chance at the right time

opportunist /ˌɒpə'tjuːnɪst/ *noun* a person who takes advantage of opportunities, especially at the expense of others (NOTE: + **opportunism** *n*)

opportunistic /ˌɒpətjuː'nɪstɪk/ *adj* trying to take advantage from an opportunity which is offered

① **opportunity** /ˌɒpə'tjuːnɪti/ (*plural* **opportunities**) *noun* a chance or circumstances which allow you to do something [~for] ○ *When you were in London, did you have much opportunity for sightseeing?* ○ *I'd like to take this opportunity to thank all members of staff for the work they have done over the past year.*

③ **oppose** /ə'pəʊz/ (**opposes, opposing, opposed**) *verb* **1.** to put yourself against someone in an election ○ *She is opposing him in the election.* **2.** to try to prevent something happening ○ *Several groups oppose the new law.*

opposed to /ə'pəʊzd tuː/ *adj* not agreeing with ○ *He is opposed to the government's policy on education.*

opposing /ə'pəʊzɪŋ/ *adj* **1.** playing, fighting or arguing against you ○ *The players on the opposing side refused to shake hands with us.* ○ *He fouled a member of the opposing team.* **2.** which is the opposite ○ *She holds quite opposing views to mine.*

② **opposite** /'ɒpəzɪt/ *prep* on the other side of, facing ○ *I work in the offices opposite the railway station.* ○ *She sat down opposite me.* ■ *adj* which is on the other side ○ *The shop's not on this side of the street – it's on the opposite side.* ○ *Her van hit a tree on the opposite side of the road.* ○ *Her van was hit by a lorry going in the opposite direction.* ■ *noun* something which is completely different ○ *'Black' is the opposite of 'white.'* ○ *She's just the opposite of her brother – he's tall and thin, she's short and fat.* ○ *He likes to say one thing, and then do the opposite.*

① **opposition** /ˌɒpə'zɪʃ(ə)n/ *noun* **1.** the action of opposing [~between/~to] ○ *There was a lot of opposition to the company's plans to build a supermarket.* **2.** (*in politics*) the party or group which opposes the government ○ *The leader of the opposition rose to speak.* ○ *The party lost the election and is now in opposition.*

oppress /ə'pres/ (**oppresses, oppressing, oppressed**) *verb* **1.** to make people suffer, especially by harsh government ○ *The barons oppressed the peasants.* **2.** to make someone feel shut in and depressed ○ *The atmosphere in this office really oppresses me.* ○ *Playing in India for the first time, the members of the team felt oppressed by the heat.* (NOTE: + **oppression** *n*)

oppressed /ə'prest/ *adj* treated in a cruel and unfair way

oppressive /ə'presɪv/ *adj* **1.** cruel and unfair in using power ○ *Under the general's oppressive regime, ordinary citizens were afraid to speak out against the government.* **2.** making someone feel trapped and depressed ○ *There's a very oppressive atmosphere in the office.* **3.** referring to unpleasant hot weather without any wind

oppressor /ə'presə/ *noun* a person who oppresses others

opt /ɒpt/ (**opts, opting, opted**) *verb* to decide in favour of something ○ *In the end, she opted for a little black dress.*

opt out③ *phrasal verb* to decide not to take part in something ○ *She decided to opt out of the pension scheme.* ○ *I think I'll opt out if you don't mind.* ○ *He opted out of the trip because he couldn't afford the price of a ticket.*

optic /'ɒptɪk/ *adj* referring to the eye or to sight

③ **optical** /'ɒptɪk(ə)l/ *adj* referring to the eyes or to eyesight

optical illusion /ˌɒptɪk(ə)l ɪ'luːʒ(ə)n/ *noun* a thing which appears different from what it really is because your eye doesn't recognise it

③ **optician** /ɒp'tɪʃ(ə)n/ *noun* a person who tests your eyes and sells glasses

optics /'ɒptɪks/ *noun* the study of sight and light rays

optimal /'ɒptɪm(ə)l/ *adj* referring to the best or most desirable (*formal*)

optimism /'ɒptɪmɪz(ə)m/ *noun* a belief or attitude that everything is as good as it can be or will work out for the best in the future

optimist /'ɒptɪmɪst/ *noun* a person who believes everything will work out for the best in the end

optimistic /ˌɒptɪ'mɪstɪk/ *adj* a feeling that everything will work out for the best

optimum /'ɒptɪməm/ *adj* best ○ *The market offers optimum conditions for sales.* ○ *What is the optimum speed for fuel consumption?*

① **option** /'ɒpʃən/ *noun* a choice, other possible action ○ *One option would be to sell the house.*

optional /'ɒpʃ(ə)n(ə)l/ *adj* which may or may not be chosen

optometrist /ɒp'tɒmətrɪst/ *noun* a person who tests your eyesight, prescribes and sells glasses or contact lenses, etc.

opulent /'ɒpjʊlənt/ *adj* rich, luxurious or splendid

① **or** /ɔː/ *conj* **1.** used for joining two parts of a sentence which show two possibilities ○ *You can come with us in the car or just take the bus.* ○ *Do you prefer tea or coffee?* ○ *Was he killed in an accident or was he murdered?* ○ *The film starts at 6.30 or 6.45, I can't remember which.* **2.** used for showing that you are not sure about an amount ○ *Five or six people came into the shop.* ○ *It costs three or four dollars.*

oral /'ɔːrəl/ *adj* spoken rather than written down ○ *There is an oral test as well as a written one.*

③ **orange** /'ɒrɪndʒ/ *noun* **1.** a sweet, brightly coloured Mediterranean fruit ○ *roast duck and orange sauce* ○ *She had a glass of orange juice and a cup of coffee* *for breakfast.* **2.** a yellowish-red colour, like that of an orange ■ *adj* of the colour of an orange

orator /ˈɒrətə/ *noun* a person who speaks well in public ○ *One of best orators in Parliament.*

oratory /ˈɒrət(ə)ri/ *noun* the art of making formal public speeches

orbit /ˈɔːbɪt/ *noun* the curved path of something moving through space ○ *The rocket will put the satellite into orbit round the earth.* ■ *verb* (**orbits, orbiting, orbited**) to move in a curved path round something ○ *The satellite orbits the earth once every five hours.*

orchard /ˈɔːtʃəd/ *noun* a field of fruit trees

orchestra /ˈɔːkɪstrə/ *noun* a large group of musicians who play together ○ *the London Symphony Orchestra*

orchestrate /ˈɔːkɪstreɪt/ (**orchestrates, orchestrating, orchestrated**) *verb* **1.** to arrange a piece of music for an orchestra ○ *Mussorgsky's 'Pictures at an Exhibition' was orchestrated by Ravel.* **2.** to organise a demonstration ○ *They orchestrated the protest marches in such a way as to get them on the TV news every evening.*

orchid /ˈɔːkɪd/ *noun* a plant with colourful showy flowers, which, in the wild, often grows on other plants

ordain /ɔːˈdeɪn/ (**ordains, ordaining, ordained**) *verb* **1.** to make someone a priest or a member of the clergy in a formal ceremony ○ *He was ordained in Canterbury Cathedral.* **2.** to order that something be done ○ *The king ordained that all children over five had to be registered with the tax authorities.* ○ *Fate ordained that the children would never see their father again.*

③ **ordeal** /ɔːˈdiːl/ *noun* a painful test or difficult time

① **order** /ˈɔːdə/ *noun* **1.** an instruction to someone to do something ○ *He shouted orders to the workmen.* ○ *If you can't obey orders you can't be a soldier.* **2.** a request to buy something, or the thing requested [~for] ○ *We've had a large order for books from Russia.* ○ *She gave the waitress her order.* **3.** a special way of organising things in a sequence ○ *Put the invoices in order of their dates.* **4.** a situation in which rules or laws are obeyed without unrest or violence ○ *Problems of law and order are important to the local authorities.* ○ *The army entered the university campus and managed to restore order.* ■ *verb* (**orders, ordering, ordered**) **1.** to tell someone to do something ○ *They ordered the protesters out of the building.* ○ *The doctor ordered him to take four weeks' holiday.* **2.** (*of a customer*) to ask for something to be served or to be sent ○ *They ordered chicken and chips and some wine.* ○ *I've ordered a new computer for the office.* ○ *They ordered a Rolls Royce for the managing director.* ◇ **out of order** not working ○ *You'll have to use the stairs, the lift is out of order.* ◇ **in order** correct, valid ○ *Are his papers in order?* ◇ **in order to** used for showing why something is done ○ *She called out all their names in order to check who was there.* ○ *He looked under the car in order to see if there was an oil leak.*

order about③ *phrasal verb* to tell someone what to do all the time

orderly /ˈɔːdəli/ *noun* a person who does general work

ordinarily /ˈɔːd(ə)n(ə)rɪli/ *adv* normally or usually ○ *Ordinarily we don't allow visitors in here.* ○ *It's not something we ordinarily do.*

① **ordinary** /ˈɔːd(ə)n(ə)ri/ *adj* not special ○ *I'll wear my ordinary suit to the wedding.* ○ *They lead a very ordinary life.* ◇ **out of the ordinary** unusual or different ○ *Their flat is quite out of the ordinary.*

ordination /ˌɔːdɪˈneɪʃ(ə)n/ *noun* the act or ceremony of ordaining someone as a priest

ore /ɔː/ *noun* a type of stone found in the earth from which metals are obtained (NOTE: Do not confuse with **oar**.)

oregano /ˌɒrɪˈɡɑːnəʊ/ *noun* a herb used in cooking

③ **organ** /ˈɔːɡən/ *noun* **1.** a part of the body with a special function, such as the heart or liver ○ *He was badly injured and some of his organs had stopped functioning.* **2.** a musical instrument which is often played in churches with one or more keyboards and many pipes through which air is pumped to make a sound ○ *She played the organ at our wedding.* ○ *The organ played the 'Wedding March' as the bride and groom walked down the aisle.*

organic /ɔːˈɡænɪk/ *adj* relating to living things

organisation /ˌɔːɡənaɪˈzeɪʃ(ə)n/, **organization** *noun* **1.** the act of arranging something ○ *The organisation of the meeting is done by the secretary.* **2.** an organised group or institution ○ *He's chairman of an organisation which looks after blind people.* ○ *International relief organisations are sending supplies.*

organisational /ˌɔːgənaɪˈzeɪʃ(ə)n(ə)l/, **organizational** *adj* relating to the way in which something is organised

organise /ˈɔːgənaɪz/ (**organises, organising, organised**), **organize** *verb* **1.** to arrange something ○ *She is responsible for organising the meeting.* ○ *We organised ourselves into two groups.* ○ *The company is organised in three sections.* **2.** to put into good order ○ *We have put her in charge of organising the city archives.*

organised /ˈɔːgənaɪzd/, **organized** *adj* **1.** (*of a person*) working efficiently and according to a plan **2.** (*of an activity*) planned carefully, and involving many different people or elements

organiser /ˈɔːgənaɪzə/, **organizer** *noun* a person who arranges things

③ **organism** /ˈɔːgənɪz(ə)m/ *noun* a living thing

organist /ˈɔːgənɪst/ *noun* a person who plays the organ

orgasm /ˈɔːgæz(ə)m/ *noun* the climax of a sexual act, when a person experiences a moment of great excitement

orgy /ˈɔːdʒi/ (*plural* **orgies**) *noun* **1.** an uncontrolled party with drinking, dancing and sexual activity ○ *The celebrations rapidly became a drunken orgy.* ○ *Jenny's birthday party turned into an all-night orgy.* **2.** an uncontrolled activity ○ *an orgy of spending*

oriental /ˌɔːriˈent(ə)l/ *adj* referring to the countries of East Asia (*dated*)

orientation /ˌɔːriənˈteɪʃ(ə)n/ *noun* **1.** the attitudes, views or aims of a person or organisation **2.** the process of helping people to get to know a place, job or subject **3.** the direction that something faces, or the line of that direction in relation to the compass

② **origin** /ˈɒrɪdʒɪn/ *noun* where something or someone comes from ○ *What is the origin of the word 'taboo'?* ○ *His family has French origins.*

① **original** /əˈrɪdʒən(ə)l/ *adj* **1.** new and interesting ○ *The planners have produced some very original ideas for the new town centre.* **2.** not a copy ○ *They sent a copy of the original invoice.* ○ *He kept the original receipt for reference.* ■ *noun* a thing from which other things are copied ○ *Send a copy of the letter but keep the original.*

originality /əˌrɪdʒɪˈnælɪti/ *noun* the fact of being original, new or different

② **originally** /əˈrɪdʒən(ə)li/ *adv* in the beginning ○ *Originally it was mine, but I gave it to my brother.* ○ *The family originally came from France in the 18th century.*

originate /əˈrɪdʒɪneɪt/ (**originates, originating, originated**) *verb* **1.** to begin, to start from or to have a beginning ○ *This strain of flu originated in Hong Kong.* ○ *His problems at work originated from home.* **2.** to make for the first time

originator /əˈrɪdʒəˌneɪtə/ *noun* someone who begins, creates or invents something

③ **ornament** /ˈɔːnəmənt/ *noun* a small object used as decoration ○ *There's a row of china ornaments on the mantelpiece.*

ornamental /ˌɔːnəˈment(ə)l/ *adj* **1.** acting as an ornament ○ *A box with ornamental carvings on its sides.* **2.** pretty rather than useful ○ *The table is purely ornamental: it's far too small to use as a dining table.*

ornate /ɔːˈneɪt/ *adj* with too much ornamentation

ornithology /ˌɔːnɪˈθɒlədʒi/ *noun* the study of birds (NOTE: + **ornithologist** *n*)

orphan /ˈɔːf(ə)n/ *noun* a child whose parents are dead ○ *She's an orphan – both her parents were killed in a car crash.* ■ *verb* (**orphans, orphaning, orphaned**) to make someone an orphan ○ *Hundreds of children were orphaned during the war.*

orphanage /ˈɔːf(ə)nɪdʒ/ *noun* a home where orphans are looked after

orthodox /ˈɔːθədɒks/ *adj* **1.** holding the generally accepted beliefs of a religion or a philosophy ○ *The Chancellor of the Exchequer is following orthodox financial principles.* **2.** observing traditional religious practices very strictly

orthodoxy /ˈɔːθədɒksi/ (*plural* **orthodoxies**) *noun* an opinion that is generally accepted at a particular time ○ *He challenged the orthodoxies of the scientific establishment.*

orthopaedic /ˌɔːθəˈpiːdɪk/ *adj* referring to the treatment of bones and joints

oscillate /ˈɒsɪleɪt/ (**oscillates, oscillating, oscillated**) *verb* to swing from one side to the other (NOTE: + **oscillation** *n*)

osmosis /ɒzˈməʊsɪs/ *noun* the movement of a solution from one part through a semi-permeable membrane to another part

ostensible /ɒˈstensɪb(ə)l/ *adj* which seems on the surface to be real, when in fact it is not

ostentatious /ˌɒstenˈteɪʃəs/ *adj* looking showy and expensive, so as to impress

osteopathy /ˌɒsti'ɒpəθi/ *noun* a treatment for some medical conditions that involves massaging and bending parts of the body

osteoporosis /ˌɒstiəʊpɔː'rəʊsɪs/ *noun* a condition where the bones become thin, porous and brittle, because of lack of calcium and lack of physical exercise

ostracise /'ɒstrəsaɪz/ (**ostracises, ostracising, ostracised**), **ostracize** *verb* to refuse to talk to somebody or allow them to be part of a group

ostrich /'ɒstrɪtʃ/ (*plural* **ostriches** or *same*) *noun* a very large bird which cannot fly but which can run fast, and is found in Africa

① **other** /'ʌðə/ *adj, pron* **1.** a different person or thing ○ *We went swimming while the other members of the group sat and watched.* ○ *I don't like chocolate cakes – can I have one of the others?* ○ *I'm fed up with that restaurant – can't we go to some other place?* **2.** second one of two ○ *He has two cars – one is red, and the other one is blue.* ○ *One of their daughters is fat, but the other is quite thin.* ■ *plural noun* **others** other people or things ○ *I'll have to ask the others if they agree.* ○ *Are there any others in the box?*

① **otherwise** /'ʌðəwaɪz/ *adv* **1.** apart from something just mentioned ○ *Your little boy can be noisy sometimes, but otherwise he's an excellent pupil.* **2.** if not, or else ○ *Are you sure you can come on Tuesday? – Otherwise I'll have to give the tickets to someone else.*

OTT *abbr* over the top (*informal*) ○ *Throwing the letter on the floor and stamping on it was a bit OTT.*

otter /'ɒtə/ *noun* a small fish-eating mammal with webbed feet living mainly by rivers

ouch /aʊtʃ/ *interj* showing that you have been hurt ○ *Ouch! That was my foot you trod on!*

① **ought** /ɔːt/ *modal verb* **1.** it would be a good thing to ○ *You ought to go swimming more often.* ○ *You ought to see the doctor if your cough doesn't get better.* ○ *He oughtn't to eat so much – he'll get fat.* ○ *The travel agent ought to have told you the hotel was full before you went on holiday.* **2.** used for showing that you expect something to happen or to be the case ○ *She ought to pass her driving test easily.* ○ *He left his office at six, so he ought to be home by now.* (NOTE: The negative is **ought not** or, especially in speaking, **oughtn't**. **Ought** is always followed by **to** and a verb in the infinitive.)

oughtn't *short for* ought not

③ **ounce** /aʊns/ *noun* a measure of weight, equal to 28 grams (NOTE: usually written **oz** after figures: *3oz of butter,* say 'three ounces of butter')

① **our** /aʊə/ *adj* belonging to us ○ *Our office is near the station.* ○ *Our cat is missing again.* ○ *Two of our children caught flu.* (NOTE: Do not confuse with **hour**.)

① **ours** /aʊəz/ *pron* a thing or person that belongs to us ○ *That house over there is ours.* ○ *Friends of ours told us that the restaurant was good.* ○ *Can we borrow your car, because ours is being serviced?* (NOTE: Do not confuse with **hours**.)

① **ourselves** /aʊə'selvz/ *pron* to for referring back to the subject pronoun 'we' ○ *We all organised ourselves into two teams.* ○ *We were enjoying ourselves when the police came.*

oust /aʊst/ (**ousts, ousting, ousted**) *verb* to force someone to leave a position

① **out** /aʊt/ *adv* **1.** away from inside ○ *How did the tiger get out of its cage?* ○ *She pulled out a box of matches.* ○ *Take the computer out of its packing case.* **2.** not at home ○ *No one answered the phone – they must all be out.*

outbid /aʊt'bɪd/ (**outbids, outbidding, outbidded**) *verb* to bid higher than someone else

outbox /'aʊtˌbɒks/ *noun US* an out tray

outbreak /'aʊtbreɪk/ *noun* a sudden series of cases of an illness or unrest ○ *the outbreak of war* ○ *There has been an outbreak of measles at the school.*

outburst /'aʊtbɜːst/ *noun* a sudden display of violent emotion ○ *The boss is prone to sudden outbursts of enthusiasm.*

outcast /'aʊtkɑːst/ *noun* a person who has been rejected by society, or driven away from a group

outclass /ˌaʊt'klɑːs/ (**outclasses, outclassing, outclassed**) *verb* to be significantly better than other people at doing something

③ **outcome** /'aʊtkʌm/ *noun* a result ○ *The outcome of the match was in doubt until the final few minutes.* ○ *What was the outcome of the appeal?*

outcrop /'aʊtkrɒp/ *noun* a rock which sticks out of the surface of the ground

outcry /'aʊtkraɪ/ *noun* a loud protest from a number of people

outdated /aʊt'deɪtɪd/ *adj* old-fashioned

outdo /aʊt'duː/ (**outdoing, outdid, outdone**) *verb* to do better than

③ **outdoor** /aʊt'dɔː/ *adj* in the open air

③ **outdoors** /aʊt'dɔːz/ *adv* in the open air, not inside a building ○ *The ceremony is usually held outdoors.* ○ *Why don't we take our coffee outdoors and sit in the sun?* ○ *The concert will be held outdoors if the weather is good.* (NOTE: You can also say **out of doors**.)

③ **outer** /'aʊtə/ *adj* on the outside ○ *Though the outer surface of the pie was hot, the inside was still cold.*

outermost /'aʊtəməʊst/ *adj* furthest out or furthest from the centre

outer space /ˌaʊtə 'speɪs/ *noun* the area beyond the Earth's atmosphere

③ **outfit** /'aʊtfɪt/ *noun* a set of clothes, often worn for a particular purpose ○ *She bought a new outfit for the wedding.* ○ *For the fancy dress party she wore a nurse's outfit.*

outflank /aʊt'flæŋk/ (**outflanks, outflanking, outflanked**) *verb* to go round the side of an enemy

outgoing /ˌaʊt'gəʊɪŋ/ *adj* **1.** referring to a phone call or post which is going out of a building ○ *an outgoing call* ○ *He hurried to catch the outgoing post.* **2.** lively, who likes to be with others ○ *He has a very outgoing personality.* **3.** referring to someone who is leaving a job ○ *She proposed a vote of thanks to the outgoing chairman.*

outgoings /'aʊtgəʊɪŋz/ *plural noun* regular expenditure

outgrow /aʊt'grəʊ/ (**outgrows, outgrowing, outgrew, outgrown**) *verb* **1.** to grow too big for clothes ○ *She's already outgrown the dress I bought her for Christmas.* **2.** to change your behaviour as you grow up ○ *We hoped they'd soon outgrow that sort of behaviour.* (NOTE: You can also say to **grow out of**.)

outing /'aʊtɪŋ/ *noun* a short trip ○ *The children went on an outing to the seaside.*

outlandish /aʊt'lændɪʃ/ *adj* strange or different from the usual

outlast /ˌaʊt'lɑːst/ (**outlasts, outlasting, outlasted**) *verb* to exist longer than another person or thing or to be successful for longer than another thing

outlaw /'aʊtlɔː/ *verb* (**outlaws, outlawing, outlawed**) **1.** to say that something is unlawful ○ *The government has proposed a bill to outlaw drinking in public.* **2.** to declare someone to be beyond the protection of the law (*old*) ○ *The leader of the bandits was outlawed and fled into the mountains.* ■ *noun* a person who has been outlawed (*dated*) ○ *They read about Robin Hood, the famous English outlaw.*

outlay /'aʊtleɪ/ *noun* money spent

outlet /'aʊtlət/ *noun* **1.** a place where something can be sold or distributed ○ *He owns a small number of clothing outlets in south-east London.* **2.** the means by which an idea or feeling can get out ○ *He did weight-lifting as an outlet for his stress at work.*

outline /'aʊtlaɪn/ *noun* a line showing the outer edge of something

outlive /aʊt'lɪv/ (**outlives, outliving, outlived**) *verb* **1.** to live longer than someone ○ *He outlived all his brothers and sisters.* ○ *She outlived her husband by twenty years.* **2.** to last longer than something □ **to outlive its usefulness** to be no longer any use ○ *Our old telephone system has outlived its usefulness.*

outlook /'aʊtlʊk/ *noun* **1.** a view of the world in general ○ *His gloomy outlook on life shows in his novels.* **2.** a view of what will happen in the future ○ *We think the outlook for the company is excellent.* ○ *The outlook for tomorrow's weather is mainly sunny with some rain.* ○ *The economic outlook is not good.*

outlying /'aʊtlaɪɪŋ/ *adj* away from a town or city

outmanoeuvre /ˌaʊtmə'nuːvə/ (**outmanoeuvres, outmanoeuvring, outmanoeuvred**) *verb* to gain an advantage over someone by acting or working more cleverly (NOTE: The US spelling is **outmaneuver**.)

outmoded /aʊt'məʊdɪd/ *adj* old-fashioned

outnumber /aʊt'nʌmbə/ (**outnumbers, outnumbering, outnumbered**) *verb* to be greater in number than something

① **out of date** /ˌaʊt əv 'deɪt/ *adj* **1.** without recent information **2.** no longer in fashion ○ *Flared trousers are rather out of date.*

out of the way /ˌaʊt əv ðə 'weɪ/ *adj* not near any main town ○ *They live in an out of the way village in the West Country.*

out-of-town /ˌaʊt əv 'taʊn/ *adj* not near to a town centre

outpatient /'aʊtpeɪʃ(ə)nt/ *noun* a person who goes to a hospital for treatment, without staying there overnight

outperform /ˌaʊtpə'fɔːm/ (**outperforms, outperforming, outperformed**) *verb* to do something better or more quickly than somebody or something else

outplay /ˌaʊt'pleɪ/ (**outplays, outplaying, outplayed**) *verb* to play better than someone else

outpost /'aʊtpəʊst/ *noun* a small town or small fort in a distant part of an occupied territory

outpouring /'aʊtˌpɔːrɪŋ/ *noun* the sudden expression of a strong emotion or production of something in large amounts

② **output** /'aʊtpʊt/ *noun* an amount which a firm, machine or person produces ○ *The factory has doubled its output in the last six months.*

outrage /'aʊtreɪdʒ/ *noun* **1.** a strong feeling of anger because something very unfair or cruel has happened [~over/at] ○ *There was outrage at the way he had been treated.* **2.** a shocking or violent event ○ *terrorist outrages* **3.** something that makes you very angry ○ *I think the extra tax on fuel is an outrage!* ■ *verb* (**outrages, outraging, outraged**) to shock, to be a cause of great indignation ○ *His behaviour outraged his parents.*

outrageous /aʊt'reɪdʒəs/ *adj* causing indignation and shock

outright /ˌaʊt'raɪt/ *adj* complete ○ *The play was an outright success.* ○ *She's the outright winner of the competition.* ■ *adv* **1.** openly ○ *He told me outright that he didn't like me.* **2.** immediately ○ *The van hit him and he was killed outright.*

③ **outset** /'aʊtset/ *noun* the beginning

① **outside** /'aʊtsaɪd/ *noun* the outer surface or the part which is not inside ○ *He polished the outside of his car.* ○ *The apple was red and shiny on the outside, but rotten inside.* ■ *adj* which is on the outer surface ○ *The outside walls of the house are made of brick.* ■ *adv* not inside a building ○ *It's beautiful and warm outside in the garden.* ○ *The dog's all wet – it must be raining outside.*

③ **outsider** /aʊt'saɪdə/ *noun* a person who does not belong to a group ○ *She has always been a bit of an outsider.*

outspoken /aʊt'spəʊkən/ *adj* speaking very frankly

③ **outstanding** /aʊt'stændɪŋ/ *adj* excellent or of a very high standard or quality ○ *an antique Chinese vase of outstanding quality* ○ *Her performance was outstanding.*

outstrip /aʊt'strɪp/ (**outstrips, outstripping, outstripped**) *verb* **1.** to go faster than someone ○ *They outstripped everybody else in their new boat.* ○ *She outstripped all the other competitors to win the race.* **2.** to do better than someone ○ *Japanese firms have been outstripping their American rivals.*

outward /'aʊtwəd/ *adj, adv* **1.** towards the outside or away from the centre or starting point ○ *The outward journey takes about six hours.* **2.** on the outside ○ *His outward appearance belies his true character.*

outwardly /'aʊtwədli/ *adv* as it seems on the outside

outwards /'aʊtwədz/ *adv* towards the outside or away from the centre or starting point

③ **outweigh** /aʊt'weɪ/ (**outweighs, outweighing, outweighed**) *verb* to be more important than something

outwit /aʊt'wɪt/ (**outwits, outwitting, outwitted**) *verb* to trick someone by being cleverer than they are

oval /'əʊv(ə)l/ *noun* a long round shape similar to an egg, but flat ■ *adj* with this shape ○ *The pie was cooked in an oval bowl.*

ovary /'əʊv(ə)ri/ (*plural* **ovaries**) *noun* one of two organs in a woman or female animal which produce ova or egg cells and secrete the female hormone oestrogen

ovation /əʊ'veɪʃ(ə)n/ *noun* great applause

③ **oven** /'ʌv(ə)n/ *noun* a metal box with a door, used for cooking ○ *Don't put that plate in the oven – it's made of plastic.* ○ *Supper is cooking in the oven.* ○ *Can you look in the oven and see if the meat is cooked?*

① **over** /'əʊvə/ *prep* **1.** above or higher than ○ *He put a blanket over the bed.* ○ *Planes fly over our house every minute.* ○ *The river rose over its banks.* **2.** on the other side or to the other side ○ *Our office is just over the road from the bank.* ○ *He threw the ball over the wall.* ○ *The children ran over the road.* **3.** from the top of ○ *He fell over the cliff.* ○ *She looked over the edge of the balcony.* **4.** during ○ *Over the last few weeks the weather has been cold and wet.* ○ *Let's discuss the problem over lunch.* **5.** more than ○ *Children over 16 years old have to pay full price.* ○ *The car costs over £40,000.* ○ *We had to wait for over two hours.* ■ *adv* **1.** down from being upright ○ *The bottle fell over and all the contents poured out.* ○ *She knocked over the plant pot.* ○ *He leaned over and picked up a pin from the floor.* **2.** more than ○ *Children of 16 and over pay full price.* ○ *There are special prices for groups of 30 and over.* **3.** not used, left behind ○ *Any food left* *over after the meal can be given to the poor.* ■ *adj* finished ○ *Is the match over yet?* ○ *When the civil war was over everyone had more food to eat.*

over- /əʊvə/ *prefix* **1.** extremely ○ *over-anxious* **2.** more than ○ *the over-60s* **3.** too much ○ *overworked* ○ *overdone*

overall[1] /ˌəʊvər'ɔːl/ *adj* covering or taking in everything ○ *The overall outlook for the country is good.* ○ *The overall impression was favourable.*

overall[2] /'əʊvərɔːl/ *noun* a light coat worn at work ○ *He was wearing a white overall as he had just come out of the laboratory.* ○ *Put an overall over your clothes before you start painting.*

overawed /ˌəʊvə'ɔːd/ *adj* surprised and impressed by something ○ *They were overawed by the immense size of the statue.*

overbearing /ˌəʊvə'beərɪŋ/ *adj* trying to dominate others

overcast /'əʊvəkɑːst/ *adj* (*of the sky*) dull and cloudy

overcharge /ˌəʊvə'tʃɑːdʒ/ (**overcharges, overcharging, overcharged**) *verb* to charge somebody too much for something

overcoat /'əʊvəkəʊt/ *noun* a thick outdoor coat which you wear over other clothes

③ **overcome** /ˌəʊvə'kʌm/ (**overcomes, overcoming, overcame, overcome**) *verb* **1.** to deal with a difficult situation ○ *Do you think the drugs problem can ever be overcome?* **2.** to make someone helpless ○ *She was overcome by fear.* ○ *Two people were overcome by smoke.* **3.** to gain victory over an enemy ○ *The boys quickly overcame their attackers.*

overcompensate /ˌəʊvə'kɒmpənseɪt/ (**overcompensates, overcompensating, overcompensated**) *verb* to try to do more than you should to make up for something

overcrowded /ˌəʊvə'kraʊdɪd/ *adj* with too many people inside

overcrowding /ˌəʊvə'kraʊdɪŋ/ *noun* having too many people or things in a small area

overdo /ˌəʊvə'duː/ (**overdoing, overdid, overdone**) *verb* to do too much, work too hard or to use too much of something ○ *They overdid the red velvet and made the sitting room look like a bar.* ○ *Don't overdo the exercises in the first few weeks.* ○ *The doctor says I've been overdoing it recently and need a rest.* ○ *He overdid it and strained his back.*

overdone /ˌəʊvə'dʌn/ *adj* **1.** exaggerated ○ *All right, it's a tragedy, but all that weeping and wailing was terribly overdone.* **2.** cooked too much ○ *I complained because my steak was overdone.*

overdose /'əʊvədəʊs/ *noun* a dose of a drug which is more than normal ○ *She went into a coma after an overdose of heroin.* (NOTE: + **overdose** *v*)

overdraft /'əʊvədrɑːft/ *noun* an amount of money which you can withdraw from your bank account with the bank's permission, which is more than there is in the account

overdue /ˌəʊvə'djuː/ *adj* **1.** which has not been paid at the correct time ○ *This invoice is overdue – please pay immediately.* **2.** which is late ○ *Her library books were overdue so she had to pay a fine.* ○ *This visit to my mother is long overdue.*

overestimate /ˌəʊvər'estɪmeɪt/ (**overestimates, overestimating, overestimated**) *verb* to think something is larger or worse than it really is

overflow[1] /əʊvə'fləʊ/ (**overflows, overflowing, overflowed**) *verb* **1.** to move out of a container or restricted space ○ *The river overflowed its banks.* ○ *The crowd was so big that it overflowed into the street outside the hall.* **2.** to be so full of things or people that there is not enough space for them all [~with] ○ *The room was overflowing with journalists.*

overflow[2] /'əʊvəfləʊ/ *noun* **1.** a liquid which has overflowed ○ *This ditch takes away the overflow from the pond.* **2.** a pipe or hole which allows a liquid to flow out of a container that is too full ○ *The overflow was blocked and water started coming through the ceiling.* **3.** an amount or number which will not fit a given space ○ *The new towns were built to house the overflow population from the capital.* ○ *The stadium was full and the overflow watched the match on giant TV screens in the park next door.*

overgrown /ˌəʊvə'grəʊn/ *adj* (*of e.g. a garden*) covered with plants and long grass because of not being looked after

overhang /ˌəʊvə'hæŋ/ (**overhangs, overhanging, overhung**) *verb* to stick out above something else ○ *The upper storey of the house overhangs the street.*

overhaul[1] /əʊvə'hɔːl/ (**overhauls, overhauling, overhauled**) *verb* **1.** to examine something carefully and make changes so that it works better ○ *We need to overhaul the company's union agreements.* **2.** to overtake another ship or car ○ *From being* *last in the race he gradually moved up and in the end overhauled the leaders.*

overhaul² /'əʊvəhɔːl/ *noun* the act of examining and improving or repairing something ○ *a long overdue overhaul of our safety procedures* ○ *My car's in the garage for a complete overhaul.*

overhead /ˌəʊvə'hed/ *adv* above you ○ *Look at that plane overhead.* ○ *Please put your hand luggage in the lockers overhead.*

overhear /ˌəʊvə'hɪə/ (**overhears, overhearing, overheard**) *verb* to hear accidentally something which you are not meant to hear ○ *I couldn't help overhearing what you said just then.*

overheat /ˌəʊvə'hiːt/ (**overheats, overheating, overheated**) *verb* to get too hot

overjoyed /ˌəʊvə'dʒɔɪd/ *adj* extremely happy

overkill /'əʊvəkɪl/ *noun* more of something than is wanted or appropriate

overlap¹ /'əʊvəlæp/ (**overlaps, overlapping, overlapped**) *verb* to cover part of something else ○ *Try not to let the pieces of wallpaper overlap.*

overlap² /ˌəʊvə'læp/ *noun* an amount by which something overlaps

overleaf /ˌəʊvə'lif/ *adv* referring to the other side of a page of a book or other publication

overload /ˌəʊvə'ləʊd/ (**overloads, overloading, overloaded**) *verb* to put too heavy a load on something

overlook /ˌəʊvə'lʊk/ (**overlooks, overlooking, overlooked**) *verb* not to notice something ○ *She overlooked several mistakes when she was correcting the exam papers.*

overnight /ˌəʊvə'naɪt/ *adv* for the whole night ○ *We will stay overnight in France on our way to Italy.* ○ *Will the food stay fresh overnight?* ■ *adj* lasting all night ○ *They took an overnight flight back from China.* ○ *There are three sleeping cars on the overnight express.*

overpower /ˌəʊvə'paʊə/ (**overpowers, overpowering, overpowered**) *verb* to control someone by force

overpowering /ˌəʊvə'paʊərɪŋ/ *adj* very strong ○ *an overpowering smell of cheese*

overrated /ˌəʊvə'reɪtɪd/ *adj* said to be better than it really is

overreact /ˌəʊvəri'ækt/ (**overreacts, overreacting, overreacted**) *verb* to react to something with too much emotion or action

③ **override** /ˌəʊvə'raɪd/ (**overrides, overriding, overrode, overridden**) *verb* **1.** to cancel an instruction ○ *The chairman decided to override the committee's decision.* **2.** to be more important than other things ○ *The group's safety overrides any other considerations.*

overriding /ˌəʊvə'raɪdɪŋ/ *adj* more important than all others

overrule /ˌəʊvə'ruːl/ (**overrules, overruling, overruled**) *verb* (*in a meeting*) not to allow a decision because you are more powerful than the person who took the decision ○ *Mr Smith tried to object but his objection was overruled by the chairman.* ○ *The committee overruled the decision made by the secretary.*

overrun /ˌəʊvə'rʌn/ (**overruns, overrunning, overran, overrun**) *verb* **1.** to go beyond a certain time limit ○ *The meeting overran by thirty minutes.* **2.** to beat someone or occupy their territory very quickly ○ *The enemy overran our coastal defences and began advancing inland.* **3.** to be filled with a crowd of people, animals or things ○ *The city centre is overrun with tourists every summer.*

overseas¹ /ˌəʊvə'siːz/ *adv* in or to a foreign country ○ *Sue's gone overseas to work for a few years.*

overseas² /'əʊvəsiːz/ *adj* relating to foreign countries ○ *Overseas sales are important for our company.*

oversee /ˌəʊvə'siː/ (**oversees, overseeing, oversaw, overseen**) *verb* to supervise something

overshadow /ˌəʊvə'ʃædəʊ/ (**overshadows, overshadowing, overshadowed**) *verb* to make someone or something less conspicuous by being more brilliant yourself

overshoot /ˌəʊvə'ʃuːt/ (**overshoots, overshooting, overshot**) *verb* to go further than you are supposed to

oversight /'əʊvəsaɪt/ *noun* a mistake made by not doing something because you forgot it or did not notice it

overspend /ˌəʊvə'spend/ (**overspends, overspending, overspent**) *verb* to spend more than you should

overstep /ˌəʊvə'step/ (**oversteps, overstepping, overstepped**) *verb* to go further than you ought to

overt /əʊ'vɜːt/ *adj* open and not hidden

overtake /ˌəʊvə'teɪk/ (**overtakes, overtaking, overtook, overtaken**) *verb* to go past someone travelling in front of you

overthrow /ˌəʊvə'θrəʊ/ (**overthrows, overthrowing, overthrew, overthrown**) *verb* to defeat ○ *Do you think the rebels can overthrow the military government?* ○ *The former régime was overthrown and the President fled.*

③ **overtime** /'əʊvətaɪm/ *noun* hours worked more than the usual working time ○ *He worked six hours' overtime.* ○ *The overtime rate is one and a half times normal pay.* ○ *The basic wage is £110 a week, but you can expect to earn more than that with overtime.*

overtone /'əʊvəˌtəʊn/ *noun* a meaning or quality which is suggested and not stated openly or made obvious in something

overture /'əʊvətjʊə/ *noun* a short piece of music played at the beginning of an opera or a concert ○ *The orchestra played the overture to 'The Magic Flute'.* ◇ **to make overtures to someone** to try to begin negotiations with someone ○ *The socialists made overtures to the communists with the aim of forming a left-wing alliance.*

overturn /ˌəʊvə'tɜːn/ (**overturns, overturning, overturned**) *verb* **1.** to make something fall over or to turn upside down ○ *The baby accidentally overturned the goldfish bowl.* ○ *The fishing boat overturned in the storm.* **2.** to vote against a previous decision ○ *The decision to raise subscriptions was overturned by the council.*

overvalue /ˌəʊvə'væljuː/ (**overvalues, overvaluing, overvalued**) *verb* to give something a higher value than is right

③ **overview** /'əʊvəvjuː/ *noun* a general view of a subject [~of] ○ *His book gives a good overview of the history of the period.*

overweight /əʊvə'weɪt/ *adj* having a body that weighs too much

③ **overwhelm** /ˌəʊvə'welm/ (**overwhelms, overwhelming, overwhelmed**) *verb* **1.** to conquer something completely ○ *The enemy was overwhelmed by our troops.* ○ *His enthusiasm overwhelms me.* **2.** to have more of something than you can do or cope with ○ *The new receptionist was overwhelmed by her job.*

overwhelming /ˌəʊvə'welmɪŋ/ *adj* enormous ○ *There was an overwhelming response to their appeal for money.* ○ *They got an overwhelming 'yes' vote.*

overwrite /ˌəʊvə'raɪt/ (**overwrites, overwriting, overwrote, overwritten**) *verb* to delete computer data or a computer file and replace it with other data or a file with the same name

ow /aʊ/ *interj* an expression of pain

② **owe** /əʊ/ (**owes, owing, owed**) *verb* **1.** to be in a situation where you will have to pay someone money, either because you have borrowed some from them, or because you have bought something from them ○ *He still owes me the £50 he borrowed last month.* **2.** □ **to owe something to something or someone** to have something because of something or someone else ○ *He owes his good health to taking a lot of exercise.* **3.** to feel that something should be done ○ *He owes her an apology.* ○ *I owe my sister a letter.*

③ **owing to** /'əʊɪŋ tuː/ *prep* because of ○ *The plane was late owing to fog.*

owl /aʊl/ *noun* a large bird which hunts small animals, mainly at night

① **own** /əʊn/ *adj* belonging to you alone ○ *I don't need to borrow a car – I have my own car.* ○ *He has his own book shop.* ■ *noun* □ **of my** *or* **his own** belonging to me or to him alone ○ *He has an office of his own.* ○ *I have a car of my own.* ■ *verb* (**owns, owning, owned**) to have or possess something ○ *I don't own a car.* ◇ **(all) on my** *or* **his** *or* **her, etc own** alone ○ *I'm on my own this evening – my girlfriend's gone out with her family.* ○ *He built the house all on his own.* ◇ **to get your own back** to have revenge on someone (*informal*) ○ *He got his own back on her for telling the teacher what he did.* ◇ **to hold your own** to remain firm against a threat ○ *He held his own during the interview by the police.*

② **owner** /'əʊnə/ *noun* a person who owns something ○ *The police are trying to find the owner of the stolen car.* ○ *Insurance is necessary for all house owners.*

③ **ownership** /'əʊnəʃɪp/ *noun* a situation where someone owns something

own goal /əʊn 'gəʊl/ *noun* **1.** a goal scored against your own side by mistake ○ *He tried to pass back to the goalkeeper and scored an own goal.* **2.** something that is intended to help you do something but has the opposite effect ○ *Their attempts to show that the government was financially incompetent led to a spectacular own goal.*

ox /ɒks/ (*plural* **oxen**) *noun* male or female domestic cattle or a castrated bull used as a draught animal

oxide /ˈɒksaɪd/ *noun* a chemical compound formed of oxygen and another element

oxygen /ˈɒksɪdʒən/ *noun* a common gas which is present in the air and is essential for plant and animal life

oyster /ˈɔɪstə/ *noun* a type of shellfish with two shells, highly valued as food

③ **oz** *abbr* ounce(s) (NOTE: say 'twelve ounces of flour', 'five ounces of butter')

ozone /ˈəʊzəʊn/ *noun* a harmful form of oxygen, which is found in the atmosphere and which is poisonous to humans when concentrated

ozone layer /ˈəʊzəʊn ˌleɪə/ *noun* a layer of ozone in the upper atmosphere, formed by the action of sunlight on oxygen, which acts as protection against harmful rays from the Sun

P

p[1] /piː/, **P** *noun* the sixteenth letter of the alphabet, between O and Q

p[2] /piː/ *abbr* pence ○ *This book costs 99p.* ○ *You should get a 60p ticket from the machine.* ○ *I bought the children 50p ice creams each.* ◊ **penny**

pa /pɑː/ *noun* a child's name for father (*informal*)

PA *abbr* personal assistant

③ **pace** /peɪs/ *noun* **1.** the distance covered by one step ○ *Walk thirty paces to the north of the stone.* ○ *Step three paces back.* **2.** speed ○ *The car was travelling at quite a pace.* ■ *verb* (**paces, pacing, paced**) **1.** to walk ○ *He paced backwards and forwards in front of the door.* **2.** to measure by walking [~about/around] ○ *He paced out the distance between the tree and the house.* ◇ **to keep pace with** to keep up with ○ *She kept pace with the leaders for the first three laps.* ○ *Wages haven't kept pace with inflation.* ◇ **to set the pace** to set the standard for something to be done

pacemaker /ˈpeɪsmeɪkə/ *noun* an electronic device which is implanted in a patient's chest and which stimulates and regulates the heartbeat

pacifism /ˈpæsɪfɪz(ə)m/ *noun* opposition to war

pacifist /ˈpæsɪfɪst/ *noun* a person who supports pacifism ○ *My father was a pacifist and refused to do military service.*

pacify /ˈpæsɪfaɪ/ (**pacifies, pacifying, pacified**) *verb* to make someone calm

② **pack** /pæk/ *noun* **1.** a set of things put together in a box [~of] ○ *He bought a pack of chewing gum.* **2.** a set of playing cards [~of] ○ *a pack of cards* ○ *Shuffle the pack.* **3.** a group of wild animals together [~of] ○ *a pack of wild dogs* **4.** a bag which you can carry on your back [~of] ○ *Will you be able to manage this walk with a heavy pack on your back?* ■ *verb* (**packs, packing, packed**) **1.** to put things into a suitcase ready for travelling ○ *The taxi's arrived and she hasn't packed her suitcase yet.* ○ *I've finished packing, so we can start.* ○ *He packed his toothbrush at the bottom of the bag.* **2.** to put things in containers ready for sending ○ *The books are packed in boxes of twenty.* ○ *Fish are packed in ice.* **3.** to put a lot of people or things into something ○ *How can you pack ten adults into one tent?* ○ *The streets are packed with Christmas shoppers.* ○ *The supermarket shelves are packed with fruit and vegetables.*

pack in *phrasal verb* □ **to pack it in** to stop whatever you are doing (*informal*) ○ *It's getting dark, let's pack it in for the day.* ○ *He packed in his job and bought a farm.*

pack off *phrasal verb* to send someone away (*informal*) ○ *We've packed the children off to their grandparents for the summer holidays.*

pack up③ *phrasal verb* **1.** to put things into a box before going away ○ *They packed up all their equipment and left.* **2.** to stop working ○ *I'll pack up now and finish the job tomorrow morning.* **3.** to break down ○ *One of the plane's engines packed up when we were taking off.*

② **package** /ˈpækɪdʒ/ *noun* **1.** a parcel which has been wrapped up for sending ○ *There was a package for you in the post.* ○ *We mailed the package to you yesterday.* **2.** a box or bag in which goods are sold ○ *Instructions for use are printed on the package.* **3.** a set of goods or services offered together at one time ○ *a software package*

package holiday /ˌpækɪdʒ ˈhɒlɪdeɪ/ *noun* a holiday where everything including a hotel, food and travel is arranged and paid for before you leave

③ **packaging** /ˈpækɪdʒɪŋ/ *noun* **1.** paper, cardboard or plastic used to wrap goods ○ *The boxes are sent in dust-proof packaging.* **2.** the act of wrapping of goods ○ *The packaging is all done by machines.*

③ **packed** /pækt/ *adj* **1.** full of people ○ *The restaurant was packed and there were no free tables.* **2.** put in a container ○ *a packed lunch*

② **packet** /ˈpækɪt/ *noun* a small bag, parcel or box [~of] ○ *a packet of cigarettes* ○ *a packet of soup*

③ **packing** /ˈpækɪŋ/ *noun* **1.** putting things into suitcases or bags ○ *My wife's in the hotel room doing our packing.* **2.** material used to protect goods which are being packed ○ *The goods are sealed in airtight packing.*

pact /pækt/ *noun* an agreement or treaty

③ **pad** /pæd/ *noun* **1.** a soft cushion which protects a person or thing from something ○ *Put a pad of cotton on your knee.* **2.** a set of sheets of paper attached together ■ *verb* (**pads, padding, padded**) to walk softly with regular steps [~across/down/into etc] ○ *The tiger was padding up and down in its cage.*

pad out *phrasal verb* to add text to a speech or article, just to make it longer

padding /ˈpædɪŋ/ *noun* **1.** a soft material which protects, used in dressmaking, or to make things like cushions or chairs ○ *The tailor put some more padding in the shoulders of the jacket.* ○ *We put cotton wool under the bandage as padding.* **2.** words added to a speech or article to make it longer ○ *The speech was over an hour long, but most of it was just padding.* ○ *Your essay has got too much padding in it.*

paddle /ˈpæd(ə)l/ *noun* a walk in shallow water ○ *The little children went for a paddle in the sea.* ■ *verb* (**paddles, paddling, paddled**) to make a boat move forward using a paddle ○ *We stopped paddling and let the canoe drift with the current.*

paddock /ˈpædək/, **puddock** *noun* a small enclosed field, where horses can run

paddy field /ˈpædi fiːld/ *noun* a field filled with water, in which rice is grown

padlock /ˈpædlɒk/ *noun* a small lock with a hook ○ *The gate is fastened with a padlock.* (NOTE: + **padlock** *v*)

paediatrician /ˌpiːdiəˈtrɪʃ(ə)n/ *noun* a doctor who specialises in treating children

paediatrics /ˌpiːdiˈætrɪks/ *noun* the study of the treatment of children's diseases

pagan /ˈpeɪgən/ *adj* believing in a form of religion which is not one of the main formal religions ○ *The missionaries tried to ban pagan religious practices.* ○ *The explorers visited a pagan temple.*

① **page** /peɪdʒ/ *noun* a side of a sheet of paper used in a book, newspaper or magazine ○ *It's a short book, it only has 64 pages.* ○ *The crossword is on the back page.* ○ *Start reading at page 34.* ○ *Look at the picture on page 6.* (NOTE: With numbers the word **the** is left out: *on the next page* but *on page 50.*) ■ *verb* (**pages, paging, paged**) to call someone by radio, over a loudspeaker, etc. ○ *Mr Smith isn't in his office at the moment – I'll page him for you.*

pageant /ˈpædʒənt/ *noun* a grand display of people in historical costumes

pager /ˈpeɪdʒə/ *noun* a small electronic device that makes a noise or displays a message when someone is trying to contact you

pagoda /pəˈgəʊdə/ *noun* a tall tower with several storeys, used as a temple, found in the Far East, e.g. in China, Korea and Japan

① **paid** /peɪd/ past tense and past participle of **pay**

pail /peɪl/ *noun* an old-fashioned word for a bucket (NOTE: Do not confuse with **pale**.)

② **pain** /peɪn/ *noun* a feeling in your body of being hurt or ill ○ *If you have a pain in your chest, you ought to see a doctor.* ○ *She had to take drugs because she could not stand the pain.* ○ *I get pains in my teeth when I eat ice cream.*

pained /peɪnd/ *adj* annoyed or upset

③ **painful** /ˈpeɪnf(ə)l/ *adj* hurting, causing pain ○ *She got a painful blow on the back of the head.* ○ *I have very painful memories of my first school.*

painfully /ˈpeɪnf(ə)li/ *adv* **1.** in a way which hurts ○ *He twisted his ankle painfully.* ○ *I am painfully aware that most people are blaming me for the accident.* **2.** used for emphasising how difficult or unpleasant something is ○ *So far, progress on building the dam has been painfully slow.*

painkiller /ˈpeɪnˌkɪlə/ *noun* a drug which stops someone feeling pain

painstaking /ˈpeɪnzteɪkɪŋ/ *adj* (*of a person*) done slowly and carefully in order to avoid mistakes ○ *The design is the result of years of painstaking effort.*

② **paint** /peɪnt/ *noun* a coloured liquid which you use to give something a colour or to make a picture ○ *We gave the ceiling two coats of paint.* ○ *I need a two-litre tin of green paint.* ○ *The paint's coming off the front door.* (NOTE: no plural) ■ *verb* (**paints, painting, painted**) **1.** to cover something with paint ○ *We got someone in to paint the house.* ○ *They painted their front door blue.* ○ *She painted her toenails bright red.* **2.** to make a picture of something using paint ○ *She painted a picture of the village.* ○ *He's painting his mother.* ○ *The sky is not easy to paint.*

paintbrush /ˈpeɪntbrʌʃ/ *noun* a brush used to put paint on something

painter /ˈpeɪntə/ *noun* **1.** a person who paints something such as a house ○ *The painter is coming next week to paint the kitchen.* **2.** a person who paints pictures ○ *He collects pictures by 19th-century French painters.*

② **painting** /ˈpeɪntɪŋ/ *noun* **1.** the act of putting paint on something or of making pictures with paint ○ *Painting and decorating is my trade* **2.** a picture done with paints ○ *Do you like this painting of the old church?*

paintwork /ˈpeɪntwɜːk/ *noun* a surface which has been painted

② **pair** /peə/ *noun* **1.** two things taken together [~of] ○ *a pair of socks* ○ *a pair of gloves* ○ *She's bought a new pair of boots.* **2.** two things joined together to make a single one [~of] ○ *He took a pair of binoculars with him when he went out walking.* ○ *I'm looking for a clean pair of trousers.* ○ *Where's my pair of green shorts?* ○ *This pair of scissors is blunt.*

pal /pæl/ *noun* a friend (*informal*)

③ **palace** /ˈpælɪs/ *noun* a large building where a king, queen, president, etc., lives

palatable /ˈpælətəb(ə)l/ *adj* nice to eat, tasting good

palate /ˈpælət/ *noun* **1.** the top part of the inside of the mouth ○ *I burnt my palate with the hot soup.* **2.** being able to judge the quality of food or drink ○ *A trained palate easily distinguishes different types of wine.* (NOTE: Do not confuse with **palette, pallet**.)

palatial /pəˈleɪʃ(ə)l/ *adj* magnificent, like a palace

② **pale** /peɪl/ (**paler, palest**) *adj* **1.** light-coloured ○ *What colour is your hat? – It's a pale blue colour.* **2.** not looking healthy, with a white face ○ *She's always pale and that worries me.* ○ *When she read the letter she went pale.* (NOTE: Do not confuse with **pail**.)

palette /ˈpælət/ *noun* **1.** a flat board on which an artist mixes his or her colours ○ *She squeezed a blob of paint onto her palette.* **2.** a range of colours available, especially on a computer graphics program ○ *You can create your own colours and add them to the palette.* (NOTE: Do not confuse with **palate, pallet**.)

pall /pɔːl/ *noun* a cloth put over a coffin ■ *verb* (**palls, palling, palled**) to become less interesting ○ *Her bright chatter began to pall after a while.*

pallid /ˈpælɪd/ *adj* sickly pale

pallor /ˈpælə/ *noun* paleness of the face

palm /pɑːm/ *noun* **1.** the soft inside surface of your hand ○ *She held out some crumbs in the palm of her hand and the birds came and ate them.* **2.** a tall tropical tree with long leaves ○ *an oasis surrounded by date palms* ○ *The boy climbed a coconut palm and brought down a nut.*

palm off *phrasal verb* □ **to palm something off on someone** to give something worthless to someone hoping that he or she won't notice (*informal*) ○ *We tried to palm off our old sofa onto my brother.*

palm tree /pɑːm triː/ *noun* a tall tropical tree with long leaves

paltry /ˈpɔːltri/ (**paltrier, paltriest**) *adj* very small

pamper /ˈpæmpə/ (**pampers, pampering, pampered**) *verb* to treat someone too well, by giving him or her too much food or making his or her life too comfortable

③ **pamphlet** /ˈpæmflət/ *noun* a small booklet giving information about something

③ **pan** /pæn/ *noun* a metal cooking container with a handle ○ *Boil the potatoes in a pan of water.* ○ *She burnt her hand on the hot frying pan.* ◊ **frying pan**, **saucepan**

pan out *phrasal verb* to turn out, to succeed (*informal*)

panache /pəˈnæʃ/ *noun* a confident and showy way of doing things

pancake /ˈpænkeɪk/ ◇ **as flat as a pancake** very flat ○ *The country round Cambridge is as flat as a pancake.*

panda /ˈpændə/ *noun* a large black and white animal found in China, which looks like a bear (NOTE: do not confuse with **pander**)

pandemonium /ˌpændəˈməʊniəm/ *noun* great uproar and confusion

pander /ˈpændə/ (**panders, pandering, pandered**) *verb* □ **to pander to something** to try to satisfy something ○ *The book panders to the low taste of the reading public.*

p & p *abbr* postage and packing

pane /peɪn/ *noun* a sheet of glass, e.g. in a window or door (NOTE: Do not confuse with **pain**.)

① **panel** /ˈpæn(ə)l/ *noun* **1.** a flat piece of something such as wood or metal, which forms part of something ○ *Unscrew the panel at the back of the washing machine.* **2.** a group of people who answer questions or who judge a competition ○ *She's on the panel that will interview candidates for the post.*

panelling /ˈpæn(ə)lɪŋ/ *noun* sheets of wood, used especially to cover walls (NOTE: The US spelling is **paneling**.)

pang /pæŋ/ *noun* a sudden strong feeling

③ **panic** /ˈpænɪk/ *noun* sudden great fear ○ *The forecast of flooding caused panic in towns near the river.* ■ *verb* (**panics, panicking, panicked**) to become very frightened ○ *Don't panic, the fire engine is on its way.*

panic-stricken /ˈpænɪk ˌstrɪkən/ *adj* mad with fright

panorama /ˌpænəˈrɑːmə/ *noun* a view over a wide expanse of landscape

pansy /ˈpænzi/ *noun* a small garden plant with large brightly coloured petals ○ *She planted pansies in her window boxes.*

pant /pænt/ (**pants, panting, panted**) *verb* to breathe fast ○ *He was red in the face and panting as he crossed the finishing line.*

panther /ˈpænθə/ *noun* a large black leopard from North America

panties /ˈpæntiz/ *plural noun* women's brief knickers ○ *A pair of panties were left on the washing line.* ○ *She carries a spare pair of panties in her handbag.*

pantomime /ˈpæntəmaɪm/ *noun* a funny Christmas play for children, with songs and dances on a traditional fairy-tale subject (*informal*)

pantry /ˈpæntri/ *noun* a cool cupboard or small room for keeping food in

③ **pants** /pænts/ *plural noun* **1.** briefs, shorts worn on the lower part of the body under other clothes ○ *She was standing by the window in her bra and pants.* ○ *I put on clean pants and socks every morning.* **2.** *US* trousers ○ *The waiter was wearing a black jacket and a pair of striped pants.* ○ *I need a belt to keep my pants up.*

paparazzi /ˌpæpəˈrætsi/ *plural noun* photographers who follow famous people to take pictures of them for newspapers ○ *The paparazzi were lying in wait for the couple as they left the hotel.*

papaya /pəˈpaɪə/ *noun* a green tropical fruit with yellow flesh

① **paper** /ˈpeɪpə/ *noun* **1.** thin, often white, material, which you write on, and which is used for wrapping or to make books, newspapers and magazines [~on] ○ *He got a letter written on pink paper.* ○ *I need another piece of paper* or *sheet of paper to finish my letter.* ○ *There was a box of paper handkerchiefs by the bed.* (NOTE: no plural for this meaning: *some paper, a piece of paper, a sheet of paper*) **2.** a newspaper [~on] ○ *I buy the paper to read on the train every morning.* ○ *My photo was on the front page of today's paper.* ○ *Our local paper comes out on Fridays.* ○ *The Sunday papers are so big that it takes me all day to read them.* **3.** an exam [~on] ○ *The English paper was very difficult.*

paperback /ˈpeɪpəbæk/ *noun* a cheap book with a paper cover

paper boy /ˈpeɪpə bɔɪ/ *noun* a boy whose job is to deliver newspapers to houses

paperclip /ˈpeɪpəklɪp/ *noun* a piece of bent wire for holding pieces of paper together

paper girl /ˈpeɪpə gɜːl/ *noun* a girl whose job is to deliver newspapers to houses

paperweight /ˈpeɪpəweɪt/ *noun* a heavy block put on papers to prevent them from being blown away

③ **paperwork** /ˈpeɪpəwɜːk/ *noun* office work

paprika /ˈpæprɪkə/ *noun* a red spice made from powdered sweet peppers

par /pɑː/ *noun* **1.** the fact of being equal **2.** (*in golf*) the number of strokes usually needed by a good golfer to hit the ball into the hole ○ *He went round in five under par.* ◇ **below par** not very well ○ *He's feeling a bit below par after his illness.* ◇ **par for the course** what usually happens (*informal*) ○ *Jack forgot my birthday again, but that's par for the course.* ◇ **to be on a par with something** *or* **someone** to be equal to something or someone ○ *It isn't really on a par with their previous performances.*

parable /ˈpærəb(ə)l/ *noun* a short story with a religious or moral point

③ **paracetamol** /ˌpærəˈsiːtəmɒl/ *noun* a common drug, used to stop symptoms, e.g. of flu, colds and headaches (NOTE: no plural: *take two paracetamol before breakfast*)

parachute /ˈpærəʃuːt/ (**parachutes, parachuting, parachuted**) *verb* to drop something attached to a parachute ○ *They parachuted supplies to the villages.*

parade /pəˈreɪd/ *noun* a public display of soldiers ○ *A sergeant inspects the men before they go on parade.*

paradigm /ˈpærədaɪm/ *noun* an example which others can copy

paradise /ˈpærədaɪs/ *noun* **1.** a wonderful place where good people are supposed to live after death ○ *For a moment, I thought I must have died and gone to paradise.* **2.** any beautiful place or a place where you feel very happy ○ *Their grandparents' farm was a paradise for the children.*

paradox /'pærədɒks/ *noun* a thing which appears to contradict itself but may really be true

paradoxical /ˌpærə'dɒksɪk(ə)l/ *adj* contradictory like a paradox

paraffin /'pærəfɪn/ *noun* a thin liquid used as a fuel, e.g. for lamps and heaters

paragon /'pærəgən/ *noun* a perfect human being

③ **paragraph** /'pærəgrɑːf/ *noun* a section of several written sentences starting on a new line ○ *to answer the first paragraph of your letter* or *paragraph one of your letter* ○ *Please refer to the paragraph headed 'Shipping Instructions'.*

③ **parallel** /'pærəlel/ *adj* (*of lines*) which are side by side and remain the same distance apart without ever touching ○ *Draw two parallel lines three millimetres apart.* ○ *The road is parallel to* or *with the railway.*

parallelogram /ˌpærə'leləgræm/ *noun* a shape with four sides in which each side is parallel to the one opposite

paralyse /'pærəlaɪz/ (**paralyses, paralysing, paralysed**) *verb* **1.** to cause paralysis in someone **2.** to make someone or something unable to move or function normally for a short time ○ *The strike paralysed the country.* (NOTE: The US spelling is **paralyze**.)

paralysis /pə'ræləsɪs/ *noun* **1.** a condition where the muscles of part of the body cannot move because of damage to the nerves **2.** an inability to move or function normally

paramedic /ˌpærə'medɪk/ *noun* a person who works in a medical profession linked to that of a nurse or doctor, such as an ambulance driver or therapist

③ **parameter** /pə'ræmɪtə/ *noun* a value which shows the limits of something

paramilitary /ˌpærə'mɪlɪt(ə)ri/ *adj* organised in the same way as the army, but not a part of it ○ *Members of paramilitary organisations were asked to surrender their arms.*

paramount /'pærəmaʊnt/ *adj* most important

paranoia /ˌpærə'nɔɪə/ *noun* a mental disorder in which the patient imagines things, usually that he or she is being persecuted or attacked

paranoid /'pærənɔɪd/ *adj* suffering from a fixed delusion

paraphernalia /ˌpærəfə'neɪliə/ *noun* a mass of bits and pieces of equipment

paraphrase /'pærəfreɪz/ (**paraphrases, paraphrasing, paraphrased**) *verb* to repeat what someone has said or written, using different words

paraplegic /ˌpærə'pliːdʒɪk/ *adj* paralysed in the part of the body below the waist

parasite /'pærəsaɪt/ *noun* **1.** an animal or plant which lives on or inside another organism and draws nourishment from it ○ *Many diseases are carried by parasites.* **2.** a person who does no useful work and gets money from others ○ *He is a parasite on society.*

parasol /'pærəsɒl/ *noun* a light umbrella to protect you from the rays of the Sun

paratrooper /'pærətruːpə/ *noun* a soldier who is a parachutist (NOTE: often shortened to **para**)

paratroops /'pærətruːps/ *plural noun* paratroopers ○ *A small group of paratroops led the attack.*

③ **parcel** /'pɑːs(ə)l/ *noun* something that is wrapped in paper and sent by post ○ *The postman has brought a parcel for you.* ○ *The parcel was wrapped up in brown paper.* ○ *If you're going to the post office, can you post this parcel for me?*

parcel out *phrasal verb* to divide something up among several people

parched /pɑːtʃt/ *adj* very dry due to lack of rain

② **pardon** /'pɑːd(ə)n/ *noun* the act of forgiving someone ■ *verb* (**pardons, pardoning, pardoned**) to forgive someone for having done something wrong ○ *Pardon me for interrupting, but you're wanted on the phone.* ○ *Please pardon my rudeness in not answering your call earlier.* ◇ **I beg your pardon!** excuse me! forgive me! ○ *I beg your pardon, I didn't hear what you said.* ○ *I do beg your pardon – I didn't know you were busy.*

pare /peə/ (**pares, paring, pared**) *verb* to make something smaller by cutting off a small amount ○ *He managed to pare three seconds off his previous best time.*

① **parent** /'peərənt/ *noun* **1.** a father or mother **2.** an organisation which owns or rules another ○ *Our parent company is based in Switzerland.*

parentage /'peərəntɪdʒ/ *noun* someone's origin

parentheses /pə'renθəsiːz/ *plural noun* a printing symbol ( ) which encloses words or characters and separates them from the rest of the text ○ *She put the phrase in parentheses.*

parenthood /'peərənthʊd/ *noun* the state of being a parent

parenting /'peərəntɪŋ/ *noun* the activity of looking after children

parents /'peərənts/ *noun* your mother and father ○ *His parents live in Manchester.* ○ *Did your parents tell you I had met them in London?*

parish /'pærɪʃ/ *noun* **1.** an area served by a church ○ *He's the vicar of a country parish.* ○ *They worship regularly in their local parish church.* ○ *Father Thomas is our parish priest.* **2.** an administrative district in a county with a church as its centre ○ *He's going through the local parish records to try to establish when his family first came to the village.*

parishioner /pə'rɪʃ(ə)nə/ *noun* a person who lives in or belongs to a parish

parity /'pærɪti/ *noun* the fact of being equal, especially having the same rates of pay and conditions as others

① **park** /pɑːk/ *noun* an open space with grass and trees ○ *Hyde Park and Regents Park are in the middle of London.* ○ *You can ride a bicycle across the park but cars are not allowed in.* ■ *verb* (**parks, parking, parked**) to leave your car somewhere while you are not using it ○ *You can park your car in the street next to the hotel.* ○ *You mustn't park on a double yellow line.*

parka /'pɑːkə/ *noun* a warm waterproof jacket with a hood

② **parking** /'pɑːkɪŋ/ *noun* the act of leaving a car somewhere when you are not using it

parking lot /'pɑːkɪŋ lɒt/ *noun US* an area where you can leave a car when you are not using it

parking meter /'pɑːkɪŋ ˌmiːtə/ *noun* a device into which you put money to pay for parking for a certain time

parking ticket /'pɑːkɪŋ ˌtɪkɪt/ *noun* a paper which you get when you leave a car parked wrongly, telling you that you will have to pay a fine

Parkinson's disease /'pɑːkɪnsənz dɪ ˌziːz/ *noun* a disease which affects the parts of the brain which control movement, making the hands and legs shake

② **parliament** /'pɑːləmənt/ *noun* a group of elected representatives who decide on the laws of a country ○ *Parliament has passed a law forbidding the sale of these drugs.*

Parmesan /ˌpɑːmɪ'zæn/ *noun* a type of hard Italian cheese that is often grated and sprinkled on pasta dishes

parody /'pærədi/ *noun* (*plural* **parodies**) poetry, a play or a song which imitates someone to make fun ○ *He wrote a parody of Wodehouse.* ■ *verb* (**parodies, parodying, parodied**) to imitate someone in order to make fun ○ *His writing style is very easy to parody.*

parole /pə'rəʊl/ *noun* the act of allowing a prisoner who has behaved well to be released from prison early on condition that he or she continues to behave well outside prison ○ *She will be eligible for parole in three weeks' time.* ○ *He was let out on parole and immediately offended again.* ■ *verb* (**paroles, paroling, paroled**) to let a prisoner out of prison on condition that he or she behaves well ○ *After six months he was paroled.*

parrot /'pærət/ *noun* a brightly coloured tropical bird with a large curved beak ○ *He keeps a green parrot in a cage in his living room.*

parsley /'pɑːsli/ *noun* a green herb with flat or curly leaves, used in cooking

parsnip /'pɑːsnɪp/ *noun* a plant with a thick white root which is eaten boiled or roasted as a vegetable and has a sweet taste

① **part** /pɑːt/ *noun* **1.** a piece or section [~of] ○ *Parts of the film were very good.* ○ *They live in the downstairs part of a large house.* ○ *They spend part of the year in France.* **2.** a person that an actor plays, e.g. in a play or film [~of] ○ *He played the part of Hamlet.* ■ *verb* (**parts, parting, parted**) to separate or move apart ○ *The curtains parted and the show began.* ◇ **to play a part** to be one of several people or things which do something ○ *The guests played an important part in putting out the hotel fire.* ◇ **to take part in something** to join in an activity ○ *They all took part in the game.* ○ *Did he take part in the concert?*

part with③ *phrasal verb* to give or sell something to someone ○ *He refused to part with his old bicycle.*

part exchange /ˌpɑːt ɪks'tʃeɪndʒ/ *noun* giving an old product as part of the payment for a new one

③ **partial** /'pɑːʃ(ə)l/ *adj* **1.** not complete ○ *He got partial compensation for the damage to his house.* ○ *The treatment was only a partial success.* **2.** with a liking for something [~to] ○ *Everyone knows he is partial* *to a slice of cake.* **3.** biased ○ *The judge was accused of being partial.*

③ **participant** /pɑːˈtɪsɪpənt/ *noun* a person who takes part [~in]

③ **participate** /pɑːˈtɪsɪpeɪt/ (**participates, participating, participated**) *verb* to take part in something

③ **participle** /pɑːˈtɪsɪp(ə)l/ *noun* a word formed from a verb, used either to form perfect or progressive forms or as an adjective or noun. The present participle of 'to go' is 'going' and the past participle is 'gone'.

particle /ˈpɑːtɪk(ə)l/ *noun* a very small piece

① **particular** /pəˈtɪkjʊlə/ *adj* special, referring to one thing or person and to no other ○ *The photocopier only works with one particular type of paper.*

① **particularly** /pəˈtɪkjʊləli/ *adv* specially ○ *I particularly asked them not to walk on the lawn.* ○ *It's a particularly difficult problem.* ○ *He isn't particularly worried about the result.*

particulars /pəˈtɪkjʊləz/ *plural noun* details ○ *the sheet which gives particulars of the house for sale* ○ *The inspector asked for particulars of the missing car.*

parting /ˈpɑːtɪŋ/ *noun* **1.** the act of leaving someone ○ *Our final parting took place outside the railway station.* **2.** the line which marks where your hair is separated when you comb it ○ *My parting is on the left side.*

parting shot /ˌpɑːtɪŋ ˈʃɒt/ *noun* the last, often unpleasant, words spoken when leaving someone

partisan /ˈpɑːtɪz(ə)n, ˌpɑːtɪˈzæn/, **partizan** *noun* **1.** a person who supports a policy forcefully ○ *She's a partisan of having more women Members of Parliament.* **2.** a member of a local armed resistance movement, fighting against an occupying army ○ *The town was captured by partisans.*

partition /pɑːˈtɪʃ(ə)n/ *noun* **1.** a division of a country into separate parts ○ *Did you agree with the partition of the country after the war?* **2.** a thin wall between two spaces, especially one splitting a large room into sections ○ *We put a partition across the centre of the room to make two separate bedrooms for the boys.* (NOTE: + **partition** *v*)

② **partly** /ˈpɑːtli/ *adv* not completely ○ *The house is partly furnished.* ○ *I'm only partly satisfied with the result.* ○ *We're selling our house in London, partly because we need the money, but also because we want to move nearer to the sea.*

② **partner** /ˈpɑːtnə/ *noun* **1.** a person who plays games or dances with someone ○ *Take your partners for the waltz.* ○ *Sally is my usual tennis partner.* **2.** a person with whom you are in a relationship, especially one you live with ○ *We invited him and his partner for drinks.* **3.** a person who owns and works in a business together with one or more others ○ *He became a partner in a firm of solicitors.*

③ **partnership** /ˈpɑːtnəʃɪp/ *noun* a business relationship between two or more people in which the risks and profits are shared according to a letter of agreement between the partners [~between] □ **to go into partnership (with someone)** to join with someone to form a partnership ○ *He went into partnership with his brother to market his new invention.*

③ **part-time** /ˌpɑːt ˈtaɪm/ *adj, adv* not for the whole working day or week ○ *He is trying to find part-time work when the children are in school.* ○ *We are looking for part-time staff to keyboard data.* ○ *She works part-time in the local supermarket.*

① **party** /ˈpɑːti/ (*plural* **parties**) *noun* a special occasion when several people meet, usually in someone's house, in order to celebrate something such as a birthday ○ *We're having a party on New Year's Eve.* ○ *Our family Christmas party was a disaster as usual.* ○ *She invited twenty friends to her birthday party.*

① **pass** /pɑːs/ *noun* (*in football, etc.*) the act of sending the ball to another player ○ *He sent a long pass across the field and Smith headed it into goal.* ■ *verb* (**passes, passing, passed**) **1.** to move something towards someone [~to] ○ *Can you pass me the salt, please?* ○ *He passed the ball back to the goalkeeper.* **2.** to be successful in a test or examination [~to] ○ *He passed in English, but failed in French.* ○ *She passed her driving test first time!*

pass away③ *phrasal verb* to die (NOTE: also **pass on**)

pass off③ *phrasal verb* **1.** to take place ○ *The meeting passed off without any problems.* **2.** □ **to pass something off as something else** to pretend that something is another thing in order to cheat ○ *He passed the wine off as French.* □ **to pass yourself off as something** to pretend to be something ○ *He passed himself off as a rich banker from South America.*

pass on③ *phrasal verb* **1.** to move something on to someone else ○ *She passed on the information to her boss.* **2.** to die ○ *My* *father passed on two years ago.* (NOTE: also **pass away** in the same meaning)

pass out③ *phrasal verb* to become unconscious for a short time ○ *He passed out when he saw the blood.*

pass round③ *phrasal verb* to hand something to various people ○ *She passed the box of chocolates round the table.* ○ *The steward passed round immigration forms.*

pass up③ *phrasal verb* not to make use of a chance or opportunity which is offered

passable /ˈpɑːsəb(ə)l/ *adj* fairly good ○ *He did a passable imitation of the prime minister.*

② **passage** /ˈpæsɪdʒ/ *noun* **1.** a long narrow space with walls on either side [~through/~to] ○ *She hurried along the passage.* ○ *There's an underground passage between the two railway stations.* **2.** a section of a piece of writing [~through/~to] ○ *She quoted passages from the Bible.* ○ *I photocopied a particularly interesting passage from the textbook.*

passageway /ˈpæsɪdʒweɪ/ *noun* a corridor

② **passenger** /ˈpæsɪndʒə/ *noun* a person who is travelling, e.g. in a car, bus, train or plane, but who is not the driver or one of the people who works on it ○ *His car's quite big – it can take three passengers on the back seat.* ○ *The plane was carrying 104 passengers and a crew of ten.*

passer-by /ˌpɑːsə ˈbaɪ/ (*plural* **passers-by**) *noun* a person who is walking past

③ **passing** /ˈpɑːsɪŋ/ *adj* **1.** existing for a short time only ○ *It's just a passing fashion.* **2.** which is going past ○ *The driver of a passing car saw the accident.*

③ **passion** /ˈpæʃ(ə)n/ *noun* a very strong feeling of love, especially sexual love ○ *He couldn't hide the passion he felt for her.*

passionate /ˈpæʃ(ə)nət/ *adj* strongly emotional

passive /ˈpæsɪv/ *adj* allowing things to happen to you and not taking any action yourself ○ *He wasn't one of the ringleaders, he only played a passive role in the coup.* ■ *noun* the form of a verb which shows that the subject is being acted upon (NOTE: If you say 'the car hit him' the verb is active, but 'he was hit by the car' is passive.)

passive smoking /ˌpæsɪv ˈsməʊkɪŋ/ *noun* the act of breathing in smoke from other people's cigarettes, when you do not smoke yourself

Passover /ˈpɑːsəʊvə/ *noun* a Jewish spring festival which celebrates the release of Jews from captivity in Egypt

③ **passport** /ˈpɑːspɔːt/ *noun* an official document allowing you to travel from one country to another ○ *If you are going abroad you need to have a valid passport.* ○ *We had to show our passports at customs.* ○ *His passport is out of date.*

③ **password** /ˈpɑːswɜːd/ *noun* a secret word which you need to know to be allowed to do something such as use a particular computer

① **past** /pɑːst/ *prep* **1.** later than, after ○ *It's past the children's bedtime.* ○ *It's ten past nine (9.10) – we've missed the TV news.* **2.** passing in front of something ○ *If you go past the bank, you'll see the shop on your left.* ○ *She walked past me without saying anything.* ○ *The car went past at at least 60 miles an hour.* (NOTE: **Past** is used for times between o'clock and the half-hour: **3.05** = five past three; **3.15** = a quarter past three; **3.25** = twenty-five past three; **3.30** = half past three. For times after **half past** see **to**. **Past** is also used with many verbs: **to go past**, **to drive past**, **to fly past**, etc.) ■ *adj* happening in a time which his finished ○ *He has spent the past year working in France.* ○ *The time for talking is past – what we need is action.* ■ *noun* the time before now ○ *In the past we always had an office party just before Christmas.*

pasta /ˈpæstə/ *noun* an Italian food made of flour and water, and sometimes eggs, cooked by boiling, and eaten with oil or sauce (NOTE: no plural: *some pasta, a bowl of pasta;* note that **pasta** takes a singular verb: *the pasta is very good here*)

paste /peɪst/ *noun* **1.** a thin liquid glue ○ *Spread the paste evenly over the back of the wallpaper.* **2.** soft food ○ *The cake is covered with almond paste.* ○ *Mix the flour, eggs and milk to a smooth paste.* ○ *Add tomato paste to the soup.* ■ *verb* (**pastes, pasting, pasted**) to glue something such as paper ○ *She pasted a sheet of coloured paper over the front of the box.* ○ *He pasted the postcards into his scrapbook.* ◊ **cut**

pastime /ˈpɑːstaɪm/ *noun* a hobby, something you do to pass your spare time

pastor /ˈpɑːstə/ *noun* a member of the Protestant clergy

pastoral /ˈpɑːst(ə)rəl/ *adj* **1.** referring to country life ○ *Virgil was famous for his pastoral poetry.* **2.** referring to guidance in connection with someone's personal problems ○ *There's an important pastoral side to a teacher's job.*

past participle /pɑːst pɑː'tɪsɪp(ə)l/ *noun* a word formed from a verb, used either to form a past tense or as an adjective. The past participle of 'go' is 'gone'.

③ **pastry** /'peɪstri/ *noun* a mixture of flour, fat and water, used to make pies ○ *She was in the kitchen making pastry.*

pasture /'pɑːstʃə/ *noun* a grassy area where animals such as horses, cows and sheep can graze

pasty[1] /'pæsti/ (*plural* **pasties**) *noun* a pastry folded round a filling of meat and vegetables

pasty[2] /'peɪsti/ (**pastier, pastiest**) *adj* white and unhealthy

pat /pæt/ *noun* a gentle touch with the hand ○ *I didn't hit her – I just gave her a little pat.* ■ *verb* (**pats, patting, patted**) to give someone or something a pat ○ *He patted his pocket to make sure that his wallet was still there.* ◇ **to pat someone on the back** to praise someone ◇ **a pat on the back** praise ○ *The committee got a pat on the back for having organised the show so well.*

③ **patch** /pætʃ/ *noun* **1.** a small piece of material used for covering up a hole, e.g. in clothes ○ *His mother sewed a patch over the hole in his trousers.* **2.** a small area of something ○ *They built a shed on a patch of ground by the railway line.* ○ *There's a patch of rust on the car door.*

patch up③ *phrasal verb* **1.** to mend something with difficulty ○ *The mechanics managed to patch up the engine.* ○ *The surgeon patched him up but warned him not to fight with knives again.* **2.** □ **to patch up a quarrel** to become more friendly again after quarrelling ○ *They had a bitter argument, but patched up their quarrel in time for the party.*

patchwork /'pætʃwɜːk/ *noun* **1.** a piece of needlework made by sewing small pieces of material together in patterns ○ *All the women in the family came together to sew a patchwork quilt.* **2.** an area which looks like a patchwork quilt ○ *a typical English landscape with a patchwork of small fields*

patchy /'pætʃi/ *adj* not the same everywhere ○ *If you don't prepare the surface properly, the paint will look patchy.*

pâté /'pæteɪ/ *noun* a paste made of cooked meat or fish finely minced

patent /'peɪtənt, 'pætənt/ *noun* an official confirmation that you have the sole right to make or sell a new invention ○ *to take out a patent for a new type of light bulb* ○ *They have applied for a patent for their new invention.*

patent leather /ˌpeɪtənt 'leðə/ *noun* leather with an extremely shiny surface

paternal /pə'tɜːn(ə)l/ *adj* referring to a father

paternity /pə'tɜːnɪti/ *noun* **1.** the fact of being a father **2.** the identity of a father ○ *The court had first to establish the child's paternity.*

paternity leave /pə'tɜːnɪti liːv/ *noun* permission for a man to be away from work when his wife has a baby

② **path** /pɑːθ/ *noun* a narrow track for walking [~of/~through/~to] ○ *There's a path across the field.* ○ *Follow the path until you get to the sea.*

③ **pathetic** /pə'θetɪk/ *adj* making you feel either sympathy or a lack of respect ○ *He made a pathetic attempt at a joke.* ○ *She looked a pathetic figure standing in the rain.*

pathological /ˌpæθə'lɒdʒɪk(ə)l/ *adj* referring to a disease or which is caused by a disease ○ *a pathological condition*

pathologist /pə'θɒlədʒɪst/ *noun* **1.** a doctor who specialises in the study of diseases and the changes in the body caused by disease ○ *A pathologist took samples for examination in the laboratory.* **2.** a doctor who examines dead bodies to find out the cause of death ○ *The pathologist found traces of poison in the corpse.*

pathology /pə'θɒlədʒi/ *noun* the study of diseases and the changes in structure and function which diseases cause in the body

pathos /'peɪθɒs/ *noun* a quality in something which makes you feel pity (NOTE: The adjective is **pathetic**.)

pathway /'pɑːθweɪ/ *noun* a track for walking along

③ **patience** /'peɪʃ(ə)ns/ *noun* the quality of being patient ○ *With a little patience, you'll soon learn how to ride a bike.* ○ *I don't have the patience to wait that long.* ◇ **to try someone's patience** to make someone impatient ○ *Looking after a class of thirty little children would try anyone's patience.*

① **patient** /'peɪʃ(ə)nt/ *adj* the ability to wait a long time without getting annoyed ○ *You must be patient – you will get served in time.* ■ *noun* a sick person who is in hospital or who is being treated by a doctor, dentist, psychiatrist, etc. ○ *There are three oth-*

er patients in the ward. ○ *The nurse is trying to take the patient's temperature.*

① **patiently** /ˈpeɪʃ(ə)ntli/ *adv* without getting annoyed

patio /ˈpætiəʊ/ (*plural* **patios**) *noun* a paved area outside a house or other building for sitting or eating

patriotic /ˌpætriˈɒtɪk/ *adj* proud of your country and willing to defend it

patrol /pəˈtrəʊl/ *noun* **1.** the act of keeping guard by walking or driving in one direction and then back again ○ *They make regular patrols round the walls of the prison.* ○ *He was on patrol in the centre of town when he saw some youths running away from a bank.* **2.** a group of people keeping guard ○ *Each time a patrol went past we hid behind a wall.* ■ *verb* (**patrols, patrolling, patrolled**) to keep guard on a place by walking or driving up and down ○ *Armed security guards are patrolling the warehouse.*

③ **patron** /ˈpeɪtrən/ *noun* **1.** a person who protects or supports someone or something [~of] ○ *She's a great patron of the arts.* **2.** a person who goes regularly to a place, e.g. a shop, hotel, restaurant or theatre [~of] ○ *The car park is for the use of hotel patrons only.*

patronage /ˈpætrənɪdʒ/ *noun* the practice of giving support or encouragement to someone, e.g. an artist

patron saint /ˌpeɪtrən ˈseɪnt/ *noun* a saint who is believed to protect a particular group of people

patter /ˈpætə/ *noun* **1.** a light tapping noise ○ *the patter of raindrops on the roof* ○ *I heard a patter of feet in the corridor.* **2.** rapid talk by someone such as a salesman or trickster, to keep your attention ○ *He kept up a continuous patter as he shuffled the cards.* ■ *verb* (**patters, pattering, pattered**) to make a light tapping noise ○ *The rain pattered on the windows.*

① **pattern** /ˈpæt(ə)n/ *noun* **1.** instructions which you follow to make something [~of] ○ *She copied a pattern from a magazine to knit her son a pullover.* **2.** a design of something, e.g. lines or flowers, repeated again and again on cloth, wallpaper, etc. [~of] ○ *She was wearing a coat with a pattern of black and white spots.* ○ *Do you like the pattern on our new carpet?*

paunch /pɔːntʃ/ *noun* a man's fat stomach

③ **pause** /pɔːz/ *noun* a short stop during a period of activity such as work [~for/~in] ○ *Walk quickly and then have a short pause after every 100 steps.* ○ *He read his speech slowly, with lots of pauses.* ■ *verb* (**pauses, pausing, paused**) to stop or rest for a short time before continuing [~for] ○ *She paused for a second to look at her watch.*

pave /peɪv/ (**paves, paving, paved**) *verb* to cover a road or path, etc., with a hard surface ○ *In the old town, the streets are paved with cobblestones.* ○ *There is a paved courtyard behind the restaurant.* ◇ **to pave the way for something** to prepare the way for something to happen ○ *The election of the new president paves the way for a change of government.*

③ **pavement** /ˈpeɪvmənt/ *noun* **1.** a hard path for people to walk on at the side of a road ○ *Walk on the pavement, not in the road.* ○ *Look out; the pavement is covered with ice!* **2.** *US* a hard road surface

pavilion /pəˈvɪliən/ *noun* **1.** a small building for people playing sport to rest in between games ○ *The rest of the team watched from the pavilion as he scored the winning run.* **2.** a separate building at a large exhibition ○ *Have you seen the Canadian pavilion yet?*

paving stone /ˈpeɪvɪŋ stəʊn/ *noun* a large flat stone slab used for making paths and patios

③ **paw** /pɔː/ *noun* the foot of an animal such as a cat or dog ○ *The bear held the fish in its paws.*

③ **pawn** /pɔːn/ *noun* **1.** the smallest piece on the chessboard [~in] ○ *He took two of my pawns.* ○ *She sacrificed a pawn in order to put his king in check.* **2.** a person who is controlled by someone more powerful [~in] ○ *He was just a pawn in the hands of powerful bankers.* ■ *verb* (**pawns, pawning, pawned**) to leave an object in exchange for borrowing money: you claim back the object when you pay back the money ○ *I was so desperate that I pawned my mobile phone.* ○ *He was in a bad state – even his dinner jacket had been pawned.* ○ *She pawned her ring to get money for food.*

pawnbroker /ˈpɔːnbrəʊkə/ *noun* a person who lends money in exchange for valuables left with him or her

① **pay** /peɪ/ *noun* the money you receive for working ○ *They're on strike for more pay.* ○ *I can't afford luxuries on my miserable pay.* ■ *verb* (**pays, paying, paid**) **1.** to give someone money for something [~to/~with//] ○ *How much did you pay for your car?* ○ *We pay £100 a week in rent.* ○ *Please pay the waiter for your drinks.* ○ *She paid him £10 for his old bike.* **2.** to give money to someone for doing something

[~to/~with//] ○ *We pay secretaries £10 an hour.* ○ *I paid them one pound each for washing the car.* ○ *I'll pay you a pound to wash my car.* (NOTE: You **pay someone to wash the car** before he or she washes it, but you **pay someone for washing the car** after he or she has washed it.)

pay back③ *phrasal verb* to give someone money which you owe them ○ *He borrowed £10 last week and hasn't paid me back.* ◇ **to pay someone back for something** to take revenge on someone for having done something ○ *'That will pay them back for ruining our party', he said as he smashed their car window.*

pay in③ *phrasal verb* to put money into an account

pay off③ *phrasal verb* **1.** to finish paying money which is owed ○ *He's aiming to pay off his mortgage in ten years.* ○ *She said she couldn't pay off the loan.* **2.** to pay all the money owed to someone and end his or her employment ○ *When the company was taken over the factory was closed and all the workers were paid off.* **3.** to be successful ○ *Their more cautious approach eventually paid off.* ○ *All that hard work paid off when she came top of her class.*

pay out③ *phrasal verb* **1.** to give money to someone ○ *The insurance company paid out thousands of pounds to claimants after the storm.* ○ *We have paid out half our profits in dividends.* **2.** to unroll a rope ○ *They paid out the rope gradually as I climbed down the cliff.*

pay up③ *phrasal verb* to pay all the money which you owe ○ *The tourist paid up quickly when the taxi driver called the police.*

payee /peɪˈiː/ *noun* a person who is paid money

① **payment** /ˈpeɪmənt/ *noun* the fact of giving money for something [~for] ○ *I make regular monthly payments into her account.* ○ *She made a payment of £10,000 to the solicitor.*

payphone /ˈpeɪfəʊn/ *noun* a public phone in which you insert money to make a call

payroll /ˈpeɪrəʊl/ *noun* **1.** the people employed by a company and paid by it ○ *The company has 250 people on the payroll.* **2.** the total wages paid by a company

③ **PC** /ˌpiː ˈsiː/ *abbr* personal computer, police constable, politically correct

PE *abbr* physical education ○ *a PE class*

③ **pea** /piː/ *noun* a climbing plant of which the round green seeds are eaten as vegetables

② **peace** /piːs/ *noun* **1.** the state of not being at war [~with/] ○ *The UN troops are trying to keep the peace in the area.* ○ *Both sides are hoping to reach a peace settlement.* **2.** a calm quiet state [~with/] ○ *Noisy motorcycles ruin the peace and quiet of the village.*

③ **peaceful** /ˈpiːsf(ə)l/ *adj* enjoyable because there is very little noise or activity ○ *We spent a peaceful afternoon by the river.*

peacekeeper /ˈpiːskiːpə/ *noun* a person who tries to maintain peace

peacetime /ˈpiːstaɪm/ *noun* a period when a country is not fighting in a war

③ **peach** /piːtʃ/ *noun* a sweet fruit with a large stone and very soft skin [~of] ○ *We had peaches and cream for dessert.*

peacock /ˈpiːkɒk/ *noun* a type of common brown butterfly with round purple spots on its wings

③ **peak** /piːk/ *noun* **1.** the top of a mountain ○ *Can you see that snow-covered peak in the distance? – It's Mont Blanc.* **2.** the highest point ○ *The team has to reach a peak of fitness before the match.* ○ *The graph shows the peaks and troughs of pollution over the last month.* **3.** the front part of a cap, which sticks out ○ *He wore a white cap with a dark blue peak.*

peal /piːl/ *noun* the sound of bells ringing ○ *Peals rang out from the church tower on Christmas morning.*

peanut /ˈpiːnʌt/ *noun* a nut which grows under the ground in a shell

peanut butter /ˌpiːnʌt ˈbʌtə/ *noun* a paste made from crushed peanuts

③ **pear** /peə/ *noun* a fruit like a long apple, with one end wider than the other

③ **pearl** /pɜːl/ *noun* a valuable round white jewel formed inside an oyster ○ *She wore a string of pearls which her grandmother had given her.*

pear-shaped /ˈpeə ʃeɪpt/ ◇ **to go pear-shaped** to go wrong, not to work properly (*informal*) ○ *Since the shop opened, everything seems to be going pear-shaped.*

peasant /ˈpez(ə)nt/ *noun* a farm labourer or farmer living in a backward region

peat /piːt/ *noun* wet soil in a bog, made from partly decayed mosses and other plants

pebble /ˈpeb(ə)l/ *noun* a small round stone

pecan /'piːkən, pɪ'kæn/ *noun* a sweet nut from a tree which grows in the south of the USA

peck /pek/ (**pecks, pecking, pecked**) *verb* (*of a bird*) to bite with a beak ○ *Hens were pecking around in the yard.*

peckish /'pekɪʃ/ *adj* slightly hungry (*informal*)

③ **peculiar** /pɪ'kjuːliə/ *adj* **1.** strange [~that] ○ *There's a peculiar smell coming from the kitchen.* ○ *It's peculiar that she never opens the curtains in her house.* **2.** only found in one particular place or person [~to] ○ *He apologised to her in his own peculiar way.* ○ *French fries with mayonnaise is a dish which is peculiar to Belgium.*

peculiarity /pɪˌkjuːli'ærɪti/ (*plural* **peculiarities**) *noun* an odd feature or detail which makes something different

pedagogical /ˌpedə'gɒdʒɪk(ə)l/ *adj* referring to teaching

③ **pedal** /'ped(ə)l/ *noun* **1.** an object worked by the foot to make a machine operate ○ *If you want to stop the car put your foot down on the brake pedal.* **2.** a flat rest which you press down on with your foot to make a bicycle go forwards ○ *He stood up on the pedals to make the bike go up the hill.* ■ *verb* (**pedals, pedalling, pedalled**) to make a bicycle go by pushing on the pedals ○ *He had to pedal hard to get up the hill.*

pedantic /pɪ'dæntɪk/ *adj* who worries too much about small details

peddle /'ped(ə)l/ (**peddles, peddling, peddled**) *verb* **1.** to sell goods from door to door or in the street ○ *He makes a living peddling cleaning products door to door.* ○ *She tried to peddle the information to various newspapers.* **2.** to sell illegal drugs ○ *He was accused of peddling drugs.* (NOTE: Do not confuse with **pedal**.)

pedestal /'pedɪst(ə)l/ *noun* a base for a statue ◇ **to put someone on a pedestal** to treat someone as if he or she were very special or important, even if they have faults ○ *He had always put his wife on a pedestal and was horrified to hear the stories about her which came out in court.*

③ **pedestrian** /pə'destriən/ *noun* a person who walks, rather than drives along, in a street ○ *Two pedestrians were also injured in the accident.*

pedestrian crossing /pɪˌdestriən 'krɒsɪŋ/ *noun* a place where pedestrians can cross a road (NOTE: Another US term is **crosswalk**.)

pedicure /'pedɪkjʊə/ *noun* the act of looking after the feet

pedigree /'pedɪgriː/ *noun* a table showing the ancestors of an animal bred by a breeder

pee /piː/ *noun* **1.** waste water from the body (*informal*) ○ *This drink's horrible, it tastes like pee!* **2.** the act of passing waste water from the body ○ *I need to go for a pee.* ○ *He had a quick pee and then went back to the meeting.* ■ *verb* (**pees, peeing, peed**) to pass waste water from the body ○ *The cat's peed all over my flowerbed.*

peek /piːk/ *noun* a quick look ○ *He opened the fridge door and had a peek at the dessert.* (NOTE: Do not confuse with **peak**.) ■ *verb* (**peeks, peeking, peeked**) to look at something quickly ○ *She peeked through the window and saw there was no one in the kitchen.*

peel /piːl/ *noun* the outer skin of a fruit or a vegetable ○ *Throw the banana peel into the rubbish bin.* ○ *This orange has got very thick peel.* (NOTE: no plural. Do not confuse with **peal**.) ■ *verb* (**peels, peeling, peeled**) to take the outer skin off a fruit or a vegetable ○ *He was peeling a banana.* ○ *If the potatoes are very small you can boil them without peeling them.*

peep /piːp/ *noun* a quick look ○ *He opened the fridge door and had a peep inside.* ■ *verb* (**peeps, peeping, peeped**) to look quickly and secretly at something ○ *She peeped into the box.* ○ *We found him peeping through the keyhole.*

peer /pɪə/ *noun* a member of the a high social class in the UK ○ *Peers sit in the House of Lords.*

peeved /piːvd/ *adj* annoyed and bothered

peg /peg/ *noun* **1.** a small wooden or metal object used for holding something in place ○ *The children hang their coats on pegs in the cloakroom.* ○ *They used no nails in building the roof – it is all held together with wooden pegs.* **2.** □ **clothes peg** little wooden clip, used to attach wet clothes to a washing line. ◊ **off-the-peg** ■ *verb* (**pegs, pegging, pegged**) to attach something with a peg ○ *She pegged the washing out on the line.*

pelican /'pelɪkən/ *noun* a large water bird, which catches fish and keeps the fish in a bag of skin under its beak ○ *The zoo keeper brought a bucket of fish to feed the pelicans.*

pellet /'pelɪt/ *noun* **1.** a small ball of lead, used in shotguns ○ *There may still be pellets left in the pheasant so be careful when* *you eat it.* **2.** a small ball of something ○ *The boys made bread pellets and threw them across the room.* ○ *The cattle feed comes in the form of pellets.*

pelt /pelt/ *noun* a skin of an animal with fur on it ○ *The trappers sold the pelts at the trading post.* ■ *verb* (**pelts, pelting, pelted**) **1.** □ **to pelt someone with something** to throw things at someone ○ *The crowd pelted the speaker with rotten tomatoes.* **2.** to run very fast ○ *I pelted after her to try to catch her up.* **3.** □ **the rain was pelting down** it was raining very hard

pelvis /ˈpelvɪs/ (*plural* **pelvises** or **pelves**) *noun* the group of bones and cartilage which forms a ring and connects the thigh bones to the spine

② **pen** /pen/ *noun* an object for writing with, using ink ○ *I've lost my red pen – can I borrow yours?* ○ *If you haven't got a pen you can always write in pencil.*

penal /ˈpiːn(ə)l/ *adj* referring to punishment

penalise (**penalises, penalising, penalised**), **penalize** (**penalizes, penalizing, penalized**) *verb* to punish someone

③ **penalty** /ˈpen(ə)lti/ (*plural* **penalties**) *noun* **1.** a punishment for breaking a law or rule [~for/~of/for] ○ *The maximum penalty for this offence is two years' imprisonment.* ○ *The coup failed and the leaders had to pay the penalty.* **2.** in sport, an advantage given to one side who has broken a rule, especially a kick directly at goal awarded to the opposite side in football [~for/~of/for] ○ *He was awarded a penalty kick.* ○ *They scored from a penalty.* □ **to take** or **miss a** or **the penalty** in football, to be the person who kicks the ball to try to score a goal when a penalty is given or who does not score in this situation

penance /ˈpenəns/ *noun* punishment which someone accepts as a way of acknowledging a bad action

③ **pence** /pens/ plural of **penny**

penchant /ˈpɒŋʃɒŋ/ *noun* a special liking for something

② **pencil** /ˈpensəl/ *noun* an object for writing or drawing with, made of wood, with a long piece of black or coloured material through the middle

pencil sharpener /ˈpensəl ˌʃɑːpnə/ *noun* an instrument for sharpening pencils

pendant /ˈpendənt/ *noun* a piece of jewellery which hangs from a chain round your neck

pending /ˈpendɪŋ/ *prep* while waiting for something to happen (*formal*) ○ *pending advice from our lawyers* ○ *He has been suspended on full pay, pending an inquiry.*

pendulum /ˈpendjʊləm/ *noun* **1.** a weight on the end of a chain which swings from side to side, making a clock work ○ *If you look in the clock case, you can see the pendulum swinging back and forth.* **2.** a trend from one extreme to another ○ *A few years ago every household had two cars, now the pendulum has swung in the opposite direction and more people are using public transport.*

penetrate /ˈpenɪtreɪt/ (**penetrates, penetrating, penetrated**) *verb* to go into or through something (NOTE: + **penetration** *n*)

penetrating /ˈpenɪtreɪtɪŋ/ *adj* deep and searching

penfriend /ˈpenfrend/ *noun* someone, often in another country, whom you write to regularly without ever meeting him or her

penguin /ˈpeŋgwɪn/ *noun* a black and white bird found in the Antarctic, which swims well but cannot fly

penicillin /ˌpenɪˈsɪlɪn/ *noun* a common antibiotic, made from a mould

peninsula /pəˈnɪnsjʊlə/ *noun* a large piece of land which goes out into the sea

penis /ˈpiːnɪs/ (*plural* **penises** or **penes**) *noun* the male organ used for passing urine and for sexual intercourse

penitent /ˈpenɪt(ə)nt/ *adj* being sorry for having done something wrong ○ *If you are penitent, God will forgive you.*

penitentiary /ˌpenɪˈtenʃəri/ (*plural* **penitentiaries**) *noun US* a prison

penknife /ˈpennaɪf/ (*plural* **penknives**) *noun* a small pocket knife which folds up

pen name /ˈpen neɪm/ *noun* a name used by a writer which is not his or her own

penniless /ˈpenɪləs/ *adj* with no money

① **penny** /ˈpeni/ (*plural* **pennies** or **pence**) *noun* the smallest British coin, one hundredth of a pound ○ *It cost £4.99, so I paid with a £5 note and got a penny change.* ○ *I came out without my purse and I haven't got a penny on me.* (NOTE: **Pennies** is used to refer to several coins, but **pence** refers to the price. In prices, **pence** is always written **p** and often said as /piː/ : *This book only costs 60p.*: say 'sixty p' or 'sixty pence'.) ◇ **not have a penny** not have any money

② **pension** /ˈpenʃən/ *noun* money paid regularly, e.g. to someone who has retired from work ○ *He has a good pension from* *his firm.* ○ *She finds her pension is not enough to live on.*

② **pensioner** /ˈpenʃənə/ *noun* a person who gets a pension

pensive /ˈpensɪv/ *adj* thoughtful

pentagon /ˈpentəgən/ *noun* a geometrical figure with five sides ○ *He drew a pentagon on the blackboard.*

pentathlon /penˈtæθlən/ *noun* an athletic competition in which competitors have to compete in five different sports

penthouse /ˈpenthaʊs/ *noun* a flat on the top floor of a high building

penultimate /pəˈnʌltɪmət/ *adj* next to last

① **people** /ˈpiːp(ə)l/ *noun* men, women or children considered as a group ○ *There were at least twenty people waiting to see the doctor.* ○ *So many people wanted to see the film that there were queues every night.* ○ *A group of people from our office went to Paris by train.*

③ **pepper** /ˈpepə/ *noun* **1.** a strong-tasting powder used in cooking, made from the whole seeds of a plant (**black pepper**) or from seeds with the outer layer removed (**white pepper**) ○ *Add salt and pepper to taste.* (NOTE: no plural in this sense) **2.** a hollow green, red or yellow fruit used as a vegetable ○ *We had stuffed peppers for lunch.*

③ **peppermint** /ˈpepəmɪnt/ *noun* a herb which is grown to produce an oil used in sweets, drinks and toothpaste ○ *I always use peppermint-flavoured toothpaste.*

pep talk /ˈpep tɔːk/ *noun* a talk designed to encourage people, e.g. to work hard or to win a match (*informal*)

① **per** /pɜː, pə/ *prep* for each ○ *I can't cycle any faster than fifteen miles per hour.* ○ *Potatoes cost 10p per kilo.* ○ *We paid our secretaries £10 per hour.*

per annum /pɜː ˈænəm/ *adv* for each year

③ **perceive** /pəˈsiːv/ (**perceives, perceiving, perceived**) *verb* to notice or realise something [~that] ○ *The changes are so slight that they're almost impossible to perceive with the naked eye.* ○ *I perceived a worsening in his condition during the night.*

per cent /pə ˈsent/, **percent** *noun* out of each hundred ○ *Fifty per cent of staff are aged over 40.* (NOTE: The symbol % is used after numbers: 50%.)

③ **percentage** /pəˈsentɪdʒ/ *noun* an amount considered in relation to 100 ○ *A low percentage of the population voted.* ○ *'What percentage of businesses are likely to be affected?' – 'Oh, about 40 per cent'.*

perceptible /pəˈseptɪb(ə)l/ *adj* which can be noticed by the senses, i.e. seen, heard, smelled, tasted or touched

③ **perception** /pəˈsepʃən/ *noun* the ability to notice or realise something [~of]

perceptive /pəˈseptɪv/ *adj* showing that you understand something clearly

perch /pɜːtʃ/ *noun* a type of small freshwater fish ■ *verb* (**perches, perching, perched** or **perched**) (*of a person or a building*) to place someone or something high up ○ *a castle perched high on the mountainside* ○ *She was sitting perched on a bar stool.*

percolate /ˈpɜːkəleɪt/ (**percolates, percolating, percolated**) *verb* to filter through

perennial /pəˈreniəl/ *noun* a plant which flowers every year without needing to be sown again ○ *Most of the plants in this bed are perennials.* Compare **annual, biennial**

perfect¹ /ˈpɜːfɪkt/ *adj* **1.** good in every way ○ *Your coat is a perfect fit.* ○ *Don't change anything – the room is perfect as it is.* **2.** completely suitable ○ *She's the perfect secretary.* ○ *George would be perfect for the job of salesman.* ○ *I was in a perfect position to see what happened.*

perfect² /pəˈfekt/ (**perfects, perfecting, perfected**) *verb* to make something new and perfect ○ *She perfected a process for speeding up the bottling system.*

perfection /pəˈfekʃən/ *noun* the state of being perfect ◇ **to perfection** perfectly ○ *He timed his kick to perfection.*

perfectionist /pəˈfekʃənɪst/ *noun* a person who demands that everything has to be perfect

② **perfectly** /ˈpɜːfɪktli/ *adv* very well ○ *That dress fits you perfectly.*

perforated /ˈpɜːfəreɪtɪd/ *adj* which has a hole or holes in it, especially with a line of small holes designed to make tearing easy

② **perform** /pəˈfɔːm/ (**performs, performing, performed**) *verb* **1.** to do an action ○ *She performed a perfect dive.* ○ *It's the sort of task that can be performed by any computer.* **2.** to do something such as acting, dancing or singing in public ○ *The dance group will perform at the local theatre next week.* ○ *The play will be performed in the village hall.*

① **performance** /pəˈfɔːməns/ *noun* **1.** the way in which someone or something works, e.g. how successful they are or how much they achieve ○ *We're looking for ways to improve our performance.* ○ *After last night's miserable performance I don't think the team is likely to reach the semi-finals.* **2.** a public show for entertainment ○ *The next performance will start at 8 o'clock.* ○ *There are three performances a day during the summer.*

③ **performer** /pə'fɔːmə/ *noun* a person who gives a public show in order to entertain people

perfume /'pɜːfjuːm/ *noun* **1.** a liquid which smells nice, and which you put on your skin **2.** a pleasant smell, especially of flowers ○ *the strong perfume of the roses*

① **perhaps** /pə'hæps/ *adv* possibly ○ *Perhaps the train is late.* ○ *They're late – perhaps the snow's very deep.* ○ *Is it going to be fine? – Perhaps not, I can see clouds over there.*

peril /'perɪl/ *noun* great danger ◇ **at your peril** you risk everything if you do this ○ *You disregard your doctor's advice at your peril.* ◇ **in peril** facing a risk ○ *The ship was on the rocks and the lives of the crew were in peril.*

perilous /'perɪləs/ *adj* very dangerous

perimeter /pə'rɪmɪtə/ *noun* the outside edge of an enclosed area

① **period** /'pɪəriəd/ *noun* **1.** an amount of time ○ *She swam under water for a short period.* ○ *The offer is open for a limited period only.* ○ *It was an unhappy period in her life.* **2.** the time during which a lesson is given in school ○ *We have three periods of English on Thursdays.*

periodic /ˌpɪəri'ɒdɪk/ *adj* repeated after a regular period of time ○ *periodic attacks of the illness* ○ *We carry out periodic reviews of the company's financial position.*

periodical /ˌpɪəri'ɒdɪk(ə)l/ *noun* a magazine which appears regularly ○ *He writes for several London periodicals.*

periphery /pə'rɪf(ə)ri/ *noun* an edge, not the centre

perish /'perɪʃ/ (**perishes, perishing, perished**) *verb* **1.** to die ○ *The ship sank and twenty-five sailors perished.* **2.** to decay ○ *The rubber has perished and the lid isn't airtight any more.*

perishable /'perɪʃəb(ə)l/ *adj* which can go bad easily ○ *Perishable food like pâté must be kept in a fridge.*

perjury /'pɜːdʒəri/ *noun* a crime of telling lies when you have sworn to tell the truth in court

perk /pɜːk/ *noun* something extra such as company cars or private health insurance given by a company to employees in addition to their salaries

perm /pɜːm/ *noun* curls or a wave put into your hair artificially ○ *She's had a perm and it's changed her appearance.*

② **permanent** /'pɜːmənənt/ *adj* lasting or intended to last, for ever ○ *He has found a permanent job.* ○ *She is in permanent employment.* ○ *They are living with her parents temporarily – it's not a permanent arrangement.*

permanently /'pɜːmənəntli/ *adv* for ever; always

permeate /'pɜːmieɪt/ (**permeates, permeating, permeated**) *verb* to move right through something

permissible /pə'mɪsɪb(ə)l/ *adj* which can be allowed

② **permission** /pə'mɪʃ(ə)n/ *noun* the freedom which you are given to do something by someone in authority ○ *You need permission from the boss to go into the storeroom.* ○ *He asked the manager's permission to take a day off.*

permissive /pə'mɪsɪv/ *adj* allowing people a large amount of freedom in the way they behave, especially in sexual matters

permit[1] /'pɜːmɪt/ *noun* an official paper which allows you to do something ○ *You have to have a permit to sell ice cream from a van.*

permit[2] /pə'mɪt/ (**permits, permitting, permitted**) *verb* to allow someone to do something ○ *This ticket permits three people to go into the exhibition.* ○ *Smoking is not permitted in underground stations.*

permutation /ˌpɜːmjʊ'teɪʃ(ə)n/ *noun* the act of putting several things together in various combinations

perpetrate /'pɜːpɪtreɪt/ (**perpetrates, perpetrating, perpetrated**) *verb* to commit a crime (NOTE: + **perpetrator** *n*)

perpetual /pə'petʃuəl/ *adj* continuous, without any end

perpetuate /pə'petʃueɪt/ (**perpetuates, perpetuating, perpetuated**) *verb* to make something continue

perplexed /pə'plekst/ *adj* feeling confused

persecute /'pɜːsɪkjuːt/ (**persecutes, persecuting, persecuted**) *verb* to treat someone badly on political or religious beliefs or because of their race (NOTE: + **persecutor** *n*)

perseverance /ˌpɜːsɪ'vɪərəns/ *noun* the act of persevering

persevere /ˌpɜːsɪˈvɪə/ (**perseveres, persevering, persevered**) *verb* to continue doing something even if it is difficult [~with/in] ○ *If you persevere with your exercises you should lose weight.* ○ *He persevered in denying his involvement.*

persist /pəˈsɪst/ (**persists, persisting, persisted**) *verb* to continue to exist □ **to persist in doing something** to continue doing something, even if you should not ○ *He will persist in singing while he works although we've told him many times to stop.* ○ *She persists in refusing to see a doctor.*

③ **persistent** /pəˈsɪstənt/ *adj* continuing to do something, even though people want you to stop

① **person** /ˈpɜːs(ə)n/ (*plural* **people** or **persons**) *noun* a man or woman ○ *The police say a person entered the house by the window.* ○ *His father's a very interesting person.* ◇ **in person** used to emphasise that someone is physically present ○ *Several celebrities were at the first night in person.*

persona /pəˈsəʊnə/ *noun* a person's character as seen by other people

personable /ˈpɜːs(ə)nəb(ə)l/ *adj* attractive, good-looking or having a pleasant character

① **personal** /ˈpɜːs(ə)n(ə)l/ *adj* **1.** belonging or referring to a particular person or people ○ *They lost all their personal property in the fire.* **2.** relating to something that you would not like to discuss with most people ○ *Can I ask you a personal question?* ○ *That's personal – I'd rather not tell you.*

personal computer /ˌpɜːs(ə)n(ə)l kəmˈpjuːtə/ *noun* a small computer used by a person at home. Abbreviation **PC**

③ **personality** /ˌpɜːsəˈnælɪti/ *noun* **1.** character ○ *He has a strange personality.* **2.** a famous person, especially a TV or radio star ○ *The new supermarket is going to be opened by a famous sporting personality.*

② **personally** /ˈpɜːs(ə)n(ə)li/ *adv* **1.** from your own point of view ○ *Personally, I think you're making a mistake.* **2.** in person ○ *He is sorry that he can't be here to accept the prize personally.* ◇ **don't take it personally** don't think it was meant to criticise you

personal pronoun /ˌpɜːs(ə)n(ə)l ˈprəʊnaʊn/ *noun* (*in grammar*) a pronoun which refers to a person, such as 'I', 'he', 'she', 'him', 'her', etc.

personal trainer /ˌpɜːs(ə)n(ə)l ˈtreɪnə/ *noun* a person whose job is to help someone become fit, e.g. by teaching them a set of physical exercises and advising them what to eat

personify /pəˈsɒnɪfaɪ/ (**personifies, personifying, personified**) *verb* **1.** to be a good example of something ○ *He seemed to personify all that was best in American life.* **2.** to use a character in art to represent a quality ○ *The artist personified the wind as a fat red-faced man, blowing hard.* (NOTE: + **personification** *n*)

③ **personnel** /ˌpɜːsəˈnel/ *noun* staff, the people employed by a company

③ **perspective** /pəˈspektɪv/ *noun* **1.** (*in art*) a way of drawing objects or scenes, so that they appear to have depth or distance ○ *He's got the perspective wrong – that's why the picture looks so odd.* **2.** a way of looking at something ○ *A French politician's perspective on the problem will be completely different from mine.* ○ *She was looking at the situation from the perspective of a parent with two young children.* □ **to put** *or* **keep things in perspective** to show or react to events in a balanced way ○ *You must put the sales figures in perspective – they look bad, but they're much better than last year.*

perspiration /ˌpɜːspəˈreɪʃ(ə)n/ *noun* the drops of liquid which come to the surface of your skin when you are hot

perspire /pəˈspaɪə/ (**perspires, perspiring, perspired**) *verb* to cause small drops of liquid to come to the surface of your skin because you are feeling hot

② **persuade** /pəˈsweɪd/ (**persuades, persuading, persuaded**) *verb* to get someone to do what you want by explaining or asking ○ *She managed to persuade the bank manager to give her a loan.* ○ *After ten hours of discussion, they persuaded him to leave.*

③ **persuasion** /pəˈsweɪʒ(ə)n/ *noun* **1.** the act of persuading ○ *It took a lot of persuasion on his part to get her to change her mind.* ○ *With a bit of gentle persuasion, he agreed to be chairman.* **2.** a firm, usually religious, belief ○ *People of that persuasion refuse to do military service.* ○ *People of varying political persuasions have signed the petition.*

persuasive /pəˈsweɪsɪv/ *adj* able to make people agree to accept something ○ *They employed some very persuasive arguments to get us to support their proposal.*

pertinent /ˈpɜːtɪnənt/ *adj* which is relevant

perturbed /pə'tɜːbd/ *adj* made to feel worried or frightened

peruse /pə'ruːz/ (**peruses, perusing, perused**) *verb* to read something carefully (NOTE: + **perusal** *n*)

pervade /pə'veɪd/ (**pervades, pervading, pervaded**) *verb* to spread everywhere

perverse /pə'vɜːs/ *adj* continuing to do something even if it is wrong

perversion /pə'vɜːʃ(ə)n/ *noun* **1.** behaviour that is considered not natural and possibly immoral ○ *sexual perversion* **2.** the act of changing something to make it bad or wrong ○ *Her story is a perversion of the truth.*

pervert[1] /'pɜːvɜːt/ *noun* a person who commits sexual acts which are thought to be not natural or normal ○ *a sexual pervert*

pervert[2] /pə'vɜːt/ (**perverts, perverting, perverted**) *verb* to change someone or something to make them evil

perverted /pə'vɜːtɪd/ *adj* which has been made bad or wrong

pessimism /'pesɪmɪz(ə)m/ *noun* the state of believing that only bad things will happen

pessimist /'pesɪmɪst/ *noun* a person who thinks only bad things will happen

pessimistic /ˌpesɪ'mɪstɪk/ *adj* believing that only bad things will happen

pest /pest/ *noun* **1.** a plant, animal or insect which causes problems ○ *Many farmers look on rabbits as a pest.* **2.** a person who annoys someone ○ *That little boy is an absolute pest – he won't stop whistling.*

pester /'pestə/ (**pesters, pestering, pestered**) *verb* to keep annoying someone or asking them for something □ **to pester someone into doing something** to keep asking or telling someone to do something until they do what you want ○ *She pestered him into getting his hair cut.*

pesticide /'pestɪsaɪd/ *noun* a poison to kill pests

pet /pet/ *noun* an animal kept in the home ○ *The family has several pets – two cats, a dog and a hamster.*

petal /'pet(ə)l/ *noun* the colourful part of a flower

peter *verb*

peter out *phrasal verb* to come to an end, to gradually stop

petite /pə'tiːt/ *adj* (*of a woman*) small and delicate

petition /pə'tɪʃ(ə)n/ *noun* an official request, often signed by many people ○ *She wanted me to sign a petition against the building of the new road.* ○ *We went to the town hall to hand the petition to the mayor.* ■ *verb* (**petitions, petitioning, petitioned**) to ask someone for something officially, to make an official request for something ○ *They petitioned the town council for a new library.* ○ *He petitioned the government to provide a special pension.* ○ *She is petitioning for divorce.*

petrified /'petrɪfaɪd/ *adj* **1.** changed to stone ○ *You can find petrified trees at the bottom of the gorge.* **2.** unable to move because you are afraid ○ *I thought he was going to shoot me, I was absolutely petrified.*

③ **petrol** /'petrəl/ *noun* a liquid used as a fuel for engines ○ *This car doesn't use very much petrol.* ○ *The bus ran out of petrol on the motorway.* ○ *Petrol prices are lower at supermarkets.* (NOTE: no plural: *some petrol, a litre of petrol*)

petroleum /pə'trəʊliəm/ *noun* raw mineral oil which comes from under the earth or sea

③ **petrol station** /'petrəl ˌsteɪʃ(ə)n/ *noun* a place where you can buy petrol for your car

petty /'peti/ *adj* **1.** unimportant ○ *I haven't time to deal with petty points of detail.* **2.** with a narrow point of view ○ *It was very petty of her to ask for her money back.*

petulant /'petjʊlənt/ *adj* feeling annoyed

pew /pjuː/ *noun* a long wooden seat in a church

pH /ˌpiː 'eɪtʃ/ *noun* a measure of the concentration of hydrogen ions in a solution, which shows how acid or alkaline it is

phantom /'fæntəm/ *noun* an imaginary creature thought to be the spirit of a dead person ○ *Phantoms were supposed to have been seen in the churchyard at dead of night.* ■ *adj* not real but imaginary, especially in a way which is frightening ○ *She felt a phantom presence standing beside her.*

pharmaceutical /ˌfɑːmə'sjuːtɪk(ə)l/ *adj* referring to medicines

pharmacist /'fɑːməsɪst/ *noun* a person who prepares and sells medicines

pharmacology /ˌfɑːmə'kɒlədʒi/ *noun* the study of drugs and medicines

pharmacy /'fɑːməsi/ (*plural* **pharmacies**) *noun* **1.** a shop which makes and sells medicines ○ *He runs the pharmacy in the High Street.* **2.** the study of medicines ○ *She's studying pharmacy.* ○ *He has a diploma in pharmacy.*

② **phase** /feɪz/ *noun* a stage in the development of something ○ *The project is now in its final phase.* ○ *It's a phase she's going through and hopefully she will grow out of it.* ○ *I'm sure dyeing his hair green is just a phase.* ■ *verb* (**phases, phasing, phased**) to introduce something gradually ○ *The changes will be phased over three years.*

phase in *or* **out** *phrasal verb* to introduce or remove something gradually ○ *The new telephone system will be phased in over the next two months.*

PhD /ˌpiː eɪtʃ 'diː/ *noun* an advanced degree from a university in an arts subject. Full form **Doctor of Philosophy** (NOTE: written after the name: *Alec Smart PhD*)

pheasant /'fez(ə)nt/ *noun* a large brightly coloured bird with a long tail, shot for sport and food

phenomenal /fə'nɒmɪn(ə)l/ *adj* surprising

③ **phenomenon** /fə'nɒmɪnən/ (*plural* **phenomena**) *noun* something very surprising or unusual which happens and which people cannot explain [~of]

phew /fjuː/ *interj* showing surprise or showing pleasure that you have avoided something unpleasant

philanthropist /fɪ'lænθrəpɪst/ *noun* a person who does good things to help people

philistine /'fɪlɪstaɪn/ *noun* a person who is not sympathetic to the arts ○ *He thinks people who don't appreciate modern jazz are simply philistines.*

philosopher /fɪ'lɒsəfə/ *noun* a person who studies the meaning of human existence; a person who teaches philosophy

philosophical /ˌfɪlə'sɒfɪk(ə)l/ *adj* **1.** carefully calm in the face of problems ○ *to take a philosophical attitude* ○ *It's best to be philosophical about it and not get too upset.* **2.** referring to philosophy ○ *She was involved in a philosophical argument.*

③ **philosophy** /fɪ'lɒsəfi/ (*plural* **philosophies**) *noun* **1.** the study of the meaning of human existence ○ *He's studying philosophy.* **2.** a general way of thinking ○ *My philosophy is that you should treat people as you would want them to treat you.*

phlegm /flem/ *noun* an unpleasant thick liquid substance which you get in the nose and throat when you have a cold ○ *She sneezes a lot and coughs up phlegm from the throat.* ○ *The cough mixture should loosen the phlegm on your chest.*

phlegmatic /fleg'mætɪk/ *adj* calm, not flustered

phobia /'fəʊbiə/ *noun* extreme fear of a particular thing

① **phone** /fəʊn/ *noun* a telephone ○ *If someone rings, can you answer the phone for me?* ○ *She lifted the phone and called the ambulance.* □ **by phone** using the telephone ○ *to place an order by phone* ■ *verb* (**phones, phoning, phoned**) to speak to someone using a telephone ○ *Your wife phoned when you were out.* ○ *Can you phone me at ten o'clock tomorrow evening?* ○ *I need to phone our office in New York.* □ **to phone for something** to make a phone call to ask for something ○ *He phoned for a taxi.* □ **to phone about something** to make a phone call to speak about something ○ *He phoned about the message he had received.*

phone back *phrasal verb* to reply by telephone; to call again ○ *The manager is out – can you phone back in about fifteen minutes?* ○ *She phoned back three minutes later to ask me my address.*

③ **phone book** /'fəʊn bʊk/ *noun* a book which gives the names of people and businesses in a town in alphabetical order, with their addresses and phone numbers

③ **phone call** /'fəʊn kɔːl/ *noun* an occasion on which you speak to someone by telephone

③ **phonecard** /'fəʊnkɑːd/ *noun* a plastic card which you use to pay for calls on a public telephone

phone-in /'fəʊn ɪn/ *noun* a radio show, where members of the public telephone a speaker to ask questions or put their points of view

③ **phone number** /'fəʊn ˌnʌmbə/ *noun* a series of numbers that you press on a telephone to contact a particular person

phonetic /fə'netɪk/ *adj* referring to spoken sounds

phonetics /fə'netɪks/ *noun* **1.** the study of the sounds of a language ○ *Every linguist has to take a course in basic phonetics.* **2.** written signs which show how words are pronounced ○ *Each word is followed by its phonetics which show you how the word should be pronounced.*

phoney /'fəʊni/ *adj* not real, not what it seems to be ○ *He gave a phoney address in Paris.* ○ *She made a lot of phoney claims in her story in the newspaper.* ■ *noun* a person who is not what he or she seems to be ○ *He's just an old phoney – he doesn't have any experience of TV reporting at all.*

② **photo** /'fəʊtəʊ/ (*plural* **photos**) *noun* a photograph; a picture taken using a camera

○ *Here's a photo of the village in the snow.* ○ *I've brought some holiday photos to show you.*

③ **photocopier** /ˈfəʊtəʊkɒpiə/ *noun* a machine which makes photocopies

③ **photocopy** /ˈfəʊtəʊkɒpi/ *noun* (*plural* **photocopies**) a copy of a document made by photographing it ○ *She made six photocopies of the contract.* ■ *verb* (**photocopies, photocopying, photocopied**) to copy something and make a print of it ○ *Can you photocopy this letter, please?*

photogenic /ˌfəʊtəʊˈdʒenɪk/ *adj* who looks well in photographs

② **photograph** /ˈfəʊtəgrɑːf/ *noun* a picture taken with a camera [~of] ○ *I've found an old black and white photograph of my parents' wedding.* ○ *She's trying to take a photograph of the cat.* ○ *He kept her photograph in his wallet.* ○ *You'll need two passport photographs to get your visa.* ■ *verb* (**photographs, photographing, photographed**) to take a picture with a camera ○ *She was photographing the flowers in the public gardens.*

photographer /fəˈtɒgrəfə/ *noun* a person who takes photographs, especially as a job

③ **photography** /fəˈtɒgrəfi/ *noun* the practice of taking pictures on sensitive film with a camera

photo opportunity /ˈfəʊtəʊ ˌɒpətjuːnɪti/ *noun* an arranged situation where a famous person can be filmed or photographed by journalists

phrasal verb /ˌfreɪz(ə)l ˈvɜːb/ *noun* a type of verb which has two or three parts, which together have a meaning different from that of the main verb, such as 'tell off', 'look after' and 'put up with'

① **phrase** /freɪz/ *noun* a short sentence or group of words ○ *Try to translate the whole phrase, not just one word at a time.* ○ *I'm trying to remember a phrase from 'Hamlet'.*

phrase book /ˈfreɪz bʊk/ *noun* a book of translations of common expressions

① **physical** /ˈfɪzɪk(ə)l/ *adj* relating to the human body ○ *The illness is mental rather than physical.* ○ *He has a strong physical attraction for her.*

physical education /ˌfɪzɪk(ə)l ˌedjʊˈkeɪʃ(ə)n/ *noun* physical exercise taught as part of the school curriculum. Abbreviation **PE**

③ **physically** /ˈfɪzɪkli/ *adv* **1.** relating to the body ○ *I find him physically very attractive.* **2.** relating to the laws of nature ○ *It is physically impossible to get a piano into that little car.*

physical science /ˌfɪzɪk(ə)l ˈsaɪəns/ *noun* a science that deals with subjects such as physics or chemistry, rather than with the science of living creatures

physician /fɪˈzɪʃ(ə)n/ *noun US* a doctor

③ **physics** /ˈfɪzɪks/ *noun* the study of things such as heat, light and sound, and the way in which they affect objects ○ *She teaches physics at the local college.* ○ *It's a law of physics that things fall down to the ground and not up into the sky.*

physiology /ˌfɪziˈɒlədʒi/ *noun* the study of the way in which living things work

physiotherapy /ˌfɪziəʊˈθerəpi/ *noun* a treatment for problems with joints, muscles and nerves, e.g. by exercise, massage or heat treatment (NOTE: + **physiotherapist** *n*)

physique /fɪˈziːk/ *noun* the shape of a person's body, especially the muscles

③ **pianist** /ˈpiːənɪst/ *noun* a person who plays the piano, especially as their job

③ **piano** /piˈænəʊ/ *noun* a large musical instrument with black and white keys which you press to make music ○ *She's taking piano lessons.* ○ *She played the piano while her brother sang.*

piccolo /ˈpɪkələʊ/ (*plural* **piccolos**) *noun* a small wind instrument, like a little flute

① **pick** /pɪk/ (**picks, picking, picked**) *verb* **1.** to choose something ○ *The captain picks the football team.* ○ *She was picked to play the part of the victim's mother.* ○ *The Association has picked Paris for its next meeting.* **2.** to take fruit or flowers from plants ○ *They've picked all the strawberries.* ○ *Don't pick the flowers in the public gardens.* ◇ **take your pick** choose which one you want ○ *We've got green, red and blue balloons – just take your pick!*

pick on *phrasal verb* to choose someone to attack or criticise

pick out① *phrasal verb* to choose something or someone

pick up① *phrasal verb* **1.** to take something that is lying on a surface and lift it in your hand ○ *She dropped her handkerchief and he picked it up.* ○ *He bent down to pick up a pound coin which he saw on the pavement.* ○ *I picked up some holiday brochures at the travel agent's.* **2.** to learn something easily without being taught ○ *She never took any piano lessons, she just picked it up.* ○ *He picked up some German when he was working in Germany.* **3.** to give someone a lift in a vehicle ○ *We will pick you up from the hotel.* ○ *Can you send a taxi to pick us up at seven o'clock?* **4.** to meet someone by chance and start a relationship with them ○ *She's a girl he picked up in a bar.* **5.** to arrest somebody ○ *He was picked up by the police at the airport.* **6.** to improve, to get better ○ *She's been in bed for weeks, but is beginning to pick up.* ○ *Business is picking up after the Christmas holiday.*

picket /ˈpɪkɪt/ *noun* **1.** a worker who refuses to go into work and stands at the gate of a factory to try to persuade other workers to not go to work, because of a disagreement with their employers ○ *The pickets at the main gate tried to stop lorries from entering.* **2.** a group of pickets ○ *They organised a picket of the factory.* **3.** a person who stands outside a place to protest against what is going on inside ○ *Pickets stood outside the laboratory.*

pickle /ˈpɪk(ə)l/ (**pickles, pickling, pickled**) *verb* to preserve vegetables in vinegar ○ *She bought some small onions for pickling.*

③ **pickpocket** /ˈpɪkpɒkɪt/ *noun* a person who steals things from people's pockets

pick-up /ˈpɪk ʌp/ *noun* a light van with an open back ○ *They loaded all their gear into the back of a pick-up.*

picky /ˈpɪki/ *adj* hard to please

③ **picnic** /ˈpɪknɪk/ *noun* a meal eaten outdoors away from home ○ *If it's fine, let's go for a picnic.* ○ *They stopped by a wood, and had a picnic lunch.* ■ *verb* (**picnics, picnicking, picnicked**) to eat a picnic ○ *People were picnicking on the bank of the river.*

pictorial /pɪkˈtɔːriəl/ *adj* referring to pictures

① **picture** /ˈpɪktʃə/ *noun* a drawing, a painting or a photograph ○ *She drew a picture of the house.* ○ *The book has pages of pictures of wild animals.* ○ *She cut out the picture of the President from the magazine.*

picturesque /ˌpɪktʃəˈresk/ *adj* (*of places*) attractive, like in a picture

② **pie** /paɪ/ *noun* meat or fruit cooked in a pastry case ○ *For pudding, there's apple pie and ice cream.* ○ *If we're going on a picnic, I'll buy a big pork pie.*

① **piece** /piːs/ *noun* a bit of something or one of a number of similar things [~of] ○ *Would you like another piece of cake?* ○ *I need two pieces of black cloth.*

piecemeal /ˈpiːsmiːl/ *adj, adv* separately, done bit by bit ○ *The work was carried out on a piecemeal basis.* ○ *They had bought all sorts of paintings piecemeal.*

pie-chart /ˈpaɪ tʃɑːt/ *noun* a diagram shaped like a circle with pieces cut out showing how something is divided up

③ **pier** /pɪə/ *noun* **1.** a structure built from the land out into the sea, often with entertainments on it ○ *If you go to Brighton, you must go on the pier.* ○ *We went for a stroll along the pier.* ○ *He spent his holiday fishing from the end of the pier.* **2.** one of the tall strong structures holding up a bridge ○ *The boat collided with one of the piers of the railway bridge.* (NOTE: Do not confuse with **peer**.)

pierce /pɪəs/ (**pierces, piercing, pierced**) *verb* to make a hole in something

piercing /ˈpɪəsɪŋ/ *adj* (*of a sound*) unpleasantly high and loud ○ *They suddenly heard a piercing cry.* ○ *He let out a piercing yell.*

② **pig** /pɪɡ/ *noun* a pink or black farm animal with short legs kept for its meat (NOTE: Fresh meat from a **pig** is called **pork**. **Bacon**, **gammon** and **ham** are types of smoked or cured meat from a **pig**.)

③ **pigeon** /ˈpɪdʒən/ *noun* a fat grey bird which is common in towns

pigeonhole /ˈpɪdʒənhəʊl/ *noun* one of a series of small square spaces in shelves, used to put away things such as papers or letters ○ *I looked in my pigeonhole to see if there were any messages for me.* ■ *verb* (**pigeonholes, pigeonholing, pigeonholed**) **1.** to file letters or papers, often as the best way to forget about them **2.** to say that someone or something belongs to a particular group or class ○ *As an artist he is not easy to pigeonhole.*

pigeon-toed /ˌpɪdʒ(ə)n ˈtəʊd/ *adj* walking with the toes turning in

piggyback /ˈpɪɡibæk/ *noun* carrying someone on your back with his arms round your neck

piglet /ˈpɪɡlət/ *noun* a little pig

pigment /ˈpɪɡmənt/ *noun* a substance which colours

pigmentation /ˌpɪɡmenˈteɪʃ(ə)n/ *noun* the colouring of the skin

pigsty /ˈpɪɡstaɪ/ (*plural* **pigsties**) *noun* **1.** a little building where a pig is kept **2.** an untidy place

pike /paɪk/ *noun* a large fish which lives in rivers and lakes

② **pile** /paɪl/ *noun* a large mass of things [~of] ○ *Look at that pile of washing.* ○ *The pile of plates crashed onto the floor.* ○ *The* *wind blew piles of dead leaves into the road.* ○ *He was carrying a huge pile of books.*

pile-up /ˈpaɪl ʌp/ *noun* a serious accident involving a series of vehicles which have crashed into each other (*informal*)

pilfer /ˈpɪlfə/ (**pilfers, pilfering, pilfered**) *verb* to steal small objects or small amounts of money from the office or shop where you work

pilgrim /ˈpɪlgrɪm/ *noun* a person who goes to visit a holy place

pilgrimage /ˈpɪlgrɪmɪdʒ/ *noun* **1.** a journey to an important religious place for religious reasons ○ *The church is organising a pilgrimage to Rome in April.* ○ *All Muslims should make the pilgrimage to Mecca at least once.* **2.** a journey to any important place, especially one connected with a famous person ○ *Many tourists make the pilgrimage to Dickens' house in London.*

③ **pill** /pɪl/ *noun* medicine in solid form, usually in a small round shape [~for] ○ *Take two pills before breakfast.*

pillage /ˈpɪlɪdʒ/ (**pillages, pillaging, pillaged**) *verb* to damage buildings and steal goods from a place, especially in a war ○ *The invaders pillaged the monastery buildings, then set fire to them.*

pillar /ˈpɪlə/ *noun* a strong tall object which supports part of a building

③ **pillow** /ˈpɪləʊ/ *noun* a cloth bag full of soft material which you put your head on in bed

③ **pilot** /ˈpaɪlət/ *noun* a person who flies a plane or other aircraft ○ *He's training to be an airline pilot.* ○ *He's a helicopter pilot for an oil company.*

pimp /pɪmp/ *noun* a man who makes money by finding customers for prostitutes ○ *The pimps are supposed to protect the girls if customers turn nasty.* (NOTE: + **pimp** *v*)

pimple /ˈpɪmpəl/ *noun* a small lump on the surface of the skin, containing pus

③ **pin** /pɪn/ *noun* a small thin sharp metal object with a round piece at the top, used for fastening things such as pieces of cloth or paper ○ *She fastened the ribbons to her dress with a pin before sewing them on.* ■ *verb* (**pins, pinning, pinned**) to attach something with a pin ○ *She pinned up a notice about the meeting.* ○ *He pinned her photograph on the wall.* ○ *He pinned the calendar to the wall by his desk.*

pin down③ *phrasal verb* □ **to pin someone down** to get someone to say what he or she really thinks, to get someone to make his or her mind up ○ *I'm trying to pin the chairman down to make a decision.* ○ *She's very vague about dates – it's difficult to pin her down.*

pinball /ˈpɪnˌbɔːl/ *noun* an indoor game played on a sloping electronic table in which a player makes a ball move quickly past obstacles to score points

pinch /pɪntʃ/ *noun* **1.** the action of squeezing something between your finger and thumb ○ *He gave her arm a pinch.* **2.** a small quantity of something held between finger and thumb ○ *Add a pinch of salt to the boiling water.* ■ *verb* (**pinches, pinching, pinched**) **1.** to squeeze something tightly, using the finger and thumb ○ *Ow! You're pinching me!* **2.** to steal something, especially something that is not very valuable (*informal*) ○ *Someone's pinched my pen!*

pine /paɪn/ *noun* **1.** □ **pine (tree)** a type of evergreen tree with needle-shaped leaves ○ *They planted a row of pines along the edge of the field.* **2.** wood from a pine tree ○ *We've bought a pine table for the kitchen.* ○ *There are pine cupboards in the children's bedroom.* ■ *verb* to feel sad because you do not have something any more [~for] ○ *She's miserable because she's pining for her cat.*

pineapple /ˈpaɪnæp(ə)l/ *noun* a large sweet tropical fruit, with stiff leaves with sharp points on top

pine cone /ˈpaɪn kəʊn/ *noun* the hard case containing the fruit of a pine tree

ping /pɪŋ/ (**pings, pinging, pinged**) *verb* to make a ping ○ *A little bell pings when the oven reaches the right temperature.* (NOTE: + **ping** *n*)

② **pink** /pɪŋk/ *adj* pale red or flesh coloured ○ *Your cheeks look pink and healthy now.* ■ *noun* a pale red colour ○ *The bright pink of those flowers shows clearly across the garden.*

pinkish *adj* of a colour that is close to pink

pinnacle /ˈpɪnək(ə)l/ *noun* **1.** the highest point of someone's career ○ *By becoming Lord Chief Justice he reached the pinnacle of his legal career.* **2.** the highest point of a pointed rock ○ *A narrow ridge connected the two pinnacles.* **3.** a tall, thin stone tower ○ *looking down on the domes and pinnacles of the old Italian city*

pinpoint /ˈpɪnpɔɪnt/ (**pinpoints, pinpointing, pinpointed**) *verb* to show exactly where something is ○ *We can pinpoint the ship's exact position by radar.*

pinstripe /ˈpɪnstraɪp/ *noun* a thin light line on a dark cloth

② **pint** /paɪnt/ *noun* a liquid measure, equal to 0.568 of a litre

pin-up /ˈpɪn ʌp/ *noun* a picture of a person, especially one of a sexually attractive person or in which the person is wearing very few clothes

pioneer /ˌpaɪəˈnɪə/ *noun* **1.** a person who is among the first to try to do something ○ *the pioneers in the field of laser surgery* ○ *He was one of the pioneers of radar.* **2.** a person who is among the first to discover or settle in a new land ○ *The first pioneers settled in this valley in about 1860.* ■ *verb* (**pioneers, pioneering, pioneered**) to be the first to do something ○ *The company pioneered developments in the field of electronics.*

pious /ˈpaɪəs/ *adj* showing great respect for religion

pip /pɪp/ *noun* a small seed in some fruits ○ *Take out all the pips when you cut up the grapefruit.* (NOTE: Fruits such as apples, pears, oranges and lemons all have pips.)

② **pipe** /paɪp/ *noun* **1.** a tube, especially one that carries a liquid or a gas from one place to another ○ *He's clearing a blocked pipe in the kitchen.* ○ *The water came out of the hole in the pipe.* ◊ **drainpipe 2.** a tube for smoking tobacco, with a small bowl at one end in which the tobacco burns

pipeline /ˈpaɪplaɪn/ *noun* a very large tube for carrying oil, natural gas, etc., over long distances ○ *An oil pipeline crosses the desert.* ◇ **in the pipeline** being worked on, coming ○ *The company has a series of new products in the pipeline.* ○ *She has two new novels in the pipeline.*

piping /ˈpaɪpɪŋ/ *noun* tubes in general ○ *The old lead piping was removed and replaced with plastic.*

piping hot /ˌpaɪpɪŋ ˈhɒt/ *adv* extremely hot ○ *Porridge should be served piping hot.*

piqued /piːkd/ *adj* feeling annoyed or angry about something

piracy /ˈpaɪrəsi/ *noun* **1.** the crime of attacking ships at sea and stealing what is in them ○ *Piracy is on the increase in the South China Sea.* **2.** the illegal copying of things such as books, records or computer programs ○ *The government is trying to stamp out video piracy.*

piranha /pəˈrɑːnə/ *noun* a small tropical fish which attacks animals, including man

pirate /ˈpaɪrət/ *noun* a person who makes illegal copies of things such as books or videos ■ *verb* (**pirates, pirating, pirated**) to make an illegal copy of something such as a book, disk or design ○ *The designs for the new dress collection were pirated in the Far East.* ○ *I found a pirated copy of my book on sale in a street market.*

Pisces /ˈpaɪsiːz/ *noun* one of the signs of the zodiac, shaped like fish, covering the period 19th February to 20th March

piss off *phrasal verb* **1.** to leave somewhere (*offensive slang*) **2.** to annoy someone ◇ **piss off!** go away!

pistol /ˈpɪstəl/ *noun* a small gun which is held in the hand

piston /ˈpɪstən/ *noun* (*in an engine*) a round flat piece of metal which moves up and down in a cylinder

pit /pɪt/ *noun* **1.** a deep dark hole in the ground ○ *They dug a pit to bury the rubbish.* **2.** a mine; a place where substances such as coal are dug out of the ground ○ *My grandfather spent his whole life working down a pit.*

③ **pitch** /pɪtʃ/ *noun* **1.** the ground on which a game is played [~of] ○ *I'll time you, if you run round the football pitch.* ○ *The pitch is too wet to play on.* ○ *He dribbled the ball the whole length of the pitch and scored.* **2.** the level of a period of anger or excitement [~of] ○ *Excitement was at fever pitch.* ■ *verb* (**pitches, pitching, pitched**) to put up a tent [~for/~with] ○ *They pitched their tent in a field by the beach.*

pitcher /ˈpɪtʃə/ *noun* **1.** a large container for liquids, with a handle and a specially shaped part on the top edge for pouring the liquid out ○ *My aunt brought out a pitcher of lemonade.* **2.** a person who throws the ball in baseball ○ *The Dodgers are without their regular pitcher this afternoon.*

pitfall /ˈpɪtfɔːl/ *noun* a hidden danger

pithy /ˈpɪθi/ *adj* full of serious meaning ○ *He made some pithy remarks.*

pitiful /ˈpɪtɪf(ə)l/ *adj* **1.** making you feel sorry for someone or something **2.** not at all good ○ *His attempts at singing were pitiful.*

pitiless /ˈpɪtɪləs/ *adj* not showing any pity ○ *His voice was harsh and pitiless.*

pitta bread /ˈpɪtə ˌbred/ *noun* a type of flat bread

pittance /ˈpɪt(ə)ns/ *noun* a very low amount that someone earns

pitted /ˈpɪtɪd/ *adj* with the stones removed

③ **pity** /ˈpɪti/ *noun* a feeling of sympathy for someone who is in a bad situation [~about] ○ *Have you no pity for the homeless?* ■ *verb* (**pities, pitying, pitied**) to feel sympathy for someone ○ *I pity those children.* ◇ **to take pity on someone** to feel sorry for someone ○ *At last someone took pity on her and showed her how to work the machine.*

pivot /'pɪvət/ *noun* a point on which something turns

pivotal /'pɪvət(ə)l/ *adj* central, of great importance

pixel /'pɪksəl/ *noun* a single point on a computer display

② **pizza** /'piːtsə/ *noun* an Italian food, consisting of a flat round piece of bread cooked with things such as cheese, tomatoes and onions on top

placard /'plækɑːd/ *noun* **1.** a notice on a large piece of thin board ○ *The protesters carried placards bearing anti-government slogans.* **2.** a large notice, picture or advertisement stuck on a wall ○ *Placards appeared in shop windows announcing that the circus was coming to town.*

placate /plə'keɪt/ (**placates, placating, placated**) *verb* to calm someone, to make someone less angry

① **place** /pleɪs/ *noun* **1.** where something is, or where something happens [~for/~on] ○ *We found a nice place for a picnic.* **2.** where something is usually kept [~for/~on] ○ *Make sure you put the file back in the right place.* **3.** a seat [~for/~on] ○ *I'm keeping this place for my sister.* ○ *I'm sorry, but this place has been taken.* **4.** a position in a race ○ *The British runners are in the first three places.* ■ *verb* (**places, placing, placed**) to put something somewhere ○ *The waitress placed the teapot on the table.* ○ *Please place the envelope in the box.* ◇ **all over the place** everywhere ○ *There were dead leaves lying all over the place.* ◇ **to change places with someone** to take each other's seat ○ *If you can't see the screen, change places with me.*

placebo /plə'siːbəʊ/ (*plural* **placebos** or **placeboes**) *noun* a pill which appears to be a drug, but has no medicine in it

placement /'pleɪsmənt/ *noun* the action of finding a job for someone

placid /'plæsɪd/ *adj* calm

plagiarise /'pleɪdʒəraɪz/ (**plagiarises, plagiarising, plagiarised**), **plagiarize** *verb* to copy the work of another author and pretend it is your own

plagiarism /'pleɪdʒərɪz(ə)m/ *noun* copying another person's written work and passing it off as your own

plague /pleɪg/ *noun* a great quantity of unpleasant things ○ *We've had a plague of ants in the garden.* ■ *verb* (**plagues, plaguing, plagued**) to annoy someone or cause them problems ○ *We were plagued with wasps last summer.* ○ *She keeps plaguing me with silly questions.*

plaice /pleɪs/ (*plural same*) *noun* a common flat sea fish

plaid /plæd/ *noun* a type of cloth which has a pattern of different coloured lines on it ○ *He wore plaid trousers.*

① **plain** /pleɪn/ *adj* **1.** simple and not complicated ○ *We put plain wallpaper in the dining room.* ○ *The outside is decorated with leaves and flowers, but the inside is quite plain.* **2.** easy to understand ○ *The instructions are written in plain English.* **3.** obvious ○ *It's perfectly plain what he wants.* ○ *We made it plain to them that this was our final offer.* **4.** a more polite word than "unattractive", used for describing a person ○ *His two daughters are rather plain.* ■ *noun* a flat area of country ○ *a broad plain bordered by mountains* (NOTE: Do not confuse with **plane**.)

plain chocolate /pleɪn 'tʃɒklət/ *noun* a dark bitter chocolate

plainclothes /'pleɪnkləʊðz/ *adj* wearing ordinary clothes, not a uniform

plainly /'pleɪnli/ *adv* **1.** in a way that is easy to see ○ *He's plainly bored by the French lesson.* ○ *Plainly, the plan is not working.* **2.** clearly ○ *It is plainly visible from here.* ○ *The sounds of a violent argument could be heard plainly from behind the door.* **3.** without much decoration ○ *a plainly decorated room* ○ *She always dresses very plainly.*

③ **plaintiff** /'pleɪntɪf/ *noun* a person who starts a legal action against someone in the civil courts (*dated*) (NOTE: This is an old term; it has now been replaced by **claimant**. The other party in an action is the **defendant**.)

plaintive /'pleɪntɪv/ *adj* (*of sounds*) sad and complaining

plait /plæt/ (**plaits, plaiting, plaited**) *verb* to form someone's hair into a plait ○ *My mother used to plait my hair before I went to school in the morning.*

① **plan** /plæn/ *noun* **1.** an organised way of doing things [~for] ○ *He made a plan to get up earlier in future.* ○ *She drew up plans for the village fair.* **2.** a drawing of the way something is arranged [~for] ○ *Here are the plans for the kitchen.* ○ *The fire exits are shown on the plan of the office.* ■ *verb* (**plans, planning, planned**) **1.** to arrange how you are going to do something ○ *She's busy planning her holiday in Greece.* **2.** to intend to do something ○ *They are planning to move to London next month.* ○ *We weren't planning to go on holiday this year.* ○ *I plan to take the 5 o'clock flight to New York.* ◇ **according to plan** in the way it was arranged ○ *The party went off according to plan.*

② **plane** /pleɪn/ *noun* **1.** an aircraft with wings ○ *When is the next plane for Glasgow?* ○ *How are you getting to Paris? – We're going by plane.* ○ *Don't panic, you've got plenty of time to catch your plane.* ○ *He was stuck in a traffic jam and missed his plane.* **2.** a tool with a sharp blade for making wood smooth ○ *He smoothed off the rough edges with a plane.*

planet /ˈplænɪt/ *noun* **1.** one of the objects in space which move round the Sun ○ *Is there life on any of the planets?* ○ *Earth is the third planet from the Sun.* **2. the planet** the planet Earth ○ *an environmental disaster which could affect the whole planet*

plank /plæŋk/ *noun* a long flat piece of wood used in building

plankton /ˈplæŋktən/ *plural noun* very small animals and plants which live and move about slowly in the sea, and are the food of large animals

③ **planner** /ˈplænə/ *noun* a person who draws up plans ○ *The planners made the car park too small.*

① **planning** /ˈplænɪŋ/ *noun* the act or practice of making plans ○ *The trip will need very careful planning.* ○ *The project is still in the planning stage.*

① **plant** /plɑːnt/ *noun* **1.** a living thing which grows in the ground and has leaves, a stem and roots ○ *He planted a row of cabbage plants.* ○ *Sunflower plants grow very tall.* **2.** a large factory ○ *They are planning to build a car plant near the river.* ■ *verb* (**plants, planting, planted**) to put a plant in the ground ○ *We've planted two pear trees and a peach tree in the garden.*

plantation /plɑːnˈteɪʃ(ə)n/ *noun* **1.** an area of trees planted as a crop ○ *a plantation of pines* **2.** a tropical farm growing a particular crop ○ *a coffee plantation* ○ *a rubber plantation*

plaque /plæk, plɑːk/ *noun* **1.** a flat plate made of a hard substance such as stone or metal and with some writing on the surface ○ *They put up a plaque to commemorate the soldiers who died.* ○ *The Princess unveiled a plaque commemorating her visit and the opening of the new library.* **2.** a substance which forms on the teeth ○ *Use dental floss every morning to control plaque.*

plasma /ˈplæzmə/ *noun* a thin yellow liquid which makes up the main part of blood

plasma screen /ˈplæzmə skriːn/ *noun* a very thin television or computer screen which shows extremely clear images

plaster /ˈplɑːstə/ *noun* **1.** a mixture of sand and a white substance called 'lime', which is mixed with water and used for covering the inside walls of houses ○ *The flat hasn't been decorated yet and there is still bare plaster in most of the rooms.* **2.** a white substance which becomes hard when it dries, used to cover a broken arm or leg and hold it in place ○ *He had an accident skiing and now has his leg in plaster.* **3.** □ **sticking plaster** adhesive tape used for covering small wounds ○ *She put a piece of sticking plaster on my cut.*

② **plastic** /ˈplæstɪk/ *noun* a strong material made from chemicals, used to make many things ○ *We take plastic plates when we go to the beach.* ○ *The supermarket gives you plastic bags to put your shopping in.* ○ *We cover our garden furniture with plastic sheets when it rains.* (NOTE: no plural: *a bowl made of plastic*)

plastic surgery /ˌplæstɪk ˈsɜːdʒəri/ *noun* a medical treatment to repair damaged parts of the body

COMMENT: Plastic surgery is used especially to treat accident victims or people who have suffered burns. When surgery is used simply to improve your appearance in some way, it is called cosmetic surgery.

② **plate** /pleɪt/ *noun* **1.** a flat round dish for putting food on ○ *Put one pie on each plate.* ○ *Pass all the plates down to the end of the table.* **2.** a flat piece of something such as metal or glass ○ *The dentist has a brass plate on his door.*

plateau /ˈplætəʊ/ (*plural* **plateaus** or **plateaux**) *noun* **1.** an area of high flat land ○ *the high plateau region of southern Argentina* ○ *The town lies on a plateau about 2000 feet above sea level.* **2.** the highest point that will be reached ○ *House prices seem to have reached a plateau.*

plateful /ˈpleɪtfʊl/ *noun* the quantity held by a plate

③ **platform** /ˈplætfɔːm/ *noun* **1.** a high flat structure by the side of the railway lines at a station, to help passengers get on or off the trains easily ○ *The train for Liverpool will leave from platform 10.* **2.** a high wooden floor for speakers to speak from ○ *The main speakers sat in a row on the platform.*

platinum /ˈplætɪnəm/ *noun* a valuable metal which does not corrode, and is used in jewellery

platitude /ˈplætɪtjuːd/ *noun* a remark considered to be ordinary and of little interest

platonic /pləˈtɒnɪk/ *adj* (*of a relationship*) which is not sexual

platoon /pləˈtuːn/ *noun* a small group of soldiers with a lieutenant in charge, part of a company

platter /ˈplætə/ *noun* **1.** a large flat serving plate ○ *A huge joint of meat was carried in on a platter.* **2.** a large plate of prepared food, arranged in an attractive way ○ *We ordered a seafood platter.*

plausible /ˈplɔːzɪb(ə)l/ *adj* **1.** which sounds as though it could be correct or true ○ *He couldn't produce any plausible excuse to explain why he was in the warehouse.* **2.** good at telling lies so that people believe what you say ○ *He sounds very plausible over the phone.*

① **play** /pleɪ/ *noun* a story which is acted in a theatre or on TV ○ *Did you see the play on TV last night?* ○ *We went to the National Theatre to see the new play.* ○ *Two of Shakespeare's plays are on the list for the English exam.* ■ *verb* (**plays, playing, played**) **1.** to take part in a game [~for/~against/~with] ○ *He plays rugby for the university.* ○ *Have you ever played against him before?* ○ *I played tennis with the children.* **2.** to make music on a musical instrument or to put a recording on a machine such as a CD player ○ *He can't play the violin very well.* ○ *Let me play you my new CD.* **3.** to enjoy yourself [~with] ○ *He doesn't like playing with other children.* ○ *When you've finished your lesson you can go out to play.*

play back③ *phrasal verb* to listen to something which you have just recorded

play down *phrasal verb* to make something seem less important

play off *phrasal verb* □ **to play someone off against someone** to try to benefit by making two people compete against each other ○ *Children try to get what they want by playing their parents off against each other.*

play up *phrasal verb* to cause trouble

playboy /ˈpleɪbɔɪ/ *noun* a rich man who spends his time enjoying himself rather than working

① **player** /ˈpleɪə/ *noun* **1.** a person who plays a game ○ *You only need two players for chess.* ○ *Rugby players have to be fit.* ○ *Four of the players in the opposing team are ill.* **2.** a person who plays a musical instrument ○ *a famous horn player*

playful /ˈpleɪf(ə)l/ *adj* lively and enjoying playing

playground /ˈpleɪgraʊnd/ *noun* a place, at a school or in a public area, where children can play

playgroup /ˈpleɪgruːp/ *noun* a group of small children who play together, looked after by a teacher

playing field /ˈpleɪɪŋ fiːld/ *noun* a large field where sports can be played

playmate /ˈpleɪˌmeɪt/ *noun* a child who regularly plays with another

playoff /ˈpleɪɒf/ *noun* a game to decide the final result, played between two players or teams that have the same score

playroom /ˈpleɪruːm/ *noun* a room in which children can play

plaything /ˈpleɪθɪŋ/ *noun* **1.** something or someone that a person uses simply for his own pleasure ○ *Luxury yachts are the playthings of the rich.* **2.** a toy for a child to play with (*old*) ○ *I keep all the children's playthings in this cupboard.*

playtime /ˈpleɪtaɪm/ *noun* a time in school when children can play

playwright /ˈpleɪraɪt/ *noun* a person who writes plays

Plc *abbr* public limited company

plea /pliː/ *noun* **1.** an answer to a charge in court **2.** a request

plead /pliːd/ (**pleads, pleading, pleaded**) *verb* **1.** to answer a charge in a law court **2.** to give an excuse **3.** to try to change someone's mind by asking again and again [~with] ○ *I pleaded with her not to go.*

③ **pleasant** /ˈplez(ə)nt/ *adj* enjoyable or attractive ○ *What a pleasant garden!* ○ *How pleasant it is to sit here under the trees!*

① **please** /pliːz/ *interj* used when you are making a polite request or accepting an offer ○ *Can you close the window, please?* ○ *Please sit down.* ○ *Can I have a ham sandwich, please?* ○ *Do you want some more tea? – Yes, please!* Compare **thank you** ■ *verb* (**pleases, pleasing, pleased**) to make someone happy or satisfied ○ *She's not difficult to please.* ◇ **please yourself** do as you like ○ *Shall I take the red one or the green one? – Please yourself.*

② **pleased** /pliːzd/ *adj* happy ○ *We're very pleased with our new house.* ○ *I'm pleased to hear you're feeling better.* ○ *He wasn't pleased when he heard his exam results.*

③ **pleasing** /ˈpliːzɪŋ/ *adj* which pleases

pleasurable /ˈpleʒ(ə)rəb(ə)l/ *adj* pleasant, which gives pleasure

② **pleasure** /ˈpleʒə/ *noun* a pleasant feeling ○ *His greatest pleasure is sitting by the river.* ○ *It gives me great pleasure to be able to visit you today.* ◇ **with pleasure** used for saying that you are happy to do something for someone ○ *I'll do the job with pleasure.*

plebiscite /ˈplebɪsaɪt/ *noun* a type of vote, where the whole population of a town, region or country is asked to vote to decide a particular issue

pledge /pledʒ/ (**pledges, pledging, pledged**) *verb* **1.** to promise something formally **2.** to give something as a pledge when borrowing money

plentiful /ˈplentɪf(ə)l/ *adj* in large quantities

① **plenty** /ˈplenti/ *noun* a large quantity ○ *You've got plenty of time to catch the train.* ○ *Plenty of people complain about the bus service.* ○ *Have you got enough bread? – Yes, we've got plenty.* (NOTE: no plural)

plight /plaɪt/ *noun* a bad situation or condition (*dated*) ○ *You must pity the plight of the people made homeless by the war.*

plod /plɒd/ (**plods, plodding, plodded**) *verb* **1.** to walk slowly and with heavy steps ○ *The camels plodded across the desert.* ○ *He plodded round the department stores but didn't find anything he wanted.* **2.** to work steadily ○ *The police plodded slowly through a list of people who had to be interviewed.*

plonk /plɒŋk/ *noun* cheap wine (*informal*) ○ *I bought a bottle of Spanish plonk from the supermarket.* ■ *verb* (**plonks, plonking, plonked**) to put something down in a careless way ○ *The waiter just plonked the plates down in front of us and went off.* ○ *A big fat man plonked himself down in the seat next to me and went to sleep.*

plop /plɒp/ *noun* the noise made by something falling into water ○ *There was a little plop as the frog jumped into the lake.* ■ *verb* (**plops, plopping, plopped**) **1.** to make a noise like a stone falling into water **2.** to sit down heavily; to put something down ○ *She plopped herself down on the settee.* ○ *He plopped the letter into the pillar box.*

plot /plɒt/ *noun* **1.** a small area of land, e.g. used for building or for growing vegetables ○ *They own a plot of land next to the river.* ○ *The plot isn't big enough to build a house on.* **2.** the basic story of a book, play or film ○ *The novel has a complicated plot.* ○ *I won't tell you the plot of the film – I don't want to spoil it for you.* **3.** a secret and evil plan ○ *They hatched a plot to hold up the security van.*

plough /plaʊ/ *noun* a farm machine for turning over soil ○ *The plough is pulled by a tractor.* (NOTE: The US spelling is **plow**.)

plough on *verb* to continue doing something difficult ○ *If I want to finish today I'd better plough on.*

plough through /ˈplaʊ ˈɒn/ *verb* to continue doing something unpleasant until it is finished ○ *It took me four hours to plough through the pile of complaints.*

plow /plaʊ/ *noun, verb* US spelling of **plough**

ploy /plɔɪ/ *noun* a clever trick

③ **pluck** /plʌk/ (**plucks, plucking, plucked**) *verb* **1.** to pull out feathers from a bird ○ *to pluck a chicken* ○ *Ask the butcher to pluck the pheasants for you.* **2.** to pull and let go of the strings of a guitar or other musical instrument, in order to make a sound ○ *He was gently plucking the strings of his guitar.*

plucky /ˈplʌki/ (**pluckier, pluckiest**) *adj* brave

③ **plug** /plʌg/ *noun* **1.** a flat round rubber object which covers the hole in a bath or sink ○ *Can you call reception and tell them there's no plug in the bath?* ○ *She pulled out the plug and let the water drain away.* **2.** an object attached to the end of a wire, which you push into a hole in the wall to make a piece of electrical equipment work ○ *The vacuum cleaner is supplied with a plug.*

plug in ③ *phrasal verb* to connect a piece of electrical equipment to an electricity supply by pushing the plug into a hole in the wall ○ *The computer wasn't plugged in – that's why it wouldn't work.*

plughole /ˈplʌghəʊl/ *noun* a hole in a bath or washbasin through which the dirty water runs away

③ **plum** /plʌm/ *noun* a gold, red or purple fruit with a smooth skin and a large stone ○ *She bought a pound of plums to make a pie.*

plumage /ˈpluːmɪdʒ/ *noun* feathers on a bird

plumb (**plumbs, plumbing, plumbed**) *verb* **1.** to measure the depth of water by using a plumb line ○ *to plumb the ocean's depths* **2.** to try to understand something fully ○ *Scientists are still trying to plumb the mysteries of the beginning of the universe.*

plumber /'plʌmə/ *noun* a person whose job is to install or repair things such as water pipes and heating systems

plumbing /'plʌmɪŋ/ *noun* a system of water pipes in a house

plume /pluːm/ *noun* **1.** a long feather, especially one worn in a hat ○ *a hat with ostrich plumes* **2.** a long cloud of smoke from a factory chimney or volcano ○ *A plume of smoke rose from the burning oil depot.*

plummet /'plʌmɪt/ (**plummets, plummeting, plummeted**) *verb* to fall sharply

plump /plʌmp/ *adj* (*of a person*) slightly fat in an attractive way ○ *He's a short man with a plump red face.* ○ *Is she pregnant or is she just plumper than she was?*

plunder /'plʌndə/ (**plunders, plundering, plundered**) *verb* to take or use something that belongs to someone else

plunge /plʌndʒ/ (**plunges, plunging, plunged**) *verb* **1.** to throw yourself into water ○ *He plunged into the river to rescue the little boy.* **2.** to fall sharply ○ *Share prices plunged on the news of the devaluation.*

plural /'plʊərəl/ *adj, noun* (*in grammar*) (which is) the form of a word showing that there is more than one ○ *Does 'government' take a singular or plural verb?* ○ *What's the plural of 'mouse'?* ○ *The verb should be in the plural after 'programs'.*

① **plus** /plʌs/ *prep* **1.** added to ○ *His salary plus bonus comes to more than £30,000.* (NOTE: In calculations **plus** is usually shown by the sign + : **10 + 4 = 14:** say 'ten plus four equals fourteen'.) **2.** more than ○ *houses valued at £200,000 plus*

plush /plʌʃ/ *adj* luxurious (*informal*) ○ *The car's got a very plush interior.* ○ *They always stay at the plushest hotel they can find.*

plus sign /'plʌs saɪn/ *noun* a sign (+) meaning more than

plutonium /pluː'təʊniəm/ *noun* a radioactive element, also used to produce nuclear power

ply /plaɪ/ (**plies, plying, plied**) *verb* to go backwards and forwards ○ *The little ferry plies between Birkenhead and Liverpool.* ◇ **to ply someone with something** to keep giving someone something to eat, drink, etc ○ *They plied the boys with drink and cigarettes, and then started asking them questions.*

plywood /'plaɪwʊd/ *noun* a sheet of wood made of several thin layers of wood stuck together

PM *abbr* prime minister, post mortem

① **p.m.** /ˌpiː 'em/ *adv* in the afternoon, after midday ○ *The exhibition is open from 10 a.m. to 5.30 p.m.* ○ *If you phone New York after 6 p.m. the calls are at a cheaper rate.* (NOTE: The US spelling is **P.M. a.m.** is usually used to show the exact hour and the word **o'clock** is left out. The US spelling is **A.M.**)

PMS /ˌpiː em 'es/ *abbr* premenstrual syndrome

PMT *abbr* premenstrual tension

pneumonia /njuː'məʊniə/ *noun* an illness caused by inflammation of a lung, where the lung becomes filled with fluid

③ **PO** *abbr* post office

poach /pəʊtʃ/ (**poaches, poaching, poached**) *verb* to persuade an employee to leave his or her job and work for another employer ○ *They poached our best salesman.*

poacher /'pəʊtʃə/ *noun* a person who catches game illegally

② **pocket** /'pɒkɪt/ *noun* one of several little bags sewn into the inside of a piece of clothing such as a coat, in which you can keep things, e.g. money, handkerchief or keys ○ *She looked in all her pockets but couldn't find her keys.* ○ *He was leaning against a fence with his hands in his pockets.*

pocketful /'pɒkɪtfʊl/ *noun* an amount contained in a pocket

③ **pocket money** /'pɒkɪt ˌmʌni/ *noun* money which parents give to their children each week

pod /pɒd/ *noun* a long green case in which some small vegetables such as peas or beans grow ○ *Mangetout peas are eaten in their pods.*

podiatrist /pəʊ'daɪətrɪst/ *noun* a person who looks after people's feet and diseases of the feet

podium /'pəʊdiəm/ *noun* a small raised platform, e.g. for winning sportsmen or orchestral conductors, to stand on

③ **poem** /'pəʊɪm/ *noun* a piece of writing with words carefully chosen to sound attractive or interesting, set out in lines usually of a regular length which sometimes end in words which sound the same ○ *He wrote a long poem about an old sailor.* ○ *The poem about the First World War was set to music by Britten.*

③ **poet** /'pəʊɪt/ *noun* a person who writes poems

③ **poetry** /'pəʊɪtri/ *noun* poems in general ○ *Reading poetry makes me cry.* ○ *This is a good example of German poetry.* (NOTE: no plural)

poignant /'pɔɪnjənt/ *adj* making you sad

① **point** /pɔɪnt/ *noun* **1.** a sharp end of something long ○ *The point of my pencil has broken.* ○ *The stick has a very sharp point.* **2.** a particular place ○ *The path led us for miles through the woods and in the end we came back to the point where we started from.* ○ *We had reached a point 2,000m above sea level.* **3.** a particular moment in time ○ *From that point on, things began to change.* ○ *At what point did you decide to resign?* □ **at that point** at that time ○ *All the lights went off at that point.* □ **at this point in time** at this particular moment ○ *At this point in time, it is not possible for me to answer reporters' questions.* **4.** a meaning or reason [/~in] ○ *The main point of the meeting is to see how we can continue to run the centre without a grant.* □ **I see your point** I see what you mean ○ *I see your point, but there are other factors to be considered.* ○ *I can't see the point of doing that.* **5.** a score in a game ○ *Their team scored three points.* ○ *In rugby, a try counts as five points.* ■ *verb* (**points, pointing, pointed**) to aim a gun or your finger at something [~at/~to] ○ *It's rude to point at people.* ○ *Don't point that gun at me – it might go off.* ○ *The guide pointed to the map to show where we were.* ◇ **it's beside the point** it's got nothing to do with the main subject ○ *Whether or not the coat matches your hat is beside the point – it's simply too big for you.* ◇ **on the point of doing something** just about to do something ○ *I was on the point of phoning you.*

point out③ *phrasal verb* **1.** to show something ○ *The tour guide will point out the main things to see in the town.* ○ *The report points out the mistakes made by the agency over the last few years.* **2.** to give a point of view ○ *She pointed out that the children in her class were better behaved than in previous years.*

point up *phrasal verb* to make something seem very obvious

point-blank /ˌpɔɪnt 'blæŋk/ *adv* sharply, directly and rudely ○ *I told him point-blank that his work was no good.* ◇ **at point-blank range** at very close range ○ *He was shot at point-blank range.*

② **pointed** /'pɔɪntɪd/ *adj* with a sharp point at one end ○ *a pointed stick*

pointer /'pɔɪntə/ *noun* **1.** something which points ○ *The pointer moved quickly around the dial.* ○ *He used a pointer to show us our positions on the wall map.* **2.** a piece of advice or information ○ *She asked her teacher for some pointers to help her with her project.*

pointless /'pɔɪntləs/ *adj* with no sense

poise /pɔɪz/ *noun* balance, a graceful way of holding your head or of standing upright ○ *She has the grace and poise of a ballet dancer.*

③ **poison** /'pɔɪz(ə)n/ *noun* a substance which kills you or makes you ill if it is swallowed or if it gets into the blood ○ *There's enough poison in this bottle to kill the whole town.* ○ *Don't drink that – it's poison.*

③ **poisoning** /'pɔɪz(ə)nɪŋ/ *noun* an occasion when someone is made ill or killed by something poisonous

③ **poisonous** /'pɔɪz(ə)nəs/ *adj* able to kill or harm people or animals with poison

③ **poke** /pəʊk/ *noun* a quick push with a finger or something sharp ○ *He got a poke in the eye from someone's umbrella.* ■ *verb* (**pokes, poking, poked**) to push something or someone quickly with a finger or with something sharp ○ *He poked the heap with his stick.* ◇ **to poke fun at someone *or* something** to laugh at someone *or* something in an unkind way ○ *He poked fun at the maths teacher.* ○ *She poked fun at his odd hat.*

poker /'pəʊkə/ *noun* **1.** a long metal rod for stirring up a fire ○ *She stirred the dying fire with the poker.* **2.** a card game in which the players gamble on the cards in their hands, at the same time trying to hide their position from the other players ○ *They played poker until 3 o'clock in the morning.* ○ *He won £25 at poker.*

poky /'pəʊki/ *adj* cramped or small ○ *They have a poky little flat in the centre of London.*

③ **polar** /'pəʊlə/ *adj* referring to the North Pole or the South Pole

① **pole** /pəʊl/ *noun* a long wooden or metal stick

① **Pole** /pəʊl/ *noun* a person from Poland

polemic /pə'lemɪk/ *noun* **1.** a fierce written or spoken attack **2.** a style of making fierce attacks ○ *His very effective use of polemic in his speeches.*

① **police** /pə'liːs/ *noun* the people whose job is to control traffic, to try to stop crime and to catch criminals ○ *The police are looking for the driver of the car.* ○ *The police emergency number is 999.* ○ *Call the police – I've just seen someone drive off in my car.*

③ **police constable** /pə'liːs ˌkʌnstəb(ə)l/ *noun* an ordinary member of the police (NOTE: also used as a title before a name: *Police Constable John Smith*; usually shortened to **PC** or **WPC** for women police constables: *PC John Smith*)

police force /pə'liːs fɔːs/ *noun* the group of police in a certain area

policeman /pə'liːsmən, pə'liːswʊmən/ (*plural* **policemen**) *noun* a man who is an ordinary member of the police

③ **police officer** /pə'liːs ˌɒfɪsə/ *noun* a member of the police

police state /pə'liːs steɪt/ *noun* a country whose government controls the freedom of the people through the police

③ **police station** /pə'liːs ˌsteɪʃ(ə)n/ *noun* a building with the offices of a particular local police force

policewoman /pə'liːswʊmən/ (*plural* **policewomen**) *noun* a woman who is an ordinary member of the police

① **policy** /'pɒlɪsi/ (*plural* **policies**) *noun* decisions on the general way of doing something [~on] ○ *government policy on wages* or *government wages policy* ○ *It is not our policy to give details of employees over the phone.* ○ *People voted Labour because they liked their policies.*

polio /'pəʊliəʊ/ *noun* an illness caused by a virus which can cause muscles to stop working ○ *She caught polio when she was ten years old.*

③ **polish** /'pɒlɪʃ/ *noun* a substance used to make things shiny ○ *Wash the car thoroughly before you put the polish on.* ■ *verb* (**polishes, polishing, polished**) to rub something in order to make it shiny ○ *He polished his shoes until they shone.*

polish off *phrasal verb* **1.** to finish off a job quickly ○ *He polished off his essay in half an hour.* **2.** to eat a meal quickly ○ *They polished off the scrambled eggs and then asked for baked beans.*

polish up *phrasal verb* to improve a skill

① **Polish** /'pəʊlɪʃ/ *adj* relating to Poland ○ *The Polish Army joined in the manoeuvres.* ■ *noun* the language spoken in Poland ○ *I know three words of Polish.* ○ *You will need an English-Polish phrase book if you're visiting Warsaw.*

③ **polite** /pə'laɪt/ (**politer, politest**) *adj* pleasant towards other people, not rude ○ *Sales staff should be polite to customers.*

politely /pə'laɪtli/ *adv* in a polite way ○ *Ask the lady politely if you can have a sweetie.*

politeness /pə'laɪtnəs/ *noun* the practice of being polite

① **political** /pə'lɪtɪk(ə)l/ *adj* referring to government or to party politics ○ *I don't want to get involved in a political argument.* ○ *She gave up her political career when she had the children.*

political prisoner /pəˌlɪtɪk(ə)l 'prɪz(ə)nə/ *noun* a person kept in prison because he or she is an opponent of the political party in power

political science /pəˌlɪtɪk(ə)l 'saɪəns/ *noun* the study of governments and their use of political power

② **politician** /ˌpɒlɪ'tɪʃ(ə)n/ *noun* a person who works in politics, especially a member of parliament ○ *Politicians from all parties have welcomed the report.*

② **politics** /'pɒlɪtɪks/ *plural noun* the ideas and methods used in governing a country ■ *noun* the study of how countries are governed ○ *He studied politics and economics at university.* (NOTE: takes a singular verb)

polka /'pɒlkə/ *noun* a type of lively dance

③ **poll** /pəʊl/ *noun* **1.** a vote or the act of voting ○ *We are still waiting for the results of yesterday's poll.* ○ *A poll of factory workers showed that more than 50% supported the union's demands.* **2.** the number of votes cast in an election ○ *The poll was lower than usual – only 35% of the voters bothered to vote.*

pollen /'pɒlən/ *noun* a yellow powder on the stamens of a flower which touches part of a female flower and so creates seeds

pollen count /'pɒlən kaʊnt/ *noun* a number showing the amount of pollen in the air, which can cause hay fever

polling station /'pəʊlɪŋ ˌsteɪʃ(ə)n/ *noun* a place where you vote in an election, usually in a public building such as a library or school

pollster /'pəʊlstə/ *noun* an expert in understanding what polls mean

pollutant /pə'luːt(ə)nt/ *noun* a substance which pollutes

③ **pollute** /pə'luːt/ (**pollutes, polluting, polluted**) *verb* to make the environment dirty by discharging harmful substances into it

polluted /pəˈluːtɪd/ *adj* made dirty

② **pollution** /pəˈluːʃ(ə)n/ *noun* **1.** the process of making the environment dirty ○ *Pollution of the atmosphere has increased over the last 50 years.* **2.** chemicals and other substances that harm people and the environment ○ *It took six months to clean up the oil pollution on the beaches.* ○ *The pollution in the centre of town is so bad that people have started wearing face masks.*

polo /ˈpəʊləʊ/ *noun* a ball game in which two teams ride on ponies, trying to hit a small hard ball with clubs like long hammers ○ *There's a polo match in the park this afternoon.* ○ *He plays polo every Saturday.*

polo shirt /ˈpəʊləʊ ʃɜːt/ *noun* a shirt with short sleeves, a collar and three or four buttons at the neck

polyester /ˌpɒliˈestə/ *noun* a type of synthetic fibre used especially to make clothing

polystyrene /ˌpɒliˈstaɪriːn/ *noun* a light plastic used as a heat insulator or as packing material

polythene /ˈpɒlɪθiːn/ *noun* a type of strong transparent plastic used in thin sheets

pomegranate /ˈpɒmɪɡrænɪt/ *noun* a tropical fruit with many black seeds covered in juicy red flesh

pomp /pɒmp/ *noun* a splendid ceremony

pompous /ˈpɒmpəs/ *adj* using very dignified language to make yourself sound more important (*disapproving*)

③ **pond** /pɒnd/ *noun* a small lake

ponder /ˈpɒndə/ (**ponders, pondering, pondered**) *verb* to think deeply about something

pontificate /pɒnˈtɪfɪˌkeɪt/ (**pontificates, pontificating, pontificated**) *verb* to give your opinion on something in a way which suggests that you believe your opinion is the only right one (*formal*)

pony /ˈpəʊni/ (*plural* **ponies**) *noun* a small horse

ponytail /ˈpəʊniteɪl/ *noun* a hairstyle where your hair is tied at the back and falls loosely

poo /puː/ *noun* faeces, solid waste matter passed from the body (*informal; children's slang*)

poodle /ˈpuːd(ə)l/ *noun* a type of curly-haired dog, with its fur usually cut in a curious way

② **pool** /puːl/ *noun* **1.** a small lake ○ *He dived in and swam across the mountain pool.* ○ *We looked for shrimps in the rock pools.* **2.** a large bath of water for swimming in ○ *an outdoor pool* ○ *a heated pool* ○ *We have a little swimming pool in the garden.* ○ *He swam two lengths of the pool.* **3.** a game rather like snooker, where you hit balls into pockets using a long stick called a 'cue' ○ *We were playing pool in the bar.*

① **poor** /pɔː/ *adj* **1.** with little or no money ○ *The family is very poor now that both parents have no work.* ○ *This is one of the poorest countries in Africa.* **2.** of not very good quality ○ *Vines can grow even in poor soil.* ○ *They were selling off poor quality vegetables at a cheap price.* ○ *She's been in poor health for some months.* **3.** used for showing you are sorry ○ *Poor old you, having to stay at home and finish your homework while we go to the cinema.* ○ *My poor legs, after climbing up the mountain!*

poorly /ˈpɔːli/ *adv* in quite a bad way ○ *The offices are poorly laid out.* ○ *The job is very poorly paid.* ■ *adj* ill (*informal*) ○ *She felt quite poorly and had to go home.* ○ *He was very poorly on Monday, but by the end of the week he was a little better.*

③ **pop** /pɒp/ *noun* a noise like a cork coming out of a bottle ○ *There was a 'pop' as she lit the gas.* ■ *verb* (**pops, popping, popped**) **1.** to go somewhere quickly ○ *I'll just pop down to the town.* ○ *He popped into the chemist's.* ○ *I'm just popping round to Jane's.* ○ *I'd only popped out for a moment.* **2.** to put something somewhere quickly (*informal*) ○ *Pop the pie in the microwave for three minutes.*

popcorn /ˈpɒpkɔːn/ *noun* the seed of a type of maize plant which is heated until it bursts and is eaten as a snack

Pope /pəʊp/ *noun* the head of the Roman Catholic Church

poplar /ˈpɒplə/ *noun* a common tall and slender tree

③ **pop music** /ˈpɒp ˌmjuːzɪk/ *noun* modern popular music

poppy /ˈpɒpi/ (*plural* **poppies**) *noun* a common red wild flower which often grows in fields

populace /ˈpɒpjʊləs/ *noun* the ordinary people (*formal*) ○ *The rest of the populace envied the privileges of the rich.*

① **popular** /ˈpɒpjʊlə/ *adj* liked by a lot of people ○ *The department store is popular with young mothers.* ○ *The South Coast is the most popular area for holidays.*

popularity /ˌpɒpjʊ'lærɪti/ *noun* the fact of being liked by a lot of people

popularly /'pɒpjʊləli/ *adv* by most people ○ *She was popularly supposed to possess magic powers.*

populate /'pɒpjʊleɪt/ (**populates, populating, populated**) *verb* **1.** to go and live in an area ○ *Settlers moved away from the coast and began to populate the interior.* ○ *The area is populated by peasant farmers.* **2.** to put people to live in an area ○ *The king decided to populate the colony with retired soldiers.*

① **population** /ˌpɒpjʊ'leɪʃ(ə)n/ *noun* the number of people who live in a place ○ *The population of the country is 60 million.* ○ *Paris has a population of over three million.*

populous /'pɒpjʊləs/ *adj* densely populated

porcelain /'pɔːs(ə)lɪn/ *noun* fine china

porch /pɔːtʃ/ *noun* **1.** a sheltered area joined onto a doorway ○ *You weren't in when I called, so I left the parcel in the porch.* **2.** *US* a balcony at ground level around a house ○ *They like to sit out on the porch on summer evenings.*

pore /pɔː/ *noun* a tiny hole in the skin or in a leaf, through which moisture such as sweat passes ○ *I was sweating from every pore as I waited for the results of the test.* ○ *Water evaporates from the pores of the leaves.*

pork /pɔːk/ *noun* fresh meat from a pig, eaten cooked (NOTE: no plural. Note also that salted or smoked meat from a pig is **ham** or **bacon**.)

porn /pɔːn/ *noun* pornography (*informal*)

pornography /pɔː'nɒgrəfi/ *noun* books, films, etc., with obscene subject matter

porous /'pɔːrəs/ *adj* which has many little holes in it, allowing water or air to seep through slowly

porpoise /'pɔːpəs/ *noun* a sea animal similar to a dolphin, which swims in groups (NOTE: A group of them is a **school of porpoises**.)

porridge /'pɒrɪdʒ/ *noun* oatmeal cooked in water or milk, eaten for breakfast

② **port** /pɔːt/ *noun* **1.** a place along a coast where boats can stop, or a town with a place like this ○ *a fishing port* ○ *The ship is due in port on Tuesday.* ○ *We left port at 12.00.* **2.** an opening in a computer for plugging in an attachment ○ *a mouse port*

③ **portable** /'pɔːtəb(ə)l/ *adj* which can be carried ○ *He used his portable computer on the plane.* ○ *Portable phones won't work in the Underground.*

portal /'pɔːt(ə)l/ *noun* an imposing entrance (*literary*)

porter /'pɔːtə/ *noun* a doorkeeper in a building such as a hotel or a block of flats ○ *Ask the porter if there have been any messages for us.*

③ **portfolio** /pɔːt'fəʊliəʊ/ *noun* **1.** a collection of work such as drawing or writing that one person has done, or a large flat case in which it is carried ○ *He brought a portfolio of samples of his work.* **2.** □ **a portfolio of investments** or **shares** all the shares owned by someone **3.** a minister's job in a government

porthole /'pɔːthəʊl/ *noun* a round window in the side of a ship

portion /'pɔːʃ(ə)n/ *noun* **1.** a part ○ *This is only a small portion of the material we collected.* ○ *Our carriage was in the rear portion of the train.* **2.** a serving of food, usually for one person ○ *The portions in that restaurant are tiny.* ○ *Ask the waiter if they serve children's portions.*

portly /'pɔːtli/ (**portlier, portliest**) *adj* rather fat

portrait /'pɔːtrɪt/ *noun* a painting or photograph of a person ○ *He has painted a portrait of the Queen.* ○ *Old portraits of members of the family lined the walls of the dining room.*

portray /pɔː'treɪ/ (**portrays, portraying, portrayed**) *verb* to paint or to describe a scene or a person (NOTE: + **portrayal** *n*)

③ **pose** /pəʊz/ *noun* **1.** a way of standing sitting or lying ○ *She is painted standing in an elegant pose.* ○ *He struck a funny pose as I was taking the photo.* **2.** a way of behaving which is just a pretence ○ *He'd like you to think he's an expert but it's just a pose.* ■ *verb* (**poses, posing, posed**) **1.** to set a problem or put a question ○ *Violent children pose a problem for schools.* **2.** to stand or sit still while someone paints or photographs you [~for] ○ *He posed for her in his uniform.* **3.** to pretend to be something [~as] ○ *He got into the prison by posing as a doctor.*

posh /pɒʃ/ *adj* expensive and attractive; suitable for special occasions ○ *I decided I'd better wear my poshest frock to the wedding.* ○ *We ate in a really posh restaurant.*

① **position** /pə'zɪʃ(ə)n/ *noun* **1.** a place where someone or something is ○ *From his* *position on the roof he can see the whole of the street.* ○ *The ship's last known position was 200 miles east of Bermuda.* **2.** a job ○ *The sales manager has a key position in the firm.* ○ *He's going to apply for a position as manager.* ○ *We have several positions vacant.* **3.** a situation or state of affairs ○ *What is the company's cash position?* **4.** someone's opinion [~on] ○ *I've made my position on suitable payment quite clear.* **5.** □ **to be in a position to do something** to be able to do something ○ *I am not in a position to answer your question at this point in time.* ■ *verb* (**positions, positioning, positioned**) to put or place someone or something in a position ○ *She positioned herself near the exit.*

② **positive** /ˈpɒzɪtɪv/ *adj* **1.** certain or sure ○ *I'm positive I put the key in my pocket.* ○ *Are you positive he said six o'clock?* **2.** (*in a test*) showing that the person tested has a particular condition ○ *The cancer test was positive.*

③ **possess** /pəˈzes/ (**possesses, possessing, possessed**) *verb* to own something ○ *They possess several farms in the south of the country.* ○ *He lost all he possessed in the fire.*

③ **possession** /pəˈzeʃ(ə)n/ *noun* ownership ○ *When he couldn't keep up the mortgage payments the bank took possession of the house.* ◇ **in someone's possession** being held by someone ○ *The jewellery came into my possession when my mother died.*

possessive /pəˈzesɪv/ *adj* who treats someone or something as if he or she owns him, her or it ○ *His girlfriend's very possessive and hates it when he goes out with his mates.* ○ *He gets very possessive about his gold pen and won't let anyone else use it.*

② **possibility** /ˌpɒsɪˈbɪlɪti/ *noun* the fact of being likely to happen [~of/~(that)] ○ *Is there any possibility of getting a ticket to the show?* ○ *There is always the possibility that the plane will be early.*

① **possible** /ˈpɒsɪb(ə)l/ *adj* able to be done ○ *She agreed that the changes were possible.*

① **possibly** /ˈpɒsɪbli/ *adv* **1.** perhaps ○ *The meeting will possibly finish late.* ○ *January had possibly the worst snowstorms we have ever seen.* **2.** used with 'can' or 'can't' to make a phrase stronger ○ *You can't possibly eat 22 pancakes!* ○ *How can you possibly expect me to do all that work in one day?*

① **post** /pəʊst/ *noun* **1.** a long piece of wood or metal put in the ground ○ *The fence is attached to concrete posts.* ○ *His shot hit the goalpost.* ◊ **goalpost 2.** a job ○ *He applied for a post in the sales department.* ○ *We have three posts vacant.* ○ *They advertised the post in 'The Times'.* **3.** letters and parcels that are sent and received ○ *The morning post comes around nine o'clock.* ○ *There were no cheques in this morning's post.* ○ *Has the post arrived yet?* **4.** the system of sending letters and parcels ○ *It is easier to send the parcel by post than to deliver it by hand.* ■ *verb* (**posts, posting, posted**) to send a letter or parcel ○ *Don't forget to post your Christmas cards.* ○ *The letter should have arrived by now – we posted it ten days ago.* ◇ **to keep someone posted** to keep someone informed ○ *Please keep us posted about your holiday arrangements.*

post- /pəʊst/ *prefix* later than or after ○ *post Christmas sales* ○ *post-holiday gloom*

③ **postage** /ˈpəʊstɪdʒ/ *noun* money which you pay to send something by post

postage stamp /ˈpəʊstɪdʒ stæmp/ *noun* a piece of paper which you buy and stick on a letter or parcel to pay for it to be sent on by the post office

postal order /ˈpəʊst(ə)l ˌɔːdə/ *noun* a paper which you can buy for sending small amounts of money through the post

③ **postbox** /ˈpəʊstbɒks/ *noun* a box into which you can put letters, which will then be collected and sent on by the post office

③ **postcard** /ˈpəʊstkɑːd/ *noun* a piece of card often with a picture on one side, which you send to someone with a short message on it

③ **postcode** /ˈpəʊstkəʊd/ *noun* a series of letters and numbers given at the end of an address, to help the people whose job is to sort letters

③ **poster** /ˈpəʊstə/ *noun* a large notice, picture or advertisement stuck on a wall

posterity /pɒˈsterɪti/ *noun* the generations which will follow this one

postgraduate /pəʊstˈɡrædʒʊət/ *noun* a person who has a first degree from a university and who is studying for a further degree ○ *He's taking a postgraduate course in physics.*

posthumous /ˈpɒstjʊməs/ *adj* after death

posting /ˈpəʊstɪŋ/ *noun* a new job with the same organisation, for which you have to move to a different country or district

Post-it /ˈpəʊst ɪt/ *trademark* a small piece of gummed coloured paper which you can write a note on and stick onto something

postman /ˈpəʊstmən/ (*plural* **postmen**) *noun* a person who delivers letters to houses

postmark /ˈpəʊstmɑːk/ *noun* a mark stamped on a letter to show when and where it was posted ○ *a letter with a London postmark* ○ *You can see from the postmark that it was posted two weeks ago.* (NOTE: + **postmark** *v*)

post mortem /ˌpəʊst ˈmɔːtəm/ *noun* **1.** the examination of a corpse to find out the cause of death ○ *The post mortem revealed that she had been poisoned.* **2.** an examination of something which has happened ○ *The government is carrying out a post mortem on the result of the elections.* Abbreviation **PM**

postnatal /ˌpəʊstˈneɪt(ə)l/ *adj* which happens after childbirth

post office /ˈpəʊst ˌɒfɪs/ *noun* a building where you can do such things as buying stamps, sending letters and parcels and paying bills ○ *The main post office is in the High Street.* ○ *There are two parcels to be taken to the post office.*

postpone /pəʊstˈpəʊn/ (**postpones, postponing, postponed**) *verb* to change the time or date of an event so that it will happen a later date or time ○ *The meeting has been postponed until next week.* (NOTE: + **postponement** *n*)

posture /ˈpɒstʃə/ *noun* a way of sitting or standing ○ *She does exercises to improve her posture.*

postwar /ˌpəʊstˈwɔː/ *adj* referring to the period after a war

② **pot** /pɒt/ *noun* **1.** a glass or china container, usually without a handle ○ *The plant is too big – it needs a bigger pot.* ○ *She made ten pots of strawberry jam.* ◊ **teapot** **2.** a deep metal container with a long handle, used for cooking ○ *Do I have to wash all the pots and pans by hand?*

potassium /pəˈtæsiəm/ *noun* soft metal found in rocks, essential to biological life

② **potato** /pəˈteɪtəʊ/ (*plural* **potatoes**) *noun* a common white or yellow root vegetable which grows under the ground ○ *boiled potatoes* ○ *mashed potatoes* ○ *roast potatoes* ○ *Do you want any more potatoes?* ○ *We're having roast lamb and potatoes for Sunday lunch.*

potent /ˈpəʊt(ə)nt/ *adj* which has a strong effect ○ *Don't drink too much of that beer – it's terribly potent.* ○ *People don't realise how potent these drugs are.*

② **potential** /pəˈtenʃəl/ *adj* possible ○ *He's a potential world champion.* ○ *The potential profits from the deal are enormous.* ■ *noun* the possibility of developing into something useful or valuable ○ *The discovery has enormous potential.* ○ *She doesn't have much experience, but she has a lot of potential.* ○ *The whole area has great potential for economic growth.*

pothole /ˈpɒthəʊl/ *noun* **1.** a hole in a road surface ○ *The council still hasn't filled in the potholes in our street.* **2.** a deep hole in rock worn away by water ○ *They were exploring a pothole in the Mendip Hills.*

potholing /ˈpɒthəʊlɪŋ/ *noun* the sport of exploring potholes in rock

potion /ˈpəʊʃ(ə)n/ *noun* a liquid mixture of medicine (*dated*)

potluck /pɒtˈlʌk/ *noun* □ **to take potluck** to take whatever comes, with no possibility of choosing anything different

potter /ˈpɒtə/ *noun* a person who makes pots out of clay ○ *a potter's wheel* ○ *The potter makes cups and bowls to sell in craft shops.* ■ *verb also* **potter about** not to do anything in particular or to do little jobs here and there ○ *He spent Saturday morning pottering about in the garden.* (NOTE: The US term is **putter around**)

③ **pottery** /ˈpɒtəri/ *noun* **1.** a place where pots are made ○ *There are several local potteries where you can buy dishes.* ○ *I bought this vase from the pottery where it was made.* (NOTE: The plural in this sense is **potteries**.) **2.** objects such as pots and plates, made of clay ○ *There's a man in the market who sells local pottery.* ○ *She brought me some Spanish pottery as a present.*

potty /ˈpɒti/ *noun* a small pot where a young child can urinate or defecate

pouch /paʊtʃ/ *noun* **1.** a small bag for carrying objects such as coins ○ *She carried the ring in a small leather pouch round her neck.* **2.** a bag in the skin in front of some animals, where the young are carried ○ *The kangaroo carries its young in its pouch.*

poultry /ˈpəʊltri/ *noun* common farm birds such as ducks or hens, reared for eggs or to be eaten

pounce /paʊns/ (**pounces, pouncing, pounced**) *verb* **1.** to jump quickly to catch something ○ *The cat was watching the bird, ready to pounce.* **2.** to criticise something strongly [~on] ○ *He pounced on the only mistake I'd made.*

① **pound** /paʊnd/ *noun* **1.** a measure of weight, equal to about 450 grams (NOTE: **pound** is usually written **lb** after figures: *It weighs 26lb.*; *Take 6lb of sugar.* say 'twenty-six pounds, six pounds'.) **2.** a unit of money used in Britain and several other countries ○ *He earns more than six pounds an hour.* ○ *The price of the car is over £50,000 (fifty thousand pounds).* ○ *He tried to pay for his bus ticket with a £20 note (twenty-pound note).* (NOTE: **pound** is usually written **£** before figures: *£20, £6,000*: say 'twenty pounds, six thousand pounds'. With the word **note**, **pound** is singular: *twenty pounds* but *a twenty-pound note*.) ■ *verb* (**pounds, pounding, pounded**) **1.** to hit something hard ○ *He pounded the table with his fist.* **2.** to smash something into little pieces ○ *The ship was pounded to pieces by heavy waves.*

② **pour** /pɔː/ (**pours, pouring, poured**) *verb* **1.** to make a liquid flow [~over/into/down etc] ○ *The waiter poured water all over the table.* ○ *He poured the wine into the glasses.* ○ *She poured water down his neck as a joke.* **2.** to flow out or down [~out of/into etc] ○ *Crowds of people poured into the stadium* ○ *Smoke was pouring out of the house.*

pour down③ *phrasal verb* to rain very hard ○ *Don't go out without an umbrella – it's pouring down.*

pout /paʊt/ (**pouts, pouting, pouted**) *verb* to make a sulky expression with your lips ○ *When she pouts she looks very sexy.* (NOTE: + **pout** *n*)

③ **poverty** /ˈpɒvəti/ *noun* the fact of being poor ○ *He lost all his money and died in poverty.* ○ *Poverty can drive people to crime.*

powder /ˈpaʊdə/ *noun* a substance like flour with very small dry grains ○ *The drug is available in the form of a white powder.* ○ *This machine grinds pepper corns to powder.*

① **power** /ˈpaʊə/ *noun* **1.** the ability to control people or happenings [~over] ○ *the power a parent has over their child* ○ *He is the official leader, but his wife has all the real power.* ○ *I haven't the power* or *it isn't in my power to ban the demonstration.* **2.** a driving force ○ *They use the power of the waves to generate electricity.* ○ *The engine is driven by steam power.* **3.** electricity used to drive machines or devices ○ *Turn off the power before you try to repair the TV set.* **4.** political control ○ *The socialists came to power in 1997.* ○ *During the period when he was in power the country's economy was ruined.* **5.** an important, powerful country ○ *China is one of the great powers.*

power base /ˈpaʊə beɪs/ *noun* a group or area which supports a politician

power cut /ˈpaʊə kʌt/ *noun* same as **power failure**

power failure /ˈpaʊə ˌfeɪljə/ *noun* a breakdown in electricity supplies

② **powerful** /ˈpaʊəf(ə)l/ *adj* having a lot of force, influence or capability ○ *This model has a more powerful engine.* ○ *The treasurer is the most powerful person in the organisation.* ○ *The raft was swept away by the powerful current.* ○ *This is the most powerful personal computer on the market.*

powerless /ˈpaʊələs/ *adj* unable to do anything because of not having any power or authority

power steering /ˈpaʊə ˌstɪərɪŋ/ *noun* steering in a car, which is powered by the engine

power tool /ˈpaʊə tuːl/ *noun* a powerful electrical tool

pp *abbr* pages

③ **PR** *abbr* public relations

practicable /ˈpræktɪkəb(ə)l/ *adj* which can be done or can be put into practice

② **practical** /ˈpræktɪk(ə)l/ *adj* **1.** referring to real actions and events rather than ideas or plans ○ *She needs some practical experience.* ○ *I need some practical advice on how to build a wall.* **2.** possible or sensible ○ *It isn't practical to plug the computer into the same socket as the TV.* ○ *Has anyone got a more practical suggestion to make?* ○ *You need practical clothing for camping.* ○ *We must be practical and not try anything too ambitious.*

practicality /ˌpræktɪˈkælɪti/ (*plural* **practicalities**) *noun* **1.** a way in which something works in practice ○ *We haven't yet got down to discussing the practicalities of selling the shop.* **2.** a way in which something is practical or possible ○ *I have doubts about the practicality of the scheme.*

practical joke /ˌpræktɪk(ə)l ˈdʒəʊk/ *noun* a trick played on someone to make other people laugh

② **practically** /ˈpræktɪkli/ *adv* almost ○ *Practically all the students passed the test.* ○ *The summer is practically over.* ○ *His suit is such a dark grey it is practically black.*

① **practice** /ˈpræktɪs/ *noun* **1.** the act of doing something, as opposed to thinking about it or planning it **2.** a repeated activity done so that you can improve ○ *You need more practice before you're ready to enter the competition.* ○ *He's at football practice this evening.* ○ *The cars make several practice runs before the race.* **3.** a way of doing something, especially a way that is regularly used ○ *It's a standard practice for shops to open late one day a week for staff training.* ○ *It's been our practice for many years to walk the dogs before breakfast.* ■ *verb* US spelling of **practise** ◇ **in practice** when something is done or carried out ○ *The plan seems very interesting, but what will it cost in practice?* ◇ **out of practice** not able to do something because of not having done it recently ○ *I used to be able to play quite well, but I'm a bit out of practice.* ◇ **to put something into practice** to apply or use something ○ *I hope soon to be able to put some of my ideas into practice.*

① **practise** /ˈpræktɪs/ (**practises, practising, practised**) *verb* **1.** to do something many times in order to become better at it ○ *He's practising catching and throwing.* **2.** to work as a doctor, dentist or lawyer ○ *He's officially retired but still practises part-time.*

practised /ˈpræktɪst/ *adj* skilful at doing something because you have had a lot of practice (NOTE: The US spelling is **practiced**.)

③ **practitioner** /prækˈtɪʃ(ə)nə/ *noun* a person who does a skilled job. ◊ **GP**

pragmatic /prægˈmætɪk/ *adj* dealing with facts or practical matters, not concerned with theories

prairie /ˈpreəri/ *noun* an area of grass-covered plain in North America, mainly without trees, where most of the world's grain is produced

praise /preɪz/ *noun* admiration, the act of showing approval ○ *The rescue team earned the praise of the survivors.* ■ *verb* (**praises, praising, praised**) to express strong approval of something or someone ○ *The mayor praised the firemen for their efforts in putting out the fire.*

praiseworthy /ˈpreɪzwɜːði/ *adj* which should be praised

pram /præm/, **praam** *noun* a light carriage for pushing a baby in

prance /prɑːns/ (**prances, prancing, pranced**) *verb* to jump about, to move fast and lightly

prank /præŋk/ *noun* a trick

prattle /ˈpræt(ə)l/ (**prattles, prattling, prattled**) *verb* to chatter a lot about things which aren't important

prawn /prɔːn/ *noun* a shellfish like a large shrimp

③ **pray** /preɪ/ (**prays, praying, prayed**) *verb* to speak to God, asking for something, or asking for someone to be helped or protected [~for] ○ *The men were praying in front of the shrine.* ○ *We've been praying for you.*

③ **prayer** /preə/ *noun* the act of speaking to God [~for] ○ *They said prayers for the sick.* ○ *She says her prayers every night before going to bed.*

pre- /priː/ *prefix* before ○ *the pre-Christmas rush* ○ *We have been invited for pre-lunch drinks.*

preach /priːtʃ/ (**preaches, preaching, preached**) *verb* **1.** to give a sermon in church **2.** to recommend or advise something

preacher /ˈpriːtʃə/ *noun* a person who gives a sermon in church

precarious /prɪˈkeəriəs/ *adj* not safe, likely to fall off or to fail

③ **precaution** /prɪˈkɔːʃ(ə)n/ *noun* care taken in advance to avoid something unpleasant

③ **precede** /prɪˈsiːd/ (**precedes, preceding, preceded**) *verb* to take place before something

precedence /ˈpresɪd(ə)ns/ *noun* □ **to take precedence over someone or something** to be more important than, when considered as part of a hierarchy ○ *Presidents take precedence over prime ministers.*

③ **precedent** /ˈpresɪd(ə)nt/ *noun* a thing which has happened before, and which can be a guide as to what should be done [~for] ○ *The trial has set a precedent for future libel cases.*

③ **preceding** /prɪˈsiːdɪŋ/ *adj* which comes before something

precinct /ˈpriːsɪŋkt/ *noun US* an administrative district in a town ○ *the 16th precinct*

③ **precious** /ˈpreʃəs/ *adj* **1.** worth a lot of money ○ *a precious stone* **2.** of great value to someone ○ *All her precious photographs were saved from the fire.* ○ *The memories of that holiday are very precious to me.*

precious metal /ˌpreʃəs ˈmet(ə)l/ *noun* a metal, such as gold, which is worth a lot of money

precious stone /'preʃəs stəʊn/ *noun* a stone such as a diamond, which is rare and very valuable

precipice /'presɪpɪs/ *noun* a high cliff on the side of a mountain, not usually near the sea

precipitate /prɪ'sɪpɪteɪt/ (**precipitates, precipitating, precipitated**) *verb* to make something happen suddenly ○ *The assassination precipitated a political crisis.*

precipitation /prɪˌsɪpɪ'teɪʃ(ə)n/ *noun* a quantity of rain, snow, etc., which falls on a certain place ○ *The north-west of the country experienced higher precipitation than normal.*

précis /'preɪsiː/ (*plural* **précis**) *noun* a summary of the main points of a text ○ *I made a précis of the report for my boss.*

③ **precise** /prɪ'saɪs/ *adj* exact ○ *We need to know the precise measurements of the box.* ○ *At that precise moment my father walked in.* ○ *Can you be more precise about what the men looked like?*

② **precisely** /prɪ'saɪsli/ *adv* exactly ○ *The train arrived at 12.00 precisely.* ○ *I don't know precisely when it was, but it was about three months ago.* ○ *How, precisely, do you expect me to cope with all this work?*

precision /prɪ'sɪʒ(ə)n/ *noun* accuracy

preclude /prɪ'kluːd/ (**precludes, precluding, precluded**) *verb* to prevent something taking place (*formal*)

precocious /prɪ'kəʊʃəs/ *adj* (*of a child*) surprisingly advanced for its age

preconception /ˌpriːkən'sepʃən/ *noun* an idea which is formed in advance, without the benefit of information or experience

precondition /ˌpriːkən'dɪʃ(ə)n/ *noun* a condition which is set in advance

precursor /prɪ'kɜːsə/ *noun* a thing which leads to something more important

predate /ˌpriː'deɪt/ (**predates, predating, predated**) *verb* to come before something in time

③ **predator** /'predətə/ *noun* an animal which kills and eats other animals

③ **predecessor** /'priːdɪsesə/ *noun* a person who has held the same job, etc., before you

predicament /prɪ'dɪkəmənt/ *noun* trouble or a difficult situation

③ **predict** /prɪ'dɪkt/ (**predicts, predicting, predicted**) *verb* to foretell something or tell in advance what will happen [~(that)] ○ *He predicted correctly that oil prices would rise.* ○ *The weather forecasters have predicted rain.* ○ *Everything happened exactly as I had predicted.*

predictable /prɪ'dɪktəb(ə)l/ *adj* which could be predicted

prediction /prɪ'dɪkʃən/ *noun* an instance of foretelling something

predisposition /ˌpriːdɪspə'zɪʃ(ə)n/ *noun* the fact of being predisposed

predominant /prɪ'dɒmɪnənt/ *adj* most striking or obvious

predominantly /prɪ'dɒmɪnəntli/ *adv* mainly

predominate /prɪ'dɒmɪneɪt/ (**predominates, predominating, predominated**) *verb* to be more powerful than others

preeminent /pri'emɪnənt/ *adj* excellent, much better than everything else

pre-empt /ˌpriː 'empt/ (**pre-empts, pre-empting, pre-empted**) *verb* to get an advantage over somebody by doing something quickly before anyone else

preen /priːn/ (**preens, preening, preened**) *verb* (*of a bird*) to smooth its feathers

prefabricated /priː'fæbrɪkeɪtɪd/ *adj* (*of a building*) built from sections which are easy to put together

preface /'prefəs/ *noun* the text at the beginning of a book, after the title page, in which the author introduces the book and thanks people for helping make it ○ *She explains in a preface what motivated her to write the book.* Compare **foreword**

prefect /'priːfekt/ *noun* an older school pupil chosen to be in charge of others ○ *The prefects help to maintain discipline in the school.*

② **prefer** /prɪ'fɜː/ (**prefers, preferring, preferred**) *verb* to like one thing better than another [~to] ○ *Which do you prefer -butter to margarine?* ○ *She prefers walking to going on the Underground.* ○ *We went to the pub, but she preferred to stay at home and watch TV.* ○ *I'd prefer not to go to Germany this summer.*

preferable /'pref(ə)rəb(ə)l/ *adj* which you would prefer

preferably /'pref(ə)rəbli/ *adv* expressing something that would be preferred ○ *I'd like to book a seat, preferably one next to a window.*

③ **preference** /'pref(ə)rəns/ *noun* a liking for one thing more than another [~for] ○ *The children all showed a marked preference for chocolate ice cream.*

preferential /ˌprefəˈrenʃəl/ *adj* showing that one person or thing is preferred to another

③ **prefix** /ˈpriːfɪks/ *noun* a group of letters put in front of another to form a new word

pregnancy /ˈpregnənsi/ *noun* the state of being pregnant

③ **pregnant** /ˈpregnənt/ *adj* (*of a woman or female animal*) carrying a developing baby inside the body ○ *Don't carry heavy weights when you're pregnant.* ○ *She hasn't told her family yet that she's pregnant.* ○ *There are three pregnant women in my office.*

preheat /priːˈhiːt/ (**preheats, preheating, preheated**) *verb* to make an oven hot before putting something to cook in it

prehistoric /ˌpriːhɪˈstɒrɪk/ *adj* belonging to the time before there was a written history

prejudge /priːˈdʒʌdʒ/ (**prejudges, prejudging, prejudged**) *verb* to judge something or someone without hearing all the facts

prejudice /ˈpredʒʊdɪs/ *noun* an unfair feeling of not liking someone or something ○ *The committee was accused of prejudice against older candidates.* ■ *verb* (**prejudices, prejudicing, prejudiced**) to make someone have less friendly feelings towards someone or something

prejudiced /ˈpredʒʊdɪst/ *adj* unfairly biased against someone

preliminary /prɪˈlɪmɪn(ə)ri/ *adj* which goes before something ○ *The executive committee will hold a preliminary meeting the day before the conference opens.* ○ *This is only the preliminary report – the main report will be published later.* ■ *noun* (*plural* **preliminaries**) something which is done as a preparation for something else

prelude /ˈpreljuːd/ *noun* **1.** something which takes place before something more important ○ *Putting tanks near the border is a prelude to a full-scale invasion.* **2.** a short introductory piece of music on one theme

premature /ˈpremətʃə/ *adj* **1.** which happens before the right time ○ *Celebrating victory before the votes have been counted is a little premature.* ○ *This can be a cause of premature death.* **2.** (*of a baby*) born less than nine months after conception ○ *Little John was six weeks premature and only weighed three pounds when he was born.*

premeditated /priːˈmedɪteɪtɪd/ *adj* (*of a crime*) planned before it is committed

premier /ˈpremiə/ *noun* a prime minister or head of government ○ *The French premier is visiting London.*

première /ˈpremieə/ *noun* the first performance of something, e.g. a film or a play

premiership /ˈpremiəʃɪp/ *noun* **1.** the time when someone is Prime Minister ○ *The introduction of income tax was the most important event of his premiership.* **2.** a premier league, the group of top football clubs who play against each other ○ *a premiership match*

③ **premise** /ˈpremɪs/, **premiss** *noun* an assumption, a thing which you assume to be true

③ **premises** /ˈpremɪsɪz/ *plural noun* a building and the land it stands on ○ *Smoking is not allowed on the premises.* ○ *There is a doctor on the premises at all times.*

premium /ˈpriːmiəm/ *noun* **1.** an amount paid for an insurance policy ○ *The house insurance premium has to be paid this month.* ○ *We pay a monthly premium of £5.* **2.** an extra amount ○ *They pay a premium for work completed ahead of schedule.* ■ *adj* higher quality and therefore more expensive than other similar things ◇ **at a premium** scarce, and therefore valuable ○ *Fresh vegetables were at a premium during the winter months.*

premonition /ˌpreməˈnɪʃ(ə)n/ *noun* a feeling that something is going to happen

preoccupation /priːˌɒkjʊˈpeɪʃ(ə)n/ *noun* something that you think about a lot, usually so much that you ignore other things ○ *his preoccupation with his business*

preoccupied /priˈɒkjʊpaɪd/ *adj* worried and thinking only about one thing

② **preparation** /ˌprepəˈreɪʃ(ə)n/ *noun* **1.** the action of getting ready [~for] ○ *The preparations for the wedding went on for months.* ○ *We've completed our preparations and now we're ready to start.* □ **in preparation for something** getting ready for something ○ *She bought a hat in preparation for the wedding.* **2.** a substance which has been mixed ○ *a chemical preparation*

preparatory /prɪˈpærət(ə)ri/ *adj* which prepares someone for something ○ *This is a preparatory course in Chinese for beginners.*

① **prepare** /prɪˈpeə/ (**prepares, preparing, prepared**) *verb* **1.** to get something ready [~for] ○ *We have prepared the hall for the school play.* ○ *I have some friends coming to dinner and I haven't prepared the meal.* **2.** to get ready for something [~for] ○ *He is preparing for his exam.* ○ *You'd better prepare yourself for some bad news.*

① **prepared** /prɪ'peəd/ *adj* ready ○ *Be prepared, you may get quite a shock.* ○ *Six people are coming to dinner and I've got nothing prepared.*

preponderance /prɪ'pɒnd(ə)rəns/ *noun* a greater number of one type of people or things than any other in a group

③ **preposition** /ˌprepə'zɪʃ(ə)n/ *noun* a word used with a noun or pronoun to show place or time

preposterous /prɪ'pɒst(ə)rəs/ *adj* silly or absurd

prerequisite /priː'rekwəzɪt/ *noun* a thing which you must have before you can do something

prescribe /prɪ'skraɪb/ (**prescribes, prescribing, prescribed**) *verb* **1.** to order that something should be done ○ *Three days' notice has been given, as prescribed by law.* ○ *We have to study two prescribed texts for our exam.* **2.** (*of a doctor*) to tell someone to use something ○ *He prescribed a course of injections.* ○ *She prescribed some antibiotics.*

③ **prescription** /prɪ'skrɪpʃən/ *noun* an order written by a doctor to a pharmacist asking for a drug to be prepared and sold to a patient [~for] ○ *The doctor has given him a prescription for painkillers.* □ **available on prescription** available from a chemist only when prescribed by a doctor ○ *This medicine is only available on prescription.*

② **presence** /'prez(ə)ns/ *noun* **1.** the fact of being present ○ *The presence of both his wives in court was noted.* ○ *Your presence is requested at a meeting of the committee on June 23rd.* **2.** an effect you have on other people ○ *The general has a commanding presence.*

present[1] /'prez(ə)nt/ *noun* **1.** something which you give to someone, e.g. on their birthday ○ *I got a watch as a Christmas present.* ○ *How many birthday presents did you get?* ○ *Her colleagues gave her a present when she got married.* **2.** the time we are in now ○ *The novel is set in the present.* **3.** the form of a verb showing that the action is happening now ○ *The present of the verb 'to go' is 'he goes' or 'he is going'.* ■ *adj* at a place when something happens there ○ *How many people were present at the meeting?* ◇ **at present** now ○ *The hotel still has some vacancies at present.* ◇ **for the present** for now ○ *That will be enough for the present.*

present[2] /prɪ'zent/ (**presents, presenting, presented**) *verb* **1.** to give something formally to someone as a present ○ *When he retired after thirty years, the firm presented him with a large clock.* **2.** to introduce a show on TV or radio ○ *She's presenting a programme on gardening.*

presentable /prɪ'zentəb(ə)l/ *adj* clean and tidy, suitable to appear in public

② **presentation** /ˌprez(ə)n'teɪʃ(ə)n/ *noun* **1.** the act of giving something to someone ○ *The chairman will make the presentation to the retiring sales manager.* **2.** a formal occasion on which something is given to someone **3.** a formal occasion on which someone tells other people about their work ○ *The company made a presentation of the services they could offer.*

③ **present-day** /ˌprez(ə)nt 'deɪ/ *adj* modern

③ **presenter** /prɪ'zentə/ *noun* a person who presents a TV or radio show

presently /'prez(ə)ntli/ *adv* **1.** soon ○ *I'll be there presently.* ○ *He'll be making a speech presently.* **2.** *US* now, at the present time ○ *He's presently working for a chemical company.* ○ *She's presently in England.* ○ *What is presently being done to correct the problem?*

present participle /ˌprez(ə)nt pɑː'tɪsɪp(ə)l/ *noun* a word formed by adding '-ing' to a verb, used either to form the present continuous tense, e.g. I am reading, or as an adjective or noun

③ **preservation** /ˌprezə'veɪʃ(ə)n/ *noun* the action of protecting [~of] ○ *The trust is mainly concerned with the preservation of historic buildings.*

preservative /prɪ'zɜːvətɪv/ *noun* a substance added to food to stop it from going bad

③ **preserve** /prɪ'zɜːv/ (**preserves, preserving, preserved**) *verb* **1.** to look after something and keep it in the same state ○ *Our committee aims to preserve the wildlife in our area.* ○ *The doctors' aim is to preserve the life of the unborn child.* ○ *They would like to preserve their own alphabet rather than use the Roman one.* **2.** to treat something so that it does not decay ○ *Meat can be preserved in salt.* ○ *Freezing is a common method of preserving meat.*

preside /prɪ'zaɪd/ (**presides, presiding, presided**) *verb* **1.** to be the person in charge of a meeting or event [~at/over] ○ *The meet-*

ing was held in the town hall, with the mayor presiding. ○ *The deputy presided in the absence of the chairperson.* ○ *Maureen usually presides over our book club meetings.* **2.** to be in power during a particular period ○ *He presided over a period of radical change.*

presidency /ˈprezɪdənsi/ *noun* the job of being president ○ *He has been proposed as a candidate for the presidency.*

① **president** /ˈprezɪd(ə)nt/, **President** *noun* the head of a republic ○ *President Bush was elected in 2000.* ○ *The French president came on an official visit.* (NOTE: also used as a title before a surname: *President Wilson*)

presidential /ˌprezɪˈdenʃəl/ *adj* relating to a president

① **press** /pres/ *noun* **1.** newspapers taken as a group ○ *The election wasn't reported in the British press.* ○ *There has been no mention of the problem in the press.* (NOTE: no plural) **2.** journalists and other people who work for newspapers, or on radio and TV ○ *Everywhere she went she was followed by the press.* ○ *Press photographers were standing outside Number 10.* ■ *verb* (**presses, pressing, pressed**) **1.** to push or squeeze something **2.** to iron something ○ *His jacket needs to be pressed.*

press on *or* **forward** *phrasal verb* to continue ○ *In spite of the weather they pressed on with the preparations for the village fair.*

③ **press conference** /ˈpres ˌkɒnf(ə)rəns/ *noun* a meeting where newspaper, radio and TV reporters are invited to hear news of a new product or a takeover bid, or to talk to a famous person

③ **pressing** /ˈpresɪŋ/ *adj* urgent, which needs to be done quickly

press office /ˈpres ˌɒfɪs/ *noun* an office in an organisation which is responsible for relations with the media

③ **press release** /ˈpres rɪˌliːs/ *noun* a sheet giving news about something which is sent to newspapers and TV and radio stations

press-up /ˈpres ʌp/ *noun* an exercise where you lie on the floor and push yourself up with your arms

① **pressure** /ˈpreʃə/ *noun* **1.** something which forces you to do something [~on] ○ *There's pressure on the journalist to reveal his source.Pressure from farmers forced the minister to change his mind.* □ **to put pressure on someone to do something** to try to force someone to do something ○ *They put pressure on the government to build a new motorway.* **2.** the force of something such as air which is pushing or squeezing ○ *There is not enough pressure in your tyres.* ◇ **under pressure** feeling that you are being forced to do something ○ *He did it under pressure.* ○ *We're under pressure to agree to a postponement.*

③ **pressure group** /ˈpreʃə ɡruːp/ *noun* a group of people who try to influence an organisation, e.g. the government or the local town council

③ **prestige** /preˈstiːʒ/ *noun* importance, e.g. because of high quality or high value

prestigious /preˈstɪdʒəs/ *adj* which brings prestige

① **presumably** /prɪˈzjuːməbli/ *adv* expressing something that is likely ○ *Presumably this is what she wanted us to do.*

③ **presume** /prɪˈzjuːm/ (**presumes, presuming, presumed**) *verb* **1.** to suppose or assume something [~(that)] ○ *I presume this little bridge is safe for cars?* ○ *The jury has to presume he is innocent until he is proved guilty.* ○ *She is presumed to have fled to South America.* **2.** □ **not** *or* **never to presume to do something** not to do something because it would be rude to do it (*formal*) ○ *I wouldn't presume to contradict her – she's the expert.*

presumption /prɪˈzʌmpʃən/ *noun* a thing which is assumed to be correct ○ *We are working on the presumption that what he has said is in fact true.*

presumptuous /prɪˈzʌmptʃuəs/ *adj* rude or bold

presuppose /ˌpriːsəˈpəʊz/ (**presupposes, presupposing, presupposed**) *verb* to depend on something having already happened

pretence /prɪˈtens/ *noun* the act of making someone believe something which is untrue, the action of pretending ○ *They made a pretence of being interested.* ○ *All this talk about his aristocratic connections is mere pretence* or *is just a pretence.* ◇ **by false pretences** by doing or saying something to cheat someone ○ *He was sent to prison for obtaining money by false pretences.*

② **pretend** /prɪˈtend/ (**pretends, pretending, pretended**) *verb* to make someone believe you are something else, so as to trick them [~(that)] ○ *She pretended she had flu and phoned to say she was having the day off.* ○ *He got into the house by pretending to be a telephone engineer.*

pretentious /prɪ'tenʃəs/ *adj* claiming to be more important than you are

pretext /'pri:tekst/ *noun* an excuse for doing something which is not the real reason for doing it

② **pretty** /'prɪti/ *adj* (**prettier, prettiest**) **1.** a pretty woman or girl has a face that is quite attractive ○ *Her daughters are very pretty.* (NOTE: Usually **pretty** is used of things or girls, not of boys or men.) **2.** quite pleasant to look at ○ *That's a pretty necklace.* ■ *adv* fairly (*informal*) ○ *The patient's condition is pretty much the same as it was yesterday.* ○ *I'm pretty sure I'm right.* ○ *You did pretty well, considering it was the first time you had tried rock-climbing.*

③ **prevail** /prɪ'veɪl/ (**prevails, prevailing, prevailed**) *verb* **1.** to exist [~upon] ○ *A positive attitude prevails in the team.* **2.** to be widely accepted ○ *A feeling that we were persuaded by doubtful evidence prevails.* **3.** to win or succeed in something **4.** □ **to prevail upon someone to do something** to persuade someone to do something (*formal*) ○ *Can I prevail on you to make a speech?*

prevailing /prɪ'veɪlɪŋ/ *adj* usual, common

prevailing wind /prɪˌveɪlɪŋ 'wɪnd/ *noun* a wind which usually blows from a certain direction

prevalent /'prevələnt/ *adj* common, occurring frequently

① **prevent** /prɪ'vent/ (**prevents, preventing, prevented**) *verb* to stop something happening ○ *We must try to prevent any more flooding.*

③ **prevention** /prɪ'venʃən/ *noun* the process of stopping something from happening [~of]

preview /'pri:vju:/ *noun* a private showing of a film or exhibition before it is open to the public

① **previous** /'pri:viəs/ *adj* happening or existing at an earlier time ○ *The letter was sent to my previous address.* ○ *The gang of workers had arrived the previous night and started work first thing in the morning.* ○ *I had spent the previous day getting to know my way round the town.*

① **previously** /'pri:viəsli/ *adv* at a time before ○ *This is my first train trip to Paris – previously I've always gone by plane.* ○ *The arrangements had been made six weeks previously.* ○ *At that time they were living in New York, and previously had lived in London.*

prey /preɪ/ *noun* an animal eaten by another animal ○ *Mice and small birds are the favourite prey of owls.*

① **price** /praɪs/ *noun* money which you have to pay to buy something ○ *The price of petrol is going up.* ○ *I don't want to pay such a high price for a hotel room.* ○ *There has been a sharp increase in house prices during the first six months of the year.* □ **to increase in price** to become more expensive

priceless /'praɪsləs/ *adj* **1.** extremely valuable ○ *His priceless collection of paintings was destroyed in the fire.* ○ *This ring is quite priceless.* **2.** very funny ○ *Some of the things she said were absolutely priceless.*

③ **price tag** /'praɪs tæg/ *noun* **1.** a ticket with a price written on it ○ *How much is this shirt? – The price tag has come off it.* **2.** a price at which something is for sale ○ *car with a £50,000 price tag*

pricey /'praɪsi/ (**pricier, priciest**) *adj* expensive (*informal*)

prick /prɪk/ (**pricks, pricking, pricked**) *verb* to make a very small hole with a sharp point in the outer layer of something such as skin ○ *She pricked her finger when she was picking roses.* ○ *Prick the sausages before you fry them to stop them from bursting.*

prickle /'prɪk(ə)l/ *noun* a sharp point on a plant or animal

prickly /'prɪkli/ *adj* **1.** covered with prickles ○ *a prickly holly bush* ○ *a prickly hedgehog* **2.** (*of a person*) who takes offence easily ○ *Be careful what you say to her – she's very prickly.*

③ **pride** /praɪd/ *noun* **1.** a pleasure in your own ability or possessions ○ *He takes great pride in his garden.* **2.** a feeling of respect for yourself that is sometimes too strong, making you behave wrongly ○ *His pride would not let him admit that he had made a mistake.*

③ **priest** /pri:st/ *noun* a person who carries out formal religious duties

priestess /pri:'stes/ *noun* a female priest in a non-Christian religion

priesthood /'pri:sthʊd/ *noun* all priests considered as a group ○ *The priesthood refused to accept the government's decree.*

prima donna /ˌpri:mə 'dɒnə/ (*plural* **prima donnas**) *noun* **1.** the main female singer in an opera company **2.** a person who thinks he or she is extremely important and makes a fuss if things are not done in the way they want ○ *He's a real prima donna* *when it comes to choosing flowers for his office.*

③ **primarily** /ˈpraɪm(ə)rɪli/ *adv* mainly, mostly

② **primary** /ˈpraɪməri/ *adj* main, basic ○ *Our primary concern is the safety of our passengers.*

② **primary school** /ˈpraɪməri skuːl/ *noun* a school for children up to the age of eleven

primate /ˈpraɪmeɪt/ *noun* an archbishop ○ *The Archbishop of Canterbury is the Primate of all England.*

prime /praɪm/ *adj* most important ○ *The prime suspect in the case is the dead woman's husband.* ○ *This is a prime example of what is wrong with this country.*

prime minister /ˌpraɪm ˈmɪnɪstə/, **Prime Minister** *noun* the head of the government in Britain and other countries ○ *the Australian Prime Minister* or *the Prime Minister of Australia* ○ *She cut out the picture of the Prime Minister from the newspaper.* ○ *The Prime Minister will address the nation at 6 o'clock tonight.* ○ *He was determined to become prime minister before the age of 40.* (NOTE: Use initial capitals when you are talking about a particular prime minister.)

primer /ˈpraɪmə/ *noun* **1.** a special paint which is put on bare wood before giving the top coats **2.** a book with simple instructions or that is an introduction to a subject

primeval /praɪˈmiːv(ə)l/ *adj* referring to the period at the beginning of the world's existence ○ *the primeval forest*

primitive /ˈprɪmɪtɪv/ *adj* **1.** referring to the very early stages in the development of something such as a plant or animal ○ *primitive life forms* **2.** rough or crude ○ *They live in a primitive hut in the woods.* ○ *The system is a bit primitive but it works.*

primrose /ˈprɪmrəʊz/ *noun* a small pale yellow spring flower

③ **prince** /prɪns/ *noun* the son of a king or queen

③ **princess** /prɪnˈses/ (*plural* **princesses**) *noun* the daughter of a king or queen ○ *Once upon a time a beautiful princess lived in a castle by the edge of the forest.*

② **principal** /ˈprɪnsɪp(ə)l/ *adj* most important ○ *The country's principal products are paper and wood.* ○ *She played a principal role in setting up the organisation.* ■ *noun* the head of a school or college ○ *The principal wants to see you in her office.* (NOTE: Do not confuse with **principle**.)

principality /ˌprɪnsɪˈpælɪti/ (*plural* **principalities**) *noun* a country ruled by a prince ○ *the Principality of Monaco*

principally /ˈprɪnsɪp(ə)li/ *adv* mainly

① **principle** /ˈprɪnsɪp(ə)l/ *noun* **1.** a general rule [~of/~that] ○ *the principles of nuclear physics* ○ *It is a principle in our system of justice that a person is innocent until he is proved guilty.* **2.** a personal sense of what is right ○ *She's a woman of very strong principles.* ○ *It's against my principles to work on a Sunday.* (NOTE: do not confuse with **principal**) ◇ **on principle** because of what you believe ○ *She refuses to eat meat on principle.* ◇ **in principle** in agreement with the general rule ○ *I agree in principle, but we need to discuss some of the details more thoroughly.* ○ *In principle, the results should be the same every time you do the experiment.*

principled /ˈprɪnsɪp(ə)ld/ *adj* based or acting on firmly held moral principles

② **print** /prɪnt/ *verb* (**prints, printing, printed**) **1.** to mark letters or pictures on paper with a machine, and so produce a book, leaflet or newspaper etc. ○ *The book is printed directly from a computer disk.* ○ *We had five hundred copies of the leaflet printed.* **2.** to write capital letters or letters which are not joined together ○ *Print your name in the space below.* ■ *noun* **1.** letters printed on a page ○ *I can't read this book – the print is too small.* **2.** a photograph ○ *If you are not happy with your colour prints, we can guarantee a full refund.*

print out③ *phrasal verb* to print information from a computer through a printing machine ○ *She printed out three copies of the letter.*

③ **printer** /ˈprɪntə/ *noun* **1.** a person or company that prints things such as books and newspapers ○ *The book has gone to the printer, and we should have copies next week.* **2.** a machine for printing documents

③ **printing** /ˈprɪntɪŋ/ *noun* **1.** the art, business and process of printing books, newspapers, etc. ○ *Errors may have crept into the text during printing.* **2.** a number of copies of a book printed at the same time ○ *The book was published with a first printing of 5,000 copies.* ○ *The second printing has sold out and a third has been ordered.*

printing press /ˈprɪntɪŋ pres/ *noun* a machine for printing books, newspapers, etc.

③ **printout** /ˈprɪntaʊt/ *noun* paper printed with information from a computer

prior /'praɪə/ *adj* **1.** previous ○ *The house can be visited by prior arrangement with the owner.* ○ *I had to refuse her invitation because I had a prior engagement in London.* **2.** □ **prior to something** before (*formal*) ○ *They had left prior to my arrival.* ○ *I received the bill prior to receiving the goods.*

prioritise /praɪ'ɒrɪˌtaɪz/ (**prioritises, prioritising, prioritised**), **prioritize** *verb* to rank things according to importance or urgency

② **priority** /praɪ'ɒrɪti/ (*plural* **priorities**) *noun* **1.** a right to be first ○ *Children have priority in the waiting list.* □ **to have *or* take priority over sth** to be more important than something and need to be done first ○ *People with serious injuries have priority over those with only cuts and bruises.* □ **to give something top priority** to make something the most important item ○ *We should give top priority to solving our own financial problems.* ○ *The President wants us to give the problem top priority.* **2.** a thing which has to be done first ○ *Finding somewhere to stay the night was our main priority.*

prism /'prɪz(ə)m/ *noun* a glass block, usually with a cross-section shaped like a triangle, which splits white light up into the colours of the rainbow

② **prison** /'prɪz(ə)n/ *noun* a building where people are kept when they are being punished for a crime ○ *The judge sent him to prison for five years.* ○ *His father's in prison for burglary.* (NOTE: **Prison** is often used without the article **the**.)

② **prisoner** /'prɪz(ə)nə/ *noun* a person who is in prison ○ *The prisoners were taken away in a police van.*

pristine /'prɪstiːn/ *adj* fresh like new

privacy /'prɪvəsi/ *noun* not being disturbed by other people

① **private** /'praɪvət/ *adj* **1.** which belongs to one person, and is not available to everyone ○ *He flew there in his private jet.* **2.** that you would not like to discuss with most people ○ *You have no right to interfere in my private affairs.* ○ *This is a private discussion between me and my son.* ◇ **in private** away from other people ○ *She asked to see the teacher in private.*

③ **private detective** /ˌpraɪvət dɪ'tektɪv/, **private investigator** *noun* a detective who is not part of a police force, and works for a fee

private enterprise /ˌpraɪvət 'entəpraɪz/ *noun* businesses that are owned and run by individuals or groups, not by the state

private practice /ˌpraɪvət 'præktɪs/ *noun* a doctor's or dentist's practice where the clients pay, as opposed to one which is part of the National Health Service

private school /'praɪvət skuːl/ *noun* a school that is not run by the state and which the students have to pay to attend. Compare **public school**, **state school**

private secretary /ˌpraɪvət 'sekrɪt(ə)ri/ *noun* someone who deals with an important person's correspondence and affairs

privet /'prɪvət/ *noun* a common shrub with small green or yellow leaves, used for garden hedges

③ **privilege** /'prɪvɪlɪdʒ/ *noun* a favour or right granted to some people but not to everyone

privileged /'prɪvɪlɪdʒd/ *adj* who has a special advantage

② **prize** /praɪz/ *noun* a reward given to someone who has won a competition ○ *He won first prize in the music competition.* ○ *He answered all the questions correctly and claimed the prize.* ○ *The prize was awarded jointly to the young British and Russian competitors.*

pro /prəʊ/ *noun* (*informal*) **1.** a professional sportsperson, actor or musician **2.** someone who does something very well because they have been doing it for a long time

proactive /prəʊ'æktɪv/ *adj* working by starting actions yourself, rather than reacting to what other people do

③ **probability** /ˌprɒbə'bɪlɪti/ *noun* the quality of being probable [~of/~that] ○ *There is little probability of the work being finished on time.* ○ *The probability is that there will be no outright winner.* ◇ **in all probability** very probably ○ *In all probability they will get married at Easter.*

probable /'prɒbəb(ə)l/ *adj* likely ○ *It's probable that the ship sank in a storm.*

① **probably** /'prɒbəbli/ *adv* used for saying that something is likely to happen ○ *We're probably going to Spain for our holidays.* ○ *My father is probably going to retire next year.* ○ *Are you going to Spain as usual this year? – Very probably.*

③ **probation** /prə'beɪʃ(ə)n/ *noun* **1.** a legal system for dealing with criminals where they are not sent to prison provided that they continue to behave well under the supervision of a probation officer ○ *She was put on probation for one year* or *was put on one year's probation.* **2.** a period when a new employee is being tested before being given a permanent job □ **on probation** being tested ○ *We are employing him on three months' probation.* ○ *She can't have a pay rise as she is still on probation.*

probationary /prəˈbeɪʃ(ə)n(ə)ri/ *adj* referring to a time when a person is on probation

probation officer /prəˈbeɪʃ(ə)n ˌɒfɪsə/ *noun* an official of the social services who supervises young people on probation

③ **probe** /prəʊb/ *noun* a thorough investigation [~into] ○ *a police probe into organised crime* ■ *verb* (**probes, probing, probed**) to examine something deeply [~into] ○ *I don't want the police to start probing into my financial affairs.* ○ *The surgeon probed the wound to try to find the bullet.*

① **problem** /ˈprɒbləm/ *noun* **1.** something or someone that causes difficulty ○ *We're having problems with the new computer system.* □ **to pose a problem** to be something that is difficult to change or improve ○ *What to do with truants poses a problem for the schools.* □ **to solve a problem** to find an answer to a problem ○ *The police are trying to solve the problem of how the thieves got into the house.* ○ *We have called in an expert to solve our computer problem.* **2.** a question in a test, especially in mathematics ○ *Most of the students could do all the problems in the maths test.* ◇ **no problem** used for giving an informal agreement to a request

② **procedure** /prəˈsiːdʒə/ *noun* **1.** the way in which something ought to be carried out ○ *To obtain permission to build a new house you need to follow the correct procedure.* **2.** a medical treatment ○ *a new procedure for treating burns*

③ **proceed** /prəˈsiːd/ (**proceeds, proceeding, proceeded**) *verb* **1.** to go further ○ *He proceeded down the High Street towards the river.* **2.** to do something after something else [~with] ○ *The students then proceeded to shout and throw bottles at passing cars.*

② **proceedings** /prəˈsiːdɪŋz/ *plural noun* a report of what takes place at a meeting ○ *the proceedings of the Archaeological Society*

③ **proceeds** /ˈprəʊsiːdz/ *plural noun* money which you receive when you sell something ○ *She sold her house and invested the proceeds in a little shop.* ○ *All the proceeds of the village fair go to charity.*

① **process**[1] /prəʊˈses/ *noun* **1.** the method of making something ○ *a new process for extracting oil from coal* **2.** □ **in the process of doing something** while doing something ○ *She interrupted me while I was in the process of writing my report.* ○ *We were in the process of moving to London when I had the offer of a job in Australia.* ■ *verb* (**processes, processing, processed**) **1.** to make goods from raw materials ○ *The uranium has to be processed before it can be used in a nuclear reactor.* **2.** to deal with a claim or bill in the usual way ○ *to process an insurance claim* ○ *Orders are processed in our warehouse.*

process[2] /prəʊˈses/ (**processes, processing, processed**) *verb* to walk in a procession ○ *The peers and peeresses processed into Westminster Abbey.*

procession /prəˈseʃ(ə)n/ *noun* a group of people walking in line, sometimes with music playing □ **in procession** in a line as part of a ceremony ○ *The people who have received their degrees will walk in procession through the university grounds.*

processor /ˈprəʊsesə/ *noun* **1.** a machine that processes ○ *Mix the ingredients in a food processor.* **2.** a computer which processes information

③ **proclaim** /prəˈkleɪm/ (**proclaims, proclaiming, proclaimed**) *verb* to make an official statement in public

proclamation /ˌprɒkləˈmeɪʃ(ə)n/ *noun* an official public statement

procrastinate /prəʊˈkræstɪneɪt/ (**procrastinates, procrastinating, procrastinated**) *verb* to delay, to postpone something until later

procure /prəˈkjʊə/ (**procures, procuring, procured**) *verb* (*formal*) **1.** to obtain something ○ *Somehow he had managed to procure the equipment he needed without anyone knowing.* ○ *We need to procure a map of the area.* **2.** to arrange for a woman to provide sexual intercourse for money

prod /prɒd/ (**prods, prodding, prodded**) *verb* **1.** to poke somebody or something with a finger or stick ○ *He prodded the pig with his stick.* **2.** □ **to prod someone into doing something** to do something to persuade someone to take action ○ *The group tried to prod the government into action* or *into taking some sort of action.*

prodigy /ˈprɒdɪdʒi/ *noun* a remarkable person, usually a young person ○ *By the age of ten he was already a mathematical prodigy.*

produce[1] /prə'djuːs/ (**produces, producing, produced**) *verb* **1.** to show something or bring something out of e.g. your pocket ○ *The tax office asked him to produce the relevant documents.* ○ *He produced a bundle of notes from his inside pocket.* ○ *The factory produces cars and trucks.* **2.** to organise a play or film ○ *She is producing 'Hamlet' for the local drama club.* **3.** to make something, especially in a factory ○ *The factory produces cars and trucks.* **4.** to give birth to young ○ *Our cat has produced six kittens.* **5.** to grow crops ○ *The region produces enough rice to supply the needs of the whole country.*

produce[2] /'prɒdjuːs/ *noun* things that have been grown in a garden or on a farm ○ *vegetables and other garden produce* (NOTE: Do not confuse with **product**.)

③ **producer** /prə'djuːsə/ *noun* a company or country which makes or grows something ○ *an important producer of steel* ○ *The company is a major car producer.*

① **product** /'prɒdʌkt/ *noun* **1.** a thing which is manufactured ○ *The government is helping industry to sell more products abroad.* (NOTE: Do not confuse with **produce**.) **2.** something that happens or exists as a result of something else [~of] **3.** (*in mathematics*) a number which is the result when numbers are multiplied ○ *The product of 4 times 10 is 40.*

① **production** /prə'dʌkʃən/ *noun* **1.** the making of something ○ *We are trying to step up production.* ○ *Production will probably be held up by the strike.* **2.** putting on a play or film ○ *The film is currently in production at Teddington Studios.*

production line /prə'dʌkʃən laɪn/ *noun* a system of making a product, where each item such as a car moves slowly through the factory with new sections being added to it as it goes along

productive /prə'dʌktɪv/ *adj* which produces results

productivity /ˌprɒdʌk'tɪvɪti/ *noun* the rate of output, rate of production in a factory

Prof *abbr* professor ○ *Prof Stanley Ridge*

profess /prə'fes/ (**professes, professing, professed**) *verb* to declare something

③ **profession** /prə'feʃ(ə)n/ *noun* work which needs special training, skill or knowledge ○ *the legal profession* ○ *the medical profession* ○ *the teaching profession* ○ *She is an accountant by profession.*

① **professional** /prə'feʃ(ə)n(ə)l/ *adj* **1.** relating to a profession ○ *He keeps his professional life and his private life completely separate.* **2.** expert or skilled ○ *They did a very professional job in designing the new office.* **3.** (*of sportsmen*) who is paid to play ○ *a professional footballer* ■ *noun* an expert ○ *Don't try to deal with the problem yourself – get a professional in.*

professionalism /prə'feʃ(ə)nəlɪz(ə)m/ *noun* being an expert, having skill ○ *People admired the professionalism with which he dealt with the problem.*

professor /prə'fesə/ *noun* **1.** the most senior teacher in a particular subject at a university ○ *a professor of English* ○ *an economics professor* **2.** the title taken by some teachers of music and art ○ *She goes to Professor Smith for piano lessons.* (NOTE: used as a title before a name: *Professor Smith*.)

proffer /'prɒfə/ (**proffers, proffering, proffered**) *verb* to offer something

proficiency /prə'fɪʃ(ə)nsi/ *noun* a skill in doing something

proficient /prə'fɪʃ(ə)nt/ *adj* able to do something very well [~at/in] ○ *I'm not very proficient at mental arithmetic.* ○ *By the summer I had become reasonably proficient in German.*

③ **profile** /'prəʊfaɪl/ *noun* **1.** a view of someone's head, seen from the side ○ *a photograph showing her in profile* **2.** □ **to keep *or* maintain a low profile** to be quiet, not to be obvious ○ *It would be better if you kept a low profile until all the fuss has died down.* □ **to keep *or* maintain a high profile** to keep yourself in the view of the public ○ *A politician needs to keep a high profile.* ○ *Advertising helps to maintain the company's high profile.* **3.** a short biography of a famous person in a newspaper ○ *There's a profile of the Chancellor in the Sunday paper.*

① **profit** /'prɒfɪt/ *noun* money you gain from selling something which is more than the money you paid for it [~from/~on] ○ *All the profits from the sale of her paintings go to charity.* ○ *We're unlikely to make a profit on the house.* ○ *The sale produced a good profit* or *a handsome profit.* □ **to make a profit** to have more money as a result of a deal ○ *We aim to make a quick profit.* ○ *We made a large profit when we sold our house.* ○ *It you don't make a profit you will soon be out of business.* ■ *verb* (**profits, profiting, profited**) to produce a benefit [~from] (*formal*) ○ *These measures will profit the business in the longer term.*

profit from *phrasal verb* to gain from something [~from] ○ *We have profited from his knowledge and experience.*

profitable /'prɒfɪtəb(ə)l/ *adj* likely to produce a profit

profound /prə'faʊnd/ *adj* very serious, very deep

profuse /prə'fjuːs/ *adj* abundant, excessive

profusion /prə'fjuːʒ(ə)n/ *noun* a very large quantity □ **in profusion** in large quantities ○ *There are wild flowers in profusion in the countryside in early summer.*

prognosis /prɒg'nəʊsɪs/ (*plural* **prognoses**) *noun* an opinion of how something, such as a disease, will develop

① **program** /'prəʊgræm/ *noun* instructions given to a computer ○ *to load a program* ○ *to run a program* ○ *a graphics program* ○ *a word-processing program* ■ *verb* (**programs, programming, programmed**) to give instructions to a computer ○ *They can program the computer to produce those results for you.*

① **programme** /'prəʊgræm/ *noun* **1.** a TV or radio show [~on] ○ *We watched a programme on life in the 17th century.* ○ *There's a football programme on after the news.* ○ *I want to listen to the phone-in programme at 9.15.* ○ *There are no good television programmes tonight.* ○ *The programme gives a list of the actors.* **2.** a paper in a theatre or at a sports event, which gives information about the show ■ *verb* (**programmes, programming, programmed**) to arrange programmes on TV or radio ○ *The new chat show is programmed to compete with the gardening programme on the other channel.*

③ **programmer** /'prəʊgræmə/ *noun* **1.** a person who programs a computer ○ *The programmers made a few alterations to our software.* **2.** a person who programmes TV or radio shows ○ *Programmers are always trying to win audiences from other channels.*

programming /'prəʊgræmɪŋ/ *noun* the process of creating computer programs

progress¹ /'prəʊgres/ *noun* a movement forwards ○ *The traffic is still making pretty slow progress.* (NOTE: no plural) ◇ **in progress** which is happening or being done ○ *The meeting is still in progress.* ○ *We still have a lot of work in progress.*

progress² /prəʊ'gres/ (**progresses, progressing, progressed**) *verb* to advance ○ *Work on the new road is progressing slowly.*

③ **progression** /prəʊ'greʃ(ə)n/ *noun* a slow change to a better or later stage

progressive /prə'gresɪv/ *adj* **1.** (*of movement*) in stages ○ *I have noticed a progressive improvement in your work.* **2.** (*of ideas*) advanced ○ *They elected a leader with progressive views on education.*

prohibit /prəʊ'hɪbɪt/ (**prohibits, prohibiting, prohibited**) *verb* to say that something must not be done (NOTE: + **prohibition** *n*)

prohibitive /prəʊ'hɪbɪtɪv/ *adj* so expensive that you cannot afford it

project¹ /'prɒdʒekt/ *noun* work planned by students on their own ○ *She asked her teacher for some pointers to help her with her project.*

project² /prə'dʒekt/ (**projects, projecting, projected**) *verb* to send a picture onto a screen ○ *The lecturer projected slides of his visit to the Arctic.*

projectile /prə'dʒektaɪl/ *noun* a thing which is thrown, or fired from a gun

③ **projection** /prə'dʒekʃən/ *noun* **1.** a calculation of something which is forecast for the future ○ *We have made a projection of the additional housing needed in this area by the year 2010.* ○ *Computer projections forecast an easy win for the government.* **2.** a thing which sticks out ○ *She gashed her arm on a sharp projection of rock.* **3.** the action of projecting a picture onto a screen

projector /prə'dʒektə/ *noun* a machine which sends pictures onto a screen

proliferate /prə'lɪfəreɪt/ (**proliferates, proliferating, proliferated**) *verb* to increase quickly in number (*formal*)

proliferation /prəˌlɪfə'reɪʃ(ə)n/ *noun* a rapid spread

prolific /prə'lɪfɪk/ *adj* **1.** producing many children, fruit or other offspring ○ *Rabbits are notoriously prolific.* **2.** producing a lot of something ○ *He's a prolific writer of travel guides.*

prologue /'prəʊlɒg/ *noun* **1.** a piece spoken as the introduction of a play or poem ○ *The prologue sets the scene and introduces the main characters.* Compare **epilogue 2.** a preliminary event that leads on to something else ○ *The discussions between Foreign Ministers are a prologue to the signing of a full-scale treaty.* (NOTE: [all senses] The US spelling is **prolog**.)

prolong /prə'lɒŋ/ (**prolongs, prolonging, prolonged**) *verb* to make something longer

prolonged /prə'lɒŋd/ *adj* lasting for a long time

prom /prɒm/ *noun* **1.** a promenade ○ *Let's go for a stroll along the prom.* **2.** *US* a school dance ○ *They met at the High School prom.*

promenade /ˌprɒmə'nɑːd/ *noun* a walkway built along the side of the sea ○ *We stood on the promenade and looked out to sea.* ○ *Our hotel was right on the promenade.*

prominence /'prɒmɪnəns/ *noun* **1.** being important or famous ○ *He first rose to prominence in the 1960s.* **2.** □ **to give prominence to sth** to emphasise something ○ *The newspapers gave too much prominence to that part of the speech.*

prominent /'prɒmɪnənt/ *adj* **1.** standing out, easily seen ○ *She has a very prominent nose.* **2.** famous or important ○ *a prominent trade union leader* ○ *They assassinated a prominent member of the ruling party.*

promiscuous /prə'mɪskjuəs/ *adj* who has sexual relations with many people

② **promise** /'prɒmɪs/ *noun* the act of saying that you will definitely do something [~to] ○ *my promise to the children to play with them later* ○ *But you made a promise not to tell anyone else and now you've told my mother!* ○ *I'll pay you back on Friday – that's a promise.* □ **to go back on a promise, to break a promise** not to do what you said you would do ○ *The management went back on its promise to increase salaries.* ○ *He broke his promise to take her to Mexico on holiday.* □ **to keep a promise** to do what you said you would do ○ *He says he will pay next week, but he never keeps his promises.* ○ *She kept her promise to write to him every day.* ■ *verb* (**promises, promising, promised**) to give your word that you will definitely do something ○ *They promised to be back for supper.* ○ *You must promise to bring the computer back when you have finished with it.* ○ *He promised he would look into the problem.* ○ *She promised the staff an extra week's holiday but it never materialised.*

② **promising** /'prɒmɪsɪŋ/ *adj* **1.** who is likely to succeed ○ *She's the most promising candidate we have interviewed so far.* **2.** good, and likely to become much better ○ *The results of the antibiotic have been very promising.* ○ *The economic situation looks much more promising than it did a year ago.*

promontory /'prɒmənt(ə)ri/ (*plural* **promontories**) *noun* a piece of high land jutting out into the sea

② **promote** /prə'məʊt/ (**promotes, promoting, promoted**) *verb* **1.** to give someone a better job ○ *He was promoted from salesman to sales manager.* **2.** to make sure that people know about a product or service, by advertising it ○ *There are posters all over the place promoting the new night club.* **3.** to encourage something ○ *The club's aim is to promote gardening.*

③ **promotion** /prə'məʊʃ(ə)n/ *noun* **1.** a move to a better job ○ *He ruined his chances of promotion when he argued with the boss.* **2.** advertising of a new product ○ *We're giving away small bottles of shampoo as a promotion.*

promotional /prə'məʊʃ(ə)n(ə)l/ *adj* used in an advertising campaign

prompt /prɒmpt/ *adj* done immediately ○ *Thank you for your prompt reply.* ■ *verb* (**prompts, prompting, prompted**) to tell an actor words which he or she has forgotten ○ *He had to be prompted in the middle of a long speech.*

③ **promptly** /'prɒmptli/ *adv* very soon after an event, in a way that is helpful or efficient

prone /prəʊn/ *adj* **1.** likely to do something, or likely to be affected by something such as an illness [~to] ○ *When you're tired you are prone to make mistakes.* ○ *He's prone to chest infections.* ○ *My brother is really accident-prone!* **2.** lying flat ○ *They found her lying prone on the floor.*

prong /prɒŋ/ *noun* one of the sharp points of a fork

③ **pronoun** /'prəʊnaʊn/ *noun* a word used instead of a noun, such as 'I', 'you', 'he', 'she' and 'it'

pronounce /prə'naʊns/ (**pronounces, pronouncing, pronounced**) *verb* **1.** to speak sounds, especially in a particular way ○ *How do you pronounce 'Paris' in French?* **2.** to state something officially ○ *He was pronounced dead on arrival at hospital.* ○ *The priest pronounced them man and wife.*

pronounced /prə'naʊnst/ *adj* noticeable

pronouncement /prə'naʊnsmənt/ *noun* an official or formal statement

pronunciation /prəˌnʌnsi'eɪʃ(ə)n/ *noun* a way of saying words ○ *What's the correct pronunciation of 'controversy'?* ○ *You should try to improve your pronuncia-*

tion by taking lessons from native speakers.

② **proof** /pruːf/ *noun* a thing which proves or which shows that something is true [~that/~of] ○ *The police have no proof that he committed the murder.There's no real proof of his guilt.*

-proof /pruːf/ *suffix* which prevents something getting in, getting out or harming ○ *a soundproof studio*

proofread /ˈpruːfriːd/ (**proofreads, proofreading, proofread**) *verb* to read proofs and make corrections to them

prop /prɒp/ *noun* a support or stick which holds something up ○ *I used a piece of wood as a prop to keep the window open.*

propaganda /ˌprɒpəˈgændə/ *noun* the spreading of false or biased information about something which you want the public to believe

propagate /ˈprɒpəgeɪt/ (**propagates, propagating, propagated**) *verb* **1.** to produce new plants ○ *I tried to propagate the plants by taking cuttings.* **2.** to spread ideas ○ *It's a view being propagated by certain sections of the press.* (NOTE: + **propagation** *n*)

propel /prəˈpel/ (**propels, propelling, propelled**) *verb* to push something forward

propensity /prəˈpensɪti/ *noun* a tendency to do something

① **proper** /ˈprɒpə/ *adj* right and correct; in the way that things are normally done ○ *She didn't put the sugar back into its proper place in the cupboard.* ○ *This is the proper way to use a knife and fork.* ○ *The parcel wasn't delivered because it didn't have the proper address.*

① **properly** /ˈprɒpəli/ *adv* correctly ○ *The accident happened because the garage hadn't fitted the wheel properly.* ○ *The parcel wasn't properly addressed.*

③ **proper noun** /ˌprɒpə ˈnaʊn/, **proper name** *noun* a word which is the name of a place, a person, a building or a title, etc

① **property** /ˈprɒpəti/ *noun* **1.** something that belongs to a particular person ○ *The furniture is the property of the landlord.* ○ *The hotel guests lost all their property in the fire.* ○ *The management is not responsible for property left in the restaurant.* **2.** buildings and land ○ *The family owns property in West London.* ○ *A lot of industrial property was damaged in the war.* (NOTE: [all senses] no plural)

prophecy /ˈprɒfəsi/ *noun* **1.** the practice of saying what will happen in the future ○ *He had the gift of prophecy.* **2.** a thing which you say will happen in the future ○ *None of his gloomy prophecies has come true.* ○ *She made a prophecy that they would be married within a month.*

prophesy /ˈprɒfəsaɪ/ (**prophesies, prophesying, prophesied**) *verb* to say what will happen in the future

prophet /ˈprɒfɪt/ *noun* **1.** a person who says what will happen in the future **2.** a great religious leader

prophetic /prəˈfetɪk/ *adj* which says what will happen in the future

proponent /prəˈpəʊnənt/ *noun* a person who supports something

② **proportion** /prəˈpɔːʃ(ə)n/ *noun* a part of a whole ○ *Only a small proportion of his income comes from his TV appearances.*

proportional /prəˈpɔːʃ(ə)n(ə)l/ *adj* which is directly related to something ○ *The amount you get in interest is proportional to the amount invested.*

① **proposal** /prəˈpəʊz(ə)l/ *noun* a plan which has been suggested [~for] ○ *proposals for changes to the rules* ○ *The committee made a proposal to rebuild the clubhouse.* ○ *His proposal was accepted by the committee.* ○ *She put forward a proposal but it was rejected.*

① **propose** /prəˈpəʊz/ (**proposes, proposing, proposed**) *verb* to make a suggestion [~that] ○ *I propose that we all go for a swim.*

proposition /ˌprɒpəˈzɪʃ(ə)n/ *noun* a thing which has been proposed ○ *We discussed the proposition that all people are equal.The proposition is not very attractive.*

proprietor /prəˈpraɪətə/ *noun* an owner

propriety /prəˈpraɪəti/ *noun* correct behaviour in society

propulsion /prəˈpʌlʃən/ *noun* the force of moving something forward

prosaic /prəʊˈzeɪɪk/ *adj* ordinary and rather dull, not poetic or imaginative or romantic

prose /prəʊz/ *noun* something written in ordinary language, not poetry

prosecute /ˈprɒsɪkjuːt/ (**prosecutes, prosecuting, prosecuted**) *verb* to bring someone to court to answer a criminal charge ○ *People found stealing from the shop will be prosecuted.*

③ **prosecution** /ˌprɒsɪˈkjuːʃ(ə)n/ *noun* **1.** the process of bringing someone to court to answer a criminal charge [~for] ○ *He faces prosecution for fraud.* **2.** the lawyers who represent the party who brings a charge against someone ○ *The costs of the case will be borne by the prosecution.* ○ *The prosecution argued that the money had been stolen.*

prospect /'prɒspekt/ *noun* a future possibility ○ *There is no prospect of getting her to change her mind.* ○ *What are the prospects for peace in the region?* ■ *plural noun* **prospects** future opportunities, especially in your work ○ *His job prospects are very good.* ○ *What are our prospects of success in this business deal?*

prospective /prə'spektɪv/ *adj* who or which may do something in the future

prospectus /prə'spektəs/ *noun* a document which gives information to attract customers

prosper /'prɒspə/ (**prospers, prospering, prospered**) *verb* to succeed; to become rich

prosperity /prɒ'sperɪti/ *noun* being rich and successful

prosperous /'prɒsp(ə)rəs/ *adj* wealthy, rich

prostitute /'prɒstɪtjuːt/ *noun* a woman who receives money for sexual intercourse

prostitution /ˌprɒstɪ'tjuːʃ(ə)n/ *noun* the practice of providing sexual intercourse in return for payment

prostrate /'prɒstreɪt/ *adj* lying flat on your face ○ *He was lying prostrate on the floor.* (NOTE: Do not confuse with **prostate**.)

protagonist /prəʊ'tægənɪst/ *noun* the main character in a story ○ *The protagonist is a Danish prince.*

② **protect** /prə'tekt/ (**protects, protecting, protected**) *verb* to keep someone or something safe from harm or danger [~against/~from] ○ *The cover protects the machine from dust.* ○ *The injection is supposed to protect you against the disease.*

protected /prə'tektɪd/ *adj* (*of species of animals or plants*) classified as being in danger of extinction

② **protection** /prə'tekʃən/ *noun* shelter, the process of being protected [~from/~against] ○ *The trees give some protection from the rain.* ○ *The injection gives some protection against cholera.* ○ *The legislation offers no protection to temporary workers.*

③ **protective** /prə'tektɪv/ *adj* who or which protects

protégé /'prɒtəʒeɪ/ *noun* a person, usually a young person, who is supported in artistic work with money or advice, by someone else

② **protein** /'prəʊtiːn/ *noun* a substance in food such as meat, eggs and nuts which is one of the elements in food which you need to keep your body working properly

protest[1] /'prəʊtest/ *noun* a statement that you object or disapprove of something ○ *She resigned as a protest against the change in government policy.* ○ *The new road went ahead despite the protests of the local inhabitants.* □ **in protest at** showing that you do not approve of something ○ *The staff occupied the offices in protest at their low pay.*

protest[2] /prə'test/ (**protests, protesting, protested**) *verb* **1.** to say or show that you do not approve of something [~against/at] ○ *Some of the workers are protesting against poor working conditions.* ○ *After being stuck in the train for twenty minutes, the passengers began to protest.* **2.** to insist that something is true, when others think it isn't ○ *She went to prison still protesting her innocence.*

③ **Protestant** /'prɒtɪstənt/ *noun* a member of a Christian Church which separated from the Catholic Church at the time of the Reformation

protestation /ˌprɒtɪ'steɪʃ(ə)n/ *noun* a strong or firm statement that something is true

protester /prə'testə/, **protestor** *noun* a person who protests in a public way about something they don't agree with ○ *Several protesters stood outside the bank's offices handing out leaflets.*

protocol /'prəʊtəkɒl/ *noun* correct diplomatic behaviour ○ *Diplomatic protocol dictates which ambassador sits next to the Queen.*

prototype /'prəʊtətaɪp/ *noun* the first model of a new machine

protracted /prə'træktɪd/ *adj* very lengthy

protrude /prə'truːd/ (**protrudes, protruding, protruded**) *verb* to stick out

protrusion /prə'truːʒ(ə)n/ *noun* something which protrudes

② **proud** /praʊd/ *adj* showing pleasure in what you or someone else has done or in something which belongs to you ○ *We're proud of the fact we did it all without help from anyone else.*

proudly /'praʊdli/ *adv* showing that you are proud of something

① **prove** /pruːv/ (**proves, proving, proved** or **proven**) *verb* to show that something is true [~(that)] ○ *The experiment proves that light travels in a straight line.* ○

The police think he stole the car but they can't prove it. ○ *I was determined to prove him wrong* or *that he was wrong.* ◊ **proof**

proven /'pruːv(ə)n/ *adj* tested and shown to be correct

proverb /'prɒvɜːb/ *noun* a saying which teaches you something

① **provide** /prə'vaɪd/ (**provides, providing, provided**) *verb* to supply [~for] ○ *We provide free travel for all our members.* ○ *Medical help was provided by the Red Cross.* ○ *Our hosts provided us with a car and driver.*

provided (that) /prə'vaɪdɪd ðæt/, **providing** /prə'vaɪdɪŋ/ *conj* on condition that; as long as, so long as ○ *It's nice to go on a picnic provided it doesn't rain.* ○ *You can all come to watch the rehearsal providing you don't interrupt.*

providence /'prɒvɪd(ə)ns/ *noun* a lucky force which protects you (*literary*)

provider /prə'vaɪdə/ *noun* a person who provides material support for someone or something, especially a family

② **province** /'prɒvɪns/ *noun* **1.** a large administrative division of a country ○ *the provinces of Canada* **2.** an area of knowledge or of responsibility ○ *That's not my province – you'll have to ask the finance manager.*

provision /prə'vɪʒ(ə)n/ *noun* **1.** the act of providing something □ **to make provision for** to see that something is allowed for in the future ○ *We've made provision for the computer network to be expanded.* ○ *There is no provision for* or *no provision has been made for car parking in the plans for the office block.* **2.** a condition in a contract

③ **provisional** /prə'vɪʒ(ə)n(ə)l/ *adj* temporary ○ *A provisional government was set up by the army.*

proviso /prə'vaɪzəʊ/ (*plural* **provisos** or **provisoes**) *noun* a condition

provocation /ˌprɒvə'keɪʃ(ə)n/ *noun* the action of making someone annoyed

provocative /prə'vɒkətɪv/ *adj* **1.** likely to make someone annoyed ○ *His provocative remarks did not go down well with the management.* **2.** likely to make someone sexually excited ○ *In some countries it is considered provocative for women to wear short skirts.*

provoke /prə'vəʊk/ (**provokes, provoking, provoked**) *verb* **1.** to make someone angry ○ *She provoked him into throwing a brick through her front window.* **2.** to make a reaction take place ○ *His reply provoked an angry response from the crowd.*

prow /praʊ/ *noun* the front end of a boat

prowess /'praʊes/ *noun* great skill

prowl /praʊl/ *verb* (**prowls, prowling, prowled**) to move about quietly ○ *She thinks she saw someone prowling about in the undergrowth.* ○ *The police are on the lookout for looters prowling around the deserted town.* ■ *noun* □ **on the prowl** moving quietly looking for something ○ *a tiger on the prowl in the jungle*

prowler /'praʊlə/ *noun* a person who moves about an area looking for an opportunity to commit a criminal act

proximity /prɒk'sɪmɪti/ *noun* the fact of being close to something

proxy /'prɒksi/ (*plural* **proxies**) *noun* **1.** a document which gives someone the power to act on behalf of someone else ○ *If you are away from home on voting day, you can cast your vote by proxy.* **2.** a person who acts on behalf of someone else ○ *to act as a proxy for someone*

prude /pruːd/ *noun* a prudish person

prudent /'pruːdənt/ *adj* showing good sense and using good judgement ○ *It would be prudent to consult a lawyer before you sign the contract.*

prune /pruːn/ (**prunes, pruning, pruned**) *verb* **1.** to cut back a tree or shrub, to keep it in good shape ○ *That bush is blocking the window – it needs pruning.* **2.** to reduce the size of something such as expenditure or parts of a book ○ *We had to prune about half the text.*

pry /praɪ/ (**pries, prying, pried**) *verb* **1.** to look inquisitively into something [~into] ○ *She accused the press of prying into her private life.* **2.** □ **to pry something open** *or* **apart** *US* to use force to open or split something ○ *He pried the lid open.*

PS /ˌpiː 'es/ *noun* an additional note at the end of a letter ○ *Did you read the PS at the end of the letter?* Full form **post scriptum**

psalm /sɑːm/, **Psalm** *noun* a religious poem or song from the Bible

pseudonym /'sjuːdənɪm/ *noun* a false or invented name used by an author

psyche /'saɪki/ *noun* the subconscious mind

psychiatrist /saɪ'kaɪətrɪst/ *noun* a person who studies and treats mental disease

psychiatry /saɪ'kaɪətri/ *noun* the study of mental disease

psychic /'saɪkɪk/ *adj* referring to supernatural forces ○ *He spends his time investi-*

gating reports of psychic phenomena. ○ *She must be psychic if she can tell the result of the lottery in advance.*

psychoanalysis /ˌsaɪkəʊə'næləsɪs/ *noun* a treatment of mental disorder where a specialist talks to patients and analyses their condition

psychoanalyst /ˌsaɪkəʊ'æn(ə)lɪst/ *noun* a doctor who is trained in psychoanalysis (NOTE: also shortened to **analyst**)

③ **psychologist** /saɪ'kɒlədʒɪst/ *noun* a person who studies the human mind

③ **psychology** /saɪ'kɒlədʒi/ *noun* the study of the human mind ○ *the psychology department in the university* ○ *She's taking a psychology course.*

psychopath /'saɪkəpæθ/ *noun* a criminal who is dangerous and mentally unstable

psychosis /saɪ'kəʊsɪs/ (*plural* **psychoses**) *noun* any serious mental disorder in which someone can no longer tell what is real

psychosomatic /ˌsaɪkəʊsə'mætɪk/ *adj* describing a physical illness that is caused by a mental problem

psychotherapy /ˌsaɪkəʊ'θerəpi/ *noun* a treatment of mental disorders by psychological methods, as when a psychotherapist talks to patients and encourages them to talk about their problems (NOTE: ı **psychotherapist** *n*)

psychotic /saɪ'kɒtɪk/ *adj* referring to or experiencing psychosis

③ **pt** *abbr* pint

③ **PTO** *interj* 'please turn over', letters written at the bottom of a page, showing that there is something written on the other side

② **pub** /pʌb/ *noun* a place where you can buy beer and other alcoholic drinks, and sometimes meals ○ *I happened to meet him at the pub.* ○ *We had a sandwich and some beer in the pub.*

puberty /'pju:bəti/ *noun* the time of life when childhood ends and adolescence and sexual maturity begin

pubic /'pju:bɪk/ *adj* referring to the area around the sexual organs

① **public** /'pʌblɪk/ *adj* relating to the people in general ○ *The crown jewels are on public display in the Tower of London.* ○ *It's in the public interest that the facts should be known.* ■ *noun* people in general ○ *The public have the right to know what is going on.*

public-address system /ˌpʌblɪk ə 'dres/ *noun* full form of **PA**

publican /'pʌblɪkən/ *noun* a person who manages a pub

② **publication** /ˌpʌblɪ'keɪʃ(ə)n/ *noun* **1.** the process of making something public ○ *The publication of the official figures has been delayed.* **2.** a book or newspaper which has been published ○ *He asked the library for a list of gardening publications.*

public figure /ˌpʌblɪk 'fɪgə/ *noun* a well-known person such as an actor or politician

③ **public holiday** /ˌpʌblɪk 'hɒlɪdeɪ/ *noun* a day when most businesses and banks are closed

publicise /'pʌblɪsaɪz/ (**publicises, publicising, publicised**), **publicize** *verb* to attract people's attention to something; to make publicity for something

publicist /'pʌblɪsɪst/ *noun* a person who attracts people's attention to something through advertising

② **publicity** /pʌ'blɪsɪti/ *noun* advertising which attracts people's attention to something ○ *We're trying to get publicity for our school play.* ○ *The failure of the show was blamed on bad publicity.*

publicly /'pʌblɪkli/ *adv* in public ○ *The Prime Minister publicly denied the accusations.*

public school /ˌpʌblɪk 'sku:l/ *noun* **1.** (*in Britain*) a private fee-paying secondary school which is not part of the state education system ○ *Eton and Winchester are two famous British public schools.* Compare **private school**, **state school** **2.** (*in the USA*) a school which is paid for by public taxes ○ *The state has decided to spend more money on its public school system.*

public sector /'pʌblɪk ˌsektə/ *noun* the nationalised industries and the civil service

public service /'pʌblɪk 'sɜ:vɪs/ *noun* **1.** the practice of working for the state **2.** all government agencies and their personnel ○ *He's hoping for a job in the public service.*

③ **public transport** /ˌpʌblɪk 'trænspɔ:t/ *noun* transport such as buses and trains which can be used by everyone

① **publish** /'pʌblɪʃ/ (**publishes, publishing, published**) *verb* **1.** to bring out a book or newspaper for sale ○ *The company publishes six magazines for the business market.* ○ *We publish dictionaries for students.* **2.** to make something publicly known ○ *The government has not published the figures yet.*

③ **publisher** /'pʌblɪʃə/ *noun* a person or company that produces books or newspapers for sale

③ **publishing** /'pʌblɪʃɪŋ/ *noun* the process of producing books or newspapers for sale

③ **pudding** /'pʊdɪŋ/ *noun* **1.** a sweet dish at the end of the meal ○ *I'll have ice cream for my pudding.* **2.** a sweet cooked food

puddle /'pʌd(ə)l/ *noun* a small pool of water, e.g. on the ground after it has rained

puff /pʌf/ *noun* a small breath of air or smoke ○ *He took a puff on his cigarette.* ○ *Little puffs of smoke came out of the chimney.* ■ *verb* (**puffs, puffing, puffed**) **1.** to blow ○ *White smoke was puffing out of the engine.* ○ *He sat in a corner, puffing on his pipe.* **2.** to breathe with difficulty ○ *He was puffing and panting and he'd only run fifty yards.*

puffy /'pʌfi/ *adj* swollen

pugnacious /pʌg'neɪʃəs/ *adj* ready to argue or fight

puke /pjuːk/ (**pukes, puking, puked**), **puke up** *verb also* **puke up** to bring up partly digested food into your mouth (*informal*) ○ *The baby puked all over the carpet.* □ **to make someone (want to) puke** to make someone feel angry and upset ○ *All these stories about lottery millionaires make me puke.*

① **pull** /pʊl/ (**pulls, pulling, pulled**) *verb* to move something towards you or after you ○ *Pull the door to open it, don't push it.* ○ *The truck was pulling a trailer.* ○ *She pulled an envelope out of her bag.*

pull down① *phrasal verb* to knock down a building

pull off① *phrasal verb* **1.** to take off a piece of clothing by pulling ○ *He sat down and pulled off his dirty boots.* **2.** to succeed in doing something very good, especially if it is unexpected ○ *The deal will be great for the company, if we can pull it off.* **3.** to drive off a road and stop ○ *He pulled off the road and lit a cigarette.*

pull out① *phrasal verb* **1.** to take something out by pulling ○ *They used a rope to pull the car out of the river.* **2.** to drive a car away from the side of the road ○ *He forgot to signal as he was pulling out.* ○ *Don't pull out into the main road until you can see that there is nothing coming.* **3.** to stop being part of a deal or agreement ○ *Our Australian partners pulled out at the last moment.*

pull over① *phrasal verb* to drive a car towards the side of the road and stop ○ *The police car signalled to him to pull over.*

pull together① *phrasal verb* **1.** to work with someone else to achieve something **2.** □ **to pull yourself together** to become more calm ○ *Although he was shocked by the news he soon pulled himself together.*

pull up① *phrasal verb* **1.** to bring something closer ○ *Pull your chair up to the window.* **2.** (*of a vehicle*) to stop ○ *A car pulled up and the driver asked me if I wanted a lift.* ○ *He didn't manage to pull up in time and ran into the back of the car in front.*

pull-down menu /'pʊl daʊn ˌmenjuː/ *noun* a menu which appears as a list on part of a computer screen

pulley /'pʊli/ *noun* apparatus for lifting heavy weights with a rope that runs round several wheels

① **pullover** /'pʊləʊvə/ *noun* a piece of clothing made of wool, which covers the top part of your body

pulmonary /'pʌlmən(ə)ri/ *adj* referring to the lungs

pulp /pʌlp/ *noun* a squashy mass ○ *Cook the apples to a pulp.* ○ *If you don't do as I say I'll beat you to a pulp.*

pulpit /'pʊlpɪt/ *noun* the raised platform in a church where the priest preaches

pulsate /pʌl'seɪt/ (**pulsates, pulsating, pulsated**) *verb* to throb regularly

③ **pulse** /pʌls/ *noun* a regular beat of your heart ○ *The doctor took his pulse.* ○ *Her pulse is very weak.*

pulverise /'pʌlvəraɪz/ (**pulverises, pulverising, pulverised**), **pulverize** *verb* to crush something to powder

pummel /'pʌm(ə)l/ (**pummels, pummelling, pummelled**) *verb* to hit something hard repeatedly

③ **pump** /pʌmp/ *noun* a machine for forcing liquids or air into something ○ *a bicycle pump* ■ *verb* (**pumps, pumping, pumped**) to force in something such as liquid or air with a pump ○ *Your back tyre needs pumping up.* ○ *The heart pumps blood round the body.*

pumpkin /'pʌmpkɪn/ *noun* a large round orange-coloured vegetable

pun /pʌn/ *noun* a play with words which have several different meanings ○ *He made an awful pun about 'ploughing on' with his book on agriculture.*

③ **punch** /pʌntʃ/ *noun* **1.** a blow with the fist ○ *She landed two punches on his head.* **2.** a metal tool for making holes ○ *The* *holes in the belt are made with a punch.* ■ *verb* (**punches, punching, punched**) **1.** to hit someone with your fist ○ *He punched me on the nose.* **2.** to make holes in something with a punch ○ *The conductor punched my ticket.*

punchline /ˈpʌntʃlaɪn/ *noun* the last part of a joke, which is the part that makes you laugh

punctual /ˈpʌŋktʃuəl/ *adj* on time ○ *He was punctual for his appointment with the dentist.*

punctuate /ˈpʌŋktʃueɪt/ (**punctuates, punctuating, punctuated**) *verb* **1.** to interrupt something ○ *Their conversation was punctuated with long silences.* **2.** to add punctuation marks to a text ○ *The sentence was not punctuated correctly.*

punctuation /ˌpʌŋktʃuˈeɪʃ(ə)n/ *noun* the practice of dividing up groups of words using special printed symbols

puncture /ˈpʌŋktʃə/ *noun* a hole in a tyre ○ *I've got a puncture in my back tyre.* ■ *verb* (**punctures, puncturing, punctured**) to make a small hole in something ○ *The tyre had been punctured by a nail.*

pundit /ˈpʌndɪt/ *noun* an expert, especially in political matters

pungent /ˈpʌndʒənt/ *adj* **1.** with a strong taste or smell ○ *a particularly pungent type of goat's cheese* ○ *The pungent odour of curry came from the kitchen.* **2.** (*of comments*) strong and sharp ○ *She reserved her most pungent criticism for the way we performed the musical numbers.*

③ **punish** /ˈpʌnɪʃ/ (**punishes, punishing, punished**) *verb* to make someone suffer because of something they have done ○ *The children must be punished for stealing apples.* ○ *The simplest way to punish them will be to make them pay for the damage they caused.*

punishable /ˈpʌnɪʃəb(ə)l/ *adj* for which you can be punished

punishing /ˈpʌnɪʃɪŋ/ *adj* exhausting, which makes you tired

③ **punishment** /ˈpʌnɪʃmənt/ *noun* a treatment given to punish someone [~for] ○ *As a punishment for your behaviour, you'll wash the kitchen floor.*

punitive /ˈpjuːnɪtɪv/ *adj* which aims to punish

③ **punk** /pʌŋk/ *noun* a person who dresses in unconventional clothes, has brightly coloured hair and pins through parts of the body

punter /ˈpʌntə/ *noun* **1.** a person who gambles ○ *Most of the punters had backed the favourite.* ○ *Punters lost thousands when the favourite fell at the last fence.* **2.** a person who uses a service ○ *We have to keep the punters happy.*

puny /ˈpjuːni/ (**punier, puniest**) *adj* **1.** weak and feeble ○ *The puny body of the baby piglet.* ○ *Their puny efforts were totally unequal to the task.* **2.** very small ○ *This year's pay rise is the puniest we've ever had.*

pup /pʌp/ *noun* the young of certain animals, especially a young dog or seal ○ *Our bitch has had pups.* ○ *They went out onto rocky islands looking for seal pups.*

① **pupil** /ˈpjuːp(ə)l/ *noun* **1.** a child at a school ○ *There are twenty-five pupils in the class.* ○ *The piano teacher thinks she is her best pupil.* **2.** a black hole in the central part of the eye, through which the light passes ○ *The pupil of the eye grows larger when there is less light.*

puppet /ˈpʌpɪt/ *noun* a doll which moves, used to give a show

puppeteer /ˌpʌpɪˈtɪə/ *noun* a person who gives a performance using puppets

③ **puppy** /ˈpʌpi/ (*plural* **puppies**) *noun* a young dog ○ *Our dog has had six puppies*

③ **purchase** /ˈpɜːtʃɪs/ *noun* something that has been bought ○ *She had difficulty getting all her purchases into the car.* □ **to make a purchase** to buy something ○ *We didn't make many purchases on our trip to Oxford Street.* ■ *verb* (**purchases, purchasing, purchased**) to buy something ○ *They purchased their car in France and brought it back to the UK*

purchaser /ˈpɜːtʃɪsə/ *noun* a person who buys something

② **pure** /pjʊə/ (**purer, purest**) *adj* **1.** not spoiled by being mixed with other things or substances of a lower quality ○ *a bottle of pure water* ○ *a pure silk blouse* ○ *a pure mountain stream* **2.** total, complete ○ *This is pure nonsense.* ○ *It is pure extortion.* ○ *It is pure spite on his part.* ○ *It was by pure good luck that I happened to find it.*

② **purely** /ˈpjʊəli/ *adv* only, solely ○ *He's doing it purely for the money.* ○ *This is a purely educational visit.*

purgatory /ˈpɜːgət(ə)ri/ *noun* **1.** a place where some people believe your soul will suffer temporarily after you die, before entering heaven ○ *Masses were said for the souls in purgatory.* **2.** an experience which makes you suffer ○ *It was sheer purgatory listening to her singing out of tune.*

purge /pɜːdʒ/ (**purges, purging, purged**) *verb* **1.** to remove something bad or harmful from your mind or body ○ *I want you to purge your minds of any unhappy memories.* ○ *This special diet is designed to purge the toxins from your body.* **2.** to remove opponents or other unacceptable people from a group ○ *The activists have purged the party of moderates* or *have purged the moderates from the party.* **3.** to make a patient have a bowel movement ○ *Old-fashioned doctors frequently purged their patients.*

purify /ˈpjʊərɪfaɪ/ (**purifies, purifying, purified**) *verb* to make something or someone pure (NOTE: + **purification** *n*)

purist /ˈpjʊərɪst/ *noun* a person who insists that everything has to be done in the correct way

puritan /ˈpjʊərɪt(ə)n/ *noun* a puritanical person

③ **purity** /ˈpjʊərɪti/ *noun* the quality of being pure

purple /ˈpɜːp(ə)l/ *noun* a bluish-red colour ■ *adj* bluish red

purplish[1] *adj* similar to purple

purplish[2] *adj* of a colour that is close to purple

purport /pəˈpɔːt/ (**purports, purporting, purported**) *verb* to claim something ○ *He purported to be a friend of the princess.*

① **purpose** /ˈpɜːpəs/ *noun* an aim or plan ○ *The purpose of the meeting is to plan the village fair.*

purpose-built /ˌpɜːpəs ˈbɪlt/ *adj* made specially for a purpose

purposeful /ˈpɜːpəsf(ə)l/ *adj* with a specific aim in view

purposely /ˈpɜːpəsli/ *adv* intentionally

purr /pɜː/ *noun* **1.** the noise made by a cat when pleased ○ *The cat rubbed against my leg with a loud purr.* **2.** a steady low noise made by a machine or engine ○ *the purr of the boat's engine* ■ *verb* (**purrs, purring, purred**) **1.** (*of a cat*) to make a noise to show pleasure ○ *He purrs when you tickle his stomach.* **2.** (*of an engine*) to make a steady low noise as it operates ○ *We purred along at seventy miles an hour.*

③ **purse** /pɜːs/ *noun* a small bag for carrying money ○ *I know I had my purse in my pocket when I left home.* ○ *She put her ticket in her purse so that she wouldn't forget where it was.*

② **pursue** /pəˈsjuː/ (**pursues, pursuing, pursued**) *verb* to go after someone in order to try to catch him or her (*formal*) ○ *The police pursued the stolen car across London.* ○ *The boys fled, pursued by their older brother.*

pursuit /pəˈsjuːt/ *noun* **1.** a chase after someone □ **in pursuit of** looking for ○ *We set off in pursuit of our friends who had just left the hotel.* ○ *The robbers left in a stolen car with the police in pursuit.* **2.** the process of trying to find something, or trying to do something ○ *Her aim in life is the pursuit of pleasure.* **3.** an occupation or pastime (*dated*)

pus /pʌs/ *noun* a yellow liquid formed in the body as a reaction to infection

① **push** /pʊʃ/ *noun* the action of making something move forwards ○ *He gave the pram a little push and sent it out into the road.* ○ *Can you give the car a push? – It won't start.* ■ *verb* (**pushes, pushing, pushed**) to make something move away from you or in front of you ○ *We'll have to push the car to get it to start.* ○ *The piano is too heavy to lift, so we'll have to push it into the next room.* ○ *Did she fall down the stairs or was she pushed?*

push off③ *phrasal verb* to start on a journey (*informal*) ◇ **push off!** go away!

pushbutton /ˈpʊʃbʌt(ə)n/ *adj* operated by a button which can be pushed ○ *a pushbutton timer*

pusher /ˈpʊʃə/ *noun* a person who sells drugs illegally (*slang*)

pushover /ˈpʊʃˌəʊvə/ *noun* **1.** something that is easy to do **2.** a person who is easily tricked

pushy /ˈpʊʃi/ *adj* always trying to push yourself forward, trying too hard to achieve success (*informal*)

pussyfoot /ˈpʊsifʊt/ (**pussyfoots, pussyfooting, pussyfooted**) *verb also* **pussyfoot about** to be unable to decide what to do or how to do something (*informal*) ○ *Stop pussyfooting about and make your mind up!*

① **put** /pʊt/ (**puts, putting, put**) *verb* to place something somewhere ○ *Did you remember to put the milk in the fridge?* ○ *Where do you want me to put this book?*

put away③ *phrasal verb* to clear things away

put back① *phrasal verb* to put something where it was before

put by *phrasal verb* to save money

put down① *phrasal verb* **1.** to place something lower down onto a surface ○ *He put his suitcase down on the floor beside him.* **2.** to write something down **3.** to charge something ○ *Put that book down on my account.* **4.** to let passengers get off

○ *The taxi driver put me down outside the hotel.* **5.** to make a deposit ○ *to put down money on a house* **6.** to kill an animal that is old or ill, painlessly using drugs ○ *The cat will have to be put down.* **7.** to defeat a group of people who make an attack against people in authority

put forward① *phrasal verb* **1.** to suggest something ○ *I put forward several suggestions for plays we might go to see.* **2.** to change an arrangement to meet someone to a earlier time ○ *Can we put forward the meeting from Thursday to Wednesday?* **3.** to change the time on a clock to a later one ○ *You have to put the clocks forward by one hour in March.*

put in① *phrasal verb* **1.** to place something inside something ○ *I forgot to put in my pyjamas when I packed the case.* **2.** to fix something such as a system or a large piece of equipment in place so that it can be used ○ *The first thing we have to do with the cottage is to put in central heating.* **3.** to do work ○ *She put in three hours' overtime work yesterday evening.* **4.** □ **to put in for** to apply for ○ *She put in for a job in the accounts department.* ○ *He has put in for a grant to study in Italy.*

put off① *phrasal verb* **1.** to arrange for something to take place later ○ *We have put the meeting off until next month.* **2.** to take someone's attention so that they cannot do things properly ○ *Stop making that strange noise, it's putting me off my work.* **3.** to say something that makes someone decide not to do something ○ *He told a story about cows that put me off my food.* ○ *I was going to see the film, but my brother said something which put me off.*

put on① *phrasal verb* **1.** to place something on top of something, on a surface ○ *Put the lid on the saucepan.* ○ *He put his hand on my arm.* ○ *Put the suitcases down on the floor.* **2.** to dress yourself in a certain piece of clothing ○ *I put a clean shirt on before I went to the party.* ○ *Put your gloves on, it's cold outside.* ○ *Put on your wellies if you're going out in the rain.* **3.** to switch something on ○ *Can you put the light on, it's getting dark?* ○ *Put on the kettle and we'll have some tea.* **4.** to add something ○ *She has put on a lot of weight since I saw her last.*

put out① *phrasal verb* **1.** to place something outside ○ *Did you remember to put the cat out?* **2.** to stretch out a part of your body, e.g. your hand or foot ○ *She put out her hand to stop herself from falling.* **3.** to switch something off ○ *He put the light out and went to bed.* **4.** □ **to put out to sea** (*of ships*) to leave harbour

put through *phrasal verb* **1.** □ **to put someone through to someone** to connect them on the phone ○ *Peter is out so I'll put you through to Simon.* ○ *I asked to speak to the accounts department and they put me through to sales.* **2.** to make someone experience something unpleasant ○ *I don't want to be put through that treatment again.*

put up① *phrasal verb* **1.** to attach something to a wall, to attach something high up ○ *I've put up the photos of my family over my desk.* ○ *They are putting up Christmas decorations all along Regent Street.* **2.** to build something ○ *They put up a wooden shed in their garden.* **3.** to lift something up ○ *The gunman told us to put our hands up.* **4.** to increase something, to make something higher ○ *The shop has put up all its prices by 5%.* **5.** to give someone a place to sleep in your house ○ *They've missed the last train, can you put them up for the night?*

put up with① *phrasal verb* to accept someone or something unpleasant ○ *I don't think I can put up with that noise any longer.*

putrid /ˈpjuːtrɪd/ *adj* decayed; which smells extremely unpleasant

putt /pʌt/ *noun* a short shot on a green in golf ○ *He sank a fifteen-foot putt to win the game.* (NOTE: + **putt** *v*)

putty /ˈpʌti/ *noun* a soft substance which becomes hard after a time, used especially for fixing the glass in windows

puzzle /ˈpʌz(ə)l/ *noun* **1.** a game where you have to find the answer to a problem ○ *I can't do today's crossword puzzle.* **2.** something that is hard to understand ○ *It's a puzzle to me why they don't go to live in the country.* ■ *verb* (**puzzles, puzzling, puzzled**) to be difficult to understand ○ *It puzzles me how the robbers managed to get away.*

puzzled /ˈpʌz(ə)ld/ *adj* confused, not understanding something

puzzling /ˈpʌz(ə)lɪŋ/ *adj* which is difficult to understand and does not seem reasonable

PVC *noun* a strong plastic material, used in floor coverings, water pipes and clothing

③ **pyjamas** /pəˈdʒɑːməz/ *plural noun* a light shirt and trousers which you wear in bed ○ *I bought two pairs of pyjamas in the* *sale. ○ When fire broke out in the hotel, the guests ran into the street in their pyjamas.*

pylon /ˈpaɪlən/ *noun* a tall metal tower for carrying electric wires

③ **pyramid** /ˈpɪrəmɪd/ *noun* a shape with a square base and four sides rising to meet at a point

pyre /paɪə/ *noun* a large fire which is burned as part of a ceremony

python /ˈpaɪθ(ə)n/ *noun* a large snake which kills animals by crushing them

Q

q /kjuː/, **Q** *noun* the seventeenth letter of the alphabet, between P and R

QC /ˌkjuː ˈsiː/ *noun* a senior British barrister. Full form **Queen's Counsel**

quack /kwæk/ *noun* **1.** a sound made by a duck ○ *I heard a quack in the reeds.* **2.** a bad doctor (*disapproving*) ○ *I went to see the quack and he gave me some pills.* ■ *verb* (**quacks, quacking, quacked**) to make a noise like a duck ○ *We could hear the ducks quacking on the lake.*

quadruple /ˈkwɒdrʊp(ə)l/ (**quadruples, quadrupling, quadrupled**) *verb* to multiply four times ○ *Our profits have quadrupled in the last three years.*

quagmire /ˈkwægmaɪə/ *noun* **1.** an area of extremely wet ground, where you may be in danger of sinking or of becoming stuck ○ *Be careful when you take the path across the quagmire.* ○ *After the rain, the football pitch was like a quagmire.* **2.** a situation which is very complicated ○ *The project got bogged down in a quagmire of government restrictions.*

quaint /kweɪnt/ *adj* attractive in a way which is strange or unusual

quake /kweɪk/ *verb* (**quakes, quaking, quaked**) **1.** to shake ○ *The explosion made the buildings quake.* **2.** to shake because you have a strong feeling such as fear or because you are very cold [~with] ○ *She was quaking with fear at the thought of going for an interview.* ■ *noun* an occasion when there is a violent shaking of the earth, caused by volcanic activity or movement of the Earth's crust (*informal*) ○ *Thousands of buildings were flattened in the San Francisco quake of 1906.*

② **qualification** /ˌkwɒlɪfɪˈkeɪʃ(ə)n/ *noun* **1.** something necessary for a job, such as proof that you have completed a particular course of study [~for/~in] ○ *Does she have the right qualifications for the job?I don't have any qualifications in computing.* **2.** something which limits the meaning of a statement, or shows that you do not agree with something completely ○ *I want to add one qualification to the agreement: if the goods are not delivered by the 30th of June, then the order will be cancelled.* **3.** being successful in a test or competition which takes you on to the next stage ○ *She didn't reach the necessary standard for qualification.*

③ **qualified** /ˈkwɒlɪfaɪd/ *adj* **1.** with the right qualifications ○ *She's a qualified doctor.* **2.** not complete, with conditions attached ○ *The committee gave its qualified approval.* ○ *The school fair was only a qualified success.*

qualifier /ˈkwɒlɪfaɪə/ *noun* **1.** a person who qualifies in a sports competition ○ *How many qualifiers were there from the first round?* **2.** a round of a sports competition which qualifies a team to go to the next round ○ *They won their qualifier and went through to the semi-final.*

② **qualify** /ˈkwɒlɪfaɪ/ (**qualifies, qualifying, qualified**) *verb* **1.** to study for and obtain a qualification which allows you to do a certain type of work [~as] ○ *When I first qualified I worked as a solicitor.* ○ *He has qualified as an engineer.* **2.** to attach conditions to something ○ *I must qualify the offer by saying that your proposals still have to be approved by the chairman.* **3.** to be in the right position for something, or have the right to have something [~for] ○ *The project does not qualify for a government grant.* **4.** to pass a test or one section of a competition and so go on to the next stage [~for] ○ *She qualified for round two of the competition.*

① **quality** /ˈkwɒlɪti/ (*plural* **qualities**) *noun* **1.** how good something is ○ *We want to measure the air quality in the centre of town.* ○ *There are several high-quality restaurants in the West End.* (NOTE: no plural) **2.** something which is part of a person's character ○ *She has many good qualities, but unfortunately is extremely lazy.* ○ *What qualities do you expect in a good salesman?*

quantifier /ˈkwɒntɪˌfaɪə/ *noun* a word such as 'all' or 'some' that shows the range of things referred to

quantify /ˈkwɒntɪfaɪ/ (**quantifies, quantifying, quantified**) *verb* to measure something in quantities

② **quantity** /ˈkwɒntɪti/ (*plural* **quantities**) *noun* an amount [~of]

quantum leap /ˌkwɒntəm ˈliːp/ *noun* a big improvement in knowledge or a big change, especially to something better

quarantine /ˈkwɒrəntiːn/ *noun* a period of time when an animal or a person, usually coming from another country, has to be kept apart from others to avoid the risk of passing on diseases ○ *The animals were put in quarantine on arrival at the port.* (NOTE: + **quarantine** *v*)

quarrel /ˈkwɒrəl/ *noun* an argument ○ *I think the quarrel was over who was in charge of the cash desk.* ○ *He's had a quarrel with his wife.*

quarry /ˈkwɒri/ *noun* an animal or person who is being hunted ○ *Gunmen surrounded the building where the kidnappers were, but their quarry managed to escape.* ■ *verb* (**quarries, quarrying, quarried**) to dig stone out of the ground ○ *The stone used to build the castle was quarried locally.*

quart /kwɔːt/ *noun* a measure of liquid equal to two pints or one quarter of a gallon

① **quarter** /ˈkwɔːtə/ *noun* one of four parts, a fourth, 25% ○ *She cut the pear into quarters.* ○ *The jar is only a quarter empty.* ○ *He paid only a quarter of the normal fare because he works for the airline.*

③ **quarter-final** /ˌkwɔːtə ˈfaɪn(ə)l/ *noun* (*in sport*) one of four matches in a competition, in which the person or team which wins goes into the semi-finals

③ **quarterly** /ˈkwɔːtəli/ *adj, adv* which happens every three months ○ *a quarterly payment* ○ *There is a quarterly charge for electricity.* ○ *We pay the rent quarterly* or *on a quarterly basis.* ■ *noun* (*plural* **quarterlies**) a magazine which appears every three months ○ *He writes for one of the political quarterlies.*

③ **quarters** /ˈkwɔːtəz/ *plural noun* places where people live ○ *When they come off duty the staff go back to their quarters.* ◇ **at close quarters** close to, very near ○ *I had seen her often on TV, but this was the first time I had seen her at close quarters.*

quartet /kwɔːˈtet/, **quartette** *noun* **1.** four musicians playing together ○ *She plays the cello in a string quartet.* **2.** a piece of music for four musicians ○ *a Beethoven string quartet* **3.** four people or four things ○ *A quartet of British archaeologists discovered the tomb.* ○ *Have you read his quartet of novels about Egypt?*

quartz /kwɔːts/ *noun* a hard mineral often found as crystals in rocks and which makes up the major part of sand

quash /kwɒʃ/ (**quashes, quashing, quashed**) *verb* **1.** to make a judgment or ruling no longer valid ○ *The appeal court quashed the verdict.* ○ *He applied for judicial review to quash the order.* **2.** to make something end ○ *The government moved quickly to quash rumours of a split in the Cabinet.*

quaver /ˈkweɪvə/ (**quavers, quavering, quavered**) *verb* (*of voice*) to shake slightly ○ *A quavering voice answered the telephone.*

quay /kiː/ *noun* the part of a harbour or port where boats stop (NOTE: Do not confuse with **key**.)

queasy /ˈkwiːzi/ *adj* feeling sick

② **queen** /kwiːn/ *noun* **1.** the wife of a king ○ *King Charles I's queen was the daughter of the king of France.* **2.** a woman who rules a country ○ *The Queen sometimes lives in Windsor Castle.* ○ *Queen Victoria was queen for many years.* **3.** in the game of chess, the second most important piece, after the king ○ *In three moves he had captured my queen.*

queer /kwɪə/ *noun* a homosexual man (*offensive; unless used by people who are gay*)

quell /kwel/ (**quells, quelling, quelled**) *verb* **1.** to calm a situation in which there is a lot of noise and fighting ○ *Extra police were drafted in to quell the disturbances.* **2.** to hold back feelings ○ *She tried to quell her fears about the journey.* ○ *It was difficult to quell a feeling of resentment.*

quench /kwentʃ/ (**quenches, quenching, quenched**) *verb* □ **to quench your thirst** to have a drink when you are thirsty ○ *I expect you would like something to quench your thirst.*

query /ˈkwɪəri/ (*plural* **queries**) *noun* a question ○ *She had to answer a mass of queries about the tax form.*

③ **quest** /kwest/ *noun* a search

① **question** /ˈkwestʃ(ə)n/ *noun* **1.** a sentence which needs an answer ○ *The teacher couldn't answer the children's questions.* ○ *Some of the questions in the exam were too difficult.* ○ *The manager refused to answer questions from journalists about the fire.* **2.** a problem or matter ○ *The question is, who do we appoint to run the shop when we're* *on holiday?* ○ *The main question is that of cost.* ○ *He raised the question of moving to a less expensive part of town.* ■ *verb* (**questions, questioning, questioned**) to ask questions ○ *The police questioned the driver for four hours.* ◇ **in question** under discussion ○ *Please keep to the matter in question.* ◇ **it is out of the question** it cannot possibly be done ○ *You cannot borrow any more money – it's out of the question.* ○ *It's out of the question for her to have any more time off.*

questionable /'kwestʃənəb(ə)l/ *adj* which is not completely honest or straightforward

questioning /'kwestʃ(ə)nɪŋ/ *noun* a situation in which someone is asked a lot of questions, especially formally or officially, or an instance of this

② **question mark** /'kweʃtʃən mɑːk/ *noun* a sign (?) used in writing to show that a question is being asked

③ **questionnaire** /ˌkwestʃə'neə/ *noun* a printed list of questions given to people to answer, usually questions about what they like or what they buy

question tag /'kwestʃ(ə)n tæg/ *noun* a short phrase at the end of a statement that changes it into a question. In English, examples are the phrases 'isn't it?' and 'have you?'

③ **queue** /kjuː/ *noun* a line of people or things such as cars, waiting one behind the other for something [~for] ○ *We joined the queue for tickets at the entrance to the stadium.* ○ *There was a queue of people waiting to get into the exhibition.* □ **to form a queue** to stand in line ○ *Please form a queue to the left of the door.* ○ *Queues formed at ticket offices when the news of cheap fares became known.* □ **to jump the queue** to go in front of other people standing in a queue ○ *Are you trying to jump the queue? – Go to the back!* ■ *verb* (**queueing** or **queuing, queued**) *also* **queue up** to stand in a line waiting for something [~for] ○ *We spent hours queuing for tickets.*

quibble /'kwɪb(ə)l/ *verb* (**quibbles, quibbling, quibbled**) to argue about the details of something which is extremely unimportant [~about] ○ *They spent hours quibbling about who should pay the bill.* ■ *noun* a minor argument ○ *I have only a few quibbles about the style, but basically I like the book.*

quiche /kiːʃ/ *noun* an open pastry case with a filling of food such as eggs or vegetables

① **quick** /kwɪk/ *adj* done with speed or in a short time ○ *I'm trying to work out the quickest way to get to the Tower of London.* ○ *We had a quick lunch and then went off for a walk.* ○ *He is much quicker at calculating than I am.* ○ *I am not sure that going by air to Paris is quicker than taking the train.*

quicken /'kwɪkən/ (**quickens, quickening, quickened**) *verb* **1.** to make something go faster ○ *He quickened his steps as he neared the house.* **2.** to make more active, to become more active ○ *The decision is bound to quicken racial tensions.* ○ *The interest of the public began to quicken as it came closer to the time for the festival.*

quickie /'kwɪki/ *noun* something which takes only a short time to deal with, e.g. a drink or question

① **quickly** /'kwɪkli/ *adv* very fast, without taking much time ○ *He ate his supper very quickly because he wanted to watch the match on TV.* ○ *The firemen came quickly when we called 999.*

② **quid** /kwɪd/ (*plural same*) *noun* a pound (*informal*)

② **quiet** /'kwaɪət/ *adj* **1.** without any noise ○ *a house in a quiet street* ○ *I wish the children would be quiet. – I'm trying to work.* **2.** with no great excitement ○ *We had a quiet holiday by the sea.* ○ *It's a quiet little village.* ○ *The hotel is in the quietest part of the town.*

quieten /'kwaɪət(ə)n/ (**quietens, quietening, quietened**) *verb* to make somebody quiet, to calm somebody down

③ **quietly** /'kwaɪətli/ *adv* without making any noise ○ *The burglar climbed quietly up to the window.* ○ *She shut the door quietly behind her.*

quilt /kwɪlt/ *noun* a thick cover for a bed. ◊ **patchwork**

quintessential /ˌkwɪntɪ'senʃəl/ *adj* which is a perfect example of something

quintet /kwɪn'tet/, **quintette** *noun* **1.** five musicians playing together ○ *She plays the cello in a string quintet.* **2.** a piece of music for five musicians ○ *a Mozart flute quintet*

quip /kwɪp/ (**quips, quipping, quipped**) *verb* to make a joke or a clever remark ○ *'Hey, big spender!' she quipped as she saw him staggering out of the supermarket laden with plastic bags.*

quirk /kwɜːk/ *noun* an unusual or strange thing

quirky /'kwɜːki/ *adj* strange, unusual

② **quit** /kwɪt/ (**quits, quitting, quitted** or **quit**) *verb* **1.** to leave something such as a job or a place and not return ○ *When the boss criticised her, she quit.* ○ *I'm fed up with the office, I'm thinking of quitting.* **2.** *US* to stop doing something ○ *Will you quit bothering me!* ○ *He quit smoking.*

① **quite** /kwaɪt/ *adv* **1.** to some degree ○ *It's quite a long play.* ○ *She's quite a good writer.* ○ *The book is quite amusing but I liked the TV play better.* **2.** to a great degree ○ *You're quite mad to go walking in a snowstorm.* ○ *He's quite right.* ○ *I don't quite understand why you want to go China.* □ **not quite** not completely ○ *The work is not quite finished yet.* ○ *Have you eaten all the bread? – Not quite.*

quiver /ˈkwɪvə/ (**quivers, quivering, quivered**) *verb* to shake slightly ○ *The dog watched the snake, quivering with fear.* ○ *The children rushed to the Christmas tree, quivering with excitement.* (NOTE: + **quiver** *n*)

③ **quiz** /kwɪz/ *noun* a game where you are asked a series of questions ○ *She got all the questions right in the quiz.* ○ *They organised a general knowledge quiz.*

quizzical /ˈkwɪzɪk(ə)l/ *adj* showing that you think something is surprising or funny

quorum /ˈkwɔːrəm/ *noun* the number of people who have to be present at a meeting to make it official or legal

quota /ˈkwəʊtə/ *noun* **1.** a fixed amount of things that should be supplied or received according to official rules **2.** an amount of something that someone has to do, e.g. a share of work

quotation /kwəʊˈteɪʃ(ə)n/ *noun* the words of one person which are repeated by another person

quotation marks /kwəʊˈteɪʃ(ə)n mɑːks/ *plural noun* printed or written marks ( ) showing that a quotation starts or finishes

② **quote** /kwəʊt/ *noun* a quotation [~from] ○ *I need some good quotes from his speech to put into my report.* ■ *verb* (**quotes, quoting, quoted**) to repeat what someone has said or written ○ *He started his speech by quoting lines from Shakespeare's 'Hamlet'.*

R

r /ɑː/, **R** *noun* the eighteenth letter of the alphabet, between Q and S

rabbi /ˈræbaɪ/ *noun* a Jewish religious leader or teacher (NOTE: also used as a title before a name: *Rabbi Jonathan Sacks*)

③ **rabbit** /ˈræbɪt/ *noun* a common wild animal with grey fur, long ears and a short white tail ○ *The rabbit ran down its hole.* ○ *She keeps a pet rabbit in a cage.*

rabbit warren /ˈræbɪt ˌwɒrən/ *noun* **1.** a series of underground tunnels where rabbits live ○ *There are many rabbit warrens in the park.* **2.** an area where there are a lot of narrow streets ○ *We got lost in the rabbit warren of old streets behind the market.*

rabble /ˈræb(ə)l/ *noun* a crowd, a large violent mass of people

rabies /ˈreɪbiːz/ *noun* a serious disease which can cause death and which is passed to humans by infected animals

② **race** /reɪs/ *noun* a competition to see which person, animal or vehicle is the fastest ○ *She was second in the 200 metres race.* ○ *The bicycle race goes round the whole country.* ■ *verb* (**races, racing, raced**) **1.** to run fast ○ *They saw the bus coming and raced to the bus stop.* ○ *He snatched some watches from the shop window and then raced away down the street.* **2.** to compete in a race ○ *I'll race you to see who gets to school first.*

③ **racecourse** /ˈreɪskɔːs/ *noun* a grass-covered track where horse races are held

racehorse /ˈreɪshɔːs/ *noun* a horse bred and trained especially to run in horse races

race relations /ˌreɪs rɪˈleɪʃ(ə)nz/ *plural noun* relations between different groups of races in the same country ○ *Race relations officers have been appointed in some police forces.*

③ **racetrack** /ˈreɪstræk/ *noun* a track where races are run

racial /ˈreɪʃ(ə)l/ *adj* referring to different races

③ **racing** /ˈreɪsɪŋ/ *noun* competitions to see who is fastest

racism /ˈreɪsɪz(ə)m/ *noun* the belief that a group of people are not as good as others because they are of a different race, and treating them differently

racist /ˈreɪsɪst/ *noun* a person who treats someone differently because of race ○ *He's an old racist and you won't change his views.* ○ *The former regime was full of racists.*

③ **rack** /ræk/ *noun* a frame for holding things, e.g. letters, tools or suitcases ○ *He put the envelope in the letter rack on his desk.*

③ **racket** /ˈrækɪt/ *noun* **1.** a light frame with tight strings, used for hitting the ball in games ○ *She bought a new tennis racket at the start of the summer season.* ○ *She asked if she could borrow his badminton racket for the tournament.* **2.** a loud noise (*informal*) ○ *Stop that racket at once!* ○ *The people next door make a terrible racket when they're having a party.*

racy /ˈreɪsi/ *adj* (*of behaviour*) slightly shocking

radiance /ˈreɪdiəns/ *noun* the quality of shining extremely brightly

radiant /ˈreɪdiənt/ *adj* **1.** very happy ○ *a radiant smile* ○ *She looked radiant in her wedding photos.* **2.** very bright or shining ○ *radiant blue* **3.** (*of heat*) sent out in the form of rays

radiate /ˈreɪdieɪt/ (**radiates, radiating, radiated**) *verb* **1.** to send out rays or heat ○ *The Sun radiates heat.* **2.** to spread out from a central point ○ *The paths radiated from the tree in the centre of the garden.* ○ *The pain can radiate down both arms and up into the neck and jaw.*

radiation /ˌreɪdiˈeɪʃ(ə)n/ *noun* the process of sending out rays or heat

radiator /ˈreɪdieɪtə/ *noun* **1.** a metal object, usually fixed to a wall, which is filled with hot water for heating a room ○ *Turn the radiator down – it's boiling in here.* ○ *When we arrived at the hotel our room was cold, so we switched the radiators on.* **2.** a metal container filled with cold water for preventing a car engine from becoming too hot ○ *The radiator overheated causing the car to break down.*

③ **radical** /ˈrædɪk(ə)l/ *noun* a member of a radical party ○ *Two Radicals voted against the government.*

① **radio** /ˈreɪdiəʊ/ *noun* **1.** a method of sending out and receiving messages using air waves ○ *They got the news by radio.* ○ *We always listen to BBC radio when we're on holiday.* **2.** a machine which sends out and receives messages using air waves ○ *Turn on the radio – it's time for the weather forecast.* ○ *I heard the news on the car radio.* ○ *Please, turn the radio down – I'm on the phone.*

③ **radioactive** /ˌreɪdiəʊˈæktɪv/ *adj* (*of a substance*) which, as its nucleus breaks up, gives off energy in the form of radiation which can pass through other substances

radioactivity /ˌreɪdiəʊækˈtɪvɪti/ *noun* energy in the form of radiation from radioactive substances

radiography /ˌreɪdiˈɒgrəfi/ *noun* the practice or process of making X-ray photographs

radish /ˈrædɪʃ/ *noun* a small red root vegetable, eaten raw in salads

③ **radius** /ˈreɪdiəs/ *noun* **1.** a line from the centre of a circle to the outside edge ○ *We were all asked to measure the radius of the circle.* **2.** the distance in any direction from a particular central point ○ *People within a radius of twenty miles heard the explosion.* ○ *The school accepts children living within a two-mile radius.*

③ **raffle** /ˈræf(ə)l/ *noun* a game where you buy a ticket with a number on it, in the hope of winning a prize ○ *She won a bottle of perfume in a raffle.*

raft /rɑːft/ *noun* many, a lot of ○ *They had to answer a raft of questions about government policy.*

rafter /ˈrɑːftə/ *noun* one of the long straight pieces of wood which hold up a roof

rag /ræg/ *noun* a piece of torn cloth ○ *He used an old oily rag to clean his motorbike.*

rage /reɪdʒ/ *noun* sudden extreme anger ○ *Her face was red with rage.* □ **to fly into a rage** to get very angry suddenly ○ *When he phoned her she flew into a rage.* ■ *verb* (**rages, raging, raged**) to be violent ○ *The storm raged all night.*

ragged /ˈrægɪd/ *adj* **1.** (*of clothes*) torn ○ *The old photographs showed poor children standing in ragged clothes.* **2.** (*of edge of paper or cloth*) not straight ○ *If you'd used scissors to cut the wrapping paper you wouldn't have made the edge all ragged.*

raid /reɪd/ *noun* a sudden attack; a sudden visit by the police ■ *verb* (**raids, raiding, raided**) to make a sudden attack on a place ○ *The police raided the club.* ○ *We caught the boys raiding the fridge.*

raider /ˈreɪdə/ *noun* a person who takes part in a raid

② **rail** /reɪl/ *noun* **1.** a straight metal or wooden bar ○ *The pictures all hang from a picture rail.* ○ *Hold onto the rail as you go down the stairs.* ○ *There is a heated towel rail in the bathroom.* **2.** one of two parallel metal bars on which trains run ○ *Don't try to cross the rails – it's dangerous.* **3.** the railway, a system of travel using trains ○ *Six million commuters travel to work by rail each day.* ○ *We ship all our goods by rail.* ○ *Rail travellers are complaining about rising fares.* ○ *Rail travel is cheaper than air travel.*

railroad /ˈreɪlrəʊd/ *noun US* same as **railway**

② **railway** /ˈreɪlweɪ/ *noun* a way of travelling which uses trains to carry passengers and goods ○ *The railway station is in the centre of town.* ○ *The French railway system has high-speed trains to all major cities.*

railway embankment /ˌreɪlweɪ ɪmˈbæŋkmənt/ *noun* a raised bank of earth to carry a railway

① **rain** /reɪn/ *noun* drops of water which fall from the clouds ○ *The ground is very dry – we've had no rain for days.* ○ *Yesterday we had 3cm of rain* or *3cm of rain fell here yesterday.* ○ *If you have to go out in the rain take an umbrella.* ○ *All this rain will help the plants grow.* ■ *verb* (**rains, raining, rained**) to fall as drops of water from the clouds ○ *As soon as we sat down and took out the sandwiches it started to rain.* ○ *Look at the clouds, it's going to rain.*

rainbow /ˈreɪnbəʊ/ *noun* a shape like half a circle which shines with many colours in the sky when it is sunny and raining at the same time

raincoat /ˈreɪnkəʊt/ *noun* a coat which keeps off water, which you wear when it is raining

raindrop /ˈreɪndrɒp/ *noun* a drop of water which falls from a cloud

rainfall /ˈreɪnfɔːl/ *noun* the amount of rain which falls in a place over a certain period

rain forest /ˈreɪn ˌfɒrɪst/ *noun* a thick forest which grows in tropical regions where there is a lot of rain

rainstorm /ˈreɪnstɔːm/ *noun* a storm with a lot of rain

rainwater /ˈreɪnwɔːtə/ *noun* water which has fallen as rain

① **raise** /reɪz/ (**raises, raising, raised**) *verb* **1.** to put something in a higher position or at a higher level ○ *He picked up the flag and raised it over his head.* ○ *Air fares will be raised on June 1st.* **2.** to mention a subject which could be discussed ○ *No one raised the subject of politics.* ○ *The manager tried to prevent the question of pay being raised.* **3.** to obtain money ○ *The hospital is trying to raise £2m to finance its building programme.* ○ *Where will he raise the money from to start up his business?* **4.** to look after a child ○ *She was raised by her aunt in Canada.* (NOTE: Do not confuse with **raze**. Note also: **raises – raising – raised**.)

raisin /ˈreɪz(ə)n/ *noun* a dried grape

rake /reɪk/ *noun* the angle of a slope ○ *The rake of the stage is quite steep.* ■ *verb* (**rakes, raking, raked**) to move a camera or gun slowly sideways so that it covers a wide area ○ *From their lookout post they were able to rake the whole square with machine-gun fire.*

rake in *phrasal verb* to gather something together (*informal*)

rake up *phrasal verb* **1.** to pull dead leaves together with a rake ○ *She raked the dead leaves up into a pile.* **2.** to bring together ○ *We had difficulty in raking up the money to buy the house.* **3.** to bring back something unpleasant from the past ○ *The newspapers tried to rake up the old scandal.*

rally /ˈræli/ (*plural* **rallies**) *noun* a large meeting of members of a group or political party ○ *We are holding a rally to protest against the job cuts.*

ram /ræm/ (**rams, ramming, rammed**) *verb* to move or hammer something down hard

RAM /ræm/ *noun* random access memory, computer memory that allows access to any part of the memory in any order without having to access the rest of memory

Ramadan /ˈræmədæn/ *noun* a Muslim religious festival, the ninth month of the Muslim year, during which believers are not allowed to eat or drink during the day

ramble /ˈræmbəl/ *noun* a walk for pleasure in the countryside ○ *We're going for a ramble through the woods.* ■ *verb* (**rambles, rambling, rambled**) **1.** to go for a walk for pleasure in the countryside ○ *We went rambling last weekend.* **2.** *also* **ramble on** to talk on and on in a confused way ○ *He has a tendency to ramble, and his phone calls never last less than half an hour.* ○ *She went rambling on about her 'boy', and it wasn't until later that I realised she was talking about her cat.*

ramp /ræmp/ *noun* a small curved shape across the surface of a road ○ *Drive carefully – ramps ahead!*

rampage /ˈræmpeɪdʒ/ *noun* □ **to go on the rampage** to go about breaking things or creating a lot of noise and mess ○ *After their team's defeat the fans went on the rampage around the town.* ■ *verb* (**rampages, rampaging, rampaged**) *also* **rampage about** to create a lot of mess and noise ○ *She was rampaging about, throwing books and pictures all over the place.*

rampant /ˈræmpənt/ *adj* existing everywhere without being controlled

ramshackle /ˈræmʃæk(ə)l/ *adj* badly damaged and falling to pieces

ran /ræn/ past tense of **run**

ranch /rɑːntʃ/ *noun* (*in North or South America*) a farm where horses or cows are kept, especially in North or South America ○ *The cowboys returned to the ranch each evening.* ○ *They left the city and bought a ranch in Colorado.*

rancour /ˈræŋkə/ *noun* an angry feeling against someone or something (NOTE: The US spelling is **rancor**.)

random /ˈrændəm/ *adj* done without any planning ◇ **at random** without choosing carefully ○ *Pick any card at random.*

rang /ræŋ/ past tense of **ring**

① **range** /reɪndʒ/ *noun* **1.** a choice or series of things which are available ○ *We have a range of holidays at all prices.* ○ *I am looking for something in the £20–£30 price range.* **2.** a distance which you can go; a distance over which you can see or hear ○ *The missile only has a range of 100 km.* ○ *The police said the man had been shot at close range.* ○ *The optician told her that her range of vision would be limited.* **3.** a series of buildings or mountains in line ○ *There is a range of outbuildings next to the farmhouse which can be converted into holiday cottages.* ○ *They looked out at the vast mountain range from the plane window.* ■ *verb* (**ranges, ranging, ranged**) to include all things within a range [~from] ○ *Sizes range from small to extra large.*

② **rank** /ræŋk/ *noun* **1.** a position in society or in a service such as the army or police ○ *What rank does he hold in the police force?* ○ *She rose to the rank of captain.* **2.** a row of people, especially soldiers ○ *The soldiers kept rank as they advanced towards the enemy.* **3.** a row of things ○ *The room was full of people watching ranks of computer screens.* ■ *verb* (**ranks, ranking, ranked**) to be placed in order of importance ○ *Shakespeare ranks among the greatest world authors.* ○ *As an artist he doesn't rank as highly as his sister.* ◇ **the rank and file** ordinary people

ranking /'ræŋkɪŋ/ *noun* a position in order of importance

rankle /'ræŋk(ə)l/ (**rankles, rankling, rankled**) *verb* to cause continuing bitter feelings

ransack /'rænsæk/ (**ransacks, ransacking, ransacked**) *verb* to cause a lot of damage and mess while searching a place to find something

ransom /'ræns(ə)m/ *noun* money paid to get back someone who is being held prisoner ○ *The daughter of the banker was held by kidnappers who asked for a ransom of £1m.*

rant /rænt/ (**rants, ranting, ranted**) *verb* to complain or shout loudly

rap /ræp/ *noun* a form of African Caribbean music where the singer speaks words quickly over a strong beat, improvising as he or she goes along ○ *The club played rap all evening.* ■ *verb* (**raps, rapping, rapped**) to sing rap music ○ *Although he couldn't play the guitar or the drums he was great at rapping.*

rape /reɪp/ *noun* the offence of attacking a person and forcing them to have sex ○ *There's been a dramatic increase in the number of rapes in this area over the past year.* ○ *He was in court, charged with rape.*

③ **rapid** /'ræpɪd/ *adj* done very quickly or happening very quickly ○ *There has been a rapid rise in property prices this year.* ○ *The rapid change in the weather forced the yachts to turn for home.*

③ **rapidly** /'ræpɪdli/ *adv* quickly

rapist /'reɪpɪst/ *noun* a person who has raped someone

rapper /'ræpə/ *noun* a person who speaks words to rap music

rapport /ræ'pɔː/ *noun* an understanding, a close connection between two people or groups

rapture /'ræptʃə/ *noun* a state of great happiness or enthusiasm

② **rare** /reə/ *adj* not usual or common ○ *It's very rare to meet a foreigner who speaks perfect Chinese.* ○ *Experienced sales staff are rare these days.* ○ *The forest is the habitat of a rare species of frog.*

② **rarely** /'reəli/ *adv* almost never ○ *I rarely buy a Sunday newspaper.* ○ *He is rarely in his office on Friday afternoons.*

rarity /'reərɪti/ *noun* **1.** the state of being rare ○ *The rarity of the species means that it must be protected.* **2.** a rare thing ○ *Hot sunny days are a rarity in November.* ○ *We get so few tourists that a coachload of them is a real rarity.*

rash /ræʃ/ *noun* a mass of red spots on your skin, which stays for a time and then disappears ○ *She had a rash on her arms.* ■ *adj* done without thinking carefully or sensibly ○ *It was a bit rash of him to suggest that he would pay for everyone.* (NOTE: **rasher – rashest**)

③ **rasher** /'ræʃə/ *noun* a thin piece of bacon

rasp /rɑːsp/ (**rasps, rasping, rasped**) *verb* to make a grating noise ○ *The steel bolt rasped as he slid it back.*

raspberry /'rɑːzb(ə)ri/ (*plural* **raspberries**) *noun* a rude noise made with the mouth to show that you think something is rubbish ○ *Instead of replying, she blew him a raspberry.*

Rastafarian /ˌræstə'feəriən/ *noun* a member of an Afro-Caribbean religious group that considers the former emperor of Ethiopia, Haile Selassie, to be God

rat /ræt/ *noun* a small furry animal like a large mouse which has a long tail and can carry disease ○ *The city's sewers are full of rats.*

① **rate** /reɪt/ *noun* **1.** a number shown as a proportion of another **2.** how frequently something is done ○ *There has been a sharp increase in the country's birth rate* ○ *His heart was beating at a rate of only 59 per minute.* **3.** a level of payment ○ *He immediately accepted the rate offered.* ○ *Before we discuss the project further, I would like to talk about the rates of payment.* ○ *Their rate of pay is lower than ours.* **4.** speed ○ *At the rate he's going, he'll be there before us.* ○ *If you type at a steady rate of 70 words per minute you'll finish copying the text today.*

① **rather** /'rɑːðə/ *adv* to a slight degree ○ *Their house is rather on the small side.* ○ *Her dress is a rather pretty shade of blue.*

ratify /ˈrætɪfaɪ/ (**ratifies, ratifying, ratified**) *verb* to approve something officially (NOTE: + **ratification** *n*)

rating /ˈreɪtɪŋ/ *noun* **1.** the act or practice of giving a score or mark for something ○ *What rating would you give that film?* **2.** (*in the navy*) an ordinary seaman ○ *The new commander joined the navy 20 years ago as a rating.*

③ **ratio** /ˈreɪʃiəʊ/ *noun* an amount of something measured in relation to another amount ○ *the ratio of successes to failures* ○ *Our athletes beat theirs by a ratio of two to one (2:1).*

ration /ˈræʃ(ə)n/ *noun* an amount of food or supplies allowed ○ *The rations provided for the expedition were more than sufficient.* ○ *The prisoners had to survive on meagre rations.* ■ *verb* (**rations, rationing, rationed**) to allow only a certain amount of food or supplies ○ *Petrol may be rationed this winter.* ○ *During the war we were rationed to one ounce of cheese per person per week.*

③ **rational** /ˈræʃ(ə)n(ə)l/ *adj* sensible, based on reason

rationale /ˌræʃəˈnɑːl/ *noun* a set of reasons for which something is done

rationalise /ˈræʃ(ə)nəlaɪz/ (**rationalises, rationalising, rationalised**), **rationalize** *verb* **1.** to find a reason for actions which do not appear to be rational ○ *He tried to rationalise what he had done.* **2.** to make something such as a system or a business work in a more effective way ○ *The rail company is trying to rationalise its freight services.*

rattle /ˈræt(ə)l/ (**rattles, rattling, rattled**) *verb* to make a repeated noise like two pieces of wood hitting each other ○ *The wind made the windows rattle.*

rattle off *phrasal verb* to say something very quickly

raucous /ˈrɔːkəs/ *adj* loud and unpleasant to listen to ○ *the raucous cries of the birds* ○ *Raucous laughter greeted his appearance on stage.* ○ *A raucous crowd gathered in front of the palace.*

ravage /ˈrævɪdʒ/ (**ravages, ravaging, ravaged**) *verb* to damage or to destroy a place ○ *The countryside had been ravaged by years of civil war.*

rave /reɪv/ *verb* (**raves, raving, raved**) **1.** to speak in an excited way ○ *He ranted and raved until someone came to see what was the matter.* **2.** to be very enthusiastic about something ○ *She raves about this little restaurant in the West End.* ■ *noun* a very large party for young people, with bright lights, loud music and usually drugs

raven /ˈreɪv(ə)n/ *noun* a big black bird like a very large crow

ravenous /ˈræv(ə)nəs/ *adj* very hungry

ravine /rəˈviːn/ *noun* a deep narrow valley

ravishing /ˈrævɪʃɪŋ/ *adj* very beautiful

③ **raw** /rɔː/ *adj* not cooked ○ *Don't be silly – you can't eat raw potatoes!* ○ *We had a salad of raw cabbage and tomatoes.* ○ *Sushi is a Japanese dish of raw fish.* ○ *They served the meat almost raw.*

③ **raw materials** /ˌrɔː məˈtɪəriəlz/ *plural noun* substances such as wool, wood or sand which are still in their natural state and have not yet been made into manufactured goods

ray /reɪ/ *noun* a beam of light or heat ○ *A ray of sunshine hit the window pane and lit up the gloomy room.*

raze /reɪz/ (**razes, razing, razed**) *verb* to destroy a building or a town completely ○ *The office block will be razed to the ground to make way for the new road.*

③ **razor** /ˈreɪzə/ *noun* an instrument with a very sharp blade for removing hair from the face or body

razor blade /ˈreɪzə bleɪd/ *noun* a blade for a razor, which can be used several times before being thrown away

③ **Rd** *abbr* road ○ *Our address is 1 Cambridge Rd.*

re /riː/ *prep* concerning

re- /riː/ *prefix* again

① **reach** /riːtʃ/ *noun* how far you can stretch out your hand ○ *Keep the medicine bottle out of the reach of the children.* ■ *verb* (**reaches, reaching, reached**) **1.** to stretch out your hand to ○ *She reached across the table and took some meat from my plate.* ○ *He's quite tall enough to reach the tool cupboard.* ○ *Can you reach me down the suitcase from the top shelf?* **2.** to arrive at a place ○ *We were held up by fog and only reached home at midnight.* ○ *The plane reaches Hong Kong at midday.* ○ *We wrote to tell her we were coming to visit, but the letter never reached her.* **3.** to get to a certain level ○ *The amount we owe the bank has reached £100,000.*

③ **react** /riˈækt/ (**reacts, reacting, reacted**) *verb* **1.** to do or to say something in response to words or an action [~ to] ○ *How will he react to the news?* ○ *When she heard the rumour she didn't react at all.* **2.** to behave in a particular way as a result of something [~to] ○ *How did he react to the news of her death?* ○ *He didn't react at all well to the injection.* **3.** to show opposition to something [~against] ○ *The farmers reacted against the new law by blocking the roads with their tractors.* **4.** (*of a chemical*) to change chemical composition because of a substance [~with] ○ *Acids react with metals.*

② **reaction** /ri'ækʃən/ *noun* **1.** a thing done or said as a result of something else [~to] ○ *His immediate reaction to the news was to burst into laughter.* ○ *There was a very negative reaction to the proposed building development.* **2.** a process of chemical change ○ *A chemical reaction takes place when the acid is added.*

reactionary /ri'ækʃən(ə)ri/ *adj* extremely conservative, opposed to any change ○ *Reactionary elements in the government may try to block the president's plan.*

① **read** /riːd/ (**reads, reading, read**) *verb* **1.** to look at and understand written words [~about] ○ *We're reading about the general election.* ○ *She was reading a book when I saw her.* ○ *What are you reading at the moment?* **2.** to look at and understand written music ○ *She can play the piano by ear, but can't read music.* **3.** to understand the meaning of data from something such as a computer disk or a piece of electronic equipment ○ *My PC cannot read these old disks.* ○ *The scanner reads the code on each product.* **4.** to speak the words of something which is written ○ *The chairman read a message from the president during the meeting.* ○ *She reads a story to the children every night.* ○ *Can you read the instructions on the medicine bottle? – The print is too small for me.*

read aloud, read out③ *phrasal verb* to speak the words you are reading

② **reader** /'riːdə/ *noun* **1.** a person who reads, especially a person who reads regularly or who reads a particular newspaper or type of book ○ *a message from the editor to all our readers* ○ *She's a great reader of science fiction.* **2.** a school book to help children to learn to read ○ *The teacher handed out the new readers to the class.* ○ *I remember one of my first readers – it was about pirates.*

readership /'riːdəʃɪp/ *noun* all the people who regularly read a particular magazine or newspaper, or read the books of a particular writer ○ *The paper is targeting a younger readership.*

③ **readily** /'redɪli/ *adv* **1.** easily and quickly ○ *This product is readily available in most shops.* **2.** willingly ○ *Is there anyone readily available to help me this weekend?* ○ *She came readily when I asked her to help me.*

readiness /'redinəs/ *noun* being ready or willing

② **reading** /'riːdɪŋ/ *noun* **1.** the act of looking at and understanding written words ○ *Reading and writing should be taught early.* **2.** an occasion when someone speaks the words of something which is written ○ *They gave a poetry reading in the bookshop.*

readjust /ˌriːə'dʒʌst/ (**readjusts, readjusting, readjusted**) *verb* to adjust again

read-out /'riːd aʊt/ *noun* the data produced by electronic equipment, e.g. a computer, and which you can read or hear

① **ready** /'redi/ (**readier, readiest**) *adj* **1.** prepared for something or to do something [~for] ○ *Hold on – I'll be ready in two minutes.* ○ *Are all the children ready for school?* ○ *Why isn't the coach here? – The group are all ready to go.* **2.** available and suitable to be used or eaten ○ *Don't sit down yet – the meal isn't ready.* ○ *Is my dry cleaning ready yet?* **3.** willing ○ *She's always ready to help in the garden.*

ready-made /ˌredi 'meɪd/ *adj* which is mass-produced and ready to use

① **real** /rɪəl/ *adj* **1.** not false or artificial ○ *Is that watch real gold?* ○ *That plastic apple looks very real* or *looks just like the real thing.* ○ *He has a real leather case.* **2.** used for emphasising something ○ *That car is a real bargain at £300.* ○ *Their little girl is going to be a real beauty.* ○ *Wasps can be a real problem on picnics.* ○ *There's a real danger that the shop will be closed.* **3.** which exists in the world, not only in someone's imagination or in stories ○ *She believes fairies are real.*

real estate /'rɪəl ɪˌsteɪt/ *noun* land or buildings which are bought or sold

① **realise** /'rɪəlaɪz/ (**realises, realising, realised**), **realize** *verb* **1.** to understand clearly something that you did not understand before ○ *He didn't realise what he was letting himself in for when he said he would paint the house.* ○ *We soon realised we were on the wrong road.* ○ *When she went into the manager's office she did not realise she was going to be sacked.* **2.** to make something become real ○ *After four years of hard work, the motor racing team realised their dream of winning the Grand*

Prix. ○ *By buying a house by the sea he realised his greatest ambition.*

③ **realism** /ˈrɪəlɪz(ə)m/ *noun* **1.** behaviour which faces facts, accepting things as they are and not trying to change them or fight against them ○ *My job is to try to bring some realism to their proposals.* ○ *With the arrival of the new managing director an air of realism has finally entered the company.* **2.** the fact or practice of showing things in writing or painting as they really are ○ *He brought piles of sand and a deckchair into the studio to lend realism to the photos for the holiday brochure.* ○ *Realism dominated French painting in the latter part of the 19th century.*

realist /ˈrɪəlɪst/ *noun* **1.** a person who accepts life as it really is, and does not try to change it or fight it ○ *He told me that he didn't believe in love at first sight as he was a realist.* **2.** an artist or writer who shows things as they really are ○ *Realist painters were popular in the 19th century.*

③ **realistic** /rɪəˈlɪstɪk/ *adj* **1.** which looks as if it is real ○ *These flowers look so realistic. I can't believe they're made of plastic.* **2.** accepting life as it really is ○ *Let's be realistic – you'll never earn enough money to buy this house.* ○ *I'm just being realistic when I say that you should reconsider the offer.*

② **reality** /riˈælɪti/ (*plural* **realities**) *noun* what is real and not imaginary ○ *the grim realities of life in an industrial town* ○ *He worked hard, and his dreams of wealth soon became a reality.* ◇ **in reality** in fact ○ *She always told people she was poor, but in reality she was worth millions.*

① **really** /ˈrɪəli/ *adv* **1.** in fact ○ *The building really belongs to my father.* **2.** used to show surprise ○ *She's not really French, is she?* ○ *She doesn't like apples. – Really, how strange!* ○ *Did you really mean what you said?*

realm /relm/ *noun* **1.** a kingdom, especially the United Kingdom ○ *defence of the realm* **2.** an area of experience ○ *It is quite within the realms of possibility.*

real time /ˈrɪəl taɪm/ *noun* an action of a computer which takes place at the same time as the problem it is solving

reap /riːp/ (**reaps, reaping, reaped**) *verb* to cut a grain crop ○ *In September everyone went to the farm to help reap the corn.*

reappear /ˌriːəˈpɪə/ (**reappears, reappearing, reappeared**) *verb* to appear again

rear /rɪə/ *noun* the part at the back ○ *The rear of the car was damaged in the accident.* ○ *They sat towards the rear of the cinema.* ■ *adj* at the back ○ *The children sat in the rear seats in the car.* ○ *He wound down the rear window.* ■ *verb* (**rears, rearing, reared**) **1.** to look after animals or children as they are growing up ○ *They rear horses on their farm.* ○ *They stopped rearing pigs because of the smell.* **2.** to rise up, or to lift something up ○ *A rhino suddenly reared up out of the long grass.* ○ *The walls of the castle reared up before them.* ○ *The spectre of inflation reared its ugly head.*

rearrange /ˌriːəˈreɪndʒ/ (**rearranges, rearranging, rearranged**) *verb* **1.** to arrange something again ○ *She rearranged the furniture so that the room looked quite different.* **2.** to change the time of a meeting ○ *Can I rearrange my appointment for next week?*

rear-view mirror /ˌrɪə vjuː ˈmɪrə/ *noun* a mirror in the centre of the front of a car, so that the driver can see what is behind him without turning round

① **reason** /ˈriːz(ə)n/ *noun* **1.** a thing which explains why something has happened [~for/~that] ○ *The airline gave no reason for the plane's late arrival.* ○ *The boss asked him for the reason why he was behind with his work.* **2.** the ability to make sensible judgments ○ *She wouldn't listen to reason.* ■ *verb* (**reasons, reasoning, reasoned**) to think or to plan something carefully and sensibly [~(that)] ○ *He reasoned that any work is better than no work, so he took the job.* ○ *If you take the time to reason it out, you'll find a solution to the problem.* ◇ **it stands to reason** it is reasonable ○ *It stands to reason that he wants to join his father's firm.* ◇ **to see reason** to see that someone's argument is right or reasonable ○ *She was going to report her neighbours to the police, but in the end we got her to see reason.* ◇ **within reason** to a sensible degree, in a sensible way ○ *The children get £5 pocket money each week, and we let them spend it as they like, within reason.* ◇ **for some reason** in a way which you cannot explain ○ *For some reason (or other) the builders sent us two invoices.*

① **reasonable** /ˈriːz(ə)nəb(ə)l/ *adj* **1.** sensible ○ *The manager of the shop was very reasonable when she tried to explain that she had left her credit cards at home.* **2.** not expensive ○ *The hotel's charges are quite reasonable.* ○ *The restaurant offers good food at reasonable prices.*

② **reasonably** /ˈriːz(ə)nəbli/ *adv* **1.** in a reasonable way ○ *The meals are very rea-*

sonably priced. ○ *Very reasonably, he asked for a check on the brakes of the car before buying it.* **2.** quite ○ *It is reasonably easy.*

reasoned /'riːz(ə)nd/ *adj* carefully thought out

reasoning /'riːz(ə)nɪŋ/ *noun* opinions, views, or decisions

reassure /ˌriːə'ʃʊə/ (**reassures, reassuring, reassured**) *verb* to make someone less afraid or less worried (NOTE: + **reassurance** *n*)

reassuring /ˌriːə'ʃʊərɪŋ/ *adj* which reassures, which makes you less worried

rebate /'riːbeɪt/ *noun* a reduction in the amount of money to be paid ○ *We are offering a 10% rebate on selected goods.*

rebel[1] /'reb(ə)l/ *noun* a person who fights against a government or against those who are in authority ○ *The rebels fled to the mountains after the army captured their headquarters.* ○ *He considers himself something of a rebel because he wears his hair in a ponytail.*

rebel[2] /rɪ'bel/ (**rebels, rebelling, rebelled**) *verb* to fight against someone or something ○ *The peasants were rebelling against the king's men.* ○ *The class rebelled at the idea of doing extra homework.*

rebellion /rɪ'beljən/ *noun* a fight against the government, against the people in authority

rebellious /rɪ'beljəs/ *adj* fighting against authority

rebirth /riː'bɜːθ/ *noun* being born again, starting again

reboot /riː'buːt/ (**reboots, rebooting, rebooted**) *verb* to start a computer again

rebound[1] /'riːbaʊnd/ *noun* bouncing back ○ *The rebound was so fast that he missed the ball altogether.* ○ *There was a rebound in Tokyo share prices yesterday.*

rebound[2] /rɪ'baʊnd/ (**rebounds, rebounding, rebounded**) *verb* **1.** to move back after hitting something ○ *The ball rebounded off the goalpost.* **2.** to have a bad effect on you instead of the person the action was directed at [~on] ○ *His attacks on local shopkeepers rebounded on him when they all voted against him in the elections.*

rebuff /rɪ'bʌf/ (**rebuffs, rebuffing, rebuffed**) *verb* to refuse something sharply ○ *They rebuffed all offers of help.* (NOTE: + **rebuff** *n*)

rebuild /riː'bɪld/ (**rebuilds, rebuilding, rebuilt**) *verb* to build again

rebuke /rɪ'bjuːk/ (**rebukes, rebuking, rebuked**) *verb* to criticise someone sharply ○ *She rebuked the MD for not doing enough for the shareholders.* (NOTE: + **rebuke** *n*)

rebut /rɪ'bʌt/ (**rebuts, rebutting, rebutted**) *verb* to state that something such as an argument is not true

recalcitrant /rɪ'kælsɪtrənt/ *adj* determined not to change your mind, behaving in a difficult way

② **recall**[1] /'riːkɔːl/ *noun* the act of asking for products to be returned, or the act of ordering someone to return ○ *The recall of the faulty goods caused the manufacturers some serious 3problems.* ○ *The recall of the ambassador is expected any time now.*

recall[2] /rɪ'kɔːl/ (**recalls, recalling, recalled**) *verb* **1.** to remember something ○ *I seem to recall that you promised to do it.* ○ *I don't recall having met her before.* ○ *She couldn't recall any details of the accident.* **2.** (*of a manufacturer*) to ask for products to be returned because of possible faults ○ *They recalled 10,000 washing machines because of a faulty electrical connection.* ○ *They have recalled all their 2001 models as there is a fault in the steering.* **3.** to tell a government official to come home from a foreign country ○ *The United States recalled their representatives after the military coup.*

recap /riː'kæp/ (**recaps, recapping, recapped**) *verb* to state the main points of something again

③ **recede** /rɪ'siːd/ (**recedes, receding, receded**) *verb* to go away or to move back

② **receipt** /rɪ'siːt/ *noun* a piece of paper that shows you have paid for something or have received something [~for] ○ *We can't give you your money back if you don't have a receipt.* ○ *Would you like a receipt for the petrol?*

① **receive** /rɪ'siːv/ (**receives, receiving, received**) *verb* **1.** to get something which has been sent ○ *We received a parcel from the supplier this morning.* ○ *We only received our tickets the day before we were due to leave.* ○ *The staff have not received any wages for six months.* **2.** to meet or to welcome a visitor ○ *The group was received by the mayor.*

③ **receiver** /rɪ'siːvə/ *noun* **1.** the part of a telephone which you hold to your ear and listen through ○ *He shouted 'get stuffed!' and slammed down the receiver.* **2.** the part of a radio or television which receives broadcast programmes ○ *Our radio receiver picked up your signal quite clearly.*

① **recent** /ˈriːs(ə)nt/ *adj* taking place not very long ago ○ *We will mail you our most recent catalogue.* ○ *The changes are recent – they were made only last week.*

① **recently** /ˈriːs(ə)ntli/ *adv* only a short time ago ○ *I've seen him quite a lot recently.* ○ *They recently decided to move to Australia*

receptacle /rɪˈseptək(ə)l/ *noun* a container

③ **reception** /rɪˈsepʃən/ *noun* **1.** the way in which people react to something that happens or to someone who arrives ○ *The committee gave the proposal a favourable reception.* ○ *The critics gave the play a warm reception.* ○ *The minister had a rowdy reception at the meeting.* **2.** the place in a hotel where guests go when they arrive or leave, e.g. to get the key to their room ○ *Let's meet at reception at 9.00 am tomorrow.* **3.** a place in a large building where visitors go when they arrive and say who they have come to see ○ *There's a parcel waiting for you in reception.* **4.** a big party held to welcome special guests ○ *He hosted a reception for the prince.* **5.** the quality of the sound on a radio or the sound and picture of a TV broadcast ○ *Perhaps you'd get better reception if you moved the aerial.*

③ **receptionist** /rɪˈsepʃənɪst/ *noun* a person in a place such as a hotel or doctor's office who meets visitors and answers the telephone

receptive /rɪˈseptɪv/ *adj* **1.** interested in what is being presented **2.** willing to accept an idea or proposal [~to] ○ *The management was not at all receptive to the employee's suggestions.*

recess /rɪˈses/ *noun* **1.** an alcove or part of the wall of a room which is set back ○ *The large stone urn stands in the recess by the doorway.* **2.** an official holiday of the law courts or parliament ○ *The decision was taken when parliament was in recess.* **3.** *US* a recreation period at school ○ *They had a game during the recess.*

② **recession** /rɪˈseʃ(ə)n/ *noun* a situation when a country's economy is doing badly

recharge /riːˈtʃɑːdʒ/ (**recharges, recharging, recharged**) *verb* to put an electric charge into something again

③ **recipe** /ˈresəpi/ *noun* instructions for cooking food ○ *I copied the recipe for leek soup from the newspaper.* ○ *You can buy postcards with recipes of local dishes.*

recipient /rɪˈsɪpiənt/ *noun* a person who receives something

reciprocal /rɪˈsɪprək(ə)l/ *adj* which is done by two people, groups of people or by such things as countries or companies, to each other

reciprocate /rɪˈsɪprəkeɪt/ (**reciprocates, reciprocating, reciprocated**) *verb* to do the same thing to someone in return for something he or she has done to you

recital /rɪˈsaɪt(ə)l/ *noun* a performance of music by a musician or a small group of musicians

recite /rɪˈsaɪt/ (**recites, reciting, recited**) *verb* to speak a poem or other piece of writing aloud in public (NOTE: + **recitation** *n*)

reckless /ˈrekləs/ *adj* risky or done without thinking

② **reckon** /ˈrekən/ (**reckons, reckoning, reckoned**) *verb* **1.** to calculate, or to estimate [~(that)] ○ *We reckon we'll be there before lunch.* ○ *I reckon the costs to be about £25,000.* **2.** to think [~(that)] ○ *I reckon we should have stayed at home.*

reckoning /ˈrekənɪŋ/ *noun* a calculation

reclaim /rɪˈkleɪm/ (**reclaims, reclaiming, reclaimed**) *verb* **1.** to claim something which you owned before ○ *After he stopped paying the hire purchase instalments, the finance company tried to reclaim his car.* ○ *His car was towed away and he had to go to the pound to reclaim it.* (NOTE: also **claim back** in this sense) **2.** to take land, such as a marsh or waste sites, and make it suitable for use ○ *They reclaimed a whole stretch of land along the banks of the river.* ○ *The airport was built on reclaimed land in the bay.*

recline /rɪˈklaɪn/ (**reclines, reclining, reclined**) *verb* **1.** to lie back ○ *She reclined on the sofa and closed her eyes.* **2.** to make something lie further back ○ *If you feel tired during the plane journey, recline your seat and try to sleep.*

recluse /rɪˈkluːs/ *noun* a person who lives all alone and does not see anyone else

recognisable /ˈrekəgnaɪzəb(ə)l/ *adj* who can be recognised

① **recognise** /ˈrekəgnaɪz/ (**recognises, recognising, recognised**), **recognize** *verb* **1.** to know someone or something because you have seen him or her or it before ○ *He'd changed so much since I last saw him that I hardly recognised him.* ○ *He didn't recognise his father's voice over the phone.* ○ *Do you recognise the handwriting on the* *letter?* **2.** to admit something that has gone wrong or is bad ○ *I recognise that we should have acted earlier.* **3.** to approve of something or someone officially ○ *The language school has been recognised by the Ministry of Education.* ○ *She is recognised as an expert in the field of genetics.* **4.** to express praise for something which has been done ○ *They recognised her years of service.*

② **recognition** /ˌrekəg'nɪʃ(ə)n/ *noun* the fact that someone recognises or acknowledges something [~of] ○ *In recognition of his services he was given a watch.*

recoil /'riːkɔɪl/ (**recoils, recoiling, recoiled**) *verb* **1.** to move backwards suddenly ○ *The gun recoils at least two metres after being fired.* **2.** to move away quickly from something unpleasant ○ *When she saw the dead dog in the road she recoiled in disgust.* **3.** to feel strongly that something is unpleasant and want to avoid it ○ *He recoiled from carrying out the captain's orders.*

recollect /ˌrekə'lekt/ (**recollects, recollecting, recollected**) *verb* to remember something from the past

recollection /ˌrekə'lekʃən/ *noun* remembering something from the past

② **recommend** /ˌrekə'mend/ (**recommends, recommending, recommended**) *verb* **1.** to tell someone that it would be good to do something [~(that)] ○ *I would recommend that you talk to the bank manager.* ○ *This restaurant was recommended by a friend.* **2.** to praise something or someone ○ *She was highly recommended by her boss.* ○ *I certainly would not recommend Miss Smith for the job.* ○ *Can you recommend a good hotel in Amsterdam?*

③ **recommendation** /ˌrekəmen'deɪʃ(ə)n/ *noun* **1.** advice ○ *My recommendation is that you shouldn't sign the contract.* ○ *He's staying in bed at the doctor's recommendation.* **2.** giving praise

recompense /'rekəmpens/ (**recompenses, recompensing, recompensed**) *verb* to give compensation, payment or reward to someone or for something

reconcile /'rekənsaɪl/ (**reconciles, reconciling, reconciled**) *verb* **1.** to make two different things agree ○ *We can't reconcile her story with the facts we already knew.* **2.** □ **to reconcile yourself to something** to accept something that you do not like ○ *She seems reconciled to staying at home and looking after her mother.* **3.** □ **to reconcile someone with someone else** to make two people become friendly ○ *Social workers managed to reconcile him with his family.*

reconciliation /ˌrekənsɪli'eɪʃ(ə)n/ *noun* **1.** the bringing together of two people to become friends again ○ *Do you think a reconciliation is at all possible between the two brothers?* **2.** making two accounts agree ○ *The reconciliation of the accounts may take a long time.*

reconnaissance /rɪ'kɒnɪs(ə)ns/ *noun* a survey of enemy territory to get military information

reconsider /ˌriːkən'sɪdə/ (**reconsiders, reconsidering, reconsidered**) *verb* to think something over again

reconstitute /riː'kɒnstɪtjuːt/ (**reconstitutes, reconstituting, reconstituted**) *verb* to form something again as it was before

reconstruct /ˌriːkən'strʌkt/ (**reconstructs, reconstructing, reconstructed**) *verb* **1.** to construct something again ○ *The centre of the town was reconstructed using old photographs.* **2.** to work out how a crime must have been committed by taking all the known facts and using actors to play the parts of the people involved ○ *The police are trying to reconstruct the crime, in the hope that it will produce new evidence.*

③ **reconstruction** /ˌriːkən'strʌkʃən/ *noun* **1.** the act of reconstructing, of building again ○ *the economic reconstruction of the area after the earthquake* ○ *They're planning the reconstruction of the old fortress as a tourist attraction.* **2.** a thing reconstructed ○ *This is not the original building, it's a modern reconstruction.* **3.** working out how a crime must have been committed by examining all known facts and using an actor to play the part of the victim, etc. ○ *The police are hoping that the reconstruction of the crime will jog people's memories.*

record[1] /'rekɔːd/ *noun* **1.** a success in sport which is better than any other ○ *She holds the world record for the 100 metres.* ○ *He broke the world record* or *he set up a new world record at the last Olympics.* ○ *The college team is trying to set a new record for eating tins of beans.* **2.** written evidence of something which has happened ○ *We have no record of the sale.* **3.** a flat round piece of usually black plastic on which sound is stored ○ *She bought me an old Elvis Presley record for Christmas.* ○ *Burglars broke into his flat and stole his record collection.* ◇ **off the record** in private and not to be made public ○ *She spoke off the record about her marriage.*

record² /rɪ'kɔːd/ (**records, recording, recorded**) *verb* **1.** to report something or to make a note of something ○ *First, I have to record the sales, then I'll post the parcels.* **2.** to put sounds or images onto something such as a film, tape or disc ○ *The police recorded the whole conversation on a hidden tape-recorder.* ○ *This song has been badly recorded.*

record-breaking /'rekɔːd ˌbreɪkɪŋ/ *adj* which breaks records

recorder /rɪ'kɔːdə/ *noun* **1.** an instrument which records sound ○ *My tape recorder doesn't work, so I can't record the concert.* **2.** a musical instrument that you play by blowing ○ *Like most children, I learnt to play the recorder at school.*

③ **recording** /rɪ'kɔːdɪŋ/ *noun* **1.** the action of putting sounds or images onto something such as a film, tape or disc ○ *the recording of a video* ○ *The recording session starts at 3pm.* **2.** music or speech which has been recorded ○ *Did you know there was a new recording of the concerto?*

recount¹ /'riːkaʊnt/ *noun* the act of counting again, especially counting votes again ○ *The vote was very close, so the loser asked for a recount.* ○ *After three recounts Edward Jones was declared the winner by eleven votes.*

recount² /rɪ'kaʊnt/ (**recounts, recounting, recounted**) *verb* to tell a story ○ *He recounted his story to the police.*

recount³ /riː'kaʊnt/ (**recounts, recounting, recounted**) *verb* to count something again ○ *All the votes had to be recounted.*

② **recover¹** /rɪ'kʌvə/ (**recovers, recovering, recovered**) *verb* to get back something which has been lost or stolen ○ *You must work much harder if you want to recover the money you invested in your business.* ○ *She's trying to recover damages from the driver of the car.*

recover² /riː'kʌvə/ (**recovers, recovering, recovered**) *verb* to put a new cover on a piece of furniture ○ *Instead of buying a new chair, I had the old one recovered.*

③ **recovery** /rɪ'kʌv(ə)ri/ *noun* **1.** the fact that someone gets well again after being ill [~from] ○ *her recovery from a knee injury* ○ *She made a quick recovery and is now back at work.* **2.** getting back something which has been lost or stolen [~of] ○ *The TV programme led to the recovery of all the stolen goods.* ○ *We are aiming for the complete recovery of the money invested.*

re-create /ˌriːkri'eɪt/ *verb* to make something that used to exist appear or happen again in a similar way

recreation¹ /ˌrekri'eɪʃ(ə)n/ *noun* enjoyable activities that people do for fun ○ *The park is used for sport and recreation.* ○ *The survey shows that fishing and gardening are people's favourite recreations.*

recreation² /ˌriːkri'eɪʃ(ə)n/ *noun* creating again ○ *We have been given a grant to help pay for the recreation of the 19th-century flower garden.*

recrimination /rɪˌkrɪmɪ'neɪʃ(ə)n/ *noun* blaming someone else for something

recruit /rɪ'kruːt/ *noun* a new soldier or a new member of staff or member of a club ○ *Recruits are not allowed in the officers' mess.* ○ *The club needs new recruits.* ■ *verb* (**recruits, recruiting, recruited**) to encourage someone to join the army, a company or a club ○ *They have sent teams to universities to recruit new graduates.* (NOTE: + **recruitment** *n*)

rectangle /'rektæŋgəl/ *noun* a shape with four sides and right angles at the corners, with two long sides and two short sides

rectify /'rektɪfaɪ/ (**rectifies, rectifying, rectified**) *verb* to correct something

rectum /'rektəm/ *noun* the end part of the large intestine leading from the colon to the anus

recuperate /rɪ'kuːpəreɪt/ (**recuperates, recuperating, recuperated**) *verb* to get better after an illness (NOTE: + **recuperation** *n*)

③ **recur** /rɪ'kɜː/ (**recurs, recurring, recurred**) *verb* to happen again

recycle /riː'saɪk(ə)l/ (**recycles, recycling, recycled**) *verb* to process waste material so that it can be used again

① **red** /red/ *adj* (**redder, reddest**) coloured like the colour of blood ○ *She turned bright red when we asked her what had happened to the money.* ○ *Don't start yet – the traffic lights are still red.* ■ *noun* a colour like the colour of blood ○ *I would like a darker red for the door.*

red card /red 'kɑːd/ *noun* a card displayed by the referee when dismissing a player for doing something against the rules

redcurrant /red'kʌrənt/ *noun* a garden fruit in the form of little red berries ○ *a jar of redcurrant jelly* ○ *The redcurrants need more sugar – they're very sour.*

redden /'red(ə)n/ (**reddens, reddening, reddened**) *verb* **1.** to become red ○ *The* *trees stood out dark against the reddening evening sky.* ○ *His eyes were reddened from lack of sleep.* **2.** to go red in the face because you are ashamed or embarrassed ○ *She reddened slightly as he gave her a kiss.*

reddish /'redɪʃ/ *adj* of a colour that is close to red

redeem /rɪ'diːm/ (**redeems, redeeming, redeemed**) *verb* to make something better than it seemed to be at first ○ *The playing by the orchestra was redeemed by the singing of the soprano and tenor.* □ **to redeem yourself** to do something good to remove the bad effect of something you did previously

redemption /rɪ'dempʃən/ *noun* **1.** the action of redeeming a debt ○ *The bond is due for redemption.* **2.** being saved from sin

redeploy /ˌriːdɪ'plɔɪ/ (**redeploys, redeploying, redeployed**) *verb* to use people or equipment in a different area or for a different activity

redevelop /ˌriːdɪ'veləp/ (**redevelops, redeveloping, redeveloped**) *verb* to improve a run down area by renovating old buildings and building new ones

red-handed /red 'hændɪd/ *adj* in the act of committing a crime

redhead /'redhed/ *noun* a person with red hair

red herring /red 'herɪŋ/ *noun* a piece of information which is not important, and is given to someone to distract attention from what is really important

③ **red hot** /red 'hɒt/ *adj* very hot ○ *Watch out – that pan is red hot!*

redial /riː'daɪəl/ (**redials, redialling, redialled**) *verb* to dial a number on a telephone again

redirect /ˌriːdaɪ'rekt/ (**redirects, redirecting, redirected**) *verb* **1.** to send a letter on to another address or a phone call to another number ○ *We have asked the post office to redirect all our mail when we are away.* ○ *Phone calls can be redirected to our office number.* ○ *He redirected the email to his boss.* **2.** to use something in another way ○ *We are trying to get him to redirect his energy towards some more constructive work.*

redistribute /ˌriːdɪ'strɪbjuːt/ (**redistributes, redistributing, redistributed**) *verb* to share something out again in a different way

red meat /red 'miːt/ *noun* meat such as lamb or beef which is red in colour before it is cooked

redo /riː'duː/ (**redoes, redoing, redid, redone**) *verb* to do something again

redress /rɪ'dres/ (**redresses, redressing, redressed**) *verb* to correct something or to compensate ○ *They plan to redress the wrongs of society by taxing the rich.* (NOTE: + **redress** *n*) □ **to redress the balance** to make something fair again ○ *Last year I gave my daughter some money, so this year I'll give the same amount to my son to redress the balance.*

③ **red tape** /ˌred 'teɪp/ *noun* official paperwork which takes a long time to complete (*informal*)

① **reduce** /rɪ'djuːs/ (**reduces, reducing, reduced**) *verb* to make something smaller or less ○ *The police are fighting to reduce traffic accidents.* ○ *Prices have been reduced by 15 per cent.* ○ *I'd like to reduce the size of the photograph so that we can use it as a Christmas card.*

② **reduction** /rɪ'dʌkʃən/ *noun* the act of making something smaller in size or number ○ *Price reductions start on 1st August.* ○ *The company was forced to make job reductions.*

② **redundancy** /rɪ'dʌndənsi/ *noun* being no longer employed, because the job is no longer needed

② **redundant** /rɪ'dʌndənt/ *adj* not needed □ **to be made redundant** to lose your job because you are not needed any more ○ *Five employees were made redundant this week.* ○ *My son thinks he'll be made redundant, so he's already looking for another job.*

redwood /'redwʊd/ *noun* a very tall conifer which grows on the West Coast of the United States

reed /riːd/ *noun* a thin piece of wood or metal inside a musical instrument, which vibrates when you blow on it (NOTE: Do not confuse with **read**.)

③ **reef** /riːf/ *noun* a long line of rocks just above or below the surface of the sea ○ *The yacht hit a reef and sank.* ○ *The Great Barrier Reef is a reef off the north-east coast of Australia.*

reek /riːk/ (**reeks, reeking, reeked**) *verb* to smell strongly of something (NOTE: + **reek** *n*)

reel /riːl/ (**reels, reeling, reeled**) *verb* to stagger

reel in *phrasal verb* to pull in a line round a reel

reel off③ *phrasal verb* to give a list of names or figures rapidly

re-elect /ˌriːɪ'lekt/ *verb* to elect someone again

ref /ref/ *noun* **1.** same as **referee** ○ *Come on ref – that was a foul!* **2.** same as **reference**

③ **refer** /rɪ'fɜː/ (**refers, referring, referred**) *verb* **1.** to be about something or someone ○ *Do you think he was referring to me when he said some staff would have to leave?* **2.** to look into something for information ○ *He referred to his diary to see if he had a free afternoon.* **3.** to pass a problem to someone to decide ○ *We have referred your complaint to our head office.* ○ *He was referred to an ear specialist by his GP.*

② **referee** /ˌrefə'riː/ *noun* (*in sports*) a person who makes sure that a game is played according to the rules ○ *When fighting broke out between the players, the referee stopped the match.* ○ *The referee sent several players off.*

① **reference** /'ref(ə)rəns/ *noun* an act of mentioning something or someone [~to] ○ *She made a reference to her brother-in-law.* ○ *The report made no reference to the bank.* ◇ **with reference to** concerning something ○ *With reference to your letter of May 25th.*

reference book /'ref(ə)rəns bʊk/ *noun* a book, such as a dictionary or an encyclopedia, where you can look for information

referendum /ˌrefə'rendəm/ (*plural* **referendums** or **referenda**) *noun* a vote where all the people of a country are asked to vote on a single question

refill[1] /riː'fɪl/ (**refills, refilling, refilled**) *verb* to fill a container that has become empty ○ *The waiter refilled our glasses.* ○ *We stopped twice to refill the car on the way to Scotland.*

refill[2] /'riːfɪl/ *noun* another amount of a drink that you have finished ○ *Your glass is empty – can I get you a refill?*

refine /rɪ'faɪn/ (**refines, refining, refined**) *verb* **1.** to make something more pure ○ *Juice from sugar cane is refined by boiling.* **2.** to make something better ○ *The process needs to be further refined before we can introduce it nationally.* ○ *The company needs to refine its sales techniques.*

refined /rɪ'faɪnd/ *adj* **1.** which has been made pure ○ *white refined sugar* **2.** very elegant and polite ○ *In refined society, you don't slurp your soup.*

refinement /rɪ'faɪnmənt/ *noun* **1.** elegance ○ *The drawing room of the old house gives an idea of the refinement of life in the 18th century.* **2.** improvement ○ *The latest model has various refinements which the earlier models lacked.* ○ *This is a refinement of our previous word-processing program.*

refinery /rɪ'faɪnəri/ (*plural* **refineries**) *noun* a plant where a raw material, such as ore, oil or sugar is processed to remove impurities

① **reflect** /rɪ'flekt/ (**reflects, reflecting, reflected**) *verb* to send back light, heat or an image of something [~off] ○ *a picture of snow-capped mountains reflected in a clear blue lake* ○ *The light reflected off the top of the car.* ○ *White surfaces reflect light better than dark ones.*

reflective /rɪ'flektɪv/ *adj* **1.** thoughtful ○ *The poem was written when the poet was in a reflective mood.* **2.** which reflects ○ *Cyclists should wear reflective armbands when cycling in the dark.*

reflector /rɪ'flektə/ *noun* apparatus which reflects

reflex /'riːfleks/ *noun* an automatic reaction to something ○ *The doctor tested his reflexes by tapping on his knee with a little hammer.* ○ *By stopping the car when the little girl ran into the road she showed how good her reflexes were.*

reflexive /rɪ'fleksɪv/ *adj* (*in grammar*) a verb or pronoun which refers back to the subject

reflexive verb /rɪ'fleksɪv vɜːb/ *noun* a transitive verb whose subject and object both refer to the same person or thing

reflexology /ˌriːflek'sɒlədʒi/ *noun* a treatment to relieve tension by massaging the soles of the feet and toes to stimulate the nerves and increase the blood supply

② **reform** /rɪ'fɔːm/ *noun* the act of changing something to make it better [~to/~of] ○ *The government is planning a series of reforms to the benefit system.the reform of the armed forces* ■ *verb* (**reforms, reforming, reformed**) **1.** to change something in order to make it better ○ *They want to reform the educational system.* **2.** to stop committing crimes, or to stop having bad habits and to become good ○ *After her time in prison she became a reformed character.* ○ *He used to drink a lot, but since he got married he has reformed.*

reformer /rɪ'fɔːmə/ *noun* a person who tries to make something better

refrain /rɪ'freɪn/ *verb* to keep yourself from doing something [~from] (*formal*) ○ *Please refrain from smoking during dinner.*

○ *We must ask everyone to refrain from applauding until the signal is given.*

refresh /rɪ'freʃ/ (**refreshes, refreshing, refreshed**) *verb* **1.** to make fresh again ○ *A coat of paint will refresh the room.* **2.** to make someone less tired ○ *After a good night's sleep she felt refreshed.* □ **to refresh yourself** to do something to make yourself less tired ○ *I need a drink to refresh myself before the second half.*

refreshing /rɪ'freʃɪŋ/ *adj* something which is refreshing makes you feel fresh or full of energy again ○ *I had a refreshing drink of cold water.* ○ *A refreshing shower of rain cooled the air.*

③ **refreshments** /rɪ'freʃmənts/ *plural noun* food and drink ○ *Light refreshments will be served after the concert.* ○ *Refreshments are being offered in a tent on the lawn.*

refrigerate /rɪ'frɪdʒəreɪt/ (**refrigerates, refrigerating, refrigerated**) *verb* to keep food cold so that it will not go bad

③ **refrigerator** /rɪ'frɪdʒəreɪtə/ *noun* an electrical machine used in the kitchen for keeping food and drink cold ○ *There's some orange juice in the refrigerator.* (NOTE: often called a **fridge**)

refuel /riː'fjuːəl/ (**refuels, refuelling, refuelled**) *verb* to put more fuel into a ship, plane, car or other vehicle

③ **refuge** /'refjuːdʒ/ *noun* □ **to take refuge** to shelter ○ *When the tornado approached, they took refuge in the cellar.* ○ *We took refuge from the rain under a covered bus shelter.*

③ **refugee** /ˌrefjʊ'dʒiː/ *noun* a person who has left his or her country because of war or because the government did not like allow his or her religious or political beliefs

refund¹ /'riːfʌnd/ *noun* money paid back ○ *She got a refund after she complained to the manager.*

refund² /rɪ'fʌnd/ (**refunds, refunding, refunded**) *verb* to pay money back ○ *We will refund the cost of postage.* ○ *The tour company only refunded £100 of the £400 I had paid.*

refurbish /riː'fɜːbɪʃ/ (**refurbishes, refurbishing, refurbished**) *verb* to make something like new

refusal /rɪ'fjuːz(ə)l/ *noun* saying that you do not accept something ○ *His refusal to help was unexpected.* ○ *Did you accept? – no! I sent a letter of refusal.*

refuse¹ /rɪ'fjuːz/ (**refuses, refusing, refused**) *verb* **1.** to say that you will not do something ○ *His father refused to lend him any more money.* ○ *He asked for permission to see his family, but it was refused.* **2.** □ **the car refused to start** the car would not start ○ *Once again this morning the car refused to start.*

refuse² /'refjuːs/ *noun* rubbish and things which are not wanted ○ *Please put all refuse in the bin.* ○ *Refuse collection on our road is on Thursdays.* (NOTE: no plural)

refute /rɪ'fjuːt/ (**refutes, refuting, refuted**) *verb* **1.** to prove that something is wrong ○ *He has tried to refute Einstein's theory.* **2.** to show that something is untrue ○ *He refuted her allegations completely.*

regain /rɪ'geɪn/ (**regains, regaining, regained**) *verb* to get something back which was lost

regal /'riːg(ə)l/ *adj* referring to a king or queen ○ *The regal splendour of the state opening of parliament.*

① **regard** /rɪ'gɑːd/ *verb* (**regards, regarding, regarded**) **1.** to have an opinion about someone [~as] ○ *She is highly regarded by the manager.* ○ *They regarded their neighbour with suspicion.* □ **to regard someone *or* something as** to consider someone or something to be something ○ *The police are regarding the case as attempted murder.* ○ *The others regarded him as a nuisance.* **2.** to look at someone or something (*formal*) ■ *noun* **1.** the extent to which you consider something or care about it [~for] ○ *She had little regard for our safety.* **2.** an opinion of someone that shows how much you respect them [~for] ○ *We have a very high regard for your system of government.He is held in high regard by his staff.* ■ *plural noun* **regards** best wishes ○ *She sends her (kind) regards.* ○ *Please give my regards to your mother.* ◇ **as regards** relating to ○ *As regards the cost of the trip, I'll let you know soon what the final figure is.* ◇ **with regard to** relating to ○ *With regard to your request for extra funds.*

③ **regarding** /rɪ'gɑːdɪŋ/ *prep* relating to, concerning ○ *He left instructions regarding his possessions.* ○ *Regarding your offer, I think we will have to say no.*

③ **regardless** /rɪ'gɑːdləs/ *adv* without paying any attention to □ **regardless of** in spite of ○ *They drove through the war zone regardless of the danger.* □ **to carry on regardless** to continue in spite of everything ○ *Although the temperature was well over 40°, they carried on working regardless.*

regenerate /rɪ'dʒenəreɪt/ (**regenerates, regenerating, regenerated**) *verb* to make something grow strong again

reggae /'regeɪ/ *noun* a type of West Indian music

regime /reɪ'ʒiːm/, **régime** *noun* **1.** a usually harsh type of government or administration ○ *Under a military regime, civil liberties may be restricted.* **2.** the government of a country ○ *The former régime was overthrown and the President fled.*

regiment /'redʒɪmənt/ *noun* a group of soldiers, usually commanded by a colonel or lieutenant-colonel

regimented /'redʒɪmentɪd/ *adj* strictly organised or kept under strict discipline

① **region** /'riːdʒən/ *noun* a large area of a country ○ *The South-West region is well known for its apples.*

① **regional** /'riːdʒ(ə)nəl/ *adj* relating to a region ○ *The recession has not affected the whole country – it is only regional.* ○ *After the national news, here is the regional news for the South West.*

③ **register** /'redʒɪstə/ *noun* **1.** a list of names ○ *I can't find your name in the register.* ○ *His name was struck off the register.* **2.** a book in which you sign your name ○ *After the wedding, the bride and groom and witnesses all signed the register.* ○ *Please sign the hotel register when you check in.* ■ *verb* (**registers, registering, registered**) to write a name officially in a list [~with/~for] ○ *Babies have to be registered with the registrar as soon as they are born.* ○ *Students are registering for their courses this week.* ○ *If you don't register, we won't be able to get in touch with you.*

register office /ˌredʒɪstə 'ɒfɪs/ *noun* an office where records of births, marriages and deaths are kept and where you can be married in a civil ceremony

registrar /ˌredʒɪ'strɑː/ *noun* **1.** a person who keeps official records ○ *The registrar of births, marriages and deaths.* ○ *They were married by the registrar.* **2.** a qualified doctor or surgeon in a hospital who supervises house doctors ○ *She's a registrar at our local hospital.*

③ **registration** /ˌredʒɪ'streɪʃ(ə)n/ *noun* the act of registering

registration number /ˌredʒɪ 'streɪʃ(ə)n ˌnʌmbə/ *noun* the official number of a car

registry /'redʒɪstri/ *noun* a place where official records are kept

registry office /'redʒɪstri ˌɒfɪs/ *noun* an office where records of births, marriages and deaths are kept and where you can be married in a civil ceremony

regress /rɪ'gres/ (**regresses, regressing, regressed**) *verb* to return to an earlier stage or condition (NOTE: + **regression** *n*)

regret /rɪ'gret/ *noun* the feeling of being sorry that something has happened ○ *I have absolutely no regrets about what we did.* ■ *verb* (**regrets, regretting, regretted**) to be sorry that something has happened ○ *I regret that I cannot be with you this evening.* ○ *I regret the trouble this has caused you.* ○ *We regret the delay in the arrival of our flight from Amsterdam.*

regrettable /rɪ'gretəb(ə)l/ *adj* which must be regretted

② **regular** /'regjʊlə/ *adj* **1.** done at the same time each day ○ *His regular train is the 12.45.* ○ *The regular flight to Athens leaves at 06.00.* **2.** usual or standard ○ *The regular price is £1.25, but we are offering them at 99p.*

③ **regularly** /'regjʊləli/ *adv* on most occasions ○ *She is regularly the first person to arrive at the office each morning.*

regulate /'regjʊˌleɪt/ (**regulates, regulating, regulated**) *verb* **1.** to adjust a machine so that it works in a certain way ○ *The heater needs to be regulated to keep the temperature steady.* ○ *Turn this knob to regulate the volume.* ○ *Her heartbeat is regulated by the pacemaker.* **2.** to maintain something by law ○ *Speed on the motorway is strictly regulated.*

② **regulation** /ˌregjʊ'leɪʃ(ə)n/ *plural noun* **regulations** laws or rules controlling something ○ *The restaurant broke the fire regulations.* ○ *Safety regulations were not being properly followed.*

rehab /'riːˌhæb/ *noun* the process of curing someone of an addiction to drugs or alcohol

rehabilitate /ˌriːə'bɪlɪteɪt/ (**rehabilitates, rehabilitating, rehabilitated**) *verb* **1.** to train a disabled person or an ex-prisoner to lead a normal life and fit into society ○ *Prisoners need special training in order to be rehabilitated.* **2.** to cure someone of an addiction to drugs or alcohol (NOTE: + **rehabilitation** *n*)

rehash /riː'hæʃ/ (**rehashes, rehashing, rehashed**) *verb* to bring out an old story, book, idea, or other work in more or less the same form as before ○ *Her recent article just rehashed the same themes as her book.*

③ **rehearsal** /rɪˈhɜːs(ə)l/ *noun* a practice of a play or concert before the first public performance. ◊ **dress rehearsal**

③ **rehearse** /rɪˈhɜːs/ (**rehearses, rehearsing, rehearsed**) *verb* to practise a play or a concert before a public performance

rehouse /riːˈhaʊz/ (**rehouses, rehousing, rehoused**) *verb* to move somebody to other, often better, housing

③ **reign** /reɪn/ *noun* a period when a king, queen or emperor rules ○ *during the reign of Elizabeth I* ■ *verb* (**reigns, reigning, reigned**) to rule ○ *Queen Victoria reigned between 1837 and 1901.* ○ *She reigned during a period of great prosperity.* (NOTE: Do not confuse with **rain**.)

reimburse /ˌriːɪmˈbɜːs/ (**reimburses, reimbursing, reimbursed**) *verb* to pay someone the money he or she has spent for a particular purpose [~for] (*formal*) ○ *You will be reimbursed for your expenses* or *your expenses will be reimbursed.*

reincarnation /ˌriːɪnkɑːˈneɪʃ(ə)n/ *noun* **1.** a person's soul born again in another body or animal after death ○ *The ancient Egyptians believed that the owl was the reincarnation of the god Horus.* **2.** reappearance of someone in another form ○ *His latest reincarnation was as an insurance salesman.*

③ **reinforce** /ˌriːɪnˈfɔːs/ (**reinforces, reinforcing, reinforced**) *verb* to make stronger or more solid

reinforcement /ˌriːɪnˈfɔːsmənt/ *noun* the act of reinforcing ○ *One of the walls needs reinforcement.*

reinstate /ˌriːɪnˈsteɪt/ (**reinstates, reinstating, reinstated**) *verb* to put someone back into a job from which he or she was dismissed (NOTE: + **reinstatement** *n*)

reinvent /ˌriːɪnˈvent/ (**reinvents, reinventing, reinvented**) *verb* to make something popular again after it has been out of fashion for a time

reiterate /riːˈɪtəreɪt/ (**reiterates, reiterating, reiterated**) *verb* to say again (NOTE: + **reiteration** *n*)

reject[1] /rɪˈdʒekt/ (**rejects, rejecting, rejected**) *verb* **1.** to refuse to accept something ○ *She rejected my suggestion that we changed our plans.* ○ *The proposals for the new project were rejected.* **2.** to refuse to accept something because it is not satisfactory ○ *Poles shorter than the standard size are rejected.*

reject[2] /ˈriːdʒekt/ *noun* something which is not accepted because it is not satisfactory

③ **rejection** /rɪˈdʒekʃən/ *noun* a refusal to accept

rejoice /rɪˈdʒɔɪs/ (**rejoices, rejoicing, rejoiced**) *verb* to be very happy ○ *We all rejoiced to hear the news that the baby had been found.*

rejoin /riːˈdʒɔɪn/ (**rejoins, rejoining, rejoined**) *verb* to join again (*formal*)

rejuvenate /rɪˈdʒuːvɪneɪt/ (**rejuvenates, rejuvenating, rejuvenated**) *verb* **1.** to make someone young again ○ *She came back from the health farm completely rejuvenated.* **2.** to give something new vigour and strength ○ *He hopes to rejuvenate the club by attracting younger members.*

rekindle /riːˈkɪnd(ə)l/ (**rekindles, rekindling, rekindled**) *verb* to start again or to make something happen again

relapse /ˈriːlæps, rɪˈlæps/ *noun* (*of patient or disease*) becoming worse after seeming to be getting better ○ *He had a relapse and had to go back into hospital.* (NOTE: + **relapse** *v*)

① **relate** /rɪˈleɪt/ (**relates, relating, related**) *verb* **1.** to have or make a connection with something else [~to] ○ *They have related the rise in standards to better teaching.* ○ *They say a happy childhood and success in life are related.* **2.** to understand someone and be able to communicate with them [~to/with] ○ *Do you find it difficult to relate to him?* ○ *The children relate well with their grandparents.* **3.** to tell a story (*formal*) ○ *It took him half an hour to relate what had happened.*

relate to *phrasal verb* **1.** to be concerned with something ○ *The regulations relate to the movement of boats in the harbour.* **2.** to be able to understand something ○ *The book deals with people's feelings in a way I can relate to.*

① **related to** /rɪˈleɪtɪd tʊ/ *adj* **1.** belonging to the same family as ○ *Are you related to the Smith family in London Road?* **2.** connected in some way with ○ *The disease is related to the weakness of the heart muscle.* ○ *He has a drug-related illness.* ○ *There are several related items on the agenda.*

③ **relating to** /rɪˈleɪtɪŋ tuː/ *adv* relating to or connected with ○ *documents relating to the sale of the house*

① **relation** /rɪˈleɪʃ(ə)n/ *noun* **1.** a member of a family ○ *All my relations live in Canada.* ○ *Laura's no relation of mine, she's just* *a friend.* **2.** a link between two things [~between] ○ *Is there any relation between wealth and happiness?* ■ *plural noun* **relations** the way that people or organizations behave towards each other ○ *We try to maintain good relations with our customers.* ○ *Relations between the two countries have become tense.* ◇ **in relation to** relating to or connected with ○ *Documents in relation to the sale.*

③ **relationship** /rɪ'leɪʃ(ə)nʃɪp/ *noun* **1.** a close friendship, especially one in which two people are involved in a romantic or sexual way with each other ○ *She decided to end the relationship when she found he had been seeing other women.* **2.** the way that people or organisations behave towards each other [/~with] ○ *We try to have a good working relationship with our staff.* **3.** a link or connection [~between] ○ *There is a proven relationship between smoking and lung cancer.*

② **relative** /'relətɪv/ *noun* a person who is related to someone ○ *We have several relatives living in Canada.* ○ *He has no living relatives.*

relative clause /'relətɪv klɔːz/ *noun* a subordinate clause that provides additional information about person or thing and which is joined to the previous clause by words like 'which', 'who' or 'that '

② **relatively** /'relətɪvli/ *adv* to some extent ○ *The children have been relatively free from colds this winter.* ○ *We are dealing with a relatively new company.*

relative pronoun /ˌrelətɪv 'prəʊnaʊn/ *noun* a pronoun, such as 'who' or 'which', which connects two clauses

③ **relax** /rɪ'læks/ (**relaxes, relaxing, relaxed**) *verb* to rest from work or to be less tense ○ *They spent the first week of their holiday relaxing on the beach.* ○ *Guests can relax in the bar before going to eat in the restaurant.* ○ *Just lie back and relax – the injection won't hurt.*

③ **relaxed** /rɪ'lækst/ *adj* not upset or nervous ○ *Even if he failed his test, he's still very relaxed about the whole thing.*

③ **relaxing** /rɪ'læksɪŋ/ *adj* which makes you less tense

relay¹ /'riːleɪ/ *noun* a group of people working in turn with other groups ○ *A shift is usually composed of groups of workers who work in relays.* ○ *All the work had been done by the time the next relay arrived.*

relay² /rɪ'leɪ/ (**relays, relaying, relayed**) *verb* **1.** to pass on a message ○ *She relayed the news to the other members of her family.* ○ *All messages are relayed through this office.* **2.** to pass on a TV or radio broadcast through a secondary station ○ *The programmes are received in the capital and then relayed to TV stations round the country.*

② **release** /rɪ'liːs/ (**releases, releasing, released**) *verb* **1.** to stop holding something, or to stop keeping someone prisoner ○ *The hostages were released last night.* ○ *Pull that lever to release the brakes.* **2.** to make something public ○ *The government has released figures about the number of people out of work.*

relegate /'relɪgeɪt/ (**relegates, relegating, relegated**) *verb* **1.** (*in sports*) to move a team down from a higher division to a lower one ○ *They were relegated from the premier division.* **2.** to put into a worse position ○ *On the arrival of the new manager, I was relegated to the accounts department.* (NOTE: + **relegation** *n*)

relent /rɪ'lent/ (**relents, relenting, relented**) *verb* to be less strict; to decide to be less strict than before

relentless /rɪ'lentləs/ *adj* continuing without giving up

③ **relevance** /'reləv(ə)ns/ *noun* the fact that something is relevant

② **relevant** /'reləv(ə)nt/ *adj* if something is relevant, it has something to do with the thing being mentioned ○ *Which is the relevant government department?* ○ *Can you give me the relevant papers?* ○ *Is this information at all relevant?*

reliable /rɪ'laɪəb(ə)l/ *adj* which can be relied on or which can be trusted ○ *It is a very reliable car.* ○ *The sales manager is completely reliable.*

reliance /rɪ'laɪəns/ *noun* the fact that someone relies on something

reliant /rɪ'laɪənt/ *adj* which relies on something

relic /'relɪk/ *noun* something which remains from the past ○ *That cap is a relic of my time as a naval cadet.*

② **relief** /rɪ'liːf/ *noun* **1.** the reduction of pain or stress [~from] ○ *medicines that bring relief from pain* ○ *He breathed a sigh of relief when the police car went past without stopping.* ○ *What a relief to have finished my exams!* **2.** help given to people who need it urgently ○ *The Red Cross is organising relief for the flood victims.*

③ **relieve** /rɪ'liːv/ (**relieves, relieving, relieved**) *verb* **1.** to make something unpleasant better or easier ○ *He took aspirins to re-*

lieve the pain. **2.** to take over from someone ○ *You can go and have something to eat – I'm here to relieve you for an hour.*

③ **relieved** /rɪ'liːvd/ *adj* glad to be rid of a problem

② **religion** /rɪ'lɪdʒən/ *noun* a belief in gods or in one God ○ *Does their religion help them to lead a good life?* ○ *It is against my religion to eat meat on Fridays.*

② **religious** /ˌrə'lɪdʒəs/ *adj* relating to religion ○ *There is a period of religious study every morning.*

religiously /rə'lɪdʒəsli/ *adv* regularly and carefully ○ *He followed all their instructions religiously.*

relinquish /rə'lɪŋkwɪʃ/ (**relinquishes, relinquishing, relinquished**) *verb* to leave or to let go of something

relish /'relɪʃ/ *noun* **1.** spicy pickles or spicy sauce ○ *Eat your sausages with mustard or relish.* **2.** enjoyment ○ *She argued with him with great relish.* ■ *verb* (**relishes, relishing, relished**) to enjoy ○ *I don't relish having to take my exam again.*

relive /riː'lɪv/ (**relives, reliving, relived**) *verb* to go through something again, especially in your mind

relocate /ˌriːləʊ'keɪt/ (**relocates, relocating, relocated**) *verb* to move an office, factory or staff to a different place (NOTE: + **relocation** *n*)

reluctant /rɪ'lʌktənt/ *adj* not willing to do something ○ *He seemed reluctant to help.* (NOTE: + **reluctance** *n*)

reluctantly /rɪ'lʌktəntli/ *adv* not willingly

rely *verb*

rely on② *phrasal verb* to believe or know that something will happen or that someone will do something ○ *We can rely on him to finish the work on time.* ○ *Can these machines be relied on?*

① **remain** /rɪ'meɪn/ (**remains, remaining, remained**) *verb* **1.** to stay ○ *We expect it will remain fine for the rest of the week.* ○ *She remained behind at the office to finish her work.* **2.** to be left ○ *Half the food remained uneaten and had to be thrown away.* ○ *After the accident not much remained of the car.*

③ **remainder** /rɪ'meɪndə/ *noun* what is left after everything else has gone ○ *What shall we do for the remainder of the holidays?* ○ *After the bride and groom left, the remainder of the party stayed in the hotel to have supper.*

① **remaining** /rɪ'meɪnɪŋ/ *adj* which is left

③ **remains** /rɪ'meɪnz/ *plural noun* **1.** things left over or left behind ○ *The remains of the evening meal were left on the table until the next morning.* ○ *We're trying to save the Roman remains from total obliteration by the construction company.* **2.** the body of a dead person ○ *The emperor's remains were buried in the cathedral.*

remake /'riːmeɪk/ *noun* new film with the same story as an old film ○ *They're planning yet another remake of 'David Copperfield'.*

remand /rɪ'mɑːnd/ *noun* sending a prisoner away for a time when a case is adjourned to be heard at a later date ■ *verb* (**remands, remanding, remanded**) **1.** to send a prisoner away to reappear later to answer a case which has been adjourned **2.** *US* to send a case back to a lower court

③ **remark** /rɪ'mɑːk/ *noun* a comment [~about/on] ○ *He made some remark about my being late.* □ **to make *or* pass remarks about** to make sharp or rude comments about ○ *She made some remarks about the dirty tablecloth.* ■ *verb* (**remarks, remarking, remarked**) to notice and comment on [~on/upon/~that] ○ *She remarked on how dirty the café was.* ○ *Customers remarked that the shop looked brighter.*

③ **remarkable** /rɪ'mɑːkəb(ə)l/ *adj* very unusual ○ *She's a remarkable woman.* ○ *It's remarkable that the bank has not asked us to pay back the money.*

remarkably /rɪ'mɑːkəbli/ *adv* to an unusually great degree, or in an unusual way ○ *She remained remarkably calm.*

remarry /riː'mæri/ (**remarries, remarrying, remarried**) *verb* to marry again

remedial /rɪ'miːdiəl/ *adj* which cures or which makes something better

③ **remedy** /'remədi/ *noun* a thing which may cure [~for] ○ *It's an old remedy for hayfever.*

① **remember** /rɪ'membə/ (**remembers, remembering, remembered**) *verb* to bring back into your mind something which you have seen or heard before [/~when/where/how etc] ○ *Do you remember when we got lost in the fog?* ○ *My grandmother can remember seeing the first television programmes.* ○ *She remembered seeing it on the dining room table.* ○ *She can't remember where she put her umbrella.* ○ *I don't remember having been in this hotel before.* ○ *I remember my grandmother very well.* ○ *It's strange that I can never* *remember my father's birthday.* ○ *Did you remember to switch off the kitchen light?* (NOTE: You **remember doing something** which you did in the past; you **remember to do something** in the future.)

remembrance /rɪ'membrəns/ *noun* memory

① **remind** /rɪ'maɪnd/ (**reminds, reminding, reminded**) *verb* to make someone remember something [~that] ○ *She reminded him that the meeting had to finish at 6.30.* ○ *Now that you've reminded me, I do remember seeing him last week.* ○ *Remind me to book the tickets for New York.*

reminder /rɪ'maɪndə/ *noun* **1.** a thing which reminds you of something ○ *Keep this picture as a reminder of happier days.* ○ *He tied a knot in his handkerchief as a reminder of what he had to do.* **2.** a letter to remind a customer to do something

reminisce /ˌremɪ'nɪs/ (**reminisces, reminiscing, reminisced**) *verb* to talk about memories of the past (NOTE: + **reminiscence** *n*)

reminiscent /ˌremɪ'nɪs(ə)nt/ *adj* which reminds you of the past

remission /rɪ'mɪʃ(ə)n/ *noun* **1.** a reduction of a prison sentence ○ *He was sentenced to five years, but should only serve three with remission.* ○ *He earned remission for good behaviour.* **2.** a period when an illness is less severe ○ *The cancer is in remission.*

remittance /rɪ'mɪt(ə)ns/ *noun* money which is sent

remnant /'remnənt/ *noun* a quantity or piece left over

remonstrate /'remənstreɪt/ (**remonstrates, remonstrating, remonstrated**) *verb* to reason with someone about something they have done (*formal*)

remorse /rɪ'mɔːs/ *noun* regret about something wrong which you have done

remorseless /rɪ'mɔːsləs/ *adj* **1.** which cannot be stopped ○ *The Green Belt is supposed to stop the remorseless advance of houses into the countryside.* ○ *There's nothing you can do to hold back the remorseless advance of old age.* **2.** cruel, showing no pity ○ *A remorseless artillery bombardment pounded the town.*

③ **remote** /rɪ'məʊt/ *adj* **1.** far away from towns and places where there are lots of people ○ *The hotel is situated in a remote mountain village.* **2.** not very likely ○ *There's a remote chance of finding a cure for his illness.* ○ *The possibility of him arriving on time is remote.*

③ **remote control** /rɪˌməʊt kən'trəʊl/ *noun* a small piece of electronic equipment which you use for controlling something such as a TV or CD player from a distance

remotely /rɪ'məʊtli/ *adv* **1.** very slightly, or not even very slightly ○ *I'm not remotely interested in meeting him.* **2.** at a great distance from a town ○ *a remotely situated farm* **3.** without direct physical contact ○ *They were able to set the controls remotely.*

removable /rɪ'muːvəb(ə)l/ *adj* designed so as to be easily taken off and put back on again

③ **removal** /rɪ'muːv(ə)l/ *noun* **1.** taking something or someone away ○ *the removal of the ban on importing computers* ○ *Refuse collectors are responsible for the removal of household waste.* ○ *The opposition called for the removal of the Foreign Secretary.* **2.** the process of moving to a new home, new office, etc.

① **remove** /rɪ'muːv/ (**removes, removing, removed**) *verb* to take something away ○ *You can remove his name from the mailing list.* ○ *The waitress removed the dirty plates and brought us some tea.*

remover /rɪ'muːvə/ *noun* **1.** a person who moves furniture from one house to another ○ *We're moving house tomorrow – the removers will be here at 7.30 am.* **2.** a thing which removes

remuneration /rɪˌmjuːnə'reɪʃ(ə)n/ *noun* payment for services done (NOTE: + **remunerate** *v*)

③ **renaissance** /rɪ'neɪs(ə)ns/, **renascence** *noun* a rebirth or a starting again ○ *British cinema has undergone a renaissance in recent years.*

rename /riː'neɪm/ (**renames, renaming, renamed**) *verb* to give something a new name

render /'rendə/ (**renders, rendering, rendered**) *verb* **1.** to translate ○ *The text was badly rendered in Italian.* **2.** to provide ○ *services rendered to the country* **3.** to make someone or something change into a particular state ○ *She was rendered speechless by their letter.* ○ *The experts rendered the bomb safe.*

rendezvous /'rɒndeɪvuː/ *noun* (*plural same*) **1.** an appointment or meeting ○ *He arranged a rendezvous with her.* **2.** a place where a meeting takes place ■ *verb* (**rendezvouses, rendezvousing, rendezvoused**) to arrange to meet, or meet somewhere ○ *You go north, and we'll go west and we'll all rendezvous at the camp at 16.00.*

rendition /ren'dɪʃ(ə)n/ *noun* a performance of a song, etc.

renege /rɪ'neɪɡ, rɪ'niːɡ/ (**reneges, reneging, reneged**) *verb* not to do something which you had promised to do (*formal*)

renew /rɪ'njuː/ (**renews, renewing, renewed**) *verb* **1.** to start again ○ *Renew your efforts and don't lose hope.* **2.** to replace something old with something new ○ *We need to renew the wiring in the kitchen.* **3.** to continue something for a further period of time ○ *Don't forget to renew your insurance policy.* (NOTE: + **renewal** *n*)

renewable /rɪ'njuːəb(ə)l/ *adj* which can be renewed ○ *The season ticket is renewable for a further year.*

renewed /rɪ'njuːd/ *adj* continuing with new energy, strength or enthusiasm

renounce /rɪ'naʊns/ (**renounces, renouncing, renounced**) *verb* **1.** to give up a right or a claim ○ *She renounced her claim to the property.* **2.** to state publicly that you are going to stop believing in something or are not going to behave in a certain way ○ *The government has renounced the use of force in dealing with international terrorists.* ○ *They called on the extremists to renounce violence.* (NOTE: + **renunciation** *n*)

renovate /'renəveɪt/ (**renovates, renovating, renovated**) *verb* to make a building like new again (NOTE: + **renovation** *n*)

renowned /rɪ'naʊnd/ *adj* known and admired by many people ○ *the renowned Italian conductor* ○ *Rome is renowned as the centre of Catholicism.*

② **rent** /rent/ *noun* money paid to live in a flat or house or to use an office or car ○ *Rents are high in the centre of the town.* ○ *The landlord asked me to pay three months' rent in advance.* ■ *verb* (**rents, renting, rented**) to pay money to use a house, flat, office or car ○ *He rents an office in the centre of town.* ○ *He rented a villa by the beach for three weeks.*

rental /'rent(ə)l/ *noun* rent, money paid to use a room, flat, office, car, etc.

③ **rep** /rep/ *noun* a salesman who visits clients, trying to sell them something ○ *They have vacancies for reps in the north of the country.* ○ *We have a reps' meeting every three months.*

③ **repair** /rɪ'peə/ *verb* (**repairs, repairing, repaired**) to make something work which is broken or damaged ○ *I dropped my watch on the pavement, and I don't think it can be repaired.* ○ *She's trying to repair the washing machine.* ○ *The photocopier is being repaired.* ■ *noun* mending something which is broken or has been damaged [~to] ○ *The hotel is closed while they are carrying out repairs to the kitchens.* ○ *His car is in the garage for repair.*

repatriate /riː'pætrieɪt/ (**repatriates, repatriating, repatriated**) *verb* to bring or to send someone back to their home country (NOTE: + **repatriation** *n*)

repay /rɪ'peɪ/ (**repays, repaying, repaid**) *verb* **1.** to pay back ○ *I'll try to repay what I owe you next month.* ○ *Thank you for your help – I hope to be able to repay you one day.* **2.** to be worth

repayment /rɪ'peɪmənt/ *noun* paying back

repeal /rɪ'piːl/ (**repeals, repealing, repealed**) *verb* to end a law officially ○ *The Bill seeks to repeal the existing legislation.* (NOTE: + **repeal** *n*)

② **repeat** /rɪ'piːt/ (**repeats, repeating, repeated**) *verb* to say something again [~that] ○ *She kept on repeating that she wanted to go home.* ○ *Could you repeat what you just said?* ○ *He repeated the address so that the policeman could write it down.* ◇ **to repeat yourself** to say the same thing over and over again ○ *He's getting old – he keeps repeating himself.*

repeated /rɪ'piːtɪd/ *adj* happening again and again

③ **repeatedly** /rɪ'piːtɪdli/ *adv* very many times, often so many that it is annoying

repel /rɪ'pel/ (**repels, repelling, repelled**) *verb* **1.** to drive back an attack ○ *The army easily repelled the invaders.* **2.** to drive something away ○ *The paint has an ingredient that repels water.* ○ *She sprayed the kitchen with a spray to repel flies.* **3.** to be so unpleasant that it drives people away ○ *The taste repelled me so much that I could not finish my meal.*

repent /rɪ'pent/ (**repents, repenting, repented**) *verb* to be very sorry for what you have done, or for what you have not done (NOTE: + **repentance** *n*)

repercussions /ˌriːpə'kʌʃ(ə)nz/ *plural noun* a result or effect, usually unpleasant ○ *The government decision on pensions will have widespread repercussions.* ○ *The BBC is trying to deal with the repercussions of the critical programme on India.*

③ **repertoire** /'repətwɑː/ *noun* the plays, songs or pieces of music which someone has learned ○ *She has an extensive repertoire, covering most of the important soprano roles.*

③ **repetition** /ˌrepɪ'tɪʃ(ə)n/ *noun* **1.** the act of repeating, of saying the same thing again ○ *Constant repetition of the song made sure we all knew it by heart.* **2.** a thing which is repeated ○ *The police will try to prevent a repetition of the ugly scenes at the football ground.*

repetitive /rɪ'petɪtɪv/ *adj* which is repeated very frequently and is boring

rephrase /riː'freɪz/ (**rephrases, rephrasing, rephrased**) *verb* to say something again, but in a different way

① **replace** /rɪ'pleɪs/ (**replaces, replacing, replaced**) *verb* to put something back where it was before ○ *Please replace the books correctly on the shelves.*

③ **replacement** /rɪ'pleɪsmənt/ *noun* **1.** a thing which is used to replace something [~for] ○ *An electric motor was bought as a replacement for the old one.* **2.** the action of replacing something with something else [~for] ○ *The mechanics recommended the replacement of the hand pump with an electric model.*

replay[1] /'riːpleɪ/ *noun* a match which is played again because the first match was a draw ○ *They drew 2–2 so there will be a replay next week.*

replay[2] /riː'pleɪ/ (**replays, replaying, replayed**) *verb* to play again ○ *He replayed the message on the answerphone several times, but still couldn't understand it.* ○ *The match will be replayed next week.*

replenish /rɪ'plenɪʃ/ (**replenishes, replenishing, replenished**) *verb* to fill up again

replica /'replɪkə/ *noun* an exact copy

replicate /'replɪkeɪt/ (**replicates, replicating, replicated**) *verb* to do or make something in exactly the same way as before

② **reply** /rɪ'plaɪ/ *noun* (*plural* **replies**) **1.** an answer, especially to a letter or telephone call [~to] ○ *We wrote last week, but haven't had a reply yet.* ○ *We had six replies to our advertisement.* **2.** □ **in reply** as an answer ○ *In reply to my letter, I received a fax two days later.* ○ *She just shook her head in reply and turned away.* ■ *verb* (**replies, replying, replied**) to answer [~to] ○ *He never replies to my letters.* ○ *We wrote last week, but he hasn't replied yet.* ○ *He refused to reply to questions until his lawyer arrived.*

① **report** /rɪ'pɔːt/ *noun* a description of what has happened or what will happen [~of/~that] ○ *We read the reports of the accident in the newspaper.* ○ *Can you confirm the report that the council is planning to sell the old town hall?* ■ *verb* (**reports, reporting, reported**) to present yourself officially [~for/~to] ○ *to report for work* ○ *Candidates should report to the office at 9.00.*

reportedly /rɪ'pɔːtɪdli/ *adv* according to what has been reported

reported speech /rɪˌpɔːtɪd 'spiːtʃ/ *noun* same as **indirect speech**

③ **reporter** /rɪ'pɔːtə/ *noun* a journalist who writes reports of events for a newspaper or for a TV news programme

③ **reporting** /rɪ'pɔːtɪŋ/ *noun* the action of reporting something in the press

repose /rɪ'pəʊz/ *noun* calm, resting ○ *a state of repose*

repossess /ˌriːpə'zes/ (**repossesses, repossessing, repossessed**) *verb* to take back an item which someone is buying under a hire-purchase agreement, or a house which someone is buying under a mortgage agreement, because the purchaser cannot continue the payments (NOTE: + **repossession** *n*)

reprehensible /ˌreprɪ'hensɪb(ə)l/ *adj* which can be criticised

① **represent** /ˌreprɪ'zent/ (**represents, representing, represented**) *verb* **1.** to speak or act on behalf of someone or of a group of people ○ *He asked his solicitor to represent him at the meeting.* **2.** to mean something, or to be a symbol of something ○ *The dark green on the map represents woods.*

② **representation** /ˌreprɪzen'teɪʃ(ə)n/ *noun* **1.** the act of selling goods for a company ○ *We can provide representation throughout Europe.* **2.** having someone to act on your behalf ○ *The residents' association wants representation on the committee.* **3.** a way of showing ○ *The design on the Lebanese flag is a representation of a cedar tree.*

② **representative** /ˌreprɪ'zentətɪv/ *adj* typical of all the people or things in a group ○ *The sample isn't representative of the whole batch.* ■ *noun* a person who represents, who speaks on behalf of someone else [~of/from] ○ *Representatives of the workforce have asked to meet the management.* ○ *He asked his solicitor to act as his representative.*

repress /rɪ'pres/ (**represses, repressing, repressed**) *verb* **1.** to control a natural impulse ○ *She had difficulty in repressing a smile.* **2.** to restrict people's freedom, etc. ○ *The ordinary people have been repressed for so long that they do not know what it is to be free.* (NOTE: + **repression** *n*)

repressed /rɪ'prest/ *adj* suppressed

repressive /rɪ'presɪv/ *adj* severe, strict or using force to keep people under control

reprieve /rɪ'priːv/ *noun* **1.** temporarily stopping a sentence or order by a court ○ *He was granted a last-minute reprieve.* **2.** saving something which was planned for demolition ○ *This magnificent building was to be demolished, but the reprieve came just in time to save it.* (NOTE: + **reprieve** *v*)

reprimand /'reprɪmɑːnd/ (**reprimands, reprimanding, reprimanded**) *verb* to criticise someone severely for doing something wrong ○ *The report reprimanded the directors for their negligence.* (NOTE: + **reprimand** *n*)

reprint[1] /'riːprɪnt/ *noun* the printing of copies of a book again after a first printing ○ *The mistake on the title page will be corrected in the reprint.*

reprint[2] /riː'prɪnt/ (**reprints, reprinting, reprinted**) *verb* to print more copies of a document or book ○ *The book is being reprinted.*

reprisal /rɪ'praɪz(ə)l/ *noun* punishment of someone in revenge for something

reproach /rɪ'prəʊtʃ/ *noun* **1.** a statement of blame or a criticism □ **beyond reproach** blameless **2.** a thing which is a disgrace ■ *verb* (**reproaches, reproaching, reproached**) to criticise someone for something for having done something [~for/with]

reprocess /riː'prəʊses/ (**reprocesses, reprocessing, reprocessed**) *verb* to process again

reproduce /ˌriːprə'djuːs/ (**reproduces, reproducing, reproduced**) *verb* **1.** to make a copy of something such as artistic material or musical sounds ○ *It is very difficult to reproduce the sound of an owl accurately.* ○ *Some of the paintings have been reproduced in this book.* ○ *His letters have been reproduced in the biography.* **2.** to produce babies or young animals

③ **reproduction** /ˌriːprə'dʌkʃən/ *noun* **1.** a copy of a painting or other work of art **2.** the action of reproducing **3.** the production of young ○ *The rate of reproduction of mice is incredible.*

reptile /'reptaɪl/ *noun* a cold-blooded animal which has skin covered with scales and which lays eggs

② **republic** /rɪ'pʌblɪk/ *noun* a system of government in which elected representatives have power and the leader is an elected or nominated president ○ *France is a republic while Spain is a monarchy.*

republican /rɪ'pʌblɪkən/ *noun* a person who believes that a republic is the best form of government ○ *Some republicans made speeches against the emperor.*

③ **Republican** /rɪ'pʌblɪkən/ *noun US* a member of the Republican Party, one of the two main political parties in the USA

repudiate /rɪ'pjuːdieɪt/ (**repudiates, repudiating, repudiated**) *verb* to reject or to refuse to accept (NOTE: + **repudiation** *n*)

repugnant /rɪ'pʌgnənt/ *adj* very unpleasant, offensive or unacceptable

repulse /rɪ'pʌls/ (**repulses, repulsing, repulsed**) *verb* to push back someone who is attacking

repulsion /rɪ'pʌlʃən/ *noun* **1.** a feeling of dislike ○ *He looked at the plate of snails with repulsion.* **2.** (*in physics*) the act of pushing something away ○ *Magnetic repulsion can be demonstrated by trying to join the negative ends of two magnets.*

repulsive /rɪ'pʌlsɪv/ *adj* unpleasant, which makes you disgusted

reputable /'repjʊtəb(ə)l/ *adj* well thought of, with a good reputation

③ **reputation** /ˌrepjʊ'teɪʃ(ə)n/ *noun* an opinion that people have of someone [~as/~for] ○ *He has a reputation as a strict teacher.* ○ *His bad reputation won't help him find a suitable job.*

repute /rɪ'pjuːt/ *noun* a reputation or general opinion (*formal*)

reputed /rɪ'pjuːtɪd/ *adj* supposed, said to be

② **request** /rɪ'kwest/ *noun* asking for something [~for] ○ *They've made a request for extra funding.Your request will be dealt with as soon as possible.* ■ *verb* (**requests, requesting, requested**) to ask for something politely or formally [~that] ○ *The police are requesting that everyone stays inside the building.* ○ *I am enclosing the leaflets you requested.* ○ *Guests are requested to leave their keys at reception.* ◇ **on request** if asked for ○ *'catalogue available on request'*

① **require** /rɪ'kwaɪə/ (**requires, requiring, required**) *verb* to need something ○ *The disease requires careful nursing.* ○ *Writing the program requires a computer specialist.*

required /rɪ'kwaɪəd/ *adj* which must be done or provided ○ *We can cut the wood to the required length.* ○ *We can't reply because we don't have the required information.*

② **requirement** /rɪ'kwaɪəmənt/ *noun* what is necessary ○ *It is a requirement of the job that you should be able to drive.*

requisite /'rekwɪzɪt/ *adj* necessary (*formal*) ○ *Does he have the requisite government permits?* ○ *We need someone with the requisite skills to run the bar.*

re-release /reɪ rɪ'liːs/ *verb* to make a music recording or a film available again some time after it first came out

re-route /ˌriː 'ruːt/ *verb* to send people or vehicles along a route which is different to the usual one

rerun /'riːrʌn/ *noun* **1.** the second showing of a programme or film on TV ○ *During the summer all the TV channels show reruns of old sitcoms.* **2.** a thing which happens again ○ *We want to avoid a rerun of the trouble we had at the last meeting.*

resale /'riːseɪl/ *noun* the act of selling of something again

reschedule /riː'ʃedjuːl/ (**reschedules, rescheduling, rescheduled**) *verb* to arrange an appointment again for a later time ○ *My plane was delayed by fog, so I had to reschedule all my meetings.*

rescue /'reskjuː/ *verb* (**rescues, rescuing, rescued**) to save someone from a dangerous or difficult situation ○ *The lifeboat rescued the crew of the sinking ship.When the river flooded, the party of tourists had to be rescued by helicopter.* ○ *The company nearly collapsed, but was rescued by the bank.* (NOTE: + **rescuer** *n*) ■ *noun* the action of saving someone or something in a difficult or dangerous situation ○ *Mountain rescue requires well-trained people.* ○ *No one could swim well enough to go to her rescue.*

① **research** /rɪ'sɜːtʃ/ *noun* scientific study, which tries to find out facts [~into/~on] ○ *The company is carrying out research into the condition.* ○ *Our laboratories are conducting important research on patient responses.* ○ *Our researches proved that the letter was a forgery.* ■ *verb* (**researches, researching, researched**) to study something in order to find out facts ○ *Research your subject thoroughly before you start writing about it.*

③ **resemblance** /rɪ'zembləns/ *noun* the fact of looking like someone [~to/~between] ○ *She bears a strong resemblance to her father.* ○ *The resemblance between the two brothers is remarkable.*

③ **resemble** /rɪ'zembəl/ (**resembles, resembling, resembled**) *verb* to look like someone or something

resent /rɪ'zent/ (**resents, resenting, resented**) *verb* to feel annoyed because of something that you think is unfair ○ *She resents having to do other people's work.*

resentful /rɪ'zentf(ə)l/ *adj* feeling anger or bitterness about something someone has done

resentment /rɪ'zentmənt/ *noun* the feeling of being angry and upset about something that someone else has done ○ *There is lot of resentment at* or *over the decision to close the school.* ○ *The decision caused a lot of resentment among local people.*

③ **reservation** /ˌrezə'veɪʃ(ə)n/ *noun* the act of booking something, e.g. a seat or table ○ *I want to make a reservation on the train to Plymouth tomorrow evening.*

③ **reserve** /rɪ'zɜːv/ *verb* (**reserves, reserving, reserved**) to book a seat or a table ○ *I want to reserve a table for four people.* ○ *Can you reserve two seats for me for the evening performance?* ○ *We're very busy this evening. Have you reserved?* ■ *noun* an amount kept back in case it is needed in the future ○ *Our reserves of coal were used up during the winter.* ◇ **in reserve** waiting to be used ○ *We're keeping the can of petrol in reserve.*

③ **reserved** /rɪ'zɜːvd/ *adj* **1.** booked ○ *There are two reserved tables and one free one.* ○ *Is this seat reserved?* **2.** who does not reveal his or her thoughts and feelings ○ *Clare is very reserved and doesn't talk much.* ○ *He's a very reserved man and does not mix with other members of staff.*

reservoir /'rezəvwɑː/ *noun* a large, usually artificial, lake where drinking water is kept for pumping to a city

reset /riː'set/ (**resets, resetting, reset**) *verb* to set something again ○ *The local time is 12.15: please reset your watches.* ○ *His broken leg was set badly, and the doctors had to reset it.*

resettle /riː'set(ə)l/ (**resettles, resettling, resettled**) *verb* to settle someone in another place

reshape /riː'ʃeɪp/ (**reshapes, reshaping, reshaped**) *verb* to shape something again, to give something a different shape

reside /rɪ'zaɪd/ (**resides, residing, resided**) *verb* to live somewhere (*formal*)

③ **residence** /'rezɪd(ə)ns/ *noun* **1.** a large house ○ *They have a country residence where they spend their weekends.* **2.** the act of living in a place

residency /'rezɪd(ə)nsi/ *noun* the fact of being legally entitled to love in a country

② **resident** /ˈrezɪd(ə)nt/ *noun* a person who lives in a place, e.g. a country or a hotel ○ *You need an entry permit if you're not a resident of the country.* ○ *Only residents are allowed to park their cars here.* ■ *adj* who lives permanently in a place ○ *There is a resident caretaker.*

residual /rɪˈzɪdjuəl/ *adj* remaining after everything else has gone

residue /ˈrezɪdjuː/ *noun* what is left after a process has taken place ○ *After the sugar has been refined the residue is used for cattle feed.*

③ **resign** /rɪˈzaɪn/ (**resigns, resigning, resigned**) *verb* to give up a job ○ *He resigned with effect from July 1st.* ○ *She has resigned (her position) as finance director.*

③ **resignation** /ˌrezɪɡˈneɪʃ(ə)n/ *noun* **1.** the act of giving up a job ○ *His resignation was accepted by the Prime Minister.* ○ *Have you written your letter of resignation?* **2.** the attitude of accepting an unpleasant or unwanted situation ○ *a look of resignation on his face*

resigned /rɪˈzaɪnd/ *adj* accepting something unpleasant

resilient /rɪˈzɪliənt/ *adj* **1.** which easily returns to its original shape after being squashed ○ *Cork is a surprisingly resilient material.* **2.** (*of a person*) who is strong or able to recover easily from a shock (*person*) ○ *She is a very resilient person, in spite of her age, and has gone back home from hospital to look after herself.*

resin /ˈrezɪn/ *noun* **1.** a sticky oil which comes from some types of pine tree ○ *Amber is a yellow stone which is fossilised resin.* **2.** a solid or liquid organic compound, a polymer used in the making of plastic ○ *He made some interesting table decorations with gold coins in blocks of transparent resin.*

③ **resist** /rɪˈzɪst/ (**resists, resisting, resisted**) *verb* to oppose or fight against something ○ *He resisted all attempts to make him sell the house.* ○ *Bands of guerrillas resisted doggedly in the mountains.* ○ *They resisted the enemy attacks for two weeks.*

② **resistance** /rɪˈzɪstəns/ *noun* opposition to or fighting against something ○ *The patients had no resistance to disease.* ○ *Skiers crouch down low to minimise wind resistance.* ○ *There was a lot of resistance to the new plan from the local residents.*

resistant /rɪˈzɪst(ə)nt/ *adj* which resists something

resit /riːˈsɪt/ (**resits, resitting, resat**) *verb* to take an examination again after having failed

resolute /ˈrezəluːt/ *adj* determined, having made up your mind

resolution /ˌrezəˈluːʃ(ə)n/ *noun* **1.** a decision to be decided at a meeting **2.** the fact of being determined to do something ○ *Her resolution to succeed is so strong that I am sure she will get through.* **3.** (*of a TV or computer image*) clearness of a picture on a screen, calculated as the number of pixels per unit of area

③ **resolve** /rɪˈzɒlv/ (*formal*) *verb* (**resolves, resolving, resolved**) to strongly decide to do something ○ *We all resolved to avoid these mistakes next time.* ■ *noun* a strong decision to do something ○ *The head teacher encouraged him in his resolve to go to university.*

③ **resort** /rɪˈzɔːt/ *noun* **1.** a place where people go on holiday ○ *a famous Swiss ski resort* ○ *Crowds have been flocking to the resorts on the south coast.* **2.** □ **as a** or **in the last resort** when everything else fails ○ *Having tried everything without success, he accepted her offer as a last resort.* ■ *verb* □ **to resort to** to do something in a difficult situation, when everything else has failed ○ *In the end the police had to resort to lifting the protestors out the road.*

resounding /rɪˈzaʊndɪŋ/ *adj* **1.** great or complete ○ *The exhibition was a resounding success.* **2.** loud ○ *a resounding bang*

① **resource** /rɪˈzɔːs/ *noun* a source of supply for what is needed or used ○ *financial resources* ○ *The country is rich in oil, minerals and other natural resources.*

resourceful /rɪˈzɔːsf(ə)l/ *adj* good at looking after yourself or at dealing with problems

① **respect** /rɪˈspekt/ *noun* admiration for someone [~for] ○ *He showed very little respect for his teacher.* ○ *No one deserves more respect than her mother for the way she coped with the bad news.* ■ *verb* (**respects, respecting, respected**) to admire someone, especially because of his or her achievements or status ○ *Everyone respected her for what she said.*

respectable /rɪˈspektəb(ə)l/ *adj* considered by people to be good, and deserving to be respected ○ *She's marrying a very respectable young engineer.* ○ *I don't want to bring up my children here, it is not a respectable area.*

③ **respected** /rɪˈspektɪd/ *adj* admired by many people

respectful /rɪ'spektf(ə)l/ *adj* full of respect

respective /rɪ'spektɪv/ *adj* referring separately to each of the people just mentioned

③ **respectively** /rɪ'spektɪvli/ *adv* in the order just mentioned

respirator /'respəreɪtə/ *noun* a machine which is used in hospital to help patients to breathe when they cannot breathe by themselves

respiratory /rɪ'spɪrət(ə)ri/ *adj* referring to breathing

respite /'respaɪt/ *noun* a rest, a period when things are slightly better ◇ **without respite** without stopping ○ *Rescue teams worked without respite for three days in their search for survivors.*

② **respond** /rɪ'spɒnd/ (**responds, responding, responded**) *verb* **1.** to give a reply ○ *She shouted at him, but he didn't respond.* **2.** to show a favourable reaction to something [~to] ○ *I hope the public will respond to our new advertisement.* ○ *The government has responded to pressure from industry.*

① **response** /rɪ'spɒns/ *noun* something that you do or say as a reaction to something [~to/~from] ○ *There was no response to our call for help.* ○ *The changes produced an angry response from customers.* □ **in response to something** as an answer or reaction to something ○ *In response to the United Nations' request for aid, the government has sent blankets and tents.*

① **responsibility** /rɪˌspɒnsɪ'bɪlɪti/ (*plural* **responsibilities**) *noun* **1.** the fact of being in a position in which you look after or deal with something [~for] ○ *The management accepts no responsibility for customers' property.* ○ *There is no responsibility on his part for the poor results.* ○ *Who should take responsibility for the students' welfare?* **2.** something that someone is responsible for

① **responsible** /rɪ'spɒnsɪb(ə)l/ *adj* **1.** looking after something and so likely to be blamed if something goes wrong ○ *He is not responsible for the restaurant next door to his hotel.* ○ *Customers are responsible for all breakages.* ○ *He is responsible for a class of 25 children.* □ **responsible to someone** under the authority of someone ○ *She's directly responsible to the sales manager.* **2.** (*of a person*) reliable and able to be trusted to be sensible

responsibly /rɪ'spɒnsɪbli/ *adv* in a responsible way

responsive /rɪ'spɒnsɪv/ *adj* **1.** showing sympathy or reacting favourably to something ○ *The management was not very responsive to the demands of the staff.* **2.** reacting to something ○ *The cat is very responsive to being stroked.* ○ *His flu seems to be responsive to antibiotics.*

① **rest** /rest/ *noun* **1.** a period of being quiet and peaceful, being asleep or doing nothing ○ *All you need is a good night's rest and you'll be fine again tomorrow.* ○ *We took a few minutes' rest and started running again.* ○ *I'm having a well-earned rest after working hard all week.* **2.** what is left ○ *Here are the twins, but where are the rest of the children?* ○ *I drank most of the milk and the cat drank the rest.* ○ *Throw the rest of the food away – it will go bad.* (NOTE: **Rest** takes a singular verb when it refers to a singular: *Here's the rest of the milk; Where's the rest of the string? The rest of the money has been lost.* It takes a plural verb when it refers to a plural: *Here are the rest of the children; Where are the rest of the chairs? The rest of the books have been lost.*) ■ *verb* (**rests, resting, rested**) **1.** to spend time relaxing or not using energy ○ *Don't disturb your father – he's resting.* ○ *They ran for ten miles, rested for a few minutes, and then ran on again.* **2.** to lean something against something ○ *She rested her bike against the wall.*

② **restaurant** /'rest(ə)rɒnt/ *noun* a place where you can buy and eat a meal ○ *I don't want to stay at home tonight – let's go out to the Italian restaurant in the High Street.* ○ *She's was waiting for me at the restaurant.*

rested /'restɪd/ *adj* feeling calm and relaxed after a rest

restful /'restf(ə)l/ *adj* which makes you feel calm and relaxed

restless /'restləs/ *adj* too nervous, worried or full of energy to keep still

③ **restore** /rɪ'stɔː/ (**restores, restoring, restored**) *verb* to repair something and make it seem new again ○ *The old house has been restored and is now open to the public.*

restrain /rɪ'streɪn/ (**restrains, restraining, restrained**) *verb* to prevent or try to stop someone doing something ○ *It took six policemen to restrain him.*

restrained /rɪ'streɪnd/ *adj* controlled or calm

restraint /rɪ'streɪnt/ *noun* control

③ **restrict** /rɪ'strɪkt/ (**restricts, restricting, restricted**) *verb* to limit someone or something ○ *You are restricted to two bottles per person.*

③ **restricted** /rɪ'strɪktɪd/ *adj* limited

② **restriction** /rɪ'strɪkʃən/ *noun* a limitation [~on] ○ *The police have placed restrictions on his movements.*

restrictive /rɪ'strɪktɪv/ *adj* which limits

③ **restructure** /riː'strʌktʃə/ (**restructures, restructuring, restructured**) *verb* to reorganise something, especially the financial basis of a company

① **result** /rɪ'zʌlt/ *noun* **1.** something which happens because of something else ○ *What was the result of the police investigation?* □ **as a result (of something)** because of something ○ *There was a traffic jam and as a result, she missed her plane.* **2.** the final score in a game, the final marks in an exam, etc. ○ *What was the result of the last race?She isn't pleased with her exam results.* ○ *I had great fun making the rug but I'm only partly happy with the result.* ○ *He listened to the football results on the radio.*

resume /rɪ'zjuːm/ (**resumes, resuming, resumed**) *verb* **1.** to start something again after stopping ○ *The meeting resumed after a short break.* ○ *Normal train services will resume after the track has been repaired.* ○ *After the fire, the staff resumed work as normal.* **2.** to go back to a place ○ *resume your places*

③ **résumé** /'rezjuːˌmeɪ/ *noun* **1.** a short summing-up of the main points of a discussion or of a book ○ *I can't attend the meeting, but I would like a résumé of the discussion.* ○ *A brief résumé of the contents of the book is all I need.* **2.** *US* a summary of a person's life story with details of education and work experience ○ *Attach a résumé to your application form.*

resumption /rɪ'zʌmpʃən/ *noun* the act of starting again

resurface /riː'sɜːfɪs/ (**resurfaces, resurfacing, resurfaced**) *verb* **1.** to put a new surface on a road ○ *No one can park on our street because they are resurfacing it today.* **2.** to come back to the surface again or appear again ○ *The bird dived into the water and resurfaced several minutes later in a different part of the river.* ○ *He disappeared for a time, then resurfaced as managing director of a TV company.*

resurrect /ˌrezə'rekt/ (**resurrects, resurrecting, resurrected**) *verb* **1.** to bring something back to use ○ *He resurrected his old plan for rebuilding the town centre.* **2.** to start something up again (NOTE: + **resurrection** *n*)

resuscitate /rɪ'sʌsɪteɪt/ (**resuscitates, resuscitating, resuscitated**) *verb* to make someone who appears to be dead start breathing again, and to restart the circulation of blood (NOTE: + **resuscitation** *n*)

retail /'riːteɪl/ *noun* the business of selling small quantities of goods direct to the public ○ *We specialise in the retail of ordinary household goods.* ○ *The goods in stock have a retail value of £10,000.* ■ *verb* (**retails, retailing, retailed**) to sell goods direct to customers who do not sell them again

retailer /'riːteɪlə/ *noun* a shopkeeper who sells goods directly to the public. Compare **wholesaler**

retailing /'riːteɪlɪŋ/ *noun* the business of selling goods at full price to the public

② **retain** /rɪ'teɪn/ (**retains, retaining, retained**) *verb* to keep something ○ *Please retain this invoice for tax purposes.* ○ *One book especially retained my attention – so I bought it.* ○ *He managed to retain his composure in spite of being constantly heckled.*

retaliate /rɪ'tælieɪt/ (**retaliates, retaliating, retaliated**) *verb* to attack someone in revenge (NOTE: + **retaliation** *n*)

retention /rɪ'tenʃən/ *noun* **1.** the act of keeping something ○ *The committee voted for the retention of the existing system.* **2.** the act of holding something back

rethink /'riːθɪŋk/ (**rethinks, rethinking, rethought**) *verb* to think again about or reconsider something ○ *We should rethink the whole plan now that the council has refused planning permission.*

reticent /'retɪs(ə)nt/ *adj* not willing to talk about something

retina /'retɪnə/ *noun* an inside layer of the eye, which is sensitive to light

retinue /'retɪnjuː/ *noun* a group of people following an important person

② **retire** /rɪ'taɪə/ (**retires, retiring, retired**) *verb* **1.** to stop work and take a pension [~from] ○ *He will retire from his job as manager next April.* ○ *She's retiring this year.* **2.** to make an employee stop work and take a pension ○ *They decided to retire all staff over 50.*

② **retired** /rɪ'taɪəd/ *adj* who has stopped work and draws a pension

② **retirement** /rɪ'taɪəmənt/ *noun* **1.** the act of retiring from work ○ *He was given a watch as a retirement present.* ○ *He claims that the pension he'll get on his retirement* *won't be sufficient.* **2.** a period of life when you are retired ○ *He spent his retirement in his house in France.* ○ *Most people look forward to their retirement.*

retiring /rɪ'taɪərɪŋ/ *adj* shy, quiet and reserved

retort /rɪ'tɔːt/ (**retorts, retorting, retorted**) *verb* to reply sharply (*literary*) ○ *She retorted that she had plenty of money and didn't want any gifts from him.* (NOTE: + **retort** *n*)

retract /rɪ'trækt/ (**retracts, retracting, retracted**) *verb* **1.** to pull back ○ *The landing gear retracted after take-off.* **2.** to withdraw something which has been said ○ *He refuses to retract a single word of his statement.*

retreat /rɪ'triːt/ *verb* (**retreats, retreating, retreated**) if soldiers retreat, they stop fighting and move back and away from the battle ○ *Napoleon retreated from Moscow in 1812.* ■ *noun* the act of moving back and away from a battle ○ *The army's retreat was swift and unexpected.*

retrial /'riːˌtraɪəl/ *noun* a second trial of a case when the first trial was not conducted properly or no verdict was reached

retribution /ˌretrɪ'bjuːʃ(ə)n/ *noun* a well-deserved punishment

③ **retrieve** /rɪ'triːv/ (**retrieves, retrieving, retrieved**) *verb* **1.** to get back something which was lost ○ *He retrieved his umbrella from the lost-property office.* **2.** to bring back something which has been stored in a computer ○ *She retrieved the address files which she thought had been deleted.*

retrospect /'retrəʊspekt/ *noun* □ **in retrospect** when you look back ○ *In retrospect, our decision to make him finance director was quite wrong.*

retrospective /ˌretrəʊ'spektɪv/ *noun* an exhibition of works of art covering the whole career of an artist ○ *This has been the first Henry Moore retrospective for some years.*

retry /ˌriː'traɪ/ (**retries, retrying, retried**) *verb* to have a retrial of a case which has already been tried once

① **return** /rɪ'tɜːn/ *noun* **1.** the act of going or coming back to a place [~from/] ○ *It snowed on the day of her return from Canada.* ○ *I'll come and see you on my return.* **2.** the key on a keyboard which you press when you have finished keying something, or when you want to start a new line ○ *To change directory, type C: and press return.* ■ *verb* (**returns, returning, returned**) **1.** to come back or go back [~from/~to] ○ *When she returned from lunch she found two messages waiting for her.* ○ *When do you plan to return to Paris?* **2.** to give or send something back [~to] ○ *The letter was returned to the sender.*

reunification /ˌriːjuːnɪfɪ'keɪʃ(ə)n/ *noun* the act of joining again something which has been split. Compare **unification**

reunion /riː'juːnjən/ *noun* a meeting of people who have not met for a long time

reunite /ˌriːjuː'naɪt/ (**reunites, reuniting, reunited**) *verb* to join people or things together again

reuse /riː'juːs/ (**reuses, reusing, reused**) *verb* to use again something which has already been used

revamp[1] /riː'væmp/ (**revamps, revamping, revamped**) *verb* to improve the appearance of something which is slightly old-fashioned ○ *The whole image of the company needs revamping.*

revamp[2] /'riːvæmp/ *noun* a complete change of the appearance of something ○ *Our headed notepaper has had a complete revamp.*

① **reveal** /rɪ'viːl/ (**reveals, revealing, revealed**) *verb* to show or mention something which was hidden [~(that)] ○ *He revealed that he actually knew very little about cars.* ○ *An unexpected fault was revealed during the test.* ○ *The X-ray revealed a brain tumour.*

revealing /rɪ'viːlɪŋ/ *adj* which shows something which is usually hidden

revelation /ˌrevə'leɪʃ(ə)n/ *noun* **1.** the act of showing or mentioning something which was secret ○ *Her revelation that she had two children took everyone by surprise.* **2.** something which was a secret which now everyone knows ○ *His singing was a revelation.*

reveller /'rev(ə)lə/ *noun* a person who is having a good time (NOTE: The US spelling is **reveler**.)

③ **revenge** /rɪ'vendʒ/ *noun* the act of punishing someone in return for harm he or she has caused you [~for] ○ *They attacked the police station in revenge for the arrest of three members of the gang.* ○ *All the time he spent in prison, his only thought was of revenge.* ○ *He had his revenge in the end, when her car broke down and she had to phone for help.*

revenue /'revənjuː/ *noun* **1.** money which is received ○ *His only source of revenue is his shop.* **2.** money received by a government in tax

reverberate /rɪˈvɜːbəreɪt/ (**reverberates, reverberating, reverberated**) *verb* to echo or to ring out loudly and repeatedly

revere /rɪˈvɪə/ (**reveres, revering, revered**) *verb* to worship someone or to respect someone very highly

reverence /ˈrev(ə)rəns/ *noun* great respect

reverie /ˈrevəri/ *noun* a dream which you have during the day when you are not asleep

reversal /rɪˈvɜːs(ə)l/ *noun* a change to the opposite

③ **reverse** /rɪˈvɜːs/ *adj* opposite to the front ○ *The reverse side of the carpet is made of foam rubber.* ○ *The conditions are printed on the reverse side of the invoice.* ■ *noun* **1.** the opposite side ○ *Didn't you read what was on the reverse of the label?* **2.** a car gear which makes you go backwards ○ *Put the car into reverse and back very slowly into the garage.* ○ *The car's stuck in reverse!* ■ *verb* (**reverses, reversing, reversed**) **1.** to make something do the opposite ○ *The page order was reversed by mistake.* ○ *Don't try to reverse the trend, go along with it.* **2.** to make a car go backwards ○ *Reverse as far as you can, then go forward.* ○ *Be careful not to reverse into that lamppost.* ◇ **in reverse order** backwards ○ *They called out the names of the prize-winners in reverse order.*

reversible /rɪˈvɜːsɪb(ə)l/ *adj* which can be worn with either side out

reversing light /rɪˈvɜːsɪŋ ˌlaɪt/ *noun* a light on the back of a car which lights up when the car is put into reverse gear

③ **revert** /rɪˈvɜːt/ (**reverts, reverting, reverted**) *verb* to go back or come back to an earlier state

② **review** /rɪˈvjuː/ *noun* **1.** written comments on something, e.g. a book, play or film, published in a newspaper or magazine ○ *Did you read the review of her latest film in today's paper?* ○ *His book got some very good reviews.* **2.** a monthly or weekly magazine which contains articles of general interest ○ *His first short story appeared in a Scottish literary review.* **3.** an examination of several things together ○ *The company's annual review of each department's performance.* ■ *verb* (**reviews, reviewing, reviewed**) **1.** to read a book, see a film, etc., and write comments about it in a newspaper or magazine ○ *Her exhibition was reviewed in today's paper.* ○ *Whoever reviewed her latest book, obviously didn't like it.* **2.** to examine something in a general way ○ *The bank will review our overdraft position at the end of the month.* ○ *Let's review the situation in the light of the new developments.* **3.** *US* to study a lesson again ○ *You must review your geography before the exam.*

reviewer /rɪˈvjuːə/ *noun* a person who writes comments on something, e.g. books, plays or films

revile /rɪˈvaɪl/ (**reviles, reviling, reviled**) *verb* to criticise someone or something harshly

② **revise** /rɪˈvaɪz/ (**revises, revising, revised**) *verb* **1.** to study a lesson again [~for] ○ *I'm revising for my history test.* ○ *There isn't enough time to revise before the exam.* **2.** to change something or make something correct ○ *He is revising the speech he is due to give this evening.* ○ *These figures will have to be revised, there seems to be a mistake.*

③ **revision** /rɪˈvɪʒ(ə)n/ *noun* the action of revising something

③ **revival** /rɪˈvaɪv(ə)l/ *noun* the act of bringing something back into existence

revive /rɪˈvaɪv/ (**revives, reviving, revived**) *verb* **1.** to recover, to get well again ○ *After drinking some water he had revived enough to go on with the marathon.* **2.** to bring someone back to life again ○ *The paramedics managed to revive her on the way to the hospital.* **3.** to make something popular again ○ *It won't be easy to revive people's interest in old country crafts.*

revoke /rɪˈvəʊk/ (**revokes, revoking, revoked**) *verb* to cancel something, e.g. a right, agreement or permission

revolt /rɪˈvəʊlt/ (**revolts, revolting, revolted**) *verb* **1.** to rise up against authority ○ *The prisoners revolted against the harsh treatment they were receiving.* (NOTE: In this sense the noun is also **revolt**.) **2.** to disgust someone ○ *It revolted me to see all that food being thrown away.* (NOTE: in this sense the noun is **revulsion**.)

revolting /rɪˈvəʊltɪŋ/ *adj* extremely unpleasant, often so unpleasant as to make you feel ill ○ *a revolting smell*

② **revolution** /ˌrevəˈluːʃ(ə)n/ *noun* **1.** an armed rising against a government ○ *He led an unsuccessful revolution against the last president.* ○ *During the French Revolution many aristocrats were executed.* **2.** a change in the way things are done [~in] ○ *a revolution in data processing*

revolutionary /ˌrevəˈluːʃ(ə)n(ə)ri/ (*plural* **revolutionaries**) *noun* a person who takes part in an uprising against a government ○ *The captured revolutionaries were shot when the army took control.*

③ **revolve** /rɪ'vɒlv/ (**revolves, revolving, revolved**) *verb* to turn round a fixed point [~around] ○ *The Earth revolves around the Sun.*

revolver /rɪ'vɒlvə/ *noun* a small hand gun in which the chamber for cartridges turns after each shot is fired, so that another shot can be fired quickly

revulsion /rɪ'vʌlʃən/ *noun* disgust

③ **reward** /rɪ'wɔːd/ *noun* money given to someone for work done or as a prize for finding something, or for information about something ○ *When she took the purse she had found to the police station she got a £25 reward.* ○ *He is not interested in money – the Olympic gold medal will be reward enough.* ■ *verb* (**rewards, rewarding, rewarded**) to give someone money as a prize for finding something, or for doing something ○ *He was rewarded for finding the box of papers.* ○ *All her efforts were rewarded when she won first prize.*

rewarding /rɪ'wɔːdɪŋ/ *adj* which gives satisfaction

rewind /ˌriː'waɪnd/ *noun* the action of winding something back ■ *verb* (**rewinds, rewinding, rewound**) to wind something back ○ *After playing the cassette he rewound it.* ○ *The flex will rewind automatically when you press the red button.*

rework /riː'wɜːk/ (**reworks, reworking, reworked**) *verb* to work on something again

rewrite /riː'raɪt/ (**rewrites, rewriting, rewrote, rewritten**) *verb* to write something again in different words ○ *She rewrote the essay, adding more references.*

③ **rhetoric** /'retərɪk/ *noun* the art of speaking in a way which is intended to make people change their minds ○ *She came away from the meeting enthused by the Prime Minister's rhetoric.*

rhetorical question /rɪˌtɒrɪk(ə)l 'kwestʃən/ *noun* a question which makes a statement, rather than expecting an answer

③ **rheumatism** /'ruːmətɪz(ə)m/ *noun* a disease which gives painful or stiff joints or muscles

rhododendron /ˌrəʊdə'dendrən/ *noun* a large evergreen shrub with clusters of huge pink, red or purple flowers

rhombus /'rɒmbəs/ (*plural* **rhombuses** or **rhombi**) *noun* a shape with four equal sides but with no right angles

rhubarb /'ruːbɑːb/ *noun* a plant of which the thick red leaf stalks are cooked and eaten as a dessert

rhyme /raɪm/ *noun* the way in which some words end in the same sound ○ *Can you think of a rhyme for 'taught'?* ■ *verb* (**rhymes, rhyming, rhymed**) to end with the same sound as another word [~with] ○ *'Mr' rhymes with 'sister'*

rhythm /'rɪð(ə)m/ *noun* a strong regular beat in music or poetry ○ *They stamped their feet to the rhythm of the music.*

rib /rɪb/ *noun* one of 24 curved bones which protect your chest ○ *He fell down while skiing and broke two ribs.*

ribbed /rɪbd/ *adj* with a pattern of raised lines (*of knitting*)

ribbon /'rɪbən/ *noun* a long thin strip of material for tying things or used as decoration

③ **rice** /raɪs/ *noun* the seeds of a tropical plant which are cooked and eaten ○ *She only had a bowl of rice for her evening meal.* ○ *Cook the rice with some saffron to make it yellow.*

② **rich** /rɪtʃ/ *adj* **1.** who has a lot of money ○ *If only we were rich, then we could buy a bigger house.* ○ *He never spends anything, and so he gets richer and richer.* **2.** made with a lot of cream, butter, or eggs ○ *This cream cake is too rich for me.*

riches /'rɪtʃɪz/ *plural noun* wealth ○ *In spite of all their riches they are not a happy family.*

rickety /'rɪkɪti/ *adj* wobbly, likely to fall down

rickshaw /'rɪkˌʃɔː/, **ricksha** *noun* a vehicle which people sit in and which is pulled by a person

ricochet /'rɪkəʃeɪ/ (**ricochets, ricocheting** or **ricochetting, ricocheted** or **ricochetted**) *verb* to bounce off a surface at an angle

① **rid** /rɪd/ *adj* □ **to get rid of something** to throw something away ○ *Do you want to get rid of that old bookcase?* ○ *We have been told to get rid of twenty staff.* ○ *She doesn't seem able to get rid of her cold.*

ridden /'rɪd(ə)n/ past participle of **ride**

riddle /'rɪd(ə)l/ *noun* a puzzling question to which you have to find the answer ○ *Here's a riddle for you: 'what's black and white and red all over?'.*

① **ride** /raɪd/ *noun* a pleasant trip, e.g. on a horse or a bike or in a car [~on/~in] ○ *Can I have a ride on your motorbike?* ○ *He took us all for a ride in his new car.* ○ *The sta-*

tion is only a short bus ride from the college. ■ *verb* (**rides, riding, rode, ridden**) to go on a horse, on a bike, etc. ○ *He rode his bike across the road without looking.* ○ *She's never ridden (on) an elephant.* ○ *My little sister is learning to ride, but she's frightened of big horses.*

rider /'raɪdə/ *noun* a person who rides ○ *The rider of the black horse fell at the first fence.* ○ *Motorcycle riders must wear helmets.*

ridge /rɪdʒ/ *noun* a long narrow raised part

ridicule /'rɪdɪkjuːl/ *noun* mocking, laughing at someone ○ *She was afraid of the ridicule of her colleagues.* ■ *verb* (**ridicules, ridiculing, ridiculed**) to laugh at someone or something ○ *She ridiculed his attempts at speaking Italian.*

② **ridiculous** /rɪ'dɪkjʊləs/ *adj* extremely silly or unreasonable

riding /'raɪdɪŋ/ *noun* the sport of going on horseback ○ *He loves riding.* ○ *Let's go riding in the park.*

rife /raɪf/ *adj* common ○ *Crime is rife in some parts of the town.*

rifle /'raɪf(ə)l/ *noun* a gun with a long barrel which you hold with two hands, against your shoulder ○ *The gunman was on a roof with a rifle.* ○ *He was shooting at a target with an air rifle.*

rift /rɪft/ *noun* a split or crack

rig /rɪg/ (**rigs, rigging, rigged**) *verb* to arrange a dishonest result (*informal*) ◊ **rig up**

rig up *phrasal verb* to arrange something or construct something quickly

rigging /'rɪgɪŋ/ *noun* **1.** the ropes on a ship ○ *The rigging creaked in the storm.* ○ *Sailors ran up the rigging to wave to the crowds on the quayside.* **2.** the practice of arranging a vote to give a dishonest result ○ *Vote rigging is very common here.*

① **right** /raɪt/ *adj* **1.** correct ○ *She didn't put the bottles back in the* ○ *You're right – the number 8 bus doesn't go to Marble Arch.* ○ *She gave the right answer every time.* ○ *He says the answer is 285 – quite right!* ○ *Is the station clock right?* ○ *Is this the right train for Manchester?* ◊ **all right 2.** on the same side as the hand which most people use to write with ○ *In England cars don't drive on the right side of the road.* ○ *The keys are in the top right drawer of my desk.* ○ *He was holding the suitcase in his right hand.* ■ *noun* the side opposite to the left [~of] ○ *Who was that girl sitting on the right of your father?* ○ *When driving in France remember to keep to the right.* ○ *When you get to the next crossroads, turn to the right.* ○ *Go straight ahead, and take the second road on the right.* ■ *adv* **1.** directly, or in a straight line ○ *Instead of stopping at the crossroads, he drove right on across the main road and* ○ *To get to the police station, keep right on to the end of the road, and then turn left.* ○ *Go right along to the end of the corridor, you'll see my office in front of you.* **2.** exactly ○ *The pub is right at the end of the road.* ○ *The phone rang right in the middle of the TV programme.* ○ *She stood right in front of the TV and no one could see the screen.* **3.** towards the right-hand side ○ *To get to the station, turn right at the traffic lights.* ○ *Children should be taught to look right and left before crossing the road.* ■ *interj* agreed, OK ○ *Right, so we all meet again at 7 o'clock?*

③ **right-hand** /ˌraɪt 'hænd/ *adj* on the right side

③ **right-handed** /ˌraɪt 'hændɪd/ *adj* using the right hand more often than the left for things like writing and eating

right-hand man /ˌraɪt hænd 'mæn/ (*plural* **right-hand men**) *noun* the main assistant

right-wing /ˌraɪt 'wɪŋ/ *adj* belonging or relating to the conservative political parties

rigid /'rɪdʒɪd/ *adj* stiff and not bending much

rigmarole /'rɪgməˌrəʊl/ *noun* a process which is unnecessarily complicated

rigorous /'rɪgərəs/ *adj* very thorough

rigour /'rɪgə/ *noun* the fact of being strict or severe ○ *We will pursue the case with the full rigour of the law.* (NOTE: The US spelling is **rigor**.)

rile /raɪl/ (**riles, riling, riled**) *verb* to make someone angry or annoyed

③ **rim** /rɪm/ *noun* **1.** the edge of something round, like a wheel or a cup ○ *The rim of the glass is chipped.* **2.** a frame of spectacles ○ *He wears glasses with steel rims.*

rind /raɪnd/ *noun* a skin on fruit, bacon or cheese

① **ring** /rɪŋ/ *noun* **1.** a round shape, e.g. of metal ○ *She has a gold ring in her nose.* ○ *He wears a ring on his little finger.* **2.** a circle of people or things ○ *The teacher asked the children to sit in a ring round her.* **3.** the noise of an electric bell ○ *There was a ring at the door.* **4.** a space where a circus show takes place or where a boxing match is held ○ *The horses galloped round the ring.* ○ *The ringmaster came into the ring with his top hat and whip.* ■ *verb* (**rings, ringing,**

rang, rung) **1.** to make a sound with a bell ○ *The postman rang the doorbell.* ○ *Is that your phone ringing?* **2.** to telephone someone ○ *He rang me to say he would be late.* ○ *Don't ring tomorrow afternoon – the office will be closed.* ○ *Don't ring me, I'll ring you.* ◇ **to ring a bell** to remind someone of something ○ *The name rings a bell.* ○ *Does the name Arbuthnot ring any bells?*

ring back③ *phrasal verb* to telephone to answer someone (*informal*)

ring off③ *phrasal verb* to put down the phone

ring up③ *phrasal verb* to speak to someone using a telephone

ringleader /ˈrɪŋliːdə/ *noun* a person who organises a revolt or some crime

ring road /ˈrɪŋ rəʊd/ *noun* a road which goes right round a town

rink /rɪŋk/ *noun* a large enclosed area, e.g. for ice skating, playing ice hockey or roller skating

rinse /rɪns/ *verb* (**rinses, rinsing, rinsed**) to put things covered with soap or dirty things into clean water to remove the soap or the dirt ○ *Rinse the dishes before putting them on the draining board to dry.* ■ *noun* the act of washing something in clean water to get rid of soap ○ *Give your shirt a good rinse.*

③ **riot** /ˈraɪət/ *noun* noisy and usually violent behaviour by a crowd of people ○ *The protesters started a riot.*

rioter /ˈraɪətə/ *noun* a person who takes part in a riot

riotous /ˈraɪətəs/ *adj* disorderly, as in a riot

rip /rɪp/ *noun* a tear in cloth ○ *He lost the race because of a rip in his sail.* ■ *verb* (**rips, ripping, ripped**) **1.** to tear something roughly ○ *I ripped my sleeve on a nail.* ○ *She ripped open the parcel to see what he had given her.* ○ *The old bathroom is being ripped out and new units put in.* **2.** to go through something violently ○ *The fire ripped through the building.*

rip off *phrasal verb* **1.** to tear something off something else ○ *It's the last day of the month so you can rip the page off the calendar.* ○ *Someone has ripped off the book's cover.* **2.** □ **to rip someone off** to cheat someone or to make someone pay too much (*slang*) ○ *They were ripped off in the market.*

③ **ripe** /raɪp/ *adj* ready to eat or to be picked ○ *Don't eat that apple – it isn't ripe yet.*

ripen /ˈraɪpən/ (**ripens, ripening, ripened**) *verb* to become ripe

rip-off /ˈrɪp ɒf/ *noun* a bad deal (*informal*)

ripple /ˈrɪp(ə)l/ *noun* a little wave

① **rise** /raɪz/ *noun* a movement or slope upwards [~in] ○ *Salaries are increasing to keep up with the rise in the cost of living.* ○ *There is a gentle rise until you get to the top of the hill.* ■ *verb* (**rises, rising, rose, risen**) to go up ○ *The sun always rises in the east.* ○ *The road rises steeply for a few miles.* ○ *Prices have been rising steadily all year.* ○ *If you open the oven door, the cake won't rise properly.*

① **risk** /rɪsk/ *noun* a possible bad result ○ *There is not much risk of rain in August.* ○ *At the risk of looking foolish, I'm going to ask her to come out with me.* ○ *The risk of going blind is very remote.* ○ *There is a financial risk attached to this deal.* ■ *verb* (**risks, risking, risked**) to do something which may possibly harm you ○ *The fireman risked his life to save her.* ○ *He risked all his savings on buying the bookshop.*

risky /ˈrɪski/ (**riskier, riskiest**) *adj* which is dangerous

risqué /ˈrɪskeɪ/ *adj* slightly indecent

rite /raɪt/ *noun* a religious ceremony

ritual /ˈrɪtʃuəl/ *noun* **1.** a religious ceremony ○ *the ritual of the mass* **2.** something which you do regularly in the same way ○ *Every evening it's the same ritual: he puts the cat out and locks the door.* ○ *We don't follow any particular ritual on Christmas Day, we take the day as it comes.*

rival /ˈraɪv(ə)l/ *adj* who competes ○ *Two rival companies are trying to win the contract.* ○ *Is this the rival product you were talking about?* ○ *Simon and I are friends but we play for rival teams.* ■ *noun* a person or a company that competes ○ *H538* ○ *We keep our prices low to compete with our rivals.*

rivalry /ˈraɪv(ə)lri/ *noun* competition

② **river** /ˈrɪvə/ *noun* a large mass of fresh water which runs across the land and goes into the sea or into a large lake ○ *London is on the River Thames.* ○ *The river is very deep here, so it's dangerous to swim in it.* (NOTE: With names of rivers, you usually say **the River**: *the River Thames*; *the River Amazon*; *the River Nile*.)

rivet /ˈrɪvɪt/ *noun* a large metal pin which fastens metal plates together ○ *The workers were driving rivets into the metal sheets with huge hammers.* ■ *verb* (**rivets, riveting, riveted**) **1.** to fasten metal plates together ○ *Workmen riveted the sheets of* *metal together.* **2.** to attract the attention of someone ○ *The audience was riveted by his stories.* ○ *He sat riveted to the TV set.* ○ *Her eyes were riveted on the door, as if she expected someone to come in.*

riveting /ˈrɪvɪtɪŋ/ *adj* which holds everyone's attention (*informal*)

① **road** /rəʊd/ *noun* a hard surface which vehicles travel on ○ *The road to York goes directly north from London.* ○ *Drivers must be careful because roads are icy.* ○ *Children are taught to look both ways before crossing the road.* ○ *Our office address is: 26 London Road.* (NOTE: often used in names: *London Road, York Road*, etc., and usually written **Rd**: *London Rd*, etc.)

roadblock /ˈrəʊdblɒk/ *noun* a barrier put across a road by the police

road map /rəʊd mæp/ *noun* a map which shows the roads in a certain area

③ **road rage** /ˈrəʊd reɪdʒ/ *noun* a violent attack by a driver on another car or its driver, caused by anger at the way the other driver has been driving

roadside /ˈrəʊdsaɪd/ *noun* the side of a road ○ *We couldn't find a picnic area, so in the end we picnicked on the roadside.* ○ *They had a puncture so they stopped by the roadside to change the wheel.*

roadway /ˈrəʊdweɪ/ *noun* a main surface of a road (NOTE: The US term is **pavement**.)

roadworks /ˈrəʊdwɜːks/ *plural noun* repairs to a road ○ *It took longer than normal to get to Birmingham because of all the roadworks.*

roadworthy /ˈrəʊdwɜːði/ *adj* in a fit state to be driven on a road

roam /rəʊm/ (**roams, roaming, roamed**) *verb* to wander about a place without any particular destination

roar /rɔː/ (**roars, roaring, roared**) *verb* to make a deep loud noise ○ *He roared with laughter at the film.* ○ *The lion roared and then attacked.*

③ **roast** /rəʊst/ *verb* (**roasts, roasting, roasted**) to cook food over a fire or in an oven ○ *If you want the meat thoroughly cooked, roast it for a longer period at a lower temperature.* ○ *You can either roast pigeons or cook them in a casserole.* ■ *adj* which has been roasted ○ *What a lovely smell of roast meat!* ○ *We had roast chicken for dinner.*

③ **rob** /rɒb/ (**robs, robbing, robbed**) *verb* to attack and steal from someone

③ **robber** /ˈrɒbə/ *noun* a person who attacks and steals from someone

robbery /ˈrɒbəri/ (*plural* **robberies**) *noun* the act of attacking and stealing someone

robe /rəʊb/ *noun* a long, loose dress for men or women ○ *The professors came onto the platform in their academic robes.* ○ *The Arab sheikh rode up on a camel in his flowing robes.*

robin /ˈrɒbɪn/ *noun* a common small brown bird with a red breast

③ **robot** /ˈrəʊbɒt/ *noun* a machine which is designed to work like a person automatically

robust /rəʊˈbʌst/ *adj* **1.** strong and healthy **2.** not likely to fail or break ○ *a robust system* **3.** vigorous and determined ○ *He gave some robust answers to the journalists' questions.*

② **rock** /rɒk/ *noun* **1.** a large stone or a large piece of stone ○ *The ship was breaking up on the rocks.* **2.** a hard pink sweet shaped like a stick, often with the name of a town printed in it, bought mainly by tourists ○ *a stick of Brighton rock* **3. rock music** loud popular music with a strong rhythm ○ *Rock is the only music he listens to.* ■ *verb* (**rocks, rocking, rocked**) to move from side to side, or to make something move from side to side ○ *The little boat rocked in the wake of the ferry.* ○ *The explosion rocked the town.*

③ **rock bottom** /ˌrɒk ˈbɒtəm/ *noun* the lowest point

rocket /ˈrɒkɪt/ *noun* **1.** a type of space vehicle that looks like a tall tower **2.** a type of firework which flies up into the sky ○ *We stood in the square and watched the rockets lighting up the sky.* **3.** a type of bomb which is shot through space at an enemy ○ *They fired a homemade rocket into the police station.*

rocking chair /ˈrɒkɪŋ tʃeə/ *noun* a chair which rocks backwards and forwards on rockers

rock music /ˈrɒk ˌmjuːzɪk/ *noun* loud popular music with a strong rhythm

rocky /ˈrɒki/ *adj* **1.** full of rocks and large stones ○ *They followed a rocky path up the mountain.* **2.** difficult ○ *The company has had a rocky year.* ○ *My brother and sister-in-law are going through a rocky patch at the moment.* **3.** not steady ○ *My chair is a bit rocky.*

rod /rɒd/ *noun* a long stick ○ *You need something rigid like a metal rod to hold the tent upright.*

③ **rode** /rəʊd/ past tense of **ride**

rodent /ˈrəʊd(ə)nt/ *noun* an animal which chews and gnaws, such as a mouse or a rat

rodeo /ˈrəʊdiəʊ, rəʊˈdeɪəʊ/ (*plural* **rodeos**) *noun* a display of skill by cowboys

roe /rəʊ/ *noun* the eggs of fish ○ *They ate salmon roe on toast.* (NOTE: Do not confuse with **row**.)

rogue /rəʊɡ/ *noun* a wicked or dishonest person ○ *That car dealer is a bit of a rogue – you shouldn't really trust him.*

① **role** /rəʊl/, **rôle** *noun* **1.** a part played by someone in a play or film ○ *He plays the role of the king.* **2.** a part played by someone in real life [~in] ○ *He played an important role in getting the project off the ground.* ○ *Sleep has an important role in good health.* (NOTE: Do not confuse with **roll**.)

③ **role model** /ˈrəʊl ˌmɒd(ə)l/ *noun* a person who should be taken as an example which others can copy

role play /ˈrəʊl pleɪ/ *noun* an activity in which people each play the part of another person, as part of a training exercise

① **roll** /rəʊl/ *noun* **1.** a tube of something which has been turned over and over on itself ○ *a roll of fax paper* ○ *a roll of toilet paper* or *a toilet roll* **2.** a very small loaf of bread for one person, sometimes cut in half and used to make a sandwich ○ *a bowl of soup and a bread roll* ■ *verb* (**rolls, rolling, rolled**) **1.** to make something go forward by turning it over and over ○ *He rolled the ball to the other player.* **2.** to go forward by turning over and over ○ *The ball rolled down the hill.* ○ *My pound coin has rolled under the piano.* **3.** to make something move on wheels or rollers ○ *The table is fitted with wheels, just roll it into the room.* ○ *The patient was rolled into the operating theatre ten minutes ago.* **4.** to turn something flat over and over so that it forms a cylinder ○ *He rolled the poster into a tube.*

roll up③ *phrasal verb* **1.** to turn something flat over and over until it is a tube ○ *He rolled up the carpet* or *rolled the carpet up.* ○ *A hedgehog will roll up into a ball if you touch it.* **2.** to arrive ○ *They just rolled up and asked if we could put them up for the night.* ○ *The bridegroom finally rolled up an hour late and said he'd had a puncture.*

rollcall /ˈrəʊlkɔːl/ *noun* the act of reading a list of names

③ **roller** /ˈrəʊlə/ *noun* **1.** a heavy round object which rolls, e.g. one used for making lawns or cricket pitches flat ○ *The ground is so bumpy, you'll need a roller to flatten it.* ○ *They used the roller just before the match started.* ◊ **steamroller 2.** a plastic tube used for rolling hair into curls ○ *She came to the door in her dressing gown and rollers.*

rollerblades /ˈrəʊləbleɪdz/ *trademark* roller skates with a single set of wheels placed in line on the sole of each skate

rollerblading /ˈrəʊləbleɪdɪŋ/ *noun* the sport of going on rollerblades

roller coaster /ˌrəʊlə ˈkəʊstə/ *noun* **1.** a fairground railway which goes up and down steep slopes ○ *We all went for a ride on the roller coaster.* **2.** a dangerous or risky series of events that cannot be controlled ○ *The government had a roller coaster ride during its first weeks in office.*

rolling pin /ˈrəʊlɪŋ pɪn/ *noun* a wooden roller with handles, for flattening pastry

Roman /ˈrəʊmən/ *noun* **1.** a person who lives or lived in Rome ○ *The Romans invaded Britain in AD 43.* **2.** a printing type with straight letters ○ *The book is set in Times Roman.* Compare **italic**

Roman Catholic /ˌrəʊmən ˈkæθ(ə)lɪk/ *noun* a person who belongs to the Christian Church of which the Pope is the head ○ *When the Pope visited the country thousands of Roman Catholics attended mass.*

③ **romance** /rəʊˈmæns/ *noun* **1.** a love affair ○ *She told us all about her holiday romance.* ○ *Their romance didn't last.* **2.** a love story ○ *You'll enjoy this book if you like romances.*

Roman numeral /ˌrəʊmən ˈnjuːmərəl/ *noun* a number belonging to the set written with the symbols I, V, X, C, D and M. Compare **Arabic numeral**

② **romantic** /rəʊˈmæntɪk/ *adj* **1.** full of mystery and love ○ *romantic music* ○ *The atmosphere in the restaurant was very romantic.* **2.** used to describe something, often a literary or artistic style, which is based on personal emotions or imagination (*of a literary or artistic style*) ○ *His style is too romantic for my liking.* ○ *She has a romantic view of life.*

Romany /ˈrɒməni/ *noun* a member of a people originally from India, who travel from place to place rather than live in a permanent home

romp /rɒmp/ (**romps, romping, romped**) *verb* to play about energetically ○ *She was romping with her friends on the sofa when her mother came in.*

② **roof** /ruːf/ *noun* **1.** a part of a building which covers it and protects it ○ *The cat* *walked across the roof of the greenhouse.* ○ *She lives in a little cottage with a thatched roof.* **2.** the top of the inside of the mouth ○ *I burnt the roof of my mouth drinking hot soup.* **3.** the top of a vehicle, e.g. a car, bus or lorry ○ *We had to put the cases on the roof of the car.*

roofing /'ru:fɪŋ/ *noun* material which is used to make roofs

roof rack /'ru:f ræk/ *noun* a frame fixed to the roof of a car for carrying luggage

rooftop /'ru:ftɒp/ *noun* the top of a roof ○ *The plane flew low over the rooftops of the village.*

rook /rʊk/ *noun* **1.** a large black bird ○ *What is the difference between a rook and a crow? – Crows usually live in pairs, while rooks live in colonies.* **2.** (*in chess*) one of two pieces used in chess, shaped like a little castle tower ○ *She took my last rook.*

rookie /'rʊki/ *noun* a new recruit in the armed forces or in the police (*informal*)

① **room** /ru:m/ *noun* **1.** a part of a building, divided from other parts by walls ○ *The flat has six rooms, plus kitchen and bathroom.* ○ *We want an office with at least four rooms.* **2.** a bedroom in a hotel ○ *Your room is 316 – here's your key.* ○ *His room is just opposite mine.* **3.** a space for something [~for] ○ *There isn't enough room in the car for six people.* ○ *The table is too big – it takes up a lot of room.* □ **to make room for someone** *or* **something** to squeeze up to give space for someone or something ○ *There is no way we can make room for another passenger.*

room-mate /'ru:m meɪt/ *noun* a person who shares a room with you, especially at college

room service /'ru:m ˌsɜ:vɪs/ *noun* an arrangement in a hotel where food or drink can be served in a guest's bedroom

roomy /'ru:mi/ (**roomier, roomiest**) *adj* with plenty of space inside

② **root** /ru:t/ *noun* **1.** a part of a plant which goes down into the ground, and which takes nourishment from the soil ○ *I'm not surprised the plant died – it has hardly any roots.* **2.** the part of a hair or a tooth which goes down into the skin ○ *He pulled her hair out by the roots.* ◇ **to put down roots** to live somewhere long enough to feel that you belong there ◇ **to take root 1.** (*of an idea*) to become established **2.** (*of part of a plant*) to make roots ○ *The cuttings died – none of them took root.*

② **rope** /rəʊp/ *noun* a very thick cord ○ *You'll need a rope to pull the car out of the ditch.* ○ *The burglar climbed down from the balcony on a rope.* ■ *verb* (**ropes, roping, roped**) to tie together with a rope ○ *The climbers roped themselves together.* ○ *We roped the sofa onto the roof of the car.*

rosary /'rəʊzəri/ *noun* a string of beads which Catholics use to count out a set of prayers

③ **rose** /rəʊz/ *noun* a common garden flower with a strong pleasant smell ○ *He gave her a bunch of red roses.* ○ *These roses have a beautiful scent.* ■ past tense of **rise**

rosé /'rəʊzeɪ/ *noun* a pink wine which gets its colour from the black grape skins being left only for a short time in the fermenting mixture

rosemary /'rəʊzməri/ *noun* a bush herb with spiky green leaves, used in cooking

rosette /rəʊ'zet/ *noun* a ribbon bunched to look like a flower, used as a decoration or as a badge

roster /'rɒstə/ *noun* a list of duties which have to be done and the people who have to do them

rostrum /'rɒstrəm/ *noun* a raised stand for a speaker

rosy /'rəʊzi/ (**rosier, rosiest**) *adj* **1.** bright pink and healthy ○ *The children had rosy cheeks when they came in from their walk.* **2.** very favourable ○ *Our future is looking rosier than it has done for years.*

rot /rɒt/ (**rots, rotting, rotted**) *verb* to decay ○ *The wooden fence is not very old but it has already started to rot.* ◊ **rotten**

rota /'rəʊtə/ *noun* a roster, a list of duties which have to be done and the people who have to do them

rotary /'rəʊtəri/ *adj* which turns round

rotate /rəʊ'teɪt/ (**rotates, rotating, rotated**) *verb* to turn round or turn something round an axis like a wheel

rotation /rəʊ'teɪʃ(ə)n/ *noun* **1.** movement around a central point ○ *the rotation of the earth round the sun* **2.** the act of taking turns ○ *the rotation of players in a team*

rote /rəʊt/ *noun* learning by heart, often without understanding it

③ **rotten** /'rɒt(ə)n/ *adj* **1.** decayed ○ *The apple looked nice on the outside, but inside it was rotten.* ○ *Don't walk on that plank, I think it is rotten.* **2.** unpleasant ○ *I had a rotten time at the party – no one would dance with me.* ○ *We had rotten weather on holiday.*

rottweiler /ˈrɒtˌwaɪlə/ *noun* a large powerful dog with a black smooth coat with brown

② **rough** /rʌf/ *adj* **1.** not smooth ○ *Rub down any rough edges with sandpaper.* **2.** not very accurate ○ *I made some rough calculations on the back of an envelope.* **3.** not finished, or with no details ○ *He made a rough draft of the new design.* **4.** not gentle ○ *Don't be rough when you're playing with the puppy.*

rough-and-tumble /ˌrʌf ən ˈtʌmbəl/ *noun* a way of living that involves a lot of conflict

roughen /ˈrʌf(ə)n/ (**roughens, roughening, roughened**) *verb* to become rough, or make something become rough

② **roughly** /ˈrʌfli/ *adv* **1.** in a way that is not gentle enough ○ *Don't play so roughly with the children.* ○ *The men threw the boxes of china roughly into the back of their van.* **2.** approximately ○ *There were roughly one hundred people in the audience.* ○ *Ten euros make roughly six pounds.* ○ *The cost of building the new kitchen will be roughly £25,000.*

roughshod /ˈrʌfʃɒd/ *adv* □ **to ride roughshod over somebody *or* something** to treat somebody with no justice or consideration, or disregard something completely

roulette /ruːˈlet/ *noun* a game of chance where bets are made on the numbers in boxes on a flat rotating wheel where a small ball will lodge when the wheel stops turning

① **round** /raʊnd/ *adj* **1.** with a shape like a circle ○ *In Chinese restaurants, you usually sit at round tables.* **2.** with a shape like a sphere ○ *Soccer is played with a round ball, while a Rugby ball is oval.* ○ *People used to believe that the Earth was flat, not round.* ■ *adv, prep* **1.** in a circular way or movement ○ *The wheels of the lorry went round and round.* ○ *The Earth goes round the Sun.* ○ *He was the first person to sail round the world single-handed.* ○ *We all sat round the table chatting.* ○ *He ran down the street and disappeared round a corner.* **2.** towards the back ○ *She turned round when he tapped her on the shoulder.* ○ *Don't look round when you're driving on the motorway.* **3.** from one person to another ○ *They passed round some papers for everyone to sign.* ○ *Can you pass the plate of cakes round, please?* **4.** in various places ○ *They spent the afternoon going round the town.*

round down *phrasal verb* to decrease to the nearest full figure

round on *phrasal verb* to start to criticise someone suddenly

round up *phrasal verb* **1.** to gather people or animals together ○ *The secret police rounded up about fifty suspects and took them off in vans.* ○ *She rounded up the children and took them into the museum.* ○ *The farmer is out in the fields rounding up his sheep.* **2.** to increase to the nearest full figure ○ *The figures have been rounded up to the nearest dollar.* ○ *I owed him £4.98 so I rounded it up to £5.00.*

③ **roundabout** /ˈraʊndəbaʊt/ *noun* **1.** a place where several roads meet, and traffic has to move in a circle ○ *When you get to the next roundabout, turn right.* **2.** (*in a children's playground*) a heavy wheel which turns, and which children ride on in a park ○ *The children all ran to get on the roundabout.* ○ *A small child fell from the roundabout and hurt his leg badly.* **3.** (*in a fairground*) a large machine in a fairground which turns round and plays music, usually with horses to sit on which move up and down

rounded /ˈraʊndɪd/ *adj* with a smooth or round shape

roundly /ˈraʊndli/ *adv* strongly and clearly

round-the-clock /raʊnd ðiː/ *adj* throughout the day and night

③ **round trip** /ˈraʊnd trɪp/ *noun* a journey from one place to another and back again

roundup /ˈraʊndʌp/ *noun* a summary

rouse /raʊz/ (**rouses, rousing, roused**) *verb* **1.** to wake someone who is sleeping ○ *The shouts of the firemen roused the sleeping patients.* **2.** to get someone to act ○ *The difficulty will be to rouse the chairman into action:* Compare **arouse**

rousing /ˈraʊzɪŋ/ *adj* loud and noisy

rout /raʊt/ *noun* the complete defeat of an army or a team ○ *The final match of the series ended in a rout for the home side.* ■ *verb* (**routs, routing, routed**) to defeat someone completely ○ *The enemy army was routed.* (NOTE: + **rout** *n*)

② **route** /ruːt/ *noun* a way to be followed to get to a destination ○ *We still have to decide which route we will take.*

③ **routine** /ruːˈtiːn/ *noun* the usual, regular way of doing things ○ *He doesn't like his daily routine to be disturbed.* ○ *A change of routine might do you good.* ■ *adj* done as part of a regular pattern of activities ○ *He went to the doctor for a routine examination.*

roving /ˈrəʊvɪŋ/ *adj* going from place to place

② **row¹** /rəʊ/ *noun* a line of things, side by side or one after the other ○ *He has a row of cabbages in the garden.* ○ *They pulled down an old house to build a row of shops.* ○ *I want two seats in the front row.*

row² /raʊ/ *noun (informal)* **1.** a serious argument ○ *They had a row about who was responsible for the accident.* **2.** a loud noise ○ *Stop making that dreadful row!*

rowdy /ˈraʊdi/ (**rowdier, rowdiest**) *adj* involving people who are making a great deal of noise ○ *A rowdy party in the flat next door kept us all awake.* ○ *The minister had a rowdy reception at the meeting.*

① **royal** /ˈrɔɪəl/ *adj* relating to a king or queen

royal blue /ˌrɔɪəl ˈbluː/ *noun* a deep blue

royalist /ˈrɔɪəlɪst/ *noun* a person supporting rule by a king or queen

royalty /ˈrɔɪəlti/ (*plural* **royalties**) *noun* **1.** members of a king's or queen's family ○ *Please dress formally, there will be royalty present.* **2.** money paid to the author of a book or an actor in a film as a percentage of sales ○ *Do you receive royalties on the sales of your book?* ○ *All royalty cheques are paid direct to my account in Switzerland.*

③ **RSVP** *abbr* letters printed on an invitation asking the person invited to reply. Full form **répondez s'il vous plaît**

③ **rub** /rʌb/ (**rubs, rubbing, rubbed**) *verb* to move something across the surface of something else ○ *He rubbed his hands together to get them warm.* ○ *These new shoes have rubbed against my heel and given me a blister.* ○ *The cat rubbed herself against my legs.*

rub in③ *phrasal verb* to make an ointment or cream enter the skin by rubbing ○ *She rubbed the ointment into her skin.*

rub out③ *phrasal verb* to remove a pencil mark with a rubber

rub up *phrasal verb* □ **to rub someone up the wrong way** to annoy someone (*informal*) ○ *She's in a bad mood, someone must have rubbed her up the wrong way.*

③ **rubber** /ˈrʌbə/ *noun* **1.** a strong substance that bends easily, made from the sap of a tropical tree ○ *Car tyres are made of rubber.* ○ *Many years ago, we visited a rubber plantation in Malaysia.* **2.** a piece of rubber used for removing pencil marks ○ *He used a rubber to try to rub out what he had written.*

rubber band /ˌrʌbə ˈbænd/ *noun* same as **elastic band**

③ **rubbish** /ˈrʌbɪʃ/ *noun* **1.** waste, things which are no use and are thrown away ○ *We had to step over heaps of rubbish to get to the restaurant.* **2.** worthless nonsense ○ *Have you read his new book? – It's rubbish!* ○ *He's talking rubbish, don't listen to him.*

rubble /ˈrʌb(ə)l/ *noun* small stones or broken bricks from damaged buildings, also used in making such things as paths

rubella /ruːˈbelə/ *noun* a usually mild disease which gives a red rash but which can affect an unborn child if caught by a pregnant woman

ruby /ˈruːbi/ (*plural* **rubies**) *noun* a red precious stone ○ *A necklace of rubies and pearls.*

rucksack /ˈrʌksæk/ *noun* a large bag carried on the back when walking

③ **rude** /ruːd/ *adj* not polite and likely to offend people ○ *Don't point at people – it's rude.* ○ *The teacher asked who had written rude words on the board.* ○ *He was rude to the teacher.* (NOTE: **ruder – rudest**)

rudely /ˈruːdli/ *adv* in a rude way

rudimentary /ˌruːdɪˈment(ə)ri/ *adj* basic; not fully developed

rudiments /ˈruːdɪmənts/ *plural noun* simple basic facts ○ *He went on a short course so he's learnt the rudiments of sailing.*

ruffle /ˈrʌf(ə)l/ (**ruffles, ruffling, ruffled**) *verb* to disturb feathers or water or someone's hair ○ *The breeze ruffled the surface of the lake.* ○ *She ruffled his hair.*

rug /rʌg/ *noun* **1.** a small carpet ○ *This beautiful rug comes from the Middle East.* **2.** a thick blanket, especially one used when travelling ○ *Put a rug over your knees if you're cold.* ○ *We spread rugs on the grass to have our picnic.*

③ **rugby** /ˈrʌgbi/, **rugby football** /ˌrʌgbi ˈfʊtbɔːl/ *noun* a type of football played with an oval ball which is thrown as well as kicked

rugged /ˈrʌgɪd/ *adj* **1.** rough, rocky, uneven ○ *The rugged landscape of the moon.* **2.** tough and sturdy ○ *At school, he rapidly developed a rugged independence.*

③ **ruin** /ˈruːɪn/ (**ruins, ruining, ruined**) *verb* to spoil something completely ○ *Our picnic was ruined by the rain.*

③ **ruins** /ˈruːɪnz/ *plural noun* remains of old or damaged buildings □ **in ruins** destroyed ○ *The town was in ruins after the war.* ○ *After being arrested at the night club, his career was in ruins.*

② **rule** /ruːl/ *noun* a statement of the right things to do or the right way to behave ○ *There are no rules that forbid parking here at night.* ○ *According to the rules, your ticket must be paid for two weeks in advance.* □ **against the rules** not as the rules say ○ *You can't hold the football in your hands – it's against the rules.* ■ *verb* (**rules, ruling, ruled**) to govern or to control ○ *The president rules the country according to very old-fashioned principles.*

rule out *phrasal verb* to leave something out, not to consider something

③ **ruler** /ˈruːlə/ *noun* **1.** a person who governs ○ *A ruler should be fair.* ○ *He's the ruler of a small African state.* **2.** a long piece of wood or plastic with measurements marked on it, used for measuring and drawing straight lines ○ *You need a ruler to draw straight lines.*

③ **ruling** /ˈruːlɪŋ/ *noun* a legal decision made by a judge or other arbitrator ○ *The judge will give a ruling on the case next week.* ○ *According to the ruling of the court, the contract was illegal.*

rum /rʌm/ *noun* an alcoholic drink made from the juice of sugar cane ○ *She had a glass of rum and pineapple juice.*

rumble /ˈrʌmbəl/ (**rumbles, rumbling, rumbled**) *verb* to make a low rolling noise ○ *Wooden carts full of stone rumbled past.* ○ *Thunder rumbled in the distance.* ○ *I'm so hungry my tummy's rumbling.*

rumbling /ˈrʌmblɪŋ/ *noun* a low rolling noise

ruminate /ˈruːmɪneɪt/ (**ruminates, ruminating, ruminated**) *verb* to think over a problem ○ *He spent the weekend ruminating on what to do next.*

rummage /ˈrʌmɪdʒ/ (**rummages, rummaging, rummaged**) *verb* to search about for something ○ *She rummaged in her drawer until she found the pair of gloves.*

rumour /ˈruːmə/ *noun* a story spread from one person to another but which may not be true ○ *People have been spreading rumours about his private life.There's a rumour going around that John's getting married.* (NOTE: The US spelling is **rumor**.)

rump /rʌmp/ *noun* the back part of an animal

rumpled /ˈrʌmpəld/ *adj* creased or untidy

① **run** /rʌn/ *verb* (**runs, running, ran, run**) **1.** to go quickly on foot ○ *When she heard the telephone, she ran upstairs.* ○ *Children must be taught not to run across the road.* ○ *She's running in the 200 metre race.* **2.** (*of buses, trains, etc.*) to be operating ○ *All underground trains are running late because of the accident.* ○ *This bus doesn't run on Sundays.* **3.** (*of vehicles*) to work ○ *He left his car in the street with the engine running.* ○ *My car's not running very well at the moment.* **4.** to direct or organise an organisation ○ *He runs a chain of shoe shops.* ○ *I want someone to run the sales department for me when I'm away on holiday.* ○ *He runs the local youth club.* ○ *The country is run by the army.* **5.** to drive someone by car ○ *Let me run you to the station.* **6.** (*of liquid*) to flow, to move along smoothly ○ *The river runs past our house.* ■ *noun* **1.** the act of going quickly on foot, usually as a sport ○ *She entered for the 10-mile run.* ○ *I always go for a run before breakfast.* ○ *You must be tired out after that long run.* **2.** a score of 1 in cricket ○ *He made 45 runs before he was out.*

run across③ *phrasal verb* **1.** to cross something quickly on foot ○ *The little boy ran across the road after his ball.* **2.** to find or to meet someone by accident ○ *I ran across it in a secondhand bookshop.*

run after① *phrasal verb* to follow someone fast

run away① *phrasal verb* **1.** to escape or to go away fast ○ *They were running away from the police.* ○ *She ran away from school when she was 16.* ○ *The youngsters ran away to Paris.* **2.** □ **to run away with someone** to go away from your family to live with someone or to marry someone ○ *She ran away with her German teacher.*

run down① *phrasal verb* **1.** to go down quickly on foot ○ *She ran down the stairs two at a time.* ○ *Can you run down to the village and buy me some bread?* **2.** (*of clock, machine*) to stop working or go slower because of lack of power ○ *The clock has run down – it needs a new battery.* **3.** to criticise someone ○ *It's not fair to run him down when he's not there to defend himself.* **4.** to reduce the quantity of something ○ *We're running down our stocks of coal before the summer.* **5.** to knock down with a vehicle ○ *She was run down by a car which did not stop.*

run into③ *phrasal verb* **1.** to go into a place fast ○ *She ran into the street, shouting 'Fire!'.* **2.** to go fast and hit something, usually in a vehicle ○ *He didn't look where he was going and ran into an old lady.* ○ *The bus turned the corner too fast and ran into a parked van.* **3.** to amount to something ○ *Costs have run into thousands of pounds.* ○ *Her income runs into five figures.* **4.** to find someone by chance ○ *I ran into him again in a café on the South Bank.* **5.** to flow ○ *The river runs into the sea.*

run off③ *phrasal verb* **1.** to go away fast ○ *He grabbed the watch and ran off down the street.* **2.** to print using a machine ○ *She ran off a few photocopies of the leaflet.*

run off with③ *phrasal verb* **1.** to go away with someone ○ *He ran off with the girl next door and phoned his parents to say they had gone to Paris.* **2.** to steal something and go away ○ *She ran off with our petty cash.*

run on① *phrasal verb* **1.** to continue ○ *The text runs on to the next page.* ○ *Does the play run on until very late?* **2.** to use something as a fuel ○ *The machine runs on electricity.*

run out① *phrasal verb* to have nothing left of something ○ *The car ran out of petrol on the motorway.* ○ *I must go to the supermarket – we're running out of butter.*

run over① *phrasal verb* **1.** to knock someone down by hitting them with a vehicle ○ *She was run over by a taxi.* ○ *The car ran over a dog.* **2.** to continue ○ *The description of the accident runs over two pages.*

run through③ *phrasal verb* **1.** to read a list rapidly ○ *Let's run through the agenda before the meeting starts to see if there are any problem areas.* ○ *She ran through the paragraph again to make sure she understood what it meant.* **2.** to use up ○ *We have run through our entire stock of wine in one weekend.* **3.** to repeat ○ *Just run through that scene again to see if you all know your lines.*

run up① *phrasal verb* **1.** to go somewhere quickly on foot [~to] ○ *She ran up and asked if we were ready.* ○ *He ran up to the policeman and asked him to call an ambulance.* **2.** to make debts go up quickly ○ *The business was running up debts of thousands of pounds each week.*

run up against③ *phrasal verb* to find your way blocked by something

runaway /ˈrʌnəweɪ/ *noun* a person who has run away from home ○ *The police are looking for the runaways.*

rundown[1] /rʌnˈdaʊn/ *adj* **1.** unwell or tired ○ *If you feel run down, ask the chemist for vitamins.* **2.** dilapidated, not looked after ○ *He drives a run-down old car.*

rundown[2] /ˈrʌndaʊn/ *noun* a summary ○ *Give me a quick run-down on what happened at the meeting.*

③ **rung** /rʌŋ/ *noun* one of the bars on a ladder ○ *Put your foot on the bottom rung to hold the ladder steady.* ■ past participle of **ring**

run-in /ˈrʌn ɪn/ *noun* an argument (*informal*)

③ **runner** /ˈrʌnə/ *noun* a person or horse running in a race ○ *My horse came in last of seven runners.* ○ *There are 30,000 runners in the London Marathon.*

runner bean /ˌrʌnə ˈbiːn/ *noun* a type of climbing bean

③ **runner-up** /ˌrʌnər ˈʌp/ (*plural* **runners-up**) *noun* a person who comes after the winner in a race or competition

③ **running** /ˈrʌnɪŋ/ *adj* □ **for three days running** one day after another for three days ○ *The company have made a profit for six years or the sixth year running.* ■ *noun* **1.** the activity of running, as a sport or a leisure activity **2.** the action of managing ○ *I now leave the running of the firm to my daughter.* ◇ **to be in the running** to be a candidate for something ○ *Three people are in the running for the post of chairperson.* ◇ **to be out of the running** to no longer be a candidate for something ○ *She's out of the running for the job in France.*

running battle /ˌrʌnɪŋ ˈbæt(ə)l/ *noun* a battle which moves around from place to place

running costs /ˈrʌnɪŋ kɒsts/ *noun* the money spent regularly on operating a business

running total /ˌrʌnɪŋ ˈtəʊt(ə)l/ *noun* a total which is carried from one column of figures to the next

running water /ˌrʌnɪŋ ˈwɔːtə/ *noun* water which is available in a house through water mains and taps

runny /ˈrʌni/ *adj* in liquid form

run-of-the-mill /ˌrʌn əv ðə ˈmɪl/ *adj* ordinary

run-up /ˈrʌn ʌp/ *noun* a period leading up to some event ○ *In the run-up to the election.*

③ **runway** /ˈrʌnweɪ/ *noun* a track on which planes land and take off at an airport

rupture /ˈrʌptʃə/ (**ruptures, rupturing, ruptured**) *verb* to break or burst ○ *A water main ruptured and the centre of town was flooded.* (NOTE: + **rupture** *n*)

② **rural** /ˈrʊərəl/ *adj* relating to the countryside ○ *Rural roads are usually fairly narrow.* ○ *We live quite close to a town but the country round us still looks very rural.*

ruse /ruːz/ *noun* a clever trick

② **rush** /rʌʃ/ *noun* a fast movement [~of] ○ *There was a rush of hot air when they opened the door.* ○ *There has been a rush to change pounds to euros.* ○ *When the film ended there was a rush for the toilets.* ■ *verb* (**rushes, rushing, rushed**) to hurry, to go forward fast ○ *The ambulance rushed to the accident.* ○ *Crowds of shoppers rushed to the shops on the first day of the sales.*

rush into *phrasal verb* **1.** to go into a place quickly ○ *He rushed into the room waving a piece of paper.* **2.** to get into a situation too quickly, without really thinking ○ *They rushed into an alliance with the socialists and regretted it immediately.* ○ *Don't rush into marriage if you're doubtful about your partner.*

rushed /rʌʃt/ *adj* done very quickly

③ **rush hour** /ˈrʌʃ aʊə/ *noun* a time of day when traffic is bad and when trains are full

rust /rʌst/ *noun* a reddish-brown substance formed on iron and steel when left in damp air ○ *There is a bit of rust on the bonnet of the car.* ■ *verb* (**rusts, rusting, rusted**) to form rust ○ *Don't leave the hammer and screwdriver in the rain – they'll rust.*

rustic /ˈrʌstɪk/ *adj* **1.** of country style ○ *They live in a little rustic cottage on the edge of a lake.* **2.** rough, not elegant ○ *We bought a rustic bench and table for eating in the garden.*

rustle /ˈrʌs(ə)l/ *verb* (**rustles, rustling, rustled**) to make a soft noise like dry surfaces rubbing against each other ○ *Her long skirt rustled as she sat down.* ○ *Don't rustle the newspaper when the radio is on, I can't hear it properly.* ■ *noun* the noise of dry leaves or pieces of paper rubbing together ○ *Listen to the rustle of the dry leaves in the hedge.*

rustle up *phrasal verb* to get something ready quickly (*informal*)

rusty /ˈrʌsti/ *adj* covered with rust ○ *She tried to cut the string with a pair of rusty old scissors.* ○ *He has a rusty old fridge in his front garden.*

rut /rʌt/ *noun* a deep track made in soft earth by the wheels of vehicles ○ *The front wheel of the car was stuck in a deep rut.*

ruthless /ˈruːθləs/ *adj* cruel, with no pity for anyone

rye /raɪ/ *noun* **1.** a type of dark brown cereal, used to make bread and American whiskey ○ *They are harvesting the rye today.* **2.** rye whiskey or American whiskey; a glass of this whiskey ○ *A large rye and soda, please.* (NOTE: Do not confuse with **wry**.)

S

s /es/, **S** *noun* the nineteenth letter of the alphabet, between R and T

's *short for* **1.** is **2.** has ■ *suffix* used on the end of a noun to show possession or relationship between things ○ *Judy's book* ○ *the dog's puppies* ○ *the rose's scent* ○ *a day's holiday*

S *abbr* **1.** south **2.** southern

sabbatical /sə'bætɪk(ə)l/, **sabbatic** *noun* leave granted to people such as teachers for study and travel after a period of work

sabotage /'sæbətɑːʒ/ (**sabotages, sabotaging, sabotaged**) *verb* to destroy something, to render something useless deliberately ○ *He sabotaged the whole plan by passing the details to the police.* (NOTE: + **sabotage** *n*)

saboteur /ˌsæbə'tɜː/ *noun* a person who commits sabotage

sabre /'seɪbə/ *noun* a sword with a curved blade (NOTE: The US spelling is **saber**.)

sabre-rattling /'seɪbə ˌræt(ə)lɪŋ/ *noun* an aggressive display or threat of force or military action (NOTE: The US spelling is **saber-rattling**.)

saccharin /'sækərɪn/ *noun* a substance used as a substitute for sugar

sachet /'sæʃeɪ/ *noun* a small plastic or paper bag containing something

sack /sæk/ *noun* a large bag made of strong cloth or paper, used for carrying heavy things ○ *a sack of potatoes* ■ *verb* (**sacks, sacking, sacked**) to force someone to leave his or her job ○ *He was sacked because he was always late for work.*

sacking /'sækɪŋ/ *noun* dismissal from a job ○ *The union protested against the sackings.*

sacrament /'sækrəmənt/ *noun* a Christian religious ceremony ○ *the sacrament of marriage*

sacred /'seɪkrɪd/ *adj* **1.** associated with religion ○ *The sacred texts were kept locked away.* **2.** respected ○ *Nothing is sacred to a reporter chasing a good story.* ○ *She believed it was her sacred duty to look after his garden while he was away.*

sacred cow /ˌseɪkrɪd 'kaʊ/ *noun* a belief or idea which is not to be criticised

sacrifice /'sækrɪfaɪs/ *noun* **1.** something which you give up to achieve something more important ○ *He finally won the competition, but at great personal sacrifice.* ○ *She made many financial sacrifices to get her children through university.* □ **to make sacrifices** to not have or do something for yourself so that someone else can benefit or you can do something better later **2.** the act of making an offering to a god by killing an animal or person ○ *He ordered the sacrifice of two lambs to please the gods.* ■ *verb* (**sacrifices, sacrificing, sacrificed**) **1.** to give something up ○ *I have sacrificed my career to be able to stay at home and bring up my children.* ○ *She has sacrificed herself for the cause of animal welfare.* **2.** to kill an animal or person to please a god ○ *The priests sacrificed a goat to the goddess.*

sacrilege /'sækrɪlɪdʒ/ *noun* behaviour towards something holy or important to other people which lacks respect

sacrosanct /'sækrəsæŋkt/ *adj* not to be criticised or changed

② **sad** /sæd/ *adj* not happy ○ *He's sad because the holidays have come to an end.* ○ *What a sad film – everyone was crying.* ○ *Reading his poems makes me sad.* ○ *It was sad to leave the house for the last time.* ○ *He felt sad watching the boat sail away.* ○ *It's sad that he can't come to see us.*

sadden /'sæd(ə)n/ (**saddens, saddening, saddened**) *verb* to make someone unhappy

saddle /'sæd(ə)l/ *noun* **1.** a rider's seat on a bicycle or motorbike **2.** a rider's seat on a horse ○ *He leapt into the saddle and rode away.*

sadhu /'sɑːduː/, **saddhu** *noun* in Hinduism, a holy man

sadist /ˈseɪdɪst/ *noun* a person who gets pleasure from being cruel (NOTE: + **sadism** *n*)

③ **sadly** /ˈsædli/ *adv* **1.** in a sad way ○ *She smiled sadly.* **2.** used for saying that something makes you sad ○ *Sadly, John couldn't join us for my birthday party.*

sadness /ˈsædnəs/ *noun* a feeling of being very unhappy

s.a.e. *abbr* self-addressed envelope, stamped addressed envelope

safari /səˈfɑːri/ *noun* an expedition to photograph or kill wild animals, especially in Africa

② **safe** /seɪf/ *adj* (**safer, safest**) not in danger, or not likely to be hurt ○ *In this cave, we should be safe from the thunderstorm.* ○ *All the children are safe, but the school was burnt down.* ○ *Is it safe to touch this snake?* ■ *noun* a strong box for keeping things such as documents, money or jewels in ○ *Put your valuables in the hotel safe.* ○ *The burglars managed to open the safe.*

safe deposit box /ˌseɪf dɪˈpɒzɪt ˌbɒks/ *noun* a small box which you can rent to hold jewellery or documents in a bank's strongroom

safeguard /ˈseɪfɡɑːd/ (**safeguards, safeguarding, safeguarded**) *verb* to protect something ○ *Our aim is to safeguard the interests of the widow and children.* (NOTE: + **safeguard** *n*)

safe haven /ˌseɪf ˈheɪv(ə)n/ *noun* a place which is safe from attack, where someone is protected from danger

safe keeping /ˌseɪf ˈkiːpɪŋ/ *noun* the care of something in a safe place

② **safely** /ˈseɪfli/ *adv* without being hurt ○ *The rescue services succeeded in getting all the passengers safely off the burning train.* ○ *We were shown how to handle explosives safely.* ○ *'Drive safely!' she said as she waved goodbye.*

safe sex /seɪf ˈseks/ *noun* having sex in a way that avoids transmission of a sexual disease, e.g. by using a condom and only having one sexual partner

② **safety** /ˈseɪfti/ *noun* **1.** being safe ○ *Our main concern is the safety of the children.* **2.** □ **for safety** in order to make something safe ○ *Put the money in the office safe for safety.* ○ *Keep a note of the numbers of your traveller's cheques for safety.*

safety belt /ˈseɪfti belt/ *noun* a belt which you wear in a plane to stop you being hurt if there is an accident

safety net /ˈseɪfti net/ *noun* **1.** a net stretched under someone such as a tightrope walker to catch him or her if he or she falls ○ *He was killed when he walked the tightrope without a safety net.* **2.** something which protects you if things go wrong ○ *He has a second job, which is a useful safety net if he is made redundant.*

safety pin /ˈseɪfti pɪn/ *noun* a pin whose point fits into a cover when it is fastened, and so can't hurt you

saffron /ˈsæfrən/ (*plural* **saffrons** or *same*) *noun* an orange-coloured powder made from crocus flowers, used in cooking to give colour and flavour to food ○ *She made rice with saffron.*

sag /sæɡ/ (**sags, sagging, sagged**) *verb* to sink or bend in the middle under weight or pressure

saga /ˈsɑːɡə/ *noun* **1.** an old story of heroic achievement or adventure, especially in Norway and Iceland ○ *the sagas of ancient kings of Iceland* **2.** a long story ○ *I don't want to hear her tell the saga of the accident all over again.*

sage /seɪdʒ/ *noun* **1.** an aromatic herb with silvery-green leaves used in cookery **2.** an old wise man ○ *The king invited sages to his castle to give him advice.*

Sagittarius /ˌsædʒɪˈteəriəs/ *noun* one of the signs of the Zodiac, shaped like an archer, covering the period from 22nd November to 21st December

③ **said** /sed/ past tense and past participle of **say**

② **sail** /seɪl/ *noun* a piece of cloth which catches the wind and drives a boat along ○ *The wind dropped so they lowered the sail and started to row.* ○ *They hoisted the sail and set out across the Channel.* ■ *verb* (**sails, sailing, sailed**) **1.** to travel on water ○ *The ship was sailing towards the rocks.* ○ *We were sailing east.* ○ *He was the first person to sail across the Atlantic single-handed.* ○ *She's planning to sail round the world.* **2.** to leave a harbour ○ *The ferry sails at 12.00.*

sailboard /ˈseɪlbɔːd/ *noun* a board with a sail, used for travelling across water

③ **sailing** /ˈseɪlɪŋ/ *noun* travel in a ship

sailing boat /ˈseɪlɪŋ bəʊt/ *noun* a boat which uses mainly sails to travel

sailor /ˈseɪlə/ *noun* a person who works on a ship ○ *The sailors were washing down the deck of the ship.*

saint /seɪnt/ *noun* **1.** a person who led a very holy life, and is recognised by the Christian Church ○ *There are more than 50 statues of saints on the west front of the cathedral.* ○ *St Peter was a fisherman.* ○ *Will*

Mother Teresa be made a saint? **2.** a very good or devoted person ○ *She has the patience of a saint and never shouts at the children.* ○ *He may be no saint in his personal life but he has the support of the voters.* (NOTE: abbreviated with names to **St** /sənt/)

② **sake**[1] /seɪk/ ◇ **for the sake of something, for something's sake** for certain reasons or purposes, or because of something ○ *They gave the children sweets, just for the sake of a little peace and quiet.* ○ *The muggers killed the old lady, just for the sake of £20.* ◇ **for the sake of someone, for someone's sake** because you want to help someone or to please someone ○ *Will you come to the party for my sake?* ○ *The president decided to resign for the sake of the country.* ◇ **for old times' sake** in order to remember a relationship or activity from the past ○ *We always send them a Christmas card, just for old times' sake.* ◇ **for heaven's sake, for goodness' sake** used for showing you are annoyed or worried ○ *What's all the fuss? It's only a little scratch, for heaven's sake.* ○ *For goodness' sake try to be quiet, we don't want wake everyone!*

sake[2] /'sɑːki/ *noun* a Japanese rice wine ○ *We had a glass of sake with our meal.*

③ **salad** /'sæləd/ *noun* a mixture of cold vegetables eaten raw, or a meal that includes such a mixture ○ *a chicken salad sandwich* ○ *We found some ham, tomatoes and lettuce in the fridge, and made ourselves a salad.*

salad dressing /'sæləd ˌdresɪŋ/ *noun* a sauce consisting of a mixture of oil, vinegar and herbs or spices, used on salad

salami /sə'lɑːmi/ *noun* a large dry Italian-style sausage eaten cold in thin slices

③ **salary** /'sæləri/ (*plural* **salaries**) *noun* payment for work, especially in a professional or office job ○ *She started work at a low salary, but soon went up the salary scale.* ○ *I expect a salary increase as from next month.*

① **sale** /seɪl/ *noun* **1.** the act of selling, the act of giving an item or doing a service in exchange for money ○ *The sale of the house produced £200,000.* ○ *The shop only opened this morning and we've just made our first sale.* **2.** an occasion when things are sold at cheaper prices ○ *There's a sale this week in the department store along the High Street.* ○ *I bought these plates for £1 in a sale.* ○ *The sale price is 50% of the normal price.*

③ **sales assistant** /'seɪlz əˌsɪstənt/ *noun* a person who sells goods to customers in a shop

③ **salesman** /'seɪlzmən/ (*plural* **salesmen**) *noun* a person who represents a company, selling its products or services to other companies

salesperson /'seɪlzˌpɜːs(ə)n/ (*plural* **salespeople** or **salespersons**) *noun* a person who sells goods in a shop

③ **saleswoman** /'seɪlzwʊmən/ (*plural* **saleswomen**) *noun* a woman who sells goods to customers in a shop

saline /'seɪlaɪn/ *adj* containing salt

saliva /sə'laɪvə/ *noun* a fluid in the mouth, secreted by the salivary glands, which starts the process of digesting food

salivate /'sælɪveɪt/ (**salivates, salivating, salivated**) *verb* to produce saliva

sallow /'sæləʊ/ *adj* slightly yellow, unhealthy looking

salmon /'sæmən/ *noun* a large fish with silver skin and pink flesh that lives in the sea, but swims up rivers to produce young in the winter

salon /'sælɒn/ *noun* a shop where people can have their hair cut or styled, or have beauty treatments

saloon /sə'luːn/ *noun* **1.** *US* a place where alcoholic drinks are sold (*dated*) ○ *The conversation stopped when the stranger walked into the saloon.* **2.** same as **car**

salsa /'sælsə/ *noun* **1.** a spicy sauce made with chopped vegetables, of Mexican origin **2.** Latin American dance music combining jazz and rock

② **salt** /sɔːlt/ *noun* a white substance that you put on food to make it taste better or put on roads to make snow or ice melt

salt cellar /'sɒlt ˌselə/ *noun* a small pot containing salt usually with a hole in the top so that it can be sprinkled on food

saltwater /'sɔːltwɔːtə/ *adj* referring to water which contains salt

salty /'sɔːlti/ (**saltier, saltiest**) *adj* tasting of salt

salute /sə'luːt/ *noun* a movement which expresses respect or recognition, especially the movement of putting your right hand up to touch the side of your forehead ○ *The officer returned the soldier's salute.* ■ *verb* (**salutes, saluting, saluted**) to give a salute to someone ○ *Ordinary soldiers must salute their officers.*

salvage /'sælvɪdʒ/ (**salvages, salvaging, salvaged**) *verb* **1.** to save from a wreck or a fire ○ *We are selling off a warehouse full of salvaged goods.* ○ *We managed to salvage the computer discs from the fire.* **2.** to save something from loss ○ *The company is trying to salvage its reputation after the managing director was sent to prison for fraud.* ○ *The receiver managed to salvage something from the collapse of the company.* (NOTE: + **salvage** *n*)

③ **salvation** /sæl'veɪʃ(ə)n/ *noun* the action of saving a person's soul from sin

① **same** /seɪm/ *adj, pron* **1.** being, looking, sounding, etc. exactly alike ○ *These two beers taste the same.* ○ *You must get very bored doing the same work every day.* ○ *She was wearing the same dress as me.* ○ *This book is not the same size as that one.* **2.** showing that two or more things are in fact one ○ *They all live in the same street.* ○ *Should we all leave at the same time?* ○ *Our children go to the same school as theirs.* ◇ **same again, please!** please serve us the same drinks or food as before (*informal*)

② **sample** /'sɑːmpəl/ *noun* a specimen, a small part which is used to show what the whole is like ○ *a sample of the cloth* or *a cloth sample* ○ *We interviewed a sample of potential customers.* ○ *He gave a blood sample.*

sanatorium /ˌsænə'tɔːriəm/ (*plural* **sanatoriums** or **sanatoria**) *noun* a hospital for the treatment of invalids, especially people suffering from tuberculosis

sanction /'sæŋkʃən/ *noun* approval, permission ○ *You will need the sanction of the local authorities before you can knock the house down.* ■ *verb* (**sanctions, sanctioning, sanctioned**) to approve something ○ *The committee sanctioned the expenditure of £1.2m on the development project.*

sanctity /'sæŋktɪti/ *noun* holiness

sanctuary /'sæŋktʃuəri/ (*plural* **sanctuaries**) *noun* **1.** a place of safety ○ *The church became a sanctuary for illegal immigrants.* ○ *People escaping from the revolutionary troops sought sanctuary in the church.* **2.** a place for the protection of wild animals or birds ○ *They established several bird sanctuaries near the sea.*

② **sand** /sænd/ *noun* a mass of very small bits of rock found on beaches and in the desert ○ *a beach of fine white sand* ○ *the black sand beaches of the Northern coast of New Zealand*

sandal /'sænd(ə)l/ *noun* a light shoe with an open top

sandbag /'sændbæg/ *noun* a bag filled with sand and used as a protection

sand dune /'sænd djuːn/ *noun* an area of sand blown by the wind into small hills and ridges which have very little soil or vegetation

sandpaper /'sændpeɪpə/ *noun* thick paper covered with sand used for smoothing rough surfaces ○ *Use fine sandpaper if you want to get a very smooth finish.* (NOTE: + **sandpaper** *v*)

sandpit /'sændpɪt/ *noun* a place in a garden, with sand where children can play

sandstone /'sændstəun/ *noun* a type of reddish brown rock, formed of tiny pieces of sand

sandstorm /'sændstɔːm/ *noun* a high wind in the desert, which carries large amounts of sand with it

② **sandwich** /'sænwɪdʒ/ *noun* a light meal made with two pieces of bread with other food between them ○ *She ordered a cheese sandwich and a cup of coffee.* ○ *What sort of sandwiches do you want to take for your lunch?* ○ *I didn't have a big meal – just a sandwich with some beer in the pub.*

sane /seɪn/ (**saner, sanest**) *adj* not mad

③ **sang** /sæŋ/ past tense of **sing**

sanguine /'sæŋgwɪn/ *adj* confident, optimistic

sanitary /'sænɪt(ə)ri/ *adj* referring to hygiene or to health

sanitary towel /'sænɪt(ə)ri ˌtauəl/, **sanitary napkin** *noun* a pad of absorbent cotton used by a woman to absorb blood during her period

sanitation /ˌsænɪ'teɪʃ(ə)n/ *noun* being hygienic, especially referring to public hygiene and the removal of household waste and sewage

sanity /'sænɪti/ *noun* the state of being sane

③ **sank** /sæŋk/ past tense of **sink**

sap /sæp/ *noun* the liquid which flows inside plants and trees ○ *They cut a notch in the bark of the tree and the sap ran out.* ■ *verb* (**saps, sapping, sapped**) to make something weaker ○ *His strength was sapped by the cold.*

sapling /'sæplɪŋ/ *noun* a young tree

sapphire /'sæfaɪə/ *noun* a bright blue precious stone

sarcasm /'sɑːkæz(ə)m/ *noun* sharp unpleasant remarks which mean the opposite of what they say

sardine /sɑː'diːn/ *noun* a small silvery fish which can be eaten fresh, or commonly bought in tins

sardonic /sɑː'dɒnɪk/ *adj* scornful, showing you feel superior to someone

sari /'sɑːri/, **saree** *noun* a long piece of cloth, especially silk, which Indian women wear wrapped round their bodies

sash /sæʃ/ *noun* **1.** an ornamental scarf or belt ○ *In France, mayors wear a red, white and blue sash.* **2.** a wooden frame holding panes of glass

③ **sat** /sæt/ past tense and past participle of **sit**

SAT /sæt/ *noun US* in the USA, a pre-college test (*trademark of the College Entrance Examination Board*) Full form **Scholastic Aptitude Test**. ◊ **SATs**

Satan /'seɪt(ə)n/ *noun* the Devil

satanism /'seɪt(ə)nˌɪz(ə)m/ *noun* the worship of Satan

③ **satellite** /'sætəlaɪt/ *noun* **1.** an object in space which goes round the Earth and sends and receives signals, pictures and data ○ *The signals are transmitted by satellite all round the world.* **2.** an object like a planet which goes round a planet ○ *The Moon is the only satellite of the Earth.*

satellite dish /'sætəlaɪt dɪʃ/ *noun* an aerial, shaped like a large saucer, used to capture satellite broadcasts

satellite television /ˌsæt(ə)laɪt 'telɪvɪʒ(ə)n/ *noun* television programmes broadcast using satellite technology

satin /'sætɪn/ *noun* a silk material with a glossy surface ○ *She bought some black satin to make a dress.*

satire /'sætaɪə/ *noun* **1.** a way of attacking people in speaking or writing by making them seem ridiculous ○ *his use of satire in his weekly political column* **2.** a piece of writing which criticises people by making them seem ridiculous ○ *'Gulliver's Travels' is a satire on 18th-century England.*

satirist /'sætərɪst/ *noun* a person who writes or performs satires

③ **satisfaction** /ˌsætɪs'fækʃən/ *noun* a good feeling; a sense of comfort or happiness ○ *We got a lot of satisfaction from beating our old rivals.*

satisfactory /ˌsætɪs'fækt(ə)ri/ *adj* good enough, or quite good

③ **satisfied** /'sætɪsfaɪd/ *adj* accepting that something is enough, is good or is correct

② **satisfy** /'sætɪsfaɪ/ (**satisfies, satisfying, satisfied**) *verb* to make someone pleased with what he or she has received or achieved ○ *The council's decision should satisfy most people.* ○ *Our aim is to satisfy our customers.*

③ **satisfying** /'sætɪsfaɪɪŋ/ *adj* which satisfies

SATs /sæts/ *noun* in the UK, national tests taken at various ages during secondary school. Full form **Standard Assessment Tests**

satsuma /sæt'suːmə/ *noun* a type of small orange, with peel which is easily removed

saturate /'sætʃəreɪt/ (**saturates, saturating, saturated**) *verb* to fill something with the maximum amount of a liquid or substance which can be absorbed (NOTE: + **saturation** *n*)

saturated fat /ˌsætʃəreɪtɪd 'fæt/ *noun* butter and other types of animal fat, which contain the largest amount of hydrogen possible

① **Saturday** /'sætədeɪ/ *noun* the sixth day of the week, the day between Friday and Sunday ○ *He works in a shop, so Saturday is a normal working day for him.* ○ *We go shopping in London most Saturdays.* ○ *Saturday is the Jewish day of rest.* ○ *Today is Saturday, November 15th.* ○ *The 15th is a Saturday, so the 16th must be a Sunday.* ○ *We arranged to meet up on Saturday.*

③ **sauce** /sɔːs/ *noun* a liquid with a particular taste, poured over food ○ *ice cream with chocolate sauce* ○ *We had chicken with a barbecue sauce.* ○ *The waitress put a bottle of tomato sauce on the table.*

③ **saucepan** /'sɔːspən/ *noun* a deep metal cooking pan with a lid and a long handle

③ **saucer** /'sɔːsə/ *noun* a shallow dish which a cup stands on

saucy /'sɔːsi/ (**saucier, sauciest**) *adj* cheeky

sauna /'sɔːnə/ *noun* **1.** a bath taken by sitting in a room filled with very hot steam ○ *We all had a sauna and then went for a swim in the lake.* **2.** a room where you can have a very hot steam bath ○ *There is a sauna in the basement of the hotel.*

saunter /'sɔːntə/ (**saunters, sauntering, sauntered**) *verb* to walk slowly, to stroll ○ *She sauntered into the bar and ordered a whisky.*

③ **sausage** /'sɒsɪdʒ/ *noun* a food which is a tube of skin full of a mixture of meat and spices

sausage roll /ˌsɒsɪdʒ ˈrəʊl/ *noun* a small roll of pastry with a piece of sausage or some sausagemeat inside

sauté /ˈsəʊteɪ/ (**sautés, sautéing, sautéed**) *verb* to fry something in a little fat ○ *She sautéed some potatoes to go with the meat.*

savage /ˈsævɪdʒ/ *noun* a person from a culture that is not considered civilised (*dated offensive*) ○ *How could he turn into such a savage and attack her like that?* ■ *verb* (**savages, savaging, savaged**) to attack somebody with teeth ○ *He was savaged by an Alsatian.*

savagery /ˈsævɪdʒ(ə)ri/ *noun* being savage

savanna /səˈvænə/, **savannah** *noun* a dry grass-covered plain with few trees, usually referring to the grasslands of South America and Africa

① **save** /seɪv/ (**saves, saving, saved**) *verb* **1.** to stop something from being damaged [~from] ○ *We managed to save most of the paintings from the fire.* **2.** to keep things such as money, food or other articles so that you can use them later [~for] ○ *Save those bones for the dog.* ○ *If you save £10 a week, you'll have £520 at the end of a year.* ○ *I'm saving to buy a new computer.* **3.** not to waste something such as time or money ○ *By walking to work, he saves £25 a week in bus fares.* ○ *If you have your car checked regularly it will save you a lot of expense in the future.* ○ *Going by air saves a lot of time.* **4.** to stop someone from being hurt or killed [~from] ○ *The firefighters saved six people from the burning house.* ○ *How many passengers were saved when the ferry sank?* **5.** to store data on a computer disk ○ *Don't forget to save your files when you have finished working on them.*

saver /ˈseɪvə/ *noun* **1.** a person who saves money ○ *All savers will receive a bonus this year.* **2.** a special offer or ticket which allows you to buy something at a lower price ○ *Among this week's savers are baked beans at 50p.* ○ *Saver tickets are not valid on trains before 9.30.*

③ **saving** /ˈseɪvɪŋ/ *noun* using less [/~on] ○ *We could make a saving of 10% on fuel costs.* ■ *suffix* which uses less ○ *energy-saving light bulbs*

saving grace /ˈseɪvɪŋ greɪs/ *noun* a quality or feature which makes a situation less bad than it seemed

saviour /ˈseɪvjə/ *noun* a person who saves people ○ *He was called the Saviour of the West.* (NOTE: The US spelling is **savior**.)

savour /ˈseɪvə/ *verb* to appreciate or enjoy something ○ *He ate slowly, savouring his meal.* ○ *The general stood at the top of the hill, savouring his victory.* (NOTE: The US spelling is **savor**.)

savoury /ˈseɪvəri/ *adj* with a salty taste, or other taste which is not sweet ○ *I don't particularly like sweets, I prefer savoury things.* (NOTE: The US spelling is **savory**.) ■ *noun* a food that is salty or spicy, served as a snack often with an alcoholic drink ○ *They served little savouries with the drinks before dinner.*

savvy /ˈsævi/ *noun* practical knowledge

③ **saw** /sɔː/ past tense of **see** ■ *noun* a tool with a long metal blade with teeth along its edge, used for cutting ○ *He was cutting logs with a saw.* ■ *verb* (**saws, sawing, sawed, sawed** or **sawn**) to cut something with a saw ○ *She was sawing wood.* ○ *You will need to saw that piece of wood in half.*

sawdust /ˈsɔːdʌst/ *noun* powder produced when you saw wood

sawmill /ˈsɔːmɪl/ *noun* a factory where wood is cut into planks by machines

sax /sæks/ *noun* a saxophone (*informal*)

saxophone /ˈsæksəfəʊn/ *noun* a large brass musical instrument with keys

① **say** /seɪ/ (**says, saying, said**) *verb* **1.** to speak words [~(that)/~how/what/who etc] ○ *She says the weather will be fine tomorrow.* ○ *Did she say how many chairs she wanted?* ○ *What's she saying? – I don't know, I don't understand Dutch.* ○ *Don't forget to say 'thank you' after the party.* **2.** to give information in writing [~(that)] ○ *The letter says that we owe the bank £200.* ○ *The notice says that you are not allowed to walk on the grass.*

③ **saying** /ˈseɪɪŋ/ *noun* a phrase which is often used to describe an aspect of everyday life

scab /skæb/ *noun* **1.** a crust of dry blood which forms over a wound and protects it ○ *The scab fell off where he had grazed his knee.* **2.** a worker who goes on working when there is a strike ○ *We don't want scabs here.*

scaffold /ˈskæfəʊld/ *noun* a wooden platform on which an execution takes place

scaffolding /ˈskæfəldɪŋ/ *noun* a construction of poles and planks which make a series of platforms for workmen to stand on while working

scald /skɔːld/ (**scalds, scalding, scalded**) *verb* to burn a part of the body with hot liquid or steam

scalding /ˈskɔːldɪŋ/ *adj* very hot

② **scale** /skeɪl/ *noun* **1.** a proportion used to show a large object in a smaller form ○ *a map with a scale of 1 to 100,000* ○ *a scale model of the new town centre development* ○ *The architect's design is drawn to scale.* **2.** a measuring system which is graded into various levels ○ *The Richter scale is used to measure earthquakes.*

scallop /ˈskɒləp/, **scollop** *noun* a type of shellfish with a pair of semicircular flat shells ○ *We had scallops fried in butter.*

scalp /skælp/ *noun* the skin which covers the skull ○ *He was taken to hospital with a scalp wound.* ○ *Rubbing the scalp will encourage your hair to grow.*

scalpel /ˈskælpəl/ *noun* a sharp pointed knife used in surgery

scam /skæm/ *noun* a case of fraud (*slang*)

scamper /ˈskæmpə/ (**scampers, scampering, scampered**) *verb* to run fast with little steps

scampi /ˈskæmpi/ *plural noun* large prawns

③ **scan** /skæn/ *noun* **1.** the examination of part of the body by passing X-rays through the body and analysing the result in a computer ○ *She went to have a scan after ten weeks of pregnancy.* **2.** a picture of part of the body shown on a screen, derived by computers from X-rays **3.** the examination of an image or an object to obtain data ○ *A heat scan will quickly show which component is overheating.*

③ **scandal** /ˈskænd(ə)l/ *noun* **1.** talk about wrong things someone is supposed to have done ○ *This latest scandal could bring the government down.* **2.** something unfair or cruel that makes people very angry ○ *It's a scandal that she was never allowed to see her children.*

scandalous /ˈskændələs/ *adj* which is shameful and wrong

③ **scanner** /ˈskænə/ *noun* **1.** a machine which scans part of the body ○ *The hospital has acquired the most up-to-date scanner.* **2.** an electronic device that scans, especially a device that scans images or text and converts them to computer data ○ *We used a small hand-held scanner to get the photos onto our computer system.*

scant /skænt/ *adj* not enough

scapegoat /ˈskeɪpgəʊt/ *noun* a person who is blamed instead of someone else

③ **scar** /skɑː/ *noun* a mark left on the skin after a wound has healed ○ *He still has the scars of his operation.* ■ *verb* (**scars, scarring, scarred**) **1.** to leave a mark on the skin after a wound has healed ○ *His arm was scarred as a result of the accident.* **2.** to affect someone's feelings badly ○ *The bullying she received at school has scarred her for life.*

scarce /skeəs/ *adj* if something is scarce, there is much less of it than you need ○ *This happened at a period when food was scarce.* ○ *Good designers are getting scarce.*

③ **scarcely** /ˈskeəsli/ *adv* almost not

scarcity /ˈskeəsɪti/ *noun* a lack of something, the state of being scarce

scare /skeə/ *verb* (**scares, scaring, scared**) to make someone feel fear ○ *The thought of travelling alone across Africa scares me.* ○ *She was scared by the spider in the bathroom.* ■ *noun* a fright ○ *What a scare you gave me – jumping out at me in the dark like that!*

③ **scared** /skeəd/ *adj* feeling or showing fear ○ *Don't be scared – the snake is harmless.* ○ *She was too scared to answer the door.* ○ *I'm scared at the idea of driving in London's rush-hour traffic.* ○ *She looked round with a scared expression.*

③ **scarf** /skɑːf/ (*plural* **scarves**) *noun* a long piece of cloth which is worn round your neck to keep yourself warm ○ *Take your scarf – it's snowing.*

scarlet /ˈskɑːlət/ *adj* brilliant red

scarves /skɑːvz/ plural of **scarf**

scary /ˈskeəri/ (**scarier, scariest**) *adj* frightening (*informal*)

scathing /ˈskeɪðɪŋ/ *adj* very critical

scatter /ˈskætə/ (**scatters, scattering, scattered**) *verb* **1.** to throw something in various places ○ *The crowd scattered flowers all over the path.* **2.** to run in different directions ○ *When the police arrived, the children scattered.*

③ **scattered** /ˈskætəd/ *adj* spread out over a wide area

③ **scattering** /ˈskætərɪŋ/ *noun* a small quantity or number of things

scavenge /ˈskævɪndʒ/ (**scavenges, scavenging, scavenged**) *verb* **1.** to feed on dead and decaying matter ○ *Vultures live by scavenging on the corpses of animals which have died in the desert.* **2.** to get food or other useful items from rubbish ○ *Children were scavenging for food in the heaps of rubbish round the city.* (NOTE: + **scavenger** *n*)

scenario /sɪˈnɑːriəʊ/ (*plural* **scenarios**) *noun* the general way in which you think something may happen ○ *The worst scenario would be if she wanted to come on holiday with us.*

② **scene** /siːn/ *noun* **1.** a place where something has happened ○ *It took the ambulance ten minutes to get to the scene of the accident.* ○ *The fire brigade were on the scene very quickly.* ○ *A photographer was at the scene to record the ceremony.* **2.** a short part of a play or film ○ *Did you like the scene where he is trying to climb up the skyscraper?* ○ *It was one of the funniest scenes I have ever seen.*

③ **scenery** /ˈsiːnəri/ *noun* **1.** the features of the countryside ○ *the beautiful scenery of the Lake District* **2.** the objects and backgrounds on a theatre stage that make it look like a real place ○ *They lowered the scenery onto the stage.* ○ *In between the acts all the scenery has to be changed.* (NOTE: no plural)

scenic /ˈsiːnɪk/ *adj* referring to beautiful scenery

scent /sent/ *noun* **1.** a pleasant smell of a particular type ○ *the scent of roses in the cottage garden* **2.** perfume ○ *That new scent of yours makes me sneeze.* (NOTE: Do not confuse with **cent, sent**.)

sceptic /ˈskeptɪk/ *noun* a person who always doubts the truth of what he or she is told ○ *I am a sceptic when it comes to astrology.* (NOTE: The US spelling is **skeptic**.)

③ **sceptical** /ˈskeptɪk(ə)l/ *adj* thinking that something is probably not true or good ○ *You seem sceptical about his new plan.* ○ *I'm sceptical of the need for these changes.*

scepticism /ˈskeptɪˌsɪz(ə)m/ *noun* doubt or uncertainty (NOTE: The US spelling is **skepticism**.)

③ **schedule** /ˈʃedjuːl/ *noun* **1.** a list of times of departure and arrival of forms of transport such as trains, planes or coaches ○ *The summer schedules have been published.* **2.** a programme or list of events ○ *the schedule of events for the music festival* ■ *verb* (**schedules, scheduling, scheduled**) **1.** to put something on an official list ○ *See the list of scheduled prices.* ○ *The house has been scheduled as an ancient monument.* **2.** to arrange the times for something ○ *The building is scheduled for completion in May.* ○ *The flight is scheduled to arrive at six o'clock.* ○ *We have scheduled the meeting for Tuesday morning.*

① **scheme** /skiːm/ *noun* a plan for making something work ○ *She joined the company pension scheme.* ○ *He has thought up some scheme for making money very quickly.*

schizophrenia /ˌskɪtsəʊˈfriːniə/ *noun* a mental disorder where the patient withdraws from other people, has delusions and seems to lose contact with the real world

scholar /ˈskɒlə/ *noun* **1.** a learned person ○ *He is a well-known scholar of medieval French history.* **2.** a student at school or university who has a scholarship ○ *Because I was a scholar my parents didn't have to pay any fees.*

scholarly /ˈskɒləli/ *adj* referring to serious study at a high level

scholarship /ˈskɒləʃɪp/ *noun* **1.** money given to someone to help pay for the cost of his or her study ○ *The college offers scholarships to attract the best students.* ○ *She got* or *won a scholarship to carry out research into causes of cancer.* **2.** a deep learning ○ *The article shows sound scholarship.*

scholastic /skəˈlæstɪk/ *adj* referring to schools or teaching methods

① **school** /skuːl/ *noun* **1.** a place where students, usually children, are taught ○ *Our little boy is four, so he'll be going to school this year.* ○ *Some children start school younger than that.* ○ *What did the children do at school today?* ○ *When he was sixteen, he left school and joined the army.* ○ *Which school did you go to?* **2.** a section of a college or university ○ *The school of medicine is one of the largest in the country.* ○ *She's studying at law school.* ■ *verb* (**schools, schooling, schooled**) to train someone in a particular skill

schoolboy /ˈskuːlbɔɪ/ *noun* a boy who goes to school

schoolchild /ˈskuːlˌtʃaɪld/ (*plural* **schoolchildren**) *noun* a child who goes to school

schooldays /ˈskuːldeɪz/ *plural noun* the time when you are at school

schoolgirl /ˈskuːlgɜːl/ *noun* a girl who goes to school

schooling /ˈskuːlɪŋ/ *noun* education at school level

school leaver /ˈskuːl ˌliːvə/ *noun* a young person who has just left secondary school

③ **schoolteacher** /ˈskuːltiːtʃə/ *noun* a person who teaches in a school

① **science** /ˈsaɪəns/ *noun* the study of natural physical things, based on observation and experiment ○ *She took a science course* or *studied science.* ○ *We have a new* *science teacher this term.* ○ *He has a master's degree in marine science.* ◊ **social science**

③ **science fiction** /ˌsaɪəns ˈfɪkʃən/ *noun* stories of life in the future, based on imaginary scientific developments

② **scientific** /ˌsaɪənˈtɪfɪk/ *adj* relating to science ○ *We employ hundreds of people in scientific research.* ○ *He's the director of a scientific institute.*

② **scientist** /ˈsaɪəntɪst/ *noun* a person who studies a science, often doing research ○ *Scientists have not yet found a cure for the common cold.* ○ *Space scientists are examining the photographs of Mars.*

sci-fi /ˈsaɪ faɪ/ *noun* same as **science fiction**

scintillating /ˈsɪntɪleɪtɪŋ/ *adj* sparkling

scissors /ˈsɪzəz/ *plural noun* a tool for cutting things such as paper and cloth, made of two blades attached in the middle, with handles with holes for the thumb and fingers ○ *These scissors aren't very sharp.* ○ *Have you got a pair of scissors I can borrow?*

scoff /skɒf/ (**scoffs, scoffing, scoffed**) *verb* to eat something greedily (*informal*)

scold /skəʊld/ (**scolds, scolding, scolded**) *verb* to speak to someone angrily

scone /skɒn/ *noun* a type of small round soft bread, sometimes with dried fruit in it, eaten with butter or cream and jam

scoop /skuːp/ *noun* **1.** a deep round spoon with a short handle, for serving soft food such as ice cream **2.** a portion of soft food such as ice cream ■ *verb* (**scoops, scooping, scooped**) to lift something or someone up in a single quick movement ○ *She scooped up the babies into her arms and ran upstairs.* ○ *He scooped all the newspapers off the floor.*

scooter /ˈskuːtə/ *noun* **1.** a child's two-wheeled vehicle which is pushed along with one foot while the other foot is on the board **2.** a vehicle like a small motorbike with a platform for the feet ○ *She dodged through the traffic on her scooter.*

③ **scope** /skəʊp/ *noun* **1.** the different types of thing that something deals with [~of] ○ *These matters are beyond the scope of our investigation.* **2.** an opportunity or possibility [~for] ○ *The job will give him plenty of scope for developing his talents.*

scorch /skɔːtʃ/ (**scorches, scorching, scorched**) *verb* **1.** to burn something slightly or brown something ○ *He accidentally scorched the tablecloth with the iron.* **2.** to make something very hot and dry ○ *The sun has scorched the grass.*

scorched /skɔːtʃt/ *adj* slightly burnt or browned

scorching /ˈskɔːtʃɪŋ/ *adj* very hot and dry (*informal*)

② **score** /skɔː/ *noun* the number of goals or points made in a match ○ *The final score in the rugby match was 22–10.* ○ *I didn't see the beginning of the match – what's the score?* ■ *verb* (**scores, scoring, scored**) to make a goal or point in a match ○ *They scored three goals in the first twenty minutes.* ○ *She scored sixty-five!*

scoreboard /ˈskɔːbɔːd/ *noun* a large board on which the score in a game is shown as the game progresses

scorn /skɔːn/ *noun* a feeling of thinking that someone or something is not good enough ■ *verb* (**scorns, scorning, scorned**) to refuse to accept an idea or a suggestion ○ *Most young people in the office scorn the idea that smoking can be bad for your health.* ○ *She scorned his proposal of a lift.*

scornful /ˈskɔːnf(ə)l/ *adj* considering something not good enough

Scorpio /ˈskɔːpiəʊ/ *noun* one of the signs of the Zodiac, shaped like a scorpion, covering the period 23rd October to 21st November

scorpion /ˈskɔːpiən/ *noun* a poisonous tropical animal which stings with its long curved tail

Scot /skɒt/ *noun* a person from Scotland

③ **Scotch** /skɒtʃ/ *adj* used for referring to some things, especially food and drink, from Scotland

Scotland /ˈskɒtlənd/ *noun* a country to the north of England, forming part of the United Kingdom ○ *He was brought up in Scotland.* ○ *Scotland's most famous export is whisky.*

Scots /skɒts/ *adj* Scottish ○ *'Not proven' is a decision in Scots Law.*

① **Scottish** /ˈskɒtɪʃ/ *adj* relating to Scotland

scoundrel /ˈskaʊndrəl/ *noun* a bad person, with no principles

scour /ˈskaʊə/ (**scours, scouring, scoured**) *verb* **1.** to clean something by scrubbing with a hard material ○ *Her first job was scouring dirty pans in the restaurant.* **2.** to search everywhere in a place ○ *We scoured the market and couldn't find any aubergines.* ○ *The police have been* *scouring the woods near the village where the little girl lived.*

scourge /skɜːdʒ/ *noun* a thing which causes suffering

scout /skaʊt/ *noun* a member of the Scout Association ■ *verb* (**scouts, scouting, scouted**) *also* **scout around** to look out for something [~for]

scowl /skaʊl/ (**scowls, scowling, scowled**) *verb* to make a scowl

scramble /ˈskræmbəl/ (**scrambles, scrambling, scrambled**) *verb* **1.** to climb using your hands and knees **2.** to hurry to do something (NOTE: + **scramble** *n*)

scrambled eggs /ˌskræmbəld ˈegz/ *plural noun* eggs mixed together and stirred as they are cooked in butter

scrap /skræp/ *noun* **1.** a little piece ○ *a scrap of paper* ○ *There isn't a scrap of evidence against him.* ○ *She is collecting scraps of cloth to make a quilt.* **2.** waste materials ○ *to sell a car for scrap* ○ *The scrap value of the car is £200.* ■ *verb* (**scraps, scrapping, scrapped**) **1.** to throw something away as useless ○ *They had to scrap 10,000 faulty spare parts.* **2.** to give up or stop working on a plan ○ *We've scrapped our plans to go to Greece.*

scrapbook /ˈskræpbʊk/ *noun* a book with blank pages on which you can stick pictures or stories cut from newspapers or magazines

scrape /skreɪp/ (**scrapes, scraping, scraped**) *verb* **1.** to scratch something with a hard object which is pulled across a surface **2.** to remove something from the surface of something

scrape through③ *phrasal verb* to pass an examination with difficulty

scrape together *phrasal verb* to gather things together with difficulty

scrappy /ˈskræpi/ (**scrappier, scrappiest**) *adj* made of bits and pieces; not joined up properly (*informal*)

③ **scratch** /skrætʃ/ *noun* **1.** a long wound on the skin ○ *Put some antiseptic on the scratches on your arms.* **2.** a long mark made by a sharp point ○ *I will never be able to cover up the scratches on the car door.* ■ *verb* (**scratches, scratching, scratched**) **1.** to make a long wound on the skin ○ *His legs were scratched by the bushes along the path.* **2.** to make a mark on something with a sharp point ○ *He scratched his name on the tree with a knife.* **3.** to rub a part of the body which itches with your fingernails ○ *If your head itches, just scratch it.* ○ *Stop scratching – it will make your rash worse!*

scrawl /skrɔːl/ (**scrawls, scrawling, scrawled**) *verb* to write something badly or carelessly ○ *He scrawled a few notes on a bit of paper.* (NOTE: + **scrawl** *n*)

scrawny /ˈskrɔːni/ *adj* extremely thin

scream /skriːm/ *noun* a loud cry of pain ■ *verb* (**screams, screaming, screamed**) to shout loudly or make a very loud sound ○ *She screamed at the class to stop singing.* ○ *They screamed in pain.* ○ *People on the third floor were screaming for help.*

screech /skriːtʃ/ (**screeches, screeching, screeched**) *verb* to make a piercing sound (NOTE: + **screech** *n*)

② **screen** /skriːn/ *noun* **1.** a flat panel which acts as protection against something, e.g. draughts, fire or noise ○ *The hedge acts as a screen against the noise from the motorway.* **2.** a flat glass surface on which a picture is shown ○ *a computer screen* ○ *a TV screen* ○ *I'll call the information up on the screen.* **3.** a flat white surface for projecting films or pictures ○ *a cinema complex with four screens* ○ *We'll put up the screen on the stage.* ■ *verb* (**screens, screening, screened**) to show a film in a cinema or on TV ○ *Tonight's film will be screened half an hour later than advertised.*

screenplay /ˈskriːnpleɪ/ *noun* a scenario, a written draft of a film with details, e.g., of plot, characters and scenes

screen saver /ˈskriːn ˌseɪvə/ *noun* a computer program which protects the screen by making it go black or show a picture when the computer is out of use for a while

screenwriter /ˈskriːnraɪtə/ *noun* a person who writes screenplays

③ **screw** /skruː/ *noun* a type of nail which you twist to make it go into a hard surface ○ *I need some longer screws to go through this thick plank.* ○ *The plate was fixed to the door with brass screws.* ■ *verb* (**screws, screwing, screwed**) **1.** to attach something with screws ○ *The picture was screwed to the wall.* **2.** to attach something by twisting ○ *He filled up the bottle and screwed on the top.* ○ *Screw the lid on tightly.*

screwdriver /ˈskruːdraɪvə/ *noun* a tool with a long handle and special end which is used for turning screws

screwed-up /ˌskruːd ˈʌp/ *adj* worried and unhappy

scribble /ˈskrɪb(ə)l/ (**scribbles, scribbling, scribbled**) *verb* **1.** to make marks which don't have any meaning ○ *The kids* *have scribbled all over their bedroom walls.* **2.** to write something hurriedly and badly ○ *She scribbled a few notes in the train.* (NOTE: + **scribble** *n*)

script /skrɪpt/ *noun* **1.** the written text of a film or play ○ *The actors settled down with their scripts for the first reading.* **2.** a style or system of handwriting ○ *The Germans used to write in Gothic script.*

scripture /ˈskrɪptʃə/, **Scripture** *noun* the writings regarded as holy by a religion ○ *a passage translated from Buddhist scriptures* ○ *The story of Vishnu is set down in Hindu scripture.*

scriptwriter /ˈskrɪptraɪtə/ *noun* a person who writes scripts for films or for TV or radio plays

scroll /skrəʊl/ *noun* a long piece of paper with writing on it, stored as a roll ■ *verb* (**scrolls, scrolling, scrolled**) to move displayed text up or down a computer screen, one line at a time ○ *She rapidly scrolled down until she came to the address she wanted.*

scroll bar /ˈskrəʊl bɑː/ *noun* a bar on a computer screen which is used to scroll up and down

scrooge /skruːdʒ/, **Scrooge** *noun* a mean or miserly person (*informal*)

scrounge /skraʊndʒ/ (**scrounges, scrounging, scrounged**) *verb* to try to get something without paying for it (*informal*)

scrub /skrʌb/ *verb* (**scrubs, scrubbing, scrubbed**) to clean something by rubbing it with a brush ■ *noun* **1.** an area of land with a few small bushes ○ *They walked for miles through the scrub until they came to a river.* **2.** the action of scrubbing ○ *After a game of rugby you will need a good scrub.*

scruffy /ˈskrʌfi/ (**scruffier, scruffiest**) *adj* untidy or dirty

scrum /skrʌm/ *noun* (*in rugby*) an arrangement in which the players of both teams crowd together with their heads down and try to get the ball

scrunch /skrʌntʃ/ (**scrunches, scrunching, scrunched**) *verb* to squash or crush something with your hand

scrupulous /ˈskruːpjʊləs/ *adj* **1.** very careful **2.** very honest or morally correct

scrutiny /ˈskruːtɪni/ *noun* a careful examination of facts or a very close look at something

scuba diving /ˈskuːbə ˌdaɪvɪŋ/ *noun* the activity of swimming underwater, using breathing apparatus

scuff /skʌf/ (**scuffs, scuffing, scuffed**) *verb* to scratch the surface of something

scuffle /ˈskʌf(ə)l/ *noun* a small fight ○ *Scuffles broke out in the crowd.* (NOTE: + **scuffle** *v*)

sculptor /ˈskʌlptə/, **sculptress** *noun* a person who makes figures or shapes out of wood, metal or stone

③ **sculpture** /ˈskʌlptʃə/ *noun* a piece of art that is a figure carved out of stone or wood or made out of metal

scum /skʌm/ *noun* **1.** a layer of dirty foam on the surface of a liquid ○ *As the liquid boils, a grey scum forms on the surface and should be removed.* **2.** people of the worst type (*offensive*) ○ *Those muggers are just scum, I hope they get sent to prison.*

scurry /ˈskʌri/ (**scurries, scurrying, scurried**) *verb* **1.** to hurry to do something **2.** to run fast, taking short steps

scuttle /ˈskʌt(ə)l/ (**scuttles, scuttling, scuttled**) *verb* to run fast, taking short steps

scuttle off ***or*** **away** *verb* to run away fast

scythe /saɪð/ *noun* a farming implement with a long slightly curved blade attached to a handle with two short projecting hand grips, used for cutting long grass

① **sea** /siː/ *noun* an area of salt water between continents or islands which is large but not as large as an ocean ○ *Swimming in the sea is more exciting than swimming in a river.* ○ *The sea's too rough for the ferries to operate.* ○ *His friends own a house by the sea.* ○ *The North Sea separates Britain from Denmark and Germany.*

sea change /siː tʃeɪndʒ/ *noun* a very big change

③ **seafood** /ˈsiːfuːd/ *noun* fish or shellfish which can be eaten

seafront /ˈsiːfrʌnt/ *noun* a road or wide path which runs beside the sea in a seaside town

seagull /ˈsiːgʌl/ *noun* a large white sea bird

③ **seal** /siːl/ *noun* a large animal with short smooth fur which eats fish and lives near or in the sea ■ *verb* (**seals, sealing, sealed**) to close something tightly ○ *a box carefully sealed with sticky tape*

seal off *phrasal verb* to close a place off so as to prevent anyone getting inside

sea level /ˈsiː ˌlev(ə)l/ *noun* the level of the sea, taken as a point for measuring altitude

sea lion /ˈsiː ˌlaɪən/ *noun* a large species of seal

seam /siːm/ *noun* **1.** a line where two pieces of material are attached together ○ *She sewed the seams on the sewing machine.* ○ *He's got fatter, so can you let out a seam at the back of his coat?* **2.** a layer of mineral beneath the earth's surface ○ *The coal seams are two metres thick.* ○ *The gold seam was worked out some years ago.* (NOTE: Do not confuse with **seem**.)

seaman /ˈsiːmən/ (*plural* **seamen**) *noun* a man who works on a ship (NOTE: Do not confuse with **semen**.)

seance /ˈseɪɒ̃ns/ *noun* a meeting at which people try to communicate with dead people

seaport /ˈsiːpɔːt/ *noun* a town with a large harbour

① **search** /sɜːtʃ/ *noun* the action of trying to find something [~for/~of] ○ *A search was carried out for the missing animal.* ○ *Our search of the flat revealed nothing.* ○ *I did a quick search on the Internet for references to Proust.* ■ *verb* (**searches, searching, searched**) **1.** to examine something or someone very carefully ○ *The police searched the house but didn't find any weapons.* ○ *She was stopped and searched by customs.* **2.** to look carefully to try to find something [~for/~through] ○ *We're searching for the missing files.* ○ *I searched the Internet for references to Ireland.* ○ *She searched through her papers, trying to find the document.*

③ **search engine** /ˈsɜːtʃ ˌendʒɪn/ *noun* a program which allows you to search for particular words or phrases on the Internet

searcher /ˈsɜːtʃə/ *noun* a person who searches

searching /ˈsɜːtʃɪŋ/ *adj* very detailed ○ *a searching question*

search party /ˈsɜːtʃ ˌpɑːti/ *noun* a group of people sent to look for someone

search warrant /ˈsɜːtʃ ˌwɒrənt/ *noun* an official document signed by a magistrate which allows police to go into a building and look for criminals, weapons or stolen goods

seashell /ˈsiːʃel/ *noun* a shell of a shellfish which lives in the sea

seashore /ˈsiːʃɔː/ *noun* a sandy area along the edge of the sea

③ **seasick** /ˈsiːsɪk/ *adj* ill because of the movement of a ship

③ **seaside** /ˈsiːdsaɪd/ *noun* an area near the sea where people go to have a holiday

① **season** /ˈsiːz(ə)n/ *noun* **1.** one of four parts of a year ○ *Spring is her favourite season.* **2.** a part of the year when something usually happens ○ *The tourist season is very long here – from March to September.* ○ *The football season lasts from September to May.* ○ *London is very crowded during the school holiday season.* ◊ **high season**, **low season**

③ **seasonal** /ˈsiːz(ə)n(ə)l/ *adj* **1.** which only lasts for a season, usually the holiday season ○ *Work on the island is only seasonal.* **2.** characteristic of a particular time of year ○ *In December the supermarket shelves are stocked with Christmas decorations and other seasonal goods.* ○ *We can expect seasonal weather, with temperatures about average for the time of year.*

seasoned /ˈsiːz(ə)nd/ *adj* **1.** (*of food*) which has had seasoning put on it to improve the flavour **2.** who has had a lot of experience ○ *a seasoned traveller*

seasoning /ˈsiːz(ə)nɪŋ/ *noun* spices which are added to food

② **season ticket** /ˈsiːz(ə)n ˌtɪkɪt/ *noun* a railway, bus or theatre ticket, which you can use for a whole year or a month at a time

① **seat** /siːt/ *noun* a chair, something which you sit on ○ *He was sitting in the driver's seat.* ○ *Can we have two seats in the front row?* ○ *Our kitchen chairs have wooden seats.* ○ *Bicycle seats are narrow.* ◇ **to take a seat** to sit down ○ *Please take a seat, the dentist will see you in a few minutes.* ○ *Please take your seats, the play is about to begin.* ○ *All the seats on the bus were taken so I had to stand.* ◇ **to take your seat** to sit down in a seat reserved for you, especially at the theatre ○ *Please take your seats, the play is about to begin.*

③ **seat belt** /ˈsiːt belt/ *noun* a belt which you wear in a car or plane to stop you being hurt if there is an accident

seating /ˈsiːtɪŋ/ *noun* seats for people

③ **seaweed** /ˈsiːwiːd/ *noun* a plant which grows in the sea

sec *noun* a second (*informal*)

secluded /sɪˈkluːdɪd/ *adj* quiet or away from crowds ○ *We found a secluded spot by the river for our picnic.*

seclusion /sɪˈkluːʒ(ə)n/ *noun* solitude

second[1] /ˈsekənd/ *noun* **1.** one of sixty parts which make up a minute ○ *I'll give you ten seconds to get out of my room.* ○ *They say the bomb will go off in twenty seconds.* **2.** a very short time ○ *Please wait a second.* ○ *Wait here, I'll be back in a second.* **3.** number 2 in a series (NOTE: In dates **second** is usually written **2nd** or **2**: *August 2nd, 1932, 2 July 1666* (American style is **2**

July 1666), say 'the second of July' or 'July the second' (American style is 'July second'). With the names of kings and queens **second** is usually written **II**: *Queen Elizabeth II*, say 'Queen Elizabeth the Second'.) ■ *adj* **1.** coming after the first and before the third ○ *February is the second month of the year.* ○ *It's his second birthday next week.* ○ *Women's clothes are on the second floor.* ○ *That's the second time the telephone has rung while we're eating.* **2.** next after the longest, best, tallest etc. (*followed by a superlative*) ○ *This is the second longest bridge in the world.* ○ *He's the second highest paid member of staff.*

second[2] /sɪ'kɒnd/ (**seconds, seconding, seconded**) *verb* to lend a member of staff, e.g. to another company or a government department, for a fixed period of time ○ *He was seconded to the Department of Trade for two years.* ◊ **secondment**

② **secondary** /'sekənd(ə)ri/ *adj* less important

secondary school /'sekənd(ə)ri skuːl/ *noun* a school for children after the age of eleven or twelve

second best /ˌsekʌnd 'best/ *noun* something which is not as good as the best

③ **second-class** /ˌsekənd 'klɑːs/ *adj, adv* **1.** (*of travel or hotels*) less expensive and less comfortable than first-class ○ *I find second-class hotels are perfectly adequate.* ○ *We always travel second-class because it is cheaper.* **2.** (*of a postal service*) less expensive and slower than the first-class postal service ○ *A second-class letter is cheaper than a first-class.* ○ *Send it second-class if it is not urgent.*

second cousin /ˌsekənd 'kʌz(ə)n/ *noun* a child of your mother's or father's cousin

second-guess /'sekənd ges/ *verb* to try to guess what someone will do

③ **secondhand** /ˌsekənd'hænd/ *adj* not new; which someone else has owned before ○ *We've just bought a secondhand car.*

second language /ˌsekənd 'læŋgwɪdʒ/ *noun* a language which you know but which is not the language you learned when you first started to speak

③ **secondly** /'sekəndli/ *adv* as the second item in a list. Compare **firstly**, **thirdly**

secondment /sɪ'kɒndmənt/ *noun* the fact of being seconded to another job

second-rate /ˌsekənd 'reɪt/ *adj* not of very good quality. Compare **first-rate**, **third-rate**

secrecy /'siːkrəsi/ *noun* the fact of being secret or keeping something secret

③ **secret** /'siːkrət/ *adj* not known about by other people ○ *There is a secret door into the cellar.* ■ *noun* a thing which is not known or which is kept hidden ○ *If I tell you my secret will you promise not to tell it to anyone else?* ◇ **to keep a secret** not to tell someone something which you know and no one else does ○ *Can you keep a secret?*

secret agent /ˌsiːkrət 'eɪdʒənt/ *noun* a spy

secretarial /ˌsekrɪ'teəriəl/ *adj* referring to the work of a secretary

① **secretary** /'sekrət(ə)ri/ (*plural* **secretaries**) *noun* a person who does work such as writing letters, answering the phone and filing documents for someone

Secretary of State /ˌsekrət(ə)ri əv 'steɪt/ *noun* **1.** a member of the government in charge of a department **2.** *US* a senior member of the government in charge of foreign affairs

secrete /sɪ'kriːt/ (**secretes, secreting, secreted**) *verb* **1.** to produce a liquid substance such as an oil or a hormone ○ *The gland secretes hormones.* **2.** to hide something ○ *They found packets of drugs secreted under the floor of the car.*

secretion /sɪ'kriːʃ(ə)n/ *noun* **1.** the process by which something is produced by a gland ○ *This gland stimulates the secretion of hormones.* **2.** a substance produced by a gland ○ *Penguins use a secretion from glands near their tails to make their feathers waterproof.*

secretive /'siːkrətɪv/ *adj* liking to keep things secret ○ *She's very secretive about her holiday plans.*

③ **secretly** /'siːkrətli/ *adv* without anyone knowing

secret service /ˌsiːkrət 'sɜːvɪs/ *noun* a government department which spies on other countries

sect /sekt/ *noun* a religious group

sectarian /sek'teəriən/ *adj* referring to conflicts between religious groups

① **section** /'sekʃən/ *noun* a part of something which, when joined to other parts, goes to make up a whole ○ *the brass section of the orchestra* ○ *the financial section of the newspaper* ○ *He works in a completely different section of the organisation.*

① **sector** /'sektə/ *noun* **1.** a part of the economy or of the business organisation of a country [~of] ○ *companies working in the* *financial sector* ○ *All sectors of industry suffered from the rise in the exchange rate.* **2.** a part of a circle between two lines drawn from the centre to the outside edge ○ *The circle had been divided into five sectors.*

secular /ˈsekjʊlə/ *adj* not religious, not connected with religion

② **secure** /sɪˈkjʊə/ *adj* firmly fixed ○ *Don't step on that plank, it's not secure.* ■ *verb* (**secures, securing, secured**) to be successful in getting something important ○ *He secured the support of a big bank.* ○ *They secured a valuable new contract.*

securely /sɪˈkjʊəli/ *adv* in a secure way

① **security** /sɪˈkjʊərɪti/ *noun* **1.** safety or protection against harm ○ *There were worries about security during the prince's visit.* ○ *Security in this office is nil.* ○ *Security guards patrol the factory at night.* **2.** a thing given to someone who has lent you money and which is returned when the loan is repaid ○ *He uses his house as security for a loan.* ○ *The bank lent him £20,000 without security.*

security service /sɪˌkjʊərəti ˈsɜːvɪs/ *noun* a government service which looks after the security of the country

sedan /sɪˈdæn/ *noun US* a two- or four-door car with seating for four or five people

sedate /sɪˈdeɪt/ (**sedates, sedating, sedated**) *verb* to give someone a drug to make them calm or go to sleep ○ *The patient became violent and had to be sedated.*

sedation /sɪˈdeɪʃ(ə)n/ *noun* the act of calming a patient with a drug

sedative /ˈsedətɪv/ *noun* a drug which acts on the nervous system to help a patient sleep or to relieve stress ○ *I was prescribed sedatives by my doctor.*

sediment /ˈsedɪmənt/ *noun* solid particles which fall to the bottom of a liquid

seduce /sɪˈdjuːs/ (**seduces, seducing, seduced**) *verb* **1.** to persuade someone to have sex ○ *She was seduced by her history teacher.* **2.** to persuade someone to do something which is perhaps wrong ○ *He was seduced by the idea of earning a vast salary.* (NOTE: + **seduction** *n*)

seductive /sɪˈdʌktɪv/ *adj* **1.** sexually appealing **2.** attractive

① **see** /siː/ (**sees, seeing, saw, seen**) *verb* **1.** to use your eyes to notice something [~(that)/~what/where/who etc] ○ *Can you see that this colour is slightly different?* ○ *See how the level of the water rises?* ○ *They say eating carrots helps you to see in the dark.* ○ *We ran because we could see the bus coming.* ○ *I have never seen a badger before.* **2.** to watch something such as a film ○ *I don't want to go to the cinema this week, I've seen that film twice already.* ○ *We saw the football match on TV.* **3.** to understand something [~(that)/~why/what/who/how etc] ○ *Don't you see that they're trying to trick you?* ○ *I can't see why they need to borrow so much money.* ○ *I see – you want me to help you.* **4.** to visit someone, e.g. a lawyer or doctor ○ *If your tooth aches that badly you should see a dentist.* ○ *He went to see his bank manager to arrange a mortgage.*

see off *phrasal verb* to go to the airport or station with someone who is leaving on a journey

see through③ *phrasal verb* **1.** to see from one side of something to the other ○ *I can't see through the window – it's so dirty.* **2.** not to be tricked by something or someone ○ *Won't they quickly see through such a poor excuse?* ○ *He pretended he was helping me, but I soon saw through him.*

see to *phrasal verb* to arrange something or make sure that something is done

① **seed** /siːd/ *noun* a part of a plant which is formed after the flowers die and from which a new plant will grow ○ *a packet of carrot seed* ○ *Sow the seeds in fine earth.* ○ *Can you eat pumpkin seeds?*

seedling /ˈsiːdlɪŋ/ *noun* a very young plant growing from a seed

seedy /ˈsiːdi/ *adj* poor and dirty ○ *The tour included three nights in a rather seedy hotel.*

③ **seeing** /ˈsiːɪŋ/ *conj* □ **seeing that** since ○ *Seeing that everyone's here, let's begin.*

① **seek** /siːk/ (**seeks, seeking, sought**) *verb* to look for someone or something (*formal*) ○ *The police are seeking a group of teenagers who were in the area when the attack took place.*

① **seem** /siːm/ (**seems, seeming, seemed**) *verb* to give the appearance of being something ○ *She seems to like* or *It seems that she likes her new job.* ○ *Everyone seemed to be having a good time at the party.* ○ *The new boss seems very nice.* ○ *It seems to me that the parcel has gone to the wrong house.* ○ *It seemed strange to us that no one answered the phone.* (NOTE: Do not confuse with **seam**.)

seemingly /ˈsiːmɪŋli/ *adv* apparently

③ **seen** /siːn/ past participle of **see**

seep /siːp/ (**seeps, seeping, seeped**) *verb* (*of a liquid*) to flow slowly through a substance or out of a container

seesaw /ˈsiːsɔː/ *noun* a plank with seats at each end, balanced in the middle, so that when one end goes down the other goes up ○ *The seesaw won't work properly because you're heavier than me.* ■ *verb* (**seesaws, seesawing, seesawed**) to go first one way then the other ○ *The opinion polls seesawed between the two parties.*

seethe /siːð/ (**seethes, seething, seethed**) *verb* **1.** to be very angry **2.** to move about like boiling water

segment /ˈsegmənt/ *noun* a part of something, especially something which divides naturally into different parts ○ *grapefruit segments* ○ *30– to 40-year-olds are the most affluent segment of the population.*

segregate /ˈsegrɪgeɪt/ (**segregates, segregating, segregated**) *verb* to separate people into groups (NOTE: + **segregation** *n*)

seismic /ˈsaɪzmɪk/ *adj* referring to earthquakes

③ **seize** /siːz/ (**seizes, seizing, seized**) *verb* to grab something and hold it tight ○ *She seized the bag of sweets in both hands and would not let go.*

seize up *phrasal verb* to stop working properly

seizure /ˈsiːʒə/ *noun* **1.** the act of taking possession of something ○ *The court ordered the seizure of the shipment of books.* **2.** a sudden contraction of the muscles, especially in a heart attack or an epileptic fit ○ *A member of the audience has had a seizure.* ○ *She has epileptic seizures.*

③ **seldom** /ˈseldəm/ *adv* not often (NOTE: Note the word order when **seldom** is at the beginning of a phrase: *you seldom hear* or *seldom do you hear*)

② **select** /sɪˈlekt/ (**selects, selecting, selected**) *verb* to choose something or someone carefully ○ *She looked carefully at the shelves before selecting a book.* ○ *He was selected for the England squad.* ○ *Selected items are reduced by 25%.*

② **selection** /sɪˈlekʃən/ *noun* **1.** a range ○ *There is a huge selection of hats to choose from.* **2.** a thing which has or things which have been chosen ○ *a selection of French cheeses*

③ **selective** /sɪˈlektɪv/ *adj* choosing carefully between different possibilities

selector /sɪˈlektə/ *noun* a person who chooses people to play in a national team

② **self** /self/ (*plural* **selves**) *noun* your own person or character ○ *She was ill for some time, but now she's her old self again.* ○ *She's not her usual happy self today – I think she's got something on her mind.*

② **self-** /self/ *prefix* referring to yourself

self-assured /self əˈʃɔːd/ *adj* confident and sure of yourself

self-awareness /self əˈweənəs/ *noun* the fact of having a clear and accurate knowledge of your own character

self-catering /self ˈkeɪt(ə)rɪŋ/ *noun* the practice of doing the cooking for yourself

self-centred /self ˈsentəd/ *adj* thinking only about yourself and your own concerns

self-confessed /self kənˈfest/ *adj* who admits to being something

self-confidence /self ˈkɒnfɪdəns/ *noun* the fact of being self-confident

self-conscious /self ˈkɒnʃəs/ *adj* embarrassed because you feel you have certain faults

self-control /ˌself kənˈtrəʊl/ *noun* the fact of keeping your feelings under control

self-defence /ˌself dɪˈfens/ *noun* the act of defending yourself

self-destruct /ˌself dɪˈstrʌkt/ (**self-destructs, self-destructing, self-destructed**) *verb* to destroy itself

self-destructive /self dɪˈstrʌktɪv/ *adj* doing things which are likely to cause yourself harm

self-determination /ˌself dɪtɜːmɪˈneɪʃ(ə)n/ *noun* a free choice by the people of a country as to how they should be governed

self-discipline /self ˈdɪsəˌplɪn/ *noun* the ability to control your behaviour and do what you should do

self-effacing /self ɪˈfeɪsɪŋ/ *adj* modest about your own achievements or good qualities

self-employed /ˌself ɪmˈplɔɪd/ *adj* working for yourself, not employed by a company ○ *a self-employed accountant* ○ *He worked for a bank for ten years but now is self-employed.*

③ **self-esteem** /ˌself ɪˈstiːm/ *noun* a good opinion of yourself and your ability

self-evident /self ˈevɪd(ə)nt/ *adj* obvious

self-explanatory /ˌself ɪkˈsplænət(ə)ri/ *adj* which explains itself easily

self-governing /self ˈgʌvənɪŋ/ *adj* which governs itself

self-help /self 'help/ *noun* the fact of using your own efforts to help yourself, without relying on other people or the government

self-important /self ɪm'pɔːt(ə)nt/ *adj* behaving as if you believe you are very important

self-imposed /ˌself ɪm'pəʊzd/ *adj* chosen for yourself

self-indulgent /self ɪn'dʌldʒ(ə)nt/ *adj* allowing yourself to do what you feel like without self-control

self-inflicted /self ɪn'flɪktɪd/ *adj* caused by yourself

self-interest /self 'ɪntrəst/ *noun* working for your own benefit

③ **selfish** /'selfɪʃ/ *adj* doing things only for yourself and not for other people

selfless /'selfləs/ *adj* not thinking of yourself, only of others

self-made /self meɪd/ *adj* rich and successful because of your own work, not because you inherited money or position

self-pity /self 'pɪti/ *noun* pity for yourself

self-portrait /self 'pɔːtreɪt/ *noun* a painting of the artist done by himself or herself

self-preservation /self ˌprezə'veɪʃ(ə)n/ *noun* the wish to protect yourself from harm

self-reliant /ˌself rɪ'laɪənt/ *adj* relying only on yourself to make decisions

self-respect /ˌself rɪ'spekt/ *noun* pride in yourself

self-righteous /self 'raɪtʃəs/ *adj* feeling sure that you are doing what is right

self-rule /ˌself 'ruːl/ *noun* the right of a country or a state to govern itself

self-satisfied /self 'sætɪsˌfaɪd/ *adj* feeling very pleased with yourself or with your actions

self-service /ˌself 'sɜːvɪs/ *adj* (*of a shop or restaurant*) in which you take things yourself before paying for them, rather than being served by an assistant

self-sufficient /ˌself sə'fɪʃ(ə)nt/ *adj* able to provide everything for yourself

① **sell** /sel/ (**sells, selling, sold**) *verb* **1.** to give something to someone for money [~to/~for] ○ *He sold the house to my father.* ○ *We managed to sell the car for £500.* ○ *The shop sells vegetables but not meat.* **2.** to be sold [~for] ○ *Those packs sell for £25 a dozen.* ○ *Her latest book is selling very well.*

sell off *phrasal verb* to sell goods quickly and cheaply to get rid of them ○ *At the end of the day the market stalls sell off their fruit and vegetables very cheaply.*

sell out① *phrasal verb* **1.** to sell every item of a particular type ○ *Have you got the dress in a size 12? – No, I'm afraid we've sold out.* ○ *We're selling out of these hats fast.* **2.** *US* to sell a business to someone ○ *He sold out to his partner and retired.* **3.** to give in to a group of influential people ○ *The environmental group has accused the government of selling out to the oil companies.*

sell up *phrasal verb* to sell a business ○ *He sold up and retired.*

sell-by date /'sel baɪ ˌdeɪt/ *noun* the date on a packet of food, which is the last date on which the food can be sold while it is guaranteed to be good

seller /'selə/ *noun* **1.** a person who sells something ○ *There were a few postcard sellers by the cathedral.* **2.** an item which sells ○ *This book is a steady seller.*

sell-off /'sel ɒf/ *noun* the act of selling something to private buyers

Sellotape /'seləʊteɪp/ *trademark* a type of sticky tape ○ *She put the books in a box and sealed it with Sellotape.*

sellout /'selaʊt/ *noun* **1.** a betrayal of all your principles ○ *They said his change of policy was a sellout to the forces of the right.* ○ *It's a sellout – the council should have stood up for our rights.* **2.** a performance of a play, film or concert for which all the tickets have been sold ○ *The new musical is a sellout.*

semantic /sə'mæntɪk/ *adj* referring to the meanings of words and phrases

semblance /'sembləns/ *noun* an appearance

semen /'siːmən/ *noun* a thick pale fluid containing spermatozoa, produced by the testes and ejaculated from the penis (NOTE: Do not confuse with **seaman**.)

semester /sɪ'mestə/ *noun* a term in a school or college year which only has two terms

semicircle /'semiˌsɜːk(ə)l/ *noun* half a circle

semicolon /ˌsemi'kəʊlɒn/ *noun* a punctuation mark (;) used to separate two parts of a sentence and also used to show a pause

semi-conscious /ˌsemi 'kɒnʃəs/ *adj* not fully conscious

③ **semi-final** /ˌsemi 'faɪn(ə)l/ *noun* one of the last two matches in a competition, the winners of which go into the final game

seminar /ˈsemɪnɑː/ *noun* the meeting of a small group of university students to discuss a subject with a teacher

seminary /ˈsemɪnəri/ *noun* a college where people train to become priests

semitone /ˈsemitəʊn/ *noun* the smallest interval between notes in music, the interval between two keys on a piano

senate /ˈsenət/ *noun* the upper house of the legislative body in some countries ○ *She was first elected to the Senate in 2001.*

senator /ˈsenətə/ *noun* a member of a senate (NOTE: written with a capital letter when used as a title: *Senator Jackson*)

① **send** /send/ (**sends, sending, sent**) *verb* **1.** to make someone or something go from one place to another ○ *My mother sent me to the baker's to buy some bread.* ○ *I was sent home from school because I had a headache.* ○ *He sent the ball into the net.* ○ *The firm is sending him out to Australia for six months.* **2.** to use the postal services to get something to someone ○ *The office sends 200 Christmas cards every year.* ○ *Send me a postcard when you get to Russia.* ○ *Send the letter by air if you want it to arrive next week.* ○ *Send your donations to the following address.*

send for *phrasal verb* to ask someone to come

send in *phrasal verb* to send a letter to an organisation

send off *phrasal verb* **1.** (*in games*) to tell someone to go off the field ○ *The referee sent both players off.* **2.** to post something ○ *He sent the postcard off without a stamp.*

send up *phrasal verb* **1.** to make something go up ○ *They sent up an emergency flare.* ○ *The cold weather has sent up the price of vegetables.* **2.** to make jokes about someone (*informal*) ○ *In one of his TV sketches, he sends up the Foreign Minister.*

sender /ˈsendə/ *noun* a person who sends something, especially a letter ○ *The letter was returned to the sender.*

senile /ˈsiːnaɪl/ *adj* referring to someone whose is forgetful and confused because of old age

② **senior** /ˈsiːniə/ *adj* **1.** older ○ *the senior members of the tribe* **2.** more important, e.g. in rank ○ *A sergeant is senior to a corporal.* ○ *My senior colleagues do not agree with me.*

senior citizen /ˌsiːniə ˈsɪtɪz(ə)n/ *noun* an old person who does not work

seniority /ˌsiːniˈɒrɪti/ *noun* **1.** the fact of being older or more important **2.** the fact of being a member of a group longer than someone else ○ *He has several years' seniority over me as a member of the club.*

③ **sensation** /senˈseɪʃ(ə)n/ *noun* **1.** a general feeling ○ *I felt the curious sensation that I had been in the room before.* **2.** a physical feeling ○ *She had a burning sensation in her arm.* **3.** a thing or person that causes great excitement ○ *The new ballet was the sensation of the season.*

sensational /senˈseɪʃ(ə)n(ə)l/ *adj* **1.** which causes great excitement ○ *His sensational discovery shocked the world of archaeology.* **2.** very good ○ *A sensational new film – don't miss it!* ○ *You look sensational in that outfit.*

sensationalism /senˈseɪʃ(ə)nəˌlɪz(ə)m/ *noun* the practice of making things seem especially exciting or shocking, e.g. in newspaper reporting

① **sense** /sens/ *noun* **1.** one of the five ways in which you notice something (sight, hearing, smell, taste, touch) ○ *Dogs have a good sense of smell.* ○ *His senses had been dulled by the drugs he was taking.* **2.** a meaning ○ *He was using 'bear' in the sense of 'to carry'.* **3.** the fact of being sensible ○ *At least someone showed some sense and tried to calm the situation.* ○ *She didn't have the sense to refuse.* ○ *I thought Patrick would have had more sense than that.*

senseless /ˈsensləs/ *adj* done for no good reason ○ *a senseless attack on a little old lady* ○ *It's senseless to buy clothes you don't need, just because they are in the sales.*

③ **sensible** /ˈsensɪb(ə)l/ *adj* **1.** showing good judgment and wisdom ○ *Staying indoors was the sensible thing to do.* ○ *Try and be sensible for once!* **2.** (*of shoes*) strong and comfortable for walking, rather than fashionable

③ **sensitive** /ˈsensɪtɪv/ *adj* **1.** easily upset ○ *She's a very sensitive young woman.* ○ *Some actors are extremely sensitive to criticism.* **2.** which measures very accurately ○ *a very sensitive light meter*

③ **sensitivity** /ˌsensɪˈtɪvɪti/ *noun* sensitive feelings

sensor /ˈsensə/ *noun* an electronic device that reacts to something such as heat, light or smoke

sensory /ˈsensəri/ *adj* referring to the senses

sensual /ˈsensjuəl/ *adj* referring to pleasures of the body, not of the mind

sensuous /ˈsensjuəs/ *adj* which gives pleasure to the senses

③ **sent** /sent/ past tense and past participle of **send**

① **sentence** /ˈsentəns/ *noun* **1.** a series of words put together to make a complete statement, usually ending in a full stop ○ *I don't understand the second sentence in your letter.* ○ *Begin each sentence with a capital letter.* **2.** a judgment of a court ○ *He was given a six-month prison sentence.* ○ *The judge passed sentence on the accused.* ■ *verb* (**sentences, sentencing, sentenced**) to give someone an official legal punishment ○ *She was sentenced to three weeks in prison.* ○ *He was sentenced to death for murder.*

sentiment /ˈsentɪmənt/ *noun* a general feeling ○ *The government had to take public sentiment into account.*

③ **sentimental** /ˌsentɪˈment(ə)l/ *adj* showing emotions of love or pity, not reason

sentry /ˈsentri/ (*plural* **sentries** /ˈsentrɪ(ə)l/), **sentinel** *noun* a soldier on duty, e.g. at a gate

separate[1] /ˈsep(ə)rət/ *adj* not together or attached ○ *They are in separate rooms.* ○ *The house has one bathroom with a separate toilet.* ○ *The dogs were kept separate from the other pets.* ○ *Can you give us two separate invoices?*

separate[2] /ˈsepəreɪt/ (**separates, separating, separated**) *verb* **1.** to divide people or things ○ *The employees are separated into permanent and temporary staff.* ○ *The teacher separated the class into two groups.* **2.** to keep people or things apart ○ *The police tried to separate the two gangs.* ○ *Is it possible to separate religion from politics?*

separated /ˈsepəreɪtɪd/ *adj* not living together any more

② **separately** /ˈsep(ə)rətli/ *adv* individually, rather than together or as a group

separation /ˌsepəˈreɪʃ(ə)n/ *noun* **1.** the act of dividing people or things **2.** the fact of living apart ○ *A six-month separation of mother and child may have long-term effects.* ○ *After my parents' separation I lived with my father.*

separatist /ˈsep(ə)rətɪst/ *noun* a person who believes that part of the country should become separate and independent

① **September** /sepˈtembə/ *noun* the ninth month of the year, between August and October ○ *September 3* ○ *The weather is usually good in September.* ○ *Her birthday is in September.* ○ *Today is September 3rd.* ○ *We always try to take a short holiday in September.* (NOTE: **September 3rd** *or* **September 3**: say 'September the third' or 'the third of September' or in US English 'September third'.)

septic /ˈseptɪk/ *adj* (*of a part of a body or a wound*) infected with bacteria

sequel /ˈsiːkwəl/ *noun* **1.** the continuation of something, such as a story or a play ○ *The sequel will be screened tomorrow night.* **2.** a result, something which follows ○ *The sequel to the discovery was that the driver of the truck was arrested.*

② **sequence** /ˈsiːkwəns/ *noun* a series of things which happen or follow one after the other ○ *The sequence of events which led to the accident.*

sequin /ˈsiːkwɪn/ *noun* a small round shiny metal ornament, sewn onto clothes

serene /səˈriːn/ *adj* calm, not worried

③ **sergeant** /ˈsɑːdʒənt/ *noun* a non-commissioned officer in the army, or an officer of low rank in the police (NOTE: also used as a title before a surname: *Sergeant Jones*)

sergeant major /ˌsɑːdʒənt ˈmeɪdʒə/ *noun* a non-commissioned officer of middle rank in the army and some other armed forces

serial /ˈsɪəriəl/ *noun* a story that is broadcast on TV or radio in separate parts ○ *an Australian police serial* (NOTE: Do not confuse with **cereal**.)

serial number /ˈsɪəriəl ˌnʌmbə/ *noun* a number that is given to something such as a piece of equipment or a bank note so that it can be identified

① **series** /ˈsɪəriːz/ (*plural same*) *noun* **1.** a group of things which come one after the other in order ○ *We had a series of phone calls from the bank.* **2.** TV or radio programmes which are broadcast at the same time each week ○ *There's a new wildlife series starting this week.*

① **serious** /ˈsɪəriəs/ *adj* **1.** not funny or not joking ○ *a very serious play* ○ *He's such a serious little boy.* ○ *Stop laughing – it's very serious.* ○ *He's very serious about the proposal.* ○ *The doctor's expression was very serious.* **2.** important and possibly dangerous ○ *There was a serious accident on the motorway.* ○ *The storm caused serious damage.* ○ *There's no need to worry – it's nothing serious.* **3.** carefully planned ○

The management is making serious attempts to improve working conditions.

① **seriously** /ˈsɪəriəsli/ *adv* **1.** in a serious way ○ *She should laugh more – she mustn't always take things so seriously.* **2.** to a great extent ○ *The cargo was seriously damaged by water.* ○ *Her mother is seriously ill.*

seriousness /ˈsiːriəsnəs/ *noun* the fact of being serious

sermon /ˈsɜːmən/ *noun* a talk given by a priest in church ○ *He gave a sermon about the need to love your neighbours.*

serotonin /ˌsɪərəˈtəʊnɪn/ *noun* a chemical in your body which affects your moods and the sending of messages through your nerves

serpent /ˈsɜːpənt/ *noun* a snake (*literary or dated*)

② **servant** /ˈsɜːvənt/ *noun* a person who is paid to work for a family ○ *They employ two servants in their London home.* ○ *Get it yourself – I'm not your servant!*

① **serve** /sɜːv/ (**serves, serving, served**) *verb* **1.** to give food or drink to someone ○ *She served the soup in small bowls.* ○ *Just take a plate and serve yourself.* ○ *Has everyone been served?* **2.** to go with a dish [~with] ○ *Fish is served with a white sauce.* ○ *You usually serve red wine with meat.* **3.** to help a customer, e.g. in a shop ○ *Are you being served?* ○ *The manager served me himself.* **4.** (*in games like tennis*) to start a point by hitting the ball, in sports such as tennis and squash ○ *She served two faults in a row.* ○ *He served first.*

③ **server** /ˈsɜːvə/ *noun* a dedicated computer or program which provides a function to a network

① **service** /ˈsɜːvɪs/ *noun* **1.** a facility which the public needs ○ *Our train service to London is very bad.* ○ *The postal service is efficient.* ○ *The hotel provides a laundry service.* **2.** the act of serving or helping someone in a shop or restaurant ○ *The food is good here, but the service is very slow.* ○ *The bill includes an extra 10% for service.* ○ *Is the service included?* ○ *The bill does not include service.* **3.** a regular check of a machine ○ *The car has had its 20,000-kilometre service.* **4.** a group of people working together ○ *the ambulance service* **5.** a time when you work for a company or organisation or in the armed forces ○ *She did six years' service in the police.* ○ *He was awarded a gold watch for his long service to the company.* ○ *As a soldier, he saw service in Northern Ireland.* **6.** a religious ceremony ○ *My mother never misses the nine o'clock service on Sundays.* **7.** (*in games like tennis*) the action of hitting the ball first ○ *She has a very powerful service.* ■ *verb* (**services, servicing, serviced**) to keep a machine in good working order ○ *The car needs to be serviced every six months.*

service charge /ˈsɜːvɪs tʃɑːdʒ/ *noun* a charge added to a bill in a restaurant to pay for service

serviceman /ˈsɜːvɪsmən/ (*plural* **servicemen**) *noun* a male member of the army, navy or air force

③ **services** /ˈsɜːvɪsɪz/ *noun* an area next to a motorway with a service station, restaurants and sometimes a hotel

③ **service station** /ˈsɜːvɪs ˌsteɪʃ(ə)n/ *noun* a garage where you can buy petrol and have small repairs done to a car

servicewoman /ˈsɜːvɪsˌwʊmən/ (*plural* **servicewomen**) *noun* a woman member of the army, navy or air force

serviette /ˌsɜːviˈet/ *noun* a square piece of cloth or paper used to protect clothes and wipe your mouth at meals (NOTE: Although **serviette** is perfectly correct English, some people prefer to use the word **napkin**.)

③ **serving** /ˈsɜːvɪŋ/ *noun* an amount of food served to one person

sesame /ˈsesəmi/ *noun* a plant with small flat seeds that are used in cooking, sometimes scattered on top of bread or cakes, or to make oil

② **session** /ˈseʃ(ə)n/ *noun* the time when an activity is taking place ○ *All these long sessions in front of the computer screen are ruining my eyesight.*

① **set** /set/ *noun* a group of things which go together, which are used together or which are sold together ○ *He carries a set of tools in the back of his car.* ○ *The six chairs are sold as a set.* ■ *verb* (**sets, setting, set**) **1.** to put something somewhere, usually carefully ○ *She set the plate of biscuits down on the table next to her chair.* **2.** to fix something ○ *When we go to France we have to set our watches to French time.* ○ *The price of the new computer has been set at £500.* **3.** to make something happen ○ *He went to sleep smoking a cigarette and set the house on fire.* ○ *All the prisoners were set free.* ○ *I had been worried about her, but her letter set my mind at rest.* **4.** to go down ○ *The sun rises in the east and sets in the west.* ■ *adj* ready ○ *We're all set for a swim.* ○ *My bags are packed and I'm all set to leave.* ○ *The government is set to intro-*

duce new anti-smoking laws. ○ *Her latest novel is set to become the best-selling book of the year.*

set about *phrasal verb* to start to do something

set aside *phrasal verb* **1.** to dismiss or reject something ○ *The proposal was set aside by the committee.* **2.** to save something and keep it for future use ○ *We set money aside every month for the children's holidays.*

set back *phrasal verb* **1.** to delay something or make something late ○ *The bad weather has set the harvest back by two weeks.* **2.** to place something further back ○ *The house is set back from the road.*

set down *phrasal verb* **1.** to let passengers get off ○ *The bus set down several passengers and two others got on.* **2.** to put something in writing ○ *The rules are set down in this booklet.*

set in *phrasal verb* to start and become permanent

set off① *phrasal verb* **1.** to begin a trip ○ *We're setting off for Germany tomorrow.* ○ *They all set off on a long walk after lunch.* **2.** to start something happening ○ *They set off a bomb in the shopping centre.* ○ *If you touch the wire it will set off the alarm.* ○ *Being in the same room as a cat will set off my asthma.*

set out *phrasal verb* **1.** to begin a journey ○ *The hunters set out to cross the mountains.* ○ *We have to set out early tomorrow.* **2.** to explain something clearly ○ *We asked her to set out the details in her report.* **3.** to aim to do something ○ *He set out to ruin the party.*

set to *phrasal verb* to start to work hard (*dated*)

set up *phrasal verb* **1.** to establish something ○ *to set up a committee* or *a working party* ○ *A fund has been set up to receive donations from the public.* ○ *He set himself up as an estate agent.* **2.** to deceive someone deliberately (*informal*) ○ *We were set up by the police.*

③ **setback** /ˈsetbæk/ *noun* a problem which makes something late or stops something going ahead

set piece /set piːs/ *noun* an action which is carefully planned in advance

settee /seˈtiː/ *noun* a long seat with a soft back where several people can sit

② **setting** /ˈsetɪŋ/ *noun* the background for a story ○ *The setting for the story is Hong Kong in 1935.*

② **settle** /ˈset(ə)l/ (**settles, settling, settled**) *verb* **1.** to arrange or agree something [~on] ○ *Have you settled on a title for the new film yet?* ○ *Well, I'm glad everything's settled at last.* ○ *Will these two sides ever settle their differences?* **2.** to place yourself in a comfortable position ○ *She switched on the television and settled in her favourite armchair.* **3.** to fall to the ground, or to the bottom of something, gently ○ *Wait for the dust to settle.* ○ *A layer of mud settled at the bottom of the pond.*

settle down *phrasal verb* **1.** to place yourself in a comfortable position ○ *After dinner, she likes to settle down in a comfortable chair with a good book.* **2.** to change to a calmer way of life without many changes of house or much travelling ○ *He has worked all over the world, and doesn't seem ready to settle down.* ○ *She had lots of boyfriends, and then got married and settled down in Surrey.*

settle for *phrasal verb* to choose or to decide on something which is not quite what you want

settle in *phrasal verb* to become accustomed to something new such as a house or job

② **settlement** /ˈset(ə)lmənt/ *noun* **1.** the payment of a bill ○ *This invoice has not been paid – can you arrange for immediate settlement?* **2.** an agreement in a dispute ○ *In the end a settlement was reached between management and workers.* **3.** a place where a group of people come to live ○ *a mining settlement in the hills*

③ **settler** /ˈset(ə)lə/ *noun* a person who goes to live in a new country

set-top box /set tɒp ˈbɒks/ *noun* a device shaped like a box, which is used to operate cable television

setup /ˈsetʌp/ *noun* **1.** the way something is organised **2.** an action taken to deceive someone

① **seven** /ˈsev(ə)n/ *noun* the number 7

① **seventeen** /ˌsev(ə)nˈtiːn/ *noun* the number 17

① **seventeenth** /ˌsev(ə)nˈtiːnθ/ *adj, noun* number 17 in a series ■ *noun* number 17 in a series

① **seventh** /ˈsevənθ/ *adj* relating to number 7 in a series ■ *noun* number 7 in a series

① **seventy** /ˈsev(ə)nti/ *noun* the number 70 □ **seventies** the numbers between 70 and 79

sever /ˈsevə/ (**severs, severing, severed**) *verb* to cut off

① **several** /'sev(ə)rəl/ *adj, pron* more than a few, but not a lot ○ *Several buildings were damaged in the storm.* ○ *We've met several times.* ○ *Several of the students are going to Italy.* ○ *Most of the guests left early but several stayed on till midnight.*

② **severe** /sɪ'vɪə/ *adj* **1.** very strict ○ *He was very severe with any child who did not behave.* ○ *Discipline in the school was severe.* **2.** having a very bad effect ○ *The government imposed severe financial restrictions on importers.* ○ *The severe weather has closed several main roads.* (NOTE: **severity** *n*)

③ **severely** /sɪ'vɪəli/ *adv* **1.** strictly ○ *She was severely punished for being late.* **2.** to a great extent ○ *a severely injured survivor* ○ *Train services have been severely affected by snow.*

③ **sew** /səʊ/ (**sews, sewing, sewed, sewn** or **sewed**) *verb* to attach, make or repair something by using a needle and thread (NOTE: Do not confuse with **sow**.)

sewage /'suːɪdʒ/ *noun* waste water and other waste from toilets, carried away in pipes under the ground

sewer /'suːə/ *noun* a large pipe which takes waste water and refuse away from buildings

③ **sewing** /'səʊɪŋ/ *noun* things such as clothes which someone is in the process of sewing

sewn /səʊn/ past participle of **sew**

① **sex** /seks/ *noun* **1.** one of two groups, male and female, into which animals and plants can be divided ○ *They've had a baby, but I don't know what sex it is.* ○ *There is no discrimination on the grounds of sex, race and religion.* **2.** physical activity which, between a man and a woman, could cause a baby to develop ○ *a film full of sex and violence* ○ *Sex was the last thing on her mind.* □ **to have sex with someone** to perform a sexual act with someone

sex appeal /'seks əˌpiːl/ *noun* the fact of being attractive to the opposite sex

sexism /'seksɪz(ə)m/ *noun* unfair treatment because of a person's sex

sex life /'seks laɪf/ *noun* the part of someone's life that involves their sexual relationships

sex offender /'seks əˌfendə/ *noun* a person who commits a crime involving sex

② **sexual** /'sekʃuəl/ *adj* relating to the activity of having sex ○ *Their relationship was never sexual.*

sexual intercourse /ˌsekʃuəl 'ɪntəkɔːs/ *noun* the act in which a man puts his penis inside a woman's vagina

③ **sexuality** /ˌsekʃu'ælɪti/ *noun* sexual feelings or activity

sexually /'sekʃʊəli/ *adv* in a sexual way

sexual orientation /ˌsekʃuəl ˌɔːriən 'teɪʃ(ə)n/ *noun* attraction to someone of the opposite sex, of the same sex or both

sex worker /seks 'wɜːkə/ *noun* a person who gets paid to have sex with people or who appears in pornographic films or photographs

② **sexy** /'seksi/ (**sexier, sexiest**) *adj* sexually attractive

SGML /ˌes dʒiː em'el/ *noun* a computer language which uses a system of codes to create files

sh /ʃ/ *interj* used to ask for silence

shabby /'ʃæbi/ *adj* (*of clothes*) used about clothes which are of poor quality or look worn out ○ *He wore a shabby coat with two buttons missing.*

shack /ʃæk/ *noun* a rough wooden shelter ○ *He lived for years in a little shack in the woods.*

shackle /'ʃæk(ə)l/ (**shackles, shackling, shackled**) *verb* to fasten someone to something or to another person with a chain ○ *The slaves were shackled together.*

shade /ʃeɪd/ *noun* **1.** a variety of a particular colour ○ *Her hat is a rather pretty shade of green.* **2.** a dark place which is not in the sun ○ *We sat in the shade of a tree.* ○ *Let's try and find some shade – it's too hot in the sun.*

② **shadow** /'ʃædəʊ/ *noun* a dark place behind an object where light is cut off by the object ○ *In the evening, the trees cast long shadows across the lawn.* ○ *She saw his shadow move down the hall.* ○ *They rested for a while, in the shadow of a large tree.*

shadowy /'ʃædəʊi/ (**shadowier, shadowiest**) *adj* not easily seen or not well known

shady /'ʃeɪdi/ *adj* **1.** out of the light of the sun ○ *At midday in Madrid, it's better to walk on the shady side of the street.* **2.** not honest ○ *He made several shady deals.*

③ **shaft** /ʃɑːft/ *noun* **1.** the long handle of a tool such as a spade ○ *The shaft of the spade was so old it snapped in two.* **2.** a thin beam of light ○ *Tiny particles of dust were dancing in a shaft of sunlight.* **3.** a deep hole connecting one place to another

○ *The shaft had become blocked with rubbish.*

shaggy /ˈʃæɡi/ *adj* long and untidy

② **shake** /ʃeɪk/ (**shakes, shaking, shook, shaken**) *verb* to move something from side to side or up and down ○ *Shake the bottle before pouring.* ○ *The house shakes every time a train goes past.* ○ *His hand shook as he opened the envelope.* ◇ **to shake your head** to move your head from side to side to mean 'no' ○ *When I asked my dad if I could borrow the car he just shook his head.*

shake off③ *phrasal verb* to get rid of something, usually something unpleasant

shakeup /ˈʃeɪkʌp/ *noun* a total reorganisation

shaky /ˈʃeɪki/ (**shakier, shakiest**) *adj* **1.** not very safe, not very reliable ○ *Be careful, that ladder is a bit shaky.* ○ *The champion driver got off to a shaky start.* ○ *Your argument sounds a bit shaky to me.* **2.** feeling weak ○ *He's still shaky after his operation.*

① **shall** /ʃəl, ʃæl/ *modal verb* **1.** used to make the future tense ○ *We shall be out on Saturday evening.* ○ *I shan't say anything – I shall keep my mouth shut!* ○ *Tomorrow we shan't be home until after 10 o'clock.* **2.** used to show a suggestion ○ *Shall we open the windows?* ○ *Shall I give them a ring?* (NOTE: **shall** is mainly used with **I** and **we**. The negative is **shan't** and the past tense is **should**.)

shallot /ʃəˈlɒt/ *noun* a type of small onion

③ **shallow** /ˈʃæləʊ/ *adj* not far from top to bottom ○ *Children were playing in the shallow end of the pool.* ○ *The river is so shallow in summer that you can walk across it.*

sham /ʃæm/ *noun* a person or thing which is false ○ *Her claim to be a great pianist is just a sham.* ○ *The government's promises were just a sham.*

shambles /ˈʃæmbəlz/ *noun* **1.** a complete lack of organisation ○ *The whole trip to Paris was a shambles – lost tickets, no hotel booking, everything that could go wrong did go wrong.* **2.** a mess ○ *She stood at the door looking at the shambles after the office party.* ○ *Tidy up your bedroom – it is an absolute shambles.*

② **shame** /ʃeɪm/ *noun* the bad feeling you get when you know you have done something wrong or cruel which you should not have done ○ *She went bright red with shame.* ○ *To my shame, I did nothing to help.*

shameful /ˈʃeɪmf(ə)l/ *adj* extremely immoral or dishonest, causing shame

shameless /ˈʃeɪmləs/ *adj* not ashamed

③ **shampoo** /ʃæmˈpuː/ *noun* **1.** liquid soap for washing your hair or for washing things such as carpets or cars ○ *There are sachets of shampoo in the bathroom.* **2.** the action of washing the hair ○ *She went to the hairdresser's for a shampoo.*

③ **shan't** /ʃɑːnt/ *short form* shall not

shanty town /ˈʃænti taʊn/ *noun* a large group of huts belonging to poor people

② **shape** /ʃeɪp/ *noun* the form of how something looks ○ *A design in the shape of a letter S.* ○ *The old table was a funny shape.* ■ *verb* (**shapes, shaping, shaped**) to make into a certain form ○ *He shaped the pastry into the form of a little boat.*

shape up *phrasal verb* to result, to end up ○ *Things are shaping up as we expected.* ○ *It's shaping up to be a fine day.*

② **shaped** /ʃeɪpt/ *adj* with a certain shape

shapeless /ˈʃeɪpləs/ *adj* with no definite shape

shapely /ˈʃeɪpli/ *adj* with an attractive shape

① **share** /ʃeə/ *noun* a part of something that is divided between two or more people ○ *Did he get his share of the prize money?* ○ *There's a lot of work to do, so everyone must do their share.* □ **to have a share in** to take part in, to have a part of ○ *All the staff should have a share in decisions about the company's future.* ○ *She has her share of the responsibility for the accident.* ■ *verb* (**shares, sharing, shared**) **1.** *also* **share out** to divide up something among several people [~among/between] ○ *The money will be shared out among her sons.* ○ *Let's share the cost.* **2.** to use something which someone else also uses ○ *We share an office.* ○ *We shared a taxi to the airport.*

shareholder /ˈʃeəhəʊldə/ *noun* a person who owns shares in a company

shareware /ˈʃeəˌweə/ *noun* computer software which you try for short period before deciding if you want to buy the right to use it

sharia /ʃəˈriːə/ *noun* Islamic religious law, based on the teaching of the Koran

③ **shark** /ʃɑːk/ *noun* a large dangerous fish which lives in the sea and can kill people ○ *The lifeguards shouted when a shark was spotted in the water.*

② **sharp** /ʃɑːp/ *adj* **1.** with an edge or point which can easily cut or pass through something ○ *For injections, a needle has to have a very sharp point.* ○ *The beach is covered with sharp stones.* ○ *This knife is useless – it isn't sharp enough.* **2.** sudden and great ○ *There was a sharp drop in interest rates.* ○ *The road makes a sharp right-hand bend.* ○ *He received a sharp blow on the back of his head.* ○ *We had a sharp frost last night.* **3.** bitter ○ *Lemons have a very sharp taste.* **4.** quick to notice things ○ *He has a sharp sense of justice.* ○ *She has a sharp eye for a bargain.* ○ *He's pretty sharp at spotting mistakes.* ■ *adv* **1.** exactly ○ *The coach will leave the hotel at 7.30 sharp.* **2.** suddenly, at an angle ○ *The road turned sharp right.*

sharpen /ˈʃɑːpən/ (**sharpens, sharpening, sharpened**) *verb* to make something sharp

③ **shatter** /ˈʃætə/ (**shatters, shattering, shattered**) *verb* **1.** to break into little pieces ○ *He knocked the vase with his elbow and it shattered onto the floor.* ○ *The bomb shattered the windows of several houses.* **2.** to destroy, to upset violently ○ *His hopes of going to university were shattered when he failed the exam.* ○ *A loud sneeze shattered the silence in the library.*

shattered /ˈʃætəd/ *adj* **1.** very upset ○ *She was shattered when the result of the court case was announced.* **2.** very tired (*informal*) ○ *He looked shattered after the marathon.*

③ **shave** /ʃeɪv/ *noun* the act of cutting off the hair on your face with a razor ○ *He decided to have a shave before going out to dinner.* ■ *verb* (**shaves, shaving, shaved, shaved** or **shaven**) **1.** to cut off the hair on your face with a razor ○ *He cut himself shaving.* **2.** to cut the hair on your head or, on a part of your body, so that it is very short ○ *I didn't recognise him with his head shaved.*

shaver /ˈʃeɪvə/ *noun* an electrical tool used for cutting hair off your body

shavings /ˈʃeɪvɪŋz/ *plural noun* small thin slices of something such as wood or cheese, cut off with a knife ○ *They packed the china in a box of wood shavings.*

shawl /ʃɔːl/ *noun* a large square of warm material for wearing around the shoulders or head

① **she** /ʃiː/ *pron* used for referring to a female person, a female animal and sometimes to cars, ships and countries ○ *She's my sister.* ○ *She and I are going on holiday to France together.* ○ *I'm angry with her – she's taken my motorbike.* ○ *She's a sweet little cat, but she's no good at catching mice.* ○ *The customs officers boarded the ship when she docked.* (NOTE: When it is the object, **she** becomes **her**: *She hit the ball* or *the ball hit her.* When it follows the verb to **be**, **she** usually becomes **her**: *Who's that? – It's her, the girl we met yesterday.*)

sheaf /ʃiːf/ (*plural* **sheaves**) *noun* **1.** a large pile of papers ○ *He threw a sheaf of papers onto my desk and told me to sort them out.* ○ *The jury had to examine sheaves of evidence collected by the fraud squad.* **2.** a collection of the stems of plants such as wheat tied together after cutting ○ *They spent all day picking up sheaves and loading them on carts.*

shears /ʃɪəz/ *plural noun* very large scissors, used for cutting plants or for cutting the wool off sheep ○ *He's cutting the hedge with the shears.*

sheath /ʃiːθ/ *noun* a cover for a weapon such as a knife ○ *Put your knife back in its sheath.*

sheaves /ʃiːvz/ plural of **sheaf**

shed /ʃed/ *noun* a small wooden building ○ *They kept the mower in a shed at the bottom of the garden.* ○ *She's in the garden shed putting geraniums into pots.* ■ *verb* (**sheds, shedding, shed**) to lose something which you are carrying or wearing ○ *In autumn, the trees shed their leaves as soon as the weather turns cold.* ○ *A lorry has shed its load of wood at the roundabout.* ○ *We shed our clothes and dived into the cool water.*

① **she'd** /ʃiːd/ *short form* **1.** she had **2.** she would

sheen /ʃiːn/ *noun* an extremely shiny surface

② **sheep** /ʃiːp/ (*plural same*) *noun* a common farm animal, which gives wool and meat ○ *a flock of sheep* ○ *The sheep are in the field.*

sheepdog /ˈʃiːpdɒg/ *noun* a dog trained and used to control sheep

sheepish /ˈʃiːpɪʃ/ *adj* embarrassed and showing that you are ashamed

sheepskin /ˈʃiːpskɪn/ *noun* the skin of a sheep, with the wool still on it, used to make something such as a coat or a floor covering

sheer /ʃɪə/ *adj* **1.** used for emphasizing something ○ *It was sheer heaven to get into a hot bath after skiing.* ○ *She was crying out of sheer frustration.* ○ *It's sheer madness to go out without a coat in this weath-*

er. **2.** very steep ○ *It was a sheer drop to the beach below.*

② **sheet** /ʃiːt/ *noun* **1.** a large piece of thin cloth which is put on a bed, either to lie on or to cover you ○ *She changed the sheets on the bed.* **2.** a large flat piece of something such as paper, metal, ice or plastic ○ *Can you give me another sheet of paper?* ◊ **balance sheet**

sheeting /ˈʃiːtɪŋ/ *noun* thin material used for covering things

② **shelf** /ʃelf/ (*plural* **shelves**) *noun* a flat piece of wood attached to a wall or in a cupboard on which things can be put ○ *He put up* or *built some shelves in the kitchen.* ○ *The shelves were packed with books.* ○ *Put that book back on the shelf.* ○ *Can you reach me down the box from the top shelf?* ○ *The plates are on the top shelf in the kitchen cupboard.*

shelf life /ˈʃelf laɪf/ *noun* the number of days or weeks that a product can be kept in a shop and still be good to use

③ **shell** /ʃel/ *noun* **1.** the hard outside part which covers some animals such as snails or tortoises ○ *The children spent hours collecting shells on the beach.* **2.** the hard outside part of an egg or a nut ○ *I found a big piece of shell in my omelette.* ◊ **eggshell**, **nutshell 3.** a metal tube which is fired from a gun and explodes when it hits something ○ *A shell landed on the hospital.*

③ **she'll** /ʃiːl/ *short form* she will

③ **shellfish** /ˈʃelfɪʃ/ *noun* sea animals such as crabs and oysters which have a hard outer covering and which you can eat

shelter /ˈʃeltə/ *noun* **1.** protection ○ *We stood in the shelter of a tree waiting for the rain to stop.* ○ *On the mountain there was no shelter from the pouring rain.* □ **to take shelter** to go somewhere for protection ○ *When the gunmen started to shoot we all took shelter behind a wall.* **2.** a structure or building which protects you from bad weather or danger ○ *People stood in the bus shelter out of the rain as they waited for the bus to come.* ■ *verb* (**shelters, sheltering, sheltered**) to go somewhere for protection ○ *Sheep were sheltering from the snow beside the hedge.*

shelve /ʃelv/ (**shelves, shelving, shelved**) *verb* **1.** to put back to a later date ○ *The project was shelved for lack of money.* ○ *Discussion of the problem has been shelved.* **2.** to slope down ○ *The beach shelves gently so it is safe for little children.*

③ **shelves** /ʃelvz/ plural of **shelf**

shelving /ˈʃelvɪŋ/ *noun* **1.** rows of shelves ○ *I've installed metal shelving in the garden shed.* **2.** the act of delaying something such as a plan to do something ○ *The shelving of the project has resulted in chaos.*

shenanigans /ʃɪˈnænɪgənz/ *plural noun* behaviour that is dishonest or immoral, but often in a way that can interesting or funny

shepherd /ˈʃepəd/ (**shepherds, shepherding, shepherded**) *verb* to take people somewhere moving them as a group ○ *The children were shepherded into the building.* ○ *The police were shepherding the crowds away from the scene of the accident.*

sheriff /ˈʃerɪf/ *noun US* an official in charge of justice in a particular part of a state ○ *the sheriff of Orange County*

sherry /ˈʃeri/ *noun* a type of strong wine, made in Spain ○ *She brought two bottles of sherry back from Spain.*

she's /ʃiːz/ *short for* **1.** she has **2.** she is

shh /ʃ/ *interj* another spelling of **sh** (NOTE: also spelt **sh!**)

② **shield** /ʃiːld/ *noun* a large flat object carried by people such as police officers for protection from attack ○ *Our police officers carry riot shields.* ■ *verb* (**shields, shielding, shielded**) to protect someone or something from being reached or seen ○ *He tried to shield her from the wind.*

② **shift** /ʃɪft/ *noun* a change of something such as position or direction [~in/~towards/to] ○ *a shift in policy* ○ *There is a shift in the market towards higher priced goods.* ○ *There has been a shift of emphasis from opposition to partnership.* ■ *verb* (**shifts, shifting, shifted**) to change position or direction ○ *We've shifted the television from the kitchen into the dining room.* ○ *My opinion has shifted since I read the official report.*

shift key /ˈʃɪft kiː/ *noun* the key which changes characters on a keyboard to capital letters

shifty /ˈʃɪfti/ *adj* not looking honest

Shiite /ˈʃiːaɪt/, **Shi'ite** *noun* a follower of the Shia branch of Islam

shimmer /ˈʃɪmə/ (**shimmers, shimmering, shimmered**) *verb* to shine softly with light in a way which is not steady ○ *The lake shimmered in the moonlight.*

shin /ʃɪn/ *noun* the front part of your leg below the knee ○ *He scraped his shin climbing over the wall.* ○ *They kicked him in the shins.*

③ **shine** /ʃaɪn/ (**shines, shining, shone**) *verb* **1.** to be bright with light ○ *The sun is shining and they say it'll be hot today.* ○ *She polished the table until it shone.* ○ *The wine glasses shone in the light of the candles.* ○ *Why do cats' eyes shine in the dark?* ○ *The moon shone down on the waiting crowd.* **2.** to make light fall on something ○ *He shone his torch into the cellar.*

shingle /ˈʃɪŋgəl/ *noun* **1.** a mass of small stones on a beach ○ *A shingle beach is quite hard to walk on in your bare feet.* **2.** a small flat piece of something such as wood which is fixed on a wall or roof as a covering ○ *I must get up on the roof, some of the shingles need replacing.*

Shinto /ˈʃɪntəʊ/ *noun* a Japanese religion with many gods and spirits of the natural world

③ **shiny** /ˈʃaɪni/ (**shinier, shiniest**) *adj* which shines

① **ship** /ʃɪp/ *noun* a large boat for carrying passengers and goods on the sea ○ *She's a fine ship.* ○ *How many ships does the Royal Navy have?* ○ *The first time we went to the United States, we went by ship.* (NOTE: A **ship** is often referred to as **she** or **her**.)

shipbuilder /ˈʃɪpˌbɪldə/ *noun* a person or business that makes ships

③ **shipment** /ˈʃɪpmənt/ *noun* **1.** the sending of goods **2.** goods which are sent somewhere by ship or other means of transport

③ **shipping** /ˈʃɪpɪŋ/ *noun* **1.** the sending of goods ○ *Shipping by rail can often work out cheaper.* **2.** ships ○ *They attacked enemy shipping in the Channel.*

shipwreck /ˈʃɪprek/ *noun* an accident which sinks a ship

shipyard /ˈʃɪpjɑːd/ *noun* a factory where ships are built

shirk /ʃɜːk/ (**shirks, shirking, shirked**) *verb* to try not to do something, especially work

① **shirt** /ʃɜːt/ *noun* a light piece of clothing which you wear on the top part of the body ○ *The teacher wore a blue suit and a white shirt.* ○ *When he came back from the trip he had a suitcase full of dirty shirts.* ○ *It's so hot that the workers in the fields have taken their shirts off.*

shiver /ˈʃɪvə/ *verb* (**shivers, shivering, shivered**) to shake with cold or fear ○ *She shivered in the cold night air.* ○ *He was coughing and shivering, so the doctor told him to stay in bed.* ■ *noun* the action of shaking because of feeling cold or frightened

shoal /ʃəʊl/ *noun* **1.** a bank of sand under the water ○ *The shoals are clearly marked on the chart of the harbour.* **2.** a group of fish swimming about ○ *a shoal of herring*

② **shock** /ʃɒk/ *noun* a sudden unpleasant surprise ○ *It gave me quite a shock when you walked in.* ○ *He's in for a nasty shock.* □ **in a state of shock** reacting badly to a sudden unpleasant surprise ○ *She was in a state of shock after hearing of the accident.* ■ *verb* (**shocks, shocking, shocked**) to give someone a sudden unpleasant surprise ○ *The conditions in the hospital shocked the inspectors.*

③ **shocked** /ʃɒkt/ *adj* having an unpleasant surprise

③ **shocking** /ˈʃɒkɪŋ/ *adj* very unpleasant, which gives someone a sudden surprise

shock wave /ˈʃɒk weɪv/ *noun* a strong emotional feeling after something has happened ○ *The shock waves from the collapse of the government will be felt for some time.*

shoddy /ˈʃɒdi/ *adj* badly done, badly made ○ *The shoddy workmanship of these shoes.* ○ *They're selling off shoddy goods at cheap prices.*

① **shoe** /ʃuː/ *noun* a piece of clothing which is worn on your foot ○ *She's bought a new pair of shoes.* ○ *He put his shoes on and went out.* ○ *Take your shoes off if your feet hurt.*

shoelace /ˈʃuːleɪs/ *noun* a string for tying up shoes

shoestring /ˈʃuːstrɪŋ/ *noun* □ **on a shoestring** done with only a little money ○ *We're trying to run this business on a shoestring.* ○ *They're living on a shoestring.*

③ **shone** /ʃɒn/ past tense and past participle of **shine**

shoo /ʃuː/ (**shoos, shooing, shooed**) *verb* to make an animal or a person go somewhere by waving your hands at them ○ *She shooed her group of four-year-olds into the bus.*

③ **shook** /ʃʊk/ past tense of **shake**

② **shoot** /ʃuːt/ *noun* a new growth of a plant, growing from a seed or from a branch ○ *One or two green shoots are already showing where I sowed my lettuces.* ○ *After pruning, the roses will send out a lot of strong new shoots.* ■ *verb* (**shoots, shooting, shot**) **1.** to fire a gun [~at] ○ *Enemy troops were shooting at us.* ○ *Don't shoot – we're coming out.* **2.** to hit or kill by firing a gun ○ *One of the robbers was shot by a police officer.* ○ *We went out hunting* *and shot two rabbits.* **3.** to go very fast ○ *When the bell rang she shot down the stairs.* ○ *He started the engine and the car shot out of the garage.* **4.** to aim a ball at the goal ○ *He shot, and the ball bounced off the post.*

shoot down *phrasal verb* to make an aircraft crash by hitting it with bullets from a gun

shoot up *phrasal verb* **1.** to go up fast ○ *Prices shot up during the strike.* **2.** to grow fast ○ *These tomatoes have shot up since I planted them.* ○ *She used to be such a small child but she's really shot up in the last couple of years.*

③ **shooting** /ˈʃuːtɪŋ/ *noun* the action of shooting or killing with a gun

shooting star /ˌʃuːtɪŋ ˈstɑː/ *noun* a small rock which travels very fast through space and shines brightly

shoot-out /ˈʃuːt aʊt/ *noun* a fight with guns

① **shop** /ʃɒp/ *noun* a place where you can buy things ○ *Quite a few shops are open on Sundays.* ○ *I never go to that shop – it's much too expensive.* ○ *The sweet shop is opposite the fire station.* ■ *verb* (**shops, shopping, shopped**) to look for and buy things in shops [~for] ○ *She's out shopping for his birthday present.* ○ *Mum's gone shopping.* ○ *They went shopping in Oxford Street.* ○ *Do you ever shop locally?*

shop around *phrasal verb* to go to various shops to find which one has the cheapest goods before you buy anything

shop assistant /ˈʃɒp əˌsɪstənt/ *noun* a person who serves the customers in a shop

shopkeeper /ˈʃɒpkiːpə/ *noun* a person who owns a shop

shoplifter /ˈʃɒplɪftə/ *noun* a person who steals things from shops

shoplifting /ˈʃɒplɪftɪŋ/ *noun* stealing from shops (NOTE: + **shoplifter** *n*)

③ **shopper** /ˈʃɒpə/ *noun* a person who buys things from shops

② **shopping** /ˈʃɒpɪŋ/ *noun* **1.** the activity of buying things in a shop ○ *We do all our shopping at the weekend.* ○ *He's gone out to do the weekly shopping.* **2.** things which you have bought in a shop ○ *Put all your shopping on the table.* ○ *She was carrying two baskets of shopping.* (NOTE: no plural: *some shopping, a lot of shopping*)

③ **shopping centre** /ˈʃɒpɪŋ ˌsentə/ *noun* a building with several different shops and restaurants, together with a car park ○ *We must stop them from building any more out-of-town shopping centres.*

shopping mall /ˈʃɒpɪŋ mɒl/ *noun* an enclosed covered shopping area with shops, restaurants, banks and other facilities

shore /ʃɔː/ *noun* land at the edge of the sea or a lake ○ *She stood on the shore waving as the boat sailed away.*

shore up *phrasal verb* to hold something up which might fall down ○ *They had to put in metal beams to shore up the ceiling.* ○ *The army is trying to shore up the president's regime.*

shoreline /ˈʃɔːlaɪn/ *noun* the area along the edge of the sea or a lake, where water meets land

① **short** /ʃɔːt/ *adj* **1.** (*of size or length*) not long ○ *Have you got a short piece of wire?* **2.** (*of distance*) not far ○ *She only lives a short distance away.* ○ *The taxi driver wanted to take me through the high street, but I told him there was a shorter route.* ○ *The shortest way to the railway station is to go through the park.* **3.** (*of time*) not lasting a long time ○ *He phoned a short time ago.* ○ *We had a short holiday in June.* ○ *She managed to have a short sleep on the plane.* **4.** (*of height*) not tall ○ *He is only 1m 40 – much shorter than his brother.*

shortage /ˈʃɔːtɪdʒ/ *noun* the fact that you do not have something you need ○ *a shortage of skilled staff* ○ *During the war, there were food shortages.*

shortcoming /ˈʃɔːtkʌmɪŋz/ *noun* a fault that reduces the effectiveness of something or someone

short cut /ʃɔːt ˈkʌt/ *noun* **1.** a way which is shorter than usual ○ *We can take a short cut through the park.* **2.** a quicker way of doing something ○ *There are no short cuts to learning Russian.*

shorten /ˈʃɔːt(ə)n/ (**shortens, shortening, shortened**) *verb* to make shorter

shortfall /ˈʃɔːtfɔːl/ *noun* an amount which is missing from a total

shorthand /ˈʃɔːthænd/ *noun* a way of writing using a system of signs

shortlist /ˈʃɔːtlɪst/ *noun* a list of some of the people who have applied for a job, and who have been chosen to come for an interview ○ *He's on the shortlist for the job.* (NOTE: + **shortlist** *v*)

shortlived /ˌʃɔːtˈlɪvd/ *adj* which does not last for a long time

③ **shortly** /ˈʃɔːtli/ *adv* soon

short-range /ˈʃɔːt ˌreɪndʒ/ *adj* which covers a short distance or a short time

③ **shorts** /ʃɔːts/ *plural noun* short trousers for men or women, that stop above the knees ○ *He was wearing a pair of green running shorts.* ○ *They won't let you into the church in shorts.*

shortsighted /ʃɔːt'saɪtɪd/ *adj* **1.** able to see close objects clearly, but not objects which are further away ○ *I'm shortsighted and have to wear glasses.* **2.** not thinking about what may happen in the future ○ *It is very shortsighted of him to spend all the money on a new car.* ○ *The government has adopted a very shortsighted policy.*

③ **short story** /ʃɔːt 'stɒri/ *noun* a piece of fiction which is much shorter than a novel

short-term /ˌʃɔːt 'tɜːm/ *adj* for a short period only

short wave /'ʃɔːt weɪv/ *noun* a radio communications frequency below 60 metres. ◊ **long wave**, **medium wave**

① **shot** /ʃɒt/ *noun* **1.** the action of shooting [~at] ○ *The police fired two shots at the car.* ○ *Some shots were fired during the bank robbery.* **2.** a kick or hit to try to score a goal ○ *His shot was saved by the goalkeeper.* ■ past tense and past participle of **shoot** ◇ **like a shot** very rapidly ○ *He heard a noise and was off like a shot.*

shotgun /'ʃɒtgʌn/ *noun* a gun which fires small pellets

① **should** /ʃʊd/ *modal verb* **1.** used in giving advice or warnings for saying what is the best thing to do ○ *You should go to the doctor if your cough gets worse.* ○ *I should have been more careful.* ○ *She shouldn't eat so much if she's trying to lose weight.* ○ *Should I ask for more coffee?* ○ *Why should I clean up your mess?* (NOTE: **Ought to** can be used instead of **should**.) **2.** used to say what you expect to happen ○ *If you leave now you should be there by 4 o'clock.* ○ *Their train should have arrived by now.* ○ *There shouldn't be any more problems now.* (NOTE: **Ought to** can be used instead of **should**.) **3.** used to show a possibility ○ *If the President should die in office, the Vice-President automatically takes over.* ○ *I'll be in the next room should you need me.* **4.** same as **would** (*formal*) ○ *We should like to offer you our congratulations.* ○ *If I had enough money I should like to buy a new car.* (NOTE: The negative is **should not** or, especially in speaking, **shouldn't**. Note also that **should** is used as the past tense of **shall**: *I suggested we should go to an Indian restaurant.*)

① **shoulder** /'ʃəʊldə/ *noun* the part of the body at the top of the arm ○ *The policeman hurt me on the shoulder.* ○ *He fell and dislocated his shoulder.* ○ *Look over your shoulder, he's just behind you.*

shoulder blade /'ʃəʊldə bleɪd/ *noun* one of two large flat bones covering the top part of your back

② **shouldn't** /'ʃʊd(ə)nt/ *short for* should not

② **shout** /ʃaʊt/ *noun* a loud cry ○ *She gave a shout and dived into the water.* ○ *People came running when they heard the shouts of the children.* ■ *verb* (**shouts, shouting, shouted**) to make a loud cry or to speak very loudly ○ *They stamped on the floor and shouted.* ○ *I had to shout to the waitress to get served.* ○ *They were shouting greetings to one another across the street.*

③ **shove** /ʃʌv/ *noun* a sudden push ○ *She gave the car a shove and it rolled down the hill.* ■ *verb* (**shoves, shoving, shoved**) to push someone or something roughly ○ *He shoved the papers into his pocket.* ○ *Stop shoving – there's no more room on the bus.*

shove off *phrasal verb* (*informal*) **1.** to leave ○ *It's time we shoved off.* **2.** to go away ○ *Shove off and let me finish my meal.*

shovel /'ʃʌv(ə)l/ *noun* a tool with a long handle and a wide flat part for picking up things such as earth or stones ○ *The workmen picked up shovels and started to clear the pile of sand.* (NOTE: + **shovel** *v*)

① **show** /ʃəʊ/ *noun* **1.** an exhibition, things which are arranged for people to look at ○ *a fashion show* **2.** something which is on at a theatre ○ *We're going to a show tonight.* ○ *What time does the show start?* ■ *verb* (**shows, showing, showed, shown**) **1.** to let someone see something ○ *He wanted to show me his holiday photos.* ○ *You have to show your passport at the check-in desk.* **2.** to point something out to someone [~what/how/why etc] ○ *Show me where the accident happened.* ○ *He asked me to show him the way to the railway station.* ○ *The salesman showed her how to work the photocopier.* ○ *My watch shows the date as well as the time.* **3.** to be seen, to be obvious ○ *The repairs were badly done and it shows.* ○ *Her rash has almost disappeared and hardly shows at all.* ◇ **on show** arranged for everyone to see ○ *Is there anything new on show in this year's exhibition?*

show off *phrasal verb* **1.** to show how

much better than other people you think you are ○ *Don't watch her dancing about like that – she's just showing off.* **2.** to let a lot of people see something which you are proud of ○ *He drove past with the radio on very loud, showing off his new car.* **show up**③ *phrasal verb* **1.** to do something which shows other people to be worse than you ○ *She dances so well that she shows us all up.* **2.** to be seen clearly ○ *When I ride my bike at night I wear an orange jacket because it shows up clearly in the dark.* **3.** to come to or arrive in a place (*informal*) ○ *We invited all our friends to the picnic but it rained and only five of them showed up.*

showbiz /ˈʃəʊbɪz/ *noun* same as **show business** (*informal*)

show business /ˈʃəʊ ˌbɪznəs/ *noun* the business of providing entertainment for people

showcase /ˈʃəʊkeɪs/ *noun* **1.** a cupboard with a glass front or top to arrange objects for sale ○ *The thieves smashed the showcase and went off with a tray of rings.* **2.** an event designed to make someone or something known to the public ○ *The computer show is a showcase for the latest developments in information technology.*

showdown /ˈʃəʊdaʊn/ *noun* a final argument which will solve a serious disagreement

② **shower** /ˈʃaʊə/ *noun* **1.** a slight fall of rain or snow ○ *In April there's usually a mixture of sunshine and showers.* ○ *There were snow showers this morning, but it is sunny again now.* **2.** a piece of equipment in a bathroom, usually fixed high up on the wall, which sends out water to wash your whole body **3.** an occasion when you wash your body with a shower ○ *She went up to her room and had a shower.* ○ *He has a cold shower every morning.* ○ *You can't take a shower now, there's no hot water.* ■ *verb* (**showers, showering, showered**) to wash yourself under a shower ○ *He showered and went down to greet his guests.*

showing /ˈʃəʊɪŋ/ *noun* a result which shows how well or badly you are doing

showman /ˈʃəʊmən/ *noun* an entertainer, especially one who performs in very skilled and exciting way

shown /ʃəʊn/ past participle of **show**

show-off /ˈʃəʊ ɒf/ *noun* a person who shows off (*informal*)

showpiece /ˈʃəʊpiːs/ *noun* the most important object in a collection or an exhibition of its type

showroom /ˈʃəʊruːm/ *noun* a room or shop where goods are arranged for sale

showy /ˈʃəʊi/ *adj* which attracts attention because of its bright colours or shiny surface

shrank /ʃræŋk/ past tense of **shrink**

shrapnel /ˈʃræpn(ə)l/ *noun* pieces of metal from a shell or bomb which has exploded

shred /ʃred/ *noun* a long narrow piece torn off something ○ *She tore his newspaper to shreds.* ■ *verb* (**shreds, shredding, shredded**) **1.** to tear or cut paper into long thin pieces, which can then be thrown away or used as packing material ○ *They sent a pile of old invoices to be shredded.* ○ *She told the police that the manager had told her to shred all the documents in the file.* **2.** to cut something into very thin pieces ○ *Here's a utensil for shredding vegetables.* ○ *Add a cup of shredded carrot.*

shredder /ˈʃredə/ *noun* a machine for shredding paper

shrewd /ʃruːd/ *adj* clever or wise

shriek /ʃriːk/ (**shrieks, shrieking, shrieked**) *verb* to make the sound of a shriek ○ *She ran shrieking into the street.* ○ *The children were shrieking with laughter.* (NOTE: + **shriek** *n*)

shrill /ʃrɪl/ (**shriller, shrillest**) *adj* **1.** which has a harsh high sound ○ *The engine has started to make a shrill whistle when I change gear.* **2.** loud and complaining ○ *The art gallery is making increasingly shrill complaints about lack of government funding.*

shrimp /ʃrɪmp/ *noun* an almost transparent little shellfish with a tail

shrine /ʃraɪn/ *noun* a place which is visited to remember a holy person or someone who has died ○ *Someone had put flowers at the roadside shrine.* ○ *The bedroom had become a shrine to her dead son.*

③ **shrink** /ʃrɪŋk/ (**shrinks, shrinking, shrank** or **shrunk, shrunk** or **shrunken**) *verb* **1.** to make something smaller ○ *The water must have been too hot – it's shrunk my shirt.* **2.** to get smaller ○ *My shirt has shrunk in the wash.* ○ *The market for typewriters has shrunk almost to nothing.*

shrinkage /ˈʃrɪŋkɪdʒ/ *noun* the action of shrinking ○ *I have noticed some shrinkage in the pullover after washing.*

shrivel /ˈʃrɪv(ə)l/ (**shrivels, shrivelling, shrivelled**) *verb* to make the surface of something become dry and creased, or to become like this

shroud /ʃraʊd/ *noun* a long cloth covering a dead body ○ *The corpse was wrapped in a white shroud.* ■ *verb* (**shrouds, shrouding, shrouded**) to cover ○ *Thick fog shrouded the town.* ○ *Clouds of smoke shrouded the factory.*

shrub /ʃrʌb/ *noun* a small plant with stiff stems

shrubbery /ˈʃrʌbəri/ (*plural* **shrubberies**) *noun* a part of a garden where shrubs grow

③ **shrug** /ʃrʌg/ (**shrugs, shrugging, shrugged**) *verb* to make the movement of a shrug with your shoulders ○ *When I asked him what he thought about it all, he just shrugged or shrugged his shoulders and walked off.*

shrug off *phrasal verb* to treat something as if it is not something to worry about

shrunk /ʃrʌŋk/ past participle of **shrink**

shrunken /ˈʃrʌŋkən/ *adj* wrinkled and dried up

③ **shudder** /ˈʃʌdə/ (**shudders, shuddering, shuddered**) *verb* to shake violently with fear ○ *The thought of eating worms makes me shudder.* ○ *She shuddered at the thought of spending Christmas with his parents.* ○ *I shudder to think how much money she spends on clothes each month.*

shuffle /ˈʃʌf(ə)l/ (**shuffles, shuffling, shuffled**) *verb* **1.** to walk dragging your feet along the ground ○ *He shuffled into the room in his slippers.* **2.** to mix the playing cards before starting a game ○ *I think he must have done something to the cards when he was shuffling them.*

shun /ʃʌn/ (**shuns, shunning, shunned**) *verb* to avoid

shunt /ʃʌnt/ (**shunts, shunting, shunted**) *verb* **1.** to put someone or something into a less important place ○ *The carriages will be shunted into a siding.* ○ *He was shunted off to our office in Bordeaux.* **2.** to move a vehicle backwards and forwards ○ *She shunted backwards and forwards until she was parked close to the pavement.*

shush /ʃʊʃ/ *interj* be quiet!

① **shut** /ʃʌt/ *adj* not open ○ *Some shops are shut on Sundays, but most big stores are open.* ○ *We tried to get into the museum but it was shut.* ○ *She lay with her eyes shut.* ○ *Come in – the door isn't shut!* ■ *verb* (**shuts, shutting, shut**) **1.** to close something which is open ○ *Can you please shut the window – it's getting cold in here.* ○ *Here's your present – shut your eyes and guess what it is.* **2.** to close for business ○ *In Germany, shops shut on Saturday afternoons.* ○ *The restaurant shuts at midnight.*

shut down③ *phrasal verb* **1.** to close completely ○ *The factory shut down for the holiday weekend.* **2.** to switch off an electrical system ○ *They had to shut down the factory because pollution levels were too high.*

shut in *phrasal verb* to lock someone inside a place

shut off *phrasal verb* **1.** to switch something off ○ *Can you shut off the water while I mend the tap?* **2.** to stop access to ○ *We can shut off the dining room with folding doors.* ○ *The house is shut off from the road by a high wall.*

shut out *phrasal verb* **1.** to lock someone outside a place ○ *I was shut out of the house because I'd left my keys inside.* ○ *If the dog keeps on barking you'll have to shut him out.* **2.** to stop light getting inside, or to stop people seeing inside ○ *Those thick curtains should shut out the light from the children's room.* ○ *A high wall shuts out the view of the factory.* **3.** to stop thinking about something ○ *Try to shut out the memory of the accident.*

shut up① *phrasal verb* **1.** to close something inside a place ○ *I hate being shut up indoors on a sunny day.* **2.** an impolite way of telling someone to stop talking or to stop making a noise ○ *Tell those children to shut up – I'm trying to work.* ○ *Shut up! – we're tired of listening to your complaints.* ○ *Once he starts talking it's impossible to shut him up.*

shutdown /ˈʃʌtˌdaʊn/ *noun* the action of shutting down

③ **shutter** /ˈʃʌtə/ *noun* **1.** a folding wooden or metal cover for a window ○ *Close the shutters if the sunlight is too bright.* **2.** the part of a camera which opens and closes very quickly to allow the light to go on to the film ○ *He released the shutter and took the picture.*

shuttle /ˈʃʌt(ə)l/ *noun* **1.** a means of transport which goes frequently from one place to another and back again ○ *There's a shuttle bus from the hotel to the exhibition grounds.* **2.** a small object for holding thread and which takes the thread backwards and forwards when weaving or sewing with a machine ■ *verb* (**shuttles, shuttling, shuttled**) to go between two places frequently ○ *Waiters were shuttling backwards and forwards from the kitchen to the dining room.*

shuttlecock /ˈʃʌt(ə)lkɒk/ *noun* a light little object with feathers stuck in it, which players hit over a net in badminton

shy /ʃaɪ/ *adj* nervous and afraid to speak or do something ○ *He's so shy he sat in the back row and didn't speak to anyone.*

③ **sibling** /ˈsɪblɪŋ/ *noun* a brother or sister

① **sick** /sɪk/ *adj* **1.** not in good health ○ *He's been sick for months.* ○ *We have five staff off sick.* **2.** □ **to be sick** to bring up food from the stomach into the mouth ○ *The last time I ate oysters I was sick all night.* □ **to feel sick** to feel ill because you want to bring up food from the stomach ○ *When I got up this morning I felt sick and went back to bed.* ○ *The greasy food made her feel sick.* **3.** involving subjects or behaviour that many people are upset or offended by ○ *a sick joke* ■ *noun* the contents of the stomach when they come out through the mouth (*informal*) ◇ **to make someone sick** to make someone very annoyed ○ *All my friends earn more than I do – it makes me sick!*

sick up *phrasal verb* to bring up food from your stomach into your mouth (*informal*)

sicken /ˈsɪkən/ (**sickens, sickening, sickened**) *verb* to make someone feel extremely upset ○ *It sickens me to think of foxes being killed.*

sickening /ˈsɪk(ə)nɪŋ/ *adj* making you upset or nervous ◇ **to be sickening for something** to have the first signs of an illness (*informal*) ○ *She's looking pale – she must be sickening for something.*

sick leave /ˈsɪk liːv/ *noun* a period when an employee is away from work because of illness

sickly /ˈsɪkli/ *adj* not healthy ○ *Your plants are looking rather sickly, do they need more fertiliser?* ○ *He turned a sickly yellow colour, and we rushed him to the doctor.*

② **sickness** /ˈsɪknəs/ *noun* **1.** the feeling of wanting to bring up food from the stomach into the mouth **2.** not being well ○ *There is a lot of sickness about during the winter months.*

① **side** /saɪd/ *noun* **1.** one of the four parts which with the top and bottom make a solid object such as a box ○ *Stand the box upright – don't turn it onto its side.* **2.** one of the two parts which with the front and back make a building ○ *The garage is attached to the side of the house.* **3.** one of the surfaces of a flat object ○ *Please write on both sides of the paper.* **4.** one of two or more parts or edges of something ○ *Our office is on the opposite side of the street to the bank.* ○ *London's Heathrow Airport is on the west side of the city.* ○ *The hitch-hikers were standing by the side of the road.* ○ *She sat to one side of the fireplace.* **5.** one of two parts separated by something ○ *In the UK, cars drive on the left-hand side of the road.* ○ *She jumped over the fence to get to the other side.* **6.** a sports team ○ *The local side was beaten 2 – 0.* **7.** the part of the body between the top of the legs and the shoulder ○ *I can't sleep when I'm lying on my right side.* ○ *The policemen stood by the prisoner's side.* ○ *They all stood side by side.* ■ *adj* which is at the side ○ *There is a side entrance to the shop.* ○ *Can you take that bucket round to the side door?*

sideboard /ˈsaɪdbɔːd/ *noun* a large piece of furniture made like a table with a cupboard underneath and used for storing objects such as plates, cups and glasses

② **side effect** /ˈsaɪd ɪˌfekt/ *noun* an effect produced by a medical treatment such as a drug, which is not the main effect intended

sidekick /ˈsaɪdkɪk/ *noun* someone who works as a helper for another person (*informal*)

sidelight /ˈsaɪdlaɪt/ *noun* one of the small lights on each side of the front of a car ○ *Switch your sidelights on – it's beginning to get dark.*

sideline /ˈsaɪdlaɪn/ *noun* a business which you carry out in addition to your usual job ○ *He runs a profitable sideline selling postcards to tourists.*

sidelong /ˈsaɪdlɒŋ/ *adj* from one side

sideshow /ˈsaɪdʃəʊ/ *noun* **1.** a small stall with a game of skill at an event such as a fair ○ *Among the sideshows were stalls selling candy floss and a shooting gallery.* **2.** an activity that is less important than another activity connected with it ○ *The European Parliament is just a sideshow – the real decisions are taken by the Council of Ministers.*

sidestep /ˈsaɪdstep/ (**sidesteps, sidestepping, sidestepped**) *verb* to avoid something unpleasant (*informal*)

side street /ˈsaɪd striːt/ *noun* a small street which leads off a main street

sidetrack /ˈsaɪdtræk/ (**sidetracks, sidetracking, sidetracked**) *verb* to attract someone's attention away from a more important problem

sidewalk /ˈsaɪdwɔːk/ *noun US* a pavement ○ *A girl was walking slowly along the sidewalk.* ○ *We sat at a sidewalk café.*

③ **sideways** /ˈsaɪdweɪz/ *adv* to the side or from the side ○ *Crabs walk sideways.* ○ *Take a step sideways and you will be able to see the castle.* ○ *If you look at the post sideways you'll see how bent it is.*

sidle /ˈsaɪd(ə)l/ (**sidles, sidling, sidled**) *verb* to walk in a way which shows you are slightly afraid and not go directly forwards

siege /siːdʒ/ *noun* an act of surrounding an enemy town or castle with an army to prevent supplies getting in, and so force the people inside to come out and stop fighting

siesta /siˈestə/ *noun* a rest period in the middle of the day, especially common in Mediterranean countries

sieve /sɪv/ *noun* an object used in the kitchen, made of a frame with a metal or plastic net, used to pour through liquids or substances such as flour, in order to remove lumps or separate some of the parts ○ *Put the flour through a sieve.* ○ *Boil the peas for a few minutes and put in a sieve to strain.*

sift /sɪft/ (**sifts, sifting, sifted**) *verb* to sieve something

sift through *phrasal verb* to examine something carefully ○ *The police sifted through the rubble to see if they could find traces of the bomb.*

sigh /saɪ/ *noun* a long deep breath, showing feelings such as sadness or showing that you feel tired ○ *She gave a deep sigh and put the phone down.* ○ *You could hear the sighs of relief from the audience when the hero was saved.* ■ *verb* (**sighs, sighing, sighed**) to breathe with a sigh ○ *He sighed and wrote out another cheque.*

② **sight** /saɪt/ *noun* **1.** one of the five senses, being able to see ○ *My grandfather's sight isn't very good any more.* **2.** the fact of being able to see something ○ *He can't stand the sight of blood.* ○ *We caught sight of an eagle up in the mountains.* ○ *She kept waving until the car disappeared from sight.* ○ *The fog cleared and the mountains came into sight.* ○ *They waved until the boat was out of sight.* **3.** something, especially something famous, which you ought to see ○ *They went off to see the sights of Beijing.* ◇ **at first sight** when you see something for the first time ○ *At first sight I thought he was wearing a wig.*

sighted /ˈsaɪtɪd/ *adj* able to see

sighting /ˈsaɪtɪŋ/ *noun* an occasion when you see someone or something

sightseeing /ˈsaɪtsiːɪŋ/ *noun* visiting the sights of a town as a tourist

① **sign** /saɪn/ *noun* **1.** a movement of the hand which means something ○ *He made a sign to us to sit down.* **2.** something such as a drawing or a notice which advertises something ○ *The shop has a big sign outside it saying 'for sale'.* ○ *A 'no smoking' sign hung on the wall.* **3.** something which shows that something is happening or has happened [~of/~that] ○ *There is no sign of the rain stopping.* ○ *We're waiting for signs that the economy is improving.* ○ *He should have arrived by now, but there's no sign of him.* **4.** a printed character ○ *the pound sign (£)* ○ *the dollar sign ($)* ○ *the hash sign (£)* ■ *verb* (**signs, signing, signed**) to write your name in a special way on a document to show that you have written it or that you have approved it [~for] ○ *Who signed for the parcel?* ○ *Sign on the dotted line, please.* ○ *The letter is signed by the managing director.*

sign on *phrasal verb* **1.** to start work ○ *He signed on and started work immediately.* **2.** to start drawing unemployment benefit ○ *She signed on after losing her job.*

② **signal** /ˈsɪgn(ə)l/ *noun* **1.** a sign or movement which tells someone to do something [~for] ○ *I'll give you a signal to start singing.* ○ *This was the signal for the army to advance.* **2.** a device used to tell someone to do something ○ *The signal was at red so the train had to stop.* ■ *verb* (**signals, signalling, signalled**) to make signs to tell someone to do something [~that] ○ *The driver signalled that he was turning right.* ○ *She signalled to me that we were running out of time.*

signatory /ˈsɪgnət(ə)ri/ (*plural* **signatories**) *noun* a person who signs a contract

③ **signature** /ˈsɪgnɪtʃə/ *noun* a name written in a special way by someone to show that a document has been authorised or accepted [~of] ○ *We need the signatures of two members.* ○ *He found a pile of cheques on his desk waiting for his signature.*

② **significance** /sɪgˈnɪfɪkəns/ *noun* **1.** meaning ○ *What is the significance of your logo of a ship?* **2.** importance ○ *We didn't understand the significance of this sudden change of temperature.* □ **of great significance** very important ○ *The contents of the letter were of great significance.*

① **significant** /sɪgˈnɪfɪkənt/ *adj* important or noticeable ○ *It is highly significant that everyone else was asked to the meet-*

ing, but not the finance director. ○ *There has been a significant improvement in his condition.*

③ **signify** /ˈsɪgnɪfaɪ/ (**signifies, signifying, signified**) *verb* **1.** to mean ○ *The letter seems to signify that they have accepted our terms.* **2.** to be important ○ *It doesn't signify in the least.*

③ **signing** /ˈsaɪnɪŋ/ *noun* **1.** the action of putting your signature on a document ○ *The signing of the peace treaty took place in the Palace of Versailles.* **2.** a footballer who has just moved to a new club ○ *The only goal was by their new signing.*

sign language /ˈsaɪn ˌlæŋgwɪdʒ/ *noun* signs made with the hands and fingers, used for communicating by people who are not able to hear or speak very well

signpost /ˈsaɪnpəʊst/ *noun* a post with signs showing directions to places ○ *You should have turned right at that last signpost.* ○ *The signpost said it was 20 miles to Bristol.* ■ *verb* (**signposts, signposting, signposted**) to put signposts along a road to show directions ○ *The way to the harbour is clearly signposted.*

② **silence** /ˈsaɪləns/ *noun* a situation which is quiet, without any noise ○ *I love the silence of the countryside at night.* ○ *The crowds waited in silence.* ○ *There was a sudden silence as she came in.*

③ **silent** /ˈsaɪlənt/ *adj* not talking or making any noise ○ *He kept silent for the whole meeting.* ○ *This new washing machine is almost silent.* ○ *They showed some old silent films.*

silhouette /ˌsɪluˈet/ *noun* a black shape of a person or thing against a light background ○ *We could see two silhouettes in the background, but couldn't make out who they were.*

silicon /ˈsɪlɪkən/ *noun* a chemical element which is used in the electronics industry because of its semiconductor properties

silicon chip /ˈsɪlɪkən tʃɪp/ *noun* a small piece of silicon able to store data, used in a computer

③ **silk** /sɪlk/ *noun* cloth made from fibres produced by insects ○ *She was wearing a beautiful silk scarf.* ○ *I bought some blue silk to make a dress.*

sill /sɪl/ *noun* a flat shelf below a window, either inside or outside

③ **silly** /ˈsɪli/ (**sillier, silliest**) *adj* stupid in an annoying way ○ *Don't be silly – you can't go to the party dressed like that!* ○ *She asked a lot of silly questions.* ○ *Of all the silly newspaper articles that must be the silliest.*

silo /ˈsaɪləʊ/ (*plural* **silos**) *noun* **1.** a large container for storing crops such as grain ○ *They are building huge grain silos near the port.* ○ *The hay is stored in silos until it is needed.* **2.** a deep hole in the ground in which missiles are kept ○ *The missiles were taken out of their silos and destroyed.*

silt /sɪlt/ *noun* soft mud which settles at the bottom of water ○ *The silt was several inches deep in places.*

③ **silver** /ˈsɪlvə/ *noun* **1.** a precious grey metal often used for making jewellery ○ *Gold is worth more than silver.* ○ *How much is an ounce of silver worth?* **2.** a shiny grey colour, like silver ■ *adj* of a shiny grey colour, like silver ○ *The car has been resprayed with silver paint.* ○ *She wore silver sandals to match her handbag.*

silver medal /ˌsɪlvə ˈmed(ə)l/ *noun* the prize given to someone who finishes in second place in a race or competition

silverware /ˈsɪlvəˌweə/ *noun* silver objects, especially things such as knives and forks

silver wedding /ˌsɪlvə ˈwedɪŋ/ *noun* an anniversary of 25 years of marriage

SIM card /ˈsɪm ˌkɑːd/ *noun* a special type of plastic card put into a mobile phone, which contains the personal information relating to the person who owns the phone, including things such as their PIN number or stored phone numbers

① **similar** /ˈsɪmɪlə/ *adj* very much like someone or something but not exactly the same ○ *The two cars are very similar in appearance.* ○ *Our situation is rather similar to yours.*

② **similarity** /ˌsɪmɪˈlærɪti/ (*plural* **similarities**) *noun* being similar [~to/~between] ○ *He bears an astonishing similarity to the Prince of Wales.* ○ *There is no similarity whatsoever between the two cases.* ○ *The two children are fair with blue eyes, but the similarity stops there.*

③ **similarly** /ˈsɪmɪləli/ *adv* in a similar way ○ *All these infections must be treated similarly.* ○ *He always writes a nice thank you letter, and similarly so does his sister.*

simile /ˈsɪmɪli/ *noun* a comparison of one thing to another, using 'like' or 'as', e.g. 'as flat as a pancake.' Compare **metaphor**

simmer /ˈsɪmə/ (**simmers, simmering, simmered**) *verb* to cook by boiling gently ○ *We left the soup to simmer gently.*

simmer down *phrasal verb* to become calmer after being very annoyed

① **simple** /ˈsɪmpəl/ *adj* **1.** easy to do or understand ○ *The machine is very simple to use.* **2.** not unusual, special or complicated ○ *They had a simple meal of bread and soup.* ○ *It's a very simple pattern of lines and squares.* (NOTE: **simpler – simplest**)

③ **simplicity** /sɪmˈplɪsɪti/ *noun* the quality of being simple

③ **simplify** /ˈsɪmplɪfaɪ/ (**simplifies, simplifying, simplified**) *verb* to make something simple

simplistic /sɪmˈplɪstɪk/ *adj* too simple, so simple as to seem foolish

① **simply** /ˈsɪmpli/ *adv* **1.** in a simple way ○ *He described very simply how the accident had happened.* ○ *She always dresses very simply.* **2.** only ○ *He did it simply to annoy everyone.* ○ *She gave a new look to the room simply by painting one wall red.* **3.** used for emphasis ○ *Your garden is simply beautiful.* ○ *It's simply terrible – what shall we do?*

simulate /ˈsɪmjʊleɪt/ (**simulates, simulating, simulated**) *verb* to copy the way something behaves, or the way something happens

③ **simulation** /ˌsɪmjʊˈleɪʃ(ə)n/ *noun* an operation in which a computer is made to copy a real life situation or a machine, showing how something works or will work in the future

simulator /ˈsɪmjʊleɪtə/ *noun* a piece of equipment that simulates something else

simultaneous /ˌsɪm(ə)lˈteɪniəs/ *adj* happening at the same time as something else

② **sin** /sɪn/ *noun* **1.** an evil action which goes against the rules of a religion ○ *Greed is one of the seven deadly sins.* **2.** something bad ○ *It would be a sin to waste all that meat.* ■ *verb* (**sins, sinning, sinned**) to commit a sin, to do something evil ○ *The priest told him he had sinned.*

① **since** /sɪns/ *prep* during the period after ○ *She's been here since Monday.* ○ *We've been working non-stop since four o'clock – can't we have a rest?* ■ *conj* **1.** during the period after ○ *He has had trouble borrowing money ever since he was rude to the bank manager.* ○ *Since we got to the hotel, it has rained every day.* **2.** because ○ *Since he's ill, you can't ask him to help you.* ○ *Since it's such a fine day, let's go for a walk.* ■ *adv* during the period until now ○ *She phoned on Sunday and we haven't heard from her since.* ○ *He left England in 1990 and has lived abroad ever since.*

③ **sincere** /sɪnˈsɪə/ *adj* very honest and real, not false or pretended

③ **sincerely** /sɪnˈsɪəli/ *adv* honestly or really ◇ **Yours sincerely, Sincerely yours** words used as an ending to a letter addressed to a named person

sincerity /sɪnˈserɪti/ *noun* honesty

① **sing** /sɪŋ/ (**sings, singing, sang, sung**) *verb* to make music with your voice ○ *She was singing as she worked.* ○ *Please sing another song.* ○ *The birds were singing in the garden.*

singe /sɪndʒ/ (**singes, singeing, singed**) *verb* to burn the outside of something

③ **singer** /ˈsɪŋə/ *noun* a person who sings

① **single** /ˈsɪŋg(ə)l/ *adj* **1.** one alone ○ *He handed her a single sheet of paper.* ○ *There wasn't a single person I knew at the party.* ○ *The single most important fact about him is that he has no money.* **2.** for one person only ○ *Have you got a single room for two nights, please?* ○ *We prefer two single beds to a double bed.* **3.** not married ○ *She's twenty-nine and still single.* ○ *Are there any single men on the course?*

single out *phrasal verb* to notice or choose one person or thing among several

single currency /ˌsɪŋg(ə)l ˈkʌrənsi/ *noun* one system of money which is shared by several countries

single-handed /ˌsɪŋg(ə)l ˈhændɪd/ *adj, adv* all by yourself ○ *a single-handed yacht race* ○ *He sailed single-handed round the world.* ○ *I can't do all this work single-handed.*

single-minded /ˌsɪŋg(ə)l ˈmaɪndɪd/ *adj* thinking only of one thing

single parent /ˌsɪŋg(ə)l ˈpeərənt/ *noun* one parent who is bringing up a child or children alone

singly /ˈsɪŋgli/ *adv* one by one

singular /ˈsɪŋgjʊlə/ *adj* showing that there is only one thing or person ○ *'She' is a singular pronoun.*

singularly /ˈsɪŋgjʊləli/ *adv* **1.** strangely **2.** particularly

sinister /ˈsɪnɪstə/ *adj* which looks evil, which suggests that something bad will happen

② **sink** /sɪŋk/ *noun* a fixed container for water in which you wash things such as dishes in a kitchen ○ *The sink was piled high with dirty dishes.* ○ *He was washing his hands at the kitchen sink.* ■ *verb* (**sinks, sinking, sank, sunk**) **1.** to go down to the bottom of something such as water or mud

○ *The ferry sank in 30m of water.* **2.** to fall suddenly [~to] ○ *House prices have sunk to an all-time low.* ○ *She was so upset that she just sank into an armchair and closed her eyes.* ○ *My heart sank when I heard the news.*

sink in *phrasal verb* to become fixed in the mind

sinking feeling /ˈsɪŋkɪŋ ˌfiːlɪŋ/ *noun* a sudden feeling of disappointment you get when you realise that something has gone wrong

sinner /ˈsɪnə/ *noun* someone who does something that is morally wrong

sinus /ˈsaɪnəs/ *noun* an empty space inside the body, especially the spaces inside your head behind the cheekbone and nose

sip /sɪp/ *noun* the act of drinking a small amount ○ *She took a sip of water, and went on with her speech.* ■ *verb* (**sips, sipping, sipped**) to drink something taking only a small amount at a time ○ *The girl was sipping her drink quietly.*

siphon /ˈsaɪf(ə)n/ (**siphons, siphoning, siphoned**), **syphon** (**syphons**) *verb* to remove liquid by using a bent tube to direct it to another place ○ *Petrol had been siphoned from the tanks of cars parked in the car park.*

③ **sir** /sɜː/ *noun* **1.** a polite way of speaking to a man, e.g. a man who is a customer in a shop (*usually used by someone serving in a shop or restaurant*) ○ *Would you like a drink with your lunch, sir?* ○ *Please come this way, sir.* **2.** the title given to a knight ◇ **Dear Sir** a polite way of beginning a letter to a man you do not know

siren /ˈsaɪrən/ *noun* a piece of equipment which makes a loud warning signal

① **sister** /ˈsɪstə/ *noun* **1.** a girl or woman who has the same father and mother as someone else ○ *His three sisters all look alike.* ○ *My younger sister Louise works in a bank.* ○ *Do you have any sisters?* **2.** a senior female nurse in charge of a ward ○ *The sister told me my son was getting better.* (NOTE: The male equivalent is **charge nurse**.)

sister-in-law /ˈsɪstər ɪn lɔː/ (*plural* **sisters-in-law**) *noun* **1.** the wife of your brother **2.** the sister of your husband or wife ○ *My sister-in-law is always telling us funny stories about things my husband did when he was a little boy.*

sisterly /ˈsɪstəli/ *adj, adv* relating to or characteristic of a sister, especially in a kind or caring way

① **sit** /sɪt/ (**sits, sitting, sat**) *verb* **1.** to be resting with your bottom on something ○ *Mother was sitting in bed reading.* ○ *There were no seats left, so they had to sit on the floor.* **2.** (*of a bird*) to rest ○ *The robin always comes and sits on the fence when I'm digging.*

sit back *phrasal verb* **1.** to rest your back against the back of a chair when sitting ○ *Just sit back and enjoy the film.* **2.** to do nothing ○ *He just sat back and watched everyone else do the work.*

sit down *phrasal verb* to sit on a seat

sit on *phrasal verb* **1.** to be a member of a committee ○ *She sat on the local choral society committee for fifteen years.* **2.** to do nothing about something that should have been dealt with ○ *They sat on the report for three months.*

sit up *phrasal verb* **1.** to sit with your back straight ○ *Sit up straight!* **2.** to move from a lying to a sitting position ○ *He's too weak to sit up.* ○ *He sat up in bed to eat his breakfast.* **3.** to delay going to bed or to go to bed later than usual ○ *We sat up playing cards until 2 a.m.*

sitcom /ˈsɪtkɒm/ *noun* a TV comedy series which always takes place in the same place, with the same characters, each week (*informal*) (NOTE: short for **situation comedy**)

② **site** /saɪt/ *noun* **1.** a place where something is or will be [~for] ○ *a building site* ○ *This is the site for the new factory.* **2.** a place where something happened, where something once existed ○ *This was the site of the Battle of Hastings in 1066.*

sitter /ˈsɪtə/ *noun* **1.** a person who looks after children in a house, while their parents are out ○ *We won't be able to go to the cinema because I can't find a sitter.* **2.** a person who poses, while someone paints or photographs him or her ○ *The sitter was his mother.*

③ **sitting** /ˈsɪtɪŋ/ *noun* a time when a group of people eat together ○ *Take your seats for the second sitting.*

③ **sitting room** /ˈsɪtɪŋ ruːm/ *noun* a comfortable room in a house for sitting in

① **situation** /ˌsɪtʃuˈeɪʃ(ə)n/ *noun* **1.** the position which someone or something is in because of things which have happened ○ *What's your opinion of the company's present situation?* ○ *I wonder how she got herself into this situation?* **2.** a place where something is ○ *The hotel is in a very pleasant situation by the sea.*

① **six** /sɪks/ *noun* the number 6

① **sixteen** /ˌsɪks'tiːn/ *noun* the number 16

① **sixteenth** /sɪks'tiːnθ/ *adj* relating to number 16 in a series ■ *noun* number 16 in a series

① **sixth** /sɪksθ/ *adj* relating to number 6 in a series ■ *noun* **1.** number 6 in a series **2.** one part of six equal parts ○ *Ten minutes is a sixth of an hour.*

sixth form /'sɪksθ fɔːm/ *noun* the final two years in a secondary school, with students between 16 and 18 years old

sixtieth /'sɪkstɪəθ/ *adj* relating to number 60 in a series ■ *noun* number 60 in a series

① **sixty** /'sɪksti/ *noun* the number 60 □ **sixties** the numbers between 60 and 69

① **size** /saɪz/ *noun* the measurements of something, how big something is, or how many there are of something ○ *The size of the staff has doubled in the last two years.* ○ *Their garage is about the same size as our house.* ○ *The school has an Olympic size swimming pool.* ○ *He takes size ten in shoes.*

size up *phrasal verb* to judge someone's qualities ○ *She quickly sized him up.*

sizeable /'saɪzəb(ə)l/ *adj* quite big

sizzle /'sɪz(ə)l/ (**sizzles, sizzling, sizzled**) *verb* to make a sound like food cooking in oil or fat

sizzling /'sɪzlɪŋ/ *adj* very hot (*informal*)

③ **skate** /skeɪt/ *noun* a boot with a blade attached to the bottom which you wear for sliding over ice ○ *a pair of skates* ■ *verb* (**skates, skating, skated**) to move wearing skates ○ *She skated across the frozen lake.*

skateboard /'skeɪtbɔːd/ *noun* a board with two pairs of wheels underneath, which you stand on to move about

skating rink /'skeɪtɪŋ rɪŋk/ *noun* a special area for skating, or for playing games such as hockey on skates

skeletal /'skelɪt(ə)l/ *adj* very thin, like a skeleton

③ **skeleton** /'skelɪt(ə)n/ *noun* all the bones which make up a body ○ *They found the skeleton of a rabbit in the garden shed.* ○ *He demonstrated joints using the skeleton in the biology lab.* ◇ **the skeleton in the cupboard** an embarrassing secret that a family is trying to keep hidden

skeptical /'skeptɪk(ə)l/ *adj* US spelling of **sceptical**

③ **sketch** /sketʃ/ *noun* a rough quick drawing ○ *He made a sketch of the church.* ■ *verb* (**sketches, sketching, sketched**) to make a rough quick drawing of something ○ *She was sketching the old church.* ○ *He sketched out his plan on the back of an envelope.*

sketchbook /'sketʃbʊk/, **sketchpad** *noun* a book of drawing paper for sketching

sketchy /'sketʃi/ (**sketchier, sketchiest**) *adj* not complete, not full

skewed /skjuːd/ *adj* unbalanced

skewer /'skjuːə/ *noun* a long thin metal or wooden rod for putting through pieces of meat, fish or vegetables when cooking or grilling ○ *She put some pieces of chicken and onion on the skewer.*

ski /skiː/ *noun* (*plural* **skis**) one of two long flat objects which are attached to your boots for sliding over snow ○ *We always hire skis when we get to the ski resort.* ○ *Someone stole my new pair of skis.* ■ *verb* (**skis, skiing, skied** or **ski'd**) to travel on skis ○ *The mountain rescue team had to ski to the site of the avalanche.* ○ *We skied down to the bottom of the slope without falling.* ○ *She broke her arm skiing.*

skid /skɪd/ (**skids, skidding, skidded**) *verb* to slide sideways in a vehicle suddenly because the wheels do not grip the surface ○ *He skidded to a halt.* ○ *If you brake too hard on ice you're likely to skid.*

skier /'skiːə/ *noun* a person who goes skiing

③ **skiing** /'skiːɪŋ/ *noun* the sport of sliding on skis

skilful /'skɪlf(ə)l/ *adj* showing a lot of skill

skilfully /'skɪlfʊli/ *adv* in a skilful way ○ *It was difficult but he did it very skilfully.*

① **skill** /skɪl/ *noun* the ability to do something well ○ *Portrait painting needs a lot of skill.* ○ *This job will help you develop management skills.* ○ *He's a craftsman of great skill.*

① **skilled** /skɪld/ *adj* **1.** able to do something well, using a particular skill ○ *She's a skilled therapist.* ○ *We need skilled programmers.* **2.** needing a particular skill ○ *nursing and other skilled professions*

skillful /'skɪlf(ə)l/ *adj* US spelling of **skilful**

skim /skɪm/ (**skims, skimming, skimmed**) *verb* **1.** to remove things floating on a liquid **2.** to move quickly over the surface of something

skimmed milk /skɪmd 'mɪlk/ *noun* milk from which most of the fat has been removed

skimpy /ˈskɪmpi/ (**skimpier, skimpiest**) *adj* small, not big enough

② **skin** /skɪn/ *noun* **1.** the outer surface of the body ○ *The baby's skin is very smooth.* **2.** the outer surface of a fruit or vegetable ○ *This orange has a very thick skin.* ○ *You can cook these new potatoes with their skins on.*

skinhead /ˈskɪnhed/ *noun* a young man with very short hair or a shaved head, often considered as behaving in an aggressive manner

③ **skinny** /ˈskɪni/ (**skinnier, skinniest**) *adj* too thin to be attractive ○ *A tall skinny guy walked in.* ○ *She has very skinny legs.*

③ **skip** /skɪp/ (**skips, skipping, skipped**) *verb* **1.** to run along partly hopping and partly jumping ○ *The children skipped happily down the lane.* **2.** to jump over a rope which you turn over your head ○ *Some girls were skipping in the playground.* **3.** to miss part of something (*informal*) ○ *She skipped the middle chapters and went on to read the end of the story.* ○ *I'm not hungry, I'll skip the pudding.*

③ **skipper** /ˈskɪpə/ *noun* **1.** the captain of a ship ○ *We reported to the skipper that there was water in the ship's engine room.* **2.** the captain of a team ○ *He's the youngest skipper ever of the national rugby team.*

skirmish /ˈskɜːmɪʃ/ *noun* a minor fight between opposite sides ○ *There were several skirmishes between rival fans, but no serious fighting.*

② **skirt** /skɜːt/ *noun* a piece of clothing worn by women over the lower part of the body from the waist down ○ *She started wearing jeans to work, but was told to wear a skirt.*

ski slope /ˈskiː sləʊp/ *noun* a specially prepared and marked slope for skiing down a mountain

skulk /skʌlk/ (**skulks, skulking, skulked**) *verb* to creep about mysteriously because you are planning something wrong

③ **skull** /skʌl/ *noun* the bones which are joined together to form the head

① **sky** /skaɪ/ *noun* a space above the earth which is blue during the day and where the moon and stars appear at night ○ *What makes the sky blue?* ○ *It's going to be a beautiful day – there's not a cloud in the sky.* ○ *The wind carried the glider high up into the sky.*

skydiving /ˈskaɪˌdaɪvɪŋ/ *noun* the sport of jumping out of a plane with a parachute

skylight /ˈskaɪlaɪt/ *noun* a window in a roof or ceiling

skyline /ˈskaɪlaɪn/ *noun* the shape of buildings seen against the sky

skyscraper /ˈskaɪskreɪpə/ *noun* a very tall building

slab /slæb/ *noun* a flat square or rectangular block of stone or concrete

slack /slæk/ *adj* **1.** not pulled tight or not fitting tightly ○ *The wind had dropped and the sails were slack.* ○ *The ropes are slack – pull on them to make them tight.* **2.** not busy ○ *Business is slack at the end of the week.* ○ *January is always a slack period for us.*

slacken /ˈslækən/ (**slackens, slackening, slackened**) *verb* **1.** to make something looser **2.** *also* **slacken off** to become slower or less busy ○ *You've been working too hard – you need to slacken off* ○ *Trade slackened during January.*

slag /slæg/ *noun* the waste material left after metal has been extracted from ore, or after coal has been mined

slain /sleɪn/ past participle of **slay**

slalom /ˈslɑːləm/ *noun* a type of race where you have to zigzag fast between a series of posts

slam /slæm/ (**slams, slamming, slammed**) *verb* **1.** to bang a door shut ○ *When he saw me, he slammed the door in my face.* **2.** to shut with a bang ○ *The door slammed and I was locked out.* **3.** to move or hit something with great force ○ *The car slammed into a tree.* ○ *He slammed his fist on the desk.*

③ **slander** /ˈslɑːndə/ *noun* an untrue spoken statement which damages a person's reputation ○ *to sue somebody for slander* ○ *What she said about me is slander.*

③ **slang** /slæŋ/ *noun* popular words or phrases used by certain groups of people, but which are not used in formal situations ○ *Don't use slang in your essay.* ○ *Slang expressions are sometimes difficult to understand.*

slant /slɑːnt/ *noun* a slope ○ *The garden is on a slant, which makes cutting the lawn difficult.* ■ *verb* (**slants, slanting, slanted**) to slope ○ *The path slants down the side of the hill.* ○ *The picture seems to be slanting to the right.*

slanted /ˈslɑːntɪd/ *adj* **1.** sloping **2.** biased

slap /slæp/ *noun* a blow given with your hand flat ○ *She gave him a slap in the face.* ■ *verb* (**slaps, slapping, slapped**) **1.** to hit someone or something with your hand flat ○ *She slapped his face.* **2.** to tap someone or something as a friendly gesture ○ *They all* *slapped him on the back to congratulate him.* ◇ **a slap on the wrist** a small punishment, a slight criticism ○ *The department had a slap on the wrist from the inspectors, but nothing serious.*

slapstick /ˈslæpstɪk/ *noun* a rough comedy which involves such things as knocking people over and throwing water over them

③ **slash** /slæʃ/ (**slashes, slashing, slashed**) *verb* to make a long cut in something with a knife, often violently ○ *He slashed the painting with a kitchen knife.*

slat /slæt/ *noun* a thin flat piece of wood

slate /sleɪt/ *noun* a thin piece of this stone used to cover a roof ○ *The slates were already piled up on the roof ready for fixing.*

slaughter /ˈslɔːtə/ *noun* **1.** the killing of many people ○ *the terrible slaughter of innocent people in the riots* **2.** the killing of animals ○ *These lambs will be ready for slaughter in a week or so.* ■ *verb* (**slaughters, slaughtering, slaughtered**) **1.** to kill many people or animals at the same time ○ *Thousands of civilians were slaughtered by the advancing army.* **2.** to kill animals for their meat

slaughterhouse /ˈslɔːtəhaʊs/ *noun* a place where animals are killed for meat (*dated*)

③ **slave** /sleɪv/ *noun* a person who belongs to someone legally and works for him or her without pay ■ *verb* (**slaves, slaving, slaved**) *also* **slave away** to work hard (*informal*)

slavery /ˈsleɪvəri/ *noun* **1.** the state of being a slave ○ *Girls were kidnapped and sold into slavery.* **2.** the buying and selling of slaves ○ *In Britain, slavery was abolished in the 19th century.*

slay /sleɪ/ (**slays, slaying, slew, slain**) *verb* to kill someone or something (*formal or literary*) (NOTE: Do not confuse with **sleigh**.)

sleaze /sliːz/ *noun* behaviour which is disreputable

sleazy /ˈsliːzi/ (**sleazier, sleaziest**) *adj* dirty or disreputable

sled /sled/ *noun* same as **sledge**

sledge /sledʒ/ *noun* a small vehicle with long pieces of wood or metal underneath, for sliding fast over snow ○ *Children dragged their sledges to the top of the snow-covered hill.* ■ *verb* (**sledges, sledging, sledged**) to go on a sledge; to play at sliding on the snow on a sledge ○ *The children were sledging down the hill.*

sleek /sliːk/ *adj* smooth and shiny ○ *the cat's sleek coat* ○ *After dinner we walked across the sleek lawns to the river.*

① **sleep** /sliːp/ (**sleeps, sleeping, slept**) *verb* to rest with your eyes closed not knowing what is happening around you ○ *She never sleeps for more than six hours each night.* ○ *He slept through the whole of the TV news.* ○ *Don't make any noise – Daddy's trying to sleep.*

sleep around *phrasal verb* to have sexual intercourse with various people (*informal*)

sleep in *phrasal verb* to sleep later than usual in the morning

sleep off *phrasal verb* to get rid of an illness by sleeping

sleeper /ˈsliːpə/ *noun* **1.** a person who sleeps ○ *Electrodes are attached to sleepers to record brain waves.* □ **he's a heavy sleeper** he always sleeps deeply **2.** a carriage on a train where passengers sleep on long journeys ○ *The last two carriages of the train were sleepers.* **3.** an overnight train with sleeping cars ○ *The Edinburgh sleeper leaves at 11.30 p.m.*

sleeping bag /ˈsliːpɪŋ bæg/ *noun* a comfortable warm bag for sleeping in, often used by campers

sleepover /ˈsliːpˌəʊvə/ *noun* a child's party involving an overnight stay at somebody else's house

sleepwalking /ˈsliːpwɔːkɪŋ/ *noun* getting up and walking about even though you are still asleep

② **sleepy** /ˈsliːpi/ *adj* feeling ready to go to sleep ○ *The children had a busy day – they were very sleepy by 8 o'clock.* ○ *The injection will make you feel sleepy.* ○ *If you feel sleepy, don't try to drive the car.* ○ *Sitting in front of the TV made him sleepier and sleepier.*

sleet /sliːt/ *noun* snow mixed with rain ○ *The temperature fell and the rain turned to sleet.* (NOTE: + **sleet** *v*)

② **sleeve** /sliːv/ *noun* the part of a piece of clothing which covers your arm ○ *The sleeves on this shirt are too long.* ○ *He was wearing a blue shirt with short sleeves.*

sleight of hand /ˌslaɪt əv ˈhænd/ *noun* the quick movements of a conjurer when performing a card trick

slender /ˈslendə/ *adj* long and thin, or tall and slim ○ *slender fingers* ○ *a slender flower stem* ○ *a girl with a slender figure*

③ **slept** /slept/ past tense and past participle of **sleep**

slew /sluː/ past tense of **slay**

③ **slice** /slaɪs/ *noun* a thin piece cut off something to eat ○ *Can you cut some more slices of bread?* ○ *Have a slice of chocolate cake.* ■ *verb* (**slices, slicing, sliced**) **1.** to cut something into thin pieces ○ *Would you slice some more bread?* **2.** to cut or move through something easily [~through/~into] ○ *The blade sliced through the thick layers.* ○ *The car sliced through the fence and overturned.*

③ **slide** /slaɪd/ *noun* **1.** a slippery metal or plastic structure for children to slide down ○ *There are swings and a slide in the local playground.* **2.** a small piece of film which can be projected onto a screen ○ *She showed us the slides of her last trip.* ○ *There will be a slide show in the village hall.* ■ *verb* (**slides, sliding, slid**) to move smoothly over a slippery surface ○ *The drawer slides in and out easily.* ○ *The car slid to a stop.* ○ *The children were sliding on the ice when it broke.*

② **slight** /slaɪt/ *adj* **1.** not very big or noticeable ○ *There was only a slight difference between the two colours.* ○ *I've noticed a slight improvement in the students' results this month.* **2.** (*of people*) small and thin ○ *Their daughter's a slight young girl.* ◇ **not (in) the slightest** not in any way ○ *'Are you worried about passing your exam?' 'Not in the slightest!'* ○ *She wasn't (in) the slightest bit nervous.*

① **slightly** /ˈslaɪtli/ *adv* to only a small extent ○ *He was only slightly hurt in the car crash.* ○ *The American bank is offering a slightly better interest rate.* ○ *I only know him slightly.*

② **slim** /slɪm/ *adj* (**slimmer, slimmest**) with a body that is thin in an attractive way ○ *How do you manage to stay so slim?* ○ *She looks slimmer in that dress.* ■ *verb* (**slims, slimming, slimmed**) to eat less food, or eat only special foods, in order to become thin ○ *She started slimming before her summer holidays.*

slime /slaɪm/ *noun* a slippery substance, which covers surfaces

slimming /ˈslɪmɪŋ/ *noun* the process of trying to lose weight, especially by eating less

slimy /ˈslaɪmi/ *adj* covered with something that is unpleasant and slippery ○ *Watch out, the rocks are slimy.* ○ *What's this slimy mess at the bottom of the fridge?*

sling /slɪŋ/ *noun* an apparatus made of ropes and pulleys for lifting and carrying goods ○ *They arranged a sling to lift the piano into the upstairs flat.* ■ *verb* (**slings, slinging, slung**) to throw ○ *Little boys were slinging snowballs at passing cars.* ○ *He slung his briefcase into the back of the car.*

slink /slɪŋk/ (**slinks, slinking, slunk**) *verb* to creep about in order to avoid being noticed

② **slip** /slɪp/ *verb* (**slips, slipping, slipped**) **1.** to push something without being seen ○ *The postman slipped the letters through the letter box.* ○ *He slipped the keys into his pocket.* **2.** to go quickly ○ *I'll just slip down to the post office with this letter.* ■ *noun* a small, often careless mistake ○ *Don't worry about that. It was just a slip.* ○ *He made a few slips in his calculations.*

slip up *phrasal verb* to make a silly mistake (*informal*)

slipper /ˈslɪpə/ *noun* a soft indoor shoe

slippers /ˈslɪpəz/ *noun* light comfortable shoes worn indoors ○ *He ran out into the street in his dressing gown and slippers.* ○ *They put their slippers on when they come into the house.*

slippery /ˈslɪp(ə)ri/ *adj* so smooth that one can easily slip and fall

slippery slope /ˈslɪpəri sləʊp/ *noun* a dangerous situation that can get very bad if it is not stopped

slip road /ˈslɪp rəʊd/ *noun* a small road which leads to or from a motorway

slit /slɪt/ *noun* a long cut or narrow opening ○ *She peeped through a slit in the curtains.*

slither /ˈslɪðə/ (**slithers, slithering, slithered**) *verb* **1.** to slide about in various directions **2.** to move over a surface like a snake

sliver /ˈslɪvə/ *noun* a long thin piece

slob /slɒb/ *noun* a lazy, dirty person

slobber /ˈslɒbə/ (**slobbers, slobbering, slobbered**) *verb* to let saliva come out of your mouth

slog /slɒg/ *noun* a difficult job ○ *Building the wall was quite a slog.* ○ *It's a hard slog from here to the top of the mountain.* ■ *verb* (**slogs, slogging, slogged**) to walk with difficulty ○ *They had to slog through miles of jungle to get to the temple.*

slogan /ˈsləʊgən/ *noun* a phrase which is easy to remember and is used in publicity for a product or for a political party

slop /slɒp/ (**slops, slopping, slopped**) *verb* (*of liquid*) to spill

③ **slope** /sləʊp/ *noun* a surface or piece of ground that has one end higher than the other ○ *The land rises in a gentle slope to* *the church.* ○ *They stopped halfway down the slope.* ■ *verb* (**slopes, sloping, sloped**) to have one end higher than the other ○ *The road slopes down to the sea.*

sloppy /ˈslɒpi/ (**sloppier, sloppiest**) *adj* **1.** untidy ○ *He's such a sloppy eater, he's made a mess all over his pullover.* **2.** loose and untidy ○ *She was wearing a sloppy jumper.* **3.** badly done ○ *They said her work was sloppy and had to be done again.* **4.** stupidly sentimental ○ *She's a sloppy old dog, she's no good at guarding.* ○ *What a sloppy film!*

slosh /slɒʃ/ (**sloshes, sloshing, sloshed**) *verb* **1.** to splash ○ *We sloshed through the mud to get to the cottage.* **2.** to hit someone or something (*informal*) ○ *She suddenly sloshed him with her umbrella.*

slot /slɒt/ *noun* a long thin hole ○ *A coin has got stuck in the slot of the parking meter.* ○ *Put the system disk into the slot on the front of your computer.*

slot machine /ˈslɒt məˌʃiːn/ *noun* **1.** a machine for gambling **2.** a machine which provides something such as drinks, food or cigarettes when you put a coin into a slot

slouch /slaʊtʃ/ (**slouches, slouching, slouched**) *verb* to stand, sit or walk in a bad position, with bent shoulders

① **slow** /sləʊ/ *adj* **1.** needing a long time to do something ○ *Luckily, the car was only going at a slow speed.* ○ *She is the slowest walker of the group.* ○ *The company is very slow at answering my letters.* ○ *Sales got off to a slow start but picked up later.* **2.** showing a time which is earlier than the right time ○ *The office clock is four minutes slow.*

slow down③ *phrasal verb* **1.** to go more slowly ○ *The van had to slow down as it came to the traffic lights.* ○ *Please slow down, I can't keep up with you.* **2.** to make something go more slowly ○ *The snow slowed the traffic down on the motorway.*

slowdown /ˈsləʊdaʊn/ *noun* a slowing down of business activity

② **slowly** /ˈsləʊli/ *adv* at a slow speed ○ *Luckily, the car was going very slowly when it hit the fence.* ○ *The group walked slowly round the exhibition.* ○ *Speak more slowly so that everyone can understand.*

slow motion /ˌsləʊ ˈməʊʃ(ə)n/ *noun* showing a film at a slower speed than it was filmed at, so that the action seems to have slowed down

sludge /slʌdʒ/ *noun* **1.** soft muddy material in a liquid ○ *There's some black sludge at the bottom of the petrol tank.* **2.** the thick soft part of sewage

slug /slʌg/ *noun* a small bullet (*informal*) ○ *A slug from the rifle hit the wall above my head.*

sluggish /ˈslʌgɪʃ/ *adj* **1.** reacting slowly **2.** slow-moving ○ *a sluggish stream*

sluice /sluːs/ *noun* a gate which closes a channel for water, especially through a dam ○ *They opened the sluices to release the water behind the dam.* ■ *verb* (**sluices, sluicing, sluiced**) to wash something with lots of water ○ *You'll have to sluice out the pig sty.* ○ *She sluiced the dirty bucket under the tap.*

slum /slʌm/ *noun* a crowded, dirty district inside a large town. ◊ **shanty town**

slumber /ˈslʌmbə/ *noun* sleep (*literary*) ○ *His peaceful slumbers were rudely disturbed by the telephone.*

slump /slʌmp/ *noun* **1.** a rapid fall **2.** a period of economic collapse with high unemployment and loss of trade ■ *verb* (**slumps, slumping, slumped**) **1.** to lose value fast or reduce suddenly ○ *The pound slumped on the foreign exchange markets.* **2.** to sit or lie down clumsily or heavily ○ *He sat slumped on a chair doing his homework.* ○ *At the end of the day, she just slumped down onto the sofa.*

slung /slʌŋ/ past tense and past participle of **sling**

slur /slɜː/ *noun* an insult ○ *The report cast a slur on his integrity.* ■ *verb* (**slurs, slurring, slurred**) to speak words indistinctly ○ *You could tell he had been taking drugs by the way he slurred his words.*

slurp /slɜːp/ (**slurps, slurping, slurped**) *verb* to drink and make a noise

slush /slʌʃ/ *noun* **1.** melting snow ○ *The snow has started to melt and the roads are covered with slush.* **2.** sentimental writing (*informal*) ○ *Her latest novel is just slush.*

sly /slaɪ/ *adj* good at doing secret or slightly dishonest things

smack /smæk/ *verb* (**smacks, smacking, smacked**) to hit someone with your hand flat ■ *noun* an act of hitting someone, especially a child, with your hand flat

① **small** /smɔːl/ *adj* not large in size or amount ○ *Small cars are more economical than large ones.* ○ *The house is too big for us, so we're selling it and buying a smaller one.* ○ *She only paid a small amount for that clock.* ○ *The guidebook isn't small enough to carry in your pocket.* ○ *These trousers are already too small for him.*

small intestine /ˌsmɔːl ɪn'testɪn/ *noun* the top section of the intestines, leading down from the stomach

smallpox /'smɔːlpɒks/ *noun* formerly a very serious, usually fatal, contagious disease, with a severe rash which leaves many small scars on the skin

small-scale /'smɔːl skeɪl/ *adj* working in a small way, with few staff and not much money

small talk /'smɔːl tɔːk/ *noun* informal conversation

② **smart** /smɑːt/ *adj* **1.** having a neat appearance ○ *A smart young man asked me if he could use my mobile phone.* ○ *He looked very smart in his uniform.* **2.** intelligent ○ *It was smart of her to note the car's number plate.* ■ *verb* (**smarts, smarting, smarted**) to hurt with a burning feeling

smart card /'smɑːt kɑːd/ *noun* a credit card with a microchip, used for withdrawing money from cash machines or buying things

smarten *verb*

smash /smæʃ/ (**smashes, smashing, smashed**) *verb* **1.** to break into pieces ○ *He dropped the plate and it smashed to pieces.* **2.** to break something into pieces, often using force or violence ○ *Demonstrators smashed the windows of police cars.* **3.** to do better than the previous best performance ○ *She smashed the world record.* ○ *Six records were smashed at the Olympics.* **4.** to hit against something violently ○ *The train smashed into the car.* ○ *The crowd smashed through the railings.*

smash up *phrasal verb* to break everything in a place

smashing /'smæʃɪŋ/ *adj* very good, fantastic (*dated informal*)

smear /smɪə/ *noun* **1.** a dirty mark ○ *Waiter, there's a lipstick smear on this cup!* **2.** a small amount of something put on glass for examining under a microscope **3.** words about someone which are not true but which are meant to harm his or her reputation ○ *The report about my wife was just a dirty smear.* ■ *verb* (**smears, smearing, smeared**) **1.** to spread something roughly over a surface ○ *She smeared glue all over the piece of wood* or *she smeared the piece of wood with glue.* ○ *How did your shirt get smeared with paint?* **2.** to make dirty marks ○ *He smeared the kitchen table with his dirty fingers.* **3.** to hurt someone's reputation by saying things which are not true ○ *The report was just an attempt to smear her.*

② **smell** /smel/ *noun* **1.** one of the five senses, which you can feel through your nose ○ *Animals have a better sense of smell than humans.* **2.** something which you can sense with your nose ○ *I love the smell of coffee.* ○ *There's a smell of burning* or *there's a burning smell coming from the kitchen.* ■ *verb* (**smells, smelling, smelt** or **smelled**) **1.** to notice the smell of something ○ *Can you smell gas?* ○ *My nose is so blocked that I can"t smell.* **2.** to make a smell [~like/~of] ○ *This cheese smells like soap.* ○ *His breath smelt of garlic.* ○ *What's for dinner? – it smells very good!* **3.** to bring your nose close to something to smell it ○ *She bent down to smell the flowers.*

smelly /'smeli/ (**smellier, smelliest**) *adj* which has a nasty smell

smelt /smelt/ past tense and past participle of **smell**

① **smile** /smaɪl/ *noun* a way of showing that you are pleased, by turning your mouth up at the corners ○ *The dentist gave me a friendly smile.* ○ *She had a big smile as she told them the good news.* ■ *verb* (**smiles, smiling, smiled**) to show that you are pleased by turning your mouth up at the corners [~at] ○ *That girl has just smiled at me.* ○ *Everyone smile please – I'm taking a picture!*

smirk /smɜːk/ (**smirks, smirking, smirked**) *verb* to give an unpleasant smile that shows that you think you are superior to someone else ○ *She smirked as the other girls all heard they'd lost their jobs.*

smock /smɒk/ *noun* a long loose overall worn over clothes to protect them

smog /smɒg/ *noun* pollution of the atmosphere in towns, caused by warm damp air combined with waste gases from cars

② **smoke** /sməʊk/ *noun* a white, grey or black substance produced by something that is burning ○ *The restaurant was full of cigarette smoke.* ○ *Clouds of smoke were pouring out of the upstairs windows.* ○ *Two people died from inhaling toxic smoke.* ○ *Smoke detectors are fitted in all the rooms.* ■ *verb* (**smokes, smoking, smoked**) **1.** to produce smoke ○ *Two days after the fire, the ruins of the factory were still smoking.* **2.** to breathe in smoke from something such as a cigarette ○ *Everyone was smoking even though the signs said 'no smoking'.* ○ *She doesn't smoke much.* ○ *You shouldn't smoke if you want to play football.* ○ *I've never seen her smoking a cigar before.*

smoker /ˈsməʊkə/ *noun* a person who smokes

smokescreen /ˈsməʊkˌskriːn/ *noun* something said or done to mislead somebody

② **smoking** /ˈsməʊkɪŋ/ *noun* the action of smoking cigarettes, cigars or a pipe ◇ **'no smoking'** do not smoke here ○ *I always sit in the 'no smoking' part of the restaurant.*

② **smooth** /smuːð/ *adj* **1.** with no bumps or rough parts ○ *the smooth surface of a polished table* ○ *The baby's skin is very smooth.* ○ *Velvet has a smooth side and a rough side.* **2.** with no sudden unpleasant movements ○ *Dirt in the fuel tank can prevent the smooth running of the engine.* ○ *We had a very smooth ride.*

smoothie /ˈsmuːði/ *noun* **1.** a charming man who is good at persuading people to do what he wants **2.** a drink made with milk, fruit, yoghurt or ice cream

smoothly /ˈsmuːðli/ *adv* in a smooth way

smoothness /ˈsmuːðnəs/ *noun* the state of being smooth ○ *The fabric has all the smoothness of a baby's skin.* ○ *The smoothness of the ride makes up for the high fare.*

smother /ˈsmʌðə/ (**smothers, smothering, smothered**) *verb* **1.** to kill someone by stopping them from breathing ○ *They took the kittens and smothered them.* ○ *Never put a pillow over someone's face – you may smother them!* **2.** to cover something completely ○ *a chocolate cake simply smothered in cream* ○ *The firemen put out the fire by smothering it with foam.* **3.** to show too much love towards someone, especially your children

smoulder /ˈsməʊldə/ (**smoulders, smouldering, smouldered**) *verb* **1.** to burn slowly ○ *The incense sticks smouldered in the entrance to the temple.* **2.** to feel strong emotion but keep it hidden **3.** (*of emotions*) to be strong but hidden

SMS *noun* a system for sending text messages between mobile phones

smudge /smʌdʒ/ *noun* a dirty mark ○ *There is a smudge on the top corner of the photograph.* ○ *He had a black smudge on his cheek.* ■ *verb* (**smudges, smudging, smudged**) to make a dirty mark, e.g. by rubbing ink which is not dry ○ *Don't touch the print with your wet hands, or you'll smudge it.*

smug /smʌg/ (**smugger, smuggest**) *adj* pleased about something, especially your own achievements, in a way that is annoying

smuggle /ˈsmʌg(ə)l/ (**smuggles, smuggling, smuggled**) *verb* **1.** to take goods into a country secretly and illegally ○ *They tried to smuggle cigarettes into the country.* ○ *We had to smuggle the spare parts over the border.* **2.** to take something into or out of a place secretly and dishonestly ○ *The knives were smuggled into the prison by a someone visiting a prisoner.* ○ *We'll never know how they smuggled the letter out.* (NOTE: + **smuggling** *n*)

③ **snack** /snæk/ *noun* a light meal, or a small amount of food eaten between meals ○ *We didn't have time to stop for a proper lunch, so we just had a snack on the motorway.*

snag /snæg/ *noun* a little problem which prevents you from doing something ○ *We've run into a snag: there are no flights to the island on Sundays.* ○ *The only snag is that he's not a very good driver.*

snail /sneɪl/ *noun* a small animal which moves slowly along the ground, which has a soft body and a spiral-shaped shell on its back ◇ **at a snail's pace** extremely slowly ○ *Negotiations over the sale of the flat have been progressing at a snail's pace.*

snail mail /ˈsneɪl meɪl/ *noun* mail sent using the postal system, rather than being sent electronically as email

③ **snake** /sneɪk/ *noun* a long thin animal which has no legs and moves along the ground by wriggling ○ *Is this snake safe to handle?*

③ **snap** /snæp/ *noun* a photograph taken quickly (*informal*) ○ *She showed me an old black-and-white snap of the house.* ○ *He took a lot of snaps of his children.* ■ *adj* sudden ○ *They carried out a snap check* or *a snap inspection of the passengers' luggage.* ○ *The government called a snap election.* ■ *verb* (**snaps, snapping, snapped**) **1.** to break sharply with a dry noise ○ *The branch snapped as he fell against it.* **2.** to move or be moved with a sudden sharp noise [~at] ○ *The handle snapped off.* □ **to snap your fingers** to make a clicking noise with your middle finger and thumb ○ *They sat snapping their fingers in time to the music.* ◇ **to snap out of it** to stop being depressed (*informal*) ○ *He told her to snap out of it.*

snap up *phrasal verb* to buy quickly

snappy /ˈsnæpi/ (**snappier, snappiest**) *adj* **1.** sharp and fashionable (*dated informal*) ○ *She's wearing a very snappy* *outfit.* **2.** irritable, short-tempered ○ *He tends to be snappy towards the end of the day.*

snapshot /ˈsnæpʃɒt/ *noun* a photograph taken quickly without special equipment

snare /sneə/ *noun* a trap ○ *His offer of a well-paid job in Luxembourg was just a snare.* ■ *verb* (**snares, snaring, snared**) to catch with a snare ○ *We snared three rabbits.*

snarl /snɑːl/ *verb* (**snarls, snarling, snarled**) to growl angrily ○ *The leopard snarled as he approached its cage.* ○ *'Take your money, and get out' he snarled.* ■ *noun* an angry growl ○ *As she opened the door of the cage she heard a snarl.*

snatch /snætʃ/ (**snatches, snatching, snatched**) *verb* to grab something suddenly and quickly ○ *He came beside her on his bike and snatched her handbag.*

sneak /sniːk/ *verb* (**sneaks, sneaking, sneaked**) **1.** to go or do something quietly without being seen ○ *She sneaked into the room while he was asleep.* ○ *He sneaked the book out of the library.* **2.** to tell an adult that another child has done something wrong ■ *noun* a person who tells an adult what another child has done (*informal*) ○ *You promised not to say anything, you little sneak!*

sneak up *phrasal verb* to creep up behind someone without being noticed

sneakers /ˈsniːkəz/ *plural noun US* soft sports shoes with rubber soles ○ *She came to work in sneakers.*

sneaky /ˈsniːki/ *adj* deceitful and secret

sneer /snɪə/ *noun* an unpleasant smile ○ *He held the whip in his hand and looked at her with a sneer.* ■ *verb* (**sneers, sneering, sneered**) to give someone a sarcastic smile or to speak in a contemptuous way

③ **sneeze** /sniːz/ *noun* the uncontrolled action of blowing air suddenly out through your mouth and nose because of an irritation inside your nose ○ *Coughs and sneezes spread diseases.* ■ *verb* (**sneezes**) to make a sneeze ○ *The smell of roses makes me sneeze.* ○ *He has hayfever and can't stop sneezing.*

snide /snaɪd/ *adj* unkind, often in a clever or indirect way

sniff /snɪf/ *noun* the act of breathing in air through your nose ○ *The dog gave a sniff at the plate before licking it.* ○ *He gave a little sniff and walked out of the shop.* ■ *verb* (**sniffs, sniffing, sniffed**) to breathe in air through your nose ◇ **it's not to be sniffed at** you should not refuse it (*informal*) ○ *A free ticket with Air Canada is not to be sniffed at.*

sniffle /ˈsnɪf(ə)l/ (**sniffles, sniffling, sniffled**) *verb* to keep on sniffing because of a cold, or because you want to cry ○ *He was sniffling and sneezing, and in the end I told him to go home early.* ○ *Stop sniffling! Blow your nose!*

snigger /ˈsnɪgə/ (**sniggers, sniggering, sniggered**) *verb* to laugh quietly in an unpleasant way ○ *They sniggered as the teacher came into the room.*

snip /snɪp/ (**snips, snipping, snipped**) *verb* to cut something quickly with scissors ○ *She snipped two inches off the hem of the dress.*

sniper /ˈsnaɪpə/ *noun* a hidden soldier who shoots at the enemy (NOTE: + **snipe** *v*)

snippet /ˈsnɪpɪt/ *noun* a little bit of information

snivel /ˈsnɪv(ə)l/ (**snivels, snivelling, snivelled**) *verb* to cry or complain in an annoying way

snob /snɒb/ *noun* **1.** a person who likes people who are of a higher social class than himself or herself ○ *Don't ask him to your party, he's such a snob.* **2.** a person who thinks he or she knows much more about art or is better-educated than other people ○ *an art snob* ○ *an intellectual snob*

snobbery /ˈsnɒbəri/ *noun* the behaviour of a snob

snog /snɒg/ (**snogs, snogging, snogged**) *verb* to kiss and hug someone (*slang*)

snooker /ˈsnuːkə/ *noun* a game for two players played on a table with twenty-two balls of different colours which you hit with a long thin stick

snoop /snuːp/ (**snoops, snooping, snooped**) *verb* to investigate something or someone secretly (*informal*)

snooze /snuːz/ (**snoozes, snoozing, snoozed**) *verb* to sleep lightly for a short time (*informal*) ○ *The dog was snoozing on the rug in front of the fire.* (NOTE: + **snooze** *n*)

snore /snɔː/ *noun* a loud noise which someone who is sleeping produces in his or her nose and throat ○ *His snores kept her awake.* ■ *verb* (**snores, snoring, snored**) to make a snore ○ *I can't get to sleep because my husband snores.*

snorkel /ˈsnɔːk(ə)l/ *noun* a tube which allows an underwater swimmer to breathe in air ○ *She could still see Brian's snorkel on the surface of the water.*

snorkelling /ˈsnɔːk(ə)lɪŋ/ *noun* swimming with a snorkel (NOTE: The US spelling is **snorkeling**.)

snort /snɔːt/ (**snorts, snorting, snorted**) *verb* **1.** to make a loud noise blowing air out through the nose ○ *The horses snorted and pawed the ground.* **2.** to take a powdered drug such as cocaine by breathing them through the nose (NOTE: + **snort** *n*)

snot /snɒt/ *noun* mucus in the nose (*offensive informal*)

snotty /ˈsnɒti/ *adj* **1.** covered with mucus (*offensive informal*) **2.** looking down on others who you think are inferior (*informal*) ○ *Don't be so snotty! I know how to do it, just as much as you do!*

snout /snaʊt/ *noun* the nose and mouth of some animals such as pigs

① **snow** /snəʊ/ *noun* water which falls as light white pieces of ice in cold weather ○ *Two metres of snow fell during the night.* ○ *The highest mountains are always covered with snow.* ○ *Children were out playing in the snow.* ○ *We went for a skiing holiday and there was hardly any snow.* ■ *verb* (**snows, snowing, snowed**) to fall as snow ○ *Look – it's started to snow!* ○ *It snowed all day, and the streets were blocked.* ○ *It hardly ever snows here in March.* (NOTE: The verb **snow** is always used with the subject **it**.)

③ **snowball** /ˈsnəʊbɔːl/ (**snowballs, snowballing, snowballed**) *verb* to get steadily bigger ○ *The protests started slowly and then snowballed into mass demonstrations.*

snowboarding /ˈsnəʊbɔːdɪŋ/ *noun* the sport of sliding down a snow-covered slope while standing on a board with both feet

snowdrift /ˈsnəʊdrɪft/ *noun* snow which has been blown into a heap by the wind

snowdrop /ˈsnəʊdrɒp/ *noun* a bulb with little white bell-shaped flowers in the early spring

snowfall /ˈsnəʊfɔːl/ *noun* the amount of snow which has fallen

snowflake /ˈsnəʊfleɪk/ *noun* a small piece of snow formed of a number of ice crystals

snowman /ˈsnəʊmæn/ (*plural* **snowmen**) *noun* a model of a man made of snow

snowplough /ˈsnəʊplaʊ/ *noun* a heavy vehicle with a plough on the front used to clear snow off roads and railway tracks

snowstorm /ˈsnəʊstɔːm/ *noun* a storm when the wind blows and snow falls

snub /snʌb/ (**snubs, snubbing, snubbed**) *verb* to insult someone by refusing to speak to them or by not paying any attention to them ○ *He snubbed all her attempts to be friendly.*

snuck /snʌk/ *US* past tense and past participle of **sneak**

snuff /snʌf/ *noun* powdered tobacco which is sniffed into the nose

snug /snʌg/ (**snugger, snuggest**) *adj* warm and comfortable

snuggle /ˈsnʌg(ə)l/ (**snuggles, snuggling, snuggled**) *verb* to get yourself into a warm and comfortable position

① **so** /səʊ/ *adv* **1.** showing how much ○ *It's so cold that the lake is covered with ice.* ○ *We liked Greece so much that we're going there again on holiday next year.* ○ *The soup was so salty that I couldn't eat it.* **2.** also ○ *She was late and so was I.* ○ *The children all caught flu, and so did their teacher.* ○ *I like apples. – So do I.* ○ *He's a good cook and so is his wife.* ○ *The teacher will be late and so will everyone else.* **3.** showing that the answer is 'yes' ○ *Does this train go to London? – I think so.* ○ *Was your car completely smashed? – I'm afraid so.* ○ *Will you be coming to the party? – I hope so!* ○ *Are they going to be at the meeting? – I suppose so.* ■ *conj* and this is the reason why ○ *It was snowing hard so we couldn't go for a walk.* ○ *She's got flu so she can't come to the office.* ◇ **so what** what does it matter?

③ **soak** /səʊk/ (**soaks, soaking, soaked**) *verb* **1.** to put something in a liquid for a time ○ *Dry beans should be soaked in cold water for 24 hours.* **2.** to make something or someone very wet ○ *I forgot my umbrella and got soaked.* ○ *The rain soaked the soil.*

soaked /səʊkt/ *adj* very wet

soaking /ˈsəʊkɪŋ/ *adj, adv* very wet ○ *Don't let the dog into the kitchen – he's soaking* or *he's soaking wet.*

so-and-so /ˈsəʊ ən səʊ/ *noun* **1.** an unpleasant person **2.** *also* **Mr/Mrs/Miss So-and-so** a person whose name is not mentioned ○ *It's the usual story – so-and-so buys a green car, and suddenly everyone has green cars.*

② **soap** /səʊp/ *noun* a substance which you wash with, made from oils and usually with a pleasant smell ○ *There's no soap left in the bathroom.* ○ *I've put a new bar of soap in the kitchen.* ○ *There is a liquid soap dispenser in the gents' toilets.*

soap opera /ˈsəʊp ˌɒp(ə)rə/ *noun* a serial story on television about the daily lives of a set of characters

soap powder /ˈsəʊp ˌpaʊdə/ *noun* soap in the form of powder, used in washing machines or dishwashers

③ **soar** /sɔː/ (**soars, soaring, soared**) *verb* **1.** to go up very quickly ○ *Food prices soared during the cold weather.* **2.** to fly high up into the sky ○ *The rocket went soaring into the night sky.* (NOTE: Do not confuse with **sore**.)

③ **sob** /sɒb/ *verb* (**sobs, sobbing, sobbed**) to cry, taking short breaths like hiccups ○ *She lay sobbing on the bed.* ○ *The little girl sobbed herself to sleep.* ■ *noun* a short breath like a hiccup, made by someone who is crying ○ *You could hear the sobs as she lay on her bed.* ○ *He gave a sob, and put the phone down.*

③ **sober** /ˈsəʊbə/ *adj* **1.** not drunk ○ *I wasn't drunk after the party – I was stone cold sober.* **2.** serious, not frivolous ○ *The sober truth is that we can't afford it.* ○ *It was a very sober gathering, nobody laughed or made a joke.* **3.** dark with no bright colours ○ *She was wearing a sober dark grey suit.*

sobering /ˈsəʊbərɪŋ/ *adj* which makes you think seriously

③ **so-called** /ˈsəʊ kɔːld/ *adj* called by a wrong name

soccer /ˈsɒkə/ *noun* a game played between two teams of eleven players with a round ball which can be kicked or hit with the head, but not carried (NOTE: The game is called **football** in most countries, but is generally called **soccer** in the USA to distinguish it from American football.)

sociable /ˈsəʊʃəb(ə)l/ *adj* friendly, liking the company of other people

① **social** /ˈsəʊʃ(ə)l/ *adj* relating to people as a group, or to human society in general ○ *an area with very serious social problems* ○ *Inequality leads to social conflict.*

socialism /ˈsəʊʃəlɪz(ə)m/ *noun* **1.** the ideas and beliefs of socialists, that the means of production and distribution should belong to the people, that people should be cared for by the state and that all wealth should be shared equally ○ *His book explains the principles of socialism.* **2.** a political system where the state is run on socialist principles ○ *Under socialism, this factory was owned by the state.* (NOTE: + **socialist** *n*)

socially /ˈsəʊʃ(ə)li/ *adv* **1.** in a friendly situation ○ *I know her from work but I've never met her socially.* ○ *They get on very well socially.* **2.** with respect to other people or society ○ *the socially unacceptable behaviour of some football fans* ○ *These policies are socially divisive.*

social science /ˌsəʊʃ(ə)l ˈsaɪəns/ *noun* the study of people and the society they live in, including such subjects as sociology, history and economics

③ **social security** /ˌsəʊʃ(ə)l sɪ ˈkjʊərɪti/ *noun* money or help provided by the government to people who need it

social services /ˌsəʊʃ(ə)l ˈsɜːvɪsɪz/ *plural noun* government services to help people with family problems ○ *The children are being looked after by social services.*

social worker /ˈsəʊʃ(ə)l ˌwɜːkə/ *noun* a person who works to help people with family or financial problems (NOTE: + **social work** *n*)

① **society** /səˈsaɪəti/ *noun* **1.** a large group of people, usually all the people living in a country, considered as an organised community ○ *a free and democratic society* ○ *a member of society* ○ *Society needs to be protected against these criminals.* (NOTE: no plural) **2.** a club or association of people who have the same interests ○ *He belongs to the local drama society.* ◊ **building society**

socio-economic /ˌsəʊʃiəʊ iːkə ˈnɒmɪk/ *adj* referring to social and economic conditions

sociology /ˌsəʊsiˈɒlədʒi/ *noun* the study of social systems and how people live in society (NOTE: + **sociologist** *n*)

③ **sock** /sɒk/ *noun* a piece of clothing worn on your foot inside a shoe ○ *a pair of socks* ◇ **to pull your socks up** to try to do better (*informal*) ○ *He'll have to pull his socks up or he'll lose his job.*

socket /ˈsɒkɪt/ *noun* **1.** a set of holes into which an electric plug can be fitted ○ *There is a socket on the wall that you can plug the vacuum cleaner into.* ○ *This plug doesn't fit that socket.* **2.** a hollow part in a bone, into which another bone fits

sodden /ˈsɒd(ə)n/ *adj* as full of a liquid or other substance as can be absorbed

sodium /ˈsəʊdiəm/ *noun* a soft white metal, which can catch fire, and is only found combined with other substances

③ **sofa** /ˈsəʊfə/ *noun* a long comfortable seat with a soft back

so far /səʊ ˈfɑː/ *adv* until now

① **soft** /sɒft/ *adj* **1.** which moves easily when pressed ○ *There are big soft arm-*

chairs in the lobby of the hotel. ○ *I don't like soft seats in a car.* ○ *Do you like soft ice cream?* **2.** not loud ○ *When she spoke, her voice was so soft that we could hardly hear her.* ○ *Soft music was playing in the background.* **3.** not bright ○ *Soft lighting makes a room look warm.*

soft copy /ˌsɒft ˈkɒpi/ *noun* data stored on a computer, rather than being printed on paper

③ **soft drink** /ˈsɒft drɪŋk/ *noun* a drink which is not alcoholic

soften /ˈsɒf(ə)n/ (**softens, softening, softened**) *verb* to make something soft, to become soft

soften up *verb* to make someone weaker before asking for something, or before launching an attack ○ *Can you try and soften him up a bit before I ask to borrow the car?* ○ *Bombing raids were made to soften up the enemy defences.*

soft-spoken /sɒft ˈspəʊkən/ *adj* having a quiet gentle voice

soft touch /ˌsɒft ˈtʌtʃ/ *noun* a person who can be easily persuaded to do something for you

③ **software** /ˈsɒftweə/ *noun* computer programs which are put into a computer to make it work, as opposed to the computer itself ○ *What word-processing software do you use?* Compare **hardware** (NOTE: no plural)

soggy /ˈsɒgi/ (**soggier, soggiest**) *adj* wet and soft to an unpleasant degree

① **soil** /sɔɪl/ *noun* the earth in which plants grow ○ *Put some soil in the plant pot and then sow your flower seeds.* ○ *This soil's too poor for growing fruit trees.* ○ *The farm has fields of rich black soil.*

soiled /sɔɪld/ *adj* spoiled by dirt or other unpleasant substances ○ *The sheets on the bed were soiled.*

solace /ˈsɒləs/ *noun* comfort

solar /ˈsəʊlə/ *adj* relating to the sun (NOTE: The similar word relating to the moon is **lunar** and to the stars is **stellar**.)

solar energy /ˈsəʊlə ˌenədʒi/, **solar power** /ˈsəʊlə ˌpaʊə/ *noun* electricity produced from the radiation of the sun

solar panel /ˌsəʊlə ˈpæn(ə)l/ *noun* a group of special electric cells used to turn the sun's energy into electricity

sold /səʊld/ past tense and past participle of **sell**

① **soldier** /ˈsəʊldʒə/ *noun* a member of an army ○ *Here's a photograph of my father as a soldier.* ○ *We were just in time to see the soldiers march past.* ○ *Enemy soldiers blew up the bridge.* ○ *The children are playing with their toy soldiers.*

soldier on *phrasal verb* to continue doing something, in spite of difficulties ○ *Even though sales are down, we must soldier on.* ○ *She's soldiering on with her preparations for the exam.*

sold out /ˌsəʊld ˈaʊt/ *adj* no longer in stock, because all the stock has been sold

③ **sole** /səʊl/ *adj* only; belonging to one person ○ *Their sole aim is to make money.* ○ *She was the sole survivor from the crash.* ○ *I have sole responsibility for what goes on in this office.* ■ *noun* **1.** the underneath side of your foot ○ *He tickled the soles of her feet.* **2.** the main underneath part of a shoe, but not the heel ○ *These shoes need mending – I've got holes in both soles.*

solely /ˈsəʊlli/ *adv* **1.** only ○ *The machine was designed solely for that purpose.* **2.** without other people being involved ○ *He was solely to blame for what happened.*

solemn /ˈsɒləm/ *adj* **1.** serious and formal ○ *The doctor looked very solemn and shook his head.* ○ *At the most solemn moment of the ceremony someone's mobile phone rang.* **2.** which should be treated as very serious ○ *He made a solemn promise never to smoke again.*

solicit /səˈlɪsɪt/ (**solicits, soliciting, solicited**) *verb* **1.** to ask someone for something such as business or financial support (*formal*) **2.** to offer sex to people ○ *Prostitutes were openly soliciting outside the station.*

② **solicitor** /səˈlɪsɪtə/ *noun* a lawyer who gives advice to members of the public and acts for them in legal matters

① **solid** /ˈsɒlɪd/ *adj* **1.** hard and not liquid ○ *a solid lump of fat* ○ *She is allowed some solid food.* **2.** firm or strong ○ *Is the table solid enough to stand on?* ○ *His wealth is built on a solid base of property and shares.* **3.** not hollow ○ *Cricket is played with a solid ball.* **4.** made only of one material ○ *The box is made of solid silver.* ■ *noun* a hard substance which is not liquid ○ *Many solids melt when heated and become liquids.*

solidarity /ˌsɒlɪˈdærɪti/ *noun* a general common interest with other people

solidify /səˈlɪdɪfaɪ/ (**solidifies, solidifying, solidified**) *verb* to become solid

solitary /ˈsɒlɪt(ə)ri/ *adj* **1.** one only ○ *It was late November, and a solitary tourist was sitting in the waterfront café.* ○ *I don't remember one solitary occasion when he* *helped with the washing up.* **2.** being alone ○ *My sister lives a solitary life in the country.*

solitary confinement /ˌsɒlɪt(ə)ri kən ˈfaɪnmənt/ *noun* being kept alone in a cell, without being able to see or speak to other prisoners

solitude /ˈsɒlɪtjuːd/ *noun* the state of being alone

solo /ˈsəʊləʊ/ *noun* (*plural* **solos** or **soli**) a piece of music played or sung by one person alone ○ *She played a violin solo.* ■ *adj* done by one person alone ○ *a piece for solo trumpet* ○ *Our daughter gave a solo performance at the school concert.* ○ *He crashed on his first solo flight.*

soloist /ˈsəʊləʊɪst/ *noun* a musician who plays a solo

soluble /ˈsɒljʊb(ə)l/ *adj* **1.** which can be dissolved ○ *a tablet of soluble aspirin* ○ *The pill is soluble in water.* **2.** which can be solved ○ *The problem is simply not soluble.* ○ *The difficulties are soluble, given a little money.*

① **solution** /səˈluːʃ(ə)n/ *noun* **1.** the action of solving a problem [~to] ○ *Finding a solution to this problem is taking longer than expected.* **2.** a mixture of a solid substance dissolved in a liquid ○ *Bathe your eye in a weak salt solution.*

① **solve** /sɒlv/ (**solves, solving, solved**) *verb* to find an answer to a problem or question ○ *The loan will solve some of his financial problems.* ○ *He tried to solve the riddle.*

solvent /ˈsɒlv(ə)nt/ *noun* a liquid in which a solid substance can be dissolved

sombre /ˈsɒmbə/ *adj* dark and gloomy (NOTE: The US spelling is **somber**.)

① **some** /səm, sʌm/ *adj, pron* **1.** a certain number of ○ *Some young drivers drive much too fast.* ○ *Some books were damaged in the fire.* ○ *Some days it was so hot that we just stayed by the swimming pool all day.* ○ *Can you cut some more slices of bread?* ○ *She bought some oranges and bananas.* ○ *We've just picked some strawberries.* □ **some of** a few ○ *Some of the students are ill.* ○ *Some of these apples are too green.* **2.** a certain amount of ○ *Can you buy some bread when you go to town?* ○ *Can I have some more coffee?* ○ *Her illness is of some concern to her family.* **3.** used for referring to a person or thing you cannot identify (*followed by a singular noun*) ○ *Some man just knocked on the door and tried to sell me a magazine.* ○ *I read it in some book I borrowed from the library.* ○ *We saw it in some shop or other in Regent Street.* **4.** relating to a period of time or a distance ○ *Don't wait for me, I may be some time.* ○ *Their house is some way away from the railway station.*

somebody /ˈsʌmbədi/ *pron* **1.** same as **someone 2.** someone who is considered to be important

some day /ˈsʌm deɪ/ *adv* at a time in the future that is not specified ○ *Some day I'll get round to cleaning out the garage.*

① **somehow** /ˈsʌmhaʊ/ *adv* by some means that are not yet known ○ *Somehow we must get back home by 6 o'clock.*

① **someone** /ˈsʌmwʌn/ *pron* a person who is not identified or referred to in particular way ○ *Can someone answer the phone?* ○ *I know someone who can fix your car.* ○ *I need someone tall who can reach the top shelf for me.* □ **someone else** an extra person, or a different person ○ *I've got four volunteers already, but I still need someone else.* ○ *If Jo is ill, could someone else help you?*

someplace /ˈsʌmpleɪs/ *adv US* somewhere (*informal*)

somersault /ˈsʌməsɔːlt/ *noun* a movement in which you roll over, head first ○ *He did a couple of somersaults on the mat.* (NOTE: + **somersault** *v*)

① **something** /ˈsʌmθɪŋ/ *pron* **1.** a thing which is not identified or referred to in particular ○ *There's something soft at the bottom of the bag.* ○ *Something's gone wrong with the TV.* ○ *Can I have something to drink, please?* ○ *There's something about her that I don't like.* **2.** an important thing ○ *Come in and sit down, I've got something to tell you.*

sometime /ˈsʌmtaɪm/ *adv* at a time which is not specified ○ *The accident happened sometime after midnight.* ○ *Let's meet sometime next week.*

① **sometimes** /ˈsʌmtaɪmz/ *adv* on some occasions but not on others ○ *Sometimes the car starts easily, and sometimes it won't start at all.* ○ *She sometimes comes to see us when she's in town on business.*

② **somewhat** /ˈsʌmwɒt/ *adv* to a fairly great degree (*formal*)

① **somewhere** /ˈsʌmweə/ *adv* in or at a place which is not identified ○ *I left my umbrella somewhere when I was in London.* ○ *Let's go somewhere else, this pub is full.* ○ *His parents live somewhere in Germany.*

① **son** /sʌn/ *noun* a male child of a father or mother ○ *He's the son of the famous run-*

ner. ○ *They have a large family – two sons and four daughters.*

sonata /sə'nɑːtə/ *noun* a piece of music in three or four movements for one or more instruments, accompanied by an orchestra, piano, harpsichord, etc.

① **song** /sɒŋ/ *noun* a set of words which are sung, usually to music ○ *She was singing a song in the bath.* ○ *The group's latest song has just come out on CD.* ○ *The soldiers marched along, singing a song.*

songwriter /'sɒŋraɪtə/ *noun* a person who writes popular songs

sonic /'sɒnɪk/ *adj* referring to sound that can be heard by the human ear

son-in-law /'sʌn ɪn lɔː/ (*plural* **sons-in-law**) *noun* the husband of a daughter

sonnet /'sɒnɪt/ *noun* a poem with fourteen lines and one of several rhyming patterns

① **soon** /suːn/ *adv* in a short time from now ○ *Don't worry, we'll soon be in Oxford.* ○ *It will soon be time to go to bed.* ○ *The fire started soon after 11 o'clock.*

② **sooner** /'suːnə/ *adv* earlier ○ *Can't we meet any sooner than that?*

soot /sʊt/ *noun* a black deposit of carbon which rises in the smoke produced by burning coal, wood and oil and which collects on the inside surfaces of chimneys

soothe /suːð/ (**soothes, soothing, soothed**) *verb* to make something less painful or to calm

③ **sophisticated** /sə'fɪstɪkeɪtɪd/ *adj* **1.** knowing a lot about the way people behave, and what is stylish or fashionable ○ *They think smoking makes them look sophisticated.* **2.** cleverly designed and complicated ○ *His office is full of the latest and most sophisticated computer equipment.*

sopping /'sɒpɪŋ/ *adj* very wet

soprano /sə'prɑːnəʊ/ *adj* relating to a high-pitched woman's singing voice ○ *She sings soprano in the local choir.* ■ *noun* a woman with a high-pitched singing voice ○ *The sopranos are too feeble – I can hardly hear them.*

sorcery /'sɔːsəri/ *noun* (*in fairy tales*) wicked magic

sordid /'sɔːdɪd/ *adj* unpleasant or dirty

① **sore** /sɔː/ (**sorer, sorest**) *adj* rough and swollen or painful ○ *He can't play tennis because he has a sore elbow.* (NOTE: Do not confuse with **soar**.)

sorely /'sɔːli/ *adv* very much (*formal*)

sorrow /'sɒrəʊ/ *noun* sadness

① **sorry** /'sɒri/ *adj* feeling unhappy, ashamed or disappointed about something ■ *interj* used to excuse yourself ○ *Sorry! I didn't see that table had been reserved.* ○ *Can I have another mint, please? – sorry, I haven't any left.* ◇ **to feel sorry for someone** to be sympathetic about someone's problems ○ *We all feel sorry for her – her family is always criticising her.* ◇ **to feel sorry for yourself** to be miserable ○ *He's feeling very sorry for himself – he's just been made redundant.*

① **sort** /sɔːt/ *noun* a type ○ *There were all sorts of people at the meeting.* ○ *I had an unpleasant sort of day at the office.* ○ *What sorts of ice cream have you got?* ○ *Do you like this sort of TV show?* ■ *verb* (**sorts, sorting, sorted**) to arrange in order or groups ○ *The apples are sorted according to size before being packed.* ○ *The votes are sorted then counted.*

sort out① *phrasal verb* **1.** to settle a problem ○ *Did you sort out the hotel bill?* **2.** to put things in order or in groups ○ *I must sort out the papers in this drawer.* ○ *Until they're sorted out, we shan't know which are our files and which are theirs.* **3.** to collect or select things of a particular kind from a mixed group of things ○ *Sort out all the blue folders and bring them to me, please.*

so-so /ˌsəʊ 'səʊ/ *adj, adv* not very good or not very well ○ *How are you today? – only so-so.* ○ *The results of the test were only so-so.*

soufflé /'suːfleɪ/ *noun* **1.** a light cooked dish, made from eggs beaten up with a savoury flavouring, eaten hot ○ *a cheese soufflé* **2.** a cold dessert made from beaten eggs, whipped cream and gelatine ○ *a lemon soufflé*

③ **sought** /sɔːt/ past tense and past participle of **seek**

sought-after /'sɔːt ˌɑːftə/ *adj* wanted by many people

③ **soul** /səʊl/ *noun* the spirit in a person, which is believed by some people to go on existing after the person dies ○ *Do you believe your soul lives on when your body dies?* ○ *From the depths of his soul he longed to be free.* (NOTE: Do not confuse with **sole**.)

soul-searching /'səʊl ˌsɜːtʃɪŋ/ *noun* an examination of your own motives or conscience

① **sound** /saʊnd/ *noun* a noise, something which you can hear ○ *Sounds of music came from the street.* ○ *I thought I heard* *the sound of guns.* ○ *Please can you turn down the sound on the TV when I'm on the phone?* ○ *She crept out of her bedroom and we didn't hear a sound.* ■ *verb* (**sounds, sounding, sounded**) **1.** to make a noise, or to cause something to make a noise [~like] ○ *The noise sounds like wind blowing in the trees.* ○ *They sounded the alarm after two prisoners escaped.* **2.** to seem ○ *It sounds as if he's made an unfortunate choice.* ○ *The book sounds interesting according to what I've heard.* ■ *adv* deeply ○ *The children were sound asleep when the police came.*

sound off *phrasal verb* to start talking loudly about something (*informal*)

sound out③ *phrasal verb* to ask someone's opinion about something ○ *I'll sound out the other members of the committee to see what they think.*

soundbite /ˈsaʊndbaɪt/ *noun* a short phrase, usually spoken by a politician, especially made so as to be broadcast on radio or TV

sound card /ˌsaʊnd ˈkɑːd/ *noun* a circuit board that allows a computer to produce sound

sound effects /ˈsaʊnd ɪˌfekts/ *plural noun* the artificial sounds used to give an impression of the real thing ○ *All the sound effects for the film were produced electronically.*

soundly /ˈsaʊndli/ *adv* deeply or thoroughly

soundtrack /ˈsaʊndtræk/ *noun* the track of a film on which the sound is recorded

③ **soup** /suːp/ *noun* a liquid food which you eat hot from a bowl at the beginning of a meal, usually made from meat, fish or vegetables ○ *We have onion soup or mushroom soup today.* ○ *Does anyone want soup?* ○ *A bowl of hot soup is always welcome on a cold day.* ○ *If you're hungry, open a tin of soup.*

soup kitchen /suːp ˈkɪtʃən/ *noun* a place that serves free hot meals to people who have no money to buy food

sour /ˈsaʊə/ *adj* with a sharp bitter taste ○ *If the cooked fruit is too sour, you can add some sugar.* ○ *Nobody likes sour milk.*

① **source** /sɔːs/ *noun* a place where something comes from [~of] ○ *I think the source of the infection is in one of your teeth.* ○ *The source of the river is in the mountains.* ○ *You must declare income from all sources to the tax office.*

sourness /ˈsaʊənəs/ *noun* the state of being sour

① **south** /saʊθ/ *noun* the direction facing towards the sun at midday ○ *Look south from the mountain, and you will see the city in the distance.* ○ *The city is to the south of the river.* ○ *The wind is blowing from the south.* ■ *adj* relating to the south ○ *The south coast is popular for holidaymakers.* ○ *Cross to the south side of the river.* ■ *adv* towards the south ○ *Many birds fly south for the winter.* ○ *The river flows south into the Mediterranean.*

southbound /ˈsaʊθbaʊnd/ *adj* travelling towards the south

③ **south-east** /ˌsaʊθ ˈiːst/ *adj, adv, noun* the direction between south and east ○ *South-East Asia is an important trading area.* ○ *The river runs south-east from here.* ○ *House prices are higher in the south-east than anywhere else in England.*

southerly /ˈsʌðəli/ *adj* **1.** towards the south **2.** (*of a wind*) blowing from the south

② **southern** /ˈsʌð(ə)n/ *adj* from, of or in the south ○ *The southern part of the country is warmer than the north.*

southerner /ˈsʌð(ə)nə/ *noun* a person who lives in or comes from the south of a country or region

southern hemisphere *noun* the part of the earth below the equator

southernmost /ˈsʌð(ə)nməʊst/ *adj* furthest to the south

South Pole /ˈsaʊθ ˈpəʊl/ *noun* the furthest point south on the earth

southward /ˈsaʊθwəd/ *adj* towards the south

southwards /ˈsaʊθwədz/ *adv* towards the south

③ **south-west** /ˌsaʊθ ˈwest/ *adj, adv, noun* the direction between south and west

souvenir /ˌsuːvəˈnɪə/ *noun* a thing bought to remind you of the place where you bought it

sovereign /ˈsɒvrɪn/ *noun* a king or queen ○ *The sovereign is not supposed to become involved in party politics.*

③ **sovereignty** /ˈsɒvrɪnti/ (*plural* **sovereignties**) *noun* the total power of a government

Soviet /ˈsəʊviət/ *adj* of the former Soviet Union its people, culture, or political system

sow /səʊ/ (**sows, sowing, sowed, sown** or **sowed**) *verb* to put seeds into soil so that they become plants ○ *Peas and beans should be sown in April.* ○ *Sow the seed* *thinly in fine soil.* (NOTE: Do not confuse with **sew**.)

soya bean /ˈsɔɪə biːn/ *noun* a bean from a plant used for food and oil

spa /spɑː/ *noun* **1.** a place where mineral water comes out of the ground naturally and where people go to drink or bathe because of its medicinal properties ○ *He spends two weeks every summer at a French spa.* **2.** an exercise and health centre in a hotel

① **space** /speɪs/ *noun* **1.** an empty place between other things ○ *There's a space to park your car over there.* ○ *Write your name and reference number in the space at the top of the paper.* **2.** an area which is available for something [~for] ○ *Is there space in your car for another passenger?* ○ *His desk takes up too much space.* **3.** *also* **outer space** the area beyond the earth's atmosphere ○ *the knowledge of the universe gained from exploring outer space* ○ *space vehicles* ○ *This is a photograph of the earth taken from space.*

space probe /ˈspeɪs prəʊb/ *noun* a spacecraft sent into space for scientific purposes

space shuttle /ˈspeɪs ˌʃʌt(ə)l/ *noun* a type of plane which is launched by a rocket, flies in space and then returns eventually to earth so that it can be used for another trip

space station /ˈspeɪs ˌsteɪʃ(ə)n/ *noun* a satellite which orbits the earth in which people can live and carry out scientific experiments

spacious /ˈspeɪʃəs/ *adj* very large, with plenty of space

③ **spade** /speɪd/ *noun* **1.** a tool with a wide square blade at the end of a long handle, used for digging or moving something such as soil or sand **2.** a similar small plastic tool, used by children ○ *The children took their buckets and spades to the beach.*

spaghetti /spəˈgeti/ *noun* long thin strips of pasta, cooked and eaten with a sauce

spam /spæm/ *noun* unwanted commercial e-mails

span /spæn/ *noun* the width of wings or of an arch ○ *Each section of the bridge has a span of fifty feet.* ■ *verb* (**spans, spanning, spanned**) to stretch across space or time ○ *Her career spanned thirty years.* ○ *A stone bridge spans the river.*

spaniel /ˈspænjəl/ *noun* a type of dog with large ears that droop down

spank /spæŋk/ (**spanks, spanking, spanked**) *verb* to hit a child's bottom as a punishment

spanner /ˈspænə/ *noun* a metal tool with an opening which fits round a nut and which can be twisted to undo the nut or tighten it

spar /spɑː/ (**spars, sparring, sparred**) *verb* to practise boxing with someone ○ *He sparred every morning before the fight.*

② **spare** /speə/ *adj* available but not being used ○ *I always take a spare pair of shoes when I travel.* ■ *plural noun* **spares** spare parts or pieces used to mend broken parts of a car or other machine ○ *We can't get spares for that make of washing machine.* ○ *It's difficult to get spares for the car because they don't make this model any more.* ■ *verb* (**spares, sparing, spared**) to give something or to do without something ○ *Can you spare your assistant to help me for a day?* ○ *Can you spare about five minutes to talk about the problem?* ○ *If you have a moment to spare, can you clean the car?*

spark /spɑːk/ *noun* a little flash of fire or of light ○ *Sparks flew as the train went over the junction.* ■ *verb* (**sparks, sparking, sparked**) **1.** to send out sparks or to make electric sparks **2.** to make something start suddenly ○ *The proposed closure of the station sparked anger among travellers.* ○ *The shooting of the teenager sparked off a riot.*

spark off *phrasal verb* same as **spark** *verb* **2**

sparkle /ˈspɑːk(ə)l/ (**sparkles, sparkling, sparkled**) *verb* to shine brightly ○ *Her jewels sparkled in the light of the candles.* ○ *His eyes sparkled when he heard the salary offered.*

sparkling /ˈspɑːklɪŋ/ *adj* **1.** shining with little lights ○ *a necklace of sparkling diamonds* **2.** which has bubbles in it, which is fizzy ○ *a bottle of sparkling water*

spark plug /ˈspɑːk plʌg/ *noun* a part of an engine which produces sparks that ignite the fuel

sparrow /ˈspærəʊ/ *noun* a very common small brown and grey bird

sparse /spɑːs/ (**sparser, sparsest**) *adj* not thick or not in large quantities (NOTE: + **sparsely** *adv*)

spartan /ˈspɑːt(ə)n/ *adj* harsh or hard

spasm /ˈspæz(ə)m/ *noun* a sudden, usually painful, involuntary contraction of a muscle, such as when you have cramp

spat /spæt/ past tense and past participle of **spit**

spate /speɪt/ *noun* a sudden rush of something ○ *We had a spate of inquiries after our ad in 'the Times'.*

spatial /ˈspeɪʃ(ə)l/ *adj* referring to space

spatter /ˈspætə/ (**spatters, spattering, spattered**) *verb* to splash with little spots of liquid

spawn /spɔːn/ *noun* a mass of eggs of a fish or a frog ○ *The children could see the frog spawn floating on the surface of the pond.* ■ *verb* (**spawns, spawning, spawned**) **1.** (*of fish*) to produce a mass of eggs ○ *Salmon swim up the river to spawn.* **2.** to produce a mass of things ○ *The meetings of the committee spawned a huge amount of documents.*

① **speak** /spiːk/ (**speaks, speaking, spoke** or **spake, spoken**) *verb* **1.** to say words [~to/~with/~about] ○ *She spoke to me just before the meeting.* ○ *I've been speaking with my colleagues about the problem.* ○ *The manager wants to speak to you about sales in Africa.* ○ *He walked past me without speaking.* **2.** to be able to say things in a particular language ○ *We need someone who can speak Russian.* ○ *He speaks English with an American accent.* ○ *You will have to brush up your Japanese as my mother speaks hardly any English.* ◇ **to speak your mind** to say exactly what you think ◇ **speak for yourself** that's what you think, I don't agree ○ *We both think the decision is crazy. – Speak for yourself!*

speak out *phrasal verb* to make your opinions or feelings known strongly

speak up *phrasal verb* **1.** to speak louder; to say what you have to say in a louder voice ○ *Can you speak up please – we can't hear you at the back!* **2.** to make your opinions known strongly ○ *He's not afraid to speak up when he thinks someone's been unfairly treated.*

speak up for *verb* to show your support for ○ *He was the only person who spoke up for me at the inquiry.*

② **speaker** /ˈspiːkə/ *noun* **1.** a person who speaks ○ *We need an English speaker to help with the tour.* **2.** a loudspeaker ○ *One of the speakers doesn't work.*

spear /spɪə/ *noun* a long pointed throwing stick, formerly used as a weapon ○ *They kill fish with spears.* ■ *verb* to push something sharp into something to catch it ○ *Spearing fish is not easy.* ○ *She managed to spear a sausage on the barbecue with her fork.*

spearhead /ˈspɪəhed/ (**spearheads, spearheading, spearheaded**) *verb* to be in the front of an attacking force ○ *The minister has spearheaded the attack on the newspapers.*

① **special** /ˈspeʃ(ə)l/ *adj* having a particular importance or use ○ *a report from our special correspondent in Hong Kong* ○ *This is a very special day for us – it's our twenty-fifth wedding anniversary.* ○ *He has a special pair of scissors for cutting metal.*

special effects /ˌspeʃ(ə)l ɪˈfekts/ *plural noun* the impression of something like a fire, a snowstorm or an earthquake, made artificially in a film or play ○ *The special effects in the film were created by computers.*

③ **specialise** /ˈspeʃəlaɪz/ (**specialises, specialising, specialised**), **specialize** *verb* **1.** to study one particular subject ○ *At university, she specialised in marine biology.* **2.** to produce one thing in particular ○ *The company specialises in electronic components.*

③ **specialist** /ˈspeʃəlɪst/ *noun* **1.** a person who knows a lot about something ○ *You should go to a tax specialist for advice.* **2.** a doctor who specialises in a certain branch of medicine ○ *He was referred to a heart specialist.*

speciality /ˌspeʃiˈæləti/ *noun* **1.** a thing you are very good at doing ○ *The speciality of the restaurant is its fish soup.* ○ *Finding the right partners for people is my speciality.* **2.** a particular interest, knowledge or study ○ *The company's speciality is computer programmes for schools.* ○ *His speciality is the history of Wales in the 15th century.* (NOTE: [all senses] The US term is **specialty**.)

② **specially** /ˈspeʃ(ə)li/ *adv* in particular or more than usual

special needs /ˌspeʃ(ə)l ˈniːdz/ *plural noun* the needs of a person with mental or physical disabilities, which are different from the needs of most people

specialty /ˈspeʃ(ə)lti/ *noun US* same as **speciality**

③ **species** /ˈspiːʃiːz/ *noun* a group of living things such as animals or plants which can breed with each other ○ *Several species of butterfly are likely to become extinct.*

① **specific** /spəˈsɪfɪk/ *adj* relating to something in particular ○ *Can you be more specific about what you're trying to achieve?* ○ *I gave specific instructions that I was not to be disturbed.* ○ *Is the money intended for a specific purpose?*

① **specifically** /spəˈsɪfɪkli/ *adv* particularly ○ *I specifically said I didn't want a* *blue door.* ○ *The advertisement is specifically aimed at people over 50.*

specification /ˌspesɪfɪˈkeɪʃ(ə)n/ *noun* detailed information about what is needed

specifics /spəˈsɪfɪks/ *plural noun* the particular details of something ○ *The minister outlined the plan but refused to go into specifics.*

③ **specify** /ˈspesɪˌfaɪ/ (**specifies, specifying, specified**) *verb* to give clear details of what is needed

specimen /ˈspesɪmɪn/ *noun* a sample of something taken as standard

speck /spek/ *noun* a tiny spot of colour

③ **specs** /speks/ *plural noun* same as **spectacles** (*informal*) ○ *I can't see anything without my specs!*

③ **spectacle** /ˈspektək(ə)l/ *noun* something very impressive to look at ○ *The firework display is a spectacle not to be missed.* ○ *For sheer spectacle you can't beat a military parade.*

spectacles /ˈspektək(ə)lz/ *plural noun* glass lenses worn in front of your eyes to correct vision ○ *I can't remember where I put my spectacles.* ○ *He's worn spectacles since he was a child.*

spectacular /spekˈtækjʊlə/ *adj* very impressive to see or watch ○ *The display was even more spectacular than last year.* ○ *She was very ill, but has made a spectacular recovery.* ■ *noun* an impressive show ○ *a firework spectacular on November 5th* ○ *A musical spectacular featuring over a hundred singers and dancers.*

③ **spectator** /spekˈteɪtə/ *noun* a person who watches an event like a football match or a horse show

spectre /ˈspektə/ *noun* **1.** a ghost (*literary*) **2.** an image of something which may cause problems in the future ○ *The spectre of mass unemployment loomed over the country.*

③ **spectrum** /ˈspektrəm/ *noun* **1.** a range of colours from red to violet as seen in a rainbow **2.** a range of something ○ *The bank tries to offer a wide spectrum of services.*

speculate /ˈspekjʊleɪt/ (**speculates, speculating, speculated**) *verb* **1.** to make guesses about something (NOTE: + **speculator** *n*) **2.** to take a risk in business which you hope will bring profit

③ **speculation** /ˌspekjʊˈleɪʃ(ə)n/ *noun* **1.** trying to guess what will happen [~about] ○ *There's been a lot of speculation in the press about who might get the job.* **2.** a risky deal which may produce a short-term profit

speculative /ˈspekjʊlətɪv/ *adj* made by guessing

sped /sped/ past tense and past participle of **speed**

② **speech** /spiːtʃ/ *noun* **1.** a formal talk given to an audience ○ *She made some notes before giving her speech.* ○ *He wound up his speech with a story about his father.* ○ *Who will be making the speech at the prize giving?* **2.** the ability to say words, or the act of saying words ○ *His speech has been affected by brain damage.* ○ *Some of these expressions are only used in speech, not in writing.*

speech-impaired /spiːtʃ ɪmˈpeəd/ *adj* not able to speak

speechless /ˈspiːtʃləs/ *adj* very angry or surprised

① **speed** /spiːd/ *noun* the rate at which something moves or is done [~of] ○ *The train travels at speeds of over 200 km per hour.* ○ *The coach was travelling at a high speed when it crashed.* ○ *The speed with which they repaired the gas leak was incredible.* ■ *verb* (**speeds, speeding, sped** or **speeded**) to move quickly ○ *The ball sped across the ice.*

speed up *phrasal verb* **1.** to go faster ○ *She speeded up because she was late.* **2.** to make something happen faster ○ *Can't we speed up production?* ○ *We are aiming to speed up our delivery times.*

speedboat /ˈspiːdbəʊt/ *noun* a small fast motorboat

speeding /ˈspiːdɪŋ/ *noun* the offence of driving a vehicle faster than the speed limit

speed limit /ˈspiːd ˌlɪmɪt/ *noun* the fastest speed at which vehicles are allowed to go legally

speedometer /spɪˈdɒmɪtə/ *noun* an instrument which shows how fast a vehicle is travelling

speedy /ˈspiːdi/ (**speedier, speediest**) *adj* very fast

② **spell** /spel/ *verb* (**spells, spelling, spelt** or **spelled**) to write or say correctly the letters that make a word ○ *W-O-R-R-Y spells 'worry'* ○ *How do you spell your surname?* ○ *We spelt his name wrong on the envelope.* ■ *noun* words which are intended to have a magic effect when they are spoken ○ *The wicked witch cast a spell on the princess.*

spell out *phrasal verb* to explain very clearly ○ *Let me spell out the consequences of this course of action.*

spellbinding /ˈspelbaɪndɪŋ/ *adj* referring to something which is so interesting it holds your attention completely

spellbound /ˈspelbaʊnd/ *adj* so interested in something that it holds your attention completely

spellchecker /ˈspeltʃekə/ *noun* a computer program which checks the spelling of text and suggests corrections

② **spelling** /ˈspelɪŋ/ *noun* the correct way in which words are spelt

③ **spelt** /spelt/ past tense and past participle of **spell**

① **spend** /spend/ (**spends, spending, spent**) *verb* **1.** to pay money ○ *I went shopping and spent a fortune.* ○ *Why do we spend so much money on food?* **2.** to use time doing something ○ *He wants to spend more time with his family.* ○ *She spent months arguing with the income tax people.* ○ *Don't spend too long on your homework.* ○ *Why don't you come and spend the weekend with us?*

spending /ˈspendɪŋ/ *noun* money spent

spending money /ˈspendɪŋ ˌmʌni/ *noun* money for ordinary personal expenses

spendthrift /ˈspendθrɪft/ *noun* a person who spends money fast

spent /spent/ *adj* used

sperm /spɜːm/ *noun* a male sex cell which fertilises female eggs ○ *Out of millions of sperm only one will fertilise an egg.*

spew /spjuː/ (**spews, spewing, spewed**) *verb* to pour out ○ *Gallons of toxic waste spewed into the river.* ○ *He spewed out a stream of racial abuse.*

SPF *noun* the amount of protection from the sun a sun cream or other sunscreen will give to your skin. Full form **sun protection factor**

sphere /sfɪə/ *noun* an object which is perfectly round like a ball ○ *The earth is not quite a perfect sphere.*

spherical /ˈsferɪk(ə)l/ *adj* shaped like a sphere, perfectly round

sphinx /sfɪŋks/ *noun* in ancient Egyptian and Greek mythology, a creature with a lion's body and the head of a man

spice /spaɪs/ *noun* a substance made from the roots, flowers, seeds or leaves of plants, which is used to flavour food ○ *Add a blend of your favourite spices.* ○ *You need lots of different spices for Indian cookery.*

spick-and-span /ˌspɪk ən ˈspæn/ *adj* very neat and clean

spicy /ˈspaɪsi/ (**spicier, spiciest**) *adj* **1.** with a lot of spices ○ *He loves spicy Indian food.* ○ *Mexican cooking is hot and spicy.* **2.** including something which excites sexual interest (*informal*) ○ *The paper published a spicy story about the MP and two girls.*

③ **spider** /ˈspaɪdə/ *noun* a small animal with eight legs which makes a web and eats insects

spike /spaɪk/ *noun* a piece of metal or wood wit ha sharp point ○ *The wall was topped with a row of metal spikes.*

③ **spill** /spɪl/ *verb* (**spills, spilling, spilt** or **spilled**) to pour a liquid or a powder out of a container by mistake ○ *That glass is too full – you'll spill it.* ○ *He spilt soup down the front of his shirt.* ○ *She dropped the bag and some of the flour spilled out onto the floor.* ■ *noun* the act of pouring a liquid by accident ○ *The authorities are trying to cope with the oil spill from the tanker.*

③ **spilt** /spɪlt/ ♦ **spill**

③ **spin** /spɪn/ *verb* (**spins, spinning, spun**) **1.** to move round and round very fast ○ *The earth is spinning in space.* ○ *The plane was spinning out of control.* **2.** to make something turn round and round ○ *The washing machine spins the clothes to get the water out of them.* ○ *He spun the wheel to make sure it turned freely.* **3.** (*of a spider*) to make a web ○ *The spider has spun a web between the two posts.* ■ *noun* the turning movement of a ball as it moves ○ *He put so much spin on the ball that it bounced sideways.* ○ *He jammed on the brakes and the car went into a spin.*

spin out *phrasal verb* to make something last as long as possible

spinach /ˈspɪnɪdʒ/ *noun* an annual plant grown for its green leaves eaten raw as salad or cooked as a vegetable

spinal cord /ˈspaɪn(ə)l kɔːd/ *noun* a part of the central nervous system which runs down the centre of the spine

spin doctor /ˈspɪn ˌdɒktə/ *noun* a person who explains news in a way that makes it flattering to the person or organisation employing him

spine /spaɪn/ *noun* **1.** a series of bones joined together from your skull down the middle of your back ○ *He injured his spine playing rugby.* (NOTE: The bones in the spine are the **vertebrae**.) **2.** a sharp part like a pin, on a plant, animal or fish ○ *The porcupine has dangerous spines.* ○ *Did you know that lemon trees had spines?* **3.** the back edge of a book, which usually has the title printed on it ○ *The title and the author's name are printed on the front of the book and also on the spine.*

spineless /ˈspaɪnləs/ *adj* who is weak and cowardly ○ *He's so spineless – he should say what he thinks to the manager himself.*

spinoff /ˈspɪnɒf/ *noun* a useful thing which comes from a process, but is not the main aim of the process

spiral /ˈspaɪrəl/ *noun* a shape which is twisted round and round like a spring ○ *He drew a spiral on the sheet of paper.* ■ *adj* which twists round and round ○ *A spiral staircase leads to the top of the tower.*

spire /ˈspaɪə/ *noun* a pointed top of a church tower

② **spirit** /ˈspɪrɪt/ *noun* **1.** the mental attitude which controls how someone behaves generally ○ *She has a great spirit of fun.* ○ *He had an independent spirit.* **2.** feelings which are typical of a particular occasion **3.** the part of a person that is said to still exist after death **4.** alcohol (NOTE: usually plural)

spirited /ˈspɪrɪtɪd/ *adj* very lively

③ **spiritual** /ˈspɪrɪtʃuəl/ *adj* relating to the spirit or the soul ○ *The church's main task is to give spiritual advice to its members.*

spiritualism /ˈspɪrɪtʃuəˌlɪz(ə)m/ *noun* the belief in the possibility of communication with people who have died

spit /spɪt/ (**spits, spitting, spit, spat**) *verb* **1.** to push liquid or food out of your mouth ○ *He took a mouthful and immediately spat it out.* **2.** to send liquid out of the mouth to show contempt ○ *He spat on or at the car as it drove away.* **3.** to rain a little ○ *It isn't really raining – it's just spitting.*

③ **spite** /spaɪt/ *noun* bad feeling ○ *They sprayed his car with white paint out of spite.* ■ *verb* (**spites, spiting, spited**) to annoy someone on purpose ○ *He did it to spite his sister.* ◇ **in spite of** although something happened or was done ○ *In spite of all his meetings, he still found time to ring his wife.* ○ *We all enjoyed ourselves, in spite of the awful weather.*

spiteful /ˈspaɪtf(ə)l/ *adj* full of a nasty feelings against someone

spitting image /ˌspɪtɪŋ ˈɪmɪdʒ/ *noun* someone who looks exactly like someone else (*informal*) ○ *He's the spitting image of his father.*

splash /splæʃ/ *noun* a sound made when something falls into a liquid or when a liquid hits something hard ○ *She fell into the pool with a loud splash.* ○ *Listen to the splash of the waves against the rocks.* ■ *verb* (**splashes, splashing, splashed**) **1.** (*of liquid*) to make a noise when something is dropped into it or when it hits something ○ *I missed the ball and it splashed into the pool.* ○ *The rain splashed against the windows.* **2.** to make someone wet by sending liquid on to him ○ *The car drove past through a puddle and splashed my trousers.* **3.** to move through water, making a noise ○ *He splashed his way through the shallow water to the rocks.* ○ *The little children were splashing about in the paddling pool.*

splatter /ˈsplætə/ (**splatters, splattering, splattered**) *verb* to splash drops of liquid

splay /spleɪ/ (**splays, splaying, splayed**) *verb* to spread fingers or legs apart

splendid /ˈsplendɪd/ *adj* extremely good or impressive

splendour /ˈsplendə/ *noun* magnificence (NOTE: The US spelling is **splendor**.)

splice /splaɪs/ (**splices, splicing, spliced**) *verb* to join two pieces of rope or film together

splint /splɪnt/ *noun* a stiff bar tied to a broken part of the body to prevent the bone from moving

splinter group /ˈsplɪntə gruːp/ *noun* a group of people who have separated from a main group ○ *The protesters are from a splinter group which broke away from the party some years ago.*

② **split** /splɪt/ (**splits, splitting, split**) *verb* **1.** to divide something into parts ○ *He split the log into small pieces with an axe.* **2.** to divide or come apart ○ *My trousers were too tight – they split when I bent down.* ○ *After they lost the election, the party split into various factions.*

split up *phrasal verb* **1.** to divide ○ *We must try to split up the class into groups of three or four.* **2.** to start to live apart ○ *They had a row and split up.*

split second /splɪt ˈsekənd/ *noun* a very short space of time

splutter /ˈsplʌtə/ (**splutters, spluttering, spluttered**) *verb* **1.** to speak rapidly, using very short phrases, especially when angry ○ *'what, what, what ... do you mean by that?' he spluttered in fury.* **2.** to make a hissing sound ○ *The wet logs were spluttering on the fire.*

② **spoil** /spɔɪl/ (**spoils, spoiling, spoiled** or **spoilt**) *verb* **1.** to change something which was good so that it is no longer good ○ *We had such bad weather that our camp-*

ing holiday was spoilt. ○ *Half the contents of the warehouse were spoiled by floodwater.* **2.** to be too kind to someone, especially a child, so that he or she sometimes becomes badly behaved ○ *You'll spoil that child if you always give in to him.* ○ *Grandparents are allowed to spoil their grandchildren a little.*

spoils /spɔɪlz/ *noun* things bought ○ *She came back from the jumble sale, laden with spoils.*

spoilsport /ˈspɔɪlspɔːt/ *noun* a person who spoils other people's enjoyment

spoilt /spɔɪlt/ *adj* (*of a child*) treated in a way which is too kind, and so is badly behaved

spoke /spəʊk/ past tense of **speak**

spoken /ˈspəʊkən/ past participle of **speak** ■ *adj* said aloud

sponge /spʌndʒ/ *noun* **1.** a soft material full of small holes used to make things like cushions ○ *The sofa has sponge cushions.* **2.** a sea animal with a skeleton which is full of holes ○ *Diving down into the Red Sea you could see sponges on the sea floor.* ■ *verb* (**sponges, sponging, sponged**) to wipe clean with a sponge ○ *He sponged the kitchen table.*

sponge bag /spʌndʒ bæg/ *noun* a bag used to hold toiletries, especially when travelling

sponge cake /ˈspʌndʒ keɪk/ *noun* a light soft cake

spongy /ˈspʌndʒi/ *adj* soft and full of holes

sponsor /ˈspɒnsə/ *noun* **1.** a person or company that pays to financially help a sport, an exhibition or a music festival, in return for the right to advertise at sporting events, on sports clothes or programmes **2.** a company which pays part of the cost of making a TV or radio programme by advertising on the programme **3.** a person who pays money to a charity when someone else walks, swims, or runs a certain distance **4.** a person who takes responsibility for someone ■ *verb* (**sponsors, sponsoring, sponsored**) **1.** to be a sponsor ○ *The company has sponsored the football match.* ○ *Will you sponsor me if I apply to join the club?* ○ *I sponsored her to take part in a marathon for charity.* **2.** to be the god-parent of a child and promise to help the child to lead a Christian life (NOTE: + **sponsorship** *n*)

spontaneous /spɒnˈteɪniəs/ *adj* which happens of its own accord, which is not forced or prepared in advance

spoof /spuːf/ *noun* an amusing imitation to trick someone

spooky /ˈspuːki/ (**spookier, spookiest**) *adj* frightening and which makes you think there may be ghosts around (*informal*)

spool /spuːl/ *noun* a cylinder round which you wind something

③ **spoon** /spuːn/ *noun* an object used for eating liquids and soft food, or for stirring food which is being cooked, with a handle at one end and a small bowl at the other, ○ *Use a spoon to eat your pudding.* ○ *We need a big spoon to serve the soup.*

spoon-feed /ˈspuːn fiːd/ *verb* **1.** to give someone food with a spoon **2.** to provide everything for people so that they need do nothing to help themselves

spoonful /ˈspuːnfʊl/ *noun* an amount which a spoon can hold

sporadic /spəˈrædɪk/ *adj* happening at irregular intervals

① **sport** /spɔːt/ *noun* a game or games involving physical activity and competition ○ *Do you like watching sport on TV?* ○ *The world of sport is mourning the death of the racing driver.* ○ *The only sport I play is tennis.* ○ *She doesn't play any sport at all.*

sporting /ˈspɔːtɪŋ/ *adj* **1.** referring to sport ○ *a big sporting weekend on TV, with tennis matches, the World Cup and a golf tournament* **2.** pleasant and willing to help, especially when playing a sport ○ *He's a very sporting chap.*

sports car /ˈspɔːts kɑː/ *noun* a fast open car

sports centre /ˈspɔːts ˌsentə/ *noun* a place where several different sports can be played

sportsman /ˈspɔːtsmən/ (*plural* **sportsmen**) *noun* a man who plays a sport

sportsmanlike /ˈspɔːtsmənlaɪk/ *adj* fair and polite

sportsmanship /ˈspɔːtsmənʃɪp/ *noun* fair and polite behaviour when playing sport

sportswear /ˈspɔːtsweə/ *noun* clothes worn to play sport (NOTE: no plural)

sportswoman /ˈspɔːtsˌwʊmən/ (*plural* **sportswomen**) *noun* a woman who plays a sport

sporty /ˈspɔːti/ *adj* interested in sport and enjoying sport

① **spot** /spɒt/ *noun* **1.** a coloured mark, usually round ○ *Her dress has a pattern of white and red spots.* ○ *He wore a blue tie with white spots.* **2.** a particular place ○ *This is the exact spot where the queen died.*

3. a small round mark or pimple on the skin ○ *She suddenly came out in spots after eating fish.* ■ *verb* (**spots, spotting, spotted**) to notice something or someone ○ *The teacher didn't spot the mistake.* ○ *We spotted him in the crowd.* ◇ **on the spot 1.** at a particular place where something happens ○ *I happened to be on the spot when the incident took place.* **2.** immediately ○ *I gave her his number and she phoned him on the spot.*

spot check /ˈspɒt tʃek/ *noun* a check made suddenly and at random

spotless /ˈspɒtləs/ *adj* completely clean, with no dirty marks at all

spotlight /ˈspɒtlaɪt/ *noun* a bright light which shines on one small area ○ *She stood in the spotlights on the stage.* ■ *verb* (**spotlights, spotlighting, spotlit** or **spotlighted**) to draw attention to something clearly ○ *We want to spotlight the dangers of riding bicycles without lights.*

spot-on /spɒt ˈɒn/ *adj* absolutely correct (*informal*) ○ *His analysis of the situation was spot-on.*

spotty /ˈspɒti/ (**spottier, spottiest**) *adj* covered with pimples

spouse /spaʊs/ *noun* a husband or wife

spout /spaʊt/ *noun* a tube on a container which is shaped for pouring liquid out of the container ○ *You fill the kettle through the spout.* ○ *Cut here and pull out to form a spout.*

sprain /spreɪn/ *verb* (**sprains, spraining, sprained**) to damage a joint of the body by twisting it suddenly and violently ○ *He sprained his ankle jumping over the fence.* ■ *noun* a condition where a joint is injured because of a sudden violent movement ○ *He is walking with a stick because of an ankle sprain.*

sprang /spræŋ/ past tense of **spring**

sprawl /sprɔːl/ (**sprawls, sprawling, sprawled**) *verb* to lie with your arms and legs spread out ○ *He sprawled in his armchair and turned on the TV.* ○ *The boy on the bike hit her and sent her sprawling.*

③ **spray** /spreɪ/ *noun* a mass of tiny drops of liquid ○ *The waves crashed against the sea wall sending spray over the road.* ○ *An aerosol sends out a liquid in a fine spray.* ○ *She uses a nasal spray to clear her catarrh.* ■ *verb* (**sprays, spraying, sprayed**) to send out liquid in fine drops ○ *He sprayed water all over the garden with the hose.* ○ *They sprayed the room with disinfectant.*

② **spread** /spred/ *verb* (**spreads, spreading, spread**) **1.** to arrange over a wide area ○ *Spread the paper flat on the table.* **2.** to move over a wide area [~to] ○ *The fire started in the top floor and soon spread to the roof.* ○ *The flu epidemic spread rapidly.* **3.** to cover with a layer of something [~over/~on] ○ *She spread a white cloth over the table.* ○ *He was spreading butter on a piece of bread.* ■ *noun* **1.** the action of moving over a wide area ○ *Doctors are trying to check the spread of the disease.* **2.** a soft food consisting of meat, fish or cheese, which you can spread on something such as bread ○ *As snacks, they offered us water biscuits with cheese spread.*

spreadsheet /ˈspredʃiːt/ *noun* a display of columns of figures produced by a computer

spree /spriː/ *noun* a short time of doing something enjoyable

sprig /sprɪɡ/ *noun* a little branch

sprightly /ˈspraɪtli/ (**sprightlier, sprightliest**) *adj* lively and energetic

① **spring** /sprɪŋ/ *noun* **1.** the season of the year between winter and summer ○ *In spring all the trees start to grow new leaves.* ○ *We always go to Greece in the spring.* ○ *They started work last spring* or *in the spring of last year and they still haven't finished.* **2.** a wire which is twisted round and round and which goes back to its original shape after you have pulled it or pushed it ○ *The mattress is so old the springs have burst through the cover.* ○ *There's a spring to keep the door shut.* **3.** a place where a stream of water rushes out of the ground ○ *The town of Bath was built in Roman times around hot springs.* ■ *verb* (**springs, springing, sprang, sprung**) to move suddenly ○ *Everyone sprang to life when the officer shouted.* ○ *The door sprang open without anyone touching it.*

spring from *verb* to come suddenly from ○ *Where on earth did you spring from?*

springboard /ˈsprɪŋbɔːd/ *noun* **1.** a long flexible board used to dive or jump off **2.** a thing used to help you start something ○ *He bought a small company and used it as a springboard to enter the US market.*

spring-clean /ˌsprɪŋ ˈkliːn/ *verb* to clean a house thoroughly ○ *It took me a week to spring-clean the house.* (NOTE: + **spring-clean** *n*)

spring onion /sprɪŋ ˈʌnjən/ *noun* a very small onion with long green leaves, used in salads and in cooking (NOTE: The US term is **scallions**.)

springtime /ˈsprɪŋtaɪm/ *noun* the time of year when it is spring

sprinkle /ˈsprɪŋkəl/ (**sprinkles, sprinkling, sprinkled**) *verb* to put small amounts of a liquid or powder over a surface by shaking

sprinkler /ˈsprɪŋklə/ *noun* a device for sprinkling water

sprinkling /ˈsprɪŋklɪŋ/ *noun* a small or thin scattering

sprint /sprɪnt/ (**sprints, sprinting, sprinted**) *verb* to run very fast over a short distance ○ *I had to sprint to catch the bus.* ○ *She sprinted down the track.* (NOTE: + **sprint** *n*)

sprinter /ˈsprɪntə/ *noun* a runner who runs in sprint races

sprout /spraʊt/ *noun* a new shoot of a plant ○ *The vine is covered with new sprouts.* ■ *verb* (**sprouts, sprouting, sprouted**) to produce new shoots ○ *Throw those old potatoes away, they're starting to sprout.* ○ *The bush had begun to sprout fresh green leaves.*

spruce /spruːs/ (*plural same* or **spruces**) *noun* a softwood tree growing in cold forests ○ *a forest of spruce*

sprung /sprʌŋ/ past participle of **spring**

spry /spraɪ/ *adj* agile and lively

spud /spʌd/ *noun* a potato (*informal*)

spun /spʌn/ past participle of **spin**

spur /spɜː/ *noun* something which stimulates an action ○ *The letter from the university was the spur that encouraged him to work harder.* ■ *verb* (**spurs, spurring, spurred**) to urge someone on ○ *The runners were spurred on by the shouts of the crowd.*

spurious /ˈspjʊəriəs/ *adj* not based on facts

spurn /spɜːn/ (**spurns, spurning, spurned**) *verb* to reject an offer scornfully

spurt /spɜːt/ *verb* **1.** *also* **spurt out** to come out in a strong jet ○ *Oil spurted out of the burst pipe.* **2.** to run fast suddenly ○ *He spurted past two runners and came in first.* ■ *noun* **1.** a strong flow of liquid ○ *They tried to block the spurts of water coming out of the pipe.* **2.** a sudden sudden effort ○ *He put on a spurt and won the race.*

sputter /ˈspʌtə/ (**sputters, sputtering, sputtered**) *verb* to send out sparks or small drops

spy /spaɪ/ *noun* (*plural* **spies**) a person who is paid to try to find out secret information about the enemy or a rival group [~for] ○ *He was a spy for the Russians.* ■ *verb* (**spies, spying, spied**) **1.** to work as a spy [~for] ○ *He spied for the Russians.* **2.** to watch someone in secret, to find out what they are planning to do [~on] ○ *Their neighbours had been spying on them and told the police.*

spyhole /ˈspaɪˌhəʊl/ *noun* a small hole in a door for looking through to see who is there

sq *abbr* square

squabble /ˈskwɒb(ə)l/ (**squabbles, squabbling, squabbled**) *verb* to argue ○ *They spent the whole evening squabbling over money.* (NOTE: + **squabble** *n*)

③ **squad** /skwɒd/ *noun* **1.** a small group of soldiers who perform duties together ○ *Corporal, take your squad and guard the prisoners.* **2.** a department in the police service ○ *He's the head of the drugs squad.* ○ *She's investigating on behalf of the fraud squad.* **3.** a group of players from whom a sports team will be chosen ○ *The England squad for the World Cup has been selected.*

squad car /ˈskwɒd kɑː/ *noun* a police car on patrol duty

③ **squadron** /ˈskwɒdrən/ *noun* a group of aircraft or of naval ships

squalid /ˈskwɒlɪd/ *adj* referring to a room or building that is dirty and unpleasant ○ *The prisoners are kept in squalid conditions.*

squall /skwɔːl/ *noun* a sudden gust of wind ○ *A sudden squall capsized the boat.*

squalor /ˈskwɒlə/ *noun* dirty conditions

squander /ˈskwɒndə/ (**squanders, squandering, squandered**) *verb* to waste money, energy or opportunity

① **square** /skweə/ *noun* **1.** a shape with four equal sides and four right-angled corners ○ *The board on which you play chess is made up of black and white squares.* ○ *Graph paper is covered with small squares.* **2.** an open space in a town, with big buildings all round ○ *The hotel is in the main square of the town, opposite the town hall.* ○ *Red Square is in the middle of Moscow.* **3.** (*in mathematics*) a number that is the result of multiplying another number by itself ○ *9 is the square of 3.* ■ *adj* **1.** shaped like a square, with four equal sides and four right-angled corners ○ *You can't fit six people round a small square table.* ○ *An A4 piece of paper isn't square.* **2.** multiplied by itself ◇ **back to square one** to start again from the point you originally started from (*informal*) ○ *The test plane crashed, so it's back to square one again.*

squarely /ˈskweəli/ *adv* in a direct and straightforward way ○ *He looked her squarely in the face.*

square meal /skweə ˈmiːl/ *noun* a large meal

square root /skweə ˈruːt/ *noun* a number which, multiplied by itself, will produce a particular number ○ *3 is the square root of 9.*

squash /skwɒʃ/ *verb* (**squashes, squashing, squashed**) to crush or to squeeze something ○ *Hundreds of passengers were squashed into the train.* ○ *He sat on my hat and squashed it flat.* ■ *noun* a fast game for two players played in an enclosed court, with a small, squashy rubber ball and light, long-handled rackets ○ *He plays squash to unwind after a day at the office.* ○ *Let's play a game of squash.*

③ **squat** /skwɒt/ (**squats, squatting, squatted**) *verb* to move your body close to the ground so that you are sitting on your heels ○ *She squatted on the floor, trying to get the stains out of the carpet.*

squatter /ˈskwɒtə/ *noun* a person who squats in someone else's property or illegally on waste ground

squawk /skwɔːk/ (**squawks, squawking, squawked**) *verb* to make short harsh cries ○ *The eagle brought back some food for her squawking chicks.* (NOTE: + **squawk** *n*)

squeak /skwiːk/ *noun* a quiet high sound like the sound that a mouse makes ○ *You can tell when someone comes into the garden by the squeak of the gate.* ■ *verb* (**squeaks, squeaking, squeaked**) to make a squeak ○ *That door squeaks – the hinges need oiling.*

squeaky clean /ˌskwiːki ˈkliːn/ *noun* **1.** extremely clean ○ *All the work surfaces have to be squeaky clean.* **2.** morally pure ○ *The minister's squeaky clean image has been tarnished by the scandal.*

squeal /skwiːl/ *noun* a loud high noise ○ *The children let out squeals of delight when they saw the presents under the Christmas tree.* ○ *The car turned the corner with a squeal of tyres.* ■ *verb* (**squeals, squealing, squealed**) to make a loud high-pitched noise ○ *She squealed when she heard she had won first prize.* ○ *As the car turned the corner its tyres squealed.*

squeamish /ˈskwiːmɪʃ/ *adj* likely to be upset by nasty things

③ **squeeze** /skwiːz/ *noun* the act of pressing or crushing ○ *I gave her hand a squeeze.* ■ *verb* (**squeezes, squeezing, squeezed**) **1.** to press on something or to press or crush something like a fruit or a tube to get something out of it ○ *She squeezed my arm gently.* ○ *He squeezed an orange to get the juice.* ○ *She squeezed some toothpaste out onto her brush.* **2.** to force something, or to force your own body, into a small space ○ *You can't squeeze six people into that little car.* ○ *More people tried to squeeze on the train even though it was full already.* ○ *The cat managed to squeeze through the window.*

squelch /skweltʃ/ (**squelches, squelching, squelched**) *verb* to make a wet sucking noise ○ *He squelched through the mud.* (NOTE: + **squelch** *n*)

squid /skwɪd/ (*plural same* or **squids**) *noun* a sea animal with eight long arms or tentacles, smaller than an octopus

squiggle /ˈskwɪɡ(ə)l/ *noun* a curved, irregular line or mark

squint /skwɪnt/ (**squints, squinting, squinted**) *verb* **1.** to have eyes which look in different directions ○ *He squints badly, which makes it difficult to know who he is looking at.* **2.** to half-close your eyes to look at a something ○ *The picture shows him squinting at the sun.* ○ *He squinted through the keyhole but couldn't see anything.* (NOTE: + **squint** *n*)

squirm /skwɜːm/ (**squirms, squirming, squirmed**) *verb* **1.** to wriggle about **2.** to feel very embarrassed

squirrel /ˈskwɪrəl/ *noun* a small red or grey wild animal with a large tail which lives in trees and eats nuts ○ *The squirrel sat up on a branch nibbling a nut.* ○ *Squirrels hoard nuts for the winter.*

squirt /skwɜːt/ (**squirts, squirting, squirted**) *verb* to send out a thin powerful flow of liquid ○ *Don't squirt so much washing-up liquid into the bowl.* ○ *She squeezed the tube hard and masses of toothpaste squirted out.* (NOTE: + **squirt** *n*)

squish /skwɪʃ/ (**squishes, squishing, squished**) *verb* to press, squeeze or crush something soft

squishy /ˈskwɪʃi/ *adj* soft, squashy and wet

③ **St** *abbr* **1.** street **2.** saint

③ **stab** /stæb/ *verb* (**stabs, stabbing, stabbed**) to push a sharp knife with force into someone or something ○ *He was stabbed in the chest.* ■ *noun* a deep wound made by the point of a knife ○ *He died of stab wounds.* ◇ **to have a stab at something** to try to do something ○ *I'm keen to have a stab at driving the tractor.* ◇ **stab in the back** an attack by someone who is thought to be a friend ○ *His speech was a stab in the back for the party leader.* ◇ **to**

stab someone in the back to do something unpleasant to someone who thinks you are a friend ○ *She was stabbed in the back by people who owed their success to her.*

stabbing /'stæbɪŋ/ *noun* an attack where someone is stabbed ○ *The stabbing of the young nurse shocked everyone.*

③ **stability** /stə'bɪlɪti/ *noun* being stable or steady

③ **stable** /'steɪb(ə)l/ *adj* which does not change ○ *The hospital said his condition was stable.* ■ *noun* a building for keeping a horse ○ *My horse is not in his stable, who's riding him?*

stack /stæk/ *noun* a pile or heap of things one on top of the other ○ *a stack of books and papers* □ **a stack of, stacks of** lots of (*informal*) ○ *You can charge the tourists what you like – they've got stacks of money.* ■ *verb* (**stacks, stacking, stacked**) to pile things on top of each other ○ *The skis are stacked outside the chalet.* ○ *She stacked up the dirty plates.* ○ *The warehouse is stacked with boxes.*

stadium /'steɪdiəm/ *noun* a large building where crowds of people watch sport, with seats arranged around a sports field

① **staff** /stɑːf/ *noun* all the people who work in a company, school, college, or other organisation ○ *She's on the school staff.* ○ *Only staff can use this lift.* ○ *A quarter of our staff are ill.* ○ *That firm pays its staff very badly.* ○ *He joined the staff last Monday.* ○ *Three members of staff are away sick.* (NOTE: **staff** refers to a group of people and so is often followed by a verb in the plural.)

staffing /'stɑːfɪŋ/ *noun* the process of providing workers for an organisation

stag /stæg/ *noun* **1.** an adult male deer ○ *Don't approach the stags in the autumn – they can be very dangerous.* (NOTE: Female deer are **does**.) **2.** a person who buys a new issue of shares and sells them immediately to make a profit

① **stage** /steɪdʒ/ *noun* **1.** a raised floor, especially where the actors perform in a theatre ○ *The pop group came onto the stage and started to sing.* **2.** one of several points of development [~of/in] ○ *the different stages of a production process* ○ *The first stage in the process is to grind the rock to powder.* □ **in stages** in different steps ○ *The company has agreed to repay the loan in stages.* **3.** a section of a long journey ○ *Stage one of the tour takes us from Paris to Bordeaux.* ■ *verb* (**stages, staging, staged**) to put on or arrange a play, a show, a musical or other performance or event ○ *The exhibition is being staged in the college library.*

stagecoach /'steɪdʒkəʊtʃ/ *noun* (*in the 18th and 19th centuries*) a horse-drawn passenger coach which used to run regularly along certain routes

stage fright /'steɪdʒ fraɪt/ *noun* nervousness which actors feel before going onto the stage

stage manager /steɪdʒ 'mænɪdʒə/ *noun* a person who organises a performance of a play, opera or other performance

stagger /'stægə/ *verb* (**staggers, staggering, staggered**) **1.** to walk unsteadily, almost falling down ○ *She managed to stagger across the road and into the police station.* ○ *Three men staggered out of the pub.* **2.** to surprise someone very much ○ *I was staggered at the amount they charge for service.* **3.** to arrange something such as holidays or working hours, so that they do not all begin and end at the same time ○ *We have to stagger the lunch hour so that there is always someone on the switchboard.* ■ *noun* the movement of someone who is staggering ○ *He walked with a noticeable stagger.*

staggered /'stægəd/ *adj* **1.** shocked or very surprised at something **2.** not in a consecutive sequence or in a straight line

staggering /'stægərɪŋ/ *adj* very surprising

stagnant /'stægnənt/ *adj* **1.** (*of water*) which does not flow, which is not pure enough to drink ○ *The marsh was full of stagnant pools of brown water.* ○ *Mosquitoes breed in stagnant water.* **2.** (*of business*) not active, not increasing ○ *Turnover was stagnant for the first half of the year.* ○ *There is a danger of the economy becoming stagnant.*

stagnate /stæg'neɪt/ (**stagnates, stagnating, stagnated**) *verb* not to increase, not to make progress

staid /steɪd/ *adj* serious and solemn

③ **stain** /steɪn/ *noun* a mark which is difficult to remove, e.g. ink or blood ○ *It is difficult to remove coffee stains from the tablecloth.* ○ *There was a round stain on the table where he had put his wine glass.* ■ *verb* (**stains, staining, stained**) to make a mark of a different colour on something ○ *If you eat those berries they will stain your teeth.* ○ *His shirt was stained with blood.*

stained glass /ˌsteɪnd ˈglɑːs/ *noun* glass which has been coloured, used for making church windows

stainless steel /ˌsteɪnləs ˈstiːl/ *noun* a type of steel with a high percentage of chromium in it, which makes it less likely to rust

② **stair** /steə/ *noun* one step in a series of steps, going up or down inside a building ○ *He was sitting on the bottom stair.* ■ *plural noun* **stairs** steps which go up or down inside a building. ◊ **downstairs**, **upstairs**

staircase /ˈsteəkeɪs/ *noun* a set of stairs which go from one floor in a building to another

stairway /ˈsteəweɪ/ *noun* a set of stairs which go from one floor inside or outside a building to another

③ **stake** /steɪk/ *noun* a strong pointed piece of wood or metal, pushed into the ground to mark something, or to hold something up [~in/into] ○ *They hammered stakes into the ground to put up a wire fence.* ○ *The apple trees are attached to stakes.*

stale /steɪl/ *adj* food which is stale is old and no longer fresh (NOTE: **staler – stalest**)

stalemate /ˈsteɪlmeɪt/ *noun* **1.** (*in chess*) a situation where neither player can make any move permitted by the rules, and so no one wins **2.** a situation where neither side will compromise ○ *The discussions have reached a stalemate.* ○ *Negotiations are continuing to try to break the stalemate* or *to find a way out of the stalemate.*

stalk /stɔːk/ *noun* the stem of a plant which holds a leaf, a flower or a fruit ○ *Roses with very long stalks are more expensive.* ■ *verb* (**stalks, stalking, stalked**) to stay near someone and watch him or her all the time, especially in a way that is frightening or upsetting ○ *She told the police that a man was stalking her.* ○ *The hunters stalked the deer for several miles.*

stalker /ˈstɔːkə/ *noun* a person who follows people or animals

stall /stɔːl/ *noun* a place in a market where one person sells his or her goods ○ *He has a flower stall at Waterloo Station.* ○ *We wandered round the market looking at the stalls.* ■ *verb* (**stalls, stalling, stalled**) (*of a car engine*) to stop unintentionally, often when trying to drive off without accelerating ○ *If he takes his foot off the accelerator, the engine stalls.* ○ *The car stalled at the traffic lights and he couldn't restart it.*

stallion /ˈstæljən/ *noun* an adult male horse, especially one kept for breeding

stamina /ˈstæmɪnə/ *noun* the strength to do something over a long period

stammer /ˈstæmə/ *verb* (**stammers, stammering, stammered**) to repeat sounds when speaking, e.g. because of feeling nervous ○ *He stammers badly when making speeches.* ○ *She rushed into the police station and stammered out 'he's – he's – he's after me, he's got – got – a knife'.* ■ *noun* a speech problem that involves hesitating and repeating sounds when speaking ○ *Because of his stammer he was shy and reserved at school.*

① **stamp** /stæmp/ *noun* **1.** a little piece of paper with a price printed on it which you stick on a letter to show that you have paid for it to be sent by post ○ *a first-class stamp* ○ *She forgot to put a stamp on the letter before she posted it.* ○ *He wants to show me his stamp collection.* **2.** a mark made on something ○ *The invoice has the stamp 'received with thanks' on it.* ○ *The customs officer looked at the stamps in his passport.* ■ *verb* (**stamps, stamping, stamped**) **1.** to mark something with a stamp ○ *They stamped my passport when I entered the country.* **2.** to walk heavily, banging your feet on the ground [~on] ○ *They stamped on the ants to kill them.* ○ *He was so angry that he stamped out of the room.*

stamp out *phrasal verb* to stop something

stampede /stæmˈpiːd/ *noun* an uncontrolled movement of many animals or people ○ *After the film finished there was a stampede for the doors.* (NOTE: + **stampede** *v*)

stance /stæns/ *noun* **1.** the position of someone when standing ○ *His stance is so awkward I'm surprised he can even hit the ball.* **2.** a point of view or opinion ○ *Her stance on environmental issues is surprising.* ○ *The Conservative Party takes a different stance towards health.*

① **stand** /stænd/ *verb* (**stands, standing, stood**) **1.** to be upright on your feet, the opposite of sitting or lying down ○ *She stood on a chair to reach the top shelf.* ○ *They were so tired they could hardly keep standing.* ○ *If there are no seats left, we'll have to stand.* ○ *Don't just stand there doing nothing – come and help us.* **2.** to be upright ○ *Only a few houses were still standing after the earthquake.* ○ *The jar was standing in the middle of the table.* **3.** to accept something bad that continues ○ *The office is filthy – I don't know how you can stand working here.* ○ *She can't stand all this noise.* ○ *He stopped going to French* *lessons because he couldn't stand the teacher.* ■ *noun* something which holds something up ○ *The pot of flowers fell off its stand.*

stand by *phrasal verb* **1.** to refuse to change something you have said ○ *I stand by what I said in my statement to the police.* **2.** to stand and watch, without getting involved ○ *Several people just stood by and made no attempt to help.* **3.** to be ready ○ *We have several fire engines standing by.* **4.** to give help ○ *She stood by him while he was in prison.*

stand down *phrasal verb* to agree not to stay in a position or not to stand for election

stand for *phrasal verb* **1.** to have a meaning ○ *What do the letters BBC stand for?* **2.** to be a candidate in an election ○ *She's standing for parliament.* **3.** to accept ○ *They will never stand for that.* ○ *I won't stand for any nonsense from the children.*

stand out *phrasal verb* **1.** to be easily seen ○ *Their house stands out because it is painted pink.* ○ *Her red hair makes her stand out in a crowd.* **2.** to be very clear against a background ○ *That picture would stand out better against a white wall.* **3.** to be much better than others ○ *Two of the young musicians stood out for their interpretations of Bach.*

stand up③ *phrasal verb* **1.** to get up from sitting ○ *When the teacher comes into the room all the children should stand up.* ○ *He stood up to offer his seat to the old lady.* **2.** to stand upright, to hold yourself upright ○ *Stand up straight and face forward.* **3.** to put something in an upright position ○ *Stand the books up on the shelf.* ○ *She stood her umbrella up by the door.* **4.** □ **to stand someone up** not to meet someone even though you had arranged to (*informal*) ○ *We were going to have dinner together and he stood me up.*

stand up for *phrasal verb* to try to defend someone or something in a difficult situation ○ *He stood up for the rights of children.*

stand up to *phrasal verb* **1.** to oppose someone bravely ○ *No one was prepared to stand up to the head of department.* **2.** to be able to resist difficult conditions ○ *A carpet in a shop has to stand up to a lot of wear.*

③ **standard** /ˈstændəd/ *noun* **1.** the level of quality something has ○ *The standard of service in this restaurant is very high.* ○ *This piece of work is not up to your usual standard.* **2.** an excellent quality which is set as a target ○ *This product does not meet our standards.* ○ *She has set a standard which it will be difficult to match.* **3.** a large official flag ○ *The royal standard flies over Buckingham Palace.* ■ *adj* **1.** usual, not special ○ *She joined on a standard contract.* ○ *You will need to follow the standard procedure to join the association.* **2.** on a tall pole

standby /ˈstændbaɪ/ *noun* a thing which is ready to be used if necessary ○ *I always have bread in the freezer as a standby.* □ **on standby** waiting and ready to act if needed ○ *We have a doctor on standby.* ○ *Army reservists have been put on standby.*

stand-in /ˈstænd ɪn/ *noun* a person who takes the place of someone else

standing /ˈstændɪŋ/ *noun* **1.** the position of being upright on your feet ○ *Standing all day at the exhibition is very tiring.* **2.** reputation ○ *a hotel of good standing* ○ *His standing in the community has never been higher.*

standing army /ˌstændɪŋ ˈɑːmi/ *noun* a professional military force which exists in times of peace as well as war

standing joke /ˈstændɪŋ dʒəʊk/ *noun* something that people often make jokes about ○ *His style of dancing is a bit of a standing joke with us.*

standing order /ˌstændɪŋ ˈɔːdə/ *noun* an order written by a customer asking a bank to pay money regularly to an account, or to a company to send something regularly

standing ovation /ˌstændɪŋ əʊ ˈveɪʃ(ə)n/ *noun* applause at the end of a performance where all the audience stand up and clap and cheer

stand-off /ˈstænd ɒf/ *noun* a situation where two sides cannot agree and neither can win

standpoint /ˈstændpɔɪnt/ *noun* a position from which you look at a problem

standstill /ˈstændstɪl/ *noun* a situation where nothing moves

stank /stæŋk/ past tense of **stink**

stanza /ˈstænzə/ *noun* a section of a poem made up of a series of lines

staple /ˈsteɪp(ə)l/ *noun* a piece of wire which is pushed through papers and bent over to hold them together ○ *He used some scissors to take the staples out of the papers.* ■ *verb* (**staples, stapling, stapled**) to fasten papers together with a staple or with staples ○ *Don't staple the cheque to the order form.*

staple diet /ˌsteɪp(ə)l ˈdaɪət/ *noun* the main part of what you eat

stapler /ˈsteɪplə/ *noun* a device used to attach papers together with staples

③ **star** /stɑː/ *noun* **1.** a bright object which can be seen in the sky at night like a very distant bright light ○ *On a clear night you can see thousands of stars.* ○ *The pole star shows the direction of the North Pole.* **2.** a shape that has several points like a star ○ *Draw a big star and colour it red.* **3.** a famous person who is very well known to the public ○ *football stars* ○ *She's one of the stars of the latest Spielberg movie.* ○ *Who is your favourite film star?* ■ *verb* (**stars, starring, starred**) to appear as a main character in a film or play [~in/~opposite/~with/alongside] ○ *He starred opposite Meg Ryan in 'When Harry Met Sally'* ○ *She starred in 'Gone with the Wind'.* ○ *He'll be starring with such big names as Tom Cruise and Gene Hackman.* ○ *Mike Myers stars as the bungling hero.* ○ *He has a starring role in the new production of 'Guys and Dolls'.*

starboard /ˈstɑːbəd/ *noun* the right-hand side of a ship or aircraft when facing the front

starch /stɑːtʃ/ *noun* the usual form in which carbohydrates exist in food, especially in bread, rice and potatoes ○ *To get a balanced diet you need to eat both protein and starch.*

starchy /ˈstɑːtʃi/ *adj* **1.** (*of food*) which contains a lot of starch ○ *Children eat too much starchy food.* **2.** very formal ○ *His starchy manner put everyone off.*

stardom /ˈstɑːdəm/ *noun* the state of being a film star, a football star etc.

② **stare** /steə/ *verb* (**stares, staring, stared**) to look at someone or something for a long time [~at] ○ *It's rude to stare at people.* ○ *She stared sadly out of the window at the rain.* ■ *noun* a long fixed look ○ *He gave her a stare and walked on.*

starfish /ˈstɑːfɪʃ/ (*plural same* or **starfishes**) *noun* a flat sea animal, with five arms branching like a star from a central body

stark /stɑːk/ *adj* (**starker, starkest**) **1.** complete ○ *He stared at the figures in stark disbelief.* **2.** bare and simple ○ *the stark outline of the rocks* ○ *a stark lunar landscape* ■ *adv* completely ○ *I don't usually walk round the house stark naked.*

starlight /ˈstɑːlaɪt/ *noun* the light from the stars

starling /ˈstɑːlɪŋ/ *noun* a common dark European bird with a green gloss to its feathers

starry-eyed /ˈstɑːri aɪd/ *adj* unrealistically optimistic about your future life or career

star sign /ˈstɑː saɪn/ *noun* the sign of the zodiac which marks your birth

star-studded /stɑː ˈstʌdɪd/ *adj* including many film or stage stars

① **start** /stɑːt/ *noun* the beginning of something ○ *It's the start of the fishing season tomorrow.* ○ *Building the house took only six months from start to finish.* ○ *Things went wrong from the start.* ○ *Let's forget all you've done up to now, and make a fresh start.* ■ *verb* (**starts, starting, started**) **1.** to begin to do something [~as/~by] ○ *He didn't start as an actor – he was a director first.* ○ *When you learn Russian, you have to start by learning the alphabet.* ○ *The babies all started to cry* or *all started crying at the same time.* ○ *He started to eat* or *he started eating his dinner before the rest of the family.* ○ *Take an umbrella – it's starting to rain.* **2.** (*of a machine*) to begin to work ○ *The car won't start – the battery must be flat.* ○ *The engine started beautifully.* ◇ **to start with** first of all ○ *We have lots to do but to start with we'll do the washing up.* ◇ **for a start** as the first point ○ *For a start, tell me the exact time when you made the phone call.*

start off *phrasal verb* **1.** to begin ○ *We'll start off with soup and then have a meat dish.* **2.** to leave on a journey ○ *You can start off now, and I'll follow when I'm ready.*

start out *phrasal verb* **1.** to leave on a journey ○ *She started out for home two hours ago, so I am surprised she hasn't arrived.* **2.** to begin ○ *I'd like to start out by saying how pleased I am to be here.*

start up *phrasal verb* **1.** to make a business begin to work ○ *She started up a restaurant, but it failed.* **2.** to make a machine start to work ○ *He started up the tractor.*

starter /ˈstɑːtə/ *noun* **1.** a person who starts doing something ○ *There were sixty starters in the race, but only twenty finished.* **2.** a person who organises the start of something ○ *The starter fired his pistol and the race started.* **3.** the first part of a meal ○ *What do you all want as starters?* ○ *I don't want a starter – just the main course.* ◇ **for starters** as the first thing to be done ○ *We need to get the room cleaned for starters.*

starting point /ˈstɑːtɪŋ pɔɪnt/ *noun* a place where something begins

startle /ˈstɑːt(ə)l/ (**startles, startling, startled**) *verb* to make someone suddenly surprised

starvation /stɑːˈveɪʃ(ə)n/ *noun* illness through lack of food

③ **starve** /stɑːv/ (**starves, starving, starved**) *verb* not to have enough food ○ *Many people starved to death in the desert.*

starving /ˈstɑːvɪŋ/ *adj* **1.** not having enough to eat to stay healthy ○ *Relief workers tried to bring supplies to the starving people.* **2.** very hungry (*informal*) ○ *Isn't dinner ready yet, I'm absolutely starving!*

stash /stæʃ/ *verb* (**stashes, stashing, stashed**) **1.** *also* **stash away** to store in a safe place ○ *He has thousands of dollars stashed away in overseas bank accounts.* **2.** to put ○ *Make sure you stash all items of hand luggage in the rack above your seat.* ■ *noun* a hidden store of things ○ *We found a stash of old love letters in a secret drawer.*

① **state** /steɪt/ *noun* **1.** the way something or someone is at a specific time ○ *The children are in a state of excitement.* ○ *They left the flat in a terrible state.* ○ *She's not in a fit state to receive visitors.* **2.** the government of a country ○ *We all pay taxes to the state.* ○ *The state should pay for the upkeep of museums.* **3.** an independent country ○ *The member states of the European Union.* **4.** one of the parts of a federal country ○ *the State of Arizona* ○ *New South Wales has the largest population of all the Australian states.* ■ *verb* (**states, stating, stated**) to give information clearly [~that] ○ *Please state your name and address.* ○ *It states in the instructions that you must not open the can near a flame.* ○ *The document states that all revenue has to be declared to the tax office.* ◇ **in a state 1.** in a very unhappy, worried or upset condition ○ *She's in such a state that I don't want to leave her alone.* ○ *He was in a terrible state after the phone call.* **2.** in a dirty or bad condition ○ *Look at the state of your trousers.* ○ *They left our flat in a terrible state.*

stateless /ˈsteɪtləs/ *adj* who is not a citizen of any country

stately home /ˌsteɪtli ˈhəʊm/ *noun* a palace or large house, usually belonging to an aristocratic family

① **statement** /ˈsteɪtmənt/ *noun* **1.** something that is spoken or written publicly [~on/about] ○ *a statement about or on the new procedures* ○ *She refused to issue a statement to the press.* **2.** same as **bank statement**

state-of-the-art /ˌsteɪt əv ði ˈɑːt/ *adj* technically as advanced as possible

state school /ˈsteɪt skuːl/ *noun* a school which is funded by the state. Compare **private school**, **public school**

statesman /ˈsteɪtsmən/ (*plural* **statesmen**) *noun* an experienced political leader or representative of a country (NOTE: + **statesmanship** *n*)

static /ˈstætɪk/ *noun* **1.** electrical interference in the air which disturbs a radio signal **2.** same as **static electricity** ○ *When I touched the car door the static gave me a shock.*

static electricity /ˌstætɪk ɪlekˈtrɪsɪti/ *noun* an electric charge that does not flow, as opposed to electricity which is flowing in a current

① **station** /ˈsteɪʃ(ə)n/ *noun* **1.** a place where trains stop and passengers get on or off ○ *The train leaves the Central Station at 14.15.* ○ *This is a fast train – it doesn't stop at every station.* ○ *We'll try to get a sandwich at the station buffet.* **2.** a large main building for a service ○ *The fire station is just down the road from us.* ○ *He was arrested and taken to the local police station.*

stationary /ˈsteɪʃ(ə)n(ə)ri/ *adj* not moving (NOTE: Do not confuse with **stationery**.)

stationer /ˈsteɪʃ(ə)nə/ *noun* a person who has a shop which sells stationery

stationery /ˈsteɪʃ(ə)n(ə)ri/ *noun* things such as paper, envelopes, pens and ink which you use for writing (NOTE: no plural. Do not confuse with **stationary**.)

statistic /stəˈtɪstɪk/ *noun* a fact given in the form of numbers

statistician /ˌstætɪˈstɪʃ(ə)n/ *noun* a person who studies or analyses statistics

② **statistics** /stəˈtɪstɪks/ *noun* the study of facts in the form of numbers

statue /ˈstætʃuː/ *noun* a solid image of a person or animal made from a substance such as stone or metal

stature /ˈstætʃə/ *noun* **1.** height ○ *her imposing stature* **2.** importance ○ *His stature in the party has never been greater.*

② **status** /ˈsteɪtəs/ *noun* **1.** social importance when compared to other people ○ *He has a low-status job on the Underground.* ○ *His status in the company has been rising steadily.* **2.** a general position

status symbol /ˈsteɪtəs ˌsɪmbəl/ *noun* a thing which you use which shows that you are more important than someone else

③ **statute** /ˈstætʃuːt/ *noun* a written law, established in an Act of Parliament

statutory /ˈstætʃʊt(ə)ri/ *adj* imposed by law

staunch /stɔːntʃ/ *verb* to stop blood flowing ○ *They tried to staunch the blood by putting ice on the wound.* ○ *They tied a bandage tightly round his arm in an attempt to staunch the flow of blood.*

① **stay** /steɪ/ (**stays, staying, stayed**) *verb* **1.** not to change ○ *The temperature stayed below zero all day.* ○ *In spite of the fire, he stayed calm.* ○ *I won't be able to stay awake until midnight.* **2.** to stop in a place ○ *They came for lunch and stayed until after midnight.* ○ *I'm rather tired so I'll stay at home tomorrow.* ○ *He's ill and has to stay in bed.* **3.** to stop in a place as a visitor ○ *They stayed two nights in Edinburgh on their tour of Scotland.* ○ *Where will you be staying when you're in New York?* ○ *My parents are staying at the Hotel London.*

stay out *phrasal verb* to remain away from home

stay up③ *phrasal verb* not to go to bed

STD *abbr* sexually transmitted disease

stead /sted/ *noun* **1.** □ **it stood him in good stead** it was very useful to him ○ *Being able to speak Japanese stood him in good stead.* **2.** □ **in your stead** in place of you (*formal*) ○ *When he was ill, she took the chair in his stead.* ◊ **instead**

steadily /ˈstedɪli/ *adv* regularly or continuously

③ **steady** /ˈstedi/ *adj* (**steadier, steadiest**) **1.** firm and not moving or shaking ○ *You need a steady hand to draw a straight line without a ruler.* ○ *He put a piece of paper under the table leg to keep it steady.* **2.** continuing in a regular way ○ *There is a steady demand for computers.* ○ *The car was doing a steady seventy miles an hour.* ○ *She hasn't got a steady boyfriend.* ■ *verb* (**steadies, steadying, steadied**) to keep something firm ○ *He put out his hand to steady the ladder.*

steak /steɪk/ *noun* **1.** a thick piece of meat, usually beef ○ *He ordered steak and chips.* ○ *I'm going to grill these steaks.* **2.** a thick piece of a big fish ○ *A grilled salmon steak for me, please!* (NOTE: Do not confuse with **stake**.)

② **steal** /stiːl/ (**steals, stealing, stole, stolen**) *verb* **1.** to take and keep something that belongs to another person without permission [~from] ○ *He stole some CDs from a music shop.* ○ *Someone tried to steal my handbag.* **2.** to move quietly ○ *He stole into the cellar and tried to find the safe.* (NOTE: Do not confuse with **steel**.)

stealth /stelθ/ *noun* □ **by stealth** in a secret way, without anyone knowing ○ *They tried to get into the government laboratory by stealth.*

③ **steam** /stiːm/ *noun* the substance like clouds which comes off hot or boiling water ○ *Clouds of steam were coming out of the kitchen.*

steam up *phrasal verb* to become covered with steam ○ *My glasses got all steamed up when I went into the Palm House at Kew Gardens.*

steamer /ˈstiːmə/ *noun* **1.** a pan with holes in the bottom which is placed over boiling water to cook food by steaming ○ *The best way to cook vegetables is in a steamer.* **2.** a large ship powered by steam ○ *We took the steamer from Cape Town to Mombasa.*

steamroller /ˈstiːmrəʊlə/ *noun* a very heavy vehicle with a large cylinder as a front wheel, used to flatten new road surfaces ■ *verb* (**steamrollers, steamrollering, steamrollered**) to force everyone to do what you want ○ *They steamrollered the bill through Congress.*

steamship /ˈstiːmʃɪp/ *noun* a large ship powered by steam

steamy /ˈstiːmi/ (**steamier, steamiest**) *adj* **1.** hot and humid, as if full of steam ○ *She chose a steamy summer day to visit London.* **2.** full of descriptions of sex ○ *This is her steamiest novel yet.*

② **steel** /stiːl/ *noun* a strong metal made from iron and carbon ○ *Steel knives are best for the kitchen.* ○ *The door is made of solid steel.*

steelworks /ˈstiːlˌwɜːks/ (*plural same*) *noun* a factory where steel is made

steely /ˈstiːli/ *adj* **1.** strongly determined **2.** grey-blue

③ **steep** /stiːp/ *adj* **1.** which rises or falls quickly ○ *The car climbed the steep hill with some difficulty.* ○ *The steps up the church tower are steeper than our stairs at home.* **2.** very sharply increasing or falling ○ *a steep increase in interest charges* ○ *a steep fall in share prices*

steeple /ˈstiːp(ə)l/ *noun* a church tower with a spire on top

steer /stɪə/ (**steers, steering, steered**) *verb* to make a vehicle go in a particular direction ○ *She steered the car into the garage.*

steering /ˈstɪərɪŋ/ *noun* the parts of a vehicle which control the direction in which it travels

stem /stem/ *noun* the tall thin part of a plant which holds a leaf, a flower or a fruit ○ *Trim the stems before you put the flowers in the vase*

stench /stentʃ/ *noun* an unpleasant strong smell

stencil /ˈstensəl/ *noun* a design which is painted in this way ○ *The bathroom is decorated with stencils of fish and shellfish.* ■ *verb* (**stencils, stencilling, stencilled**) to mark with a stencil ○ *His name was stencilled on each piece of luggage.*

③ **step** /step/ *noun* **1.** a movement of your foot when walking ○ *I wonder when the baby will take his first steps.* ○ *Take a step sideways and you will be able to see the castle.* **2.** a regular movement of feet at the same time as other people **3.** one stair, which goes up or down ○ *There are two steps down into the kitchen.* ○ *I counted 75 steps to the top of the tower.* ○ *Be careful, there's a step up into the bathroom.* **4.** an action which is done or has to be done out of several ○ *The first and most important step is to find out how much money we can spend.* ■ *verb* (**steps, stepping, stepped**) to walk in a particular direction ○ *He stepped out in front of a bicycle and was knocked down.* ○ *She stepped off the bus into a puddle.* ○ *Don't step back, there's a child behind you.* ◇ **in step** moving your feet at the same rate as everybody else ○ *I tried to keep in step with him as we walked along.* ○ *The recruits can't even march in step.* ◇ **out of step** moving your feet at a different rate from everyone else ○ *One of the squad always gets out of step.* ◇ **to take steps to** to act to encourage or prevent something ○ *We should take steps to encourage female applicants.* ○ *The museum must take steps to make sure that nothing else is stolen.*

step in *phrasal verb* **1.** to enter ○ *Please step in and see what we have to offer.* **2.** to do something in an area where you were not involved before ○ *Everything was working fine until the manager stepped in.* ○ *Fortunately a teacher stepped in to break up the fight.*

step up *phrasal verb* **1.** to walk onto something higher ○ *He stepped up onto the platform.* **2.** to increase the quantity of something ○ *The company wants to step up production to 2,000 units a day.*

stepbrother /ˈstepbrʌðə/ *noun* the son of a stepfather or stepmother

step-by-step /ˌstep baɪ ˈstep/ *adj* gradual ○ *a step-by-step process*

stepchild /ˈstepˌtʃaɪld/ (*plural* **stepchildren**) *noun* a stepdaughter or stepson

stepdaughter /ˈstepdɔːtə/ *noun* the daughter of a wife or husband from another marriage

stepfather /ˈstepfɑːðə/ *noun* the husband of a mother, who is not a person's father

stepladder /ˈsteplædə/ *noun* a small ladder in two parts, hinged together, which is steady when opened up and does not need to lean on anything

stepmother /ˈstepmʌðə/ *noun* the wife of a father, who is not a person's mother

stepping-stone /ˈstepɪŋ stəʊn/ *noun* **1.** one of a series of large stones placed to allow you to cross a stream ○ *I lost my balance going over the stepping-stones.* **2.** a useful stage in your career ○ *Working in head office is a useful stepping-stone to becoming a manager.*

stepsister /ˈstepsɪstə/ *noun* the daughter of a stepfather or stepmother

stepson /ˈstepsʌn/ *noun* the son of a wife or husband from another marriage

③ **stereo** /ˈsteriəʊ/ *noun* a machine which plays music or other sound through two different loudspeakers ○ *I bought a new pair of speakers for my stereo.* □ **in stereo** using two speakers to produce sound

stereotype /ˈsteriətaɪp/ *noun* a pattern for a certain type of person

sterile /ˈsteraɪl/ *adj* **1.** free from infectious organisms ○ *She put a sterile dressing on the wound.* **2.** infertile, not able to produce offspring ○ *The flowers on some plants are sterile.* **3.** not producing any useful results ○ *They engaged in a sterile debate about human rights.*

sterilise /ˈsterɪlaɪz/ (**sterilises, sterilising, sterilised**), **sterilize** (**sterilizes, sterilizing, sterilized**) *verb* **1.** to make something sterile by killing infectious organisms ○ *Surgical instruments must be sterilised before used.* ○ *The soil needs to be sterilised before being used for greenhouse cultivation.* **2.** to make a person unable to have children ○ *A vasectomy is a surgical operation to sterilise men.*

sterility /steˈrɪlɪti/ *noun* being unable to produce offspring ○ *Increased sterility has been found in men living near the nuclear site.*

sterling /ˈstɜːlɪŋ/ *noun* British currency ○ *The prices are quoted in sterling.*

stern /stɜːn/ *adj* serious and strict ○ *The judge addressed some stern words to the boys.*

steroid /ˈstɪərɔɪd/ *noun* **1.** one of several natural chemical compounds which affect the body and its functions **2.** a synthetic chemical used to treat some disorders and also used by some athletes to improve their strength ○ *The random sample of urine obtained from the athlete proved that he had been taking steroids.* ○ *She was banned from competing after tests showed that she had taken steroids.*

stethoscope /ˈsteθəskəʊp/ *noun* an instrument consisting of a tube with a metal disc at one end and two parts that go in the ears at the other, used by doctors to listen to sounds made inside the body by organs such as the heart or lungs

stew /stjuː/ *noun* a dish of meat and vegetables cooked together for a long time ○ *This lamb stew is a French recipe.* ■ *verb* (**stews, stewing, stewed**) to cook food for a long time in liquid ○ *Stew the apples until they are completely soft.*

steward /ˈstjuːəd/ *noun* **1.** a man who looks after passengers, and serves meals or drinks on a ship, aircraft, train or in a club ○ *The steward served us tea on deck.* **2.** a person who organises public events such as races etc. ○ *The stewards will inspect the course to see if the race can go ahead.*

stewardess /ˌstjuːəˈdes/ *noun* a woman who looks after passengers and serves food and drinks on a ship or aircraft (*dated*)

① **stick** /stɪk/ *noun* **1.** a thin piece of wood ○ *He jabbed a pointed stick into the hole.* ○ *I need a strong stick to tie this plant to.* **2.** a thin branch of a tree **3.** anything long and thin ○ *carrots cut into sticks* ■ *verb* (**sticks, sticking, stuck**) **1.** to attach something somewhere firmly, especially with glue [~on/~together] ○ *She stuck the stamp on the letter.* ○ *Can you stick the pieces of the cup together again?* **2.** to be fixed or not to be able to move [~to/~in] ○ *Some of the sauce stuck to the pan.* ○ *The car was stuck in the mud.* ○ *The door sticks – you need to push it hard to open it.* ○ *He was stuck in Italy without any money.* **3.** to push something into something [~in/into] ○ *He stuck his hand into the hole.* ○ *She stuck her finger in the jam to taste it.* **4.** to stay in a place [~to] ○ *Stick close to your mother and you won't get lost.* **5.** to put up with ○ *I don't know how she can stick working in that office.* ○ *I'm going, I can't stick it here any longer.* ◇ **to stick together** to stay together ○ *If we stick together they should let us into the club.*

stick out *phrasal verb* **1.** to push something out **2.** to be further forward or further away from something ○ *Your wallet is sticking out of your pocket.* ○ *The balcony sticks out over the road.*

stick up *phrasal verb* **1.** to be further up above a surface or to extend beyond a surface ○ *The aerial sticks up above the roof of the car.* **2.** to attach something to something such as a wall or noticeboard for people to see ○ *She stuck up a notice about the village fête.* ◇ **to stick up for someone *or* something** to defend someone or something against criticism ○ *He stuck up for his rights and in the end won the case.* ○ *Will you stick up for me if I get into trouble at school?*

③ **sticker** /ˈstɪkə/ *noun* a small piece of paper or plastic which you can stick on something to show a price, as a decoration or to advertise something

stickler /ˈstɪklə/ *noun* someone who insists on the correctness of details

③ **sticky** /ˈstɪki/ *adj* **1.** covered with something which sticks like glue ○ *My fingers are all sticky.* ○ *This stuff is terribly sticky – I can't get it off my fingers.* **2.** with glue on one side so that it sticks easily

② **stiff** /stɪf/ *adj* **1.** which does not move easily ○ *The lock is very stiff – I can't turn the key.* ○ *I've got a stiff neck.* ○ *She was feeling stiff all over after running in the race.* **2.** with hard bristles ○ *You need a stiff brush to get the mud off your shoes.*

stiffen /ˈstɪf(ə)n/ (**stiffens, stiffening, stiffened**) *verb* **1.** to become or make stiff **2.** to become cautious or unfriendly **3.** (*of wind*) to become stronger **4.** to make stronger ○ *The TV broadcasts helped to stiffen resistance to the government's new measures.*

stiffness /ˈstɪfnəs/ *noun* **1.** having muscle pains after doing exercise, or being unable to move easily because of damaged joints ○ *Arthritis accompanied by a certain amount of stiffness in the joints.* **2.** the quality of being stiff ○ *The stiffness of the material makes it unsuitable for a dress.*

stifle /ˈstaɪf(ə)l/ (**stifles, stifling, stifled**) *verb* **1.** to make someone not able to breathe, not to be able to breathe because of heat or smoke ○ *The firemen were almost stifled by the toxic gas.* **2.** to prevent something ○ *The plan of the authorities is* *to stifle any protests before they start.* □ **to stifle a yawn** to try to prevent yourself from yawning ○ *He had difficulty in stifling a yawn.*

stifling /ˈstaɪf(ə)lɪŋ/ *adj* extremely hot ○ *He stepped off the plane into the stifling heat of the Louisiana sunshine.*

stigma /ˈstɪgmə/ *noun* **1.** a feeling of shame **2.** a part of the female organ of a flower that forms seeds after receiving pollen

① **still** /stɪl/ *adj* not moving ○ *Stand still while I take the photo.* ○ *There was no wind, and the surface of the lake was completely still.* ■ *adv* **1.** continuing until now or until then ○ *I thought he had left, but I see he's still there.* ○ *They came for lunch and were still sitting at the table at eight o'clock in the evening.* ○ *Weeks afterwards, they're still talking about the accident.* **2.** in spite of everything ○ *It wasn't sunny for the picnic – still, it didn't rain.* ○ *He still insisted on going on holiday even though he had broken his leg.*

still life /stɪl ˈlaɪf/ (*plural* **still lifes**) *noun* a painting of objects such as fruit, bottles, flowers or food

stilted /ˈstɪltɪd/ *adj* forced and unnatural

stimulant /ˈstɪmjʊlənt/ *noun* **1.** a substance which makes the body function faster ○ *Caffeine is a stimulant.* **2.** something which encourages more activity ○ *Tax cuts should act as a stimulant to the economy.*

stimulate /ˈstɪmjʊleɪt/ (**stimulates, stimulating, stimulated**) *verb* to encourage someone or an organ to be more active (NOTE: + **stimulation** *n*)

stimulating /ˈstɪmjʊleɪtɪŋ/ *adj* causing interest, excitement or enthusiasm

stimulus /ˈstɪmjʊləs/ (*plural* **stimuli**) *noun* an encouragement or incentive that leads to greater activity

③ **sting** /stɪŋ/ *noun* a wound made by an insect or plant ○ *Bee stings can be very painful.* ○ *Have you anything for wasp stings?* ■ *verb* (**stings, stinging, stung**) **1.** to wound someone with an insect's or plant's sting ○ *I've been stung by a wasp.* ○ *The plants stung her bare legs.* **2.** to give a burning feeling ○ *The antiseptic may sting a little at first.*

stingy /ˈstɪndʒi/ *adj* not very generous (*informal*)

③ **stink** /stɪŋk/ (*informal*) *noun* a very unpleasant smell ○ *the stink of cigarette smoke* ■ *verb* (**stinks, stinking, stank** or **stunk, stunk**) to have a nasty smell ○ *The office stinks of gas.*

stint /stɪnt/ *noun* a period of working ○ *It's your turn to help now, I've done my stint.* ○ *She had a long stint as a sister in a London hospital.*

stipulate /ˈstɪpjʊleɪt/ (**stipulates, stipulating, stipulated**) *verb* to insist, to make it a condition that (NOTE: + **stipulation** *n*)

③ **stir** /stɜː/ (**stirs, stirring, stirred**) *verb* to move a liquid or powder or something which is cooking, to mix it up ○ *He was stirring the sugar into his coffee.* ○ *Keep stirring the porridge, or it will stick to the bottom of the pan.*

stir up③ *phrasal verb* to encourage strong emotions or reactions ○ *The fans came with the deliberate intention of stirring up trouble.*

stir-fry /ˈstɜː fraɪ/ *verb* to cook vegetables or meat quickly in hot oil, while continuously stirring ○ *Stir-fry the vegetables separately, not all together.* (NOTE: + **stir-fry** *n*)

stirring /ˈstɜːrɪŋ/ *adj* making you feel strong emotions, especially pride or enthusiasm

stirrup /ˈstɪrəp/ *noun* a metal loop hanging from the saddle into which a rider puts his foot

② **stitch** /stɪtʃ/ *noun* **1.** a little loop of thread made with a needle in sewing or with knitting needles when knitting ○ *She used very small stitches in her embroidery.* ○ *Very fine wool will give you more stitches than in the pattern.* **2.** a small loop of thread used by a surgeon to attach the sides of a wound together to help it to heal ○ *She had three stitches in her arm.* ○ *Come back in ten days' time to have the stitches removed.* ■ *verb* (**stitches, stitching, stitched**) to attach something with a needle and thread ○ *She stitched the badge to his jacket.*

② **stock** /stɒk/ *noun* **1.** a supply of something kept to use when needed ○ *I keep a good stock of printing paper at home.* ○ *Our stocks of food are running low.* **2.** a liquid made from boiling bones in water, used as a base for soups and sauces ○ *Fry the onions and pour in some chicken stock.* ■ *verb* (**stocks, stocking, stocked**) to keep goods for sale in a shop or warehouse ○ *They don't stock this book.* ○ *We try to stock the most popular colours.*

stock up *phrasal verb* to buy supplies for use in the future

stockade /stɒˈkeɪd/ *noun* a strong fence made of thick upright poles

stockbroker /ˈstɒkbrəʊkə/ *noun* a person who buys or sells shares for clients

stocking /ˈstɒkɪŋ/ *noun* a long light piece of women's clothing which covers all of a leg and foot

stockist /ˈstɒkɪst/ *noun* a person or shop which stocks a certain product

stock market /ˈstɒk ˌmɑːkɪt/ *noun* a place where shares are bought and sold

stockpile /ˈstɒkpaɪl/ (**stockpiles, stockpiling, stockpiled**) *verb* to collect large supplies of something that you will need in the future ○ *We started to stockpile raw materials in case there was a rail strike.* (NOTE: + **stockpile** *n*)

stocktaking /ˈstɒkteɪkɪŋ/ *noun* counting and listing the existing stock in a shop or business

stocky /ˈstɒki/ (**stockier, stockiest**) *adj* with large shoulders, a strong body and short, strong legs

stodgy /ˈstɒdʒi/ (**stodgier, stodgiest**) *adj* (*of food*) heavy and filling

stoical /ˈstəʊɪk(ə)l/ *adj* accepting what happens without complaining

stoke /stəʊk/ (**stokes, stoking, stoked**) *verb* to put wood or coal into a fire

stole /stəʊl/ past tense of **steal**

③ **stolen** /ˈstəʊlən/ past participle of **steal**

stolid /ˈstɒlɪd/ *adj* serious, not easily excited

② **stomach** /ˈstʌmək/ *noun* **1.** a part of the body shaped like a bag, into which food passes after being swallowed and where it continues to be digested ○ *I don't want anything to eat – my stomach's upset* or *I have a stomach upset.* ○ *He has had stomach trouble for some time.* **2.** the front of your body between your chest and your waist ○ *He had been kicked in the stomach.*

stomach ache /ˈstʌmək eɪk/ *noun* a pain in the abdomen

stomp /stɒmp/ (**stomps, stomping, stomped**) *verb* to walk with heavy steps

① **stone** /stəʊn/ *noun* **1.** a very hard material, found in the earth, used for building ○ *All the houses in the town are built in the local grey stone.* ○ *The stone carvings in the old church date from the 15th century.* ○ *Stone floors can be very cold.* (NOTE: no plural: *some stone, a piece of stone, a block of stone*) **2.** a small piece of stone ○ *The children were playing at throwing stones into the pond.* ○ *The beach isn't good for bathing as it's covered with very sharp stones.* **3.** a British measure of weight equal to 14 pounds or 6.35 kilograms ○ *She's trying to lose weight and so far has lost a stone and a half.* ○ *He weighs twelve stone ten (i.e. 12 stone 10 pounds).* (NOTE: no plural in this sense: *He weighs ten stone.* In the USA, human body weight is always given only in pounds.)

stoned /stəʊnd/ *adj* **1.** (*of fruit*) with the stone removed ○ *We only buy stoned olives.* **2.** high on drugs (*informal*) ○ *He was completely stoned when I met him.*

stony /ˈstəʊni/ *adj* made of lots of stones ○ *They walked carefully across the stony beach.*

③ **stood** /stʊd/ past tense and past participle of **stand**

③ **stool** /stuːl/ *noun* a small seat with no back ○ *When the little girl sat on the piano stool her feet didn't touch the floor.* ◊ **footstool**

stoop /stuːp/ (**stoops, stooping, stooped**) *verb* to bend forward

① **stop** /stɒp/ *verb* (**stops, stopping, stopped**) **1.** not to move any more, e.g. in order to let people get on or off [~at] ○ *The motorcycle didn't stop at the red light.* ○ *This train stops at all stations to London Waterloo.* ○ *The bus went right past without stopping.* **2.** to make something not move any more ○ *The policeman stopped the traffic to let the lorry back out of the garage.* ○ *Stop that boy! – he's stolen my purse.* **3.** not to do something any more ○ *The office clock has stopped at 4.15.* ○ *At last it stopped raining and we could go out.* ○ *She spoke for two hours without stopping.* ○ *We all stopped work and went home.* ○ *The restaurant stops serving meals at midnight.* **4.** □ **to stop someone *or* something (from) doing something** to make someone *or* something not do something any more ○ *The rain stopped us from having a picnic.* ○ *How can the police stop people stealing cars?* ○ *Can't you stop the children from making such a noise?* ○ *The plumber couldn't stop the tap dripping.* **5.** to stay as a visitor in a place [~in] ○ *They stopped for a few days in Paris.* ■ *noun* **1.** the end of something, especially of movement ○ *The police want to put a stop to car crimes.* □ **to come to a stop *or* a full stop** to stop moving or continuing ○ *The car rolled on without the driver, and finally came to a stop at the bottom of the hill.* ○ *All the building work came to a stop when the money ran out.* **2.** a place where you break a journey ○ *We'll make a stop at the next service station.* **3.** a place where a bus or train lets passengers get on or off ○ *We have been waiting at the bus stop for twenty minutes.* ○ *There are six stops between here and Marble Arch.*

stop by *phrasal verb* to visit someone for a short time

stop off *phrasal verb* to stop for a time in a place before going on with your journey

stopgap /ˈstɒpgæp/ *noun* something used for a short time, while waiting for something better to be found

stoplight /ˈstɒpˌlaɪt/ *noun US* a traffic light

stop over /ˌstɒp ˈəʊvə/ *verb* to spend a night in a place on a long journey ○ *We'll stop over in Rome on the flight to Hong Kong.*

stopover /ˈstɒpəʊvə/ *noun* a short overnight stop on a long journey by air

stoppage /ˈstɒpɪdʒ/ *noun* **1.** the action of stopping something from moving ○ *Deliveries will be late because of stoppages on the production line.* **2.** money taken from an employee's wages to pay for insurance and tax

stopper /ˈstɒpə/ *noun* an object that you put into the mouth of a bottle or jar to close it

stopwatch /ˈstɒpwɒtʃ/ *noun* a watch which can be started and stopped by pressing a button, used for timing races

③ **storage** /ˈstɔːrɪdʒ/ *noun* the act of keeping something in a store or warehouse ○ *We put our furniture into storage.* ○ *We don't have enough storage space in this house.*

① **store** /stɔː/ *noun* a shop, usually a big shop ○ *You can buy shoes in any of the big stores in town.* ○ *Does the store have a food department?* ■ *verb* (**stores, storing, stored**) **1.** to keep food etc. to use later ○ *We store (away) all our vegetables in the garden shed.* **2.** to keep something in a computer file ○ *We store all our personnel records on computer.*

③ **storey** /ˈstɔːri/ *noun* a whole floor in a building

stork /stɔːk/ *noun* a large white bird with long legs and a long thin red beak

② **storm** /stɔːm/ *noun* a high wind and very bad weather ○ *Several ships got into difficulties in the storm.* ○ *How many trees were blown down in last night's storm?*

stormy /ˈstɔːmi/ *adj* when there are storms ○ *They are forecasting stormy weather for the weekend.*

① **story** /ˈstɔːri/ (*plural* **stories**) *noun* **1.** a description that tells things that did not really happen but are invented by someone [~of/about] ○ *The book is the story of two children during the war.* ○ *She writes children's stories about animals.* **2.** a description that tells what really happened ○ *She told her story to the journalist.*

storyteller /ˈstɔːritelə/ *noun* a person who tells a story

stout /staʊt/ *adj* **1.** (*of a person*) quite fat ○ *He has become much stouter and has difficulty going up stairs.* **2.** (*of material*) strong or thick ○ *Take a few sheets of stout paper.* ○ *Find a stout branch to stand on.*

③ **stove** /stəʊv/ *noun* a piece of equipment for heating or cooking

stow /stəʊ/ (**stows, stowing, stowed**) *verb* to put away ○ *He had stowed all the luggage in the boot of the car.*

stow away *phrasal verb* **1.** to put away ○ *It's June – time you stowed away your skis.* **2.** to travel secretly on a ship or aircraft without paying the fare ○ *They found two students stowing away in a lifeboat.*

stowaway /ˈstəʊəweɪ/ *noun* a person who travels secretly on a ship or aircraft without paying

straddle /ˈstræd(ə)l/ (**straddles, straddling, straddled**) *verb* **1.** to stand with legs apart, on either side of something ○ *He straddled the ditch.* **2.** be on both sides of something ○ *The town straddles the main highway to the north.*

straggle /ˈstræg(ə)l/ (**straggles, straggling, straggled**) *verb* **1.** to move in various directions, not in an orderly fashion ○ *After the flood went down a few people straggled back to their villages each day.* **2.** to grow or lie in various directions ○ *Her hair was straggling over her face.* (NOTE: + **straggler** *n*)

① **straight** /streɪt/ *adj* **1.** not curved ○ *a long straight street* ○ *The line isn't straight.* ○ *She has straight black hair.* ○ *Stand up straight!* **2.** not sloping ○ *Is the picture straight?* ○ *Your tie isn't straight.* ■ *adv* **1.** in a straight line, not curving ○ *The road goes straight across the plain for two hundred kilometres.* ○ *She was sitting straight in front of you.* **2.** immediately ○ *Wait for me here – I'll come straight back.* ○ *If there is a problem, you should go straight to the manager.* **3.** without stopping or changing ○ *She drank the milk straight out of the bottle.* ○ *The cat ran straight across the road in front of the car.* ○ *He looked me straight* *in the face.* ○ *The plane flies straight to Washington.*

straightaway /ˌstreɪtə'weɪ/ *adv* at once

straighten /'streɪt(ə)n/ (**straightens, straightening, straightened**) *verb* to make something straight

straighten up *phrasal verb* **1.** to stand straight after bending ○ *He straightened up and looked at me.* **2.** to make something tidy ○ *I must straighten up my bedroom before I leave.*

③ **straightforward** /streɪt'fɔːwəd/ *adj* easy to understand or carry out ○ *The instructions are quite straightforward.*

strain /streɪn/ *noun* **1.** nervous tension and stress ○ *Can she stand the strain of working in that office?* **2.** a variety, breed ○ *They are trying to find a cure for a new strain of the flu virus.* ■ *verb* (**strains, straining, strained**) **1.** to injure part of your body by pulling too hard ○ *He strained a muscle in his back* or *he strained his back.* ○ *The effort strained his heart.* **2.** to make great efforts to do something ○ *They strained to lift the piano into the van.* **3.** to pour liquid through a sieve to separate solids from it

strained /streɪnd/ *adj* tense or unfriendly ○ *Relations between them became strained.*

strainer /'streɪnə/ *noun* a kitchen utensil with metal or nylon mesh, used to separate solids from a liquid

straitjacket /'streɪtdʒækɪt/, **straightjacket** *noun* something which prevents you from acting freely

strand /strænd/ *noun* one piece of hair or thread ○ *Strands of hair kept blowing across her forehead.*

stranded /'strændɪd/ *adj* alone and unable to move

① **strange** /streɪndʒ/ *adj* **1.** not usual ○ *Something is the matter with the engine – it's making a strange noise.* ○ *She told some very strange stories about the firm she used to work for.* ○ *It felt strange to be sitting in the office on a Saturday afternoon.* ○ *It's strange that no one spotted the mistake.* **2.** which you have never seen before or where you have never been before ○ *I find it difficult getting to sleep in a strange room.* ○ *We went to Korea and had lots of strange food to eat.* (NOTE: **stranger – strangest**)

③ **stranger** /'streɪndʒə/ *noun* **1.** a person whom you have never met [~to] ○ *He's a complete stranger to me.* ○ *Children are told not to accept lifts from strangers.* **2.** a person in a place where he has never been before [~to] ○ *He's a stranger to these parts.* ○ *I can't tell you how to get to the post office – I'm a stranger here myself.*

strangle /'stræŋgəl/ (**strangles, strangling, strangled**) *verb* **1.** to kill by squeezing the throat so that someone cannot breathe or swallow ○ *The marks on his neck showed that he had been strangled.* **2.** to slow the development of something ○ *The company's expansion is being strangled by lack of funds.*

stranglehold /'stræŋgəlˌhəʊld/ *noun* control which prevents you doing what you want to do

strap /stræp/ *noun* a long flat piece of material used to attach something ○ *Can you do up the strap of my bag for me?* ○ *I put a strap round my suitcase to make it more secure.* ■ *verb* (**straps, strapping, strapped**) to fasten something with a strap ○ *He strapped on his rucksack.* ○ *The patient was strapped to a stretcher.* ○ *Make sure the baby is strapped into her seat.*

strata /'strɑːtə/ plural of **stratum**

strategic /strə'tiːdʒɪk/ *adj* **1.** done with the intention of achieving a specific aim **2.** attacking an enemy from a long distance ○ *strategic weapons*

strategist /'strætədʒɪst/ *noun* someone who makes business, military or other plans

② **strategy** /'strætədʒi/ (*plural* **strategies**) *noun* the decisions you make about how you are going to do something ○ *Their strategy is to note which of their rival's models sells best and then copy it.* ○ *The government has no long-term strategy for dealing with crime.*

stratum /'strɑːtəm/ (*plural* **strata** or **stratums**) *noun* a layer, especially of rock ○ *As they dug down, they exposed several strata of rock.*

straw /strɔː/ *noun* **1.** dry stems and leaves of crops, used for animals to sleep on ○ *You've been lying on the ground – you've got bits of straw in your hair.* ○ *The tractor picked up bundles of straw and loaded them onto a truck.* **2.** a thin plastic tube for sucking up liquids ○ *She was drinking orange juice through a straw.*

strawberry /'strɔːb(ə)ri/ (*plural* **strawberries**) *noun* a common soft red summer fruit which grows on low plants

stray /streɪ/ *verb* (**strays, straying, strayed**) to move away from the place where something is expected to be, or from a subject being discussed ○ *She told the* *children not to stray too far.* ■ *noun* a pet animal which is lost or without a home ○ *We have two female cats at home and they attract all the strays in the district.* ■ *adj* **1.** not where it should be ○ *He was killed by a stray bullet from a sniper.* **2.** (*(of a pet animal)*) lost or without a home ○ *We found a stray cat and brought it home.*

streak /striːk/ *noun* **1.** a line of colour ○ *The cloth is blue with streaks of red in it.* ○ *She's had blonde streaks put in her hair.* **2.** a particularly characteristic type of behaviour **3.** a period when a series of things happens ○ *I hope our streak of bad luck is coming to an end.* ■ *verb* (**streaks, streaking, streaked**) **1.** to go very fast ○ *The rocket streaked across the sky.* **2.** to run about naked in public (*informal*)

③ **stream** /striːm/ *noun* **1.** a small river ○ *Can you jump across that stream?* **2.** things which pass continuously ○ *Crossing the road is difficult because of the constant stream of traffic.*

streamer /ˈstriːmə/ *noun* a long paper strip used for decoration

streaming /ˈstriːmɪŋ/ *noun* a method of sending a continuous stream of data over the Internet to a computer, providing live video or sound

streamline /ˈstriːmlaɪn/ (**streamlines, streamlining, streamlined**) *verb* **1.** to design a car, plane or boat so that it can move easily through water or air ○ *The body of the car was streamlined to make it faster.* **2.** to make something more efficient or more simple ○ *We are trying to streamline the accounting system.*

① **street** /striːt/ *noun* **1.** a road in a town, usually with houses on each side ○ *It is difficult to park in our street on Saturday mornings.* ○ *Her flat is on a noisy street.* ○ *The school is in the next street.* **2.** used with names ○ *What's your office address? – 16 Cambridge Street.* ○ *Oxford Street, Bond Street and Regent Street are the main shopping areas in London.* (NOTE: When used in names, **street** is usually written **St**: *Oxford St.*)

streetwise /ˈstriːtwaɪz/ *adj* able to deal with difficult and dangerous situations in a modern city

② **strength** /streŋθ/ *noun* the quality of being physically strong ○ *She hasn't got the strength to lift it.* ○ *You should test the strength of the rope before you start climbing.*

③ **strengthen** /ˈstreŋθ(ə)n/ (**strengthens, strengthening, strengthened**) *verb* **1.** to make something stronger ○ *The sea wall is being strengthened to prevent another flood.* ○ *This will only strengthen their determination to oppose the government.* ○ *We are planning to strengthen airport security.* **2.** to become stronger ○ *The wind is strengthening from the south-west.*

strenuous /ˈstrenjuəs/ *adj* requiring a lot of physical effort or energy ○ *The doctor has told him to avoid strenuous exercise.* ○ *It's a very strenuous job.*

③ **stress** /stres/ *noun* **1.** nervous strain caused by an outside influence ○ *She's suffering from stress.* ○ *How will he cope with the stress of working in an office?* **2.** the force or pressure on something ○ *Stresses inside the earth create earthquakes.* ■ *verb* (**stresses, stressing, stressed**) to put emphasis on something [~that] ○ *She stressed that the work must be completed on time.* ○ *I must stress the importance of keeping the plan secret.*

stressed /strest/ *adj* worried and tense

stressful /ˈstresf(ə)l/ *adj* (*of a situation*) which causes stress

stress mark /stres mɑːk/ *noun* a mark showing which syllable of a word should be stressed

③ **stretch** /stretʃ/ *verb* (**stretches, stretching, stretched**) **1.** to spread out for a great distance ○ *The line of cars stretched for three miles from the accident.* ○ *The queue stretched from the door of the cinema right round the corner.* ○ *White sandy beaches stretch as far as the eye can see.* **2.** to push out your arms or legs as far as they can ○ *The cat woke up and stretched.* **3.** to pull out so that it becomes loose ○ *Don't hang your jumper up like that – you will just stretch it.* ○ *These trousers are not supposed to stretch.* ■ *noun* **1.** a long piece of land, water or road ○ *Stretches of the river have been so polluted that bathing is dangerous.* **2.** a long period of time ○ *For long stretches we had nothing to do.* ◇ **at a stretch** without a break ○ *He played the piano for two hours at a stretch.* ◇ **to stretch your legs** to go for a short walk after sitting for a long time ○ *In the coffee break I went out into the garden to stretch my legs.*

stretcher /ˈstretʃə/ *noun* a folding bed with handles, on which an injured person can be carried by two people

strew /struː/ (**strews, strewing, strewed, strewn**) *verb* to scatter over a wide area

③ **strict** /strɪkt/ *adj* **1.** which must be obeyed ○ *I gave strict instructions that no one was to be allowed in.* ○ *The rules are* *very strict and any bad behaviour will be severely punished.* **2.** expecting people to obey rules ○ *Our parents are very strict with us about staying up late.*

③ **strictly** /ˈstrɪktli/ *adv* in a strict way ○ *All staff must follow strictly the procedures in the training manual.*

stride /straɪd/ *noun* a long step ○ *In three strides he was across the room and out of the door.* ■ *verb* (**strides, striding, strode, stridden**) to walk with long steps ○ *He strode into the room.* ○ *We could see him striding across the field to take shelter from the rain.* ◇ **to make great strides** to advance quickly ○ *Researchers have made great strides in the treatment of asthma.* ◇ **to take something in your stride** to deal with something easily ○ *Other people always seem to have problems, but she just takes everything in her stride.*

strident /ˈstraɪd(ə)nt/ *adj* unpleasantly loud and harsh

strife /straɪf/ *noun* trouble between people

② **strike** /straɪk/ *noun* the stopping of work by workers because of lack of agreement with management or because of orders from a trade union ○ *They all voted in favour of a strike.* ○ *A strike was avoided at the last minute.* ■ *verb* (**strikes, striking, struck**) **1.** to stop working because of disagreement with management ○ *The workers are striking in protest against bad working conditions.* **2.** to hit something hard ○ *She struck her head on the low door.* ○ *He struck a match and lit the fire.* **3.** (*of a clock*) to ring to mark an hour ○ *The clock had just struck one when she heard a noise in the corridor.* **4.** to come to someone's mind ○ *A thought just struck me.* ○ *It suddenly struck me that I had seen him somewhere before.*

strike off *phrasal verb* to remove a name from a list because of bad behaviour

strike up *phrasal verb* to start playing a piece of music ○ *The band struck up, and everyone settled in their seats.*

striker /ˈstraɪkə/ *noun* **1.** a worker who is on strike ○ *Strikers picketed the factory.* **2.** a football player whose main task is to score goals ○ *His pass back to the goalkeeper was intercepted by the opposition striker who promptly scored.*

③ **striking** /ˈstraɪkɪŋ/ *adj* noticeable, unusual ○ *She bears a striking resemblance to the Queen.* ○ *It is a very striking portrait of Winston Churchill.*

② **string** /strɪŋ/ *noun* **1.** a strong thin fibre used for tying up things such as parcels ○ *This string isn't strong enough to tie up that big parcel.* ○ *She bought a ball of string.* ○ *We've run out of string.* (NOTE: no plural in this sense: *some string; a piece of string*) **2.** one of the long pieces of fibre or wire on a musical instrument which makes a note when you hit it ○ *a guitar has six strings* ○ *He was playing the violin when one of the strings broke.* **3.** one of the strong pieces of fibre which form the flat part of a tennis racket ○ *One of the strings has snapped.*

string along *phrasal verb* **1.** to walk along in a line behind someone ○ *The teachers walked in front and the children strung along behind.* **2.** to promise someone something to get him or her to agree to do what you want ○ *He was just stringing her along – he never intended to marry her, but just wanted to get at her money.*

stringed instrument /ˈstrɪŋd ˌɪnstrʊmənt/ *noun* a musical instrument where the notes are played on strings

stringent /ˈstrɪndʒənt/ *adj* strict or severe

③ **strip** /strɪp/ *noun* a long narrow piece of something ○ *He tore the paper into strips.* ○ *Houses are to be built along the strip of land near the church.* ■ *verb* (**strips, stripping, stripped**) to take off your clothes ○ *Strip to the waist for your chest X-ray.* ○ *He stripped down to his underpants.*

stripe /straɪp/ *noun* a long line of colour ○ *He has an umbrella with red, white and blue stripes.*

stripper /ˈstrɪpə/ *noun* a person who performs a striptease

striptease /ˈstrɪptiːz/ *noun* an entertainment where someone takes their clothes off piece by piece

strive /straɪv/ (**strives, striving, strove, striven**) *verb* to try very hard to do something, especially over a long period of time ○ *Everyone is striving for a solution to the dispute.* ○ *He always strove to do as well as his brother.*

strode /strəʊd/ past tense of **stride**

③ **stroke** /strəʊk/ *noun* **1.** a serious medical condition in which someone suddenly becomes unconscious because blood has stopped flowing normally to the brain ○ *He was paralysed after his stroke.* ○ *She had a stroke and died.* **2.** the act of hitting something such as a ball ○ *It took him three strokes to get the ball onto the green.* **3.** a style of swimming ○ *She won the 200m* *breast stroke.* ■ *verb* (**strokes, stroking, stroked**) to run your hands gently over something or someone ○ *She was stroking the cat as it sat in her lap.*

stroll /strəʊl/ (**strolls, strolling, strolled**) *verb* to walk slowly as a way of relaxing ○ *People were strolling in the park.* ○ *On Sunday evenings, everyone strolls along the boulevard.* (NOTE. + **stroll** *n*)

① **strong** /strɒŋ/ *adj* **1.** who has a lot of strength ○ *I'm not strong enough to carry that box.* **2.** which has a lot of force or strength ○ *The string broke – we need something stronger.* ○ *The wind was so strong that it blew some tiles off the roof.* **3.** having a powerful smell, taste or effect ○ *I don't like strong cheese.* ○ *You need a cup of strong black coffee to wake you up.* ○ *There was a strong smell of gas in the kitchen.* ◊ **strength**

stronghold /ˈstrɒŋhəʊld/ *noun* **1.** a place such as a castle which is difficult for an enemy to defeat ○ *The enemy stronghold finally surrendered.* **2.** a place which is famous for something ○ *Rome is renowned as the stronghold of Catholicism.* ○ *The club is a stronghold of male chauvinism.*

strongly /ˈstrɒŋli/ *adv* in a strong way

stroppy /ˈstrɒpi/ *adj* behaving in a rude and angry way (*informal*)

strove /strəʊv/ past tense of **strive**

③ **struck** /strʌk/ past tense and past participle of **strike**

③ **structural** /ˈstrʌktʃ(ə)rəl/ *adj* referring to a structure

② **structure** /ˈstrʌktʃə/ *noun* a building or something else that is built

③ **struggle** /ˈstrʌg(ə)l/ *noun* a fight ○ *After a short struggle the burglar was arrested.* ■ *verb* (**struggles, struggling, struggled**) to try hard to do something difficult [~with/for] ○ *She's struggling with her maths homework.* ○ *The industry is struggling for survival.* ○ *He struggled to carry all the shopping to the car.*

strum /strʌm/ (**strums, strumming, strummed**) *verb* to play a stringed instrument by running your fingers across the strings in an informal way

strut /strʌt/ (**struts, strutting, strutted**) *verb* to walk in a proud and important way ○ *She strutted across the stage to collect her prize.* ○ *He refused to accept their offer and strutted out of the room.*

stub /stʌb/ *noun* a small piece left after something has been used ○ *He walked along the gutter looking for cigarette stubs.*

stubble /ˈstʌb(ə)l/ *noun* **1.** short stems left in the ground after a crop such as wheat has been cut **2.** short hairs which grow on a man's chin if he does not shave for several days ○ *She told him to shave, as she didn't like his stubble.*

stubborn /ˈstʌbən/ *adj* determined not to change your mind ○ *He's so stubborn – he only does what he wants to do.*

stuck /stʌk/ past tense and past participle of **stick**

③ **stud** /stʌd/ *noun* **1.** a small round piece of metal jewellery worn in the ear, nose or elsewhere on the body ○ *She wears a stud in her nose.* **2.** a young man who is extremely sexually attractive (*informal*) **3.** a nail with a head that stands out above a surface ○ *He had a pattern of studs on his belt.*

① **student** /ˈstjuːd(ə)nt/ *noun* a person who is studying at a college, university or school ○ *All the science students came to my lecture.* ○ *She's a brilliant student.* ○ *Two students had to sit the exam again.*

③ **studio** /ˈstjuːdiəʊ/ *noun* **1.** a room where an artist paints ○ *She uses this room as a studio because of the good light.* **2.** a place where things such as films or broadcasts are made ○ *And now, back to the studio for the latest news and weather report.* ○ *They spent the whole day recording the piece in the studio.* **3.** a very small flat for one person, usually one room with a small kitchen and bathroom ○ *You can rent a studio overlooking the sea for £300 a week in high season.*

studious /ˈstjuːdiəs/ *adj* enjoying study, spending a lot of time studying

② **study** /ˈstʌdi/ *noun* (*plural* **studies**) the work of examining something carefully to learn more about it [~on/~on] ○ *The review has published studies on the new drug.* ○ *I'm preparing a study of new production techniques.* ■ *verb* (**studies, studying, studied**) **1.** to learn about a subject at college or university ○ *I plan to study for a law degree.* ○ *He is studying medicine at university.* **2.** to look at something carefully ○ *She was studying the guidebook.*

① **stuff** /stʌf/ *noun* **1.** a substance, especially something unpleasant ○ *You've got some black stuff stuck to your shoe.* **2.** equipment or possessions ○ *Dump all your stuff in the living room.* ○ *Take all that stuff and put it in the dustbin.* ○ *All your photographic stuff is still in the back of my car.* ■ *verb* (**stuffs, stuffing, stuffed**) **1.** to push something into something to fill it ○ *He stuffed his pockets full of peppermints.* ○

The £20 notes were stuffed into a small plastic wallet. **2.** to put small pieces of food such as bread, meat or herbs inside meat or vegetables before cooking them ○ *We had roast veal stuffed with mushrooms.*

stuffing /ˈstʌfɪŋ/ *noun* **1.** a mixture of small pieces of food such as bread, fat, onions and herbs put inside a chicken, fish or vegetables before cooking them ○ *I prepared the stuffing for the fish according to my mother's recipe.* **2.** a soft material used to fill things such as children's toys or chair seats ○ *The stuffing's coming out of this cushion.*

stuffy /ˈstʌfi/ (**stuffier, stuffiest**) *adj* without any fresh air ○ *Can't you open a window, it's so stuffy in here?*

stumble /ˈstʌmbəl/ (**stumbles, stumbling, stumbled**) *verb* **1.** to almost fall by hitting your foot against something **2.** to make mistakes when reading aloud or speaking

stumbling block /ˈstʌmblɪŋ blɒk/ *noun* something which prevents you doing what you want to do

stump /stʌmp/ *noun* **1.** a short piece of something left sticking up, such as the main stem of a tree that has been cut down ○ *After cutting down the trees, we need to get rid of the stumps.* **2.** one of the three sticks placed in the ground in cricket ○ *The ball hit the stumps and the last man was out.*

stump up *phrasal verb* to pay money (*informal*)

stun /stʌn/ (**stuns, stunning, stunned**) *verb* **1.** to make someone become unconscious with a blow to the head **2.** to shock someone completely ○ *She was stunned when he told her that he was already married.*

stung /stʌŋ/ past tense of **sting**

stunk /stʌŋk/ past tense and past participle of **stink**

stunning /ˈstʌnɪŋ/ *adj* impressive, extremely beautiful

stunt /stʌnt/ *noun* a trick or dangerous act done to attract attention ○ *Climbing up the outside of the building was just a publicity stunt.* ○ *He's so fit that he insists on doing all the stunts in his films himself.*

stupendous /stjuːˈpendəs/ *adj* extremely unusual, very large or impressive

① **stupid** /ˈstjuːpɪd/ *adj* **1.** not very intelligent ○ *What a stupid man!* **2.** behaving in a way that is not sensible ○ *It was stupid of her not to wear a helmet when riding on her scooter.* ○ *He made several stupid mistakes.*

stupor /ˈstjuːpə/ *noun* the state of being almost unconscious

sturdy /ˈstɜːdi/ (**sturdier, sturdiest**) *adj* well made and not easily damaged

stutter /ˈstʌtə/ *noun* a speech problem where you repeat the sound at the beginning of a word several times ○ *He is taking therapy to try to cure his stutter.* ■ *verb* (**stutters, stuttering, stuttered**) to repeat the same sounds when speaking ○ *He stuttered badly when making his speech.*

sty /staɪ/ *noun* a little building where a pig is kept. ◊ **pigsty**

① **style** /staɪl/ *noun* **1.** a way of doing something, especially a way of designing, drawing or writing [~of] ○ *his original style of painting* ○ *The room is decorated in Chinese style.* **2.** a fashionable way of doing things ○ *She always dresses with style.* ○ *They live in grand style.* ◊ **hairstyle**

stylised /ˈstaɪlaɪzd/, **stylized** *adj* drawn or designed in a fixed way that does not look natural

stylish /ˈstaɪlɪʃ/ *adj* attractive and fashionable

stylistic /staɪˈlɪstɪk/ *adj* referring to style in art

suave /swɑːv/ (**suaver, suavest**) *adj* extremely polite with very good manners, though often with an unpleasant character

sub /sʌb/ *abbr* **1.** submarine **2.** subscription **3.** substitute

sub- /sʌb/ *prefix* below, under

subcommittee /ˈsʌbkəmɪti/ *noun* a small committee which is set up by a main committee and deals with a specific matter

subconscious /sʌbˈkɒnʃəs/ *noun* a part of your mind which has ideas or feelings which you do not realise are there ○ *Somewhere, deep in his subconscious, was a feeling of hatred for his family.*

subcontinent /sʌbˈkɒntɪnənt/ *noun* a large mass of land which is a separate part of a continent

subcontract /ˈsʌbˌkɒntrækt/ *noun* a contract between the main company managing a whole project and another firm who will do part of the work

subculture /ˈsʌbˌkʌltʃə/ *noun* a separate social group within a larger culture

subdivide /ˌsʌbdɪˈvaɪd/ (**subdivides, subdividing, subdivided**) *verb* to divide up something which has already been divided

subdivision /ˈsʌbdɪvɪʒ(ə)n/ *noun* the division of something into smaller parts

subdue /səbˈdjuː/ (**subdues, subduing, subdued**) *verb* to defeat, to bring under control

subdued /səbˈdjuːd/ *adj* **1.** very quiet, not excited ○ *The audience was very subdued.* **2.** not bright, not loud ○ *The room has been painted in subdued colours.* ○ *A subdued discussion was going on in a far corner of the restaurant.*

subgroup /ˈsʌbˌgruːp/ *noun* a small separate group within a larger group

subheading /ˈsʌbhedɪŋ/ *noun* a heading used to divide something such as a long document into smaller sections

① **subject** /ˈsʌbdʒɪkt/ *noun* **1.** the thing which you are talking about or writing about ○ *The debate is on the subject of pollution.He suddenly changed the subject of the conversation.* **2.** an area of knowledge which you are studying ○ *Maths is his weakest subject.* ○ *You can take up to five subjects at 'A' Level.* **3.** □ **to be the subject of** to be the person or thing talked about or studied ○ *The painter Chagall will be the subject of our lecture today.* ○ *Advertising costs are the subject of close examination by the auditors.* **4.** (*in grammar*) a noun or pronoun which comes before a verb and shows the person or thing that does the action expressed by the verb ○ *In the sentence 'the cat sat on the mat' the word 'cat' is the subject of the verb 'sat'.*

subjective /səbˈdʒektɪv/ *adj* seen from your own point of view, and therefore possibly influenced by your feelings or beliefs

subject line /ˈsʌbdʒɪkt laɪn/ *noun* the part at the top of an e-mail where the subject of the message is written

subject matter /ˈsʌbdʒɪkt ˌmætə/ *noun* the subject dealt with in something such as a book or TV programme

subjunctive /səbˈdʒʌŋktɪv/ *noun* the form of a verb used to express something such as a doubt, suggestion or wish

sublime /səˈblaɪm/ (**sublimer, sublimest**) *adj* impressive, beautiful ○ *the sublime music of Beethoven's Ninth Symphony* ○ *the sublime sight of snow-capped mountains towering above the lake*

submarine /ˌsʌbməˈriːn/ *noun* a special type of ship which can travel under water ○ *The submarine dived before she was spotted by enemy aircraft.* ■ *adj* under the water ○ *a submarine pipeline*

submerge /səbˈmɜːdʒ/ (**submerges, submerging, submerged**) *verb* **1.** to cover with something, especially with water ○ *At high tide the rocks are completely submerged.* **2.** to go under water ○ *The submarine submerged and disappeared from view.*

submission /səbˈmɪʃ(ə)n/ *noun* **1.** the state of giving in or having to obey someone **2.** a piece of evidence, a document or an argument used in court

submissive /səbˈmɪsɪv/ *adj* (*of a person*) who obeys all orders, or who gives in easily

③ **submit** /səbˈmɪt/ (**submits, submitting, submitted**) *verb* **1.** to put something forward for someone to examine [~to] ○ *You are requested to submit your proposal to the planning committee.* **2.** to accept that someone has the power to make you do something you don't want to do

subordinate /səˈbɔːdɪnət/ *noun* a person who is under the direction of someone else ○ *His subordinates find him difficult to work with.*

subordinate clause /səˌbɔːdɪnət ˈklɔːz/ *noun* a clause in a sentence which depends on the main clause

subpoena /səˈpiːnə/ *noun* a court order telling someone to appear in court ○ *She has been served a subpoena to appear in court next month.* (NOTE: + **subpoena** *v*)

subscribe /səbˈskraɪb/ (**subscribes, subscribing, subscribed**) *verb* to give money to ○ *He subscribes to several charities.*

subscription /səbˈskrɪpʃən/ *noun* **1.** the amount of money which someone pays to a magazine for a series of issues ○ *Did you remember to pay the subscription to the computer magazine?* **2.** money paid to a club for a year's membership ○ *He forgot to renew his club subscription.*

subsection /ˈsʌbˌsekʃ(ə)n/ *noun* a division of a section such as in a document

subsequent /ˈsʌbsɪkwənt/ *adj* which comes later (*formal*) ○ *The rain and the subsequent flooding disrupted the match.* ○ *All subsequent reports must be sent to me immediately they arrive.*

subsequently /ˈsʌbsɪkwəntli/ *adv* happening later or following something which has already happened ○ *I subsequently discovered that there had been a mistake.*

subset /ˈsʌbˌset/ *noun* a mathematical set whose elements are contained in another set

subside /səbˈsaɪd/ (**subsides, subsiding, subsided**) *verb* **1.** to go down, to become less loud or strong ○ *After the rain-*

storms passed, the flood waters gradually subsided. ○ *His anger subsided and he began to try to find out what had happened.* ○ *He waited for the noise to subside before going on with his speech.* **2.** (*of a piece of ground or a building*) to fall to a lower level ○ *The office block is subsiding because it is built on clay.*

subsidence /'sʌbsɪd(ə)ns/ *noun* (*of a piece of ground or a building*) an act of sinking or falling to a lower level

subsidiary /səb'sɪdiəri/ (*plural* **subsidiaries**) *noun* a company which is owned by a parent company ○ *Most of the profit comes from subsidiaries in the Far East.*

subsidise /'sʌbsɪdaɪz/ (**subsidises, subsidising, subsidised**), **subsidize** *verb* to help by giving money

subsidy /'sʌbsɪdi/ (*plural* **subsidies**) *noun* money given to help pay for something which does not make a profit

subsist /səb'sɪst/ (**subsists, subsisting, subsisted**) *verb* **1.** to stay alive, to manage **2.** to continue to exist (*formal*) (NOTE: + **subsistence** *n*)

① **substance** /'sʌbstəns/ *noun* a solid or liquid material, especially one used in chemistry ○ *A secret substance is added to the product to give it its yellow colour.* ○ *Toxic substances got into the drinking water.*

substandard /sʌb'stændəd/ *adj* not up to the usual standard

② **substantial** /səb'stænʃəl/ *adj* **1.** large or important ○ *She was awarded substantial damages.* ○ *He received a substantial sum when he left the company.* ○ *A substantial amount of work remains to be done.* **2.** large enough to satisfy someone ○ *We had a substantial meal at the local pub.* **3.** solid or strong ○ *This wall is too flimsy, we need something much more substantial.*

substantially /səb'stænʃəli/ *adv* **1.** mainly, mostly ○ *Their forecast was substantially correct.* **2.** by a large amount ○ *The cost of raw materials has risen substantially over the last year.*

substantiate /səb'stænʃieɪt/ (**substantiates, substantiating, substantiated**) *verb* to prove that something which has been stated is true

③ **substitute** /'sʌbstɪtjuːt/ *noun* a person or thing that takes the place of someone or something else [~for] ○ *This type of plastic can be used as a substitute for leather.* ○ *The substitute teacher was very good.* ○ *When the goalkeeper was injured they sent on a substitute.* ■ *verb* □ **to substitute something *or* someone for something *or* someone else** to put something or someone in the place of something or someone else ○ *He secretly substituted the fake diamond for the real one.* □ **to substitute for someone** to replace someone ○ *Who will be substituting for the sales manager when she's away on holiday?*

substitution /ˌsʌbstɪ'tjuːʃ(ə)n/ *noun* the act of substituting someone or something for someone or something else

subsume /səb'sjuːm/ (**subsumes, subsuming, subsumed**) *verb* to include something in a larger group or set (*formal*)

subterfuge /'sʌbtəfjuːdʒ/ *noun* a trick or clever way of doing something

subterranean /ˌsʌbtə'reɪniən/ *adj* under the ground

subtitle /'sʌbtaɪt(ə)l/ *noun* a translation of the words spoken in a film which are shown at the bottom of the screen

subtle /'sʌt(ə)l/ (**subtler, subtlest**) *adj* **1.** not obvious or easily seen ○ *There's a subtle difference between the two political parties.* **2.** complicated or delicate ○ *a sauce with a subtle taste of lemon* ○ *A subtler shade would be better than that bright colour.*

subtlety /'sʌt(ə)lti/ *noun* careful thought processes which are difficult to explain

subtract /səb'trækt/ (**subtracts, subtracting, subtracted**) *verb* to take one number away from another (NOTE: **Subtracting** is usually shown by the minus sign – : **10 – 4 = 6:** say 'ten subtract four equals six'.)

subtraction /səb'trækʃən/ *noun* the act of subtracting one number from another

suburb /'sʌbɜːb/ *noun* an area on the edge of a town where there are houses and shops but not usually factories or other large industries

suburban /sə'bɜːbən/ *adj* referring to the suburbs

suburbia /sə'bɜːbiə/ *noun* the middle-class suburban districts around a city

subversive /səb'vɜːsɪv/ *adj* acting secretly against the government or people in authority ○ *The police are investigating subversive elements in the student organisations.*

subvert /səb'vɜːt/ (**subverts, subverting, subverted**) *verb* to make something such as a system fail, or to damage or destroy the existing political system (NOTE: + **subversion** *n*)

subway /'sʌbweɪ/ *noun* **1.** an underground passage along which people can walk, e.g. so that they do not have to cross a busy road ○ *There's a subway from the bus station to the shopping centre.* **2.** *US* an underground railway system ○ *the New York subway* ○ *It will be quicker to take the subway to Grand Central Station.* (NOTE: The London equivalent is the **tube** *or* **Underground**.)

sub-zero /sʌb 'zɪərəʊ/ *adj* below zero degrees in temperature

① **succeed** /sək'siːd/ (**succeeds, succeeding, succeeded**) *verb* to do well in a particular activity [~in] ○ *We hope you succeed in your chosen career.* ○ *His business succeeded better than he expected.*

① **success** /sək'ses/ *noun* **1.** the fact that you achieve what you have been trying to do ○ *She's been looking for a job in a library, but without any success so far.* **2.** the fact that something or someone does well ○ *the success of the car in the Japanese market* ○ *Her photo was in the newspapers after her Olympic success.*

① **successful** /sək'sesf(ə)l/ *adj* who or which does well ○ *He's a successful business man.* ○ *She's very successful at hiding her real age.* ○ *Their trip to German proved successful.*

① **successfully** /sək'sesf(ə)li/ *adv* achieving what was intended

succession /sək'seʃ(ə)n/ *noun* **1.** a series of the same type of thing ○ *I had a succession of phone calls from my relatives.* □ **in succession** one after the other ○ *Three people in succession have asked me the same question.* ○ *He won the title five times in succession.* **2.** taking a property or a title from someone who has died ○ *The question of the succession to the throne is often mentioned in the newspapers.*

successive /sək'sesɪv/ *adj* which come one after the other

successor /sək'sesə/ *noun* a person who takes over from someone

success story /sʌk'ses ˌstɔːri/ *noun* a person or something such as an invention that has been a great success

succinct /sək'sɪŋkt/ *adj* exact, not using many words

succumb /sə'kʌm/ (**succumbs, succumbing, succumbed**) *verb* (*formal*) **1.** to accept defeat **2.** to die from an illness or injury [~to] ○ *The heroine of the book succumbed to tuberculosis.*

① **such** /sʌtʃ/ *adj* **1.** of this type ○ *The police are looking for such things as drugs or stolen goods.* **2.** very; so much ○ *There was such a crowd at the party that there weren't enough chairs to go round.* ○ *It's such a shame that she's ill and has to miss her sister's wedding.* ◇ **such as** used for giving an example ○ *Some shops such as food stores are open on Sundays.* ◇ **no such (person or thing)** a person or thing like that is not in existence ○ *There is no such day as April 31st.* ○ *Someone was asking for a Mr Simpson but there is no such person working here.*

③ **suck** /sʌk/ (**sucks, sucking, sucked**) *verb* **1.** to hold something with your mouth and pull at it with your tongue ○ *The baby didn't stop sucking his thumb until he was six.* **2.** to have something in your mouth which makes your mouth produce water ○ *He bought a bag of sweets to suck in the car.*

sucker /'sʌkə/ *noun* **1.** a part of an animal which sticks to a surface by sucking ○ *An octopus has rows of suckers on its arms.* **2.** a little plastic cup which sticks to a surface by suction ○ *Some hooks can be glued to the wall, others stick with suckers.* **3.** a person who is easily tricked into doing something **4.** a person who cannot resist something ○ *He's a sucker for chocolate desserts.* ○ *He's a sucker for any pretty girl.* **5.** (*of a plant*) a shoot which comes from the bottom of the stem or from a root ○ *You need to cut all those suckers off the roses.*

suction /'sʌkʃən/ *noun* the action of sucking out air, so that two surfaces stick together

② **sudden** /'sʌd(ə)n/ *adj* which happens very quickly or unexpectedly ○ *The sudden change in the weather caught us unprepared.* ○ *The bus came to a sudden stop.* ○ *His decision to go to Canada was very sudden.* ◇ **all of a sudden** suddenly ○ *All of a sudden the room went dark.*

① **suddenly** /'sʌd(ə)nli/ *adv* quickly and giving you a shock ○ *The car in front stopped suddenly and I ran into the back of it.* ○ *Suddenly the room went dark.* ○ *She suddenly realised it was already five o'clock.*

sue /sjuː/ (**sues, suing, sued**) *verb* to take someone to court, to start a legal case against someone to get payment for the harm or damage they have caused

suede /sweɪd/ *noun* leather with a soft surface that looks like velvet

suet /'suːɪt/ *noun* the hard fat from around an animal's kidneys, used in cooking

① **suffer** /ˈsʌfə/ (**suffers, suffering, suffered**) *verb* **1.** to receive an injury ○ *He suffered multiple injuries in the accident.* **2.** □ **to suffer from something** to have an illness or a fault ○ *She suffers from arthritis.* ○ *The company's products suffer from bad design.* ○ *Our car suffers from a tendency to overheat.*

sufferer /ˈsʌfərə/ *noun* a person who has a particular disease

suffering /ˈsʌf(ə)rɪŋ/ *noun* feeling pain over a long period of time

suffice /səˈfaɪs/ (**suffices, sufficing, sufficed**) *verb* to be enough (*formal*)

② **sufficient** /səˈfɪʃ(ə)nt/ *adj* as much as is needed ○ *Does she have sufficient funds to pay for her trip?* ○ *There isn't sufficient room to put the big sofa in here.* ○ *Allow yourself sufficient time to get to the airport.* ◊ **self-sufficient**

suffix /ˈsʌfɪks/ *noun* letters added to the end of a word to make another word. Compare **prefix**

suffocate /ˈsʌfəkeɪt/ (**suffocates, suffocating, suffocated**) *verb* **1.** to make someone stop breathing by cutting off the supply of air, or to die from lack of air to breathe ○ *She was accused of suffocating the baby.* ○ *The family suffocated in the smoke-filled room.* **2.** to be uncomfortable because of heat and lack of air (*informal*) ○ *We're suffocating in this little room.* (NOTE: + **suffocation** *n*)

suffrage /ˈsʌfrɪdʒ/ *noun* a right to vote in elections

② **sugar** /ˈʃʊɡə/ *noun* a substance that you use to make food sweet ○ *How much sugar do you take in your tea?* ○ *A spoonful of sugar will be enough.* ○ *Can you pass me the sugar, please?*

① **suggest** /səˈdʒest/ (**suggests, suggesting, suggested**) *verb* to mention an idea to see what other people think of it [~(that)/~what/why/where etc] ○ *The chairman suggested that the next meeting should be held in October.* ○ *What does he suggest we do in this case?* ○ *I suggested a visit to the museum.*

① **suggestion** /səˈdʒestʃən/ *noun* an idea that you mention for people to think about [~for] ○ *Do you have any suggestions for how we could improve things?* ○ *Whose suggestion was it that we should go out in a boat?* ○ *I bought those shares at the stockbroker's suggestion.*

suggestive /səˈdʒestɪv/ *adj* **1.** relating to sex ○ *He sang some very suggestive songs.* **2. suggestive of** suggesting something [~of] ○ *The music is suggestive of a calm evening in the country.*

suicidal /ˌsuːɪˈsaɪd(ə)l/ *adj* wanting to kill yourself ○ *He has suicidal tendencies.* ○ *After her son's death she became suicidal.*

suicide /ˈsuːɪsaɪd/ *noun* **1.** the act of killing yourself ○ *Whether her death was murder or suicide is not yet known.* □ **to commit suicide** to kill yourself ○ *He killed his two children and then committed suicide.* **2.** a person who has killed himself

suicide note /ˈsuːɪsaɪd nəʊt/ *noun* a letter left by someone who has committed suicide

② **suit** /suːt/ *noun* **1.** a set of pieces of clothing made of the same cloth and worn together, e.g. a jacket and trousers or skirt ○ *A dark grey suit will be just right for the interview.* ○ *The pale blue suit she was wearing was very chic.* **2.** one of the four sets of cards with the same symbol in a pack of cards ○ *Clubs and spades are the two black suits and hearts and diamonds are the two red suits.* ■ *verb* (**suits, suiting, suited**) **1.** to look good when worn by someone ○ *Green usually suits people with red hair.* ○ *That hat doesn't suit her.* **2.** to be convenient for someone ○ *He'll only do it when it suits him to do it.* ○ *Thursday at 11 o'clock will suit me fine.* ◇ **suit yourself** do what you want

suitability /ˌsuːtəˈbɪlɪti/ *noun* the degree to which someone or something is suitable

② **suitable** /ˈsuːtəb(ə)l/ *adj* which fits or which is convenient ○ *I'm looking for a suitable present* ○ *We advertised the job again because there were no suitable candidates.* ○ *A blue dress would be more suitable for an interview.*

③ **suitcase** /ˈsuːtkeɪs/ *noun* a box with a handle which you carry your clothes in when you are travelling

suite /swiːt/ *noun* **1.** a set of rooms, especially expensive rooms ○ *Their offices are in a suite of rooms on the eleventh floor.* ○ *They booked a suite at the Savoy Hotel.* **2.** a set of pieces of furniture

suitor /ˈsuːtə/ *noun* a person who wants to marry a girl (*old*)

sulk /sʌlk/ (**sulks, sulking, sulked**) *verb* to show you are annoyed by not saying anything ○ *They're sulking because we didn't invite them.*

sulky /ˈsʌlki/ (**sulkier, sulkiest**) *adj* showing that you are annoyed

sullen /ˈsʌlən/ *adj* silent and sulky

sulphur /ˈsʌlfə/ *noun* a non-metallic element, which is usually found in the form of yellow powder, and smells of rotten eggs (NOTE: The US or technical spelling is **sulfur**.)

sulphur dioxide /ˌsʌlfə daɪˈɒksaɪd/ *noun* a colourless gas which has a strong unpleasant smell and causes serious air pollution (NOTE: The US or technical spelling is **sulfur dioxide**.)

sultan /ˈsʌltən/ *noun* a Muslim prince

sultana /sʌlˈtɑːnə/ *noun* a type of pale seedless raisin. Compare **currant**, **raisin**

sultry /ˈsʌltri/ (**sultrier, sultriest**) *adj* **1.** (*of weather*) hot and making you feel uncomfortably sticky ○ *A massive thunderstorm brought the sultry weather to an end.* **2.** attractive in a dark and passionate way ○ *Her sultry good looks attracted the eye of her boss.*

② **sum** /sʌm/ *noun* **1.** a quantity of money ○ *A large sum of money was stolen from his safe.* ○ *We are owed the sum of £500.* ○ *He only paid a small sum for the car.* **2.** a simple problem in arithmetic ○ *She tried to do the sum in her head.* **3.** the total of two or more numbers added together ○ *The sum of all four sides will give you the perimeter of the field.*

sum up *phrasal verb* **1.** to make a summary of what has been said ○ *I'd just like to sum up what has been said so far.* ○ *Can you sum up the most important points in the speech for me?* **2.** (*of a judge*) to speak at the end of a trial and go over all the evidence and arguments for the benefit of the jury ○ *I was surprised the judge did not mention that when he summed up.*

summarily /ˈsʌmərɪli/ *adv* immediately and without discussion or attention to the usual way of doing things

③ **summarise** /ˈsʌməraɪz/ (**summarises, summarising, summarised**), **summarize** *verb* to make a short account of what has happened or what has been said

summary /ˈsʌməri/ *noun* a short description of what has been said or written, or of what happened, without giving all the details ○ *She gave a summary of what happened at the meeting.* ○ *Here's a summary of the book in case you don't have time to read it.*

① **summer** /ˈsʌmə/ *noun* the hottest season of the year, between spring and autumn ○ *Next summer we are going to Greece.* ○ *The summer in Australia coincides with our winter here in England.* ○ *I haven't any summer clothes – it's never hot enough here.*

summer camp /ˈsʌmə kæmp/ *noun* a place where children go for a holiday without their parents in the summer, usually in the country

summer holiday /ˌsʌmə ˈhɒlɪdeɪ/ *noun* a holiday which you have in the summer (NOTE: The US term is **summer vacation**.)

summer school /ˈsʌmə skuːl/ *noun* classes held at a school, college or university during the summer holiday

summertime /ˈsʌmətaɪm/ *noun* the time of year when it is summer

③ **summit** /ˈsʌmɪt/ *noun* the top of a mountain ○ *It took us three hour's hard climbing to reach the summit.*

summon /ˈsʌmən/ (**summons, summoning, summoned**) *verb* to tell people to come to a meeting (*formal*) ○ *The president summoned a meeting of the supreme council.* ○ *She was summoned to appear before the committee.*

summons /ˈsʌmənz/ *noun* **1.** an official order to go to see someone ○ *He received a summons to see the president.* **2.** an official order or document telling someone to appear in court to be tried for a criminal offence or to defend a civil action ○ *He threw away the summons and went on holiday to Spain.*

sumo /ˈsuːməʊ/ *noun* a Japanese style of wrestling, where two very large wrestlers try to throw each other out of a ring

sumptuous /ˈsʌmptʃuəs/ *adj* very expensive or impressive

① **sun** /sʌn/ *noun* **1.** a very bright star round which the earth travels and which gives light and heat ○ *The sun was just rising when I got up.* ○ *I'll try taking a photograph now that the sun's come out.* **2.** the light from the sun ○ *I'd prefer a table out of the sun.* ○ *She spent her whole holiday just sitting in the sun.*

sunbathe /ˈsʌnbeɪð/ (**sunbathes, sunbathing, sunbathed**) *verb* to lie in the sun to get your skin brown (NOTE: + **sunbather** *n*)

sunbed /ˈsʌnˌbed/ *noun* **1.** a piece of equipment which you use to make your skin look brown by means of ultraviolet light **2.** a piece of furniture on which you lie in the sun

sunburn /ˈsʌnbɜːn/ *noun* damage to the skin caused by being in the sun for too long

sunburnt /ˈsʌnbɜːnt/ *adj* (*of the skin*) damaged or made red by the sun

① **Sunday** /ˈsʌndeɪ/ *noun* the seventh day of the week, the day between Saturday and Monday ○ *Last Sunday we went on a picnic.* ○ *Most shops are now open on Sundays.* ○ *Can we fix a lunch for next Sunday?* ○ *The 15th is a Saturday, so the 16th must be a Sunday.* ○ *Today is Sunday, November 19th.*

Sunday school /ˈsʌndeɪ skuːl/ *noun* classes held on a Sunday, where children are taught about the Christian religion

sundial /ˈsʌndaɪəl/ *noun* a type of outdoor clock with a central piece whose shadow points to the time when the sun shines on it

sundown /ˈsʌndaʊn/ *noun* the time when the sun goes down in the evening

sundry /ˈsʌndri/ *adj* various ○ *The tourists made sundry purchases in the market.*

sunflower /ˈsʌnflaʊə/ *noun* a very large yellow flower on a very tall stem

sung /sʌŋ/ past participle of **sing**

③ **sunglasses** /ˈsʌŋglɑːsɪz/ *plural noun* dark glasses worn to protect your eyes from the sun ○ *I always wear sunglasses when I'm driving.*

sunk /sʌŋk/ past participle of **sink**

③ **sunlight** /ˈsʌnlaɪt/ *noun* the light which comes from the sun (NOTE: no plural)

sunlit /ˈsʌnlɪt/ *adj* bright with the light of the sun

Sunni /ˈsʊni/ *noun* **1.** one of the main branches of Islam **2.** a member of the Sunni branch of Islam

③ **sunny** /ˈsʌni/ *adj* **1.** with the sun shining ○ *Another sunny day!* ○ *They forecast that it will be sunny this afternoon.* **2.** where the sun often shines ○ *We live on the sunny side of the street.* ○ *Their sitting room is bright and sunny, but the dining room is dark.*

sunrise /ˈsʌnraɪz/ *noun* the time when the sun comes up in the morning

sunroof /ˈsʌnruːf/ *noun* a part of the roof of a car which opens to let in light and air

sunscreen /ˈsʌnskriːn/ *noun* a cream which you put on your skin to prevent sunburn

sunset /ˈsʌnset/ *noun* the time when the sun goes down in the evening

③ **sunshine** /ˈsʌnʃaɪn/ *noun* a pleasant light from the sun (NOTE: no plural)

suntan /ˈsʌntæn/ *noun* the brown colour of skin caused by sunlight

super /ˈsuːpə/ *adj* very good (*dated*)

superb /sʊˈpɜːb/ *adj* extremely good

supercomputer /ˌsuːpəkəmˈpjuːtə/ *noun* a high-speed computer

③ **superficial** /ˌsuːpəˈfɪʃ(ə)l/ *adj* **1.** affecting only the top surface ○ *The damage was only superficial.* ○ *She had a few superficial cuts on her skin but nothing serious.* **2.** dealing only with the most obvious and simple matters ○ *I can't answer your question because I only have a very superficial knowledge of the subject.* **3.** not serious or important ○ *My brother and I only discuss superficial topics like the weather and sport.* ○ *He's very superficial, you can't have a serious conversation with him.*

superfluous /suːˈpɜːfluəs/ *adj* which is more than is needed; not necessary, not needed

superhuman /ˌsuːpəˈhjuːmən/ *adj* beyond what humans are usually able to do, or having unusually great abilities

superimpose /ˌsuːpərɪmˈpəʊz/ (**superimposes, superimposing, superimposed**) *verb* to lay one picture over another so that they are both visible; to print one thing on top of another ○ *If you superimpose one picture on the other you get the impression of a ghost in the room.*

superintendent /ˌsuːpərɪnˈtendənt/ *noun* a person who is responsible for work, or for a place ○ *Go and see the building superintendent if a pipe is leaking.*

superior /sʊˈpɪəriə/ *noun* a person in a higher rank ○ *Each manager is responsible to his superior.*

superiority /sʊˌpɪəriˈɒrɪti/ *noun* being more important, more intelligent, better than someone else ○ *The superiority of the Brazilians in the World Cup was obvious.* ○ *He gives the impression of effortless superiority.*

superlative /sʊˈpɜːlətɪv/ *adj* extremely good ○ *He's a superlative goalkeeper.* ■ *noun* the form of an adjective or adverb showing the highest level when compared with another ○ *'Biggest' is the superlative of 'big.'* ○ *Put a few superlatives in the ad to emphasise the superiority of the product.*

③ **supermarket** /ˈsuːpəmɑːkɪt/ *noun* a large store selling mainly food and goods for the house, where customers serve themselves and pay at a checkout ○ *We've got no tea left, can you buy some from the supermarket?*

supermodel /ˈsuːpəmɒd(ə)l/ *noun* a famous fashion model who earns a lot of money

supernatural /ˌsuːpəˈnætʃ(ə)rəl/ *adj* which cannot be explained by the laws of nature ○ *He believes in supernatural occurrences like ghosts.*

superpower /ˈsuːpəpaʊə/ *noun* an extremely powerful country with great economic strength and large armed forces

supersede /ˌsuːpəˈsiːd/ (**supersedes, superseding, superseded**) *verb* to take the place of something which has become old and no longer useful

supersonic /ˌsuːpəˈsɒnɪk/ *adj* going faster than the speed of sound

superstar /ˈsuːpəstɑː/ *noun* an extremely famous film actor or other performer

superstition /ˌsuːpəˈstɪʃ(ə)n/ *noun* a belief in magic and that some things are lucky and others unlucky

superstore /ˈsuːpəstɔː/ *noun* a very large self-service store selling a wide range of goods or selling a variety of things of the same type

③ **supervise** /ˈsuːpəvaɪz/ (**supervises, supervising, supervised**) *verb* to watch carefully, to see that work is well done

③ **supervisor** /ˈsuːpəvaɪzə/ *noun* a person whose job is making sure that other people are working well

supper /ˈsʌpə/ *noun* the meal which you eat in the evening

supplant /səˈplɑːnt/ (**supplants, supplanting, supplanted**) *verb* to take the place of someone or something

supple /ˈsʌp(ə)l/ *adj* who or which bends easily

supplement¹ /ˈsʌplɪmənt/ *noun* **1.** a thing which is in addition, especially an additional amount ○ *The company gives him £200 per month as a supplement to his pension.* ○ *You need to take a vitamin supplement every morning.* **2.** a magazine which is part of a newspaper ○ *I read his article in the Sunday supplement.* **3.** an additional section at the back of a book ○ *Look in the supplement at the back of the book.*

supplement² /ˈsʌplɪment/ (**supplements, supplementing, supplemented**) *verb* to add to ○ *We will supplement the ordinary staff with six part-timers during the Christmas rush.*

supplementary /ˌsʌplɪˈment(ə)ri/ *adj* in addition to what is already there

supplier /səˈplaɪə/ *noun* a person, company or country that supplies something

① **supply** /səˈplaɪ/ *noun* (*plural* **supplies**) a store of something which is needed ○ *We have two weeks' supply of coal.* ■ *verb* (**supplies, supplying, supplied**) to provide something which is needed ○ *Details of addresses and phone numbers can be supplied by the store staff.* ○ *He was asked to supply a blood sample.* ○ *She was asked to supply the names of two referees.* ○ *They have signed a contract to supply online information.* ◇ **in short supply** not available in large enough quantities to meet people's needs ○ *Fresh vegetables are in short supply during the winter.*

① **support** /səˈpɔːt/ *noun* **1.** an object or structure which stops something from falling ○ *They had to build wooden supports to hold up the wall.* **2.** help or encouragement ○ *We have had no financial support from the bank.* **3.** an act of encouraging and helping someone, or of agreeing with their plans ○ *The chairman has the support of the committee.* ○ *She spoke in support of our plan.* ■ *verb* (**supports, supporting, supported**) **1.** to hold something up to stop it falling down ○ *The roof is supported on ten huge pillars.* **2.** to provide money to help someone or something ○ *We hope the banks will support us during the development period.* **3.** to encourage someone or something ○ *Which football team do you support?* ○ *She hopes the other members of the committee will support her.*

② **supporter** /səˈpɔːtə/ *noun* a person who encourages someone or something ○ *It sounds a good idea to me – I'm surprised it hasn't attracted more supporters.*

support group /səˈpɔːt gruːp/ *noun* a group of people who meet to discuss their problems and help one another

supportive /səˈpɔːtɪv/ *adj* who supports, helps or encourages

① **suppose** /səˈpəʊz/ (**supposes, supposing, supposed**) *verb* **1.** to think something is likely to be true or to happen [~(that)] ○ *I suppose you've heard the news?* ○ *Will you be coming to the meeting this evening? – I suppose I'll have to.* ○ *I don't suppose many people will come.* **2.** (*showing doubt*) what happens if? [~(that)] ○ *Suppose it rains tomorrow, do you still want to go for a walk?* ○ *He's very late – suppose he's had an accident?* ○ *Suppose I win the lottery!* ◇ **I suppose so** used to give a doubtful 'yes' ○ *Please can I go to the party? – Oh, I suppose so.*

supposed /səˈpəʊzt/ *adj* accepted as true but not definitely true

supposedly /səˈpəʊzɪdli/ *adv* as we suppose

supposition /ˌsʌpəˈzɪʃ(ə)n/ *noun* something which is thought to be true or correct, but cannot be proved

suppress /səˈpres/ (**suppresses, suppressing, suppressed**) *verb* **1.** to limit something such as a person's freedom ○ *The rebellion was ruthlessly suppressed and its leaders executed.* **2.** to stop something being made public ○ *All opposition newspapers have been suppressed.* ○ *They tried to suppress the evidence but it had already got into the newspapers.* **3.** to stop yourself showing what you really feel ○ *She suppressed her feeling of annoyance and tried to look happy.* ○ *He couldn't suppress a smile.* (NOTE: + **suppression** *n*)

supremacy /sʊˈpreməsi/ *noun* the position of being the strongest power

supreme /sʊˈpriːm/ *adj* greatest, in the highest position ○ *Her dog was supreme champion.* ○ *It meant one last supreme effort, but they did it.*

supremely /sʊˈpriːmli/ *adv* to the greatest degree

surcharge /ˈsɜːtʃɑːdʒ/ *noun* an extra charge ○ *There is a 10% surcharge on goods that are delivered.*

① **sure** /ʃʊə/ *adj* without any doubt ○ *Is he sure he can borrow his mother's car?* ○ *I'm sure I left my wallet in my coat pocket.* ○ *It's sure to be cold in Russia in December.* ○ *Make sure* or *be sure that your computer is switched off before you leave.* ■ *adv mainly US* meaning yes ○ *Can I borrow your car? – sure, go ahead!* ○ *I need someone to help with this computer program – sure, I can do it.*

sure-footed /ʃɔː ˈfʊtɪd/ *adj* **1.** unlikely to trip or fall **2.** confident and not likely to make mistakes

① **surely** /ˈʃʊəli/ *adv* of course, certainly (*used mostly in questions where a certain answer is expected*) ○ *Surely they can't expect us to work on Sundays?* ○ *But surely their office is in London, not Oxford?* ○ *They'll surely complain about the amount of work they have to do.*

surf /sɜːf/ *noun* **1.** a mass of white foam coming onto a beach on large waves ○ *The surf is too rough for children to bathe.* **2.** waves breaking along a shore (NOTE: Do not confuse with **serf**.) ■ *verb* (**surfs, surfing, surfed**) to ride on large waves coming onto a beach on a surf board ○ *I'd like to be able to surf.* ○ *It's too dangerous to go surfing today.*

① **surface** /ˈsɜːfɪs/ *noun* the top part of something ○ *When it rains, water collects on the surface of the road.* ○ *The surface of the water was completely still.* ○ *He stayed a long time under water before coming back to the surface.* ○ *Dinosaurs disappeared from the surface of the earth millions of years ago.* ■ *verb* (**surfaces, surfacing, surfaced**) to come up to the surface ○ *The captain gave orders for the submarine to surface.* ○ *His fear of failure has surfaced again.*

surfboard /ˈsɜːfbɔːd/ *noun* a long board made especially for standing on to ride on top of large waves coming onto a beach

surfing /ˈsɜːfɪŋ/ *noun* **1.** to ride waves on a surfboard as a sport or for fun **2.** to keep switching from channel to channel on a television or from site to site on the Internet in no particular order

surge /sɜːdʒ/ *noun* a sudden increase in the quantity of something ○ *The fine weather has brought a surge of interest in camping.* ○ *The TV commercials generated a surge of orders.* ■ *verb* (**surges, surging, surged**) **1.** to rise suddenly ○ *The waves surged up onto the rocks.* **2.** to move in a mass ○ *The crowd surged (forward) onto the football pitch.* ○ *The fans surged around the pop star's car.*

surgeon /ˈsɜːdʒən/ *noun* a doctor who performs medical operations

surgery /ˈsɜːdʒəri/ (*plural* **surgeries**) *noun* **1.** treatment of disease in which doctors cut into or remove part of the body ○ *She had surgery to straighten her nose.* ○ *The patient will need surgery to remove the scars left by the accident.* (NOTE: no plural in this sense) **2.** a room where a doctor or dentist sees and examines patients ○ *I phoned the doctor's surgery to make an appointment.*

surgical /ˈsɜːdʒɪk(ə)l/ *adj* referring to surgery

surly /ˈsɜːli/ (**surlier, surliest**) *adj* extremely unfriendly

surmise /səˈmaɪz/ (**surmises, surmising, surmised**) *verb* to make a guess about something

surmount /səˈmaʊnt/ (**surmounts, surmounting, surmounted**) *verb* **1.** to overcome an obstacle ○ *It took us some time to surmount the obstacles in our path.* **2.** to be on top of ○ *The summit is surmounted by an observatory.*

③ **surname** /ˈsɜːneɪm/ *noun* the name of someone's family, shared by all people in the family. Compare **first name**

surpass /səˈpɑːs/ (**surpasses, surpassing, surpassed**) *verb* to do better than

surplus /'sɜːpləs/ *noun* more goods than are needed

② **surprise** /sə'praɪz/ *noun* **1.** the feeling you get when something happens which you did not expect to happen ○ *He expressed surprise when I told him I'd lost my job.* ○ *To his great surprise, a lot of people bought his book.* ○ *What a surprise to find that we were at school together!* **2.** an unexpected event ○ *They baked a cake for her birthday as a surprise.* ○ *What a surprise to see you again after so long!* ■ *verb* (**surprises, surprising, surprised**) to make someone surprised ○ *It wouldn't surprise me if it rained.* ○ *What surprises me is that she left without saying goodbye.*

② **surprised** /sə'praɪzd/ *adj* feeling or showing surprise ○ *She was surprised to see her former boyfriend at the party.* ○ *We were surprised to hear that he's got a good job.*

③ **surprising** /sə'praɪzɪŋ/ *adj* which you do not expect ○ *There was a surprising end to the story.* ○ *Wasn't it surprising to see the two sisters together again?* ○ *It's hardly surprising she doesn't want to meet you again after what you said.*

surreal /sə'rɪəl/ *adj* extremely unusual, as if in a dream

surrender /sə'rendə/ *noun* giving in to an enemy because you have lost ○ *the surrender of the enemy generals* ■ *verb* (**surrenders, surrendering, surrendered**) to accept that you have been defeated by someone else ○ *Our troops were surrounded by the enemy and were forced to surrender.*

surreptitious /ˌsʌrəp'tɪʃəs/ *adj* done in secret

surrogate mother /ˌsʌrəgət 'mʌðə/ *noun* a woman who becomes pregnant and has a baby for a woman who is not able to do this herself,

② **surround** /sə'raʊnd/ (**surrounds, surrounding, surrounded**) *verb* to be all round something or someone ○ *The house is surrounded by beautiful countryside.* ○ *The President has surrounded himself with experts.*

③ **surroundings** /sə'raʊndɪŋz/ *plural noun* the area around a person or place ○ *The surroundings of the hotel are very peaceful.* ○ *She found herself in very unpleasant surroundings.*

surveillance /sə'veɪləns/ *noun* a careful watch over someone or something

survey[1] /'sɜːveɪ/ *noun* **1.** a way of finding out about something by asking people questions **2.** the careful examination of a building to see if it is in good enough condition

survey[2] /sə'veɪ/ (**surveys, surveying, surveyed**) *verb* **1.** to ask people questions to get information about something ○ *Roughly half the people we surveyed were in favour of the scheme.* ○ *They're surveying the site.* **2.** to measure land in order to produce a plan or map ○ *They're surveying the area where the new runway will be built.*

surveyor /sə'veɪə/ *noun* **1.** a person who examines buildings to see if they are in good condition **2.** a person who surveys land

③ **survival** /sə'vaɪv(ə)l/ *noun* the state of continuing to exist ○ *The survival of the crew depended on the supplies carried in the boat.* ○ *The survival rate of babies has started to fall.*

② **survive** /sə'vaɪv/ (**survives, surviving, survived**) *verb* to continue to be alive after an experience such as accident, attack or serious illness ○ *It was such a terrible crash, it was miracle that anyone survived.* ○ *He survived a massive heart attack.*

survivor /sə'vaɪvə/ *noun* a person who is still alive after an experience such as an accident, attack or serious illness

susceptible /sə'septɪb(ə)l/ *adj* **1.** likely to catch a disease ○ *She is susceptible to colds and throat infections.* **2.** easily influenced ○ *He's very susceptible to pretty women.* **3.** able to be dealt with in a particular way

sushi /'suːʃi/ *noun* small cakes of rice mixed with fish or vegetables and wrapped in seaweed

suspect[1] /sə'spekt/ (**suspects, suspecting, suspected**) *verb* **1.** to think that something is likely ○ *I suspect it's going to be more difficult than we thought at first.* ○ *We suspected all along that something was wrong.* **2.** □ **to suspect someone of doing something** to think that someone may have done something wrong ○ *I suspect him of being involved in the robbery.* ○ *They were wrongly suspected of taking bribes.*

suspect[2] /'sʌspekt/ *noun* a person who is thought to have committed a crime ○ *The police arrested several suspects for questioning.* ■ *adj* **1.** which is not reliable ○ *Such high figures for exports look a bit suspect to me.* **2.** which might be dangerous or illegal ○ *a suspect package*

suspend /sə'spend/ (**suspends, suspending, suspended**) *verb* **1.** to hang something ○ *The ham is suspended over a smoky fire for some time, which gives it a particular taste.* **2.** to stop something for a time ○ *Work on the construction project has been suspended.* ○ *Sailings have been suspended until the weather gets better.* **3.** to stop someone from doing something, such as working ○ *He has been suspended on full pay while investigations are continuing.*

suspenders /sə'spendəz/ *plural noun* *US* long narrow bands of material which go over your shoulders to hold up your trousers ○ *He wore bright red suspenders with his jeans.* (NOTE: The British term is **braces**.)

suspense /sə'spens/ *noun* nervous excitement experienced while waiting for something to happen or for someone to do something

suspension /sə'spenʃən/ *noun* **1.** a system of springs which supports a car and helps it to move smoothly ○ *Hydraulic suspension gives you a very smooth ride.* **2.** the action of hanging from something **3.** the action of stopping something for a time ○ *suspension of payments by the bank* ○ *There has been a temporary suspension of deliveries.*

suspension bridge /sə'spenʃən brɪdʒ/ *noun* a bridge which hangs from strong ropes, chains or wires attached to tall towers

suspicion /sə'spɪʃ(ə)n/ *noun* **1.** a feeling that something is wrong or that someone has committed a crime ○ *His behaviour confirmed my suspicion that he was lying.* ○ *They were arrested on suspicion of exporting stolen goods.* ○ *His actions immediately aroused suspicion on the part of the police.* ○ *The bank regards his business deals with considerable suspicion.* **2.** a general feeling that something is going to happen ○ *I have a suspicion that he's coming to see me because he wants to borrow some money.* ○ *Her suspicions proved to be correct when she saw the wedding announced in the paper.*

③ **suspicious** /sə'spɪʃəs/ *adj* which seems to be wrong, dangerous or connected with a crime ○ *The police found a suspicious package on the station platform.* ○ *We became suspicious when we realised we hadn't seen him for three days.*

suss /sʌs/ (**susses, sussing, sussed**) *verb* to discover or understand something such as somebody's reason for doing something, a situation or the correct way to use something (*informal*)

suss out *phrasal verb* to discover something (*informal*)

③ **sustain** /sə'steɪn/ (**sustains, sustaining, sustained**) *verb* **1.** to make something continue ○ *How long can this level of activity be sustained?* **2.** to receive an injury (*formal*) ○ *He sustained severe head injuries.* **3.** to give you strength ○ *You need a good breakfast to sustain you through the day.* **4.** to support something ○ *Will the roof sustain the weight of the snow?*

sustainable /sə'steɪnəb(ə)l/ *adj* which does not damage natural resources and which leaves the environment in good condition

sustained /sə'steɪnd/ *adj* which continues for a long time

sustenance /'sʌstənəns/ *noun* food

swab /swɒb/ *noun* **1.** a thick piece of soft cloth, often attached to a small stick, used for cleaning a cut in your body or for taking samples of infection for analysis **2.** a sample of infection taken for analysis ○ *The swabs from his mouth were sent away to the laboratory.* **3.** a cloth for wiping floors clear of water

swagger /'swægə/ (**swaggers, swaggering, swaggered**) *verb* to walk in a proud way, swinging your shoulders ○ *He swaggered into the office, showing off his new suntan.* (NOTE: + **swagger** *n*)

Swahili /swɑː'hiːli/ *noun* the language of the Swahili people

③ **swallow** /'swɒləʊ/ (**swallows, swallowing, swallowed**) *verb* to make food or liquid pass down your throat from your mouth to the stomach ○ *He swallowed his beer and ran back to the office.* ○ *She swallowed hard and knocked on the door to the interview room.*

swam /swæm/ past tense of **swim**

swan /swɒn/ *noun* a large white water bird with a long curved neck

swansong /'swɒnsɒŋ/ *noun* a last performance or appearance

③ **swap** /swɒp/ (**swaps, swapping, swapped**) *verb* to exchange something for something else ○ *Can I swap my tickets for next Friday's show?* ○ *Let's swap places, so that I can talk to Susan.* ○ *After every game the players swapped jerseys with the other team.*

swarm /swɔːm/ *noun* a large group of insects flying around together ○ *A swarm of flies buzzed around the meat.*

swat /swɒt/ (**swats, swatting, swatted**) *verb* to hit and kill a fly

swathe /sweɪð/ *noun* a long wide band of land, grass or trees ○ *Great swathes of forest were destroyed in the fire.*

sway /sweɪ/ (**sways, swaying, swayed**) *verb* **1.** to move slowly and smoothly from side to side ○ *The crowd swayed in time to the music.* ○ *The palm trees swayed in the breeze.* **2.** to have an influence on someone ○ *The committee was swayed by a letter from the president.*

swear /sweə/ (**swears, swearing, swore, sworn**) *verb* **1.** to make a serious public promise ○ *He swore he was telling the truth.* ○ *Do you swear never to go there again?* □ **to swear someone to secrecy** to make someone swear not to tell a secret ○ *He was sworn to secrecy.* **2.** to shout offensive or rude words ○ *They were shouting and swearing at the police.* ○ *Don't let me catch you swearing again!* ◇ **I could have sworn** I was completely sure ○ *I could have sworn I put my keys in my coat pocket.*

swear by *phrasal verb* to believe completely in something (*informal*) ○ *He swears by Chinese herbal medicine.*

swear word /sweə/ *noun* an offensive or rude word, which most people think should not be spoken

sweat /swet/ *noun* drops of salt liquid which come through your skin when you are hot or when you are afraid ○ *After working in the vineyard he was drenched with sweat.* ○ *He broke out into a cold sweat when they called his name.* ■ *verb* (**sweats, sweating, sweated**) to produce sweat ○ *He ran up the hill, sweating and red in the face.*

sweater /ˈswetə/ *noun* a thick piece of clothing with sleeves that covers your upper body

sweatshirt /ˈswetʃɜːt/ *noun* a thick cotton shirt with long sleeves

sweatshop /ˈswetʃɒp/ *noun* a small factory where people work for long hours and get paid very little money

sweaty /ˈsweti/ *adj* feeling slightly wet with sweat

swede /swiːd/ *noun* a common vegetable with a round root and yellow flesh, used mainly in soups and stews

③ **sweep** /swiːp/ (**sweeps, sweeping, swept**) *verb* **1.** to clear up dust and dirt from the floor with a brush ○ *Have you swept the kitchen floor yet?* **2.** to move rapidly ○ *She swept into the room with a glass of wine in her hand.* ○ *The party swept to power in the general election.* ○ *A feeling of anger swept through the crowd.*

sweep away *phrasal verb* to carry something away very quickly ○ *The river flooded and swept away part of the village.*

sweepstake /ˈswiːpsteɪk/ *noun* a form of gambling on a horse race where each person bets on a certain horse, and the holder of the winning ticket takes all the money which has been bet

② **sweet** /swiːt/ *adj* **1.** tasting like sugar, and neither sour nor bitter ○ *These apples are sweeter than those green ones.* **2.** very kind or pleasant ○ *He sent me such a sweet birthday card.* ○ *It was sweet of her to send me flowers.* ○ *What a sweet little girl!* ○ *How sweet of you to help me with my luggage!* ■ *noun* **1.** a small piece of sweet food, made with sugar ○ *She bought some sweets to eat in the cinema.* ○ *He likes to suck sweets when he is driving.* **2.** sweet food eaten at the end of a meal ○ *What's on the menu for sweet?* ○ *I'm afraid I haven't made a sweet.* ○ *I won't have any sweet, thank you, just some coffee.* ◇ **to have a sweet tooth** to like sweet food ○ *He's very fond of puddings – he's got a real sweet tooth!*

sweet chestnut /swiːt ˈtʃesnʌt/ *noun* a chestnut from a sweet chestnut tree, which produces edible fruit (*fruit*)

sweetcorn /ˈswiːt kɔːn/ *noun* the large yellow seeds of a type of maize, eaten cooked

sweeten /ˈswiːt(ə)n/ (**sweetens, sweetening, sweetened**) *verb* to make something sweet ○ *Use honey to sweeten your cereal instead of sugar.*

sweetener /ˈswiːt(ə)nə/ *noun* **1.** an artificial substance such as saccharin added to food to make it sweet **2.** a bribe ○ *She was accused of taking sweeteners from building contractors.*

sweetheart /ˈswiːthɑːt/ *noun* a boyfriend or girlfriend (*old*) ○ *They were sweethearts when they were at school* or *They were childhood sweethearts.*

sweetness /ˈswiːtnəs/ *noun* a state of being sweet

sweet pepper /swiːt ˈpepə/ *noun* a red, yellow or green vegetable, eaten raw in salads, fried, or baked in the oven

sweet potato /swiːt pəˈteɪtəʊ/ *noun* a vegetable like a long red potato with sweet yellow flesh

swell /swel/ *verb* (**swells, swelling, swelled, swollen** or **swelled**) to become larger, usually because of an illness or injury ○ *Her feet started to swell.* ○ *More people arrived to swell the crowd outside the shop.* ■ *noun* the movement of large waves in the open sea ○ *The boat rose and fell with the swell.* ○ *There's a heavy swell running.*

swelling /'swelɪŋ/ *noun* a condition where liquid forms in part of the body, making that part swell up

swell up *verb* to become larger or to increase in size ○ *She was bitten by an insect and her hand swelled up.*

sweltering /'swelt(ə)rɪŋ/ *adj* very hot

swept /swept/ past tense and past participle of **sweep**

swerve /swɜːv/ (**swerves, swerving, swerved**) *verb* to move suddenly to one side ○ *They think the car swerved to the left and hit a wall.* ○ *She had to swerve to avoid the bicycle.* (NOTE: + **swerve** *n*)

swift /swɪft/ *adj* very fast ○ *Their phone call brought a swift response from the police.*

swig /swɪg/ (**swigs, swigging, swigged**) *verb* to drink something in large mouthfuls (*informal*) ○ *They stopped and swigged water from a bottle.*

swill /swɪl/ (**swills, swilling, swilled**) *verb* **1.** to wash a floor with a lot of water **2.** to drink a lot of alcohol ○ *swilling pints of beer*

② **swim** /swɪm/ *verb* (**swims, swimming, swam, swum**) to move in the water using your arms and legs to push you along ○ *She can't swim, but she's taking swimming lessons.* ○ *She swam across the English Channel.* ○ *Salmon swim upstream to get to their spawning grounds.* ■ *noun* an occasion when you swim ○ *What about a swim before breakfast?* ○ *It's too cold for a swim.*

swimmer /'swɪmə/ *noun* a person who is swimming

② **swimming** /'swɪmɪŋ/ *noun* the activity or sport of moving through water using your arms and legs

swimming costume /'swɪmɪŋ ˌkɒstjuːm/ *noun* a piece of clothing worn by women or girls when swimming

swimming pool /'swɪmɪŋ puːl/ *noun* a large pool for swimming

swimming trunks /'swɪmɪŋ trʌŋks/ *plural noun* short trousers worn by men and boys when swimming

swimsuit /'swɪmsuːt/ *noun* a one-piece swimming costume for women and girls

swindle /'swɪnd(ə)l/ (**swindles, swindling, swindled**) *verb* to get money from someone by a trick ○ *She said she had been swindled by the bank.* ○ *He swindled the old lady out of £10,000.* (NOTE: + **swindle** *n*)

swine /swaɪn/ *noun* **1.** pigs (*old*) **2.** an unpleasant man (*insult*) ○ *He's a swine – he keeps us working all day long and pays us peanuts.* ○ *You rotten swine!*

② **swing** /swɪŋ/ *verb* (**swings, swinging, swung**) to move from side to side or forwards and backwards, while hanging from a central point ○ *Swing your arms round to warm up the muscles.* ○ *He swung up and down on the garden swing.* ○ *A window swung open and a man looked out.* ■ *noun* a seat held by two ropes or chains, to sit on and move backwards and forwards, usually outdoors ○ *a garden swing*

swipe /swaɪp/ *noun* a punch ○ *He took a swipe at the man who tried to steal his wallet.* ■ *verb* (**swipes, swiping, swiped**) **1.** to steal (*informal*) **2.** to pass a credit card or charge card through a machine that reads its details **3.** to hit someone or or something or try to hit someone or something

swipe card /'swaɪp kɑːd/ *noun* a credit card or charge card which can be read by an electronic machine

swirl /swɜːl/ *noun* a twisting movement ○ *Swirls of smoke came out of the chimney.* ■ *verb* (**swirls, swirling, swirled**) to move with a twisting motion ○ *Clouds of smoke were swirling round the factory.*

swish /swɪʃ/ (**swishes, swishing, swished**) *verb* to move making a regular quiet sound ○ *We sat by the motorway, listening to the cars swishing past.* (NOTE: + **swish** *n*)

② **switch** /swɪtʃ/ *noun* a small object which you push up or down to stop or start a piece of electrical equipment ○ *The switch to turn off the electricity is in the cupboard.* ○ *There is a light switch by the bed.* ■ *verb* (**switches, switching, switched**) **1.** to do something different suddenly [~from/to/~between] ○ *We decided to switch from gas to electricity.* ○ *He likes to switch between working in television and the theatre.* **2.** to change or exchange something ○ *Let's switch places.* ○ *He switched flights in Montreal and went on to Calgary.*

switch off *phrasal verb* **1.** to make an piece of electrical equipment stop ○ *Don't forget to switch off the TV before you go to bed.* ○ *She forgot to switch her car lights off* or *switch off her car lights.*

○ *The kettle switches itself off automatically when it boils.* **2.** to stop listening to what someone is saying (*informal*) ○ *If you talk too slowly, everyone starts to switch off.* ○ *I just switched off once the discussion started getting too technical.*

switch on *phrasal verb* to make a piece of electrical equipment start ○ *Can you switch the radio on – it's time for the evening news.* ○ *When you put the light on in the bathroom, the fan switches itself on automatically.*

switchboard /ˈswɪtʃbɔːd/ *noun* a central point in a telephone system, where all internal and external lines meet

swivel /ˈswɪv(ə)l/ (**swivels, swivelling, swivelled**) *verb* to turn around a point ○ *Swivel your chair to face the monitor.* ○ *He swivelled round in his chair and looked out of the window.*

③ **swollen** /ˈswəʊlən/ past participle of **swell** ■ *adj* much bigger than usual

swoop /swuːp/ (**swoops, swooping, swooped**) *verb* to come down quickly ○ *The planes swooped (down) low over the enemy camp.*

swop /swɒp/ *noun, verb* same as **swap**

sword /sɔːd/ *noun* a weapon with a handle and a long sharp blade

swordfish /ˈsɔːdfɪʃ/ *noun* a fish with a long pointed upper jaw like a sword

swore /swɔː/ past tense of **swear**

swot /swɒt/ *verb* (**swots, swotting, swotted**) to study hard ■ *noun* a person who you dislike because they study very hard

swum /swʌm/ past participle of **swim**

swung /swʌŋ/ past tense and past participle of **swing**

sycamore /ˈsɪkəmɔː/ *noun* a large tree of the maple family

③ **syllable** /ˈsɪləb(ə)l/ *noun* a whole word or part of a word which has one single sound. ◊ **monosyllable**

syllabus /ˈsɪləbəs/ (*plural* **syllabi** or **syllabuses**) *noun* a list of subjects to be studied

③ **symbol** /ˈsɪmbəl/ *noun* a sign, letter, picture or shape which means something or shows something [~of/~for] ○ *The crown was the symbol of the empire.* ○ *The olive branch is a symbol of peace.* ○ *Pb is the chemical symbol for lead.* (NOTE: Do not confuse with **cymbal**.)

symbolism /ˈsɪmbəlɪz(ə)m/ *noun* **1.** using symbols to express things such as feelings ○ *The symbolism of chopping down the orchard as the old man watched was obvious.* **2.** a movement in literature and art in the 19th century in which feelings were not expressed in a straightforward way

symmetrical /sɪˈmetrɪk(ə)l/ *adj* with two sides exactly the same

③ **symmetry** /ˈsɪmətri/ *noun* a state where two sides of something are exactly the same

③ **sympathetic** /ˌsɪmpəˈθetɪk/ *adj* showing that you understand someone's problems

sympathise /ˈsɪmpəθaɪz/ (**sympathises, sympathising, sympathised**), **sympathize** *verb* **1.** to show that you understand someone's problems [~with] ○ *My husband snores too – I sympathise!* ○ *I get back pains, and I sympathise with all fellow sufferers.* **2.** to agree with or support someone or something [~with] ○ *I sympathise with their goals but not their methods of achieving them*

③ **sympathy** /ˈsɪmpəθi/ *noun* a feeling of understanding for someone else's problems, or after someone's death [~for] ○ *I have no sympathy for those students who didn't work hard.* ○ *We received many messages of sympathy when my wife died.*

symphony /ˈsɪmfəni/ (*plural* **symphonies**) *noun* a long piece of music in several parts, called 'movements', played by a full orchestra

③ **symptom** /ˈsɪmptəm/ *noun* **1.** a change in the body, showing that a disease is present ○ *He has all the symptoms of flu.* **2.** a visible sign which shows that something is happening ○ *Factory closures are seen as a symptom of economic failure.*

symptomatic /ˌsɪmptəˈmætɪk/ *adj* showing that something exists (*formal*)

synagogue /ˈsɪnəgɒg/ *noun* a building where people of the Jewish faith pray and study their religion

syndicate /ˈsɪndɪkət/ *noun* a group of people or companies working together to make money ○ *a German finance syndicate*

syndrome /ˈsɪndrəʊm/ *noun* **1.** a group of symptoms which, taken together, show that a particular disease is present ○ *Their daughter has Down's syndrome.* **2.** a general feeling or way of approaching a situation ○ *It's an example of the 'let's go home early on Friday afternoon' syndrome.*

synonym /ˈsɪnənɪm/ *noun* a word which means almost the same as another word

synonymous /sɪˈnɒnɪməs/ *adj* meaning the same

synopsis /sɪ'nɒpsɪs/ (*plural* **synopses**) *noun* a short text, giving the basic details of something

③ **syntax** /'sɪntæks/ *noun* the grammatical rules for putting words together into phrases

synthesis /'sɪnθəsɪs/ (*plural* **syntheses**) *noun* producing something by combining a number of smaller elements

③ **synthetic** /sɪn'θetɪk/ *adj* made from artificial materials ○ *The coat she was wearing was made of synthetic fur.*

syphilis /'sɪfəlɪs/ *noun* a serious sexually transmitted disease

syphon /'saɪf(ə)n/ another spelling of **siphon**

syringe /sɪ'rɪndʒ/ *noun* a surgical instrument made of a tube with a plunger which slides down inside it, forcing the contents out through a needle to give an injection ○ *I close my eyes when I see the dentist's syringe ready.*

syrup /'sɪrəp/ *noun* a sweet liquid ○ *To make syrup, dissolve sugar in a cup of boiling water.*

① **system** /'sɪstəm/ *noun* **1.** a group of things which work together ○ *the system of motorways* or *the motorway system* ○ *the London underground railway system* **2.** a way in which things are organised [~for] ○ *I've got my own system for dealing with invoices.*

systematic /ˌsɪstə'mætɪk/ *adj* well-organised

systems analyst /'sɪstəmz ˌænəlɪst/ *noun* a person who examines computer systems

T

t /tiː/, **T** *noun* the twentieth letter of the alphabet, between S and U

ta /tɑː/ *interj* thank you (*informal*)

tab /tæb/ *noun* **1.** a small piece of paper or cloth which sticks out from a surface, used, e.g., for pulling open a box ○ *Pull the tab up to lift the cover off the box.* **2.** a piece of metal which you pull to open a drinks can ○ *The tab of the beer can came off when I tried to open it.* **3.** □ **to pick up the tab** to pay the bill (*informal*) ○ *I'll take you all out to lunch – the company will pick up the tab.* **4.** the tab key on a keyboard ◇ **to keep tabs on someone** to keep watch on someone ○ *I'm not too happy about the performance of our new representative in the Far East – you had better keep tabs on him for a while.*

tabby /ˈtæbi/ *noun* a cat with brown or orange stripes

tab key /ˈtæb kiː/ *noun* a key on a keyboard which you press to jump forward to a set place on the line

① **table** /ˈteɪb(ə)l/ *noun* **1.** a piece of furniture with a flat top and legs, used to eat or work at ○ *We had breakfast sitting round the kitchen table.* ○ *He asked for a table by the window.* ○ *She says she booked a table for six people for 12.30.* **2.** a list of numbers, facts, or information set out in an organised way

tablecloth /ˈteɪb(ə)lˌklɒθ/ *noun* a cloth which covers a table during a meal

tablespoon /ˈteɪb(ə)lspuːn/ *noun* **1.** a large spoon for serving food at table **2.** an amount held in a tablespoon ○ *Add two tablespoons of sugar.*

tablet /ˈtæblət/ *noun* a small round pill taken as medicine ○ *Take two tablets before meals.*

table tennis /ˈteɪb(ə)l ˌtenɪs/ *noun* a game similar to tennis, but played on a large table with a net across the centre, with small round bats and a very light white ball

tabloid /ˈtæblɔɪd/ *noun* a newspaper with a small page size, usually containing a lot of information about famous people, and not much serious news (NOTE: Large format newspapers are called **broadsheets**.)

taboo /təˈbuː/ *adj* not talked about because of being rude or embarrassing ○ *Talking about pay rises is taboo in this office.* ○ *Money used to be a taboo subject at home.* ■ *noun* a custom which forbids something ○ *There is a taboo against eating pork in the Muslim religion.*

tack /tæk/ *noun* **1.** a small nail with a wide head **2.** (*in sewing*) a loose stitch used to hold cloth in place when making clothes, which can be removed later ○ *She put in a row of tacks to show where the pockets were to go.* **3.** a movement of a sailing boat in a certain direction as it sails against the wind ■ *verb* (**tacks, tacking, tacked**) **1.** to nail something down using tacks ○ *He tacked down the edge of the carpet.* **2.** to make a loose stitch which will be taken out later ○ *She tacked up the hem of her skirt.* ◇ **to change tack** to start doing something different ○ *Originally he offered to pay all the costs of the party and then changed tack and asked everyone to pay for themselves.*

tack on *phrasal verb* to add something at the end

③ **tackle** /ˈtæk(ə)l/ *verb* (**tackles, tackling, tackled**) **1.** to try to deal with a problem or job ○ *You can't tackle a job like changing the central heating system on your own.* ○ *You start cleaning the dining room and I'll tackle the washing up.* **2.** (*in football, etc.*) to try to get the ball from an opposing player ○ *He was tackled before he could score.* ■ *noun* equipment ○ *He brought his fishing tackle with him.*

tacky /ˈtæki/ (**tackier, tackiest**) *adj* looking cheap and of bad quality ○ *The decorations were expensive, but they just look tacky.*

taco /ˈtækəʊ/ *noun* a Mexican savoury pastry that is filled with meat and vegetables, and cooked until it is hard

tact /tækt/ *noun* being careful not to offend people, being careful to say the right thing

tactful /ˈtæktf(ə)l/ *adj* showing tact

tactic /ˈtæktɪk/ *noun* a way of doing something so as to get an advantage (*often plural*) ○ *His tactic is to wait until near closing time, when the supermarket reduces the price of bread.*

tactless /ˈtæktləs/ *adj* offensive, not always intentionally

tad /tæd/ □ **a tad** a little, a bit ○ *I'll have a tad more, if I may.* ○ *I thought that lesson was a tad boring.*

tadpole /ˈtædpəʊl/ *noun* a frog in its first stage after hatching, when it has a body and tail

taffeta /ˈtæfɪtə/ *noun* a stiff shiny material often used to make women's clothes

tag /tæg/ *noun* **1.** a label or a piece of paper or plastic attached to something to show e.g. a price, contents, or someone's name and address **2.** a children's game where the first child has to try to touch another one who then chases the others in turn ○ *They were playing tag in the school playground.* ■ *verb* (**tags, tagging, tagged**) to attach a label to something

t'ai chi /ˌtaɪ ˈtʃiː/ *noun* a Chinese form of very slow physical exercise aimed at assisting relaxation and improving balance

② **tail** /teɪl/ *noun* **1.** a long thin part at the end of the body of an animal or bird, which can move ○ *All you could see was a slight movement of the cat's tail.* ○ *The dog rushed up to him, wagging its tail.* **2.** an end or back part of something ○ *The tail of the queue stretched round the corner and into the next street.* ○ *I prefer to sit near the tail of the aircraft.*

tail off *phrasal verb* to become fainter or less

tailback /ˈteɪlbæk/ *noun* a long line of cars that is moving very slowly, or not moving at all

tailgate /ˈteɪlgeɪt/ *noun US* a door at the back of a car, that opens to give access to the storage space ○ *He had difficulty shutting the tailgate over the box.*

tail light /ˈteɪl laɪt/ *noun* a back light of a vehicle

tailor /ˈteɪlə/ *noun* a person who makes clothes for men ○ *He gets all his clothes made by a tailor in Oxford Street.* ■ *verb* (**tailors, tailoring, tailored**) to adapt something to fit a particular need ○ *The payments can be tailored to suit your requirements.* ○ *This course is tailored to the needs of women going back to work.*

tailor-made /ˌteɪlə ˈmeɪd/ *adj* made to fit certain needs

① **take** /teɪk/ (**takes, taking, took, taken**) *verb* **1.** to lift and move something ○ *She took the pot of jam down from the shelf.* ○ *The waiter took the tablecloth off the table.* **2.** to carry something to another place ○ *Can you take this cheque to the bank for me, please?* **3.** to go with someone or something to another place ○ *He's taking the children to school.* ○ *They took the car to the garage.* ○ *We took a taxi to the hotel.* **4.** to steal something ○ *Someone's taken my watch.* **5.** to go away with something which someone else was using ○ *Someone has taken the newspaper I was reading.* ○ *Who's taken my cup of coffee?* **6.** to use or occupy something ○ *Sorry, all these seats are taken.* **7.** to do a test ○ *You must go to bed early because you'll be taking your exams tomorrow morning.* ○ *She had to take her driving test three times before she finally passed.* **8.** to accept something ○ *If they offer you the job, take it immediately.* **9.** to do certain actions ○ *We took our holiday in September this year.* ○ *She's taking a shower after going to the beach.* ○ *She took a photograph* or *took a picture of the Tower of London.* ○ *She needs to take a rest.* **10.** to need a certain amount of time or number of people ○ *It took three strong men to move the piano.* ○ *They took two days* or *it took them two days to get to London.* ○ *When he wants to watch a TV programme it never seems to take him long to finish his homework.* ◇ **to take place** to happen ○ *The reception will take place on Saturday.*

take after *phrasal verb* to look like a parent or relative

take away③ *phrasal verb* **1.** to remove something or someone ○ *Take those scissors away from little Nicky – he could cut himself.* ○ *The ambulance came and took her away.* ○ *The police took away piles of documents from the office.* **2.** to subtract one number from another (NOTE: **Take away** is usually shown by the sign – : *10 – 4 = 6*: say 'ten take away four equals six'.)

take back③ *phrasal verb* **1.** to go back with something ○ *If the trousers are too short you can take them back to the shop.* **2.** to accept something which someone has brought back ○ *I took my trousers to the shop where I had bought them, but they wouldn't take them back because I didn't have a receipt.* **3.** to withdraw something which has been said, and apologise for it ○ *I take it all back – they're a marvellous team.*

take down *phrasal verb* **1.** to reach up and bring something down ○ *I took the jar down from the shelf.* **2.** to bring something down which had been put up ○ *On January 6th we take down the Christmas decorations.* ○ *They have finished the roof and are taking down the scaffolding.* **3.** to write down ○ *The policeman took down his name and address.*

take in③ *phrasal verb* **1.** to bring inside something which was outside ○ *In October they took in the lemon trees from the gardens.* **2.** to understand something ○ *I don't think she took in anything of what you said.* **3.** to deceive someone ○ *Thousands of people were taken in by the advertisement.* **4.** to make a piece of clothing smaller ○ *Can you take these trousers in? They're much too loose round the waist.*

take off③ *phrasal verb* **1.** to remove something, especially your clothes ○ *He took off all his clothes or he took all his clothes off.* ○ *Take your dirty boots off before you come into the kitchen.* ◊ **hat 2.** to make an amount smaller ○ *He took £25 off the price.* **3.** (*of a plane*) to leave the ground ○ *The plane took off at 4.30.* **4.** to start to rise fast ○ *Sales took off after the TV commercials.* **5.** to imitate someone in a funny way ○ *He likes to make everyone laugh by taking off the head teacher.*

take on *phrasal verb* **1.** to agree to do a job ○ *She's taken on a part-time job in addition to the one she's already got.* **2.** to agree to have someone as a worker ○ *The shop has taken on four trainees.* ○ *We need to take on more staff to cope with the work.* **3.** to fight someone ○ *It seems he is taking on the whole government.*

take out③ *phrasal verb* **1.** to pull something out ○ *He took out a gun and waved it around.* ○ *The dentist had to take my tooth out.* **2.** to invite someone to go out ○ *I'm taking all the office staff out for a drink.* ◇ **to take it out on someone** to make someone suffer because you are upset or worried ○ *He keeps on taking it out on his secretary.*

take over *phrasal verb* **1.** to start to do something in place of someone else ○ *Miss Black took over from Mr Jones on May 1st.* ○ *Thanks for looking after the switchboard for me – I'll take over from you now.* ○ *When our history teacher was ill, the English teacher had to take over his classes.* ○ *The Socialists took over from the Conservatives.* **2.** to buy a business by buying most of its shares ○ *The company was taken over by a big group last month.*

take to *phrasal verb* **1.** to start to do something as a habit ○ *He's taken to looking under his bed every night to make sure no one is hiding there.* ○ *She's recently taken to wearing trousers to work.* **2.** to start to like someone ○ *She took to her boss right away.*

take up *phrasal verb* **1.** to fill a space or time ○ *This settee takes up too much room.* ○ *Being in charge of the staff sports club takes up too much of my time.* **2.** to remove something which was on a floor or other low surface ○ *You will need to take up the rugs if you want to polish the floor.* **3.** to start to do a certain activity ○ *She was over fifty when she took up long-distance running.* **4.** □ **to take someone up on something** to accept an offer made by someone ○ *He asked me if I wanted two tickets to Wimbledon and I took him up on his offer.* **5.** to make something such as a skirt or dress shorter ○ *Can you take up the hem of this coat?*

takeaway /ˈteɪkəweɪ/ *noun* a shop where you can buy cooked food to eat somewhere else ○ *There's an Indian takeaway round the corner.* ○ *We had a Chinese takeaway.* ■ *noun, adj* a hot meal that you buy in a shop and eat somewhere else ○ *We had a takeaway Chinese meal.*

taken /ˈteɪkən/ past participle of **take**

takeoff /ˈteɪkɒf/ *noun* **1.** (*of an aircraft*) the act of leaving the ground ○ *The takeoff was without any problems.* ○ *I always ask for a seat by the window, so that I can watch the takeoff.* **2.** an amusing imitation of someone ○ *He did a wonderful takeoff of the head teacher.*

takeover /ˈteɪkəʊvə/ *noun* **1.** the buying of a controlling interest in a business by buying more than 50% of the shares ○ *The takeover may mean that a lot of people will lose their jobs.* **2.** occupying a country and removing the government ○ *Many people were killed during the military takeover.*

talcum powder /ˈtælkəm ˌpaʊdə/ *noun* soft scented powder, used to soften the skin or reduce rubbing

③ **tale** /teɪl/ *noun* a story (*literary*)

③ **talent** /ˈtælənt/ *noun* an ability or skill [~for] ○ *At university, he showed a talent for* *acting.* ○ *Her many talents include singing and playing the piano.*

talented /ˈtæləntɪd/ *adj* with a lot of talent

talisman /ˈtælɪzmən/ *noun* an object believed to give protection to somebody carrying or wearing it

① **talk** /tɔːk/ *verb* (**talks, talking, talked**) to say things, to speak [~about/~to/with] ○ *I didn't understand what he was talking about.* ○ *We must talk to the neighbours about their noisy dog – it kept me awake again last night.* ○ *We talked for hours.* ■ *noun* **1.** a conversation, a discussion [~with] ○ *I had a long talk with my father about what I should study at university.* ○ *We had a little talk, and she agreed with what the committee had decided.* **2.** a lecture about a subject [~on] ○ *He gave a short talk on the history of the town.*

talk into *phrasal verb* □ **to talk someone into doing something** to persuade someone to do something ○ *The salesman talked us into buying a new car.*

talk over③ *phrasal verb* to discuss something

talk round *phrasal verb* to persuade someone to change their mind

talkative /ˈtɔːkətɪv/ *adj* liking to talk a lot, or sometimes too much

talker /ˈtɔːkə/ *noun* a person who talks a lot

② **tall** /tɔːl/ *adj* high, usually higher than normal ○ *the tallest building in London* ○ *Can you see those tall trees over there?* ○ *He's the tallest boy in his class.* ○ *How tall are you? – I'm 1 metre 68 centimetres.* ○ *His brother is over six feet tall.* (NOTE: **Tall** is used with people and thin things like trees or skyscrapers; for things which are a long way above the ground use **high**: *high clouds, a high mountain.*)

tally /ˈtæli/ *noun* a note, account or score ○ *What's the tally in the race so far? – We've had two crashes and four retirements through mechanical failure.* ○ *The scorer keeps a tally of the runs scored.* ○ *Did you keep a tally of all your expenses?* ■ *verb* (**tallies, tallying, tallied**) to agree ○ *The totals in the two columns don't tally.* ○ *The figures in my notebook tally with the computer figures.*

talon /ˈtælən/ *noun* the big claw of a bird of prey

tambourine /ˌtæmbəˈriːn/ *noun* a small drum with metal discs attached to the rim, so that they jangle when it is hit

tame /teɪm/ (**tamer, tamest**) *adj* a tame animal can live with people because it is no longer wild ○ *Don't be afraid of that fox – he's perfectly tame.*

tamper /ˈtæmpə/ (**tampers, tampering, tampered**) *verb* □ **to tamper with something** to change something that you should not touch ○ *Someone has been tampering with the weighing machine.* ○ *I hope no one tampered with the test sample.*

tampon /ˈtæmpɒn/ *noun* a tube of absorbent material placed inside the vagina to soak up menstrual blood ○ *I need to buy a packet of tampons from the chemist.*

tan /tæn/ *noun* a brownish-yellow colour of the skin after being in the sun ○ *She got a tan from spending each day on the beach.* ◊ **suntan** ■ *verb* (**tans, tanning, tanned**) to get brown from being in the sun ○ *She tans easily – just half an hour in the sun and she's quite brown.*

tandem /ˈtændəm/ *noun* a bicycle for two people ○ *I'm sure that's the second time today we've passed that couple on their tandem.* ◇ **in tandem** together, in pairs ○ *They worked in tandem for many years.*

tandoori /tænˈdʊəri/ (*plural* **tandooris**) *noun* **1.** a method of Indian cooking where the food is usually marinated in yoghurt and spices, then cooked in a traditional clay oven **2.** food cooked in this way

tangent /ˈtændʒənt/ *noun* a line which touches a curve without cutting through it ○ *The line AB forms a tangent to the circle at the point P.* ◇ **to fly** *or* **to go off at a tangent, to go off on a tangent** to start talking about something quite different ○ *He suddenly flew off at a tangent and started talking about his car.* ○ *She went off at a tangent almost from the beginning of the discussion.*

tangerine /ˌtændʒəˈriːn/ *noun* a kind of small orange with soft skin which peels easily

tangible /ˈtændʒəb(ə)l/ *adj* which is real or noticeable

tangle with *phrasal verb* to get into an argument with someone ○ *Tourists are advised not to tangle with the local football supporters.*

tango /ˈtæŋgəʊ/ *noun* a South American dance for two people, where you glide sideways

② **tank** /tæŋk/ *noun* **1.** a large container for liquids ○ *How much oil is left in the tank?* **2.** an army vehicle which is covered in strong metal, has tracks instead of wheels and has powerful guns ○ *Tanks rolled along the main streets of the town.*

tankard /ˈtæŋkəd/ *noun* a large mug for drinking beer

tanker /ˈtæŋkə/ *noun* a ship or lorry for carrying liquids, especially oil

tanned /tænd/ *adj* brown from having been exposed to the sun

tantrum /ˈtæntrəm/ *noun* a sudden attack of uncontrollable bad temper

③ **tap** /tæp/ *noun* an object which you turn in order to let liquid or gas come out of a pipe ○ *He washed his hands under the tap in the kitchen.* ■ *verb* (**taps, tapping, tapped**) to hit something gently [~on] ○ *Someone tapped me on the shoulder.* ◇ **on tap** available when you need it ○ *We should have all this information on tap.*

② **tape** /teɪp/ *noun* **1.** a long narrow piece of cloth or plastic ○ *She stitched tape along the bottom of the sleeves to stop it fraying.* **2.** same as **magnetic tape** □ **magnetic tape** special plastic tape on which sounds and pictures can be recorded, also used for recording computer data □ **on tape** recorded on magnetic tape ○ *We have the whole conversation on tape.* ■ *verb* (**tapes, taping, taped**) **1.** to record something on tape or on video ○ *The whole conversation was taped by the police.* ○ *I didn't see the programme because I was at work, but I've taped it.* **2.** to attach something with sticky tape ○ *She taped up the box before taking it to the post office.*

tape deck /ˈteɪp dek/ *noun* a part of a stereo system, which plays tapes

tape measure /ˈteɪp ˌmeʒə/ *noun* a measuring tape, a long strip marked in centimetres or inches, used for measuring

taper /ˈteɪpə/ (**tapers, tapering, tapered**) *verb* **1.** to make something thinner at the end ○ *You will need to taper the piece of wood to make it fit into the hole.* **2.** to become thinner at the end ○ *Her new shoes taper to a point.*

taper off *phrasal verb* to become less thick, strong, large, etc. ○ *Interest in the project seems to have tapered off.*

tapestry /ˈtæpɪstri/ (*plural* **tapestries**) *noun* a thick woven cloth with a picture or design, usually hung on walls or used to cover chairs ○ *The walls were hung with tapestries.*

tap water /ˈtæp ˌwɔːtə/ *noun* water which comes through pipes into a building

tar /tɑː/ *noun* a similar black oily substance which comes from burning tobacco ○ *cigarettes with low tar content* or *low tar cigarettes* ■ *verb* (**tars, tarring, tarred**) to cover with melted tar ○ *a special machine for tarring roads*

tarantula /təˈræntjʊlə/ *noun* a large mildly poisonous tropical spider

② **target** /ˈtɑːɡɪt/ *noun* **1.** an object which you aim at e.g. with a gun ○ *His last shot missed the target altogether.* ○ *She hit the target three times in all.* **2.** a goal which you try to reach [~of] □ **to set targets** to fix quantities of work which employees have to produce □ **to meet a target** to produce the quantity of goods or sales which is expected ○ *We need to set targets for our sales staff to meet.* □ **to miss a target** not to produce the amount of goods or sales which is expected ○ *The factory missed its production targets again this year.*

tariff /ˈtærɪf/ *noun* **1.** a tax to be paid for importing or exporting goods **2.** a list of prices for things such as electricity, gas or water ○ *The new winter tariff will be introduced next week.*

Tarmac /ˈtɑːmæk/ *trademark* a trademark for a hard road surface made of tar mixed with small stones ○ *The sun was so hot, the Tarmac was starting to melt.*

tarnish /ˈtɑːnɪʃ/ (**tarnishes, tarnishing, tarnished**) *verb* **1.** (*of metal*) to become discoloured ○ *Silver tarnishes easily on contact with the air.* **2.** to ruin a reputation ○ *The sex scandal has irreparably tarnished his reputation as a politician.*

tarot /ˈtærəʊ/ *noun* a special set of cards with pictures on them, such as the Emperor, the Pope, the Hanged Man and the Fool, used in telling fortunes

tarpaulin /tɑːˈpɔːlɪn/ *noun* a piece of thick waterproof canvas, used to cover things left outside

tart /tɑːt/ *noun* a woman who looks or dresses like a prostitute (*offensive*)

tartan /ˈtɑːt(ə)n/ *noun* a distinctive pattern in such a cloth, worn by members of a Scottish clan ○ *My Scottish grandmother gave me a rug with the Mackay tartan on it* or *a Mackay tartan rug.*

① **task** /tɑːsk/ *noun* something, especially a piece of work, that has to be done ○ *He had the unpleasant task of telling his mother about it.*

taskbar /ˈtɑːskbɑː/ *noun* a display on a computer screen with symbols showing which programs are open and operating

task force /ˈtɑːsk fɔːs/ *noun* a special group of people chosen to carry out a difficult task

tassel /ˈtæs(ə)l/ *noun* a group of threads tied together to form a ball, with the ends hanging free

② **taste** /teɪst/ *noun* **1.** one of the five senses, by which you can tell differences of flavour between things you eat, using your tongue ○ *She loves the taste of oranges.* ○ *I've got a cold, so I've lost all sense of taste.* **2.** a flavour of something that you eat or drink ○ *The pudding has a funny* or *strange taste.* ○ *Do you like the taste of garlic?* ○ *This milk shake has no taste at all.* ■ *verb* (**tastes, tasting, tasted**) **1.** to notice the taste of something with your tongue ○ *Can you taste the garlic in this soup?* ○ *She's got a cold so she can't taste anything.* **2.** to have a certain taste ○ *This cheese tastes like soap.* ○ *The bread tastes vaguely of onions.* ○ *The pudding tastes very good.* **3.** to try food or drink to see if you like it ○ *Would you like to taste the wine?*

taste buds /ˈteɪst bʌdz/ *plural noun* areas on your tongue which enable you to tell differences in flavour

tasteful /ˈteɪstf(ə)l/ *adj* showing good taste

tasteless /ˈteɪstləs/ *adj* **1.** with no special flavour ○ *Chicken can be quite tasteless unless you add herbs to it.* **2.** showing bad taste ○ *a restaurant with tasteless decorations* ○ *She made a tasteless remark about her mother's dress.*

③ **tasty** /ˈteɪsti/ (**tastier, tastiest**) *adj* with a pleasant taste

tattoo /tæˈtuː/ *noun* **1.** a decoration on skin made by pricking with a needle and putting colour into the wound ○ *She has a little tattoo of a rose on her left shoulder.* **2.** a military parade ○ *Crowds went to see the tattoo last night.*

tatty /ˈtæti/ *adj* worn out, in bad condition

③ **taught** /tɔːt/ past tense and past participle of **teach**

taunt /tɔːnt/ (**taunts, taunting, taunted**) *verb* to jeer at someone sarcastically ○ *He taunted the minister with* or *about his financial problems.* (NOTE: + **taunt** *n*)

Taurus /ˈtɔːrəs/ *noun* one of the signs of the Zodiac, shaped like a bull, covering the period 20th April to 20th May

taut /tɔːt/ *adj* stretched tight

① **tax** /tæks/ *noun* money taken by the government from things such as people's incomes and sales, to pay for government services [~on] ○ *The government is planning to introduce a tax on food.* ○ *You must pay your tax on the correct date.* ○ *The newspaper headline says 'TAXES TO GO UP'.*

③ **taxation** /tækˈseɪʃ(ə)n/ *noun* the action of imposing taxes

tax evasion /ˈtæks ɪˌveɪʒ(ə)n/ *noun* illegally trying not to pay tax

③ **taxi** /ˈtæksi/ *noun* a car which you can hire with a driver ○ *Can you call a taxi to take me to the airport?* ○ *Why aren't there any taxis at the station today?* ○ *There are no buses on Sunday afternoons, so we had to take a taxi to the party.* (NOTE: also often called a **cab** and sometimes **taxicab**)

taxi rank /ˈtæksi ræŋk/ *noun* a place in the street where taxis can wait

taxpayer /ˈtækspeɪə/ *noun* a person who pays tax, especially income tax

tax return /ˈtæks rɪˌtɜːn/ *noun* a form to be filled in to inform the tax office of your earnings and allowances

① **tea** /tiː/ *noun* **1.** a drink made from hot water which has been poured onto the dried leaves of a tropical plant ○ *Can I have another cup of tea* or *some more tea?* ○ *I don't like tea – can I have coffee instead?* **2.** a cup of tea ○ *Can we have two teas and two cakes, please?* **3.** the dried leaves of a tropical plant used to make a warm drink ○ *We've run out of tea, can you put it on your shopping list?* ○ *Put a spoonful of tea into the pot and add boiling water.* **4.** a meal eaten in the late afternoon or early evening ○ *The children have had their tea.*

teabag /ˈtiːbæg/, **tea bag** *noun* a small paper bag with tea leaves in it which you put into the pot with hot water

① **teach** /tiːtʃ/ (**teaches, teaching, taught**) *verb* to show someone how to do something ○ *She taught me how to dance.* ○ *He teaches maths in the local school.*

① **teacher** /ˈtiːtʃə/ *noun* a person who teaches, especially in a school ○ *Mr Jones is our maths teacher.* ○ *The French teacher is ill today.* ○ *He trained as a primary school teacher.* ◊ **pet**

① **teaching** /ˈtiːtʃɪŋ/ *noun* the work of being a teacher or of giving lessons ○ *The report praised the high standard of teaching at the college.* ○ *He was working in a bank, but has decided to go into teaching instead.*

teacup /ˈtiːkʌp/ *noun* a cup for drinking tea out of

teak /tiːk/ *noun* **1.** the hard wood of a tropical tree, which is resistant to water, and is used for making things such as outdoor furniture ○ *We bought some teak furniture for the patio.* ○ *The table is solid teak.* **2.**

the large tropical tree which produces this wood ○ *the teak forests of Indonesia*

① **team** /tiːm/ *noun* **1.** a group of people who play a game together ○ *There are eleven people in a football team and fifteen in a rugby team.* ○ *She's in the team for next Saturday's game.* **2.** a group of people who work together [~of] ○ *We have a team of scientists tracking the animals' movements.* ○ *They make a very effective team.*

team-mate /'tiːmmeɪt/ *noun* someone in the same team as you

teamwork /'tiːmwɜːk/ *noun* working together as a group

teapot /'tiːpɒt/ *noun* a container which is used for making tea in

② **tear[1]** /tɪə/ *noun* a drop of salt water which forms in your eye when you cry ○ *Tears were running down her cheeks.* □ **to burst into tears** to suddenly start crying ◇ **in tears** crying ○ *All the family were in tears.*

tear[2] /teə/ *verb* (**tears, tearing, tore, torn**) **1.** to make a hole in something by pulling ○ *He tore his trousers climbing over the fence.* ○ *My coat is torn – can it be mended?* **2.** to pull something into small pieces ○ *He tore the letter in half.* ○ *She tore up old newspapers to pack the cups and saucers.* ■ *noun* a place where something has a hole in it from being torn ○ *Can you mend the tear in my jeans?* ◊ **wear and tear**

tear apart *phrasal verb* to pull something to pieces

tear down *phrasal verb* **1.** to knock something down ○ *They tore down the old town hall and replaced it with a supermarket.* **2.** to remove a piece of paper or cloth which is hanging up ○ *The crowd tore down the pictures of the president.* ○ *The police tore down the opposition party's election posters.*

tearful /'tɪəf(ə)l/ *adj* sad, crying

tear gas /'tɪə gæs/ *noun* gas which makes your eyes burn, used by police to control crowds

tear up *phrasal verb* to destroy something such as a document by tearing it into small pieces ○ *She tore up all her father's letters.* □ **to tear up an agreement** to refuse to do what you have agreed to do

tease /tiːz/ (**teases, teasing, teased**) *verb* to say or do something to annoy someone on purpose ○ *He teased her about her new haircut.* ○ *Stop teasing that poor cat.*

tea set /'tiː set/, **tea service** /'tiː ˌsɜːvɪs/ *noun* a set of matching china, used for serving tea ○ *Get out the best tea set because Aunt Flora is coming.*

COMMENT: A tea set will include cups, saucers, small plates, a large plate for cakes, a teapot, milk jug and sugar basin.

teaspoon /'tiːspuːn/ *noun* a small spoon for stirring tea or other liquid ○ *Can you bring me a teaspoon, please?*

tea towel /'tiː ˌtaʊəl/ *noun* a cloth which you use for drying plates and dishes

techie /'teki/, **tekkie** *noun* a person who understands the more technical aspects of things such as computers (*Informal*)

② **technical** /'teknɪk(ə)l/ *adj* relating to industrial processes or practical work ○ *Don't bother with the technical details of how the machine works, just tell me what it does.* ○ *The instructions are too technical for the ordinary person to understand.*

technicality /ˌteknɪ'kælɪti/ *noun* a little, usually unimportant, detail which relates to something

technician /tek'nɪʃ(ə)n/ *noun* a person who is a specialist in a particular area of industry or science

① **technique** /tek'niːk/ *noun* a way of doing something [~for/~of] ○ *modern techniques of firefighting* ○ *He developed a new technique for processing steel.*

techno /'teknəʊ/ *noun* a type of fast dance music using electronic instruments

① **technology** /tek'nɒlədʒi/ *noun* the use or study of industrial or scientific skills ○ *We already have the technology to produce such a machine.* ○ *The government has promised increased support for science and technology.*

teddy bear /'tedi 'beə/, **teddy** (*plural* **teddies**) *noun* a child's toy bear ○ *The little boy was clutching his old teddy bear.*

tedious /'tiːdiəs/ *adj* boring

tee /tiː/ *noun* **1.** a raised grass area on a golf course where the ball is placed when you begin to play each hole ○ *He is walking towards the sixteenth tee.* **2.** a little peg which is pushed into ground, on which the golf ball is placed to start playing a hole ○ *The ground is so hard I can hardly stick my tee in.*

teenage /'tiːneɪdʒ/ *adj* referring to young people aged between 13 and 19 ○ *the teenage years* ○ *The teenage market for their records is enormous.*

③ **teenager** /'tiːneɪdʒə/ *noun* a young person aged between 13 and 19 ○ *She writes stories for teenagers.*

teens /tiːnz/ *plural noun* the age between 13 and 19

teeny /ˈtiːni/ *adj* very small (*informal*)

③ **teeshirt** /ˈtiːʃɜːt/, **T-shirt** *noun* a light shirt with a round neck and no buttons or collar, usually with short sleeves

teeter /ˈtiːtə/ (**teeters, teetering, teetered**) *verb* to wobble, to be very unstable

② **teeth** /tiːθ/ plural of **tooth**

teethe /tiːð/ (**teethes, teething, teethed**) *verb* (*of a baby*) to have the first teeth starting to grow ○ *The baby wakes up at night because he is teething.*

teething problems /ˈtiːθɪŋ ˌprɒbləmz/, **teething troubles** /ˈtiːθɪŋ ˌtrʌb(ə)lz/ *plural noun* problems which happen when a new process or system is being introduced ○ *We are experiencing some teething problems with the new software system.*

teetotal /ˌtiːˈtəʊt(ə)l/ *adj* who never drinks alcohol

TEFL *abbr* teaching of English as a foreign language

tel *abbr* telephone

telecommunications /ˌtelikəˌmjuːnɪˈkeɪʃ(ə)nz/ *plural noun* a communication system using e.g. telephone, radio, TV, satellites ○ *Thanks to modern telecommunications, the information can be sent to our office in Japan in seconds.* (NOTE: also shortened to **telecoms** /ˈtelɪkɒmz/)

telecommuter /ˈtelikəmjuːtə/ *noun* a person who works from home, using email and telephone as their main means of communicating with the company they work for

teleconference /ˈteliˌkɒnf(ə)rəns/ *noun* a meeting held by people in different places using telephone and television

telegram /ˈtelɪgræm/ *noun* a message sent by telegraph

telegraph pole /ˈtelɪgrɑːf pəʊl/, **telegraph post** *noun* a pole which holds up a telephone line

telemarketing /ˈtelɪˌmɑːkɪtɪŋ/ *noun* the activity of selling goods and services by telephone

telepathy /təˈlepəθi/ *noun* sending thoughts or mental images from one person to another without using the senses

① **telephone** /ˈtelɪfəʊn/ *noun* a machine which you use to speak to someone who is some distance away ○ *I was in the garden when you called, but by the time I got to the house the telephone had stopped ringing.* ○ *She lifted the telephone and called the ambulance.* ■ *verb* (**telephones, telephoning, telephoned**) to call someone using a telephone ○ *Your wife telephoned when you were out.* ○ *Can you telephone me at ten o'clock tomorrow evening?* ○ *I need to telephone our office in New York.* (NOTE: **Telephone** is often shortened to **phone**: *phone call, phone book*, but not in the expressions **telephone switchboard**, **telephone operator**, **telephone exchange**.)

telephone box /ˈtelɪfəʊn bɒks/ *noun* a shelter with windows round it containing a public telephone (NOTE: often shortened to **phone box**)

telephone directory /ˈtelɪfəʊn daɪˌrekt(ə)ri/ *noun* a book which lists names of people and businesses in alphabetical order with their phone numbers and addresses

telephone exchange /ˈtelɪfəʊn ɪksˌtʃeɪndʒ/ *noun* a central telephone switchboard

③ **telephone number** /ˈtelɪfəʊn ˌnʌmbə/ *noun* the number of a particular telephone (NOTE: often shortened to **phone number**)

telesales /ˈteliˌseɪlz/ *noun* same as **telemarketing**

③ **telescope** /ˈtelɪskəʊp/ *noun* a piece of equipment for looking at objects which are very far away, consisting of a long tube with a series of lenses in it ○ *With a telescope you can see the ships very clearly.* ○ *He watched the stars using a telescope in his back garden.*

televise /ˈtelɪvaɪz/ (**televises, televising, televised**) *verb* to broadcast something by television

① **television** /ˌtelɪˈvɪʒ(ə)n/ *noun* **1.** sound and pictures which are sent through the air or along cables and appear on a special machine ○ *television programmes* ○ *He stayed in his room all evening, watching television.* **2.** a piece of electrical equipment which shows television pictures ○ *I switched off the television before going to bed.* (NOTE: **Television** is often written or spoken as **TV** /ˌtiː ˈviː/ .)

teleworker /ˈteliwɜːkə/ *noun* a person who works from home, using telephone and email as their principal way of communicating with the company they work for

① **tell** /tel/ (**tells, telling, told**) *verb* **1.** to communicate something to someone, e.g. a story or a joke ○ *She told me a long story about how she got lost in London.* ○ *I don't think they are telling the truth.* **2.** to give information to someone [~how/what/whether etc/~(that)/~about] ○ *She told me how to get* *there.* ○ *He told the police that he had seen the accident take place.* ○ *Don't tell my mother you saw me at the pub.* ○ *Nobody told us about the picnic.* **3.** □ **to tell someone what to do** to give someone instructions ○ *The teacher told the children to stand in a line.* ○ *Give a shout to tell us when to start.* **4.** to notice something [~(that)] ○ *You can tell he is embarrassed because his face goes red.* ○ *He can't tell the difference between butter and margarine.*

tell off③ *phrasal verb* to speak to someone angrily about something wrong he or she has done (*informal*)

teller /'telə/ *noun* a clerk in a bank who takes in money or pays it out to customers ○ *The teller told me that I couldn't cash the cheque.*

telling /'telɪŋ/ *adj* which has a certain effect

telltale /'telteɪl/ *adj* which shows something

telly /'teli/ *noun* a television (*informal*)

temp /temp/ *noun* a worker who is appointed for a short time ○ *We have two temps working in the office this week.* ■ *verb* (**temps, temping, temped**) to work as a temp ○ *She has done some temping jobs.* ○ *I'm temping for the moment until I can find something permanent.*

temper /'tempə/ *noun* the state of becoming angry ○ *You have to learn to control your temper.* ○ *He has a violent temper.* ○ *She got into a temper.*

temperament /'temprəmənt/ *noun* the nature of a person

temperate /'temp(ə)rət/ *adj* which is neither very hot nor very cold ○ *The temperate forests of northern Europe have been badly affected by acid rain.*

② **temperature** /'temprɪtʃə/ *noun* **1.** heat measured in degrees ○ *The temperature of water in the swimming pool is 25°.* ○ *Temperatures at night can fall well below zero.* ○ *We use this thermometer to take the patient's temperature.* **2.** an illness where your body is hotter than normal ○ *The doctor says he's got a temperature and has to stay in bed.*

tempest /'tempɪst/ *noun* a big storm (*literary*)

template /'tem,pleɪt/ *noun* something that is used as a pattern to make other similar things

temple /'tempəl/ *noun* a building for worship, usually Hindu or Buddhist, or ancient Greek or Roman ○ *We visited the Greek temples on the islands.*

tempo /'tempəʊ/ *noun* **1.** a rhythm or the beat of music ○ *The tempo of the band speeded up as midnight approached.* **2.** the speed at which something happens ○ *He found it difficult to keep up with the tempo of life in the City.*

temporarily /ˌtemp(ə)'rerəli/ *adv* for a short time only

② **temporary** /'temp(ə)rəri/ *adj* existing or lasting only for a limited time ○ *She has a temporary job with a construction company.* ○ *This arrangement is only temporary.*

③ **tempt** /tempt/ (**tempts, tempting, tempted**) *verb* to try to persuade someone to do something, especially something pleasant or wrong ○ *Can I tempt you to have another cream cake?* ○ *They tried to tempt him to leave his job and work for them.*

temptation /temp'teɪʃ(ə)n/ *noun* **1.** the state of being tempted **2.** something which attracts people ○ *Putting chocolates near the cash desk is just a temptation for little children.*

tempting /'temptɪŋ/ *adj* which attracts

① **ten** /ten/ *noun* the number 10

tenacious /tɪ'neɪʃəs/ *adj* holding on to an idea tightly ○ *her tenacious belief in socialist principles*

tenancy /'tenənsi/ *noun* a period during which a tenant has an agreement to rent a property

tenant /'tenənt/ *noun* a person or company that rents e.g. a room, a flat, a house, an office or land in which to live or work

① **tend** /tend/ (**tends, tending, tended**) *verb* **1.** to look after something ○ *His job is to tend the flower beds in front of the town hall.* **2.** □ **to tend to do something** to be likely to do something ○ *She tends to lose her temper very easily.*

③ **tendency** /'tendənsi/ *noun* the way in which someone or something is likely to act ○ *The photocopier has a tendency to break down if you try to do too many copies at the same time.* ○ *He has an unfortunate tendency to sit in a corner and go to sleep at parties.*

tender /'tendə/ *adj* **1.** (*of food*) easy to cut or chew ○ *a plate of tender young beans* ○ *The meat was so tender, you hardly needed a knife to cut it.* **2.** showing love ○ *The plants need a lot of tender loving care.* **3.** painful when touched

tendon /ˈtendən/ *noun* a piece of strong tissue which attaches a muscle to a bone

tenement /ˈtenəmənt/ *noun* a large old building which is divided into flats

tenet /ˈtenɪt/ *noun* a basic principle or belief

tenner /ˈtenə/ *noun* a ten pound note (*informal*)

tennis /ˈtenɪs/ *noun* a game for two or four players who use rackets to hit a ball over a net ○ *He's joined the local tennis club.* ○ *Would you like a game of tennis?*

tenor /ˈtenə/ *adj* with a high pitch, similar to that of a tenor ○ *He plays the tenor saxophone.* ○ *He has a pleasant tenor voice.* Compare **bass** ■ *noun* a man who sings with the highest male voice ○ *The tenors start the song, followed by the sopranos.*

ten-pin bowling /ˌten pɪn ˈbəʊlɪŋ/ *noun* a game where you roll a large ball and try to knock down ten targets, shaped like bottles

② **tense** /tens/ *adj* (**tenser, tensest**) nervous and worried ○ *I always get tense before going to an interview.* ○ *The atmosphere in the hall was tense as everyone waited for the result of the vote.* ■ *noun* the form of a verb which shows the time when the action takes place

② **tension** /ˈtenʃən/ *noun* **1.** a state of nervous anxiety ○ *Tension built up as we waited for the result.* **2.** a state of hostility between countries, races, or groups [~between] ○ *The talks are aimed at reducing tension between these neighbouring republics.* **3.** the state of being tight ○ *There's a lot of tension in your muscles.*

tent /tent/ *noun* a shelter made of cloth, held up by poles and attached to the ground with ropes

tentacle /ˈtentək(ə)l/ *noun* a long arm with suckers, such as that of an octopus

① **tenth** /tenθ/ *adj* relating to number 10 in a series ■ *noun* number 10 in a series

tenuous /ˈtenjuəs/ *adj* not strong, very slight

tenure /ˈtenjə/ *noun* **1.** a right to hold property or a position ○ *Freehold farmers have tenure of their land.* **2.** a period when you hold an office ○ *during his tenure as honorary secretary* **3.** (*in a college or university*) a right to hold a job permanently ○ *He's on a contract but hopes to get tenure next year.*

tepid /ˈtepɪd/ *adj* **1.** slightly warm ○ *There was no hot water left so my bath was only tepid.* ○ *There's only a bit of coffee left in your mug and it's probably tepid.* **2.** not very enthusiastic ○ *His tepid reaction to my great plan disappointed me.*

tequila /tɪˈkiːlə/ *noun* a strong Mexican alcoholic drink

① **term** /tɜːm/ *noun* **1.** one of the parts of a school or university year ○ *The autumn term ends on December 15th.* ○ *Next term I'll be starting to learn the piano.* **2.** a word or phrase which has a particular meaning ○ *He used several technical terms which I didn't understand.* ○ *Some people use 'darling' as a term of affection.*

terminal /ˈtɜːmɪn(ə)l/ *noun* a building at an airport where planes arrive or leave ○ *The flight leaves from Terminal 4.* ■ *adj* referring to the last period of a serious illness that will lead to death ○ *terminal cancer* ○ *The condition is terminal.*

terminate /ˈtɜːmɪneɪt/ (**terminates, terminating, terminated**) *verb* to end something (NOTE: + **termination** *n*)

③ **terminology** /ˌtɜːmɪˈnɒlədʒi/ *noun* special words or phrases used in a particular subject area

terminus /ˈtɜːmɪnəs/ (*plural* **termini** or **terminuses**) *noun* **1.** a station at the end of a railway line ○ *Waterloo Station is the terminus for Eurostar trains from Paris and Brussels.* **2.** the place at the end of a journey by bus or coach ○ *We got off two stops before the terminus.*

termite /ˈtɜːmaɪt/ *noun* a tropical white insect, like a large ant, which eats wood

③ **terrace** /ˈterəs/ *noun* **1.** a flat outdoor area which is raised above another area ○ *The guests had drinks on the terrace before going in to dinner.* **2.** a row of similar houses connected together

terracotta /ˌterəˈkɒtə/ *noun* **1.** a red clay used to make little statues, pots and tiles ○ *Terracotta flowerpots can crack in very cold weather.* **2.** a dull red-brown colour

terrain /təˈreɪn/ *noun* a particular type of land surface

terrestrial /təˈrestriəl/ *adj* **1.** referring to the planet Earth **2.** (*of an animal or plant*) which lives on land, not in water ○ *Mice and rats are terrestrial animals.* (NOTE: Animals and plants that live in water are **aquatic**.)

① **terrible** /ˈterɪb(ə)l/ *adj* very bad ○ *We shouldn't have come to this party – the music's terrible.* ○ *There was a terrible storm last night.*

② **terribly** /ˈterɪbli/ *adv* **1.** very ○ *I'm terribly sorry to have kept you waiting.* ○ *The situation is terribly serious.* **2.** in a very bad way ○ *The farmers suffered terribly from drought.*

terrier /ˈteriə/ *noun* a small dog, originally one used in hunting

③ **terrific** /təˈrɪfɪk/ *adj* **1.** extremely good ○ *We had a terrific time at the party.* **2.** very big or loud ○ *There was a terrific bang and the whole building collapsed.*

terrified /ˈterɪfaɪd/ *adj* very frightened

terrify /ˈterɪfaɪ/ (**terrifies, terrifying, terrified**) *verb* to make someone very frightened ○ *The sound of thunder terrifies me.*

② **territory** /ˈterɪt(ə)ri/ (*plural* **territories**) *noun* **1.** a large area of land ○ *They occupied all the territory on the east bank of the river.* **2.** land which belongs to a country ○ *A group of soldiers had wandered into enemy territory.* **3.** an area which an animal or bird thinks belongs only to it ○ *Animals often fight to defend their territories.*

③ **terror** /ˈterə/ *noun* great fear ○ *They live in constant terror of terrorist attacks.*

terrorism /ˈterərɪz(ə)m/ *noun* a policy of using violence in a political cause ○ *Acts of terrorism continued during the whole summer.* ○ *The government has said that it will not give in to terrorism.*

terrorist /ˈterərɪst/ *noun* a person who practises terrorism ○ *Terrorists hijacked a plane and told the pilot to fly to Rome.* ■ *adj* referring to terrorism ○ *Terrorist attacks have increased over the last few weeks.*

terse /tɜːs/ *adj* concise, short, using few words

tertiary /ˈtɜːʃəri/ *adj* referring to a third stage, especially to the level of education after the secondary ○ *She's studying at the local tertiary college.*

TESOL *abbr* Teaching of English to Speakers of Other Languages

① **test** /test/ *noun* **1.** an examination to see if you know something ○ *We had an English test yesterday.* ○ *She passed her driving test.* **2.** an examination to see if something is working well ○ *The doctor will have to do a blood test.* ○ *It is a good test of the car's ability to brake fast.* ■ *verb* (**tests, testing, tested**) **1.** to find out how well someone can do something or how well someone knows something ○ *The teacher tested my spoken German.* **2.** to examine someone or something to see if everything is working well ○ *We need to test your reactions to noise and bright lights.* ○ *He has to have his eyes tested.* ○ *She tested her new car in the snow.*

test case /ˈtest keɪs/ *noun* a court case in which the decision will establish a principle which other cases can follow

testify /ˈtestɪfaɪ/ (**testifies, testifying, testified**) *verb* to give evidence in court

testimony /ˈtestɪməni/ *noun* a statement given in court about what happened

test tube /ˈtest tjuːb/ *noun* a small glass tube, open at the top and with a rounded bottom, used in laboratories to hold liquids during experiments ○ *Position the base of the test tube over the flame.*

tetanus /ˈtet(ə)nəs/ *noun* a serious disease caused by infection of a wound by bacteria in the soil, which affects the spinal cord and causes the jaw muscles to stiffen

tether /ˈteðə/ *noun* a rope which attaches an animal to a post ○ *The horse had slipped its tether and was galloping away down the street.* ■ *verb* (**tethers, tethering, tethered**) to attach an animal to a post with a rope ○ *He tethered his horse to a post.* ◇ **to be at the end of your tether** to be unable to stand any more, to have lost all patience ○ *He was at the end of his tether and resigned after just one month in the job.*

① **text** /tekst/ *noun* the written parts of a document or book, not the pictures ○ *It's a book for little children, with lots of pictures and very little text.*

textbook /ˈtekstbʊk/ *noun* a book which students use to learn about the subject they are studying

textile /ˈtekstaɪl/ *noun* cloth

text message /ˈtekst ˌmesɪdʒ/ *noun* a message sent by telephone, using short forms of words, which appear on the screen of a mobile phone

text messaging /ˈtekst ˌmesɪdʒɪŋ/ *noun* the action of sending text messages

texture /ˈtekstʃə/ *noun* the way in which the surface of a material can be felt ○ *the soft texture of velvet*

textured /ˈtekstʃəd/ *adj* with a certain texture

① **than** /ðən, ðæn/ *conj* used to show a comparison ○ *It's hotter this week than it was last week.* ■ *prep* used to link two parts of a comparison ○ *His car is bigger than mine.* ○ *She was born in London, so she knows it better than any other town.* ○ *You can't get more than four people into this lift.* ○ *It's less than five kilometres to the nearest station.*

① **thank** /θæŋk/ (**thanks, thanking, thanked**) *verb* to say or do something that shows you are grateful to someone for doing something for you ○ *She thanked the* *policeman for helping her to cross the street.* ○ *Don't forget to thank Aunt Ann for her present.*

thankful /'θæŋkf(ə)l/ *adj* glad because a worry has gone away. ◊ **mercy**

① **thanks** /θæŋks/ *noun* a word showing that you are grateful ○ *We sent our thanks for the gift.* ○ *We did our best to help but got no thanks for it.* ○ *The committee passed a vote of thanks to the school for having organised the meeting.* ○ *Many thanks for your letter of the 15th.* ■ *interj* used to show you are grateful ○ *Do you want some more tea? – No thanks. I've had two cups already.* ○ *Anyone want a lift to the station? – Thanks, it's a long walk from here.*

Thanksgiving /'θæŋks,gɪvɪŋ/ *noun* an American festival, celebrating the first harvest of the Pilgrims who settled in the United States, on the fourth Thursday in November

COMMENT: The traditional menu for Thanksgiving dinner is roast turkey with cranberry sauce, followed by pumpkin pie.

① **thanks to** /'θæŋks tuː/ *prep* used for saying that someone or something is responsible for something or to blame for something

① **thank you** /'θæŋk juː/ *interj* showing that you are grateful ○ *Thank you very much for your letter of the 15th.* ○ *Did you remember to say thank you to your grandmother for the present?* ○ *Would you like another piece of cake? – No thank you, I've had enough.* ■ *noun* something that you do or say to show you are grateful ○ *Let's say a big thank you to the people who organised the show.*

① **that** /ðæt/ *adj* used to show something or someone that is further away or in the past ○ *Can you see that white house on the corner over there?* ○ *Do you remember the name of that awful hotel in Brighton?* Compare **this** ■ *pron* something or someone that is further away ○ *That's the book I was talking about.* ○ *Do you know who that is sitting at the next table?* ○ *Is that the one? – Yes, that's it.* Compare **this** ■ *relative pronoun* used to give more information about someone or something just mentioned ○ *Where is the parcel that she sent you yesterday?* ○ *Can you see the man that sold you the ticket?* ○ *There's the suitcase that you left on the train!* (NOTE: When it is the object of a relative clause, **that** can sometimes be left out: *Where's the letter he sent you? Here's the box you left in the bedroom.* When it is the subject, **that** can be replaced by **which** *or* **who**: *a house that has red windows or a house which has red windows; the man that stole the car or the man who stole the car.*) ■ *conj* used after verbs like 'say' or 'think' and adjectives like 'glad' or 'disappointed', and after 'so' or 'such' (*after verbs like; and adjectives like*) ○ *The restaurant was so expensive that we could only afford one dish.* ○ *It rained so hard that the street was like a river.* ○ *We had such a lot of work that we didn't have any lunch.* ○ *There was such a long queue that we didn't bother waiting.* ○ *They told me that the manager was out.* ○ *I don't think they knew that we were coming.* ○ *I'm glad that the weather turned out fine.* (NOTE: **That** is often left out: *He didn't know we were coming; It's so hot in here we all want a drink of water.*) ■ *adv* to such a degree ○ *You must remember him, it's not all that long ago that we had a drink with him.* ○ *His new car is not really that big.*

thaw /θɔː/ *noun* a time of warm weather which makes snow and ice melt ○ *The thaw came early this year.* ■ *verb* (**thaws, thawing, thawed**) to melt ○ *The ice is thawing on the village pond.*

① **the** /ðə/; *before a vowel* /ðɪ/ *article* **1.** meaning something in particular, as opposed to 'a' ○ *Where's the book you brought back from the library?* ○ *That's the cat from next door.* ○ *The town centre has been made into a pedestrian zone.* **2.** used with something of which only one exists, e.g. in the names of places ○ *an expedition to the Antarctic* ○ *A spacecraft landed on the moon.* ○ *The sun came up over the hills.* **3.** used for referring to a thing in general ○ *born on the 31st of January* ○ *There's nothing interesting on the television tonight.* ○ *She refuses to use the telephone.* ○ *The streets are crowded at lunchtime.* ○ *Many people were out of work during the 1990s.* ○ *Both sisters play the flute.* **4.** meaning something special ○ *It's the shop for men's clothes.* ○ *She's the doctor for children's diseases.* ○ *That's not the Charlie Chaplin, is it?* **5.** used to compare ○ *The more he eats the thinner he seems to get.* ○ *The sooner you do it the better.* ○ *This is by far the shortest way to London.* ○ *She's the tallest person in the office.*

the Antarctic *noun* the area round the South Pole

theater /'θɪətə/ *noun* US spelling of **theatre**

② **theatre** /ˈθɪətə/ *noun* a building in which plays are shown ○ *I'm trying to get tickets for the theatre tonight.* ○ *What is the play at the local theatre this week?* ○ *We'll have dinner early and then go to the theatre.* (NOTE: The US spelling is **theater**.)

theatrical /θiˈætrɪk(ə)l/ *adj* **1.** referring to the theatre ○ *She had a distinguished theatrical career before going into films.* **2.** exaggerated, dramatic and not natural ○ *Throwing the letter on the floor and stamping on it was a bit theatrical.*

theft /θeft/ *noun* **1.** the practice of stealing **2.** an act of stealing ○ *Thefts in supermarkets have increased enormously.*

① **their** /ðeə/ *adj* belonging to them ○ *After the film, we went to their house for supper.* (NOTE: Do not confuse with **there, they're**.)

① **theirs** /ðeəz/ *pron* the one that belongs to them ○ *Which car is theirs – the Ford?* ○ *She's a friend of theirs.* ○ *The girls wanted to borrow my car – theirs wouldn't start.*

① **them** /ðəm, ðem/ *pron* **1.** referring to people or things that have been mentioned before ○ *Do you like cream cakes? – No, I don't like them very much.* ○ *There's a group of people waiting outside. – Tell them to come in.* ○ *She saw her friends and asked them to help her.* **2.** referring to a single person, used instead of **him** or **her** ○ *If someone phones, ask them to call back later.*

② **theme** /θiːm/ *noun* the main subject of a book or article ○ *The theme of the book is how to deal with illness in the family.*

theme park /ˈθiːm pɑːk/ *noun* an amusement park based on a single theme such as a medieval castle

① **themselves** /ðəmˈselvz/ *pron* referring to the same people or things that are the subject of the verb ○ *Cats always spend a lot of time cleaning themselves.* ○ *It's no use going to the surgery – the doctors are all ill themselves.*

① **then** /ðen/ *adv* **1.** at that time in the past or future ○ *He had been very busy up till then.* ○ *Ever since then I've refused to eat oysters.* ○ *We're having a party next week. – What a pity! I'll be in Scotland then.* **2.** after that ○ *We all sat down, and then after a few minutes the waiter brought us the menu.* ○ *It was a busy trip – he went to Greece, then to Italy and finally to Spain.*

theology /θiˈɒlədʒi/ *noun* the study of religion and the belief in God

theorem /ˈθɪərəm/ *noun* a statement which can be proved in mathematics

theoretical /ˌθɪəˈretɪk(ə)l/ *adj* **1.** referring to theories ○ *a theoretical study of the universe* **2.** not proved in practice ○ *She has the theoretical power to dismiss any of the staff.*

theorist /ˈθɪərɪst/ *noun* a person who develops theories

① **theory** /ˈθɪəri/ (*plural* **theories**) *noun* **1.** an explanation of something which has not been proved but which you believe is true [~that/~about] ○ *I have this theory that the criminal wanted to be caught.She doesn't have any theories about why he never came back.* **2.** a careful scientific explanation of why something happens ○ *Galileo put forward the theory that the earth turns round the sun.* **3.** a statement of general principles which may not apply in practice ○ *In theory the treatment should work, but no one has ever tried it.*

therapist /ˈθerəpɪst/ *noun* a person who is specially trained to give therapy

therapy /ˈθerəpi/ *noun* the treatment of a patient to help cure a disease or condition

① **there** /ðeə/ *adv* **1.** in that place ○ *Is that black van still there parked outside the house?* ○ *Where have you put the tea? – There, on the kitchen counter.* **2.** to that place ○ *We haven't been to the British Museum yet. – Let's go there tomorrow.* ○ *Have you ever been to China? – Yes, I went there last month.* **3.** used when giving something to someone ○ *There you are: two fish and chips and a pot of tea.* (NOTE: Do not confuse with **their, they're**.) ■ *pron* used usually before the verb when the real subject follows the verb ○ *There's a little door leading onto the patio.* ○ *There's someone at the door asking for you.* ○ *There are some pages missing in my newspaper.* ○ *Were there a lot of people at the cinema?* ○ *There seems to have been a lot of rain during the night.*

thereabouts /ˌðeərəˈbaʊts/ *adv* **1.** near that place ○ *They live in Glasgow or thereabouts.* **2.** about that number ○ *They owe us £250 or thereabouts.*

① **therefore** /ˈðeəfɔː/ *adv* for this reason ○ *I therefore have decided not to grant his request.* ○ *They have reduced their prices, therefore we should reduce ours if we want to stay competitive.*

thermal /ˈθɜːm(ə)l/ *adj* referring to heat ■ *noun* a rising current of warm air ○ *Hang-gliders rose into the air on thermals.*

thermometer /θəˈmɒmɪtə/ *noun* an instrument for measuring temperature

thermostat /ˈθɜːməʊstæt/ *noun* an instrument which controls heating according to a set temperature

thesaurus /θɪˈsɔːrəs/ (*plural* **thesauruses** or **thesauri**) *noun* a book with words collected into groups of similar meaning

① **these** /ðiːz/ plural of **this**

thesis /ˈθiːsɪs/ (*plural* **theses**) *noun* **1.** a long piece of written research prepared by a candidate for a higher university degree ○ *She is writing her thesis on the place of women in Spanish literature.* **2.** a particular point of view ○ *His thesis is that, the lower the income tax rate, the more people will spend.*

① **they** /ðeɪ/ *pron* **1.** referring to people or things ○ *Where do you keep the spoons? – They're in the right-hand drawer.* ○ *Who are those people in uniform? – They're traffic wardens.* ○ *The children played in the sun and they all got sunburnt.* **2.** referring to people in general ○ *They say it's going to be fine this weekend.*

③ **they'd** /ðeɪd/ *short form* **1.** they had **2.** they would

② **they'll** /ðeɪl/ *short form* they will

① **they're** /ðeə/ *short form* they are (NOTE: Do not confuse with **their, there**.)

① **they've** /ðeɪv/ *short form* they have

② **thick** /θɪk/ *adj* **1.** bigger than usual when measured from side to side ○ *He cut a slice of bread which was so thick it wouldn't go into the toaster.* ○ *The walls of the castle are three metres thick.* ○ *Some oranges have very thick skins.* ○ *He took a piece of thick rope.* **2.** growing close together ○ *They tried to make their way through thick jungle.* ○ *The field was covered with thick grass.* **3.** (*of a liquid*) which cannot flow easily ○ *If the paint is too thick add some water.* ○ *A bowl of thick soup is just what we need on a cold day like this.*

thicken /ˈθɪkən/ (**thickens, thickening, thickened**) *verb* **1.** to make something thick ○ *Thicken the sauce with cornflour.* **2.** to become thick ○ *The custard will thicken when you heat it.*

thicket /ˈθɪkɪt/ *noun* a small wood of trees and bushes growing close together

thickness /ˈθɪknəs/ *noun* **1.** the state of being thick or the extent to which something is thick **2.** a layer of something

thick-skinned /ˌθɪk ˈskɪnd/ *adj* able to stand a lot of criticism ○ *Luckily he's a thick-skinned individual or he would be very upset at what the tabloids say about him.*

thief /θiːf/ (*plural* **thieves**) *noun* a person who steals. ◊ **thick**

thigh /θaɪ/ *noun* the part at the top of the leg between your knee and your hip

thimble /ˈθɪmb(ə)l/ *noun* a small cup worn to protect the end of your finger when sewing

② **thin** /θɪn/ (**thinner, thinnest**) *adj* **1.** not fat ○ *The table has very thin legs.* ○ *He looks too thin – he should eat more.* **2.** not thick ○ *a plate of thin sandwiches* ○ *The book is printed on very thin paper.* ○ *The parcel was sent in a thin cardboard box.* **3.** (*of a liquid*) which flows easily, often because of containing too much water ○ *All we had for lunch was a bowl of thin soup.* ○ *Add water to make the paint thinner.*

① **thing** /θɪŋ/ *noun* **1.** an object ○ *Can you see that black thing in the pan of soup?* ○ *What do you use that big blue thing for?* **2.** something in general ○ *They all just sat there and didn't say a thing.* ○ *The first thing to do is to call an ambulance.* ○ *That was a stupid thing to do!* ◇ **a good thing** something lucky ○ *It's a good thing there was no police officer on duty at the door.*

thingy /ˈθɪŋi/ *noun* something whose name you don't know or can't remember

① **think** /θɪŋk/ (**thinks, thinking, thought**) *verb* **1.** to consider something, e.g. in order to make a decision [~about/of] ○ *She never thinks about how other people might feel.* ○ *Whenever I think of him, I smile.* ○ *You need to think carefully before making your choice.* **2.** to have an opinion or belief [~(that)/~of/about] ○ *I think London is a nicer town to live in than Frankfurt.* ○ *Everyone thinks we're mad to go on holiday in December.* ○ *What did you think of the film?* ○ *What will he think about my new haircut?* ○ *The gang is thought to be based in Spain.* **3.** to make a plan to do something [~(that)/~of/about] ○ *We're thinking we might open an office in New York.* ○ *I've been thinking about going to art college.* ◇ **to think twice** to consider very carefully ○ *Think twice before you sign that contract.* ○ *I'd think twice about spending all the money you've saved.*

think about *phrasal verb* **1.** to have someone or something in your mind ○ *I was just thinking about you when you phoned.* ○ *All she thinks about is food.* **2.** to have an opinion about something ○ *What do you think about the government's plans to increase taxes?*

think of *phrasal verb* **1.** to consider a plan in your mind ○ *We are thinking of going* *to Greece on holiday.* **2.** to have an opinion about something ○ *What do you think of the government's plans to increase taxes?* ○ *I didn't think much of the play.* ○ *She asked him what he thought of her idea.* ◇ **to think better of something** to change your mind about something ○ *He was going to pay the whole cost himself, and then thought better of it.* ◇ **to tell someone what you think of something** to criticise something ○ *He went up to her and told her exactly what he thought of her stupid idea.* ◇ **to think highly of someone** to have a high opinion of someone ◇ **to think nothing of doing something** to consider something normal or easy ○ *She thinks nothing of working ten hours a day.* ◇ **think nothing of it!** please don't bother to thank me for it

think out *phrasal verb* to consider something carefully in all its details

think over *phrasal verb* to consider a plan or proposal very carefully

think through *phrasal verb* to consider something carefully in all its details

think up *phrasal verb* to invent a plan or new idea

thinker /ˈθɪŋkə/ *noun* a person who thinks

thinking /ˈθɪŋkɪŋ/ *noun* the process of reasoning about something

think tank /ˈθɪŋk tæŋk/ *noun* a group of advisers who are appointed to discuss important problems and suggest how they should be solved

① **third** /θɜːd/ *adj* relating to number 3 in a series ○ *She came third in the race.* ○ *The cake shop is the third shop on the right.* ○ *It will be her third birthday next Friday.* ■ *noun* **1.** number 3 in a series ○ *Her birthday is on the third of March* or *March the third (March 3rd).* **2.** one of three equal parts of something ○ *A third of the airline's planes are jumbos.* ○ *Two-thirds of the staff are part-timers.*

thirdly /ˈθɜːdli/ *adv* as the third item on a list. Compare **firstly, secondly**

third party /ˌθɜːd ˈpɑːti/ *noun* any person other than the two main parties involved in a contract or a civil case

third-rate /ˌθɜːd ˈreɪt/ *adj* quite bad. Compare **first-rate, second-rate**

thirst /θɜːst/ *noun* **1.** a feeling of wanting to drink ○ *Digging the garden has given me such a thirst!* ○ *They ran to the mountain stream to quench their thirst.* **2.** a feeling of wanting something ○ *He studied at night to satisfy his thirst for knowledge.*

① **thirsty** /ˈθɜːsti/ *adj* feeling that you want to drink ○ *It's so hot here that it makes me thirsty.*

① **thirteen** /ˌθɜːˈtiːn/ *noun* the number 13

thirteenth /θɜːˈtiːnθ/ *adj* relating to number 13 in a series ■ *noun* number 13 in a series

thirtieth /ˈθɜːtiəθ/ *adj* relating to number 30 in a series (NOTE: With dates **thirtieth** is usually written **30th**: *May 30th, 1921*; *June 30th, 1896* (American style is *30 June 1896*): say 'the thirtieth of June' or 'June the thirtieth' (American style is 'June thirtieth').) ■ *noun* number 30 in a series

① **thirty** /ˈθɜːti/ *noun* the number 30 ○ *He's thirty (years old).* □ **thirties** the numbers between 30 and 39

① **this** /ðɪs/ *adj, pron* used to show something which is nearer or in the present, in contrast to something else ○ *This is the shop I was telling you about.* ○ *I prefer these earrings to those ones.* ○ *I saw him on the train this morning.* ○ *My mother is coming for tea this afternoon.* ○ *I expect to hear from him this week.* ■ *adv* so much ○ *I knew you were going to be late, but I didn't expect you to be this late.*

thistle /ˈθɪs(ə)l/ *noun* a large wild plant with prickly leaves and purple flowers

THNQ *abbr* thank you

thong /θɒŋ/ *noun* a rubber sandal held on by a strap between the toes

③ **thorn** /θɔːn/ *noun* a thin pointed part on some plants ○ *Most roses have thorns.*

③ **thorough** /ˈθʌrə/ *adj* **1.** including everything that needs to be dealt with very carefully ○ *The police have carried out a thorough search of the woods.* **2.** used for emphasis ○ *They made a thorough mess of it.* ○ *It was a thorough waste of time.*

thoroughbred /ˈθʌrəbred/ *noun* a horse of high quality whose parents and other relatives are all known

thoroughfare /ˈθʌrəfeə/ *noun* a main road through a town, usually where there is a lot of traffic

thoroughly /ˈθʌrəli/ *adv* **1.** in a complete and careful way ○ *We searched the garden thoroughly but couldn't find his red ball.* **2.** used for emphasis ○ *I'm thoroughly fed up with the whole business.*

① **those** /ðəʊz/ plural of **that**

① **though** /ðəʊ/ *adv, conj* **1.** used for mentioning something that makes something else seem surprising ○ *Though tired, she still kept on running.* ○ *We don't em-*

ploy a computer programmer, though many companies do. **2.** but ○ *It is unlikely though possible.* ◇ **as though** as if ○ *His voice sounded strange over the telephone, as though he was standing in a cave.* ○ *That shirt doesn't look as though it has been ironed.* ○ *It looks as though there is no one in.* ◇ **even though** in spite of the fact that ○ *He didn't wear a coat, even though it was snowing.*

① **thought** /θɔːt/ past tense and past participle of **think** ■ *noun* an idea which you have when thinking [~of] ○ *I was terrified at the thought of doing the exam.* ○ *He had an awful thought – suppose they had left the bathroom taps running?*

thoughtful /ˈθɔːtf(ə)l/ *adj* **1.** thinking about something a lot ○ *He looked thoughtful, and I wondered if there was something wrong.* **2.** being sensitive to what other people want ○ *It was very thoughtful of you to come to see me in hospital.*

thoughtless /ˈθɔːtləs/ *adj* without thinking about other people

① **thousand** /ˈθaʊz(ə)nd/ *noun* the number 1,000 ○ *We paid two hundred thousand pounds for the house (£200,000).* □ **thousands of** a large number of ○ *Thousands of people lost money in the scheme.*

thousandth /ˈθaʊzənθ/ *adj* relating to number 1,000 in a series ■ *noun* **1.** number 1,000 in a series **2.** one part out of a thousand ○ *a thousandth of a second*

thrash /θræʃ/ (**thrashes, thrashing, thrashed**) *verb* to defeat another person or team easily (*informal*) ○ *She expects to be thrashed by the champion.*

thrash out *phrasal verb* **1.** to try to hit wildly in all directions ○ *He thrashed out at the youths with his stick.* **2.** to discuss something until a solution is found ○ *We sat down with the management and thrashed out a compromise.* ○ *They spent all day thrashing out a solution to the problem.*

thrashing /ˈθræʃɪŋ/ *noun* **1.** a severe beating **2.** an easy defeat in a game

thread /θred/ *noun* a long strand of cotton, silk, or other fibre ○ *A spider spins a thread to make its web.* ○ *Wait a moment, there's a white thread showing on your coat.*

threadbare /ˈθredbeə/ *adj* very worn

② **threat** /θret/ *noun* a warning to someone that you are going to do something unpleasant, especially if he or she does not do what you want [~of/~to] ○ *The company made numerous threats of legal action.* ○ *The police took the threat to the Prime Minister very seriously.* ○ *Do you think they will carry out their threat to bomb the capital if we don't surrender?*

② **threaten** /ˈθret(ə)n/ (**threatens, threatening, threatened**) *verb* to warn that you are going to do something unpleasant, especially if someone does not do what you want ○ *She threatened to go to the police.* ○ *The teacher threatened her with punishment.*

threatening /ˈθret(ə)nɪŋ/ *adj* suggesting that something unpleasant will happen

① **three** /θriː/ *noun* the number 3 (NOTE: **three** (3) but **third** (3rd))

3-D /ˌθriː ˈdiː/ *noun* vision in three dimensions

③ **three-quarters** /θriː ˈkwɔːtəz/ *plural noun* three fourths, 75%

threshold /ˈθreʃhəʊld/ *noun* **1.** a bar across the floor of a doorway ○ *She stopped at the threshold and looked back into the room.* **2.** a point where something begins ○ *She's on the threshold of a great career in teaching.*

① **threw** /θruː/ past tense of **throw** (NOTE: Do not confuse with **through**.)

thrill /θrɪl/ *noun* a feeling of great excitement ○ *It gave me a thrill to see you all again after so many years.* ○ *I experienced the thrill of sailing near to a waterfall.* ■ *verb* (**thrills, thrilling, thrilled**) to make someone very excited ○ *We were thrilled to get your letter.*

thriller /ˈθrɪlə/ *noun* an exciting work of art, e.g. a crime novel or a film

thrilling /ˈθrɪlɪŋ/ *adj* which makes you very excited

③ **thrive** /θraɪv/ (**thrives, thriving, thrived**) *verb* to grow well and be strong ○ *a thriving community*

② **throat** /θrəʊt/ *noun* **1.** the tube which goes from the back of your mouth down the inside of your neck ○ *I've got a sore throat.* ○ *She got a fish bone stuck in her throat.* **2.** your neck, especially the front part ○ *He put his hands round her throat and pressed hard.* ◇ **to clear your throat** to give a little cough ○ *He cleared his throat and started to speak.*

throb /θrɒb/ (**throbs, throbbing, throbbed**) *verb* **1.** to beat fast ○ *She stopped running, and stood still with her heart throbbing.* ○ *The engine started to throb more regularly and the great ship started to move.* **2.** to have a pain which comes regularly like a heartbeat ○ *When I woke up I* *had a sore throat and my head was throbbing.*

throne /θrəʊn/ *noun* a chair on which a king or queen sits during ceremonies

throng /θrɒŋ/ *noun* a large crowd of people (*literary*) ○ *The stars had difficulty making their way through the throng of fans outside the cinema.* ■ *verb* (**throngs, thronging, thronged**) to crowd together ○ *The children thronged round the TV star.* ○ *The shopping precinct was thronged with shoppers in the days before Christmas.*

throttle /'θrɒt(ə)l/ *noun* a valve on a pipe in an engine, which allows variable quantities of fuel to pass into an engine ○ *He had to retire from the race when his throttle jammed.* ■ *verb* (**throttles, throttling, throttled**) to strangle someone by squeezing the neck, and preventing him or her breathing ○ *I could throttle him sometimes when he gives me that sort of answer.*

① **through** /θruː/ *prep* **1.** across to the inside of something ○ *The bullet went straight through the door.* ○ *She looked through the open door.* ○ *Cold air is coming in through the hole in the wall.* ○ *The street goes straight through the centre of the town.* ○ *She pushed the needle through the ball of wool.* **2.** during a period of time ○ *They insisted on talking all through the film.* ○ *Snow accumulated through the winter.* ■ *adv* going in at one side and coming out of the other side ○ *Someone left the gate open and all the sheep got through.*

① **throughout** /θru'aʊt/ *prep, adv* in all or several parts of ○ *Throughout the country floods are causing problems on the roads.* ○ *Heavy snow fell throughout the night.*

① **throw** /θrəʊ/ (**throws, throwing, threw, thrown**) *verb* to send something through the air ○ *How far can he throw a cricket ball?* ○ *They were throwing stones through car windows.* ○ *She threw the letter into the wastepaper basket.* ○ *He was thrown into the air by the blast from the bomb.*

throw away *phrasal verb* to get rid of something which you do not need any more

throw in *phrasal verb* to add something extra as a bargain ○ *When we bought our new oven, they threw in a set of saucepans as a free gift.*

throw off *phrasal verb* **1.** to remove something quickly ○ *She threw off the bedclothes and ran out of the room.* **2.** to recover from an illness ○ *She's had a cough for several days, and can't throw it off.*

throw out *phrasal verb* **1.** to push someone outside ○ *When they started to fight, they were thrown out of the restaurant.* **2.** to get rid of something which you do not need ○ *I'm throwing out this old office desk.* **3.** to refuse to accept something ○ *The proposal was thrown out by the planning committee.*

throw up *phrasal verb* **1.** to let food come up from your stomach and out through your mouth (*informal*) ○ *The cat threw up all over the sofa.* **2.** to give up something ○ *She's thrown up her job and gone to live in Australia.*

throwback /'θrəʊ,bæk/ *noun* a person or thing that seems to belong to a time in the past

throw-in /'θrəʊ ɪn/ *noun* (*in football*) the act of throwing the ball back into play from the touchline

① **thrown** /θrəʊn/ past participle of **throw** (NOTE: Do not confuse with **throne**.)

thru /θruː/ *prep, adv, adj US* same as **through**

thrush /θrʌʃ/ (*plural* **thrushes** or *same*) *noun* a common brown bird with brown spots on its light-coloured breast

thrust /θrʌst/ *verb* (**thrusts, thrusting, thrust**) to push something somewhere suddenly and hard ○ *He thrust the newspaper into his pocket.* ○ *She thrust the documents into her briefcase.* ■ *noun* **1.** the act of suddenly pushing something strongly ○ *He was killed with a thrust of his opponent's sword.* **2.** a force which pushes someone or something ○ *The thrust of the engines pushed him back in his seat.* ◇ **the thrust of something** the important or main part of the content of a report, speech or discussion

thud /θʌd/ *noun* a dull, heavy noise ○ *His head hit the ground with a sickening thud.* ○ *They could hear the thud of the guns in the distance.* ■ *verb* (**thuds, thudding, thudded**) to make a dull noise ○ *A stone thudded into the wall behind him.*

thug /θʌg/ *noun* a violent person

③ **thumb** /θʌm/ *noun* a part on the side of your hand that looks like a short thick finger ○ *The baby was sucking its thumb.* ○ *How she cried when she hit her thumb with the hammer!*

thumbnail /'θʌm,neɪl/ *noun* the nail on your thumb

③ **thump** /θʌmp/ *noun* a dull noise ○ *There was a thump from upstairs as if someone had fallen out of bed.* ■ *verb* (**thumps, thumping, thumped**) to hit someone hard with your fist

thunder /'θʌndə/ *noun* a loud noise in the air following a flash of lightning ○ *a tropical storm accompanied by thunder and lightning* ○ *He was woken by the sound of thunder.* ■ *verb* (**thunders, thundering, thundered**) to make a loud noise in the air following lightning ○ *It thundered during the night.*

thunderstorm /'θʌndəstɔːm/ *noun* a storm with rain, thunder and lightning

Thurs. *abbr* Thursday

① **Thursday** /'θɜːzdeɪ/ *noun* the day between Wednesday and Friday, the fourth day of the week ○ *Last Thursday was Christmas Day.* ○ *Shall we arrange to meet next Thursday?* ○ *Today is Thursday, April 14th.* ○ *The club meets on Thursdays* or *every Thursday.* ○ *The 15th is a Wednesday, so the 16th must be a Thursday.*

① **thus** /ðʌs/ *adv* **1.** in this way ○ *The two pieces fit together thus.* ○ *She is only fifteen, and thus cannot vote.* **2.** as a result ○ *She is only fifteen, and thus is not able to take part in the over-sixteens competition.*

thwart /θwɔːt/ (**thwarts, thwarting, thwarted**) *verb* to prevent someone doing something ○ *He was thwarted by the police in his attempt to get into the building.* ○ *His career move was thwarted by the new manager.*

thyme /taɪm/ *noun* a common herb used as flavouring

tiara /ti'ɑːrə/ *noun* a small jewelled crown

tic /tɪk/ *noun* a twitch of the muscles, usually in the face, which cannot be controlled

tick /tɪk/ *noun* **1.** a sound made every second by a clock ○ *The only sound we could hear in the room was the tick of the grandfather clock.* **2.** a mark written to show that something is correct ○ *Put a tick in the box marked 'R'.* ■ *verb* (**ticks, ticking, ticked**) **1.** to mark something with a tick to show that you approve ○ *Tick the box marked 'R' if you require a receipt.* **2.** to make a quiet regular sound noise like a clock ○ *All you could hear was the clock ticking in the corner of the library.* ○ *Watch out! That parcel's ticking!*

tick off *phrasal verb* **1.** to mark something with a tick ○ *She ticked off the names on the list.* **2.** □ **to tick someone off** to say that you are annoyed with someone (*informal*) ○ *The policeman ticked them off for running across the road in front of a bus.*

① **ticket** /'tɪkɪt/ *noun* **1.** a piece of paper or card which allows you to travel ○ *They won't let you get onto the train without a ticket.* ○ *We've lost our plane tickets – how can we get to Chicago?* **2.** a piece of paper which allows you to go into a place, e.g. a cinema or an exhibition [~for] ○ *Can I have three tickets for the 8.30 show please?* ○ *We tried several theatres but there were no tickets left anywhere.*

tickle /'tɪk(ə)l/ (**tickles, tickling, tickled**) *verb* **1.** to touch someone in a sensitive part of the body in order to make him or her laugh ○ *She tickled his toes and made him laugh.* **2.** to cause a slight uncomfortable feeling on the skin of part of the body, or to have that feeling

tidal wave /'taɪd(ə)l weɪv/ *noun* a huge wave in the sea, caused by an underwater earthquake and not by the tide

tide /taɪd/ *noun* the regular rising and falling movement of the sea ○ *The tide came in and cut off the children on the rocks.* ○ *The tide is out – we can walk across the sand.*

tidily /'taɪdɪli/ *adv* in a tidy way

tidy /'taɪdi/ (**tidier, tidiest**) *adj* with everything arranged in the correct way or in an organised way ○ *I want your room to be completely tidy before you go out.* ○ *She put her clothes in a tidy pile.*

② **tie** /taɪ/ *noun* **1.** a long piece of coloured cloth which men wear round their necks under the collar of their shirts ○ *He's wearing a blue tie with red stripes.* ○ *They won't let you into the restaurant if you haven't got a tie on.* **2.** a result in a competition or election where both sides have the same score ○ *The result was a tie and the vote had to be taken again.* ■ *verb* (**ties, tying, tied**) **1.** to attach something with string, rope or twine ○ *The parcel was tied with a little piece of string.* ○ *He tied his horse to the post.* ○ *The burglars tied his hands behind his back.* **2.** to have the same score as another team in a competition ○ *They tied for second place.*

tie down *phrasal verb* **1.** to attach something to the floor, to the ground, etc. **2.** to make someone accept certain conditions

tie up *phrasal verb* **1.** to put string or rope round something ○ *The parcel was tied up with thick string.* ○ *You should tie that dog up or it will bite someone.* **2.** to buy something, so that the money is not available for other purposes ○ *All his fortune is tied up in property.* ◇ **to be tied up** to be busy ○ *I'm rather tied up at the moment – can we try to meet next week some* *time?*

tiebreaker /ˈtaɪˌbreɪkə/, **tiebreak** *noun* a way of deciding the winner of a game or a competition, e.g. by asking an extra question

tie-in *noun* something such as a book, which is brought out in connection with a successful film or television programme

tier /tɪə/ *noun* one of a series of steps, usually a row of seats in a theatre ○ *They sat on the topmost tier of seats.*

tiff /tɪf/ *noun* a small argument or quarrel (*informal*)

tiger /ˈtaɪɡə/ *noun* a large wild animal of the cat family which is yellow with black stripes and lives mainly in India and China (NOTE: The female is a **tigress**.)

② **tight** /taɪt/ *adj* **1.** fitting too closely ○ *These shoes hurt – they're too tight.* **2.** holding firmly ○ *Keep a tight hold of the bag, we don't want it stolen.*

tighten /ˈtaɪt(ə)n/ (**tightens, tightening, tightened**) *verb* to make tight or become tight

tighten up /ˌtaɪt(ə)n ˈʌp ɒn/ *verb* to control something more carefully [~on] ○ *They have tightened up on parking in this area.*

tight-knit /taɪt nɪt/ *adj* (*of a group of people*) who are good friends together

tight-lipped /taɪt ˈlɪpt/ *adj* not prepared to comment on a subject

② **tightly** /ˈtaɪtli/ *adv* in a tight way

tightrope /ˈtaɪtrəʊp/ *noun* a rope stretched between two poles on which someone can walk or perform tricks

tights /taɪts/ *plural noun* a piece of clothing made of thin material, covering your hips, and your legs and feet separately, worn especially by girls, women and dancers ○ *Look – you've got a hole in your tights!*

tile /taɪl/ *noun* **1.** a flat piece of baked clay used as a covering for floors, walls or roofs ○ *The floor is covered with red tiles.* ○ *We are putting white tiles on the bathroom walls.* **2.** a similar piece of another kind of material used to cover floors or walls ○ *They put cork tiles on the walls.* ■ *verb* (**tiles, tiling, tiled**) to cover the surface of a roof, a floor or a wall with tiles ○ *a white-tiled bathroom* ○ *They have tiled the kitchen with red floor tiles.*

① **till** /tɪl/ *prep, conj* up to the time when ○ *I don't expect him to be home till after nine o'clock.* ○ *They worked from morning till night to finish the job.* ○ *We worked till the sun went down.* ■ *noun* a drawer for keeping cash in a shop ○ *There was not much money in the till at the end of the day.*

tilt /tɪlt/ (**tilts, tilting, tilted**) *verb* **1.** to slope ○ *The shelf is tilting to the right.* ○ *You'll have to change places – the boat is tilting.* **2.** to put something in a sloping position ○ *He tilted the barrel over to get the last drops of beer out.*

③ **timber** /ˈtɪmbə/ *noun* wood cut ready for building ○ *These trees are being grown to provide timber for houses.*

① **time** /taɪm/ *noun* **1.** a particular point in the day shown in hours and minutes ○ *What time is it* or *what's the time?* ○ *Can you tell me the time please?* ○ *The time is exactly four thirty.* ○ *Departure times are delayed by up to fifteen minutes because of the volume of traffic.* □ **to tell the time** to read the time on a clock or watch ○ *She's only three so she can't tell the time yet.* **2.** the hour at which something usually happens [~for] ○ *The closing time for the office is 5.30.* ○ *It's must be nearly time for dinner – I'm hungry.* ○ *Is it time for the children to go to bed?* ◊ **bedtime, lunchtime 3.** an amount of hours, days, weeks, months or years that is available for someone to do something [~for] ○ *Do you have time for a cup of coffee?* ○ *There's no need to hurry – we've got plenty of time.* ○ *He spent all that time watching the TV.* ○ *If the fire alarm rings, don't waste time putting clothes on – run out of the hotel fast.* **4.** a certain period ○ *We haven't been to France for a long time.* ○ *We had a letter from my mother a short time ago.* **5.** a particular moment when something happens ○ *They didn't hear anything as they were asleep at the time.* ○ *By the time the ambulance arrived the man had died.* ○ *You can't do two things at the same time.* **6.** a period when things are pleasant or bad ○ *Everyone had a good time at the party.* ○ *We had an awful time on holiday – the hotel was dreadful, and it rained solidly for ten days.* **7.** one of several moments or periods when something happens ○ *I've seen that film on TV four times already.* ○ *That's the last time I'll ask them to play cards.* ○ *Next time you come, bring your swimming things.* □ **time after time, time and again** repeatedly, again and again ○ *I've told her time after time not to do it.* **8.** the rhythm of a piece of music ○ *It's difficult keeping time in a modern piece like this.* ○ *He tapped his foot in time to the music.* ■ *verb* (**times, timing, timed**) to count something in hours, minutes and seconds ○ *I timed him as he ran* *round the track.* ○ *Don't forget to time the eggs – they have to cook for only three minutes.* ◇ **find time** /ˈfaɪnd taɪm/ to do something even though you are busy ○ *In the middle of the meeting he still found time to phone his girlfriend.* ○ *We must find time to visit the new staff sports club.* ◇ **for the time being** temporarily ○ *We will leave the furniture as it is for the time being.* ◇ **in ... time** after a particular period from now ○ *We're going on holiday in four weeks' time.* ◇ **to take time** to need a certain amount of time ○ *It didn't take you much time to get dressed.* ○ *Don't hurry me, I like to take my time.* ◇ **at times** on some occasions ○ *At times I think he's quite mad.* ◇ **at all times** always ○ *Passengers should keep hold of their baggage at all times.*

time bomb /ˈtaɪm bɒm/ *noun* **1.** a bomb with a clock attached, which can be set to explode at a certain time ○ *They said that they had left a time bomb in the railway station.* **2.** a difficult situation which will happen in the future ○ *The rapid increase in the world's population is a time bomb for future governments.*

time-consuming /ˈtaɪm kənˌsjuːmɪŋ/ *adj* which takes a lot of time to do

time frame /ˈtaɪm freɪm/ *noun* the period of time during which something should take place

timeless /ˈtaɪmləs/ *adj* which is not affected by time

③ **time limit** /ˈtaɪm ˌlɪmɪt/ *noun* a point in time by which something should be done

timely /ˈtaɪmli/ *adj* which happens at the right moment

time off /taɪm ˈɒf/ *noun* time away from work or school

time out /ˌtaɪm ˈaʊt/ *noun* □ **to take time out from something** to take a rest from some activity ○ *She took time out from her work to come and say hello to the visitors.*

timer /ˈtaɪmə/ *noun* a device which times things ○ *The timer buzzed to show that the five minutes were up.*

timescale /ˈtaɪmskeɪl/ *noun* the period of time during which something should be completed

timetable /ˈtaɪmteɪb(ə)l/ *noun* a printed list which shows the times at which something such as classes in school or trains leaving will happen ○ *We have two English lessons on the timetable today.* ○ *According to the timetable, there should be a train to London at 10.22.* ■ *verb* (**timetables, timetabling, timetabled**) to arrange the times for something to happen ○ *You are timetabled to speak at 4.30.*

③ **time zone** /ˈtaɪm zəʊn/ *noun* one of 24 bands in the world in which the same standard time is used

timid /ˈtɪmɪd/ *adj* afraid to do something

timing /ˈtaɪmɪŋ/ *noun* the act of arranging the time at which something happens

③ **tin** /tɪn/ *noun* **1.** a silver-coloured soft metal ○ *Bronze is a mixture of copper and tin.* ○ *There have been tin mines in Cornwall since Roman times.* **2.** a metal container in which food or another substance is sold and can be kept for a long time ○ *I'm lazy – I'll just open a tin of soup.* ○ *She bought three tins of cat food.* ○ *We'll need three tins of white paint for the ceiling.* **3.** any metal box ○ *Keep the biscuits in a tin or they'll go soft.* ○ *She puts her spare coins into a tin by the telephone.*

tinfoil /ˈtɪnfɔɪl/ *noun* a thin sheet of aluminium, used to cover food

tinge /tɪndʒ/ *noun* a slight colour or feeling of something ○ *She has has blonde hair with tinges of red.* ○ *The fabric is red with a blue tinge.* ○ *There was a slight tinge of sadness in the air as they left the house for the last time.*

tingle /ˈtɪŋgəl/ *noun* a feeling like a lot of small sharp things sticking into your skin ○ *It didn't hurt, I just felt a tingle in my leg.* ○ *We felt a tingle of excitement as we queued for the roller coaster.* ■ *verb* (**tingles, tingling, tingled**) to have a sharp prickling feeling ○ *'Are your fingers tingling?' asked the doctor.* ○ *It will tingle when I put the antiseptic on your cut.*

tinker /ˈtɪŋkə/ (**tinkers, tinkering, tinkered**), **tinker around** *verb* to try to make something work better, but not very successfully [~with] ○ *He spent Saturday morning tinkering about with his car.* ○ *The government are just tinkering with the economy when they should be taking strong action.*

tinkle /ˈtɪŋkəl/ *noun* a noise like the ringing of a little bell ■ *verb* (**tinkles, tinkling, tinkled**) to make a little ringing noise ○ *The little bell tinkled as she went into the shop.*

tinned /tɪnd/ *adj* preserved and sold in a tin

tin opener /ˈtɪn ˌəʊp(ə)nə/ *noun* an object used for opening tins of food

tinsel /ˈtɪnsəl/ *noun* thin strips of glittering metal used as Christmas decorations

tint /tɪnt/ *noun* a slight shade of colour ○ *A rosy tint in the eastern sky was the first sign of dawn.* ○ *Do you prefer this blue* *with a tint of grey in it?* ■ *verb* (**tints, tinting, tinted**) to give something a slight shade of colour ○ *tinted glass* ○ *Windows of aircraft are tinted to reduce the glare from the sun.* ○ *He was wearing tinted spectacles.* ○ *How much would it cost to have my hair tinted?*

② **tiny** /ˈtaɪni/ (**tinier, tiniest**) *adj* very small ○ *Can I have just a tiny bit more pudding?* ○ *The spot is so tiny you can hardly see it.* ○ *She lives in a tiny village in the Welsh mountains.*

② **tip** /tɪp/ *noun* **1.** the end of something long [~of] ○ *You have to touch the tip of your nose with your finger.* **2.** money given to someone who has provided a service ○ *The service hasn't been very good – should we leave a tip for the waiter?* ○ *The staff are not allowed to accept tips.* **3.** advice on something which could be profitable [~on] ○ *He gave me some tips on training my dog.* **4.** a place where household rubbish is taken to be thrown away ■ *verb* (**tips, tipping, tipped**) **1.** to pour something out ○ *He picked up the box and tipped the contents out onto the floor.* ○ *She tipped all the food out of the bag.* **2.** to give money to someone who has helped you ○ *I tipped the waiter £1.* ○ *Should we tip the driver?*

tip off *phrasal verb* to warn someone about something (*informal*) ○ *We think he tipped the burglars off that the police were outside.*

tip up *phrasal verb* **1.** to lean and fall over ○ *The cup tipped up and all the tea went into the saucer.* **2.** to turn something over so that the contents fall out ○ *He tipped up the bottle to see if there was any tomato sauce left inside.*

tip-off /ˈtɪp ɒf/ *noun* a piece of useful information, given secretly (*informal*)

tipsy /ˈtɪpsi/ *adj* rather drunk

tiptoe /ˈtɪptəʊ/ (**tiptoes, tiptoeing, tiptoed**) *verb* to walk quietly on the tips of your toes ○ *She tiptoed into the room and looked at the baby.*

tirade /taɪˈreɪd/ *noun* a long speech attacking something

tire /ˈtaɪə/ (**tires, tiring, tired**) *verb* **1.** to become tired ○ *He is getting old and tires easily.* **2.** to make someone become tired ○ *We went for a long cycle ride to tire the children out.* ◇ **to tire of something or someone** to lose interest in something or someone ○ *The children soon tired of playing with their toy soldiers.*

① **tired** /ˈtaɪəd/ *adj* **1.** feeling that you want to sleep ○ *I'm tired – I think I'll go to bed.* ○ *If you feel tired, lie down on my bed.* **2.** feeling that you need rest ○ *We're all tired after a long day at the office.*

tireless /ˈtaɪələs/ *adj* full of energy, never needing to rest

tiresome /ˈtaɪəs(ə)m/ *adj* annoying

tiring /ˈtaɪərɪŋ/ *adj* which makes you tired

③ **tissue** /ˈtɪʃuː/ *noun* a soft paper handkerchief ○ *There is a box of tissues beside the bed.*

tit /tɪt/ *noun* a woman's breast (*informal*)

titbit /ˈtɪtbɪt/ *noun* a special little piece of food or of gossip (NOTE: The US spelling is **tidbit**.)

① **title** /ˈtaɪt(ə)l/ *noun* **1.** the name of something, e.g. a book, play, painting or film ○ *He's almost finished the play but hasn't found a title for it yet.* **2.** a word such as Dr, Mr, Professor, Lord, Sir or Lady put in front of a name to show an honour or a qualification

title role /ˈtaɪt(ə)l rəʊl/ *noun* the part in a play or film which gives the name to the play or film

titter /ˈtɪtə/ (**titters, tittering, tittered**) *verb* to give a little laugh (NOTE: + **titter** *n*)

T-junction /ˈtiː ˌdʒʌŋkʃən/ *noun* a junction where one road joins another at right angles

① **to** /tə, tʊ, tuː/ *prep* **1.** showing direction or place ○ *They went to the police station.* ○ *Do you know the way to the beach?* ○ *The river is to the north of the town.* ○ *Everyone take one step to the right, please.* **2.** showing a period of time ○ *The office is open from 9.30 to 5.30, Monday to Friday.* ○ *She slept from 11.30 to 8.30 the following morning.* **3.** showing time in minutes before an hour ○ *Get up – it's five to seven (6.55).* ○ *The train leaves at a quarter to eight (7.45).* (NOTE: **To** is used for times between the half hour and o'clock: *3.35* = twenty-five to four; *3.45* = a quarter to four; *3.55* = five minutes to four. For times after the hour see **past**.) **4.** showing a person or animal that receives something ○ *Take the book to the librarian.* ○ *Pass the salt to your grandfather.* ○ *You must be kind to cats.* **5.** showing a connection or relationship ○ *They lost by twelve to nine.* ○ *There are four keys to the office.* ○ *In this class there are 28 children to one teacher.*

toadstool /ˈtəʊdstuːl/ *noun* a small fungus shaped like an umbrella, but usually not edible, and sometimes poisonous (NOTE: White edible fungi are called **mushrooms**.)

toast /təʊst/ *noun* pieces of bread which have been heated at a high temperature until they are brown ○ *Can you make some more toast?* ○ *She asked for scrambled eggs on toast.*

toaster /'təʊstə/ *noun* an electric device for toasting bread

tobacco /tə'bækəʊ/ *noun* the dried leaves of a plant used to make cigarettes and cigars, and for smoking in pipes (NOTE: no plural)

toboggan /tə'bɒgən/ *noun* a sledge made of a long flat piece of wood curved upwards at the front, designed for sliding downhill on snow or ice ○ *The children pulled their toboggans to the hill.*

① **today** /tə'deɪ/ *noun* this day ○ *Today's her sixth birthday.* ○ *What's the date today?* ○ *There's a story in today's newspaper about a burglary in our road.* ■ *adv* on this day ○ *He said he wanted to see me today, but he hasn't come yet.*

③ **toddler** /'tɒdlə/ *noun* a child who has just learnt to walk

③ **toe** /təʊ/ *noun* one of the five parts like fingers at the end of the foot ○ *She trod on my toe and didn't say she was sorry.* ◇ **to keep someone on their toes** to keep someone ready or alert ○ *My job is to make sure the staff are always on their toes.*

TOEFL /'təʊf(ə)l/ *trademark* Test of English as a Foreign Language

TOEIC /'təʊɪk/ *trademark* Test of English for International Communication

toenail /'təʊneɪl/ *noun* a nail covering the end of a toe

toffee /'tɒfi/ *noun* a sticky sweet made by cooking sugar and butter

tofu /'təʊfuː/ *noun* bean curd, a soft white paste made from soya beans

① **together** /tə'geðə/ *adv* **1.** doing something with someone else or in a group ○ *Tell the children to stay together or they'll get lost.* ○ *Why don't we all go to the cinema together?* **2.** joined with something else or with each other ○ *Tie the sticks together with string.* ○ *Do you think you can stick the pieces of the cup together again?* ○ *If you add all the figures together, you'll get the total sales.* ○ *We've had three sandwiches and three beers – how much does that come to all together?*

togetherness /tə'geðənəs/ *noun* a feeling of friendliness and closeness with a person or people you know well

toggle /'tɒg(ə)l/ (**toggles, toggling, toggled**) *verb* (*in computers*) to change between two states ○ *The symbol can be toggled on and off the display.*

toil /tɔɪl/ (**toils, toiling, toiled**) *verb* to work hard ○ *They toiled for months to try to improve the conditions of the workers.* ○ *She was toiling away at a hot stove.* (NOTE: + **toil** *n*)

② **toilet** /'tɔɪlət/ *noun* **1.** a bowl with a seat on which you sit to get rid of waste from your body ○ *There is a shower and toilet in the bathroom.* □ **to flush a toilet** to press a handle to make water flow through the toilet bowl to clear it ○ *Don't forget to flush the toilet.* **2.** a room with a toilet bowl in it ○ *The ladies' toilet is at the end of the corridor.* ○ *The gents' toilets are downstairs and to the right.* ○ *There's a public toilet at the railway station.*

toilet paper /'tɔɪlət ˌpeɪpə/ *noun* soft paper for wiping your bottom after going to the toilet

toiletries /'tɔɪlətriz/ *plural noun* things, e.g. soap, cream and perfume,which are used in washing the body or making yourself smell nice

toilet roll /'tɔɪlət rəʊl/ *noun* a roll of toilet paper

token /'təʊkən/ *noun* **1.** a thing which is a sign or symbol of something ○ *Please accept this small gift as a token of our gratitude.* **2.** a piece of paper or card, which is used in the place of money ○ *You can use these tokens to pay for meals.* **3.** a plastic or metal disc, which is used instead of money ○ *She put a token into the slot machine.*

① **told** /təʊld/ past tense and past participle of **tell**

tolerance /'tɒlərəns/ *noun* **1.** the practice of accepting or allowing something which you do not agree with ○ *tolerance of other people's views* **2.** the ability of the body to stand the effect of a drug or a poison

tolerant /'tɒlərənt/ *adj* who shows tolerance

tolerate /'tɒləreɪt/ (**tolerates, tolerating, tolerated**) *verb* **1.** to allow something which you do not like to happen without complaining about it ○ *She does not tolerate singing in the classroom.* **2.** to allow something which you do not agree with to exist ○ *Opposition parties are not tolerated in that country.* ○ *He is not known for tolerating people with opposing views to his.* **3.** to accept the effect of a drug or a poison ○ *The body can tolerate small amounts of poison.* (NOTE: + **toleration** *n*)

toll /təʊl/ *noun* **1.** a payment for using a service, usually a road, bridge or ferry **2.** the number of people hurt, of buildings damaged, etc. **3.** the solemn ringing of a bell ○ *The toll of the great bell could be heard across the marshes.* ■ *verb* (**tolls, tolling, tolled**) to ring a bell slowly, as for a funeral ○ *The bell was tolling as the coffin arrived at the church.*

③ **tomato** /tə'mɑːtəʊ/ (*plural* **tomatoes**) *noun* a small round red fruit used in salads and cooking ○ *Tomatoes cost 30p per kilo.* ○ *We had a salad of raw cabbage and tomatoes.* ○ *Someone in the crowd threw a tomato at the speaker on the platform.*

③ **tomb** /tuːm/ *noun* a grave, sometimes one with an underground vault

tomboy /'tɒmbɔɪ/ *noun* a girl who enjoys playing boys' games

tombstone /'tuːmstəʊn/ *noun* a large stone placed on a grave with the name of the dead person written on it

tomcat /'tɒmkæt/ *noun* a male cat

tome /təʊm/ *noun* a large book

① **tomorrow** /tə'mɒrəʊ/ *adv* on to the day after today ○ *Are you free for lunch tomorrow?* ○ *I mustn't forget I have a dentist's appointment tomorrow morning.* ○ *We are going to an Italian restaurant tomorrow evening.* ■ *noun* the day after today ○ *Today's Monday, so tomorrow must be Tuesday.* ○ *Tomorrow is our tenth wedding anniversary.*

③ **ton** /tʌn/ *noun* a measure of weight equal to 2240 pounds ○ *a ship carrying 1000 tons of coal*

② **tone** /təʊn/ *noun* a way of saying something, or of writing something, which shows a particular feeling ○ *His tone of voice showed he was angry.* ○ *She said hello in a friendly tone of voice.* ○ *You could tell from the tone of his letter that he was annoyed.*

tone down *phrasal verb* to make something less offensive

tone up *phrasal verb* to make your body firmer or fitter

toner /'təʊnə/ *noun* **1.** a black powder, like dry ink, used in photocopiers and laser printers ○ *The printer has run out of toner.* **2.** a substance used on your skin to make it look nicer or smoother (NOTE: no plural)

② **tongue** /tʌŋ/ *noun* **1.** the long organ in your mouth which can move and is used for tasting, swallowing and speaking ○ *The soup was so hot it burnt my tongue.* **2.** a language (*literary*) ○ *They spoke to each other in a strange foreign tongue.* ○ *It was clear that English was not his native tongue.* **3.** a long loose piece of leather under the laces in a shoe

tongue-in-cheek /ˌtʌŋ ɪn 'tʃiːk/ *adj* not meant seriously

tongue-tied /'tʌŋ taɪd/ *adj* so shy as to be unable to say anything

tongue-twister /'tʌŋ ˌtwɪstə/ *noun* a phrase like 'red lorry, yellow lorry,' which is difficult to say quickly

tonic /'tɒnɪk/ *noun* something which makes you stronger ○ *He's taking a course of iron tonic tablets.* ○ *Going on holiday will be a tonic for you.*

① **tonight** /tə'naɪt/ *adv, noun* the night or the evening of today ○ *I can't stop – we're getting ready for tonight's party.* ○ *I'll be at home from eight o'clock tonight.* ○ *I don't suppose there's anything interesting on TV tonight.*

③ **tonne** /tʌn/ *noun* a metric ton, a weight of 1,000 kilograms ○ *People in the region need over 900 tonnes of wheat to survive the winter.*

tonsil /'tɒns(ə)l/ *noun* one of two soft lumps of tissue at the back of the throat

tonsillitis /ˌtɒnsɪ'laɪtɪs/ *noun* an inflammation of the tonsils

① **too** /tuː/ *adv* **1.** more than necessary ○ *There are too many people to fit into the lift.* ○ *I think we bought too much bread.* ○ *It's too hot for us to sit in the sun.* **2.** (*often at the end of a clause*) also ○ *She had some coffee and I had some too.* ○ *She comes from Scotland too.*

① **took** /tʊk/ past tense of **take**

② **tool** /tuːl/ *noun* an instrument which you hold in your hand to do specific work, such as a hammer or a spade ○ *a set of gardening tools*

toolbar /'tuːlbɑː/ *noun* a line of icons on a computer screen which you click on to get the computer to do certain things

tool shed /tuːl ʃed/ *noun* a small wooden shed in a garden where tools are kept

toot /tuːt/ (**toots, tooting, tooted**) *verb* to blow a horn sharply ○ *She tooted as she turned the corner.* (NOTE: + **toot** *n*)

② **tooth** /tuːθ/ (*plural* **teeth**) *noun* one of a set of hard white objects in the mouth which you use to bite or chew food ○ *Children must learn to clean their teeth twice a day.* ○ *The dentist took one of her teeth out.*

toothache /'tuːθeɪk/ *noun* a pain in a tooth (NOTE: no plural)

toothbrush /'tuːθbrʌʃ/ *noun* a small brush which you use to clean your teeth

toothpaste /'tu:θpeɪst/ *noun* a soft substance which you spread on a toothbrush and then use to clean your teeth (NOTE: no plural: *some toothpaste, a tube of toothpaste*)

toothpick /'tu:θpɪk/ *noun* a little pointed piece of wood, used for cleaning between the teeth

① **top** /tɒp/ *noun* **1.** the highest place or highest point of something ○ *He climbed to the top of the stairs and sat down.* ○ *The bird is sitting on the top of the apple tree.* ○ *There is a roof garden on top of the hotel.* ○ *Look at the photograph at the top of page four.* ○ *Manchester United are still at the top of the league table.* □ **on top of the world** very healthy or very happy **2.** the flat upper surface of something ○ *a birthday cake with sugar and fruit on top* ○ *Do not put coffee cups on top of the computer.* ○ *The desk has a black top.* **3.** a cover for a container ○ *Take the top off the jar, and see what's inside.* ○ *She forgot to screw the top back on the bottle.* **4.** a piece of clothing covering the upper part of the body ○ *She wore jeans and a yellow top.* ■ *adj* **1.** in the highest place ○ *The restaurant is on the top floor of the building.* ○ *Jams and marmalades are on the top shelf.* **2.** best ○ *She's one of the world's top tennis players.* ◇ **on top of** /ɒn 'tɒp ɒv/ **1.** on the top surface of ○ *He put the book down on top of the others he had bought.* **2.** in addition to ○ *On top of all my office work, I have to clean the house and look after the baby.* ◇ **at the top of her voice** in a very loud voice ◇ **from top to bottom** completely

top up *phrasal verb* to add liquid to fill completely something which is half empty

top-down /ˌtɒp 'daʊn/ *adj* working from general things to more specific ones

top hat /ˌtɒp 'hæt/ *noun* a tall cylindrical hat with a narrow brim which is worn by a man on formal occasions

top-heavy /ˌtɒp 'hevi/ *adj* with the top part heavier than the bottom, and so likely to fall over

② **topic** /'tɒpɪk/ *noun* the subject of a discussion or conversation ○ *Can we move on to another topic?* □ **to bring up a topic** to start to discuss something ○ *She brought up the topic of where to go on holiday.*

③ **topical** /'tɒpɪk(ə)l/ *adj* interesting at the present time

topless /'tɒpləs/ *adj* not wearing any clothes on the top part of your body

topmost /'tɒpməʊst/ *adj* highest or nearest the top

topography /tə'pɒgrəfi/ *noun* the study or description of the physical features of a place and its rivers, mountains, and valleys

topping /'tɒpɪŋ/ *noun* things such as cream or melted cheese, put on the top of food such as cakes, pizzas, or ice cream

topple /'tɒp(ə)l/ (**topples, toppling, toppled**) *verb* ○ *He lost his balance and toppled forwards.*

topple over *phrasal verb* to fall down

top secret /'tɒp ˌsi:krət/ *adj* absolutely secret

topsy-turvy /ˌtɒpsi 'tɜ:vi/ *adj* in disorder or all upside down

③ **torch** /tɔ:tʃ/ *noun* a small electric light that you can carry ○ *Take a torch if you're going into the cave.* ○ *I always carry a small torch in the car.*

③ **tore** /tɔ:/ past tense of **tear**

torment[1] /'tɔ:ment/ *noun* extreme pain ○ *the torment of parents who are separated from their children*

torment[2] /tɔ:'ment/ (**torments, tormenting, tormented**) *verb* to make someone suffer ○ *The old couple were tormented by their neighbours' children and in the end moved to a different street.* ○ *He was constantly tormented by doubt.*

③ **torn** /tɔ:n/ past participle of **tear**

tornado /tɔ:'neɪdəʊ/ (*plural* **tornados** or **tornadoes**) *noun* a violent storm with a whirlwind

torpedo /tɔ:'pi:dəʊ/ *noun* (*plural* **torpedoes**) a missile like a shell which travels under the water ○ *The submarine fired a torpedo.* ○ *The ship was hit by three torpedoes and sank immediately.* ■ *verb* (**torpedoes, torpedoing, torpedoed**) **1.** to sink a ship using a torpedo ○ *The ship was torpedoed by an enemy submarine.* **2.** to ruin someone's plans ○ *His grandiose scheme for a leisure complex was torpedoed by the council planning department.*

torrent /'tɒrənt/ *noun* **1.** a fast rushing stream ○ *To get to the farm we had to cross a mountain torrent.* **2.** a fast flow ○ *The rain came down in torrents.*

torrential /tə'renʃəl/ *adj* like a torrent ○ *torrential rain*

torso /'tɔ:səʊ/ (*plural* **torsos** or **torsi**) *noun* the main part of the body, not including the head, arms and legs

tortilla /tɔ:'ti:ə/ *noun* **1.** a type of Spanish omelette, often made with potato and onion **2.** a round, flat bread made of corn or wheat flour ○ *Tortillas are part of Mexican food.*

tortoise /ˈtɔːtəs/ *noun* a reptile covered with a hard shell which moves very slowly on land and can live to be very old

torture /ˈtɔːtʃə/ *noun* **1.** making someone suffer pain as a punishment or to make them reveal a secret ○ *They accused the police of using torture to get information about the plot.* **2.** extreme mental or physical pain ■ *verb* (**tortures, torturing, tortured**) to inflict mental or physical pain on someone ○ *was tortured with doubts* ○ *The soldiers tortured their prisoners.*

Tory /ˈtɔːri/ (*plural* **Tories**) *noun* a member of the Conservative party ○ *The Tories have recently elected a new leader.*

③ **toss** /tɒs/ *verb* (**tosses, tossing, tossed**) **1.** to throw something up into the air ○ *He tried to toss the pancake and it fell on the kitchen floor.* ○ *She tossed me her car keys.* **2.** to move something about ○ *The waves tossed the little boat up and down.* ○ *The horse tossed its head.* ■ *noun* **1.** the act of throwing something into the air **2.** a sharp movement of the head up and down ○ *With a toss of its head, the horse galloped off.* ◇ **to toss and turn** to move about in bed, not able to sleep

tot /tɒt/ *noun* **1.** a little child ○ *She took the tot by the hand and led him back into the house.* ○ *There are special classes where they teach tiny tots to swim.* **2.** a small glass of alcohol ○ *A tot of whisky before dinner won't do you any harm.*

① **total** /ˈtəʊt(ə)l/ *adj* complete or whole ○ *The expedition was a total failure.* ○ *Their total losses come to over £400,000.* ■ *noun* the whole amount ○ *The total comes to more than £1,000.*

totalitarian /təʊˌtælɪˈteəriən/ *adj* having total power and not allowing any opposition or personal freedom

① **totally** /ˈtəʊt(ə)li/ *adv* used for emphasis ○ *The house was totally destroyed in the fire.* ○ *I had totally forgotten that I had promised to be there.* ○ *He disagrees totally with what the first speaker said.*

totter /ˈtɒtə/ *noun* to walk unsteadily or to wobble ○ *I cannot bear to look at her tottering along in those platform shoes.* ○ *The old lady manages to totter over to the bakery to get some fresh bread every day.*

① **touch** /tʌtʃ/ *noun* **1.** one of the five senses, the sense of feeling with the fingers ○ *The sense of touch becomes very strong in the dark.* **2. in touch with** having contact with □ **to get in touch with someone** to contact someone ○ *I'll try to get in touch with you next week.* □ **to put someone in touch with someone** to arrange for someone to have contact with someone ○ *The bank put us in touch with a local lawyer.* □ **to stay in touch with someone** to keep contact with someone ○ *We met in Hong Kong thirty years ago but we have still kept in touch.* **3.** a gentle physical contact [~of] ○ *the touch of his hand on my face* **4.** a very small amount [~of] ○ *He added a few touches of paint to the picture.* ○ *There's a touch of frost in the air this morning.* ■ *verb* (**touches, touching, touched**) **1.** to feel something with your fingers ○ *The policeman touched him on the shoulder.* ○ *Don't touch that cake – it's for your mother.* **2.** to be so close to something that you press against it ○ *His feet don't touch the floor when he sits on a big chair.* ○ *There is a mark on the wall where the sofa touches it.* ◇ **to lose touch with someone** to lose contact with someone ○ *They used to live next door, but we've lost touch with them now that they've moved to London.*

touch down *phrasal verb* **1.** to land ○ *The plane touched down at 13.20.* **2.** to score a try in rugby, by touching the ground behind the opponents' line with the ball ○ *He touched down behind the posts.*

touch up *phrasal verb* to add a small amount of paint to a surface

touch-and-go /ˌtʌtʃ ən ˈgəʊ/ *adj* possible that anything can happen

touchdown /ˈtʌtʃdaʊn/ *noun* **1.** the landing of a plane or spacecraft ○ *The plane veered across the runway as one of its tyres burst on touchdown.* **2.** (*in rugby*) scoring a try by touching the ground behind the opponents' line with the ball ○ *He burst through for a touchdown between the posts.* **3.** *US* scoring a goal in American football by taking the ball over the opponents' line ○ *He completed a pass for the winning touchdown.*

touched /tʌtʃt/ *adj* grateful, pleased with

touching /ˈtʌtʃɪŋ/ *adj* making you feel emotion, especially affection or sympathy ○ *I had a touching letter from my sister, thanking me for my help when she was ill.*

touchline /ˈtʌtʃlaɪn/ *noun* a white line along the side of a football field

touch screen /ˈtʌtʃ skriːn/ *noun* a computer screen which you operate by touching displayed options with your finger

touchstone /ˈtʌtʃˌstəʊn/ *noun* s[illegible] thing which is an excellent examp[illegible] a standard by which to judge o[illegible]

touchy /ˈtʌtʃi/ *adj* **1.** easily offended ○ *Don't mention his red hair – he's very touchy about it.* **2.** which is likely to cause offence ○ *Don't mention his divorce- it's a very touchy subject at the moment.*

② **tough** /tʌf/ *adj* **1.** (*of meat*) difficult to chew or to cut ○ *My steak's a bit tough – how's yours?* **2.** requiring a lot of physical effort, or a lot of bravery or confidence ○ *She's very good at taking tough decisions.* ○ *You have to be tough to succeed in business.*

toughen /ˈtʌf(ə)n/ (**toughens, toughening, toughened**) *verb* **1.** to make tough or harder ○ *Cooking the meat too much will simply toughen it.* **2.** to make more strict or severe ○ *The aim is to toughen university entrance requirements.*

toupee /ˈtuːpeɪ/ *noun* artificial hair worn to cover a bald area on a man's head

② **tour** /tʊə/ *noun* a holiday journey to various places coming back eventually to the place you started from [~of] ○ *She gave us a tour of the old castle.* ■ *verb* (**tours, touring, toured**) to go on holiday, visiting various places ○ *They toured the south of France.*

tourism /ˈtʊərɪz(ə)m/ *noun* the business of providing travel, accommodation, food and entertainment for tourists

③ **tourist** /ˈtʊərɪst/ *noun* a person who goes on holiday to visit places away from their home ○ *The tourists were talking German.* ○ *There were parties of tourists visiting all the churches.* ○ *Trafalgar Square is always full of tourists.*

tournament /ˈtʊənəmənt/ *noun* a sporting competition with many games where competitors who lose drop out until only one is left

tourniquet /ˈtɔːnɪkeɪ/ *noun* a tight bandage put round an arm or leg to stop bleeding

tout /taʊt/ (**touts, touting, touted**) *verb* **1.** to praise something in the hope that people will believe you ○ *The book was touted as a masterpiece.* **2.** to try to persuade people to buy something

tow /təʊ/ *verb* (**tows, towing, towed**) to pull something behind a vehicle ○ *The motorways ... crowded with cars towing ... ey towed the ship into port.* ... on of pulling something ○ ... *r to give us a tow to the* ... NOTE: Do not confuse with ... ccompanied by someone ... *were approached by a* ... *ith children in tow.*

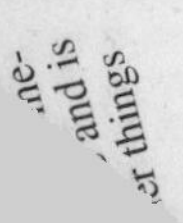

① **towards** /təˈwɔːdz/ *prep* **1.** in the direction of ○ *The crowd ran towards the police station.* ○ *The bus was travelling south, towards London.* ○ *The ship sailed straight towards the rocks.* **2.** near in time ○ *Do you have any free time towards the end of the month?* ○ *The exhibition will be held towards the middle of October.* **3.** as part of the money to pay for something ○ *He gave me £100 towards the cost of the hotel.* **4.** in relation to ○ *She always behaved very kindly towards her father.*

towel /ˈtaʊəl/ *noun* a large piece of soft cloth for drying something, especially your body ○ *There's only one towel in the bathroom.* ○ *After washing her hair, she wound the towel round her head.* ○ *I'll get some fresh towels.*

③ **tower** /ˈtaʊə/ *noun* a tall structure ○ *The castle has thick walls and four square towers.*

tower block /ˈtaʊə blɒk/ *noun* a very tall block of flats

① **town** /taʊn/ *noun* a place, larger than a village, where people live and work, with houses, shops, offices, factories and other buildings ○ *There's no shop in our village, so we do our shopping in the nearest town.* ○ *They moved their office to the centre of town.*

town hall /ˌtaʊn ˈhɔːl/ *noun* the main building in a town, where the town council meets, and where many of the council departments are

toxic /ˈtɒksɪk/ *adj* harmful

toxin /ˈtɒksɪn/ *noun* a poisonous substance produced inside the body by germs

② **toy** /tɔɪ/ *noun* a thing for children to play with ○ *We gave him a box of toy soldiers for Christmas.* ○ *The children's toys are all over the sitting room floor.*

③ **trace** /treɪs/ *noun* something which shows that something existed [~of] ○ *The police found traces of blood in the kitchen.* ■ *verb* (**traces, tracing, traced**) to find where someone or something is ○ *They couldn't trace the letter.* ○ *The police traced him to Dover.*

② **track** /træk/ *noun* a rough path ○ *We followed a track through the forest.* ■ *plural noun* **tracks** a series of footprints left by an animal or marks left by things like wheels □ **to make tracks for** to go towards ○ *They made tracks for the nearest hotel.* ■ *verb* (**tracks, tracking, tracked**) to follow someone or an animal ○ *The hunters tracked the bear through the forest.* ○ *The police tracked the gang to a flat in south London.*

track down *phrasal verb* □ **to track someone down** to follow and catch something, e.g. a criminal ○ *Did you track down your old boss?* □ **to track something down** to manage to find something ○ *I finally tracked down that file which you were looking for.*

trackball /ˈtrækbɔːl/ *noun* a ball used instead of a computer mouse to control the cursor on a computer screen

track record /ˈtræk ˌrekɔːd/ *noun* the success or failure of someone or a business in the past

③ **tracksuit** /ˈtræksuːt/ *noun* a pair of matching trousers and top, in warm material, worn when practising sports

tract /trækt/ *noun* **1.** a large area of land ○ *Whole tracts of forest have been contaminated by acid rain.* **2.** a system of organs and tubes in the body which are linked together ○ *The respiratory tract takes air into the lungs.*

traction /ˈtrækʃən/ *noun* **1.** the gripping power between one surface and another, e.g. between a tyre and the road ○ *These tyres are so old they have no traction at all on ice.* **2.** the force used in pulling a load

① **trade** /treɪd/ *noun* the business of buying and selling [~in/~with] ○ *the illegal trade in ivory* ○ *Britain's trade with the rest of Europe is up by 10%.* ■ *verb* (**trades, trading, traded**) to buy and sell, to carry on a business [~in/~with] ○ *They trade in furs.* ○ *The company has ceased trading with Europe.*

trade in *phrasal verb* to give in an old item, such as a car or washing-machine, as part of the payment for a new one

trade on *phrasal verb* to exploit or to use something to your advantage

trade deficit /ˈtreɪd ˌdefɪsɪt/ *noun* the difference between the value of a country's exports and the value of its imports

trade fair /ˈtreɪd feə/ *noun* an occasion when manufacturers and producers exhibit their products and services to try to sell them

trademark /ˈtreɪdmɑːk/ *noun* a particular name, design, etc., which has been registered by the manufacturer and which cannot be used by other manufacturers

trade name *noun* same as **brand name**

trade-off /ˈtreɪd ɒf/ *noun* exchanging one thing for another as part of a deal

trader /ˈtreɪdə/ *noun* a person who does business

tradesman /ˈtreɪdzmən/ (*plural* **tradesmen**) *noun* a person who runs a shop (*dated*)

② **tradition** /trəˈdɪʃ(ə)n/ *noun* beliefs, stories and ways of doing things which are passed from one generation to the next ○ *It's a family tradition for the eldest son to take over the business.* ○ *According to local tradition, the queen died in this bed.*

① **traditional** /trəˈdɪʃ(ə)n(ə)l/ *adj* done in a way that has been used for a long time ○ *On Easter Day it is traditional to give chocolate eggs to the children.* ○ *Villagers still wear their traditional costumes on Sundays.*

traditionalist /trəˈdɪʃ(ə)nəlɪst/ *noun* a person who does things in a traditional way

traditionally /trəˈdɪʃ(ə)nəli/ *adv* according to tradition

① **traffic** /ˈtræfɪk/ *noun* cars, buses and other vehicles which are travelling on a street or road ○ *I leave the office early on Fridays because there is so much traffic leaving London.* ○ *The lights turned green and the traffic moved forward.* ○ *Rush-hour traffic is worse on Fridays.*

traffic jam /ˈtræfɪk dʒæm/ *noun* a situation where cars, buses and other vehicles cannot move forward on a road because there is too much traffic, because there has been an accident or because of roadworks

③ **tragedy** /ˈtrædʒədi/ *noun* **1.** a serious play, film, or novel which ends sadly ○ *Shakespeare's tragedy 'King Lear' is playing at the National Theatre.* **2.** a very unhappy event ○ *Tragedy struck the family when their mother was killed in a car crash.*

③ **tragic** /ˈtrædʒɪk/ *adj* very sad ○ *a tragic accident on the motorway*

③ **trail** /treɪl/ *noun* **1.** tracks left by an animal or by a criminal ○ *We followed the trail of the bear through the forest.* ○ *The burglars left in a red sports car, and a police car was soon on their trail.* **2.** a path or track ○ *Keep to the trail otherwise you will get lost.* ■ *verb* □ **to trail behind someone** to follow slowly after someone ○ *She came third, trailing a long way behind the first two runners.* ○ *The little children trailed behind the older ones.*

trailer /ˈtreɪlə/ *noun* **1.** a small goods vehicle pulled behind a car ○ *We carried all our camping gear in the trailer.* **2.** *US* a van with beds, a table, and washing facilities, which can be towed by a car **3.** parts of a full-length film shown as an advertisement for it ○ *We saw the trailer last week, and it put me off the film.*

① **train** /treɪn/ *noun* an engine pulling a group of coaches on the railway ○ *The train to Paris leaves from platform 1.* ○ *Hundreds of people go to work every day by train.* ○ *We'll be changing trains at Crewe.* ■ *verb* (**trains, training, trained**) **1.** to teach someone or an animal how to do a particular activity [~in/~as] ○ *He trained as a doctor.* ○ *She's being trained in self-defence.* ○ *The dogs are trained to smell and find illegal substances.* **2.** to become fit by practising for a sport [~for] ○ *He's training for the 100 metres.* ○ *She's training for the Olympics.*

trained /treɪnd/ *adj* who has been through a course of training

trainee /treɪ'niː/ *noun* a person who is being trained

③ **trainer** /'treɪnə/ *noun* a person who trains an athlete ○ *His trainer says he's in peak condition for the fight.* ■ *plural noun* **trainers** light sports shoes

trainers /'treɪnəz/ *plural noun* light sports shoes ○ *She needs a new pair of trainers for school.* ○ *He comes to work every morning in trainers.*

① **training** /'treɪnɪŋ/ *noun* **1.** the process of being taught a skill or being trained ○ *The shop is closed on Tuesday mornings for staff training.* ○ *There is a short training period for new staff.* **2.** practise for a sport □ **to be in training** to practise for a sport ○ *She's in training for the Olympics.*

③ **trait** /treɪt/ *noun* a particular characteristic of someone

traitor /'treɪtə/ *noun* a person who betrays his or her country, especially by giving secret information to the enemy

trajectory /trə'dʒekt(ə)ri/ *noun* the curving movement of something which has been thrown or shot through the air

tramp /træmp/ *noun* **1.** a person who has nowhere to live and walks from place to place looking for work or begging for food or money ○ *The farmer was surprised to find a tramp asleep in one of his barns.* **2.** a long walk ○ *We went for a tramp along the cliffs last Sunday.* **3.** the noise made by of feet hitting the ground regularly as someone walks ○ *the tramp of marching soldiers* ■ *verb* (**tramps, tramping, tramped**) **1.** to walk with a regular heavy step ○ *You could hear soldiers tramping through the streets at night.* **2.** to walk for a long way, or walk with difficulty ○ *They tramped for miles before they came to a little inn.* ○ *They tramped through the snow to get to the camp.*

trampoline /'træmpəliːn/ *noun* a large sheet of elastic material stretched across a frame, which you can bounce or jump on

trance /trɑːns/ *noun* a state when you are not alert but not asleep, and do not notice what is going on around you

tranquil /'træŋkwɪl/ *adj* calm or peaceful

transaction /træn'zækʃən/ *noun* a piece of business

transatlantic /ˌtrænzət'læntɪk/ *adj* **1.** across the Atlantic ○ *Transatlantic flights take about six hours depending on the wind.* ○ *Prices for transatlantic phone calls have been reduced.* **2.** on the other side of the Atlantic ○ *our transatlantic trading partners*

transcend /træn'send/ (**transcends, transcending, transcended**) *verb* to go better or further than something or to be much more important than something

transcribe /træn'skraɪb/ (**transcribes, transcribing, transcribed**) *verb* to write out the text of something which is heard ○ *His speech was transcribed from the radio tape.* ○ *The sound of each word has been transcribed into phonetic characters.*

transcript /'trænskrɪpt/ *noun* a written record of something which has been noted in shorthand, or text of what was said on a radio programme, at a meeting, etc.

② **transfer** (**transfers, transferring, transferred**) *verb* **1.** to move something or someone to another place [~to] ○ *The money will be transferred directly to your bank account.* ○ *She transferred her passport from her handbag to her jacket pocket.* ○ *He's been transferred to our New York office.* **2.** to change from one type of travel to another [~to] ○ *They transferred us to another plane at London.*

③ **transform** /træns'fɔːm/ (**transforms, transforming, transformed**) *verb* to change the appearance or character of someone or something completely ○ *The outside of the building has been transformed by cleaning.* ○ *The book has transformed my views on medical care.*

transformer /træns'fɔːmə/ *noun* a device for changing the voltage of an alternating current

transgress /trænz'gres/ (**transgresses, transgressing, transgressed**) *verb* to go against a rule (NOTE: + **transgression** *n*)

transient /'trænziənt/ *adj* which will not last ○ *Fame for most pop groups is very transient.*

transit /'trænsɪt/ *noun* the movement of passengers or goods on the way to a destination □ **in transit** in the process of being moved from one place to another ○ *The police seized the goods when they were in transit between London and Manchester.*

transition /træn'zɪʃ(ə)n/ *noun* the process of moving from one situation to another

transitory /'trænsɪt(ə)ri/ *adj* not lasting for a long time

translate /træns'leɪt/ (**translates, translating, translated**) *verb* to put written or spoken words into another language ○ *Can you translate what he said?* ○ *He asked his secretary to translate the letter from the German agent.* ○ *She translates mainly from Spanish into English, not from English into Spanish.*

translation /træns'leɪʃ(ə)n/ *noun* writing or speech which has been translated ○ *I read Tolstoy's 'War and Peace' in translation.* ○ *She passed the translation of the letter to the accounts department.*

translator /træns'leɪtə/ *noun* a person who translates

translucent /træns'lu:s(ə)nt/ *adj* which light can pass through, but which you cannot see through clearly

transmission /trænz'mɪʃ(ə)n/ *noun* **1.** passing of disease from one person to another ○ *Patients must be isolated to prevent transmission of the disease to the general public.* **2.** a radio or TV broadcast ○ *We interrupt this transmission to bring you a news flash.* **3.** (*in a car*) a series of moving parts which pass the power from the engine through the gearbox and clutch to the axles ○ *There's a strange noise coming from the transmission.*

transmit /trænz'mɪt/ (**transmits, transmitting, transmitted**) *verb* **1.** to pass a disease from one person to another ○ *The disease was transmitted to all the people he came into contact with.* ○ *The disease is transmitted by fleas.* **2.** to send out a programme or a message by radio or TV ○ *The message was transmitted to the ship by radio.*

transmitter /trænz'mɪtə/ *noun* apparatus for sending out radio or TV signals

transparency /træns'pærənsi/ *noun* **1.** the quality of being transparent ○ *The transparency of the water allows you to see the coral reefs.* **2.** being clear when making decisions, and being open to the public about official actions ○ *The government insists on the importance of transparency in all its actions.* **3.** a photograph which is printed on transparent film so that it can be projected on to a screen ○ *Transparency is another name for 'slide'.* ○ *Do you want to have prints or transparencies?*

transparent /træns'pærənt/ *adj* which you can see through ○ *The meat is wrapped in transparent plastic film.*

transpire /træn'spaɪə/ (**transpires, transpiring, transpired**) *verb* **1.** to become obvious ○ *It transpired that she had never seen the letter.* **2.** (*of a plant*) to lose water through the surface of a leaf ○ *In tropical rainforests, up to 75% of rainfall will transpire into the atmosphere.*

transplant[1] /'trænsplɑ:nt/ *noun* **1.** the act of replacing a damaged organ or part of the body with a part from another body, or with a part from somewhere else on the same body ○ *He had a heart transplant.* **2.** an organ or piece of tissue which is transplanted ○ *The kidney transplant was rejected.*

transplant[2] /træns'plɑ:nt/ (**transplants, transplanting, transplanted**) *verb* **1.** to move a plant from one place to another ○ *You should not transplant trees in the summer.* **2.** to replace a damaged organ or other body part with a healthy part ○ *They transplanted a kidney from his brother.*

transport[1] /'trænspɔ:t/ *noun* the movement of goods or people in vehicles ○ *Air transport is the quickest way to travel from one country to another.* ○ *Rail transport costs are getting lower.* ○ *What means of transport will you use to get to the hotel?*

transport[2] /træns'pɔ:t/ (**transports, transporting, transported**) *verb* to move goods or people from one place to another in a vehicle ○ *The company transports millions of tons of goods by rail each year.* ○ *The visitors will be transported to the factory by helicopter.*

③ **transportation** /ˌtrænspɔ:'teɪʃ(ə)n/ *noun* the action or means of moving goods or people ○ *The company will provide transportation to the airport.*

transpose /træns'pəʊz/ (**transposes, transposing, transposed**) *verb* to make two things change places

transvestite /trænz'vestaɪt/ *noun* a person who wears the clothes of the opposite sex. ◊ **drag**

③ **trap** /træp/ *noun* an object used for catching an animal ○ *We have a mouse in the kitchen so we will put down a trap.* ■ *verb* (**traps, trapping, trapped**) to catch or hold someone or something ○ *Several peo-*

ple were trapped in the wreckage of the plane. ○ *He was trapped on video as he entered the bank.*

trapezium /trəˈpiːziəm/ *noun* **1.** a flat four-sided geometric shape, where two of the sides are parallel and the other two sides are not (NOTE: The US term is **trapezoid.**) **2.** *US* a flat four-sided geometric shape, where none of the sides are parallel (NOTE: The British term is **trapezoid.**)

trash /træʃ/ *noun* **1.** *US* useless things ○ *Throw out all that trash from her bedroom.* **2.** something of bad quality, e.g. a newspaper ■ *verb* (**trashes, trashing, trashed**) **1.** to smash up ○ *Someone trashed the telephones.* **2.** to ruin someone's reputation ○ *She wrote an article trashing the pop singer.*

trashcan /ˈtræʃkæn/ *noun US* a large plastic or metal container for household rubbish (*informal*)

trashy /ˈtræʃi/ *adj* of bad quality

trauma /ˈtrɔːmə/ *noun* a mental shock caused by a sudden unpleasant experience, which was not expected to take place

traumatic /trɔːˈmætɪk/ *adj* which gives a sharp and unpleasant shock

② **travel** /ˈtræv(ə)l/ *noun* the action of moving from one country or place to another ○ *Air travel is the only really fast method of going from one country to another.* ■ *verb* (**travels, travelling, travelled**) to move from one country or place to another ○ *He travels fifty miles by car to go to work every day.* ○ *He has travelled across the United States several times on his motorbike.* ○ *The bullet must have travelled several metres before it hit the wall.* (NOTE: The US spelling is **traveling – traveled.**)

travel agency /ˈtræv(ə)l ˌeɪdʒənsi/ *noun* an office which arranges tickets and accommodation for travellers

travel agent /ˈtræv(ə)l ˌeɪdʒənt/ *noun* a person or company that arranges tickets and accommodation for its customers

traveller /ˈtræv(ə)lə/ *noun* **1.** a person who travels ○ *travellers on the 9 o'clock train to London* ○ *Travellers to France are experiencing delays because of the dock strike.* **2.** a person who has no fixed home and who travels around the country ○ *The fields were full of hippies and travellers.*

traveller's cheque /ˈtræv(ə)ləz tʃek/ *noun* a cheque which you buy at a bank before you travel and which you can then use in a foreign country

traverse /trəˈvɜːs/ (**traverses, traversing, traversed**) *verb* to go across

travesty /ˈtrævəsti/ *noun* a ridiculous or poor imitation ○ *It's a travesty of the truth.*

trawl /trɔːl/ (**trawls, trawling, trawled**) *verb* to search something large in order to get something ○ *We trawled the files for a recent photo of the businessman.* □ **to trawl through something for something** to search through something ○ *He spent hours trawling through boxes until he found the letter he was looking for.*

trawler /ˈtrɔːlə/ *noun* a fishing boat which pulls a net behind it

tray /treɪ/ *noun* a flat board for carrying food, and things like glasses, cups and saucers ○ *He had his lunch on a tray in his bedroom.* ○ *She bumped into a waitress who was carrying a tray of glasses.*

treacherous /ˈtretʃərəs/ *adv* **1.** dangerous ○ *There are treacherous reefs just offshore.* ○ *Black ice is making the roads very treacherous.* **2.** not to be trusted ○ *His treacherous behaviour led to the loss of the town to the enemy.*

treachery /ˈtretʃəri/ *noun* the act of betraying or of being a traitor to your country, friends, etc.

treacle /ˈtriːk(ə)l/ *noun* a thick dark-brown liquid produced when sugar is being refined ○ *You can use treacle in Christmas cakes and Christmas puddings.*

tread /tred/ *verb* (**treads, treading, trod**) to step or to walk, especially with force ○ *She trod on my toe and didn't say she was sorry.* ○ *Watch where you're treading – there's broken glass on the floor.* ■ *noun* the top part of a stair or step which you stand on ○ *The carpet on the bottom tread is loose.* ○ *Metal treads are noisy.*

treadmill /ˈtredmɪl/ *noun* **1.** an exercise machine with a moving belt on which you walk or jog without actually moving forward **2.** dull work which has to be done every day

treason /ˈtriːz(ə)n/ *noun* the crime of betraying your country, by giving your country's secrets to the enemy or by helping the enemy during wartime

treasure /ˈtreʒə/ *noun* jewels, gold, or other valuable things ○ *the treasures in the British Museum* ○ *They are diving in the Caribbean looking for pirates' treasure.*

treasurer /ˈtreʒərə/ *noun* a person who looks after the money of a club, society or other organisation ○ *Please send your subscriptions to the treasurer by May 1st.*

① **treat** /triːt/ *noun* a special thing which gives pleasure ○ *It's always a treat to sit down quietly at home after a hard day in* *the shop.* ■ *verb* (**treats, treating, treated**) **1.** to deal with someone or something ○ *She was badly treated by her uncle.* ○ *It you treat the staff well they will work well.* ○ *He didn't treat my suggestion seriously.* **2.** to give medical help to a sick or injured person ○ *After the accident some of the passengers had to be treated in hospital for cuts and bruises.* ○ *She is being treated for rheumatism.*

treatise /'triːtɪz/ *noun* a long piece of formal writing on a specialised subject

① **treatment** /'triːtmənt/ *noun* **1.** a way of behaving towards something or someone ○ *The report criticised the treatment of prisoners in the jail.* ○ *What sort of treatment did you get at school?* **2.** a way of looking after a sick or injured person [~for] ○ *The treatment for skin cancer is very painful.* ○ *He is having a course of heat treatment.*

treaty /'triːti/ *noun* a written legal agreement between two or more countries ○ *The treaty was signed in 1845.* ○ *Countries are negotiating a treaty to ban nuclear weapons.*

treble /'treb(ə)l/ *noun* **1.** a boy's high-pitched soprano voice ○ *The treble solo rose above the sound of the basses.* **2.** a high-pitched musical instrument ○ *The school has six recorders: two bass, two tenors and two trebles.* ■ *verb* (**trebles, trebling, trebled**) to increase by three times ○ *The council is planning to treble the amount it spends on education.* ○ *The value of our house has trebled in the last fifteen years.*

① **tree** /triː/ *noun* a very large plant, with a thick trunk, branches and leaves ○ *The cat climbed up an apple tree and couldn't get down.* ○ *In autumn, the leaves on the trees in the park turn brown and red.* ○ *He was sheltering under a tree and was struck by lightning.*

trek /trek/ *noun* a long hard journey ○ *It's quite a trek to the centre of town from here.* (NOTE: + **trek** *v*)

trellis /'trelɪs/ *noun* a frame of criss-crossed pieces of light wood, used for plants to climb up

tremble /'trembəl/ (**trembles, trembling, trembled**) *verb* to shake because you are cold or afraid, or worried by something ○ *She was trembling with cold.* ○ *I tremble at the thought of how much the meal will cost.*

② **tremendous** /trɪ'mendəs/ *adj* very big ○ *There was a tremendous explosion and all the lights went out.* ○ *There's tremendous excitement here in Trafalgar Square as we wait for the election result.*

tremor /'tremə/ *noun* a slight shaking ○ *They noticed a tremor in her hands.*

trench /trentʃ/ *noun* a long narrow ditch ○ *They dug trenches for drainage round the camp.* ○ *He fought in the trenches during the First World War.*

② **trend** /trend/ *noun* a general tendency [~towards] ○ *There is a trend towards shopping in smaller local stores.* ○ *The government studies economic trends to decide whether to raise taxes or not.*

trendy /'trendi/ (**trendier, trendiest**) *adj* very fashionable (*informal*) ○ *She's always wearing the trendiest clothes.* ○ *It's trendy nowadays to care about the environment.*

trepidation /ˌtrepɪ'deɪʃ(ə)n/ *noun* nervous worry

② **trial** /'traɪəl/ *noun* **1.** a court case held before a judge ○ *The trial will be heard next week.* **2.** the act of testing something ○ *The new model is undergoing its final trials.* ◇ **on trial** being tested to see if it is acceptable ○ *The system is still on trial.*

trial run /ˌtraɪəl 'rʌn/ *noun* a test of something which is new to see how good it is

③ **triangle** /'traɪæŋgəl/ *noun* a shape with three straight sides and three angles ○ *The end of the roof is shaped like a triangle.*

triathlon /traɪ'æθlən/ *noun* an Olympic endurance sport in which competitors must complete a 1,500-metre swim, then cycle 40 kilometres and finally run 10,000 metres

tribe /traɪb/ *noun* a group of people with the same race, language and customs ○ *She went into the jungle to study the jungle tribes.*

tribunal /traɪ'bjuːn(ə)l/ *noun* a specialist court outside the main judicial system which examines special problems and makes judgments

tribute /'trɪbjuːt/ *noun* words or gifts to show respect to someone, especially someone who has died

tribute band /'trɪbjuːt ˌbænd/ *noun* a musical group that tries to look and sound like and performs songs and music made popular by a famous predecessor

② **trick** /trɪk/ *noun* a clever act to deceive or confuse someone ○ *The recorded sound of barking is just a trick to make burglars think there is a dog in the house.* ■ *verb* (**tricks, tricking, tricked**) to deceive someone ○ *We've been tricked, there's nothing in the box.* □ **to trick someone into doing something** to make someone do something which they did not mean to do by means of a trick ○ *He tricked the old lady into giving him all her money.* □ **to trick someone out of something** to get someone to lose something by a trick ○ *She tricked the bank out of £100,000.*

trickery /ˈtrɪkəri/ *noun* deceiving by using tricks

trickle /ˈtrɪk(ə)l/ (**trickles, trickling, trickled**) *verb* to flow gently

trick question /trɪk ˈkwestʃən/ *noun* a question which is intended to deceive people

③ **tricky** /ˈtrɪki/ *adj* requiring a lot of skill, patience or intelligence ○ *Getting the wire through the little hole is quite tricky.*

tried /⌐(ˋ ₌ₒ ˋ/ past tense and past participle of **try**

tries /traɪz/ plural of **try**. 3rd person singular present of **try**

trifle /ˈtraɪf(ə)l/ *noun* a small thing which is not important (*literary*) ○ *The president does not bother himself with trifles.*

trigger /ˈtrɪgə/ *noun* a little lever which you pull to fire a gun

trilogy /ˈtrɪlədʒi/ (*plural* **trilogies**) *noun* a novel or play in three separate parts which are linked together

trim /trɪm/ *verb* (**trims, trimming, trimmed**) to cut something to make it tidy ○ *Ask the hairdresser to trim your beard.* ■ *adj* (**trimmer, trimmest**) **1.** cut short to give a tidy appearance ○ *She always keeps her hedges trim.* **2.** slim and fit ○ *He keeps himself trim by going for a long walk every day.*

trinket /ˈtrɪŋkɪt/ *noun* a cheap ornament

trio /ˈtriːəʊ/ (*plural* **trios**) *noun* a group of three people, especially a group of three musicians

② **trip** /trɪp/ *noun* a short journey [~to] ○ *Our trip to Paris was cancelled.* ○ *We're going on a trip to the seaside.* ■ *verb* (**trips, tripping, tripped**) to catch your foot in something so that you stagger and fall down [~on/over] ○ *She tripped over a cable as she was coming out of the workshop.*

trip over *phrasal verb* to catch your foot in something so that you fall ○ *She was running away from him when she tripped over.*

triple /ˈtrɪp(ə)l/ (**triples, tripling, tripled**) *verb* to become three times as large; to make something three times as large ○ *Output has tripled over the last year.* ○ *We've tripled the number of visitors to the museum since we reduced the entrance fee.*

tripod /ˈtraɪpɒd/ *noun* a stand with three legs

trite /traɪt/ *adj* very ordinary and unexciting or used too often

③ **triumph** /ˈtraɪʌmf/ *noun* a great victory or great achievement [~over/~of] ○ *their recent triumph over the French* ○ *The bridge is a triumph of modern engineering.* ■ *verb* (**triumphs, triumphing, triumphed**) [~over] □ **to triumph over something** to be successful in spite of difficulties which could have stopped you ○ *He triumphed over his disabilities to become world champion.* □ **to triumph over someone** to win a victory over someone ○ *Our local team triumphed over their old rivals.*

triumphant /traɪˈʌmfənt/ *adj* happy or proud because you have won

trivia /ˈtrɪviə/ *noun* details which are not important

trivial /ˈtrɪviəl/ *adj* not important

trod /trɒd/ past tense of **tread**

trodden /ˈtrɒd(ə)n/ past participle of **tread**

③ **trolley** /ˈtrɒli/ *noun* a small vehicle on wheels which is designed to be pushed ○ *They put the piano onto a trolley to move it out of the house.*

trombone /trɒmˈbəʊn/ *noun* a brass musical instrument like a large trumpet, where different notes are made by sliding a tube in or out

② **troop** /truːp/ *noun* a large group of people ○ *She took a troop of schoolchildren to visit the museum.* (NOTE: Do not confuse with **troupe**.) ■ *plural noun* **troops** soldiers ○ *Enemy troops occupied the town.*

trophy /ˈtrəʊfi/ *noun* a prize given for winning a competition ○ *His mantelpiece is full of trophies which he won at golf.* ○ *Our team carried off the trophy for the third year in a row.*

② **tropical** /ˈtrɒpɪk(ə)l/ *adj* relating to hot countries ○ *In tropical countries it is always hot.*

③ **trot** /trɒt/ *noun* the action of running with short regular steps, like a horse does ○ *Let's start today's exercises with a short trot round the football field.* ■ *verb* (**trots, trotting, trotted**) to run with short regular steps ○ *We've got no butter left, so I'll trot off to the shop to buy some.* ○ *She trotted down the path to meet us.*

① **trouble** /ˈtrʌb(ə)l/ *noun* problems or worries ○ *The trouble with old cars is that sometimes they don't start.* ○ *The children were no trouble at all.* ○ *We are having some computer trouble* or *some trouble with the computer.* ■ *verb* (**troubles, troubling, troubled**) to make someone feel worried ○ *I can see that there's something troubling him.* ◇ **asking for trouble** likely to cause problems ○ *If you don't take out insurance, it's just asking for trouble.* ◇ **it's no trouble** it is easy to do, it won't cause any problems ○ *Looking after your cat is no trouble – I like animals.*

troubled /ˈtrʌb(ə)ld/ *adj* **1.** where there are problems ○ *He comes from a troubled family background.* ○ *We live in troubled times.* **2.** worried ○ *He has a troubled look on his face.* ○ *They seem troubled but I don't know why.*

troublemaker /ˈtrʌb(ə)lmeɪkə/ *noun* a person who causes problems for other people

troubleshooting /ˈtrʌb(ə)lʃuːtɪŋ/ *noun* sorting out problems, in business or in technology

troublesome /ˈtrʌb(ə)ls(ə)m/ *adj* which causes trouble or which is annoying

trouble spot /ˈtrʌb(ə)l spɒt/ *noun* a place where trouble, especially political unrest or violence, occurs

trough /trɒf/ *noun* **1.** a long narrow open container for food or water for farm animals ○ *The pigs were so greedy for their food, some of them even got into the trough.* **2.** a low point between two higher points of something that rises and falls regularly ○ *The graph shows the peaks and troughs of the number of births in different months.*

trounce /traʊns/ (**trounces, trouncing, trounced**) *verb* to defeat someone easily

troupe /truːp/ *noun* a group of actors or other performers who perform together (NOTE: Do not confuse with **troop**.)

② **trousers** /ˈtraʊzəz/ *plural noun* clothes which cover your body from the waist down, each leg separately ○ *He tore his trousers climbing over the fence.* ○ *She was wearing a red jumper and grey trousers.* ○ *He bought two pairs of trousers in the sale.*

trout /traʊt/ *noun* a type of edible freshwater fish

trowel /ˈtraʊəl/ *noun* a hand tool, like a large spoon, used in gardening

truancy /ˈtruːənsi/ *noun* the action of not going to school when you should

truant /ˈtruːənt/ *noun* □ **to play truant** not to go to school when you should ○ *They didn't go to school, but played truant and went fishing instead.*

truce /truːs/ *noun* an agreement between two armies or enemies to stop fighting for a time

② **truck** /trʌk/ *noun* a goods vehicle used for carrying heavy loads (*informal*) ○ *Trucks thundered past the house all night.* ○ *They loaded the truck with bricks.*

① **true** /truː/ *adj* **1.** correct according to facts or reality ○ *What he says is simply not true.* ○ *It's quite true that she comes from Scotland.* ○ *Is it true that he's been married twice?* ◊ **truth 2.** faithful or loyal ○ *an expression of true love* ○ *She's a true friend.* ◇ **to come true** to happen as was predicted ○ *Her forecast of bad storms came true.* ◇ **true to life** like things really are

truffle /ˈtrʌf(ə)l/ *noun* **1.** a type of round black edible fungus found under the earth near trees ○ *Specially trained pigs are trained to sniff out the best truffles.* **2.** a soft sweet made of chocolate, often flavoured with rum ○ *We bought our hosts a bottle of wine and a box of chocolate truffles.*

③ **truly** /ˈtruːli/ *adv* used for emphasis ○ *He truly believes that was what happened.* ○ *I'm truly grateful for all your help.* ○ *Do you love me, really and truly?*

trump card /ˈtrʌmp kɑːd/ *noun* an advantage which is kept ready for use in an emergency

trumpet /ˈtrʌmpɪt/ *noun* a brass musical instrument which is played by blowing, with three parts which you press with your fingers ○ *He plays the trumpet in the school orchestra.* ○ *She practises the trumpet in the evenings.*

truncheon /ˈtrʌntʃən/ *noun* a short, thick stick used by policemen as a weapon

trundle /ˈtrʌnd(ə)l/ (**trundles, trundling, trundled**) *verb* to push or roll along something heavy or to move in a heavy way

③ **trunk** /trʌŋk/ *noun* **1.** the thick stem of a tree ○ *Ivy was climbing up the trunk of the oak tree.* **2.** an elephant's long nose **3.** a large box for storing or sending clothes ○ *They sent a trunk of clothes in advance to the new house.*

trunk road /ˈtrʌŋk rəʊd/ *noun* a main road

trunks /trʌŋks/ *plural noun* shorts worn by a man when swimming

① **trust** /trʌst/ *verb* (**trusts, trusting, trusted**) to be confident that someone is reliable ○ *You can trust his instructions – he* *knows a lot about computers.* ○ *I wouldn't trust him farther than I could kick him.* ■ *noun* a belief that something will work well or that someone will do something [~in] ○ *Don't put too much trust in his navigating skills.* □ **to take something on trust** to take something without looking to see if it is all right ○ *We took his statement on trust.*

trustee /trʌ'stiː/ *noun* a person who administers a trust or who directs a charity or other public institution

trust fund /'trʌst fʌnd/ *noun* an investment fund which is managed on behalf of another person

trustworthy /'trʌstwɜːði/ *adj* who can be depended upon

① **truth** /truːθ/ *noun* being true; a true story [~about] ○ *The police are trying to work out the truth about what happened.* ○ *Do you think he is telling the truth?* ○ *I don't think there is any truth in his story.* ◊ **home truths**

truthful /'truːθf(ə)l/ *adj* **1.** who always tells the truth ○ *She's a very truthful child.* **2.** giving true facts ○ *To be truthful, I'm not quite sure where we are.* ○ *The young man gave a truthful account of what happened.*

① **try** /traɪ/ *verb* (**tries, trying, tried**) **1.** to make an effort to do something ○ *You have to try hard if you want to succeed.* ○ *Don't try to ride a motorbike if you've never ridden one before.* **2.** to test or to see if something is good ○ *I tried the new toothpaste and I didn't like the taste.* **3.** to hear a civil or criminal case in court ○ *The case will be tried by a judge and jury.* ■ *noun* (*plural* **tries**) an attempt to do something ○ *She's going to have a try at water skiing.* ○ *He had two tries before he passed his driving test.* □ **let's give it a try** let's see if it works

try on *phrasal verb* **1.** to put on a piece of clothing to see if it fits ○ *You must try the trousers on before you buy them.* ○ *Did you try on the shoes at the shop?* **2.** □ **to try it on** to try to trick someone (*informal*) ○ *Don't believe him – he's just trying it on.*

try out *phrasal verb* to test something, to see if it is good

trying /'traɪɪŋ/ *adj* annoying and difficult to deal with

T-shirt /'tiːʃɜːt/ *noun* another spelling of **teeshirt** ○ *She was wearing jeans and a T-shirt.* ○ *No wonder you're cold if you went out in just a T-shirt.*

tsp. *abbr* teaspoon

tub /tʌb/ *noun* **1.** a round container with straight sides, often used for growing plants ○ *a tub of daffodils* **2.** a small, round container for food, usually with a lid ○ *a tub of coleslaw* **3.** a bath

tuba /'tjuːbə/ *noun* a large bass brass instrument

③ **tube** /tjuːb/ *noun* **1.** a long pipe for carrying liquids or gas ○ *He was lying in a hospital bed with tubes coming out of his nose and mouth.* ○ *Air flows down this tube to the face mask.* **2.** a soft container for a soft substance like toothpaste, which you squeeze to get the substance out ○ *I forgot to pack a tube of toothpaste.* ○ *I need a tube of glue to mend the cup.* ○ *She bought a tube of mustard.* **3.** (*in London*) the underground railway system ○ *It's quicker to take the tube to Oxford Circus than to go by bus.* ○ *You'll have to go by bus because there's a tube strike.*

tuberculosis /tjʊˌbɜːkjʊ'ləʊsɪs/ *noun* an infectious disease caused by a bacillus, where infected lumps form in the lungs

tubing /'tjuːbɪŋ/ *noun* tubes in general

tuck /tʌk/ (**tucks, tucking, tucked**) *verb* to put something carefully into a narrow or small place ○ *She tucked the blanket around the baby.* ○ *He tucked the note into his shirt pocket.*

tuck in *phrasal verb* **1.** to fold something carefully around someone or something and push the ends in ○ *She tucked the baby in* or *She tucked the blanket in (around the baby).* **2.** to start eating enthusiastically ○ *The food's ready, everyone can tuck in.* ○ *We all tucked in to a huge lunch.*

tuck up /ˌtʌk 'ʌp/ *verb* to push the edge of the bedclothes around someone to keep them warm ○ *By eight o'clock the children were all tucked up in bed.*

Tues. *abbr* Tuesday

① **Tuesday** /'tjuːzdeɪ/ *noun* the second day of the week, the day between Monday and Wednesday ○ *I saw him in the office last Tuesday.* ○ *The club always meets on Tuesdays.* ○ *Shall we meet next Tuesday evening?* ○ *Today is Tuesday, April 30th.* ○ *The 15th is a Monday, so the 16th must be a Tuesday.* ○ *We went to the cinema last Tuesday.*

tuft /tʌft/ *noun* a small bunch of something like grass or feathers

tug /tʌg/ *verb* (**tugs, tugging, tugged**) to give something a sudden hard pull ○ *He tugged on the rope and a bell rang.* ■ *noun* a sudden pull ○ *He felt a tug on the line – he had caught a fish!*

tug-of-war /ˌtʌɡ əv ˈwɔː/ *noun* a bitter struggle between two sides ○ *After the divorce the children were caught in a tug-of-war between their parents.*

③ **tuition** /tjuˈɪʃ(ə)n/ *noun* the teaching of students

tulip /ˈtjuːlɪp/ *noun* a common spring bulb with flowers in brilliant colours, shaped like cups

tumble /ˈtʌmbəl/ (**tumbles, tumbling, tumbled**) *verb* to fall ○ *He tumbled down the stairs head first.* ○ *She arrived home late after the party and just tumbled into bed.* (NOTE: + **tumble** *n*)

tumbler /ˈtʌmblə/ *noun* a glass with a flat base and straight sides, used for serving drinks

tummy /ˈtʌmi/ (*plural* **tummies**) *noun* the stomach (*informal; children's language*)

tumour /ˈtjuːmə/ *noun* an unusual swelling or growth of new cells in the body (NOTE: The US spelling is **tumor**.)

tuna /ˈtjuːnə/ (*plural same* or **tunas**) *noun* a very large sea fish used for food

③ **tune** /tjuːn/ *noun* a series of musical notes which have a pattern ○ *He wrote some of the tunes for the musical.* ○ *She walked away whistling a little tune.*

tune in *phrasal verb* to adjust a radio so that it takes broadcasts from a particular station

tunic /ˈtjuːnɪk/ *noun* **1.** a long loose shirt ○ *She was wearing a matching tunic and skirt.* **2.** a short uniform jacket worn by soldiers, policemen and others ○ *The guardsmen spent hours polishing the buttons on their tunics.*

③ **tunnel** /ˈtʌn(ə)l/ *noun* a long passage under the ground ○ *The Channel Tunnel links Britain to France.* ○ *The road round Lake Lucerne goes through six tunnels.* ○ *They are digging a new tunnel for the underground railway.*

tunnel vision /ˌtʌn(ə)l ˈvɪʒ(ə)n/ *noun* **1.** seeing only the area immediately in front of the eye **2.** having the tendency to concentrate on only one aspect of a problem

turban /ˈtɜːbən/ *noun* a long piece of cloth worn wrapped round your head

turbine /ˈtɜːbaɪn/ *noun* a machine which produces power from the action of water, gas or steam turning a wheel with blades which runs a generator

turbulence /ˈtɜːbjʊləns/ *noun* a disturbance in air or water currents

turbulent /ˈtɜːbjʊlənt/ *adj* **1.** which is moving violently ○ *Watch out for turbulent water near the rocks.* **2.** likely to have riots or civil war ○ *It was a turbulent period in the country's history.*

turf /tɜːf/ *noun* **1.** an area of grass which is mown and looked after ○ *After the rain, the dry springy turf suddenly turned wet and sticky underfoot.* **2.** a piece of grass and soil which can be planted to form a lawn ○ *Make sure the ground is flat before laying the strips of turf.* ○ *It is quicker to lay turfs than to sow grass seed.*

③ **turkey** /ˈtɜːki/ *noun* a large farm bird, similar to a chicken but much bigger, often eaten at Christmas ○ *We had roast turkey and potatoes.* ○ *Who's going to carve the turkey?*

③ **Turkey** /ˈtɜːki/ *noun* a country in the eastern Mediterranean, south of the Black Sea (NOTE: capital: **Ankara**; people: **the Turks**; language: **Turkish**; currency: **Turkish lira**)

turmoil /ˈtɜːmɔɪl/ *noun* a state of disorder and confusion

① **turn** /tɜːn/ *noun* **1.** a change of direction, especially of a vehicle ○ *The bus made a sudden turn to the left.* ◊ **U-turn 2.** a road which leaves another road ○ *Take the next turn on the right.* ■ *verb* (**turns, turning, turned**) **1.** to go round in a circle ○ *The wheels of the train started to turn slowly.* ○ *Be careful – the machine goes on turning for a few seconds after it has been switched off.* **2.** to make something go round ○ *Turn the handle to the right to open the safe.* **3.** to change direction, to go in another direction ○ *Turn left at the next traffic lights.* ○ *The car turned the corner too fast and hit a lamppost.* ○ *The path turns to the right after the pub.* **4.** to move your head or body so that you face in another direction ○ *Can everyone turn to look at the camera, please.* **5.** to change into something different ○ *Leaves turn red or brown in the autumn.* ○ *When he was fifty, his hair turned grey.*

turn away *phrasal verb* **1.** to send people away ○ *The restaurant is full, so we have had to turn people away.* **2.** to turn so as not to face someone ○ *He turned away because he didn't want to be photographed.*

turn back③ *phrasal verb* **1.** to turn round and go back in the opposite direction **2.** to tell someone to go back ○ *The police tried to turn back the people who had no tickets.*

turn down *phrasal verb* **1.** to refuse something which is offered ○ *He was offered a* *job in Australia, but turned it down.* ○ *She has turned down a job* or *turned a job down in the town hall.* **2.** to make something less noisy or less strong ○ *Can you turn down the radio – I'm trying to work.* ○ *Turn down the gas* or *turn the gas down – the soup will burn.* **3.** to fold back a sheet on a bed, so that the pillow is uncovered

turn in *phrasal verb* **1.** to take someone or something to someone in authority ○ *Everyone was asked to turn in their guns.* ○ *He caught the thief and turned him in to the police.* **2.** to go to bed ○ *It's after eleven o'clock – time to turn in!*

turn into③ *phrasal verb* **1.** to change to become something different ○ *The witch turned the prince into a frog.* ○ *We are planning to turn this room into a museum.* **2.** to change direction and go into something ○ *We went down the main road for a short way and then turned into a little lane on the left.*

turn off *phrasal verb* **1.** to make a piece of electrical equipment stop working ○ *Don't forget to turn the TV off when you go to bed.* ○ *Turn off the lights* or *turn the lights off – father's going to show his holiday films.* **2.** to leave a road you are travelling on ○ *You can turn off the main street into one of the car parks.* ○ *Here's where we turn off.*

turn on *phrasal verb* **1.** to make a piece of electrical equipment start working ○ *Can you turn the light on* or *turn on the light – it's too dark to read.* **2.** to attack someone suddenly ○ *The dog suddenly turned on the girl.* ○ *The newspapers suddenly turned on the prime minister.*

turn out *phrasal verb* **1.** to force someone to go out ○ *They were turned out of their house when they couldn't pay the rent.* **2.** to produce or make ○ *The factory turns out more than 10,000 cars a week.* **3.** to switch off ○ *Please turn out all the lights* or *turn all the lights out before you go up to bed.* **4.** to happen in the end ○ *We got talking, and it turned out that she was at school with my brother.* ○ *The party didn't start very well, but everything turned out all right in the end.* **5.** to come out ○ *The whole town turned out to watch the cycle race.*

turn over *phrasal verb* **1.** to roll over ○ *The lorry went round the corner too fast and turned over.* ○ *Their boat turned over in the storm.* **2.** to show the other side ○ *He turned over the burger to see if it was done.* **3.** to have a certain amount of sales ○ *We turn over about three million pounds per annum.*

turn round③ *phrasal verb* to move your head or body so that you face in another direction

turn up③ *phrasal verb* **1.** to arrive ○ *The food was spoiled because half the guests didn't turn up until nine o'clock.* ○ *He turned up unexpectedly just as I was leaving the office.* **2.** to be found in a particular place ○ *The police searched everywhere, and the little girl finally turned up in Edinburgh.* ○ *The keys turned up in my trouser pocket.* **3.** to make something louder or stronger ○ *Can you turn up the radio* or *turn the radio up – I can't hear it.* ○ *Turn up the gas* or *turn the gas up, the potatoes aren't cooked yet.* **4.** to unfold ○ *To keep warm he turned up his coat collar.*

turnaround /ˈtɜːnəraʊnd/ *noun* same as **turnround**

③ **turning** /ˈtɜːnɪŋ/ *noun* a road which goes away from another road

turning point /ˈtɜːnɪŋ pɔɪnt/ *noun* the time when an important or decisive change takes place

turnip /ˈtɜːnɪp/ *noun* a common vegetable, with a round white root

turnout /ˈtɜːnaʊt/ *noun* a crowd of people who come to a show or a meeting ○ *The football match attracted only a small turnout.* ○ *There was a record turnout for the flower show.*

③ **turnover** /ˈtɜːnəʊvə/ *noun* the amount of sales of goods or services by a business ○ *Our turnover is rising each year.*

turnround /ˈtɜːnraʊnd/ *noun* the process of receiving orders and sending out goods (NOTE: The US term is **turnaround**.)

turnstile /ˈtɜːnstaɪl/ *noun* a little revolving gate which has a counter to record the number of people going through it

turntable /ˈtɜːnteɪb(ə)l/ *noun* a flat part of a record player which turns with the record on it ○ *I don't think the turntable is aligned correctly – the records seem to turn at the wrong speed.*

turquoise /ˈtɜːkwɔɪz/ *adj* blue-green ○ *I bought a pale turquoise silk dress to go to the wedding.* ○ *From the top of the cliff the sea looked turquoise in the sunshine.*

turret /ˈtʌrɪt/ *noun* **1.** a small tower ○ *From here, you can see the castle's pointed turrets.* **2.** a small armoured structure with a gun inside, on a ship or tank ○ *The turret of the tank swung round until the barrel of* *the gun was pointing directly at the president's palace.*

tusk /tʌsk/ *noun* the long tooth of some animals such as elephants and walruses

tussle /ˈtʌs(ə)l/ *noun* a fight or argument ○ *He got into a tussle with two men outside a pub.* ○ *After a short tussle with the manager she got a refund.* (NOTE: + **tussle** *v*)

tutor /ˈtjuːtə/ *noun* a teacher, especially a person who teaches only one student or a small group of students ○ *His first job was as private tutor to some German children.* ■ *verb* (**tutors, tutoring, tutored**) to teach a small group of students (*formal*) ○ *She earns extra money by tutoring foreign students in English.*

tutorial /tjuːˈtɔːriəl/ *noun* a teaching session between a tutor and one or more students

tuxedo /tʌkˈsiːdəʊ/ *noun US* a man's formal black or white jacket, worn with a bow tie

① **TV** /ˌtiː ˈviː/ *noun* a television ○ *They watch TV every night.* ○ *The TV news is usually at nine o'clock.* ○ *Some children's TV programmes are very dull.* ○ *The daughter of a friend of mine was on TV last night.*

twang /twæŋ/ *noun* a sound made when the string of a musical instrument or a taut wire is pulled and released ○ *You could hear the twang of his guitar.* ○ *There was a loud twang as the cable snapped.*

tweak /twiːk/ (**tweaks, tweaking, tweaked**) *verb* **1.** to pinch and pull with your finger and thumb ○ *She tweaked his nose.* **2.** to adjust something carefully ○ *With a little tweaking we got the graphics right.*

tweed /twiːd/ *noun* a usually rough woollen cloth made with strands of different coloured wool

tweezers /ˈtwiːzəz/ *plural noun* little metal pincers for pulling out a hair or splinter ○ *She pulled the hair out with her tweezers.*

① **twelfth** /twelfθ/ *adj* relating to number 12 in a series ■ *noun* number 12 in a series

① **twelve** /twelv/ *noun* the number 12

twentieth /ˈtwentiəθ/ *adj* relating to number 20 in a series (NOTE: With dates **twentieth** is usually written **20th**: *May 20th, 1921*; *June 20th, 1896* (American style is *20 June 1896*): say 'the twentieth of June' or 'June the twentieth' (American style is 'June twentieth').) ■ *noun* number 20 in a series

① **twenty** /ˈtwenti/ *noun* the number 20 (NOTE: **twenty-one (21), twenty-two (22)** etc., but **twenty-first (21st), twenty-second (22nd),** etc.) □ **twenties** the numbers between 20 and 29

twenty-first /ˈtwenti fɜːst/ *adj, noun* referring to 21

24/7 /ˌtwenti fɔː ˈsev(ə)n/ *adv* 24 hours a day, 7 days a week without stopping

20/20 vision /ˌtwenti twenti ˈvɪʒ(ə)n/ *noun* perfect eyesight

③ **twice** /twaɪs/ *adv* two times ○ *Turn it off – I've seen that programme twice already.* ○ *Twice two is four, twice four is eight.* ○ *I'm fifteen, she's thirty, so she's twice as old as I am.*

twiddle /ˈtwɪd(ə)l/ (**twiddles, twiddling, twiddled**) *verb* to twist something aimlessly ○ *She twiddled the knobs, hoping to find a German radio station.*

twig /twɪg/ *noun* a little branch of a tree or bush ○ *There is a bud at the end of each twig.* ○ *The bird made its nest of twigs and leaves.*

twilight /ˈtwaɪlaɪt/ *noun* a time when the light is weak, between sunset and night

③ **twin** /twɪn/ *adj, noun* one of two babies born at the same time to the same mother ○ *he and his twin brother* ○ *She's expecting twins.*

twin beds /ˌtwɪn ˈbedz/ *plural noun* two single beds placed in a bedroom

twinge /twɪndʒ/ *noun* a short sharp pain

twinkle /ˈtwɪŋkəl/ (**twinkles, twinkling, twinkled**) *verb* to shine with a little moving light ○ *His eyes twinkled as he showed the children the sweets he had bought.* ○ *We could see the lights of the harbour twinkling in the distance.* (NOTE: + **twinkle** *n*)

twirl /twɜːl/ (**twirls, twirling, twirled**) *verb* **1.** to twist something round in your hand ○ *I wish I could twirl a baton like those girls in the procession.* **2.** to spin round ○ *Models twirled round on the catwalk.* (NOTE: + **twirl** *n*)

③ **twist** /twɪst/ (**twists, twisting, twisted**) *verb* **1.** to wind something round something ○ *She twisted the string round a piece of stick.* **2.** to turn in different directions ○ *The path twisted between the fields.*

twitch /twɪtʃ/ (**twitches, twitching, twitched**) *verb* to make small movements of the muscles (NOTE: + **twitch** *n*)

2 /tuː/ *prep* to (*informal*)

① **two** /tuː/ *noun* the number 2 ◇ **to put two and two together** to draw a conclusion from something ○ *They put two and two together and decided she must be pregnant.*

2.1 /ˌtuːˈwʌn/ *noun* an upper second class university degree

2.2 /ˌtuːˈtuː/ *noun* a lower second class university degree

two-dimensional /ˌtuː daɪˈmenʃən(ə)l/ *adj* with two dimensions, flat

twofold /ˈtuːfəʊld/ *adv, adj* twice as much

two-time /ˈtuː taɪm/ *verb* to be unfaithful to your marriage partner or lover (*informal*)

tycoon /taɪˈkuːn/ *noun* a very rich businessman

tying /ˈtaɪɪŋ/ present participle of **tie**

① **type** /taɪp/ *noun* a group of people, animals or things that are similar to each other [~of] ○ *This type of bank account pays 10% interest.* ○ *What type of accommodation are you looking for?* ■ *verb* (**types, typing, typed**) to write with a computer or typewriter ○ *Please type your letters – your writing's so bad I can't read it.* ○ *She only typed two lines and made six mistakes.*

typeface /ˈtaɪpfeɪs/ *noun* a set of printed characters which have been designed with a certain style and have a certain name

typewriter /ˈtaɪpraɪtə/ *noun* a machine which prints letters or numbers on a piece of paper when keys are pressed

② **typical** /ˈtɪpɪk(ə)l/ *adj* having the usual qualities of a particular group or occasion ○ *Describe a typical day at school.* ○ *He's definitely not a typical bank manager.*

typify /ˈtɪpɪfaɪ/ (**typifies, typifying, typified**) *verb* to be a good example of something

typing /ˈtaɪpɪŋ/ *noun* the action of writing letters with a typewriter

typist /ˈtaɪpɪst/ *noun* a person whose job is to type letters on a typewriter

tyrant /ˈtaɪrənt/ *noun* a ruler who rules by force and fear

① **tyre** /ˈtaɪə/ *noun* a ring made of rubber which is put round a wheel ○ *Check the pressure in the car tyres before starting a journey.* ○ *They used an old tyre to make a seat for the garden swing.*

U

u /juː/, **U** *noun* the twenty-first letter of the alphabet, between T and V

ubiquitous /juː'bɪkwɪtəs/ *adj* which is or which seems to be everywhere

udder /'ʌdə/ *noun* a gland which produces milk, a bag which hangs under the body of a cow or female goat

UFO /juː ef 'əʊ, 'juːfəʊ/ *abbr* unidentified flying object

ugh /ʊx/ *interj* showing a feeling that something is unpleasant

② **ugly** /'ʌgli/ *adj* unpleasant to look at ○ *What an ugly pattern!* ○ *The part of the town round the railway station is even uglier than the rest.*

uh huh /ʌ 'hʌ/ *interj* showing that you agree or that you are listening

uh-oh /ʌ 'əʊ/ *interj* used as the written form of an exclamation made to express worry or a warning

UK *abbr* United Kingdom ○ *Exports from the UK* or *UK exports rose last year.*

ulcer /'ʌlsə/ *noun* an open sore on or inside the body

ulterior motive /ʌlˌtɪəriə 'məʊtɪv/ *noun* a hidden reason for doing something which will give you an advantage

③ **ultimate** /'ʌltɪmət/ *noun* the most valuable or desirable thing ○ *Our first-class cabins are the ultimate in travelling luxury.*

③ **ultimately** /'ʌltɪmətli/ *adv* in the end

ultimatum /ˌʌltɪ'meɪtəm/ *noun* a final demand, proposal sent to someone stating that unless he does something within a period of time, action will be taken

ultra- /ʌltrə/ *prefix* more than normal, excessively

ultrasonic /ˌʌltrə'sɒnɪk/ *adj* relating to frequencies above the range of human hearing

ultrasound /'ʌltrəsaʊnd/ *noun* a very high frequency sound wave, used to detect objects in the body or under water

um /ʌm/ *interj* showing that you are not sure what to say ○ *Um, perhaps it's – no I don't know the answer.*

umbilical cord /ʌm'bɪlɪk(ə)l kɔːd/ *noun* a cord which links the foetus to the placenta inside the womb

umbrage *noun* □ **take umbrage (at something)** to be offended by someone

③ **umbrella** /ʌm'brelə/ *noun* a round frame covered with cloth which you hold over your head to keep off the rain ○ *Can I borrow your umbrella?* ○ *As it was starting to rain, he opened his umbrella.* ○ *The wind blew my umbrella inside out.*

umpire /'ʌmpaɪə/ *noun* a person who acts as a judge in a game to see that the game is played according to the rules ○ *The umpire ruled that the ball was out.* ○ *He was disqualified for shouting at the umpire.* (NOTE: + **umpire** *v*)

umpteen /ˌʌmp'tiːn/ *adj* a large number (*informal*) ○ *I've been to France umpteen times.* ○ *There are umpteen forms to fill in.*

UN *abbr* United Nations ○ *UN peacekeeping forces are in the area.* ○ *The British Ambassador to the UN spoke in the debate.*

un- /ʌn/ *prefix* not

② **unable** /ʌn'eɪb(ə)l/ *adj* not able to do something ○ *I regret that I am unable to accept your suggestion.* ○ *She was unable to come to the meeting.* (NOTE: **be unable to** is a rather formal way of saying **can't**.)

unaccompanied baggage /ˌʌnəˌkʌmpənid 'bægɪdʒ/ *noun* cases which are sent by air, with no passenger travelling with them

unanimous /juː'nænɪməs/ *adj* with everyone agreeing

unasked /ʌn'ɑːskt/ *adj* without having been asked ○ *Our unasked questions would always remain so now.*

unassuming /ˌʌnə'sjuːmɪŋ/ *adj* quiet or modest

unattached /ˌʌnə'tætʃt/ *adj* not married, or not in a sexual relationship with anyone

unattainable /ˌʌnə'teɪnəb(ə)l/ *adj* impossible to achieve or reach

unattractive /ˌʌnəˈtræktɪv/ *adj* not attractive ○ *Her husband is a rather unattractive man.* ○ *The house is unattractive from the outside.*

unaware /ˌʌnəˈweə/ *adj* not knowing or realising something [~of/~that] ○ *He said he was unaware of any rule forbidding animals in the restaurant.* ○ *She walked out of the shop with her boyfriend, unaware that the photographers were waiting outside.*

unawares /ˌʌnəˈweəz/ *adv* without being expected ◇ **to catch someone unawares** to catch someone by surprise ○ *The TV cameras caught her unawares as she slept through the reception.* ○ *The security cameras caught him unawares as he was putting a packet in the rubbish bin.*

unbearable /ʌnˈbeərəb(ə)l/ *adj* so bad that you cannot accept it or deal with it

③ **unbelievable** /ˌʌnbɪˈliːvəb(ə)l/ *adj* which is difficult to believe

unbending /ʌnˈbendɪŋ/ *adj* not flexible in opinions or attitudes

unbiased /ʌnˈbaɪəst/ *adj* without any bias

unblock /ʌnˈblɒk/ (**unblocks, unblocking, unblocked**) *verb* to remove something that is stopping something from flowing

unborn /ʌnˈbɔːn/ *adj* not yet born

unbreakable /ʌnˈbreɪkəb(ə)l/ *adj* which cannot be broken

unbroken /ʌnˈbrəʊkən/ *adj* which has not been broken

unbutton /ʌnˈbʌt(ə)n/ (**unbuttons, unbuttoning, unbuttoned**) *verb* to undo buttons

uncalled-for /ʌnˈkɔːld fɔː/ *adj* not deserved

uncanny /ʌnˈkæni/ *adj* mysterious, which seems unnatural

uncaring /ʌnˈkeərɪŋ/ *adj* without having any sympathy

uncertain /ʌnˈsɜːt(ə)n/ *adj* not sure, or not decided ○ *She is uncertain whether to accept the job.* ○ *He's uncertain about what to do next.* ○ *Their plans are still uncertain.*

③ **uncle** /ˈʌŋk(ə)l/ *noun* a brother of your father or mother ○ *He was brought up by his uncle in Scotland.* ○ *We had a surprise visitor last night – old Uncle Charles.*

unclear /ʌnˈklɪə/ *adj* not clear

uncomfortable /ʌnˈkʌmftəb(ə)l/ *adj* not comfortable ○ *What a very uncomfortable bed!* ○ *Plastic seats are very uncomfortable in hot weather.*

uncommon /ʌnˈkɒmən/ *adj* strange or unusual

uncommunicative /ˌʌnkəˈmjuːnɪkətɪv/ *adj* not saying much, or not answering people

uncomplicated /ʌnˈkɒmplɪkeɪtɪd/ *adj* easy to deal with or understand ○ *In children's books, the writing should be clear and uncomplicated.* ○ *The procedure is relatively quick and uncomplicated.*

uncompromising /ʌnˈkɒmprəmaɪzɪŋ/ *adj* unwilling to give in or to change your ideas

unconcerned /ˌʌnkənˈsɜːnd/ *adj* not worried, not bothered

unconditional /ˌʌnkənˈdɪʃ(ə)nəl/ *adj* with no conditions attached

unconfirmed /ˌʌnkənˈfɜːmd/ *adj* which has not been confirmed

unconnected /ˌʌnkəˈnektɪd/ *adj* not related or connected to anything else or each other

③ **unconscious** /ʌnˈkɒnʃəs/ *adj* **1.** in a physical condition in which you are not aware of what is happening ○ *He was found unconscious in the street.* ○ *She was unconscious for two days after the accident.* **2.** not realising something [~of] ○ *He was quite unconscious of how funny he looked.* ■ *noun* □ **the unconscious** the part of the mind which stores thoughts, memories or feelings which you are not conscious of, but which influence what you do

uncontrolled /ˌʌnkənˈtrəʊld/ *adj* which has not been controlled

unconventional /ˌʌnkənˈvenʃ(ə)n(ə)l/ *adj* not usual

uncork /ʌnˈkɔːk/ (**uncorks, uncorking, uncorked**) *verb* to remove the cork from a bottle

uncountable /ʌnˈkaʊntəb(ə)l/ *adj* describing a noun that does not refer to a single object

uncover /ʌnˈkʌvə/ (**uncovers, uncovering, uncovered**) *verb* **1.** to take a cover off something ○ *Leaving the pots of jam uncovered will simply attract wasps.* **2.** to find something which was hidden ○ *They uncovered a secret store of gold coins.* ○ *The police have uncovered a series of secret financial deals.*

① **under** /ˈʌndə/ *prep* **1.** in or to a place where something else is on top or above ○ *We all hid under the table.* ○ *My pen rolled under the sofa.* **2.** less than a number ○ *The old table sold for under £10.* ○ *The train goes to Paris in under three hours.* ○ *Under half of the members turned up for the meet-*

ing. **3.** according to ○ *Under the terms of the agreement, the goods should be delivered in October.* ■ *adv* in a lower place

underage /ˌʌndərˈeɪdʒ/ *adj* younger than the legal age

underarm /ˈʌndərˌɑːm/ *noun* the area under the shoulder joint

undercarriage /ˈʌndəkærɪdʒ/ *noun* the landing gear of an aircraft, the aircraft's wheels and their supports

underclass /ˈʌndəklɑːs/ *noun* the lowest class in society

undercover /ˌʌndəˈkʌvə/ *adj* acting in disguise ○ *Two undercover policemen were sent to the night club to monitor the sale of drugs.* ■ *adv* in secret ○ *He was working undercover for the British government at the time.*

undercurrent /ˈʌndəkʌrənt/ *noun* **1.** a current of water under the surface **2.** hidden feelings

undercut /ˌʌndəˈkʌt/ (**undercuts, undercutting, undercut**) *verb* to sell more cheaply than someone

underdog /ˈʌndədɒg/ *noun* the person or team that is weaker, that is going to lose

underdone /ˌʌndəˈdʌn/ *adj* not cooked enough, or not overcooked

underestimate[1] /ˌʌndərˈestɪmət/ *noun* an estimate which is less than the actual figure ○ *The figure of £50,000 was a considerable underestimate.*

underestimate[2] /ˌʌndərˈestɪmeɪt/ (**underestimates, underestimating, underestimated**) *verb* to think that something is smaller or not as bad as it really is ○ *He underestimated the amount of time needed to finish the work.* ○ *Don't underestimate the intelligence of the average voter.*

underfund /ˌʌndəˈfʌnd/ (**underfunds, underfunding, underfunded**) *verb* to provide too little money to enable something to happen or operate satisfactorily

undergo /ˌʌndəˈgəʊ/ (**undergoes, undergoing, underwent, undergone**) *verb* to suffer, to have something happen to you

undergraduate /ˌʌndəˈgrædʒʊət/ *noun* a student at university who is studying for his or her first degree

underground[1] /ˌʌndəˈgraʊnd/ *adv* under the ground ○ *The ordinary railway line goes underground for a short distance.* ○ *Worms live all their life underground.* ■ *adj* built under the ground ○ *There's an underground passage to the tower.* ○ *The hotel has an underground car park.*

underground[2] /ˈʌndəgraʊnd/ *noun* a railway in a town, which runs under the ground ○ *Thousands of people use the underground to go to work.* ○ *Take the underground to go to Oxford Circus.* ○ *It's usually quicker to get across town by underground.* (NOTE: The London Underground is often called the **Tube**. In the United States, an underground railway is called a **subway**.)

undergrowth /ˈʌndəgrəʊθ/ *noun* plants which grow thickly under large trees

underhand /ˌʌndəˈhænd/ *adj* not honest

underlie /ˌʌndəˈlaɪ/ (**underlying, underlay, underlain**) *verb* to be beneath, to be the basic cause of something

③ **underline** (**underlines, underlining, underlined**) *verb* to write a line under a word or figure ○ *He wrote the title and then underlined it in red.*

③ **underlying** /ˌʌndəˈlaɪɪŋ/ *adj* which is the reason for everything

undermine /ˌʌndəˈmaɪn/ (**undermines, undermining, undermined**) *verb* to make weaker

② **underneath** /ˌʌndəˈniːθ/ *prep* under ○ *She wore a long green jumper underneath her coat.* ○ *Can you see if my pen is underneath the sofa?* ■ *adv* under ○ *He put the box of books down on the kitchen table and my sandwiches were underneath!*

underpants /ˈʌndəpænts/ *plural noun* men's short underwear for the part of the body from the waist to the top of the legs ○ *The doctor told him to strip down to his underpants.* ○ *His wife gave him a pair of bright red white and blue underpants for his birthday.*

underpass /ˈʌndəpɑːs/ *noun* a road which is built under another

underpin /ˌʌndəˈpɪn/ (**underpins, underpinning, underpinned**) *verb* to support

underprivileged /ˌʌndəˈprɪvɪlɪdʒd/ *adj* not having the same opportunities as other people

underrated /ˌʌndəˈreɪtɪd/ *adj* deserving to be valued more

③ **underscore** /ˌʌndəˈskɔː/ (**underscores, underscoring, underscored**) *verb* to emphasise

③ **undershirt** /ˈʌndəʃɜːt/ *noun US* a light piece of underclothing for the top half of the body (NOTE: The British term is **vest**.)

underside /ˈʌndəsaɪd/ *noun* a side that is underneath

① **understand** /ˌʌndəˈstænd/ (**understands, understanding, understood**) *verb* **1.** to know what something means ○ *Don't* *try to talk English to Mr Yoshida – he doesn't understand it.* **2.** to have sympathy for someone ○ *She's a good teacher – she really understands children.* **3.** to know why something happens or how something works [~how/why/what etc] ○ *I can easily understand why his wife left him.* ○ *I still don't understand how to operate the new laser printer.*

understandable /ˌʌndəˈstændəb(ə)l/ *adj* normal, which is easy to understand

③ **understanding** /ˌʌndəˈstændɪŋ/ *noun* **1.** the fact that someone understands something [~of] ○ *My understanding of how the Internet works is limited.* **2.** sympathy for someone else and their problems ○ *The aim is to promote understanding between the two countries.* **3.** a private agreement ○ *We reached an understanding with the lawyers.* ○ *The understanding was that we would all go to the office after lunch.* **4.** □ **on the understanding that** on condition that, provided that ○ *We accept the terms of the treaty, on the understanding that it has to be passed by Parliament.* ■ *adj* sympathetic ○ *His understanding attitude was much appreciated.*

understatement /ˈʌndəˌsteɪtmənt/ *noun* a statement which does not tell the facts forcefully enough

① **understood** /ˌʌndəˈstʊd/ past tense and past participle of **understand**

understudy /ˈʌndəstʌdi/ *noun* an actor who learns a part in the play so as to be able to act it if the usual actor cannot perform ○ *The understudy had to take over last night when the male lead fell and broke his arm.*

③ **undertake** /ˌʌndəˈteɪk/ (**undertakes, undertaking, undertook, undertaken**) *verb* **1.** to agree to do something ○ *He has undertaken to pay her £100 a week for twelve weeks.* **2.** to do something ○ *They undertook a survey of the market on our behalf.*

undertaker /ˈʌndəteɪkə/ *noun* a person who organises funerals

③ **undertaking** /ˈʌndəteɪkɪŋ/ *noun* **1.** a business ○ *The Post Office must be considered as a commercial undertaking, not as a public service.* **2.** a promise ○ *She gave him an undertaking that she would continue to work for a further six months.* ○ *They have given us a written undertaking that they will not play loud music after ten o'clock at night.* **3.** a large-scale job

undertone /ˈʌndətəʊn/ *noun* **1.** a quiet voice **2.** a hidden feeling

undertook /ˌʌndəˈtʊk/ past tense of **undertake**

underused /ˌʌndəˈjuːzd/ *adj* not used enough

undervalue /ˌʌndəˈvæljuː/ (**undervalues, undervaluing, undervalued**) *verb* to value at less than the true rate

underwater /ˌʌndəˈwɔːtə/ *adj* below the surface of the water ○ *How long can you stay underwater?* ○ *He dived and swam underwater for several seconds.* ○ *She goes on holiday to the Red Sea to do underwater photography.*

under way /ˌʌndə ˈweɪ/ *adv* in progress ○ *The show finally got under way after a lot of delays.*

③ **underwear** /ˈʌndəweə/ *noun* clothes worn next to your skin under other clothes (NOTE: no plural)

underweight /ˌʌndəˈweɪt/ *adj* not heavy enough, which weighs less than usual

③ **underwent** /ˌʌndəˈwent/ past tense of **undergo**

underworld /ˈʌndəwɜːld/ *noun* **1.** (*in mythology*) a place inhabited by the dead ○ *Orpheus went down into the Underworld to search for his wife.* **2.** the world of criminals ○ *The police superintendent is an expert on London's underworld gangs.*

undesirable /ˌʌndɪˈzaɪərəb(ə)l/ *adj* not wanted ○ *It's highly undesirable that they should build a factory in the national park.*

③ **undid** /ʌnˈdɪd/ past tense of **undo**

undies /ˈʌndiz/ *plural noun* underwear, especially women's underwear (*informal*) ○ *I've just washed my undies, I hope they'll be dry by the morning.*

③ **undo** /ʌnˈduː/ (**undoes, undoing, undid, undone**) *verb* to open something which is tied or fastened ○ *The first thing he did on getting home was to undo his tie.* ○ *Undo your top button if your collar is too tight.*

undoubtedly /ʌnˈdaʊtɪdli/ *adv* certainly

undress /ʌnˈdres/ (**undresses, undressing, undressed**) *verb* to take your clothes off

undressed /ʌnˈdrest/ *adj* having just taken off your clothes ○ *The children are getting undressed ready for bed.* ○ *Are you undressed yet?*

unearth /ʌnˈɜːθ/ (**unearths, unearthing, unearthed**) *verb* to dig up; to discover

uneasy /ʌnˈiːzi/ (**uneasier, uneasiest**) *adj* nervous and worried

② **unemployed** /ˌʌnɪm'plɔɪd/ *adj* without a job ○ *The government is encouraging unemployed teenagers to apply for training grants.*

② **unemployment** /ˌʌnɪm'plɔɪmənt/ *noun* a lack of work ○ *The unemployment figures* or *the figures for unemployment are rising.*

unemployment benefit /ˌʌnɪm 'plɔɪmənt ˌbenɪfɪt/ *noun* money paid by the government to someone who is unemployed

unending /ʌn'endɪŋ/ *adj* which is going on for ever, with no end

unenviable /ʌn'enviəb(ə)l/ *adj* difficult or unpleasant

unequal /ʌn'iːkwəl/ *adj* not equal ○ *The management was accused of applying unequal conditions to male and female employees.*

uneven /ʌn'iːv(ə)n/ *adj* not smooth or flat

unexpected /ˌʌnɪk'spektɪd/ *adj* which is surprising and not what was expected ○ *We had an unexpected visit from the police.* ○ *His failure was quite unexpected.*

unexpectedly /ˌʌnɪk'spektɪdli/ *adv* in an unexpected way

unfailing /ʌn'feɪlɪŋ/ *adj* which never changes, which is always there

③ **unfair** /ʌn'feə/ *adj* not fair ○ *It's unfair to expect her to do all the housework while her sisters don't lift a finger to help.*

unfairly /ʌn'feəli/ *adv* in an unfair way

unfairness /ʌn'feənəs/ *noun* lack of justice or fairness

unfamiliar /ˌʌnfə'mɪljə/ *adj* not knowing at all well

unfashionable /ʌn'fæʃ(ə)nəb(ə)l/ *adj* not fashionable

unfasten /ʌn'fɑːs(ə)n/ (**unfastens, unfastening, unfastened**) *verb* to undo a belt, tie or button etc. which is fastened

unfeeling /ʌn'fiːlɪŋ/ *adj* not caring or sympathetic

unfinished /ʌn'fɪnɪʃt/ *adj* which has not been finished

unfit /ʌn'fɪt/ *adj* not fit, not in good physical condition ○ *I used to play a lot of tennis but I've got unfit during the winter.* ○ *He's so unfit, he goes red in the face if he simply bends down to pick something up off the floor.*

unfold /ʌn'fəʊld/ (**unfolds, unfolding, unfolded**) *verb* **1.** to spread out something which is folded, such as a newspaper ○ *She unfolded the tablecloth and put it on the table.* **2.** (*of a story*) to become clear ○ *As the full extent of the disaster unfolded, so it became clear that the emergency services could not cope.*

unforgettable /ˌʌnfə'getəb(ə)l/ *adj* which cannot be forgotten

unforgivable /ˌʌnfə'gɪvəb(ə)l/ *adj* impossible to forgive

③ **unfortunate** /ʌn'fɔːtʃ(ə)nət/ *adj* which makes you sad ○ *It was very unfortunate that she couldn't come to see us.*

① **unfortunately** /ʌn'fɔːtʃ(ə)nətli/ *adv* which you wish was not true ○ *Unfortunately the train arrived so late that she missed the meeting.*

unfounded /ʌn'faʊndɪd/ *adj* without any basis in truth

unfriendly /ʌn'frendli/ (**unfriendlier, unfriendliest**) *adj* not acting like a friend

unfulfilled /ˌʌnfʊl'fɪld/ *adj* which has not been carried out

unfurl /ʌn'fɜːl/ (**unfurls, unfurling, unfurled**) *verb* to unroll like a flag

ungainly /ʌn'geɪnli/ *adj* moving without grace

ungracious /ʌn'greɪʃəs/ *adj* not well-mannered

ungrammatical /ˌʌngrə'mætɪk(ə)l/ *adj* using incorrect grammar

ungrateful /ʌn'greɪtf(ə)l/ *adj* not grateful

unhappily /ʌn'hæpɪli/ *adv* in a sad way

③ **unhappy** /ʌn'hæpi/ (**unhappier, unhappiest**) *adj* sad, not happy ○ *He's unhappy in his job because his boss is always criticising him.* ○ *She looked very unhappy when she came out of the hospital.* ○ *The children had an unhappy childhood.* (NOTE: + **unhappiness** *n*)

unhealthy /ʌn'helθi/ *adj* not healthy, especially often ill ○ *I thought her face was an unhealthy colour.*

unheard of /ʌn'hɜːd ɒv/ *adj* strange or odd

unhurried /ʌn'hʌrid/ *adj* done in a quiet, relaxed way

unicorn /'juːnɪkɔːn/ *noun* an imaginary animal, a white horse with one long, straight horn growing from the centre of its head

unidentified /ˌʌnaɪ'dentɪfaɪd/ *adj* which you do not recognise, which you cannot identify

unification /ˌjuːnɪfɪ'keɪʃ(ə)n/ *noun* the act of joining two countries together to form one. Compare **reunification**

③ **uniform** /ˈjuːnɪfɔːm/ *noun* special clothes worn by all members of an organisation or group ○ *He went to the fancy dress party dressed in a policeman's uniform.* ○ *Who are those people in French army uniform?* ○ *What colour is her school uniform?* ○ *The holiday camp staff all wear yellow uniforms.* ◇ **in uniform** wearing a uniform ○ *The policeman was not in uniform at the time.*

uniformed /ˈjuːnɪfɔːmd/ *adj* wearing a uniform

unify /ˈjuːnɪfaɪ/ (**unifies, unifying, unified**) *verb* to join separate countries or groups together to form a single one

unilateral /ˌjuːnɪˈlæt(ə)rəl/ *adj* done by one side only, not taken jointly

unimportant /ˌʌnɪmˈpɔːt(ə)nt/ *adj* not important

unintentional /ˌʌnɪnˈtenʃ(ə)n(ə)l/ *adj* which is not intended

uninterested /ʌnˈɪntrəstɪd/ *adj* not having any interest in something

① **union** /ˈjuːnjən/ *noun* the state of being joined together, or the process of joining together

③ **Union Jack** /ˌjuːnjən ˈdʒæk/ *noun* the national flag of the United Kingdom ○ *The Union Jack was flying over the embassy.* ○ *The streets were decorated with Union Jacks.*

② **unique** /juːˈniːk/ *adj* different to anything else and therefore the only on of its type ○ *The stamp is unique, and so is worth a great deal.* ○ *He's studying the unique vegetation of the island.*

unisex /ˈjuːnɪseks/ *adj* which can be used by both men and women

③ **unit** /ˈjuːnɪt/ *noun* **1.** one part of something larger ○ *If you pass three units of the course you can move to the next level.* **2.** one piece of furniture, such as a cupboard or set of shelves which can be matched with others ○ *The kitchen is designed as a basic set of units with more units which can be added later.* **3.** the amount used to measure something ○ *Kilos and pounds are units of weight.* **4.** a single number less than ten ○ *63 has six tens and three units.*

③ **unite** /juːˈnaɪt/ (**unites, uniting, united**) *verb* to join together into a single body

③ **united** /juːˈnaɪtɪd/ *adj* joined together as a whole ○ *Relief workers from various countries worked as a united team.* ○ *They were united in their desire to improve their working conditions.*

③ **unity** /ˈjuːnɪti/ *noun* being one whole

③ **universal** /ˌjuːnɪˈvɜːs(ə)l/ *adj* which is understood or experienced by everyone in the world ○ *There is a universal hope for peace in the region.*

③ **universe** /ˈjuːnɪvɜːs/ *noun* all space and everything that exists in it, including the earth, the planets and the stars

① **university** /ˌjuːnɪˈvɜːsɪti/ (*plural* **universities**) *noun* an educational institution where students study for degrees and where students and teachers do research ○ *You need to do well at school to be able to go to university.* ○ *My sister is at university.*

unjust /ʌnˈdʒʌst/ *adj* not fair

unkempt /ʌnˈkempt/ *adj* not looked after, especially referring to things which need cutting

unkind /ʌnˈkaɪnd/ (**unkinder, unkindest**) *adj* acting in an unpleasant way to someone ○ *It was unkind of him to keep talking about her weight.*

unkindness /ʌnˈkaɪndnəs/ *noun* the action of treating someone unpleasantly

② **unknown** /ʌnˈnəʊn/ *adj* not known ○ *She was killed by an unknown attacker.* ○ *The college received a gift of money from an unknown person.*

unleash /ʌnˈliːʃ/ (**unleashes, unleashing, unleashed**) *verb* to allow a violent force to become free ○ *The government's decision unleashed a wave of protests throughout the country.*

① **unless** /ənˈles/ *conj* except if ○ *Unless we hear from you within ten days, we will start legal action.* ○ *I think they don't want to see us, unless of course they're ill.*

③ **unlike** /ʌnˈlaɪk/ *adj, prep* **1.** totally different from ○ *He's quite unlike his brother.* **2.** not normal or typical □ **it is unlike him to be rude** he is not usually rude

② **unlikely** /ʌnˈlaɪkli/ *adj* **1.** not likely ○ *It's unlikely that many people will come to the show.* **2.** which is probably not true ○ *He trotted out some unlikely excuse about how his train ticket had been eaten by the dog.*

unlimited /ʌnˈlɪmɪtɪd/ *adj* with no limits

unload /ʌnˈləʊd/ (**unloads, unloading, unloaded**) *verb* to remove a load from a vehicle

③ **unlock** /ʌnˈlɒk/ (**unlocks, unlocking, unlocked**) *verb* to open something which was locked

unluckily /ʌnˈlʌkɪli/ *adv* with bad luck

unlucky /ʌnˈlʌki/ (**unluckier, unluckiest**) *adj* not lucky, or bringing bad luck

unnatural /ʌn'nætʃ(ə)rəl/ *adj* **1.** which is not as it is in nature ○ *His face was an unnatural blue colour.* **2.** which does not follow the usual pattern ○ *It seems unnatural that he should take his father to court.* ○ *Their behaviour seemed unnatural to me.*

③ **unnecessary** /ʌn'nesəs(ə)ri/ *adj* which is not needed, or which does not have to be done ○ *It is unnecessary for you to wear a suit to the party.* ○ *She makes a lot of unnecessary phone calls.*

unobtrusive /ˌʌnəb'truːsɪv/ *adj* not obvious; not easily noticed

unoccupied /ʌn'ɒkjʊpaɪd/ *adj* not being used by anyone

unofficial /ˌʌnə'fɪʃ(ə)l/ *adj* not approved by an administration or by people in power

unorthodox /ʌn'ɔːθədɒks/ *adj* not usual

unpack /ʌn'pæk/ (**unpacks, unpacking, unpacked**) *verb* to take things out of cases in which they were sent or carried

③ **unpleasant** /ʌn'plez(ə)nt/ *adj* not pleasant ○ *There's a very unpleasant smell in the kitchen.* ○ *Try not to be unpleasant to the waitress.* (NOTE: + **unpleasantly** *adv*; **unpleasantness** *n*)

unplug /ʌn'plʌɡ/ (**unplugs, unplugging, unplugged**) *verb* to remove a plug from a socket

unpopular /ʌn'pɒpjʊlə/ *adj* not liked by many people

unpredictable /ˌʌnprɪ'dɪktəb(ə)l/ *adj* which cannot be predicted or forecast

unprepared /ˌʌnprɪ'peəd/ *adj* not ready □ **unprepared to do something** not willing to do something ○ *The students are unprepared to pay the increased tuition fees.*

unprofessional /ˌʌnprə'feʃ(ə)n(ə)l/ *adj* not according to professional standards

unreal /ʌn'rɪəl/ *adj* not like the real world

unrealistic /ˌʌnrɪə'lɪstɪk/ *adj* not taking into account the true facts of a situation

unreasonable /ʌn'riːz(ə)nəb(ə)l/ *adj* not reasonable or fair

unrelated /ˌʌnrɪ'leɪtɪd/ *adj* **1.** not related, with no connection ○ *Two unrelated incidents occurred during the night.* ○ *The sudden increase in temperature is quite unrelated to her heart condition.* **2.** not belonging to the same family ○ *They have the same surname, but as far as I know are unrelated.*

unrest /ʌn'rest/ *noun* a situation where people protest to try to get political or industrial change

unroll /ʌn'rəʊl/ (**unrolls, unrolling, unrolled**) *verb* to undo something which is rolled up

unruly /ʌn'ruːli/ (**unrulier, unruliest**) *adj* wild, with no discipline

unsafe /ʌn'seɪf/ *adj* dangerous □ **to feel unsafe** to feel you are in danger ○ *She doesn't like to be alone at night, she says she feels unsafe.*

unsatisfactory /ˌʌnsætɪs'fækt(ə)ri/ *adj* not satisfactory

unscrew /ʌn'skruː/ (**unscrews, unscrewing, unscrewed**) *verb* **1.** to open by twisting a top which screws on ○ *The top of this bottle opens by unscrewing so you don't need a bottle opener.* **2.** to unfasten by taking out screws ○ *My screwdriver is much too big to unscrew the back of the TV.*

unscrupulous /ʌn'skruːpjʊləs/ *adj* not worrying too much about honesty

unseen /ʌn'siːn/ *adj* not seen, invisible

unselfish /ʌn'selfɪʃ/ *adj* thinking only of other people

unsettled /ʌn'set(ə)ld/ *adj* **1.** (*of weather*) which changes often ○ *Unsettled weather is forecast for the next few days.* **2.** not calm ○ *The present unsettled market shows no sign of becoming more stable.*

unsettling /ʌn'set(ə)lɪŋ/ *adj* which makes you nervous and worried

unshaven /ʌn'ʃeɪvən/ *adj* without having shaved

unsightly /ʌn'saɪtli/ *adj* very unpleasant to look at ○ *She has an unsightly scar on her face.*

unsociable /ʌn'səʊʃəb(ə)l/ *adj* not friendly, not wanting to meet other people

unsophisticated /ˌʌnsə'fɪstɪkeɪtɪd/ *adj* simple; not sophisticated

unsound /ʌn'saʊnd/ *adj* not based on fact or logic ○ *His reasoning is unsound.*

unstable /ʌn'steɪb(ə)l/ *adj* **1.** not secure or firm ○ *The platform had become unstable.* **2.** likely to change suddenly ○ *The economic situation has become very unstable.* ○ *Neighbouring states were worried that the unstable military regime could be overthrown.* **3.** with a mental state that is likely to change quickly

unsteady /ʌn'stedi/ *adj* not steady; wobbly

unsubscribe /ˌʌnsəb'skraɪb/ *verb* to ask not to receive something any longer

unsubstantiated /ˌʌnsəb'stænʃieɪtɪd/ *adj* not having any supporting evidence

③ **unsuccessful** /ˌʌnsək'sesf(ə)l/ *adj* which does not succeed

unsuitable /ʌn'suːtəb(ə)l/ *adj* not suitable

unsure /ʌn'ʃʊə/ *adj* not sure ○ *She was unsure whether to go to work or to stay at home.* ○ *I'm unsure as to which route is the quickest.*

untangle /ʌn'tæŋg(ə)l/ (**untangles, untangling, untangled**) *verb* **1.** to separate and free from tangles **2.** to make simpler and clearer

untidy /ʌn'taɪdi/ (**untidier, untidiest**) *adj* not tidy

untie /ʌn'taɪ/ (**unties, untying, untied**) *verb* to open something which is tied with a knot

① **until** /ʌn'tɪl/ *conj* up to the time when ○ *She was perfectly well until she ate the strawberries.* ○ *He blew his whistle until the police came.* ■ *prep, conj* up to the time when ○ *I don't expect to be back until after ten o'clock.* ○ *Until yesterday, I felt very well.*

untold /ʌn'təʊld/ *adj* very large; so large that it cannot be counted ○ *The lottery offers people the possibility of untold wealth.* ○ *The new treatment should help untold numbers of asthma sufferers.*

untrue /ʌn'truː/ *adj* not true

untruth /ʌn'truːθ/ *noun* a lie (*literary*) ○ *His statement was an untruth.*

② **unusual** /ʌn'juːʒʊəl/ *adj* not normal or expected ○ *It is unusual to have rain at this time of year.* ○ *She chose a very unusual colour scheme for her sitting room.*

unveil /ʌn'veɪl/ (**unveils, unveiling, unveiled**) *verb* **1.** to take a cover off something, to open it formally ○ *The statue was unveiled by the mayor.* **2.** to reveal details of a new plan etc. ○ *The committee will unveil its proposals next week.*

③ **unwell** /ʌn'wel/ *adj* in a bad state of health (NOTE: not used before a noun: *the baby was unwell* but *a sick baby*)

unwieldy /ʌn'wiːldi/ *adj* large and awkward

unwilling /ʌn'wɪlɪŋ/ *adj* not wanting to do something

unwind /ʌn'waɪnd/ (**unwinds, unwinding, unwound**) *verb* **1.** to undo something which has been wound ○ *Pull to unwind the flex – it will rewind automatically when you press the red button.* **2.** to relax ○ *Gardening at the weekend helps him to unwind.*

unwise /ʌn'waɪz/ *adj* rash or not prudent; not wise

unworkable /ʌn'wɜːkəb(ə)l/ *adj* which will not work

unwound /ʌn'waʊnd/ past tense and past participle of **unwind**

unwrap /ʌn'ræp/ (**unwraps, unwrapping, unwrapped**) *verb* to take the wrapping off something

unzip /ʌn'zɪp/ (**unzips, unzipping, unzipped**) *verb* to undo a zip fastener

① **up** /ʌp/ *adv* **1.** in or to a high place ○ *Put your hands up above your head.* ○ *What's the cat doing up there on the cupboard?* (NOTE: **up** is often used after verbs: *to keep up, to turn up.*) **2.** to a higher position ○ *His temperature went up suddenly.* ○ *The price of petrol seems to go up every week.* **3.** not in bed ○ *The children were still up when they should have been in bed.* ○ *They stayed up all night watching films on TV.* ○ *He got up at six because he had an early train to catch.* ○ *It's past eight o'clock – you should be up by now.* **4.** completely, entirely ○ *The puddles dried up quickly in the sun.* **5.** happening in an unpleasant or dangerous way ○ *Something's up – the engine has stopped!* ■ *prep* **1.** in or to a high place ○ *They ran up the stairs.* ○ *She doesn't like going up ladders.* **2.** along ○ *Go up the street to the traffic lights and then turn right.* ○ *The house is about two hundred metres up the road.* ◇ **what's up?** what's the matter? ◇ **what's up with him?** what is the matter with him? ○ *What's up with the cat? – It won't eat anything.*

③ **up-and-coming** /ˌʌp ən 'kʌmɪŋ/ *adj* becoming fashionable and likely to succeed

upbeat /'ʌpbiːt/ *adj* feeling optimistic and happy (*informal*) ○ *The conference ended on a very upbeat note.* ○ *We're all very upbeat about the potential sales of the new model.*

③ **upbringing** /'ʌpbrɪŋɪŋ/ *noun* the way a child is brought up

upcoming /'ʌpkʌmɪŋ/ *adj* approaching soon, forthcoming

update[1] /'ʌpdeɪt/ *noun* the latest information ○ *The manager gave us an update on the latest sales figures.*

update[2] /ʌp'deɪt/ (**updates, updating, updated**) *verb* to add the latest information to something so that it is quite up-to-date ○ *She was asked to update the telephone list.* ○ *The figures are updated annually.* ○ *They have updated their guidebook to Greece to include current prices.*

upend /ʌp'end/ (**upends, upending, upended**) *verb* to turn something over on its end

③ **up front** /ˌʌp 'frʌnt/ *adv* in advance

upgrade /ʌp'greɪd/ *verb* (**upgrades, upgrading, upgraded**) **1.** to improve the quality or performance of something such as a computer **2.** to give someone a higher position or better facilities ■ *noun* software or equipment that will make a computer system more powerful or up to date

upheaval /ʌp'hiːv(ə)l/ *noun* a great change

uphold /ʌp'həʊld/ (**upholds, upholding, upheld**) *verb* to reject an appeal and support an earlier judgment ○ *The appeal court upheld the decision of the lower court.*

upholstery /ʌp'həʊlst(ə)ri/ *noun* covers for chairs; padded seats and cushions ○ *The upholstery matches the colour scheme in the sitting-room.*

upkeep /'ʌpkiːp/ *noun* **1.** the cost and process of keeping property such as a house, garden or car in good order **2.** the cost of paying for children's clothes, food, etc.

upload /'ʌpˌləʊd/ (**uploads, uploading, uploaded**) *verb* to send information or programs from your computer to a larger system, e.g. over the Internet

up-market /ʌp 'mɑːkɪt/ *adj* more expensive, appealing to the wealthy section of the market

① **upon** /ʌ'pɒn/ *prep* **1.** on ○ *The church was built upon a grassy hill.* **2.** likely to happen soon ○ *The summer holidays will soon be upon us again.*

② **upper** /'ʌpə/ *adj* higher or further up ○ *The upper slopes of the mountain are covered in snow.* ○ *He had a rash on his right upper arm.*

upper case /ˌʌpə'keɪs/ *noun* (*in printing*) capital letters

uppermost /'ʌpəməʊst/ *adj* **1.** highest ○ *The birds are nesting in the uppermost branches of the apple tree.* **2.** most important ○ *Which plan has the uppermost significance for you?* ■ *adv* in the top position ○ *Carry the box with this side uppermost.* ○ *Which side of the painting should be uppermost?*

③ **upright** /'ʌpraɪt/ *adj* straight up ○ *He got dizzy as soon as he stood upright.* ○ *Put the backs of your seats into the upright position for landing.* ○ *She picked up the vase and placed it upright on the table.*

uprising /'ʌpraɪzɪŋ/ *noun* a rebellion or revolt

uproar /'ʌprɔː/ *noun* **1.** a loud noise **2.** angry criticism by a lot of people ○ *There was an uproar over the increase in fares.*

uproot /ʌp'ruːt/ (**uproots, uprooting, uprooted**) *verb* **1.** to pull a plant out of the ground with its roots ○ *Everywhere you could see trees uprooted by the storm.* **2.** to make a family move to a totally new area ○ *Families were uprooted from their homes and taken to camps many miles away.*

upset[1] /ʌp'set/ *adj* very worried or unhappy ○ *His parents get upset if he comes home late.* ■ *verb* (**upsets, upsetting, upset**) **1.** to make someone worried or unhappy ○ *Don't upset your mother by telling her you're planning to go to live in Russia.* **2.** to knock something over ○ *He upset all the coffee cups.*

upset[2] /'ʌpset/ *noun* **1.** an unexpected defeat ○ *There was a major upset in the tennis tournament when the number three seed was beaten in the first round.* **2.** a slight illness because of something you have eaten or drunk ○ *a stomach upset*

upsetting /ʌp'setɪŋ/ *adj* which causes you to feel worried, unhappy or anxious

upshot /'ʌpʃɒt/ *noun* a result

upside /'ʌpsaɪd/ *noun* the positive side of a situation

③ **upside down** /ˌʌpsaɪd 'daʊn/ *adv* with the top underneath ○ *Don't turn the box upside down – all the papers will fall out.* ○ *The car shot off the road and ended up upside down in a ditch.* ○ *Bats were hanging upside down from the branches.*

upstage /ʌp'steɪdʒ/ (**upstages, upstaging, upstaged**) *verb* to take attention away from someone who should be more important ○ *In last night's performance, the prima ballerina was completely upstaged by the youngest dancer.*

② **upstairs** /ˌʌp'steəz/ *adv* on or to the upper part of something, e.g. a building or bus ○ *She ran upstairs with the letter.* ○ *I left my glasses upstairs.* ○ *Let's go upstairs onto the top deck – you can see London much better.* ■ *adj* on the upper floors of a building ○ *We have an upstairs kitchen.* ○ *We let the one of the upstairs offices to an accountant.*

upstart /'ʌpstɑːt/ *noun* an inexperienced person who has just started a job and feels he knows everything about it

upsurge /'ʌpsɜːdʒ/ *noun* a sudden increase

uptake /ˈʌpteɪk/ ◇ **slow *or* quick on the uptake** slow or quick to understand

uptight /ʌpˈtaɪt/ *adj* nervous and angry (*informal*)

② **up to date** /ˌʌp tə ˈdeɪt/, **up-to-date** *adv* with the latest information ○ *I keep myself up to date on the political situation by reading the newspaper every day.*

up-to-the-minute /ˌʌp tə ðə ˈmɪnɪt/ *adj* very recent

uptown /ˈʌptaʊn/ *adv US* in or to the outer residential parts of a town

upturn /ˈʌptɜːn/ *noun* a movement towards higher sales or profits

③ **upward** /ˈʌpwəd/ *adj* moving towards a higher level ○ *The spacecraft's engines generate enormous upward thrust.* ■ *adv US* same as **upwards**

③ **upwards** /ˈʌpwədz/ *adv* towards the top ○ *The path went upwards for a mile then levelled off.*

uranium /jʊˈreɪniəm/ *noun* a radioactive metal used in producing atomic energy

② **urban** /ˈɜːbən/ *adj* **1.** relating to towns ○ *They enjoy an urban lifestyle.* **2.** living in towns ○ *The urban fox has become a menace in parts of London.*

urbane /ɜːˈbeɪn/ *adj* having an easy relaxed manner

③ **urge** /ɜːdʒ/ *noun* a strong wish to do something ○ *She felt an urge to punch him on the nose.* ■ *verb* (**urges, urging, urged**) to advise someone strongly to do something ○ *He urged her to do what her father said.*

urgency /ˈɜːdʒənsi/ *noun* the fact of being very important or needing to be done quickly

③ **urgent** /ˈɜːdʒənt/ *adj* which is important and needs to be done quickly ○ *He had an urgent message to go to the police station.* ○ *She had an urgent operation.* ○ *The leader of the council called an urgent meeting.* ○ *This parcel is urgent and needs to get there tomorrow.*

urinate /ˈjʊərɪneɪt/ (**urinates, urinating, urinated**) *verb* to pass waste liquid from the body

urine /ˈjʊərɪn/ *noun* a yellowish liquid which is passed out of the body, containing water and waste matter

URL /ˌjuː ɑː ˈel/ *abbr* Uniform Resource Locator

urn /ɜːn/ *noun* a very large vase

① **us** /əs, ʌs/ *object pronoun* meaning me and other people ○ *Mother gave us each 50p to buy ice cream.* ○ *Who's there? – It's us!* ○ *The company did well last year – the management have given us a bonus.*

usable /ˈjuːzəb(ə)l/ *adj* which can be used

③ **usage** /ˈjuːsɪdʒ/ *noun* **1.** a way of using a word ○ *It is a technical term that is now in common usage.* ○ *The book clearly explains common legal terms and their usage.* **2.** the amount of something that is used ○ *Our usage of electricity is too high.*

use[1] /juːz/ (**uses, using, used**) *verb* **1.** to take something such as a tool and do something with it ○ *Did you use a sewing machine to make your curtains?* ○ *The car's worth quite a lot of money – it's hardly been used.* ○ *Do you know how to use a computer?* ○ *Can I use this knife for cutting meat?* **2.** to take a substance and do something with it ○ *Don't use the tap water for drinking.* ○ *Does this car use much petrol?* ○ *Turn down the heating – we're using too much gas.*

use up① *phrasal verb* to use all of something

use[2] /juːs/ *noun* **1.** a purpose ○ *Can you find any use for this piece of cloth?* **2.** the fact of being used ○ *The coffee machine has been in daily use for years.* ◇ **to make use of something** to use something ○ *You should make more use of your bicycle.*

① **used** /juːzd/ *adj* which is not new ○ *a shop selling used clothes* ○ *a used-car salesman*

① **used to** /ˈjuːzt tuː/ *adj* **1.** □ **to be used to something *or* to doing something** not to worry about doing something, because you do it often ○ *Farmers are used to getting up early.* ○ *We're used to hard work in this office.* ○ *I'm not used to eating such a large meal at lunchtime.* **2.** showing that something happened often or regularly in the past ○ *There used to be lots of small shops in the village until the supermarket was built.* ○ *When we were children, we used to go to France every year for our holidays.* ○ *The police think he used to live in London.* ○ *He used not to smoke a pipe.* (NOTE: The forms used in the negative and questions: *He used to work in London, He didn't use to work in London* or *He used not to work in London, Didn't he use to work in London?*)

① **useful** /ˈjuːsf(ə)l/ *adj* who or which can help you do something ○ *I find these scissors very useful for opening letters.* ○ *She's a very useful person to have in the office.* □ **to make yourself useful** to do something to help

③ **useless** /ˈjuːsləs/ *adj* which is not useful

③ **user** /ˈjuːzə/ *noun* a person who uses a tool or a service ○ *We have mailed the users of our equipment about the possible design fault.*

user-friendly /ˌjuːzə ˈfrendli/ *adj* easy to use without special training

username /ˈjuːzəneɪm/ *noun* a name which you use when operating a computer program

usher /ˈʌʃə/ *noun* a man who shows people to their seats in a cinema or at a wedding

usher in *phrasal verb* **1.** to bring someone in ○ *They were ushered into the chairman's office.* **2.** to be the beginning of ○ *The end of the war ushered in a period of great prosperity.*

② **usual** /ˈjuːʒuəl/ *adj* done or used on most occasions ○ *She took her usual bus to the office.* ○ *Is it usual for him to arrive so late?*

① **usually** /ˈjuːʒuəli/ *adv* in most cases or on most occasions

usurp /juːˈzɜːp/ (**usurps, usurping, usurped**) *verb* to take and use a right which is not yours, especially to take the throne from a king

utensil /juːˈtens(ə)l/ *noun* a tool or object used when cooking ○ *knives, bowls and other kitchen utensils*

uterus /ˈjuːt(ə)rəs/ *noun* the hollow organ in a woman's body where a fertilised egg is lodged and an unborn baby is carried (*technical*)

utilise /ˈjuːtɪlaɪz/ (**utilises, utilising, utilised**), **utilize** *verb* to use something (*formal*) ○ *He's keen to utilise his programming skills.*

utmost /ˈʌtməʊst/ *noun* the greatest action possible ○ *They did their utmost to save the children from the fire.*

utopia /juːˈtəʊpiə/, **Utopia** *noun* an imaginary perfect world

utter /ˈʌtə/ (**utters, uttering, uttered**) *verb* to speak; to make a sound ○ *She only uttered a few words during the whole evening.*

③ **utterance** /ˈʌt(ə)rəns/ *noun* something which is said

utterly /ˈʌtəli/ *adv* completely

③ **U-turn** /ˈjuː tɜːn/ *noun* **1.** the act of turning round to go back in the opposite direction ○ *The police car did* or *made a U-turn and went back to the hotel.* ○ *U-turns are not allowed on motorways.* **2.** a complete change in policy

V

v[1] /ˈvɜːsəs, viː/ *abbr* versus

v[2] /viː/, **V** *noun* the twenty-second letter of the alphabet, between U and W. ◊ **V-neck**

V /viː/ *noun* the Roman numeral for five or fifth ○ *King George V*

③ **vacancy** /ˈveɪkənsi/ *noun* **1.** a job for which there is no employee [~for] ○ *We advertised a vacancy for a receptionist in the local paper.* **2.** a room in a hotel which is available to stay in ○ *All the hotels had signs saying 'No vacancies'.*

③ **vacant** /ˈveɪkənt/ *adj* empty and available for you to use ○ *There are six rooms vacant in the new wing of the hotel.* ○ *Is the toilet vacant yet?*

vacate /vəˈkeɪt/ (**vacates, vacating, vacated**) *verb* to leave something empty

② **vacation** /vəˈkeɪʃ(ə)n/ *noun* **1.** *especially US* a holiday ○ *The family went on vacation in Canada.* **2.** a period when the universities and law courts are closed ○ *I'm spending my vacation working on a vineyard in Italy.*

vaccinate /ˈvæksɪneɪt/ (**vaccinates, vaccinating, vaccinated**) *verb* to use a vaccine to give a person immunisation against a specific disease [~against] ○ *Make sure you are vaccinated before you travel to Africa.* ○ *She was vaccinated against smallpox as a child.*

vaccine /ˈvæksiːn/ *noun* a substance which contains the germs of a disease and which is injected into a patient to prevent him or her from catching the disease

vacuum /ˈvækjuəm/ *noun* **1.** a space which is completely empty of all matter, including air ○ *The experiment has to be carried out in a vacuum.* **2.** *US* same as **vacuum cleaner** ■ *verb* (**vacuums, vacuuming, vacuumed**) to clean a carpet or a room using a vacuum cleaner ○ *She vacuums the hall every day.* ○ *I must vacuum the living room before my mother arrives.*

③ **vacuum cleaner** /ˈvækjuəm ˌkliːnə/ *noun* a machine which cleans by sucking up dust

vacuum flask /ˈvækjuəm flɑːsk/ *noun* a type of bottle which keeps liquids hot or cold (NOTE: also commonly called by a trade name, **thermos**)

vagina /vəˈdʒaɪnə/ *noun* a passage in a female body connecting the uterus to the vulva and through which a baby is born

vagrant /ˈveɪgrənt/ *noun* a tramp, a person who travels from place to place with no home or work

③ **vague** /veɪg/ *adj* with no details

vain /veɪn/ *adj* very proud of your appearance or achievements ○ *He's always combing his hair – he's very vain.* (NOTE: Do not confuse with **vein**.)

valentine /ˈvæləntaɪn/ *noun* the person you say you love particularly (*old*) ○ *He asked her to be his valentine.*

Valentine's Day /ˈvæləntaɪnz deɪ/ *noun* 14th February, a day when people send cards and flowers to loved ones

valet /ˈvælɪt/ *noun* **1.** a servant who looks after a man's clothes **2.** a person who parks your car at a restaurant or hotel

valiant /ˈvæliənt/ *adj* brave

③ **valid** /ˈvælɪd/ *adj* **1.** which can be lawfully used for a particular time ○ *Travellers must have a valid ticket before boarding the train.* ○ *I have a season ticket which is valid for one year.* ○ *He was carrying a valid passport.* **2.** which is acceptable because it is true ○ *That is not a valid argument* or *excuse.* ○ *She made several valid points in her speech.*

validate /ˈvælɪdeɪt/ (**validates, validating, validated**) *verb* **1.** to check to see if something is correct ○ *The document has to be validated by the bank.* **2.** to make something valid ○ *The ticket has to be stamped to validate it.* **3.** to certify officially that something is acceptable ○ *The new course has not yet been validated by the academic board.*

③ **valley** /ˈvæli/ *noun* a long piece of low land through which a river runs ○ *Fog forms in the valleys at night.* ○ *A lot of com-*

puter companies are based in the Thames Valley.

③ **valuable** /'væljʊəb(ə)l/ *adj* **1.** worth a lot of money ○ *Be careful, that glass is valuable!* ○ *The burglars stole everything that was valuable.* **2.** useful or helpful ○ *She gave me some very valuable advice.*

valuables /'væljʊəb(ə)lz/ *plural noun* items which are worth a lot of money ○ *You can deposit valuables in the hotel safe.*

③ **valuation** /ˌvælju'eɪʃ(ə)n/ *noun* **1.** an estimate of the worth of something ○ *A £350 valuation for this ring is much too low.* **2.** the act of estimating the worth of something ○ *At the end of a financial year, we have to do a stock valuation.* ○ *We asked for a valuation of the property* or *for a property valuation.*

① **value** /'vælju:/ *noun* an amount of money which something is worth ○ *the fall in the value of the yen* ○ *He imported goods to the value of £500.* ○ *Items of value can be deposited in the hotel safe overnight.* ■ *verb* (**values, valuing, valued**) to consider something as being valuable ○ *She values her friendship with him.* ◇ **good value (for money)** a bargain, something which is worth the price paid for it ○ *That restaurant gives value for money.* ○ *Holidays in Italy are good value because of the exchange rate.*

values /'vælju:z/ *plural noun* principles, important things in life ○ *He's a believer in traditional family values.*

valve /vælv/ *noun* a device in a tube which allows liquid or air to pass through in one direction only

vampire /'væmpaɪə/ *noun* an evil person who supposedly sucks blood from his or her victims

③ **van** /væn/ *noun* a covered goods vehicle ○ *A delivery van ran into the back of my car.* ○ *Our van will call this afternoon to pick up the goods.*

vandal /'vænd(ə)l/ *noun* a person who takes pleasure in destroying property, especially public property

vandalism /'vændəˌlɪz(ə)m/ *noun* the meaningless destruction of property

vanilla /və'nɪlə/ *noun* a flavouring made from the seed pods of a tropical plant

vanish /'vænɪʃ/ (**vanishes, vanishing, vanished**) *verb* to disappear suddenly ○ *The magician made the rabbit vanish.*

vanity /'vænɪti/ *noun* the fact of being excessively proud of your appearance, feeling that you are very handsome or beautiful

vantage point /'vɑ:ntɪdʒ ˌpɔɪnt/ *noun* a place from which you can see well

vapour /'veɪpə/ *noun* a substance in the form of a gas, usually caused by heating (NOTE: The US spelling is **vapor**.)

variable /'veəriəb(ə)l/ *noun* a thing which varies ○ *We have to take a great many variables into account.*

variance /'veəriəns/ *noun* the amount of difference between two things ◇ **to be at variance with something** not to agree or to be slightly different from something ○ *The actual sales are at variance with the sales reported by the reps.*

variant /'veəriənt/ *noun* the spelling of a word or name which is slightly different

② **variation** /ˌveəri'eɪʃ(ə)n/ *noun* a change from one state or level to another ['~in] ○ *The variation in colour* or *the colour variation is because the cloth has been dyed by hand.*

② **varied** /'veərɪd/ *adj* made up of different sorts and kinds

① **variety** /və'raɪəti/ (*plural* **varieties**) *noun* **1.** frequent differences or changes that make something interesting ○ *Her new job, unlike the old one, doesn't lack variety.* □ **a variety of things or people** a lot of different sorts of things or people ○ *She's had a variety of boyfriends.* ○ *We had a variety of visitors at the office today.* ○ *We couldn't go on holiday this year for a variety of reasons.* **2.** a different type of plant or animal in the same species ○ *Do you have this new variety of rose?* ○ *Is this a new variety of potato?* ◇ **variety is the spice of life** if you meet lots of different people, visit lots of different places, etc., then this makes your life exciting

① **various** /'veəriəs/ *adj* several different ○ *The shop sells goods from various countries.* ○ *I'll be out of the office today – I have to see various suppliers.*

variously /'veəriəsli/ *adv* in different ways

varnish /'vɑ:nɪʃ/ *noun* a liquid which when painted on something gives it a shiny surface ○ *He applied two coats of varnish to the door.* ■ *verb* (**varnishes, varnishing, varnished**) to paint something with a liquid varnish, to give a shiny surface to something ○ *Can you varnish our front door?*

② **vary** /'veəri/ (**varies, varying, varied**) *verb* **1.** to change what you do often ○ *The temperature varies from 8 degrees C at night to 18 degrees C during the day.* **2.** to be different [~from] ○ *Prices of flats vary from a few thousand pounds to millions.*

③ **vase** /vɑːz/ *noun* a container used for cut flowers, or simply for decoration

vasectomy /və'sektəmi/ *noun* a surgical operation to sterilise a man

② **vast** /vɑːst/ *adj* extremely big, often extremely wide ○ *A vast area of the region was affected by the flood.* ○ *There are vast differences in price between the two shops.*

vastly /'vɑːstli/ *adv* very much

vat /væt/ *noun* a large container for liquids

① **VAT** /ˌviː eɪ 'tiː, væt/ *abbr* value added tax ○ *VAT is an indirect tax.* ○ *The invoice includes VAT at 17.5%.* ○ *Hotels and restaurants have to charge VAT like any other business.* ○ *In Britain there is no VAT on books.*

vault /vɔːlt/ *noun* **1.** an arched stone ceiling ○ *The 11th-century vault of the chapel in the Tower of London.* **2.** an underground room for burying people ○ *She is buried in the family vault.* **3.** a high jump

VCR /ˌviː siː 'ɑː/ *abbr* video cassette recorder

VDU *abbr* visual display unit

've /əv/ *short form* have

veal /viːl/ *noun* meat from a calf

veer /vɪə/ (**veers, veering, veered**) *verb* **1.** to turn in a direction suddenly ○ *The car suddenly veered to the right and crashed through a wall.* ○ *She veered away off the main road into a little lane.* **2.** to change plans or ideas ○ *The government seems to be veering towards the left.*

veg /vedʒ/ *noun* vegetables (*informal*)

vegan /'viːgən/ *noun* a person who does not eat meat, dairy produce, eggs or fish, but only eats vegetables and fruit

③ **vegetable** /'vedʒtəb(ə)l/ *noun* a plant which is grown to be eaten but which is not usually sweet ○ *We grow potatoes, carrots and other sorts of vegetables in the garden.* ○ *The soup of the day is vegetable soup.* ○ *Green vegetables are a good source of dietary fibre.*

vegetarian /ˌvedʒɪ'teəriən/ *adj* not containing meat, or for people who do not eat meat ○ *a vegetarian dish* ○ *He is on a vegetarian diet.* ○ *She asked for the vegetarian menu.* ■ *noun* a person who eats only fruit, vegetables, bread, eggs, etc., but does not eat meat, and sometimes not fish

vegetation /ˌvedʒɪ'teɪʃ(ə)n/ *noun* plants

veggie /'vedʒi/ *noun* (*informal*) **1.** a vegetarian **2.** a vegetable

vehement /'viːəmənt/ *adj* forceful

② **vehicle** /'viːɪk(ə)l/ *noun* a machine which carries passengers or goods, e.g. a car, lorry or bus ○ *a three-wheeled vehicle* ○ *Goods vehicles can park at the back of the building.*

veil /veɪl/ *noun* **1.** a light cloth which can cover a woman's head or face ○ *At the funeral she wore a hat with a black veil.* ○ *The bride lifted her veil as she came out of the church.* **2.** something which stops you seeing or understanding ○ *A veil of mist lay over the valley.* ○ *A veil of secrecy has prevented us finding out what really happened.*

vein /veɪn/ *noun* a small tube in the body which takes blood from the tissues back to the heart (NOTE: Do not confuse with **vain**.)

Velcro /'velkrəʊ/ *trademark* a material with stiff fibres which cling tight when pressed together ○ *Her sandals have Velcro straps.* ○ *The rucksack fastens with Velcro.*

velocity /və'lɒsɪti/ *noun* speed

velvet /'velvɪt/ *noun* a cloth made from silk, with a soft pile surface on one side

vendetta /ven'detə/ *noun* a private quarrel between families or persons

vendor /'vendə/, **vender** *noun* a person who sells a property (*formal*) ○ *The vendor's solicitor is trying to get the purchaser to hurry up.*

veneer /və'nɪə/ *noun* **1.** a thin layer of expensive wood glued to the surface of ordinary wood ○ *The table has a mahogany veneer.* **2.** behaviour or an appearance which hides the truth [~of] ○ *His veneer of politeness soon disappeared as the old lady asked more and more questions.*

venetian blind /vəˌniːʃ(ə)n 'blaɪnd/ *noun* a blind to shut out light, made of horizontal strips, e.g. of plastic or wood, which can be opened or shut or raised and lowered by pulling a string

vengeance /'vendʒəns/ *noun* harm caused to someone in return for harm he or she has caused you ○ *He has vowed to exact vengeance for the wrong done to his family.* ○ *She is seeking vengeance for the killing of her child.* ◇ **with a vengeance** very strongly (*informal*) ○ *The rain came down again with a vengeance.*

venison /'venɪs(ə)n/ *noun* meat from a deer

venom /'venəm/ *noun* **1.** poison, e.g. from the bite of a snake ○ *The venom of certain snakes may cause paralysis.* **2.** bitter hatred ○ *The venom in her reply was obvious.*

venomous /ˈvenɪməs/ *adj* **1.** with poison in its bite ○ *This snake is particularly venomous.* ○ *She was bitten by a venomous spider.* **2.** showing bitter hatred ○ *She gave him a venomous look.* ○ *His venomous letter was printed in the newspaper.*

vent /vent/ *noun* **1.** a hole through which air or gas can escape ○ *The gas heater is connected to a vent in the wall.* **2.** a slit in the back of a coat or jacket allowing you to sit down more easily ○ *He always wears jackets with double vents.*

ventilate /ˈventɪleɪt/ (**ventilates, ventilating, ventilated**) *verb* to allow fresh air to come into a place ○ *The freshly painted kitchen needs to be ventilated for several hours.* ○ *Children tend to fall asleep in poorly ventilated classrooms.*

ventilation /ˌventɪˈleɪʃ(ə)n/ *noun* the process of bringing fresh air into a place

venture /ˈventʃə/ *noun* a new activity, especially in business, which involves some risk ○ *She has started a new venture – a computer shop.* ■ *verb* (**ventures, venturing, ventured**) **1.** to say something cautiously or reluctantly **2.** to go somewhere when it may be exciting or unpleasant ○ *We couldn't wait any longer, so we ventured out into the rain.*

venture capital /ˌventʃə ˈkæpɪt(ə)l/ *noun* money which you invest in a new business when there is a high risk of failure

venue /ˈvenjuː/ *noun* an agreed place where an event such as a meeting will be held

③ **verb** /vɜːb/ *noun* (*in grammar*) a word which shows an action, being or feeling, such as 'to hit' or 'to thank'

verbal /ˈvɜːb(ə)l/ *adj* spoken and not written down ○ *She gave me a verbal account of what had happened.* ○ *It was a verbal agreement between the two of us.*

verbal noun /ˌvɜːb(ə)l ˈnaʊn/ *noun* a gerund, a noun formed from the present participle of a verb (NOTE: In English, gerunds are formed from the '-ing' form of verbs, as in *Cycling is good exercise*; *Choral singing is very popular in Wales.*)

verbatim /vɜːˈbeɪtɪm/ *adj* using exactly the same words ○ *a verbatim account* ○ *That was what she said, verbatim.*

verdict /ˈvɜːdɪkt/ *noun* a decision made in a court □ **to come to *or* reach a verdict** to decide whether the accused is guilty or not

verge /vɜːdʒ/ *noun* **1.** a border of grass along the side of a road ○ *You can park on the verge outside the house.* ○ *Wild flowers were growing all along the motorway verges.* **2.** the edge ◇ **on the verge of something** about to experience something ○ *The company is on the verge of bankruptcy.* ○ *She was on the verge of a nervous breakdown.*

verify /ˈverɪfaɪ/ (**verifies, verifying, verified**) *verb* to check to see if documents or a statement are correct (NOTE: + **verification** *n*)

vermin /ˈvɜːmɪn/ *noun* animals or insects, e.g. mice, fleas or cockroaches, which eat crops, bring disease into houses, live on other animals, etc.

versatile /ˈvɜːsətaɪl/ *adj* **1.** good at doing various things equally well **2.** (*of a machine, material, etc.*) which is suitable for various uses ○ *The car is extremely versatile: it can be used on rough mountain tracks, but is equally suitable for town use.*

verse /vɜːs/ *noun* **1.** a group of lines which form a part of a song or poem ○ *We sang all the verses of the National Anthem.* ○ *She read the first verse to the class.* **2.** poetry ○ *He published a small book of verse.* Compare **prose** (NOTE: no plural in this sense)

① **version** /ˈvɜːʃ(ə)n/ *noun* **1.** a description of what happened as seen by one person ○ *The victim told her version of events to the jury.* **2.** a type of something, e.g. a work of art or model of car ○ *This is the film version of the novel.* ○ *He bought the cheapest version available.*

versus /ˈvɜːsəs/ *prep* (*in a sports match or a civil court case*) against (NOTE: usually written **v**, sometimes also **vs**: *Manchester United v Arsenal; Smith vs the Inland Revenue*)

vertebra /ˈvɜːtɪbrə/ (*plural* **vertebrae**) *noun* one of the 24 bones which form the vertebral column or backbone

vertical /ˈvɜːtɪk(ə)l/ *adj* standing or rising straight up ○ *He drew a few vertical lines to represent trees.* ○ *We looked at the vertical cliff and wondered how to climb it.*

vertigo /ˈvɜːtɪgəʊ/ *noun* dizziness or loss of balance where everything seems to rush round you, especially when you are in a high place ○ *Some ear conditions may cause vertigo.*

verve /vɜːv/ *noun* enthusiasm, a feeling of liveliness

① **very** /ˈveri/ *adv* used to make an adjective or adverb stronger ○ *It's very hot in the car – why don't you open a window?* ○ *Can you see that very tall pine tree over there?* ○ *The time seemed to go very quickly when* *we were on holiday.* ■ *adj* used to make a noun stronger ○ *He did his very best to get tickets.* ○ *The scene takes place at the very beginning of the book.*

vessel /ˈves(ə)l/ *noun* a ship ○ *Vessels from all countries crowded into the harbour.*

vest /vest/ *noun* **1.** a light piece of underclothing for the top half of the body ○ *He wears a thick vest in winter.* ○ *If you don't have a clean vest, wear a T-shirt instead.* **2.** *US* a short coat with buttons and without any sleeves, which is worn over a shirt and under a jacket ○ *He wore a pale gray vest with a black jacket.*

vested interest /ˌvestɪd ˈɪntrəst/ *noun* a special interest in keeping an existing state of affairs

vestige /ˈvestɪdʒ/ *noun* remains

③ **vet** /vet/ (**vets, vetting, vetted**) *verb* to check someone or something carefully to see if they are suitable ○ *All candidates have to be vetted by the managing director.*

veteran /ˈvet(ə)rən/ *noun* **1.** a member of the armed forces who has fought in a war ○ *The veterans visited war graves on the 50th anniversary of the battle.* **2.** a person who has a lot of experience ○ *He is a veteran of many takeover bids.*

③ **veterinary** /ˈvet(ə)rənəri/ *adj* referring to the treatment of sick animals

veterinary surgeon /ˈvet(ə)rɪnəri ˌsɜːdʒən/ *noun* a doctor who specialises in treating animals (NOTE: always shortened to **vet** when speaking)

veto /ˈviːtəʊ/ *noun* (*plural* **vetoes**) a ban or order not to allow something to become law, even if it has been passed by a parliament ■ *verb* (**vetoes, vetoing, vetoed**) to forbid something ○ *The proposal was vetoed by the president.* ○ *The council has vetoed all plans to hold protest marches in the centre of town.*

② **via** /ˈvaɪə/ *prep* through ○ *We drove to London via Windsor.* ○ *We are sending the payment via our office in London.* ○ *The shipment is going via the Suez Canal.*

viable /ˈvaɪəb(ə)l/ *adj* **1.** able to work in practice ○ *The project is certainly viable.* ○ *It is no longer viable to extract tin from these mines.* **2.** (*of a foetus*) which can survive if born ○ *A foetus is viable after about 28 weeks of pregnancy.*

viaduct /ˈvaɪədʌkt/ *noun* a long bridge carrying a road or railway across a valley

vibe /vaɪb/ *noun* a particular kind of feeling which you connect with a certain place or person (*informal*)

vibrant /ˈvaɪbrənt/ *adj* (*of a person*) full of energy ○ *a teacher with a vibrant personality*

vibrate /vaɪˈbreɪt/ (**vibrates, vibrating, vibrated**) *verb* to move slightly, but rapidly and continuously

③ **vibration** /vaɪˈbreɪʃ(ə)n/ *noun* a fast and continuous shaking movement

vicar /ˈvɪkə/ *noun* (*in the Church of England*) a priest in charge of a parish

vicarage /ˈvɪk(ə)rɪdʒ/ *noun* a house of a vicar

③ **vice** /vaɪs/ *noun* **1.** criminal activity involving sex **2.** a tool that screws tight to hold something firm while it is being worked on

vice- /vaɪs/ *prefix* a person who is second in rank to someone

vice-president /ˌvaɪs ˈprezɪd(ə)nt/ *noun* **1.** the deputy to a president **2.** *US* one of the executive directors of a company

vice versa /ˌvaɪsi ˈvɜːsə/ *adv* the other way from what has just been mentioned

vicinity /vəˈsɪnɪti/ *noun* an area around something ○ *The police are searching the vicinity of the lake.*

③ **vicious** /ˈvɪʃəs/ *adj* cruel and violent ○ *a vicious attack on an elderly lady*

vicious circle /ˌvɪʃəs ˈsɜːk(ə)l/ *noun* a situation in which by trying to solve one problem you find yourself in another which is worse than the first

② **victim** /ˈvɪktɪm/ *noun* a person who is attacked, who is in an accident ○ *The victims of the train crash were taken to the local hospital.* ○ *She was the victim of a violent attack outside her front door.* ○ *Earthquake victims were housed in tents.*

victimise /ˈvɪktɪmaɪz/ (**victimises, victimising, victimised**), **victimize** (**victimizes, victimizing, victimized**) *verb* to treat someone more unfairly than others

victor /ˈvɪktə/ *noun* a person who wins a fight, game or battle

Victorian /vɪkˈtɔːriən/ *noun* a person living at the time of Queen Victoria ○ *He wrote the biography of several eminent Victorians.*

victorious /vɪkˈtɔːriəs/ *adj* having won a game or a battle

② **victory** /ˈvɪkt(ə)ri/ (*plural* **victories**) *noun* the fact of winning something, e.g. a battle, a fight or a game ○ *the American victory in the Olympics* ○ *They won a clear victory in the general election.* ○ *The guerrillas won a victory over the government troops.*

① **video** /ˈvɪdiəʊ/ *noun* **1.** a machine which records TV programmes ○ *Don't forget to set the video for 8 p.m. before you go out.* **2.** a magnetic tape on which you can record TV programmes or films for playing back on a television set ○ *She bought a box of blank videos.*

video game /ˈvɪdiəʊ geɪm/ *noun* an electronic game which you play on a television or computer screen

videophone /ˈvɪdiəʊˌfəʊn/ *noun* a telephone with a screen where you can see the person you are speaking to

videotape /ˈvɪdiəʊteɪp/ *noun* a magnetic tape on which pictures and sound can be recorded for playing back on a television set

vie /vaɪ/ (**vies, vying, vied**) *verb* to be in competition with someone or something [~with/~for] ○ *They vied with the German team for the gold medal.* ○ *The best students are vying for the scholarship.* ○ *The food at this little restaurant vies with that of more expensive establishments.*

① **view** /vjuː/ *noun* **1.** what you can see from a certain place ○ *You can get a good view of the sea from the church tower.* ○ *We asked for a room with a sea view and were given one looking out over the bus depot.* **2.** an opinion or a way of thinking about something [~on/about/~of/~that] ○ *What are your views on politics?* ○ *I can't accept your view of life.* ○ *It's my view that she lied to save herself.* ○ *In his view, the government ought to act now.*

③ **viewer** /ˈvjuːə/ *noun* **1.** a person who watches TV ○ *The programme attracted ten million viewers.* **2.** a small device through which you can look at colour slides ○ *She bought a little viewer to look at her slides.*

viewfinder /ˈvjuːfaɪndə/ *noun* a small window in a camera through which you look when taking a picture, and which shows the exact picture you are about to take

viewing /ˈvjuːɪŋ/ *noun* **1.** the act of inspecting something such as a house which you are thinking of buying **2.** the act of watching television

viewpoint /ˈvjuːpɔɪnt/ *noun* a point of view, a particular way of thinking about things

vigil /ˈvɪdʒɪl/ *noun* the act of staying quietly in a place to look after someone who is ill, to pray for something, or as a protest ○ *a vigil for peace* ○ *A nurse kept vigil by her bedside.* ○ *The family held a silent vigil near the place where the accident happened.*

vigilant /ˈvɪdʒɪlənt/ *adj* staying very aware of possible danger ○ *The disease particularly affects young children, so parents must remain vigilant.*

vigilante /ˌvɪdʒɪˈlænti/ *noun* a person who is a member of group which tries to enforce law and order in their area, especially when the police seem to find it impossible to do so

vigorous /ˈvɪɡərəs/ *adj* very energetic or strong

vigour /ˈvɪɡə/ *noun* energy (NOTE: The US spelling is **vigor**.)

vile /vaɪl/ *adj* extremely unpleasant or bad

vilify /ˈvɪlɪˌfaɪ/ (**vilifies, vilifying, vilified**) *verb* to criticise someone, especially unfairly (*formal*)

villa /ˈvɪlə/ *noun* a large country or seaside house, usually in a warm country ○ *He is staying in a villa on the Mediterranean.* ○ *They are renting a villa in Greece for August.*

① **village** /ˈvɪlɪdʒ/ *noun* a small group of houses in the country, like a little town, often with a church, and usually some shops ○ *They live in a mountain village.* ○ *The village shop sells just about everything we need.*

village green /ˈvɪlɪdʒ ɡriːn/ *noun* a public grassy area in the middle of a village

③ **villager** /ˈvɪlɪdʒə/ *noun* a person who lives in a village

③ **villain** /ˈvɪlən/ *noun* **1.** a wicked character in a work of art, e.g. a film or novel ○ *He plays the villain in the pantomime.* **2.** a criminal ○ *The villains must be caught.*

vindicate /ˈvɪndɪkeɪt/ (**vindicates, vindicating, vindicated**) *verb* to justify; to show that someone was right (NOTE: + **vindication** *n*)

vindictive /vɪnˈdɪktɪv/ *adj* wanting to take revenge; spiteful

vine /vaɪn/ *noun* a climbing plant which produces grapes. ◊ **grapevine**

vinegar /ˈvɪnɪɡə/ *noun* a liquid with a sour taste, usually made from wine, used in cooking and for pickling

vineyard /ˈvɪnjəd/ *noun* an area planted with vines for making wine

③ **vintage** /ˈvɪntɪdʒ/ *noun* all the wine made in a particular year ○ *1995 was a very good vintage.* ■ *adj* **1.** (*of wine*) made in a high-quality year **2.** showing the best typical qualities of someone ○ *The film is vin-*

tage Laurel and Hardy. **3.** (*of objects*) old but well-preserved and often valuable

vinyl /ˈvaɪn(ə)l/ *noun* a type of strong plastic sheet which can be made to look like other materials such as leather or tiles

viola /viˈəʊlə/ *noun* **1.** a small pansy-like garden flower **2.** a stringed instrument slightly larger than a violin ○ *She plays the viola in the city orchestra.*

violate /ˈvaɪəleɪt/ (**violates, violating, violated**) *verb* **1.** to break a rule, to go against the law ○ *The council has violated the planning regulations.* ○ *The rebels violated the conditions of the peace treaty.* **2.** to treat something or someone without respect ○ *to violate the sanctity of a church*

③ **violation** /ˌvaɪəˈleɪʃ(ə)n/ *noun* the action of violating something or someone

② **violence** /ˈvaɪələns/ *noun* action which is intended to hurt someone ○ *Acts of violence must be punished.*

② **violent** /ˈvaɪələnt/ *adj* **1.** very strong ○ *The discussion led to a violent argument.* ○ *A violent storm blew all night.* **2.** using force to hurt people ○ *Her husband was a very violent man.*

③ **violently** /ˈvaɪələntli/ *adv* **1.** with physical force, often with the intention of hurting ○ *This horse threw him violently onto the ground.* ○ *She hurled the bottle violently across the table.* **2.** with great feeling ○ *She violently rejected the accusations made against her.* ○ *He reacted violently to the injection.* ○ *The oysters made her violently sick.*

violet /ˈvaɪələt/ *noun* a bluish-purple colour ○ *Her lips turned violet as she gasped for breath.*

③ **violin** /vaɪəˈlɪn/ *noun* a musical instrument with strings that hold under your chin and play with a bow

③ **VIP** *abbr* very important person

viper /ˈvaɪpə/ *noun* a small European poisonous snake

viral /ˈvaɪrəl/ *adj* caused by or referring to a virus

virgin /ˈvɜːdʒɪn/ *noun* a person who has never had sex ○ *She was a virgin until she was married.*

virginity /vəˈdʒɪnɪti/ *noun* the fact of being a virgin

Virgo /ˈvɜːgəʊ/ *noun* one of the signs of the Zodiac, shaped like a girl, covering the period 23rd August to 22nd September

virile /ˈvɪraɪl/ *adj* with strong male characteristics

virility /vəˈrɪlɪti/ *noun* manliness; the fact of being virile

③ **virtual** /ˈvɜːtʃuəl/ *adj* almost ○ *The company has a virtual monopoly of French wine imports.* ○ *His grandfather has become a virtual recluse.*

② **virtually** /ˈvɜːtʃuəli/ *adv* almost ○ *These shirts have been reduced so much that we're virtually giving them away.* ○ *It's virtually impossible to get tickets for the concert.*

virtual reality /ˌvɜːtʃuəl riˈælɪti/ *noun* the simulation of a real-life scene or real events on a computer

③ **virtue** /ˈvɜːtʃuː/ *noun* **1.** a particular goodness of character, a good quality ○ *Honesty is his principal virtue.* **2.** a special thing which gives you an advantage ○ *The virtue of the train link to France is that you arrive right in the centre of Paris.* ◇ **by virtue of something** as a result of something (*formal*) ○ *He's eligible for British citizenship by virtue of his father who was born in Newcastle.*

virtuoso /ˌvɜːtʃʊˈəʊsəʊ/ (*plural* **virtuosos** or **virtuosi**) *noun* a person who is skilled in an art, especially one who can play a musical instrument extremely well

virtuous /ˈvɜːtʃʊəs/ *adj* **1.** very good or honest ○ *She was a virtuous old lady who never said a bad word against her neighbours.* **2.** feeling satisfied because you think that you have done something good ○ *There is nothing virtuous about going to the office on Saturday morning – we do it as a matter of course.* ○ *She said she felt virtuous doing her exercises first thing in the morning.* ○ *I won't have any pudding – I'll be virtuous.*

virulent /ˈvɪrʊlənt/ *adj* **1.** (*of a form of a disease or an organism*) strongly active ○ *The new flu virus is said to be particularly virulent.* ○ *He contracted a virulent form of the disease.* **2.** very harsh ○ *The newspaper carried a virulent attack on the Foreign Minister.*

③ **virus** /ˈvaɪrəs/ *noun* **1.** a very small living thing that causes disease by living in the bodies of people or animals ○ *Scientists have isolated a new flu virus.* ○ *Shingles is caused by the same virus as chickenpox.* **2.** a part of a computer program which is designed to destroy files on someone else's computer ○ *You must check the program for viruses.*

visa /ˈviːzə/ *noun* a special stamp on a passport allowing you to enter a country

vis-à-vis /ˌviːz ə ˈviː/ *prep* in relation to

viscous /'vɪskəs/ *adj* thick and slow-moving

visibility /ˌvɪzɪ'bɪlɪti/ *noun* an ability to see clearly

③ **visible** /'vɪzɪb(ə)l/ *adj* which can be seen

visibly /'vɪzɪbli/ *adv* in a way which everyone can see

② **vision** /'vɪʒ(ə)n/ *noun* **1.** eyesight, your ability to see ○ *After the age of 50, the vision of many people begins to fail.* **2.** a thing which you imagine ○ *He had visions of himself stuck in London with no passport and no money.* ○ *She had visions of him being arrested for drug smuggling.*

visionary /'vɪʒ(ə)n(ə)ri/ *adj* idealistic, with original ideas ○ *His visionary designs influenced a whole generation.*

① **visit** /'vɪzɪt/ *noun* a short stay with someone or in a town or a country [~to/~from] ○ *We will be making a short visit to London next week.* ○ *They had a visit from the police.* ■ *verb* (**visits, visiting, visited**) to stay a short time with someone or in a town or country ○ *I am on my way to visit my sister in hospital.* ○ *They are away visiting friends in the north of the country.* ○ *The group of tourists are going to visit the glass factory.* ○ *He spent a week in Scotland, visiting museums in Edinburgh and Glasgow.*

visitation /ˌvɪzɪ'teɪʃ(ə)n/ *noun* an instance of someone believing that he or she has seen a spirit

② **visitor** /'vɪzɪtə/ *noun* a person who comes to visit [~to] ○ *The number of visitors to the museum has risen sharply.* ○ *We had a surprise visitor yesterday – the bank manager!*

visor /'vaɪzə/, **vizor** *noun* a part of a helmet, which is hinged and can drop down to cover and protect the eyes ○ *He lifted his visor to talk to the policeman.*

vista /'vɪstə/ *noun* a wide view

③ **visual** /'vɪʒʊəl/ *adj* referring to seeing

visual aid /'vɪʒʊəl eɪd/ *noun* something, e.g. a picture or a chart, that you use to explain something to people

② **vital** /'vaɪt(ə)l/ *adj* extremely important ○ *It is vital that we act quickly.* ○ *Oxygen is vital to human life.*

vitality /vaɪ'tælɪti/ *noun* great energy

vitally /'vaɪt(ə)li/ *adv* in a very important way

vitamin /'vɪtəmɪn/ *noun* an essential substance which is found in food and is needed for growth and health

vivacious /vɪ'veɪʃəs/ *adj* full of life or excitement

vivid /'vɪvɪd/ *adj* **1.** very bright ○ *vivid yellow sunflowers* ○ *the vivid colours of the Mediterranean beach* **2.** representing real events clearly ○ *She has a vivid imagination.* ○ *The play is a vivid portrayal of country life.* ○ *I had a really vivid dream last night.* ○ *She gave a vivid account of her experiences at the hands of the kidnappers.*

vivisection /ˌvɪvɪ'sekʃən/ *noun* the practice of operating on live animals for the purpose of scientific research

vixen /'vɪksən/ *noun* a female fox

V-neck /'viː nek/ *noun* a piece of clothing, e.g. a dress, or a pullover, with a neck shaped like a V

vocab /'vəʊkæb/ *noun* vocabulary (*informal*)

vocabulary /vəʊ'kæbjʊləri/ *noun* **1.** all the words used by a person or group of persons ○ *specialist legal vocabulary* ○ *She reads French newspapers to improve her French vocabulary.* **2.** a printed list of words ○ *There is a German-English vocabulary at the back of the book.*

vocal /'vəʊk(ə)l/ *adj* **1.** referring to the voice ○ *Singers need to do vocal exercises daily.* **2.** protesting loudly ○ *The protesters were very vocal at the demonstration.*

vocal cords /'vəʊk(ə)l kɔːdz/ *plural noun* folds in the larynx which are brought together to make sounds when air passes between them

vocalist /'vəʊkəlɪst/ *noun* a singer, especially in a pop group

vocation /vəʊ'keɪʃ(ə)n/ *noun* work which you feel you have been called to do or for which you have a special talent

vocational /vəʊ'keɪʃ(ə)n(ə)l/ *adj* referring to a vocation

vociferous /vəʊ'sɪfərəs/ *adj* shouting loudly

vodka /'vɒdkə/ *noun* a strong, colourless alcohol made from grain or potatoes, originally in Russia and Poland ○ *We talked over a glass of vodka.*

vogue /vəʊg/ *noun* the fashion ◇ **in vogue** fashionable ○ *This year, black is back in vogue again.*

① **voice** /vɔɪs/ *noun* a sound made when you speak or sing ○ *I didn't recognise his voice over the telephone.* ○ *The chairman spoke for a few minutes in a low voice.*

voice-activated /vɔɪs 'æktɪˌveɪtd/ *adj* (*of a piece of equipment*) operated by the sound of your voice

voice box /'vɔɪs bɒks/ *noun* the larynx, the upper part of the windpipe, where sounds are made by the voice

voice mail /'vɔɪsmeɪl/ *noun* a type of telephone answering system, where messages can be left for a person

void /vɔɪd/ *noun* emptiness ○ *He tried to fill the void in his life caused by the death of his wife.* ○ *She stood on the bridge for a few minutes, looking down into the void.*

volatile /'vɒlətaɪl/ *adj* **1.** which can easily change into gas at normal temperatures (*of a substance*) ○ *canisters of highly volatile liquid petroleum gas* **2.** changing your mind or mood frequently ○ *The voters are very volatile.* **3.** not stable, likely to move up or down sharply ○ *a volatile stock market*

volcano /vɒl'keɪnəʊ/ *noun* a mountain which lava, ash and gas may flow out of from time to time

vole /vəʊl/ *noun* a small animal, like a mouse, but with a shorter tail

volley /'vɒli/ *noun* **1.** a series of shots fired at the same time ○ *The police fired a volley into the crowd.* ○ *Volleys of gunfire could be heard in the distance.* **2.** (*in sport*) the act of hitting the ball before it touches the ground ○ *He managed to return a very difficult volley.*

volleyball /'vɒlibɔːl/ *noun* an Olympic sport played on a rectangular court between two teams of six, in which a large inflated ball is hit over a high net with the hands, and the object is to prevent the ball touching the floor of the court

volt /vəʊlt/ *noun* the standard unit of for measuring electric force. Abbreviation **V**

voltage /'vəʊltɪdʒ/ *noun* an electric force expressed in volts

② **volume** /'vɒljuːm/ *noun* **1.** the amount of sound ○ *She turned down the volume on the radio.* ○ *He drives with the car radio on at full volume.* **2.** the capacity, the amount which is contained inside something ○ *What is the volume of this barrel?* **3.** one book, especially one in a series ○ *Have you read the third volume of his history of medieval Europe?*

③ **voluntary** /'vɒlənt(ə)ri/ *adj* **1.** done because you want to do it, and done without being paid ○ *Many retired people do voluntary work.* **2.** done willingly, without being forced ○ *He made a voluntary contribution to the fund.*

volunteer /ˌvɒlən'tɪə/ *noun* a person who offers to do something without being paid or being forced to do it ○ *The information desk is staffed by volunteers.* ■ *verb* (**volunteers, volunteering, volunteered**) to offer to do something without being paid or being forced to do it ○ *Will anyone volunteer for the job of washing up?* ○ *He volunteered to collect the entrance tickets.*

voluptuous /və'lʌptʃʊəs/ *adj* evoking sensual pleasure

vomit /'vɒmɪt/ *noun* partly digested food which has been brought up into the mouth from the stomach ○ *There was vomit all over the bathroom floor.* ○ *He choked on his own vomit.* ■ *verb* (**vomits, vomiting, vomited**) to bring up partly digested food into your mouth ○ *He vomited last night and now has a high temperature.* ○ *She vomited her breakfast.*

voodoo /'vuːduː/ *noun* witchcraft practised in the West Indies

voracious /və'reɪʃəs/ *adj* very enthusiastic ○ *a voracious reader*

① **vote** /vəʊt/ *noun* the act of marking a paper, holding up your hand, etc., to show your opinion or who you want to be elected [~for/in favour of/~against] ○ *There were only ten votes in favour of the plan.* ○ *The majority of votes were against strike action.* ○ *How many votes did the other candidate get?* ■ *verb* (**votes, voting, voted**) to mark a paper, to hold up your hand, etc., to show your opinion or who you want to be elected [~for/in favour of/~against] ○ *We all voted for the changes.* ○ *Even some of his friends voted against him.* ○ *Only forty per cent of the people were interested enough to vote.* ○ *Most of the strikers voted to go back to work.* □ **to vote for *or* against a proposal** to say that you agree or do not agree with a proposal ○ *Twenty people actually voted for the proposal to demolish the old church.*

voter /'vəʊtə/ *noun* a person who votes or who has the right to vote

vouch *verb*

vouch for *phrasal verb* to guarantee that something is true or that someone will behave well

③ **voucher** /'vaʊtʃə/ *noun* a paper which is given instead of money

vow /vaʊ/ *noun* a solemn promise ○ *He made a vow to go on a pilgrimage to Jerusalem.* ○ *She vowed to have her revenge but she died before she could keep her vow.* ■ *verb* (**vows, vowing, vowed**) to make a solemn promise to do something ○ *She vowed* *that she would never let it happen again.* ○ *He vowed to pay the money back.*

vowel /ˈvaʊəl/ *noun* one of the five letters, a, e, i, o and u, which represent sounds made without using the teeth, tongue or lips (NOTE: The letters representing sounds which are not vowels are **consonants**. Note also that in some languages 'y' is a vowel.)

voyage /ˈvɔɪɪdʒ/ *noun* a long journey, especially by ship or spacecraft

③ **vs** *abbr* versus

vulgar /ˈvʌlgə/ *adj* **1.** rude or indecent ○ *Don't use that sort of vulgar language in front of the children.* ○ *He made a vulgar gesture at the police officer.* **2.** not in good taste ○ *His pink Rolls Royce is particularly vulgar.*

③ **vulnerable** /ˈvʌln(ə)rəb(ə)l/ *adj* who or which can easily be hurt

vulture /ˈvʌltʃə/ *noun* a large bird that mainly eats dead animals ○ *Vultures live by scavenging on the bodies of animals which have died.* ○ *Scavengers like vultures wait in the trees near where the lions are hunting.*

W

w /ˈdʌb(ə)ljuː/, **W** *noun* the twenty-third letter of the alphabet, between V and X

W *abbr* **1.** west **2.** western

wacky /ˈwæki/ (**wackier, wackiest**) *adj* crazy or silly (*informal*)

wad /wɒd/ *noun* **1.** a thick piece of soft material ○ *The nurse put a sterile wad on the sore.* **2.** a thick pile of banknotes or papers ○ *He had a wad of banknotes in his hand.* ○ *The hole was blocked with a wad of old papers.*

waddle /ˈwɒd(ə)l/ (**waddles, waddling, waddled**) *verb* to walk swaying from side to side like a duck

wade /weɪd/ (**wades, wading, waded**) *verb* to walk through water ○ *They waded into the sea.*

wafer /ˈweɪfə/ *noun* a thin biscuit

waffle /ˈwɒf(ə)l/ *noun* **1.** a type of crisp pancake cooked in an iron mould and eaten with syrup ○ *We bought waffles at the stall in the fairground.* ○ *Waffles are very popular in Belgium.* **2.** unnecessary or muddled speaking or writing (*informal*) ○ *You don't need to read the article, it is just waffle.* ○ *Don't tell me you listened to all his waffle!* ■ *verb* (**waffles, waffling, waffled**) to talk too much without saying anything clearly (*informal*) ○ *What are you waffling on about?* ○ *If someone mentions the word 'ecology', our lecturer will waffle on for 20 minutes.*

waft /wɑːft/ (**wafts, wafting, wafted**) *verb* to carry something gently through the air ○ *The delicious smell of strawberry jam wafted through the window to where I was sitting.*

wag /wæg/ (**wags, wagging, wagged**) *verb* to move something from side to side or up and down ○ *The dog ran up to him, wagging its tail.* ○ *The grandmother wagged her finger at the little boy who was picking the flowers.*

wage /weɪdʒ/, **wages** *noun* money paid, usually in cash each week, to a worker for work done ○ *The company pays quite good wages.* ○ *She is earning a good wage* or *good wages in the pizza restaurant.*

wager /ˈweɪdʒə/ *noun* money which you promise to pay if something you expect to happen does not take place ○ *She made a wager that the government would lose the election.* (NOTE: + **wager** *v*)

waggle /ˈwæg(ə)l/ (**waggles, waggling, waggled**) *verb* to move from side to side quickly

wagon /ˈwægən/, **waggon** *noun* a railway truck used for carrying heavy loads ○ *The container wagons are leaving the freight terminal.*

waif /weɪf/ *noun* a person, especially a child, who is thin and does not look healthy

wail /weɪl/ (**wails, wailing, wailed**) *verb* to make a high-pitched mournful cry ○ *At the news, she just sat down and wailed.* (NOTE: + **wail** *n*)

③ **waist** /weɪst/ *noun* **1.** the narrow part of the body between the bottom of the chest and the hips ○ *She measures 32 inches round the waist* or *has a 32-inch waist.* **2.** the part of a piece of clothing, e.g. a skirt, trousers or dress, that goes round the middle of your body ○ *The waist of these trousers is too small for me.* (NOTE: Do not confuse with **waste**.)

waistband /ˈweɪs(t)ˌbænd/ *noun* a band of fabric on a piece of clothing, e.g. a skirt, trousers or dress, that goes round the middle of your body

③ **waistcoat** /ˈweɪstkəʊt/ *noun* a short coat with buttons and without any sleeves, which is worn over a shirt and under a jacket

waistline /ˈweɪstlaɪn/ *noun* a measurement around your waist, showing how fat you are

① **wait** /weɪt/ (**waits, waiting, waited**) *verb* to stay where you are, and not do anything until something happens or someone comes [~for/~until] ○ *Don't wait for me, I'll be late.* ○ *Wait here until the ambulance arrives.* ○ *They had been waiting for half an hour in the rain before the bus finally ar-*

rived. ○ *Wait a minute, my shoelace is undone.* ○ *We gave our order half an hour ago, but are still waiting.* ◇ **can't wait to do something** very eager to do something ○ *I can't wait to see what happens.*

wait up③ *phrasal verb* not to go to bed because you are waiting for someone

waiter /ˈweɪtə/ *noun* a man who brings food and drink to customers in a restaurant

③ **waiting list** /ˈweɪtɪŋ lɪst/ *noun* a list of people waiting for a service or medical treatment

③ **waiting room** /ˈweɪtɪŋ ruːm/ *noun* a room where you wait, e.g. at a doctor's, dentist's or railway station

waitress /ˈweɪtrəs/ *noun* a woman who brings food and drink to customers in a restaurant. ◊ **waiter**

waive /weɪv/ (**waives, waiving, waived**) *verb* to give up a right or a claim (NOTE: Do not confuse with **wave**.)

waiver /ˈweɪvə/ *noun* a document showing that someone is willing to give up a right or claim (NOTE: Do not confuse with **waver**.)

② **wake** /weɪk/ (**wakes, waking, woke, woken**) *verb* **1.** to stop someone's sleep ○ *The telephone woke her* or *she was woken by the telephone.* ○ *I banged on her door, but I can't wake her.* ○ *He asked to be woken at 7.00.* **2.** to stop sleeping ○ *He woke suddenly, feeling drops of water falling on his head.*

wake up② *phrasal verb* **1.** to stop someone's sleep ○ *He was woken up by the sound of the dog barking.* **2.** to stop sleeping ○ *She woke up in the middle of the night, thinking she had heard a noise.* ○ *Come on, wake up! It's past ten o'clock.* ○ *He woke up to find water coming through the roof of the tent.* ◇ **to wake up to something** to realise something ○ *When is he going to wake up to the fact that he is never going to be promoted?*

waken /ˈweɪkən/ (**wakens, wakening, wakened**) *verb* to make someone wake up

wake-up call /ˈweɪk ʌp ˌkɔːl/ *noun* a phone call from the hotel switchboard to wake a guest up

waking /ˈweɪkɪŋ/ *adj* awake, not asleep

Wales /weɪlz/ *noun* a country to the west of England, forming part of the United Kingdom ○ *There are some high mountains in North Wales.* ◊ **Welsh** (NOTE: capital: **Cardiff;** people: **the Welsh;** languages: **Welsh, English**)

① **walk** /wɔːk/ *verb* (**walks, walking, walked**) **1.** to go on foot ○ *The baby is ten months old, and is just starting to walk.* ○ *She was walking along the high street on her way to the bank.* ○ *We walked slowly across the bridge.* ○ *The visitors walked round the factory.* □ **to walk someone home** to go with someone who is walking home ○ *It was getting late, so I walked her home.* **2.** to take an animal for a walk ○ *He's gone to walk the dog in the fields.* ○ *She walks her dog every morning.* ■ *noun* **1.** a usually pleasant journey on foot ○ *Let's all go for a walk in the park.* **2.** a distance which you cover on foot ○ *It's only a short walk to the beach.* ○ *It's only five minutes' walk from the office to the bank* or *the bank is only a five minutes' walk from the office.*

walk into *phrasal verb* to enter on foot

walk off③ *phrasal verb* to go away on foot ○ *She walked off and left him holding the shopping.* ○ *The builders walked off the site because they said it was too dangerous.*

walk off with③ *phrasal verb* **1.** to win ○ *She walked off with first prize.* **2.** to steal ○ *The burglar walked off with all my silver cups.*

walk out① *phrasal verb* **1.** to go out on foot ○ *She walked out of the house and down the street.* **2.** to go out angrily ○ *He walked out of the restaurant, saying that the service was too slow.* **3.** (*of workers*) to go on strike, to stop working and leave your office or factory ○ *The office staff walked out in protest.* ◇ **to walk out on someone** to leave someone suddenly ○ *She walked out on her husband and went to live with her mother.* ○ *Our sales manager walked out on us just as we were starting our autumn sales campaign.*

③ **walker** /ˈwɔːkə/ *noun* a person who goes walking for pleasure and exercise

walkie-talkie /ˌwɔːki ˈtɔːki/ *noun* a portable two-way radio

③ **walking** /ˈwɔːkɪŋ/ *noun* going on foot as a relaxation, e.g. along paths or up mountains

walking frame /ˈwɔːkɪŋ freɪm/ *noun* a metal frame used by someone who has difficulty walking, to help him or her move about

walking stick /ˈwɔːkɪŋ stɪk/ *noun* a strong wooden or metal stick with a handle used as a support when walking

Walkman /ˈwɔːkmən/ *trademark* for a small portable cassette player which you can carry around with you and which has headphones for you to listen to music with ○ *The chap next to me in the Underground*

had his Walkman on full blast. ○ *He likes to listen to rock music on his Walkman.*

walkout /ˈwɔːkaʊt/ *noun* a strike by workers

walkover /ˈwɔːkəʊvə/ *noun* an easy victory (*informal*)

walkway /ˈwɔːkweɪ/ *noun* an outdoor path where you can walk between buildings, usually raised above ground level

① **wall** /wɔːl/ *noun* a structure made from things such as bricks or stones, built up to make one of the sides of a building, of a room or to surround a space ○ *The walls of the restaurant are decorated with pictures of film stars.* ○ *There's a clock on the wall behind my desk.* ○ *He got into the house by climbing over the garden wall.*

wall up *phrasal verb* to block something such as a door or an entrance with a wall

wallaby /ˈwɒləbi/ *noun* an Australian animal like a small kangaroo

wallet /ˈwɒlɪt/ *noun* a small flat leather case for carrying things such as credit cards and banknotes in your pocket

wallop /ˈwɒləp/ (**wallops, walloping, walloped**) *verb* to hit someone or something very hard

wallow /ˈwɒləʊ/ (**wallows, wallowing, wallowed**) *verb* **1.** (*of animals*) to roll around in mud ○ *When I hear of animals wallowing in mud, I immediately think of hippos.* **2.** (*of a person*) to take a lot of pleasure in doing something ○ *He positively wallows in gossip about media people.* ○ *It's time she stopped wallowing in self-pity.*

wallpaper /ˈwɔːlpeɪpə/ *noun* paper with different patterns on it, covering the walls of a room ○ *The wallpaper was light green to match the carpet.*

① **Wall Street** /ˈwɔːl striːt/ *noun* a street in New York where the Stock Exchange is, the American finance centre in New York ○ *He walked along Wall Street, looking for the company's offices.*

wally /ˈwɒli/ *noun* an offensive word that deliberately insults somebody's intelligence

walrus /ˈwɔːlrəs/ *noun* an animal which looks like a large seal, with two long tusks pointing downwards

waltz /wɔːls/ *noun* (*plural* **waltzes**) **1.** a slow dance in which a man and woman turn around together as they move forward ○ *The next dance is a waltz, so I'll ask her to dance.* **2.** music suitable for such a dance ○ *Listen, the orchestra is playing a waltz.* ○ *The 'Blue Danube' is one of Strauss' most famous waltzes.* ■ *verb* (**waltzes, waltzing, waltzed**) **1.** to dance a waltz **2.** to do something in a relaxed way that shows you are not worrying or not trying hard ○ *She waltzed into the bank and said she wanted to withdraw $200,000 in cash.* ○ *He waltzed off with first prize.*

③ **wander** /ˈwɒndə/ (**wanders, wandering, wandered**) *verb* to walk somewhere without any specific destination ○ *They wandered round the town in the rain.*

wander off/away *verb* to walk away from where you should be ○ *Two of the party wandered off into the market.*

wane /weɪn/ (**wanes, waning, waned**) *verb* to appear smaller; to become less effective ○ *His influence over his family is waning.* ○ *He takes vitamin tablets to boost his waning energy.*

wangle /ˈwæŋgəl/ (**wangles, wangling, wangled**) *verb* to get something by a trick (*informal*)

wanna /ˈwɒnə/ *contr* want to (*informal*)

wannabe /ˈwɒnəbi/ *noun* a person who would like to be something or someone different (*informal*)

① **want** /wɒnt/ (**wants, wanting, wanted**) *verb* **1.** to hope that you will do something, that something will happen, or that you will get something ○ *She wants a new car for her birthday.* ○ *Where do you want to go for your holidays?* ○ *He wants to be a teacher.* **2.** to ask someone to do something ○ *The manager wants me to go and see him.* ○ *I want those windows painted.* **3.** to need something ○ *With five children, what they want is a bigger house.* ○ *You want to take some rest.*

wanted /ˈwɒntɪd/ *adj* searched for by the police, usually because of a crime

wanting /ˈwɒntɪŋ/ *adj* lacking a necessary feature or quality

wanton /ˈwɒntən/ *adj* in a way which is uncontrolled or without reason

① **war** /wɔː/ *noun* a period of fighting between countries [~with/~between] ○ *the numerous wars between the English and the Scots* ○ *In 1914 Britain was at war with Germany* or *Britain and Germany were at war.* ○ *Millions of soldiers and civilians were killed during the war.*

war crime /ˈwɔː kraɪm/ *noun* a crime committed during a war which is against international agreements on the rules of war

③ **ward** /wɔːd/ *noun* a room or set of rooms in a hospital, with beds for patients ○ *The children's ward is at the end of the* *corridor.* ○ *She was taken into the accident and emergency ward.*

warder /ˈwɔːdə/, **wardress** *noun* a prison officer, a person who guards prisoners (*old*)

wardrobe /ˈwɔːdrəʊb/ *noun* a tall cupboard in which you hang your clothes ○ *He moved the wardrobe from the landing into the bedroom.*

warehouse /ˈweəhaʊs/ *noun* a large building where goods are stored ○ *Our goods are dispatched from the central warehouse to shops all over the country.*

warfare /ˈwɔːfeə/ *noun* fighting a war, especially the method of fighting

war game /ˈwɔː ɡeɪm/ *noun* a military exercise

warhead /ˈwɔːhed/ *noun* the top end of a missile which explodes when it hits something

warlord /ˈwɔːlɔːd/ *noun* a military leader who rules part of a country

② **warm** /wɔːm/ *adj* **1.** fairly hot ○ *The temperature is below freezing outside but it's nice and warm in the office.* ○ *The children tried to keep warm by playing football.* ○ *Are you warm enough, or do you want another blanket?* ○ *This coat is not very warm.* ○ *The winter sun can be quite warm in February.* **2.** pleasant and friendly ○ *We had a warm welcome from our friends.* ○ *She has a really warm personality.* ■ *verb* (**warms, warming, warmed**) to make something hotter ○ *Come and warm your hands by the fire.* ○ *I'll warm some soup.* ○ *The greenhouse effect has the result of warming the general temperature of the earth's atmosphere.*

warm up③ *phrasal verb* **1.** to make hotter ○ *A cup of coffee will soon warm you up.* ○ *I'll just warm up some soup for supper.* **2.** to practise or exercise ○ *The orchestra is just warming up before the concert.*

war memorial /ˈwɔː mɪˌmɔːriəl/ *noun* a structure built to remember soldiers who died in a war

warm-hearted /ˌwɔːm ˈhɑːtɪd/ *adj* friendly and kind

warmth /wɔːmθ/ *noun* the fact of being warm or feeling warm ○ *It was cold and rainy outside, and he looked forward to the warmth of his home.*

② **warn** /wɔːn/ (**warns, warning, warned**) *verb* **1.** to inform someone of a possible danger [~that/~against/~of] ○ *The guide warned us that there might be snakes in the grass.* ○ *Children are warned of the dangers of playing on the frozen lake.* ○ *The group was warned to look out for pickpockets.* **2.** to inform someone that something is likely to happen [~that/~of] ○ *The railway has warned that there will be a strike tomorrow.* ○ *The weather forecast warned of storms in the English Channel.* (NOTE: You warn someone **of** something, or warn someone **that** something may happen.)

warn off *phrasal verb* □ **to warn someone off something** to advise someone not to do something ○ *Two men came to see him and warned him off going to the police.* ○ *They hope that this tragedy will warn other adolescents off drugs.*

② **warning** /ˈwɔːnɪŋ/ *noun* news about a possible danger [~to/~against] ○ *He shouted a warning to the children.* ○ *The government has issued a warning against travelling in some areas of the country.* ○ *Each packet of cigarettes has a government health warning printed on it.* ■ *adj* which informs about a danger ○ *Red warning flags are raised if the sea is dangerous.* ○ *Warning notices were put up round the building site.*

warp /wɔːp/ (**warps, warping, warped**) *verb* **1.** to twist out of shape ○ *Cycling across potholes can warp your front wheel.* ○ *If you leave the planks out in the rain they will warp.* **2.** to have a bad effect on someone's mind or character ○ *The beatings he had from his father seem to have warped his mind.*

warped /wɔːpt/ *adj* strange and twisted

warrant /ˈwɒrənt/ *noun* an official document from a court giving someone permission to do something ○ *The magistrate issued a warrant for her arrest.*

warranty /ˈwɒrənti/ (*plural* **warranties**) *noun* a legal document which promises that goods you buy will work properly or that an object is of good quality

warren /ˈwɒrən/ *noun* same as **rabbit warren**

warring /ˈwɔːrɪŋ/ *adj* at war

warrior /ˈwɒriə/ *noun* a person who fights in battle

warship /ˈwɔːʃɪp/ *noun* an armed ship which is used for fighting, not for carrying passengers or goods

wart /wɔːt/ *noun* a small hard lump on the skin, which is not harmful

wartime /ˈwɔːtaɪm/ *noun* a time of war

war-torn /wɔː tɔːn/ *adj* (*of a country or area*) very badly affected by war

wary /ˈweəri/ (**warier, wariest**) *adj* aware of a possible problem with someone or something ○ *I am very wary of any of his ideas for making money.*

③ **was** /wəz, wɒz/ past tense of **be**

① **wash** /wɒʃ/ *verb* (**washes, washing, washed**) to clean something using water ○ *Cooks should always wash their hands before touching food!* ○ *I must wash the car before we go to the wedding.* ○ *The moment I had washed the windows it started to rain.* ○ *His football shirt needs washing.* ◊ **linen** ■ *noun* the action of cleaning, using water ○ *The car needs a wash.* ○ *He's in the bathroom, having a quick wash.*

wash down① *phrasal verb* **1.** to wash with a large amount of water ○ *They washed down the van with buckets of water.* ○ *The sailors were washing down the deck.* **2.** to have a drink with food ○ *He had a pizza washed down by a glass of beer.*

wash up① *phrasal verb* **1.** to clean objects such as dirty cups, plates, knives and forks with water ○ *It took us hours to wash up after the party.* ○ *My brother's washing up, while I'm sitting watching the TV.* **2.** (*of the sea*) to bring something up onto the beach ○ *It's interesting to walk along the shore to see what has been washed up onto the beach during the night.* **3.** *US* to wash your face and hands ○ *He went into the bathroom to wash up.*

washable /ˈwɒʃəb(ə)l/ *adj* (*of clothing*) which can be washed in water, as opposed to being dry-cleaned

③ **washbasin** /ˈwɒʃbeɪs(ə)n/ *noun* a container for holding water for washing the hands and face, which has taps and is usually attached to the wall of a bathroom

washed-up /wɒʃd ˈʌp/ *adj* having failed and not likely to be successful again

washer /ˈwɒʃə/ *noun* **1.** a rubber ring inside a pipe which prevents liquid escaping from a joint ○ *The tap is leaking, and I think the washer needs replacing.* **2.** a metal ring under a nut or bolt ○ *Put a washer on the bolt to make it screw tight.*

② **washing** /ˈwɒʃɪŋ/ *noun* clothes which have been washed, or which are ready to be washed ○ *Put the washing in the washing machine.* ○ *She hung out the washing to dry.* □ **to do the washing** to wash dirty clothes ○ *I'm not doing the washing today.*

washing line /ˈwɒʃɪŋ laɪn/ *noun* a long piece of rope fixed between two poles or hooks and used for hanging washing on to dry

② **washing machine** /ˈwɒʃɪŋ məˌʃiːn/ *noun* a machine for washing clothes (NOTE: A machine for washing plates and cutlery is a **dishwasher**.)

washing powder /ˈwɒʃɪŋ ˈpaʊdə/, **soap powder** /ˈsəʊp ˌpaʊdə/ *noun* soap in powder form, used in washing machines or dishwashers

② **washing up** /ˌwɒʃɪŋ ˈʌp/ *noun* **1.** the activity of washing all the objects which have been used in preparing and eating a meal ○ *Can someone help with the washing up?* ○ *It took us hours to do the washing up after the party.* ○ *Use this little brush for the washing up.* **2.** things such as dirty dishes and glasses waiting to be cleaned ○ *There is a pile of washing up waiting to be put into the dishwasher.*

washing-up liquid /ˌwɒʃɪŋ ʌp ˈlɪkwɪd/ *noun* a liquid detergent used for washing dirty dishes

washout /ˈwɒʃaʊt/ *noun* **1.** a failure because of rain ○ *The village fete was a complete washout.* **2.** a failure ○ *No one turned up for the memorial service – it was a washout.*

① **wasn't** /ˈwɒznt/ ◊ **be**

③ **wasp** /wɒsp/ *noun* an insect which has black and yellow bands of colour round its body and which can sting

wastage /ˈweɪstɪdʒ/ *noun* **1.** the act of wasting ○ *There is an enormous wastage of natural resources.* **2.** an amount lost by being wasted ○ *Allow 10% extra material for wastage.*

② **waste** /weɪst/ *noun* **1.** an unnecessary use of time or money ○ *It is a waste of time asking the boss for a rise.* ○ *That computer is a waste of money – there are plenty of cheaper models.* **2.** rubbish, things which are no use and are thrown away ○ *Put all your waste in the rubbish bin.* ■ *verb* (**wastes, wasting, wasted**) to use more of something than you need ○ *Don't waste time putting your shoes on – jump out of the window now.* ○ *We turned off all the heating so as not to waste energy.* ■ *adj* useless and ready to be thrown away ○ *Keep all your waste paper and recycle it.* ○ *Waste products need to be disposed of carefully.*

waste bin /weɪst bɪn/ *noun* a container for putting rubbish in

wasted /ˈweɪstɪd/ *adj* **1.** useless **2.** (*of a person's body*) extremely thin and weak **3.** under the influence of drink or drugs (*informal*)

wasteful /ˈweɪstf(ə)l/ *adj* which wastes a lot

wasteland /ˈweɪstlænd/ *noun* land which is not used for anything

③ **wastepaper basket** /weɪs(t)ˈpeɪpə ˌbɑːskɪt/ *noun* a small box or basket where useless papers can be put

① **watch** /wɒtʃ/ *verb* (**watches, watching, watched**) **1.** to look at and notice something [~how/who/what etc] ○ *Watch how the mother elephant feeds her babies.Did you watch the news on TV last night?* ○ *I love watching football.* ○ *Everyone was watching the children dancing.* **2.** to look at something carefully to make sure that nothing happens [~(that)] ○ *Watch the potatoes don't burn.* ○ *Can you watch the baby while I'm at the hairdresser's?* ■ *noun* **1.** an object like a little clock which you wear on your wrist ○ *She looked at her watch impatiently.* ○ *What time is it? – my watch has stopped.* **2.** the activity of watching something carefully ○ *Visitors should be on the watch for pickpockets.* ○ *Keep a watch on the potatoes to make sure they don't burn.* (NOTE: no plural)

watch out① *phrasal verb* to be careful ○ *Watch out! there's a car coming!*

watchdog /ˈwɒtʃdɒg/ *noun* **1.** a dog used to guard a house or other buildings ○ *Alsatians are often used as watchdogs.* **2.** a person or committee that examines things such as public spending or public morals ○ *The report of the watchdog committee on water pricing.*

watchful /ˈwɒtʃf(ə)l/ *adj* very careful

watchman /ˈwɒtʃmən/ (*plural* **watchmen**) *noun* a person who guards a building, usually when it is empty

watchword /ˈwɒtʃˌwɜːd/ *noun* a word or phrase which shows someone's attitude towards life in general or towards a particular subject or situation

① **water** /ˈwɔːtə/ *noun* the liquid which falls as rain and forms rivers, lakes and seas. It makes up a large part of the bodies of living creatures, and is used for drinking and in cooking; also in industrial processes. ○ *Can we have three glasses of water please?* ○ *Cook the vegetables in boiling water.* ○ *Is the tap water safe to drink?* ○ *The water temperature is 60°.* (NOTE: no plural: *some water, a drop of water*) ■ *verb* (**waters, watering, watered**) to pour water on the soil round a plant to make it grow ○ *Because it is hot we need to water the garden every day.* ○ *She was watering her pots of flowers.*

watercolour /ˈwɔːtəkʌlə/ *noun* **1.** paint which is mixed with water and used by artists ○ *He prefers using watercolours to oils.* **2.** a picture painted using watercolours ○ *There is an exhibition of Turner's watercolours in the Tate Gallery.* ○ *She bought a watercolour of the village church.* (NOTE: [all senses] The US spelling is **watercolor**.)

water cooler /ˌwɔːtə ˈkuːlə/ *noun* a machine which people can get cold drinking-water from, used in places such as offices

watercress /ˈwɔːtəkres/ *noun* a low spreading plant grown in water streams and eaten in salads and soup

③ **waterfall** /ˈwɔːtəfɔːl/ *noun* a place where a stream falls down a steep drop

waterfront /ˈwɔːtəfrʌnt/ *noun* a bank of a river or shore of the sea and the buildings along it

waterhole /ˈwɔːtəhəʊl/ *noun* a small pool in the desert or other dry area, where animals come to drink

waterlogged /ˈwɔːtəlɒgd/ *adj* waterlogged ground is full of water, so the surface stays wet for a long time ○ *After so much rain, the waterlogged golf course had to be closed.* ○ *Most plants cannot grow in waterlogged soil.*

watermark /ˈwɔːtəmɑːk/ *noun* **1.** a hidden mark in paper, usually put there to prove that the paper is legal or official ○ *If you hold a banknote up to the light you will see the watermark.* **2.** a line showing the level water has reached ○ *On the wall by the river you can see various watermarks showing the level of floods in different years.*

watermelon /ˈwɔːtəmelən/ *noun* a very large type of melon with red flesh, large black seeds and dark green skin

water polo /ˈwɔːtə ˌpəʊləʊ/ *noun* a ball game played in water by two teams, each trying to throw a ball into a goal

waterproof /ˈwɔːtəpruːf/ *adj* not letting water go through ○ *waterproof clothing* ○ *These boots aren't waterproof – my socks are soaking wet.*

watershed /ˈwɔːtəʃed/ *noun* a point where an important permanent change takes place

waterskiing /ˈwɔːtəskiːɪŋ/ *noun* the sport of moving over the surface of a lake or river on large skis, pulled by a fast boat

water table /ˈwɔːtə ˌteɪb(ə)l/ *noun* a natural level of water below the ground

watertight /ˈwɔːtətaɪt/ *adj* **1.** made so that water cannot get in or out ○ *The food has to be kept in watertight containers.* ○ *Is* *the seal round the radiator watertight?* **2.** which cannot be shown to be false ○ *She has a watertight alibi for the time when the crime was committed.*

waterway /ˈwɔːtəweɪ/ *noun* a canal or deep river along which boats can easily travel

watery /ˈwɔːt(ə)ri/ *adj* like water, which has a lot of water in it

watt /wɒt/ *noun* the standard unit of electrical power

② **wave** /weɪv/ *noun* **1.** a raised mass of water on the surface of the sea, a lake or a river ○ *Waves were breaking on the rocks.* ○ *Watch out for big waves on the beach.* ○ *The sea was calm, with hardly any waves.* ◊ **Mexican wave 2.** an up and down movement of your hand **3.** a regular curve on the surface of hair ○ *His hair has a natural wave.* **4.** a sudden increase in something ○ *A wave of anger surged through the crowd.* ■ *verb* (**waves, waving, waved**) **1.** to move up and down in the wind ○ *The flags were waving outside the town hall.* **2.** to make an up and down movement of the hand, [~to] ○ *The star waved to fans as he boarded the plane to New York.* ○ *The children waved until the car was out of sight.* ○ *They waved goodbye as the boat left the harbour.* □ **to wave to someone** to signal to someone by moving your hand up and down ○ *When I saw him I waved to him to cross the road.*

waveband /ˈweɪvbænd/ *noun* a group of radio waves which are close together

wavelength /ˈweɪvleŋθ/ *noun* the distance between similar points on radio waves ○ *They used a short wavelength for transmitting messages.*

waver /ˈweɪvə/ (**wavers, wavering, wavered**) *verb* to be unable to decide what to do (NOTE: Do not confuse with **waiver**.)

wavy /ˈweɪvi/ (**wavier, waviest**) *adj* **1.** (*(of hair)*) slightly curly **2.** curving up and down ○ *He drew a wavy line across the bottom of the page.*

wax /wæks/ *noun* a solid substance made from fat or oil, used for making things such as candles and polish ○ *She brought a tin of wax polish and started to polish the furniture.*

① **way** /weɪ/ *noun* **1.** the direction in which something can be found or in which someone or something is going [~to] ○ *Do you know the way to the post office?* ○ *The bus is going the wrong way for the station.* ○ *She showed us the way to the railway station.* ○ *They lost their way and had to ask for directions.* ○ *I'll lead the way – just follow me.* **2.** the means of doing something [~of] ○ *Isn't there a faster way of digging the hole?* ○ *My mother showed me the way to make marmalade.* ○ *The way she said it implied it was my fault.* **3.** the distance between one place and another ○ *The nearest bank is quite a long way away.* ○ *He's got a long way to go before he qualifies as a doctor.* **4.** a path or road which goes somewhere ○ *Our neighbours across the way.* ○ *I'll walk the first part of the way home with you.* **5.** a particular direction from here ○ *a one-way street* ○ *Can you tell which way the wind is blowing?* ○ *This way please, everybody!* **6.** a space where someone wants to be or which someone wants to use ○ *Get out of my way – I'm in a hurry.* ○ *It's best to keep out of the way of the police for a moment.* ○ *I wanted to take a short cut, but there was a lorry in the way.* ◇ **to get your own way** to do what you want to do, even if other people don't want you to do it (*informal*) ○ *She always seems to get her own way.* ◇ **to make your way** to go to a place with some difficulty ○ *Can you make your way to passport control?* ○ *He made his way to the tourist information office.*

① **way in** /ˌweɪ ˈɪn/ *noun* an entrance

waylay /weɪˈleɪ/ (**waylays, waylaying, waylaid**) *verb* **1.** to stop and attack someone ○ *The gang waylaid the cashier as she was walking back to the office.* **2.** to stop someone to talk to them ○ *I was waylaid by an old friend on my way to the Post Office.*

① **way out** /ˌweɪ ˈaʊt/ *noun* an exit ○ *This is the way out of the car park.* ○ *He couldn't find the way out in the dark.*

way-out /ˌweɪ ˈaʊt/ *adj* strange, exciting (*dated informal*) ○ *They played some really way-out music.*

wayside *noun* □ **fall by the wayside** to fail or to stop before something is completed

③ **way up** /ˌweɪ ˈʌp/ *noun* a way in which something stands

wayward /ˈweɪwəd/ *adj* tending to do what he or she wants rather than what is expected

WC *noun* same as **toilet** (NOTE: mainly used on signs)

① **we** /wiː/ *pron* used by someone speaking or writing to refer to himself or herself and others ○ *He said we could go into the exhibition.* ○ *We were not allowed into the restaurant in jeans.* ○ *We had a wonderful holiday – we all enjoyed ourselves enormously.* (NOTE: When it is the object **we** becomes **us**: *We gave it to him; He gave it to* *us.* When it follows the verb to **be**, **we** usually becomes **us**: *Who is it? – It's us!*)

② **weak** /wiːk/ *adj* **1.** not strong ○ *After his illness he is still very weak.* ○ *I don't like weak tea.* **2.** not effective ○ *a weak leader* ○ *a weak argument* **3.** not having knowledge or skill ○ *She's weaker at science than at maths.* ○ *French is his weakest subject.* (NOTE: + **weakly** *adv.* Do not confuse with **week**.)

weaken /ˈwiːkən/ (**weakens, weakening, weakened**) *verb* to make or to become weak

weakling /ˈwiːklɪŋ/ *noun* a person who lacks physical strength

③ **weakness** /ˈwiːknəs/ *noun* **1.** the state of being weak ○ *The doctor noticed the weakness of her pulse.* **2. weakness for** a liking for something [~for] (*informal*) ○ *I have a weakness for Danish pastries.*

② **wealth** /welθ/ *noun* a large amount of money and property which someone owns ○ *His wealth was acquired in business.*

wealthy /ˈwelθi/ (**wealthier, wealthiest**) *adj* (*of a person*) very rich

wean /wiːn/ (**weans, weaning, weaned**) *verb* to make a baby start to eat solid food after only drinking mother's milk ○ *At what age should you start to wean a baby?* ◇ **to wean someone off** *or* **away from something** to get someone to drop a bad habit (*informal*) ○ *We must try to wean him off the TV for a period.*

② **weapon** /ˈwepən/ *noun* an object such as a gun, sword or bomb, which you fight other people with ○ *nuclear and biological weapons* ○ *The crowd used sticks and iron bars as weapons.*

weaponry /ˈwepənri/ *noun* weapons

① **wear** /weə/ (**wears, wearing, wore, worn**) *verb* **1.** to have something such as clothes or jewellery on your body ○ *What dress are you wearing to the party?* ○ *When last seen, he was wearing a blue raincoat.* ○ *She's wearing her mother's earrings.* ○ *She wears her hair very short.* **2.** to damage something or make it thin through using it ○ *The tread on the car tyres is worn.* ○ *I've worn a hole in the heel of my sock.*

wear down *phrasal verb* **1.** to disappear gradually, or make something disappear by much use **2.** to make someone gradually lose their confidence or effectiveness ○ *They wore down the enemy's resistance.*

wear off① *phrasal verb* to disappear gradually

wear out① *phrasal verb* **1.** to use something so much that it becomes broken and useless ○ *Walking across the USA, he wore out three pairs of boots.* **2.** □ **to wear yourself out** to become very tired through doing something ○ *She wore herself out looking after the old lady.*

wear and tear /ˌweər ən ˈteə/ *noun* the action of damaging something through use □ **fair wear and tear** damage through normal use which is accepted by an insurance company ○ *The policy covers most forms of damage but not wear and tear to the machine.*

wearing /ˈweərɪŋ/ *adj* tiring

weary /ˈwɪəri/ *adj* very tired

weasel /ˈwiːz(ə)l/ *noun* a small thin furry wild animal which kills and eats birds and other small animals ○ *The weasel chased the rabbit into its burrow.*

① **weather** /ˈweðə/ *noun* conditions outside, e.g. if it is raining, hot, cold or sunny ○ *What's the weather going to be like today?* ○ *If the weather gets any better, then we can go out in the boat.* ◇ **under the weather** miserable or unwell ○ *She's feeling a bit under the weather.*

weatherbeaten /ˈweðəbiːt(ə)n/ *adj* **1.** (*of a face*) made brown by the wind and sun ○ *The weatherbeaten faces of the old mountain farmers.* **2.** worn and marked by rain, sun and wind ○ *There are a few weatherbeaten fishermen's cottages down by the harbour.*

weave /wiːv/ (**weaves, weaving, wove, woven**) *verb* **1.** to make cloth by twisting fibres over and under each other ○ *The cloth is woven from the wool of local sheep.* ○ *The new weaving machines were installed last week.* **2.** to make something by a similar method, but using things such as very thin pieces of wood or the dried stems of plants ○ *She learnt how to weave baskets.*

③ **web** /web/ *noun* **1.** a net spun by spiders ○ *The garden is full of spiders' webs in autumn.* **2. the web** the thousands of websites and webpages within the Internet, which users can visit **3.** a set of events that cause problems [~of] ○ *The truth had been hidden by a web of lies and intrigue.*

web browser /ˈweb ˌbraʊzə/ *noun* a program for showing and using pages on the World Wide Web

webcam /ˈwebkæm/ *noun* a video camera recording pictures that are broadcast live on the Internet

webcast /ˈwebkɑːst/ *noun* a broadcast on the World Wide Web

webmaster /ˈwebmɑːstə/ *noun* a person who designs or manages a website

③ **webpage** /ˈwebpeɪdʒ/ *noun* a single file of text and graphics, forming part of a website

website /ˈwebsaɪt/ *noun* a collection of pages on the Web which have been produced by one person or organisation and are linked together

wed /wed/ (**weds, wedding, wedded** or **wed**) *verb* to marry (*formal, used mainly in newspapers*)

we'd /wiːd/ *short form* **1.** we had **2.** we would

② **wedding** /ˈwedɪŋ/ *noun* a marriage ceremony, when two people are officially made husband and wife ○ *This Saturday I'm going to John and Mary's wedding.*

wedding anniversary /ˈwedɪŋ ænɪˌvɜːs(ə)ri/ *noun* a celebration every year of the date of a wedding

wedding ring /ˈwedɪŋ rɪŋ/ *noun* a ring which is put on the finger during the wedding ceremony

wedge /wedʒ/ *noun* a solid piece of something such as wood, metal or rubber in the shape of a V ○ *Put a wedge under the door to hold it open.*

① **Wednesday** /ˈwenzdeɪ/ *noun* the day between Tuesday and Thursday, the third day of the week ○ *She came for tea last Wednesday.* ○ *Wednesdays are always busy days for us.* ○ *Can we meet next Wednesday afternoon?* ○ *Wednesday the 24th would be a good date for a meeting.* ○ *The 15th is a Tuesday, so the 16th must be a Wednesday.*

Weds abbreviation **Wednesday**

wee /wiː/ (**wees, weeing, weed**) *verb* to urinate (*child's word*) ○ *Do you want to wee, Tommy?* (NOTE: also **wee-wee**)

weed /wiːd/ *noun* a wild plant that you do not want in a garden or crop

weedy /ˈwiːdi/ *adj* **1.** thin and weak ○ *His opponent was a weedy little man who looked as though he had never had a fight before.* **2.** covered with weeds ○ *We've been away and the garden is so weedy.*

① **week** /wiːk/ *noun* a period of seven days, usually from Monday to Sunday ○ *There are 52 weeks in the year.* ○ *The firm gives us two weeks' holiday at Easter.* ○ *It's my aunt's 80th birthday next week.* ○ *I go to the cinema at least once a week.* (NOTE: Do not confuse with **weak**.)

weekday /ˈwiːkdeɪ/ *noun* any of the days from Monday to Friday, when most offices are open

① **weekend** /wiːkˈend/ *noun* Saturday and Sunday, or the period from Friday evening to Sunday evening ○ *We're going to the coast for the weekend.* ○ *Why don't you come to spend next weekend with us in the country?* ○ *At weekends, we try to spend time in the garden.*

③ **weekly** /ˈwiːkli/ *adj, adv* happening or published once a week ○ *Are you paid weekly or monthly?* ○ *We have a weekly paper which tells us all the local news.* ○ *The weekly rate for the job is £250.* (NOTE: Do not confuse with **weakly**.) ■ *noun* (*plural* **weeklies**) a magazine published once a week

weep /wiːp/ (**weeps, weeping, wept**) *verb* to produce tears

② **weigh** /weɪ/ (**weighs, weighing, weighed**) *verb* **1.** to use scales or a weighing machine to measure how heavy something is ○ *Can you weigh this parcel for me?* ○ *They weighed his suitcase at the check-in desk.* ○ *I weighed myself this morning.* **2.** to have a particular weight ○ *This piece of meat weighs 100 grams.* ○ *How much do you weigh?* ○ *She only weighs 40 kilos.*

weigh down *phrasal verb* □ **to be weighed down with** to be bent because you are carrying something heavy ○ *The car was weighed down with all our luggage.* ○ *The branches of the pear trees were weighed down with fruit.* □ **to be weighed down with** to be anxious or worried about something

weigh in *phrasal verb* **1.** (*of boxers and jockeys*) to have your weight measured before a fight or horse race ○ *The boxer weighed in at 200lbs.* **2.** to join in an argument [~with] (*informal*) ○ *He weighed in with some forceful comments.*

weigh up *phrasal verb* to form an opinion of someone or something

① **weight** /weɪt/ *noun* **1.** how heavy something is ○ *What's the maximum weight of parcel the post office will accept?* **2.** how heavy a person is ○ *His weight is less than it was a year ago.* **3.** something which is heavy ○ *If you lift heavy weights like paving stones, you may hurt your back.* (NOTE: Do not confuse with **wait**.) ◇ **that's a weight off my mind!** that is something I need not worry about any longer

weighted /ˈweɪtɪd/ *adj* changed by the addition of an amount to a total

weightlifting /ˈweɪtlɪftɪŋ/ *noun* the sport or exercise of lifting heavy weights (NOTE: + **weightlifter** *n*)

weight training /weɪt 'treɪnɪŋ/ *noun* physical training using weights to make your muscles strong

weighty /'weɪti/ (**weightier, weightiest**) *adj* **1.** important or serious ○ *We now face the weighty problem of trying to expand into new markets.* **2.** heavy ○ *She's tired after lugging her weighty bag round London.*

weir /wɪə/ *noun* a small structure built across a river to control the flow of water ○ *From here, you can see the weir and the lock.*

② **weird** /wɪəd/ *adj* strange in a way that makes you feel nervous or frightened (NOTE: **weirder – weirdest**)

weirdo /'wɪədəʊ/ (*plural* **weirdos**) *noun* a person regarded as strange (*slang*)

② **welcome** /'welkəm/ *verb* (**welcomes, welcoming, welcomed**) **1.** to greet someone in a friendly way ○ *The staff welcomed the new assistant to the office.* ○ *When we arrived at the hotel we were welcomed by a couple of barking guard dogs.* **2.** to be pleased to hear news ○ *I warmly welcome the result of the election.* ○ *I would welcome any suggestions as to how to stop the water seeping into the basement.* ■ *noun* the action of greeting someone ○ *There was not much of a welcome from the staff when we arrived at the hotel.* □ **a warm welcome** a friendly welcome ○ *They gave me a warm welcome.* □ **to outstay your welcome** to stay longer than your hosts thought you were going to stay ■ *adj* met or greeted with pleasure ○ *They made me very welcome.* ◇ **you're welcome!** a reply to 'thank you' ○ *Thanks for carrying the bags for me – you're welcome!*

weld /weld/ (**welds, welding, welded**) *verb* to join two pieces of metal together by heating them together ○ *The chassis can be repaired by welding the two pieces together.*

② **welfare** /'welfeə/ *noun* the act or practice of providing the things which people need and which help them to be healthy ○ *The club looks after the welfare of the old people in the town.* ○ *The government has taken measures to reform the welfare system.*

welfare state /ˌwelfeə 'steɪt/ *noun* a state which makes sure that all its citizens have suitable houses, education, public transport and health services

① **well** /wel/ *adv* **1.** in a way that is satisfactory ○ *He doesn't speak Russian very well.* ○ *Our business is small, but it's doing well.* ○ *Is the new computer working well?* **2.** very much ○ *He got back from the office late – well after eight o'clock.* ○ *You should go to the Tower of London – it's well worth a visit.* ○ *There were well over sixty people at the meeting.* ○ *She's well over eighty.* ■ *adj* (**better, best**) healthy ○ *She's looking well after her holiday!* ○ *The secretary's not very well today – she's had to stay off work.* ○ *It took him some weeks to get well after his flu.* ■ *interj* used for starting a sentence ○ *Well, I'll show you round the house first.* ○ *Well now, we've done the washing up so we can sit and watch TV.* ■ *noun* a very deep hole dug in the ground with water or oil at the bottom ◇ **as well** also ○ *When my aunt comes to stay she brings her two cats and the dog as well.* ○ *You can't eat fish and chips and a meat pie as well!* ◇ **as well as** in addition to ○ *Some newsagents sell groceries as well as newspapers.* ○ *She ate a slice of cheesecake as well as two scoops of ice cream.*

we'll /wiːl/ *contr* we will

well- /wel/ *prefix* in a satisfactory way ○ *well-attended* ○ *well-chosen* (NOTE: **Well-** is used in front of many adjectives, see the following words. Note also the comparative in these compounds: **well-advised – better advised**; **well-off – better off**.)

well-behaved /ˌwel bɪ'heɪvd/ *adj* having good behaviour

well-being /wel 'biːɪŋ/ *noun* a feeling of being healthy and happy

well-brought-up /ˌwel brɔːt'ʌp/ *adj* polite because of having been shown the correct way to behave when young

well-built /ˌwel 'bɪlt/ *adj* strong and solid

① **well done** /wel 'dʌn/ *interj* used for praising someone for their success ○ *Well done, the England team!* ○ *Well done to all of you who passed the exam!* ■ *adj* (*of meat*) which has been cooked a long time ○ *Can I have my steak well-done, please?*

well-heeled /ˌwel 'hiːld/ *adj* rich (*informal*)

wellie /'weli/ *noun* a wellington boot

wellington /'welɪŋtən/ *noun* a loose knee-length rubber boot

② **well-known** /ˌwel 'nəʊn/ *adj* known by a lot of people

② **well-off** /ˌwel 'ɒf/ *adj* rich

② **well-paid** /ˌwel 'peɪd/ *adj* earning a good salary

well-timed /ˌwel 'taɪmd/ *adj* happening at a favourable time

well-to-do /ˌwel tə 'duː/ *adj* rich

well-wisher /ˈwel ˌwɪʃə/ *noun* a person who is friendly towards someone

① **Welsh** /welʃ/ *adj* relating to Wales ○ *We will be going climbing in the Welsh mountains at Easter.* ■ *noun* **1.** □ **the Welsh** the people of Wales ○ *The Welsh are proud of their heritage.* ○ *The Welsh are magnificent singers.* **2.** the language spoken in Wales ○ *Welsh is used in schools in many parts of Wales.*

① **went** /went/ past tense of **go**

① **wept** /wept/ past tense and past participle of **weep**

① **were** /wə, wɜː/ 1st person plural past of **be**. 2nd person plural past of **be**. 3rd person plural past of **be**

① **we're** /ˈwiːə/ *short form* we are

② **weren't** /wɜːnt/ *short form* were not

werewolf /ˈweəwʊlf/ (*plural* **werewolves**), **werwolf** *noun* a person who is thought to change into the form of a wolf at night and back into human form in the day

① **west** /west/ *noun* **1.** the direction of where the sun sets [~of] ○ *We live in a village to the west of the town.* ○ *The sun sets in the west and rises in the east.* ○ *Their house has a garden that faces west* or *a west-facing garden.* **2. West** the countries in the western part of the world, e.g. Europe and North America ■ *adj* relating to the west ○ *She lives on the west coast of the United States.* ○ *The west part of the town is near the river.* ■ *adv* towards the west ○ *Go west for about ten kilometres, and then you'll come to the national park.* ○ *The river flows west into the ocean.*

westbound /ˈwestbaʊnd/ *adj* travelling towards the west

westerly /ˈwestəli/ *adj* **1.** towards the west **2.** (*of a wind*) blowing from the west

② **western** /ˈwestən/ *adj* from, of or in the south ○ *The western part of Canada has wonderful scenery.* ■ *noun* a book or film about life in the western USA in the nineteenth century, especially about cowboys ○ *She likes watching old westerns on TV.*

westerner /ˈwestənə/, **Westerner** *noun* **1.** a person who lives in or comes from the west of a country or region **2.** a person from Europe or North America

westernised, **westernized** *adj* accepting and using things such as the ideas, customs, and industrial methods of countries in Western Europe and the United States

westernmost /ˈwestənməʊst/ *adj* furthest to the west

Westminster /ˈwestmɪnstə/ *noun* **1.** in the area of London where Westminster Abbey and the Houses of Parliament are ○ *Tourists always go to Westminster as part of their visit to London.* **2.** the British Parliament itself ○ *The news was greeted with surprise at Westminster.* ○ *MPs returned to Westminster after the summer recess.*

② **wet** /wet/ *adj* **1.** covered in water or other liquid ○ *She forgot her umbrella and got wet walking back from the shops.* ○ *The chair's all wet where he knocked over his beer.* ○ *The baby is wet – can you change her nappy?* **2.** raining ○ *The summer months are the wettest part of the year.* ○ *There's nothing I like better than a wet Sunday in London.* **3.** not yet dry ○ *Watch out! – the paint's still wet.*

wet blanket /wet ˈblæŋkɪt/ *noun* an unhappy person who spoils social events, e.g. parties, by making other people feel unhappy (*informal*)

wetsuit /ˈwetsuːt/ *noun* a rubber suit worn by swimmers and divers to keep themselves warm in the water

① **we've** /wiːv/ *short form* we have

whack /wæk/ (**whacks, whacking, whacked**) *verb* to hit hard, making a loud noise ○ *She whacked her head on the low doorway.* ○ *He whacked the ball hard with his bat.* (NOTE: + **whack** *n*)

whacked /wækt/ *adj* feeling extremely tired

whale /weɪl/ *noun* a very large creature that lives in the sea ○ *You can take a boat into the mouth of the river to see the whales.* (NOTE: Do not confuse with **wail**.)

whaling /ˈweɪlɪŋ/ *noun* the practice of hunting whales

wham /wæm/ *noun* the loud noise produced by a solid heavy blow

wharf /wɔːf/ (*plural* **wharves** or **wharfs**) *noun* a quay where a ship can tie up to load or unload

① **what** /wɒt/ *adj* asking a question ○ *What kind of music do you like?* ○ *What type of food does he like best?* ■ *pron* **1.** the thing which ○ *Did you see what was in the box?* ○ *What we like to do most on holiday is just to visit old churches.* **2.** asking a question ○ *What's the correct time?* ○ *What did he give you for your birthday?* ○ *What happened to his car?* (NOTE: When **what** used to ask a direct question, the verb is put before the subject: *What's the time?* but not when it is used in a statement: *They don't know what the time is.*) ■ *adv* showing surprise ○ *What a huge meal!* ○ *What beauti-*

ful weather! ■ *interj* showing surprise ○ *What! did you hear what he said?* ○ *I won the lottery! – What!*

① **whatever** /wɒt'evə/ *pron* **1.** it does not matter what (*form of 'what' used for emphasis; in questions*) ○ *You can have whatever you like for Christmas.* ○ *She always does whatever she feels like doing.* ○ *I want that car whatever the price.* **2.** used instead of 'what' for emphasis in questions ○ *'I've sold the car.' 'Whatever for?'* ○ *Whatever made him do that?* ○ *Whatever does that red light mean?*

whatnot /'wɒtnɒt/ *noun* something of the same or a similar kind

what's /wɒts/ *short for* **1.** what has **2.** what is

whatsoever /ˌwɒtsəʊ'evə/ *adj, pron* used for emphasising 'whatever' ○ *There is no truth whatsoever in the report.* ○ *The police found no suspicious documents whatsoever.*

③ **wheat** /wiːt/ *noun* a plant of which the grain is used to make flour (NOTE: no plural)

wheedle /'wiːd(ə)l/ (**wheedles, wheedling, wheedled**) *verb* to try to persuade someone to do something, especially by speaking to them in a soft voice

② **wheel** /wiːl/ *noun* **1.** a round object on which a vehicle such as a bicycle, a car or a train runs ○ *The front wheel and the back wheel of the motorbike were both damaged in the accident.* ○ *We got a flat tyre so I had to get out to change the wheel.* **2.** any similar round object which turns ○ *a steering wheel* ○ *gear wheels* ■ *verb* (**wheels, wheeling, wheeled**) to push something along which has wheels ○ *He wheeled his motorbike into the garage.* ○ *She was wheeling her bike along the pavement.* ○ *The waiter wheeled in a sweet trolley.*

wheelbarrow /'wiːlbærəʊ/ *noun* a large container with one wheel at the front and two handles, used by people such as builders and gardeners for pushing heavy loads around

wheelchair /'wiːltʃeə/ *noun* a chair on wheels which people who cannot walk use to move around ○ *a special entrance for wheelchair users*

wheeler-dealer /ˌwiːlə 'diːlə/ *noun* a person who is skilled and successful, but possibly dishonest, in getting what they want, especially in business or politics

wheeze /wiːz/ (**wheezes, wheezing, wheezed**) *verb* to make a whistling sound when breathing ○ *The little boy had an attack of asthma and started to wheeze.*

① **when** /wen/ *adv* at what time (*asking a question*) ○ *When is the last train for Paris?* ○ *When did you last go to the dentist?* ○ *When are we going to get paid?* ○ *Since when has he been wearing glasses?* ○ *I asked her when her friend was leaving.* (NOTE: After **when** used to ask a direct question, the verb is put before the subject: *When does the film start?*; *When is he coming?* but not when it is used in a statement: *He doesn't know when the film starts.*; *They can't tell me when he is coming.*) ■ *conj* **1.** at the time that ○ *When he was young, the family was living in London.* ○ *When you go on holiday, leave your key with the neighbours so they can feed the cat.* ○ *Do you remember the day when we all went for a picnic in the park?* ○ *Let me know when you're ready to go.* **2.** after ○ *When the speaker had finished, he sat down.* ○ *Wash up the plates when you've finished your breakfast.* **3.** even if ○ *The salesman said the car was worth £5,000 when he really knew it was worth only half that.*

① **whenever** /wen'evə/ *adv* at any time that ○ *Come for tea whenever you like.* ○ *We try to see my mother whenever we can* or *whenever possible.*

① **where** /weə/ *adv* **1.** (*asking a question*) in what place, to what place ○ *Where did I put my glasses?* ○ *Do you know where the restaurant is?* ○ *Where are the knives and forks?* ○ *Where are you going for your holiday?* **2.** in a place in which ○ *Stay where you are and don't move.* ○ *They still live in the same house where they were living twenty years ago.* ○ *Here's where the wire has been cut.*

③ **whereas** /weər'æz/ *conj* if you compare this with the fact that ○ *He likes tea whereas she prefers coffee.*

whereupon /ˌweərə'pɒn/ *conj* at that point, after that (*literary*)

② **wherever** /weər'evə/ *adv* **1.** to or in any place ○ *You can sit wherever you want.* ○ *Wherever we go on holiday, we never make hotel reservations.* ○ *The police want to ask her questions, wherever she may be.* **2.** used instead of 'where' for emphasis ○ *Wherever did you get that hat?*

whet /wet/ (**whets, whetting, whetted**) *verb* □ **to whet your appetite** to make you more interested in something by giving you a little taste of it ○ *The brochures whet your appetite for holidays by the sea.*

① **whether** /'weðə/ *conj* **1.** (*showing doubt, or not having reached a decision*) used to mean 'if' for showing doubt, or for showing that you have not decided something ○ *Do you know whether they're coming?* ○ *I can't make up my mind whether to go on holiday now or later.* **2.** (*applying to either of two things*) used for referring to either of two things or people ○ *All employees, whether managers or ordinary staff, must take a medical test.* (NOTE: Do not confuse with **weather**.)

whew /fjuː/ *interj* used to express an emotion such as great, surprise or to show that you feel too hot, or you are very pleased that something unpleasant has not happened

① **which** /wɪtʃ/ *adj, pron* **1.** (*asking a question*) what person or thing ○ *Which dress are you wearing to the wedding?* ○ *Which boy threw that stone?* **2.** (*only used with things, not people*) that ○ *The French restaurant which is next door to the office.* ○ *They've eaten all the bread which you bought yesterday.*

③ **whichever** /wɪtʃ'evə/ *pron* **1.** any one in a group ○ *You can take several routes, but whichever you choose, the journey will still take three hours.* **2.** used for emphasising 'which' ○ *Take whichever you want.* ■ *adj* used for emphasising that it it is not important which person or thing is being referred to ○ *Whichever newspaper you read, you'll get the same story.*

whiff /wɪf/ *noun* a slight smell

① **while** /waɪl/ *conj* **1.** at the time that ○ *He tried to cut my hair while he was watching TV.* ○ *While we were on holiday someone broke into our house.* ○ *Shall I clean the kitchen while you're having a bath?* **2.** showing difference ○ *He likes meat, while his sister is a vegetarian.* ○ *Everyone is watching TV, while I'm in the kitchen making the dinner.* **3.** although (*formal*) ○ *While there may still be delays, the service is much better than it used to be.* ■ *noun* a short time ○ *It's a while since I've seen him.* ◇ **in a while** in a short time, soon ○ *I'll be ready in a while.* ◇ **to be worth someone's while** to be worth doing ○ *It's worth your while keeping copies of your work, in case your computer goes wrong.*

② **whilst** /waɪlst/ *conj* while (*formal*)

whim /wɪm/ *noun* a sudden wish or desire

whimper /'wɪmpə/ (**whimpers, whimpering, whimpered**) *verb* (*of a person or small animal*) to make low weak cries ○ *She whimpered that she would be OK.* ○ *The dog was whimpering because it was tied up.* (NOTE: + **whimper** *n*)

whimsical /'wɪmzɪk(ə)l/ *adj* unusual or strange, not very serious

whine /waɪn/ (**whines, whining, whined**) *verb* **1.** to make a loud high noise ○ *You can hear the engines of the racing cars whining in the background.* ○ *The dogs whined when we locked them up in the kitchen.* **2.** to complain frequently in a way that annoys other people (NOTE: Do not confuse with **wine**.+ **whine** *n*)

whinge /wɪndʒ/ (**whinges, whingeing, whinged**) *verb* to complain in a whining voice (*informal*)

whip /wɪp/ *noun* a long, thin piece of leather with a handle, used to hit animals to make them do what you want ○ *The rider used her whip to make the horse run faster.* ■ *verb* (**whips, whipping, whipped**) to hit someone or an animal with a whip ○ *He whipped the horse to make it go faster.*

whip up *phrasal verb* **1.** to make something increase suddenly ○ *The announcement whipped up the crowd's enthusiasm.* ○ *The wind whipped up the waves on the lake.* **2.** to get food ready quickly ○ *I'll just whip up a salad.*

whirl /wɜːl/ (**whirls, whirling, whirled**) *verb* to turn round quickly ○ *She put on her new skirt and whirled around for every one to see.* ○ *The children's paper windmills whirled in the wind.*

whirlpool /'wɜːlpuːl/ *noun* a stream of water that turns round and round very fast

whirlwind /'wɜːlwɪnd/ *noun* something which happens more quickly than usual ○ *They had a whirlwind romance, and got married on holiday.*

whirr /wɜː/ (**whirrs, whirring, whirred**) *verb* to make a low sound like something turning ○ *The journalists' cameras were whirring and clicking as she stepped out of the church.*

whisk /wɪsk/ (**whisks, whisking, whisked**) *verb* to mix food such as cream or eggs until they become thick and firm ○ *Next, whisk the mixture until it is creamy.* ○ *I always whisk egg whites by hand.*

whiskey /'wɪski/ *noun* Irish or American whisky

whisky /'wɪski/ (*plural* **whiskies**) *noun* an alcoholic drink, made in Scotland from barley ○ *The company produces thousands of bottles of whisky every year.* ○ *I don't like whisky – I prefer gin.*

② **whisper** /'wɪspə/ *verb* (**whispers, whispering, whispered**) to speak very quietly, so that only the person you are talking to can hear ○ *He whispered instructions to* *the other members of the gang.* ○ *She whispered to the nurse that she wanted something to drink.* ■ *noun* a quiet voice, or words spoken very quietly ○ *She spoke in a whisper.*

whistle /'wɪs(ə)l/ *noun* **1.** a high sound made by blowing through your lips when they are almost closed ○ *She gave a whistle of surprise.* ○ *We heard a whistle and saw a dog running across the field.* **2.** a simple instrument which makes a high sound, played by blowing ○ *He blew on his whistle to stop the match.* ■ *verb* (**whistles, whistling, whistled**) **1.** to blow through your lips to make a high sound ○ *They marched along, whistling an Irish song.* ○ *He whistled for a taxi.* **2.** to make a high sound as a signal, using a small metal instrument

① **white** /waɪt/ *adj* (**whiter, whitest**) of a colour like snow or milk ○ *A white shirt is part of the uniform.* ○ *A white car will always look dirty.* ○ *Her hair is now completely white.* ○ *Do you take your coffee black or white?* ■ *noun* **1.** the colour of snow or milk **2.** a person whose skin is pale **3.** a white part of something ○ *the white of an egg* ○ *The whites of his eyes were slightly red.* **4.** a white wine ○ *A glass of house white, please.*

whiteboard /'waɪtbɔːd/ *noun* a flat white board in a classroom, on which you can write with a special type of pen

Whitehall /'waɪthɔːl/ *noun* **1.** a street in London, leading from Trafalgar Square to the Houses of Parliament, where there are the offices of several government departments ○ *As you walk down Whitehall you pass Downing Street on your right.* **2.** the British government and civil service ○ *Whitehall sources suggest that the plan will be adopted.* ○ *There is a great deal of resistance to the idea in Whitehall.*

white lie /ˌwaɪt 'laɪ/ *noun* a lie about something unimportant, especially a lie told in order not to upset someone (*informal*)

white meat /waɪt 'miːt/ *noun* **1.** meat from the breast of chicken or turkey **2.** a pale coloured meat like veal, as opposed to red meat like beef

whiten /'waɪt(ə)n/ (**whitens, whitening, whitened**) *verb* to make whiter or to become whiter

whitewash /'waɪtwɒʃ/ *noun* **1.** a mixture of water and lime used for painting the walls of houses ○ *One coat of whitewash should be enough for this wall.* **2.** an attempt to cover up mistakes or dishonest behaviour ○ *Everyone said the report was a whitewash and nobody was ever arrested.* (NOTE: + **whitewash** *v*)

whitewater rafting /ˌwaɪtwɔːtə 'rɑːftɪŋ/ *noun* the sport of riding in small strong rubber boats down dangerous rivers

whitish /'waɪtɪʃ/ *adj* similar to white or partly white

whiz /wɪz/ *verb* (**whizzes, whizzing, whizzed**) to move very fast ○ *Someone whizzed past me but I didn't see who it was.* ○ *She's been whizzing around all afternoon trying to sort out her trip to the Caribbean.* ■ *noun* a whistling sound made by something moving very fast

whizz /wɪz/ *verb, noun* another spelling of **whiz**

① **who** /huː/ *pron* **1.** (*asking a question*) which person or persons ○ *Who phoned?* ○ *Who are you talking to?* ○ *Who spoke at the meeting?* **2.** the person or the people that ○ *The men who came yesterday morning work for the electricity company.* ○ *Anyone who didn't get tickets early won't be able to get in.* ○ *There's the taxi driver who took us home last night.* (NOTE: After an object, **who** can be left out: *There's the man I saw at the pub.* When **who** is used to ask a direct question, the verb is put after 'who' and before the subject: *Who is that man over there?*, but not when it is used in a statement: *I don't know who that man is over there.* When **who** is used as an object, it is sometimes written **whom** /huːm/ but this is formal and not common: *the man whom I met in the office*; *Whom do you want to see?*)

who'd /huːd/ *short form* **1.** who had **2.** who would

② **whoever** /huː'evə/ *pron* (*emphatic form of 'who'*) no matter who, anyone who ○ *Whoever finds the umbrella can keep it.* ○ *Go home with whoever you like.*

① **whole** /həʊl/ *adj* all of something ○ *She must have been hungry – she ate a whole apple pie.* ○ *We spent the whole winter in the south.* ○ *A whole lot of people went down with flu.* ■ *noun* all of something ○ *She stayed in bed the whole of Sunday morning and read the newspapers.* ○ *The whole of the north of the country was covered with snow.* ○ *Did you watch the whole of the programme?* (NOTE: Do not confuse with **hole**.) ■ *adv* in one piece ○ *The birds catch small fish and swallow them whole.*

wholefood /ˈhəʊlfuːd/ *noun* food that has had very little processing and has been grown or produced without the use of chemicals

wholehearted /həʊlˈhɑːtɪd/ *adj* complete or total

whole number /həʊl ˈnʌmbə/ *noun* a number such as 1, 35 or 630 which is not a fraction

wholesale /ˈhəʊlseɪl/ *adv* buying goods from manufacturers and selling them in large quantities to traders who then sell them in smaller quantities to the general public ○ *He buys wholesale.* Compare **retail** ■ *adj* **1.** in large quantities ○ *wholesale discount* **2.** on a large scale ○ *The wholesale killing of wild birds.*

③ **wholesaler** /ˈhəʊlseɪlə/ *noun* a person who buys goods in large quantities from manufacturers and sells them to retailers

wholesome /ˈhəʊls(ə)m/ *adj* **1.** good for your health ○ *a wholesome diet* **2.** having a good influence on moral behaviour ○ *wholesome entertainment*

who'll *short for* who will

wholly /ˈhəʊlli/ *adv* completely (*formal*) (NOTE: Do not confuse with **holy**.)

① **whom** /huːm/ ◊ **who**

whoop /wuːp, huːp/ (**whoops, whooping, whooped**) *verb* to make loud cries ○ *The gang ran along the main street, shouting and whooping at passers-by.* (NOTE: + **whoop** *n*)

whoops /wʊps/ *interj* used to show that an accident has almost happened ○ *Whoops! you nearly hit that tree!* ○ *She went charging across the kitchen on her trike and whoops! just missed Mum carrying a pile of plates.*

whopping /ˈwɒpiŋ/ *adj* very large (*informal*)

who's *short for* **1.** who has **2.** who is

① **whose** /huːz/ *pron* **1.** (*asking a question*) which belongs to which person ○ *Whose is that car?* ○ *Whose book is this?* ○ *Whose money was stolen?* **2.** of whom ○ *the family whose house was burgled* ○ *the man whose hat you borrowed* ○ *the girl whose foot you trod on* (NOTE: Do not confuse with **who's**.)

who've *short for* who have

① **why** /waɪ/ *adv* **1.** for what reason ○ *Why did he have to phone me in the middle of the TV film?* ○ *I asked the ticket collector why the train was late.* **2.** giving a reason ○ *She told me why she couldn't go to the party.* **3.** agreeing with a suggestion ○ *'Would you like some lunch?' 'Why not?'*

wicked /ˈwɪkɪd/ *adj* very bad ○ *What a wicked thing to say!* ○ *It was wicked of them to steal the birds' eggs.*

wicker /ˈwɪkə/ *adj* made of thin pieces of wood or sticks woven together ○ *a wicker basket* ○ *wicker furniture*

wicket /ˈwɪkɪt/ *noun* **1.** (*in cricket*) a set of three sticks put in the ground with two small sticks on top, used as the target ○ *The first ball hit his wicket.* **2.** the main playing area between two sets of these sticks

① **wide** /waɪd/ *adj* (**wider, widest**) **1.** which measures from side to side ○ *The table is three foot* or *three feet wide.* ○ *The river is not very wide at this point.* **2.** including many things ○ *The shop carries a wide range of imported goods.* ○ *She has a wide knowledge of French painting.* ◊ **width** (NOTE: **wider – widest**) ■ *adv* (**wider, widest**) as far as possible, as much as possible ○ *She opened her eyes wide.* ○ *The door was wide open so we just walked in.*

wide-eyed /waɪd aɪd/ *adj* with eyes wide open

② **widely** /ˈwaɪdli/ *adv* **1.** by a wide range of people ○ *It is widely expected that he will resign.* **2.** over a wide area ○ *Contamination spread widely over the area round the factory.* ○ *She has travelled widely in Greece.*

widen /ˈwaɪd(ə)n/ (**widens, widening, widened**) *verb* **1.** to make wider ○ *We need to widen the road to take larger lorries.* **2.** to become wider ○ *Further along, the road widens into two lanes in each direction.*

wide-ranging /ˌwaɪd ˈreɪndʒɪŋ/ *adj* which covers a wide range of subjects

widescreen /ˈwaɪdskriːn/ *adj* referring to a television whose screen is noticeably wider than average

③ **widespread** /ˈwaɪdspred/ *adj* over a large area

widow /ˈwɪdəʊ/ *noun* a woman whose husband has died and who has not married again

widowed /ˈwɪdəʊd/ *adj* who is a widow or widower

widower /ˈwɪdəʊə/ *noun* a man whose wife has died and who has not married again

③ **width** /wɪdθ/ *noun* **1.** a measurement of something from one side to another ○ *I need to know the width of the sofa.* ○ *The width of the garden is at least forty feet* or *the garden is at least forty feet in width.* **2.** the distance from one side to another of a swimming pool ○ *She swam three widths easily.*

wield /wiːld/ (**wields, wielding, wielded**) *verb* **1.** to hold something, usually by its handle, and use it ○ *Her attacker was wielding a knife.* **2.** to use or have power to control people ○ *The state wields enormous power over the ordinary citizen.*

① **wife** /waɪf/ (*plural* **wives**) *noun* a woman who is married to a man ○ *I know Mr Jones quite well but I've never met his wife.* ○ *They both came with their wives.* ◊ **old wives' tale**

wig /wɪɡ/ *noun* false hair worn on the head

wiggle /ˈwɪɡ(ə)l/ (**wiggles, wiggling, wiggled**) *verb* to move slightly up and down or from side to side

② **wild** /waɪld/ *adj* **1.** living naturally, not with people as a pet ○ *Wild dogs roam over parts of Australia.* **2.** very angry or very excited ○ *He will be wild when he sees what I have done to the car.* ○ *The fans went wild at the end of the match.* **3.** not thinking carefully ○ *She made a few wild guesses, but didn't find the right answer.* ○ *They had the wild idea of walking across the Sahara.* ■ *adv* without any control ○ *The crowds were running wild through the centre of the town.*

wild card /ˈwaɪldkɑːd/ *noun* a computer symbol that represents any character

wilderness /ˈwɪldənəs/ *noun* uncultivated and uninhabited country or desert

③ **wildlife** /ˈwaɪldlaɪf/ *noun* birds, plants and animals in their natural conditions

① **will** /wɪl/ *modal verb* **1.** used to form the future tense ○ *The party will start soon.* ○ *Will they be staying a long time?* ○ *We won't be able to come to tea.* ○ *If you ask her to play the piano, she'll say 'no'.* **2.** used as a polite way of asking someone to do something ○ *Will everyone please sit down?* ○ *Will someone close the curtains?* ○ (formal) *Won't you sit down?* **3.** used for showing that you are keen to do something ○ *Don't call a taxi – I'll take you home.* ○ *The car will never start when we want it to.* ○ *Don't worry – I will do it.* (NOTE: **will** is often shortened to **'ll**: *he'll* = he will. The negative is **will not** or, especially in speaking, **won't**. The past tense is **would**. Note also that **will** is only used with other verbs and is not followed by **to**.) ■ *noun* **1.** someone's desire that something will happen **2.** a legal document by which a person gives instructions to his or her executors as to what should happen to the property after he or she dies ○ *He wrote his will in 1984.* ○ *According to her will, all her property is left to her children.* ○ *Has she made a will yet?* ◊ **at will** whenever someone wants to ○ *Visitors can wander around the gardens at will.* ◊ **against your will** without your agreement ○ *He was forced to pay the money against his will.*

② **willing** /ˈwɪlɪŋ/ *adj* keen to help ○ *Is there anyone who is willing to drive the jeep?* ○ *I need two willing helpers to wash the car.*

willow /ˈwɪləʊ/ *noun* a tree with long thin branches often found near rivers and streams

willpower /ˈwɪlpaʊə/ *noun* mental strength that helps you to achieve something

wilt /wɪlt/ (**wilts, wilting, wilted**) *verb* to become weak and droop ○ *We've had no rain for days and the plants in the garden have started to wilt.* ○ *We all started off at a fast pace, but after the first mile or so some of us began to wilt.*

wily /ˈwaɪli/ (**wilier, wiliest**) *adj* full of tricks

wimp /wɪmp/ *noun* a person without a strong character (*insult*)

① **win** /wɪn/ *verb* (**wins, winning, won**) **1.** to beat someone in a game, or be first in a race or competition ○ *I expect our team will win tomorrow.* ○ *The local team won their match yesterday.* ○ *She won the race easily.* **2.** to get something as a prize ○ *She won first prize in the art competition.* ○ *He won two million pounds on the lottery.* ○ *She's hoping to win a new car in a competition in the paper.* ■ *noun* the act of winning a game, race or competition ○ *The local team has only had two wins so far this year.* ○ *We're disappointed, we expected a win.*

wince /wɪns/ (**winces, wincing, winced**) *verb* to show signs of pain or embarrassment, especially on your face ○ *He winced as the nurse gave him an injection.* ○ *She still winces at the memory of the awful mistake she made.*

winch /wɪntʃ/ *noun* a device which pulls things up by winding a rope around a drum ○ *The recovery vehicle has a winch at the back.* (NOTE: + **winch** *v*)

wind[1] /wɪnd/ *noun* air moving outdoors ○ *The wind blew two trees down in the park.* ○ *There's no point trying to use an umbrella in this wind.* ○ *There's not a breath of wind – the sailing boats aren't moving at all.*

wind down ③ *phrasal verb* to turn a handle to make something go down

wind² /waɪnd/ (**winds, winding, wound**) *verb* to twist something round and round ○ *He wound the towel round his waist.* ○ *She wound the string into a ball.*

wind up③ *phrasal verb* **1.** to twist round and round ○ *She was winding the string up into a ball.* **2.** to turn a key to make a machine work ○ *When did you wind up the clock* or *wind the clock up?* **3.** to turn a key to make something go up ○ *Wind up your window if it starts to rain.* **4.** to be in a situation at the end of a period (*informal*) ○ *They wound up owing the bank thousands of pounds.* **5.** to finish ○ *The meeting wound up at five o'clock.* **6.** □ **to wind up a company** to put a company into liquidation ○ *The court ordered the company to be wound up.* **7.** to make someone annoyed ○ *He only did it to wind you up.*

windfall /ˈwɪndfɔːl/ *noun* **1.** a fruit which has fallen to the ground from a fruit tree ○ *There are a lot of windfalls this year.* **2.** money which you receive unexpectedly ○ *His premium bond suddenly produced a windfall.*

wind instrument /ˈwɪnd ˌɪnstrʊmənt/ *noun* a musical instrument which you have to blow to make a note

① **window** /ˈwɪndəʊ/ *noun* **1.** an opening in a surface such as a wall or door, which is filled with glass ○ *When I fly, I always ask for a seat by the window.* ○ *It's dangerous to lean out of car windows.* **2.** any of several sections of a computer screen on which information is shown ○ *Open the command window to see the range of possible commands.*

window-pane /ˈwɪndəʊ peɪn/ *noun* a single piece of glass, used as part of a whole window

window shopping /ˈwɪndəʊ ˌʃɒpɪŋ/ *noun* the practice of looking at shop windows without buying anything

windpipe /ˈwɪndpaɪp/ *noun* the main air passage from the nose and mouth to the lungs

wind power /ˈwɪnd ˌpaʊə/ *noun* the force of the wind used to drive a windmill to produce energy

windscreen /ˈwɪndskriːn/ *noun* the glass window in the front of a vehicle

windscreen wiper /ˌwɪn(d)ˌskriːn ˈwaɪpə/, **windshield wiper** /ˌwɪn(d)ˌʃiːld ˈwaɪpə/ *noun* a device on a car which removes rainwater away from the windscreen

windshield /ˈwɪndʃiːld/ *noun* **1.** a screen on the front of a motorcycle ○ *The windshield protects the rider from the rain.* **2.** *US* the glass window in the front of a vehicle

windsurfing /ˈwɪndsɜːfɪŋ/ *noun* the sport of riding on the sea on a surfboard with a sail attached (NOTE: + **windsurfer** *n*)

windswept /ˈwɪndswept/ *adj* blown by the wind

③ **windy** /ˈwɪndi/ (**windier, windiest**) *adj* when a strong wind is blowing (*informal*)

② **wine** /waɪn/ *noun* an alcoholic drink made from grapes ○ *We had a glass of French red wine.* ○ *Two glasses of white wine, please.* ○ *Should we have some white wine with the fish?*

② **wing** /wɪŋ/ *noun* **1.** one of the two parts of the body, which a bird or butterfly etc. uses to fly ○ *The little birds were flapping their wings, trying to fly.* ○ *Which part of the chicken do you prefer: a leg or a wing?* **2.** one of the two flat parts sticking from the side of an aircraft, which hold the aircraft in the air ○ *He had a seat by the wing, so could not see much out of the window.*

wing mirror /wɪŋ ˈmɪrə/ *noun* one of a pair of mirrors attached to the outside of a vehicle and providing a view to the rear

wink /wɪŋk/ (**winks, winking, winked**) *verb* to shut and open one eye quickly, as a signal (NOTE: + **wink** *n*)

② **winner** /ˈwɪnə/ *noun* **1.** a person who wins something ○ *The winner of the race gets a silver cup.* **2.** something which is successful ○ *His latest book is a winner.*

winnings /ˈwɪnɪŋz/ *plural noun* money which has been won at betting ○ *He collected all his winnings and went to book a holiday in Spain.*

winning streak /ˈwɪnɪŋ striːk/ *noun* a period of time when a person has continuing good luck

② **winter** /ˈwɪntə/ *noun* the coldest season of the year, the season between autumn and spring ○ *It's too cold to do any gardening in the winter.* ○ *We're taking a winter holiday in Mexico.*

winter solstice /ˌwɪntə ˈsɒlstɪs/ *noun* 21st December, the shortest day in the northern hemisphere, when the sun is at its furthest point north of the equator

winter sports /ˌwɪntə ˈspɔːts/ *plural noun* sports which are done in the winter, such as skiing and skating etc.

wintry /ˈwɪntri/ *adj* **1.** cold like winter ○ *They are forecasting more wintry weather tonight.* **2.** unfriendly and cold ○ *He gave* *them a wintry smile which made conversation difficult.*

win-win /wɪn 'wɪn/ *adj* used to describe a situation which has a satisfactory outcome for all the parties involved

③ **wipe** /waɪp/ (**wipes, wiping, wiped**) *verb* to clean or dry something with a cloth ○ *Wipe your shoes with a cloth before you polish them.* ○ *Use the blue towel to wipe your hands.*

wipe out③ *phrasal verb* **1.** to kill, to destroy ○ *The tidal wave wiped out half the villages along the coast.* **2.** to remove completely ○ *The costs of moving to the new office have completely wiped out our profits.*

③ **wire** /'waɪə/ *noun* **1.** a thin piece of metal or metal thread ○ *He used bits of wire to attach the apple tree to the wall.* ○ *The chip basket is made of woven wire.* **2.** □ **(electric) wire** thin metal thread along which electricity flows, usually covered with coloured plastic ○ *The wires seem to be all right, so there must be a problem with the computer itself.*

wireless /'waɪələs/ *noun* a radio receiver (*dated; old*)

wiring /'waɪərɪŋ/ *noun* all the wires which make up a system to carry electricity round a building

wiry /'waɪəri/ (**wirier, wiriest**) *adj* **1.** (*of a person*) thin but strong **2.** (*of hair*) stiff and not easily combed

wisdom /'wɪzdəm/ *noun* general common sense and the ability to make good decisions

③ **wisdom tooth** /'wɪzdəm tuːθ/ *noun* one of the four back human teeth which only grow after the age of 20, or sometimes not at all

③ **wise** /waɪz/ *adj* having intelligence and being sensible ○ *I don't think it's wise to keep all that money in the house.* ○ *It was a wise decision to cancel the trip.* ◇ **none the wiser** still not understanding something ○ *His lengthy explanation left us none the wiser about how the system would work.*

① **wish** /wɪʃ/ *noun* what you want to happen □ **to make a wish** to think of something you would like to have or to see happen ○ *Close your eyes and make a wish.* ○ *Make a wish when you blow out the candles on your birthday cake.* ■ *plural noun* **wishes** a greeting ○ *Best wishes for the New Year!* ○ *Please give my good wishes to your family.* ■ *verb* (**wishes, wishing, wished**) **1.** to want something to happen [~(that)] ○ *She sometimes wished she could live in the country.* ○ *I wish you wouldn't be so unkind!* **2.** to hope something good will happen ○ *She wished him good luck in his interview.* ○ *He wished me a Happy New Year.* ○ *Wish me luck – it's my exam tomorrow.*

wishful thinking /ˌwɪʃf(ə)l 'θɪŋkɪŋ/ *noun* the practice of thinking that something will actually happen because you want it to

wisp /wɪsp/ *noun* a little piece

wistful /'wɪstf(ə)l/ *adj* longing for something, but sad because there is no hope of getting it

wit /wɪt/ *noun* an ability to say clever and funny things ○ *His wit comes out all through his book.* ◇ **at your wits' end** not knowing what to do next ○ *They were at their wits' end when the builders reported even more structural problems in the house.*

witch /wɪtʃ/ *noun* a woman believed to have magic powers. Compare **wizard**

witchcraft /'wɪtʃkrɑːft/ *noun* the art of magic

witch hunt /'wɪtʃ hʌnt/ *noun* persecution of people who are supposed to be politically unreliable

① **with** /wɪð, wɪθ/ *prep* **1.** showing that things or people are together ○ *She came here with her mother.* ○ *My sister is staying with us for a few days.* (NOTE: **with** is used with many adjectives and verbs: *to agree with, to be pleased with.*) **2.** something which you have ○ *The girl with fair hair.* ○ *They live in the house with the pink door.* **3.** showing something which is used ○ *He was chopping up wood with an axe.* ○ *Since his accident he walks with a stick.* ○ *The crowd attacked the police with stones and bottles.* **4.** because of ○ *Her little hands were blue with cold.* ○ *Half the people in the office are ill with flu.*

② **withdraw** /wɪð'drɔː/ (**withdraws, withdrawing, withdrew, withdrawn**) *verb* **1.** to stop offering or providing something [~from] ○ *The old coins have been withdrawn from circulation.* **2.** to stop doing something ○ *After his accident he withdrew from most public activities.* **3.** to take money out of a bank account [~from] ○ *You can withdraw up to £100 from any cash machine.* **4.** to change your mind about something which has been said or sent and say you no longer want it to be considered ○ *She withdrew her offer to provide the food for the party.* □ **to withdraw an email** to delete an email from someone's mailbox before it has been read, or say that it should not be read **5.** to move backwards ○ *The crowd slowly withdrew as the soldiers advanced.*

③ **withdrawal** /wɪð'drɔːəl/ *noun* **1.** the act of removing money from a bank account ○ *She made three withdrawals last week.* **2.** the act of going back, doing the opposite of what you had said you would do [~from] ○ *His withdrawal from the election surprised his friends.*

withdrawn /wɪð'drɔːn/ *adj* shy, not liking to meet other people

wither /'wɪðə/ (**withers, withering, withered**) *verb* (*of plants*) to grow weaker and dry up, to shrivel

withhold /wɪð'həʊld/ (**withholds, withholding, withheld**) *verb* to refuse to let someone have something

① **within** /wɪ'ðɪn/ *prep* (*in space or time*) inside an area or period of time ○ *The house is within easy reach of the station.* ○ *We are within walking distance of the shop.* ○ *I must go back for a another check within three months.* ○ *They promised to deliver the sofa within a week.*

① **without** /wɪ'ðaʊt/ *prep* **1.** not with ○ *They came on a walking holiday without any boots.* ○ *She managed to live for a few days without any food.* ○ *He was stuck in Germany without any money.* ○ *They were fined for travelling without tickets.* **2.** not doing something ○ *She sang for an hour without stopping.* ○ *They lived in the hut in the forest without seeing anybody for weeks.*

withstand /wɪð'stænd/ (**withstands, withstanding, withstood**) *verb* to resist something difficult or unpleasant

② **witness** /'wɪtnəs/ *noun* **1.** a person who sees something happen or who is present when something happens ○ *Were there any witnesses to the incident?* **2.** a person who is present when someone signs a document ○ *The contract has to be signed in front of two witnesses.* ○ *His sister signed as a witness.* ■ *verb* (**witnesses, witnessing, witnessed**) to be present when something happens, and see it happening ○ *Did anyone witness the accident?*

③ **witness box** /'wɪtnəs ˌbɒks/ *noun* a place in a courtroom where the witnesses give evidence

witty /'wɪti/ (**wittier, wittiest**) *adj* clever and funny ○ *She gave a witty and entertaining speech.*

③ **wives** /waɪvz/ plural of **wife**

wizard /'wɪzəd/ *noun* a clever person, expert ○ *He's a wizard at chess.*

wizardry /'wɪzədri/ *noun* being clever

wizened /'wɪz(ə)nd/ *adj* dried and wrinkled

③ **wobble** /'wɒb(ə)l/ (**wobbles, wobbling, wobbled**) *verb* to move from side to side in a way that is not smooth or steady ○ *The children made the jelly wobble in their bowls.* ○ *Don't wobble the table when I'm pouring coffee.*

woe /wəʊ/ *noun* sadness or trouble ○ *Money cannot cure all the woes of the world.* ○ *She stopped me and told me her tale of woe.*

wok /wɒk/ *noun* a Chinese round-bottomed frying pan used in stir-fry cooking

③ **woke** /wəʊk/, **woken** /'wəʊk(ə)n/ past tense of **wake**

woken /'wəʊk(ə)n/ past participle of **wake**

wolf /wʊlf/ (*plural* **wolves**) *noun* a wild animal like a large dog, which usually lives in groups in the forest ○ *At night the wolves came and howled outside the hut.*

① **woman** /'wʊmən/ (*plural* **women**) *noun* an adult female person ○ *The manageress is an extremely witty woman.* ○ *There were two middle-aged women in the seats next to ours.* ○ *There are very few women in government.* ○ *There are more and more women bus drivers.*

womanhood /'wʊmənhʊd/ *noun* the state of being a woman

womankind /'wʊmənkaɪnd/ *noun* all women taken as a group

womanly /'wʊmənli/ *adj* feminine, like a woman

womb /wuːm/ *noun* the hollow organ in a woman's body where a fertilised egg is lodged and an unborn baby is carried

③ **won** /wʌn/ past tense and past participle of **win**

① **wonder** /'wʌndə/ (**wonders, wondering, wondered**) *verb* **1.** to want to know something [~why/what/how etc] ○ *I wonder why the room has gone quiet.* ○ *If you don't ring home, your parents will start wondering what has happened.* **2.** to think about something [~how/what/when etc] ○ *I wonder how I can earn more money.* ○ *He's wondering what to do next.* **3.** to be surprised at something [~at] ○ *The tourists stood in groups, wondering at the size of the Pyramids.* **4.** asking a question politely [~if/whether] ○ *We were wondering if you would like to come for dinner on Saturday.*

① **wonderful** /ˈwʌndəf(ə)l/ *adj* extremely good or enjoyable ○ *They had a wonderful holiday by a lake in Sweden.* ○ *The weather was wonderful for the whole holiday.* ○ *You passed your driving test first time? – Wonderful!*

wonky /ˈwɒnki/ *adj, adv* **1.** unreliable to use **2.** not straight

③ **won't** /wəʊnt/ *contr* will not

woo /wuː/ (**woos, wooing, wooed**) *verb* **1.** to try to get someone to support you or to vote for you ○ *The government is wooing the younger voter.* ○ *The supermarket is trying to woo customers with special offers.* **2.** to try to attract a girl to marry you (*old*) ○ *Three suitors came to woo the princess, each bringing costly gifts.*

② **wood** /wʊd/ *noun* **1.** a hard material which comes from a tree ○ *The kitchen table is made of wood.* ○ *She picked up a piece of wood and put it on the fire.* ○ *A wood floor would be just right for this room.* (NOTE: no plural: *some wood, a piece of wood*) **2.** an area in which many trees are growing together ○ *The path goes straight through the wood.* ○ *Their house is on the edge of a wood.* (NOTE: Do not confuse with **would**.)

wooded /ˈwʊdɪd/ *adj* covered in trees

③ **wooden** /ˈwʊd(ə)n/ *adj* made out of wood ○ *In the market we bought little wooden dolls for the children.*

woodwind /ˈwʊdwɪnd/ *noun* smaller instruments in an orchestra such as the flute, clarinet, oboe and bassoon, which are played by blowing

woodworm /ˈwʊdwɜːm/ *noun* a little insect that eats wood

woof /wʊf/ *noun* the sound made by a dog when it barks ○ *A dog goes 'woof, woof', a cat goes 'miaow.'* ○ *Your father must be back, I've just heard a woof from the garden.*

② **wool** /wʊl/ *noun* **1.** long threads of twisted animal hair, used to make clothes or carpets etc. ○ *The carpet is made of wool.* ○ *I need an extra ball of wool to finish this pullover.* **2.** the hair growing on a sheep ○ *The sheep are sheared and the wool sent to market in early summer.*

woollen /ˈwʊlən/ *adj* made of wool (NOTE: The US spelling is **woolen**.)

woolly /ˈwʊli/ (**woollier, woolliest**) *adj* made out of wool ○ *She wore a woolly hat.*

woozy /ˈwuːzi/ *adj* feeling confused and dizzy

① **word** /wɜːd/ *noun* **1.** a separate piece of language, either written or spoken ○ *This sentence has five words.* ○ *He always spells some words wrongly, such as 'though'.* **2.** something spoken [~about/on] ○ *I'd like to say a few words about Mr Smith who is retiring today.* ○ *She passed me in the street but didn't say a word.* **3.** a promise which you have made ◇ **to have a word with** to speak to someone ○ *I must have a word with the manager about the service.* ○ *The salesgirl had made so many mistakes, I had to have a word with her.* ◇ **without a word** without saying anything ○ *She went out of the room without a word.* ◇ **word for word** exactly as it is said or written ○ *Tell me what he said word for word.* ○ *A word-for-word translation often doesn't make any sense.* ◇ **to give your word** to promise ○ *He gave his word that the matter would remain confidential.* ◇ **to keep your word** to do what you promised to do ○ *He kept his word, and the cheque arrived the next day.* ◇ **by word of mouth** spoken, not written ◇ **to take someone's word for it** to accept what someone says as being true ○ *OK, I'll take your word for it.*

wording /ˈwɜːdɪŋ/ *noun* words and phrases used in a piece of writing

wordplay /ˈwɜːdˌpleɪ/ *noun* the clever use of words

word processing /ˌwɜːd ˈprəʊsesɪŋ/ *noun* using a computer to produce, check and change texts, reports and letters etc.

word processor /ˌwɜːd ˈprəʊsesə/ *noun* **1.** a small computer which is used to produce texts, reports and letters etc. ○ *She offered to write the letter for me on her word processor.* ○ *You can use my word processor to type your letter if you like.* **2.** a word-processing program which allows you to create texts, edit them and print them

wordy /ˈwɜːdi/ (**wordier, wordiest**) *adj* using more words than necessary

③ **wore** /wɔː/ past tense of **wear**

① **work** /wɜːk/ *noun* **1.** things that you do using your strength or your brain ○ *There's a great deal of work still to be done on the project.* ○ *There's too much work for one person.* ○ *If you've finished that piece of work, there's plenty more to be done.* ○ *Cooking for two hundred people every day is hard work.* **2.** a job done regularly to earn money ○ *He goes to work every day on his bicycle.* ○ *Work starts at 9 a.m. and finishes at 5 p.m.* ○ *Her work involves a lot of travelling.* ○ *He is still looking for work.* **3.** something which has been made, painted or written by someone ○ *the complete* *works of Shakespeare* ○ *An exhibition of the work of local artists.* ■ *verb* (**works, working, worked**) **1.** to use your strength or brain to do something ○ *I can't work in the garden if it's raining.* ○ *He's working well at school, we're very pleased with his progress.* ○ *Work hard and you'll soon get a better job.* **2.** to have a job [~in/~with/~as/~for] ○ *She works in the medical profession.* ○ *He works with his father in the family business.* ○ *She's working as a teacher at the moment.* ○ *Which company do you work for?* **3.** (*of a machine*) to operate in the usual way ○ *The computers aren't working.* ○ *The machine works by electricity.* **4.** to make a machine operate ○ *She works the biggest printing machine in the factory.* ○ *Do you know how to work the microwave?* **5.** to have the desired effect or result ○ *His plan worked well.* ○ *Will the plan work?* ○ *If the cough medicine doesn't work, you'll have to see a doctor.* ◇ **at work** working ○ *The builders are still hard at work.* ○ *She's at work today, but will have the day off tomorrow.* ◇ **to set to work** to start working ○ *If we all set to work early, we should finish the job this evening.*

work on① *phrasal verb* to work hard to make something better

work out① *phrasal verb* **1.** to solve a problem by looking at information or calculating figures ○ *I'm trying to work out if we've sold more this year than last.* □ **to work out at** to amount to an amount ○ *The total works out at £10.50 per person.* **2.** to succeed ○ *Everything worked out quite well in the end.* □ **to work something out** to find a successful way of solving a problem **3.** to do exercises ○ *He works out every morning in the gym.* **4.** (*of a mine*) to exhaust a seam of coal etc., and not be able to continue working there ○ *The gold seam was worked out some years ago.*

work up③ *phrasal verb* **1.** to develop ○ *I find it difficult to work up any enthusiasm for my job.* **2.** to do some hard work to make something happen ○ *I'm doing some digging to work up an appetite.*

workaholic /ˌwɜːkəˈhɒlɪk/ *noun* a person who cannot stop working (*informal*)

workbook /ˈwɜːkbʊk/ *noun* a book in which a student can write answers to exercises printed in the book

① **worker** /ˈwɜːkə/ *noun* **1.** a person who works ○ *She's a good worker.* ○ *He's a fast worker.* **2.** a person who works in a particular job ○ *The factory closed when the workers went on strike.* ○ *Office workers usually work from 9.30 to 5.30.*

workforce /ˈwɜːkfɔːs/ *noun* all the people who work in an office or factory

① **working** /ˈwɜːkɪŋ/ *adj* relating to a job or to work ○ *the working population of a country* ○ *The unions have complained about working conditions in the factory.* ○ *He came to the party in his working clothes.* ■ *noun* a way or ways in which something works ○ *The workings of a car engine are a complete mystery to him.* ○ *I wish I could understand the workings of local government!*

working class /ˌwɜːkɪŋ ˈklɑːs/ *noun* a group in society consisting of people who work with their hands, usually earning wages not salaries

working day /ˈwɜːkɪŋ deɪ/ *noun* **1.** a day on which someone works **2.** the number of hours someone spends at work

③ **workload** /ˈwɜːkˌləʊd/ *noun* an amount of work which a person has to do

③ **workman** /ˈwɜːkmən/ (*plural* **workmen**) *noun* a man who works with his hands

workmanship /ˈwɜːkmənʃɪp/ *noun* the skill of a good workman

workout /ˈwɜːkaʊt/ *noun* exercise or sports practice

workplace /ˈwɜːkpleɪs/ *noun* a place where work is done

① **works** /wɜːks/ *plural noun* **1.** the moving parts of a machine ○ *I looked inside the clock and there seems to be dust in the works.* **2.** a factory ○ *The steel works will be closed next week for the Christmas holidays.* **3. the works** everything (*informal*) ○ *They built a conservatory with a fountain, automatic lighting, a barbecue – the works!*

worksheet /ˈwɜːkˌʃiːt/ *noun* a sheet of questions for students to answer

③ **workshop** /ˈwɜːkʃɒp/ *noun* a very small factory where things are made or repaired

③ **workstation** /ˈwɜːkˌsteɪʃ(ə)n/ *noun* a desk with terminal, monitor or keyboard etc., where a computer operator works

① **world** /wɜːld/ *noun* the earth on which we live ○ *Here is a map of the world.* ○ *She flew round the world twice last year.* ○ *He has to travel all over the world on business.* ○ *A round-the-world ticket allows several stopovers.*

world-class /ˌwɜːld ˈklɑːs/ *adj* so good as to be among the best in the world

world-famous /ˌwɜːld ˈfeɪməs/ *adj* known everywhere

worldly /ˈwɜːldli/ *adj* **1.** referring to the material world ○ *All her worldly possessions fitted into two small suitcases.* **2.** not idealistic, with a lot of experience ○ *She's worldly enough to know exactly what she's doing.*

world music /wɜːld ˈmjuːzɪk/ *noun* music from cultures outside the western world

worldwide /wɜːldˈwaɪd/; /ˈwɜːldwaɪd/ *adj, adv* over the whole world ○ *a worldwide energy crisis* ○ *The company has a worldwide network of distributors.* ○ *The TV news programme is available worldwide.*

worm /wɜːm/ *noun* a small thin animal which has no arms or legs and lives in the soil ○ *Birds were pecking at the soil for worms.*

③ **worn** /wɔːn/ past participle of **wear**

③ **worn out** /ˌwɔːn ˈaʊt/ *adj* very tired ○ *He was worn out after the game of rugby.* ○ *She comes home every evening, worn out after a busy day at the office.*

② **worried** /ˈwʌrid/ *adj* unhappy because you think something bad will happen or because something bad has happened ○ *He had a worried look on his face.* ○ *She's looking worried.* ○ *I'm worried that we may run out of petrol.*

③ **worry** /ˈwʌri/ *verb* (**worries, worrying, worried**) to feel anxious, or to make someone feel anxious [~about/~(that)] ○ *He's worrying about his driving test.* ○ *I worry that the children aren't happy.* ○ *Don't worry, I'll be back on time.* ○ *She's always looks so tired, and that worries me.* ■ *noun* (*plural* **worries**) **1.** something that makes you anxious [~about] ○ *Parents had worries about safety.* ○ *Go on holiday and try to forget your worries.* **2.** the state of being anxious ○ *She is a great source of worry for her family.* (NOTE: no plural)

③ **worrying** /ˈwʌriɪŋ/ *adj* which makes you worried

① **worse** /wɜːs/ *adj* **1.** less good than something else ○ *It rained for the first week of our holidays, and the second week was even worse.* ○ *I think this film is worse than the one I saw last week.* ○ *Both children are naughty – but the little girl is worse than her brother.* **2.** more ill ○ *He's much worse since he started taking his medicine.* ■ *adv* not as well ○ *He drives badly enough but his sister drives even worse.*

worsen /ˈwɜːs(ə)n/ (**worsens, worsening, worsened**) *verb* to become worse, to make worse

③ **worse off** /ˌwɜːs ˈɒf/ *adj* with less money than before

worship /ˈwɜːʃɪp/ (**worships, worshipping, worshipped**) *verb* **1.** to praise and respect God ○ *The ancient peoples worshipped stone statues of their gods.* **2.** to take part in a church service ○ *They worship regularly in the local church.*

① **worst** /wɜːst/ *adj* worse than anything else ○ *This summer is the worst for fifty years.* ○ *I think this is the worst film he's ever made.* ■ *adv* less well than anything or anyone else or than at any other time ○ *It's difficult to say which team played worst.* ○ *She works worst when she's tired.* ■ *noun* a very bad thing ○ *This summer is the worst for fifty years.* ◇ **to prepare for the worst** to get ready to have bad news ○ *Your father was very badly injured – you must prepare for the worst.*

① **worth** /wɜːθ/ *adj* **1.** □ **to be worth** to have a certain value or price ○ *This ring's worth a lot of money.* ○ *Gold is worth more than silver.* ○ *The house is worth more than £250,000.* ○ *The car is worth £6,000 on the secondhand market.* **2.** □ **to be worth doing something** to find something good or helpful to do ○ *It's worth taking a map with you, as you may get lost in the little streets.* ○ *His latest film is well worth seeing.* ○ *The old castle is well worth visiting* or *is well worth a visit.* ■ *noun* a value ○ *Its worth will increase each year.* ○ *She lost jewellery of great worth in the fire.* ○ *Can you give me twenty pounds' worth of petrol?*

worthless /ˈwɜːθləs/ *adj* having no worth, no use

③ **worthwhile** /wɜːθˈwaɪl/ *adj* which is worth the effort spent on it

worthy /ˈwɜːði/ (**worthier, worthiest**) *adj* deserving

① **would** /wʊd/ *modal verb* **1.** used as a polite way of asking someone to do something ○ *Would you please stop talking?* ○ *Would someone please tell me where the library is?* ○ *Would you like some more tea?* **2.** used as the past of 'will' ○ *He said he would be here for lunch.* ○ *She hoped she would be well enough to come.* ○ *He wouldn't go even if I paid him.* **3.** used as the past of 'will', showing something which often happens ○ *He would bring his dog with him, even though we asked him not to.* ○ *Naturally the car wouldn't start when we were in a hurry.* ○ *My husband* *forgot my birthday again this year – he would!* **4.** used for showing something which often happened in the past ○ *Every morning she would go and feed the chickens.* ○ *He would always be there waiting outside the station.* ○ *They would often bring us flowers.* **5.** used following a condition ○ *I'm sure that if they could come, they would.* ○ *I would've done it if you had asked me to.* ○ *If she were alive, she would* or *she'd be a hundred years old today.* ○ *If it snowed we would* or *we'd go skiing.* (NOTE: **would** is often shortened to **'d**: *she'd* = she would. The negative is **would not** or, especially in speaking, **wouldn't**. Note also that **would** is only used with other verbs and is not followed by **to**.)

would rather② *phrasal verb* to prefer

would-be /ˈwʊdbiː/ *adj* who hopes to become

② **wouldn't** /ˈwʊd(ə)nt/ *short for* would not

③ **wound**[1] /wuːnd/ *noun* a cut made on someone's body, usually in fighting ■ *verb* (**wounds, wounding, wounded**) **1.** to hurt someone badly by cutting into their flesh ○ *Two of the gang were wounded in the bank robbery.* **2.** to hurt someone's feelings ○ *She was deeply wounded by what he said.*

wound[2] /waʊnd/ past tense and past participle of **wind**

wove /wəʊv/, **woven** past tense of **weave**

woven /ˈwəʊv(ə)n/ past participle of **weave**

wow /waʊ/ *interj* showing surprise and pleasure ○ *Wow! Have you seen his new car?*

wrangle /ˈræŋgəl/ (**wrangles, wrangling, wrangled**) *verb* to argue ○ *They're always wrangling over money.* ○ *They wrangled for months before the treaty was finally signed.* (NOTE: + **wrangle** *n*)

③ **wrap** /ræp/ *vt* (**wrapping, wraps, wrapped**) to cover something by putting something over it ○ *She wrapped the parcel in paper.* ■ *noun* **1.** a type of shawl that is put round the shoulders or the top part of the body ○ *She pulled her wrap closer around her.* **2.** a piece of material used to cover something ○ *Remove the wrap before putting the dish in the microwave.*

wrap up *phrasal verb* to finish off ○ *That just about wraps up the points we have to make.*

wrapper /ˈræpə/ *noun* a piece of paper used to wrap round something

③ **wrapping** /ˈræpɪŋ/ *noun* the paper or plastic used to wrap something up

wrapping paper /ˈræpɪŋ ˌpeɪpə/ *noun* brightly coloured paper used to wrap presents

wrath /rɒθ/ *noun* great anger

wreak /riːk/ (**wreaks, wreaking, wreaked**) *verb* to do something violent

wreath /riːθ/ *noun* a circle of flowers or leaves especially given at a funeral in memory of the dead person

wreck /rek/ *noun* **1.** a ship which has been sunk or badly damaged ○ *Divers have discovered the wreck on the seabed.* ○ *The wreck of the 'Mary Rose' was found in the sea near Southampton.* **2.** anything which has been damaged and cannot be used ○ *The police towed away the wreck of the car.* ○ *Their new car is now a total wreck.* ■ *verb* (**wrecks, wrecking, wrecked**) to damage something very badly ○ *The ship was wrecked on the rocks in the storm.* ○ *The bank was wrecked by the explosion.*

③ **wreckage** /ˈrekɪdʒ/ *noun* what is left of a building, ship or plane etc. after it has been wrecked

wrench /rentʃ/ *noun* **1.** a large spanner which can be adjusted to undo various sizes of nut. ◊ **monkey wrench 2.** a feeling of sadness at leaving ○ *It will be a wrench to leave the old office.* ■ *verb* (**wrenches, wrenching, wrenched**) to twist and pull something violently ○ *She wrenched the box from his hands and ran off.*

wrest /rest/ (**wrests, wresting, wrested**) *verb* to twist, to wrench away

wrestle /ˈres(ə)l/ (**wrestles, wrestling, wrestled**) *verb* to fight with someone to try to throw him to the ground

wrestling /ˈres(ə)lɪŋ/ *noun* the sport of fighting, but without punching (NOTE: + **wrestler** *n*)

wriggle /ˈrɪg(ə)l/ (**wriggles, wriggling, wriggled**) *verb* to twist from side to side ○ *The baby wriggled in her father's arms.* ○ *The worm wriggled back into the soil.*

wring /rɪŋ/ (**wrings, wringing, wrung**) *verb* to twist something, especially to get water out of it ○ *Wring the face cloth (dry) after you have used it.* ○ *He wrung out his shirt before putting it to dry.*

wrinkle /ˈrɪŋkəl/ *noun* a fold in the skin ○ *She had an operation to remove wrinkles round her eyes.*

wrinkled /ˈrɪŋkəld/ *adj* full of lines or creases

③ **wrist** /rɪst/ *noun* the joint between the arm and the hand

wristwatch /ˈrɪstwɒtʃ/ *noun* a small clock worn on a strap around the wrist

writ /rɪt/ *noun* a legal document which starts an action in the High Court

① **write** /raɪt/ (**writes, writing, wrote, written**) *verb* **1.** to put words or numbers on paper etc., with a pen or word processor etc. ○ *She wrote the address on the back of an envelope.* ○ *Someone wrote 'down with the management' on the wall of the staff canteen.* ○ *Write the reference number at the top of the letter.* **2.** to write a letter and send it to someone [~to] ○ *I've written to my MP about the problem.* ○ *Don't forget to write as soon as you get to your hotel.* ○ *He wrote a letter to the management to complain about the service.* **3.** to be the author of a book or music etc. [~about/on/~for] ○ *He wrote a book on keeping tropical fish.* ○ *Didn't you know she used to write for the 'Sunday Times'?*

write back③ *phrasal verb* to answer by letter

write down③ *phrasal verb* to write something

write in③ *phrasal verb* to write a letter to an organisation

write off③ *phrasal verb* **1.** to cancel a debt ○ *The bank couldn't trace him so they had to write the debt off.* **2.** to remove an asset from a company's accounts because it no longer has any value

write out③ *phrasal verb* to write something in full

write up③ *phrasal verb* to write a text fully from notes which you have taken ○ *I took masses of notes, and now I have to write them up for the local newspaper.*

write-off /ˈraɪt ɒf/ *noun* a total loss, removing an asset from a company's accounts

write-protected /raɪt prəˈtektɪd/ *adj* (*of a computer disk*) which cannot be altered or erased

② **writer** /ˈraɪtə/ *noun* a person who writes ○ *Who is the writer of this letter?* ○ *She's the writer of books on gardening.*

write-up /ˈraɪt ʌp/ *noun* an article about someone or something in a newspaper

writhe /raɪð/ (**writhes, writhing, writhed**) *verb* to twist and turn when pain is very severe

② **writing** /ˈraɪtɪŋ/ *noun* something which is written ○ *Please don't phone, reply in writing.* ○ *Put everything in writing, then you have a record of what has been done.*

③ **written**[1] /ˈrɪt(ə)n/ *adj* which has been put in writing

written[2] /ˈrɪt(ə)n/ past participle of **write**

① **wrong** /rɒŋ/ *adj* **1.** not correct ○ *He gave three wrong answers and failed the test.* ○ *That's not the right time, is it? – No, the clock is wrong.* ○ *You've come to the wrong house – there's no one called Jones living here.* ○ *There is something wrong with the television.* ○ *I must have pressed the wrong button.* **2.** not suitable ○ *You came just at the wrong time, when we were bathing the children.* ○ *She was wearing the wrong sort of dress for a wedding.* **3.** not working properly ○ *There is something wrong with the television.* **4.** morally bad ○ *It's wrong to talk like that about her.* ○ *Cheating in exams is wrong.* **5.** making someone worried ■ *adv* badly ○ *Everything went wrong yesterday.* ○ *She spelt my name wrong.* ◇ **don't get me wrong** don't put the wrong meaning on what I'm trying to say ○ *Don't get me wrong, I love him dearly but at times he can be infuriating.*

wrongdoing /ˈrɒŋduːɪŋ/ *noun* a crime or unlawful act

wrongly /ˈrɒŋli/ *adv* not correctly

③ **wrote** /rəʊt/ past tense of **write**

wrought iron /ˌrɔːt ˈaɪən/ *noun* iron which is bent to make gates and fences etc. Compare **cast iron**

wrung /rʌŋ/ past tense and past participle of **wring**

wry /raɪ/ *adj* showing amusement by twisting your mouth (NOTE: Do not confuse with **rye**.)

wt *abbr* weight

www *abbr* World Wide Web

XYZ

x /eks/, **X** *noun* the twenty-fourth letter of the alphabet, between W and Y ■ *symbol* **1.** a multiplication sign ○ *3 x 3 = 9.* (NOTE: say 'three times three equals nine') **2.** showing size ○ *The table top is 24 x 36cm.* (NOTE: say 'twenty-four by thirty-six centimetres')

X /eks/ *noun* the Roman numeral for ten or tenth

xenophobia /ˌzenəˈfəʊbiə/ *noun* a dislike of foreigners

XL *abbr* extra large

③ **Xmas** /ˈkrɪsməs, ˈeksməs/ *noun* same as **Christmas** (*informal*)

XML /ˌeks em ˈel/ *noun* a computer programming language designed for web documents

X-ray /ˈeks ˌreɪ/, **x-ray** *noun* **1.** a type of radiation that doctors use for taking photographs of the inside of your body ○ *The X-ray examination showed the key was inside the baby's stomach.* ○ *The X-ray department is closed for lunch.* **2.** a photograph taken with X-rays ○ *The X-ray showed that the bone was broken in two places.* ○ *They will take an X-ray of his leg.* ○ *She was sent to hospital for an X-ray.* ■ *verb* (**X-rays, X-raying, X-rayed**) to take an X-ray photograph of someone ○ *There are six patients waiting to be X-rayed.* ○ *They X-rayed my leg to see if it was broken.*

xylophone /ˈzaɪləfəʊn/ *noun* a musical instrument consisting of wooden or metal bars of different lengths which make different notes when you tap them with a little hammer

y /waɪ/, **Y** *noun* the twenty-fifth letter of the alphabet, between X and Z

yacht /jɒt/ *noun* **1.** a sailing boat used for pleasure and sport **2.** a large comfortable boat with a motor ○ *She spent her holiday on a yacht in the Mediterranean.*

yank /jæŋk/ (**yanks, yanking, yanked**) *verb* to give something a sudden sharp pull ○ *Yank that string and it should ring a bell in the bar.* ○ *She tried to yank the pram out of the mud.*

yap /jæp/ (**yaps, yapping, yapped**) *verb* (*of a small dog*) to bark ○ *Her wretched little dog was yapping all the time.*

② **yard** /jɑːd/ *noun* **1.** a measurement of length, equal to 0.914 metres ○ *The police station is only yards away from where the fight took place.* ○ *Can you move your car a couple of yards as it is blocking the entrance to our garage?* **2.** an area of concrete at the back or side of a house ○ *We keep our bikes in the yard.*

yardstick /ˈjɑːdstɪk/ *noun* a standard for measurement

yarn /jɑːn/ *noun* a long piece of wool used in knitting or weaving ○ *She sells yarn from the wool of her sheep.*

yawn /jɔːn/ (**yawns, yawning, yawned**) *verb* to open your mouth wide and breathe in and out deeply when you are tired or bored ○ *He went on speaking for so long that half the people at the meeting started yawning* or *started to yawn.* (NOTE: + **yawn** *n*)

yd *abbr* yard

yeah /jeə/ *interj* yes

① **year** /jɪə/ *noun* **1.** a period of time lasting twelve months, from January 1st to December 31st ○ *Columbus discovered America in the year 1492.* ○ *Great celebrations which took place in the year 2000.* ○ *Last year we did not have any holiday.* ○ *Next year she's going on holiday in Australia.* ○ *The weather was very bad for most of the year.* **2.** a period of twelve months from a particular time ○ *We spent five years in Hong Kong.* ○ *He died two hundred years ago today.* ○ *She'll be eleven years old tomorrow.* ○ *How many years have you been working for the company?* ◇ **all year round** working or open for the whole year ○ *The museum is open all year round.*

yearbook /ˈjɪəbʊk/ *noun* a reference book which is published each year with updated or new information

yearly /ˈjɪəli/ *adj, adv* which happens every year or once a year ○ *They make a yearly trip to London to do their Christmas shop-*

ping. ○ *My yearly subscription to the museum is only £25.00.*

yearn /jɜːn/ (**yearns, yearning, yearned**) *verb* to want something that may not be easy to get very much ○ *She's yearning for some peace and quiet.*

yeast /jiːst/ *noun* a living fungus used to make bread and to ferment alcohol

yell /jel/ (**yells, yelling, yelled**) *verb* to shout very loudly (NOTE: + **yell** *n*)

② **yellow** /ˈjeləʊ/ *adj* of a colour like that of the sun or of gold ○ *His new car is bright yellow.* ○ *She's wearing yellow sandals.* ○ *At this time of year the fields are full of yellow flowers.* ■ *noun* the colour of the sun or gold

yellow card /ˌjeləʊ ˈkɑːd/ *noun* in football, a card that a referee shows when giving a player a warning

yellowish /ˈjeləʊɪʃ/ *adj* of a colour that is close to yellow

③ **yellow pages** /ˌjeləʊ ˈpeɪdʒɪz/ *trademark* a section of a telephone directory printed on yellow paper, which lists businesses under various headings, such as computer shops, newsagent's etc. ○ *He looked up 'airlines' in the yellow pages.*

yelp /jelp/ (**yelps, yelping, yelped**) *verb* (*usually of animals*) to give a short cry of pain or excitement ○ *The dogs were yelping in the back of the car.* (NOTE: + **yelp** *n*)

yep *adv, interj* yes

① **yes** /jes/ *adv* a word showing that you agree with someone, accept something, or give permission for something ○ *They asked her if she wanted to come and she said 'yes'.* ○ *Anyone want more coffee? – Yes, please.* ○ *You don't like living in London? – Yes I do!* ○ *Didn't you work in Scotland at one time? – Yes, I did.* ○ *I need a clear answer – is it 'yes' or 'no'?*

① **yesterday** /ˈjestədeɪ/ *adv, noun* the day before today ○ *Yesterday was March 1st so today must be the 2nd.* ○ *She came to see us yesterday evening.*

① **yet** /jet/ *adv* now, before now, or until now ○ *Has the manager arrived yet?* ○ *I haven't seen her yet this morning.* ○ *Don't throw the newspaper away – I haven't read it yet.* ■ *conj* however ○ *He's very small and yet he can kick a ball a long way.* ○ *It was starting to snow, and yet he went out without a coat.*

yield /jiːld/ *noun* the quantity of a crop or a product produced from a plant or from an area of land ○ *What is the normal yield per hectare?* ■ *verb* (**yields, yielding, yielded**) **1.** to produce a result **2.** to produce a crop or a product **3.** to do or agree to do something that you have been trying not to do

yo /jəʊ/ *interj* used as an informal greeting

yoga /ˈjəʊgə/ *noun* a system of exercises and meditation practised by Hindu thinkers, now popular in western countries as a way of keeping fit and relaxing

yoghurt /ˈjɒgət/, **yogurt** *noun* milk which has become slightly sour and thicker after bacteria are added, often flavoured with fruit ○ *a pot of raspberry yoghurt*

yolk /jəʊk/ *noun* the yellow part inside an egg (NOTE: Do not confuse with **yoke**.)

① **you** /jʊ, juː/ *pron* **1.** referring to someone being spoken to ○ *Are you ready?* ○ *You look tired, you should rest a bit.* ○ *If I give you my address will you give me yours?* ○ *Hello, how are you?* ○ *Are you both keeping well?* **2.** referring to anyone ○ *You never know when you might need a penknife.* ○ *You have to be very tall to be a policeman.*

③ **you'd** /juːd/ *short for* **1.** you had **2.** you would

③ **you'll** /juːl/ *short for* you will

① **young** /jʌŋ/ *adj* (**younger, youngest**) not old ○ *She's very young, she's only six.* ○ *He became Prime Minister when he was still a young man.* ○ *My little brother's much younger than me* or *than I am.* ○ *In the afternoon there are TV programmes for very young children.* ○ *This is where your Daddy lived when he was young.* ■ *noun* young animals or birds ○ *Animals fight to protect their young.*

youngster /ˈjʌŋstə/ *noun* a young person ○ *My grandparents don't understand today's youngsters.*

① **your** /jɔː/ *adj* belonging to you ○ *I hope you didn't forget to bring your toothbrush.* ○ *This letter is for your brother.*

① **you're** /jʊə, jɔː/ *short for* you are

① **yours** /jɔːz/ *pron* belonging to you ○ *This is my car – where's yours?* ○ *My car's in the garage, can I borrow yours?*

yourself /jəˈself/ *pron* relating to 'you' as a subject ○ *Why do you wash the car yourself, when you could easily take it to the car wash?* ○ *Watch out for the broken glass – you might hurt yourself.* ○ *I hope you are all going to enjoy yourselves.*

② **youth** /juːθ/ *noun* **1.** a young man ○ *Gangs of youths were causing trouble in the village.* ○ *A youth, aged 16, was arrested for possessing drugs.* **2.** a period when you are young, especially the time between being a child and being an adult ○ *In his* *youth he was a great traveller.* ○ *I haven't done that since the days of my youth!*

youth club /ˈjuːθ klʌb/ *noun* a club where young people meet

youthful /ˈjuːθf(ə)l/ *adj* young

youth hostel /ˈjuːθ ˌhɒst(ə)l/ *noun* a building where young travellers or walkers can stay the night cheaply

③ **you've** /juːv/ *short for* you have

yo-yo /ˈjəʊ jəʊ/ *noun* a toy made of two round pieces and a string which you make the toy run up and down ○ *Yo-yos were very popular when I was at school.*

yr *abbr* year

yuck /jʌk/ *interj* used to show that something has a nasty taste

yucky /ˈjʌki/ *adj* not nice, unpleasant

yummy /ˈjʌmi/ *adj* delicious (*informal*)

z /zed/, **Z** *noun US* the last and twenty-sixth letter of the alphabet

zany /ˈzeɪni/ (**zanier, zaniest**) *adj* wildly mad

zap /zæp/ (**zaps, zapping, zapped**) *verb* (*informal*) **1.** to hit or kill someone **2.** to shut down the television using the remote control

zeal /ziːl/ *noun* keenness or eagerness

zealous /ˈzeləs/ *adj* eager, too efficient

zebra crossing /ˌzebrə ˈkrɒsɪŋ/ *noun* a place marked with black and white lines where traffic stops to allow you to walk across a road

zenith /ˈzenɪθ/ *noun* the highest point, point of greatest achievement ○ *The soprano retired at the zenith of her career.* ○ *The British Empire reached its zenith at the beginning of the 20th century.*

③ **zero** /ˈzɪərəʊ/ *noun* **1.** the number 0 ○ *To make an international call you dial zero zero (00), followed by the number of the country.* **2.** the temperature at which water freezes ○ *The temperature stayed below zero for days.* (NOTE: no plural in this sense) **3.** nothing ○ *They stole all our stock – we were left with zero.* (NOTE: no plural in this sense)

zero in *phrasal verb* to go straight to something

zest /zest/ *noun* **1.** enthusiasm or enjoyment ○ *Her zest for playing football made her apply to join the local club.* **2.** a thin piece of orange or lemon peel ○ *Grate the zest of one lemon and add it to the cake mix.*

zigzag /ˈzɪgzæg/ *adj, noun* used to describe a line which turns one way, then the opposite way ○ *There are zigzag lines painted at pedestrian crossings to show that cars must not stop there.*

zilch /zɪltʃ/ *noun* nothing (*informal*)

zillion /ˈzɪljən/ *noun* a huge number (*informal*) ○ *Zillions of people watched the game on TV.*

zinc /zɪŋk/ *noun* a hard bright light-coloured metal

zip /zɪp/ *noun* a device for closing openings on clothes and bags, consisting of two rows of teeth which lock together (*informal*) ○ *The zip of my anorak is broken.* ○ *Can you do up the zip at the back of my dress?* ■ *verb* (**zips, zipping, zipped**) **1.** *also* **zip up** to close something using a zip ○ *He zipped up his bag.* **2.** to go fast ○ *Cars were zipping past us on the motorway.*

ZIP code /ˈzɪp kəʊd/ *noun US* a trademark for the numbers used to indicate a US postal delivery area in an address on an envelope

zip drive /ˈzɪp draɪv/ *trademark* a trademark for a piece of computer equipment that makes large computer files smaller for easier storage or faster transmission

zipper /ˈzɪpə/ *US* same as **zip**

zit /zɪt/ *noun* a pimple or spot on the skin

zombie /ˈzɒmbi/ *noun* **1.** (*in the West Indies*) a dead body which is revived and controlled by witchcraft **2.** a person who is unable to think ○ *After thirteen hours in the plane I felt like a zombie.*

③ **zone** /zəʊn/ *noun* an area ○ *Police cars are patrolling the inner city zones.*

zoo /zuː/ *noun* a place where wild animals are kept, and where people can go to see them

zoo-keeper /zuː ˈkiːpə/ *noun* a person whose job is to look after the animals in a zoo

zoologist /zuːˈɒlədʒɪst, zəʊˈɒlədʒɪst/ *noun* a person who studies animals

zoology /zuːˈɒlədʒi, zəʊˈɒlədʒi/ *noun* the study of animals

zoom /zuːm/ (**zooms, zooming, zoomed**) *verb* to go very fast ○ *Cars were zooming past me on the motorway.*

③ **zoom lens** /ˈzuːm lenz/ *noun* a camera lens which allows you to change quickly from distant to close-up shots while still keeping in focus

zzz *noun* a representation of the sound made by somebody sleeping, often used in cartoons

SUPPLEMENTS

Irregular Verbs

Verb	*Past tense*	*Past participle*
arise	arose	arisen
awake	awoke	awoken
be	was, were	been
bear	bore	borne
beat	beat	beaten
become	became	become
befall	befell	befallen
begin	began	begun
bend	bent	bent
beseech	besought, beseeched	besought, beseeched
beset	beset	beset
bet	bet	bet
bid	bid	bid
bind	bound	bound
bite	bit	bitten
bleed	bled	bled
blow	blew	blown
break	broke	broken
breed	bred	bred
bring	brought	brought
broadcast	broadcast	broadcast
build	built	built
burn	burnt, burned	burnt, burned
burst	burst	burst
buy	bought	bought
cast	cast	cast
catch	caught	caught
choose	chose	chosen
cling	clung	clung
come	came	come
cost	cost	cost
creep	crept	crept
cut	cut	cut
deal	dealt	dealt
dig	dug	dug
dive	dived, *(US)* dove	dived
do	did	done
draw	drew	drawn
dream	dreamed, dreamt	dreamed, dreamt
drink	drank	drunk
drive	drove	driven
dwell	dwelt, dwelled	dwelt, dwelled
eat	ate	eaten
fall	fell	fallen
feed	fed	fed
feel	felt	felt
fight	fought	fought
find	found	found
flee	fled	fled
fling	flung	flung
fly	flew	flown
forbid	forbade	forbidden
forecast	forecast	forecast
foresee	foresaw	foreseen
forget	forgot	forgotten
forgive	forgave	forgiven
forgo	forwent	forgone
forsake	forsook	forsaken
freeze	froze	frozen
get	got	got, *(US)* gotten
give	gave	given
go	went	gone
grind	ground	ground
grow	grew	grown
hang	hung	hung
have	had	had
hear	heard	heard
hide	hid	hidden
hit	hit	hit
hold	held	held

Irregular Verbs *continued*

Verb	*Past tense*	*Past participle*
hurt	hurt	hurt
input	inputted, input	inputted, input
interweave	interwove	interwoven
keep	kept	kept
kneel	knelt, kneeled	knelt, kneeled
knit	knit, knitted	knit, knitted
know	knew	known
lay	laid	laid
lead	led	led
lean	leant, leaned	leant, leaned
leap	leapt, leaped	leapt, leaped
learn	learnt, learned	learnt, learned
leave	left	left
lend	lent	lent
let	let	let
lie	lay	lain
light	lit	lit
lose	lost	lost
make	made	made
mean	meant	meant
meet	met	met
mislay	mislaid	mislaid
mislead	misled	misled
misspell	misspelt, misspelled	misspelt, misspelled
mistake	mistook	mistaken
misunderstand	misunderstood	misunderstood
mow	mowed	mowed, mown
outdo	outdid	outdone
outgrow	outgrew	outgrown
overcome	overcame	overcome
overdo	overdid	overdone
overdraw	overdrew	overdrawn
overeat	overate	overeaten
overhang	overhung	overhung
overhear	overheard	overheard
overpay	overpaid	overpaid
override	overrode	overridden
overrun	overrun	overrun
oversee	oversaw	overseen
overtake	overtook	overtaken
overthrow	overthrew	overthrown
pay	paid	paid
put	put	put
quit	quit	quit
read	read	read
redo	redid	redone
repay	repaid	repaid
rerun	reran	rerun
reset	reset	reset
rethink	rethought	rethought
rewind	rewound	rewound
rewrite	rewrote	rewritten
rid	rid	rid
ride	rode	ridden
ring	rang	rung
rise	rose	risen
run	ran	run
saw	sawed	sawn
say	said	said
see	saw	seen
seek	sought	sought
sell	sold	sold
send	sent	sent
set	set	set
sew	sewed	sewed, sewn
shake	shook	shaken
shear	sheared	sheared, shorn
shed	shed	shed
shine	shone	shone

Irregular Verbs *continued*

Verb	*Past tense*	*Past participle*
shoot	shot	shot
show	showed	shown
shrink	shrank	shrunk
shut	shut	shut
sing	sang	sung
sink	sank	sunk
sit	sat	sat
slay	slew	slain
sleep	slept	slept
slide	slid	slid
sling	slung	slung
slink	slunk	slunk
slit	slit	slit
smell	smelt, smelled	smelt, smelled
sow	sowed	sown
speak	spoke	spoken
speed	sped	sped
spell	spelt, spelled	spelt, spelled
spend	spent	spent
spill	spilt, spilled	spilt, spilled
spin	spun	spun
spit	spat	spat
split	split	split
spoil	spoilt, spoiled	spoilt, spoiled
spread	spread	spread
spring	sprang	sprung
stand	stood	stood
steal	stole	stolen
stick	stuck	stuck
sting	stung	stung
stink	stank	stunk
stride	strode	strode
strike	struck	struck
strive	strove	striven
swear	swore	sworn
sweep	swept	swept
swell	swelled	swelled, swollen
swim	swam	swum
swing	swung	swung
take	took	taken
teach	taught	taught
tear	tore	torn
tell	told	told
think	thought	thought
thrive	thrived, throve	thrived
throw	threw	thrown
thrust	thrust	thrust
tread	trod	trodden
understand	understood	understood
undergo	underwent	undergone
undertake	undertook	undertaken
undo	undid	undone
unwind	unwound	unwound
uphold	upheld	upheld
upset	upset	upset
wake	woke	woken
wear	wore	worn
weave	wove	woven
wet	wet, wetted	wet, wetted
weep	wept	wept
win	won	won
wind	wound	wound
withdraw	withdrew	withdrawn
withhold	withheld	withheld
withstand	withstood	withstood
wreak	wreaked, wrought	wreaked, wrought
wring	wrung	wrung
write	wrote	written

How to say ...

The Alphabet

A	/eɪ/	N	/en/
B	/biː/	O	/əʊ/
C	/siː/	P	/piː/
D	/diː/	Q	/kjuː/
E	/iː/	R	/ɑɪ/
F	/ef/	S	/es/
G	/dʒiː/	T	/tiː/
H	/eɪtʃ/	U	/juː/
I	/ɑɪ/	V	/viː/
J	/dʒeɪ/	W	/ˈdʌb(ə)ljuː/
K	/keɪ/	X	/eks/
L	/el/	Y	/waɪ/
M	/em/	Z	/zed/, *(US)* /ziː/

Numbers

1, 2, 3, 4	one, two, three, four
I,II, III, IV	
1st, 2nd, 3rd, 4th	first, second, third, fourth
5, 6, 7, 8	five, six, seven, eight
V VI, VII, VIII	
5th, 6th, 7th, 8th	fifth, sixth, seventh, eighth
9, 10, 11, 12	nine, ten, eleven, twelve
IX, X, XI, XII	
9th, 10th 11th, 12th	ninth, tenth, eleventh, twelfth
13, 14, 15, 16	thirteen, fourteen, fifteen, sixteen
XIII, XIV, XV, XVI	
13th, 14th,15th, 16th	thirtheenth, fourteenth, fifteenth, sixteenth
17, 18, 19, 20	seventeen, eighteen, nineteen, twenty
XVII, XVIII, XIX, XX	
17th, 18th,19th, 20th	seventeenth, eighteenth, nineteenth, twentieth
21, 22, 23	twenty one, twenty two, twenty-three
XX1, XXII, XXIII	
21st, 22nd, 23rd	twenty-first, twenty-second, twenty-third
30, 31, 32	thirty, thirty-one, thirty-two
XXX, XXX1, XXXII	
40, 50, 60, 70, 80, 90	forty, fifty, sixty, seventy, eighty, ninety
XL, L, LX, LXX, LXXX, XC	
40th, 50th, 60th, 70th, 80th, 90th	fortieth, fiftieth, sixtieth, seventieth, eightieth, ninetieth
100,101	one hundred, a hundred; one hundred and one,
C, CI	a hundred and one
200, 300, 400, 500	two hundred, three hundred, four hundred, five hundred
CC, CCC, CCCC, D	
1,000	one thousand, a thousand
M	
10,000	ten thousand
1,000,000	one million, a million
1,000,000,000	one billion, a billion

How to say ...

Decimals

0.5	zero point five, point five
0.25	zero point two five, point two five
2.5	two point five

Money

£1	one pound, a pound
30p	thirty pence, thirty pee
£1.25	one pound twenty-five (pee), one twenty-five
£27.36	twenty-seven pounds thirty-six (pee)
$1	one dollar, a dollar
10¢	ten cents, or *(US)* a dime
25¢	twenty-five cents, or *(US)* a quarter
$1.25	one dollar twenty-five, a dollar twenty-five, one twenty-five

Telephone numbers

020 7921 3567	oh-two-oh, seven-nine-two-one, three-five-six-seven

Years

1905	nineteen oh five, nineteen hundred and five
1998	nineteen ninety-eight
the 1900s, the 1900's	the nineteen hundreds
2000	two thousand, the year two thousand
2005	two thousand and five

Dates

2.1.98 or 2/1/98	the second of January, nineteen ninety eight, or *(US)* February first, nineteen ninety eight (NOTE: European and British dates are written with the day before the month, American dates are written with the month before the day.)

Some words with numbers

999, *(US)* 911, *(Australia)* 000	nine nine nine, *(US)* nine one one, *(Australia)* triple oh (NOTE: the number to phone in an emergency)
24/7	twenty-four seven (NOTE: means 'all the time')
9/11	nine eleven (NOTE: the eleventh of September 2001, when many people died in a terrorist attack in New York)
the big 40, 50, etc.	the big four oh, five oh, etc. (NOTE: used humorously to refer to a fortieth or fiftieth, etc. birthday)
A1	/ˌei 'wʌn/ (NOTE: means 'excellent')
A1, A12, B125, etc.	/ˌei 'wʌn/, /ˌei 'twelv/, /ˌbiː wʌn tuː 'faiv/, etc. (NOTE: the numbering system for roads in Great Britain)
4x4	four by four (NOTE: a vehicle with four-wheel drive)
4WD	four-wheel drive (NOTE: a system in which engine power drives all four wheels of a vehicle, or a vehicle with this system)
H_2O	/ˌeitʃtuː'əʊ/ (NOTE: The chemical formula is sometimes used to say 'water'.)
M1, M25, etc.	/ˌem 'wʌn/, /ˌem twenti 'faɪv/, etc. (NOTE: the numbering system for motorways in Great Britain)

Numbers are sometimes used as abbreviations in e-mails, text messages or adverts.

2day	today	CUL8R	see you later	L8R	later
4U	for you	F2F	face to face	M8	mate
B4	before	GR8	great	P2P	person to person